The
echanics'Magazine,Museum,Register,Journ and Gazette,April 7Th-
September 29Th,1838.Vol.XXIX

The

Mechanics'Magazine,Museum,Register,Journal And Gazette,April 7th-
September 29th,1838.VOL.XXIX

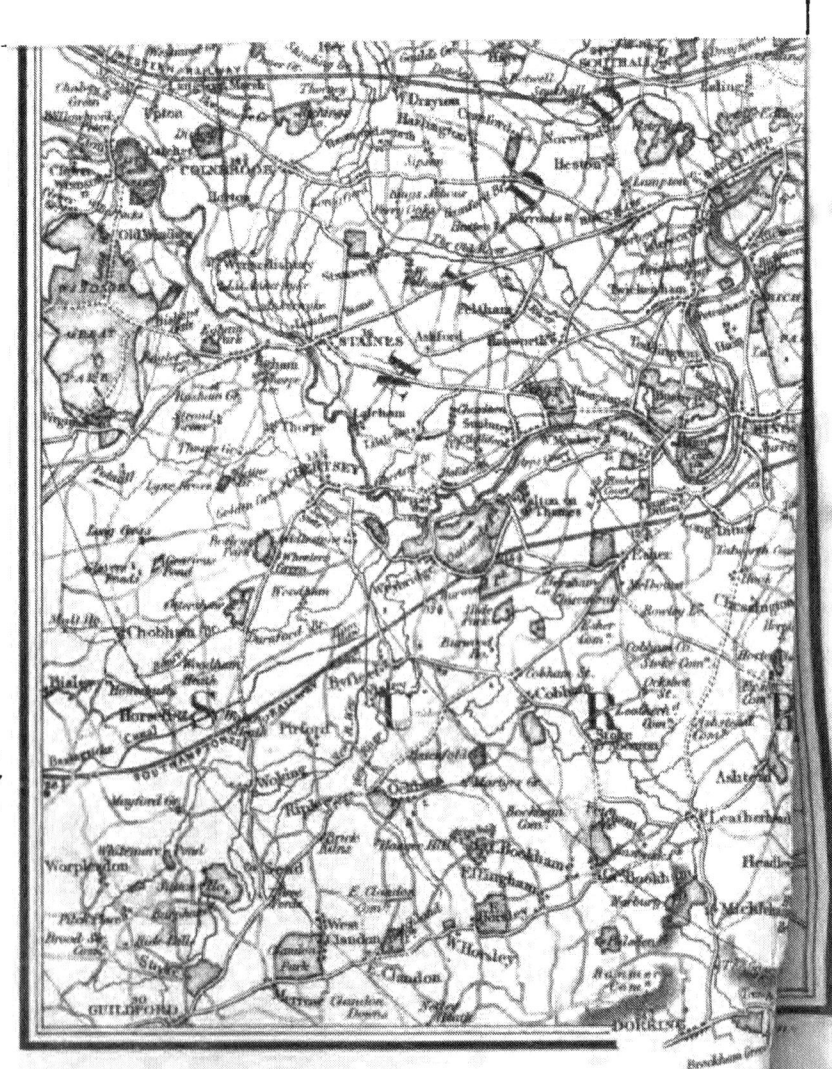

THE

MECHANICS' MAGAZINE,

MUSEUM,

Register, Journal,

AND

GAZETTE,

APRIL 7th—SEPTEMBER 29th, 1838.

VOL. XXIX.

" Here is employment enough for the vastest parts, the most indefatigable industries, the happiest opportunities. Seneca hath said, ' The people of the next age shall know many things unknown to us; many are reserved for ages then to come, when we shall be quite forgotten—no memory of us remaining. The world would be a pitiful small thing indeed, if it did not contain enough for the inquiries of the whole world.' "—RAY.

LONDON:

PUBLISHED FOR THE PROPRIETOR, BY W. A. ROBERTSON,
MECHANICS' MAGAZINE OFFICE, PETERBOROUGH-COURT.

1838.

PRINTED BY W. A. ROBERTSON, 6, PETERBOROUGH-COURT, FLEET STREET.

CONTENTS.

ORIGINAL ARTICLES.

REVIEWS AND CRITICAL NOTICES.

EXTRACTS.

NEW PATENTS.

ENGLISH.

Mechanics' Magazine,

MUSEUM, REGISTER, JOURNAL, AND GAZETTE

| No. 765.] | SATURDAY, APRIL 7, 1838. | [Price 3d. |

BARNARD AND JOY'S PATENT SELF-ROLLING MANGLE.

BARNARD AND JOY'S PATENT SELF-ROLLING MANGLE.

The engraving on our front page is a perspective view of an improved mangle patented some time ago by Messrs. Barnard and Joy, of Norwich, in which weighted rollers have been substituted successfully for the cumbrous travelling bed now in use. It is very compact, occupying not more than one-fourth the space of the ordinary clumsy machine; it has already been extensively used, and, we are informed, with equal, if not superior, efficacy to both the common, and Baker's patent, mangle.

In the view on our front page N N N is the framework of the machine; A, B and C are three rollers or cylinders; E is a cross rail at the bottom of the machine, from which is suspended the weight F. K K are vertical grooves or slots in the upright posts of the framework N, in which the ends of the axis of the roller A are free to move up and down; M M are two other vertical slots in the upright posts, in which the ends of the cross rail E are also free to move up and down; D D are bars in-

the upright posts N N. for the purpose of connecting the roller A with the cross rail E, and the weight F attached thereto. The form of one of these bars is shewn more clearly at fig. 2; d being the hole through which the axis of the roller or cylinder A passes; X X a slot to allow of the free action of the axes of the rollers or cylinders B and C, and e, the hole for receiving the end of the cross rail E. L L are slots in the upright posts of the framework, in which the ends of the axis of the middle roller B are free to move, but which slots form a segment of a circle described from the centre of the pinion H, instead of being vertical. The vertical slot K, and the curved slot L, are more clearly shewn in figure 3, which exhibits a portion of one of the posts N with the slots therein; the wheel G being removed. G is a wheel fixed to one end of the axis of the middle wheel B (outside of the framework N N N), and H, a pinion, which works into the teeth of the wheel G. C, which is the lowest or lowest of the three rollers is required to revolve at one fixed point of elevation only, and has therefore no such range of action provided for as in the cases of the rollers A and B. O is the table which carries the articles to be mangled or calendered; P, brackets supporting the table O, and projecting from the framework N. Fig. 4, is a section of the

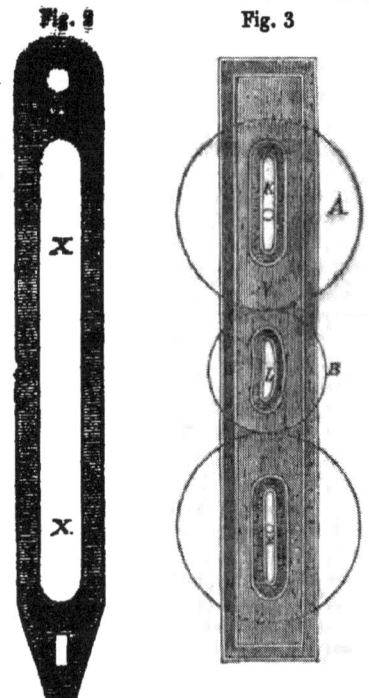

Fig. 2   Fig. 3

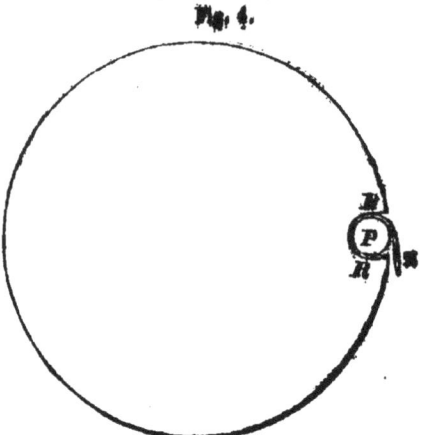

Fig. 4.

serted in grooves in the inner sides of

middle roller B, shewing the manner in which the mangle-cloth Z is attached to the roller B. A groove R is made along the whole length of the roller B, into which a rod P, of brass or other metal, is made to fit exactly. The end of the mangle-cloth is sewn so as to form a loop or hem, and the rod P being passed through, it is placed in the groove R R; the one end of the rod being secured in a hole or socket, at one end of the roller B, and the other end of the rod with a screw at the other end of the roller. By this means the mangle-cloth is made to start true, and the trouble of adjusting the same avoided.

Before setting the machine to work, the linen, or other cloth Z is attached to the middle roller B, in the manner before mentioned, and brought over on table O, and on this cloth the articles to be mangled or calendered are laid; a winch I being now applied to the axis of the pinion H, and being turned, the roller B is made to revolve, the linen or other cloth Z, to wind itself together with the articles to be mangled or calendered placed thereon, upon the roller B, and the roller B, in consequence of the circular range of action given to it by the curved slots L L, to rise in these slots in proportion as its diameter is increased by the plies or laminations of the articles to be calendered or mangled, and of the linen or cloth Z, which by the counteraction of the rollers A and B, and the weight F, the articles which have been placed on the table O, and wound round the roller or cylinder B, are mangled or calendered to any degree ordinarily required.

FRENCH INVENTION OF GAS-LIGHTING.

The French are determined to lose no time in putting in their claims to a far greater share in the invention and introduction of improvements in the useful arts than the rest of the world has hitherto been willing to give them credit for. It is now held—in France—as an established fact, that the steam-engine was brought to bear by Papin, although Newcomen and Watt are entitled to some consideration for their trouble in reviving it;—and, now that Paris is, in some degree, lighted with gas instead of oil, it has been discovered that the brilliant novelty,—which, like most brilliant novelties, has been hailed with enthusiasm by our volatile neighbours—is an emanation of Gallic genius! Henceforth, we dull islanders must hide our diminished heads!

The proofs of this startling position advanced by the French journalists are almost too ludicrous for belief. After detailing some of the earlier English experiments on coal-gas, and especially those of Bishop Watson, the account goes on to give a description of a portable lamp, invented by a Monsieur Lebon, in 1785, the flame of which was to be supported by the combustion of the gas obtained from wood. In this grand object the inventor failed,—and voilà the origin of lighting the street and shops of London and Paris by means of carburetted hydrogen conveyed through miles of iron pipes!!

It is true that the account candidly acknowledges the claims of Mr. Murdoch, to the invention of the present system of gas-lighting, and enters into a history of his exertions. In this the Frenchman is for awhile lost sight of, only to re-appear in the greater brilliancy. Murdoch, we are told, met with such difficulties in his attempts to light the Soho factory, as to begin to think of giving them up altogether. This was happily prevented by the liberal patronage of Messrs. Boulton and Watt, seconded by the encouragement afforded by the reports which reached England of the *experiments of M. Lebon! Risum teneatis, amici?* We are gravely informed that Murdoch would have most probably given up the idea of applying coal-gas to the purposes of illumination on a large scale, and left the world to the comparative darkness of oil and candles, even after he had brought his invention towards perfection, had he not happened luckily to hear, just in the nick of time, —what?—that *some twenty years before, a certain Frenchman had made an unsuccessful attempt to light a table lamp with a different kind of gas!*

On the strength of the probability of this occurrence, it is now proposed that the name of Lebon, shall be inscribed among those of Murdoch, Winsor, Clegg, and the other non-Frenchmen who have hitherto run away with the whole credit of introducing gas to the world. It is impossible to imagine a richer or more laughable specimen of that egregious national vanity which prompts our 'cross-channel friends, like the " French falconers" of Shakspeare, to " fly at every thing they see." We have never yet heard of their claiming the invention of railways and locomotives as their own, but it is by no means unlikely that they will do so. We remember in our youthful days often gazing with wonder at a street exhibition in which a magic car ran several times round a table by means of clockwork concealed between its wheels. For this machine we were said to be indebted to French ingenuity;—and what is more probable than that a sight of it gave the first impulse to the inventive faculties of a Trevithick and a Stephenson? What, in fact, have these *soi-disant* inventors done but substitute steam for clockwork, and iron rails for a mahogany table? Railway locomotion is, in point of fact, as clearly of continental origin as the system of lighting by gas!

The " new light" is at length making considerable progress in France, although its benefits are hitherto confined almost exclusively to the capital, and even there they are enjoyed but in a limited degree. Long after London had fully availed itself of its advantages, the only place where it might be seen at Paris was at a house of entertainment whose proprietor expected to make his fortune by entitling himself to write up the attractive name of "*cafe du gas.*" His speculation, however, does not seem to have answered his anticipations, and his " gaz" we are told, now that the Parisians have an opportunity of comparing it with some of better quality, burned with a very dim flame. Mr. Winsor, to whom the credit of suggesting, at least, the lighting of the streets of London with gas is due, had the principal hand in introducing it to the Parisian public, and it is now making (for France) rapid strides to general use. A company has just been formed in the south of France, for lighting the principal towns, and has made proposals to the authorities of Marseilles and Toulouse, among others, for commencing the superior enlightenment of their ways forthwith. One of the stipulations they insist upon, sounds strangely enough to English ears, and would hardly be thought of by an English company. It is that the city shall not only contract to use their lights alone, granting the requisite permission to open the streets, to lay down the pipes, but also assign over a suitable site for the erection of the works, free of expense to the company! These terms it is expected will be gladly acceded to.

PROVERBIAL INEFFICIENCY OF PA-
RISH-ENGINES—PROPOSAL FOR A
FIRE-POLICE IN THE CITY.

Sir,—I believe there is no place in the world *apparently* so well protected against the spread of conflagrations, as the metropolis of London; while at the same time, there is not another place, whose protection depends upon, and is really effected by, such very slender means. Numerically considered, fire-engines are so abundant, as to afford nearly one for every street : but the bulk of this number consists of parish-engines, which have not only dwindled down from their original importance and utility, into proverbial inefficiency—but the term has become synonymous with all that is important, ridiculous, and useless. The inimitable " Boz," in his " sketches" says, " we never saw a parish-engine at a *regular fire* but once. It came up in gallant style—three miles and a half an hour at least ; there was a plentiful supply of water, and it was first upon the spot. Bang went the pumps—the people cheered—the beadle perspired profusely ; but it was unfortunately discovered, just as they were going to put the fire out, *that nobody understood the process by which the engine was filled with water :* and that eighteen boys and a man, had exhausted themselves in pumping for twenty minutes, without producing the slightest effect !" It will most likely be imagined, by persons whose acquaintance with these matters is of necessity very limited, that this is a burlesque by our facetious friend, but it is no such thing. Scarcely a week passes in this metropolis without the rehearsal of some such absurdity, and it has been my lot to witness many scenes of this description, even more abominably ridiculous than that which has been so graphically depicted by " Boz."

Parish engine-keepers are often called a set of blundering old women ; one of the city parishes, however, is actually furnished with an *engineer* of the true *feminine gender !* As parish affairs generally are managed by *old women*, it cannot be matter of surprise, that, from sympathy " our ladye" should be permitted to hold so honourable and important an employment—or that she should be exempt from displacement—unless the buxom widow should deem it expedient to her worldly comfort to induct some " good man and true," into her hydraulic office.

Again, parish-engines are not only badly *manned*, but also very imperfectly furnished with such appurtenances as are requisite for efficient service. They are also most irregularly located; in one short street (Lombard-street, City,) there are nine fire-engines, and in the turnings out of it eight more: making in all *seventeen*, within a few square yards, while there are many spots of at least three times the extent, and containing above ten times the amount of property, without a single engine, for their protection.

Notwithstanding the proximity of the above engines to the Royal Exchange, at the late fire *one of the smallest* only was brought out, and that one, as a matter of course was not worked! A glance at these facts strongly suggests the propriety of reform—any change must be for the better. Now that the organization of a new day and night police, in the city, is under consideration, a favourable opportunity is offered for adding to their other duties, that of a *fire-police*.

This might be accomplished with far less difficulty, and at a much smaller expense, than is generally imagined. On handing over to the police committee, all the present fire-engines of the city parishes, it would be found, that the proceeds from the sale of the least useful, would suffice to put the remainder (an ample number) into an efficient working state. The equipment of every engine should be made uniform and complete, and in every respect adequate to the preservation of life, and the protection of property; the subsequent expenses necessary for maintaining such a condition would be but trifling—very much under the annual sum at present uselessly expended upon this object.

The engines would require to be stationed with discrimination, with one man on duty day and night at each engine-house to be relieved at stated intervals. Periodical drilling, under experienced instructors, would soon bring the whole force into a condition to be eminently useful. An extra gratuity to each man employed at a fire would take off much of the irksomeness of such an employment. Special rewards for extraordinary exertion, would stimulate the men to discharge their duties with skill and alacrity.

It is truely a most disgraceful circumstance, that engines are continually brought to fires by policemen and others, and there suffered to stand unemployed for want of the moderate share of knowledge needful to set them to work—yet such is a frequent occurrence, even in London A.D. 1838! Should the citizens have the good sense properly to appreciate these remarks, and adopt the suggestions I have thrown out, incalculable benefits would result. I am confident the advantages of a well disciplined system of this kind would in a very short time be so striking apparent, as to induce—nay, almost compel—the commissioners of the metropolitan police to adopt similar measures. The result of this would ultimately be, to establish such a well organized protection against both fire and thieves, as would materially abridge the depredations of the one—and limit the destructive influences of the other. I have occasion to know, that this state of things was fully contemplated by Sir Robert Peel, when the metropolitan police force was first established, and only delayed, in consequence of the great outcry every where raised against the expenses of this force at its formation.

As the government have again expressed their fixed determination not to forego the duty on fire-insurance, it might be as well to endeavour to get them to appropriate some portion of the immense revenue thus derived, towards defraying the expenses of a *fire-police*. All the protection now, afforded, is at the expense of the *insured*, and this would be but an extension of the principle. The more *equitable* method, however, would be, by means of a universal rate levied upon all property, whether insured or not.

I remain, Sir,
Your's respectfully,
Wm. BADDELEY.

London, March 27, 1838.

———

FIRE ON BOARD THE GREAT WESTERN STEAM - SHIP—MERRYWEATHER'S PORTABLE FIRE-ENGINE.

Sir,—It is a source of considerable satisfaction to me, to observe that the proprietors of steam vessels are at length manifesting a proper sense of what is due to the public as well as to themselves, by providing their vessels with suitable means of counteracting the great dangers to which they exposed, by accidents from fire. Scarcely had the "Great Western" steam ship, to which all eyes are now so anxiously directed—got under weigh on her voyage from London to New York, than this magnificient trophy of British mechanical skill, had nearly fallen a victim to devouring flames. Shortly after passing the Nore on Saturday morning, a smell of burning oil for some time attracted the attention of flames issuing from above the boilers. The dense volume of smoke that filled and issued from the engine-room, drove every person on deck, preventing any one from descending to stop the engines, or to work a powerful forcing-pump, that was there placed for the purpose of extinguishing any fire that might occur.

The most strenuous exertions, however, were made by all on board for the suppression of the flames; one of Merryweather's portable fire-engines, (described at page 236, of your xxiv, volume,) being stationed on the deck it was instantly got to work, and a powerful jet of water was by this means successfully directed into the midst of the fire, through openings speedily cut in the deck for that purpose.

The fire originated in the accidental ignition of the *patent felt*, with which the boilers and steam-pipe were covered to prevent loss by the radiation of heat, and to keep the engine-room as cool as possible. The workmen, had improperly used a quantity of red-lead and oil in coating the boilers, &c., with the felt, particularly with that part of the boilers in contact with the chimney; when the felt had once ignited the flames spread like wild-fire, and but for the precautions adopted by the Great Western Steam-Ship Company, for so speedily extinguishing fire, there is no doubt their first vessel would have been sacrificed. It is a curious circumstance, that the fire-engine was only put on board by Mr. Merryweather late on Friday night, at a very short notice; and in less than twelve hours it proved the means of saving this beautiful vessel from threatened destruction.

The "Sirius," now the aspiring rival of the "Great Western," was very near being destroyed by fire in the river a few months since, and was only preserved by the timely and efficient application of a similar portable engine, which they had on board, and was quickly brought to bear upon the flames.

The tendency of accidents of this kind is to show, that forcing-pumps fixed in the engine-rooms, which I have hitherto strongly advocated, are not always to be relied upon, as access to that part of the vessel is so extremely liable to be cut off. A portable fire-engine stationed on deck may almost always be depended upon, for should the smoke be at all overpowering, the engine can be lowered into a boat alongside, to windward, and worked with the utmost certainty and effect. The proprietors of the "Great Western" have wisely adopted both plans, and there is every reason to believe as well as to hope that the precautions they have taken will insure constant safety.

I remain, Sir,
Your's respectfully,
WM. BADDELEY.

London, April 2, 1838.

BLURTON'S PATENT APPARATUS FOR MILKING COWS.

Sir,—I was much amused (in fact I thought it was a hoax,) about two years ago, on reading in your list of English patents the announcement that one had been granted to a Mr. Blurton of Uttoxeter, Stafford, for "an improved method of, and apparatus for, extracting milk from cows and other animals." From the singularity of the thing, I was in weekly expectation of seeing an account of the invention in your useful Magazine, more particularly as I have cows not a few grazing on the pastures of Devonshire. I was, however, disappointed; and being in town a short time ago, determined to examine Mr. Blurton's specification at the patent Inrolment office. Here I paid a shilling, and was told no such specification had been inrolled, and was about to depart in high anger at you Mr. Editor, for being party (perhaps unwittingly) to what I then thought to be a deception—when a gentleman who happened to be examining a specification informed me that there were two other offices where the document I wanted might be deposited, the Rolls Chapel, and Petty Bag. Thanking him for his civility, I proceeded to the former mentioned office, and for three and sixpence, procured the information of which I was in search. Having read over the description of the invention, and seeing it was not such nonsense as I had expected, I was, in the simplicity of my heart, about to make a few notes in my pocket-book of the principal points of the description. In this I was stopped, and told that it was contrary to the rules of the office;—but that I might read it as long as I liked. Being blessed with a good memory, and having an hour or two to spare, I determined to learn the specification by heart. I very soon got the pith of it, and now send you an account of the method and apparatus, which I hope you will deem sufficiently interesting to publish in your Magazine.

In the common way of milking by the hand, the operation is simply to squeeze out as much milk at a time as the teat contains; on taking away the hand, the teat again fills from the udder, and is again squeezed out; and so on until the whole milk is drawn from the cow. Mr. Blurton's invention is to keep the hole in the teat open, by putting a tube or pipe into it, by which means, he says, the whole of the milk will run out of the cow without intermission in a continuous stream. He states that the tubes will not hurt the cow, and that she does not appear so uneasy at being milked in this way, as by the milk-maid. As, however, with a plain tube, air might get into the udder and produce pain and inflammation, Mr. B. adds, to the mouth of the tube what he calls a "liquid valve"—which consists of a little cup, into which the milk first runs, and overflows into the milk pail; the mouth of the pipe is thus always under the milk, and when it has stopped running from the cow, the cup and pipe will be full,—so that no air can get into the udder. A pipe is to be put into each teat about an inch up, and milk will flow from the whole of them at once into the pail which is to hang by ropes or straps over the cow's hind quarter. Mr. Blurton states that in this way, one person can milk nearly a dozen cows at a time.

This, Mr. Editor, is styled the age of invention, and really the term would appear to be well applied. One would have thought the milk-maid's occupation was the least likely of any to be trenched upon by the march of machinery. What a world of poetical similes and charming rural descriptions is Mr. Blurton's apparatus destined to destroy, should it ever come into general use. The milk-maid, with snow-white pail and nut-brown visage will give place to a rival of the rougher sex, armed with the Blurton tube; and the song, so musical to rustic ears, must henceforth cease. I should like to know how the cows look upon this departure from ancient practice, and whether they chew the cud of sweet or of bitter fancies over days departed. Had Mr. Blurton flourished in those unintellectual days, when great men were raised to the dignity of stars in heaven, as well as on earth, he and his apparatus would undoubtedly have obtained a prominent place in the *Via Lactea*.

I am, Sir,
Your obedient servant,
LACTARIUS.

SIMPLE LETTER-COPYING MACHINE.

Sir,—A short time since I read some papers, in your valuable Magazine of science, upon copying machines. If you deem the following account of a very simple one, which I contrived for my own use some years since, likely to interest your readers, it is much at your service.

The object of this contrivance is to afford to the traveller a portable instrument for copying letters, &c. It consists simply of a brass tube 14 inches long and 1½ diameter. One end, which has a bottom soldered into it and a cover fitted to it, contains a small bottle of copying ink. To the inside of the cover of the other end is attached a brush for the purpose of damping the paper. The space between is occupied by sheets of copying paper together with some oiled paper and thick blotting or filtering paper in a cover. To use the instrument it is only necessary to place a sheet of copying paper between the leaves of blotting paper, which have been previously wetted with the brush, and to let it remain till sufficiently damp—or, more expeditiously, to damp the copying paper itself with the brush and allow the dry blotting paper to absorb the superfluous moisture. Place the paper thus prepared upon the letter &c., and over it a piece of oiled paper and roll the whole tightly upon the outside of the brass tube which may be then rolled under the hands upon a table; a copy may thus be readily taken off. The tube also serves the purpose of a ruler.

I am, Sir, &c.

N. S. HEINEKEN.

Sidmouth.

HUMPHREY'S SLIDE VALVES.

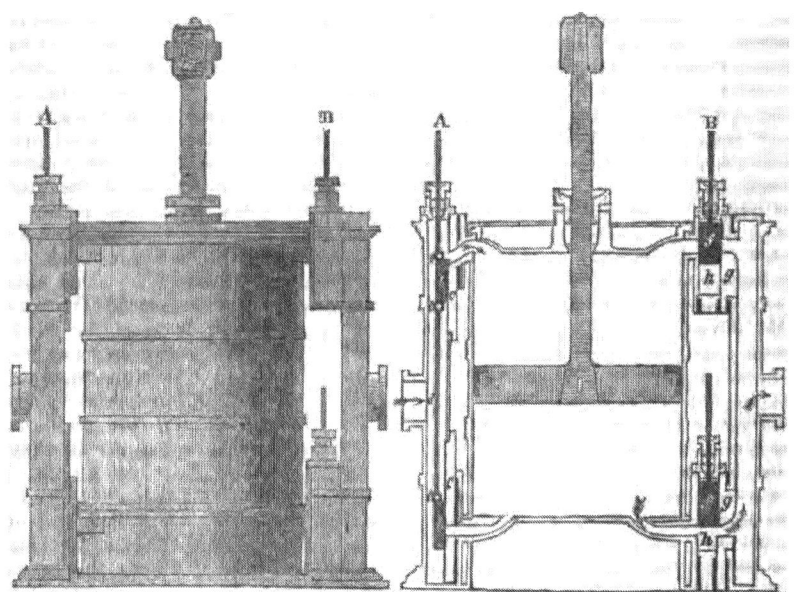

Sir,—I had just glanced at your 760th Number, when I received a note from a friend of mine, informing me that the leading article in it contained a description of Messrs. Seawards' patent slide valves; and as my friend believes I have some claim to priority in this invention, or at least of having anticipated Messrs. Seaward in pointing out the use and advantages of the scheme, I feel myself called on to say a few words regarding my claim, and Messrs. Seawards' patent, when the invention appears to be attended with such beneficial results in marine steam-engines.

In order to shew you what I claim as my invention, I beg to refer you to the accompanying drawing and specification, copied from one, made in 1832, by which I think it will be readily perceived that the engraving of Messrs. Seawards' patent slides would serve equally well to illustrate my plan without presenting any sensible difference in the respective arrangements of the several parts.

Having been taught by experience, that the many disadvantages which are enumerated in the article descriptive of Messrs. Seawards' patent steam-engine slide-valves are (particularly with large sea-going engines) fully verified in practice, I was led to devise several modes of obviating the difficulties complained of, and amongst them I invented the arrangement of nosles and slides shewn in my drawing in the *early part of the year* 1832. About this time I was engaged by the Dublin and London Steam Marine Company to furnish a design of a pair of large marine engines, for a vessel which the Company contemplated building. In this design I included my newly invented nosles, having first consulted the managing director of the company; and from the design thus prepared the drawing I now send you was copied.

As the responsibility for the due performance of these valves, being new, would have rested wholly with the company, and not with the contractors for the engines, it was proposed by the directors, that the opinion of some scientific engineer of acknowledged eminence should also be obtained on the subject, before the directors finally closed with the firm who were about to make the engines, and Mr. William Brunton was named as a gentleman whose opinion would be received with confidence by the directors. I proceeded shortly afterwards from Dublin to London for the purpose of waiting upon that gentleman with the drawings, and particularly to explain to him my views regarding the *double nosles and slide-valves.* I left the drawings with Mr. Brunton by his request, that he might have time to consider and report on the matter, and they were afterwards sent by Mr. Brunton to the care of Mr. W. I. Smith, the company's agent, 16 John-street, Crutched-friars, in a tin case (which I believe was unsealed,) to be forwarded to Dublin. Mr. Brunton reported favourably of my scheme for the double nosles and slides, and the engines would have been forthwith executed under my directions with them, had not the company at the moment, on an unexpected offer made a purchase of the "William Fawcett" steam vessel.

I have now before me a letter which I received from one of the directors of Dublin and London Steam Marine Company, *dated August* 27,1832, from which I extract the following:

"Messrs. ——— declined yesterday to come to a definite agreement regarding the new vessel, until furnished with specification, such as to enable them to judge as to the comparative expense between the engines for the new vessel, and those of the ———. I must therefore entreat your particular attention to the completion of the requisite specification of the great part of the engines with a description of the minor details, sufficient to guide their judgment as to expense. *I would not, if I was you, in the present stage of the business enter into particulars regarding the double nosles;* but in every thing else it would be desirable that you possessed them of our wishes to have a pair of engines of first-rate execution," &c.

I subsequently introduced my plan of nosles to the notice of Mr. Williams,

managing director of the City of Dublin Steam Packet Company, and left with him a moving diagram of the valves, shewing how they balanced each other, and the way in which they were actuated by one eccentric. Mr. Williams appeared to entertain the same favourable opinion regarding them as Mr. Richard Bourne had previously done. As I made no secret of the scheme, the diagram thus submitted might have been inspected by fifty persons for aught I know. I remember Mr. Williams making some proposition at the time, for applying my valves to two new cylinders which he contemplated putting in (I think) the "Leeds" steam vessel; but I was called to London on business about this time, and the subject again dropped. I thought no more of the matter until my attention was called to a pair of engines on board the "Emerald," at that time belonging to the Gravesend Diamond Company. I had occasion to go to Messrs. Seawards' works, and was met just as I was about entering the gateway by one of their foremen who knew me, and asked me if I had seen Mr. Seawards' new invented patent slide-valves? I said "No, I have not? I know nothing about them." "Well," said he, "will you come with me on board the 'Emerald' lying in the canal yonder, and look at them; the covers are off now, and you can see the inside of the nosles; we had some of the Lords of the Admiralty on board yesterday (he continued), and Mr. Ewart, and Mr. William Brunton, the civil engineer, who thinks there is nothing like them." Well, we got on board; I had a full view before me of the first practical example of my plan, both in principle and in detail; the latter of which, I confess, struck me as presenting a remarkable coincidence in mechanical design with my own. On returning to the works I briefly mentioned to Mr. Samuel Seaward that I had been upon the eve of applying precisely the same arrangement of valves to one or two pairs of marine engines, but I had not the least idea at the time that Mr. Seaward contemplated obtaining a patent for them, especially as these nosles had been publicly exhibited in action on the river, and the engines sold to the Diamond Company. Of course I can have no idea as to the period at which Messrs.

Seaward's attention began to be occupied with or when they invented that, which has brought forth such gratifying and highly interesting testimonials, as those given by the commander of H. M. steam vessel "Volcano," and Mr. John Sinclair, engineer of the Russian steam vessel "Naslednik;" but this I know, that the facts I have stated occurred at the period aforesaid, and attended with all the concomitant circumstances which I have described. But I entertained no more idea of patenting the thing than I should of patenting the double nozles of a Cornish expansive engine. In fact, after the subsidence of that enthusiasm with which most new projects are fostered by their authors, I began to look upon the arrangement as too complicated for marine purposes, and did not much regret the accidental circumstance which prevented their introduction in a pair of engines of such magnitude as those I had designed; for without being able to entertain any different opinion regarding the objections to the ordinary packed D slide-valves, particularly in very large engines, I was led to devise another description of valve of great simplicity in construction, requiring no hemp packing nor greater attention from the engineer than any other part of the engines require. These valves have lately been brought into operation in a pair of engines built by Messrs. John and Edward Hall, at the Dartford Iron Works, and now working on board the Humber Union Steam Company's new ship "Wilberforce." The cylinders of these engines are each of them 60 inches in diameter, with a stroke of 6 feet, and doing a duty of at least 300 horse power. So little friction attends the working of these valves, that one man can readily handle both engines, although the leverage power is only as 2 to 1, and the levers themselves little stronger than parlour fire-irons; notwithstanding which the valves are perfectly steam-tight. As some proof that they are so, I may mention, that the boilers by which these large engines are supplied with steam, are of no greater dimensions than the boilers in the steam-vessel "Vivid," belonging to the same company, and adapted for a pair of 90-horse engines only; yet the "Wilberforce" boilers maintain a steady and uniform pressure

of steam, keeping the pistons moving with a velocity of 360 feet per minute, and propelling the vessel when fully loaded at the rate of above twelve miles per hour through the water.

In conclusion, I beg to recapitulate the substance of the foregoing statement of facts, and to observe, that if called for, I can produce abundant testimony as to the pains I took to introduce the use of precisely the same description of actuating valves, which it appears Messrs. Seaward subsequently invented, and by the use of which, their marine engines have been so materially improved. I promulgated the plan of double nozles and slide-valves, arranged exactly as shewn in the drawing which was submitted to Mr. W. Brunton for his opinion in the early part of 1832.

I remain, Sir,

Yours, &c.

FRANCIS HUMPHREY.

Dartford, March 12, 1838.

Abstract from Specification. — "Each cylinder is to be provided with two nozles, one attached to the fore part of the cylinder, and the other to the after part, constructed in the following manner, that is to say:

"The nozle marked A in the elevation, is for the purpose of admitting the steam into the cylinder, and must be provided with *two flat cast iron sliding-valves b b*, 4 inches thick each, accurately fitted and ground upon the faces of two cast iron back plates c c, having apertures in them, of 4 inches by 24 inches, as shewn in drawing No. 2: the sliding-valves b b, are to be connected together by a rod of malleable iron d, with joints of steel, provided with steel pins, tempered and accurately fitted to the joints, cast on the sliding valves at e e, so that each valve may not only slide upon the surface of its respective back plate with accuracy, but that each valve may also be at liberty to move off the back plates by any internal and undue pressure accumulating within the cylinder.

"The nozle marked B in the elevation, is for the purpose of allowing the steam to escape from the cylinder into the condenser, and is likewise to be provided with two flat sliding-valves of cast iron f f, and two surface plates g g, fitted and ground together, precisely similar to the steam valves, but with this difference in their dimensions, namely, the valves f f, in the nozle B, must be planed or fitted by some other suitable means all over their surfaces, and so proportioned, that each valve will fit its respective box A A in thickness and in width, that there may be the least possible vacant space therein,* merely allowing a space of one-sixteenth part of an inch between the valve boxes and the valves, exclusive of the clear stroke of such valves; the plates *c c* attached to the steam nozle A, and the plates *g g*, attached to the outlet nozle B, are all to be cast of very hard close-grained iron, and each sliding valve is to be cast from metal prepared in the following manner."

DAVIES GILBERT'S HISTORY OF CORNWALL.

A county history is generally but another name for a mass of dullness and inanity. The compilers of such works generally make it a rule to pass over without notice any interesting circumstances which may happen to be connected with the places their voluminous labours refer to, in order to make room for the pedigrees at full length of the lords of the manor, with abstruse investigations as to their coats of arms, and a variety of other matters of equal importance to the world at large. How it ever came to be considered that such valueless trash as this ought to form the staple of a standard county history it might not be easy to conjecture; certain it is, however, that the notion has thriven to such an extent, that every topographical collection of any importance groans beneath the weight of a heap of "bulky tomes," so scrupulously constructed on the long pedigree and coat-of-arms system, that there are ninety-nine parts of such imponderable ponderosities to every *one* of real solid information. There are symptoms abroad which seem to indicate that the day of these abortions is going by; the sooner the better, since they only stand in the way of a superior class of works which may be expected to spring up and occupy their place as soon as they shall have quitted the scene.

From the venerable ex-president of the Royal Society we might reasonably anticipate a book of the latter rather than the former class, especially when his theme is his native county,* with whose mineral treasures he has a double connection, forming, as they have done, the basis of his fortune, and at the same time the subject of his scientific investigation. We are inclined to suspect that Mr. Gilbert has been unfortunate rather than otherwise in meeting with the MSS. of Hals and Tonkin, which form the groundwork of his history, notwithstanding he considers it a piece of singular good fortune. Certain it is that the additions made by the Editor form the most valuable portion of the whole. Hals and Tonkin, who wrote upwards of a century ago, although apparently far from the worst specimens of the county-historian genus (which has seen its palmiest days since their time), are yet too prone to enter at full length into long rambling legends of the history of saints and fabulous heroes, and similar aimless gossipry. All this Mr. Gilbert has greatly retrenched; but we cannot help thinking he would have done better to re-write the history altogether, making use of his predecessors' materials, so far as they were available, than as he has done, to begin each parish by quoting and abridging from them, and finish by filling up the canvas with his own composition. The trouble would probably not have been greater than that he has actually undergone, of which he bitterly complains; although, at the commencement, the task of writing anew four thick octavoes, might appear far more formidable than merely to edit the same quantity already written.

Had this plan been adopted, more attention would doubtless have been paid to a point in which the work is more deficient than could have been wished,—the history and description of the mining operations for which Cornwall is famous throughout the world. The form of the work is also a circumstance unfavourable to the introduction of these details; it proceeds parish by parish, so that no opportunity occurs

* By the bye, in this particular I observe there is a difference in Messrs. Seaward's arrangements and mine. Messrs. Seaward's, doubtless for some good and substantial reason, show a very considerable vacant space in each slide case, which must be filled with steam and emptied every stroke of the engine; this waste of steam I endeavoured to avoid, by proportioning the valves and boxes in the manner shewn in the drawing, and described above.

* The Parochial History of Cornwall, founded on the MS. Histories of Mr. Hals and Mr. Tonkin; with additions and various Appendices. By Davies Gilbert, some time President of the Royal Society, F.A.S., F.R.S.E., M.R.I.A., D.C.L., &c. In 4 volumes. London, 1838. Nichols and Son. 8vo. pp. 496, 582, 470, 571.

for giving a general view of the subject, and what information is afforded is necessarily split into unconnected fragments. It would surely have been worth while to have devoted a portion of one of the volumes especially to a topic of such paramount interest in a "History of Cornwall," as its mines and minerals. This, however, has not been done, but the immense hiatus which would have been left, if Hals and Tonkin had been servilely followed, is in a great measure filled up by an article on the "Geology" of each parish, for which the Editor acknowledges his obligations to his friend Dr. Boase, by whom the whole have been contributed. It is to be regretted that the Doctor has confined himself so strictly to the letter of his task, as to have favoured us with very few passing notices of mining operations, in addition to those of mining products. As it is, however, his portion of the work includes the fullest information it affords in that respect.

The following occurs in Dr. B.'s notice of the geology of St. Austell, generally considered the very centre of the mining district :—

"This parish (St. Austell) so important in an economical point of view, on account of its minal production, affords a vast fund of geological information. Its northern part is composed of granite; its southern part of various rocks belonging to the porphyritic group. Its granite, on the eastern side is like that of Alternun, and contains layers which abound in porphyritic crystals of felspar. On the western side it comprises several kinds of this rock, some characterized by the proportions of shorl that enter into their composition, and others by containing talc instead of mica, and by the felspar being prone to an extensive decay, in which state it furnishes porcelain clay (or china clay) for the potteries."—Vol. i. page 50.

"Carclaze tin mine must not be passed by, as it is one of the greatest curiosities in Cornwall. This mine is worked 'open to the day' (according to the miners' term), that is, like a quarry. It is of a considerable depth, and its superficies exceeds several acres in extent. It is excavated entirely in a white granite, somewhat similar to the disintegrating variety above alluded to; and when the sun shines, the reflection of light is so exceedingly dazzling as to be almost insupportable. The tin ore occurs here intermixed with shorl and quartz, in the form of short irregular veins, which traverse the granite in every direction, and so

abundant, that the whole rock requires to be pounded and washed to complete an entire separation of the ore."—Vol. i. page 48.

It is seldom that Dr. Boase ventures on so much description as in this instance; some of the parishes most noted for their mines are passed over with a very slight notice of their general geological features: the Doctor, indeed, probably expected that this would be made up for in the other divisions of the work. Of St. Austell, however, or its celebrated "stream-works," he favours us with a further sketch:—

"This parish has long been celebrated for its stream works, which are diluvial beds containing tin ore. They are generally found in deep valleys where rivulets flow, which are used in separating the tin ore, by its inferior specific gravity, from common stones or pebbles; hence the name of "stream works." The nature of these deposits varies according to the positions which they occupy between the sea and the granite; whence the stanniferous strata were derived.

"Pentewan stream work is one of the most interesting in the whole county. Its lowest bed consists of pebbles, gravel, and tin ore, and it rests on the solid rock. Immediately above this tin ground is a black stratum of vegetable remains, among which are stumps of trees, standing erect, with their roots penetrating downwards into the bed of gravel. This subterranean forest stands forty-eight feet above high-water mark; showing that there must have been a change in the relative sea-level. On this vegetable bed reposes a thick stratum of silt, intermixed with horns of deer, and with other relics of land animals, and also with detached pieces of timber. This silt is covered by a deep deposit of siliceous sand; and, lastly, over this lies another bed of silt like the preceding, which reaches to the surface."—Vol. i. page 50.

Taken altogether, this "History of Cornwall," notwithstanding its imperfections, will form a valuable addition to the topographical library, and Mr. Gilbert "deserves well of his *county*" for the spirit which, at the age, as he tells us, of threescore and ten, he has displayed in its production; the more especially that it appears he could not get it before the world except by making a paction with his publisher that the profits (if any) should be the publisher's, while the loss (a much greater certainty) should be borne by Mr. Gilbert!

ATLANTIC STEAM NAVIGATION.

(Abridged from the *Athenæum*.)

" *Steam Navigation to New York.*—The well-known steam-ship *Sirius*, Lieut. Roberts, R. N., Com., is intended to leave London for New York on Wednesday, the 28th of March, calling at Cork harbour, and to start from thence on Monday, the 2nd of April, returning from New York the 1st of May."—*Advertisement in the daily papers.*

There is really no mistake, then, in this long talked-of project of navigating the Atlantic Ocean by steam. The *Sirius*, being an already built, tried, and known boat, has succeeded in stealing a march on all her long-announced competitors, but it is only a start of *a few days,* which in a race, for the first time, over the Atlantic (much unlike a horse-race at Goodwood), is a trifle after all. She left this port on Wednesday of the current week ; and now the *Great Western* is roused at length. One may see her excited almost like a living thing. She heaves her huge whale-like sides with impatience. Her paddles instinctively dash into the water, as a war-horse, when he hears a trumpet, paws the ground. And see, how the fierce breath of a giant defiance pours out of her eager nostrils ! Look to it, *Sirius !*

In plain prose we mean to inform our readers that the Bristol Company, the owners of this fine boat, announce their intention of moving her from London *this day* (March 31st), round to her birthplace, and to start her thence for New York on Saturday next, April 7th. They remark, rather sharply, that " previously to her sailing, this ship will have made several trips to sea. She stows with ease sufficient coal for twenty-five days' steaming. It is unnecessary, therefore, to incur the delay of calling at Cork." Furthermore, the *Great Western* is " equipped for the sole purpose of maintaining a constant communication between England and New York." Again, " No letters will be taken, except upon payment at the rate of 1s. the single sheet, newspapers and slips 3d. each. Parcels in proportion to their size and weight, and a small quantity of light goods, at 5l. per ton. Specie and valuables a half per cent. It is intended the *Great Western* should start from New York on her return to Bristol (which port has been fixed upon as the best for a western departure and arrival, and at the same time a convenient distance from the metropolis) between the 1st and 7th of May. A surgeon of high qualifications is engaged, and a branch pilot for the Bristol Channel and Irish coast is attached to the ship," &c. &c.

For months the various papers of the town and country alike have been putting out rumours of preparations and experiments being made and tried at various points towards this grand result of establishing a regular steam communication between the two great commercial and closely-interested countries, which certainly would profit by it so much. We have endeavoured to reduce these various, vague, and often confused and contradictory statements to a summary view of the case, that may be relied on for what it does *not* assert as well as for what it does. It stands, if we understand it, pretty nearly as follows ; and we think it, as a matter of future interest, at least, enough to be put on record at the time.

The *Sirius*, then, which, though about the last introduced of the candidates for the approaching contest, seems the first to get off, is a boat belonging, we believe, to the St. George Steam Packet Company, and has therefore run, with a good reputation, between London and Cork. Though by no means an old vessel, perhaps only old enough to have been thoroughly t ied—she is, of course, not expressly built for the Atlantic route, being one of the elder and European *régime ;* her tonnage 700, with engines of 320-horse power. Her agent, we notice, is an old acquaintance of the public, Mr. Macgregor Laird. commander of the first iron-boat expedition which was fitted out to explore the interior of the African continent. Dr. Lardner—shall we say it ?—in that same memorable treatise, wherein he shows as clear as light—to all who don't think otherwise—that this project of navigating the Atlantic by steam, is, of necessity, and in plain facts and figures, the veriest humbug ever devised,—the Doctor doth so far forget himself as to say on another occasion, " Philosophy already directs her finger at sources of inexhaustible power in the phenomena of electricity and magnetism, and many causes combine to justify the expectation [*belief*] *that we are on the eve of mechanical discoveries still greater than any which have yet appeared ;* that the steam-engine itself, with the gigantic powers conferred on it by the immortal Watt, will dwindle into insignificance in comparison with the hidden powers of nature still to be revealed ; and that the day will come when that machine which is now extending the blessing of civilization to the remotest points of the globe, *will cease to exist except in the page of history !"* * * *

The *Great Western* was designed and built, and is owned wholly, we believe, at Bristol. This noble steamer has a burthen of 1,340. tons. How it compares with the class it belongs to, and with its spry little competitor before mentioned, may be judged by the least seaman-like reader we have, when we say, that, as far as we know, the largest steam-ship in her Majesty's navy, and that a new one, is the *Gorgon*, with a tonnage of 1150. The *Gorgon* is constructed to carry 20 days' coal, a crew of 150, and 1000 men besides, and stores for six months. Her engines are only of the same power with those of the *Sirius*. The largest American steam-ship we have heard of is the *Natchez*, now or lately on the stocks at New York, and intended to ply as a packet between that city and the southern port whose name she bears; her tonnage is 900. The *Wilberforce* and the *Victoria*, Hull packets, were considered to be at the head of the *old* order of boats; the former a little exceeding 200 feet in length, with paddle-wheels 24 feet in diameter, and engines second only to those used in the American scheme. There may be a farther comparison with the Bristol boat by stating that her length is about 240 feet; that each paddle-shaft, after turning, weighs 6½ tons, and the intermediate shaft 4½ tons, with diameters of 18½ and 17½ inches; that her cylinders are 73½ inches in diameter—the *Gorgon's* being 64 inches—and nearly rivalling the size of the hugest ever used in the most extensive operations of the Cornish mines; and she has four boilers, rated to weigh, with the water in them, 180 tons—bordering on a stowage-room capable of containing in iron boxes nearly 900 tons of coal; and that her two marine engines are stated to have a 225 horse-power each. To imagine, in a word, the appearance this vessel makes in the river among the myriad crafts which encircle her, one must conceive a large man-of-war of 80 guns, with the unwieldly protuberances we have mentioned at the sides, a steam apparatus of the total weight of 470 tons, a great black funnel, and volumes of smoke in due proportion; and withal, for the plan is amphibious, a complete sailing machinery—for emergencies of fair winds or accidents to machinery,—including four rather low masts, rigged somewhat in schooner style, and able to add considerably on occasion to the boat's speed. It appears that this ship is much the largest, on the whole, ever built. The fore-cabin is 46 feet long; an ample engine-room is left in the centre; and this separates the former from a state-cabin of 82 feet in length and 34 in extreme breadth, taken up, except in the centre, with berths (like the fore-cabin) at the sides, including, above and below, and fore and aft, 128 sleeping-places for one class of passengers, besides which there are 20 for servants. Of the very costly and elegant fittings-up of this grand saloon we can add nothing to the plentiful details furnished by the daily papers. Affixed to the frame-work of the engine is an index, by which the number of strokes performed by the machinery, and the rate of

their performance, is shewn with the greatest accuracy, and which, it is stated, without requiring to be again wound up, will mark as many strokes as suffice for the whole voyage to New York. * * * She is expected to make her passage out, under average circumstances, in fifteen days, and the return-voyage in twelve.

The cabin fare, we may mention, is 35 guineas out, and 30 returning, which includes bedding, provisions, and wines. This is the same as the fare of the Liners *out*. It is the same on board the *Sirius*, we see; but provision is made, by that boat, for a second class of passengers, in an inferior cabin, of the old *régime*, at twenty guineas; and for steerage passengers, like the Liners, at eight. The *Sirius* also expect to make her passage in fifteen days, from Cork.

But we are not yet done with the steamers. We promised to give a summary of all that is proposed by the various parties, and we have not yet named the greatest of all the lions by far,—we mean the *Victoria*, now on the stocks at Limehouse. This extraordinary ship is the project and property of the British and American Steam Navigation Company. Their plan, as first announced, was, to build a line, composed of two British and two American steam-ships, of great size each, as sufficient to keep up a communication twice a month to and from New York; the reason for uniting the two classes being, of course, that British ships, by treaty of commerce are not permitted to take foreign goods to the United States—they must be shipped in American bottoms; while, on the other hand, American ships are not permitted to bring foreign goods to England except for exportation only. By the union of both, all descriptions of goods are secured. These *four* were expected to make as many passages to and fro as *eight* sailing-packets would. More were to be added as required. The tonnage proposed was 1,200, and the horse power 300; and the ships were estimated to cost 40,000*l.* each. The annual expense of such a vessel was rated at 18,480*l.*, including fuel out and home for six voyages, or for 42,000 miles. This calculation, which we think worth preserving, is exclusive of the charges incident to freight. These, with the profit also on freight, are contingent. Set down this at 400 tons measurement goods, with certain prices, and 60, 80, and 100 passengers, of three different classes, and we have 4,600*l.* receipts on freight. The expenses on the same being rated at 2,520*l.*, the net freight out and home is made to amount to 3,880*l.*, or above 50 per cent. per annum on prime cost; or 30 per cent. with a net of 1,200*l.* and 800*l.* out and home. We subjoin, for reference, the following items of the annual expense of the floating establishment :—

Commander 200l.; first mate, 100l.; second mate, 80l. third mate, 60l.; surgeon, 100l.; twenty-five seamen and apprentices, 600l.; ten firemen, at 60s., 360l.; one engineer at 150l., one at 100l., and one at 80l., 330l.; one carpenter, 50l.; oil, tallow, and tow for engines, and other small stores, 1,000l.

The distance from London to New York is about 3,000 nautical, or 3,500 English miles; and the speed of the vessels is taken from an average of the Dundee and Perth ships, Dublin and Liverpool post-office packets, Clyde and Liverpool vessels, and Mediterranean packets: their averages giving a mean speed of ten statute miles per hour *in all weathers*. At this rate, the average passage will be from fourteen to fifteen days to New York; and, allowing for prevailing eastward and current winds, about eleven to twelve days home. The fuel is taken at the rate of 9lbs. per horse-power the hour. The quantity each vessel is supposed to take is for twenty days' consumption, or about 500 tons.

Such *was* the plan. On further reflection, it was so far altered, that the Company, increasing their capital from half a million to a whole one, at the same time concluded to concentrate their efforts, at present, on one grand ship, to be built in this port—and hence the origin of the *Victoria*. This mammoth craft is truly the naval curiosity of the age: her tonnage is stated at over 1,800, nearly 500 more than that of her Bristol rival. Her length on the water-line is 230 feet, the length of keel exceeding, we suppose, that of any existing man-of-war; extreme length, 253; 40 feet breadth of beam, and 27 feet depth of hold; whole breadth, including paddle-boxes, 69; displacement, 2740 tons; draught, when laden, 16 feet; cylinders, 78 inches diameter; paddle-wheel, 30 do.; with two engines of 250 horse-power each. The calculation is, that this vessel may take 500 passengers of various classes—which is mainly relied on for her chief business and support—together with 1000 tons of measurement goods, (which we consider rather a liberal scheme, considering that we have twenty-five days' fuel on board.) The cost of the *Victoria*, by the way is rated at 100,000l., which alone indicates sufficiently the power put into her. Her sailing apparatus is as unprecedented as her steam and her size; but all this is nothing, so long as *Victoria* sits at the gates of Limehouse, and the experiment remains untried. This ship will be afloat, we hear, in a few weeks, and ready for sea in the course of the summer. One of the boats talked of as meant for American commerce, is an iron one, launched lately at Birkenhead, 213 feet long, and divided below into six compartments on the

new plan. Another is the *Liverpool*, built by Sir John Tobin, of 1,040 tons measurement, with engines of 460 horse-power, rated to cost 48,000l.—rivalling the Bristol boat in some respects, and in her length, which is 240 feet, coming between her and the *Victoria*. We should here name also the *Columbus*, a small experimental boat, on the quicksilver plan, propelled by Howard's patent vapour engines, and announced to carry fifty days' fuel at the same immersion as a common steam-vessel, of equal power and tonnage, can carry twelve days' fuel. This modest candidate for the contest has been fitted up in this port—making, certainly, very little noise about it—and has already gone round, by stages, to Liverpool, trying herself on the way, with the view, it is now said, of going directly out to New York. The papers state, that she will attend one of the regular Liners.   *   *   *

Thus far England. We are permitted, active as Jonathan usually is, to establish the steam navigation—if we can—as we did that of the sailing-packets. That the Americans, unlike us, universally and implicitly believe in the practicability (we do not say the policy or present continuance) of this scheme—that they take the rival of the *Sirius* and her train, as a mere matter of course—nobody, who knows anything of their habits and notions on such subjects, can for a moment doubt. Nearly half a century ago, and twenty years before Fulton manufactured his first boats, Fitch, of Philadelphia,—who, by the way, preceded *him* in one sense, and who then made a boat that ran eight miles an hour on the Delaware,—*Fitch, in 1790, boldly predicted the future and early navigation of the Atlantic by steam.* This prophecy was in a well-known letter addressed to the astronomer Rittenhouse. He was called crazy, to be sure; but that also was a matter of course. The idea, still, was forced on the national mind, and doing and seeing what they have since, they could not but adopt it as they do. Among the rest,—let us not forget it, in our willingness to meet the opponents of the theory of this project, on their own ground—*they have seen this same thing done!* We have not lately observed any notice of the fact, but we take it to be well authenticated, *that a steam-ship arrived at Liverpool, in 1819, directly from the United States,* we believe from Savannah; and, that a boat was some years ago built in New Orleans, (*possibly* the same,) for the Emperor of Russia, and sent out to him. It is quite recently, if we mistake not, that the *Royal William* went out to Halifax—which point, Dr. Lardner allows, if we understand him rightly, is within the potential reach of a steam-ship starting from Valentia, at the western side of Ireland. * * * The practicability of steam will be established at once. Its speed and its certainty will induce interests, enough for its maintenance, to a greater or less extent, to support it. All correspondence will be conveyed by it; all mercantile travel, and some goods, Most passengers may be shy of it for a time—many for a long time (as some are of railroads still); accidents will happen, of course: still the scheme will go on to maturity. Of its influence on the other and far greater interests than yet alluded to, we cannot now speak. This is a theme not to be hastily treated. It is one, too, which may be deferred awhile. All eyes now are turned on the " *commencement* of the end." We may yet discuss, with improved data, the *end* of such a beginning.

NOTES AND NOTICES.

A Claimant to Dr. Arnott's Stove.—Sir,—Having read your pithy observations on Dr. Arnott's Thermometer Stove, &c., and his disinclination to take out a patent, inasmuch as he desires it to be widely known that the whole world may participate in the advantages it offers, allow me to observe, that Dr. Arnott ought to be just before is generous, for be it known to the Doctor that I hold a patent for burning combustible bodies for heating retorts in airtight chambers, kilns, ovens, &c. &c., admitting air by the ash pit to keep up any required or given heat; this being the principle of Dr. Arnott's Stove, I am surprised at his presuming to assume an invention not his own. My patent was taken out in the spring of 1833, and if the original drawings and specifications of this patent are of any service in your valuable work, you can have the loan of them at any time. By inserting this you will correct a misrepresentation, and do justice to an individual who wishes for nothing more than fair play. I am, Mr. Editor, your constant reader, J. I.—Kennington-lane, March 15, 1838.

[We shall be obliged to J. I. for an inspection of his specification and drawing.—ED. M. M.]

Dr. Franklin's Printing Press.—A lecture on self-education, was last week delivered at the London Mechanics' Institution, by Mr. Thatcher, of Boston, U. S., in the course of which, as might be supposed, allusions were made to that eminent countryman of the lecturer's, who may be called the great modern realization and model, practical and personal, of the philosophy of "making the most and best of one's self." After the lecture, we learned from Mr. Thatcher, that his researches after traces of Franklin's doing's in London have brought to light a relic, which few of our readers have either heard of or seen. The relic we refer to is the identical press which Franklin worked when with Mr. Watts, of Lincoln's Inn Fields. It is now the property of a member of the craft, and may be seen at Mr. Harrild's, Distaff-lane, Friday-street, who has also a complete, accurate, and well-authenticated pedigree of this precious machine. The tradition is still preserved among the trade, that when Franklin was here again in 1768, as the agent of Massachusetts, he visited his old master, who still continued the business at the same place, sought out the press, which was still doing duty too, called the workmen together, and gave them, over a good noggin of porter, an account of the article, and a few words of comment in " poor Richard's" usual manner, which made a great impression. It is no longer used; but, though clumsy and rough, does not differ so much from common presses as might be supposed,—it being now 110 years since the philosopher pulled at it himself. We may add, as a proper postscript to this reminiscence, Mr. Thatcher's statement, that a "*composing-stick*" of Franklin's was, within a year or two, sold by auction. It was authenticated clearly, and brought a high price.—*Athenæum.*

Steam Navigation in India.—The use of steam-vessels has been found by experience so well adapted to the navigation of the rivers of Hindostan, that the supply is, for the present at least, greatly inadequate to the demand. On a recent occasion, when the company announced the intended dispatch of a steamer up the Hoogly, the competition among the merchants for freighting her was so great, that it was seriously proposed to determine precedence by lottery, it being evident that only a small proportion could be accommodated! Strong representations have been sent home of the necessity for immediately placing a greatly-increased number of steamers on this service, and the greatest anxiety is evinced for the accomplishment of the object. The company have at length given orders that the experiment should be tried of building a steam-ship at Bombay, the expense of which, from the cheapness of labour and materials, is expected to be much less than that of a similar vessel built in England. Her machinery will be made by artificers sent for the purpose from home, and she is directed to be made on the model of the Berenice, who has proved herself, by the voyage out, to be one of the best steamers afloat.

"*Many a little makes a mickle*".—So important is the manufacture of that apparently insignificant article, the pin, that in some years, pins to the value of £20,000, or (at least) *three hundred million* in number, have been sent to the metropolis, from Gloucester alone, within the twelvemonth! Gloucestershire is still the chief seat of the trade, the largest pin factory in the world being that of Messrs. Tayler, and Co., near Stroud, where almost the whole of the requisite operations are performed by patent machinery.

India Rubber in the Army.—Caoutchouc is being daily applied to more and more useful purposes, abroad as well as at home. In the East Indies it has been put in requisition as a material, in lieu of leather, for the soldiers' belts and other accoutrements, an use for which it would seem particularly well adapted, as the article is to be had in abundance in India, it is probable that it will be found as preferable on the score of economy as in other, and even more essential respects.

Our engraver, Mr. W. C. Walker, has a vacancy for an apprentice. Cards of Address may be obtained from our publisher.

Mechanics' Magazine, Complete sets.—The proprietor of the Mechanics' Magazine has now effected the repurchase of the earlier portions of the stock of this journal from the parties who were possessed of the same in the right of his first publishers; and he is now able to supply several complete sets of the work. Price, twenty-seven volumes, half-cloth, £11 7s.

☞ *British and Foreign Patents taken out with economy and despatch; Specifications, Disclaimers, and Amendments, prepared or revised; Caveats entered; and generally every Branch of Patent Business promptly transacted. A complete list of Patents from the earliest period (15 Car. II. 1675,) to the present time may be examined. Fee 2s. 6d.; Clients, gratis.*

LONDON: Printed and Published for the Proprietor, by W. A. Robertson, at the Mechanics Magazine Office, No. 6, Peterborough-court between 135 and 136, Fleet-street.—Sold by A. & W. Galignani, Rue Vivienne, Paris.

Mechanics' Magazine,

MUSEUM, REGISTER, JOURNAL, AND GAZETTE

No. 766.]   SATURDAY, APRIL 14, 1838.   [Price 3*d.*

MESSRS. HERAPATH AND COX'S NEW PROCESS OF TANNING.

Fig. 1

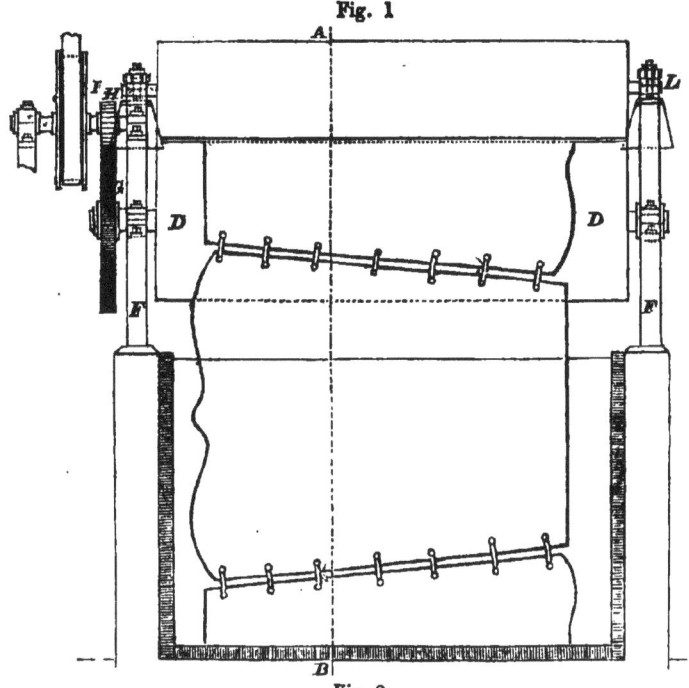

Fig. 2

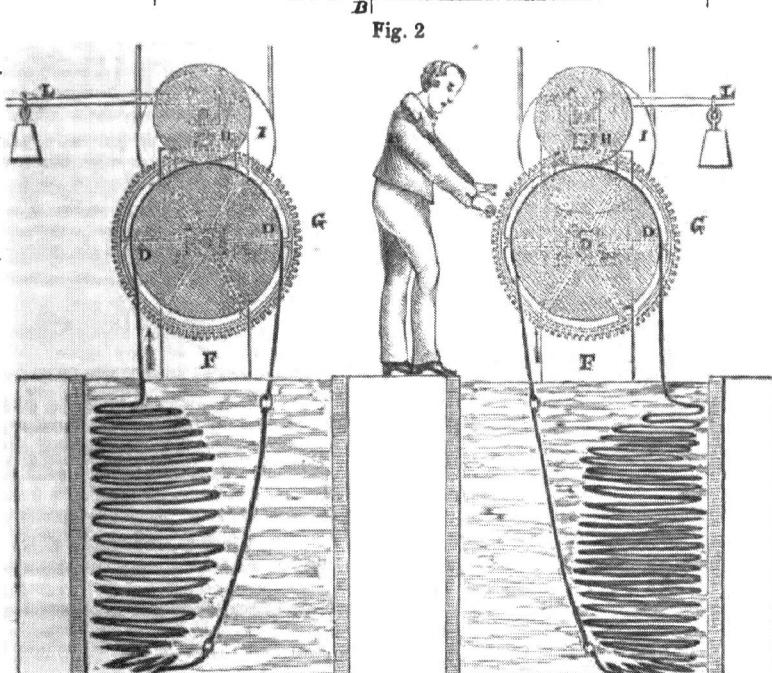

MESSRS. HERAPATH AND COX'S NEW PROCESS OF TANNING.

We have now the pleasure of laying before our readers, the first complete and authentic account yet published of this singularly valuable improvement in the art of tanning. Like most great inventions, it is of a very simple description —so simple, that, as usual, the wonder with most people will be, "how it should not have been found out long ago!" No trick of chemical magic is this—producing by some newly found out substance, or newly contrived combination of substances, a rapidity of transformation from the raw to the manufactured state, and an excellence of quality in the manufactured article, unheard of—unwitnessed before. It is simply a more judicious method of manipulation, by means of which the natural affinities of the tannin and gelatine for each other, are brought more quickly, fully and uninterruptedly into play, than by any of the processes heretofore in use. It is withal a method, the machinery requisite for which, is extremely cheap, easy of construction, and capable of universal application—to old tan pits as well as new. The general results are, that the hides and skins are converted into leather in one *fourth of the* time ordinarily required—that the tanner can of course derive from the same amount of capital embarked in his business four times his former profit, or a like profit from one-fourth the capital—that the leather in point of resistance to moisture, (the grand criterion) is better than the best leathers hitherto known in the market, in the proportion, of at least *ten to one*—and that the weight of leather produced from any given weight of hides or skins is so much greater than usual (owing to there being less waste of the constituent elements, tannin and gelatine)—that the increase is of itself nearly sufficient to defray all the cost of the new process. We would willingly dwell on the philosophy of the system by which such immense practical benefits have been realized—for it is, after all, to philosophy alone, or more properly speaking, to theory applied to practice, that we are indebted for this new process, which leaves all other processes so far behind it; but this we leave to Mr. Herapath himself (Mr. *William* He-

rapath) who in his reply to Mr. Chaplin, inserted in another part of this day's Magazine, has accounted most clearly and satisfactorily for the great superiority of the new method over all others.

After the butts have undergone the usual preparatory processes, such as unhairing, rounding, fleshing, and graining, the patentees take as many as a pit will conveniently hold, the number varying according to the size of the pit, and attach them to one another by means of ligatures of strong twine or some other suitable material, either endwise or sidewise, taking care in the former case to join the hides butt to butt and shoulder to shoulder, and in the latter to join the butt side of each hide to the shoulder side of that next to it, so that the band formed may be as nearly straight and even as the shape of the butts will allow. They then connect the said band of butts with a system of rollers such as represented in figures, 1 and 2. Figure 1 as a front view with the side of the tan-pit removed for the sake of greater clearness, and fig. 2 a transverse section of the same through the line A B of fig. 1. D D is a roller of wood supported by standards F F, which roller stretches across the top of the pit containing the tanning liquid. To one end of the axis of this roller there is affixed a cog wheel G, into which the pinion H on the shaft of the speed I is geared, which pinion is connected by a drum and strap in the usual way with a steam-engine or other moving power. The standards F F support also at top two weighted levers L L, from which levers there is suspended a second roller E of smaller dimensions than D; by adjusting the weights on which levers according to the degree of pressure required, the roller E is made to press with more or less force on the under roller D, and to derive a rotary motion therefrom. The patentees state, that they find the proportion of ten to six, a convenient one between the two rollers, but that they do not confine themselves to that or any other rate of proportion. One end of the band of butts being brought over the under roller D, is fastened to the last of the butts, at the other end of the series, by ligatures in like manner as before directed, so as to form of the whole one endless band or belt. A rotary motion being now communicated to the under roller D from the cog wheel and pinion G and H, the endless band of butts is made to revolve, and as each butt rises from the pit, and passes between the rollers D and E the partially or wholly exhausted liquor is pressed or squeezed out of it by the weighted roller, so that it descends again into the pit with its pores open for the reception of a fresh supply of tanning liquor. A boy attends to the endless band as it emerges from the pit (as shewn in fig 2,) to lay each butt smooth and even upon the under roller D; and it is found in practice that one boy can readily attend to two adjoining pits and pairs of rollers at a time. The pits the patentees have hitherto used are of the ordinary size and form, but they recommend that they should be made at bottom of a semi-cylindrical form, to allow of the endless band of butts turning round with greater ease.

MESSRS. HERAPATH AND COX'S NEW TANNING PROCESS—REPLY OF MR. HERAPATH TO MR. CHAPLIN.

Sir,—I assure Mr. Chaplin (p. 353) that I have no wish to establish my patent upon the ruin or injury of any other. I am so frequently appealed to in cases of manufactural difficulties, and have seen such vast sums thrown away from a want of chemical first principles, that I am sometimes induced to give an opinion before it is asked; for doing so in this instance, I have to apologize, as Mr. Chaplin must be the best judge of his own affairs, and my only anxiety will be to explain those parts of my communication which have been thought inconsistent.

A solution for tanning upon entering the pores of the skin, is quickly deprived of its tanning and extractive matter, but the exhausted fluid remains within the tubes of a wet hide for weeks or months, being only slowly removed by the principle of exosmosis, or partially so by the operation of " handling." The desideratum of tanners has long been to find a *cheap* and *quick* method of getting rid of this exhausted ooze, and replacing it with a stronger solution. There is no difficulty in filling these tubes when the hide has been *dried*, because then it is effected by capillary attraction. Mr. Chaplin will see then that it is possible that tanning liquor passing through a hide may tan the sides of the tubes through which it passes to the other surface and may *fill for once* the arteries and veins through which there is no current; but as the liquid cannot be renewed in the latter, the exhausted ooze remains in them until the apparently tanned hide is dry; when upon being introduced into water, the veins and arteries being untanned are immediately filled with water, and the leather is *pervious*. There is therefore no inconsistency in my statement. The eye is not a sufficient judge of the completion of the tanning process where part of the pores only have been tanned, because the distances between the tanned and untanned pores are only microscopic.

Mr. Chaplin states that the white slimy substance which oozes through the skin cannot be gelatine, because it tastes bitter and precipitates gelatine, and kindly offers me a means of satisfying myself that it is only tannin. I feel obliged, but have already analysed a portion of the white matter from a sample of the leather, and found it to be a compound of tannin, gelatine, and lime, and if that gentleman will make two more simple experiments, he will satisfy himself that I am right. First let him heat a bit on platinum foil or a glass plate; it will melt, then char, and will give off the well known smell of *burning animal matter*, which would not be produced were it only tannin, and he will find the ashes to be lime, which he may prove by a bit of moistened turmeric paper.

If the increased weight of my leather was owing to artificial or extraneous additions, it would be dishonest to take advantage of the ignorant trader by selling it as leather; but it is not so: I retain the gelatine in the hide by preventing its being dissolved in the oozes; I tan the retained gelatine by giving it its due proportion of tannin and extractive, and thus increase the real matter of the leather, and consequently its durability, and its impermeability to water. It may be said that the shoemaker will lose by paying a halfpenny a pair more for his soles, but he will have more profits from customers who will have found the benefits of dry feet, and the economy of wearing shoes which have not required constant mending.

I perfectly agree that weight alone is not a sufficient test of the value of leather, nor have I advanced such an idea—the sentence ran thus : " I will engage to use his *own liquors*, whether from bark, valonia, divi divi, or terra japonica, and to return him 3 lb. per hide more than he can make by the ordinary mode."

Mr. Chaplin has misunderstood me when he believes me to object to the system of transfusion, merely because it was a " quick process." If the sentence is read as a whole, beginning after the word " weight," it will be seen that other circumstances besides quickness are given as reasons for the deficiency of weight and the permeability of leather tanned by transfusion.

In the course of a few days my specification will be enrolled, when the public will decide whether the new plan be or not a simple and philosophical means of surmounting the difficulties which the tanner has hitherto experienced. In the mean time I invite examination and trial of the few samples sent into the London market (which have been deficient in colour, however, not as a necessary consequence of the process, but from the difficulties attendant upon first experiments) and shall feel pleasure in answering any objections which may be urged with the urbanity and intelligence displayed by my present opponent.

Yours, &c.

WILLIAM HERAPATH.

Bristol, March 1, 1838.

THE CONTROVERSY BETWEEN NAU-
TILUS, O. N., &c.

Sir,—I have sometimes been inclined to think that your able mathematical correspondent, O. N., in his first lucubrations in the *Mechanics' Magazine* was acting the character of the " Dougal creature" in Sir Walter Scott's historical novel of " Rob Roy ;" and I am pretty sure Nautilus has by this time discovered that he very much underrated his scientific attainments when he reproved Kinclaven for condescending to notice some of his first essays in the

Mechanics' Magazine. But be that as it may, my present purpose is to make some remarks on Nautilus' last, and I must also say very intemperate, letter (763) inserted in your minor correspondence In the first place I must inform Nautilus, that at the time I wrote my last letter (761) I had not seen his (758) and I will also farther inform him, that even if I had seen it I certainly would have taken no notice of it. The task I was called upon to perform was to answer a question put to me by O. N. (755). namely, "whether he, O. N., had mistaken my meaning in the answer he gave to my question" (743), which was " why the perpendicular P N must fall upon D Z′ produced, the latitude of the places of observation being 55 . . 58 N." The answer O. N. gave to this question was, " if the perpendicular P N did not fall upon D Z′ produced, then by a very simple calculation it might be shown that the zenith distance of Procyon would be greater than 90° &c." This was a simple and proper answer ; in fact it was the only true answer that could be given to my question. And further, in justice to O. N. I must also state that the answer he gave to my second question which he deduced from the principles he so ably demonstrated in his letter (732) was equally judicious, and I trust, Mr. Editor, you will believe me, when I say, that had O. N. given an improper answer to either of my questions I would have lost no time in telling him so. But right or wrong Nautilus appears to have been determined to find O. N. in error, on my first question. Accordingly, in No. 751, he makes the following most illiberal remarks :—

" O. N. has made another unfortunate slip, when he says in answer to Iver McIver's question of ' why the perpendicular P N must fall upon D Z′ produced,' that if it did not, the zenith distance of Procyon would be greater than 90°."

This was the passage that O. N. called on me for my opinion upon (755) and this I gave ; and I can with truth aver, in the most impartial way I could devise (761). Nautilus in continuation says, " now a slight consideration of the particulars before given will show that from *a* to *b* the perpendicular P N must fall inside of the triangle, and not upon D Z′ produced, and yet that the zenith distance of Procyon is less than 90° since it has already risen. It is not till after *b* that it becomes necessary to produce D Z' ".

No one can be so dull, as not to see at once that the latter part of the above quoted observations, as well as the first, was intended for the direct purpose of proving that O. N. was in error in the answer he gave to my question, and I must say, that a more disengenuous mode of going to work I have never seen (and I hope I shall never see again,) used by any of the scientific writers in the *Mechanics' Magazine*. Now what is the truth? Why simply this, that all these observations of Nautilus only hold true within the limits of the two latitudes 57..59.10 N, and 57..22..32 N. Now in O. N.'s solution of his own question, the lat. of the place was not within these limits, as it happened to be 55..58 N. So that Nautilus in his vain attempts to prove that O. N. was in error has been under the sad necessity of contradicting himself. This is really too bad.

Had Nautilus attended to the general principles demonstrated by O. N. (732), he would have discovered that all the information which he fancies he has given us (751), are only simple deductions, which necessarily follow from O. N.'s premises; the only thing new that I can discover, is in giving the lesser latitude 57..22..32, and this is found at once by calculating P Z on the supposition that D Z' is 90°.

But in the teeth of all this, Nautilus, in his last letter, now pretends to say, "that in the latitude of Edinburgh he had never denied that the perpendicular P N must fall upon D Z' produced," and this information he gave a week previously to the date of my last letter. Well, suppose I should be inclined to admit this (which I do not) to be true, then I would insist upon Nautilus telling us what slips O N in reference to my question had really made, and this Nautilus might have found would have been only leaping out of the frying pan into the fire.

In making the above remarks, Mr. Editor, I have been obliged to associate O. N. with myself, for this plain reason, that had he been wrong I must have been so too. O. N., I see from his last letter (761), intends to reply to that of Nautilus (758); he may do so, although I should imagine that both gentlemen

have already nearly exhausted all the information they can give us on that subject.

I am, Mr. Editor, yours, &c.
IVER McIVER.

PATENT WARMING-PAN.

Sir,—Some time ago, Col. Maceroni in one of his ordinary *de omnibus rebus* communications, mentioned that in 1814 he had caused to be made by an ironmonger in Bishopgate-street, a warming-pan, which was to be heated by containing hot water. One would have thought that this would have been the natural gradation from the more primitive plan of warming a bed with a bottle of boiling water: but not so, the simplest plans, sometimes leading to the *grandest* results, are often overlooked. This was evidently the case with our forefathers in the instance now under consideration; they skipped from the hot-water bottle to the burning-coal pan, leaving the honour of the invention of the hot-water warming-pan to the present enlightened generation.

Col. M. does not appear to have been aware that the invention which he thought of so little importance as to throw out as a mere hint for the benefit of a thankless public, had been the subject of a patent. Such, however, is the fact; for, be it known, that on the 24th of May 1834, his late Majesty's royal letters patent were granted to Stephen Hawkins, of Milton House, in the county of Hampshire, gentleman, for "certain improvements in warming-pans or apparatus for warming beds and other purposes." It should be observed that this grand discovery was made by a *gentleman*, enjoying probably the *otium cum dignitate*, warm in the pursuit of science, ardent in his researches into the economy of nature. It is most likely the invention was the result of much study, and that it was not a mere discovery, fallen upon by chance. Mr. Hawkins, is therefore, deserving of the greater honour. From the specification enrolled in his Majesty's High Court of Chancery, pursuant to the proviso in the patent, I have taken the following particulars of this invention. The patentee proposes that a pan should be made of copper or other suitable metal, and which he represents in an accompanying drawing as of an oblong form instead of the ordinary circular shape, for reasons no doubt most cogent, and which the scientific world is a loser by his not having stated; the handle is to be of wood, screwed into a stem fixed to the pan. The hot water is to be poured into the pan by a hole, which is to be closed with a screw. Colonel Maceroni uses a cork for this purpose.

Wishing you, Mr. Editor, and your readers the luxury of a warm bed in winter,

I remain, &c.

PAN.

Bedford.

SIR SAMUEL MORLAND'S SPEAKING TRUMPET.

Sir,—In the 764th number of your Magazine, you were obliging enough to notice a little pamphlet of mine containing a life of Sir Samuel Morland: I send you a description of one of his speaking trumpets in Trinity College library thinking it may prove interesting to some of your readers.

It consists of a large hollow copper trumpet six feet long, the diameter of the lesser end being 1¼ inches, and the diameter of the larger end 1 foot 3 inches. It is unfortunately much bent at the larger end.

If any one have the curiosity to inspect this trumpet, which is perhaps the only original one now *in esse*, I would advise him not to try its effect in *magnifying* the voice: on me it had quite a contrary effect, for my mouth was instantly filled with dust, and I was hoarse for some time afterwards. As far, however, as " carrying" the voice is concerned it succeeds excellently, for it carried mine quite away.

Your obedient servant,

H.

Cambridge. April 3.

MACERONI'S WATER-PROOF COMPOSITION—MILL BELTS—LEATHER HOSE, &c.

Sir,—Few persons can better appreciate the value of water-tight boots than myself, and I believe I have tried most of the plans that have at different times been suggested for giving them this essential quality. The last method I

have resorted to, is that recommended by Col. Maceroni at page 299 of your last volume, which I have no hesitation in saying is the very best I have met with, and I take this opportunity of returning thanks for the information. I happen to know, that many other persons have availed themselves of the publication of this simple but valuable recipe. I have not attempted to meddle with the "*wax polish*," and find that some of those who have tried it have not been successful. The plan I follow in applying this, or any similar composition, is first, thoroughly to clean the boots, to black and polish them as highly as possible and then lay on the composition as directed. By this means a good black colour is insured from the first, and in the course of a blacking or two afterwards, the boots will carry a pretty good polish.

There is one caution necessary to be given, which is, not to apply the tallow and rosin dressing to *tight boots;* for in consequence of the powerful friction-making properties of the rosin, it is next to impossible to get boots that are in any way tight, off or on, after being prepared with this composition. The adhesion occasioned, is such as to set patience, perseverance, and boot-powder at utter defiance. There are some situations where a knowledge of this property may be turned to good account—the belting of mills for instance. There is a valuable and interesting paper on this subject in your last number, in which the writer, Mr. I. H. Beard, recommends that the belts should be stuffed with bees-wax and tallow. The tallow and rosin will be found infinitely superior for this purpose; for besides the preserving properties of this preparation, the firm hold upon the drums given to the belts, will permit them to be so slack as to run very free and easy, and yet most effectually prevent slipping. As a dressing for leather previous to making up into engine-hose, &c., Col. Maceroni's composition is preferable to all others. It is a common practice to prepare such leather by well oiling it; the oil lies in the pores of the leather, whence it is is driven out the very first time the hose used under pressure, forming a scum on the outer surface. The composition, when cold, forming a tenacious substance, gives a greater body to the leather, fills up more effectually and durably the minute interstices of the skin, and renders it water-tight from the first.

Two months is, perhaps, an early period, to give any decided opinion as as to the *preservative* effects of this composition when applied to leather; but the present appearances, together with my previous knowledge of the subject, leave no doubt in my mind of the correctness of Col. Maceroni's statements respecting it.

I remain, Sir,
Your's respectfully,
WM. BADDELEY.

London, April 4, 1838.

INVENTION OF THE CAMERA OBSCURA.

Sir,—The camera obscura is now so well known, but still considered so curious and amusing, that some account of its early introduction may perhaps not be uninteresting. The invention of it has been claimed by two or three persons; it was ascribed by Vasari, to Leon Baptista Alberti, a celebrated architect of the 15th century, but there are the strongest grounds for attributing it to John Baptista Porta, who was born A.D. 1445, and was a Neapolitan; since he gives a very minute detail of it in his book entitled, " *Magia naturalis, sive de miraculis rerum naturalium, libri* 20. *Jo. Baptista Porta auctore*"—Speaking of the various effects of concave glasses he says—" Before I have done speaking about the operations of this glass, I will tell you a use of it, which is very amusing and ingenious, and by which we may observe many curious natural phenomena; it is—to see all things in the dark that are done outside in the sun, in their true colours. First, the room must be thoroughly darkened by closing up all the windows and crevices for if there be any light in the apartment, the effect of the experiment will be entirely spoiled. Make a hole, the breath and length of a person's hand; above this, place a little leaden or brass table and cover it with a thin coating of glue; make a round hole in the middle of it the size of a finger; opposite this let there be a wall of white paper or white linen, and by this means you will see all that is done

outside in the sun, those that walk in the streets like your antipodes; whatever is on the right will be seen on the left; all things will have changed their direction, and the further they are from the hole, the larger will they appear. If you bring your paper or white table nearer, they will look smaller, and more distinct, but you must wait a little, for strong similitudes sometimes cause affections in the sense, which are often so great that they trouble the organs not only while the senses are acting but after they have ceased acting. For instance, if we walk in the sun, and then suddenly go into the shade, the sensation continues, so that we can hardly see, because the affection made by the light is still in our eyes, and when that is gone, we are then able to see clearly in shadowy places. I now mention what I have hitherto concealed, and what I had some thoughts of never revealing—if you put a small centicular crystal glass to the hole, you will perceive all the figures much clearer, the countenances of people walking, &c."

The description here quoted is certainly sufficient to establish Porta's claim to the invention, since it appears that he speaks as if he had not the least idea of its being ever attempted before, and reveals it as something not previously known. It is very probable that the part of Leon Alberti's book on architecture referred to by Vasari, alludes only to an instrument for reducing drawings or views to smaller sizes, in their proper colours. Porta's description, however, is so exceedingly exact, that it is impossible to mistake the instrument he means, which answers precisely to the camera obscura now in use, having been materially improved by Gravesande, the Dutch philosopher.

Your's, &c.
J. C. W.

MESSRS. SEAWARD'S PATENT SLIDE VALVES.

Sir,—In your last number, for April 7th, I observe that Mr. Francis Humphrey lays claim to a priority of invention for the slide valves, which I have patented and used successfully these four years, without ever having had my claim for a moment disputed: he says that in the year 1832 he made a drawing which was shewn to one or two individuals, and then put into a tin case (which he believes was unsealed); and that a moving diagram was exhibited which might have been inspected by fifty persons for aught he knows.

I should not have deemed it necessary to take notice of the claim put forth by this gentleman as being also the inventor of these valves, had it not been for the inference intended to be drawn, from the tenour of his observations, regarding the originality of my idea; as well as for some misstatements which require refutation.

I believe, Mr. Editor, that nothing is now more common, directly an inventor has brought his views into successful practice, than for other persons to spring up and claim to have imagined and invented the whole before; although they have never either published or applied the invention,

As regards the observations made in reference to the "Emerald's" engines, my foreman states that he never accompanied or asked Mr. Humphrey to go on board the "Emerald" at all: and what he states about the Lords of the Admiralty, Mr. Ewart, and Mr. Brunton, must exist in his own imagination only, as at the time he speaks of, none of those gentlemen had ever been on board that vessel.

As to the conversation he alleges to have had with me, I unequivocally deny that I ever had any conversation with him upon the subject of these valves; and I further declare that nine months previous to the time he mentions having viewed the "Emerald's" engines, I had applied for the patent, and it had been then sealed for some time: and I must also observe, that the drawings of a set of slides from which those of the "Emerald's" engines were afterwards made, were prepared by me in the year 1831.

I have also by me a full description of this plan of arranging the working valves of steam-engines in my journal dated May, 1830: so much for Mr. H's originality.

I think it a little extraordinary that this gentleman should have waited till the present day to put forth his claim, when, according to his own showing, he has known of my successful application of the valves for so long a period; particularly after his "enthusiasm for the

invention had somewhat subsided, and he had been lead to devise the other valves of great simplicity, used on board the 'Wilberforce'."

In conclusion, Mr. Editor, I have only to remark that at the time I first entertained the idea of using slides in the way I have patented, I had never even heard of Mr. Humphrey, nor until this claim made by him, had I ever seen or heard of any arrangment of valves like them; either of his invention, or that of any other person whatever,;—the idea first originated with me when in Cornwall, twelve years ago, while fixing a 90 inch pumping engine for the late Mr. Woolf at the Weelalfred mine: where I had abundant opportunity of observing the great expence of manufacturing, as well as the difficulty of keeping tight the double beat lifting valves, used with that description of engine: had I remained in the county I should certainly have had these slide valves then tried upon that sort of engine, if I could have got an opportunity:—however, I am happy to say they are now likely to be applied there, as I have recently sent drawings and descriptions of them to an engine manufacturer in the county, who contemplates using them.

I am, Sir,
Your obedient servant,
SAMUEL SEAWARD.
Canal Iron Works, Limehouse.
April 11th, 1838.

PREMIUM OF TEN POUNDS FOR A MACHINE FOR WASHING AND MEASURING WINE BOTTLES.

We are authorised to offer a premium of Ten Pounds for the best design for a machine for the washing and measuring of wine bottles; the power to be used, either steam on a small scale, or horse. The great objection to the machines in common use are, that the *bristles* which are always employed do not clean *port wine crusted* bottles. It is required that the machine entitled to the premium should perfectly clean old crusted port wine bottles. The parties who offer the premium, have heard that there was a machine invented by a person in London, by which this desideratum was completely effected, and the bottles filled by their own weight. Designs to be sent free of expense to the Editor of the *Mechanics' Magazine*, on or before the 14th of May, shortly after which the premium will be awarded.

———

EXPERIMENTS ON THE STRENGH OF CAST-IRON BEAMS. BY JOHN U. RASTRICK, ESQ., C. E.

[Extracted from Report by Mr. Rastrick, to the Architects employed to examine the construction of Buckingham Palace.]

On my arrival in town, I found that the method of putting the cast-iron beams in the floors to a satisfactory proof, had particularly engaged your attention, and that it had been proposed to effect such proof by loading a carriage with a sufficient weight, and running it leisurely over the centre of each floor at right angles, to the beams; and if the floors stood this proof without failure, or any indication of weakness, it might be concluded they were perfectly secure.

On discussing this point, we were soon aware this could not be so easily effected; in the first place, it would have been necessary to have had a carriage constructed on purpose, capable of carrying twenty tons; and this weight, to produce the desired proof, must all have been concentrated in a small compass; and as the wheels of the carriage would have broken in the boarding of the floors, unless strong beams had been laid to have run the wheels upon, which beams would have taken a bearing upon not less than three cast-iron beams, it would have become necessary to have increased the weight in proportion, which would have been quite impracticable; add to which, as the weight would have been brought nearly all at once upon the beam, it would, if defective, have given way instantly, and, even with strong framing constructed under the floor, any sudden fracture might have been attended with the most serious consequences. Several other methods had also been proposed, as loading the floors with an accumulating weight of materials, such as sand, bricks, &c.; but by these methods we could not have so well decided upon the nature and quality of the castings, as it would have been difficult to have discovered what the deflection was, and it was at all events desirable that we should prove some of the beams to determine this point.

After further consultation, it was ultimately agreed, that the most effectual proof would be, to place the weight necessary for the proof in a scale, suspended from the centre of the beam to be proved, guarding the agents and workmen employed below during the proof from any risk, by having substantial wood frames covered by strong planks set up on the floor below; this method of proof had this further advantage, that as the weight would be put on gradually, it would give us the opportunity of ascertaining the deflection of the beam at any stage of the proof; should there be any appearance of failure, we could stop short, and even should the beam give way suddenly, the scale being hung within an inch of the wood wedges resting on the floor, no damage would ensue.

Having given orders for the iron-work for the scale (which was executed by Mr. Bramah, in the most satisfactory manner), while the carpenters were preparing the timber-work, I took the opportunity of examining some of the cast-iron beams, and, having discovered some defective ones in the ground-floor, of the bow room, I selected them for trial; but as the floor was laid over these beams, and they were arched between with brick coombs, it would have been impossible to have made any satisfactory proof of any one beam under these circumstances; having, therefore, applied and obtained your authority, I ordered so much of the floor to be taken up, and three of the coombings to be removed, as to set the beams completely at liberty.

The weights that were put on the scale were pigs of lead; I had them numbered from No. 1, upwards; they were accurately weighed, and the number and weight marked on each; the weight of the scale and iron-work complete, was found to be exactly one ton; a table was formed by adding the weight of the pig, No. 1, to the weight of the scale, and the weight of every other pig was added successively thereto; and as the weights were placed in the scale according to their numbers, this table gave us the total weight on the beam without further calculation, as every pig was put in the scale.

At a distance of ten or twelve feet on each side from the centre of the beam, was fixed an upright or standard, between which was stretched a fine silken line, at right angles to and over the centre of the beam; a diagonal scale of inches, divided into hundredths, was fixed to the beam itself, and adjusted to correspond with an even inch with the silken line.

I shall here state the data from which I determined the weight that this beam in question, or any other, should be proved to.

In trying experiments on cast-iron, I have found that bars one inch square and twelve inches long, supported at each end, and weighted in the middle, have taken from 2,180 to 2,600 pounds to break them, according to the quality of the iron, and some bars much more. In making such small castings as these experimented upon, you can always ensure a pretty sound casting; whereas, in making large castings, you cannot depend on its being perfectly sound throughout; neither is the iron itself so strong, the grain being generally larger and coarser.

It has therefore always been my practice, as a general average of cast-iron, to take one ton as my datum for the weight that will break a bar one inches square and one foot long, supported and weighted as above, exclusive of the effect of the weight of the bar itself in producing the fracture.

Now, although it would have been more scientific to have taken a higher number or greater weight as a datum, and considered the weight of the beam itself as a part of the weight with which it was loaded, yet this condition would have involved two considerations; for it would always have been necessary to have found the weight of the beam itself, and subtracted that portion of its weight which contributed to its load, from the calculated weight which would produce fracture before the precise weight to be applied could be determined. I therefore chose the lower number, or less weight, as we practical men wish to arrive at our conclusions with the least trouble, and by the shortest rules.

I have, however, had such extensive practice in the use of cast-iron, and had so many opportunities of breaking cast-iron beams of all sizes, from a load of one ton to twenty, that I now place the most implicit confidence in my data, having found them, on large beams in general, true to less than the twentieth of the calculated weight; and more frequently the calculation has overrated the weight that produced fracture, than come under it.

It has also been my practice, as it is of every prudent and experienced engineer, never to expose a cast-iron beam, under any circumstances, to more than one-sixth of the weight that would break it; and, from calculations I have occasionally made, on castings made by other engineers, I find it accords very nearly with their general practice.

With this object in view, and to ensure security, I always prove every casting to double the weight that I intend there should ever come upon it; for I wish it to be distinctly understood, that I consider no casting safe till it has undergone a satisfactory proof; for a casting shall appear perfect and sound on the surface, yet air-holes and such like imperfections may be within,

and nothing but a severe proof can detect them.

Having calculated the weight applied at the centre that will break the beam or casting to be proved, I take one-third, of that weight, and apply it to the centre of the beam, and while this weight is upon it, I have the beam forcibly struck all over its upper edge with a sledge-hammer, and afterwards all over its flat side with moderate blows by the same hammer. Previous to applying the weight, we strike a chalk line upon the beam, and after the weight has been applied, and the beam well hammered, we apply the chalk like again, and find what deflection has been produced by the weight. The weight is then suffered to remain upon the beam for a short time, and if the deflection does not increase, the weight is removed, and the chalk line applied again, and then, if the beam has recovered its deflection, we conclude it is perfect enough for the intended purpose, and it is accordingly sent off to its destination.

Should the beam, however, have not recovered its deflection, we conclude it has some imperfections; and it is again put to a more severe trial by hammering with the same weight upon it; and if the deflection does not increase, the beam is passed, but if the deflection does increase, the proof is continued, by adding more weight, and well hammering, till it gives way; and I seldom remember an instance of a beam giving way under such circumstances that did not turn out to have a material defect in it.

With regard to the weight of the hammer with which the beam is struck, it has been in general discretionary; but the workmen who have made the proof for me have never been very nice about it, always taking the first hammer that came to hand, and not being very ceremonious about the use of it, concluding, according to my observations to them, that it is much better that the beam should be broken in the proof, if imperfect, than be sent off, and found defective afterwards

A good general rule may be, to have the weight of the hammer one pound for every ton, applied as a proof.

The deflection which one-third of the breaking weight occasions to a beam, varies from one six-hundredth to one five-hundredth of its length, according to the quality of the iron; but as a ready means of calculation for the proof-weight, I take the one five-hundredth of the length, which I find near enough for all practical purposes, observing that the deflection is directly as the weight. When a beam is loaded with about one-half its breaking weight, permanent deflection begins to take place, consequently a beam should never be loaded to such an excess.

I need hardly observe to you, gentlemen, that the strength of any beam is directly as the square of the depth and thickness, and inversely as the length, a truth you are no doubt fully acquainted with; but I thought it best to insert it, that the report on this subject might be complete.

The proving of beams of large dimensions is a very tedious and laborious operation, and was attended with great expense, till, having so much proving to do, I contrived a method by which the business was performed with certainty and despatch, and at a comparatively trifling expense One of your association (Mr. Smirke) has seen the apparatus, and witnessed a proof, and can speak as to the efficacy of it.

I have stated, that I never exposed a beam when applied to the purpose for which it is intended to a greater load than one-sixth of its breaking weight, but that I always prove it to twice that weight; take an example: suppose I find by calculation that the strength of the given beam, or the weight that would break it, was fifteen tons; I then apply five tons on its centre as a proof: now five tons on the centre, is equal to ten tons uniformly distributed over the whole beam; but the load is to be equal to $\frac{1}{5}$ or $2\frac{1}{2}$ tons applied at the centre, which would be equal to five tons uniformly distributed over the beam; consequently, the beam having been proved with five tons on its centre, will be equal to double the weight that should ever come upon it when the load is not more than one-sixth of its breaking strength.

Having now given you a detailed account of my system of proof, and the several reasons thereof, which I considered as essentially necessary, that you might duly appreciate my proceedings, and also, that you might the better be enabled to draw your own conclusion on the following results, and further, that you might be assured I did not proceed at random, but that there was reason and method in what I did ;—

Everything having been prepared as before described, I measured the beam we were about to prove, being the first from the centre beam on the east side of it, and I found the distance between the walls on which it rested, 35 feet, from which I calculated that it would require 47 tons 17 cwt. 1 qr. 17lbs. to break it; and consequently, the proof having to be one-third of this weight, there would have to be applied 15 tons 19 cwt. 15lbs. at the centre of the beam.

All parties present being now prepared, we commenced at twelve o'clock at noon to put on the weights, taking the deflections at certain intervals (the particulars of which will be given in a table after the trial of the second beam, as one table will answer for both, and shew the effects on each at one view.) The operation was performed with as much dispatch as was possible, only just allowing time to take the various deflections ; nevertheless it was a quarter past three o'clock by the time we had got on 15 tons 13 cwt. 1 qr. 16lbs. (the time employed being three hours and a quarter) ; when a question being raised whether there was not already more than double the weight upon it that could ever be brought upon the beam, I agreed to let the weight remain upon it all night, and decide this question in the morning ; the deflection was now $\frac{89}{100}$ of an inch ; the doors were locked, and every thing made secure, and the weight left to hang upon it all night.

The same parties that met yesterday having assembled again this morning, the beam being examined the deflection was found to be exactly the same as when we left it last night ; the weight was removed, and the deflections noted with the same weights at those they were taken at in putting the weights on, when the whole of the weight was removed, and the scale taken of ; the beam regained its original position within one-tenth of an inch. It was however found, that on applying the chalk-line to a line that had been struck on the beam, before beginning the proof yesterday, that it exactly corresponded, so that it was evident no permanent deflection had taken place ; and the apparent deflection, as indicated by the diagonal scale, was accounted for, by supposing the weight to have settled the beam one-tenth of an inch closer, and more firmly down upon the wall.

The question now came to be decided, whether or not I had proved the beam to double the weight that could ever be brought upon it (for this being a very defective casting, I was desirous of proceeding to prove it up to twenty tons) ; and if so, whether it was advisable to proceed to such an extremity.

The principal difference amongst us was as to the weight that a dense mass of people would bring upon the floor: to decide this point, I had a square of ten feet struck out upon the floor, and by getting as many of the workmen together, upon a portion of it, as could stand close wedged together, it appeared that seventy people might stand upon a square of an hundred superficial feet ; this gave 1·43, or about $1\frac{1}{2}$ superficial feet for each person ; ten of the men taken promiscuously were weighed, and found to be 13 cwt. 21lbs. which gave us an average of about 147lbs. for each person, or nearly 100lbs. for the weight on each square foot of floor.

I then made a calculation of the weight of floor; but the following is a more correct account, as I have since revised and corrected it: and I give it you in detail, that if I have overrated the weight, you may yourselves correct it.

For one square foot of floor:

		Lbs.
One square foot of eight-inch coombs, with mortar, and filling the spandrils		67
Plastered ceiling under		9
Timber for bridging, flooring, joist, nails, &c.		9
Pugging; viz. boarding, fillet, mortar and nails		8
Oak boarding, nails and dowles		5
Weight of the floor and ceiling, per square foot, exclusive of any weight that may be brought upon it		98 lbs.

Note.—Consonant with the explanation I have already given, it will be observed, that I have taken no account of the weight of the beam itself as part of the load, neither shall I in any of the subsequent calculations.

To the above weight must be added the weight of the company, on a crowded floor, per square foot		100 lbs.
		198 ditto.

This I call 200lbs. per square foot for the greatest weight that can be brought upon the floor, for we must be secure against the greatest extremity; it is in such extremity, that security is most desirable; for should an accident happen in a crowded assembly, the consequences would be most deplorable.

Each beam supports a portion of the floor 35 feet long and 4 feet 9 inches wide, equal to 166¼ superficial feet, which, at 200 lbs. per square foot, will be 14 tons 16 cwt. 3 qrs. 14 lbs.; the proof I had put the beam to was 15 tons 13 cwt. 1 qr. 16 lbs. suspended at the centre, which was equal to 31 tons 6 cwt. 3 qrs. 4 lbs., equally distributed over the beam; consequently it was evident the beam had been proved to more than double the weight that could ever be brought upon it; under these circumstances, I declined going to any further proof on this beam.

I proceeded to the proof of the next beam, which is nearly in the centre of the bow. The proof was made in the same manner as with the first beam; the weight, 15 tons 13 cwt. 1 qr. 16 lbs., was suffered to remain upon it all night, under a deflection of $\frac{6}{10}$ of an inch, and next morning we found the deflection had increased the $\frac{1}{300}$ part of an inch during the night; when the weight was taken off, and the chalk line applied as in the former case, we found the beam had recovered its original

position, and we concluded that the apparent deflection had been from the beam bedding itself more firmly down upon the wall.

The following Table shows the weights upon the beams, with the deflection which those weights produced; it will be observed that the deflections on the removal of the weights did not come back to the same point as when they were put on; but this may be accounted for, first, from the beams having settled themselves a little down upon the walls; and secondly, from less time being given for the beam to recover itself, as the weights were taken off in about one-half the time in which they were put on, for the beams ultimately recovered their original position. It may be further noticed, the deflections are nearly as the weight, and if the half of the weight of the beam itself was taken into the account, the deflections would be found to agree much nearer with the ratio of the weights.

The ends of the beam, No. 1, had no weight of any importance upon them; but the ends of the beam, No. 2, were built solidly into the wall, and the iron angular pilaster, with a weight of about 100 tons upon it, rested on the top edge; this circumstance no doubt gave a greater degree of stiffness to the beam, No. 2, as it will be found, on inspection of the following Table, to have had much less deflection with the same weight than the beam, No. 1.

REMARKS.	Deflection of Beam, No. 1. In decimals of an Inch.		Number of the Pigs of Lead in the Scale.	Total Weight at each Number.				Deflection of Beam, No. 2. in decimals of an Inch.	
	Putting on the weights, May 16.	Taking off the weights, May 17.		Tons.	Cwts.	Qrs.	Lbs.	Putting on the weights, May 19.	Taking off the weights, May 20.
Beam free from all weight except its own -	.000	.000	{ No weight on the Beam - }	—	—	—	—	.000	.000
Scale attached -	not obsd.	.100	Iron work & Scale	1	—	—	—	.020	.130
	ditto	.130	No. 8. Pigs on	1	10	3	19	.040	.150
	ditto	.160	No. 13. —	2	—	—	11	.055	.180
	ditto	.180	No. 20. —	2	10	3	16	.070	.200
	ditto	.210	No. 26. —	3	—	—	20	.085	.220
	.150	.260	No. 33. —	3	10	3	22	.097	.250
	.200	.310	No. 44. —	4	7	3	18	.130	.290
	.230	.340	No. 52. —	5	—	1	8	.145	.310
	.280	.370	No 59. —	5	11	—	18	.163	.330
	.300	.400	No. 65. —	6	—	1	16	.177	.350
	.310	.430	No. 72. —	6	11	—	23	.195	.370
The Beam will have this deflection with a room full of Company	.340	.470	No. 78. —	7	—	1	21	.210	.390
	.370	.500	No. 85. —	7	11	—	25	.225	.410
	.400	.510	No. 91. —	8	—	2	7	.247	.430
	.429	.540	No. 98. —	8	11	1	6	.280	.450
	.440	.570	No. 104. —	9	—	2	—	.296	.460
* The Beam was here forcibly struck with a sledge hammer of 14lbs weight, and the deflection became 620	.470	.590	No. 111. —	9	11	1	20	.307	.480
	.510	.610	No. 117. —	10	—	2	14	.330	.490
	.540	.630	No. 123. —	10	9	3	14	.352	.500
	.570	.660	No. 130. —	11	—	2	26	.385	.520
	.640	.690	No. 136. —	11	9	3	24	.398	.530
	.670	.710	No. 143. —	12	—	3	4	.418	.550
	.690	.740	No. 149. —	12	10	—	8	.440	.575
	.710	.770	No. 156. —	13	—	3	11	.470	.590
	.740	.780	No. 162. —	13	10	—	17	.498	.600
	.780	.800	No. 169. —	14	—	3	7	.510	.610
	.810	.810	No. 175. —	14	10	—	3	.540	.615
	.850	.850	No. 182. —	15	—	3	11	.570	.635
	.880	.880	No. 188. —	15	10	—	20	.592	.650
Deflection remained the same till next morning	.890	.890	No. 190. —	15	13	1	16	.600	.650†

* I had this sledge hammer provided purposely for the trial, and meant to have proceeded in my usual way of proof by hammering, but it was objected to as an unfair mode of trial, it being urged that you could not estimate the effect of such a blow; and as both Mr. Rennie and Mr. Bramah concurred in the objection, I thought it most prudent to forbear, notwithstanding I am decidedly of opinion that hammering is a most essential part of the proof.

† Deflection increased one 500th of an inch during the night.

(To be continued.)

PREVENTING ACCIDENTS ON RAILWAYS.

The repeated accidents which have occurred on the Grand Junction Railway since its opening, have produced considerable excitement amongst those connected with the railway system, both as proprietors and travellers. It has been stated that more serious accidents have happened upon this line during the short time it has been worked, than on the Liverpool and Manchester during all the years it has been at the service of the public. Numerous plans have been from time to time suggested for the prevention of such mishaps, and not a few have been published in our pages; surely from the whole of them some efficient method could be designed. We add to the list of suggestions the following:

Plan by P. Lecount, Esq. C.E., F.A.S.
(From the Railway Times.)

"Sir—I shall be glad to lay before the public, through your valuable publication, the following plan for conducting railway travelling, which will, I think, render accidents to passengers next to impossible; and

I should be glad if those persons most interested in the question will point out any objection to it, that they may, if possible, be obviated.

"I propose, instead of attaching the engine close to the foremost carriage, to fix the train to it by a chain of a sufficient length to allow the train to be stopped by the brakesmen when any accident happens to to the engine. The engine first meeting all obstacles, and being subject to upsetting, getting off the rails, &c., is the means, as railways are now worked, of doing all the ultimate damage to the carriages; but by my plan it will be next to impossible, with a proper look out, for any damage to happen to the carriages at all. The chain should be fixed to a roller, so that it could be wound up when the engine backed astern to keep it clear of the wheels; and when the train approaches the station, the engine and train should be gradually approximated, in order that the train might be brought into the station; this can be done by the roller with ease, as I have found by trial, that I can draw up a train of loaded earth-waggons with one hand when being towed by an engine, so as to render the connecting chain quite slack.

"Yours, truly,

"P. LECOUNT."

February 26, 1838.

Plan by R. Prosser, Esq., C. E.

(From the *Birmingham Advertiser*.)

"No system of telegraphic signals of the ordinary kind can be serviceable on a railway, because that implies that the road should be divided into stations, and an accident occurring between stations could not be communicated without great loss of time, and the velocity which the trains acquire on a railway will not admit of this loss of time.

"Any system of light upon a railway would be useless in foggy weather, for no artificial light with which I am acquainted, can penetrate a dense fog; either of these methods are clearly inapplicable. In travelling by railway, it has always appeared to me that too much was exacted from the engineer, who, in my estimation, has quite sufficient to attend to in working his machine. I would therefore propose that the engineer be placed, as in steam-boats, under the control of a captain or person whose sole business should be the direction of the train. I would furnish this person with as long a speaking-trumpet as it might be found convenient to carry. I should place another person behind each train with a similar apparatus; if these trumpets were mounted upon light wheels, I believe that a velocity of at least 20 miles per hour could be communicated to the apparatus, upon the principle of the velocipede.

"In the event of an accident occurring between stations, either one or both of these apparatus could be started for assistance, and the trumpet used as a means of alarm, long before his arrival.

"By applying the ear to the small end, in the event of the train to which he belonged standing still, he would be able to hear the approach of another train in time to prevent accident, and before they hove in sight, could communicate his wants. I should also recommend that each of the stations be supplied with two speaking-trumpets, which might be used in the same manner as the others, for speaking or hearing.

"The above is merely an outline of the method I propose to your consideration: I shall now procede to give you the proofs upon which I ground its recommendation:—Soon after the accident of the 9th of September, I had a speaking-trumpet constructed, and with an assistant, I have held distinct conversations at more than a mile distance; and, judging from the effect, this was by no means the limit, but I could not conveniently command a greater distance, or spare time from other avocations; of course, any artificial sound communicated through the tube would be heard at a distance depending upon the intensity of the original sound.

"I lay no claim to discovery, because I am aware that the speaking-trumpet is of remote origin, and that useful publication, the *Mechanics' Magazine*, No. 750, contains an extract from *Blackwood's Magazine*, under the head "Acoustic Telegraph," which I enclose, because it will shorten this communication, and it contains in a short compass much which I had quoted at greater length from Nicholson, Somerville, Lieutenant Foster, M. M. Biot, Arnot, Young, Perrole, Chladin, La Grange, Derham, Morland, Gough, Hassenfratz, Dr. Moyse, Monsieur Charles, Walker, Robinson, Hutton, &c. &c. The modern application of the Stethoscope is a beautiful illustration of a mode [of rendering audible, sounds too feeble for the human ear to discriminate without artificial aid.

"This communication might be made much longer. I have said sufficient to put you in possession of my notions, and although I have apparently added to the expense of each trip, I am sure it will be found not really so; but I am quite confident that, by the adoption of this plan, a further sacrifice of life may be prevented, at a cost too trifling to form an objection, and furnishing a means of telegraphic despatch along the whole line, in any weather, thus tending to alleviate any unnecessary fears arising from the detention of a train past its usual hour.

"Whether or not the whole of my suggestions are followed out, I earnestly recommend the placing of the train under the guidance of some person to give sole orders to the engineer, and this alone would add to the safety of each trip, to the profit of the proprietors, and to the public security.

"I am, Sir,
"Yours very respectfully,
"R. PROSSER.
"Civil Engineer, Birmingham."
Birmingham, Dec. 15, 1837.

RAILWAY MILEAGE—LONDON AND BIRMINGHAM RAILWAY ACT.

Sir,—To corroborate my statements made in one of your late numbers respecting " railway mileage," I subjoin those sections of the " London and Birmingham Railway Act," that appear to have been, either misunderstood, or overlooked.

" Section 171. And be it further enacted, that all persons shall have free liberty to pass along and upon, and to use the said railway, with carriages properly constructed, as by this act directed, upon payment only of such rates and tolls as shall be demanded by the said company, not exceeding the respective rates or tolls by this act authorized, and subject to the rules and regulations which shall from time to time be made by the said company, or by the said directors, by virtue of the powers to them respectively by this act granted.

" Section 173. And be it further enacted, that it shall be lawful for the said company to demand, receive, and recover, to and for the use and benefit of the said company for and in respect of passengers, beasts, cattle, and animals conveyed in carriages any toll not exceeding the following: (that is to say,)

" For every person conveyed in or upon any such carriage, the sum of two pence per mile. For every horse, mule, ass, or other beast of draught or burthen, and for every ox, cow, bull or neat cattle, conveyed in or upon, &c. &c. &c. $1\frac{1}{2}d$. per mile. For every calf or pig, conveyed in or upon &c. &c. $\frac{1}{2}d$. per mile. For every sheep, lamb, or other small animal conveyed in or upon &c. &c. $\frac{1}{4}d$. per mile.

" For every carriage of whatever description not being a carriage adapted and used for travelling on a railway and not weighing more than one ton, carried or conveyed on a truck or platform the sum of four pence per mile.

" Section 175. And be it further enacted, that it shall be lawful for the said company, and they are hereby authorized to convey upon the said railway all such passengers cattle and other animals, goods, wares, &c., merchandize, articles, matters, and things, as shall be offered to them for that purpose, and to make such reasonable charges as they may from time to time determine upon, *in addition to the several rates or tolls by this act authorized to be taken;* provided always that it shall not be lawful for the said company, or for any persons using the said railway to charge for the conveyance of any passenger upon the said railway any greater sum than the sum of $3\frac{1}{2}d$. per mile including the rate or toll hereinbefore granted.

[By Sections 180 and 181, the company are allowed to reduce tolls but not to reduce them partially in relation to persons or things.]

" Section 216. And be it further enacted, that in all cases on which the said company of proprietors shall carry for their own profit any passengers, cattle, or other animals, goods, wares, or merchandize, articles, matters or things, a separate accompt shall be duly kept, shewing the amount of rates or tolls which would have been received by the said company for the use of the said railway in respect of such passengers, cattle or other animals, goods, wares, or merchandize, articles, matters or things if carried by any other party or parties; and the overseers of the poor of the several parishes and townships through which the said railway shall pass, shall have free access to, and liberty to inspect the same at any times during the first fourteen days in the months of February and August in each year."

I am, Sir, your's &c.
CHRIS. DAVY.

NOTES AND NOTICES.

Comparison of Speed.—The comparative speed per second is, of a man 4 feet—a horse 12—a rein-deer 26—a race horse 43—a hare 88—a good ship 19—the wind 82—a cannon ball 1,800. The comparison says the *Railway Times*, might, we think, be carried with advantage a little further. A railway steamer, travelling at the ordinary rate of 30 miles an hour, performs 44 feet per second, which is eleven times the speed of the man walking, nearly four times that of the good horse, twice that of the rein-deer, and only about one-half less than the swiftness of the wind itself. But man, horse, and rein-deer, all become soon exhausted—even Boreas is sure to " crack his cheeks" before long; while the railway steamer is as fresh and strong at the end of a long journey as at first starting. Miles to it are but as paces to others. A racer, such as the Flying Childers, might possibly rival the steamer for the last half of a single mile heat; but we know a Firefly that would do more miles in one day than 360 Flying Childerses. Again, a racer doing one mile in two minutes, and no more, can but carry a feather weight for that brief time and distance, while the steamer could draw the Grand Stand, and half the sporting world along with it, from Doncaster to Newmarket, and thence to the Hippodrome in one day.

Projected Improvements at Deal.—Strenuous exertions are to be made this summer for the revival of the prosperity of Deal, a town which has been in a declining state ever since the return of peace. The principal improvement projected is the erection of a commodious pier, giving every facility for landing and embarking, with a view of attracting some part of the shoals of Londoners, who at present get no further than Margate and Ramsgate, in their summer pleasurings. Arrangements have been made with the Commercial Steam Navigation Company, for running a packet daily to and from the metropolis, as soon as the pier—which is to be of wood—is ready to accommodate the passengers. By these means Deal hopes to recover some of its importance in the scale of towns, and commence a race with its neighbour Dover, which has sprung up into consequence as a watering-place within these few years, aided not a little, it must be acknowledged, by local advantages and poetical associations of which Deal cannot boast. Deal has indeed a castle, but she possesses no "Shakespeare's Cliff;"—nor perhaps will Dover ere long, should the South-Eastern Railway Company continue operations on the scale they have begun upon.

The "Prepared-Charcoal" Stove.—The question as to the healthfulness of the prepared fuel burned in the new stove, whose exhibition at the Jerusalem Coffee-house and the principal scientific societies of the metropolis has excited so much attention, will soon be set at rest. The patentees announce that they are now ready to supply the demands of the public; so that the new wonder will soon be brought to the test of experience, which has proved fatal to so many wonders of the kind. We shall give an engraving and description of the stove next week. The inventor, Mr. Joyce, has just taken out a second patent, for further improvements in the apparatus.

Subterranean Travelling.—The line of railway between Lyons and St. Etienne, the largest manufacturing town and richest coal district in France, is only thirty-four miles in length;—yet, such is the unevenness of the country, and so great has been the anxiety of the engineers to preserve as complete a level as possible, that there are actually no less than *twenty tunnels* between the two termini! One of these is a mile in length, while another, which is half a mile long, is carried under the bed of a river which crosses the line.

Wonderful Changes.—The Swedish City of Gottenburgh is built principally of stone from Aberdeen, and it is a well-known fact that the dust-heap which was wont to grace the top of Gray's Inn Lane, is now a component part of the city of Moscow, to which it was exported as a material for brick-making, after the conflagration of that city. Greater changes than these are daily brought about by our extended commerce. The first mile out of London of the Kingsland Road is actually macadamized with *Chinese* stone; a fact which appears incredible until it is explained that the material was brought over in the shape of ballast in the ships

of the East India Company, and disposed of to the road-contractor (who little cared how far it had come) at a cheap rate. In return for this, it is said that the Chinese are indebted for a part of the materials for their porcelain to the English ships, which take out in a similar way the fine chalk of Northfleet and its neighbourhood, which is found to be particularly well suited for the purposes of the manufactures of the Celestial Empire.

The Rocket Safety Apparatus.—A Mr. Gyngell made experiments on the Green near Brecon, with some rockets of his invention for communicating with stranded vessels. He discharged several rockets of different weights. The rope was coiled on a cone formed of light rails of wood, and was carried out the distance of from 3 to 5 hundred yards according to the size of the rocket attached to it. The 2lb. rockets carried nearly 300 yards, and one 6lbs. conveyed the rope a distance of 500 yards, into the fields over the river Usk. Mr. Byers, of Swansea, in a letter on this subject which we inserted a few weeks since, remarks that if rockets could have been obtained at the time of the wreck of the Killarney Steamer, a number of lives might have been saved and the survivors would have been delivered from their dreadful sufferings. He also adduces another case in which they would have been of great service —that of a small vessel seen in distress off the Steep Holmes, by the Lady Charlotte steamer, but after the most strenuous exertions was obliged to proceed on her voyage without being able to effect an approach. It is very seldom that an instance occurs of a vessel striking on a lee shore a greater distance than a quarter of a mile from land; a convict ship was lost about three years since off Boulogne, within 400 yards of the shore, and more than 200 lives were lost. We need hardly point out the utility of the rocket in such cases, and we hope that ere long no vessel will leave port without being provided with this simple and cheap apparatus, the outside cost of which does not exceed 2l.; indeed we do not see why the legislature should not make it compulsory.—*Silurian.*

English Linens in France.—The French manufacturers complain bitterly of the great increase which has taken place of late years in the importation of English and Irish linens and linen thread, and call loudly on their government for a higher rate of duty on the foreign goods. It appears from their statements that the quantity has increased upwards of *two hundred fold* between 1831 and 1837, and that the value in the latter year amounted to something more than seventeen millions of francs, or over seven hundred thousand pounds sterling!

A plan for copying the outline of mouldings, &c., similar to that with which Mr. Heineken has favoured us, was published in our fifth vol. p. 57.

Errata.—Page 4, 2d column, 19th line from top, for "*importent*" read "*impotent*;" page 6, first column, 15th line from top, after the word " of," supply the following omission:—"*those on board, which ended in the discovery of*" flames issuing,&c. ; page 5, 2d column, 17th line from top, for "*striking*" read "*strikingly.*"

Mechanics' Magazine, Complete sets.—The proprietor of the Mechanics' Magazine has now effected the repurchase of the earlier portions of the stock of this journal from the parties who were possessed of the same in the right of his first publishers; and he is now able to supply several complete sets of the work. Price, twenty-seven volumes, half-cloth, £11 7s.

☞ British and Foreign Patents taken out with economy and despatch; Specifications, Disclaimers, and Amendments, prepared or revised; Caveats entered; and generally every Branch of Patent Business promptly transacted. A complete list of Patents from the earliest period (15 Car. II. 1675,) to the present time may be examined. Fee 2s. 6d.; Clients, gratis.

LONDON: Printed and Published for the Proprietor, by W. A. Robertson, at the Mechanics Magazine Office, No. 6, Peterborough-court between 135 and 136, Fleet-street.—Sold by A. & W. Galignani, Rue Vivienne, Paris.

Mechanics' Magazine,

MUSEUM, REGISTER, JOURNAL, AND GAZETTE

No. 767.]   SATURDAY, APRIL 21, 1838.   [Price 3*d*.

HARPER AND JOYCE'S PATENT STOVE.

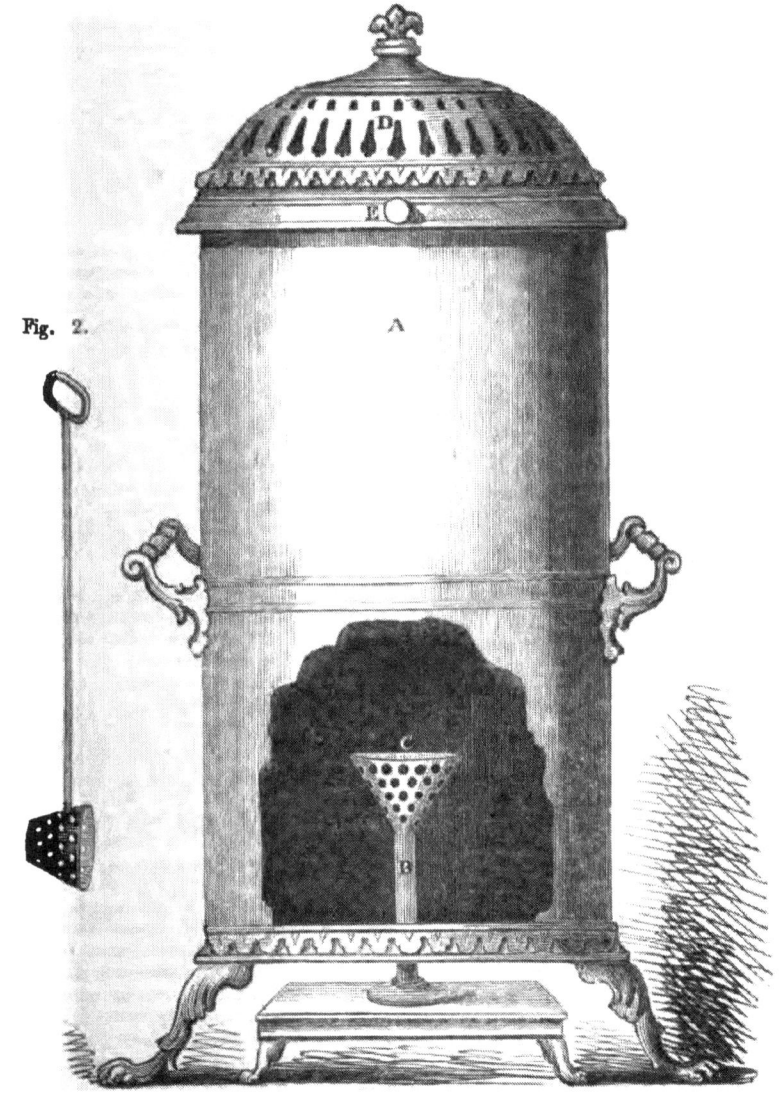

Fig. 2.

HARPER AND JOYCE'S STOVE.

We give on our front page an engraving of this much-talked-of stove, though we can add but little to the information of which our readers are in possession with respect to it, the specification of the patentees not having been as yet enrolled. A correspondent ("Honestas") very fairly expresses some surprise that the *Monthly Chronicle*, from which we extracted the laudatory notice of this invention inserted in our Journal of March 17, No. 762, did not in its last number contain any thing on the subject, "although the said stove has been on sale for some time, and consequently, the writer of the article (Dr. Lardner?) might have had it in his power to speak from actual experiment, which it appears he had not, when he penned his first notice." Our correspondent expresses also a very reasonable desire to know, whether "any experiment has been made with the stove by persons capable of passing a sound judgment upon its merits, and in particular *with respect to the gases evolved by the combustion of the (said to be) prepared fuel.*" The words we have marked in italics point to what we apprehend will be found to be the great—perhaps fatal—drawback on the value of this invention. It is not a little curious, however, that the correspondent who guesses so shrewdly where the defect of this stove lies, happens to be the same gentleman who lately quarreled with us for objecting, chiefly on the same ground, to Dr. Arnott's. Both of these "nine days' wonders" seem to us to be more or less faulty on this score. In a printed explanation which Messrs. Harper and Joyce furnish along with their stoves, some paragraphs from which we subjoin, they assert that "*it is smokeless and gives out neither smell nor vapour.*" Now this we can, of our own knowledge, attest not to be the fact. When we visited their shop and inspected the stove kept burning there, we felt instantly sensible of the escape of carbonic acid gas from the stove; and to remove all doubt on the point, we requested permission to test the vapour issuing from the dome, but this was declined—for what reason we leave our readers to judge. For our own parts, we would not, after this, sleep with one in our bedchamber for one night for ten times the sum we have heard mention-

ed as having been offered to the patentees for the invention.

The engraving on our front page is a perspective view of the stove with a part of the side removed to show the interior. A, is the body, consisting of a metallic cylinder. B, a tube for the admission of air to the fuel to support combustion. C, an inverted cone placed on the top of the tube B, perforated with holes round its sides, whereby the air is carried to the centre of the burning fuel. E, a circular regulating valve, by which the egress of the hot vapour into the interior of the dome D is controuled. The dome D is perforated with holes to allow of the escape of the hot vapour into the atmosphere. Fig. 2 is a ladle for supplying the prepared fuel in an ignited state, as mentioned in the subjoined extract from the circular:—

Extract from Messrs. Harper and Joyce's Circular.

This Apparatus is simple and economical, and possess the following advantages over all other stoves.

1. It feeds itself.

2. It is smokeless and *gives out neither smell nor noxious vapour.*

3. It is perfectly portable, and can be placed on a table or side-board, or may be suspended, as most convenient.

4. It throws out no dust whatever.

5. Nothing which may come into contact with it will burn.

6. It will continue burning from twelve to forty-eight hours, or longer if required.

7. During that time it does not require any attention whatever.

Its treatment is as follows :—If a single cylinder, place a *ladleful* of the fuel on any fire, and when it arrives at a *red heat*, which will be in three or four minutes, take off the lid of the apparatus and place the heated fuel at the bottom; then fill the apparatus to its top with the cold fuel, and replace the lid, leaving the regulator raised to its highest point till the temperature of the room be increased to the degree desired; then lower it about two-thirds of its length, and the same temperature will be preserved so long as the machine shall be in action.

Should it not be convenient to heat the ladle of fuel at a common fire, another ladle may be used of a slightly different construction, in the bottom of which place paper or shavings, and two or three small pieces of wood, and a handful of fuel on the top; and then light the shavings and wood and put the ladle in the draught of the fire place or out of doors, and it will arrive at a red heat in three or four minutes as before. Care must be taken not to light any fuel, but that prepared, because of the noxious gas and bad smell of all other. A small vessel to contain water will accompany the apparatus if desired; the heat causes the water to evaporate slowly, and supplying the air with a moderate moisture, remedies the too great dryness so generally complained of in close stoves. This vessel requires only to be filled when the apparatus is loaded.

When all the fuel of one loading is consumed, it will be necessary to reverse the apparatus in order to displace a trifling quantity of ash which remains, and which, if allowed to accumulate, might in some degree check the free burning of the fuel.

In the double cylinder the treatment is the same with that of the single, except when the apparatus is large, and then, for convenience, the inner cylinder will be made so that it can be taken out to be loaded as above and then replaced.

In the more common sort of apparatus for cellars, &c., no reversing is necessary when a charge of fuel is consumed. A small receiver will be fixed to the bottom, and in it a door, through which the ash that falls into this receiver may be raked out. But when this sort of apparatus is re-lighted, it will be advisable to place over the holes in the bottom of the cylinder, pieces of fuel a little larger than the holes in order to prevent the fall of any of the ignited fuel which is first put in, into the hot receiver.

As soon as Mr. Joyce's specification is inrolled we shall inform our readers of the method of preparing the charcoal, and correct any inaccuracies into which we may have fallen; unless we are previously enabled so to do by the inventor or some one acquainted with the details of the invention. We understand that none of the most approved construction of stoves have yet been manufactured.

THE " INDIA STEAM NAVIGATION COMPANY."

Sir,—Among the thousand and one new companies of the day the " India Steam Navigation Company" is not the least conspicuous. Its object is to establish a communication by steam with our Indian possessions, by the well known and long-used route of the Cape of Good Hope, instead of that by the Mediterranean and the Red Sea, on which the line of steam vessels supported by government and the East India Company has at length been established. The chairman of the company is no less a personage than Sir John Ross, the commander of the last North-polar Expedition; and the advantages of the proposed scheme are set forth, under the sanction of his name, with no lack of ingenuity and attractiveness. According to the prospectus, the voyage from Plymouth to Point de Galle, in the island of Ceylon, is to be effected in fifty days, the vessel stopping to take in fuel only at one intermediate station, which, it is proposed, shall be Saldanha Bay, in the Cape of Good Hope territory. The steamers are to be of gigantic size, to carry a large quantity of goods, as well as passengers, and that at so high a freight, in consequence of the *certainty* attending their transit, as to pay a dividend of nobody-knows-how-much per cent. to the fortunate shareholders, on the subscribed capital of no more than half-a-million sterling,—backed, however, by another quarter of a million to be raised in India !

All this looks very well on paper, but it is to be feared the " reverse of the medal" would be but too apt to show itself when the plan should be reduced to practice. Above all, the probability of reaching Ceylon in fifty days seems exceedingly problematical,—to say the least of it. Messrs. Seaward, who may be presumed to know as much of the matter as Sir John Ross himself, and who are enthusiastic advocates of the line of the Cape of Good Hope, in preference to that of the Red Sea, calculated upon the voyage to India occupying seventy days, and never ventured to anticipate, as the New Company do, running the whole of the distance at a quicker rate than the fastest Scotch steamers are able to maintain in their short voyages round our own coast, "with all appliances and means to boot." It remains to be proved, also, whether it will be practicable to perform the distance from England to the Cape, and the Cape to Ceylon, without once halting for coals. The Company are apparently aware that some doubt will be felt on this point, for they hasten to assure the public that they are not dependent for success on the ordinary means at present in use, but that they have secured the "exclusive right" to an invention which throws all existing marine steam machinery into the shade.

The "scantling" of the machinery, indeed, they do not give any particulars of,—the world at large is left to guess at its *modus operandi*, as the world at large best may; but meanwhile Sir John Ross and the rest of the directors are quite satisfied that, by its means, a voyage, compared to which that across the Atlantic is but a trifle, may be accomplished with the utmost ease! What more is necessary? Surely the shares of the " India Steam Navigation Company" ought to rise at once to a handsome premium, with such *satisfactory* prospects in view as these!

In a word, the proposed Company exhibits only a more decided specimen than usual of the precipitency with which a novel speculation is entered into in these exciting and excited times. It is next to impossible to carry its objects into effect in the manner held out by the " concoctors" of the scheme. Almost every paragraph in the prospectus might be met by a fatal objection. On what, then, is reliance to be placed? On the "magic in the name" of Sir John Ross, to whom the public are supposed willing to give credit for the performance of seeming impossibilities, on the score of his having commanded two unsuccessful expeditions, and found his way safe home again at last. Sir John Ross has been to the North Pole,—*argal*, he is the properest person in the world to direct a company for traversing the torrid regions of the East; Sir John Ross started on his last expedition in a steamer which became no steamer at all on the first mischance it met with; *argal*, he is the very man to preside over the " energies" of a set of steamers which are to go farther and faster than ever steamer went before!— But no matter;—Sir John is, or has been, a " lion," his name is well-known for *something*, and that is sufficient in these happy days of jointstockomania, when Signor Paganini, or any other famous first-fiddle, would be hailed with rapture as the chairman of a cemetry company, and the Right Honourable Lord Viscount Shabbysides would carry all before him as director of the Patent Steam-Hog-trough and Mousetrap-Manufacturing Association, or any equally promising affair. Name and notoriety are every thing in such cases;—the merits of the plan so bolstered—nothing.

The Red Sea line of steam-communication is going on prosperously, although complaints are ever and anon made that the conduct of the East India Company in the affair is not by any means so spirited as it ought to be. Steam committees are still kept up in India, their object being, now that the grand one is obtained, to prove the extension of the line, now reaching only to Bombay, to the other presidencies. This object, generally known as " the comprehensive plan," will doubtless sooner or later be carried, notwithstanding it seems to meet with a sort of " passive resistance" from the powers that be. It is proposed to work the extension from Bombay for the present by means of private subscriptions, no doubt being entertained that when the advantages it presents are once made manifest in practice, the Company must soon yield to the general voice, and take the maintenance of the line upon itself. There is certainly every probability of all this being effected long before the " India Steam Navigation Company" shall have made its first voyage to Ceylon " in fifty days"!

I remain, Sir,
Your very obdient servant,
H.

London, April 11, 1838.

———

DIE-SINKING AT A DISCOUNT—SIGNOR PISTRUCCI'S NEW METHOD OF MEDAL-STRIKING.

" When this process shall have been brought to the perfection of which it is capable, there can be no doubt that in the execution of works of this description, it will not only be the saving of the labour of months or years in the engraving of dies, and consequently, of great expense, but the work to be executed will in all points be, in an instant, an exact fac-simile of the original conception of the artist, instead of representing as at present, merely the handy-work of the engraver, copied from such original."—*Times.*

Sir,—At a time like the present, when the best energies of benevolent minds are directed to ameliorate the condition, and elevate the social character of man— while legislators and philanthrophists are vying with each other in the most laudable endeavours to raise the standard of public taste, by extending far and wide the beneficial influence of education in general, and a knowledge of, and love for the fine arts in particular—at such a time I say, any person who shall develope a practical method of facilitating the production, and reducing the cost, of any of the true works of art, is deserving of public gratitude.

That such a practical developement has now been achieved, will be the object of this communication to establish; and when the facts that will be adduced have been fairly and impartially considered, every honourable mind will at once admit, that in the increased facility of producing *new designs*, as well as in the faithful and unlimited multiplication of the choicest productions of antiquity, a new era has been opened by the successful labours of Signor Pistrucci, chief medallist at the Royal Mint. The brilliant talents of this foreign artist, as a *modeller*, and his skilful execution as an engreaver, have unfortunately excited the envy, and provoked a series of illiberal and unjust attacks, from individuals whose inferiority in point of real merit, is as marked as the falsehood and malignity of their attacks.

It would be both a grateful and an honourable task, to plead the cause of a foreigner, whose only bane is his *country*, and his greatest crime—his *merit ;* and whose want of proficiency in our language, compels him to endure unanswered, the base and cowardly insinuations of disappointed rivals. For my own part, however, I confess that I have neither leisure nor ability for such an employment, nor do I consider your pages properly occupied, when filled with matters that must of necessity be so strictly personal. Without further preface, therefore, I proceed to notice Signor Pistrucci's recent discovery, the first announcement of which, occasioned considerable excitement among his jealous brethren of the art, who freely lavished upon him all those expressive epithets so abundant in the English vocabulary, descriptive of fools and madmen. The line of argument pursued by all these parties, is of a very remarkable character, inasmuch as they one and all set out by denying the *novelty* of the invention, and wind up, by designating it as *absurd* and *impossible*. One illustration of this singularly honest and ingenious mode of disposing of an inventors claims, may be found at page 401, of your 27th volume.

This article, written by a namesake of mine, may be taken as a fair specimen of the class. I have suffered this communication to stand over thus long unanswered, in order to watch the progress, and see the ultimate result of Signor Pistrucci's labours ; not caring to wage a wordy war about the probability or impossibility of success. The quotation prefixed to this communication, is from a very interesting article, copied from the *Times* newspaper into the "Notes and Notices" in your 732nd Number, descriptive of Signor Pistrucci's new method of striking up medals without the aid of engraving. The paragraph I have quoted, admits that the process was not at that time brought to perfection, but the writer very confidently asserted its capability of being perfected, and briefly adverted to the incalculable advantages, that must of necessity follow the maturing of this curious process.

Since this publication took place Signor Pistrucci has perfected his process, and has recently made such a valuable practical application of his invention, as completely refutes the assertions of the impossibility-mongers ; and now with regard to originality. "*The method,*" says Mr. John Baddeley, in his communication before alluded to, "was known and practised by my grandfather *as far as it was practicable* fifty years since." He also adds, "it was carried to its utmost (*known*) extent in the coining of the old penny at Matthew Bolton's Mint, Soho, near Birmingham, in 1797." The first assertion would be a direct falsehood, but for the expressive and significant qualification, marked in italics. That it was carried to its utmost extent, as known at that time, at the Soho in 1797, is true enough, and it is just the difference between the very imperfect and inefficient process, then known and practised, and the exceedingly beautiful process now successfully, matured, that constitutes Signor Pistrucci's merit !

Can it for one moment be matter of surprise, that in all branches of practical science we surpass the knowledge of our grandfathers ? By the illuminating powers of an invisible fluid, we see things clearer than our forefathers did, and by the force of omnipotent steam we achieve many triumphs which they never dreamt of. Narrow indeed must be the intellects of that man, who can put a complacent negative on all attempts to improve what was either partially known, or imperfectly practised, some fifty years ago.

Signor Pistrucci's first application of his new process, has been in striking up a seal for the Duchy of Lancaster. This seal is four inches in diameter, of sterling silver; one side presents a very beautiful equestrian figure of her Majesty, Queen Victoria, surrounded by a bold inscription; on the reverse, the arms of the Duchy are richly emblazoned, in the midst of a profusion of scroll-work, with an inscription. To have *engraved* the two dies for striking up this seal, would have taken about fourteen or fifteen months hard labour, with the risk at the end of that time, of the dies breaking in the process of hardening. By Signor Pistrucci's method, they have been produced in less than fifteen days!

There is an exquisite softness, and a boldness of relief, in many parts of this seal not attainable in an *engraved* die; the graceful flowing of the drapery, the prominence of the arm of her Majesty, as well as the ear and hoofs of the horse, are altogether unrivalled. The fame of Signor Pistrucci's success has drawn to the Mint, most of those who are celebrated for their practical acquaintance with the powers and properties of the metals, and with mechanics generally; one and all of whom, have expressed themselves astounded at the results obtained. When such gentlemen as Bramah, Maudslay and others, state, that nothing short of seeing with their own eyes would have satisfied them of the possibility of such a work, incredulity may well be pardoned in those who have not witnessed the recent production. There are plenty of workmen in the Royal Mint, well versed in all the methods employed at the *Soho* for the last fifty years, and they all agreed in designating Mr. Pistrucci's plan, when first propounded to them,—as a *new fangled and impossible scheme*, and yet have these very workmen themselves since proved its *possibility*.

The outline of Signor Pistrucci's plan, is tolerably well explained, in the *Times* newspaper referred to; the subject is modelled in the usual way, either in wax, clay, or other fit material, from which a cast is taken in plaster of Paris. The plaster cast being hardened, is moulded in fine sand with great care, and a cast in iron is taken from it. The great *secret*—if there can be any secret in what has been published in the leading journal of the day, and thence very extensively copied into other publications—consists in the *thinness* of the *iron castings*. The plaster of Paris model is left only about one eight of an inch thick, the consequence of which is, that the *chill* which takes place on the *surface* of all iron castings, from the proximity of the two surfaces in this instance, pervades the whole mass, giving it the hardness of a hardened steel die, with a toughness, not attainable by the latter metal while in a hard state.

In all large castings, the contraction of the mass of metal in cooling causes a shrinking of all the finer lines, while in thin castings, the sharpness of every line is preserved with suprising beauty. Mr. John Baddeley says, " it is *utterly impossible* to cast any metal *hard enough for the purpose* in sand or loam or any other composition!" Verily, Mr. John Baddeley is but a poor authority in such matters—facts prove him wrong. Signor Pistrucci is his own founder, but there is no peculiarity in his mode of founding—nothing beyond the extreme care, which the delicacy of the subject in hand requires; his castings do him much credit, though they are by no means equal to the productions of the best Berlin casters.

The iron casting having been made perfectly flat at the back, a hollow is turned out in a steel bed to receive it, and when thus mounted it is ready for use. One proof among many others, of the extreme hardness of the cast-iron dies, is afforded by the fact, that no extension of the metal takes place from the severest blows : the die fitting no tighter into its bed, after striking up a medal, than it did before. The seal before alluded to, took upwards of one hundred and fifty blows from the most powerful press in the mint, and the dies appear in every respect as perfect now as when first cast.

Many persons, who, from their known celebrity and eminence in the scientific world, would be considered the very highest authorities that could be cited in a question of this kind, have not only on examination admitted the *entire novelty* and great importance of this process, but have charged Signor Pistrucci with injustice to himself, for neglecting to secure the privileges of a patent. This, however, the Signor has from the first declined to do; choosing rather to throw open the result of his (miscalled) "hours of idleness," for universal public benefit.

What the real value of this discovery is—or where the useful application of the fact thus established will stop, it is at present wholly impossible to imagine. The advantages, of being able to produce at so little cost, and in so short a space of time, the most perfect and beautiful designs—or to copy with so much facility the choicest productions of others, are altogether incalculable. One drawback, perhaps, is the power thus placed in the hands of the fraudulent copyist, and the spurious coiner; but the knowledge of an existing power to do certain mischiefs generally produces an antidote sufficient for the evil, and it is to be hoped the present case forms no exception to the rule. One happy effect of the general introduction of this method of obtaining *dies*, will be, to make the *die-sinkers* more of *artists* and less of *mechanics*, to wield the graver *less*—but the pencil *more skilfully*. Should my endeavours to render this useful process intelligible. not be sufficiently explicit I shall have much pleasure in affording any additional information that may be thought necessary, but as this communication has extended beyond a convenient limit, I shall for the present close, by subscribing myself,

Your's respectfully,
WM. BADDELEY.

London, April 6, 1838.

PREVENTION OF FIRE ON BOARD SHIPS AT SEA.

Sir,—On reading the remarks of Mr. Baddeley, in your last Number, relative to the late fire on board the "Great Western," it occurred to me, that still further precaution might be taken to prevent the spread of fire on board steam-ships at sea, by having a smoke-proof jacket, such as is used by the London Fire Engine Establishment; the engine-room might thus be entered when full of smoke, and a forcing pump put into work, which it appears could not be done in the case referred to.

An arrangement by which the engines would be as controllable on deck as in the engine-room, might also be useful in some cases of emergency, precaution being, of course, taken to prevent any except the engineers having access to the small space allotted for this purpose.

When two engineers and several stokers are employed, they should not *all* be permitted to remain in the engine-room at one time, or we may witness a repetition of the melancholy scene on board the Victoria, when every man—(if I am rightly informed) who was capable of assisting in any way in the engine-room—was suddenly deprived of the use of his limbs. Had one-half of these unfortunate men been on deck, there would have been a saving of human life, and of labour, which at sea, is unquestionably the most valuable.

I am, Sir,
Your obedient servant,
H. WALKER.

20, Maiden-lane, Wood-street.
April 11, 1838.

PORTABLE SHIPS' PUMPS.

Sir,—Mr. Baddeley, with his characteristic zeal, has lost no time in calling attention to the fact, that even the untiring energy of the steam engine cannot *at all times* be availed of on ship board, for the purpose of extinguishing fire, although fitted with apparatus which might be instantly adapted for that purpose.

The advantage of an auxiliary pump on deck has been clearly shewn in the instance of Merryweather's engine on board the "Great Western," and it would be well if every *sea-going* steam vessel were similarly supplied.

In addition to the pump worked by the engine, many vessels are fitted with Downton's rotary pumps, which are fixed on deck, and efficiently perform the several offices of fire engine, bilge, fresh, and salt-water pumps; and each may be adapted by a very simple and expeditious contrivance: but still, in case a fire were to take place in the neighbourhood of the pump, its valuable services would, in all probability be cut off.

A very compact portable pump was constructed some years since, by Mr. W. Kingston, engineer, at Portsmouth, and with very slight exception, resembling that since patented by Hearle, of Plymouth. This pump has two barrels concealed in a snug iron box, leaving only the two ends of an axis protruding, on which the handles are shipped for use, in the manner of an ordinary fire-engine—the box becoming the air vessel;—the whole is fixed on a plank, which may be placed on the thwarts of a boat, and is transported with great readiness. This pump can wash decks, wet sails, water the ship from alongside, or become a bilge pump if needful; and when watering on a dangerous coast, by mooring the boat without, and leading the hose on shore, the casks can be filled in place without the risk attendant on getting them off through the surf. As to its advantages as a fire engine, I was witness to an alarm of fire on board a vessel in harbour at eleven at night;—the crew was roused and the pump got over the side into the boat and alongside the vessel in danger, in ten or fifteen minutes from the outcry; fortunately the fire was smothered below, in time to prevent a conflagration. On another occasion, when a steam vessel was approaching her anchorage, on a still night, after a voyage of some days, the ignited soot was seen to pour out from her chimney so as to resemble a volcano, driving her crew off the deck, which they were flooding with water. The engine was instantly got out and sent to meet her, the hose being shipped during the time; but her assistance was again rendered unnecassary from the precautions taken on board the steamer.

I mention these facts, although, perhaps tedious, in order to show that the advantages of portable engines are by no means limited to the ships they are on board.

In the cases above stated, there was not one of the many vessels in the port, excited by the alarm of fire, which could bring any thing but a bucket into play. How efficient would the crowd of boats, at a distance from the shore, have been rendered, had each had a portable fire-engine on board!

Hearle's pumps are now manufactured by Mare, engineer, at Plymouth, who could best describe them and their capabilities. I am, Sir, &c.

NAUTICUS.

Woolwich, April 9, 1838.

MIXTURE OF SULPHATE OF BARYTES WITH WHITE LEAD.

Sir,—I beg leave to address the following query to your scientific correspondents through your widely-extended miscellany. Is sulphate of barytes a fit and proper ingredient to be mixed with white lead for paint? An immense quantity of this article, which does not possess the viscous properties of white lead, is ground in Montgomeryshire, North Wales, and sold in England, as well as a considerable quantity sent to America, at an immense profit to one or two parties. The colour and weight of the ground material so nearly resemble white lead, that it is difficult to discover the difference when mixed with it. If this article be not proper to mix with white lead, how may its presence be detected?

NO PAINTER.

Solop, April 12, 1838.

RIDDLE'S UNIVERSAL PEN-HOLDER.

It is highly amusing to observe the gradual progress of invention, to watch the steady progress of improvement as it advances step by step towards perfection—to see plans and contrivances that have long reigned pre-eminent, set aside one after the other by the every day "march of science."

Scarcely a number of our Magazine issues from the press that does not teem with numerous instances of this description; upon the present occasion we have to notice a new Pen-holder, lately introduced by Mr. G. Riddle, whose intimate connexion with most of the improvements in writing materials for the past fifteen or twenty years, must be well known to many of our readers.

The jointed pen-holder patented some some years ago by Mr. Bramah, hitherto the best extant, is too well known to require description, having been very extensively employed for a long time; its construction displayed much ingenuity, the smiths' tongs being its model; but the mode of application rendered this principle liable to many inconveniencies and objections. Bramah's holder was only adapted for pens of an elastic character, or of an uniform curve and thickness; the insertion of a large or thick pen caused a straining of the joint which prevented its holding a thin pen ever after. There was also considerable difficulty in guiding the slide-ring over the sharp pointed tail-piece, and as this tail-piece must always be brought close down upon the body of the tube to allow the ring to pass over it, whatever the size or curvature of the pen—the straining before alluded to was the inevitable result, which ended in the breaking of the holder. Various attempts have at different times been made, to simplify this holder and preserve its good qualities, but without success—all these attempts having been even more objectionable than their prototype. The last effort, however, now before us, is an exception; Mr. Riddle's universal pen-holder is a very simple and effective instrument adapted for either quill or metallic pens, of various curves and thicknesses. This new and highly ingenious contrivance combines all the excellences of previous inventions, and at the same time, obviates the several objections to which they have been liable. The construction of the universal pen-holder (so called from the extensive nature of its application,) will be readily understood by referring to the accompanying engravings, where it will be seen to consist of a gold or silver tube, with a handle of ebony, ivory or other suitable material; on the under side of the tube, which is semi-cylindrical for a short distance up, there is a detached limb held by a strong spring-joint exerting a constant tendency to keep the jaws of the holder apart, as shown by fig. 1.

This tendency is counteracted at pleasure, by a sliding ring, which being pushed towards the extremity of the holder, brings the jaws together until they are so closely in contact, as to embrace and hold very fast any thing that is placed between them. The appearance of the holder with a pen mounted for use is exhibited in fig. 2.

A very slight examination will suffice to shew the great superiority of this, over all preceding pen-holders. The pen, which may be of any ordinary size, is inserted without any trouble and without inking the fingers; when placed, it is held very firmly, but can never become fixed, as on withdrawing the ring the holder flies open and the pen is instantly discharged. The joint, which in other holders has always been the *weakest part*—in the above is actualy the *strongest*. Any variation in the size of

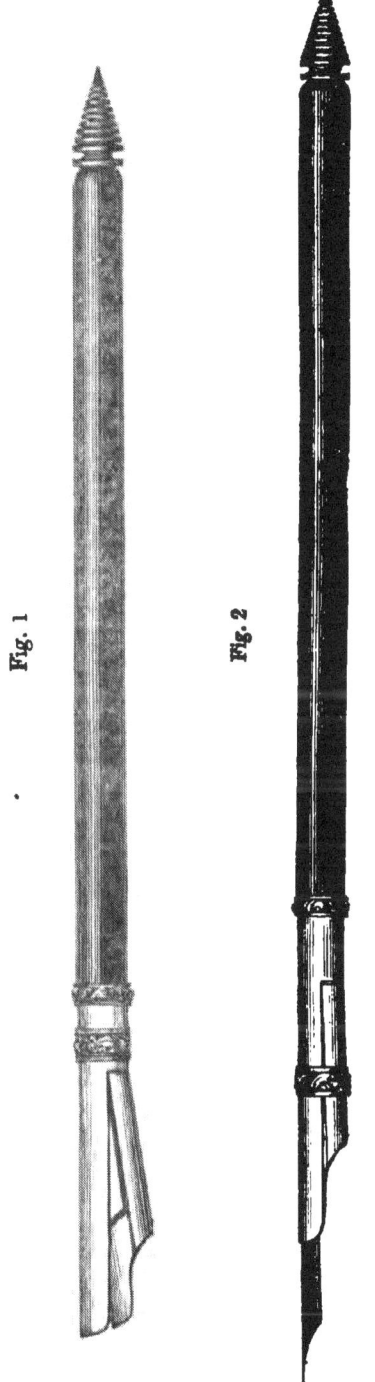

Fig. 1

Fig. 2

the pen, is met, by a proportionate shifting of the fulcrum.

This pen-holder has been pronounced by competent judges, in point of simplicity, durability, and convenience, decidedly the best hitherto produced.

METHOD OF DRAWING THE PARABOLIC CURVE BY AN APPLICATION OF THE DESCENT OF FALLING BODIES.

Fig. 1.   Fig. 2.

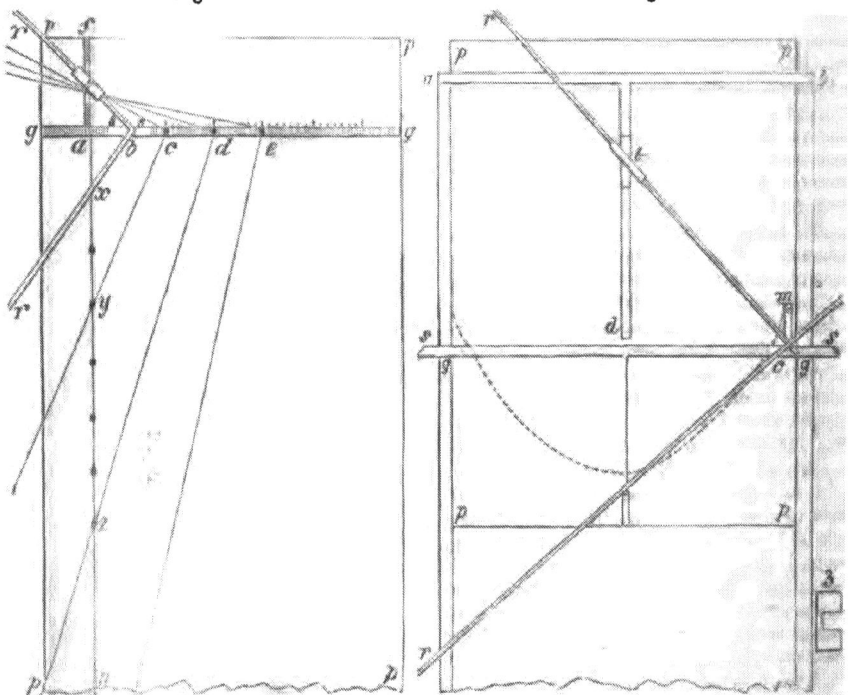

Sir,—The annexed is a description of a mechanical representation of the descent of falling bodies, and also an application of the principle to the drawing the curve of the parabola; in finding a place for the same in your scientific journal, you will oblige

Your humble servant,

J. R. ARIS.

Paterson-street, Stepney, April 14, 1838.

p p p p Fig. 1, represent a rectangular plane, the lower part of which is supposed to extend to some distance beyond the bottom of the figure. *s s,* is a short slip of wood or metal, which is made to slide in a groove *g g,* (projecting a small matter above the surface of the plane,) the latter being divided into a number of equal parts immediately above the slider;

these divisions are intended to represent any given intervals of time. *r b r* are two narrow slips joined together at *b*, forming a right angle, and attached at the angular point to the middle of the slip *s s*, by a screw at the centre on which it turns; the slip *s* on being moved in either direction, will carry the right angle with it, the upper part of it sliding through a short at *t*, which is attached to a slider which moves in the groove *a f*, and can be placed in any given position between *a* and *f*; the tube can be detached from the slider when required, and it also turns on its centre, that it may conform to the angular motion of the right angle. To represent the spaces that any body has fallen through in any given intervals of time, slide the slip *s* till the angular point of the right angle stands opposite the given intervals of time; for ample, to division marked b, which may represent any given interval and the lower part of the right angle will intersect the line a n, in x; a x representing the space fallen through in that interval of time. Again, on moving the slider s, till the angular point of the right angle coincides with the division marked c, and the lower part of the right angle will intersect the line a n, in y; d y, representing the whole space fallen through at the end of the second equal interval of time, which is equal to the square of two or four times the space a x. If the angular point be now moved to d, the point of intersection on the line a n, will be z; a z being the whole space fallen through at the end of the third equal interval of time, being equal to the square of three or nine times the space a x and so on. And if the angular point of the right angle be moved on with an uniform velocity over the space representing the progress of time, the point of intersection will move downwards on the line a n, with accelerated velocity, exactly corresponding with the accelerated motion in the descent of falling bodies. To represent the space that any body would fall through if moving with an uniform velocity equal to that which it may have acquired at the end of any given interval of time, slide the slip s s, till the angular point of the right angle coincides with the given interval of time, and the point of intersection on the line a n, will as before represent the space fallen through; now detach the tube t from the slider, and fasten the right angle by tightening the screw at the angular point, which will prevent it from having any angular motion, (thereby preventing any acceleration,) then slide the angular point till it coincides with the succeeding interval of time, and the space between the two last points of intersection (of the lower part of the right angle) on the line a n, will represent the space fallen through with the uniform velocity given; and if the last interval of time be equal to the former, it will be found that the body will fall through twice the space with the uniform velocity that it had acquired at the end of the first interval of time, (with accelerated velocity) which exactly agrees with the laws regulating the descent of falling bodies. If the tube t be placed at a greater distance from a, a similar effect well be produced; the only difference will be, that the points of intersection on the line a n, will be on a smaller scale; this principally depends on the depth of the plane; the best mode of adjusting it is, first to move the angular point of the right angle as far as it will go to the right, then slide the tube t till the lower part of the right angle intersects the line a n at the bottom; this will be found to be the most convenient. The reason of the result of the foregoing arrangment is as follows:—The motion of the slide s s producing an equal angular motion in both parts of the right angle, the angle made by the upper part with the line a t, will always be equal to the angle made by the lower part with the line a g. For example, let the centre of the right angle be moved to b, a b, representing the first interval of time, and the upper part of the right angle will make with the line a t, the angle a t b, a b being the tangent, and the angle a b x being equal to the angle a t b, and the radius a b, being equal to the radius a t; the tangent on the line a n, will be also equal. On moving the centre to c the second interval of time, the upper angle will be increased to a t c, a c being the tangent which is double that of a b, and as the angle a c y is equal to the angle a t c, the tangent of the former angle with an equal radius would be double also; but in addition to this, the radius a c is double that of a t, therefore the tangent on the line a n, is equal 2 × 2 or 4 times that of a x. Again, on moving the centre to d, the upper angle will be a t d, a d being the tangent which is now three times that of a b, and as the angle a d z, is equal to the angle a t d, the tangent of the former angle with an equal radius would be treble also, but the radius a d being equal to three times that of a t, the tangent a s, will be equal to the square, or nine times that of a x.

Fig. 2, shews the application of the same principle to the drawing of the curve of the parabola. Two sides of the plane are placed in a frame which projects above the surface; on the frame are fixed two narrow slips a b d, leaving a space underneath for the parallelogram p p p p to slide in; the paper on which the curve is to be drawn, is placed on the parallelogram; on the slip d is placed the slider with the tube t; the sliding slip s s is placed exactly under d, sliding in the two grooves g g; the length of the slip is double that of the width of the plane, the right angle being attached to the middle of it in the same manner as in fig. 1; to the middle of the slip underneath is attached the small arm m, carrying the tracing point or pencil which is placed a little above the centre; the lower part of the right angle is fixed on the upper part, in such a manner that the line forming the lower edge may pass exactly over the centre of motion, as it is also continued beyond the centre, being now in the form of a T square, that the curve may be traced at one operation. To trace the curve of a parabola of any given focus, slide the tube t till the distance from a is equal to four times the focal distance; then slide the slip s s which will carry the tracing point or pencil with it, and the lower part of the T square pressing on the projecting piece at the lower part of the parallelogram, forces it downwards to those distances which are exactly in proportion to the squares of the distances of the pencil from the middle of the parallelogram, (which are exactly equal to the ordinates); therefore, the curve traced by the pencil will be that of an inverted parabola.

In the above arrangement, it is not absolutely necessary that the pencil should be exactly in the centre of the T square, or even in the middle of the sliding slip s s; the curve drawn would still be that of a parabola; if it were placed at the end of the sliding slip s s, it would trace one side only of the parabola. When the lower part of the T square makes an angle with the axis of the curve less than 45 degrees, it will not readily push the parallelogram downwards; in this case move the parallelogram downwards by the hand, at the same time keeping the lower part of the T square in contact with the projecting piece by pressing slightly against it, by which means the curve may be easily traced. The lower part of the projecting piece is cut away (see fig. 3,) to allow the upper part of it to pass over the edge of the slip s s, and to come in direct contact with the centre of the T square, when the lower part of it is in a position parallel to the line s s.

AERIAL NAVIGATION.

Sir,—Eighteen months ago, Mr. Baddeley created no small sensation by the announcement in your pages, that he had " succeeded in contriving a balloon of an entirely new description, possessing all the requisites for efficient aerial navigation, and capable of being propelled and guided at the pleasure of the aeronauts." Had some other of your correspondents vouchsafed a similar declaration, it might, in the absence of anything in the shape of a " scantling" of the invention, have been passed without much notice; but, coming from the quarter it did, the general impression was, that there must be " something in it," and, while it was regretted that " it would not be consistent with Mr. Baddeley's personal interest" to enter into particulars at that time, the period was anxiously looked forward to, at which " your readers would have an opportunity of becoming acquainted with it."

However, the readers of the Magazine have watched in vain. A year and-a-half have since elapsed, and I do not recollect seeing a word more in relation to the matter, with the exception of a claim, in the next number, to a discovery of like nature and importance, on the part of a certain Signor Andervolti;—who has also disappeared, " and made no sign"! May I therefore be permitted to enquire, on the part of myself and the rest of the vast body of mankind who expected long ere this to have seen balloons, ·in the words of Mr. Baddeley, " propelled and guided through the air *with as much facility as boats at present are upon the surface of our river Thames*,"— what are the present state and prospects of the invention in question? Whether it is intended, in the course of the summer, to start regular stage-balloons (as *was to have been* done in the case of the aerial ship) to " Paris, Berlin, Vienna, and other principles cities of the Continent"? Or whether, (which, is just within the verge of possibility,) the scheme has turned out to be as impracticable as the many other contrivances for the same grand purposes broached from time to time in the pages of our scientific periodicals, and has been abandoned accordingly?—Even if this be the case, Mr. Baddeley surely owes it to himself and to your readers to make the result known as widely as the original announcement whose appearance raised the expectation of all so high. The world should not be any longer left in ignorance of the fate, whether good or bad, of an invention, the first rough plans of which were so satisfactory that the "scientific friends" of the author "expressed themselves perfectly convinced of their feasibility, and felt satisfied that *the time had arrived* when balloons would cease to be scientific toys, and *assume a new and useful character*." This was in, or previous to the month of October 1836, yet "the time has not yet arrived" for the public at large to have an opportunity of judging of the feasibility of a scheme so highly thought of, and balloons are at this present writing, just as mere "scientific toys" as ever. Is it not high time then for Mr. Baddeley to put an end to such a state of things, by publishing the details of his plan at once, or at least giving the reasons why he does not?

From some of the expressions in Mr. B.'s letter, it would seem that he contemplated taking out a patent, but as his name does not appear in any of your Lists of Patents up to the present date, it is evident that it is useless to expect any enlightenment on the subject from that quarter.

I beg to remain, Sir,
Your obedient humble servant,
PHILO-BADDELEY.

April 13, 1838.

DOMESTIC MANUFACTURE OF CIDER—NEW CIDER-PRESS.

(From a Paper "On the Manufacture of Cider," by Mr. Towers, C.M.H.S., in the *Journal of Agriculture*.)

The cost of the fruit must be an *ad valorem* calculation; because it must depend upon circumstances which will variously affect it. I presume that an orchard exists; and, in that case, the price will be little more than that of the labour bestowed in gathering it. The preparation of the fruit is readily submitted to calculation; provided there be a cider-press in the neighbourhood; but I shall give an estimate of the expenses incurred in that part of Berkshire where I reside, as, by it, persons at a distance may not only form an idea of the extreme cheapness of this beverage, but may be induced to introduce presses in the neighbourhood, where none are, as yet, to be found.

The writers whom I have consulted, agree in their censures of the awkward machinery which is in general employed; and I can add my testimony to the justness of their remarks, from having observed the construction of the ponderous presses that still exist in Somersetshire. These are lent out on hire, and require a waggon to remove them from place to place. Instead of encumbering the pages of the journal with any further account of them, I will attempt cursorily to describe a very compact and useful press, which I have seen at a village not remote from Windsor. It is kept by a gentleman for the express purpose of pressing apples for any one who will send them to him. Those who wish to make a certain quantity of cider, may have the fruit pressed, at the cost of twopence for every gallon of juice, at an hour's notice. My first experiment in this county was made in November 1835. I had 14 bushels of apples to spare; these were taken six miles in sacks with the barrels for receiving the juice. In a few hours, the juice was returned to me, with a charge of six shillings for 36 gallons, a surplus quantity remaining at the mill which the barrels would not contain.

This mill or press consists of two parts. The first is a sort of case or box firmly fixed to the floor of a barn; but it would stand in any common shed or outhouse, as it is little more than a yard long and two feet wide. There is at the top a wooden hopper to contain the apples; below that are two pair of cylindrical rollers which have an involute action in opposite directions, one towards the other; the upper pair are of wood full of iron nails or pegs, which rend and tear the apples to fragments, and deliver them to the lower pair of cylinders, made of stone. They are about 9-inches wide and 18-inches long, placed very near to each other.

The mill is set in motion by two winches, fixed to two heavy and broad fly-wheels which are turned by two men. The fragments of apples are carried by the tearing-rollers, and delivered at the upper surfaces of the pressing stone cylinders; which, partaking of the same simultaneous motion, crush them to a complete pulp, and deliver that into a trough at the bottom of the case or box. Such is the tremendous power of the rollers, that the pips of the apples are completely smashed; and yet there is no appearance of effort, and scarcely any noise: nothing can be more compact or convenient.

The *Pomace* (as the pulp is termed) is now put into horse-hair bags and placed on the stage of the press. This apparatus consists of a square case or frame about four feet wide, which rests upon the floor. The sides of the case are made of boards eight or nine inches wide ; the bottom is of very thick and strong plank, and upon this the hair-bags are placed. A similar board of great substance is put over the bags, and this is forced by the action of two extremely powerful iron screws upon the bags The pressure is first made by the hand, one man being employed at each screw, which he turns till juice ceases to flow. The shorter of two small levers is next passed through two of the handles of the screw, and thus an additional power is obtained. Finally, a longer lever is applied, and thus the pulp is deprived of nearly the whole of its juice. This simple and commodious press, that occupies the room of a moderately-sized table only, is capable of acting upon the pulp of 10 bushels of apples ; and as each bushel of good fruit is supposed to yield three gallons of juice, 30 gallons may be obtained in a very few minutes.

WHISHAW'S HYDRAULIC TELEGRAPH.

The uses of telegraphs in England have hitherto been exceedingly limited, from various causes, but more especially from the circumstance of the time of working them being very circumscribed, either from the total absence of light, or from hazy or foggy weather. The hydraulic telegraph is entirely free from such objections ; and on account of its simplicity and certainty is especially calculated for the speedy transmission of intelligence, whether for purposes of state, commerce, &c.

The operation of *telegraphing* by this machine is so simple, as to require no extraordinary abilities on the part of the Manipulator ; for, merely by regulating the increase or decrease of the column of water, by means of the cocks, it is either elevated or depressed *ad libitum* in the glass tubes at the different stations at the same time, to any figure of the vertical scale required.

The combination of this system are infinite ; though, for ordinary purposes, a dictionary of 12,000 words is sufficient. Each word in the dictionary is represented by a corresponding figure ; so that the Manipulator at one station has merely to telegraph the figures given to him, while the Manipulator at the other end returns each figure, as a proof of having the communication correct, and finds their meaning either by a reference to a general dictionary, or a dictionary for a particular purpose,—as for shipping, railways, elections. &c. These communications also may be carried on quite privately, if desirable, each telegraphic correspondent having his own set of figures.

Communications also may be made, through this medium, in different languages ; as between Germany and Spain,—a German and Spanish dictionary having similar numbers opposite corresponding words.

A great advantage of using figures is, that the longest words in the English language, many of which have from *eight* to *twelve* letters, are represented by four figures at most. The telegraph, on this principle, fixed at the Royal Gallery of Practical Science, is to full size, including the pipes, &c. Any one, therefore, may judge for himself of its great simplicity, and of the expense of fixing the whole apparatus to any extent.

To guard against frost, it is proposed to lay the pipes four feet below the surface of the ground ; and in passing over bridges the pipes would be fixed by collars in pipes of larger bore, and thus prevent congelation by the intervention of a non-conducting medium.

The estimated cost of a telegraph on this principle is as follows :—

1760 × 2 = 3520 yards of pipe in each mile, for two columns, at 8*d.* a yard............... £117 6 0

Laying down pipes, including digging and filling in, per mile   80 0 0

_____

£197 6 0

In London or other towns I have calculated the cost at double the above rate, from the greater difficulties which present themselves ; viz. 400*l.* per mile, including the apparatus at the stations.

The most proper routes to lay down pipes in, are railways, towing-paths of canals, turnpike-roads, and occasionally, if convenient, footways across fields.

It is to be observed, that an alarm can be sounded from one station to another. The telegraph at the Royal Gallery of Practical Science is fitted up on this principle.

It has been offered to the Admiralty, to which establishment it would be of immense use in passing the London fogs, which for weeks together impede the progress of communication beyond Chelsea by the common semaphore.

As a means of communicating between the different government offices, situated in different parts of the metropolis, it would be of great use. For purposes of state, in communicating between the government departments in London and the temporary residence of the court ; for giving alarms of fires to engine-stations in any part of London ; for sending communications from the offices of dock companies in London to their large commercial establishments eastward : for collecting the metropolitan police in any quarter of the town at a few minutes' notice; and for a variety of other purposes, the hydraulic telegraph is eminently calculated.

FRANCIS WHISHAW.

Gray's Inn, March 1838.

CAMUS ON THE TEETH OF WHEELS.

May, 4th 1768, died Charles Stephen Lewis Camus, the celebrated French geometrician, aged 69; author of a well known Treatise on the teeth of Wheels, in which the best forms to be given to them for the purpose of machinery, were for the first time determined, on true mathematical principles. An English translation of this treatise appeared in 1806, with some additions from the translator's own pen, which evinced an unfortunate ignorance of the scope of M. Camus's demonstrations; and have been a fruitful source of error in English mechanical practice. Camus proved clearly that the epicycloidal part of a tooth, designed to act on another wheel or pinion, ought to be generated by a circle equal to *the radius* of the wheel or pinion with which it is to be engaged; while his English translator represented his meaning to be, that it should be equal to *the diameter!* Mr. J. I. Hawkins, who has lately favoured the public with a more correct edition of the treatise, states, that "many of our first-rate engine manufacturers" have been so misled by this mis-conception of the original translator of Camus, that they are daily "pouring into the market multitudes of cast-iron wheels and pinions, of various magnitudes, for cotton and other machinery, with teeth formed from the epicycloid of the diameter, instead of the radius of the opposite wheel, or pinion;" and which must, in consequence, "wear out in a few years, instead of lasting the greater part of a century,—as many of them would do, if the teeth were formed on the true principles. We regret to learn, from the same authority, that there are many wheel-makers who follow no rule of proportion at all in their formation. "In Lancashire, they make the teeth of watch-wheels of what is called the bay-leaf pattern; they are formed altogether by the eye of the workman, and they would stare at you for a simpleton, to hear you talk about the epicycloidal curve. These Lancashire workmen should be called bay-leaf fanciers, because they cannot be bay-leaf copiers; since it is notorious that there are not two bay-leaves of the same figure. It is the opinion of Mr. Hawkins, that teeth accurately formed, either by the epicycloid or involute curve, will endure the wear of a century, with less damage than teeth, as usually made, suffer n ten years..—*Mechanics' Almanac.*

Manufacture of Salt for Dairy Purposes.—The Dutch are remarkably particular as to the proper quantity and quality of their salt, of which there are three kinds manufactured. The small salt for butter, which is somewhat smaller than the common salt made in this country, is boiled or evaporated in 24 hours. This kind is also used, as already mentioned, in mixing in some districts with the Kanter cheese. The second salt is evaporated by a slower process, in about three days; it is used in salting by outward application, the Edam, Gouda, and in some places, the Kanter cheeses. This kind is beautifully formed in the natural crystals of about half an inch square. The third kind is larger sized; the crystals are nearly an inch square, and the evaporation process lasts four or five days. It is sometimes used for salting the cheeses by outward application, but principally for curing fish, beef, pork, &c. The Dutch pay great attention to the exact quantity of the particular kind of salt necessary, so that we never find the cheeses made in Holland salted to an intolerable degree, as we sometimes experience in this country. I (says Mr. Mitchell) endeavoured to discover the mode of manufacture, and learned some particulars on this important subject, but there appeared to be some secret in the process, which the manufacturers were unwilling to disclose. One thing is certain, that the use of the Dutch salt is one of the causes of the sweet and delicious flavour of their butter, which, although always well flavoured, hardly tastes of salt, or rather of that acrid quality which the poisonous bittern of the muriate and sulphate of magnesia pervading our common salt imparts to our butter; and this is very obvious in comparing the Dutch butter with the best salted butter of this country. When it is considered that the health and prosperity of the people are materially concerned in the use of this article in so many various ways, the propriety, or rather necessity, of improvement in its manufacture will be more evident, and it is rather remarkable that whilst chemistry has now advanced to such perfection, no change has taken place in the mode of making salt for several centuries. The late scientific Earl of Dundonald, the late Dr. Coventry, and the Rev. James Headrick, proposed important improvements in the mode of manufacture of this article, which, however, seem never to have been adopted.—*Times.*

Machinery in Ireland.—On Tuesday the 6th ultimo, the Knight of Kerry gave a grand dinner to 200 of his quarrymen, at Valencia. Their homely substantial repast consisted of the best beef, pork, and bread, with excellent ale from Murphy's brewery at Killarney, crowned with abundance of whisky punch. One hundred and fifty of their wives and daughters joined the dance in the evening, and the festivity lasted till a late hour, when all departed satisfied and happy, without one instance of drunkenness or impropriety. The feast was to celebrate the establishment of a steam-engine and machinery for dressing the fine slate-stone of the Valencia quarries, which, by enlarging the demand for material, will have the effect of increasing considerably the number of quarrymen. It is a gratifying thing to have in our country a successful enterprise, giving employment to so large a number of fine industrious fellows, supporting their families in comfort. This is the true remedy for destitution in Ireland, and not poor-house jails. The Knight presided at the dinner, which was attended by several neighbouring clergy, Protestant and Catholic, and the repast afforded a most joyous scene of festivity and sound harmony.—*Kerry Evening Post.*—[The machinery above referred to is, we understand, that patented by our ingenious countryman, Mr. James Hunter, superintendent of Mr. Lindsay Carnegie's pavement quarries in Forfarshire.]—*Scotsman.*

Society for the Promotion of Practical Design.—A society under this title has just been set on foot by Mr. Ewart (the ex-member for Liverpool) and a select few of his *liberal* friends. It does not very clearly appear by what specific means the association proposes to accomplish its purpose, but, judging from the proceedings adopted hitherto, it is evidently considered that the vilification of the English artisan, and the exaltation of continental competitors at his expense, are among the most efficient. This can hardly be wondered at, when it is recollected that Mr. Ewart was not only the leading member of the House of Commons' Committee on the arts in connection with design, but is also the reputed author of the memorable report of that body,—memorable for the perversion of facts, even if those facts happened to militate against that same anti-English spirit which seems the essential ingredient of the new society.

Liverpool High School.—Some notion may be formed of the extent to which the Mechanics' Institution of Liverpool has swerved from its original design, from the perusal of the prospectus of the new "High School" commenced at the beginning of the present year, in the splendid building just erected for the purposes of the establishment. The course of instruction includes not only "the Belles Lettres," English style and composition, the classics, French, &c. &c., but "the entire range of pure mathematics, fitting the pupils for entrance into *the Universities*, as well as the *highest rank* in commercial life." The terms are from eight to ten guineas per annum, with a guinea extra from those parents who are not already members of the institution,—(the *Mechanics'* Institution!) The intelligent foreigner must conceive a high idea of the prosperity of the working classes of England, when he sees this *proof positive* that the mechanics of Liverpool are able to afford such a sum for the education of each of their children, as well as to indulge in the pleasing prospect of launching them into life from Oxford or Cambridge, or setting them up at once as substantial merchants of large capital! He would of course think it needless to inquire whether all the members of the Mechanics' Institution sending sons to the schools were really working mechanics; although it might not be very irrelevant to ask whether *any* of them were in that predicament!

"A Prophet is not without honour," &c.—The last number of "The Civil Engineer" contains an account of an *American invention* for the preservation of timber, extracted from the "Franklin Journal," but without the name of the inventor. That name, "Webster Flockton," certainly looks sufficiently transatlantic, but in point of fact it appertains to a countryman of our own, who has thought proper to secure his invention by an American patent, and has thereby, for a time at least, gained brother Jonathan credit for what he is not at all entitled to. The truth would have been obvious had the trouble been taken to copy the the patentee's name and designation from the *Franklin Journal*, where he is somewhat curiously described as "Webster Flockton of Great Britain, residing in Spa Road, Bermondsey, Surrey County, near London," (vide *Mec. Mag.* vol. xxviii, page 331.) Mr. F. is so far from being a Yankee, that he has just received a piece of plate from the corps of yeomanry of which he was captain, in testimony of his virtues as a "true Britain."

The "Asphalte" Mania.—Companies for the introduction of "Asphalte" into England, as a cement and material for paving, are at present quite the rage in the Share-Market. Some profess to have the exclusive right to the product of the only mines from which the genuine Asphalte is to be procured; others assert that it is to be had in Germany quite as pure as in France; while a third party proclaims that there is no necessity in the world to cross the channel for it at all; as it may be procured in abundance at home! It is taken for granted by all the speculators that "Asphalte" is to supersede granite and every other sort of pavement, on the strength of certain experiments made at Paris, and which are said to have succeeded to admiration. We believe, however, that all the experiments referred to have been made on foot-pavement, and not in the carriage-way, and it might therefore be as well to suspend judgment until a fair trial of the new material should have been made in the roadway of some such thoroughfare as Fleet-street or Cheapside. Cements of a like nature have often been tried in England, and found to succeed very well for footpaths, and where the nature of the traffic was not very heavy; but for carriage-way pavement, the result was different. A certain patent scheme which was tried opposite White-chapel Church, failed so signally that the "cement" had to be taken up and the road macadamized again immediately.

The "School of Design" at Somerset House, now numbers about a hundred pupils, most of whom are said to be master-tradesmen, as well may be the case, so long as the high charge of four shillings per week is persisted in. There is, however, an evening school now opened at one shilling per week, which may be expected to attract more of "our workmen" (for whose instruction the school was professedly established) than the older branch.

Mr. A. Symington's Plough for Tilling Steep Slopes.—Sir,—The Highland Society, taking into consideration the great loss of time incurred by the present mode of tilling steep slopes with the common plough, have offered a premium for the best form of one that will till at right angles to the slope, and lay the furrows all to the declivity. I have made a drawing of a plough with a view to accomplish this object, and shown it to a few eminent agriculturists, who highly approve of it, and recommend that one should be made for exhibition this season. It is to consist of two mould-boards set in opposite directions, both on the same-side of the plough, with coulter and sock to each, and a pair of stilts attached to both ends of the beam. The plough is to be drawn by means of an iron rod that moves upon a socket, to allow the horses to turn without turning the plough. In this way it will work in both directions, laying all the furrows to one side, doing double the work of the common plough in the same space of time.—I am, &c.

ANDREW SYMINGTON.
Kettle, April 9, 1838.   *Fife Herald.*

Scientific Holiday.—The number of visitors to the British Museum, on Easter Monday, amounted to *twenty-two thousand*, which, large as it is, falls short of last year by about two thousand. The difference may be attributed to the circumstance of the want of *entire novelty* on the present occasion: the Easter of 1837 was the first holiday-time during which the Museum had ever been open to the public.

☞ *British and Foreign Patents taken out with economy and despatch; Specifications, Disclaimers, and Amendments, prepared or revised; Caveats entered; and generally every Branch of Patent Business promptly transacted. A complete list of Patents from the earliest period (15 Car. II. 1675,) to the present time may be examined. Fee 2s. 6d.; Clients, gratis.*

LONDON: Printed and Published for the Proprietor, by W. A. Robertson, at the Mechanics Magazine Office, No. 6, Peterborough-court between 135 and 136, Fleet-street.—Sold by A. & W. Galignani, Rue Vivienne, Paris.

𝔐𝔢𝔠𝔥𝔞𝔫𝔦𝔠𝔰' 𝔐𝔞𝔤𝔞𝔷𝔦𝔫𝔢,

MUSEUM, REGISTER, JOURNAL, AND GAZETTE

No. 768.]   SATURDAY, APRIL 28, 1838.   [Price 3d.

TAYLOR AND DAVIS'S ROTARY STEAM-ENGINE.

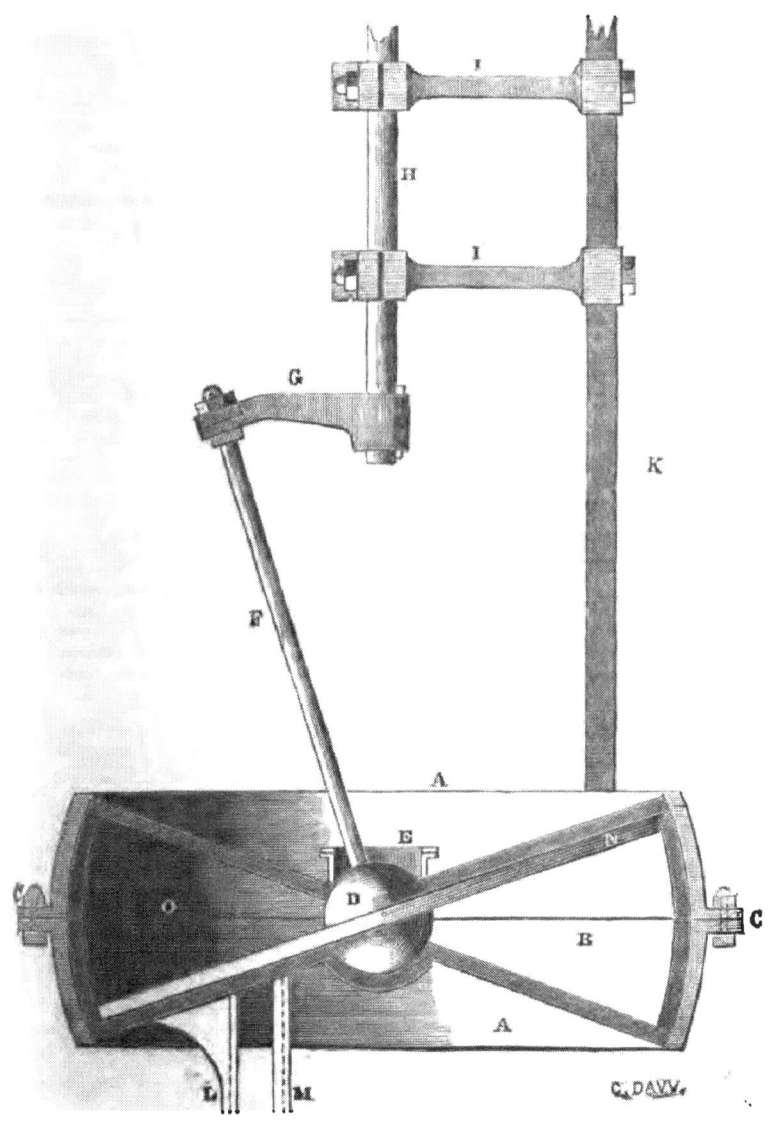

TAYLOR AND DAVIS'S ROTARY STEAM-ENGINE.

Sir,—Contemporary journals have of late been rife with an account of a new mechanical wonder that has made its appearance in the shape of a steam-engine, possessing (so say the accounts) unrivalled power, portability, and cheapness. The accounts of this new wonder have hitherto been without the aid of diagram or illustration. At all times it is a matter of considerable difficulty to represent by words alone, the mechanical construction and action of any apparatus however simple its arrangement may be. In this particular instance, however, the description alone would appear to draw largely upon the credulity of the public, and its obscurity of meaning has reminded some of the less credulous, of the story of the old lady who shewed so much anxiety to furnish her dwelling with curious and complicated articles of furniture—giving as general directions to her mechanist that all was to be accomplished " *somehow* by means of a screw." The inventor of the present notable contrivance appears to have been fully impressed with the wonder-working operations of the " screw," and has accordingly produced an apparatus which probably has not its equal for eccentricity of motion or screw-like evolutions. The following is the non-illustrated description, assisted in the present instance by the diagram accompanying this communication, which it is hoped will help to throw a little more light upon this new-born of science:—

" At the British Alkali works, Stoke Prior, near Bromsgrove, a steam-engine has been invented by a labouring mechanic, and is daily in full operation, which will certainly supersede every other now in use, and that, too, in a very short period of time; as the simplicity of its construction, the smallness of its size, and the almost nothingness of its cost, will necessarily bring it speedily into notice among all persons whose business may require the aid of so useful an auxillary. Its size is not more than twice that of a man's hat, and the expense of a five horse power will not exceed in cost half a score pounds. Its form is cylindrical being about eighteen inches diameter and twenty-two deep. The steam is admitted through a hole in a hollow circular belt (attached to a wall) upon which it revolves, and works it by a diagonal action, against an upright piston, being forced out by pressure of a diagonal plate, which divides the inte-rior into two portions. The rotary action is beautifully managed by means of a perfectly spherical steam-tight joint, at the end of a fixed inclined arm, towards which joint the upper and lower surfaces of the interior part of the cylinder are made to slope, after the form of the exterior of an hour glass. Upon these the diagonal plate performs its revolutions, such movement being permitted through an opening (from the circumference to the centre), equal in width to the thickness of the before named upright piston, up and down the sides of which it continually works. In the centre of the bottom of the cylinder is fixed a shaft, having attached to it a wheel which communicates the motion that may be required; and this is all the machinery of which it consists."*

One would imagine that the editor of the journal was making merry at the expense of the "labouring mechanic," or at any rate gving a satirical fillip to the inventor, when he says. that " our scientific friends will not consider us too bold in asserting that this invention will speedily revolutionize the whole system in this department of mechanics." When and how this will be effected I leave to the readers of the *Mechanics' Magazine* to determine. For one, I must confess a *little* scepticism on the subject. In the absence of all practical data connected with the operation of this engine, we may at least suggest that friction is not *altogether* dispensed with, and that the rotary action so " beautifully managed" with the spherical " *steam-tight joint*" is a very clumsy way of accomplishing what has hitherto been effected without that tendency to torsion which would ultimately result from its present mode of application. Appearances indicate this engine to be of the kind usually denominated " high pressure." The quantity of steam used, its pressure, work employed in, form of boiler, quantity of fuel used, quality of ditto, form and packing of piston, number of revolutions per minute, &c. &c., are so many important points of information that require to be ascertained, to do full justice to the ingenuity of the inventor. As matters stand at present, Messrs. Boulton and Watts, Maudslay's, Seaward's, Hall's, &c. &c., respective steam engine arrangements, are not likely to be affected by the revolutionary assertions of the *Engineer's Journal*.

* Civil Engineer and Architect's Journal for March 1838.

References to the Diagram.—A, outer case of cylinder; B, steam chamber (or cylinder); C, flanges to connect outer case; D, ball and socket joint; E, stuffing box &c.; F, connecting rod to crank; G, the crank; H, crank shaft; I, plummer blocks, &c.; K, standard for ditto; L, M, steam passages. N a disc fitting into the cylinder A; O, a quadrant-shaped piston, attached to the inner surface of the cylinder, the disc N having a slit therein from the rim to the centre, to allow it to reciprocate upon this quadrant. The steam is alternately brought to the upper and under surfaces of the disc N, thereby producing a circular conical motion of the disc, and turning the crank G.

Your, &c.

CHRIS. DAVY.

Note.—The diagram is intended merely to shew the form and operation of the engine—possibly there may be some slight inaccuracies, but they cannot be of sufficient importance to effect the merits of the invention. The drawing has been made from recollection.—C. D.

TAYLOR AND DAVIS'S PATENT STEAM BOILER FEEDER.

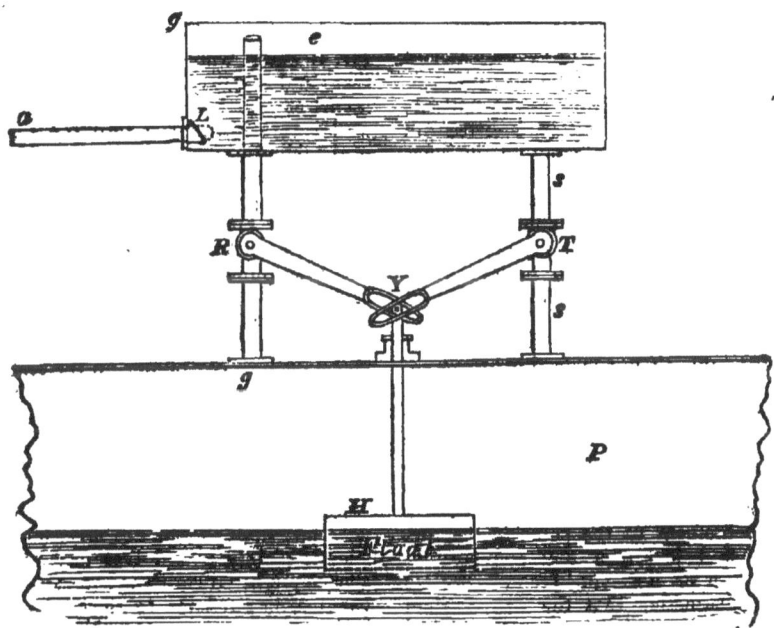

Sir,—This invention, I believe has been patented some time; it is very simple, and likely to be effective, and the only thing that can in any shape militate against it (in my humble opinion), is the possibility of the combined friction of the two cocks, and the rod working in the stuffing-box, rendering so sluggish the action of the float, as to defeat the object of the invention. In the above drawing, P shows a portion of the boiler; c, a water reservoir, made steam tight; a, a pipe, through which c is supplied with water, having a valve opening inwards, at L; g is a steam pipe, extending from the boiler, to nearly the top of the close vessel c, and s is a water-pipe extending from the bottom of the close vessel to the interior of the boiler. In both these pipes, are stop cocks R and T, with levers extending to Y, by which they are opened and closed. In these levers are two longitudinal slits, for the reception of a pin, fixed in a rod, extending from the float H, through a stuffing-box, in the top of the boiler. Now,

B 2

when the water in the boiler has evaporated, and its surface descended, the
weight of the float brings down the
levers to the position represented; the
cocks will then be opened, and the steam
will rise through the pipe *g*, by which
the pressure will be equalized in the
boiler P, and the supply vessel *c*, and
and water will descend through *s*, till
its surface in the boiler, rises sufficiently
high to raise the float, and shut the two
cocks, and then the condensation of
steam in *c*, will cause a partial vacuum,
permitting a fresh dose of water to pass
through T into the feed vessel.

I remain, your obedient servant,
RICHARD EVANS.
Swansea, Dec. 18, 1887.

MR. SEAWARD'S DOUBLE SLIDE VALVES
—MR. HUMPHREY'S REPLY.

Sir,—I am astonished at the contents
of Mr. Seaward's letter inserted in
your last number in reply to my communication of the 12th of March, in
reference to my invention of double
slide valves for steam-engines. Had
Mr. Seaward fairly met my claim after
having condescended to notice it, by
proving his priority of invention, it would
have been unnecessary to have occupied
your valuable pages with another word
on the subject; but instead of doing so,
Mr. Seaward commences his observations by endeavouring to implicate me
in falsehood by most positively denying that he had ever any conversation with me on the subject of the
valves. Now, although it is a matter
of no moment to the point in dispute,
whether I had ever any conversation
with him or not, yet, I again declare
most distinctly, that the conversation
alluded to in my letter with Mr. Samuel
Seaward, occurred in Messrs. Seaward's
office; and if it were at all necessary I
can perhaps refresh Mr. Seaward's
memory with his reply to me, nearly
word for word. With regard to "one
of Messrs. Seaward's foremen" not having asked or accompanied me on board
the "Emerald" at the time alluded to
in my letter,—I can only say, that it is
untrue. Messrs. Seaward had more than
one foreman in 1834, I certainly cannot
name the man who accompanied me on
board, but I feel pretty confident that

should this meet his eye he will not
hesitate to avow it.

If Mr. S. had read my letter with a
little more attention than he appears to
have done, he would have seen that what
I therein stated about the Lords of the
Admiralty and Mr. Brunton, was given
as I received it from the person who
accompanied me on board; I did not represent as a fact that those gentlemen
were on board the "Emerald" at any
particular time, and I have reason to
believe myself in error in stating that
Mr. Ewart name was mentioned. Indeed,
I find upon inquiry in the proper quarter,
that Mr. Ewart was not connected with
the government service at the period
alluded to, and I am sorry this gentleman's name should have been thus inadvertently introduced. It was Mr.
Kingston the engineer of Woolwich, and
Mr. Brunton who were on board together; and it was owing to the favourable
report of Mr. Kingston that the double
nosles were introduced into the service
of the admiralty.

My communication contains no allusion to the period at which Mr. Seaward
applied for his patent; indeed it is perfectly immaterial to the question; but
the first publication of Mr. Seaward's
invention, or at least so far as my knowledge of it extends, is to be traced to its
use on board the "Emerald" which
vessel commenced plying on the river in
June 1834, four months previous, I think,
to the date of Mr. Seaward's patent.

Mr. Seaward expresses astonishment
that I should have "waited till the present day to put forth my claim." I can
assure Mr. Seaward, I should not even
now have done so, had not several of my
friends plainly hinted that any further
silence might be construed to my disadvantage, in reference to the part I took
in introducing the plan. Nearly three
years ago, I received a letter from a
gentleman well-known in the scientific
world directing my attention to Mr.
Seaward's circulars respecting these
nosles, and advising me to publish my
claim to the invention.

In no part of my letter have I stated
that Mr. Seaward was not the inventor
of the nosles of which he is patentee, I
left it for Mr. Seaward to shew his claim
to priority in the invention if he thought
proper; and perhaps he may now consider he has done so by having informed

your readers that he thought of it in Cornwall twelve years ago, and that a full description of the plan is contained in his journal dated May 1830; all this I cannot dispute; the object of my letter was simply to prove, that I had anticipated Messrs. Seaward in pointing out the use and advantages of double slide valves, not to " one or two individuals only" as Mr. Seaward represents it, but to the directors of two public companies, and that I had devoted a good deal of time in endeavouring to introduce their use in marine engines, two years before the date of Mr. Seaward's patent, facts which Mr. S. has not attempted to disprove. It was by mere accident only that these valves were not in operation in a pair of engines of 220 horse power between five and six years ago. What in that case may I ask, would have become of Mr. Seaward's claim? Why, I should have been told perhaps that I had peeped into his journal of 1830!

Hoping that the introduction of double slide valves into Cornwall may fully realize Mr. Seaward's expectations, and remove all the imperfections and difficulties he complains of as arising from the use of double beat valves,

I remain, Sir,

Yours respectfully,

FRANCIS HUMPHREYS.

Dartford, April 18, 1838.

ANALYSIS OF HARPER AND JOYCE'S PATENT FUEL.

Sir,—The increasing estimation in which the *Mechanics' Magazine* is held, and the great benefit it has conferred, and is conferring on the scientific world in the improvement of the arts and sciences, induces me to trouble you with a few lines on Messrs. Harper and Joyce's stove. A few evenings ago I experienced the gratification of witnessing a series of experiments on the *material* used in this stove as fuel, and which has been kept so profound a secret. The chemical operations were conducted by the hand of a master, and according both to the analytic and synthetic methods. Before proceeding farther, however, it may be as well for the information of the general reader to explain what these methods are. The first is *analysis* or decomposition; the second *synthesis* or composition. In analysis the parts of which

bodies are composed are separated from each other : thus, if we reduce cinnabar which is composed of sulphur and mercury, and exhibit these two bodies in a separate state, we say we have decomposed or analyzed cinnabar. But if on the contrary, several bodies be mixed together and a new substance be produced, the process is then termed chemical composition or *synthesis* : thus if by fusion or sublimation we combine mercury with sulphur and produce cinnabar, the operation is termed chemical composition by *synthesis*. This explanation will clear the way for the following outline :—On the evening in question the experimenter or manipulator before commencing his operations began by enumerating the gases which experience has proved to be destructive to animal life; he extracted these gases from solid matter by chemical affinities ; a lighted wax taper when plunged into these gases was instantly extinguished and animal life expired in a few seconds when immersed in them. After these various phenomena had been exhibited, the experimenter showed how by certain tests the presence of these various deleterious gases might be detected, and also how the quantity of these gases contained in any given quantity of a solid material, might be ascertained. The gas I believe (with the exception of oxygen) which is most abundant in nature, is the carbonic acid gas, which when inhaled by animals almost immediately destroys life, and to this gas the experimenter particularly directed his attention. The material used as fuel in Joyce's stove was examined with great care and judgment, with the view of ascertaining its composition; it having been currently reported that this fuel was gifted with its extraordinary virtues by means of two, if not three new ingredients, or new combinations of old ingredients, that in fact it was charcoal combined with some substances which caused an immense volume of caloric to be thrown out when in a state of combustion. Now the carbonic acid with which charcoal is known to abound, and which is so destructive to animal life when extricated by combustion, was said to be neutralised by these hitherto unknown or newly combined ingredients. The experimenter having subjected the fuel used in Joyce's stove to analysis, proved it to be incontestibly nothing more nor less than charcoal well prepared by burning, with a portion of potass, an ingredient to be found in charcoal made from wood, though not always in the proportion required for Joyce's stove.* When the stove was in operation, and the material in a state of combustion, the gas extricated and collected, was carbonic acid gas, as proved by various tests, and by killing birds in a few seconds when exposed to it. Even when the gas obtained from this stove was mixed with (I think) one third of atmospheric air, it destroyed life. The stove experimented on was a single cylinder one. When in operation a piece of linen rag was applied to the cylinder with the view of ascertaining whether it would scorch or burn a similar substance that might either by accident or design be brought in contact with it. The result was, that the linen rag was in a few seconds so singed, that I am persuaded had it been applied a few minutes longer, it would have ignited. The gases evolved had upon myself personally, a very noxious and suffocating effect.

C. Q.

London, April 22, 1838.

———

HARPER AND JOYCE'S STOVE.

Sir,—In the very fair and impartial account of Messrs. Harper and Joyce's "much-talked-of stove," inserted in your last number, the fact of carbonic acid being evolved by the combustion therein, is very properly adverted to, and the unfitness of this stove for carriages, close apartments, and sleeping chambers, clearly and forcibly pointed out. For my own part, I entertain the highest possible opinion of the integrity of the patentees, and firmly believe that the various statements put forth by them, are the consequences of being themselves deceived, and not from any desire to deceive or impose upon others.

There are some points, however, in which they are decidedly wrong; the first mistake, rather an important one, occurs in over-rating the heat-giving powers of these stoves, and it is the more surprising that there should be ambiguity about this, inasmuch as the effect produced by the radiation of heat

of a uniform temperature (in this instance I believe about 200°) from a given surface (in these stoves only a few feet) is dependant upon long known and well established laws. This point is one in which scientific men ought not for one moment to be deceived, and yet, the most erroneous statements have been promulgated of the heating powers of this stove.

The next error—the fatal tendency of which has been more readily perceived and pointed out, is the statement, that the patent stove "is smokeless, and gives out neither smell nor noxious vapour."

The fuel employed by Messrs. Harper and Joyce is charcoal subjected to a certain preparatory process, which is said to enable it to discharge its office, free from the baneful consequences attending its ordinary combustion.

Now, charcoal varies greatly in its character, according to the kind of wood from which it is obtained, varying again not only in trees of the same class, but also in different parts of the same tree. The materials employed in the preparation, are said to be cow-dung and lime, both of them substances liable to greater variations in their component parts than even the charcoal itself. With such materials, therefore, let the operation be conducted with the greatest possible care, it is altogether impossible to prepare a fuel of such purity, with the chemical constituents in such exquisite equilibrium, as to maintain innoxious combustion. Carbonic acid gas will, in all cases, be given off, in greater or smaller quantities, according to the purity of the fuel employed, varying as the elements approach to, or recede from, that perfect theoretical "balance of power" upon which the invention is grounded.

But the greatest evil of all appears to me to be, in the temptation held out by the hope of gain, and the facility afforded to fraudulent venders of the patent fuel, for adulteration. The prepared is not to be distinguished by the eye from common charcoal, and when we see the amount of rascality practised in the vending of ordinary kinds of fuel, it is much to be feared that there are dealers base enough to mix, or substitute common, for the patent charcoal.

The consequences of such an admixture, I need hardly tell your readers, burned in a close apartment, would be

* We do not think this is the true secret.—ED. M.M.

certain death. So far as the metropolis is concerned, the patentees may, perhaps, effect the supply of fuel direct from their own depôt; but, should subsequent improvements render the apparatus eligible for general employment, persons residing in the provincial towns, &c. should have some ready means of distinguishing between genuine and spurious fuel.

I remain yours respectfully.

WM. BADDELEY.

April 23rd, 1839.

ANTI-PHLOGISTIC FLUID, FOR THE PREVENTION AND EXTINGUISHING OF FIRE.

Sir,—In the list of patents inserted at p. 464 of your last volume, there is one recently taken out by Eugene Richard Ladislas de Breza, of Paris, for a chemical combination for rendering cloth, wood, paper, &c. indestructible by fire.

As it is scarcely possible to peruse a newspaper without having the feelings harrowed up by a recital of the most appalling accidents from the ignition of female clothing, an unobjectionable mode of rendering articles of dress incombustible, must be peculiarly beneficial.

It may, perhaps, be a pity that any preventive for these heart-rending calamities should be shut up under the monopolizing influences of a patent-right. Thanks to British humanity, however, we are already in possession of some simple and tolerably efficient methods of checking the progress of combustion in certain substances. The ingenious Captain Manby, whose exertions in the cause of humanity through a long life of benevolence, entitle him to our warmest gratitude, after having perfected and successfully established his well known plan for "*saving the lives of mariners wrecked on lee-shores*," devoted a great deal of time to the investigation of the best means of extinguishing or of escaping from fire. Among other branches of inquiry, considerable attention was paid to discover a practical method of increasing the extinguishing powers of water. The result of Capt. Manby's experiments are lucidly set forth in the following extract from "An Essay on the Prevention and Extinction of Destructive Fires, &c." published by him in the year 1830:—

" The addition of *common pearl-ash*, or the pot-ash of commerce, to water, renders that fluid capable of extinguishing fire very efficaciously: indeed, such is its power, that it will instantly extinguish the flames, nor will the part where it wets re-ignite, or rather re-inflame; for, as the water evaporates, a solid incrustation of the pearl-ash is left on the surface, which by defending it from the influence of air, prevents it from burning and from communicating flame to the contiguous parts. Water thus impregnated constitutes what may be called an *antiphlogistic fluid* which is by many times more effectually extinguishing, than common water. The simple solution of pearl-ash is the one which I have constantly used, and I consider it the best, as it never fails in extinguishing active conflagration. As a demonstrative proof of the efficacy of my antiphlogistic fluid, I illustrated at a lecture, its extinguishing properties by direct experiment. On the hand I showed its power of extinguishing flames,—on the other, its property of rendering materials otherwise highly combustible, incapable of burning with flame; and, finally, I contrasted it with the effect of common water. For this purpose I exhibited its effects on the most combustible materials found in dock-yards, viz.: hemp, oakum, cordage, and deal wood; and and afterwards, with a view to diminish the the numerous fatal calamities, that have so often befallen females, from the structure of their dresses, and the inflammable materials of which they are composed—as calico, muslin, gauzes, linen, &c. Of each of these I exhibited a specimen,—the one impregnated with the solution and afterwards dried, the other dipped in common water. By applying fire to each of these specimens, there was at once manifested the value of such an agent in resisting fire."

A knowledge of these facts cannot be too extensively disseminated, as it may providentially be the means of averting some of the worst consequence arising from accidents by fire. By using more extensively *stuffs* for the external clothing of females, and protecting the linen and calico by means of the simple alkaline solution, the number of deplorable accidents now continually taking place might be materially diminished. I entertain great hopes of much being shortly achieved in this way, as there is some slight symtoms of *preventives* generally becoming fashionable.

I remain, Sir,

Your's respectfully,

WM. BADDELEY.

London, April 19, 1839.

TABLES OF WORK PERFORMED BY CORNISH STEAM-ENGINES, FOR MARCH, 1835.

MINES.	Engine & diam. of the cylinder.	Average quantity of water drawn per minute. imp. gal.	Load per square inch on the piston. Lbs.	Length of the Stroke in the Cylinder. Feet.	Number of lifts.	Depth. fms-ft.	Diameter of the pumps. Inches.	Time.	Consumption of coal in bushels.	Number of strokes.	Length of stroke in the pump. Ft.	Load in lbs.	Pounds lifted one foot high by consuming a bushel of coal.	Num. of strokes per minute.	Remarks, and Engineers names.
North Boskear.	New engine; 70 inches; single.	242.5	13.2	10.	1 1 1 1 1 1	8.3 / 40. / 41.4 / 40.0 / 20. / 18.3 / 80. / 12	11 / 18¾ / 13¾ / 8 / 7 / 16 / 6	March 1 to April 2.	1547	229390	8.0	6847	75,280,252	4.97	Drawing perpendicularly 150 fathoms, the remainder diagonally. Main beam over the cylinder, and one balance bob at the surface. John West.
Wheal Darlington.	90 inches; single.	655.49	14.74	10	4 3 2 1	89.5 / 79.8 / 7 / 9.5	19 / 12 / 10 / 8	Feb. 23 March 23.	2498	27097	8.0	93599	80,357,249	6.97	Drawing perpendicularly; main beam over the cylinder; and one bob at the surface. Eustis.
Consolidated Mines.	Davey's engine; 90 inches; single.		13.12	11.38	2 12 1	13.5 / 262.1 / 10.	14 / 12 / 10¼	March 3 to April 3.	3857	819060	8.75	86530	71,556,445	7.18	Drawing perpendicularly; main beam over cylinder; two balance bobs at the surface; two ditto under ground; and a balance lift in the shaft. Hocking and Loam.
United Mines.	30 inches; single; Eldon's engine.		17.96	9	1 1	5.1 / 34.1	12 / 14	ditto	629	401650	7.5	15219	78,945,929	8.68	Drawing perpendicularly; main beam over the cylinder. Hocking and Loam.
Ditto	Hocking's engine.		13.58	10	1 1 6 1	3.4 / 44. / 157.1 / 7.	12 / 9 / 16 / 10	ditto	3943	374600	8.5	92098	74,372,113	8.1	Drawing perpendicularly; main beam over cylinder; one balance bob at the surface; one ditto under ground. Hocking and Loam.
Fowey Consols.	Austen's engine; 90 inches; single.	454.01	10.79	10.8	3 2 1 2 1	97.3 / 51.3 / 11. / 18 / 13	15 / 10 / 10¼ / 8 / 6	March 8 to March 29.	1250	193960	9.25 / 6	58969 / 2375	86,849,585	6.4	Drawing in two shafts perpendicularly; main beam over the cylinder; and four bobs, and 130 fathoms of horizontal rods at the surface. William West.
Wheal Vor.	Borlace's engine; 90 inches; single.		14.5	10	8 1 1	222.4 / 10.3 / 5.8	14 / 8¾ / 8	Feb. 24 to March 31.	3163	339170	8.0	91364	78,144,960	6.08	Drawing in two shafts 170 fathoms perpendicularly; remainder diagonally. Main beam over the cylinder, and one balance bob at the surface, and four ditto, and a V bob under ground; and 106 fathoms horizontal, rods worked by two king posts, and three angle bobs at 174 fathoms level. Richards.
Polgooth.	66 inches.	967.68	9.2	9.8	1 1 1 1	30.3 / 20. / 20 / 20	20 / 18 / 9¼ / 12	March 8 to March 29.	1240	290050	7.4	41902	72,529,996	9.59	Drawing perpendicularly; main beam over the cylinder, and one balance bob at the surface. James Sims.

74 millions, average of eight engines.

MINES.	Engine, and the diameter of the cylinder.	Length of the crank. feet.	Length of the stroke in cylinder. feet.	Diameter of the fly wheel. feet.	Number of heads.	Time.	Consumption of coal bushels.	Average height which every head lifts in inches.	Number of times when every head lifts at stroke.	Number of strokes.	Average weight of heads and lifters, and water column, in pounds.	Pounds one foot high by consuming a bushel of coal.	Number of strokes per minute.	Engineers' name, and remarks.
Charlestown United mines.	32 inches; single.	3.5	9	18	75	March 7 March 29	527	9	5	188560	37500	50,315,464	5.9	J. Sims.
Wheal Kitty.	32 inches; single.	4.0	9	20	59.2	March 6 March 31	706	9	5	357740	29314	55,701,790	9.9	Lifts the water to supply the grates, 5 fathoms 3 feet of 14 column, and 4.75 feet lift. J. Sims.
Carn Brea.	32 inches; single.	4.0	9	20	67.8	March 1 April 4	740	9	5	305290	35602	55,079,060	6.28	Lifts the water to supply the grates 6¼ fathoms of 15 inch column, and 4.75 feet lift. J. Sims.

Extract from Duty Report of March 1838, for the purpose of showing the Depth, Number, and Diameter of the Pumps attached to several Engines in the Mines of Cornwall. As the eight highest are given, the eight lowest added, will give nearly the *average Duty*.

Inch cylinder.	Duty.	
24	23,527,908	{ Shaft 90 fathoms from the Engine ; load light, 100 fathoms.
36	28,682,917	Two shafts ; load heavy ; 18.8lb. per square inch } Same mine.
36	30,406,901	Two shafts.
60	29,415,942	} Same mines ; circumstances favourable.
70	32,597,952	
45	34,128,562	Circumstances ditto.
30	32,798,717	Three shafts.
53	26,653,138	Circumstances favourable ; load heavy.

	millions.	
No.		Above
2		80
6		70
5		60
15		50
14		40
9		30
4		20
5		1
60		

Engines pumping

8 best   74
8 worst   29
          108

Average about 51 millions.

BADDELEY'S NAVIGABLE BALLOON.

Sir,—In reply to your correspondent who exhibits such a very pardonable anxiety about a navigable balloon (*vide* page 44), the discovery of which was announced in your pages eighteen months ago, permit me to say, that I never intended taking out a patent for this invention, the magnitude and costliness of its application rendering such a procedure superfluous.

I was rather desirous of disposing of the invention to any party who would be disposed to take it up in a manner calculated to render the speculation a profitable one. Up to the present time, I have not met with any person so disposed, and the thing remains in *statu quo.* The experience of eighteen months has in no way tended to shake my confidence in the practicability of the scheme, though I must confess other more pressing engagements have permitted the navigable balloon to receive but a very small share of my attention.

I remain, Sir, yours, respectfully,

WM. BADDELEY.

April 24, 1838.

MR. UTTING'S ASTRONOMICAL TABLES.

Sir,—In No. 756 of the *Mechanics' Magazine*, the Cambridge Student has advanced some further remarks on my previous communications, on which, however, it is necessary for me to make but few observations, as the tenor of his epistles are completely on a par with those of the Scotch Dominie. One remark however I shall not pass over, viz.: "Of what use is it to give the length of the *tropical* periods? It is not from these periods (as the Scotch Dominie has fully demonstrated) that the synodic periods are computed, but from the siderial periods! Let then, Mr. Utting give us a table of the mean siderial periods of the planets, together with the precession of their respective equinoxes, such as he used in calculating his tropical periods, then we would have something to grapple with." (Vol. xxviii, p. 298.) Now in respect to the first, it is evident that the Cambridge Student, as well as the Scotch Dominie, are equally in error, as I have before asserted that the siderial and tropical periods both give the same synodic period (if stated in the same denomination of time). What is still more ludicrous, the Dominie asserts in answer to a satirical remark of mine, copied into No. 747, p. 139, " Mr. Utting," in continuation says, ' and further, you assert that in no case in the solar system is $\frac{T\ T'}{T-T'} = \frac{P\ P'}{P-P'}$;' what a display of intelligence !" " whoever contested such a point." To which the Dominie replies, " I will here tell Mr. Utting that he may now pretend to be acquainted with the above-mentioned fact," (mark) " but sure I am, he knew nothing about it until I gave him the information !" I may again here exclaim—What a display of intelligence ! These remarks fully prove that you are grounded in the false notion that the above formulas invariably give different results, and moreover, that I was of a different opinion until you gave me the information to the contrary; that is, previous to your information I believed that both formulas gave the same result ! A very unfortunate admission on your part, as it completely condemns your own arguments and establishes mine, and as I am about to prove. In answer to other remarks of the Cambridge Student, I have given the tropical periods of the planets, with the secular motion of the equinoxial points, from which he may easily compute the siderial periods of the planets, unless he, like the Scotch Dominie, quails at " the drudgery of science" !

Since writing the above I have received part 182 of the *Mechanics' Magazine*, in which is contained a letter by Kinclaven, confirming all the blunders contained in the communications of the Scotch Dominie. After all the arguments that had been advanced on the subject, he ought to have made himself thoroughly acquainted as to which of the parties was in error ; instead of which, he has by an idle calculation subjected himself to a castigation which he justly deserves. (Intended for me too, by the bye). Now the matter in dispute is simply this, whether the said two formulas give, or whether they do not give, the same results ?—which I shall now proceed to establish beyond the power of contradiction ; as follows :—

Secular Motion in 100 Years.

	seg. deg. min. sec.		seg. deg. min. sec.		deg. min. sec.
Earth	0..0..45..53..	Jupiter	5..6..18..2	Equinoxial points	1..23..30

Solar Periods. *Synodic Periods.*

Hence,
$$\frac{4330 . 59895073 \times 365 . 24224142}{4330 . 59895073 - 365 . 24224142} = 398 . 884081157$$

Siderial Periods.

And,
$$\frac{4332 . 58476000 \times 365 . 25636098}{4332 . 58476000 - 365 . 25636098} = 398 . 884081153$$

Difference = 0 . 000000004

Now as it may again be insinuated, that "I have acted wisely in not taking the data from my own tables," I shall therefore give another example as a further illustration, by making use of them as follows :—

Secular Motion in 100 Years.

	seg. deg. min. sec.		sg. deg. min. sec.		deg. min. sec.
Earth	0.0.45..52.068567	Jupiter	5..6..16..10.403513	Equinox. points	1..26..5.322195

Solar Periods.

$$\frac{4330 . 6431643117 \times 365 . 2422440456}{4330 . 6431643117 - 365 . 2422440456} = 398 . 88370918817$$

Siderial Periods.

$$\frac{4332 . 6906529242 \times 365 . 2568016772}{4332 . 6906529242 - 365 . 2568016772} = 398 . 88370918809$$

Difference = 0 . 00000000008

In the first example the two results agree to eight places of decimals; and in the latter to ten places; being in each case the number of decimals employed in the solar and siderial periods, from which the synodic periods were deduced. Hence, a nearer coincidence cannot possibly be expected. And from the above results it is perfectly evident who the persons are, that have sullied your pages, with the numerous stains, imputed to me by Kinclaven.

I am, Sir, yours, &c.

J. UTTING.

Sporle, April 12, 1838.

POISONS IN CHEMISTS SHOPS.

Sir,—Most of your readers are, no doubt familiar with the melancholy death, which has just occurred, of Mr. Bruce, butcher, Stamford, occasioned by poison administered to him, by his apprentice. When we are told that the poison was procured by this apprentice from the errand-boy of a chemist, I cannot but remark that some steps should be taken to exclude access to poisons from such hands. Surely this pitiable case is lamentable enough of itself, without mentioning others which have occurred, to call for an immediate remedy, ere another, destructive of human life should take place. I should be pleased to see some of your correspondents suggest some improvement in the shop of the chemist whereby greater safety may be ensured to the public.

I noticed a short time since, in the shop of a chemist in the West of England a simple plan by which the poisons were kept together, and distinct from the other chemicals, with the additional security of a lock and key. The plan was merely the having a cupboard in which the poisons were kept, placed in a conspicuous part of the shop with the word "Poisons" painted very large on the door, which was kept locked; thereby enabling the customer to see that poison was not administered to him by mistake, which has frequently been done from the great similarity in appearance of many chemical preparations, some of which are comparatively innoxious, while others are poisons of a very active kind :—for instance, the crystals of epsoms salts and oxalic acid are so much alike, that many persons have been poisoned in consequence of taking the latter for the former. Now it will be clearly seen, from what has been said, that an errand-boy could not have obtained poison from the shop I have alluded to; and as the plan is so simple, I cannot see the slightest reason against its adoption until a more effectual preventive is found.

    I am, Sir,
        Your's respectfully
                HY. GOOD.

Brighton, April 21, 1838.

HERAPATH AND COX'S PATENT PROCESS OF TANNING.

    Sir,—From the disposition you have exhibited to bring our specification before your readers, I take it for granted you would have no objection to take our own version of the advantages to be derived from the new process; I therefore send you the circular we have addressed to the trade, and beg you to consider, that we stand pledged to the accuracy of the statements, notwithstanding the facility we afford to every tanner to come and judge for himself.

    I remain, Sir,
      , Yours respectfully,
        WILLIAM HERAPATH.

Bristol, April 20, 1838.

    The patent process is extremely simple and economical: it has been seen in action by some of the most celebrated tanners, all of whom have spoken of it in the most favourable terms, and some have acted upon their good opinion by entering into arrangements for its immediate introduction. For 100 butts or hides a week it may be described as follows:—A pair of rollers is placed over each of eight pits, from fifty to sixty butts are then connected together by legatures for each pit, so as to form an endless belt; by turning the rollers the belt of butts is drawn between them, so that every butt, in succession, has its partially exhausted ooze squeezed out of it every few minutes, by a judiciously graduated pressure, and is immediately allowed to descend into the pit for a fresh supply of liquor. It will be seen that the rollers are constantly drawing a hide from the bottom of the pit, squeezing it, and then instantly dropping it at the top of the heap of hides, which is under the liquor on the other side of the rollers. Simple as this plan is, with a pressure and strength, of ooze suited to the state of the leather, the following extraordinary results are produced by it:—

    1st. The time of tanning is shortened, from twelve months to six weeks; from six months to one month: two months are sufficient for the stoutest and strongest butts; consequently the new tanner makes, by *time alone*, four full profits in the year instead of one.

    2nd. The leather is better tanned, while its weight is increased considerably: the patentees produce from 2 to 3 lbs. per butt on light, and from 3 to 4 lbs. on heavy butts —more than half the payable weight of a salted hide; or, the same quantities, more than the payable weight of a dry hide, in addition to the full proportion of belly and shoulder. This increase of weight is not derived from extra tan, but from a preservation of the substance of the hide (gelatine) which, in the old process, is dissolved in the enormous quantity of oozes employed during the protracted period of operation. This extra profit, of $3\frac{1}{4}$ lbs. of leather per butt, is realised also *four times a year.*

    3rd. In all past trials to tan quickly, the produce has suffered, either in quality, colour, or weight, and sometimes in all three; and this has so constantly occurred that it has grown into an adage, that " no quickly-tanned leather can be good." But the patent leather is softer, more elastic, wears better, and resists water longer than any known. If thrown into water and cut through in twelve hours, the interior is dry; and sometimes it is so after eighteen hours, which is more than ten times as long as the best tanned upon the old plans.

    4th. The work of handling is done cheaper, as one-horse power to turn eight pair of rollers, and four boys, at 2s. 6d. each, per week, to attend upon them, are all that is sufficient to turn out 100 hides per week; and the rapidity of the process is such, that one-third of the present capital will do the same extent of business; while the size of of tan-yards and quantity of oozes will be reduced in nearly a corresponding proportion.

    5th. The patent plan is applicable to existing yards at a very trifling expense; it costs about 160l. to 170l. to alter an old yard, to tan 100 hides a week; and every tanner will be able to select his tanning mixture or material, or he can follow his own peculiarities of manufacture just as much as at present; this the patentees conceive to be a great advantage, as there will be as many varieties of leather under the new system as under the old, although all the samples will be superior in quality. It will be seen that the mode of operation gives the most perfect means of working in series, or " rounds," and thus permits the progressive application of liquors from weak to strong : and those liquors are found in practice to be much more quickly exhausted.

MANUFACTURE OF ALKALI—THE QUEEN v. MUSPRATT.

On the 7th instant this very important case was tried at the Liverpool Assizes—affecting the very existence of some extensive manufactories in which great capital has been sunk, in Liverpool and its neighbourhood. The action was brought at the instance of the corporation of Liverpool, against Mr. Muspratt for a nuisance. It appeared that the works which formed the subject of the indictment were founded in 1822, shortly after the reduction of the duty on salt. The works were for the manufacture of alkali, in the course of which two processes were necessary—first of all, the manufacture of sulphuric acid, and secondly, the mixture of that acid with common salt, in the manufacture of what was called salt-cake, or black ash, for the purpose of converting it into alkali, that being used as a substitute for kelp, or Spanish barilla. The works were so conducted as to discharge into the air from the lower part of the premises more or less of sulphuric acid gas, and from the high chimney in which the other part of the process was carried on a large quantity of muriatic gas. It was stated that it injured and destroyed vegetation, tarnished and corroded all metallic substances, was particularly offensive to the senses, excited coughing, and produced a smarting of the eyes. In 1828, Mr. Muspratt was indicted, when he agreed to make such improvements as would do away with complaints. To effect this he erected a chimney 228 feet high—so that the gas might be carried to a considerable distance over Liverpool before it fell. This it appears did not have the desired effect, and in 1832 he was indicted again and acquitted. Thus matters remained until the present year.

A very great number of witnesses were called for the prosecution. They deposed that the white vapour which descended from Mr. Muspratt's chimney pained the eyes, produced cough, corroded metals, took the colour out of dyed good, and destroyed vegetation. Even forest-trees were gradually killed by it. The leaves looked as if struck by lightning, and the grass turned black and shrivelled up.

Mr. Rogerson, surgeon, stated, that salt was a compound of muriate of soda, and by pouring the sulphuric acid upon it the muriatic acid was separated from the soda, in the form of gas, leaving the sulphuric acid to combine, and form sulphate of soda. This gas was driven up the chimney and poured out in the form of a white vapour, from uniting with the moisture of the atmosphere. It was highly deleterious in a condensed form, killing both plants and animals, but he should think became innoxious in the proportion of one part of the gas to 1,500 of the atmosphere ; though then it was not good for the health, as producing a hurtful stimulant to the lungs. When in a condensed state, it greatly injured the conjunctiva, a membrane of the eye, the mucous membrane of the nose, the mouth, the throat, the lungs, and sometimes the bowels.

Mr. J. Rogerson, physician, brother of last witness, stated that the muriatic is a transparent, colourless gas, when in a pure state ; but when mixed with air, or rather with the moisture of the atmosphere, it forms the vapour spoken of. It mixes with the moisture and forms a liquid acid. It has a pungent, irritating odour, and an acidulous taste. It is rapidly absorbed by water, which, at 40 degree of Fahrenheit, takes up 480 times its bulk. It turns vegetable colours red. Besides these properties, it will not support combustion, and it is fatal both to animal and vegetable life. If a portion of muriatic acid gas flowed from the mouth of a chimney, I should consider that the effect would be that it would combine with the moisture of the atmosphere and fall to the ground in the shape of a dilute acid. It would fall more rapidly in a damp state of the atmosphere. Although, when mixed in the proportion of 1 to 1,500, it does not kill vegetables or plants, immersed in it for a certain period of time, it must still be consider injurious to health, and, on account of its irritating properties, it can be in no way useful to the growth of plants. Dr. Christieson, of Edinburgh, states that when one cubic inch is mixed with 20,000 of air it is still injurious to plants. It is also injurious to persons labouring under diseases of the lungs. In the experiments made on plants they had been confined under a glass ; the effect might be different if the plant were experimented upon in the open air and in the presence of a bright sun. Hydrogen gas is very destructive to animal life. Carburetted hydrogen comes from the gas-works. The men employed seem to inhale it without injury. Turpentine works give out acetic acid ; it will make people cough. Tanyards give out ammonia ; brimstone refining, sulphuric acid gas. The air is humid at Liverpool, on account of its proximity to the sea. This will produce rust. For the defence a great number of witnesses were called, who deposed generally that the annoyance, though considerable eight or nine years ago, was now very trifling, and that they and their families, though residing in places exposed to the action of of the vapour, suffered no serious inconvenience. The most material evidence was given by Dr. Thomas Thomson, professor of chemistry in the University of Glasgow. In the manufacture of alkali like that of Mr. Muspratts, muriatic acid gas will be evolved at one step, during the decomposition of the common salt. The first step in the manufacture is to decompose salt with sulphur, and in that process the muriatic gas is evolved. The chimney from which it issues being 228 feet high the proportion in the 100 parts of muriatic gas which escapes, I can state from experiment, to be not more than 6¼ per cent. of muriatic acid. The rest consists of carbonic acid and azotic gas, which is one of the constituents of common air. During the decomposition of the salt, for every ton of salt used there are used four tons of coals. The coal being burned, the salt is converted into water and carbonic acid gas. The water from the heat of the fire ascends in the state of steam—an invisible elastic substance, like common air, and the muriatic acid is united to it in the same form. The mixture ascends to the top of the chimney, expands, and becomes a visible smoke. The water is changed to the substance of cloud, precisely the same as you see coming from the top of a steam-engine. A cloud consists of a congeries of little bladders of water, every one at small distances from the others, in dimensions varying immensely, usually invisible, not the 1,000th part of an inch in diameter, but I have seen them as large as peas. This white vapour or cloud consists of little globes of water combined with muriatic acid. It is slightly lighter than the air, and of course floats on. As it gets through the atmosphere it gradually changes again to steam, so that it disappears; but the process is a very slow one. It never falls, but by the time it has disappeared the muriatic acid, becomes muriatic acid gas, which moves at the rate of 1,000 feet per second, so that by the time it gets to a certain distance, and all depends on the state of the atmosphere, it is impossible to detect the smallest particle of muriatic acid. On a dry day it travels before doing so a short distance, on a wet day a longer one, and cannot be detected by the most delicate tests. At the distance of a quarter of a mile from the greatest manufactory in the world I could not detect its presence by the finest tests that would have detected 1-50,000th part. That was at Glasgow. I tried it in consequence of a lawsuit like this, and I was determined not

to give my evidence until I was sure of the fact. The muriatic acid disperses itself through the atmosphere equally in every direction, and by the time it has travelled a quarter of a mile, you cannot detect it but by one test. That test is the nose. I can perceive the smell, but I cannot prove its existence by any other means. I know it then, but I cannot detect it. It is impossible that in that state of dilution, when you can smell it, but not detect it, it can do any mischief. It is impossible that this white vapour can impinge at different distances, from 100 to 1,800 yards, except there was a wind driving it down. The ultimate fate of that stream of vapour is that it resolves into steam and muriatic acid gas. Suppose, instead of the muriatic acid gas going off in in clouds, it assumed the character of drops on leaving the chimney they would immediately fall to the ground; if the diameter of the drop were the 1,000th part of an inch, they would begin to fall at the rate of ten feet the second, and the rate of their descent would increase as the square of the time, according to the well-known laws of gravitation. I have watched a chimney of the kind for twenty years, and never saw a drop of acid fall from that; if a drop did fall, it would fall at the rate I have described, if of the diameter I have assumed. The relative heights of the chimney and of Everton-hill, being, the former 250 feet above the level of the sea, and the latter 226 feet, the gas from the chimney would necessarily pass over Everton-hill; it would be contrary to a law of nature for it to do otherwise, without a vertical wind. No doubt muriatic gas will rust metals, but the effect of a quantity not detectable by reagents must be very trifling indeed. The grand cause of the rusting of metals is the moisture of the atmosphere. In a dry atmosphere they will not rust. Any acid will rust metals. Suppose a gas disengaged at the orifice of a chimney; if a persons stands at the base, there will be in the air just 1-90,000th part of the vapour that issues from the mouth of the chimney; and, in order to get the proportion of muriatic acid gas, assuming it when it issues from the chimney to be 6¼ per cent., you must divide it by 16, and the result will be less than 1,000,000th part. Supposing there is a wind, it will have a tendency to make it fall on one side; it will reduce it one-half; instead of 1,000,000th part, there may be 1-500,000th part. It is a regular law of nature, on which there can be no doubt. All gasses expand as the square of the distance. If you double the distance, you have the fourth of the proportion; if you treble it, 1-9th. If you take an immense vessel of muriatic gas and empty it, its contents may remain for a certain depth as a stratum for perhaps one minute; but it will disappear in a much shorter time than those will think who have not tried it. I have taken an immense vessel of carbonic acid, emptied it into a room, and in five minutes I could not detect the slightest trace of it, all had gone. The most injurious of all gas given out in this neighbourhood, is the sulphuretted hydrogen gas; it would kill an animal in a very short time, though much diluted; it is poisonous, and though much diluted, will readily kill a rat or any small animal immersed in it. The carbonic acid gas is one of the least injurious of all; any animal placed in it is destroyed as if plunged in water, from mere want of atmospheric air: it is not a poisonous gas. The evolution of those gasses would account for all or most of the circumstances described here, and exclusively charged on the muriatic acid gas. A moist atmosphere is the great ruster. The process of rusting is this:—moisture attaches to the iron, and carbonic acid to the moisture, and both together begin to to corrode the iron, and, whenever that process begins, it goes on with great rapidity. I don't think that any gas, unless very long applied, would have a deleterious action on meat. Muriatic acid gas produces no effect on meat at all; it washes off; it does not destroy meat; it wants that character altogether; some gases will destroy meat; acetic acid, for instance, will dissolve it—dissolve it into a jelly. Muriatic acid gas would dissolve the leaves of vegetables, cauliflowers or cabbages. Some trees are destroyed by the sea air; the beech is one, and the sycamore is another; their leaves become covered with black spots.

After a long and lucid summing up by the judge the jury consulted together for upwards of an hour, and brought in a verdict of *Guilty*.

————

LIST OF ENGLISH PATENTS GRANTED BETWEEN THE 22D MARCH, AND THE 25TH OF APRIL, 1838.

James Lowe, of King-street, Old Kent-road, mechanic, for improvements in propelling vessels. March 24; six months to specify.

Michael Wheelright Ivison, of Hailes-street, Edinburgh, silk-spinner, for an improved method of preparing and spinning silk, waste wool, flax and other fibrous substances, and for discharging the gum from silks raw and manufactured. March 26; six months.

Julius Oliver, of Queen-street, Golden-square, gent., for a certain improvement in the filtres employed in sugar refining. March 26; six months.

Auguste Coulon, of Token-house Yard, London, merchant, for improvements applicable to block-printing, being partly a communication from a foreigner residing abroad. March 26; six months.

Thomas Oram, of 27 East-street, Red Lion-square, gent., for improvements in the manufacture of fuel. March 26: six months.

Charles Hullmandel, of Great Marlborough-street, Westminster, lithographic printer, for a new mode of preparing certain surfaces for being corroded with acids, in order to produce patterns and designs for the purpose of certain kinds of printing and transparencies. March 26; six months.

Charles William Grant, captain, bombay engineers, St. Alban's-place, Westminster, for certain improved modes of exhibiting signals for the purpose of communicating intelligence, either at sea or on shore. March 26; six months.

Julius Jeffreys, of Kensington, esq., for improvements in stoves, grates, and furnaces. March 26; six months.

John Clark, of Mile-end, Glasgow, cotton-spinner, for improved machinery for turning, some part or parts of which may be made applicable to other useful purposes. April 4; six months.

William Angus Robertson, of Peterborough-court, Fleet-street, London, patent agent, for certain improvements in the manufacture of hosiery, shawls, carpets, rugs, blankets, and other fabrics, being a communication from a foreigner residing abroad. April 4; six months.

George Barnett, of 49 Jewin-street, London, tailor, for an improved button, for protecting the thread or shank from friction and wear. April 7; two months.

Joseph Rock Cooper, of Birmingham, gun-maker, for improvements in fire arms. April 10; six months.

Thomas Watson, of Addle-hill, Doctor's Commons, mechanic, for improvements in stoves. April 10; six months.

David Redmund, of Wellington Foundry, Charles-street, City-road, engineer, for certain improvements in the construction and apparatus of steam-boats or vessels, used for war or commercial purposes. April 10; six months.

Edward Cobbold, of Long Melford, Suffolk, and Peter Richold the younger, of the same place, coachmaker, for improvements in the manufacture of certain pigments or paints, or such like substances, April 10; six months.

William Fothergill Cooke, of Breeds-place, Hastings, esq., for improvements in giving signals and sounding alarms at distant places, by means of elastic currents transmitted through metallic circuits. April 18; six months.

William Barnett, of Brighton, ironfounder, for certain improvements in the production of motive power. April 18; six months.

Thomas Murray Gladstone, of Bootle-cum-Linacre, near Liverpool, chain cable and anchor manufacturer, for certain improvements in ships windlasses, which improvements are applicable to other purposes. April 21; six months.

Edward Cooper, of Haverton, Wilts, clothier, for an improvement in the making or manufacturing of soap. April 21; six months.

James Timmins Chance, of Birmingham, glass manufacturer, for improvements in the manufacture of glass. April 21; six months.

James Macnee, coachmaker, George-street, Edinburgh, for an improvement or improvements in carriages. April 21; two months.

Moses Poole, of Lincoln's-Inn, Middlesex, gent., for improvements in manufacturing of carpets, rugs, and other napped fabrics, being a communication from abroad. April 21; six months.

Christopher Nickels, of York-road, Lambeth, manufacturer, for improvements in machinery for recovering fibres, applicable to the manufacture of braid and other fabrics. April 21; six months.

Robert Finlayson, of Regent-street, Cheltenham, Gloucester, M.D., for improvements in harrows. April 21; six months.

Francis Pope, of Wolverhampton, Stafford, fancy iron worker, for certain improvements in machinery for making or manufacturing pins, bolts, nails, and rivets, applicable to various useful purposes. April 24; six months.

Thomas Vaux, of Woodford Bridge, Essex, land surveyor, for improvements in tilling and fertilizing land. April 24; six months.

Samuel Wagstaff Smith, of Leamington Priors, Warwick, iron founder, for improvements in regulating the heat of furnaces for smelting iron, which improvements may also be applicable to retorts for generating gas. April 24; six months.

Alexandre Happey, of Basing-lane, London, gent., for a new composition applicable to paving roads, streets, terraces and other places, which improvements are also applicable to the different purposes of building; and also in the apparatus for making the said composition, being a communication from a foreigner residing abroad. April 25; six months.

Richard Goodwin, of Saint Paul's Terrace, Camden Town, coal merchant, for an improved prepared fuel. April 26; six monts.

LIST OF SCOTCH PATENTS GRANTED BETWEEN THE 22D MARCH, AND THE 22D APRIL, 1838.

Henry Bessemer, of City-terrace, City-road, Middlesex, engineer, for certain improvements in machinery or apparatus for casting printing types, spaces and quadrats, and the means of breaking off and counting the same. Sealed 23rd March, 1838: four months to specify.

Richard Tappin Claridge, of 8 Regent-street, gent., in consequence of a communication from abroad, for a mastic or cement or composition applicable to paving and road-making, covering buildings and the various purposes to which cement, mastic, lead, zinc, or composition are employed. March 27.

Jeremiah Bynner, of Birmingham, Warwick, lampmaker, for improvements on lamps. March 30.

Auguste Coulon, of Token-house Yard, London, merchant, partly in consequence of a communication by a foreigner residing abroad, and partly by invention of his own, for improvements applicable to block-printing. March 30.

Joshua John Lloyd Margary, of Wellington-road, Saint John's Wood, Middlesex, esq., for a new mode of preserving animal and vegetable substances from decay. March 30.

Julius Oliver, of Queen-street, Golden-square, Middlesex, gent., in consequence of a communication from a foreign residing abroad, for a certain improvement in the filtres employed in sugar refining. April 6.

Charles Wye Williams of Liverpool, Lancaster, gent., for certain improvements in the means of preparing the vegetable material of peat moss or bog, so as to render it applicable to several useful purposes and particularly for fuel. April 6.

Alexandre Happey, of Basing-lane, London, gent., in consequence of a communication from a foreigner residing abroad; for a new composition applicable to paving roads streets, terraces and other places which improvements are also applicable to the different purposes of building, and also in the apparatus for making the said composition. April 9.

John Stewart, of Glasgow, for improvements in machinery for manufacturing ropes, lines, twines, and yarns, from hemp, flax, or tow. April 12.

Marie Claudine Veronise Lenoble, of Leicester-square, Middlesex, for certain bituminous mastics or cements, capable of receiving various colours, which compositions are applicable to various useful purposes. April 17.

Michael Wheelwright Ivison, silk-spinner, residing in Hailes-street, Edinburgh, for an improved method of consuming lime in furnaces and other places where fire is used, and for economising fuel, and also for supplying air heated or cold to blasting or smelting furnaces. 19th April.

LIST OF IRISH PATENTS GRANTED IN MARCH, 1838.

William Watson, of Temple-street, Dublin, for an improved boat or vessel to be used on canal and other inland navigation.

Moses Poole, of Lincoln's Inn, for improvements in looms for weaving figured and ornamental fabrics.

Henry Quintin Tenneson, late of Paris, but now of Leicester-square, Middlesex, for an improved construction of the portable vessels used for containing portable gas, and of the apparatus or mechanism for regulating the issue or supply of gas, either from a portable vessel, or from a fixed pipe communicating with an ordinary gasometer.

Thomas Joyce, of Camberwell New-road, gardener, for an improved apparatus for heating churches, warehouses, shops, factories, hothouses, carriages, and other places requiring artificial heat, and improved fuel to be used therewith.

Richard Burch of Haywood, Lancaster, engineer, for certain improvements in manufacturing gas from coal.

John George Bodmer, of Bolton-le-Moor, Lancaster, civil engineer, for certain improvement in machinery for spinning and doubling cotton, wool, silk, flax, and other fibrous material.

NOTES AND NOTICES.

"In America the trade of a *chimney-sweeper* is unknown. There are whole states, including some of the greatest towns, where such a creature was never heard of. To supply this defect every man sets fire to the soot in his chimney by way of clearing—a practice often productive of serious conflagrations."—*Painter's Church of England Gazette.* In several parts of England a similar practice prevails, and is often attended with the same fatal consequences. In Edinburgh and many provincial towns a check is put upon this practice by the infliction of a pecuniary fine; in London a similar fine is incurred in the shape of fees to the engine-keepers who may attend such fires.

Spontaneous Combustion.—Among the numerous bubble companies of the day, is a "Self-producing and Self-consuming Coal Company." A sort of fuel which should *produce* itself would certainly be an acquisition, were its good quality not counterbalanced by the very bad one of *self-consumption!* It is to be feared that the parties who venture to deal with so fiery a material will only *burn their fingers* for their pains.

Mechanics' Magazine, Complete sets.—The proprietor of the Mechanics' Magazine has now effected the repurchase of the earlier portions of the stock of this journal from the parties who were possessed of the same in the right of his first publishers; and he is now able to supply several complete sets of the work. Price, twenty-seven volumes, half-cloth, £11 7s.

☞ *British and Foreign Patents taken out with economy and despatch; Specifications, Disclaimers, and Amendments, prepared or revised; Caveats entered; and generally every Branch of Patent Business promptly transacted. A complete list of Patents from the earliest period (15 Car. II. 1675,) to the present time may be examined. Fee 2s. 6d.; Clients, gratis.*

LONDON: Printed and Published for the Proprietor, by W. A. Robertson, at the Mechanics Magazine Office, No. 6, Peterborough-court between 135 and 136, Fleet-street.—Sold by A. & W. Galignani, Rue Vivienne, Paris.

Mechanics' Magazine,

MUSEUM, REGISTER, JOURNAL, AND GAZETTE.

No. 769.]   SATURDAY, MAY 5, 1838.   [Price 3*d*.

WHITELAW'S PLAN FOR FEEDING STEAM-BOILERS.

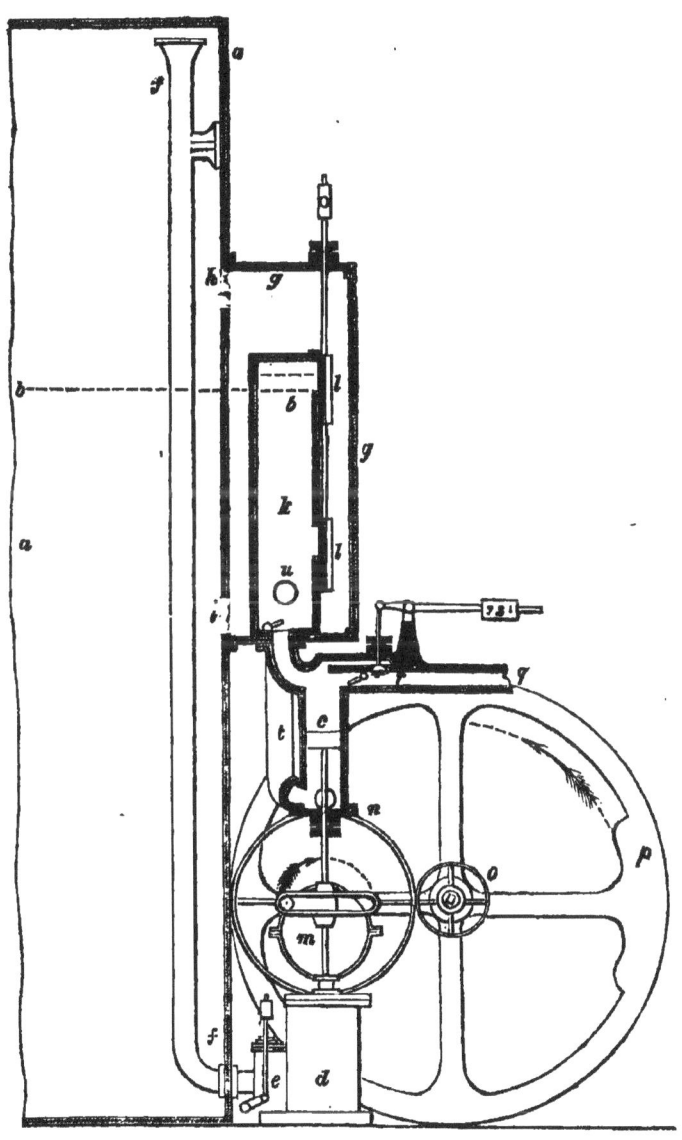

PLAN FOR KEEPING THE BOILERS OF HIGH PRESSURE STEAM- ENGINES ALWAYS FILLED WITH WATER UP TO THE REQUIRED LEVEL, BOTH WHEN THE ENGINES ARE WORKING AND WHEN THEY ARE NOT AT WORK; TOGETHER WITH DIRECTIONS HOW THE PLAN MAY BE APPLIED TO THE BOILERS OF CONDENSING STEAM-ENGINES.

Sir,—*a a a* in the figure (see front page) shows a section of one end of a high pressure boiler, and the dotted line *b b* is drawn near to the place at which the water in it should stand. The feed pump *c* is wrought by means of a small steam-engine, the cylinder, nosles, and steam pipe of which are marked by *d*, *e*, and *f f*, respectively. *g g* is a casing fixed upon this boiler, *h* and *i* are holes which allow the water always to stand at the same level in the casing as in the boiler, and these holes diminish the agitation which the water in the casing would have if the whole of one of its sides was open into the boiler. Inside of the casing a chest *k* is fixed, having a space left round its sides and top for the steam and water to get past it freely. The chest *k* has two openings, or ports in one of its sides, with one of the valves marked *l*, working upon each in such a manner as that the inside of the chest has no communication with the casing *g g*, during the time the piston of the feed pump is working upwards; but when the piston of this pump is working towards the cylinder *d*, then there is always a communication with the chest *k* and the casing. A pulley upon the crank pin of the little engine works into a horizontal slit in a frame fixed upon the top of the piston rod, and the bottom end of the rod of the feed pump is attached to the top side of the same frame : in this way the crank shaft as well as the feed pump are set in motion. The eccentric *m*, which works the valves *l l* is fixed upon the crank. Both of the valves marked *l* are attached to the same rod, and in order that the eccentric *m* may stand right under them, the steam cylinder *d* and the feed pump are placed a little towards one side of the boiler, while the casing *g g*, and the chest *k*, stand towards the other side. The fly wheel is on the second motion, and its shaft is driven by means of the spur wheel *n* and the pinion *o*, so as to make double the number of revolutions as the crank shaft. As the fly weel makes two revolutions for one of the crank shaft, its heavy side *p* will always be next the end of the boiler, and in a line level with its own shaft every time the piston is at the top or bottom end of its stroke ; by this arrangement (if the parts work in the direction of the arrows, and if the fly wheel has the position on its shaft, as per the figure,) the engine can never stand on its centres, however slow its motions, as the heavy side of the fly wheel will always be in a position to carry it past them. The slide valves *l l*, must be fitted upon the chest *k* in such a manner that they will not be forced away from their faces when the pressure inside of the chest is greater than the pressure in the boiler.

When the piston of the feed pump arrives at the top end of its stroke, as then a pump full of water has passed into the chest *k*, the steam in the top part of the chest will be compressed, and on this account it will have a greater pressure than the steam in the boiler ; and if the space in *k*, which lies above the surface of the water in the boiler is twice as large as the contents of the pump-barrel, then when a full of the pump is sent into *k*, the steam in it will be of twice the density of the steam in the boiler. If the space in *k*, which lies above the dotted line *b b*, is double that of the contents of the barrel of the feed pump, then the conical valve *r* must have its weight *s* so heavy as that it will allow the valve to open as soon as the pressure inside of the chest *k* is double of the force of the steam in the boiler. If the steam space in the chest *k* holds twice the full of the pump-barrel, and if the valve *r* is loaded to the extent now mentioned, a pump full of water will pass into the boiler after each stroke, as soon as the valves *l l* are opened, whenever the water in the boiler stands at or under the dotted line *b b*, as in this case the pressure inside of *k* will not have opened the valve *r*, and allowed part of the contents of the feed-pump to be discharged back into the hot-well of the large engine. But if the water in the boiler stands above the line *b b* then (as by this the steam space in *k* is diminished) the pressure inside of *k* will open the valve *r* before the pump has finished its stroke, and allow part of the water to escape through the communication, running betwixt the top of the pump and a part of the pipe g (behind its valve) leading to the hot well. So by this contrivance, whenever the water in the boiler stands so high as that the steam space in k is not double that of the contents of the pump barrel, then a portion of the water in the pump will be sent through the valve r back into the hotwell, and when the valves $l\ l$ are opened there will not be a barrel full of water in k to pass into the boiler. The more the steam space in k is diminished by the water rising in the boiler, a less quantity of the water from the feed pump will pass into k at each stroke, and on this account the boiler will always get less water from the feed-pump the higher the water stands in it above the line $b\ b$. If the water in the boiler stood as high as the top of the chest k, then no water would pass into it from the pump. When the water in the boiler is low, and on this account the steam space in k is made as great or greater than double the contents of the feed-pump, then a pump full of water will pass from the chest k into the boiler every time the valves $l\ l$ open. In this way, if the boiler is too full of water, it gets less feed than its average quantity at each stroke of the pump; and if there is not enough of water in it, it is supplied with more than the average quantity, and for this reason the water in it will keep always at the same level.

It is to be understood, that the feed-pump is double acting, and in its downward stroke the water is discharged through the pipe t, into a chest placed alongside of the chest k, and of the same dimensions. This chest is also to have valves working on it, like those marked l. The small circle at the bottom of the feed-pump, shows the pipe which leads the water into it: the pipe at the bottom of the pump for this purpose should have been drawn running in the same direction as this one, if it had not been wanted to show the loaded valve r, &c. I have not shown the loaded valve at the bottom of the pump, as it, and the other parts are of the same construction as shown for the top end.

It is not important that the space which is above the line $b\ b$ in the chest k, is double of the contents of the feed-pump, only if this space is made in any

other proportion to the contents of the pump; the weight s must be made to correspond to it; I may here remark, that the additional pressure given to the steam in the chest k, by the water pumped into it, helps the water to pass from the chest into the boiler as soon as the valves $l\ l$ open.

By having the cylinder d and the nozles e, as well as the feed-pump pretty large, the small engine will not require more steam to work it than if these parts were made small, as in this case, it will work slow when it is forcing the water through the loaded valve r, if this valve is fitted so that it can only open a small distance. From the manner in which the fly wheel is applied to the engine, it cannot stop, although its motion is not a quick one.

When two boilers are to be supplied with water by means of a small engine, with one feed-pump, then the chest k, and the other parts in connection with it, must be fixed upon one boiler, and the other chest of the same sort as k, and which is in connection with the bottom end of the feed-pump, must be fixed to the end of the other boiler. If four boilers are to be supplied with water by means of a small steam-engine and one feed pump, then a chest, as k, and its appendages must be fixed upon each boiler, two of them in connection with the top end of the pump, and the other two in connection with its bottom end. If two or more chests, like k, are connected to the same end of the pump, then a pipe passes from the pump to one of them, and a pipe as the one at r connects the others of the set. On the principle now explained, any number of boilers may be supplied with water by means of the same feeding apparatus. Only one loaded valve to the top of the pump, and another to the bottom are required, whatever may be the number of boilers to be fed.

The pump, for an apparatus, as now described, may be wrought by the large steam-engine in the ordinary way, if the loaded valve is very large, and if it is made to open sufficiently. In this case the pump may be single acting, and only one chest like k will be required. If the feed pump is wrought as now described, the boilers will get no water when the large engine is standing. When the feed pump is wrought by the large engine, then a ratchet should be connected to the lever of the loaded valve, so as to work a screw in order to shorten the stroke of the pump a little every time the valve opens; and a similar motion should be taken from the engine to lengthen the stroke of the pump at any time the valve r did not open.

If an apparatus, as already described, is to be put upon the boilers for a low pressure steam-engine, then the small engine, which works the feed-pump, must have an air pump and condenser to it. The only difficulty attending this arrangement is the following :—When the boiler is very full of water, and the escape at the loaded valve r is small, then the small engine will work slow, and on account of this, too much water will run into the condenser. This inconvenience can be got over by causing the injection cock to shut as soon as the engine is longer than a certain time in making a revolution. A cam or tooth fixed upon the crank shaft of the little engine, so as to lift the piston of a common cataract at each revolution, will answer the desired end; for if the piston rod of the cataract is connected to the handle of the injection cock by a proper arrangement, then if the engine is longer than a certain time in making its revolution the cataract will shut the injection cock, and it will remain shut till the cam fixed upon the crank shaft acts upon the cataract and opens it. In this way the exact quantity of water required to condense the steam can be let into the condenser at each stroke.

The arrangement of the parts, as per the figure (see front page), is for a steam boat boiler. In a boiler with a building round its end, the chest g g, and the other parts of the feeding apparatus, must be placed at a distance from it; and pipes run from the chest and join the boiler at the holes h and i. In order to avoid complexity, the framing, which supports the fly wheel shaft, as well as some of the other parts, are not put into the figure. The short dotted line running above the line b b, is intended to show the height at which the water stands in the chest k, after a full of the pump is put into it.

As in ordinary cases the common feed-pump will not be wanted, if the feeding apparatus, as now described, is used, the addition to the cost of a new engine will be trifling, and it is a very great advantage to have boilers (especially high pressure ones) regularly supplied with water.

I am, Sir, yours truly,
JAMES WHITELAW.
London, April 12, 1838.

P. S.—The steam space in the chest k, may be made of the same capacity as the barrel of the feed-pump, if the pipe, or communication, which carries the water back to the hot well of the large engine runs not from the end of the pump, but from the top of the steam-space to the same place in the pipe g, as shown in the figure. In this plan the steam is not compressed into the chest k, but it is sent into the hot-well of the large engine at each stroke, and the waste water passes along with it; the loaded valve must be made to open with a force not much greater than that of the steam in the boiler in this case; or a valve made to open and shut by means of an eccentric, will answer instead of the valve r. The remarks made in this paragraph apply when there is only one chest to each end of the pump; when there is a number of chests in connection with each end of the pump, the same remarks apply if their united capacity is equal to that of the feed-pump.

J. W.

NAUTILUS'S REPLY TO IVER MAC-IVER, &c.

Sir,—I had hoped to spare you and myself any further recurrence to the subject of the vertical stars; but I have been so directly appealed to by Iver Mac Iver in this day's Number of the *Mechanics' Magazine*, that a reply to him becomes unavoidable. Iver Mac Iver has, most undoubtedly, the best right to know what his own meaning was, in the question proposed by him; but, on any other evidence I could scarcely have believed it possible, that he could seriously mean to propose a question, which (in the confined sense in which it now appears to have been asked) is so simple as almost to border on the ridiculous. Having had a high opinion of Iver's mathematical attainments, I certainly gave him credit for having investigated the subject in its general sense, and for having, consequently, become aware that the necessity for the perpendicular being external to the triangle was so nearly a general rule, with respect to these two stars, that the smallness of the exception made it interesting, and caused him to put the question by way of drawing attention to it; when, therefore, O. N., in his answer, appeared altogether to have overlooked this exception, I conceived that he had mistaken the drift of the proposed question; it now appears that by overrating Iver Mac Iver, I did injustice to O. N., and with the full benefit of this admission, I beg to present both gentlemen.

A perfect community of feeling and expression seems now to exist between Iver, and O. N.; the same word ("disingenuous") occurs to both as applicable to my letter, but, when Iver Mac Iver, in quoting his own question in his last letter, places it between inverted commas as follows: "Why the perpendicular must fall upon D Z produced, *the latitude of the place being 55° 58'*"; and when, upon reference as directed to No. 743, or to his own original question, the *latter* portion of the question (which I have placed in italics) is found to be an interpolation, having no place in the original; then, it must be allowed, the question is, if not *ingenuous*, at least most *ingenious*. Again, they both agree in insisting, that there is nothing at all remarkable, or interesting, in the phenomenon pointed out by me in No. 752; but, if it be indeed so very obvious and common place a matter, as Iver would make it appear, he cannot refuse to explain how he would get over the following difficulty:—

Suppose Iver were to retrograde into the Highlands, and take up his abode at Dunrobin Castle, or at the village of Golspie, hard by; and suppose him ignorant or unmindful of the phenomenon that he holds so cheap. And let him, with a view to the determination of his time, observe the stars Capella and Procyon in a vertical position, and make his calculation accordingly. Then, the problem being capable of *two* solutions, both equally correct according to the conditions hitherto given, but differing from each other to the extent of sixteen or seventeen minutes; which of them would he adopt, or how avoid uncertainty? He will perhaps answer that the quality of the azimuth angle must, at the same

time, be observed; but it is obvious that this, within such narrow limits, would be quite impracticable; so that another datum, not hitherto alluded to, would become absolutely necessary.

In conclusion, I must observe, that from the manner in which Iver Mac Iver, and O. N., have expressed themselves with respect to this phenomenon, it would appear that neither, even yet, understands its true nature; it is quite absurd to assert that the double position must occur in every instance, since the very nature of the problem requires that both stars should be above the horizon.

NAUTILUS.

April, 14, 1838.

P. S.—The latitude of the locality alluded to above, is 57° 58', and on the 1st of Jan. last, the first vertical position occurred, at 52 minutes past six; and the second at 10 minutes past 7 in the evening.

—————

FIRES IN SHIPPING—MERRYWEATHER'S FIRE-ENGINES.

SIR,—In the course of last week, the brig "Charles" of 168 tons, (which left the London Docks for St. John's, Newfoundland, on Good Friday, with a general cargo and government stores,) was wholly destroyed by fire, while lying at anchor in the Downs. The "City of Aberdeen" steam-ship also, narrowly escaped a similar fate, from the spontaneous ignition of some portion of her cargo; and intelligence has just reached Lloyd's of the total loss of two vessels, and the serious damage of others, by fire. The alarming frequency of these accidents, strongly forces the subject upon our attention, and shows the propriety of fully and freely discussing, what are really the best means of guarding against the ascendancy of such calamities. I perfectly agree with the opinion expressed by your valuable correspondent "Nauticus," that it would be well if every *sea-going* vessel was provided with some sort of portable fire-engine—the advantages of such a provision having on many occasions been most strikingly exemplified.

I have observed several engines, constructed upon the plan mentioned by "Nauticus" as having been adopted by Mr. Kingston, of Portsmouth, in which the containing box becomes the air-vessel. I should imagine a *patent* for this *common contrivance* was of very little value, and the plan itself is liable to several objections ;—in the first place, it is exceedingly difficult, or next to impossible, to keep the joints air-tight where the working axis passes through the containing box : unless this can be done, the *air-vessel* becomes limited to the small portion of space situated above the working axis. In common use, as on ship-board, these joints soon cease not only to be air-tight, but even water-tight, proving a source of much annoyance whenever the engine is used.

Another serious objection to this form of engine is, that in the event of the slightest derangement of the works, the whole machine must be taken to pieces, in order to discover and remedy the defect.

In Merryweather's patent fire-engines, which are of the most compact and portable description, the form and position of the metallic valves is such, as almost to preclude the possibility of failure in this part; but should such occur, the valve-chamber covers can be unscrewed and taken off, the valve examined and adjusted, and the whole replaced in a few minutes. This may be done in the middle of working, without disturbing any other part of the machine, and without detaching either the suction or delivery hose—occasioning a delay of not more than three or four minutes. This engine was described in your 24th volume, page 226. The valves formed the subject of another communication, in Number 732 of your Magazine. The following satisfactory opinion of this particular engine is contained in a letter recently addressed to Mr. Merryweather from the "Great Western Steam Ship Office, Bristol," by Captain Claxon, managing director of the company, who says " I have great pleasure in bearing my testimony to the efficiency of your small fire-engine, which had only been on board the "Great Western" a few hours, when it was called into actual service."

Apprehension of not obtaining water, may sometimes operate, to render persons on land indifferent about providing themselves with a fire-engine : they may also hope for the timely arrival of assistance from other quarters, of which

there may be a reasonable chance ; but at sea, no extra help is to be expected, and an inexhaustible supply of a powerful *anti-phlogistic* fluid can always be depended upon. A small engine is particularly useful on board a ship for numberless ordinary purposes ; the owners, therefore, who exhibit such a recklessness of lives and property as to send a vessel on a distant voyage without a machine of this kind, are culpable in the highest degree.

I remain, Sir,
Yours respectfully,
WM. BADDELEY.
London, April 25, 1838.

SIMPLE ACCOUNT FILE.

Sir,—Vol. xxii. of your Magazine contains a description of an account file by Mr. Samuel Argell, which, though neat and ingenious, is objectionable,—first, the expense,—and next, the great inconvenience in stowing away the files upon each other.

The following is a brief description of one I have just made, which is much more simple and cheaper, but whether superior to Mr. Argell's or not I leave others to judge. It consists of two mill-boards, each 8½ inches long, and 3½ in. wide, which are covered with leather ; 2½ yards of green silk ferret, or ribbon, is attached to the centre of the bottom board. One end (2 inches) of the upper board turns up with a leather joint for the purpose of examining the endorsements. Now when the folded accounts are placed between these boards, I keep them firm by taking as many turns round the narrow part of the boards as will leave sufficient ferret, to make one turn round the long way of the board, and tie in a loop similar to the way a ream of paper is tied. When I wish to look for a particular account, I have nothing to do but untie the ferret which passes round the long-way of the boards, which at once frees the joint and enables me to withdraw the account, the remainder of the ferret still keeping the other accounts secure.

I am, Sir, yours respectfully,
H. GOOD.
Brighton, April 21, 1838.

MURPHY IN FRANCE.

By the *Constitutionnel*, for Monday the 25th of April, we find to our surprise that Murphy the weather-wise, has had the hardihood to put to the test the gullibility of another public. "'The predictions of Mr. Murphy on the daily state of the atmosphere, have," says the French newspaper, "made a great noise in London, and even produced an echo at Paris. The system of this astronomer, (we had almost said astrologer) is founded on the combination of three causes, the influence of the season, that of the locality, and that of the moon. The first labours of Mr. Murphy had England for their object,—he has since come on the continent, and devoted his time to collecting the observations necessary for applying his theory to France. The result of his investigations and calculations is embodied in a small work, which bears the title of a "*Meteorological Calendar* for the year 1838." However extraordinary this discovery may appear, we should feel scrupulous as to rejecting it *a priori*, but before we admit it as well-founded, we must be allowed to wait for it to show its effects." The *Constitutionnel* then treats its readers to a dish of the usual jargon, of which we in England have already had enough and to spare. The weather is to be fine for twenty-four days of the month of May; on the 13th, 17th, 23rd, 27th, and 28th, it is to be *variable*, and so forth. No one ever surpassed Mr. Murphy in the art of retailing fudge with a circumstance. We must own that we shall hardly be able to avoid a malicious feeling of satisfaction in case the French, by paying any attention to the nonsense of this impudent quack, redeem the English from the disgrace of having made his previous predictions the standard subject of conversation for longer than the old established period of nine days. They will have had fair warning, as it appears that in the *Meteorological Calendar* aforesaid, he absolutely commences his predictions, not having the fear of a horse-laugh before his eyes, from the *first of April!*

THE NEW COPYRIGHT BILL.

Since last session the prospects of Mr. Serjeant Talfourd's Copyright Bill appear to have clouded over to an amazing degree. "A change has come over the spirit of his dream" with a vengeance. In 1837, his proposals were received with acclamation in the legislature, with enthusiastic approbation by the press, (the *Mechanics' Magazine*, being, we verily believe, the only periodical that ventured "to spy a hole in his beautiful armour.") —In 1838, we find meeting upon meeting, held at London, at Dublin, at Edinburgh to oppose his bill in the legislature—petitions presented against it night after night, by members who avow an intention of subjecting the measure to a close and rigid scrutiny—in the press the voice of disapprobation gradually swelling from the whisper of the breeze to what bids fair to become at last a very respectable storm.

It is true, that a great deal of this opposition arises from motives of not the most disinterested nature, and views of not the most enlarged description. The parties who are warmest in their endeavours to thwart the project, are bookbinders, printers, publishers; all of whom we suspect consider the interests of their own peculiar class, as much more deserving of protection than those of authors, or of the public either. They appear to have been seized with a horrid apprehension, that in case of the success of the bill, bookbinding, printing, and publishing, will somehow or other, all be "knocked on the head"—all involved in one common ruin. It may be so, but we are rather inclined to dread they might flourish as much as ever, but with an inferior article to print, to publish, and to bind—and consequently, for the public to read, the most important feature of all in our view of the question. It must be owned that this inclination to take a narrow view of the matter in hand is not confined to one of the parties at issue, or to tradesmen alone. There seems a disposition on the part of those who support Serjeant Talfourd's bill to consider "the main chance", as the matter of main importance, the sum of money which an author puts in his pocket, as an affair both to himself and others of much higher consequence, than the influence he exerts on his readers, and on mankind. Those, who on the contrary, think there are some considerations connected with literature of a higher order, than those which relate to pounds, shillings, and pence, will rather be led, we think, on an impartial view of the whole question, to side with the prejudiced tradesmen, than the prejudiced professional author.

The readiest way of coming to a view of the question will be, to review the opinions of one of its advocates. In the last number of the *Monthly Chronicle*, there is an elaborate article on the subject, in favour of Serjeant Talfourd's views, which in spite of all its eloquence and ingenuity, will certainly induce an impartial reader to come to conclusions very different from those of the writer. It commences with an attack on the system of plunder now carried on by foreign publishers, who pirate the copyright works of English authors, with such success, that the native editions are driven, we are told, from the market, even on our own coasts. This is a fact which tells against Serjeant Talfourd's bill, not for it. How and why is it, that foreign editions take the place of our own? Because, undoubtedly, of the difference in the price of the two, caused by the monopoly, which in one case remains in the hands of one publisher. Is it not notorious in fact, that even those of the middle classes, who have a love for literature, never, with rare exceptions, purchase a copyright book,— and that for the very good reason, that they cannot afford it. Their only way of getting a sight of a new publication complete, is by obtaining it from a circulating library, and particular passages that they wish to have by them, for the purpose of reference or reperusal, they get possession of, if they get possession at all, by purchasing them extracted in some of the cheap periodicals, which subsist on extracts. The effect of this state of things is now manifesting itself in the condition of our literature, which is becoming more and more the literature of circulating libraries—a heavy mass of light reading. How indeed, can it be expected, that an author will take pains when he knows that all his pains will be of no use; that his history or his travels, will only come into the hands of those who will be compelled to rush through them at a certain rate, and return them by a certain hour. "He who runs may read" under the present system, and none but those who do run. This system has come up under the twenty-eight

years monopoly—is it likely to be improved under a law which will secure a monopoly for sixty years certain, and perhaps a hundred? We do not think it is. The advocates of the bill indeed, triumphantly refer us to the recent cheap editions of copyright authors, as proofs of the——we hardly know what; for what do they prove in their favour. The greater part of the works alluded to— the poems of Southey, the novels and poems of Walter Scott, are works of which the copyright is on the verge of expiring. Were Dr. Southey's death to occur to-morrow, (to use a favourite expression of his favourite nation, the Spaniards, "may he live a thousand years"), his Joan of Arc, his Thalaba, his Madoc, his Curse of Kehama, would become public property at once. The Lay of the Last Minstrel, and Marmion, are so already; the Lady of the Lake will become so this year; the other poems will soon follow, and Waverley lead the van of the novels in 1842. Here, then, is a very good reason for publishing cheap editions of these works. Who would buy dear ones, with, in some cases, the chance, and in others, the certainty of soon having cheap ones to choose from. But would these same cheap editions appear, if there were not the same necessity for their being cheap? If so, why have they not appeared before? These are questions, the answers to which will certainly not tell in favour of the new Copyright bill. In favour of the old law, it may be stated with truth, that it is more favourable to the public than the new one; and that it was sufficiently so to authors, may be deduced from the fact, that under it a popular author writing a work intended to be popular—Sir Walter Scott, writing the life of Napoleon, found it possible to obtain remuneration at the rate of one hundred and twenty pounds a day!

Our remarks on this branch of the subject have extended to so great a length, that we have left ourselves little room to notice the others. Suffice it to say, that the writer in the *Monthly Chronicle* is reduced to anticipate such extravagant improbabilities to support his causes, that one would almost suspect him of intentionally ridiculing his own argument—of volunteering a *reductio ad absurdum*. He speculates for instance, in the remuneration to be derived by scientific characters, from the sale of their works abroad, where he observes, that scientific readers are more numerous than in England. This may be, but then do these scientific readers all read English, or would it be considered a great point gained by the new international copyright law, if our "men of mark" were induced to give their observations to the world in French or German? The spirit of such an idea is diametrically opposed to that manifested in another part of the article, where it is stated, as an inducement to nations, to join in preventing piratical editions of foreign authors, that by heightening the price of these excited luxuries, they will foster a native literature of their own, dear in every sense. The case of Belgium is brought forward for illustration, and it is pointed out, that at present its literature does not rank among the foremost in Europe, which is sagaciously attributed to the ease with which the inhabitants can procure the productions of foreign authors, at piratical prices. Were it not for this, the writer seems to take it for granted, that Brussels would assuredly leave Paris in the shade. We should like to hear what our political economists who declaim so eloquently against the narrow spirit of nourishing a paltry national manufacture, by excluding or high-taxing superior foreign productions, would say to this.

These are some of the objections which must readily occur to those who consider the new Copyright bill, without a bias on either side; and who, therefore, while indisposed to deny that the present laws might admit of some beneficial alteration, are not willing

" to shun the ills we have"

by flying

" to others that we know not of."

HARPER AND JOYCE'S PATENT STOVE.

We hasten to lay before our readers a valuable paper on this new "wonder of the world," by which it will be seen that our suspicions as to its unhealthiness are fully confirmed. We are indebted for the complete exposé of the invention to a foreigner, M. Gay-Lussac, the first in the first rank of the living chemists of France, to whom, it appears, the subject of the stove, which has excited consider-

able attention over the water as well as at home, was referred, by the Academy of Sciences, to examine and report. It will be seen that his "report" is quite conclusive, as to the merits of the affair. It should seem, indeed, that the new stove constitutes one of the most transparent delusions of the day, and that what all the world and his wife have been running with breathless eagerness to see, is merely a common charcoal stove! The patentees might well object to allowing us to test the absence of deleterious fumes, and we might well object, in our turn, to sleep in a room warmed by the "patent stove." If the crevices of the windows and doors were sufficiently tight, there need be no doubt as to the fate of the sleeper; and the "exporters" of the stove to France may, after all, realize a handsome profit on their venture, in spite of M. Gay Lussac's exposure, by the sale of their commodity, as a fashionable instrument, of the most fashionable mode of committing suicide on the Continent. John Bull, we opine, will still continue to prefer the razor and the rope, so that the prospects of success at home are not so flattering.

It was rumoured, a short time back, that Lord Brougham had declared himself an enthusiastic admirer of the new stove, and pronounced that its inventor would be inadequately rewarded, by the transfer of the National Debt to his name. His Lordship is now on a visit to Paris, where he is being *fêted* to his heart's content; and as he is extremely proud of being a member of the Institute of France, he was most probably present at the reading of M. Gay-Lussac's report. If so, and the story as to his enthusiasm be correct, (which *may* admit of a doubt,) what must have been his sensations on hearing the contents of such a document as the following?

" *Report by M. Gay-Lussac to the Academy of Sciences of the Institute of France, 9th April, on the heating apparatus of M. Joyce, presented to the Academy at the preceding meeting.*

" Much has been said of the wonderful nature of this process; that with an expense of fifty or sixty centimes, (5d. or 6d.,) in properly prepared charcoal, a large apartment may be maintained at an agreeable temperature for twenty-four hours; and, moreover, that the carbonic acid produced by the combustion is not diffused in the apartment, being absorbed by the carbonate of soda, with which the charcoal is impregnated, the danger of suffocation being therefore no longer to be dreaded from this method of heating; it has also been said, that it has been approved of by English men of science, and even that it has been presented to the Royal Society.

"This much vaunted process has appeared to me to be deserving of my examination; and in making the results known, I believe I am doing a service to the public, and even to the exporters, who must possess too much good faith not to wish to be better informed than they have been, on the advantages and inconveniences of this process of heating.

"The fuel employed is a very light charcoal, impregnated, it is said, with carbonate of soda, to retain the carbonic acid produced in burning. I have found an authentic specimen of this fuel to contain, carbonate, not of soda, but of potash, yet in so minute a quantity, that I am certain it does not amount to 1-4000th of the weight of the charcoal; hence it burns with as much facility as the charcoals of other light woods.

"It is therefore quite evident, that this charcoal must *diffuse in the apartment as much carbonic acid during its combustion, as an equal weight of any other charcoal;* that it must *vitiate the air in the same degree,* and that *the same accidents may be produced by it as in other cases;* it is equally evident, that it can produce *no more heat* than the same quantity of common charcoal, as it contains no more combustible matter.

"Having ascertained, (along with other persons,) that the combustion of this charcoal produces no unpleasant odours, it occurred to me that the small quantity of alkali, (which I then supposed had been added to it,) might be the cause of the absence of smell. As this would have been an useful discovery, I submitted my conjecture to the test of experiment. I ascertained that ordinary charcoal contains nearly as much alkali as the new fuel; but, in order to make the experiment more conclusive, I wetted some charcoal in a weak solution of carbonate of soda, so that it became more alkaline than the English charcoal. This was dried on a stove, and two furnaces were charged, one with this prepared charcoal, and the other with the common. No appreciable difference was discovered. The experiment was repeated with different proportions of the alkali, but always with the same results.

"Having satisfied myself that the absence of smell in the English charcoal must arise from its peculiar nature, and having, as I thought, discovered that it was made from fir wood, I prepared some charcoal from pieces of deal; the result was, a coal very light, and sensibly more alkaline charcoal than the English fuel. When burned it gave, in comparison with ordinary charcoal, a less degree of smell, and appeared to resemble in all respects the English charcoal, of which, however, I did not possess a sufficient quantity to make an exact experiment.

"The importers of this new process of heating, burn the charcoal in an elegant apparatus, which it is unnecessary to describe. It is sufficient to say that it is a true brazier, diffusing all the products of combustion into the apartment where it is placed, and that it is from this circumstance that the alleged economy arises. This economy cannot be disputed; but it should not be forgotten that it is gained at the expense of vitiating the air of the apartment, and compromising the safety of ignorant persons, who may incautiously expose themselves to its effects. It is not my business to cry down this new process, but to make it thoroughly understood: I therefore state, that my observations lead me to think,

"1st—That the fuel is merely a light charcoal, well prepared, but containing no alkali besides that which it naturally possesses.

"2nd—That this fuel gives no more heat than the ordinary charcoal of wood.

"3rd—That the mode in which the combustion is conducted, diffusing its whole products, and thereby vitiating the air of the apartment in which the stove is placed, is the only real source of economy beyond other processes.

"4th—That a constructed stove, ventilated by air brought from the exterior, may be made to give out nine-tenths of the heat produced by the combustion of the fuel, without vitiating the air of the apartment, or giving out any unpleasant smell; and that its use would be safer than the new process, and nearly as economical" ! !

Thus far M. Gay-Lussac, whose report is so full and satisfactory as to leave little more to be observed. Suffice it to add, as a counterbalance to the approbation which the Royal Society of London is *said,* (in France,) to have given to the "patent stove," that the Royal Society of Edinburgh has fully confirmed the opinion of the Parisian chemists. At the meeting of the Society on Easter Monday, one of the stoves was exhibited in action, and, by way of proof positive of its deleterious effects, Sir John Robison, one of the secretaries, held a lighted match above it, which was speedily ex-

tinguished, by the invisible but nexious vapour arising from the dome!

It is certainly not a little singular, that it should have fallen to the lot of a foreign philosopher to be the first to demonstrate the utter fallacy of this domestic "nine days wonder" to the British public.

Since writing the above we have seen the report of Professor Everitt's experiments upon the subject, published in the *Athenæum*, and from which we make the following extracts :—

Of the Fuel called by the patentees "prepared fuel," he observed, that (A.) In appearance it resembled common charcoal.—(B.) On being heated in a nearly-closed vessel, it lost 8 per cent., which being collected, was found to be mostly water.—(C.) On 100 parts being burnt in an open platinum vessel, it left of ash 2.5 parts, resembling the ash of common charcoal.—(D.) On being boiled with distilled water, and the solution filtered, and evaporated to dryness, this left a small quantity of alkaline carbonate.—(E.) A portion being made quite dry, and subjected to analysis, in the apparatus of Liebeg, for determining the quantity of carbon in organic products, was found to contain from 97 to 98 per cent. of pure carbon.—(F.) On a small piece being burnt in oxygen gas, and the product tested, it was found to have become carbonic acid gas.

Hence it appeared to be only well-burnt wood charcoal, with perhaps a little additional alkaline carbonate, not containing, as common charcoal often does. portions of wood half charred, which, when the charcoal is lighted, give off some smoke, and certain vapours irritating to the eyes and nose ;—but as respects the quantity of carbonic acid and heat produced during the burning of a given weight of this, and the same weight of well prepared charcoal, there is no appreciable difference.

The Products of Combustion.—When the stove is first set in action, the hot air which arises from the upper aperture brings with it all the hydroscopic moisture of the charcoal; but so soon as this has become tolerably hot, the air comes out hot, and inconveniently dry. To avoid this, some of the boxes are provided with a small vessel for holding water, which, being placed at the top of the internal cylinder, is gently heated, and, from a small pipe, a certain quantity of aqueous vapour constantly rises, and mixes with the dry air passing by it. In order to collect specimens of the air issuing from this upper aperture for examination, the following simple method was adopted :—A small tube was provided, about twelve inches long,

and half an inch in diameter, open at both ends, one of which was nicely fitted to the aperture of the vent-hole, the tube being placed vertically, by which a stream of the air was constantly flowing from the upper end. Then any gas receiver, glass tube, or bell jar. having its lips ground flat, and provided with a piece of plate glass, which would close it air-tight, may be filled thus :—slide the glass plate just enough on one side to admit the tube; the receiver is now to be brought down upon the tube, so that the upper aperture delivers the hot air quite at the top and inside; all is allowed to remain thus for some minutes, during which the hot, and hence lighter air, flowing from the tube, gradually displaces the cold air of the receiver. This, with the glass plate, are now to be carried slowly upwards; and, just as the upper end of the tube leaves the receiver, the glass plate is to be slided so as completely to cut off all communication with the external air. The specimen of air can then be tested, or carried to the mercurial or aqueous pneumatic trough for examination. Specimens thus collected were subjected to the following trials :—(A.) A lighted taper, on being introduced, was instantly extinguished: the same with a mixture of half this and half pure air; the same with one-third this and two-thirds pure air.—(B.) On lime and baryta water being added and agitated, their becoming turbid indicated the presence of plenty of carbonic acid gas.—(C.) On five measures in a graduated tube, over mercury, being agitated with a little strong solution of caustic potassa, one measure was absorbed, indicating that the quantity of carbonic acid was one-fifth, or as much as could possibly be present; for, as atmospheric air contains, in round numbers, four measures of nitrogen to one of oxygen, and as oxygen, in unity with carbon, produces its own volume of carbonic acid, no more than one-fifth of carbonic acid can be formed.—(D.) Another fixed quantity in a graduated tube had a little piece of phosphorus melted in it. This did not become luminous, nor was there the least diminution of the volume of the gas—hence no free oxygen was left in the air. This confirms the accuracy of the preceding experiment.—(E.) Another portion, after being deprived of its carbonic acid by caustic potassa, was mixed with a little pure oxygen, and electric sparks passed frequently through the mixture. No change in bulk was seen, nor did an addition of caustic potassa occasion a further absorption—hence no carbonic oxide was present.—(F.) A bird, introduced into a quantity of the stove air, died in less than half a minute; and one introduced into a mixture of 60 cubic inches of the stove air, and 60 of pure atmospheric air, died in less than three minutes. Hence, Mr. Everitt observes, we may conclude, that *all* the air which passes through these boxes is deprived of its oxygen or vital part, this being replaced by a similar bulk of carbonic acid gas.

. Now as to the quantity produced in a given time : this of course must depend on the rate of combustion ; it is to be remarked, that it does not at all depend on the size of the box, but on the size of the lower or entrance aperture of the cone, and on the upper or exit aperture, by which the quantity of air passing through the box is regulated, and hence the rate of combustion. The one produced, being of no very great heating power, was 19 inches high, and $6\frac{3}{4}$ inches in diameter; and could contain 37,480 grains of prepared fuel: if the upper part were left quite open during the whole duration of combustion, it would burn out in about 18 hours ; but as it is rated as lasting 20 hours, it is better to take this time as the element of any calculations. Now allowing 10.5 per cent. for moisture and ash, as above determined, these 37,480 grains of fuel contain 33,544 of pure carbon, consumed in 20 hours; or, adding 1-5th, 40,253 in 24 hours : and further, every 6 grains of carbon, in passing to carbonic acid gas, during combustion, unite with 16 grains of oxygen, producing 22 grains of this ; hence 6 : 22 : 40,253 to 147,594 grains of carbonic acid ; and as 100 cubic inches of carbonic acid weigh $47\frac{1}{4}$ grains, 47.25 : 100 : : 147,594 : 312,368 cubic inches in 24 hours, or $180\frac{8}{10}$ cubic feet. It will, doubtless, be sought to estimate the per centage of this gas, which will be found in any apartment of given dimensions, after a certain number of hours burning, of a stove of the above size ; one of the elements of such a calculation—viz : ventilation, is, however, so variable, that it is impossible to make any approximate, much less, serviceable estimate, on this point. But the following comparison may be useful for medical men, and others, to found an opinion upon :—Physiologists have determined, that a healthy man produces, by respiration, in 24 hours, 38,304 cubic inches of carbonic acid (Davy); 38,232 (Allen and Pepys); the mean of which is 38,267 cubic inches. Hence $\frac{312368}{38267}$, the quantity produced by the close stove in 24 hours, gives 8.15 ; or if we put this stove into a small bed-room or other apartment, we are placed, as it respects the production of carbonic acid gas, exactly as if we had 8 full-grown individuals in the same room. Or, in order to find this relation for any other box of any size, find the number of ounces of fuel it

consumes in the 24 hours, deduct 10.5 per cent. for moisture and ash, the rest represents the *pure carbon* consumed. This divided by 10, (10 ounces of carbon being about the estimated quantity an adult gives off from his lungs in 24 hours,) the quotient will be the number of adults required to produce, in equal times, the same quantity of carbonic acid as the stove. Mr. Everitt then stated that he purposely avoided collecting himself the records of experiments, and observations, on the injurious effects of this gas, as it might be feared he had been biassed one way or other, and would therefore content himself with reading a concise summary of what has been written on the subject in Dr. Christieson's celebrated work on poisons, pages 744 to 754 inclusive, of the last edition. As general results from what precedes, Mr. Everitt deduced the following conclusions :—

1st. The fuel, called "prepared fuel," used in these boxes, differs from common charcoal in its being perfectly charred, or having no portion of wood left half-decomposed ; that it differs in no essential from well-burnt wood charcoal.

2nd. That all the air which passes through these boxes, when fairly in combustion, is entirely deprived of its oxygen, this being replaced by a bulk of carbonic acid gas.

3rd. That a stove or box 19 inches high, and $6\frac{3}{4}$ diameter, consumes about 40,253 grains ($5\frac{7}{10}$lb) of pure carbon in 24 hours, and generates $180\frac{8}{10}$ cubic feet of carbonic acid gas in that time.

4th. That this is as much, hour by hour, as is produced by eight adults by respiration.

5th. That what is implied by the following quotation from the printed circulars of the patentee—" To guard against accidents from the neglect or mistake of servants using *common charcoal*, a pipe will be attached to the apparatus for bed-rooms," viz. that if *their prepared fuel* be used no deleterious gas or vapour is produced, is incorrect.

6th. That if only a part of what is recorded relative to the noxious action of carbonic acid gas on animals be true (See Christieson, pp. 744 to 754), then in no case ought these boxes to used for heating dwelling-rooms, unless provision be made for carrying off the products of combustion.

7th. That by the combustion of any given weight of charcoal, the same quantity of heat is generated as by the combustion of the same weight of prepared fuel.

8th. That having the means to regulate the entrance of air to keep up combustion into a furnace where charcoal is burning, will effect the same end as having the means of regulating the exit after combustion.

Mr. Everitt in conclusion said, that as

soon as Mr. Harper had become acquainted with the positive results arrived at by this investigation, he expressed his determination to attach, to all boxes which he should in future sell, contrivances for carrying out of the apartment all the products of combustion, and Mr. Everitt produced a box where this was already effected. He further begged to say, that Mr. Harper expressed his readiness to adopt any suggestion which might tend to avoid the slightest injurious effects arising from the application of the invention.

HARPER AND JOYCE'S STOVE.

Sir,—Mr. Baddeley and others, who object to Joyce's stove, on account of its not being likely to give out sufficient heat, in consequence of the smallness of the metallic heating surface, have overlooked the fact, that the atmosphere of the apartment in which the stove is used is warmed by the mingling of the hot vapour issuing from the dome, therewith. If, therefore, as Professor Everitt stated at the close of his luminous exposition of the subject, at the Westminster Medical Society, Mr. Harper has devised a means by which all the products of combustion will be carried out of the apartment, it will require as much more surface, and more fuel, as will make up for the caloric carried off in such vapour. Will not this so greatly add to the original cost, and daily expense, of the apparatus, as to make the common coal fire cheaper? And if a chimney of any description is to be added, the very principal feature which made the invention popular, is lost. Lastly, supposing the use of charcoal, (prepared or otherwise, and if a chimney is to be used, where the necessity for preparation,) as a fuel, to become general, with chimneys, what would its effect be on the health of a city—London for instance? Carbonic acid gas is specifically heavier than atmospheric air; and it will not therefore ascend and pass over like the carburetted hydrogen, and other light products of the combustion of coal.

Yours,

ANTI-CARBON.

Westminster, April 30, 1838.

IMPROVEMENT IN STEAM NAVIGATION.

(From the *Edinburgh Evening Courant.*)

An improvement has lately been introduced in the method of condensing the steam in marine engines, which appears to be of great importance to the advancement of steam navigation, particularly in long voyages, such as those now proposed across the Atlantic and to India. The following account of the "Wilberforce" is from a correspondent of the *Hull Observer*, and we have also received the following letters on the subject:—

It is with pleasure we lay before our readers an account of the trials of the "William Wilberforce" steamer, which took place before she proceeded to Hull, to the great satisfaction of a number of scientific gentlemen who witnessed the performance of the engines. Nothing could surpass the beautiful style in which the vessel passed down the Thames, the engines performing in a manner beyond the expectation of every one on board. The "Wilberforce" is commanded by Captain Wilkinson, and belongs to the spirited and enterprising gentlemen forming the Humber Union Steam Company, and is for the conveyance of passengers, &c. between Hull and London. That which gives to the engines of this vessel a great superiority, and an immense additional power, is the application of Mr. Samuel Hall's, of Basford, patent condensers, which are becoming generally applied to first-rate steam-vessels, and which, no doubt, ere long, will be found in every steam packet of importance. On both of the above occasions, the barometer indicated a vacuum in one engine of 29½ inches of mercury, and in the other 29¾ inches, the engines making 21 strokes of six feet per minute. The advantages attending Mr. Hall's patent condensing engines in heavy gales and storms at sea are quite surprising, for it matters not how hard it blows or how heavy the sea rolls, the same uniform power is maintained as in a calm; and while common engines, under similar circumstances, cannot keep up the vacuum to a higher point than from 20 to 25 inches the patent engines obtain a steady vacuum of from 29 to 29¾ inches.

To the Editor of the Courant.

Sir,—As the introduction of this apparatus on board steamers promises to become pretty general, I consider it justice to state than an invention similar in principle and possessing apparently all the advantages of Mr. Hall's. was communicated to me by Mr. Buchanan, civil engineer of this city, and F.R.S.E.. in a letter dated March 29, 1834.

With regard to the method of condensation, which forms the prominent feature of Mr. Hall's invention, Mr. Buchanan, after enumerating the anticipated advantages of of his boiler, such as increased efficiency and durability, with diminished weight and bulk, also a considerable diminution of prime cost and annual expence, with increased economy of fuel, proceeds to state :—

" The above improvements are dependent on, and cannot well be introduced but in connection with, a new mode which I propose in condensing with steam, and in regard to which I have made numerous experiments, which leave no doubt of the practicabity of the plan in regard to which I undertake to satisfy any competent judges." Besides these and other advantages mentioned, he goes on,—" It would also allow the boilers to be worked with fresh water, which is far less injurious than sea water to the boiler and to the engines, where a small supply would be necessary, as what is condensed would be again returned to the boiler, and act over again continually."

It would thus appear that the idea of restoring the condensed steam to the boiler, thus rendering it possible to employ fresh water, preventing the incrustation of salt, which is found so injurious in the ordinary construction, had occurred to Mr. Buchanan independently of all knowledge of Mr. Hall's invention, and it is to be regretted that the Directors of the London and Edinburgh Steam Packet Company had not taken it up.

I am, &c.

R. W. HAMILTON.

Edinburgh, 8, Waterloo-place,
March 30, 1838.

Sir,—In reference to the above letter, which Mr. Hamilton has shown me, I may state in explanation, that ever since the introduction of steam navigation, the use of sea water in the boilers of marine engines has been felt as a serious evil. The actual deposition of salt within the boilers has, no doubt, been in a great measure prevented, by the expedient of discharging the saturated water at intervals into the sea. But the greatest evil, and which has not been got over, arises from a deposit of another kind, or rather a solid incrustation which occurs in the boilers, in spite of all the care that can be taken in blowing off the salt with the water. It is a compound of salts and metallic oxides, as hard as marble or stone, and adhering so firmly to the bottom and sides of the boilers, that it can only be removed by hammers or picks. This requires to be done at frequent intervals when the vessel is not sailing, to prevent its accumulation; and still it occasions serious inconveniences, loss of fuel, and expense in repairing and renewing the boilers, every three or four years. It also prevents the introduction of improved boilers, of less magnitude and weight, and more efficient in the generation of steam. Impressed with these considerations, and with the importance of the subject, my attention has been long directed to the prac-

ticability of condensing the steam without the introduction of the sea water, for injection, into the condenser, but by the external contact of an extensive surface of metal with the cold water. The result would be, that the water being condensed separately, would be again returned back into the boiler, and the same supply lasting for a considerable length of time, would allow pure fresh or distilled water to be used in the boiler.*

Having made numerous experiments in the year 1832, and previous to it, with an apparatus constructed on purpose, having a boiler, air-pump, and condenser, of the above description, with accurate thermometer and barometer guages, for pointing out the temperature and pressure of the steam, and degree of vacuum, I ascertained exactly the quantity of metal surface which it would be necessary to expose, in order to effect the condensation thoroughly. The result left no doubt remaining of the perfect practicability of the plan, nor have I any doubt that it will yet form one of the greatest improvements in steam navigation; and it was under this conviction that I made the proposition referred to above, to the Directors of the London and Edinburgh Steam Packet Company, through Mr. Hamilton, offering to construct a small vessel, with the improved boilers and condensers, and to answer for the success of the plan. This offer was not accepted, and owing to various other avocations, I was prevented from pursuing the subject at that time, and have not since been able to resume it. It is satisfactory, however, to find the above views so fully confirmed, by the practical results of the trials by Mr. Hall, which only require to be better known to secure the general introduction of the plan. My experiments, however, showed a much less extent of metallic surface as necessary to be exposed, in order to effect the condensation, and the method of supplying the cold water, would, I believe, be found to possess decided advantages.—I am, &c.,

GEO. BUCHANAN.

Edinburgh, 9th April. 1838.

PROPOSED MONUMENT TO SIR WALTER SCOTT.—MR. KEMP'S DESIGN.

It is generally known that about seven thousand pounds have been subscribed for the purpose of erecting a monument to Sir

---

* I am aware that the process of condensing by external contact had been tried by Watt himself, and abandoned. But this trial had reference only to land engines, supplied with fresh water. Had that illustrious inventor lived to see the full extent of his discoveries, as applied in marine engines, I feel convinced that a different system of condensation would have, ere this, been introduced.

Walter Scott in Edinburgh. A committee of the subscribers advertised for designs, with the promise of a fifty-guinea prize to each of the three which should be most approved of. Fifty-four were sent in. Two of these considered entitled to the fifty-guinea prizes, were by eminent English architects, and to the third the committee found attached the name " John Morvo," a fictitious one, adopted from an ancient inscription on Melrose Abbey, telling that such was the appellation of one who

    —— had in kepyng al mason werk
    Of Santandroys, ye hie kirk
    Of Glasgow, Melros, and Paslay,
    Of Niddisdaill, and of Galway.

The architect who had chosen it was one George Kemp, an obscure artist, recently a journeyman carpenter! Some months before, when engaged in taking drawings and plans of the Abbey of Kilwinning, in Ayrshire, Kemp had been urged by a professional architect who was aware of his merit, to furnish a design for the Scott Monument. Intermitting his task in Ayrshire, he had hurried home to Edinburgh, and, from the details of Melrose Abbey, which were strongly imprinted on his mind in consequence of having minutely surveyed the ruin some years before, he composed a tall Gothic tower or spire, of most beautiful proportions, taking, we believe, exactly five days to execute the work.

The committee being now disposed to receive additional competing designs, a few were given in, including one by Mr. Kemp, being a much improved edition of his first design. This new plan is described by the committee, as " an imposing structure of 135 feet in height, of beautiful proportions, in strict conformity with the purity in taste and style of Melrose Abbey, from which it is, in its details, derived:" at the bottom, beneath a groined arch, is an open chamber, for the reception of a statute of Scott. Mr. Burn, of Edinburgh, an architect of the first reputation, attested to the committee "his great admiration of the elegance of Mr. Kemp's design, its purity as a Gothic composition, and more particularly the constructive skill exhibited throughout, in the combination of the graceful features of that style of architecture in such a manner, as to satisfy any professional man of the correctness of its principle, and the perfect solidity which it would possess when built." The committee accordingly, in a report drawn up in February last, *recommended his design for adoption*, only two out of sixteen persons remaining dissatisfied with the resolution. One of the dissentients has since raised an opposition, (we are glad to say ineffectual,) to the design, on two grounds—first, that the artist is an obscure

man; and, second, that his design is a plagiarism. The second point has been refuted, we believe, in a satisfactory manner, by the artist himself; but the first is one which he cannot so well answer.

Mr. Kemp is the son of a shepherd, on the property of Mr. Brown of Newhall, on the southern slope of the Pentland Hills: he became an apprentice to a joiner at the Red Scaur Head, near Eddlestone, where his opportunities of seeing architectural objects were nearly as limited as at Newhall. Having served out his time, he removed to Galashiels, and wrought for nearly a year with a millwright.

The business pursued by Kemp at Galashiels led him occasionally to distant spots in Yarrow, Ettrick, and other districts of that romantic country, and enabled him to gratify his peculiar taste by an inspection of the ruined fanes of Melrose and Jedburgh. He afterwards went into England, where he wrought as a joiner for several years, never omitting an opportunity of seeing any remains of Gothic architecture. On one occasion, when settled somewhere in Lancashire, he walked fifty miles to York, spent a week in inspection of the minster, and returned on foot. Subsequently, he removed to Glasgow, where he wrought for four years, and used to employ his leisure in inspecting the cathedral. Again he spent some time in England, where it was his custom to remove as frequently as possible, that he might have opportunities of seeing fresh specimens of his favourite architecture. He thus became acquainted, amongst other remarkable structures, with the cathedral of Canterbury, so distinguished as an example of the early Gothic.

In 1824, Mr. Kemp formed the design of travelling over Europe, for the inspection of its most valuable Gothic remains, working at his trade, as he went along, for his support. He commenced at Boulogne, and thence proceeded to Abbeville and Beauvais to Paris, spending a few weeks in each place. His skill in mill-machinery, and the anxiety of the French to obtain English workmen in this department, secured him employment wherever he went; and he experienced much kindness from the various parties with whom he became connected. It was his custom to stop for employment at or near those towns in which the finest Gothic structures were to be found, and to spend his leisure hours in inspecting them. He had thus much superior opportunities of studying the features of the architecture, than the most of professional men who travel under what appears more favourable circumstances; for, while these can only pause for a day or two at each place, and in the long run bring home confused impressions of a multitude of objects seen in too rapid succession to be well individualised in recollection, Kemp was enabled to meditate upon each for weeks, and to form distinct pictures in his mind of every particular of what met his eye. Now, too, he began to use the pencil, though only for the delineation of parts of the various buildings, and with the awkwardness of one who was yet a tyro in drawing.

His designed tour of Europe was abruptly broken off, after about a twelvemonth's travel in France, by intelligence respecting the commercial embarrassments of a near relative, and he then returned to Scotland. After some time, he made an endeavour to set up in business for himself as a joiner in Edinburgh, but the effort did not succeed. In the mean time, he applied himself regularly and systematically to the study of drawing and perspective, in which he soon rendered himself a proficient. About the year 1830, he proceeded to Melrose, and took three minutely elaborate views of the ruined abbey from various points. They were purchased at a liberal price by the eminent Scottish architect, Mr. Thomas Hamilton. Mr. Kemp was next employed, by Mr. Burn, to execute a model of a splendid palace which he had designed for the Duke of Buccleugh, and which was then proposed to be built at Dalkeith, but has not as yet been commenced. The model, which was on so large a scale as to require the architect's drawing-room for the business of its construction, was completed, after sundry interruptions and alterations, in two years, and was then placed in the vestibule of the existing palace of Dalkeith, where it has been admired by all who have seen it. An engraver in Edinburgh, named Johnston, who had undertaken on his own account a splendid work, of the character of Britton's Cathedral Antiquities, now employed Mr. Kemp to take some of the requisite drawings of ground plans, elevations, and details—a task not more congenial to his taste than within the range of his ability. Mr. Johnston's premature death occasioned a transference of the undertaking to an enterprising copartnery of publishers, by whom Mr. Kemp has continued till now to be employed at intervals, in the preparation of his work. We believe some time must yet elapse ere the publication of the work will be commenced;

but when it is, we shall be much disappointed if the work fails to establish his reputation. Such of the drawings as have been shown to us are of surprising correctness and beauty, the two distinguishing characters of every thing he executes.— *Abridged from the Edinburgh Journal.*

NOTES AND NOTICES.

Copyright Law.—The Globe of April 25, speaking of the Copyright bills, says—"It has occurred to us," much meditating, "how justice to authors might be reconciled with convenience to the other classes concerned in literature, whether something analagous to the rights conceded to dramatists to a share in the profits of each representation might not answer the purpose—on the publication of each new edition of a popular work." A suggestion to the same effect was made in the *Mechanics' Magazine* when Sergeant Talfourd's Copyright bill was first brought forward last session.

A Sign of the Times.—It may be taken as a fact, in proof of the increasing tendency of education towards utilitarianism, that the directors of King's College, originally established as a peculiarly aristocratic rival to the London University, have announced for the present session a course of lectures on "Civil Engineering." This is a decided step in the march of practical science.

Steaming Extraordinary.—Yesterday afternoon, Mr. Walter Hancock, the enterprising steam-carriage engineer, accompanied by two friends, rode from Stratford and through the principal streets of the City in a steam-gig! Mr. Hancock remained a considerable time with this novelty of science in front of Guildhall, now and then guiding it adroitly round the open space. This was about a quarter past four o'clock, when a great number of persons were present. A notice was painted on the back of the gig, stating that Mr. Hancock had no connection with the "Steam Carriage and Waggon Company." Every one seemed surprised at the ease with which Mr. Hancock threaded his way through the crowd of carts, omnibuses, cabs, and other vehicles in Cheapside, Leadenhall-street, and other crowded thoroughfares. The gig stopped opposite the Bank for a few minutes, when the machinery was inspected by Mr. Oldham, the engineer, who has fitted up all the printing apparatus of that establishment to be worked by steam. During Mr. Hancock's temporary absence much amusement was caused by one of the bank porters pompously ordering the gentleman left in the gig to "move on," the latter declaring that he could not. Mr. Hancock soon returned, when the machine, obedient to the guidance of its master "moved on" in fine style, and returned without accident to Stratford.

Erratum.—Sir,—In my communication on the descent of falling bodies, which appeared in No. 767, page 42, there is a mistake in fig. 1, in the distances of the points of intersection x y z on the line a n; the distance of the point x from a should be equal to that of b from a, y four times, and z nine times that of x from a. The correct distances of x y z, viz, 1, 4 and 9 is the principal object of the arrangement.—I. R. Aris.

Complete Sets of the Mechanics' Magazine may now be had, twenty-seven volumes, half-cloth, price £11 7s.

☞ *British and Foreign Patents taken out with economy and despatch; Specifications, Disclaimers, and Amendments, prepared or revised; Caveats entered; and generally every Branch of Patent Business promptly transacted. A complete list of Patents from the earliest period (15 Car. II. 1675,) to the present time may be examined. Fee 2s. 6d.; Clients, gratis.*

LONDON: Printed and Published for the Proprietor, by W. A. Robertson, at the Mechanics Magazine Office, No. 6, Peterborough-court between 135 and 136, Fleet-street.—Sold by A. & W. Galignani, Rue Vivienne, Paris.

Mechanics' Magazine,

MUSEUM, REGISTER, JOURNAL, AND GAZETTE.

| No. 770.] | SATURDAY, MAY 12, 1838. | [Price 3*d*. |

WRIGHT'S IMPROVED GAS-STOVE.

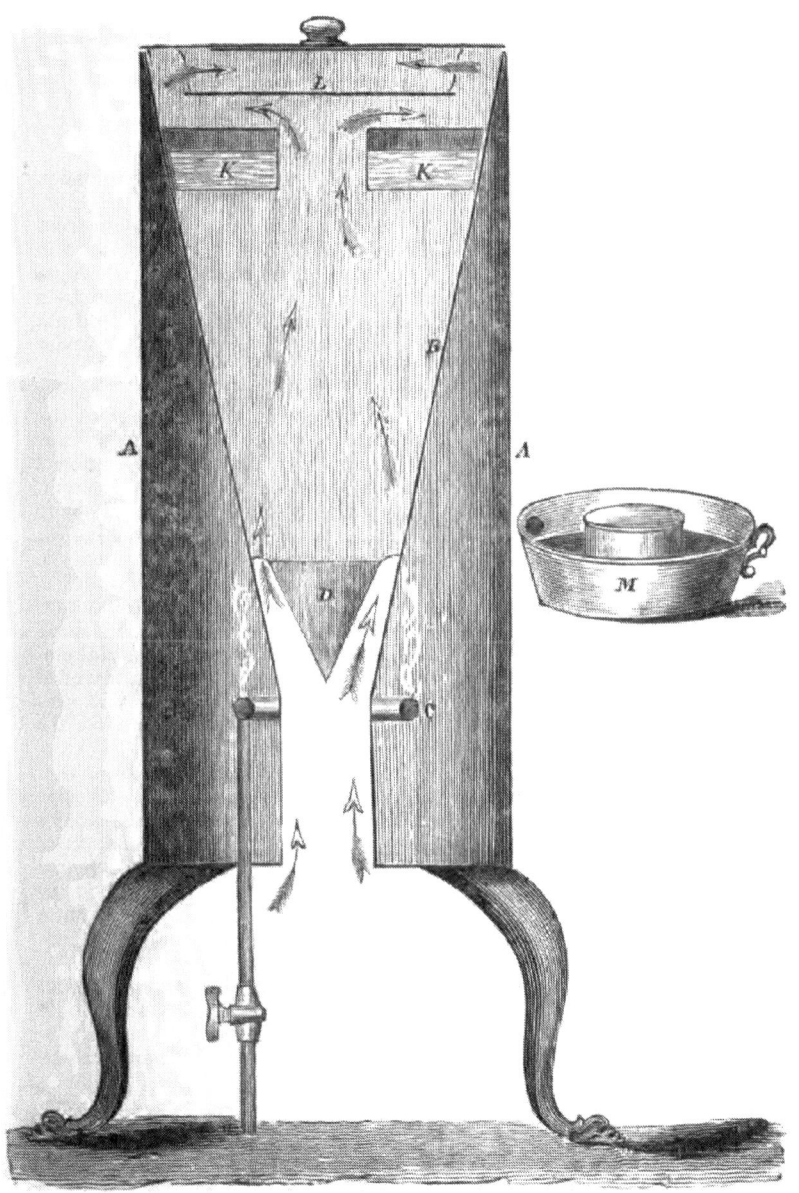

WRIGHT'S IMPROVED GAS-STOVE.

Sir,—Having invented and practically applied a modification or improvement of the gas-stove lately patented, the result of which has equalled my fullest expectation, I am induced to lay the same before the readers of your valuable Magazine, from a conviction that it only requires to be well known to be generally adopted.

It combines three most useful properties, viz. :—portability, lightness, and cheapness : at the same time it has none of the ill effects so justly attributed to dry air arising from the old gas stove. The material is entirely sheet-iron (with the exception of the copper gas-ring and fittings.)

The annexed drawing (see front page) is a vertical section of the stove now in action. A is an outer case of cylindrical form, inclosing an inverted cone B, around the lower part of which the ignited gas plays from the hollow perforated ring C. There is little novel in the general principle of these three portions of the stove, but my improvement consists 1st, in the addition of a smaller cone D, supported within the larger, leaving a space between the two for the current of air : 2nd an annular vessel K, containing water through which the hot air must pass in its passage through the stove ; and lastly above the vessel K., and between it and the damper, is placed a circular plate L rather larger than the orifice in the water vessel. The use of this plate will be seen.

The gas being ignited through an opening for that purpose, the cone immediately above the jets gets heated ; this by rarifying the air within, causes an upwards current through the stove ; the external air now rushing in is divided by the point of the lesser cone, and compelled in its passage to pass against the heated sides of the larger cone. It now rises through the opening in the water vessel, and striking against the plate passes over the surface of the water, carrying with it whatever steam or moisture is there generated ; the air being by this process rendered wholesome, passes round the edge of the plate, and out at the damper on the top into the apartment. No inconvenience is felt from the burnt air, which is suffered to escape through perforations in the upper part of stove. M represents the vessel of water seen in perspective.

It is but justice that I should mention that the plan of the small cone was proposed by Mr. W. Ashdown, of this town, the maker, in lieu of a moveable diaphragm which I thought of having.

I am, Sir,

Your obedient servant,

F. J. WRIGHT.

Hammond-place, Chatham,
Wednesday, March 3, 1838.

POISONS IN CHEMISTS' SHOPS.

Sir,—Of whatever trade or profession your correspondent Mr. Good, of Brighton, is, or has been, I am quite certain from the tenor of his letter which appeared in your last No. of the *Mechanics' Magazine*, that he has not been used to a chemist's shop : if he had, he would not propose that " poisons be kept under lock and key." If such plan was to be adopted, particularly that of having " Poison !" written on the door of the cupboard, we should soon lose our customers. Mr. Good does not know I think, that in the *greater* part of prescriptions which are brought to our shops to be made up, poison of some kind or other is ordered, such as laudanum, prussic acid, and many other kinds, to get at which the cupboard would have to be unlocked, and the person waiting for his recipe to be dispensed, would therefore very naturally suppose we intended to poison him, when he saw " in very large letters" the word poison on the door.

It is not every one who knows, that all medicines are poisonous if taken in sufficient quantities ; and if Mr. Good's suggestion were to be acted upon, there would be comparatively few things in a druggist's shop, but what would be under lock and key—a shop fitted up in this style would very soon have to be locked up altogether.

Your correspondent must also look at the great inconvenience his plan would subject us to ; for example—that of unlocking the poisonous cupboard perhaps fifty times a day to get at such common articles as verdigris, blue and white vitriol, sugar of lead, spirits of salts, &c., which he perhaps knows to be strong poisons and must be kept locked up.

H. G. says oxalic acid is sometimes taken in mistake for epsom salts, their crystals being like to one another ; perhaps if the following simple test for distinguishing them was more generally known it would prevent at least any *accident* from occurring through their being taken in mistake :—Test—to the suspected article add a few drops of common black writing ink—if its colour remains, it is epsom salts—but if the ink in a short time turns *red* it is oxalic acid. This is a very easy manner of telling one from the other, and should one life be saved by its being more generally known by means of this letter, I shall be more than repaid for any critical remarks which this my very imperfect attempt at letter writing may bring forth from any of your correspondents.

I am, Sir, &c.

A Druggist.

STEAM CARRIAGES ON COMMON ROADS.

A new company has just been started, having for its object, the not very new one of introducing "steam carriages and waggons" into general use on common roads. The company state that they have secured the right to the exercise of a patent boiler and machinery, invented by "Sir James C. Anderson, Bart.," after many years of study and research, and which are said to combine every requisite for the successful prosecution of the scheme. According to the prospectus, Sir James Anderson has succeeded in constructing a boiler capable of producing the "*most dense*" kind of steam, and at the same time of resisting any degree of pressure. From this specimen, it will be perceived that the concocters of the company have no very clear ideas of the matter they have taken in hand, and are even ignorant of the very simplest and best-known qualities of the powerful agent they intend to call into their service. As to the flourishes they indulge in with regard to the wonders of the Baronet's invention (and we perceive he is one of the directors into the bargain) they might as well be spared until a little experience has been had ; and references to the opinion of the Parliamentary Committee of 1831, in proof of the practicability and economy of common road steam travelling, are worse than useless. The seven years that have since elapsed, without any progress being made towards the state of things which the report of the committee gravely announced as close at hand, speak volumes on the reliance to be placed on their judgment. The prospectus talks of conveying goods and passengers at double the speed of horse coaches, and at one-half the expense. Let but one-half of this be actually accomplished, and there will be no necessity to raise the ghost of the committee's unlucky dictum, in order to direct the public attention to the desirableness of investing a spare half-million in a common-road-locomotive company.

SUPPLY TO HIGH-PRESSURE BOILERS —SIMPLE WATER-GAUGE — THE BLOWING-FAN.

Sir,—A method of supplying water to a high-pressure boiler appearing to be still a desideratum, the following results of a few experiments directed to that object, may, perhaps, be not unworthy of consideration ; although my situation prevents my having much contact with the mechanical world, and other circumstances confine my mechanical operations to a very small scale. The ingenious contrivance of Mr. Baddeley (page 276, vol. xxi. of your Magazine) suggested to me a more easy construction with the same principle, which is represented in the accompanying figure, and which I have had in operation for nearly a twelvemonth.

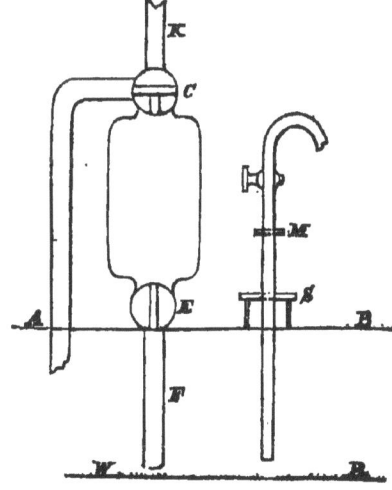

A B represents the top surface of the boiler; W R the water-line; C E cross-section of two cocks having the water-"transferrer" between them: the cock E is of the ordinary construction, that at C differing from it only by having a small hole drilled in its side so as to reach into the main passage of the plug; so that the pipe C Q being soldered to this new orifice, the cock has three ways, any two of which may be made to communicate, while the third is shut off: viz. one to a pipe K leading to an open reservoir of water; another into the transferrer, and a third to the branch-pipe C Q, which pipe descends into the boiler so far as to be just above the highest limit of the water-line. The cock E connects the transferrer with a pipe P, which descends nearly to the bottom (or flue-pipe) of the boiler. The two cocks may be supposed to have their handles connected by a bar so as to move simultaneously, so that the passages may either be in the relative positions denoted in the figure, or those obtained by turning both of them a quarter of a revolution to the left; in which latter case, it will be seen that every passage will be closed except from K to the transferrer which is full of steam, immediately to be condensed and replaced by water from the reservoir. On account of the vacuum thus formed in the transferrer, there will be no necessity (as supposed by Mr. Baddeley) for placing the reservoir *above* the water-line of the boiler, as the water will be raised by atmospheric pressure from a depth depending on the density of the steam, which, if it be considerable, will fill, and form a vacuum in a proportionate length of pipe from the reservoir to K. When the passages are in the positions represented in the figure, it is clear that the water will fall by its own gravity through the cock E into the boiler; the upward pressure of the steam being counterbalanced by the downward pressure of that admitted from the pipe Q C. But when, from a frequent repetition of this action, the water-line has reached the pipe Q, the arrangement of pipes and vessel Q C P, forms a continuous syphon, having two legs of equal altitude and pressure, from which no water can flow, and the supply consequently ceases until the water-line again descends below the pipe Q. Much more neat and compact arrange-

ments than that in the figure may be easily imagined, as well as the substitution of any description of valves for the cocks; but this represents the one I have experimented with, as it appeared to admit of the readiest and most economical construction. It was found best in practice to make the transferrer of rather large dimensions (containing about a fiftieth of the whole contents of the boiler) and to suffer the water to flow in slowly by opening the cock E to a small extent; and by a due regulation of the aperture, the strength of the steam, always under perfect controul, so as to prevent the waste of much of the heat by the safety-valve. However, the result of my experience was to regard this apparatus, not as a substitute for the forcing-pump, but as a very useful auxiliary to it, in cases of intermission of the working of the engine, or a surplus quantity of steam: and this circumstance will allow the forcing-pump to be of much smaller capacity than it usually is, so that the power required to work it may no longer be an object of consideration; and, accordingly, in one that I made conformably with this view, the loss of force was quite imperceptible.

It afterwards became an object to render the force-pump less liable to disorder than it usually is, and also to provide a test of its efficiency, which I found to be best accomplished by the following contrivance:—Let a stop-cock intervene between the force-pump and the boiler with a hole drilled in its side as above described; so that at any time the water which the pump is delivering may be shut off from the boiler and discharged into the open air; by which the quantity injected at each stroke is immediately seen, and any defective action of the valves at once detected. As long as there is no intermission in the working of the engine, and the water is obtained in a moderately clean state, there is no cause to apprehend any derangement or "choaking" of the pump; but as soon as the engine is stopped, the mud and other foreign matter deposited in the boiler, being no longer resisted by the flow of water through the supply tube, finds its way to the valves of the pump which thus frequently become choaked; on which account it is advisable to close the stop-cock just mentioned, whenever the engine is stopped.

I now come to consider the water-guage, which I have used for nearly three years with perfect success. To the right of the boiler-feeder in the above figure is represented a very slender pipe furnished with a stop-cock, and passing into the boiler through a stuffing-box, S. At M is a ring of metal encircling the pipe, and soldered to it at such a place, that when the pipe is thrust down so as to touch the bottom (or flue) of the boiler, the ring may may rest upon the stuffing-box, S. Thus, the ring M will serve as an index to denote the distance of the bottom of the pipe from that of the boiler. Now to ascertain the depth of the water above the bottom or flue of the boiler, let the pipe be drawn up through the stuffing-box as far as its length will permit; open the stop-cock and a small jet of steam will flow out; and now let the pipe be gradually pushed down through the stuffing-box until water flows from it, indicating that it has just reached the water-line in the boiler; close the stop-cock, and the distance, M S, will plainly be equal to the depth of water required.

I have read with great pleasure Dr. Ure's theory of the blowing-fan (vol. xxvii, p. 25, *Mechanics' Magazine*), the importance of which appears to be very generally acknowledged by its extensive adoption in foundries and other establishments; but the conciseness with which this is stated, together with some typographical errors,* will, I apprehend, render the calculation unintelligible to the majority of your readers.

This, together with the presumed usefulness of a practical rule for determining the power requisite to drive a given fan with a given velocity, is my apology for offering the calculations in the following form :—

If a fluid be made to issue from an aperture with an uniform velocity, by the action of any mechanical power, this action may be obviously regarded as equivalent to that of a similar stream of the fluid issuing from an orifice at the bottom of a reservoir kept filled to a constant altitude, which altitude is proved by all hydrodynamical writers to be equal to that through which any heavy body must fall to acquire the velocity which each particle of the fluid has

at the orifice: so that the question is reduced to finding the mechanical power requisite to keep such a reservoir of the fluid filled to a certain constant height. Having premised this, the theory above quoted will furnish a practical rule in the following manner :—

Let v = velocity of extremities of fan leaves in feet per second. a = area of section of discharging pipe in square feet; then $a\,v$ = cubic feet discharged per second with velocity v; and since a cubic foot of air weighs nearly $\frac{1}{13}$th of a pound $\therefore \frac{60\,a\,v}{13}$ = lbs. per minute acquiring velocity v.

Now let h = altitude through which a heavy body must fall to acquire the velocity v; then $v^2 = 2\,g\,h$ ($g = 32\frac{1}{4}$ feet)
$$\therefore h = \frac{v^2}{2g}$$
$\therefore$ the mechanical power required = that which will raise a weight $\frac{60\,a\,v}{13}$ through a height h in one minute.

$$= \frac{60\,a\,v}{13} \times \frac{v^2}{2g}$$

$$= \frac{3\,a\,v^3}{13\,g \times 3300}$$ in horses power.

$$= \frac{a\,v^3}{457600}.$$

Hence, for the same fan, the power varies directly as the cube of the velocity: and the practical rule is to multiply the cross section of the discharging-pipe in feet, by the cube of the velocity of the extremities of the leaves, and to divide by 457600 : the quotient is the number of horses power required.

Having trespassed so far on your valuable pages, I reserve the account of some experiments with the fan for my next communication, I am, Sir,
Yours respectively,
WM. COOK.

Monks, Kirby, Dec. 1837.

PRACTICAL HINTS TO BEGINNERS IN TURNING.

Sir,—To a very large portion of your readers I feel confident that any information connected with the lathe would be most interesting. On all other subjects we have treatises of great merit which readily open the richest stores of information to the aspiring inquirer, but upon practically entering on mechanics, a barrier opposes him on the very thres-

* In page 25, lines 11 and 20 from the bottom, for + read ×; line 20 for " be square feet" read " be 2 square feet"; line 22, for " &c read 80."

hold, which only long experience, much thought, and great inquiry amongst a race most tenacious of their own little stock of knowledge, can even partially remove. How sad a stain is it upon our national character, that whilst our neighbours the French, so greatly our inferiors in mechanical arts generally, should have brought the art of turning to such perfection, and can boast of such excellent works as Plumier of old, Bergeron, Desormeaux, and Dessables, of more recent date, whilst we can only produce a small work by Ibbetson, confined to the use of the excentric chuck, and one other of very little utility by Rich. Gill in his technical repository, (a work of great merit, but now unfortunately discontinued) did much to encourage and promote this art, and the perusal of your past labours convinces me that your publication is not altogether indifferent to it. Several small articles have at various times appeared evincing much ingenuity, but, alas! possibly from want of encouragement the first communications of these writers (if we except Messrs. Ibbetson, Child, and few other valuable correspondents,) have been the last. Could you not, Mr. Editor, once more rouse their dormant spirits, and under the conviction that, where all is to be discovered, and so wide and untrodden a field is open to them, every trifling hint will be of service, induce

them to communicate some, *however small*, portion of their experience. Let not the idea that the subject of their communication may possess little novelty with the more practical in the art, deter them from contributing to the information and amusement of the less experienced, for whose sake, as I apprehend, your valuable miscellany is principally undertaken.

Every beginner must lament the obscurity in which this art is involved, and feel grateful to any individual who would assist in its removal. Such at least were my feeling. As an amateur in a humble degree, the great object of my ambition was to form my own chucks, and more especially the excentric and oval, but my great stumbling block was to form the bevels of the guides and slides of those instruments. For the benefit of beginners, acting upon the suggestions I before offered, I will describe the mode I adopted. Not depending upon the file in the use of which much practice is required to ensure efficiency, I fixed the brass plate and strips of brass, which I destined to form the slide and its guides on a flanch chuck, and by means of a tool placed in a parallel rest fixed at right angles to the mandril, I turned both sides as accurately as was necessary. I then formed a brass chuck (as represented in fig. 1 in a side view, and in a front view in fig. 2) having two flat sides previously turned in the lathe of different

Fig. 1

angles meeting in a point*. Upon that

---

* In the copy, the point has been cut away, as the holes have been drilled too far from the point.

side which possessed the required angle, and at about ⅛ an inch from the point, I drilled two holes *a a* at a distance from each other, corresponding with

Fig. 2

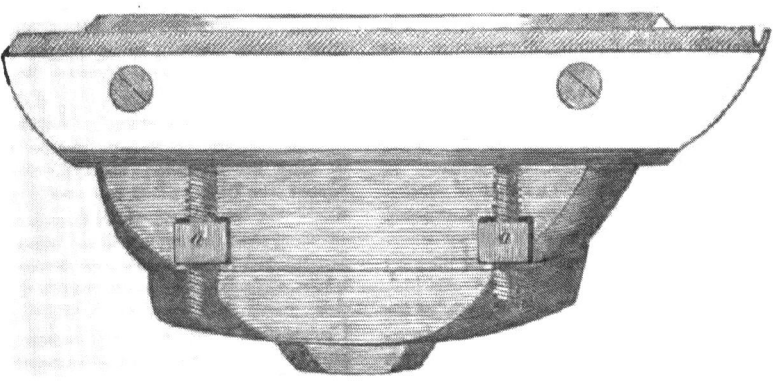

those which I should require in the guides of the chuck. These I then tapped, and drilling corresponding holes in the pieces intended for the guide, I screwed it on the chuck in such a manner that one edge might project beyond the point of the chuck as represented in fig. 2. Then screwing the chuck on the nose of the mandril, and putting it in motion whilst at the same time I moved the cutting tool fixed in the parallel rest as before, I at once cut the edge of the brass guide of the angle I required. The slide was afterwards treated in the same way, and nothing more than a little oil stone powder and oil was required, to make them work together pleasantly and with accuracy. By placing a temporary ledge or regulating screws *a a* fig. 2, at the lower part of the chuck, the same plan would also answer for the formation of the double bevelled guide which, as offering less friction is more applicable to the oval chuck.

After I had formed the double bevelled guides, I experienced great difficulty in cutting truly the groove in the sliding plate. This, however, I effected much to my satisfaction in the following manner:—Upon the nose of the mandril I screwed a flanch chuck of about five inches in diameter, in the centre of which was inserted a strong steel pin terminating in a screw and nut. Next to the plate of the chuck, and on the pin was fitted a steel collar which might form a portion of the pin correctly turned on its chuck, of about two inches in diameter, and $\frac{1}{8}$ or $\frac{1}{16}$ of an inch in

thickness. Next to this was fitted a cutter double bevelled of an angle to correspond with the guides before mentioned and about $2\frac{1}{4}$-inches in diameter. The whole is then made fast by a washer and nut on the end of the pin. After preparing the slide as before and making the edges flat and parallel, the wheel of the lathe is put in motion and by applying the edge of the slide to the cutter, the groove is cut with great accuracy; the even surface of the flanch chuck, (to which the plate is held) regulating the line of the groove, whilst the steel collar, regulates its depth.

I have now before me a translation of many of the most interesting portions of Bergeron, as well as a still more recent work by Dessables, the latter containing as an appendix a description of many excellent inventions by foreign mechanicans of later years, which if acceptable I shall be happy occasionally to offer to your interesting miscellany.

I am, Sir,
Your obedient servant,
W. KENT.

April, 1838.

———

ELMES'S SURVEY OF THE PORT OF LONDON.

The port of London has at length found an historian,—not a whit too soon, it must be confessed,—in the person of Mr. Elmes, the well-known architect, who brings to the execution of his task all the facilities afforded by the official situation he holds under the Corporation, of Surveyor to the Port. That such a work was a desideratum will be allowed on all hands; and Mr. Elmes deserves some degree of credit, if only for the attempt to furnish a literary illustration of the greatest haunt of commerce in the world : it is high time, indeed, that the " Port of London" should have a local habitation and a name in world of letters as well as that of trade : the greatest wonder is, that it should have come down to our author in all its freshness as a novel subject of literary research.

Mr. Elmes commences his work* by a view of the history, privileges, functions, and government of the port, which forms, almost necessarily, a dry and rather uninteresting division, although one which could not very well be omitted, albeit it is well worth while to give the abstracts of old charters and out-of-date legal records in as small a compass as possible. Following this, we have another on its " Extent, Division, and Commercial Regulations," to which the same remark will apply with but little diminution of force, especially as the *compressor* has not been called into play with near so much vigour here as in the preceding chapter, and a variety of mere " parish matters" are allowed to spread themselves at length over a rather imposing number of folio pages. But the third chapter, which concludes the book, is by far the most interesting and important of the whole, the matters it refers to being the " bridges, docks, piers, quays, embankments, moorings, and other scientific works" of the Port, with a series of " tidal and other observations" appended. For the latter, Mr. Elmes is indebted entirely to the essays of Messrs. Lubbock and Whewell, in the Transactions of the British Association, which have thrown more light upon the matter than all the researches—

scanty enough certainly—of previous experimenters ; while the account of the level of the bed of the Thames, from Gloucestershire to the Nore, deduced from actual survey, is, as might be expected, taken from Messrs. Rennies' valuable report in the same collection, which we noticed when the Transactions of the Association passed under review. It may be objected, indeed, that Mr. Elmes has been rather too sweeping and wholesale in his extracts from previous writers, that his accounts of the various docks, and the statistics of the port, are taken with but little alteration or addition, from M'Culloch's " Dictionary of Commerce," and a great portion of his other matter, from a very inconsiderable number of original sources,—nor can he be wholly acquitted on this score. Throughout the work the marks of haste are but too often perceptible ; in some instances so glaringly as even to become offensive to the cursory reader,—an effect, which is not pleasant, in a book which aims to become a work of standard reference on a theme of permanent importance. At one place several consecutive pages are occupied by extracts from a little volume which, the author tells us, was put into his hands by his " spirited publisher" during the progress of the work through the press; and these addititions, it is almost needless to observe, do not harmonize so well as could be desired with the more leisurely-prepared pages in which room has per force been found for them. There are other blemishes of the same description which it is to be regretted Mr. Elmes did not allow himself time enough to remove, as they of course detract in some degree from the completeness and thorough *finish* which ought to distinguish, in all its departments, an elegant and expensive book like his.

Our author has contrived to throw a certain air of novelty over the descriptions of some of the more recent public works on the banks of the river, by making use of the labours of a scientific Swedish tourist, who has paid much attention to the subject, and whose work is as yet (and perhaps likely to remain) a stranger to the English public. Notwithstanding the strong recommendation of Mr. Elmes, we fear that no publisher could be found in the metropolis, willing to adventure the publication of an Eng-

* A Scientific, Historical, and Commercial Survey of the Harbour and Port of London, containing accounts of its history, privileges, functions, and government; its extent, divisions, and jurisdictions; tidal and other scientific observations, &c. Accompanied by plans and details of the port, its docks, gates, and machinery, swivel bridges, moorings, &c., as directed by the By-Laws, its shoals, soundings, &c. Surveyed by James Elmes, Architect, and Civil Engineer, Surveyor of the Port of London, author of " Memoirs of Sir Christopher Wren," &c. London. Weale: 1838. Folio: pp. 78. (Plates.)

lish version of a book so far removed from the limits of "light reading" as that of Captain Carlsund, even had it originally appeared in French or German, instead of Swedish. Had it been written in rhyme it might have stood a better chance, if we may judge from the fact of two English translations having appeared of the "Frithioff's Saga' of Bishop Tegner; a most unusual honour indeed for a book in so little-known a language, and one, the half of which, the prose of the Captain of Engineers is by no means likely to arrive at. Mr. Elmes thus introduces him to his readers, when he arrives in due course at the Saint Katharine's Docks:—

"The following observations connected with this part of our survey, are from the pen of Captain A. G. Carlsund, a highly-talented Royal Engineer, in the Swedish naval service, who died of the malignant cholera, after publishing one volume of his 'Travels in Great Britain,' and leaving another ready for the press. It is much to be wished that a good translation of this volume, from the Swedish into the English language, was published, as the author was not only a man of practical science, but an excellent observer of whatever passed his view.

"In his eighth chapter he describes his voyage from London Bridge downwards, and notices the immense number and variety of the vessels which frequent our port from every quarter of the globe. He commends the build and trim of our wherries, and the skill of our watermen. The boats he calls excellent, of light construction and really beautiful appearance, which, he says, is not the case in general with the larger class of English vessels, which are seldom, if ever, of better construction than those of other nations. In going down the river he was astonished at the activity displayed on board of all the ships in the pool, particularly those engaged in the coal trade. He, very properly, censures the rude appearance of the shores, saying, they present a continual series of roughly-built warehouses, without symmetry, taste, or any attempt at architectural design, and consequently a wretched and ugly appearance, which seriously disappoints every foreigner, who generally arrives in London with great expectations, he says, in favour of English capital, English neatness, and English splendour. He and his companions then passed the Tower, that old fortress, he says, which is so celebrated in the history of English disturbances. Our waterman, he continues, related to us its many curiosities, and pointed out the arch-

way through which state prisoners are conducted to their prison. He told us, that he had just before been one of the boatmen who had been employed in conveying Sir Francis Burdett from his memorable imprisonment in the Tower.

"'We soon arrived,' he continues, ' at the termination of our present excursion, the new docks lately commenced under the superintendance and from the designs of Thomas Telford. On the space of ground called St. Katherine's, was still to be seen, in 1825, the ancient church or chapel of St. Katherine's, surrounded by a densely-populated neighbourhood of labourers, sailors, and publicans.' 'A few years afterwards,' he continues, ' I visited those spacious docks with their expensive stacks of warehouses finished. Large ships were now floating on the very spot where, a few years previous, no other water was visible than that furnished by the water-companies. On that spot, where formerly thousand of chimneys spread a thick, unwholesome smoke, we now witnessed only the smoke from a powerful steam-engine, working to maintain a proper depth of water in the docks. He describes the origin of those docks us arising from some merchants and men of property, who, anticipating the great benefit that would accrue to the port of London by the construction of docks higher up the river and nearer to the Royal Exchange than the other docks, formed a corporation or company for such purpose, and employed Mr. Telford, the most celebrated engineer in Great Britain, to furnish them with a design suited to the situation chosen, which was between the London Docks and the Tower. The bill met with great opposition, but was passed into an Act in 1825, and the works were begun in 1826.' 'On the site,' he observes, " was a church and a collegiate establishment, under the special protection of the Queen, and considered, from the most ancient times, as the property of the Queen Consort; yet, exclaims the Captain with surprise, she was obliged to consent to its removal.' Before commencing the works, the strata upon which they were to be constructed were examined by boring, a method which, he says, had been lately much improved by a Mr. Good. These borings were repeated all over the site, to the depth of forty feet. The houses and other buildings were pulled down, and the ground cleared during the years 1826 and 1827, the excavation for the docks were began (was begun) in May, 1826, and was finished within eighteen months from that time. During the progress of these extensive operations, says Captain Carlsund, I frequently witnessed a thousand men and several hundred of horses employed in the operations, besides several powerful steam-engines. At the beginning of the works wheelbarrows were employed to carry away the earth, but as the excavations proceeded and became deeper, iron railways and steam-engines were substituted. The earth was conveyed into barges, carried down the river, and deposited in convenient places. At the first sight, he continues, the visitor was convinced that none but experienced engineers were the conductors of the works, and such, he says, was really the case; for Mr. Logan, who, under the direction of Mr. Telford, had constructed the celebrated docks at Dundee, was here selected as the superintendent, and Mr. Rhodes, who had previously assisted Mr. Telford in the suspension bridge over the straits of Menai, was the resident engineer. The docks, of which the first stone was laid in May, 1827, were in the following October so far completed, that water was admitted from the river, and every thing ready to receive ships. He then describes the docks, the buildings, and the quays, with minute accuracy, and says, of the various stacks of warehouses, these colossal buildings are neither stuccoed nor painted, and are without architectural ornament, but the regularity of their enormous masses renders the whole sublime and imposing, and a decided acquisition to the improvements of the metropolis. He awards the credit of the architectural department to Mr. Hardwick, and describes the great utility of the two large steam-engines, which, besides being useful for emptying either or all of the basins, in the event of repairs being necessary, are applied to raise the water in the docks, so that vessels can be docked or undocked, during the night or day, at any time of the tide."—pp. 47.

We do not perceive that there is any thing very brilliant in this specimen of Captain Carlsund's talents. It is little more than a simple statement of facts, which would read much better without the continued "he says" with which Mr. Elmes has thought proper to overlay it. Moreover, it displays a blunder here and there, which a native writer would not have fallen into, and a foreign one might easily have avoided. Sir Francis Burdett's liberation from the Tower took place in 1810, and the commencement of St. Katharine's Docks in 1826, so that the waterman who talked of having "just before" set the baronet free, must have referred to an epoch at least sixteen years past and gone. Again, we have the Captain expressing his surprise at

the Queen Consort's being compelled to accede to the removal of St. Katharine's Hospital, although a slight effort of recollection would have been sufficient to recal the fact that, during the period of the projection and execution of the docks, there happened to be no Queen-Consort at all, either to give or withhold her consent. His mention of the Tower as the scene of "English disturbances" is also rather strange. It would almost seem that the Captain had forgotten its older and higher historical associations, and retained only the remembrance of the Spa-fields riots, or some event of equal importance in the records of the Tower. This seems the more probable from a paragraph which we have taken the liberty to omit, in which Captain Carlsund not only coolly proposes to demolish the Tower at once, but takes it for granted that there is no reason in the world why its site should not forthwith be converted into docks. Had all its "memorials" been present to his mind, he could hardly have spoken of the pulling-down of the Tower as such an every-day and matter-of-course affair; nor is his suggestion, we imagine, likely to find favour in the eyes of any who are "native, and to the manner born."

We have already observed that Mr. Elmes is indebted for almost all his information on the tides (as he freely confesses) to the labours of Messrs. Lubbock and Whewell. Other and fresher matter is however not wanting, as the following sketch of the effects of the removal of old London Bridge, especially in the lower parts of the river, will testify.

"On the new bridge being opened, on the 1st of August, 1831, the demolition and removal of the old bridge commenced on the 22d of November following; and on the 25th Mr. Combe (Messrs. Rennies' assistant) was instructed by those gentlemen to proceed up the river to collect information, and to make a series of observations at Putney, Kew, and Richmond bridges, and at Teddington Lock. Tide gauges, accurately adjusted by levelling to a tide gauge similarly fixed at New London Bridge, at Fresh Wharf and a little below the bridge, were fixed at those places, and experienced persons were appointed to keep a daily register of the high and low water marks as indicated by the gauges. The observations commenced on the 1st of December, and were continued till the 1st of June, 1832; at which period no more than two piers which obstructed the waterway had been removed. These removals, however, had lessened the fall at low water nearly one foot.

" In 1833, almost all the masonry and starlings were removed and the whole finally in 1834, and the results of these useful observations are, that from the substitution of the new for the old London Bridge, the drainage of districts bordering on the Thames, as well as the navigation of the river, has been greatly improved ; that barges, which used formerly to be towed up from Putney to Richmond by horses, are carried from London Bridge to Richmond in one tide ; that the fall of the low water surface *below* bridge has been so considerable, as to cause ships in many instances to ground in their tiers at low water ; and that from a register of tides kept by Captain Maugham, of the London Docks, the average depth of low water in the sill of the Shadwell Dock was one foot ten inches below the old Trinity datum ; and that, when there were formerly eight feet in depth, upon the dock sill, there were then only six feet two inches on the average. On the 5th of November, 1834, the tide fell as low as four feet three inches on the sill."

While the natural tide seems thus to be decreasing, it is no small consolation to reflect that the tide of commerce is greatly on the increase. The details on this subject are so amazing as to be almost incredible, were they not so well supported by the unerring testimony of figures. Who would be led to guess, for instance, that the commerce of London had multiplied itself to the surprising extent of nearly four times, in the short period between 1830 and 1836? Yet that such is the fact appears to be quite incontestable. Mr. Elmes observes :—

" The increase of all commercial business in our port has been of late quite extraordinary, as may be seen in the following tables, extracted from the Parliamentary Reports of August, 1836. In the year 1830, the number and tonnage of all the vessels that frequented the port were as follows :—Those engaged in the foreign

trade, 361 ships, equal to 73,634 tons, and 185 coasting ditto equal to 48,100 tons : making together 546 ships, and 121,734 tons. In 1835, the vessels in the foreign trade, 1,076 ships, and 266,684 tons ; those in the coasting trade, 699 ships, and 448,424 tons of shipping ; which gives an increase over 1830 of 326,690 tons, which is equal to 371 per cent. The increase in the number of steam-boats is equally surprising. In 1820 there were only four steam-packets ; in 1830, twenty ; in 1835, forty-three. The still further increase is to be seen in the following statistical accounts of the steam-navigation of our port."

From these accounts, which are given at full length, it appears that the "further increase"—in two years only—amounts to between three and four hundred per cent.—a list being appended of no less than a hundred and six steamers employed in the home trade, and fifty-one engaged in communicating with foreign ports ! A considerable contrast to the four vessels which formed the pigmy steam-fleet of 1820, and an instance of the rapid growth of the facilities for intercommunication which probably cannot be paralleled,—although it may perhaps be even exceeded in the course of a few years on land, when our railway-system shall have been brought into full and efficient operation.

The increase in every department of the trade of our giant port, whether in connection with steam or not, is indeed one not the least among the marvels of the day. The very last page of Mr. Elmes's work affords a proof, had any been needed after the facts advanced in our last extract. The amount even now goes on increasing, and 1836 already " pales its ineffectual fires" before the glories of 1837, itself destined, we hope and believe, to yield in its turn to the superior claims of this present 1838. The following is the statement (with which Mr. Elmes concludes) in which 1836 and 1837 are compared :—

" Ships with cargoes that entered the Port of London from Foreign parts during the years 1836 and 1837.

	British.		Foreign.		Total.	
	Vessels.	Tons.	Vessels.	Tons.	Vessels.	Tons.
1836 ..	3500	766,010	1449	249,080	4949	1,015,090
1837 ..	4058	818,179	1530	236,662	5588	4,054,841
Increase .	558	52,169	81	12,418 (less tonnage.)	639	39,751

Coasting Trade with London.

British.				Vessels.	Tons.
	Vessels.	Tons.	Increase over 1836 ..	1605	154,770
1836 ..	19,715	2,656,750	Add increase of foreign trade ..	639	39,751
1837 ..	21,390	2,811,520			
			Total increase ..	2444	194,521

" The aggregate tonnage of British ships that entered the Port of London in 1837, amounts to no less than 3,629,699 registered tons, which exceeds considerably in amount any previous year in its history, and affords additional reasons, if any were required, for extending the accommodation of the port f)r colliers, and for the removal of the shoals and other obstructions to the navigation." —p. 70.

Of what former port, in either modern or ancient times, could it ever be said that its commerce had increased in a single year by the enormous number of *two thousand four hundred and forty-four* ships, or nearly *two hundred thousand tons* of merchandize?—at this rate, London would seem to bid fair to engross the commerce of the world; yet at the same time the trade of Liverpool is augmenting in a like proportion, and numerous other outports are all pressing forward in the same race of activity and prosperity. May that activity never have occasion to be relaxed, and that prosperity prove as lasting as it is brilliant!

Of Mr. Elmes's work it only remains to say that, as regards " getting-up," it is unexceptionable. The twenty-two plates which illustrate its descriptions are good specimens of engraving, as well as valuable for the information they afford; while the printer and the binder have performed their tasks with unquestionable excellence. The size of the book—an immense folio—is, however, very inconvenient, but was probably determined on in consequence of the necessarily large dimensions of the plates, and may be further justified on the ground of the *gigantic extent* of the subject to which it refers. The graphic illustrations chiefly consist of maps, plans of the docks, and details of the machinery connected with them, and with the navigation of the port. The vignette in the engraved title is of a peculiarly appropriate and interesting character; it is composed of a neat map, in demonstration of the fact pointed out by Sir John Herschel, as affording a key to the commercial prosperity of the British metropolis, that " *the situation of London is nearly in the centre of the terrestrial hemisphere.*"

THE LOSS OF POWER BY THE CRANKS IN STEAM-ENGINES MATHEMATICALLY DEMONSTRATED AND ITS QUANTITY DETERMINED—DAVENPORT'S ELECTRO-MAGNETIC ENGINE.

Sir,—I trust to your candour to insert this letter in reply to the illiberal remarks of " Nauticus" on my calculations on Mr. Davenport's engine, to enable me to demonstrate correctly the loss of power by the crank movement in steam-engines, and to rectify as far as possible any error or miscalculation which may have taken place in my former paper relative to the working powers of Mr. Davenport's engine. The annexed diagram is supposed to refer to the crank, &c., of a steam-engine whose cylinder is perpendicular to the horizon H H or F F. Let D A represent the

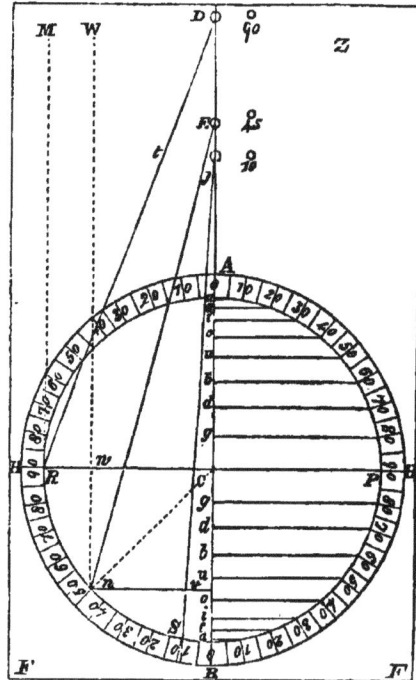

guide rods, and let C R or C n be the crank, and then will D R or E n or J S represent the connecting rod, under the several positions respectively, and then will the inner circle represent *that* which is described by the radius of the crank, the diameter of the said inner circle being equal to the length of the stroke of the piston.

Then will A be the place of the crank when it is up at the top, and B when it is down at the bottom; these two points in the circle are what the mechanics usually call the dead points, or places of *vis inertia*, for when there, however powerful the piston, it can exercise no effective force to drive the crank, but would stand still altogether, if the crank was not placed a little out of the perpendicular when the engineer opens the valve which admits the steam into the cylinder, and thereby sets the engine in motion. It is only when the crank is in the position C R or C P, or when the piston is at the half stroke, that the crank acts with the greatest force it receives from the piston, and from these two points, the power of the crank continually decreases until it arrives at A and B where its power is nothing. And as the crank is a revolving lever, it is clear from the very inspection of the diagram, that the sum total of its power will be represented by a series of levers of different lengths, and the length of these levers respectively, will be equal to the natural sines of their distances from A and B; thus when the crank was 10° 20° 30° degrees, &c., from A or B, its power would be represented by the natural sines *a* 10° *e* 20° *i* 30° &c., and by taking C R or C P to be the full power of the engine crank, and by using Sherwin's or Hutton's mathematical tables we obtain the total power, or leverage of the crank under all these different positions during its rotation.

Places or Positions of the Crank.

	Natural Sines
First Position at A or last at B	00000
Second Position at 10° from A or B	01736
Third Position at 20° from A or B	03420
Fourth Position at 30° from A or B	05000
Fifth Position at 40° from A or B	06427
Sixth Position at 50° from ·A or B	07660
Seventh Position at 60° from A or B	08660
Eighth Position at 70° from A or B	09397
Ninth Position at 80° from A or B	09848
Tenth Position at 90° from A or B	10,000
Sum of the leverage of 10 Positions	62148

which divided by 10, rejecting fractions gives 6,215 instead of 10,000 for the average power of the crank; and thus we clearly see that if 10,000 parts represented the total computed power of a steam-engine, the difference between 10,000 and 6,215 is 3785, and thus we are convinced that the crank engine loses 3785 ten thousandth parts of the power at which it is commonly reckoned, and although this is not a loss of quite one half of its power, it is yet much more than a third thereof that is lost. Or we may render this still more intelligible and familiar by taking the total power of the steam-engine at 100 equal parts, and then we shall have thirty-eight such parts very nearly, for the loss of power by the crank in converting rectilinear into circular motion; besides which there is the effect of friction which will still further diminish the commonly computed power of the steam-engine. And if we reckon the effect of friction of crank, connecting rods, &c., at so little as .02 one fiftieth part, though it is likely to be more, that would make the total loss of power by the crank, &c., equal to $\frac{40}{100}$, or to four tenths; and as I wrote from memory without referring to the notes of my calculations and experiments, not having referred to them for seven or eight years past, I certainly was not so very far wide of my reckoning, when in a former letter I stated the loss of power by the crank as being one half or five tenths; and as there is still another loss of power which I shall immediately explain. I therefore consider that there was no occasion for the empty triumph and illiberal remarks of your correspondent " Nauticus." And even if the loss of power by the crank was no more than four tenths, that would reduce the hundred horse-power steam-engine to an average of no more than a sixty horse power engine made to revolve by an equable motion.

While investigating the nature of the crank movement, there is another and very considerable source of the loss of power which we must not lose sight of, that is the angle formed by the crank and connecting rod; thus by referring to the accompanying diagram, we see that the connecting rod D R when the piston is up or down at the half stroke, forms the angle C R D, and I believe that neither Nauticus, nor any other admirer of crank movements will be bold enough to assert, that acting under such an angle, the piston would produce as great an effect, as if its force had been applied in the direction from M to R perpendicular to the crank R C !

It will be seen by this diagram, that if the angle formed by the connecting rod and crank, be a very acute angle, as for example when the crank is at *n* represented by the dotted line C *n* at forty-five degrees from B, the angle between the crank and connecting rod will be equal to C *n* E, and although the equivalent length is the natural sine of forty-five degrees and consequently equal to the line *n v*. Will Nauticus venture to affirm that the engine will have as great a power under this position, as if the force of the piston was thrown perpendicularly in the direction from W to *n* upon a lever whose length was equal to the line *n v* ?

I believe, Mr. Editor, you will agree with me in the opinion, that there are plenty of Englishmen who thoroughly understand this subject, and that it was quite unnecessary for " Nauticus" to give himself the trouble to *travel* to France for the opinion of the Chevalier de Pambour, on steam-engine cranks. The demonstration I have here given is strictly mathematical and it is not in the power of " Nauticus" to prove the contrary.

I next proceed to correct the calculations in my communication in No. 763 of your Magazine, by using four tenths for the loss of power, instead of five tenths or one half. If we reckon one horse power at 200lbs. then allowing a loss of four tenths, it is reduced to 120lbs. only ; and secondly, if the horse power be taken at 220lbs. then will it be reduced to 132lbs. only of real or effective power ; thirdly, if we reckon one horse power engine equal 230lbs., which I believe is rather more than is generally allowed by the engineers for a horse power, then 230lbs. reduced by four tenths for the loss by the crank, &c., will give 138lbs. for the real effective power by that standard. But as authors are not all agreed exactly as to what force should be reckoned a horse power, I will make corrections according to all these three standards reduced by four tenths for loss, &c., so that it shall not be said that I have overrated the capabilities of Mr. Davenport's engines to the disparagement of the crank steam-engines.

Referring to No. 763, of your Magazine, and page 427, we find that an engine on Mr. Davenport's plan with the driving wheel or first mover fifteen feet diameter, would lift of absolute weight 15,000lbs. six feet high in one second, which considered as the stroke of a steam-engine of that extent, will when computed by the third standard be equal to $108\frac{24}{27}$, or $108\frac{7}{8}$ horse power nearly, by the 2d standard $113\frac{81}{137}$, or $113\frac{7}{12}$ horse power nearly, and if compared by the first standard 125 horse power.

And if the wheel of Davenport's engine be twenty-five feet diameter it would lift 69,444lbs. six feet high per second, this power compared as before with the third standard will give $503\frac{14}{37}$ or $503\frac{7}{18}$ horse power nearly ; if we computed this by the second standard we find $526\frac{13}{137}$, or a very little more than 526 horse power for the capacity of the engine ; but if we calculate according to the first standard the answer is $578\frac{14}{25}$ = 578·7 being very nearly equal to 579 horse power.

Thus it will be seen that " Nauticus" has gained very little by his ill-natured assertion of upsetting the whole of my calculations ; and I leave it for the candid and judicious to consider how very amiable his motives must be who seeks to establish a reputation of his own skill in science by casting a slur upon the disinterested endeavours of others, who have no doubt investigated these subjects as carefully and as closely as himself can have done. It will be further seen, that an engine on Davenport's plan, with the wheel aforesaid of 25 feet diameter, and the whole space required, would only be about 25 by 25 feet or very little more for the entire apparatus, which is not a third of of the space occupied by the engine room,[*] on board the " Great Western" steam ship, whose engine is rated at 450 horses power ; but if the same space were occupied by an engine on Davenport's plan, the said apparatus would produce an effective force of more than two thousand horse power, following out the proportions given in the *Mechanics' Magazine*, No. 736. Let " Nauticus" controvert this if he can.

[*] I believe it has been stated, that the engine room on board the " Great Western," is 75 feet long, and 41 or 42 feet broad, including the stowage of about 800 tons of coals for the engine. I believe one of Davenport's of the same power would not weigh above 200 tons.

It ought to be observed that the great object of these calculations and investigations is to enable us to determine beforehand, what should be the size of an engine capable of performing any quantity of work required, and that although the steam-engines, as does hereby plainly appear, are four tenths less powerful than what they are commonly thought to be, yet this is no disparagement to the manufacturers of them, as they furnish engines that will do what is stipulated for; and for the clearer understanding of this subject, it would be well to distinguish between the computed nominal power, and the real and effective power of steam-engines. Thus for example, the engine on board the "Great Western" steam ship, is rated at 450 horse-power; but if this be reduced by allowing four tenths by the cranks and connecting rods, &c., will give 270 for the number of effective horse-power; and since in these cases, whether we calculate by the real or nominal power, we see this is sufficient to carry a ship of 1400 tons burden with rapidity through the ocean, and will therefore serve us as a standard to regulate the size of the engine and other machinery, for any other ship, whether larger or smaller than the "Great Western" steamer. And it will further be seen by referring to my corrections contained in this letter, that an electro-magnetic engine with the driving wheel 25 feet diameter would be 53 horse-power, 76 horse-power, and 129 horses power greater than the power of the engine of the "Great Western," according as we calculated by the third, second, or first standards for a horse-power beforementioned.

I will further call your attention to the important fact, that "Nauticus" has unwittingly, and no doubt quite unintentionally furnished me with one of the most powerful arguments in favour of Davenport's engines; and with the weapons he has provided me I shall proceed to combat him, and to prove their (Davenport's) vast superiority over steam-engines. In the beginning of "Nauticus's" letter he snarls at my shewing, "that Davenport's would be equal to a steam-engine whose piston has a stroke of 6 feet in length and making sixty strokes per minute; and consequently the space passed over by the piston will be 6 feet × 60 = 360 feet per

minute!" ("Nauticus" then proceeds to state,) that "the utmost limit prescribed by Watt and others is 220 feet per minute, and that this is never exceeded except in locomotives, where the rapid motion of the piston is found to be so distressing to the working parts, that those concerned therein are seriously contemplating to reduce the speed to the above standard of 220 feet per minute, and that hence the deductions referred to are totally incorrect."

Whoever will take the pains carefully to examine this quotation from "Nauticus," will soon see, that he either did not understand, or else that he has misrepresented the meaning of my communication: he has treated the whole matter as if Davenport's was a piston engine, which performed sixty strokes per minute of six feet in length each stroke. I never stated any such thing; what I stated was by way of comparison, that an electro-magnetic wheel on Davenport's plan 15 feet diameter would lift 15000lbs. 6 feet high per second; and that if the wheel was 25 feet diameter it would lift 69,444lbs. 6 feet high per second, which would of course be equal to the pistons of steam-engines, each respectively lifting the same weights and moving through the space of 6 feet per second. I did not assert that any steam-engine actually did *this*; but I shewed that Davenport's engines of the sizes I had there stated would equal steam-engines of certain dimensions that might do this; what I there stated was to enable the reader easily to understand and compare the capabilities of the electro magnetic with the powers of the common steam-engines.

To acknowledge that the velocity of the pistons must not exceed 220 feet per minute, is indeed very unfortunate for the admirers of piston and crank movements. "Nauticus" did not perceive that by this avowal he had declared that there exists a striking imperfection in steam-engines, which arises from the violent concussions of the piston upon the connecting rods and crank, which when the motion of the piston is very rapid acts like the sudden blow of a hammer, and it is this which occasions the wear and straining of the working parts. But there are no such objections against the electro-magnetic engine, the very power of which originates in a circular movement of the driving wheel itself, and has no jerking nor straining of the working, but is smooth and uniform in its motion; and moreover as a first mover is not limited in its velocity to 220 nor to 2200 feet per minute; for it appears that Mr. Davenport's wheel makes from 600 to 1000 revolutions in a minute! There is no danger of explosions, and of destruction to the vessel and passengers, as in steam-engines. These peculiar mechanical properties together with the great saving of room and expense, cannot fail in establishing the use of Davenport's invention, and ultimately throwing the common steam-engine completely into the shade.

The person who does not know that engines may be made to act by other means than by steam produced from *boiling water*, surely cannot boast of being profoundly versed in mechanical science; there are certainly many things that "Nauticus" yet never dreamt of in *his philosophy*.

I had intended to have now written something concerning a remedy or substitute for the crank in steam-engines, but must defer *this*, till some other opportunity, and in the mean time subscribe myself, as I have been for fifteen years past,

Sir, your's very respectfully,

THOMAS OXLEY.

3, Elizabeth-place, Westminster-road,
April 26, 1838.

NOTES AND NOTICES.

Great Mongolfier Balloon.—An experimental trial of an immense machine was made on Tuesday, on the borders of Epping Forest, in the presence of the constructor and several scientific gentlemen connected with the undertaking, for the purpose of trying the effect of a newly-invented furnace by which the balloon is to be filled with heated air, instead of the imperfect open brazier used by Mongolfier, Pilâtre, Rozier, and others, in their ascents from Paris some years since. By means of this invention the possibility of any spark coming in contact with the machine during the inflation is entirely avoided, and although at one period of the experiment the temperature was raised to two hundred degrees, not the slightest appearance of danger was visible. So powerful were the means used to obtain the requisite degree of rarefaction, that the vast machine was completely filled in eight minutes, and had then an ascending power of 1,200 lbs. exclusive of the furnace and car, the latter of which alone weighs, when adorned, 300 lbs., and is 15 feet long by 8 feet wide. Three persons ascended to a considerable height, but were restrained from making an aërial excursion, it being intended only to ascertain correctly the capabilities of the balloon. All the persons present expressed themselves extremely gratified with the perfect success of the experiment. The first ascent will take place from the Surrey Zoological Gardens, when the builder and two other gentlemen well versed in aërostation will ascend.—*Essex Paper.*

The Atlantic Steamers.—Much anxiety is evinced to learn the particulars of the voyage out of the Atlantic steamers, Sirius and Great Western, and especial interest is attached to the former, from the circumstance of her being furnished with Hall's condensers, which will thus undergo a decisive trial. The last news of her was on the 14th April, when she had been ten days out, and she was then gallantly steaming on at the rate (it is said) of two hundred and fifty miles a day. Both she and her opponent, it will be recollected, must have met on the outset of their passage with the strong westerly gales which prevailed in the beginning of April, and been much retarded in consequence. It is therefore tolerably certain that neither would arrive at New York within the "expected" time,—twelve days,—although it may be anticipated that they will have beaten the sailing packets by a "pretty considerable way."

French Steamer in the Thames.—Hitherto all the steam-vessels frequenting the port of London have been virtually, if not ostensibly, of British ownership and origin. The French, however, have at length resolved to enter the field, and "carry the war into the enemy's quarters." A splendid new steamer, the "Phœnix," has been built at Havre for this purpose, and has just commenced running between her native port and London Bridge, between which places she intends to take up a regular station. She belongs to a French company, who are determined, if possible, to reap some of the benefits of the immense intercourse between the two capitals of England and France, by water as well as by land.

Sir John Soane's Benefactions.—The Soane Museum has just re-opened for the season, under the same regulations as last year,—regulations which operate to prevent any thing like the free admission of "the public." The "Soane Medal" is to be adjudged by the Institute of British Architects, and the subject for the present year is "the restoration of one of the ancient Baronial Castles of Great Britain." The first annual distribution of Sir John Soane's donations by will to distressed architects and architects' widows is also on the eve of taking place.

Charcoal Fuel.—In the *London Magazine* for December, 1758, there is the following paragraph in a division of the work called the "Monthly Chronologer," under the date Tuesday, Nov. 26:—"Some persons having been almost suffocated lately by sleeping in a room wherein was a charcoal fire, it has been declared that experiment has proved, that charcoal fire wetted with salt dissolved in water will have no suffocating quality."

Complete Sets of the Mechanics' Magazine may now be had, twenty-seven volumes, half-cloth, price £11 7s.

☞ *British and Foreign Patents taken out with economy and despatch; Specifications, Disclaimers, and Amendments, prepared or revised; Caveats entered; and generally every Branch of Patent Business promptly transacted. A complete list of Patents from the earliest period (15 Car. II. 1675,) to the present time may be examined. Fee 2s. 6d.; Clients, gratis.*

LONDON: Printed and Published for the Proprietor, by W. A. Robertson, at the Mechanics' Magazine Office, No. 6, Peterborough-court between 135 and 136, Fleet-street.—Sold by A. & W. Galignani, Rue Vivienne, Paris.

𝔐𝔢𝔠𝔥𝔞𝔫𝔦𝔠𝔰' 𝔐𝔞𝔤𝔞𝔷𝔦𝔫𝔢,

MUSEUM, REGISTER, JOURNAL, AND GAZETTE.

No. 771.]	SATURDAY, MAY 19, 1838.	[Price 3*d.*

CHANTER AND CO.'S PATENT SMOKE CONSUMING FURNACE.

CHANTER AND CO.'S PATENT SMOKE BURNER.

This invention essentially consists in so arranging the form of the furnace and position of the bars, that the fuel is regularly advanced by gravitation, without the aid of machinery, or any apparatus besides the simple instruments in common use for the management of furnaces. This is effected by placing the fire-bars at an angle of about 45°, and sloping the bottom of the boiler in the same degree; the carbon and various more inflammable gases are set free at the commencement of combustion at the upper end of the furnace, and being charged with the oxygen of the atmosphere proceed through and over the fire, which increases in heat to its lower end, gradually subjecting the less combustible gases to perfect combustion. Saving in fuel is thus effected; for in the present furnaces, these latter gases are not only passed off unconsumed, but by preventing the ignition of more combustible materials necessarily waste a large portion of the fuel. Thus the effect, in the operation of this furnace, may be stated to be that of obtaining, at the termination of the furnace, that intense degree of heat indispensable to the entire combustion of the various substances emitted from the burning fuel. The invention is exhibited in Mr. Chanter's specification in twelve different forms, shewing its application to various descriptions of furnaces. The engraving on our front page shews the application of the inclined fire-bars to a locomotive-engine furnace. The secondary furnaces beneath the principal fire-bars are for the purpose of heating the air as it enters the ash-pit; a hot blast is thereby obtained to effect the more complete combustion of the fuel. It appears from numerous testimonials, given by the first engineering authorities, that the intended object is effectually performed—the most common coal being burned without any appearance of smoke from the chimney.

STEAM NAVIGATION TO INDIA.

Sir,—The pamphlet recently published by Sir John Ross for the purpose of showing the practicability of forming a steam communication with India via the Cape of Good Hope, has just come under my notice. I fully concur with him in opinion as to its practicability, but cannot yet bring myself to the belief that it can be accomplished in the short period he has stated (less than 50 days), for the following reasons:—First, assuming the distance to be about 12,000 miles by the most direct route; if the steam-vessels were able to maintain an average rate of 10 miles per hour, fifty days would be required for the voyage, exclusive of the necessary delays for receiving additional fuel on board, cleaning the machinery, &c. I have not at present met with any steam-vessel in the course of my somewhat extensive observation, that has been able to maintain such an average speed for several consecutive days, and my opportunities for acquiring information relative to the *actual* performance of steam-boats, are very frequent. Some few boats will maintain ten miles an hour for 30 or 40 hours, or even 80 hours; yet these fast vessels would not be found to maintain an average of quite ten miles an hour during the *whole* of the voyages made from the 1st of January to the 30th June, or from the 1st July to the 31st December, in the British seas, with a fair average cargo on board; although these voyages are comparatively so short that the machinery may be reasonably expected to run the whole passage without requiring to be stopped for a sufficient length of time to occasion any material reduction in their average rate. Some months since I had an opportunity of examining the account (regularly kept) of the performance of some of the fastest boats plying between Glasgow and Liverpool, which fully bears me out in the preceding statement. The reports of the speed of steam-vessels are very generally exaggerated. An instance recently came to my knowledge in which it was confidently stated that a speed of 14 miles an hour had been attained by a new steam-vessel. One of the gentlemen present at the trial proved that the speed attained was only from 11¼ to 11½ miles per hour, and this with the engines in the best possible condition. His statement was confirmed by the facts, that the number of strokes and size of the wheels would not admit of her going at a greater speed unless the resistance of the boat is reduced in the same ratio as her velocity through the water is increased. Something like this theory was advanced by a gentleman upon whose work some remarks were made by the present writer in a former number of your magazine.

It now appears highly probable that a communication by means of a line of steam-vessels with India, will be accomplished very shortly. Mr. Seaward, I am informed, has long since maintained its practicability; but not having had the opportunity of seeing his remarks upon the subject, I am unable to give you the details of his plan, which ought to be again brought under public notice.

The Dutch Government are taking measures for the introduction of steam navigation in the East Indies, and have some vessels building there for that purpose. Surely this ought to incite those who have the management of British interests in that quarter to take care that our pre-eminence there is not sacrificed through their supineness.

If we wish to carry steam navigation on to its greatest degree of perfection, there must be a cordial co-operation between the builders of the vessels and the constructors of the machinery, and the present jealous system of procedure be given up; for unless the vessel be properly constructed with regard to sailing properties, there will continue to be a vast expenditure of power to obtain speed beyond what is really required if the vessels be properly constructed for the purpose.

Another point requiring more attention than has hitherto been paid to it is, that the vessels should be constructed in such a manner as to have the necessary strength to bear the unavoidable strain arising from the unequal distribution of the weight of the machinery, in relation to the volume of water displaced. At some future period I may possibly offer some remarks upon the method by which the evils arising from this unequal distribution of weight may be avoided, without materially, if at all, increasing the expence beyond the present method of construction.

I am, Sir, your obedient servant,
GEORGE BAYLEY.

RAILWAY SIGNALS.

Sir,—The attention of the scientific world has been so engrossed by railway projects as to leave but little time for the consideration of those minor details which, however trifling they may appear at first, ultimately demand the careful attention of the engineer. Upon the perfection of the details, the ultimate success of the system depends. Already we have had painful evidence of the want of a judicious system of working day and night signals, announcing the approach to, or the departure from, stations or other parts of the line, where it appeared most requisite. There are two signals at present in use that require a passing notice. The first of these, the "whistle," certainly does possess considerable advantages; its portability, sharpness, and clearness of tone, renders it worthy of being retained in the service, and to be used on certain occasions. The other signal in use is of a far different kind; I know not what to call it. The war-whoop of the Blackfeet must be positive harmony compared with the execrable shriek caused by the rush of the steam! I should presume that a signal of this kind is likely to make matters worse—in case of an accident or alarm it would be perhaps difficult to tell which uttered the cry of danger, the engine or the passengers; add to this the alarm given to the female portion of the travellers, and there is sufficient ground for its abandonment. They manage these things better in Russia. I have lately seen an apparatus intended to be applied to the Russian locomotive engines which is well worth the attention of our railway directors. It consists of a moderate sized oblong box containing three or four "reed pipes" (as they would be technically termed by organ builders); these pipes are of brass, and shaped trumpet like. The box also contains a cylinder upon which the trumpet flourish or movement is pricked. The cylinder being put in motion by the action of the engine, the keys are raised, and act upon levers connected with the valves at the mouth end of the trumpets; the bellows attached to the apparatus (which is also worked by the same action) supply the wind to the instrument, and produce an excellent effect. A small swell might be added to increase or diminish the sound. I have had an opportunity of hearing one of these contrivances, and was much gratified with the accuracy of intonation. Near at hand the sounds were of immense volume, and I am certain fully equal to any thing required on a railroad. The apparatus was constructed by Messrs. Robson and Son, organ builders, of St. Martin's lane.

It is a matter worth serious consideration whether the *night signals* could not be so contrived as to be clearly exhibited at a considerable distance (say one mile); a revolving light might be conveniently worked by the engine—or what might perhaps be better, a preparation of strontian, to be ignited at a given time in a receptacle hoisted for that purpose, but sufficiently protected from the weather. In perfecting the details of this estimable mode of travelling, much is required to be done: let the correspondents of the *Mechanics' Magazine* render the public still further indebted to them by turning their attention to these matters, thereby ensuring greater safety to railway travelling.

Your's, &c.

CHRIS. DAVY.

P.S. I regret to hear the unfounded rumours of the failure of the Kilsby Tunnel—nothing has occurred to warrant such statements. I shall shortly resume my description of that laborious work.—C. D.

CONDENSATION BY EXTERNAL COLD.

Sir,—Observing in your last number a claim to the invention for producing a vacuum by passing cold water between a series of metallic pipes or chambers open to the steam on its exit from the eduction pipe of the cylinder of a steam-engine set up for a Mr. Buchanan, in opposition to Mr. Hall, it may be right to state that several others appear to have a prior right of claim to either. Dr. Church, it would seem, obtained a patent in 1833, from which the latter inventions differ in no essential degree; and a gentleman connected with a large engine manufactory in Scotland, so early as the year 1828, had prepared the material, consisting of half-inch tubes, &c. for a condenser, arranged in the manner of Mr. Hall's; but owing to a pressure of business, it was not completed for some time after. On reference to a memorandum, it appears that the gentleman above alluded to, informed the writer on the 2nd February, 1830, that "his mode of condensing by external cold fully succeeded;

that it materially relieved the engine (which had been some years previously in use at the works), and that it saved one-fifth of the fuel." Subsequently several steam-boats have been built at the works, fitted with these condensers, giving, I am informed, entire satisfaction; and most of them, if not owned by a London proprietary, frequent the port. No patent has been obtained by the inventor.

I remain, Sir,

Your's respectfully,

B. H.

Wapping, May 7, 1838.

DR. ARNOTT'S STOVE IMPROVED.

Sir,—As the subject of warming apartments, &c. has occupied my attention for some time, I will, with your leave, make a few remarks thereon. First, as to Messrs. Harper and Joyce's stove. Everybody knew that a shovel-ful of live charcoal will burn in a brazier or other vessel, where there is a free circulation of air. H. and J.'s stove is no more in principle than the brazier in common use in the south of Europe, only of a different shape and with an apparatus at top, to regulate the exit of heated air and of carbonic acid gas. So much for this "nine days' wonder."

Next, as to Dr. Arnott's Stove and Essay. You are too severe in your critique (March 10). True there is much in his Essay we know already: the same remark applies to his "Elements of Physic;" but it is in the agreeable and familiar style in which the latter is written, that its chief merit consists. The Doctor certainly has been a principal agent in directing public attention to the subject. His stove can only be used for warming rooms, but I think he has made it too complicated for general use. I should dispense with the fire-screen, dome, funnel, and partition in the inside, as I conceive the last rather impedes than assists the free circulation of air in the stove. To prove this, put a small quantity of powdered gum myrrh in a wine glassful of water; apply heat to the side of the glass, or to the bottom partially, and an upward and downward current will soon be perceived; then introduce a piece of tin-plate so as to fit the sides of the glass, dividing it in two, but not reaching either to the top or bottom of the liquid; apply the heat as before, and you will see that this partition proves a great obstacle to a free circulation of the fuel. The fire-screen, dome, and funnel wastes the heat, which it is the principal object of the stove to economise. The air regulator effects all the objects for which they are introduced.

The apparatus for regulating the admission of air may do very well while attended to by the Doctor himself, or any one who comprehends the principle; but suppose it in use in a nursery, and one of the little chaps hits the glass tube with the mercury, with his stick! Yet the Doctor strongly advises the thermometer to be on the outside.

Now, Sir, you will ask, after pulling the Doctor's stove to pieces, what I have to offer in its stead? Let the outer case or stove of cast or sheet-iron, with the door and ash-pit be as it is—(probably it might be better to have a small shutter in the front to be opened at the first lighting of the fire, and then to be completely shut, leaving the office of supplying the necessary air to the regulator)—the fire-pot ought to be raised about two inches from the bottom of the stove by means of three or four legs; the air regulator may be either in front or at the sides of the stove. The Doctor says, page 51, "the whole air necessary to support combustion might enter by an opening of half an inch in diameter." On the inside of the case I would have an iron-plate hung on one side by a nail, like that which covers a key-hole, and to the opposite end of the plate, from which it is hung, have it attached to a brass rod, which hangs from the top of the case, by a screw, so that by turning or returning this screw you regulate exactly the quantity of air you wish admitted—the hole to be proportioned to the size of the case. Brass expands by heat about double that of iron, so that you have now a good thermometer in the inside of the case, and which cannot by any possibility go wrong, or be put out of repair. I should also advise a throttle-valve to be placed in the flue, open when the fire is first lighted, and afterwards regulated according to circumstances. This last, I conceive, will very materially economise the heat.

S.

North Brixton.

———

ANSWER TO QUESTION UPON THE RELATIVE SIZES OF PULLEYS— MECH. MAG., VOL. XXVI, P. 249.

Sir,—As the following question (proposed some time ago, in your Magazine) has received no satisfactory answer any where, so far as I know, the accompanying solution is at your service, provided you think it worthy of a place in your useful miscellany.

Question.—If motion is to be communicated from one shaft to another, by means of a belt passing over a pulley on each shaft; to find the size of either pulley, when that of the other is increased, or diminished by any number of inches, or parts of an inch, and so that the same length of belt as before will still answer?

1st. When the belt crosses (in the form of the figure 8) the solution is very simple: for in that case you have only to increase the diameter of the pulley upon one of the shafts as much as you diminish the diameter of that upon the other shaft, and the same length of belt as before will exactly suit.

2nd. When the belt is open (that is, when it does not cross) the solution is twofold, according as the pulley, whose size is known, is greater or less than that which is unknown or required. When this point is uncertain, you add half the circumference of the known pulley to the distance between the centres of the shafts, which done, may be called the trial number; and when the trial number is greater than half the length of the belt, the required pulley is the less of the two; but if otherwise, it is the greater.

This done, suppose, 1st., that the required pulley is less than the given one. In that case, take the length of the belt from double the trial number, and divide the remainder by the distance between the centres of the shafts. Subtract this quotient from 2.4674011, and having taken the square root of the remainder, true to four or five decimal places, subtract that root from 1.5708. Multiply the remainder by the distance between the centres of the shafts, and the last product taken from the radius of the larger pulley will give that of the smaller one, near enough to the truth for all practical purposes, when the distance between the shafts is considerable with respect to the difference between the radii of the pulleys. When the distance between the centres of the shafts is inconsiderable, and one of the pulleys very much larger than the other, the following, which may be called the correcting rule, will give the required radius, as near the truth as you please.

(1st). Find an approximate value of the radius of the required pulley, by last rule, or by trial, or you may suppose it anything near to the truth you please, and having taking this approximate value from the radius of the given pulley, divide the remainder by the distance between the centres of the shafts, till you have six decimal figures in the quotient, and consider this decimal as the natural sine of an angle a, which angle, being added to 90°, find the length of the sum to unity as radius, and multiply this length by the greater or given radius.

(2nd). Find the natural cosine of the aforesaid angle a, and multiply the same by the distance between the centres of the shafts; or take the square of the difference between the radius of the given pulley and the approximate value of the required one, from the square of the distance between the centres of the shafts, and extract the square root of the remainder to six decimal places.

(3rd). Take the length of the arc whose natural sine is got by direction (1st), that is, of arc a, from 1.570796.

(4th). Add the numbers got by directions (1st) and (2d), and having subtracted the sum from half the length of the belt, divide the remainder by the number got by direction (3rd), and the quotient will be the radius of the less, or required pulley, the nearer the truth, in proportion as the approximate or supposed value was near to the truth.

Repeat the processes of directions (1st), (2nd), (3rd) and (4th), with the new or nearer value of the required radius, instead of the former approximate or supposed value, till the value come out the same, twice in succession, to five or six decimal places, which will generally happen in a few trials, and the last value will be true to the one-ten-thousandth part of an inch.

Case 2nd, or that in which the given pulley is the less, and the required pulley the greater. Add half the circumference of the given or less pulley to the distance between the centres of the shafts, and having subtracted the double of the same from the length of the belt, divide the remainder by the distance between the centres of the shafts, and to the quotient add the number 2.4674011. Let the square root of this last sum be extracted to five or six decimal places, and take 1.5708 from that root, multiply the last remainder by the distance between the centres of the shaft, and the product, increased by the radius of the less pulley, will give that of the greater, sufficiently true for all practical purposes when the difference between the sizes of the pulleys is small and the distance between the centres of the shafts considerable with respect to the diameters of the pulleys.

When the shafts are near each other, and the pulleys differ much in their diameters, the following, which may be called the correcting rule, will give the required radius as near the truth as we may wish.

(1st.) Find (as in case first) an approximate value of the radius of the required pulley by the rule immediately preceding, or by trial, or in any other way, and having subtracted from this value that of the given, or less pulley, divide the remainder by the distance between the centres of the shafts, carrying out the quotient to six decimal places; and considering this quotient as the natural sine of an angle a, subtract angle a from 90°, and find the length of the remaining angle to unity as radius; and let the length of the arc thus found be multiplied by the radius of the given or less pulley.

(2nd). Find the natural cosine of angle a to unity as radius, and multiply the same by the distance between the centres of the shafts; or take the square of the difference between the radii of the given and approximately found pulleys from the square of the distance between the centres of the shafts, and extract the square root of the remainder to six places of decimals.

(3rd). Add the length of arc a (unity being radius) to the number 1.570796, and having taken the sum of the numbers got by directions (1st) and (2nd), from half the length of the belt, divide this remainder by the aforesaid sum, and the result will be a nearer value of the radius of the larger pulley.

Repeat the processes of directions of (1st) (2nd) and (3rd), with the new or corrected value of the acquired radius, instead of the last or approximate value, and with the succeeding or more correct values, instead of the former values, till two of these come out the same to five or six decimal places, which will generally happen in two or three trials, and the final number will be the radius of the greater pulley, true to the one ten-thousandth part of an inch.

To prevent any mistake, and for the sake of those who are able to read alge-bra, I shall annex below the algebraic expressions of the preceding rules; and for this purpose let $\Pi = 3.1415926$ &c.; $D =$ the distance between the centres of the shafts in inches; $L =$ half the length of the belt; R', R'', R''' &c.; r', r'', r''' &c. the successive approximate values of the radii of the larger and smaller pulleys respectively, also in inches; then, case 1st, R and r being the correct values of the radii, we have:

$$r' = R - D \left\{ \frac{\Pi}{2} - \sqrt{\frac{\Pi^2}{4} - 2 . \frac{D + \Pi . R - L}{D}} \right\}$$

and,

$$r'' = \frac{L - \sqrt{D^2 - (R - r')^2} - R \left(\frac{\Pi}{2} + \text{arc sin.} \frac{R - r'}{D} \right)}{\frac{\Pi}{2} - \text{arc sin.} \frac{R - r'}{D}}$$

$$r''' = \frac{L - \sqrt{D^2 - (R - r'')^2} - R \left(\frac{\Pi}{2} + \text{arc sin.} \frac{R - r''}{D} \right)}{\frac{\Pi}{2} - \text{arc sin.} \frac{R - r''}{D}}$$

Case 2nd, or that in which the less pulley is given, and the greater required.

$$R' = r + D \left\{ \sqrt{\frac{\Pi^2}{4} + 2 . \frac{L - \Pi r - D}{D}} - \frac{\Pi}{2} \right\}$$

$$R'' = \frac{L - \sqrt{D^2 - (R' - r)^2} - r \left(\frac{\Pi}{2} \text{ arc sin.} \frac{R' - r}{D} \right)}{\frac{\Pi}{2} + \text{arc sin.} \frac{R' - r}{D}}$$

$$R''' = \frac{L - \sqrt{D^2 - (R'' - r)^2} - r \left(\frac{\Pi}{2} - \text{arc sin.} \frac{R'' - r}{D} \right)}{\frac{\Pi}{2} + \text{arc sin.} \frac{R'' - r}{D}}$$

A more interesting and useful case of the foregoing general question may be put as follows:—

Question.—If motion is to be communicated from one shaft to another by means of a belt passing over a pulley on each shaft, and if other pairs of pulleys are to be put upon the same shafts, of such sizes, that for m revolutions of the one shaft, the other was to perform n revolutions; to find the radii of each corresponding pair of pulleys?

Supposing m greater than n, and using the same letters in the same sense as before, we have—

$$R' = D \left\{ \sqrt{\frac{\Pi^2}{4} . \left(\frac{m + n}{m - n} \right)^2 + \frac{2m}{m - n} . \frac{L - D}{D}} - \frac{\Pi}{2} \frac{m + n}{m - n} \right\}$$

$$R'' = \frac{L - \sqrt{D^2 - \left(\frac{m - n}{m} R' \right)^2}}{\frac{\Pi}{2} . \frac{m + n}{m} + \frac{m - n}{m} \text{ arc sin.} \frac{m - n}{m} . \frac{R'}{D}}$$

$$R'' = \frac{L - \sqrt{D^2 - \left(\frac{m - n}{m} R'' \right)^2}}{\frac{\Pi}{2} . \frac{m + n}{m} + \frac{m - n}{m} \text{ arc sin.} \frac{m - n}{m} . \frac{R''}{D}}$$

The greater radius being thus found, the less is evidently equal to the $\frac{n}{m}$th part of the greater. The two annexed examples will illustrate the above rules.

1st. Let the distance between the centres of the shafts be 108 inches, half the length of the belt 163.23 inches, and the motions of the shafts as 10 to 1, to find the radii of the pulleys:

$$\frac{\Pi^2}{2} \times \left(\frac{m+n}{m-n}\right)^2 = 2.4674 \times \frac{121}{81} = \ldots\ldots\ldots\ 3.685869$$

$$\frac{2m}{m-n} \cdot \left(\frac{L}{D} - 1\right) \ldots\ldots\ldots\ldots\ \frac{1.136419}{\sqrt{4.822288}} = 2.19597$$

$$\frac{\Pi}{2} \cdot \frac{m+n}{m-n} = \ldots\ldots\ldots\ldots\ldots\ldots\ldots\ldots\ 1.91986$$

$$\times\ by\ldots\ldots\ \frac{.27611}{108}$$

$$R' = \ldots\ldots\ 29.82\ \ nearly.$$

This value differs from the truth by $\frac{84}{100}$ of an inch. To show now the operation of the correcting rule.

$$L = \ldots\ldots\ldots\ldots\ldots\ldots\ldots\ldots\ldots\ldots\ldots\ 163.23$$
$$D^2 = 108^2 = \ldots\ldots\ldots\ldots\ 11664$$
$$\left(\frac{m-n}{m} R'\right)^2 = \ldots\ldots\ldots\ \frac{720.2783}{\sqrt{10943.7217}} = 104.61$$

$$- 58.62 = \text{Numerator of the value of } R''.$$

$$\frac{m-n}{m} \cdot \frac{R'}{D} = .2485 = \text{nat. sin. of } 14°\ 23'\ \text{nearly.}$$

$$\text{Length of } 14°\ 23' = .251029$$

$$.251029 \times \frac{m-n}{m} = .225926$$

$$\frac{\Pi}{2} \cdot \frac{m+n}{m} = \ldots\ldots\ldots\ 1.727875$$

$$1.953801) 58.620000 (30.00305' = R''$$

and this value is within the one five-hundreth part of an inch of the truth.

Example 2nd. Let the distance between the centres of the shafts and half the length of the belt be the same as in the last example, but the motions of the shafts as 7 to 5—to find the radii of the pulleys?

$$\frac{\Pi^2}{4} \times \left(\frac{m+n}{m-n}\right)^2 = 2.4674 \times 36 = \ 88.8264$$

$$\frac{2m}{m-n} \cdot \left(\frac{L}{D} - 1\right) = \ldots\ldots\ \frac{3.5797}{\sqrt{92.4061}} = 9.6128$$

$$\frac{\Pi}{2} \cdot \frac{m+n}{m-n} = \ldots\ldots\ldots\ldots\ldots\ldots\ldots\ 9.4247$$

$$\times\ \ \frac{.1881}{108}$$

$$20.3148 = R'.$$

To show the operation of the correcting rule:

$$L \dots\dots\dots\dots\dots\dots\dots\dots\dots\dots\dots\dots 163.23$$

$$D^2 = \dots\dots\dots\dots\dots 11664$$

$$\left(\frac{m-n}{m} R'\right)^2 = \dots \quad 33.689069$$

$$\sqrt{11630.310931} = 107.843$$

$$55.387 = \text{Numerator of the value of } R''.$$

$$\frac{m-n}{m} \cdot \frac{R'}{D} = .053742 = \text{nat. sin. of } 3^\circ .. 5' \text{ nearly.}$$

Length of $3^\circ .. 5' = .0538128$.

and $.0538128 \times \frac{m-n}{m} = .015375$

$$\frac{\Pi}{2} \cdot \frac{m+n}{m} = \dots\dots\dots 2.692793$$

$$2.708168) 55.387 (20.451 \&c. = R''.$$

and $20.451 \times \frac{5}{7} = 14.608 = r''$; and these values are within the one five-hundredth part of an inch of the truth.

Note.—When the sizes of the pulleys, and the distance between the centres of the shafts are known, the following formula will give the length of the belt, viz. :

$$2 L = (R + r) \Pi + 2 \sqrt{D^2 - (R-r)^2} + 2 (R-r) \text{ arc sin. } \frac{R-r}{D}$$

To practical mechanics, the foregoing rules may perhaps appear complicated and tedious : it does not seem easy, however, to find anything simpler, and at the same time equally accurate, especially when tables containing the lengths of circular arcs are at hand. If they shall prove useful to any of your numerous readers, the writer will be very happy.

I am, Sir, your obedient servant,

R.

Dundee, N.B., April 16, 1838.

HARPER AND JOYCE'S STOVE.

Sir,—The public are infinitely indebted to the pages of your Magazine, for being the first to warn the public against the dangers attending the use of Harper and Joyce's stove. If these gentlemen have erred through ignorance, the useless expense which they have incurred will perhaps be a sufficient penalty; but the party, or parties, whoever they may be, through whose instrumentality this dangerous imposition originated, deserve the most severe condemnation. A gentleman called only a few days past at the establishment for the sale of the stoves, to make inquiry respecting them, when he was informed that a person had slept in a confined apartment with one of the stoves burning all night without experiencing the slightest inconvenience ; he was likewise assured, that if the prepared fuel was used, not the slightest danger was to be apprehended! Now, this, Sir, is too bad, since it has been proved beyond contradiction, that the prepared fuel is neither more nor less than charcoal, the only difference between it and common charcoal being, that it is more perfectly charred, but possesses at the same time all the deadly properties of the former.

It has been stated, that if the stove is useless as regards dwelling-houses, it is nevertheless a valuable discovery in reference to hot-houses, &c. I imagine, Sir, that carbonic acid is destructive of vegetable as well as of animal life, and that the discovery (if discovery it can be called) is altogether a failure.

I am, Sir, yours respectfully,

I. S.

12, Grafton-street, Soho, May 9, 1838.

TAYLOR'S PATENT BOILER FEEDER—
SEAWARD'S PATENT STEAM-SAVER
—WHITELAW'S FEED PUMPS.

Sir,—On inspection of the Patent Boiler Feeder in No. 768, it appears to be nearly identified, the float excepted, with an apparatus patented some time since by Mr. Samuel Seaward, as a steam-saver for marine engines, having other important objects likewise in view, but which it seems has not been brought into common use, probably on account of the personal attention required by the cocks when the apparatus is in action

The plans agree so far as the close cistern placed over the boiler, and the steam and water cocks, are concerned.

Now as to the action of the feeder, I really cannot see the advantage of its employment in land engines, unless to meet some local consideration—which requires to be stated—and in such case there will be an inevitable loss of heat from the admission of steam to the *surface* of the water while the boiler is supplied by the *lower portion*, to which the heat is slowly conducted, and whence the supply is admitted to the cistern to meet the next demand of the boiler.

What can be more simple than the long established method of regulating the supply of water in land engine boilers by the float, and valve acted on thereby? Certainly, if I understand it rightly, Taylor and Davis's patent steam boiler feeder will never supersede it, and for marine engines it is out of the question.

The inclosed sketch and description of the "steam saver" alluded to, from Mr. Seaward's specification, may be thought worth your consideration from its novelty of application, if it has not already appeared in your most useful journal.

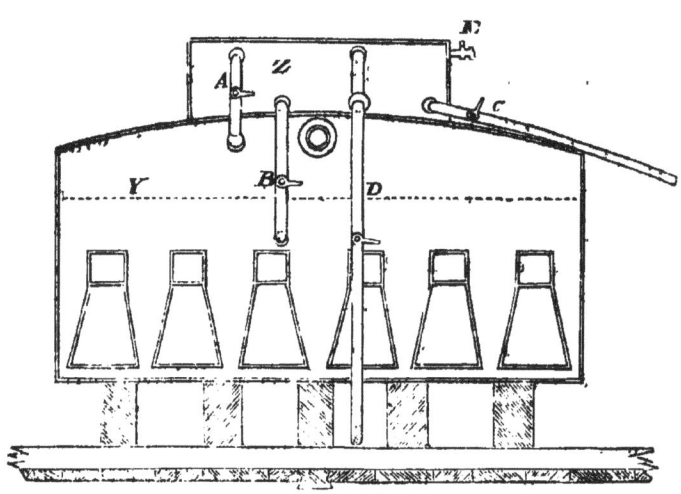

"I cause a vessel Z, of iron or other suitable material, and capable of withstanding the heat of the steam contained in the boiler Y, and of resisting the pressure of the atmosphere, and of a capacity equal to one-twentieth of the water chamber of the boiler, or thereabouts; this vessel I call a receiver, and it is to be placed on the said boiler Y, as shewn in the drawing, or any where near the boiler, of a sufficient height, that any fluid contained in the said receiver, will descend by its own gravity into the steam boiler. To this vessel I attach four cocks or valves, and as many pipes, in the following order, viz.: one pipe A, from the top of the vessel Z, to the steam chamber of the steam-boiler; one pipe B, from the bottom of the receiver Z, to the water chamber of boiler; one pipe C, from the bottom of the said receiver to the water outside the ship; and one pipe D, from the top of the said receiver, to the well or lowest part of the ship in which the boiler is placed.

"The first operation of this apparatus for the effecting the saving of fuel is as follows:—When the steam is so high as to raise the safety-valves, and escape, either in consequence of the engines standing still, or the too great quantity of fire, the cock A is to be opened, and the receiver Z filled with steam, the air rushing out by a small cock E, placed at the top. The receiver being fall, the cock A is to be shut, and also the cock E, and the cock C opened; the steam contained in the said receiver will by this operation be condensed, and a partial vacuum thereby be formed; the water will then rush from outside the ship, and fill the receiver; the cock C being then shut, and the cock B opened, the water will descend slowly by its own gravity into the water chamber of the boilers; and this can be accelerated by again opening the cock A, by which means the water will descend at a heat not much below that of boiling water. The saving of fuel will be evident, because, at all times, the boiler may be completely filled, and the water itself raised to a high temperature by the steam, which would otherwise escape at the safety valves, and be completely lost.

"The second operation is that of pumping or drawing the water from the hold of the ship. To effect this the cock A is again opened, and the receiver thereby filled with steam; upon closing the cock A, the cock D is opened, and the water will rush up from the hold of the ship, and fill the receiver; the cock D being shut, and the cock C opened, the water contained in the receiver will run overboard, by opening the small air cock E in the top. This operation can be repeated till the ship is perfectly dry: fifty or sixty tons of water per hour can be discharged with great facility in a boat of 100 horses' power, by simply employing the spare steam while the engines are at rest."

Since writing the above, I received No. 769, with a frontispiece and description of another feeding apparatus, to be worked by a separate steam-engine! with "chests," "casings," "slide valves," and other details, which are left out *to avoid complexity !* (vide sketch) which certainly displays much ingenuity, and is intended as an illustration of their application to marine engines. It would appear that Messrs. Taylor, Davis, and Whitelaw have taken a great deal of pains, the latter gentleman especially, in contriving to meet a defect in the steam-engine which exists but in imagination.

I have already remarked on the simplicity of the existing apparatus in ordinary land engines, with the feed head or equilibrium pipe; and where steam of high pressure is used, the feed-pump forces the water directly into the boiler, regulated by a stop-cock and loaded valve, through which the surplus is conveyed to waste; and in many places a cock is fitted to the suction pipe of the pump, so as to regulate the supply by admission of a portion of air, and thus dispensing with

the loaded valve, which passing into the boiler with the feed, is no doubt objectionable in condensing engines.

In many cases the height of water within the boilers is regulated by a float acting on the stop-cock before mentioned.

Now in marine engines, from the constant fluctuation of the height of water in the boilers, both from the influence of the sea, and from the necessity of accumulating water for blowing off, and diminishing the same in performing the latter operation, experience has shown that the ordinary feed pump, with its stop-cock and loaded valve, is the most simple and efficient contrivance: all schemes for regulating the feed by floats, &c., having been abandoned long since as unsafe from their liability to throw the engineer off his guard, who might place too much confidence in their doubtful performance.

It appears moreover that the precision of Mr. Whitelaw's feeder mainly depends on the compression of a certain bulk of steam, admitted at each stroke of his slide valve—compression of steam (that is, increasing its elastic force) by injection of a charge of comparatively cold water! Surely Mr. W. must have lost sight of the fact, that his feed will be cold in the case of a high pressure boiler, or nearly so, and will not be above 100° if discharged from the condenser of a low pressure engine; so that on the outset his principles are mistaken, without reference to the absurdity of employing a supplementary engine, with its additional cost and expense of maintaining.

Now Taylor and Davis's plan would effect that which Whitelaw's engine is expected to do, under all circumstances, with the advantage of greater simplicity at least, to recommend it.

I am, Sir,
Your most obedient servant,
NAUTICUS.

Woolwich, May 7, 1838.

———

MR. BADDELEY'S NAVIGABLE BALLOON.

Sir,—Will Mr. Baddeley think it "pardonable" to inquire whether the short note on the navigable balloon in your last (page 58), is all that the readers of the *Mechanics' Magazine* are to expect from him on the subject? Or, if not, at what period they may look for the appearance of those interesting particulars which Mr. B. (when he announced his discovery, eighteen months ago), led them to suppose would be published in its pages?

I cannot but express surprise at the very *nonchalant* way in which Mr. Baddeley speaks of his plan, even in the same paragraph which states his continued confidence in its perfect practicability. One would imagine that few "more pressing engagements" would be allowed to stand in the way of introducing to the world an invention which would instantly take its place as one of the most important of modern times, and infallibly immortalize the name of its discoverer into the bargain! At any rate, if only to silence the incredulous many, who may be apt, on this occasion as on others, to insinuate that what seemed perfect in theory has failed in practice, it would surely be worth Mr. Baddeley's while to make public the details of his scheme at once.

I remain, Sir,
Your obedient servant,
PHILO-BADDELEY.

London, May 2, 1838.

ARIS'S ELLIPTICAL COMPASSES.

Sir,—Having lately had occasion to draw some very small ovals, and not being able to procure any elliptical compasses small enough for that purpose, I have contrived an instrument which has answered my purpose very well, as the ovals required were not very excentric. I send you a description of it for insertion in your scientific Magazine, which I think might be acceptable to some of your readers. Your compliance will oblige,

Yours respectfully,
J. R. ARIS.

Paterson-street, Stepney, 7th May. 1838.

A B C represent an instrument similar to a pair of compasses, the legs of which are moveable on the joint C; the leg B C is somewhat longer than A C; the latter is a cylindrical piece of hard steel wire pointed at the end; *t* is a hollow tube which slides up and down the leg A C; to this tube is attached the piece D E P, having two joints to allow the pencil P to be placed in a position parallel to the leg A C; there should be a milled-headed screw at each of the two joints D and E to make them tight when adjusted to any given position.

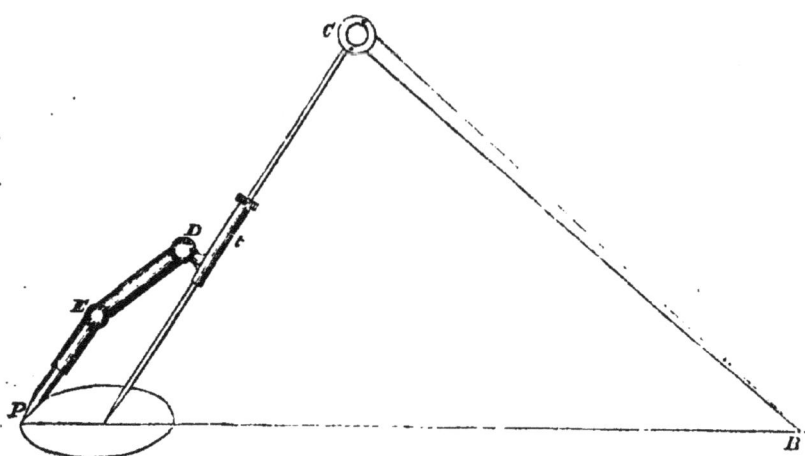

To describe an ellipsis, place the point A on the centre of the ellipsis, the point B must be placed on the continuation of the longer diameter, then open the point P till the pencil coincides with the end of the shorter diameter, turn the tube a quarter round, and if the pencil should not coincide with the end of the longer diameter, it can easily be made to do so by moving the point B either nearer to or farther from A in the line A B till it does coincide; this being done, turn the clylinder round by the milled-head; this in combination with the sliding motion will cause the pencil to describe a true ellipsis. The ellipsis described is an oblique section of a cylinder made by the plane of the paper, the point of the pencil been always in the surface of a cylinder the radius of which is equal to the distance of the pencil from the axis. The ellipsis described is as true as any one produced by the section of a cone. This plan answers very well when the ellipsis required is not very excentric, that is, when it does not require the leg A C to make an angle with the paper much less than 45 degrees, which limits its use. I send it to you, imperfect as it is, in hopes that some of your readers may improve upon it.

I. R. A.

THE LOSS OF POWER BY THE CRANKS OF STEAM-ENGINES.

Sir,—I have not read the former papers on this subject, nor do I believe it necessary, to enable me to point out an error into which Mr. Oxley appears to have fallen—his not admitting into his calculation the space moved over by the crank pin, as compared with the piston of a steam-engine, which is for a whole stroke, as much more than that moved over by the piston, as the circumference of a circle is greater than two diameters, which for half a stroke is the half of 31416 or 15708. Although Mr. Oxley may be, and is, in a rough way, correct with regard to the leverage of the crank being diminished from 100000 to 62142, yet by multiplying by 15708 we have 97612, which is within 1-25th of the whole amount. This difference arises, no doubt, from want of greater nicety in calculating the length of the leverage, or average of sines, a defect which Mr. Oxley, no doubt, with his extensive mathematical knowledge, will be able to supply.

W. H. T.

RECENT AMERICAN PATENTS.
(Selected from the *Franklin Journal* for Dec. 1837, and Jan. 1838.)

A REGISTER AND AIR BOX FOR ADMITTING THE AIR TO FIRE PLACES, *Allan Pollock, Boston, Massachusetts.*—This is a contrivance intended to regulate the admission of air from without the room, to feed the fire contained in a grate. The box described may be made of cast iron, and it is to be built into the chimney in setting the grate, in such a way that the bottom of the box shall rest upon the hearth, its front edge being even with the back of the grate, and extending up from the hearth to the grate, thus occupying the ordinary position of the chimney back under the grate; this front side of the box is entirely open. The depth of it from front to back may be about six or eight inches; the back plate is to be perforated, near its lower edge, with four holes, more or less, say of two inches in diameter, which holes may be simultaneously opened or closed by a sliding register, allowing air from without the house, or from a cellar, entry, &c., to pass through the openings in regulated quantities. A lever attached to the register extends to the front of the fire place, serving to move it at pleasure. To prevent ashes, &c., from coming into contact with the register, or from being blown into the room by the entering draught, a partition extends from the bottom along the whole length of the box, about midway of its depth, and rises to within two inches of its top.

The claim is to " the register with two or more spaces, apertures being so placed that by moving the register the corresponding apertures in the back of the box may be opened or shut simultaneously; also the air box with the middle partition intended to change the direction of the current of air, so as to prevent the dust and ashes from being blown into the room."

IMPROVEMENTS IN THE PROCESS OF BURNING LIME, *Samuel Garber, and H. Swartzengrover, Norristown, Pennsylvania.*—" We take (say the patentees,) a kiln of either of the ordinary constructions for the burning of lime, and we adapt thereto any of the various kinds of blowing apparatus used for forges, or for furnaces, and after having charged our kiln with lime-stone and fuel in the usual way, and ignited the fuel, we introduce a blast of air into the same, giving to the blast such a degree of force as may be found requisite. The blowing apparatus which we prefer, is the ordinary fan-wheel, as it affords, at once, a more diffused blast than that from bellows, or from blowing cylinders; but by the adoption of proper means, well known to machinists, as by blowing into a regulator, and by introducing the blast through several openings as large as may be found convenient, the blast may be sufficiently diffused from any blowing apparatus.

" It is well known to those persons employed in the business of burning lime, that the operation of a kiln is much influenced by the state of the weather, the fuel sometimes burning too feebly to produce a sufficiently high temperature; but by means of the artificial blast, the process is made to go on independently of the atmospheric changes, and the proper temperature is rapidly attained. By this procedure, the saving of fuel is large in amount, as the proper degree of heat can not only be produced but also maintained, until the calcination is completed; and furthermore, we are enabled to burn such fuel as would either be thrown away, or would be rejected as unsuited to the burning of lime in kilns without the blast."

The patentees claim the introduction of wind into a lime kiln, by a blowing apparatus, for regulating the combustion of the fuel, and, in consequence, the calcination of the lime.

STRAW CUTTER, *Henry Silliman, New York.*—This straw cutter is peculiar in its construction, presenting in this respect more novelty than is usual in machines for this purpose. The part in which the straw is to be placed, consists of a hollow cylinder standing horisontally upon a suitable frame. The interior of this cylinder is to be divided into several compartments, say four, by partitions running the whole length of it. The cross section of each compartment would, in this case, be a quadrant; but the inner angle of this quadrant is cut off in consequence of the passing of a screw, through a tube or case occupying the axis of the cylinder. The cutting knives are fixed upon the face of a wheel at one end of the cylinder, which is open, and as this wheel revolves, the screw with which it is connected, also revolves, and carries a nut which moves back and forth within the centre tube. From this nut, rods project out at the back end of the cylinder, which rods are received and attached to pistons, or followers which fill the compartments, and serve to force the straw forward. Each compartment is furnished with a door, which is opened to supply the straw when requisite. The cylinder may be turned round in its frame, to bring the doors successively to the top.

The claim is to the manner of acting upon the pistons, by which the straw is fed to the cutting knife, or knives, by the intervention of a revolving screw, carrying a nut backward and forward, and with it the rods and pistons, substantially in the manner and for the purpose set forth.

MANUFACTURE OF WHITE LEAD, *Peregrine Phillips, Campbell county, Kentucky.*—The lead is to be rolled into sheets, or shotted, but it is preferred to be feathered, that is, granulated, by pouring it, in a small

stream, into water. The prepared lead is then to be placed in a vat with a perforated false bottom at about its middle, where the lead is to be sustained. A pump is to be placed so as to pass through the false bottom, or in such manner as to allow the liquid contained in the vat to be pumped up. A steam pipe, of pure tin, &c., is to pass once, or more times, round within the vessel; and a tube through which air may be blown, is also to pass into the vat, below the false bottom. Distilled vinegar, or dilute acetic acid, containing about two or three per cent of dry acetic acid, is then to be poured into the vessel, to such height as not to interfere with the passage or air through the feathered lead. The pump is then to be worked, and the liquid to be so distributed by it as that the lead shall be kept constantly moistened. The acid may be kept at a temperature of 85 or 90 degrees by the passing of steam through the steam pipe. A blowing apparatus is to be kept at work at the same time, throwing in atmospheric air, to oxidize the lead as it passes up among it, which oxide will be dissolved by the acid, forming an acetate. When saturation is perfect, the fluid is to be drawn off into a cooler, and a fresh portion supplied to the lead, and this repeated until the whole is dissolved. The saturation may be judged of by the specific gravity ceasing to increase.

The saturated liquid is to be put into a vat, called a carbonating vat, constructed like that for saturating, but, instead of lead, having twigs, or pebbles, &c., upon the false bottom. Upon this brushwood, &c., the saturated liquid is to be pumped, whilst a quantity of carbonic acid, or a mixture of it with other air, is to be forced into the vat below the false bottom, which as it passes up, will convert the acetate into a carbonate, and this, being insoluble, will fall to the bottom in the form of an impalpable powder. When the precipitation ceases, the liquid is to be drawn off, and used again in the first vat, and so on continuously. The precipitated lead is to be thoroughly washed, then dried, and the process is completed.

The whole apparatus used is clearly described, and full estimates are given of the respective ingredients necessary to produce the desired reaction. The following are the claims:—

"I claim as my own invention, *first*, the oxidation of the lead, and dissolving of the said oxide by means of pumping or throwing diluted acetic acid, or vinegar over lead when in a state exposing a large proportion of surface, at the same time drawing, or forcing, a current of atmospheric air through the interstices of the said lead; and I claim this only for the purpose of preparing a liquor to be used in the manufacture of white lead.

" I claim *secondly*, the pumping or throwing the aforesaid solution of lead over any substance or materials placed in an atmosphere composed wholly, or in part, of carbonic acid gas, or for pumping or throwing the aforesaid solution into the atmosphere as before said, so that it shall fall down through the said atmosphere, for the purpose of manufacturing white lead.

" I claim *thirdly*, the purifying of the vapour of burning charcoal by causing the same to pass through a stratum of pebbles, or other substances, which substances shall be kept moist by the constant or occasional injection of water over them. And I claim this only for the purpose of assisting in the manufacture of white lead."

This latter claim refers to the removal of all dust, or other impurity, which might enter with the gas, and injure the colour of the lead.

We doubt the economy of the process of forming the acetate in the first instance, and are not aware of its superiority, in any respect, to the usual mode of manufacturing that salt from litharge. The carbonating is substantially the same with the French process described in Gray's Operative Chemist, and in other works ; the particular management described by the patentee is all that he can hold, as being the only novelty presented to us.

IMPROVEMENT IN THE TONGUES OF POWER LOOM SHUTTLES, *Comfort B. Thorp, Smithfield, Rhode Island.*—This improvement consists in a mode of more effectually securing and holding the cop, or woof, upon the tongues of the common power loom shuttle, than the mode now in use, preventing the cops, or woof, from sliding off from the tongues while weaving, especially the last part of them, which so frequently slips from the common smooth tongues, and draw into the web, injuring the cloth, and wasting yarn.

The improvement consists of ridges, or parts jutting from the surface of said tongues, protruding into the cop, against which the innermost turns or coils of the woof will lodge and prevent the cops from sliding from the tongues.

There are various ways to form or produce such projections or protuberances, such as cutting notches in of a saw tooth form, the points or cutting part of which will stand towards the heel or pivot of the tongues, and about five eighths of an inch apart on each corner, and so arranged that neither of them will come opposite to another. The square of the tongue should be equal to the hole in the cop. Also by forming a worm,

or spiral projecting lip or edge around the surface of the round tongues, or by cutting notches therein.

The most convenient way to form and use the improvement on the common smooth round tongue will be to wind a piece of wire around it, spirally, beginning at the head of the tongue near its pivot, and forming about eight turns, more or less, onward towards the point; each turn should be three eighths of an inch apart, or thereabout. The wire should be the sixteenth of an inch in diameter, and confined to the tongue by soldering. It is necessary that the tongues should be made so small in size as to protrude into the cop with ease, before the wire is put on to said tongue. The most handy way to put the cop on to the screw tongue will be, to slip the cop on to its point until it comes to the worm, and then with one hand hold the cop and whirl the shuttle round.

REVOLVING HAND RAKE FOR HAY OR GRAIN, *Stephen Coats, Shoreham, Vermont.*—This revolving hand rake consists of a rake head which is about six feet long, with teeth about two feet ten inches long, running through said head, and projecting out on opposite sides. To this head is affixed a pair of shafts, within which the person drawing the rake is to walk, a strap passing in front of him to aid him in drawing. The rake head revolves on the hind ends of the shafts, in loops formed by iron straps, there being catches to stop the head in a proper position for raking, and a lever at the command of the operator, by which the rake can be disengaged when fully loaded, and thus allowing it to revolve so as to bring the opposite row of teeth into action. The claims are to the particular mode of constructing the operating parts as described in the specification.

FURNACE FOR SMELTING IRON ORE BY THE USE OF ANTHRACITE COAL, *George E. Sellers, Pennsylvania.*—In this furnace the fuel is to be contained in a stack distant from that in which the smelting is to be effected. The latter is to contain the ore, with the necessary flux, and and such portion of coal as may be required to carbonate the iron. The tuyere is in front of the fuel stack, and on the opposite side of this is an opening, called a concentrating flue, leading into the smelting stack, and in this passage there is a depression forming a timp, or receiving chamber, into which the metal runs as it is smelted, the bottom being inclined for that purpose. The necessary devices for performing the different operations appropriate to a furnace are, of course, appended to this. It is not pretended that the placing the fuel in one stack, and the mine in the other, is by itself, new; but the novelty claimed consists in the particular construction of the furnace in its combined character. The patentee says, "I do not intend to claim the parts described in their individual characters. There is nothing new, for example, in the mode of feeding adopted by me, or in the principle of passing the blast through a stack containing fuel only, and causing the blast and heated air, thereform, to enter a second chamber containing the ore to be smelted, this having been previously performed, or essayed. But what I do claim is that particular arrangement of the respective parts of the within-described furnace by which it may be distinguished from all those which have preceded it; intending by this particular arrangement, the manner of connecting the main furnace for fuel with that containing the ore to be reduced, by a concentrating flue, within which is contained a receiving bed for the reduced metal, constructed and operating in the manner herein set forth, combining the same with the smaller flue above it, for the purpose herein fully shown. I also claim the provision for removing the slag from the fuel under the main furnace, by means of one or two openings constructed for that purpose, upon the principle, or in the manner, described."

"The smaller flue," above referred to, is one situated above the concentrating flue, and like it leading from the fuel stack into the smelting stack; its design being to conduct a portion of the heat into the smelting stack at such height above the bottom as may be useful in preparing the materials for the full action of the blast.

IMPROVEMENT IN THE SPOKE-SHAVE, *Ira L. Beckwith, Quincy, Massachusetts.*—In this spoke-shave there is a steel roller in front of the cutting edge of the knife, which roller turns freely on pivots at its ends; it extends the length of the knife, taking the place of the wood or metal which usually constitutes the front of the throat. The bearing of this roller is adjustable, so that as the knife wears away, it may be advanced towards it. A thin plate of steel, called a cap, is to be screwed on to the under side of the knife, to cause it to operate like a double iron plane, and shave against the grain. The claims are to these particular improvements.

An Electrical Lady.—A respectable physician, in the last number of *Silliman's Journal*, gives the following curious account of an *Electrical Lady*. He states, that on the evening of Jan. 28th, during a somewhat extraordinary display of the northern lights, the person in question became so highly charged with electricity, as to give out vivid electrical sparks from the end of each finger to the face of each of the company present. This did not cease with the heavenly phenomenon, but continued for several months, during which time she was constantly charged, and giving off electrical sparks to every conductor she approached. This was extremely vexatious, as she could not touch the stove nor any metallic utensils, without first giving off an electrical spark, with the consequent twinge. The state most favourable to this phenomenon, was an atmosphere of about 80 Fah., moderate exercise, and social enjoyment. It disappeared in an atmosphere approaching zero, and under the debilitating effects of fear. When seated by the stove, reading, with her feet upon the fender, she gave sparks at the rate of three or more a minute; and under the most favourable circumstances a spark that could be seen, heard, or felt, passed every second! She could charge others in the same way, when insulated, who could then give sparks to others. To make it satisfactory that her dress did not produce it, it was changed to cotton and woollen, without altering the phenomenon. The lady is about 30—of sedentary pursuits, and delicate state of health, having for two years previously suffered from acute rheumatism and neuralgic affections, with peculiar symptoms.

Lead.—Chemists have long turned their attention towards the different combinations of water and acetic acid with oxide of lead, and which are so valuable to medicine, to the arts, and to analysis but the subject is still incomplete. M. Payen, however, has been making some important progress in this branch of chemistry, and the most interesting part of his labours consists in the discovery of a new acetate of lead, and an equally new combination between water and protoxide of lead. In the course of his researches, he has been able to explain several phenomena, the causes of which have been hitherto unknown, and which are highly interesting in the matter of analysis.—*Athenæum.*

Sounds caused by Electricity.—M. Sellier has found it sufficient to place an electric diamond upon a pane of glass in order to produce sounds. When a well polished sewing needle, is suspended from a hair, is placed in a glass bowl filled with an acid sulphate of copper, the bowl crackles, even after the needle has been withdrawn and the liquid poured out. Small currents of common electricity become perceptible to the ear, by means of weathen straw, struck upon a drum of vegetable paper.—*Ib.*

Sail-worked Paddles.—Sir,—Having some time ago, observed in your valuable journal various communications on the above subject, both in favour of, and against the possibility, of propelling vessels by means of sail worked paddles, I am induced to solicit any who may feel interested in the matter, to favour me (through the medium of your publisher with their names and addresses, that I may lay before them a proposition, by which an experiment can be made, which will set at rest this contested question, I am, &c. A. B. C.

Complete Sets of the Mechanics' Magazine may now be had, twenty-seven volumes, half-cloth, price £11 7s.

☞ *British and Foreign Patents taken out with economy and despatch; Specifications, Disclaimers, and Amendments, prepared or revised; Caveats entered; and generally every Branch of Patent Business promptly transacted. A complete list of Patents from the earliest period (15 Car. II. 1675,) to the present time may be examined. Fee 2s. 6d.; Clients, gratis.*

LONDON: Printed and Published for the Proprietor, by W. A. Robertson, at the Mechanics' Magazine Office, No. 6, Peterborough-court between 135 and 136, Fleet-street.—Sold by A. & W. Galignani, Rue Vivienne, Paris.

Mechanics' Magazine,

MUSEUM, REGISTER, JOURNAL, AND GAZETTE.

| No. 772.] | SATURDAY, MAY 26, 1838. | [Price 3*d*. |

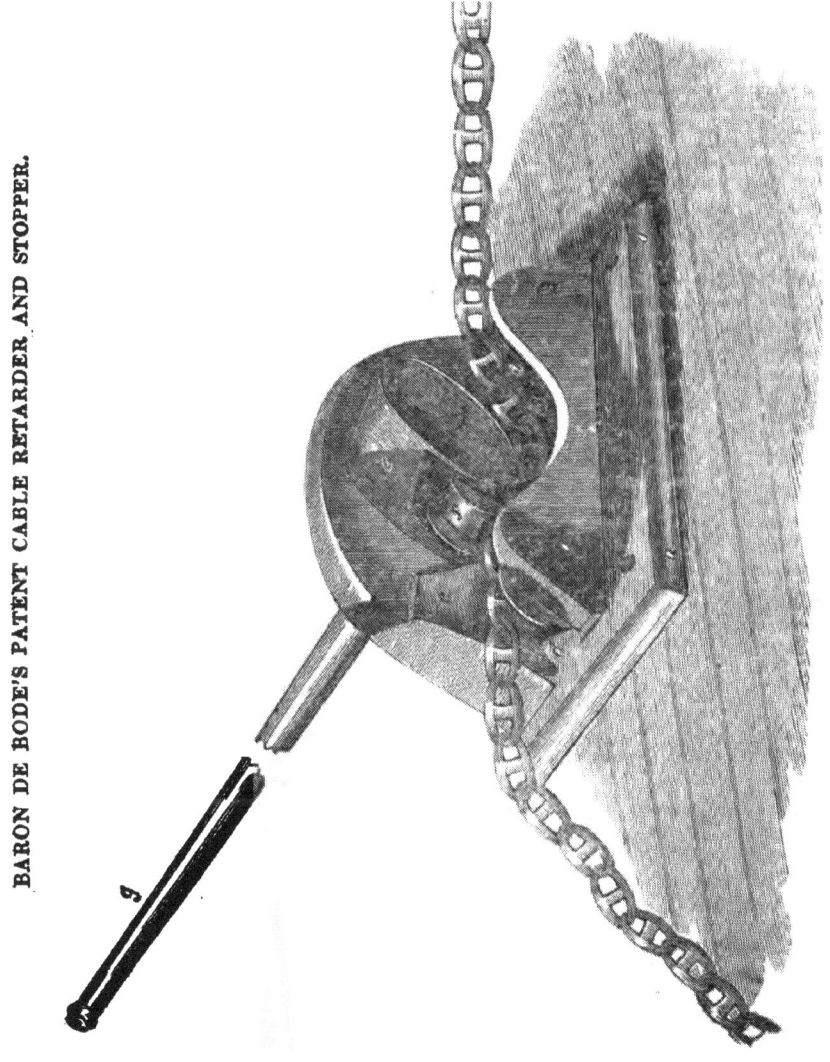

BARON DE BODE'S PATENT CABLE RETARDER AND STOPPER.

BARON DE BODE'S PATENT CABLE RETARDER AND STOPPER.

Sir,—I herewith forward you a drawing and description of this most useful nautical invention of the Baron de Bode's. I feel confident that your maritime readers will pronounce it to be the best method that has yet been devised for stopping or retarding a cable, which it has already been declared to be, by first-rate authorities upon such subjects.

The cable stopper consists of an iron bed *a a*, with upright side pieces *b c*, supporting two friction-rollers *d d;* the side piece *c*, is higher and stronger than *b*, and the short lever *e*, carrying the friction roller *f*, is connected to the handspike on lever *g* by a strong axis or pivot, through the side piece *c*. The action of the apparatus will be readily seen; the lever *g* being raised, the friction roller *f* will be above, and clear of the cable; as soon as it is desired to retard the chain, depress the lever *g*, when the cable will be clasped between the rollers *f* and *d d;* and by further depressing the lever *g*, so as to bring the roller *f* to a nearly centrical position, the chain will be stopped by being clutched between the roller *f* and a stud or elevation in the bottom of the stopper.

The following are amongst the advantages stated by the Baron to be consequent upon the use of his stopper:—

Most stoppers have not the means of retarding the speed of a running cable which is known to be so pernicious to the men, and articles on deck, and those which can partially retard, can only do it at the destructive expense of both the cable and the stopper, as the cable has to rub through fixed bodies of metal; whereas, in the Baron's it slides between rollers.

The cable being stretched whilst running, when the speed is retarded by pressing the middle roller on it, there is no risk of destructive chafing, as it never gets in contact with the small elevation on the bottom of the stopper, until the middle roller is pressed down to the degree of stopping the cable altogether.

All stoppers hitherto in use stop the cable by pressing suddenly on one link only of the chain, whilst the roller of this one, presenting a larger surface, presses on three links; and instead of stopping the cable suddenly, can but stop it gradually, however quickly the operation may be performed. This must naturally prevent many ruptures, and even the frequent partial injuries to which cables are so subject.

This stopper will answer for a hemp cable as well as any chain of whatever size or figure it may be; whilst the other stoppers in use are still more destructive to hemp cables than to chains.

As the cable never has to force its way through two fixed metal bodies, there is no reason for either stopper or cables wearing out by the operation of stopping.

Most stoppers are by their angular opposition to the strain of the cable, and by their being fixed only to one of the ship's beams, more or less exposed to be broken or torn from their holdings, or even to injure the beam they are attached to; whilst this one, presenting a large basis may easily be fixed to three or more beams, by the means of two cross beams underneath the deck; and as it works quite horizontally, it cannot be exposed to capsize, nor to be torn to pieces.

The construction being much simpler and more solid than all others, it is evident, that besides its not being so exposed to the above accidents, it must in itself be less subject to repairs.

I am, Sir, your obedient servant,

HAWSER.

March, 1838.

MIXTURE OF SULPHATE OF BARYTES WITH WHITE LEAD.

Sir,—In reply to your correspondent, who inquires whether sulphate of barytes is a fit and proper ingredient to be mixed with white lead for paint, I beg leave to say, decidedly it is not; and its effects I have found to be these: in painting which is exposed to the weather, such as greenhouse lights, &c., it eats up (if I may be allowed the expression) the oil with which it has been mixed, and remains on the surface in the form of a white powder, which may be wiped off as readily as common whitewash. In indoors painting, such as staircase walls, &c., which are intended to be left glossy, it causes the work to have a streaky appearance, very similar to what would be produced by a wet, dirty cloth being passed over its surface, which very frequently brings the innocent workman into disgrace. I am not aware that there is any test by which its presence, when ground, can be detected, but this I know by sad experience, that it is almost next to impossible to procure genuine white lead at any of the colour merchants, unless you order it to be ground on purpose, it being a well-known fact, that none of them keep a stock of the genuine article.

I remain, Sir, your obedient servant,

R. N.

Hitchin, Herts, May 17, 1838.

OBJECTIONS TO DAVENPORT'S ELECTRO-MAGNETIC ENGINE.

Sir,—In Number 763 of the *Mechanics' Magazine*, I observe a long communication from Mr. Oxley, in support of a calculation which he made in a former number, of the power of Davenport's electro-magnetic engine. I do not intend to enter on the merits of that calculation as such, but I contend that its principle is entirely erroneous. The wheel of the engine revolves by the attraction and repulsion of magnets; now, if the electro-magnet received its attractive power the instant that its wires were in the galvanic circuit, it is plain that there could be no assignable limit to the velocity of the wheel, and consequently that the power of the engine would also be unlimited. It has, however, been sufficiently demonstrated that magnetism cannot be induced instantaneously, and therefore the magnets can only attain a certain limited velocity, say 10 feet per second. It is plain, that if the circumference of the wheel revolves at a rate thus defined, no increase of power whatever will arise from the increase of the diameter of that wheel—its power will depend entirely on the size of the magnets.

This consideration makes me not quite so sanguine as Mr. Oxley of the success of the engine which is generally, I don't know how fairly, put to Mr. Davenport's credit; but *nil desparandum*, the landmark which I have pointed out, will, without doubt, by improvements in the construction of the electro-magnets, and in the generating of electricity, be obtained in such measure, that electro-magnetism will eventually supersede steam altogether.

Yours respectfully, F.

Manchester, May 15, 1838.

ON THE CONSTRUCTION OF IRON SUSPENSION BRIDGES AND CHAIN PIERS —BY MR. JAMES DREDGE.

Sir,—In hopes of your favouring me again with a place in your valuable Magazine, for the communication of my ideas on the construction of iron bridges and chain piers, I repeat the liberty of addressing you on the subject. In my former letter I told you, that if they were mathematically constructed more strength would be obtained at one-fourth the usual cost, I will now furnish you with my explanation, that your readers may have an opportunity of duly estimating the economy, utility and importance of the principle I have advanced.

The material in the arch of all bridges, is in a position of reduced power; therefore, arrangement and gravity ought to correspond; every advantage should be embraced for relieving the vertex of the arch, or ends of the levers, because requisite diminution of material toward the extremity of the lever is increase of power. This truth is clearly exemplified in the horizontal limb of the oak, the fishing-rod, and the ship's mast; these, as well as bridges, and the strength of all bodies, are obedient to the same law.

Every part of a bridge mathematically constructed, is active and powerful, and that in proportion to the strength of its materials, bulk, and versed sine. Gravity is borne by the arch commencing at the vertex or point of inflection, and progressively increasing from thence to their bases respectively, with power increasing in the same ratio; and horizontal pressure or tension is sustained by the roadway, which renders it uniformly stiff and powerful; but on the other hand, as they have hitherto been constructed, especially suspension bridges, the chains, or suspended levers, are parallel from their fulcrums throughout; half of the whole suspended weight being concentrated on the point of inflection, or centre of the bridge, and is oppressive in proportion to the deflection of the chains; the roadway is destitute of horizontal pressure or tension, therefore it is undulatory, notwithstanding two or three extra layers of thick planking, and heavy trussing are had recourse to.

In short, the section of the entire chains for a span similar to the Hammersmith Bridge, on my improved taper principle would not exceed 40 square inches at each base, and 6 square inches at the centre, which would only average 23 square inches, instead of 180,—as it now is; and for the Clifton Suspension Bridge, 70 square inches at each base, and ten at the centre, instead of 496 square inches at each base, and 458 at the centre, as proposed by Mr. Brunel, and adopted for execution.*

In corroboration of what I have stated, I have given proof by experiment before various parties, and in particular before a numerous assembly of the most influential gentlemen of Bristol and the neighbourhood, for the results of which, I must refer your readers to my last letter. Independent of all I have said, a bridge in Bath of 150 feet span is constructed on my patent principle, which demonstrates its truth better than words.

I am, Sir, your obedient servant,

JAMES DREDGE.

P.S.—My patent chain is well adapted for portable bridges for military purposes, and for spans of ten times the magnitude yet accomplished, and for sustaining a greater weight than ever was yet on any bridge.

J. D.

THE NEW LAW OF COPYRIGHT.

Mr. Serjeant Talfourd's New Copyright Bill has passed the second reading by a majority of fifty-two, and the measure may therefore be considered *safe*, so far, at least, as the House of Commons is concerned. Notwithstanding, however, the triumphant manner in which it has thus passed through the fiery ordeal, it may be doubted whether its success is attributable so much to the cogency of the arguments which its supporters brought forward in its favour, as to a certain chivalrous feeling to which the House seems to have been roused, by the eloquent speeches of the introducer of the measure, backed by the published letters of Wordsworth, Southey, and others of the *irritable genus*, in the same high-flown strain. Certain it is, at any rate, that most of the reasons advanced by the advocates of the bill are

* See Drewey's Memoir on Suspension Bridges.

anything but convincing to those not predisposed towards it,—that many of them, *tell* quite as much against as for the bill, and many more are absolutely convertible into excellent reasons for the opposite party!

Thus, Lord Mahon held forth in the most pathetic strain on the degradation of Dryden in being forced to pander to the vile taste of his age, instead of following the dictates of his own genius,—an evil which the wonder-working new bill is of course to rectify. But how? If an extended term of copyright could have effected the object, Dryden would never have suffered degradation, for in his time the term of copyright was, not for sixty-years only, but perpetual; and according to the theories now laid down, he ought to have been occupied in standard works alone, and not to have dreamt of ministering to the passing tastes of the day! If, in the time of Charles the Second copyright had only been allowed for a few years, or not at all, the case of Dryden might have been brought forward with some effect; but it is certainly rather strange that it should be adduced in support of a bill introduced as a sort of partial restoration of the extensive "common law right" under whose operation "glorious John" was the willing slave of the titled debauchees of his day. If the extent of the term of copyright he admitted to have anything to do with it, it would surely be better to shorten rather than lengthen it, since, under the present twenty-eight year system we have no author so "degraded" as poor Dryden was, in the full enjoyment of all the advantages of "perpetual" copyright.

This unhappy instance speaks volumes also, especially in conjunction with others also adduced by supporters of the bill, as to the effect it may be expected to have in stimulating the production of works of a standard order. It has been seen that Dryden, in spite of every imaginable legal "protection" for his labours, spent his energies in ephemeral productions; and Southey, we are told, has received more for his contributions to periodicals, and other temporary matter, than for all his larger works. If, therefore, as the *billites* constantly take it for granted, the great inspirer of literary genius is the hope of profit, what expectations can we indulge in under the bill? None, certainly, than that ephemeral productions will be at least as rife as ever. In the face of such facts the notion that the proposed extension of the term will encourage *solidity* in literature, must be given up at once.

The notion alluded to, that gain is, and must be the great inspirer of the highest efforts in authorship, is a favourite one with the learned serjeant and his followers, one of whom actually went so far as to assert, that the majority of our standard works had been produced by writers for their "daily bread." At this rate, we are to believe that Milton wrote "Paradise Lost" for the sake of the ten or fifteen pounds he received for the (perpetual) copyright,—that the illustrious Bacon, composed his "Essays" with a keen eye to the main chances, and that Locke produced his immortal "Treatise on the Human Understanding" from no higher motive than that which actuated the printer who set up the types! The speaker who broached the idea would, however, probably draw the facts to support it from the literary history of the last century, and rely on the names of Johnson, Goldsmith, and their contemporaries, to bear him out. But what then? These authors wrote at a time when only the *fourteen years'* copyright was in existence! The argument therefore would better apply, as in the former case, to a reduction in the length of the exclusive privilege, instead of an increase.

The speakers for the measure were very anxious to draw a distinction between the case of patents and of literary copyrights. It may be admitted that there are some points of difference between the two, but that they resemble each other in the main features is no less unquestionable. A perpetual monopoly, in either case, is not to be thought of. The public interest requires that the works of the author, as of the inventor, shall be thrown open to the enjoyment of all,—of course not without a due recompense. As to determine the measure of this recompense would be a difficult task,—as it is not practicable to set up a tribunal to judge of new performances, and, if meritorious, to reward, or, if not, to reject them,—the alternative is adopted of leaving the author, like the inventor, to bring forward his production as he pleases, and of making his recompense depend on the public opinion of his merits, by granting him a monopoly for twenty-eight years, or just double the ordinary one of an inventor. Yet authors, we are told, are not sufficiently " protected," and one of the members of the honourable house actually called upon his colleagues in the name of common justice to grant that protection to literary men which the law did not refuse to " an Arkwright"! To judge from this gentleman's speech and others of the same class, it might be supposed that at present there was no copyright law at all, and it would hardly be suspected that the privileges granted to authors were so superior, in every respect, to those charity doled out to patentees on payment of exorbitant fees.

The strangest misapprehensions seem indeed to prevail generally as to this question. One of the strangest is that the only parties interested are the authors and the booksellers—and that if the bill be thrown out, the former will suffer, that the latter may be enriched by the fruit of their labours. The third party, whose interests are not the least among those concerned,—the public,—is generally quite lost sight of. Thus it has been said, in reference to the often-quoted case of Wordsworth, that the question is, whether the heirs of the poet shall enjoy the profit of his works, or the heirs of Mr. Tegg (the bookseller who is so active in opposition to the bill.) But it is no such thing. Under the present law, at Mr. Wordsworth's death, and the consequent expiration of the copyright in his works, they would become the property, not of this or of that man's heirs, but of " all England,"—of the public at large. If Mr. Tegg or his heirs reap any profit, it will only be by the exercise of their callings,—and Mr. Wordsworth's heirs will have just the same privilege. The notion that the title of the cause now pending is only " Author v. Bookseller," has been worked upon to such an extent, that it would almost seem that the advocates of the bill see the importance of *mystifying* the public on the subject, and preventing the names of the real *defendants* from being seen. In order to do this, all the old stale stories of the poverty of authors, and the luxury of booksellers have been revived, and the bill held out as the means of reversing the picture. How it is to effect this is not indeed very perceptible, unless it were accompanied by another having for its object to compel authors to be prudent and provident. But meanwhile the very intention serves as a good stalking-horse, under which to cover the institution of a monopoly which, undisguised, would be intolerable. It is singular enough that in the midst of the denunciations of the rapacity of booksellers, and their hard treatment of authors, the case of Sir Walter Scott is continually being referred to as proving the necessity of " turning the tables" on the publishers; that case being one in which an author made immense gains by his literary exertions, only to lose them by dabbling in the lucrative business of publishing! Surely this often-adduced case of the author of Waverley, is the worst that could have been selected, in all points, to prove the necessity of the bill; especially when the immense profits of the trade which ruined him, are to be compared with the *inadequate* remuneration afforded by the existing law to " the trade" (as it seems to be considered) by which he made his fortune!

It is to be hoped that, notwithstanding the progress the bill has already made, it will receive very considerable modifications before it becomes law, or otherwise the public will probably be the greatest loser, and neither authors nor publishers the gainers. As the principle of extending the present law may now be considered as adopted, it might perhaps be as well if the adverse party turned their attention to the making of the extension as small as possible; every year added, is an evident disadvantage to the public, while it is by no means so clear that it will be an advantage to any party. The pretence that the production of more solid works than the great bulk of those now published,— the only boon held out to the public for the great deprivation they are to suffer,— is evidently untenable, for reasons before stated, as well as innumerable others. Our standard historians, for instance, required no century of monopoly; Hume, Gibbon, and Robertson wrote under the fourteen years' system, while the tribe of light and frivolous authors whose discouragement is one professed object of the

bill, have flourished since the term has been extended to " twenty-eight years at least." To lengthen the term to sixty years after the death of the author, then, will obviously be no remedy for the complaint, while the postponement of the time at which the really standard productions of recent times are to be thrown open to the public will be an undoubted and considerable evil. The very case of Wordsworth, to meet which would appear to have been Serjeant Talfourd's chief object in undertaking his bill at all, speaks trumpet-tongued to the fact that it will have no effect in improving the tone of our literature. That Wordsworth must have written for something else than the money produced by copyright, is evident from the statement made by the friends of the bill, that his poems had produced him more within the last year or two, than they ever had done during the first thirty years of their publication. He must have continued writing, therefore, from some other impulse than a pecuniary one; and is even now likely enough to make more money by his office of stamp distributor, than by his poetical works, even when the term of monopoly shall have been enlarged. Nevertheless, the case of his slow-growing popularity (a singular one, by the way) must be admitted to prove that the present term *may be* too short, in some instances, to secure due remuneration to the author, on the principle that the public are to be the judges of the extent of that remuneration. It does not follow, however, that so enormous a term as that of sixty years after the death of the author should be adopted;—an absolute term of forty years from publication would surely answer every purpose, and at the same time not deprive the public of all hope of seeing a new work added to the general stock before it became quite out of date. It may be objected that an author, under this arrangement, would often outlive the copyright of his work; but wherein consists the force of this objection? Parliament has been called upon to extend the same protection to an author as to an inventor; and what hardship is it considered that the patentee should outlive his patent?

BEATING-SPRINGS FOR FIRE-ENGINES.

Sir,—It is now nearly ten years since I first recommended the employment of *beating-springs,* to take off the violence of the concussion which occurs in working of fire-engines. A sketch of a plan for this purpose appeared at page 49, of your 11th volume, accompanied with a reference to the evils sought to be avoided, as well as an enumeration of the several advantages to be expected from the introduction of an elastic medium in this manner. In that communication, I stated, that " although I may not have chosen the best arrangement of the mechanism, still I am convinced that the principle is worth the serious consideration of all those who either use or construct these useful machines."

This principle has recently met with a practical application, having been introduced in one of the three powerful engines, on board the new floating fire-engine of the London Fire-engine Establishment, and the ingenious manner in which this has been accomplished, reflects great credit on Mr. W. J. Tilley, the engineer. A brief description of this engine, with a sketch of its general appearance, will be found in your 757th Number; the following additional particulars will still further elucidate its construction, and show the manner in which the *beating-springs* are introduced. A is one of three strong cast-iron standards, which are placed breadth-wise on the deck of the boat, and carry the main shaft of the engine. B is the middle

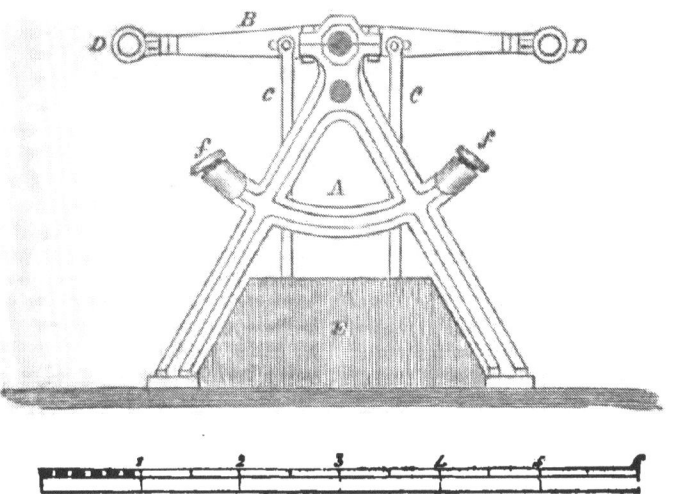

lever, pierced in three different places for the attachment of the piston-slings (*c c*), so as to give an eight, ten, or twelve inch stroke at pleasure. D D are the handles. The pumps are enclosed beneath the wooden casing E. The *beat-springs f f,* consist of strong spiral springs, working in a cylindrical cavity, cast in the standards for that purpose; a round iron buffer supported by the spiral spring receives the blow from the levers, and by its yielding, greatly reduces the shock given to the machine as well as diminishing the jar to the arms and shoulders of the persons working the engine.

The result of this experiment fully confirms my previous opinions on this subject, and proves the efficacy of an elastic medium in diminishing the violent concussions otherwise experienced in alternating machines of this description. I may also state, that I have tried square blocks of Indian-rubber for this purpose, on a smaller engine, and the effect produced was highly satisfactory; but the violence of the blows was such, that this material was completely destroyed by the working of the engine for only a few hours.

I remain, Sir, yours respectively,
WM. BADDELEY.
London, May 15, 1838.

STEAM NAVIGATION OF THE ATLANTIC —VOYAGES OF THE GREAT WESTERN AND SIRIUS.

The grand experiment of Atlantic steam navigation has at length been made—and the result is a glorious triumph for British science and enterprize. The *Sirius* left Cork on the 6th of April, and arrived at New York on the morning of the 23rd, St. George's day, performing the voyage in seventeen days. The *Great Western* left Bristol on the 7th April and arrived at New York on the 23d, only a few hours after the *Sirius*, performing the voyage in fifteen days.

" The arrival of the *Sirius* and *Great Western* steam-ships (says the *Times*) caused the greatest sensation. Thousands poured on board daily. The number of passengers coming by these and the regular packets to England was beyond all precedent. At least 100, it is said, had been entered for the 1st instant alone. The American papers, although not behind in paying a tribute to British skill and enterprize in thus extending steam navigation, are careful to note that they were the first to show the way, some years since, by the steam-ship *Savannah*, which went twice to Europe, and made a ' vast circuit of navigation.' "

On the return, the *Sirius* left New York on the 1st instant, arrived at Falmouth on the 19th, accomplishing the distance in eighteen days. The *Great Western* left New York at half-past two P.M., on the 7th instant, and arrived at Bristol at half-past ten o'clock in the morning of the 22d, thus performing her voyage across the Atlantic in *fourteen days* and *seventeen hours*.

We quote the following from the private correspondence of the *Times*:—

" King-road, Tuesday, May 22, 12 o'clock.

" It is with the greatest satisfaction that I communicate to you the safe arrival of the *Great Western* steam-ship from New York here at half-past 10 o'clock this morning. Having lain in the Roads in expectation of her, I had a full view of the majestic vessel immediately after her passing the Holmes (about twenty-one miles down the Channel), and nothing could exceed the beauty of her appearance as she gallantly breasted the waves; and although a smart breeze was blowing from the N.W., she sailed triumphantly along without rolling in the slightest degree, or appearing to be at all affected by them.

" At the time of the departure of the *Sirius* from New York on the 1st inst. she had not finished discharging her cargo, and upon departing from New York quay at half-past two o'clock p.m., on the 7th instant, upwards of 100,000 persons assembled to witness her departure with bands of music, and a variety of steam-boats attending her to Sandy Hook, which she left at five o'clock, with 68 cabin passengers at 35 guineas each (the greatest number of cabin passengers which ever came across the Atlantic in one ship), upward of 20,000 Post-office letters, and a cargo consisting of cotton for our new factory, indigo, silks, and miscellaneous articles. During her voyage home she encountered head-winds nine days out of the fourteen, and on one occasion a severe gale, yet she accomplished $7\frac{1}{4}$ knots during its greatest severity, with the wind directly in her teeth, and completed her voyage to King-road in fourteen days and $17\frac{1}{4}$ hours, her engines averaging from seventeen to nineteen strokes a-minute, and with a consumption of less than a ton of coal per hour."

The British Queen, destined for the same service, was launched on Thursday, and will shortly proceed to the North to receive her engines.

———

STEAM NAVIGATION TO INDIA AND AMERICA.

Sir,—It is rather surprising that Mr. Bayley (page 99 of your last,) should lament his ill-fortune in not having had an opportunity of seeing " the remarks of Messrs. Seaward on steam navigation to India by the Cape of Good Hope," since, had he been a constant reader of the *Mechanics' Magazine*, he could not have missed the very full and prominent article on the subject, chiefly in the words of the Messrs. Seawards' themselves, contained in your twenty-first volume, pages 298 to 303; a perusal of some more recent numbers of the same work would have also relieved Mr. B.'s mind from the apprehension he so vividly expresses, that we shall loose our dominion in the East by allowing the Duch to get the start of us in introducing steam navigation in that quarter. Its pages have already recorded that the Dutch have not the monopoly in "building vessels for that purpose," but that the English are about to reinforce the steam flotilla which they have *long ago* "introduced in the East Indies" from home, by a number of steamers built and equipped in the country itself. There is consequently no fear of British pre-eminence being sacrificed by supineness in that respect, even were it admitted, (which is not quite clear to every capacity) that the said pre-eminence depends entirely on priority in the introduction of steam navigation!

It is strange enough that Messrs. Seaward had the same fears of being outstripped in the race by Dutch activity. In their case, however, the horror was, lest the Dutch should be the first to perform a *successful* voyage by steam round the Cape. The triumphant voyages of the *Atalanta* and *Berenice* have probably relieved their minds in this respect, though the addition of those two splendid vessels to our East India steam-fleet does not seem sufficient to satisfy Mr. Bayley, that we shall not be in the background when Mynheer is prepared to "introduce" steam in the Indian seas. Even were the question of priority not already settled in our favour, there would, however, be little fear of any other nation's stealing a march upon us, now that public attention is so well awakened to the importance of the subject, both abroad and at home; as witness the various companies in England, and the enthusiastic "steam-committees" and subscriptions in India.

Mr. Bayley and the Messrs. Seaward are rather at issue as to the speed which might be kept up on the voyage to India. The latter calculated that ten miles an hour might be maintained throughout the whole distance, while the former holds this to be impossible, and, so far as present experience of long voyages goes, certainly seems to be in the right. A great deal depends, however, on the nature of the "miles" alluded to—whether common or nautical—an important distinction, the keeping of which in view often serves to clear up a good deal of mystery. Thus, in the case of the steamer alluded to by Mr. Bayley, which was said to have performed at the rate of fourteen miles an hour, and turned out to have gone only about eleven and a half, it will be perceived that the difference is not very great, if it be supposed that the speed was originally reported (by way of making the greater show) in common miles, while those who tested its correctness used the nautical as a matter of course. The distinction ought certainly to be always drawn, if fair play is intended; but our American friends, in particular, are very

fond of juggling in this respect, when the wonderful doings of their river steamers are in question. Mr. Bayley seems to be incredulous as to a speed of fourteen miles an hour having ever been attained;—but surely this is of common occurrence with the crack steamers in the Thames; and, according to the newspapers, a new vessel, *The Rainbow*, has this week made the passage from Blackwall to Gravesend, a distance of twenty-two (land) miles, in one hour and eleven minutes! This, to be sure, is not equal to a first-rate railway speed, but it is nevertheless pretty fair as times go, and, could we place implicit confidence in the "honest chroniclers" who record the fact, quite decisive against Mr. Bayley's views, especially as *The Vesper*, Gravesend boat is said to have also done the distance in only four minutes over the time stated.

Facts, those always "stubborn things," are indeed especial stumbling blocks in the way of the theorists in steam-navigation. The successful prosecution of the voyage across the Atlantic by the *Sirius* and *Great Western*, and the return of the former, must have thrown poor Dr. Lardner, one of the most confident of the tribe, on his beam-ends. Considerable curiosity has been excited to learn what the Doctor has to say to it, especially as an article on "Ocean Steamers" is announced (and had been before the arrival of the *Sirius*) to appear in the next number of *The Monthly Chronicle*, to which Dr. L. is chief scientific contributor. It is to be hoped this article will be honestly printed, without any alterations to suit it to "existing circumstances," and we dare say it will then afford some amusement, if it should fail in imparting information. It will be followed immediately, there can be no doubt, by the Doctor's plan for a "voyage to the Moon," which we now have his word for it, is perfectly practicable. Hath not the Atlantic been crossed by steam at one trip? Go to, then,—why doubt of the speedy execution of that "equal possibility," a trip to the Lunar Empire?

The enthusiasm with which the people of New York have received the intrepid navigators does them great credit, especially as it might have been anticipated that Brother Jonathan would not have been best pleased at John Bull's having so completely got the weather-gage of him, in a matter on which he is so apt to think highly of himself as steam navigation. In one point, however, the demeanour of the New Yorkers was rather novel, and more to the credit of their astuteness than their generosity. To celebrate the occasion, a dinner was of course necessary, and a dinner was accordingly had; but, instead of the inhabitants of New York giving a dinner *to*, they took a dinner *from* the captain and officers of the *Sirius*, and quaffed mighty bumpers to the success of the scheme,—at the expense of its promoters! Considering that the Americans were the parties *visited*, it seems somewhat strange that the British should have been called upon to display their " hospitality." However, all parties appear to have been quite satisfied; Jonathan not the least, at the pleasant mode he had discovered of testifying his friendly feelings, and indulging his sympathy with his hospitable guests.

There are other parties, besides Dr. Lardner, to whom recent events will be rather mortifying. Among others, Mr. Hall, who took great credit to himself for not drawing public attention to the advantage enjoyed by the *Sirius* over the *Great Western*, in the possession of his patent condensers, until after the vessels had started. Long as his forbearance was, it would have been as well could he have restrained himself a little longer, and not, by anticipating the superior steaming qualities of the *Sirius*, and taking credit beforehand for that superiority, have drawn down the world's dread laugh on the arrival of the news that the *Great Western*, *without* Hall's condenser, had performed the voyage in upwards of three days less time than the *Sirius* with them! The boastful advertisement was ill-timed, at any rate, and Mr. H. has received his proper punishment by the event. We shall now hear, probably, that it could not be expected the *Sirius*, taken as she was from a home station merely to secure the honour of first steaming across the Atlantic, could compete with a new vessel built expressly for the purpose of navigating the ocean, with all appliances and means for its accomplishment. This may be very true; but, then, why publish the advertisement,—why call attention to the comparative capabilities of

these very two vessels,—and why claim, in advance, a triumph for Hall's condensers, founded on the expected results of this identical first voyage?—The procedure altogether has been a must unfortunate one.

Most people will be inclined to regret that the race-course was not a little longer, that the *Great Western* might have given the go-by to her antagonist, and, by arriving first, secured the laurel which the *Sirius* almost literally snatched from her brows. The commander of the latter was styled by a Yankee orator " the Columbus of Steam"; but the term is hardly applicable, not only because the discoverer of America had not another Columbus only twelve hours behind him, but because he did not secure the honour by stealing a march on a competitor,—in other words, by *breaking the end of his egg* in a hurry, just as his opponent, with a little more circumspection, was showing the company how the thing might be done.

However, all parties deserve credit, though, had the *Sirius* alone made the voyage, the great superiority of steaming to sailing might still have been problematical. The *Great Western's* outward passage,—fifteen days,—is by no means bad for a beginning, and, if her return voyage should prove proportionably short, it will soon be a question, not whether the steam navigation of the Atlantic will become general, but *how long* it will take the " steam liners" to beat the old sailing packets quite out of the field.

I remain, Sir,
Very respectfully yours.

H.

May 28, 1838.

GALVANIZATION OF METALS TO PREVENT THEIR OXYDATION.

(From the Prospectus of the English, Scotch and Irish Galvanized Metal Company.)

M. Sorel, a French chemist, after many years of study and experiment, discovered an application of a scientific principle for preventing the oxydation or destruction of metals, particularly iron, as effectual as it is simple and inexpensive. His discovery is protected by a patent in France, where for some months the process has been in successful operation. Patents have also been granted for the invention in the United Kingdom.

The discovery has been submitted to the consideration of the following eminent British chemists:—W. T. Brande, F.R.S. Professor of Chemistry to the Royal Institution; J. G. Children, F.R.S.; Thomas Graham, Professor, London University; A. Garden, M.R.I.; Richard Phillips, F.R.S.; and such of the Reports of those Gentlemen as have been received are annexed.

By Professor Graham, of the London University.

The effect of zinc in protecting iron from oxydation has been known to chemists for some time. When these two metals are in contact, an electrical or galvanic relation is established between them, by which the iron ceases to be susceptible of corrosion by dilute acids, saline solutions, or atmospheric humidity. It was found in experiments lately conducted at Dublin and Liverpool, that small pieces of zinc attached to each link of a chain-cable were adequate to defend it from corrosion in sea-water. The protection was observed to be complete, even in the upper portion of the iron-chains by which buoys are moored, and which, from being alternately exposed to sea-water and air, is particularly liable to oxydation, so long as the zinc remained in contact with the iron-links. The protecting influence of the zinc could not be more certainly secured than in the articles prepared by the patent process, the iron surface being uniformly coated over by that metal. In trials, to which I have had an opportunity of subjecting them, the iron escaped untouched in acid liquids, so long as a particle of the zinc covering remained undissolved. The same protection is afforded to iron in the open atmosphere by zinc, with a loss of its own substance, which is inappreciably minute. The zinc covering has the advantage over tinning, that, although it may be worn off and the iron below it partially exposed, the iron is still secured from oxydation by the galvanic action, while the smallest quantity of zinc remains upon it. Whereas tin in common tin-plate affords no protection of this kind, and not being absolutely impermeable to air and moisture, the iron under it soon begins to rust in a damp atmosphere. The simplicity and perfect efficacy, of the means employed to defend iron from the wasting influence of air and humidity in this process of zinc-tinning, certainly entitle it to be ranked as one of the most valuable economical discoveries of the present age.

THOMAS GRAHAM,
Professor of Chemistry.

University College, London,
April 17th, 1839.

Jointly by J. G. Children, Esq. F.R.S., &c., and A. Garden, Esq. M.R.I., &c.

The so-called galvanized iron consists of iron coated by zinc. The process by which the union of these two metals is effected we are ignorant of, as we have not seen a copy of the French patent, but we conclude that it is somewhat similar to that by which iron is coated with tin, since, that zinc may be so employed instead of the latter metal was pointed out by the Messrs. Aikin in their Dictionary of Chemistry, as long ago as the years 1807. The method adopted by Sir H. Davy for protecting the copper-sheathing of ships by means of some metal whose electrical relations are positive with respect to the copper, may have suggested the idea of a similar protection to iron, and it is obvious to theory, and demonstrated by fact, that zinc is an incomparably more powerful agent in producing that effect than tin. A material difference, however, exists between the French invention and that of Sir H. Davy, since the English philosopher employed contact of the metals only in protecting copper; whereas Monsieur Sorel avails himself of the chemical (or electrical) affinity of the metals in the most extensive and perfect contact in protecting iron.

Certain specimens have been shown to us as the results of comparative experiments made by exposing articles formed of galvanized iron, and similar articles of tinned iron, and of iron in an uncovered state, for several months, to the influence of the atmosphere, in which the iron of the first remains unaffected, whilst that of the two latter is very much oxydated. Time has not been allowed us to repeat this, the most simple and most conclusive, experiment; but those which we have been able to make in the short interval that has elapsed since our opinion on the merits of this invention has been demanded, give us every reason to believe that the results alluded to have been honestly obtained, and that they afford decisive evidence of the efficacy and importance of this method of protecting iron from rusting influences.

The experiments we have made consisted in exposing plates of galvanized iron, and similar plates of tinned iron, and of iron altogether unprotected, in separate vessels, to the action of distilled water, a solution of common salt of about the same strength as sea-water, and of diluted muriatic acid. In every case the unprotected iron and the tinned iron were acted on and oxydated in a very few hours, and in three days abundance of red oxyde of iron was found to have been deposited in each vessel containing the iron plates and tinned iron plates; but in those containing the galvanized iron not the slightest trace of red oxyde could be detected, and, except an almost imperceptible discolouration of the zinc surface, which in one or two instances had become a little darker, the galvanized iron was entirely unchanged. A piece of galvanized iron plate and of simple iron plate were also placed *in contact with each other* in distilled water, and another similar pair in a solution of common salt. In three days neither plate showed any symptoms of the iron having been oxidated, so that the protecting power of the zinc of the galvanized iron plate appeared to have extended to the iron plate in external contact with it also. It had been suggested to us that perhaps accidental or partial abrasion of the zinc surface might occasion the iron to rust into holes where unprotected. We did not think this likely, nevertheless we put it to the test of experiment, and with a file cut lines into the galvanized plate entirely through the zinc, so as to leave the surface of the iron exposed, and did the same with a plate of tinned iron. In every instance the lines in the latter were filled in a day or two with red oxyde of iron, whilst those in the galvanized iron plate retained their undiminished metallic brightness. We did more,—we dissolved off every particle of zinc from two portions of the galvanized plate—in one case by very dilute muriatic acid, in the other by equally dilute sulphuric acid. As soon as the whole of the zinc was removed, the solution was poured off, and a portion of it, to which some nitric acid was previously added, was tested for iron by pure ammonia; when the only evidence that any portion of the latter metal had been dissolved was a very faint reddish tinge which prevailed through the liquid, but so slight as hardly to afford a sensible precipitate of light flocculent particles, after considerable repose. With the evidence of these facts before us, we can have no hesitation in stating our opinion that this method of protecting iron from rust will prove of infinite service in a variety of arts, and will admit of economical application in numerous ways, as the roofing of buildings, sheathing and bolting of ships, and a thousand other forms, and entirely supersede the employment of tinned iron, except in vessels used for culinary purposes, in which, we fear, it could not safely be adopted. It is possible that the objection to the use of H. Davy's protected copper for the sheathing of ships, may also prevail against the employment of the galvanized iron for the same purpose,— namely, the increased tendency to foulness from the adherence of barnacles, weeds, &c. to the ship's bottom; at the same time we think it probable that it may not be liable to that drawback; but this question must be referred to the only satisfactory solution— *experiment.*

J. G. CHILDREN.
A. GARDEN.
London, 17th April, 1838.

By William Thomas Brande, Esq., F.R.S.
Royal Mint, 26th April, 1838.

Gentlemen,—I have examined the several articles sent to me by your order under the name of *galvanized iron,* and represented as manufactured of iron in various combinations with zinc. In this way an arrangement susceptible of electric excitation is obtained, in which, consistently with the laws of electro-chemical action, a preservative power is conferred by the zinc upon the other metal; for in all cases in which two different metals are in contact, a current of electricity may be established in them in such a direction as to protect the least oxydizable of the two metals.

In common tin-plate or tinned iron the combination is such that the oxydizement or corrosion of the iron is accelerated by the tin, so that the *iron is the protecting* and the *tin* the *protected* metal; but in the case before us, in which the respective metals are iron and zinc, the reverse effect ensues,— the *iron* is here the *protected* metal and the *zinc* the *protector;* and, consequently, when these latter combinations are subjected to the action of water and other agents, the iron is preserved from corrosion so long as any zinc remains to maintain the electrical current.

I have subjected pieces of this prepared iron to the action of distilled water, or rain water, to sea-water, to the joint action of air and water, to dilute solutions of sulphuric, nitric, and muriatic acids, and to other oxydizing or corroding agents, and having compared the effects with the action of the same agents upon common tinned plate and upon wrought and cast iron, and, as was expected, the rusting and corrosion of the iron, is in all these cases entirely prevented in the zinced or patent plate; whereas, on the other hand, it goes on with more or less rapidity in regard to the unprotected and the tinned iron; and as respects the latter, the iron, whenever it is exposed, appears to be more rapidly corroded in consequence of the adjacent tin.

As far, therefore, as under these circumstances the relative durability of the patent iron as compared with either wrought or cast iron or with tinned iron is concerned, permanence is excessively in favour of the former; and there can be no doubt of the great advantage that must accrue in a vast number of the ordinary applications and uses of these substances, in the employment of the zinced or patent plate, and in its substitution for any of the usual forms of manufactured iron.

As my experiments have necessarily been limited in regard to time, I cannot speak with certainty as to effects which may possibly ensue from the protracted action of chemical agents upon the zinced iron ; but both theory and experience lead me to believe that so long as the zinc endures the protection will hold good.

Again, speaking theoretically, I should presume that the zinced plate or the other forms of the protected iron would be admirably adapted for roofing materials, gutters, water-papes, chimney-tops, packing-cases, and all analogous applications in which a light and durable material that will resist the joint action of air and water is required ; that it would also be well adapted for certain tanks and cisterns ; for the manufacture of a great variety of articles required to endure a damp atmosphere, such as locks, keys, hinges, and so forth ; for cellars, warehouses, and all exposed situation ; and for the iron-work of bridges, canal-locks, and much other machinery ; for the beams and columns of buildings ; for clamps, bars, rails, bolts, nails, screws, and nuts ; for all out-door work ; and for many implements in, and parts of chemical and other manufactories. In short these applications are as obvious as they are endless.

On the whole, I regard this as by far the most valuable practical application of the electro-chemical principle of the protection of metals which has hitherto been carried into effect.

I am, Gentlemen,
Your faithful servant,
WILLIAM THOMAS BRANDE.

In addition to which indubitable opinions, the following translated extracts from the French Society are corroborate and interesting.

" Chemists have long attempted to apply electricity by perpetual contact to the preservation of iron ; but the means employed were defective, and unsuccessful, until the recent discovery by M. Sorel. Sir H. Davy died with the conviction, that the applicacation of the principle was possible, and would some day be attained.

" Science has already given testimony in favour of M. Sorel's process. Messrs. Dulong and Dumas have frequently alluded to it in their addresses to L'Academie des Sciences.

" The following extract is from a Report made to the General Meeting of La Société d'Encouragement, at which Baron Thenard presided on the 5th July, 1837.

" ' The experiments of several members of the Committee of the Chemical Arts have proved that M. Sorel's process effectually protects iron from oxydation. It is, therefore, to be expected that the galvanic coating will soon be applied, not only to their sheet-iron but to many of the larger masses of that metal, cast or wrought, which are employed in naval architecture, military implements, and domestic building, especially to the iron-work of shipping exposed to the atmosphere or salt-water, to war projectiles, to masses of iron buried in damp situations or covered with plaister.

" ' The Galvanic Paint is well adapted to all articles of iron exposed to the action of air or water, or both alternately.' "

Extract from the Report of L'Academie des Sciences. Paris, 11th April, 1837.

" M. Dumas read a Report, by which it appeared that various trials had been made by Sir H. Davy and other chemists to preserve iron from rust, but that none had succeeded. He at the same time read a letter from Captain Born, (of the Artillery of France,) addressed to the Academy, calling their attention to the vast importance of this discovery in its applicability to military purposes only. In giving the substance of Captain Born's letter, M. Dumas said, ' the military and naval artillery had a stock of 7,734,000 projectiles of the value of 26,000,000 francs (1,100,000*l.* sterling.) According to Captain Born's estimate a pile of cannon-balls, after twenty years' exposure to the open air, are almost all unfit for service. If it be admitted, as it must be, that the value of a projectile, sold as cast iron, is not more than one-third of its cost price, then is the importance of this discovery apparent. Supposing that the Government of France should adopt M. Sorel's process, the expense of which is very trifling, it then would appear, from Captain Born's calculations, that a saving of 17,333,334 francs, for this part alone of the war department, would accrue in twenty years.' "

The Patent Process may be applied in three different ways, all equally simple :—

1. By coating iron with zinc in a fluid state.

2. By applying a paint made from zinc.

3. By covering with a powder made from zinc.

Under the first process, many articles, not already referred to, will occur to every one considering the subject. Gas-pipes, water-pipes, rails for tram-roads, iron bridges, iron boats, roof-gutters, iron railing, interior of steam-engine-boilers, iron sheathing of ships, ships' bolts, &c. On the applicability of the patent process to the three last-mentioned articles but little, if any, doubt exists in the minds of our most eminent chemists. The difference in the cost of a seventy-four gun ship between iron and copper would be as 810*l.* to 6480*l.* The saving in her Majesty's Navy and in the mercantile marine of this country would consequently be enormous.

Under the second process, zinc paint would be employed wherever the bulk of the article to be protected or the difficulty of displacing it would render an immersion of the iron into the heated metal impracticable. Bridges, therefore, already constructed, boats already built, in short all articles already fixed may be preserved from further decay by the use of the patent paint. This paint will not be dearer than white lead.

By means of the third process, the finer sorts of iron and steel will be preserved. All articles of hardware and cutlery are subject to the most serious deterioration by exposure to moisture; but by applying to them the galvanic powder, or wrapping them in paper prepared with it, they may be exposed with safety to any weather, or exported with security to any climate.

It remains only to repeat that the processes are not expensive. However numerous and important are the admitted advantages of these discoveries, they would be less striking were they to be obtained only at a high price. The process of coating with the metal in a liquid state is cheaper than tinning. Tin is worth 98*s.* per cwt., zinc 20*s.* per cwt. Supposing that galvanized sheet iron should be sold at the price of tin-plate, the profit would be at least 100 per cent.

GAS COKE AS A FUEL FOR MELTING IRON.
(From the *Franklin Journal* for Dec. 1837.)

The following communication possesses much interest for all concerned in the manufacture or use of iron casting. In the preparation of this material, time is emphatically money, and the experiments at the Franklin Works show that a saving may be effected of one-half the time usually required in melting.

Franklin Works, Philadelphia,
January 1, 1838.

Dear Sir,—At the suggestion of Mr. Cresson, Superintendent of the Gas Works, we made, some weeks since, a few trials of gas coke as a fuel for melting iron. They were not made with reference to exact results because having never heard of gas coke being used in England for this purpose, we doubted the success of the experiments.

A few days, however, convinced us that the coke presented advantages over the anthracite which would render it an important

fuel for iron founders, and we determined upon making some exact comparative experiments upon the use of the two fuels. The results of which we deem it proper to send you, with liberty to make such use of them as the Board may deem expedient.

Our cupola is thirty inches in diameter. The blast is urged into it by a fan with four wings having an aggregate area of 384 inches of fan surface moving 1800 revolutions per minute through three tuyeres, two of them 4½ inches in diameter, and one of 5 inches; the aggregate area being fifty-one inches and a half.

The trial was made in two heats with each kind of fuel, and the results given are the aggregate of both heats respectively.

1st. *Anthracite Coal*, white ash of very excellent quality,

Time of blowing 1st heat   3 hours 15′
      2nd ..   3 .. 30

   Aggregate   6hs. 45′ or 405 min.
Metal melted 15.464 lbs. or 2300 lbs. per hour.
Fuel used 2.300 lbs. or 470 lbs. to ton of iron.

2nd. *Coke.*

Time of blowing 1st heat   1 hr. 54′
      2nd ..   1   18′

   Aggregate   3 12′ or 192 min.
Metal melted 14.342 lbs. or 4450 lbs. each h.
Coke used 3.056 lbs. or 470 lbs. to ton of iron.

The weight of fuel used to each ton of iron melted, was in both cases precisely the same, but the quantity melted in the same time was nearly double. The importance of time in a shop where many hands are employed, can readily be appreciated, and would of itself be a sufficient inducement to ensure it a preference even at an advanced cost.

The capacity of a cupola for large castings is increased in proportion to the increased rapidity of melting—while with the anthracite our operations were confined to castings weighing not more than from 30 to 3500; we should have no hesitation of undertaking a piece of work weighing from three to four tons from our cupola using coke as fuel.

     MERRICK & AGNEW,
     Iron Founders, Southwark.

Dr. R. M. Huston,
President, Philadelphia Gas Works.

SPECULATIONS RESPECTING ELECTRO-MAGNETIC PROPELLING MACHINERY.
(From the *Franklin Journal* for Jan.)

In our number for November last, (*Mech. Mag.* vol. xxviii, p. 322) we published the specification of Mr. Davenport's patent for a machine intended to furnish a motive power by the agency of electro-magnetism, to which we appended some remarks upon the subject generally. We had hoped, ere now to have received more definitive information than has transpired, respecting the progress of the experiments which are being made in New York with a view to its testing the utility by applying it to drive a Napier Press, requiring a two horse power; we have hitherto learnt nothing of the result of this proposed experiment; and suppose, therefore, that the trial has not yet been made.

Since publishing the article above alluded to, it has appeared to us that should a much less power be attained by such a machine than that which is now sought for, say the power of a man only, it would still be equally valuable with the steam-engine, and would produce a great, if not a greater change, in the economy of the useful arts, as has been produced by that instrument; this, however, is under the proviso that the cost of materials consumed in performing the work of a day should be less than that giving for the labour of a man. Who is there that would not under such circumstances, need such a machine? If we hire a man by the day we must not allow him to be idle, as in that case we give our money for nothing. The current of his life flows on, and he must be fed and clothed or the stream will stop. But give us a machine which is not costly at first, and which if it works but one hour in the twenty-four, will itself be a consumer in that proportion only; a machine which we can at any moment set to turn our lathes, our grindstones, our washing machines, our churns, our circular saws, and a catalogue of other things which it would be no easy task to make out; such a machine would also perform a million of other operations by the conversion of the rotary into a reciprocating motion; and we again ask who is there among us who would not want one? our farmers, our mechanics, and our housekeepers generally, must all be supplied. We could no more submit to live without it, after it had once been introduced, than we can now submit to travel at the slow rate of ten miles an hour, an event which we have learnt to think one of the miseries of human life.

With such a machine at our command we should soon wonder how we could have lived so long without it; and if taken from us it would leave a most awful chasm in the necessaries of life, of the existence of which our fathers never dreamed, and which happily we could not be called upon to witness so long as the store house of nature would enable us to obtain zinc and sulphuric acid at a cheap rate.

The steam engine cannot be used to advantage where it has not the labour of several horses to perform, as, whether large or small, it requires the constant attention of the engineer, or of the fireman, and is kept at work at an expense which is relatively increased as its power is diminished. One giving the power of a man only would be employed, at a cost which would pay the hire of two or three men, and if used but for an hour or two in the day, the expense would be incalculably increased; of course it is not, and never will be used under such circumstances.

Let it not be said that we are prophesying about what is to happen; not so by any means; but be it remembered that we are speaking of what is a possible contingency. We have no doubt respecting the practicability of obtaining the power of a man by the agency of electro-magnetism; we believe that such a machine may be kept at work without any considerable tax upon the time of the person using it; and we further believe that the only thing which can prevent its coming into use is, the cost of the materials employed in operating it; the statements which we have heard upon this point are extremely contradictory, and upon the whole, are far from encouraging; the time, however, is not remote when this point will be determined.

————

LIST OF ENGLISH PATENTS GRANTED BETWEEN 26th OF APRIL AND THE 24th OF MAY, 1838.

John Paterson Reid, power loom manufacturer, Glasgow, and Thomas Johnson, mechanic, of the same place, for certain improvements in preparing yarn or thread by machinery, suitable for warps in preparation for weaving in looms. April 28; six months to specify.

Joseph Jepson Oddy Taylor, of Gracechurch-street, machinist, for an improved mode of propelling ships and other vessels on water. May 1; six months.

Miles Berry, of Chancery Lane, for a new and improved method, or process of alloying metals by cementation, particularly applicable to the preservation of copper, wrought or cast iron, and metals, and thereby operating a change in the appearance of their surface, and giving them more brilliancy, being a communication from a foreigner residing abroad. May 3; six months,

John Ball, of Finsbury Circus, merchant, for improvements in carriages, being a communication from a foreigner residing abroad. May 3; six months.

Edward Cobbold, M.A., of Long Melford, Somerset, for certain improvements in the manufacture of gas for affording light and heat, and in the application of certain products thereof to useful purposes. May 5; six months.

Edmund Shaw, of Fenchurch-street, stationer, for improvements in the manufacture of paper and paper boards, being a communication from a foreigner residing abroad. May 5; six months.

Thomas Joyce, of Camberwell New Road, gardener, for certain improved modes of applying prepared fuel, to the purposes of generating steam and evaporating fluids. May 5; six months.

Pierre Armand Lecomte de Fontainemoreau, of Charles-street, City Road, for an improved method of preventing the oxydation of metals, being a communication from a foreigner residing abroad. May 5; six months.

William Gossage, of Stoke Prior, Worcester, manufacturing chemist, for certain improvements in manufacturing sulphuric acid. May 8; six months.

William Henry James, late of Birmingham, and now of London, Civil Engineer, for certain improvements in machines or apparatus for weighing substances or fluids, and for certain additions thereto, applicable to other purposes. May 8; six months.

William Crofts, of Radford, machine maker, for improvements in the manufacture of lace. May 10; six months.

Miles Berry, of Chancery Lane, for a new or improved method of applying certain textile and exotic plants, as substitutes in various cases for flax, hemp, cotton, and silk, being a communication from a foreigner residing abroad. May 14; six months.

Jean Francois Isidore Caplin, of Portland-street, artist, for improvements in stays or corsets, and other parts of the dress, where lacing is employed, and in instruments for measuring for corsets or stays, and for the bodies of dresses. May 14; six months.

Alexandre Happey, of Basing-lane, London, gent., for a new and improved method of extracting tar and bitumen from all matters which contain those substances, or either of them, being a communication from a foreigner residing abroad. May 14; six months.

Thomas Mellodew, of Wallshaw Cottage, near Oldham, Lancaster, mechanic, for certain improvements in looms for weaving various kinds of cloth. May 15; six months.

James Vincent Desgrand, of Size-lane, London, merchant, for a certain new pulpy product, or material, to be used in manufacturing paper and paste board, prepared from certain substances not hitherto used for such purposes, being a communication from a foreigner residing abroad. May 15; six months.

Francis Thorpe, of Knaresborough, in the county of York, flax spinner, for certain improvements in machinery or apparatus for heckling, preparing, or dressing hemp, flax, and other such like fibrous materials. May 15; six months.

David Stead, of Great Winchester-street, London, merchant, for an invention for making or paving public streets and highways, and public and private roads, courts and bridges, with timber or wooden blocks, being a communication from a foreigner residing abroad. May 19; four months.

Samuel Seaward, of the Canal Iron Works, Poplar, for certain improvements in steam engines. May 21; six months.

Augustus Applegath, of Crayford, calico printer, for improvements in apparatus for block-printing. May 22; six months.

Henry Adcock, of Liverpool, for improvements in raising water from mines and other deep places, or from a lower level to a higher, which improvements are applicable to raising liquids generally, and to other purposes. May 22; six months.

John Ratcliff, of Birmingham, lamp manufacturer, for improvements in Lamps. May 22; six months.

Robert Martineau, of Birmingham, and Brook Smith of the same place, both in the county of Warwick, cock founders, for improvements in cocks for drawing off liquids. May 24; six months.

John Radcliffe, of Stockport, Chester, machine agent, for a new method of removing the fly droppings, waste and other matters, which, being separated from the material falls below the cylinders and beaters, in the respective processes of carding, willowing, devilling, batting, blowing, scutching, opening, or mixing of cotton-wool, silk, flax, wool, or any other fibrous material or substances. May 24; six months.

Charles Searle, of Fitzroy-street, London, for a new description of aerated water, or waters, and which method of aerating is applicable also to other fluids. May 24; six months.

————

LIST OF IRISH PATENTS GRANTED IN APRIL, 1838.

John Clarke the younger, of Mile-end, Glasgow, cotton-spinner, for improved machinery for turning, some part or parts of which may be made applicable to other useful purposes.

Sir James Caleb Anderson, bart., of Buttevant Castle, Cork, for improvements in locomotive and stationary engines, and in the mode of applying the same to tillage of land.

Luke Barton, of Arnold, Nottingham, for certain improvements in machinery for frame-work knitting.

William Fothergill Cooke, of Breeds-place, Hastings, Sussex, and Charles Wheatstone, of Conduit-street, Hanover-square, for improvement in giving signals and sounding alarms at distant places by means of electric currents, transmitted through metallic circuits.

Richard Tappin Claridge, of Regent-street, Middlesex, gen., for a mastic cement or composition applicable to paving and road-making, covering buildings, and the various purposes in which cement, mastic, lead, zinc, or composition is employed.

————

NOTES AND NOTICES.

Useful Discoveries.—The Brussels journals mention that Dr. Bernhardt has discovered processes, by means of which he is enabled to form out of the refuse of fish, a pure and limpid oil without any odour, soap of superior quality, fish glue, Prussian blue, and bone black, in quantities sufficient to produce a profit of 400 per cent.; and has founded a factory on an extensive scale for carrying his processes into effect.—*Mining Journal.*

Complete Sets of the Mechanics' Magazine may now be had, twenty-seven volumes, half-cloth, price £11 7s.

☞ *British and Foreign Patents taken out with economy and despatch; Specifications, Disclaimers, and Amendments, prepared or revised; Caveats entered; and generally every Branch of Patent Business promptly transacted. A complete list of Patents from the earliest period (15 Car. II. 1675,) to the present time may be examined. Fee 2s. 6d.; Clients, gratis.*

LONDON: Printed and Published for the Proprietor, by W. A. Robertson, at the Mechanics' Magazine Office, No. 6, Peterborough-court between 135 and 136, Fleet-street.—Sold by A. & W. Galignani Rue Vivienne, Paris.

𝕸echanics' 𝕸agazine,

MUSEUM, REGISTER, JOURNAL, AND GAZETTE.

No. 773.] SATURDAY, JUNE 2, 1838. [Price 3*d*.

BLOWING UP OF THE "WILLIAM" OFF GRAVESEND.

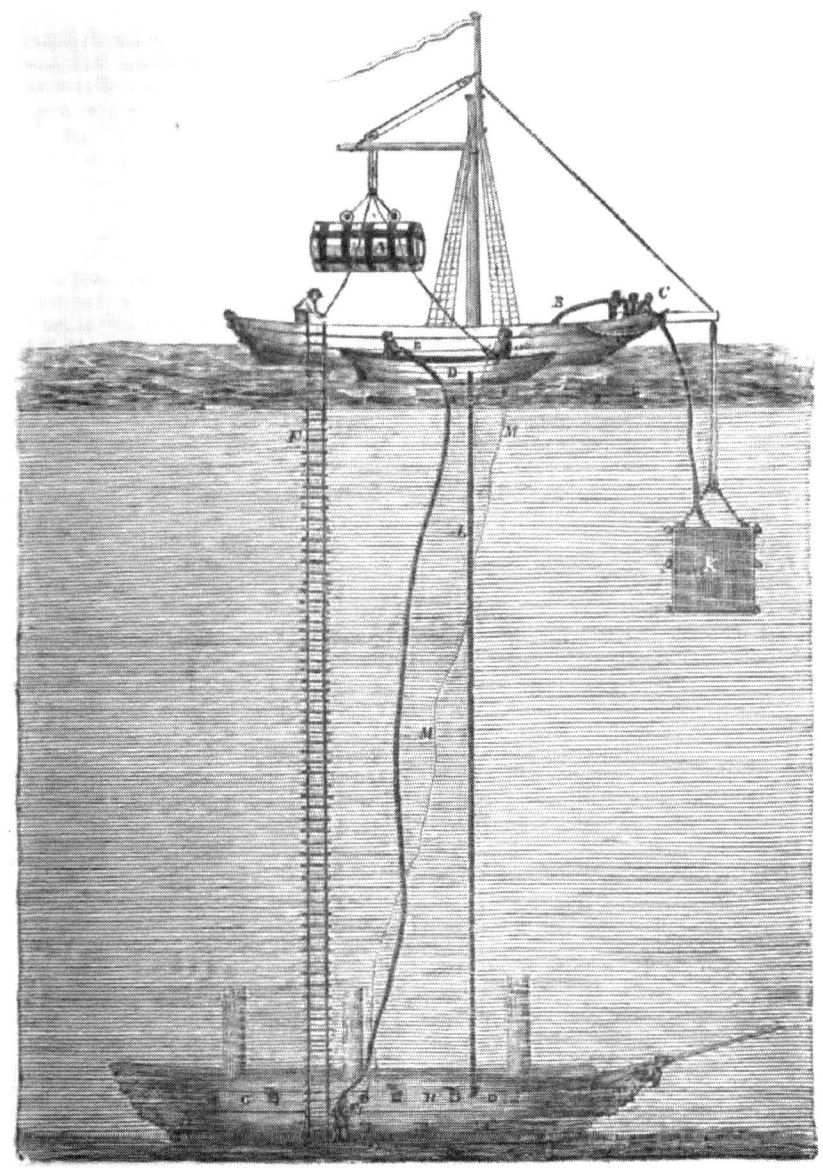

ACCOUNT OF THE BLOWING UP OF THE WRECK OF THE BRIG "WILLIAM" OFF GRAVESEND, AND OF THE APPARATUS EMPLOYED, BY COL. PASLEY.

The navigation of the Thames, it has been generally asserted, has, for a considerable time, been impeded by the wreck of a collier brig of 400 tons burthen, the *William* of Sunderland, which was run down by a steamer at Gravesend, near Tilbury Fort, in the winter of 1836. That this wreck, however, was ever found to be an actual impediment is very questionable, as at the lowest neap tide, she was covered with 23 feet of water, and lay in a spot where the sweep of the current would effectually prevent the formation of any sand bank. Various plans have been tried to raise the vessel, but owing to the weight of the cargo with which it was loaded —300 tons of coals—as well as other circumstances, all failed. Amongst other methods which were tried, was that invented and patented by Mr. Kemp, and described in our 763rd Number, and which it was expected would succeed, but the cylinders and apparatus were broken away by a vessel coming in collision with them. An attempt was also made to weigh the wreck by means of mooring chains and lighters furnished by the Admiralty, but unsuccessfully, owing entirely to the scanty material afforded by the Government. Instead of two lighters, and a few hands, there ought to have been one lighter on each bow, and one lighter on each quarter, each furnished with not fewer than thirty hands. Had these necessary means been supplied, that highly talented officer Mr. Purdo, of the Dock Yard, Chatham, would long ere this, have recovered the vessel from her bed. Under these circumstances, it was at last deemed advisable to destroy the wreck by blowing it up with gunpowder. The superintendence of this difficult and novel operation was intrusted to Colonel Pasley. The means and apparatus employed by this gentleman we shall now proceed to lay before our readers.

The wreck was proposed to be blown up by the explosion of two large leaden cylinders of gunpowder, protected by outer casings of wood, and each charged with 2500 lbs. of gunpowder, to be placed against the sides of the brig. These cylinders were constructed by the Royal Sappers and Miners at Chatham. After being filled with the powder, the two holes by which it was poured in were covered with pieces of tin, which were soldered to a flange from a leaden case inside, with red-hot iron, in a perfectly safe, and therefore, we need scarcely add, ingenious, manner.

The engraving on our front page, will give a better idea of the operation than can be conveyed by words alone. A is the exploding cylinder, ready to be lowered to the wreck, to which it is to be rove by tackle, passed through ring bolts fixed in the side of the brig by the diver; B, the air tube to supply the diving-bell K, containing men to assist the diver; C sappers, lowering the diving bell; D a small lighter to attend the diver; E the tube to supply the diver with air; F a ladder formed of rope, with wooden staves, by which the diver ascends and descends; G H the wreck of the brig; I the diver, a sapper, shown attaching the ring bolts to the hull of the brig, to secure the exploding cylinders in their proper places. This diver is equipped with Dean's diving helmet, and an India rubber dress; M the life-line, fastened round the body of the diver to haul him up in case of accident to the apparatus. The principal object in the operation is the cylinder, of which the following is a detailed description: Fig. 2 is an elevation of the cylinder. The wooden casing was made of elm, 3 inches in thickness, 10 feet in length, and 4 feet in diameter; it was bound with iron hoops 3 inches wide and ⅜ths of an inch thick, and strengthened and protected by longitudinal bars, and framed ends, as shown in fig. 2 and 4. Figure 3 is a section of the cylinder, showing the fuse. Fig. 4 an end view of cylinder. Fig. 5 the cylinder shown placed against the side of the wreck, completely prepared and ready to explode. The central hoops of the cylinder were cut nearly through on the side next the hull (see fig. 2), in order that by making this the side of least resistance, the vessel might be subject to the greater force from the powder. The cylinder was to be exploded by means of a fine powder hose in a flexible leaden pipe attached to the cylinder, the upper end of which

Fig. 4.   Fig. 2

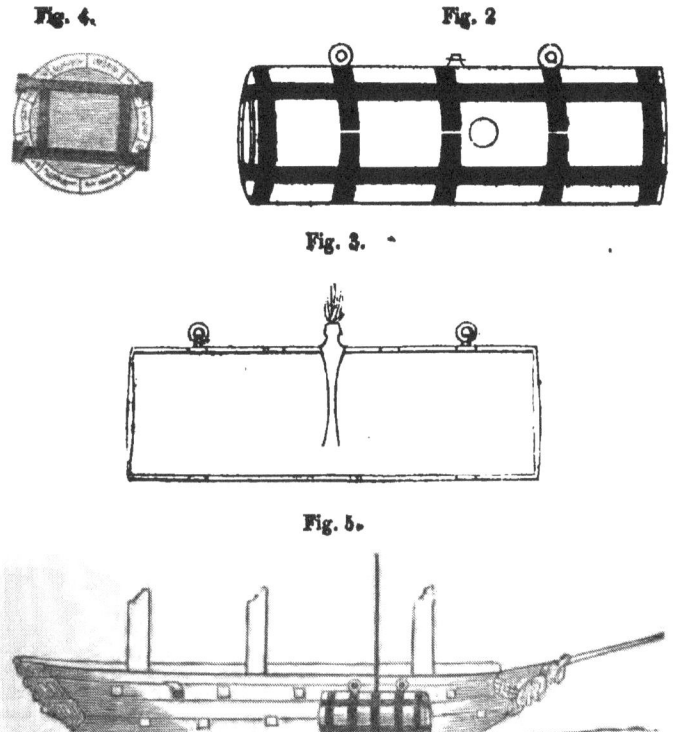

Fig. 3.

Fig. 5.

was to be moored to a red buoy. As in so very rapid a tideway it was probable that the leaden pipe might be broken by accident, and water get in, to preserve the mass of the powder from being rendered useless, the train only immediately communicated with a small tin canister in the centre of the great charge, which, on ignition would explode the whole. The cylinders were to be lowered and attached to the hull, and all preparations made at low water; and at high water the fuse was to be lighted by a man in a cutter, which was immediately to row from the spot. The explosion of the gunpowder, it was expected by Col. Pasley, would not only effect the destruction of the vessel, but form a crater of about 30 feet in diameter at top, and 10 feet deep.

On Saturday, the 19th ult., a steamer, by direction of the Lord Mayor, towed the lighter containing the cylinders, diving bell, and other apparatus from Chatham to Gravesend, with Capt. Yule of the Royal engineers, and a party of

Sappers and Miners to be employed in the operation, as also Mr. Purdo, who superintended the mooring of the lighter and other naval operations.

Preparations were commenced on Monday the 21st ult., when a Sapper descended with the diving apparatus to make preparations. Having been several hours down, and there being no indications of his return, the diving-bell was lowered, when the poor fellow was found dead—the life-line having, it is supposed with the sweep of the tide, become entangled with a broken plank projecting from the side of the hull; in the angle formed by this plank and the vessel, the unfortunate diver was found jammed, with the life-line tight round his body. A serjeant of Sappers, who went down in the bell, states that the water was so thick and muddy that he was in perfect darkness, and that he only found the body of his comrade by groping for it. It is singular that a diver, under such circumstances, should have descended without being provided with either a knife or hatchet;

K

had the unfortunate Sapper possessed what at first sight appears to be a necessary implement, it is more than probable that he would have been enabled to free himself from the entanglement which caused his destruction.

A second trial was made on Tuesday, when a few minutes before the period fixed for the explosion, one of the screws of the leaden pipe holding the fuse being detached, the water was admitted—only the fuse and a small canister of powder, however, were spoilt—that in the cylinder, from the precautions taken, was preserved quite dry.

On Tuesday night an Indiaman ran foul of the lighter, and carried away all the working gear : and it was not until the following Monday, the 28th ult., that the explosion was effected. Precisely at 28 minutes to four o'clock, the signal was given to fire the train leading to the gunpowder cylinder from Tilbury Fort, by the hoisting of red flags. All craft that were near the wreck proceeded to a great distance, and to a place of safety, with the exception of a cutter containing a party of miners, with their oars in their hands. One stood at the stern of the boat, with a lighted taper, and when the gun was fired he set fire to the fuse, which burnt for five minutes brilliantly, at the expiration of which period the explosion took place. In the interim the miners had rowed away, and attained a considerable distance from the wreck, and out of danger. The shock of the explosion was so great, that it not only was distinctly felt all over the town of Gravesend and the adjacent places, Milton, Grays, and Northfleet, but heard as far distant as Chatham and Gillingham. The houses on the high ground behind Gravesend, suffered more than those on a lower situation. The appearance from the shore, where no less than 7000 persons had assembled, was exceedingly grand, although difficult to describe. Instantly the powder in the cylinders ignited, a head of water, in the shape of a dome, and above 800 feet in circumference, was forced to the height of 70 feet. A dense black vapour, and remains of the wreck, masts, timbers, planks, &c., were completely blown out of the water to some distance. Not the least accident occurred. We subjoin the official report of Col. Pasley to the Water Bailiff of London :—

"Royal Engineer Establishment,
"Chatham, May 28, 1838.

"Sir,—I have great pleasure in stating, for the information of the Lord Mayor of London, that we succeeded in fixing one of our large powder cylinders, containing 2,500 lb., against the western side of the brig William, this afternoon, a little after high water, when the ebb-tide had just strength enough to force the cylinder against the side of the vessel a little above the bed of the river.

"The effect exceeded my expectation. A large column of water was thrown up, evidently mixed with coals, which had been the cargo of the vessel, and, on coming to the spot, we found that all or most of the fir timber floated at the surface, and as we found the step of a mast, and parts of the beams and deck, the naval officers who were present agree in opinion that the brig must have been blown entirely to pieces ; and if their opinion should be correct, which we shall be able to ascertain to-morrow morning by sounding, and by sending down the diving-bell at low water to examine the wreck, it will be unnecessary to fire the second cylinder which I had prepared with the intention of using it against the eastern side of the brig. It appears practicable that the oak timbers of the vessel being water-logged, and having their fastenings of bolts run through them, will remain at the bottom, but as there seems reason to believe that they must be all shattered and broken to pieces, it will be easy to get hold of them by creeping, and pull them up, so as to clear the bed of the river of them.

"If to-day's operation should have succeeded in effecting the complete demolition of the brig William, I have great pleasure in acknowledging how much I am indebted to the zealous, skilful, and indefatigable exertions of Mr. Purdo, Master-Attendant of Chatham Dock-yard, who conducted the naval part of the operation quite to my satisfaction ; and I could not but remark the zeal and activity of the Dock-yard riggers, and of the seamen of the Royal Navy employed under his orders. Captain Yule and Lieutenant Hornby, and a strong detachment of Captain Yule's company of Royal Sappers and Miners, not only executed the mining part of the operation, but assisted in the naval part, under the able superintendence of Mr. Purdo. The mechanical construction of the powder-cylinders, and of the lead pipes, screws, &c., and of their fitments, upon the perfection of which the success of the operation depended as much as on anything else, was executed by the master artificers of Her Majesty's dock-yard, under the able superintendence of Mr. Howe, clerk of works of the Royal Engineer Establishment, whose zeal and ability, especially in the mechanical department, are well known to the corps.

"I have the honour to be, Sir,

"Your most obedient humble servant,

"C. W. PASLEY,

"Colonel Royal Engineers."

The intention expressed by Colonel Pasley in his letter, of examining the bed of the river and state of the wreck with the diving-bell, was not thought necessary to be carried into effect. By the use of the lead-line it was found that the depth amongst the ruins ranged from five to six fathoms, with great irregularity of surface. The tide will do all that is now required for the removal of the fragments.

This is the first attempt to destroy vessels under water, and in that point of view is important. Col. Pasley proposed to the Lord Mayor to blow up the *Apollo* steamer, sunk about three miles above Gravesend, but his Lordship thought this would only remove the nuisance from one part of the river to another, as the immense masses of iron-work of which the engine was constructed, would remain, and perhaps prove more destructive than the complete hull. There are several other sunken wrecks in the river, some of which will no doubt be got rid of in this novel manner.

MR. WHITELAW'S STEAM-BOILER FEED-PUMP.

Sir,—Your correspondent "Nauticus" certainly thought very little on the subject before he wrote the remarks on my feeding apparatus, contained in No. 771 of your Magazine. He first tries to make it appear that the plan is a complex one, by saying that it is "to be worked by a separate steam-engine! with 'chests,' 'casings,' 'slide-valves,' and other details which are left out to *avoid complexity!* (vide sketch)." In answer to the first part of this assertion, I have only to state, that it is clearly shewn in the description, that my feeding apparatus can be wrought without a separate steam-engine, if it is connected to the large engine; and in answer to the second part, I may say that I neither left out a "chest," "casing," nor "valve," to *avoid complexity;* but that these parts were not put into the sketch, partly, because it was impossible to shew them all in one view, and partly, because it was not de-

sirable that they should be seen, as they were of the same construction as other parts in the figure. It is also clearly shewn in my description, that it is only when the feed-pump is made double-acting, that more "chests," "casings," and "valves," than are shewn in the figure, are needed to feed a boiler. Now every one acquainted with the subject must perceive, that this pump will answer perfectly if made single-acting, whether it is wrought by means of the large steam-engine, or a separate one. The framing, &c. of the little steam-engine are left out of the sketch, "to avoid complexity," as I said before, because their constructions are generally understood, and also because by leaving them out, the arrangement of the parts for working one modification of my plan are more distinctly shewn.

"Nauticus" is surely wrong in supposing that the old methods of feeding boilers answer well enough in all cases, and that a proper feeding apparatus for many kinds of steam-engines is not needed. I believe if he would consult Tredgold's work on the steam-engine, the reports of the Society of Arts for Scotland, and the report of the committee of the Franklin Institute on their experiments on steam, he would alter his mind on this subject.

"Nauticus" considers it a very absurd affair to employ a small steam-engine to work the feed-pump of a large engine. Now I consider that this is a very good arrangement, especially in cases where the large engine is frequently kept standing with the steam up in its boiler. Although the idea of working the feed-pump of a large engine by means of a small one, is rather new in Glasgow and its neighbourhood, yet there are there a number of boilers supplied with water in this way, and the plan is found to answer well.

"Nauticus" is of opinion, that the water pumped into the chest k (see my sketch in No. 769 of the Magazine) will condense the steam in the top part of it. I do not see how this can take place; for, from the construction of the chest, and the cold water being heavier than the hot, it will always keep at the bottom; and from the small tendency which water has to conduct heat downwards, the water in contact with the steam will always be hot. But even allowing him to be right in this particular, he should not have brought it forward as an argument against my plan, for it applies only to one modification of it: the modification given in the P.S. to my letter has not this defect (granting it to be one).

If the modification of my plan of feeding boilers, given in the P.S. to my former letter, be adopted, it will be an improvement on it to send the feed water in at the top, and not at the bottom end of the chest k; for then the steam in the chest will heat the water pumped into it. As Nauticus admits that my plan is "ingenious," it certainly would have been more to his credit if he had tried to improve it in the way here shewn, or in any other way, than to condemn the whole on account of one or two supposed faults in some of its forms. In the modification of my plan described in this paragraph, no cold water will pass into the chest k after it is filled, and displace the hot water in it, if the loaded valve and the pipe into which it is placed have a position to counteract the circulation, which is sometimes caused by hot and cold particles of water being in different parts of the same set of pipes or vessels.

"Nauticus" is certainly not in earnest when he says that he considers Taylor's plan preferable to mine; for surely, valves wrought by an eccentric will have a more certain action, than stop-cocks wrought by means of a float can have.*

I must object to the appending notes of exclamation (!) to remarks upon contributions by correspondents—a sneer is implied by them, which is not deserved by anyone who wishes to benefit your readers by publishing a useful or novel idea.

I am, Sir, yours respectfully,
JAMES WHITELAW.

———

IMPROVEMENTS IN GAS-STOVES, ETC.

Sir,—Since the "new heating apparatus" has been at such a woeful discount, gas-stoves have again been "looking up," and appear likely to recover from the *damper* put upon them by the exaggerated announcements of the Jerusalem conjurors. I think there is little doubt that before cold weather (properly so called) revisits this hemisphere, ingenuity will have devised such improvements in the management of gaseous fuel, as to render it a desirable, and in many situations an indispensable mode of house-warming.

Having worked one of Rickett's patent gas-stoves through the late severe winter, I can bear testimony to the efficiency of this apparatus; at the same time I must admit, that there is plenty of room for *actual improvement*. There is, however, so much ignorance prevailing, on the subject of heating generally, and the properties of carburetted hydrogen gas, as a source of light and heat, are so imperfectly understood by a majority of the public, that the march of real improvement in these departments, is any thing but rapid.

A plan for an *improved* gas-stove appeared at page 82, of your present volume, which is in reality a poor attempt at improvement. It is a very common error with many persons, to imagine, that atmospheric air which has been deteriorated by contact with hot metallic surfaces, may be restored to its pristine purity, by admixture with the vapour of water; it is therefore recommended to place a vessel of water upon, or within, the heating apparatus for this purpose. Whatever benefits may arise from the admixture of vapour with the arid atmosphere of an ordinary *hot-air stove*, its application to gas-stoves is highly absurd. On reference to the very interesting exposition of the phenomena of gas-stoves published at page 391 of your 26th volume, it will be found stated that, "a stove which burns 15 cubic feet of carburetted hydrogen gas per hour, forms 39 cubic inches of water (nearly a pint and a quarter) and 15 cubic feet of carbonic acid gas. There is no difficulty, then, in accounting for the fact, "that the windows where such a stove is used are covered with moisture;" for if the stove be used for fourteen hours a day, it will in that time form just two gallons of water, which must all be deposited on the windows and walls of the room, or on any other cold surfaces. There are no means of preventing this formation of water, as it has no connexion whatever with the nature of the materials of the stove; for, whenever hydrogen gas is burned with oxygen, water is necessarily formed."

* The following errors of the press appear in my last communication:—In page 67, line 3, from the top, for "pipe g," read "pipe q;" the same error is repeated in page 68, line 15 from the top. In page 7, line 19, from the bottom, "r" should read "u"; and in the same page, line 15, from the bottom, bottom" should read "top."

The demonstration of this fact is a continual source of annoyance to shop-keepers and others, whose bright steel and iron goods soon shew very plainly what is going on; besides, the windows being so dimmed by the moist deposit, as to render the goods exhibited therein, "invisible or dimly seen." A mechanic of great celebrity lately employed a gas-stove for warming one of his workshops, but was soon compelled to abandon it; his valuable and delicate machinery becoming covered with rust. The evil was attributed to the escape of uncon-sumed gas, but this was a mistake; the mischief arose from the water resulting from the combustion of the two gases. A slight glance at these facts will be suffi-cient to shew the absurdity of any scheme by which *increase of humidity* is sought to be obtained. Our friend Col. Macerone seems to have blundered in this matter; at page 369, volume 26, he alludes to the aqueous moisture generated by gas-stoves, and endeavours to explain the phenomenon, by his electrical theory of the universe. "I suppose," says Col. M., "such gas to consist of an electric or galvanic globule, inclosed in a vesicle of water. This water is set free upon the combustion of the gas, and may account for the deposit referred to." And yet, in the face of this statement, at page 298 of your last volume, we find him advising the application of a cup of water to a gas-stove to give the necessary humidity to the respiring medium!

Of all the gas-stoves I have yet seen, Rickett's is by far the best; indeed I have seen some so truly barbarous, that I should be ashamed to mention the maker's name. There is one in my own neighbourhood, made of sheet-iron, very badly put together, and constructed in direct opposition to the principles upon which the due performance of this stove entirely depends; the quantity of gas expended in producing a very small de-gree of heat is enormous. A supply of gas cannot be obtained in the day-time, or the expence of this stove would be ruinous. Should gas become generally employed for the purposes of heating, the supply must be continued throughout the twenty-four hours, which will per-haps lead to a universal system of sup-plying by meter—a system which I am well convinced would be highly advan-tageous to both buyer and seller. If the several gas companies knew their own

interest, they would not supply their commodity, except in known quantities, at a definite price; and were consumers equally enlightened, they would receive it on no other terms. Such persons as chose to be prodigal in their lights, &c. would pay accordingly; while those who chose to economise their consumption, would receive the full benefit of their frugality and care. Under such arrange-ment, less gas would be wasted; defec-tive fittings would at once be restored; and the number of serious accidents from the escape of gas, would be greatly re-duced.

Several of your correspondents have re-commended the use of sheet-iron in the formation of gas-stoves, in preference to casting: in choosing between the two materials, there is much to be said both pro and con.; different advantages and defects being peculiar to both. The cast-iron stoves being a larger mass of metal, cause the temperature to be more evenly preserved; and without any por-tion of the metal being made so hot as to decompose the air of the apartment. Mr. Ricketts is now introducing *diluted gas-stoves*, for domestic and manufacturing purposes, which offer many advantages over the original method. When carbu-retted hydrogen gas is mixed or diluted with atmospheric air, the combustion is more perfect, and the heat more intense, than when pure gas is burned. For the first practical application of this fact, we are indebted to Sir John Robison, the talented and much-respected secretary of the Royal Society of Edinburgh, who employed diluted gas-stoves, and point-ed out their great superiority several years back. The flame of diluted coal-gas is the very best heat that can be em-ployed for hardening of small steel arti-cles, as it does not black or scale the surface. From the great attention that has been paid to the subject of coal-gas in Scotland, the Scotch are far before us in a correct knowledge of its use and properties; as also in its useful applica-tion to many of the ordinary concerns of life.

Of all the methods for diffusing arti-ficial warmth within our dwellings, the radiation of heat from vessels filled with water, is by far the best. In this case the apparatus can never become so hot as to injure the wholesome character of the atmosphere; while, at the same time, the free circulation of the fluid particles ensures a constant transmission of heat, which is exceedingly effective for the purpose required. The plan which most effectually realises all the advantages of this principle, is that of Mr. Price, set forth at page 434 of your last volume.

There are many places so circumstanced, however, as to render Mr. Price's apparatus inadmissible; there being, perhaps, no convenience for the introduction of the furnace-flue. Want of space may also compel the heating to be effected within the apartment itself. It therefore only remains to modify the two plans, so as to offer a large quantity of radiating surfaces, through which the air should rapidly circulate, maintaining an uniform temperature in the transmitting fluid by means of diluted gas. A skilful and judicious combination of these valuable principles, will produce an apparatus, which for safety, efficacy, and economy, would far surpass anything hitherto achieved.

At an early opportunity, I shall return to this subject; in the meantime I shall be happy to receive the suggestions of any of your readers, as to the best method of carrying out the plan I have here proposed.

I remain, Sir, yours respectfully,
WM. BADDELEY.

London, May 23, 1838.

COLES'S PATENT RAILWAY CARRIAGES.

The object of Mr. Coles's invention is the reduction of the friction of the axles of railway carriages. This Mr. C. states that he effects by making the axletrees of the carriage-wheels bear upon the rim of large friction-wheels, and the axletrees of these large friction-wheels again to bear upon the rims of smaller friction-wheels, the axletrees of which turn in bearings attached to the carriage. The carriage-wheels revolve 60 times while the large friction-wheels revolve once; and the smaller friction-wheels revolve only once to, say 20 revolutions of the large friction-wheels. Thus the friction is transferred from where the motion is rapid, to where it is slow, which slow degree of attrition has not that destructive effect which rapid friction has been found to possess. In the annexed engraving the invention is shewn as applied to a four-wheeled railway carriage, and two two-wheeled. The latter Mr. Coles has

a peculiar way of coupling, in order to

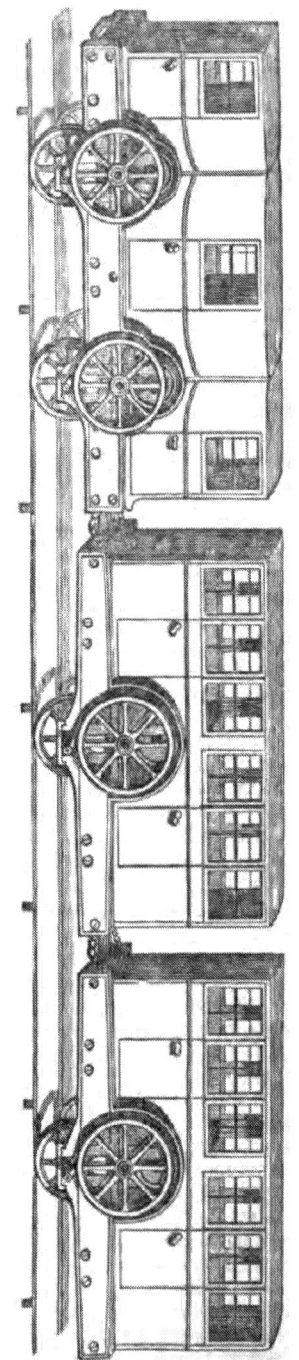

allow a train to accommodate itself to the

curves of the railway, and at the same time to keep the bodies in a horizontal position, notwithstanding any inequality in the loading.

The Patentee asserts that carriages mounted in his manner, can be propelled with not much more than half the power required to propel carriages with wheels attached in the common way.

IMPROVEMENT IN MASSEY AND WINDHAM'S SOUNDING MACHINE.

Sir,—The accompanying drawing is of an improvement upon the sounding machine described in a former number (753),

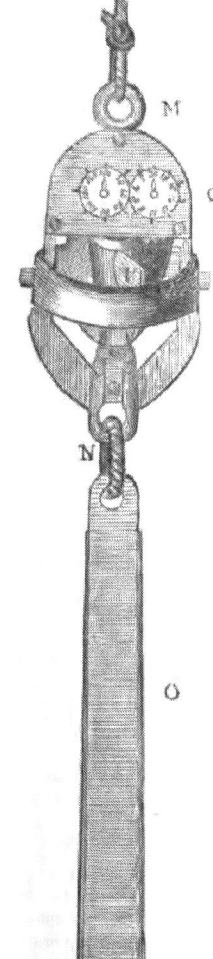

invented by Messrs. Massey and Wind-

ham. The improvement consists in placing the rotator V within a strong iron frame, which will effectually prevent any injury happening to it when the lead O strikes the ground, which might occur on a rocky bottom. The lead O, which sinks the machine, is attached to the frame-work containing the rotator and index plate C, by a piece of rope N. At the bottom of the lead is a receptacle for tallow, by which the nature of the bottom is ascertained. This machine will give correct soundings when going 9 or 10 knots through the water, without heaving-to, or deadening the ship's way, by giving it plenty of line, as it only registers the perpendicular descent, and has no connexion whatever with the quantity of line in the water. There is a flirt piece, or lock, at the back of the indexes, which is not shown in the engraving, which is kept in an upright position during the descent of the machine by the action of the water, but which immediately falls when the lead strikes the bottom; or also when the machine is hauled inboard, should the vessel not be in soundings, which prevents the rotator acting while being hauled in, which would cause an error in the soundings. I have only to add, that I have repeatedly got correct soundings at a depth of from 25 to 30 fathoms, from on board a steam-vessel at full speed, which speaks volumes for the utility and value of the machine.

I remain, Sir, your obedient servant,
AN OLD SAILOR.
Dover Road, May 22, 1838.

MR. UTTING'S ASTRONOMICAL TABLES—A SCOTCH DOMINIE IN REPLY.

Sir,—I return Kinclaven my best thanks for the assistance he has given me in his letter in No. 764; at the same time, I beg leave to inform him, that it was my intention to have replied to Mr. Utting's last letter in No. 754. Indeed I had nearly finished a reply to it, when I received the number containing Kinclaven's letter, and found that he (Kinclaven) had anticipated me in several remarks which I intended to have made; under these circumstances I thought the better way would be, to write a new one, and to go a little more into detail on some of those parts of Mr. Utting's letter which Kinclaven has only glanced at; and this I very much regret, as I am well aware that he is far better qualified for the task than I can pretend to be.

In the first place, Mr. Utting informs us in his letter above referred to, " that the motion of the equinoxial points varies in proportion to the periodical times of the planets. This is surely a most important astronomical discovery if it should be found to be true. Well we shall see : —assume 50″.1 as the precession of the equinoxial points of the earth, to determine those of Jupiter; then by Mr. Utting's simple rule we have 365.25 + &c. : 50″.1 : : 4332.60+&c. : 591″.55 ; that is, the precession of the equinoxial points of Jupiter in one periodical revolution of that planet is 591″.55 or 9′.. 51″.55.

Now suppose P and T to be the periodical and tropical periods of a planet, $360° = 1296000$ seconds $= a$, $x =$ to the precession of the equinoxial points in seconds of a circular arch, then we evidently have $a - x : T : : a : P$; hence,

$$a P - P x = a T \therefore x = \frac{a P - a T}{P} = \frac{a (P - T)}{P},$$

or if P and x are given to find T, we have $T = \frac{a P - P x}{a} = P - \frac{P x}{a}$; or lastly, if T and x are given to find P, we have $P = \frac{a T}{a - x} = T + \frac{T x}{a - x}$. According to La Place the periodical and tropical revolutions of the earth are 365.256384 and 365.242264.

Hence, $x = \frac{1296000 \times .014120}{365.256384} = 50″.100$ or 50″.1, and $T = P - \frac{P x}{a} = 365.256384 - \frac{365.256384 \times 50′.1}{1296000} = 365.242264$ and $P = 365.242264 + \frac{365.242264 \times 50′.1}{1296000} = 365.256384$; and I may here remark, that if we compute x from the periods Mr. Utting has assumed in No. 754, we find $x = 50′.169$, which is certainly above the truth ; and now for Jupiter, we have P = 4332.602173, and T = 4330.610440* ∴ P — T =

* These periods I have taken from Sir David Brewster's Astronomy, as it is the only work in my possession where all the siderial and tropical periods of the planets are calculated to hand.

1.991733 and $x = \frac{129800 \times 1.991733}{4332.602173}$ = 595″.81; and here I will admit that in the case of Jupiter Mr. Utting's general rule (perchance) is not very far from correct; and I will further allow that the nearer the results obtained from *his rule*, and those which result from the true and simple rule which I have given, the nearer will there be an equality between the expressions $\frac{P \ P'}{P - P'}$ and $\frac{T \ T'}{T - T'}$; but even in the case of Jupiter there is not an equality between the expressions.

We shall now proceed to enquire how affairs go on with some of the other planets, according to Mr. Utting's general rule. And first we shall take the planet Mercury, the periodical period of which is 87.969150; hence, according to the golden rule of Mr. Utting, 365.254, &c. : 50′.1 : : 87.969 + &c. : 12″;07.— Solution by the true rule :—The tropical period of Mercury is 87.968434; hence, P — T = .000716 and $x = \frac{1296000 \times .000716}{87.969 + \&c.} = 10″.44$; that is, the error produced by Mr. Utting's rule in a periodical revolution of Mercury is 1″.63 ; or the error for a periodical revolution of the earth will be 6″.8. Proceeding in the same way with the planet Venus, Mr. Utting's error will be found to be no less than 19″.1 in one siderial year. But surely, Mr. Editor, you, as well as your numerous scientific contributors and readers, will allow that I have advanced quite enough to show the absurdities that result from Mr. Utting's newly-discovered rule. No doubt from some of those long arithmetical calculations of which he is so fond, Mr. U. discovered that his rule was nearly true with respect to the Earth and Jupiter, and hence he very unscientifically concluded that it must universally hold good. I was very much amused (edified I cannot say) with Mr. Utting's two solutions of the question I proposed him, and inserted in No. 747 of your Magazine, the first of which he has taken from the *Philosophical Magazine*. The synodic period being found to be 399.976169 siderial days, or 398.884105 (according to Kinclaven) mean solar days. Mr. Utting, from his manufacturing system, has calculated the said period to be only

398.8837. Kinclaven seems to be surprised why Mr. U. has only extended the decimal to four places. This I can easily explain (having had a little more experience in the Uttonian system of arithmetic than Kinclaven). Mr. Utting had his eye upon the grand conjunction feat of all the planets, and he found that the grand period 91640740 was very nearly divisible by 398.8837; whereas, if he had used 6 decimal places, it would not have answered his purpose. I will ask Mr. Utting to point out his authority for having taken the tropical period of Jupiter 4330.643164 ? It is clearly above the truth. Indeed, I believe I may answer the question myself—it has been manufactured in Mr. U.'s own shop. I have now nearly exhausted the subject, Mr. Editor, but shall reserve what I have further to say for another opportunity.

I am, yours, &c.

A Scotch Dominie.

Forfarshire, April 20, 1838.

MR. UTTING'S ASTRONOMICAL TABLES —STRICTURES BY KINCLAVEN.

Sir,—Your indefatigable arithmetical calculator, Mr. Utting, in order to cram us with a belief of the vast importance of his astronomical discoveries, has, in his last letter, No. 768, given us a new set of synodic periods for Jupiter. The first he makes 398.884081157; and, the second, 398.8837091809 mean solar days. (Mr. U. has not being sparing of his decimals this time.) In the siderial and tropical periods, Mr. U. in his last communication has been under the necessity of manufacturing new periods for the Earth and Jupiter, which are considerably different from those he used in his letter in No. 654. In his first letter, he says the synodic period of Jupiter is:

$$\frac{4330.6431644 \times 365.242244}{3965.4002920} =$$

398.863709; and, in his last, he states,

$$\frac{4330.59895073 \times 365.24224142}{4330.59895073 - 365.24224142} =$$

398.88401157. In the tropical periods of the earth, Mr. Utting has made but small changes; but with regard to Jupiter he has acted (if not with perfect wisdom) very cunningly, and this I shall presently make appear. But first I must notice the synodic period of

Jupiter, which he has given us from the siderial periods, viz. :—

$$\frac{4332.584760000 \times 365.25636098}{4332.584760000 - 365.25636098} =$$

398.884081153. I shall here only remark, that the above siderial period of Jupiter is under the truth by 16 minutes $37''.7$ in time; but this I shall pass over, and suppose that the synodic period of Jupiter as derived from the siderial periods is correct. Assume, 398.884081153 = a. Then, according to Mr. Utting's system, we must force an equality right or wrong between the expressions $\frac{P\,P'}{P-P'}$ and $\frac{T\,T'}{T-T'}$. Well, acting upon the principles of this forcing system, we have $\frac{P\,P'}{P-P'} = \frac{T\,T'}{T-T'} = a$; hence, by reduction, &c., we have $T = T' + \frac{T'}{a-T'}$. But $T' = 365.242241142$; hence, $T = 365.242241142 + \frac{(365.242241142)^2}{33.641839733} =$ 4330.59895073! Hence, we have the following rule: fix upon two periods P' and P to represent the siderial periods of the earth and a planet, and prefix as many decimal places as you may think proper (100 if you please); there is no necessity for P and P' being expressed in accordance with the best authenticated authority; then find a value of a from the equation $\frac{P\,P'}{P-P'} = a$; take a value of T' somewhat less than P, and find the value of T from the expression $T + \frac{T'\,2}{a-T'}$, substitute this value of T in the expression $\frac{T\,T'}{T-T'}$. Then there will evidently be an equality between the expressions $\frac{P\,P'}{P-P'}$ and $\frac{T\,T'}{T-T'}$, whether the numbers P, P', T and T' are consistent with facts or otherwise. Here we have a precious specimen of the manufacturing system (so named by the Scotch Dominie) which Mr. U. has chosen to adopt for the purpose of veiling his astronomical blunders.

Mr. Utting has given us another value of the synodic period of Jupiter, and here he assumes the mean precession of the equinoxial points of the earth to be 51″.632; but how this change of data could produce such a change in the siderial periods of the Earth and Jupiter, or why it should produce any change at all, would be almost impossible to conceive. But Mr. U. has his motive for this also, which is easily seen through. It is, in fact, another slight of hand he has had recourse to, for the purpose of trying to reconcile the two different synodic periods which he has calculated for Jupiter. It may be further remarked, that in his last calculation he has been under the sad necessity of calling to his aid the forcing system. It does not, however, appear, that Mr. U. was acquainted with this *system* at the time he wrote his letter (No. 754); but having subsequently been informed (No. 764) that the synodic period of Jupiter which he calculated,was not in accordance with the same period as calculated in the *Philosophical Magazine* he, therefore, to save appearances found himself compelled to invent the above-named system. He has also been forced to use both tropical and siderial periods at variance with one another, and also inconsistent with well-established facts.

Mr. Utting does not say one word about the precession of the equinoxial points of Jupiter. This I suppose he considered unnecessary, as he had before informed us that the precession of the equinoxial points of the planets are in proportion to their periodic periods (!).* Supposing this proposition of Mr. Utting's to be true, the following simple formula deducible from it, will express the mean distance of any planet from the sun, viz.: $D = d \sqrt[3]{\dfrac{P+T}{P'+T'}}$; where, d is the mean distance of the earth from the sun, P and T the siderial and tropical periods of the planet, P′ and T′ the same of the earth. But whether the above formula will be found to agree with Kepler's third law, I shall not at present say any thing about.

Mr. Utting may pretend to say that he has never given any rule or formula

---

* Supposing the periodic periods of the planets to be in proportion to the precession of the equinoxial points, it by no means follows that $\dfrac{P}{P-P'} = \dfrac{T}{T-T'}$. The absurdity of this supposition I shall demonstrate in my next communication.

for his last astronomical discovery. I know he has not; but the tropical and periodical periods which he has adopted, so as to obtain his wished-for synodic periods, plainly indicate the corrupt source from which he has obtained his information.

I am, Mr. Editor, yours, &c.
                    KINCLAVEN.
May 7, 1838.

MR. UTTING'S ASTRONOMICAL TABLES.
—NAUTILUS IN DEFENCE.

Sir,—The last time Mr. Utting's name was introduced into a communication from me, it was for the purpose of proving him to have been in error, in a former discussion—my present letter has for its object the more agreeable task of defending him in a contest, in which he has, at least, the disadvantage of numbers, to contend against. Another consideration which induces me to submit to you the following remarks upon the controversy, so long pending between him and the Scotch Dominie, the Cambridge Student, and Kinclaven, is, the hope that they may tend to bring the contest to a conclusion, the question in dispute being now narrowed into the truth or falsehood of a single proposition, viz:—"In no case in the solar system is $\dfrac{T\,t}{T-t} = \dfrac{P\,p}{P-p}$," where T, and t, are the tropical, and P, and p, the siderial, periods of the planets.

On the truth of this proposition the Dominie and his followers have pinned their faith; they have erected it as the standard under which they do battle, and by the maintenance of which they must stand or fall.

The arguments for, and against, have hitherto been confined to those of a complicated arithmetical nature; these being precisely the worst possible; for, not only do their force altogether depend upon the correctness with which the calculations may be performed, but, they can, necessarily, convince those only who may be at the trouble of testing that correctness. I shall endeavour to analyse the question, and place it upon simpler grounds.

360° being the siderial revolution of a planet, performed in the time P, 360°÷P, is the mean daily angular velocity, expressed by V. If two planets, then, of different periods, set out from conjunction, $\left(\dfrac{360}{P} - \dfrac{360}{p}\right)$ or (V—v), expresses the daily difference of their velocities, or their separation; and when this separation amounts to 360° it becomes annihilated, and the planets are again in conjunction; this period of separation is called their synodical period, and is expressed by S.

Therefore, $\left(\dfrac{360}{P} - \dfrac{360}{p}\right)$ $\dfrac{360}{S}$;

whence ows the obvious equation, $\dfrac{P\,p}{P-p}$ = S, or $\dfrac{360}{V-v}$ = S.

On the other hand, the tropical period being short of 360°, by reason of the tropical point of departure receding in an opposite direction and meeting the planet before it has completed its entire circuit, the portion of the circle thus anticipated, or P—T, may be represented by the letter a; therefore, $\dfrac{360-a}{T}$ is equal and identical with $\dfrac{360}{P}$, or V. And in like manner in the case of the second planet,

the anticipated arc being represented by b, $\dfrac{360-b}{t}$ is equal to $\dfrac{360}{p}$. Now, therefore, the expressions $\left(\dfrac{360-a}{T} - \dfrac{360-b}{t}\right)$, $= \left(\dfrac{360}{P} = \dfrac{360}{p}\right)$, $= (V-v)$; are, all three, equal in every respect; but in the first, viz.: $\left(\dfrac{360-a}{T.} - \dfrac{360-b}{t}\right)$, it is evident, that since $a : b :: T : t$, the addition, subtraction, or total omission of the parts a, and b, can make no difference in the value of the result; and that, therefore, $\left(\dfrac{360}{T} - \dfrac{360}{t}\right)$ is, as an entire expression, equal to $\left(\dfrac{360-a}{T} - \dfrac{360-b}{t}\right)$, and also to $\left(\dfrac{360}{P} - \dfrac{360}{p}\right)$: finally, therefore, $\dfrac{T.\,t}{T-t} = \dfrac{P.\,p}{P-p}$.

Perhaps an arithmetical example, wherein the numbers are purposely chosen so simple, that those who run may read, may further elucidate the matter.

Let the siderial period of planet A, be.......... = 180 days.
And the recession of its equinox in its tropical year = 180 degrees.
Hence, its tropical year will be .... = 90 days.
And let the siderial period of another planet B, .. = 120 days.
Whence, its tropical revolution with respect to A, is = 72 days.
And their synodical period .... S = 360 days.

Therefore, $\dfrac{P.\,p}{P-p}$ = S, = $\dfrac{180 \times 120}{180-120}$ = 360 = $\dfrac{T.\,t}{T-t}$ = S = $\dfrac{90 \times 72}{90-72}$ = 360.

From all this, it appears that the Dominie's celebrated proposition may be directly negatived by the following counter assertion, viz.: *In no case in the solar system, is* $\dfrac{T.\,t}{T-t}$ *otherwise than equal to* $\dfrac{P.\,p}{P-p}$. But how, it may be asked, have the Dominie and his pupils been able to maintain, for so long a time, an argument to the contrary? First, because the Dominie's proposition has been mere assertion, unsupported by any argument better than an arithmetical comparison, founded, as I shall presently show, upon false principles; and, secondly, because the question has never been *directly* met by Mr. Utting, who,

himself, seems to have wavered considerably in his belief, and to be, at length, only half convinced by dint of arithmetical trials;—nay, he even at one time (in No. 741 of the *Mechanics' Magazine*) made a most unqualified admission of the *truth* of the Dominie's proposition; and although he attempts in his last letter in No. 768, to make it be believed that he meant that admission in a "satirical" (ironical?) sense, yet I must strongly protest against such an insult to the understandings of your readers.

In attempting to prove his proposition, the argument of the Dominie, if it may be so called, is as follows: he has taken the *tropical* periods from Mr. Utting's Tables, and compared results obtained from them, with results obtained from *siderial* periods, not deduced from the same tables, but taken at random from some other authority; and because such necessarily incongruous materials gave different results, he attributed to the method an error which was, in reality, due to his own choice of materials:— Thus, at pages 147, and 215, vol. xxvii, he quotes the tropical periods of Venus and Jupiter from Utting's Tables; and, in order to reduce them to siderial periods, he applies equations, arbitrarily assumed, instead of being, as they ought, deduced from the tables themselves. Yet this extraordinary error has been carried all through the discussion; and, will it be believed? is the sole and entire foundation on which the so-called *castigation* inflicted upon Mr Utting by Kinclaven, (so lately as your 764th Number) rests. Kinclaven there compares the siderial period of Jupiter, taken from the *Philosophical Magazine*, (published before Mr. U.'s Tables were heard of) with Jupiter's tropical period taken from the Tables; and because he found the result to be a difference of 32″ in the determination of the synodical period, he fancied that he had found a "pickled rod" which he most unmercifully flourishes over Mr. U.'s devoted head, as an irrefragible proof that $\frac{P \cdot p}{P-p}$ cannot be equal to $\frac{T \cdot t}{T-t}$; although, I need scarcely observe, that the said difference of 32″ is not by any means to be attributed to the use of either of these formulæ, but to the different sources whence the periods were obtained. I was sorry to observe the language in which Kinclaven allowed himself to clothe his ill-grounded triumph; had he been as certainly in the right as he was altogether wrong, it could scarcely have justified it; but when the error was wholly on his own side, it became reprehensible in the extreme.

But perhaps the most extraordinary circumstance, connected with this discussion, remains to be noticed: at page 366, vol. xxvii, the Dominie refers, in support of his views, to the treatise on astronomy published by the Society for the Diffusion of Knowledge; but in that very publication, at page 70, may be found a full refutation of his own proposition, in the shape of an ample, though rather prolix demonstration of the truth of the following equation, viz.: $q = \frac{Q \cdot s}{Q+s}$

er, using the same notation as heretofore, $t = \frac{T \cdot s}{T+s}$. Again, at page 297, vol. xxviii, the Cambridge Student writes thus: "If the Dominie is wrong, so is every writer on astronomy I have ever read." And yet, in a class-book, emanating from the very university of which he may be inferred to be a member, is this self-same equation given for finding the tropical period of the moon, viz.: $t = \frac{T \cdot s}{T+s}$, T, and t, being the tropical periods of the earth and moon; and s, their synodical revolution! Vide "Maddy's Principles of Plane Astronomy," page 200.

In thus attempting a defence of Mr. Utting, I have no ambition to be supposed an unqualified admirer of his grand conjunction; I have always looked upon it as a very ingenious arithmetical exercise, something analogous to the finding a common denominator in a series of fractions; I have little fault to find with it, with the exception of some very improper phrases, such as the *perikelion* of the *sun* and moon, &c.: but it is altogether of such questionable utility, that it would be scarcely worth one's while to test the calculations. I must, however, observe to Mr. Utting, that, the real agreement of his Tables with other authorities, is not, after all, so very remarkable, since a slight alteration in the periods (a liberty which he has amply taken) is quite sufficient, when multiplied into the little eternity of his grand conjunction, to reconcile all discrepancies.

NAUTILUS.

May 22, 1838.

───────────

RECENT AMERICAN PATENTS.
(Selected from the *Franklin Journal* for Feb.)

IRON CHEST, OR SAFE FOR THE PRESERVATION OF BOOKS, *Benjamin Sherwood, New York*.—This chest, safe, or bookcase, is to be made in the form of a vertical cylinder. Its security is to result from there being two double cases, each filled with a bad conductor of heat. The outer case is a double cylinder, with double heads, a space of about two inches between the two being filled with a mixture of prepared plaster-of-Paris, and pulverized charcoal. The inner case is similarly made, there being a space of about an inch between it and the outer; it revolves on central gudgeons, has its proper door, which when closed is to be turned round so as to be on the side opposite to that of the outer case.

The claim is to "the principle of suspending by pivots, one safe within another, that the door of the inner one may be shut, and it turned round and secured so as to place the door of the inner and outer safes in different directions from each other; that if by a fall of any great weight upon it the outer door should be thrown open, the inner one being turned round would prevent any exposure of the contents: second, the application of pulverized charcoal and boiled gypsum combined, in fire-proof chests, as a non-conductor of heat.

Double chests failed in the intense heat of the fire in New York, and there does not appear to be any thing special in that presented to us above, to protect it under similar circumstances; the mixture of charcoal and gypsum will do no more good than charcoal alone, or various other bad conductors of heat, or, in fact, than a mere air chamber.

MACHINE FOR FACING AND DRESSING STONE, *David Hull and John Critcherson, Portland, Maine.*—The cutting is to be effected by chisels, or cutters, projecting out from a quadrant of a cylinder, which is to be vibrated backward and forward above the stone, being caused to do so by the action of a crank shaft, and fly wheel. The cutters are to be forked, so as to have two edges, and it is said that they will sharpen themselves by their vibratory motion. Perhaps they may, but to us the motion seems well calculated to produce a contrary effect. The claim is to "the double edged cutters placed upon a segment of a cylinder, having a pendulous motion, for cutting and dressing stone, substantially as set forth in the specification."

MACHINE FOR CUTTING AND DRESSING GRANITE, MARBLE, OR OTHER STONE, *John D. Buzzell, Cape Elizabeth.*—The chisels for cutting, adapted in shape to the particular purpose for which they are to be used, are fixed in sockets set in spiral rows round a hollow cast iron cylinder, and these, it is said, are to "strike upon the stone in such a manner as to cut the stone and dress and polish it fit for building." The peculiar form of the chisel is described, and is such that it may be shifted in its socket as it wears, and so secured as to present a new cutting edge. There are to be cylinders of stone for grinding and polishing after the cutting; and a wooden cylinder covered with leather, to be used with emery, &c., for the same purpose. We have not seen this machine in operation; but from those who have, we have received very favourable reports. We look for one to be brought to

Washington, to be tried on stone for the public buildings.

The subject of stone cutting machines has arrested the attention of several different inventors within a short period of time, most probably in consequence of the very favourable reports of the success of the machine invented and patented by Mr. Hunter, of Scotland.

MODE OF PROPELLING BOATS, *Jesse Ong, North Huntingdon, Pennsylvania.*—The claim is to "the application of two paddle wheels for the purpose of propelling boats, at the centre of the stern, and having that centre as the common focus of their motions, which are contrary in direction, and their planes at right angles instead of parallel with the direction of the boat; and the direction and order of their strike is such, that the created currents, whilst they assist the efficacy of the wheel, are themselves dissipated and destroyed by their successive action on each other."

The paddles are set obliquely to the hub, or centre, of the propelling wheels, which are parallel to, and in the vicinity of, each other. The shaft of one wheel is hollow, to allow that of the other to pass through it, as they are to be propelled in reverse directions, the obliquity of the paddles being reversed.

Attempts have been made to propel boats by means of wheels like the foregoing, but, we believe, on separate axes. How far the reversed force acting upon the water will still the agitation, we are not prepared to say; this must be determined by experience; we, however, do not believe that it will be such as to have much effect in preventing the washing of the banks of canals; the only situation where such an affair is of importance.*

MACHINE FOR DRYING OIL CLOTHS, PAINTED FLOOR CLOTHS, &c., *Daniel Sampson, Winthrop, Maine.*—"Instead of extending out the cloth in length for the purpose of drying it, after it has received the paint (says the patentee), I wind it round a shaft, spirally, in such a way that the painted side shall be fully exposed to the action of the air, whilst it is at the same time prevented from coming into contact with the contiguous coil, or with any part of the machine.

"I construct two shafts, or cylinders, of sufficient length to have the painted cloth wound upon them, and mount them in a suitable frame parallel to each other. To wind the cloth upon these cylinders I prepare a band of slats, which slats are united together at the ends by webbing or by a leather or other strap of any convenient width. The slats are placed at any suitable distance apart, say one inch, and they must be of such length as to allow the cloth to lie upon them widthwise, between the connecting straps. The straps must be raised above the slats to a sufficient distance to allow a space for the cloth, which will prevent its painted surface from coming into contact with the contiguous slats, when wound. For this purpose I put between the strap and each slat, a thickness of sole leather, a small block of wood, or other suitable material.

" The band of slats may be fifty or sixty feet in length, or longer if desired, and their ends are fastened respectively upon the two cylinders above named. When the painted cloth is to be operated on, the whole band of slats is first wound on one of the shafts; the end of the cloth is then attached to one of the slats, or to the shaft upon which it is to be wound; this shaft is then turned by a winch, or otherwise, as the paint is spread upon cloth, and it is thus received and retained upon the slats and suffered to remain there until the drying is completed."

LIST OF SCOTCH PATENTS GRANTED BE-
TWEEN THE 22ND OF APRIL AND THE
22ND OF MAY, 1838.

William Chubb, of Portsea, Portsmouth, Southampton, umbrella manufacturer, for certain improvements in night commode pans and chamberpots. April 26; four months.

William Holme Heginbotham, of Stockport, Chester, gent., for certain improvements in the construction of gas retorts. April 26.

Pierre Armand Lecomte de Fontainemoreau, of Charles Street, City Road, Middlesex, for an improved method of preventing the oxidation of metals, being a communication from a foreigner residing abroad. May 7.

Thomas Ridgway Bridson, of Great Bolton, Lancaster, bleacher, for certain improvements in the construction and arrangement of machinery or apparatus for stretching, mangling, drying, and finishing woven goods or fabrics, and part or parts of which improvements are applicable to other useful purposes. May 11.

John White, of Haddington, in the county of Haddington, ironmonger, for certain improvements on stoves for producing heated air applicable to ovens, or where heated air is required. May 18.

Hippolyte Francois, Marquis de Bouffet Montauban, Colonel of Cavalry, now residing in Sloane Street, Chelsea, Middlesex, and John Carvalho de Medeiros, of Old London Street, London, merchant, in consequence of a communication from a foreigner residing abroad, for certain improvements in the means of producing gas for illumination, and also in the construction of burners for consuming gas. May 14.

NOTES AND NOTICES.

The Copyright Bill.—We are glad to see that Sir Edward Sugden has given notice of his intention to move the introduction of several amendments in the Copyright Bill, which, indeed, could hardly be expected to pass in the crude state in which it was brought in by Serjeant Talfourd. Among other alterations, Sir Edward proposes to limit the term to forty years, instead of sixty,—not, we believe, an absolute term of that extent from the date of publication, as proposed in our last, but from the death of the author. Another honourable member has revived the clause of the bill of last session, now abandoned by Serjeant Talfourd himself, which provides that no author shall be allowed to dispose of more than the first twenty-eight years of his copyright; so that literature will be encouraged, not by holding out the hope of additional remuneration to the author, but by giving him the prospect of possibly enriching his descendants or "next of kin." It is needless to say that there is little chance of this ridiculous clause being re-adopted.

New Steam-Plough.—The same gentleman,—an Irish Baronet—whose steam-carriage for common roads is about to be brought forward by a joint-stock company, is also the inventor of a steam-plough, of similar wonder-working capabilities, for which a patent has been secured, and which will probably soon be introduced to the agricultural interest by another company. In the meanwhile, why does not the worthy Baronet carry off the five hundred guineas offered as a premium for the first really-effective steam-plough by the Highland Society of Scotland? He would have competitors, indeed, but not near so many (reckoning the has-beens) as in the reviving of road-locomotives.

Taylor & Davis's Steam-engine.—Sir,—I have just returned from the British Alkali Works, at Stoke Prior, and have minutely inspected the new engine, described in No. 768 of the Mechanics' Magazine. The accounts hitherto published of this engine (more particularly the one inserted in the *Engineers' Journal*), are exceedingly incorrect, as is also the diagram accompanying my former communication. I shall furnish you as early as possible with a correct drawing and description of the engine. It is the intention of the patentees to prosecute a series of experiments with the new engine, in order to determine its power, economy, &c. &c.: at present, therefore, any observations on these heads would be premature. The absurd paragraph already noticed has caused them considerable annoyance. To correct any false impressions respecting the invention, and to enable the public to judge fairly of its merits and capabilities, is the earnest desire of the proprietors. I am, Sir, &c. CHRIS. DAVY.—Birmingham, May 14, 1838.

Cmplete Sets of the Mechanics' Magazine may now be had, twenty-seven volumes, half-cloth, price £11. 7s.

☞ *British and Foreign Patents taken out with economy and despatch; Specifications, Disclaimers, and Amendments, prepared or revised; Caveats entered; and generally every Branch of Patent Business promptly transacted. A complete list of Patents from the earliest period* (15 Car. II. 1675,) *to the present time may be examined. Fee 2s. 6d.; Clients, gratis.*

LONDON: Printed and Published for the Proprietor, by W. A. Robertson, at the Mechanics' Magazine Office, No. 6, Peterborough-court between 135 and 136, Fleet-street.—Sold by A. & W. Galignani, Rue Vivienne, Paris.

𝔐𝔢𝔠𝔥𝔞𝔫𝔦𝔠𝔰' 𝔐𝔞𝔤𝔞𝔷𝔦𝔫𝔢,

MUSEUM, REGISTER, JOURNAL, AND GAZETTE.

No. 774.]   SATURDAY, JUNE 9, 1838.   [Price 3*d.*

LONDON AND SOUTHAMPTON RAILWAY—LONDON STATION.

LONDON AND SOUTHAMPTON RAILWAY.

We this week present our readers with a view of the entrance to the London Station of the Southampton Railway, at Nine Elms, which we have copied from a very well-executed lithographic engraving, forming one of the illustrations accompanying a map of the line lately published.* The first portion of this railway, extending to Woking Common, a distance of 23 miles from London, commenced its work of transit on the 21st ult. Between London and Woking Heath there are five stations or places where passengers and goods are taken up or deposited. The first of these is at Wimbledon, 5¾ miles from town, whence passengers will be forwarded to London in fifteen minutes. The next is at Kingston, 10¼ miles from town, whence passengers will be conveyed in twenty-five minutes. Then we have one at Ditton Marsh, 12¾ miles from town, which will embrace Esher, Hampton, Hampton Court, Thames Ditton, Long Ditton, and East and West Moulsey, and will send passengers to town in thirty minutes. Three miles farther is the station at Hersham Green, which will embrace Hersham and Walton, and send passengers to town in thirty-seven minutes. Next we have the station at Weybridge Common, seventeen and a half miles from town, embracing Cobham, Ripley, Chertsey, Addlestone, Thorpe, Byfleet, and Weybridge, whence the traveller will find himself in London in forty-four minutes. Finally, there is the station at Woking Common, which will embrace Bagshot, Godalming, Guildford, and Cobham, and whence, at the ordinary pace, (calculated at twenty-four miles an hour,) the passenger will be transmitted to town in fifty-seven minutes. It is expected, that, by the 1st of September next, more than forty miles of the railway will be completed, to within about a mile of Murrell-Green; and that portion, also, between Winchester and Southampton about the same time.

In Mr. Jobbins's map, the towns, seats, and other prominent objects passed on the line are faithfully marked, as well as the distances of the various stations from London. The lithographic views are very faithful; so much so, that the spots they depict would be easily recognisable by a stranger, in even the passing glimpse which the speed of railway transit will allow.

SUBSTITUTE FOR PUMPS IN FILLING STEAM-BOILERS.

Sir,—Several recently invented methods of maintaining a proper supply of water to steam-boilers, have lately been described in your pages, some of which have been very justly commented upon by "Nauticus," at page 107. I think most of your readers will agree, that Mr. Whitelaw's apparatus (vide No. 769), is objectionable from its complexity, entailing great expense in its construction, with great liability to derangement. Taylor and Davis's plan, described by Mr. Evans, bears some slight resemblance to the plan which I published about four years ago, at page 277 of your 21st volume; upon this plan Mr. William Cook has suggested what he considers an improvement (vide page 83). The most simple, and the best practical method hitherto generally employed for supplying water to high-pressure boilers, has been by means of a common force-pump, wrought by connection with the engine. The principal objection to this mode of supply is, the loss of a certain quantity of power, consumed in overcoming the friction of the pump, and working it against the internal pressure of the steam, together with the impossibility of maintaining, by this means, the required uniformity of level. By the arrangement submitted as an efficient "substitute for pumps in high-pressure steam-boilers," in your 572nd number, both these desirable objects are accomplished: little or no power is required for working the apparatus, and the water is sure to be kept at any definite height that may be determined upon. In Mr. Cook's communication, before alluded to, he states that, "on account of the vacuum formed in the transferrer, there will be no necessity for placing the reservoir above the water-line of the boiler;" but I must beg to differ from him on this point, inasmuch as the condensation of the steam, and rising of the water from

---

* Map of the London and Southampton Railway, showing the situation of the stations from London to Woking Heath. Illustrated with five views from original drawings. London: J. R. Jobbins, Warwick Court, Holborn.

a lower level, by atmospheric pressure alone, will not be sufficiently rapid for the purpose, when the engine is working at any considerable speed. An elevated reservoir insures the instant condensation of the steam and filling of the transferrer, every time it is either wholly or partially emptied. My " substitute for pumps" may require a little modification to adapt it to particular employments, but I believe it will be found, in point of simplicity and efficiency, far superior to most of those contrivances for the like purpose which have been made the subject of patents.

I remain, Sir, yours respectfully,
WM. BADDELEY.
London, May 28, 1838.

CONSTRUCTION OF STEAM-VESSELS.

Sir,—Since I last addressed you on the subject of steam-navigation, the *Sirius* has accomplished the voyage out to New York and home, proving that the Atlantic is actually navigable by steam-vessels from its eastern to its western shore, and, one would think, convincing a certain learned Doctor, that there is more *duty* in coals than he calculated upon. The *Great Western*, too, has made her passage out, and before this reaches you, will most probably have arrived at Bristol,—the place where it was proved to demonstration that steam navigation to the United States was impossible !

It is gratifying to observe, how nearly the calculation made prior to her sailing, has been verified : she was, if I mistake not, 15 days on her passage out ; and the *Sirius* (a much smaller vessel) was 17 days from Cork ;—proving, too, the correctness of the opinion advanced by Messrs. Seaward, in a pamphlet published by them in 1829, that for the successful extension of steam navigation, a larger class of vessels must be introduced, in order to obtain greater speed at less cost. I most cordially concur in the statement, that the vessel should be of the greatest possible length, consistent with strength. Length has been given, but unfortunately it has been at the expence of strength, as will be apparent to any one who will take the trouble to examine many of the existing steam-vessels. Instead of presenting a regular sheer, and a fair deck-line, they will be

found depressed in that part occupied by the boiler and machinery, below a regular curve ; and, if coppered, the metal will be wrinkled, which is an unequivocal proof of an alteration in the form of the vessel. This distortion is generally most perceptible in the after body of the ship, just abaft the boiler. In some old boats, on their arrival from a voyage, after a somewhat boisterous passage, the butts and seams of the wales and upper works will be found opened to a considerable extent. If any remark be made upon these appearances, the answer almost invariably given is, " Oh, these long vessels will strain." But why should they strain thus ? Are there no means of prevention ? Or is their length so great as to produce a strain beyond the native strength of the materials to sustain, without permanent alteration ? There is, no doubt, a length which it is not prudent to exceed, in constructing a vessel ; and I think from what has passed under my observation, it will be found that this limit has been very nearly, if not quite, reached upon the present mode of constructing and fastening steam-vessels. For large ships, fir ought not to be used in those parts which are intended to bind and connect the fabric together. The soft and yielding nature of this timber renders it incapable of presenting sufficient resistance to tension or pressure, without permanent alteration in the arrangement of its fibres. I might adduce some striking illustrations of this result, were it proper to do so.

The use of oak, or other hard woods, is open to objection, on account of their greater liability to shrinkage, from the great heat. This objection is greater in appearance than in reality ; for, if they be properly seasoned before using, they will not be found to shrink more than soft woods under the same circumstances. Still, so far as the shrinkage extends, so much will the strength of the fabric be weakened ; for it is obvious, that if the several parts be not kept in actual contact, the strength of the separate parts are not rendered fully available to the general strength. Steam-boat building bears a similar relation to the building of ordinary merchant-vessels, that building a light travelling carriage does to an agricultural waggon ; and, therefore, the same principle of binding the parts together should be applied ; and instead of using fir or other soft woods in the construction of steam-vessels, nothing but oak or other hard wood should be used. The common plea for the use of fir, is its *lightness ;* but in order to obtain the requisite strength, it is used of greater substance, and therefore the total weight of the materials is increased so as to be nearly the same as if oak only were used. I very much incline to the belief, that when thoroughly saturated with water, the fir planking is equally as heavy as oak. Another plea for the extensive use of fir for planking is, the great lengths which can be obtained. This is an advantage, undoubtedly; but it is frequently completely thrown away by the exceedingly unskilful combination of the parts. There are now in existence some of the earlier steam-boats, built entirely with oak ; these vessels do not present any signs of weakness or giving way, whilst many others which have fir planking, although less than one-third their age, are yielding in several parts, and some of them either actually extensively repaired, or requiring to be so.

There can be no question but that it is contrary to sound policy to use so large a quantity of fir in the construction of steam-boats, even if cost only be taken into consideration. The difference per cent. in the prime cost between oak and fir plank, applies only to the material—the workmanship and fastening is the same in both cases; but, as experience has shewn, the durability of the one is two or three times longer than the other. If we assume the difference in cost of material to be 50 per cent., the cost of labour and fastenings will be equal to the cost of the oak, or 50 per cent. on the price of the fir ; the duration of the oak will be from 2 to 3 times longer than the fir. The account will stand thus :—

For Fir Planking.
Material 100
Labour and fastening.. 150
                       ———
                       250

For Oak Planking.
Material 150
Labour and fastening.. 150
                       ———
                       300

Assuming that fir will last half the time of oak, its cost for the same period will be 500 ; whilst oak would cost but 300, to say nothing of the loss that must ac-

crue from loss of freight during the repairs. That the practice of planking steam-boats with fir should have prevailed so extensively, can only be accounted for upon the principle that *present* advantage and saving is alone regarded.

I should be glad to see an end put to the practice of using fir for planking sea-going steamers : it is unfit for the purpose, both as it respects strength and durability ; a great number of instances might be quoted in proof of this statement : instead of the present cheap method of running these vessels up, a more careful and scientific method of construction should be adopted.

It was my intention to have suggested some improvements upon the present method of construction ; but, as I have for the present occupied too much of your space, I forbear.

I am, Sir, yours &c.
GEORGE BAYLEY.
1, Addington Place, Camberwell, May 22, 1838.

P.S. There is a material which appears exceedingly well adapted to the framing of steam-vessels, and has not yet been imported for that purpose. I refer to Saul timber, immense supplies of which could be readily obtained from the East Indies. There is another species of timber from the island of Fernando Po, which also appears extremely well suited to the purpose, some cargoes of which have already been imported into England.

———

THE IRON STEAM-BOAT "RAINBOW"
—SPEED OF THAMES STEAMERS.

Sir,—The good folks of Liverpool appear to be in a fair way to bear the palm of boasting from their hitherto successful rivals, the Americans ; indeed I think upon the subject of the above-named vessel, they have beaten them hollow.

Fame has blown herself hoarse during the last fifteen months, trumpeting the praises of this wonderful vessel ; when the keel was laid long since, various were the statements made by the friends of the builder and engineer, as to what her intended performance was to be ; fifteen miles per hour was said to be the speed contracted for, and for every mile above this small speed, some thousands per mile were to be paid. She was to be constructed of iron, instead of wood, of the great length of 190 feet, and 180 horse-power, with 5 feet draught of water only; certain it is, that the proprietors of the little slow boats on the Thames trembled when it was known that this *nonpareil* was on her way to London—the river captains were chapfallen—the owners of the steamers thought of burning them—oak was at a discount, and iron at a premium.

The *Rainbow* has at length appeared, and run the race on the Thames, firstly with the old *Emerald*, a third-rate boat, of 140 horse-power, running from France to London, heavily laden, and the deck lumbered with cargo; which vessel she passed, to the infinite delight of her owners. And shortly afterwards, to crown her triumphs, ran with the little *Vesper* of 70 horse-power only, and in a race of one hour and twelve minutes, gained, as they state, four minutes upon this vessel, of scarcely more than one-third her own power, and having passengers on board at the time; in fact, there is little doubt but the *Vesper* would have been quite a match for the *Rainbow*, had they both been in the same trim.

The people of London would have considered this performance a great failure, had the immense advantages this iron boat possesss in length and power (180 horses,) over her little opponent (70 horses) been considered; and which ought to have given her, at least, one and a half miles per hour more speed; but the Liverpool friends of the *Rainbow* think otherwise, and seem so exceedingly delighted, that newspapers detailing this glorious achievement, are being sent about the country cost free.

The truth is, her trials have only begun; there are yet three or four boats for her to run with, all faster than the *Vesper*, and of infinitely less power than the *Rainbow*. Why was she not tried with the *Ruby*, a vessel of 100 horse-power only? This boat can, and has beaten the *Vesper* from Gravesend to London, from seven to eight minutes; there are also the *Star*, the *City of Canterbury*, and the *Red Rover;* all of these boats are really very fast, and the whole of them, the *Vesper* included, will, I am confident, beat the *Rainbow* if loaded equally; that is, one passenger and luggage for every horse-power the contending vessels possess: thus the *Rainbow* should carry 180 passengers, when the *Vesper* carries seventy, and so on. Should the owners of the *Rainbow* be inclined to run her with the *Ruby*, I understand the captain of that vessel has 100*l*. at his command, to run her against any vessel in Europe, the *Rainbow*, of course, included.

By the following statement of speed, your readers will be better enabled to form an opinion of the performance of the Gravesend steamers, and thus, by comparison, what the speed of the *Rainbow* really is; (I now speak of speed through still water by the power of steam alone, as measured by a statute mile marked off on the bank of the Thames in Long Reach, where all the London vessels, as well as the Admiralty ones, have their powers tested). The *Ruby*, well known as the fastest steamer afloat, goes exactly 13½ miles per hour, as has been ascertained by repeated trials. The *Star* and *Vesper* 13¼, the *City of Canterbury* and *Red Rover* 13⅛; all the other Gravesend steamers above twelve; and I have no hesitation in saying, that the Gravesend steam boats, taking them all, are, without exception, the fastest vessels in Europe; and I fully believe, that when vessels have been successively brought from the ports of Glasgow, Liverpool, and other places, to compete with London built and fitted steamers, the different parties could not have deceived themselves and others, as they have done, had they known the real speed of these celebrated vessels.

I will now give you the performance of some of these boats, after the Yankee fashion, that is, reckoning tide and every thing in favour. On three different occasions last season, the *Ruby* made the passage from London Bridge to Gravesend with passengers, including stoppages, in one hour and thirty-five minutes; which, allowing five minutes for stoppages and interruptions, would make the time of running 1½ hours; the distance is computed to be thirty miles; here then, Mr. Editor, is twenty miles per hour! This, I think, is the greatest steam-boat performance upon record in this country. The *Star* has also done it under one hour and forty minutes; the *Vesper*, the *Diamond*, the *Gem*, and most of the other Gravesend steamers do it often in one hour and forty-five minutes, including their loading of passengers and the stoppages; this gives seventeen miles per hour. What is here stated can be substantiated by numbers of gentlemen who are daily in the habit of travelling by these splendid vessels; but the Londoners have never thought of boasting to the world as the Americans are in the habit of doing, that their vessels always go at the rates just stated, well knowing, that going through the water, and *overland*, as it is technically termed, are two totally different things.

In conclusion, Mr. Editor, I feel quite confident, that there are plenty of builders and engineers in London, who are quite competent to build and equip a vessel of timber of the power and length of the *Rainbow*, that will beat her a mile an hour.

I am, Sir, your obedient servant,
PISTON.

Limehouse, May 31, 1838.

STEAM NAVIGATION TO INDIA--SPEED
OF THAMES STEAMERS.

Sir,—It is difficult to bear the ridicule of others, without either feeling one's temper ruffled, or suspecting that there really is something in our conduct or opinions not consistent with propriety. Now it does so happen, that upon seeing the communication of your correspondent "H." in No. 772, page 120, my temper was unruffled at the sneer with which he commences his letter; and I can assure him, that until within a few days, it has never been my good fortune to meet with a copy of Messrs. Seaward's pamphlet, although I happen to have been a *constant reader*, and an occasional correspondent of the *Mechanics' Magazine* from its commencement. The assurances of your correspondent, "H.," that "a perusal of the more recent numbers of the same work" will relieve my mind from the apprehension "so vividly" expressed for the safety of our maritime pre-eminence in the East, would be, doubtless, very consolatory, if—they met the case; but, as you well know, the "pressure from without" was required to produce even a show of attention on the part of the government to this important object; and then much valuable time and talent was wasted in the attempt to render the navigation of the Tigris available to commercial purposes.

From the tenor of "H."'s remarks, he appears to be very desirous of inducing the belief that steam navigation is very general in India. If so, it is passing strange that, in common with many others who have access to the sources of early and accurate information upon maritime affairs, he should have overlooked the fact, that steam navigation in India was common *long ago*, and that we should have been impressed with the belief that steam navigation was still in its infancy in that part of the British empire,—so much so, that even the comparatively recent colony of New South Wales had made greater progress, and has actually been in possession of a more extended and frequent communication by steam-vessels, than our Indian empire.

Captain Grindlay, in his excellent remarks on steam communication with India, has most clearly shewn, that its introduction has been covertly opposed or retarded, by some influence or other, which has been too powerful for the exertions of private speculators to overcome at present. It is certainly true, that the force of public opinion is compelling the reluctant compliance with *a part* of the demands of a just and enlarged view of the necessity of commercial enterprise, by providing for the more frequent communication with the mother country *via* the Red Sea; but as floating straws indicate the direction of the current, it would seem that this communication was intended to be maintained by vessels unsuited to the purpose. The *Hugh Lindsay* has long ago received her character as an inefficient vessel, altogether unsuited to the purpose. The *Enterprize* is somewhere in India; her qualifications are tolerably well known.

The *Atalanta* and *Berenice*, sent out last year, are certainly efficient vessels, as it regards power and capacity; but it is with me a matter of great doubt whether the extensive use of fir planking was prudent for a vessel designed to navigate the Indian Seas. My reasons for doubting its propriety are deduced from the facts which frequently come under my observation. The *Semiramis*, late the *City of Waterford*, was the last sent out to reinforce the *steam flotilla*; of her excellencies it is unnecessary to speak; she is principally planked with fir, and was built for carrying a large cargo.

There are three other vessels contracted for in this country, to be built expressly for the service. I have seen the model, and from my knowledge of the constructor, I have every reason to believe that they will be really efficient and suitable ships for the purpose. Thus, Sir, this large East Indian steam flotilla at present appears to consist of *two efficient steam-vessels*;—one whose qualifications are not quite all that can be wished, and two (?) others altogether unsuited to the purpose. Whether these will be sufficient to maintain a sufficiently frequent communication with England *via* the Red Sea, and with our most distant dependencies in the East Indies, I leave to the candid judgment of your readers. The Dutch are building some steam-vessels to navigate the Indian Archipelago; and, according to present appearances, will be in possession of that field before our active Indian Government, with its "flotilla of steam-vessels," already in the East. I trust that the merchants in Calcutta will rouse themselves, and, by arrangements with their fellow-subjects in New South Wales, forthwith take measures for the establishment of a steam communication through the Indian Archipelago, and thus carry into effect the excellent suggestions of Capt. Grindlay and others, who have "long ago" suggested its propriety and necessity; and then I, for one, shall not fear the permanent maintenance of our maritime pre-eminence in those seas.

With regard to the difference between myself and the Messrs. Seaward, as to "the speed which might be kept up on the voyage to India," my calculation was made on the speed which has actually been maintained by the *Atalanta* and the *Berenice*: Messrs. Seaward, in their calculations, assumed that vessels of a much larger class should be employed. If this were the case, I have but little doubt but that they would be found to be correct.

The case referred to by me, was one in which the usual nautical miles were used; but the report was at variance with the facts, as was shewn by the gentleman at the time of the trial; and the vessel in question did not go more than from 11½ to 11¾ miles an hour, instead of 14, as the other parties asserted. Subsequent trials have confirmed the correctness of my friend's report.

I have no hesitation in repeating my conviction, that a speed of 14 miles an hour has not yet been attained by steam alone, notwithstanding the statements of "H.,"

who, by the way, seems to have fallen into the common error, as to the actual distance between Blackwall and Gravesend, which, I believe, does not exceed 18 statute miles; and I have it on unquestionable authority, that the greatest speed ever attained by means of steam alone, under the most favorable circumstances, did but just exceed 13 miles per hour.

It is far from my wish to discourage the praiseworthy efforts to increase the velocity of our steam-vessels, but, on the contrary, have every inducement, both official and private, to promote the improvement of naval architecture in all its branches, to the utmost of my ability.

It seems that "H." disapproves of the patent condensers of Mr. Hall, on board the *Sirius*, and would fain have your readers suppose that they were the cause of the difference between her speed and that of the *Great Western*, altogether overlooking the difference in size and construction of the two vessels. The smaller size of the *Sirius* would have prevented her attaining the same velocity as the *Great Western*, even if the two vessels had been constructed upon the same model; but when it is known that the *Sirius* was built for the British coasting trade, the wonder is, that she should have proved herself so formidable a competitor to the *Great Western*. It is very probable, that the *British Queen* will be a much faster vessel than the *Great Western*, notwithstanding the excellence of her machinery, which is certainly of the most perfect description, and does the greatest credit to Messrs. Maudsley and Co., by whom it was constructed.

I beg to apologize for having trespassed so much on your valuable columns, and subscribe myself, with the greatest respect,

Your obedient servant,
GEO. BAYLEY.

London, June 2, 1838.

———

DR. LARDNER AND THE ATLANTIC STEAMERS.

Since the return of the *Sirius* and *Great Western*, Dr. Lardner has evinced a very pardonable anxiety to explain away and gloss over his too-celebrated declaration against the practicability of traversing the Atlantic by steam. He now wishes it to be understood, that his opinion was, not that the scheme was impracticable, but that it would not be found to answer in a pecuniary point of view. This opinion will soon be put to the test, especially if the idea be realized, of immediately starting a regular series of steam liners from Liverpool, whose enterprising inhabitants, probably, owe their present position, so far in the rear of their ancient rivals, the Bristolians, in some degree to the circumstance of Dr. Lardner having made their town the scene of his *wet-blanket* prognostications. The *Great Western* has set out on its present voyage with more "malice prepense" than ever against the worthy Doctor, having taken from England a sufficient quantity of coals, not only to reach America —the grand difficulty, in his estimation,— but to steam all the way back again, without troubling the good folks of New York for a supply! This may almost be complained of as an offensive personality.

Another point on which the Doctor relies, on behalf of sailing-vessels, is the fact, that the regular liners which left England nearly at at the same time as the *Great Western*, arrived there nearly as soon,—to wit, in *twenty-six days*, the *Great Western* having taken fifteen: and the Doctor quotes this speed of the sailers in proof that the passage, after all, must have been a favourable one. If the same proportion between steaming and sailing continue, as it most probably will, it requires no conjuror to predict that steam will soon be "monarch of all she surveys," in the Atlantic, notwithstanding the indifference with which Dr. L. regards the *trifling* disparity. The proportion has been most admirably kept up on the return voyage,—the *Roscoe* liner having arrived at Liverpool nearly a fortnight after the arrival of the *Great Western* at Bristol, with "fresh news" from America, *one day later* than that brought by the steamer! The Liverpoolites may well be anxious to redeem their reputation by entering the field, even late as it is, as soon as possible. It is understood that the *Columbus*, a vessel on a less gigantic scale than the Bristol leviathan, and fitted with engines on Mr. Howard's principle, is now nearly ready for her first trip from their port. Meanwhile, the owners of the *Great Western* have already a second vessel on the stocks, of even larger dimensions than their first; and the *British Queen* is expected to astonish the Yankees, some time before Michaelmas, with a specimen of London ship-building.

It may be regarded as an unerring indication of Dr. Lardner's wish, "under existing circumstances," not to draw *too much* public attention to his opinions on the subject, that his intended article in the June number of the *Monthly Chronicle*, on "Ocean steam-

ers," has been *withdrawn*, at the eleventh hour, although it formed a prominent attraction in the advertised list of contents, *previous* to the arrival of the *Sirius* and *Great Western*. Alas! alas! what havoc does experience make of the *speculations of the learned!*

BILL TO REGULATE THE SPEED OF THAMES STEAMERS—WATERMEN'S WHERRIES—TURKISH CAIQUES, &C.

Sir,—I see by the papers, that a bill is being smuggled through the "honourable house," to limit the speed of steam-vessels navigating the river "below bridge" to five miles an hour. Now if this limitation of pace were declared to be enacted in order to prevent collisions, there would be some sort of sense in it; but the avowed reason is, the protection of the watermen's wherries from the swell of water, otherwise waves, caused by the steamers' speed. This piece of legislation is beautifully on a par with many others of the dull day-dreams of our night-walking legislators! Because the London watermen choose to build their boats on such a plan as to render them the most unsafe that any inventive genius could devise, the great national advantage of steam-navigation is to be cramped, and squeezed, and cut down, to suit the sea-worthiness of a London wherry! About a year ago, I addressed the *Morning Chronicle* and the *Times* newspapers on this subject, but my voice being neither gold nor silver-toned, remained unheeded. Sir, I think that you will take a proper view of this mechanical question; and if you only bestow upon it half the pains, the logic, and acumen which distinguish your excellent remarks upon the copyright bill of Mr. Talfourd, and which once did the like by the new patent law, you will confer a benefit upon those (the steam-navigators) who confer a vast benefit on society.

I am not cavilling at a regulation without being able to supply a reason and a remedy. The whole question lies *in the improper construction of the wherries*, at least as far as the proposers, or rather smugglers, of the bill moot this question. If, I repeat, they had predicated the objection to any more than a certain rate of speed to steamers, upon the plea of other vessels being unable to *avoid collision*, it would have been another affair;

but to pretend that the power of steam and quick travelling are to be foregone, because the London watermen, or any other men, choose to row about in boats with gunwales scarce an inch above the water, is nationally injurious.

It may be truly argued that boats that are to be rowed by one man only, must of necessity be constructed with a view to lightness, and to easy transit through the water, proportionate to the power of the labourer who thereby gets his bread. Far, very far, am I from being disposed to aggravate the cruel case of many thousand worthy men, whose modicum of earnings has been cut shorter, and in many cases almost extinguished, by the appliances of mighty steam. My heart almost bleeds whenever I step into a river steamer, and see the poor "watermen," listless, sitting with hands in empty pockets, in vain expecting any of the numerous arrivers at the stairs to require their services, that they may take home a shilling to their starving children. My object is to benefit all parties, by proposing an improvement in the build of wherries, which will render them secure from the swell of steamers, give confidence and security to those who use them, and obviate the necessity or pretence for any law to render nugatory the vast advantages of steam-navigation on the Thames.

After all this preamble, I fear that some grand product or project will be expected; and then, on my finishing my story, allusion may be made to the *ridiculus mus*; but I only speak of that which I have seen, and therefore brave all ridicule.

It cannot be expected that a "waterman" should be able to throw up his wherry, and build another; but, as a palliative to the unsafe construction of the existing boats, I strenuously recommend the raising of their gunwales; and of this I shall say a word, before I speak about the adoption of a build for one-man wherries, different from the existing form, and like those most beautiful light boats of analogous appliance,—the *caiques* of Constantinople.

In the first place, the larger sort of sailing *caiques*, whenever they have to navigate the Sea of Marmora, or the Black Sea, set up false moveable gunwales, of tarred or painted canvas, and these I have often seen in the roughest

weather keep the vessel dry; whereas, without them, it was every minute evident, that it must have filled and sunk. If, therefore, it be deemed too much trouble or expense to raise the sides of the London wherries permanently, in wood, cannot the ingenuity of the London boat-builders prompt them to apply so easy a contrivance, and see if then the ripple-storm of a passing steamer may not be weathered by a London wherry?

Thus far we have the expedients of the permanent or the temporary raising of the wherry's sides. But I think that if any boat-builder were to exhibit the *fac-simile* of a Constantinopolitan *caique*, he would soon have cause to thank me for the suggestion. These boats are of quite as easy pull as are the London wherries, if one may judge by the speed with which *one* Turkish boatman will row six or eight passengers to their destination. The topography of Constantinople causes a continual demand for water passage. The city in one place cut in twain by the port, or Golden Horn— in others by the Bosphorus, along which suburbs extending many miles, are far more easily approached by water than by land. The Sea of Marmora, bordering half the city, offers a brief and easy passage to the opposite half of Scutari, as well as to Galata and Pera; so that I should think ten thousand watermen a mitigated number to name as being employed in constant locomotion.* The locality of the Black Sea, Bosphorus, the Sea of Marmora, and the surrounding mountains of Olympus, and the blast that sweeps from eastern Caucasus, cause frequent gales which agitate the waters traversed by the pair-oared boats in all directions, and such as would swamp a London wherry in a minute. But the build of the *caiques* is such as to enable them to "live," when even the smaller boats of ships of war would run much danger. I have been out in Marmora, in the smallest sized *caique*, when it has

---

* Amongst other innumerable examples of the great honesty of the Turks, especially the lower orders, I will not let this occasion pass without recording, that strangers to the city are always advised by the British and French residents, to choose a Turkish boatman amongst the crowd of Turks, Greeks, and Armenians who ply for hire at the numerous stairs. "Take a Turk," they told me; "and when arrived at your journey's end, offer him a handful of coin, that he may *pay himself*, when you may depend upon paying less than you would have haggled for, with Greek or Armenian." I found it so.

blown a regular gale, and shipped less water than I surely should in any sea-going boat of equal size.

It is of equal efficacy against resistance to the water, whether the opposing surface be presented in an incline that approaches the perpendicular or horizontal—I mean, whether the head of a boat presents a very acute angle sinking into the water, or the head be broader, and the acuteness of the presented angle be horizontal to the water, like the bottom of a spoon. Such is the principle of the *caique's* construction. Their substance

is as thin as that of the London wherries, but their sides are three times as high, tapering gradually from stern to stem, so that when they are without a load, the latter sticks up in a very unsightly manner. But when the passengers are on board, the boat assumes its proper trim, presenting a line, rising a little to the head.

I herewith send you a rough sketch of something like a Turkish *caique*, which I have made rather too short for its bulk. A is the water-line when loaded; B when empty. I should be glad

to give directions to any boat-builder who may have sense enough to attend to this communication.

I think that as in the affair of the Montgolfier balloon, my suggestion may be followed, while the experimenter will disdain to seek the aid I offer, to save him from disappointment. Let your readers refer to Nos. 684, 685, and 686, of your valuable Magazine, and then look to the miserable doings of last week at the Surrey Zoological Gardens, with the grand Montgolfier balloon, the miserable failure

of which would have been prevented, had the projector consulted me, as was proposed by your correspondent in No. 685. Again I repeat, that although ballooning is a foolish thing, the Montgolfier principle is immeasurably preferable to the gas, as well in safety as in the chance of finding various currents of air, by rising and descending *ad libitum*, so as to be enabled to take, at one altitude or another, the direction desired.

I have the honour, &c.
F. MACERONI.

DESCRIPTION OF AN OIL TEST, INVENTED BY JOHN M'NAUGHT, ENGINEER, OF GLASGOW.

The oil test is an instrument for ascertaining the quality of oil, as applied to machinery, or used for burning; it shows exactly the different degrees of tenacity, and in what degree different oils lessen friction, or what the lubricating qualities of the oils submitted to trial are,—and enables any person, in a few minutes, to ascertain with certainty the relative values of that he means to purchase, and to compare the stock with the sample he has made trial of.

Description of the Engraving.—A is a cramp, with its screw for fixing the in-

strument by. P is a pulley for driving the arbor by; *d* is a piece of brass screwed upon the top of the arbor, and into which is fitted a piece of agate, or pebble; *e* is a moveable plate of brass, faced with hard steel; the top of the arbor goes through a hole in the upper plate, to keep it steady.

The agate and plate are perfectly flat, and truly ground, to fit each other, and between them the oil is put for trial; *f* is a pin, fastened into the top plate, which, when turned round against the sun, will come in contact with the pin

P, and endeavour to carry it forward towards the pin g, on the side next the cramp; the pins $g g$, in the frame, are stops to prevent its being carried too far out of the perpendicular. W is a sliding weight, being kept steady in any situation by a small spring; C is the centre upon which the lever turns, being supported in the upper part of the brass frame; the lever is divided into 150 equal parts. B is a counter-weight; when the mark upon the sliding weight corresponds with 0, the graduated leg of the lever will be horizontal, and the leg P will be perpendicular, playing freely between the pins $g g$, without touching either of them, and is then in equilibrium.

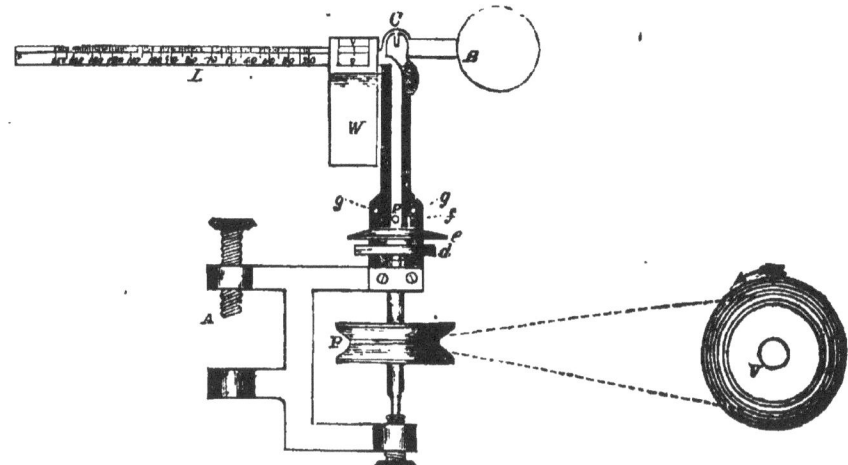

V is a pulley, with six or eight grooves, varying about one-eighth of an inch each, for the convenience of finding the desired speed, and for immediate application, is supposed to be fixed upon the point of a turning lathe spindle, the cramp being fixed to the lathe rest.

For permanent use, the instrument should be fixed in some convenient place by itself, where a steady uniform motion can be obtained; and the whole should be enclosed in a box, to keep it clean, and prevent its being hurt.

For a temporary trial, a common turning lathe will answer the purpose; let the instrument be fixed by its cramp to a T rest, or a piece of wood fixed into the socket of the rest; then fix a pulley of about $1\frac{1}{2}$ or 2 inches on the point of the lathe spindle, turning it conically, with six or eight grooves, varying about 1-8th of an inch; there will be no difficulty of finding the proper speed, by means of the different speeds of the lathe spindle, and the grooves of the small conical pulley. The rest will slide out or in, so as to make the driving band fit any of the grooves; by this means, it is easily brought to the required speed. It is preferable to give proper length of time to each trial, than to turn at a quick speed, as there can be but little chance of increase of temperature by a speed of 360 per minute, which is nearly the speed required.

To use the test, take off the top plate, wipe both plates clean, and apply about four drops of oil, or as much as will cover the piece of agate as high as the brass brim that surrounds it; more than this is needless, and less will not moisten the plates; the superfluous oil will fly off. A little experience will be the best guide in this matter. The top plate is now to be put on; set the spindle in motion, and let it run ten minutes for each trial; the motion will carry the pin in the upper plate round so as to act upon the pin in the lower part of the bent lever, and have a tendency to push it away, and lift the weight; it must therefore be shifted upon the lever, till the tenacity of the oil and the weight balance each other; or if done at the expiry of the time, it will answer the same purpose; the lower end of the lever to play freely between the stops without touching either; when it has run its time, observe the division the mark on the weight points out; mark it down; repeat the same for every trial, giving the same time. Take care to wipe the plates very clean at every trial, as the least particle of dirt, or fibre of cotton, will keep the plates off one another, and give a false result, or rather indicate nothing. The under plate will be best cleaned while running; the upper one must be done by hand. A soft rag must be used; not cotton waste. In a trial of a superior, after an inferior sort of oil, some remains of the former is apt still to adhere to the plates; it will be best, therefore, to apply a little of the oil to be tried upon the plates, wiping them well. This will take off any remains of the former; and will equally apply when inferior oil is tried after good.

To make sure, the trials may be repeated, and the average taken; but if the speed is the same, and the experiment properly made, the same result will be produced.

To ascertain what oils will last longest, the test may be charged with oil, and set on at the same time the spindles of a throstle or mule are oiled, then let it run the same as the former trial, viz. ten minutes; observe what division it points to; and afterwards, at the end of six or eight hours, it will be seen what difference in tenacity, and consequently, how much the friction of such machinery has increased by this particular oil. It is very doubtful if any vegetable oil will stand so severe a trial; but with sperm oil, it has been done, and found to alter about two divisions of the scale.

To judge of the correctness of the instrument, let a trial be made of equal parts of different oils. Suppose one of them to stand at 30, the other at 60, then the medium is 45. This will be the case if the mixtures have been equal; however, it will be sufficiently near to show that bad oil cannot be mixed with good, without being detected.

As oils sold under the same name differ so much in quality, it is impossible to state precisely the speed that will make any given oil point to a given number; but as comparative trial is all that is wanted, every person will be able to do this for themselves; but in order to make that as easy as possible, and that they may in some degree compare with one another, a small box of hog's lard accompanies each instrument sold by the inventor, as it is more uniform than oil, and easier carried. Let it be brought to such a speed as with the lard the weight will stand at 70, then good sperm oil will be 20, olive oil about 60, Neat's foot 60 to 70.

The remaining part of the scale will do for mixtures of oil and tallow, used for wheels and great geering. If any of the mixtures should be without the range of the scale, a slower motion may be given, which will have the same effect as lengthening the scale.

This description is adapted to the lever kind of tests, but will apply equally to the circular kind, with the spring: the mode of driving and application being the same in both.

From what has been explained and described, the principle upon which the instrument is constructed will be easily comprehended: thus, if with one kind of oil the tenacity will only lift the weight at 20, and another will lift it at 40, it is evident that the tenacity of the former is but one half of the latter, and will lessen friction in the same proportion, as far as oil is concerned: thereby leaving it in the option of a proprietor of machinery, whether he will save his money in oil, and waste it in the purchase of coals, or the waste of power otherwise, besides the injury of machinery.

THE "LYCEUM SYSTEM" IN AMERICA. —CONDITION OF THE WORKING CLASSES.

The second volume of the labours of the central Society of Education, just published,[*] includes, among its contents, —which consist of a variety of papers of very varying excellence, each the production of an individual, and edited only by the society in its aggregate character, —an essay on a subject which entitles it to some notice in our pages. It is from the pen of Thomas Wyse, Esq., the liberal member for Waterford, who has rendered himself rather conspicuous

* Central Society of Education, Second Publication. Papers by George Long, Esq., J. F. Duppa, Esq., Mons. de Fellenberg, G. R. Porter, Esq., F.R.S., etc.; also, the results of the Statistical Inquiries of the Society. London, 1838: Taylor and Walton: 8vo. p.p. 428.

of late by the zeal with which, at divers public meetings, he has advocated the question of National Education, and refers, as its title imports, to the " Lyceum System" in America, and its applicability to mechanics' institutions in England. He enters at considerable length into the history of the origin and progress of the associations known by the name of "Lyceums" in the United States, of which, in all their bearings, he is an enthusiastic admirer and an uncompromising champion,—while he is most strenuous in recommending the immediate adoption of some similar system in our own country, in order that we may not ere long find ourselves, to our own surprise and discomfiture, lagging far behind in the "march of intellect," and Jonathan "going a-head" at a railroad pace. This is a consummation, indeed, by no means devoutly to be wished, nor is it, we think, likely to be brought about in a very great hurry, in spite of the portentous warnings of the "Lyceum System." Mr. Wyse, in fact, in introducing the system to the acquaintance of the British public, displays infinitely more of the headlong impetuosity of the partizan, than the settled calmness of the philosopher. He can least of all be charged with understating the advantages of the system he wishes us to adopt; on the contrary, his zeal has so far outrun discretion in this respect,—he has indulged in such highflown hyperbolical flourishes as to the wonders it has effected, as to cast an air of doubt even over the more sober details of its history. Of this hyperbole we shall by-and-bye give a small specimen, extracting in the mean while a passage from Mr. W.'s sketch of the origin of "the system!"

" Like almost every thing in that country, the *Lyceum* system, as it is called, sprang from very humble beginnings. The first proposal made to the public, was in the 10th number of the American Journal of Education, in the year 1826. At this time, not even a designation by which it should be known had been adopted. A few weeks afterwards, the system was more formally proposed to the citizens of Milbury (Massachusetts); and a society organized by thirty or forty farmers and mechanics, under the name of ' The Milbury Branch of the American Lyceum,' was established. Twelve or fifteen towns in the same vicinity promptly followed their example, and united by delegates in forming ' The Worcester County Lyceum.' During the same season, several societies with similar titles and objects were constituted in the county of Windham (Connecticut); and so rapid was the progress, that already, in 1831, there existed not less than eight hundred or one thousand town Lyceums, fifty or sixty county Lyceums, and a general union of the whole, under the denomination of ' The National Lyceum.' "

All this is characteristic enough of Brother Jonathan's "slick-right away" method of doing business; but it remains to be seen what it was that he was thus pleased to *approbate* so considerably. We give Mr. Wyse's account :—

" There are three classes of Lyceums, one subordinate to the other: 1st, ' Town Lyceums;' 2nd, ' County Lyceums;' 3rd, ' State Lyceums;' finally, ' The National Lyceum ;' to which, as to a great national board for the management of subsidiary education, is entrusted the direction and controul of the entire system. The ' Town Lyceums,' which also assume the designation of ' Branches of the American Lyceum,' are usually composed of the principal inhabitants of the town ; the life subscription is twenty, the annual, two dollars; threefourths of which are applied to the purchase of apparatus, books, tools, &c., for the use of the Town Lyceum, and the remaining onefourth is forwarded to the County Lyceum, for the purpose of defraying the expenses of county libraries, apparatus, and collections too heavy for the Town Lyceums—of maps and agents for town and county surveys, statistical inquiries, &c. &c. They hold meetings for lectures and essay discussions, in literature and science, at stated periods ; and establish classes in various courses, under the superintendence of their lecturers, for the education of their junior members, and the greater improvement of the instruction pursued in schools.

" The ' County Lyceums' propose the same objects (though on a larger scale) as the Town Lyceums, promote the interests of the Lyceums generally throughout the country, and co-operate with the State and National Lyceums in the same manner as the Town Lyceums do with them, in all measures recommended for the advancement of national education and the general diffusion of knowledge. The members consist of delegates from the several Town Lyceums in the county, each Lyceum having the right of sending three. The County Lyceum holds semi-annual meetings, for the purpose of hearing reports or statements from the Town Lyceums, supporting discussions and pronouncing addresses, or reading papers upon any subject relative to the theory or practice of education. They procure, moreover, in proportion to the amount of their funds, a county library, apparatus, collection in natural history, mineralogy, models, &c.; appoint a supervisor, or civil engineer, to aid in surveys for town or county maps, &c.; agents for statistical inquiries, &c.; and, finally, carry into execution any other arrangements for the general or special objects of the Lyceum System throughout their jurisdiction."

It must be confessed that all this looks very well on paper,—above all, it must be admitted that if there be any magic in the word " Lyceum," it is put to the proof often enough. Puzzled as the originators of the plan were to find a title at first, it is evident that they had no sooner hit upon one than it " took" amazingly; to such an extent, indeed, that it would sometimes seem to be considered that the efficacy of the scheme lay in its name alone, so pertinaciously is " the Lyceum System" dragged in at every opportunity. Except in its title, a " Town Lyceum" apparently differs but little from Literary Institutions of older date; and as to the " Lyceums" of a higher grade,—the County, State, and National Lyceums,—why, sooth to say, the higher they get, the less is their utility perceptible. If the Town Lyceums were gone, there would be an end of the whole system;—the loss of the County Lyceums would derange it in some degree:—but the disappearance of the " State" and " National" institutions would have but little effect, further than in abridging the importance of the " delegates" who attend them, chiefly for no other purpose than to hear lengthy orations on new *systems* of education, or joining in wordy discussions of unprofitable questions. Such, at least, is the impression left on our minds by the little Mr. Wyse has to say on the subject, setting aside mere panegyric, of which he is never tired. The State Lyceums are so completely purposeless, that they have evidently been established for the sake of " symmetry" alone; while the most we are told of the grand National Lyceum itself, is contained in the paragraph which records the titles of three prize essays, produced under its auspices, on different abstruse points of pedagogical science!

Whatever have been the effects produced by the system, therefore, we are inclined to attribute a very minute portion to the vast organisation which Mr. Wyse holds to be the all in all, and is so earnest in recommending for immediate adoption in Great Britain, taking the already-existing mechanics' institutions as a nucleus. Why mechanics' institutions should be selected it would be difficult to guess, since in America the Town Lyceums evidently most resemble the far more numerous body of our general literary and scientific institutions, to which, indeed, the mechanics' institutions are daily more and more assimilating in every thing but name. Add a museum to be collected by the members, and an additional class or two to these already existing, and you have a " Town Lyceum" complete and perfect at once, without any further trouble. We are not sanguine enough to anticipate that the consequences of such an improvement would be so miraculous as Mr. Wyse gravely assures us those of the " Lyceum System" have been on the other side of the Atlantic. These are indeed almost quite incredible; *ex. gr.*

" Thousands of children, of not more than eight or ten years old, know now more of geology, mineralogy, botany, statistical facts, &c., &c.,—in fine, of what immediately concerns their daily interests and occupations, —than was probably known thirty years ago by any five individuals in the United States."—p. 216.

If this soberly-stated fact be not conclusive as to the merits of the Lyceum System, what will be? Of its perfect accuracy there need, of course, be no more doubt than that the knowledge of geology, botany, statistical facts, &c., is " what immediately concerns the daily interests and occupations" of the children in the States!—As, however, we could not expect such prodigious results in the old country, even were the Lyceum System adopted as fully as Mr. Wyse could wish, it may happen that the Americans will be left to the exclusive enjoyment of its exquisite organization for some time longer, maugre the efforts of the Central Society of Education. We must jog on as we best may, without the " immense advantages of Union," and even perhaps without the " Minister of Public Instruction," recommended by Mr. Wyse and his liberal compeers as the best succedaneum.

The former volume published by the Society included an interesting paper on the physical condition of the working classes in London, drawn from statistical facts, some of them of a very minute description, collected at the expense of the Society. This article is resumed in the present volume; and from its commencement, which refers to one of the Irish "rookeries" by which the metropolis is infested, we shall quote a passage, both on account of its intrinsic interest, and as a specimen of the manner in which the curious inquiry is conducted, and the economy of a human *warren* laid bare.

" The first district examined was a place called Callmel Buildings, situated within a few yards of one of the most fashionable squares in the metropolis. These buildings, comprising twenty-six houses, are almost wholly inhabited by Irish catholics. The houses contain 264 rooms; 210 of which were occupied, and fifty-four vacant, at the time of the inquiry. The smallest number of individuals then inhabiting any one of the houses, was twenty-two, and the largest number was forty-eight; the average number to each house being thirty-five persons. There were in these twenty-six houses seventy-seven families and sixty-four single persons, who severally occupied only a share in a single room; 120 families and fourteen single persons occupied severally one room, or among them 134 rooms; eleven families and one single person occupied severally two rooms, and one family occupied three rooms. The rooms which were shared in common by different families were fifty-one in number. In twenty-seven of these one family was joined by single persons, varying in number from one to six. In each of eleven rooms there were two families; in nine rooms two families, and from one to four single persons in addition. In each of two rooms there were three families. In one room were four families and one single person; and one other room was inhabited by five single persons.

" Of the 288 families inhabiting these twenty-six houses, forty-five live in apartments which may be called airy; while the remaining 243, or five-sixths of the whole, occupy close and ill-ventilated rooms, some of which, according to the report of the visitors, are unfit for human habitation. In some respects, the houses are more comfortable than those described in the former volume, the drainage being good, and the supply of water abundant; while the proportion of families whose dwellings are provided with shelves and cupboards is greater (124 out of the 288).

" As regards the intellectual condition of the parents, it was found that 203 could read, and some among that number could write; but that 244, or 55 per cent. of the whole, could neither read nor write. Of the children, 450 in number, 262, including 117 under five years of age, could neither read nor write. Only 114 of the whole number, or about one-fourth, went to school at the time the inquiry was made. * * * The sum paid for schooling appears unusually large, considering the condition of the parents; the average weekly payment for each scholar, where regular payments are made, being 5½d. There is a school in the court, attended by about fifty scholars, held in a room twelve feet square, and eight and a half high, which is the sole dwelling of the schoolmaster, his wife, and six children. The unwholesome condition of the air, under these circumstances, may be easily conceived. The mode of payment to the teacher of this school is remarkable and characteristic. A kind of club, which does not consist exclusively of the parents of the scholars, meets every Saturday evening at a public-house; when, after some hours spent in drinking and smoking, a subscription is raised, and handed over to the schoolmaster, who forms one of the company, and who is expected to spend a part of the money in regaling the subscribers."— page 253.

In the remaining part of the article, a similar examination is entered into of the condition of several country parishes, the result of which, is, of course, strikingly different. Here, however, we meet with an instance of that inaccuracy which is so common in statistical papers, and detracts so considerably from their value. The writer professes to give a view of the condition of three neighbouring parishes in the county of Essex; which, as he observes, present very great points of contrast. And well they may. One of these parishes only (St. Osyth) in point of fact, belongs to that county, the other two, Porlock and Dunster, represented as composing part of the same union, being really situated in Somerset, at a distance of between two and three hundred miles! Where such a blunder as this could creep in, what dependence can be placed on the minuter details, which cannot in their nature be so readily detected? This author, too, in his zeal to display the benefits of education, resorts to prison and workhouse returns, in order to show how few persons " superiorly educated" have been reduced to either, in comparison to those who have not had the same advantage. The fallacy of this presumed test need not be pointed out, at any rate, when it is unaccompanied by similar tables of the relative numbers of the same classes *outside* as well as *in*. While the numbers of the "superiorly educated" are comparatively so small, they may well be expected to add but little to our pauper and prisoner population, even were their circumstances similar to those of the classes by which our gaols and poorhouses are chiefly peopled. What would the author of this paper himself think of an enthusiastic dancing-master, who should insist that dancing was a sure preventative against crime ; and gravely maintain his position by statistical tables, showing the small proportion of offenders who could make a graceful figure in a quadrille or cotillion, compared to the masses who could not dance at all, or only manage to shuffle through a jig ?

Among the remaining papers in the volume, we are sorry to say, is one calling for the severest animadversion. This is a letter from M. de Fellenberg, the celebrated founder of the academy at Hofwyl, detailing his ideas on education, and written entirely in the French language ; in which language the Society have sent it forth to the *English* public, in a professedly *English* work, without a word of apology, and without the slightest whisper of a translation ! We hope, as this is the first, it will also be the last time such an occurrence will need to be complained of, as the Society cannot fail to perceive how ridiculous is such a procedure, the moment their attention is fairly called to it.

In the concluding paper, the absurdities of many of the education-mongers of the day are very happily exposed, in a manner, different indeed from that of more than one of the preceding articles, in which some of these very absurdities receive a full measure of applause, in the usual wholesale style. The infant schools, above all, come in for a full share of punishment, which is administered fairly enough, merely by means of illustrative quotations from the books in use at these crushing-mills of the infant intellect. Most of these are so exquisitely ridiculous, that they require no heightening from comment. What need have we of a "Lyceum System" in England, when our "children," not of "eight or ten years old," but of two or three, are stuffed full of knowledge by committing to memory such easy and flowing sing-song as the following, *which is actually extracted from an Infant School Manual?*

> "The organ curiously designed,
>   By which it is we hear,
> Which catches modulated wind,
>   Is simply called the ear ;
> The organ of the sense the smell
>   Resides within the nose,
> To which, unfelt, invisible,
>   The spreading odour flows !"

NOTES AND NOTICES.

French & English Railways.—The defeat of the French Ministers on the Railway question, by unsettling all affairs of that nature for the next twelve-month, has made it quite certain that the English part of the railway line from London to Paris will be ready long before the French. While our Southampton line is already opened to the extent of 23 miles from the metropolis, not a yard of that from Paris to Rouen and Havre is yet laid down ; and the South Western Railway to Dover is in a forward state, while the line on the opposite side as yet exists solely in the brains of its projectors, and seems likely to do so for some time yet to come.

Improvement in Gunnery.—We understand that Mr. Symington has invented a method of loading artillery, which diminishes the risk of accident, needs only one man instead of two to serve the gun with wadding, increases materially the projectile force of the ball, causes the common gun to act in the same manner as a rifle piece, and is applicable to guns on the present construction. Its introduction would produce an important change in the mode of naval warfare, inasmuch as that vessels during an engagement would, instead of coming to close quarters, or being carried by boarding, be enabled, by firing "long ball," as it is termed, to decide the contest scientifically—the gaining of the victory depending more on the destruction of property than the destruction of life.

Gas Stoves.—Sir,—Your intelligent correspondent, Mr. Baddeley, accuses me, in your last number, of inconsistency in recommending a cup of water to be placed over the gas-stove described by "Evander." If he will refer to the description of that stove, he will find his mistake, inasmuch as the products of the consumed gas are not, in that arrangement, evolved into the apartment, which, therefore, cannot receive the water formed by the combination of the oxygen and hydrogen.—I am, &c. F. MACERONI.

Complete Sets of the Mechanics' Magazine may now be had, twenty-seven volumes, half-cloth, price £11. 7s.

☞ *British and Foreign Patents taken out with economy and despatch ; Specifications, Disclaimers, and Amendments, prepared or revised : Caveats entered ; and generally every Branch of Patent Business promptly transacted. A complete list of Patents from the earliest period (15 Car. II. 1675,) to the present time may be examined. Fee 2s. 6d. ; Clients, gratis.*

LONDON: Printed and Published for the Proprietor, by W. A. Robertson, at the Mechanics' Magazine Office, No. 6, Peterborough-court, between 135 and 136, Fleet-street.—Sold by A. & W. Galignani, Rue Vivienne, Paris.

Mechanics' Magazine,

MUSEUM, REGISTER, JOURNAL, AND GAZETTE.

No. 775.] SATURDAY, JUNE 16, 1838. [Price 3d.

SIR JAMES ANDERSON'S STEAM-CARRIAGE BOILER.

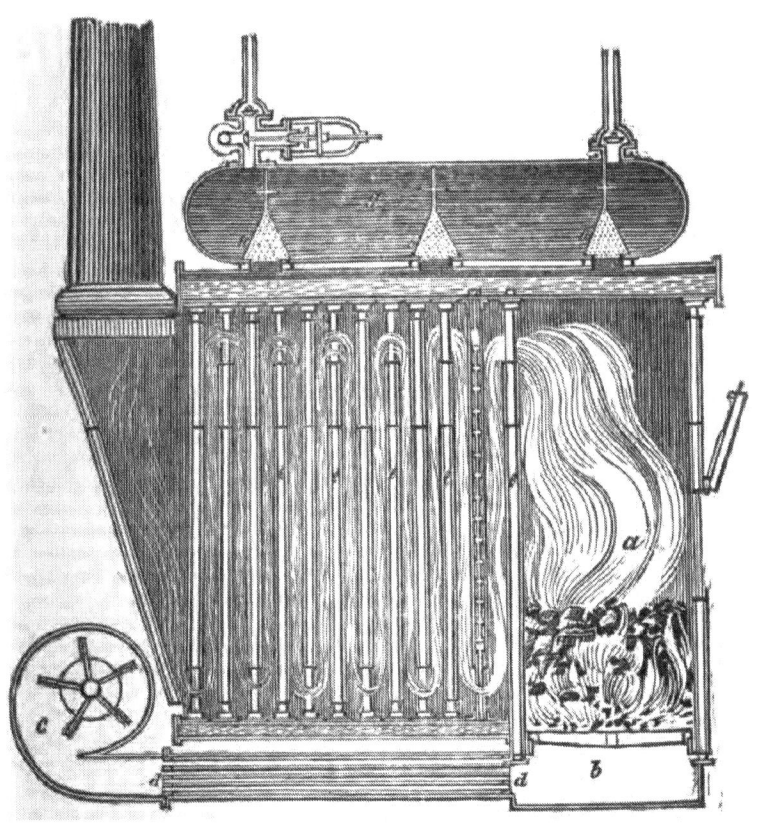

THE STEAM CARRIAGE AND WAGGON COMPANY—SIR JAMES ANDERSON'S STEAM CARRIAGE BOILER.

In a recent No. (778) we briefly noticed a company, which has lately been brought forward for the purpose of working steam carriages and waggons upon common roads. Our remarks were depreciatory of the project as a commercial enterprise, because we considered that the inventor, whose plan was advertised as being adopted by the *pseudo* Company, had done nothing to warrant the confidence of the public in his abilities to overcome the numerous difficulties which are incident to common road locomotion—and because we regarded it as a mere individual speculation, under the guise of a public undertaking, to put into temporary operation the individual speculator's patent. We considered, that if the company had been formed with the *bonâ fide* view of giving the public all the advantages that are obtainable from common road locomotion, and at the same time, with a *chance* of remunerating those who advanced the capital, the directors would have chosen their plan from amongst the inventors who have devoted their attention, time, or fortune to the attainment of the desired object, with the greatest success. As being next in importance to railways and steam navigation, we have always been anxious to make public all that has been projected and effected in this branch of commercial transit; and we may mention, as amongst those whose experiments have been recorded in our pages, and who have all done more than Sir James Anderson, the names of Gurney, Maceroni, Ogle, Maudslay and Field, the Heatons of Birmingham, Sir Charles Dance, Dr. Church, and above all, Mr. Walter Hancock. We believe, that if any thing is to be done with steam carriages on common roads, this last-named gentleman is he who is most likely to effect it. For twelve or fourteen years his undeviating aim has been the perfection of his steam carriage; he has built more carriages, travelled a far greater number of miles, and has, consequently, had far greater experience in the matter than any other engineer. In a letter detailing his travelling on the Paddington road in the autumn of 1836 (see No. 685), Mr. Hancock mentioned that he was preparing calculations, prov-

ing, that even that traffic, unfavourable as the attendant circumstances were, was carried on at a profit; and he has since that time assured us to the same effect, taking interest of capital, wear and tear, expenses of fuel, stations, steersmen, engineers, and every thing else into consideration. If then, such be the fact, and we have no reason to doubt Mr. Hancock's statement, the sooner the matter is taken up and put into practice by enterprising capitalists the better.

Our only motive in thus putting forward Mr. Hancock's steam-carriage, is a desire to see steam locomotion flourish, not only on railways, but, if practicable, on common roads. We should have thought that the course to be pursued by a *bonâ fide* public company would have been to advertise a public competition, engaging to adopt the plan which should fulfil certain fixed conditions. Every steam carriage inventor, and his backing capitalist, would then have an opportunity of putting his locomotive to the test, and with a fair prospect of remuneration in case of success. If the result of such a trial, fairly conducted, should be against Mr. Hancock, and in favour of Sir James Anderson, or any one else, we should rest content. We certainly, however, think that an undertaking, professing to be public, should either have chosen for its adoption that plan which had already been put to the most extensive and severe tests, or have left the matter open to competition.

To enable all who are interested in the matter to judge for themselves of the merits of Sir James Anderson's plan, the adopted of the Steam Carriage and Waggon Company, we give without expressing any opinion of our own, *pro* or *con.*, the following description of his boiler, in the peculiar applicability of which, to locomotives, we presume the pith of his plan lies. We extract the description from the *Farmers' Magazine* for the present month, in which it forms part of a high-flown article in favour of common road, in opposition to railway locomotion. The writer, we are sorry to say, appears to have but a very partial knowledge of either branch of the subject; in his mechanical calculations he is altogether at fault; and, moreover, we think, that the road steamer could be more favourably supported by argument, in connection with, than as a rival to the railway.

"We shall proceed to give a description of Sir James Anderson's new patent boiler. That part of a locomotive engine being, as it were, the heart, or seat of life of the machine.

"The above engraving affords a side view of the boiler, partly in section, for the better illustration of its construction. At *a* is the fire chamber, and at *b* the ash pit. A blowing machine is represented at *c* by which the air is forced through an assemblage of pipes *d d* (contained in a condensing cylinder) into the ash pit, whence it ascends between the fire bars and excites the combustion of the fuel; the current of heated gases thence ascend, and passing over the first of a series of broad flat water chambers (the edges of which *e e* are only seen in this view), it descends between the first and second, then turning under the second, it ascends between the second and third, and so upwards and downwards throught the series, as indicated by the current of flame until it reaches the chimney *f*. The sides and top cases of the fire chamber, as well as the sides and top cases of the boiler are also water chambers, in order to generate as much steam as possible within the space, and to prevent any undue radiation of caloric, so as to adapt the apparatus in an especial manner to steam boats as well as to steam carriages. One of the water chambers is shown in section for the better comprehension of their construction. They are formed of two flat plates each containing about fifteen superficial feet placed about two inches asunder, and held in this position by the interposition of peculiarly formed frames of solid iron, through which and the external plates they are strongly rivetted. The plates are thus united at about every three inches distance over the whole surface, so as to render it impossible by any force of steam that can be generated to tear them asunder. The water is supplied to the boiler by the ordinary means, which fills the lower horizontal tube and rises thence uniformly through short vertical tubes into the water chambers *e e* which are always kept full to the top and even partly filling the horizontal tube above, whence the steam enters the reservoir through the perforated caps which impede such aqueous particles as might be borne upwards along with the steam, and returns them into the boiler, while the purified yet dense vapour passes freely through into the reservoir for the supply of the engine." "A part of the steam is condensed, and returned to the boiler by the force pumps. This condensation is effected by discharging the steam into two large horizontal cylinders fixed underneath the carriage, each of them containing an as-

semblage of small tubes, through which the cold air is forced to supply the furnace."

"A boiler of this kind was, we understand, completed about fifteen months back, and has continued to work every day since most successfully, without producing a leak or the slightest derangement, and this notwithstanding the steam has frequently been raised to upwards of 500lbs. pressure upon each square inch of surface!"

MR. WOONE'S SUBSTITUTE FOR WOOD ENGRAVING, NOT A NEW INVENTION —METAL PIPE MAKING—FILE CUTTING MACHINERY—INVENTION OF STEAM NAVIGATION — LOSS OF POWER BY THE CRANK—DAVENPORT'S ENGINE.

Sir,—I have very often reflected upon the great difficulty of properly determining the priority of inventions; one thing, however, is very clear, that a person who makes any useful discovery, or brings forward an ingenious invention, must bestow much thought and trouble before he can reduce his first crude ideas into a practical form, and therefore would fain believe himself, not only as a *true* but the *first* inventor or discoverer. You will admit, however, that it is very possible that different persons may invent the same thing at the same time, or near the same time, or even at distant and different times, without the slightest knowledge, or communication of each other's discoveries, and yet each be entitled to the full honour of being an original inventor or discoverer; I will here remark that in all these cases of similar inventions by different persons, if the circumstances which originated the invention or discovery, were properly detailed, they would always be found to carry along with them internal evidence of the invention having been made by the persons claiming that honor; for it often happens that the most useful and important inventions and discoveries have had their origin in some very trivial occurrence, which has been seized at the happy moment by an ingenious mind, the idea improved upon, and ultimately turned to the advantage of himself and others. In mathematics this is indeed a very common occurrence; and speaking from experience, upwards of twenty-five years ago I thought I had made some very clever discoveries in that science, but when I became possessed of Dr. Hutton's Mathematical and Philosophical Dictionary, I found that the same things had been done by others, particularly the Hindoos, Arabians, and Italians, many hundred years ago. Although I do not go so far as to implicitly believe Solomon's proverb "that there is nothing new under the sun," yet I willingly admit that it is extremely difficult to bring forward any invention or discovery which may not have had a prototype, some faint resemblance, or which has been in some degree attempted in past years, or even in past ages.

I will begin with Mr. Woone's substitute for wood engraving, and shew you and your readers that I many times attempted a precisely similar thing about thirty-three years ago. During the years 1804 and 1805, being then intimately acquainted with some goldsmiths and silversmiths, I often went to their shops, and had frequent opportunities of observing their operations in the precious metals, and in silver plated goods. I observed that silversmiths frequently with a brush spread their work over with a white composition, which on inquiry I was informed was flour and water, with fine whiting, boiled up together and thoroughly mixed; this was always done when they soldered on borders, beads, and other devices of silver, upon silver plated goods, or when they filled hollow plated articles with soft solder to give them weight, strength, and solidness. On inquiry I was informed that the aforesaid composition was spread over the plated goods, and dried on, to prevent the solder sticking on the surface where it was not wanted; for in that case it would either eat off the silver, or spoil the colour and look of the articles. I had several times observed, that when the whiting composition did by any means get scratched or rubbed off, that the solder would immediately run into the vacancy and assume curious forms; and it was this very circumstance which suggested to me the discovery of coating over polished plates of metal with a wet composition of whiting, plaster of paris, and similar substances, and when dried to trace thereon with a needle or pointrel any letters or drawings. It was the more natural that this idea should occur to me, for there was scarcely a day passed at that period on which I was not more or less visiting printing offices, &c., and had previously seen both wood cuts and copper plate engraving, and had occasionally witnessed the casting of the metallic

types used by printers. I thought at first that I had hit upon something that would prove very useful; and made many attempts upon plates of brass and copper, and also on plates of polished steel: I tried many castings both with soft solder and with type metal, but could never get a cast to my liking of any drawing, even though it were not more than three or four inches square. I found many difficulties in the practice, that could not have been expected from the theory of the discovery; for example, if I wished to have a number of fine lines in the casting, I found it absolutely necessary that the coat of whiting composition should be spread very thin upon the metallic plates; and however thin it was spread, I found that when there was a number of fine lines to be drawn close, it would often happen that the composition would peel off for two or three lines together, so that what should have been three or four very fine lines, formed only one broad and coarse line; and I found that this difficulty was always increased with the increase of thickness in the composition spread over the plates of metal. For coarse lines, a greater thickness of the composition was necessary than when fine lines were desired, which still increased the difficulty; and by having the composition spread very thin, although fine lines were produced, there was then so little of depth or boldness in the casting, that the balls in spreading the printing ink over these fine lines, were liable to fill them up, and to touch upon the bottom of the open spaces where the lines were far apart, and thus produce imperfect impressions. And again, after having completed drawings without any of the composition peeling off under the operation of the tracing needle, I have known when the melted metal came to be cast upon it for the intended type plate, that while one part thereof was beautifully cast, in other places large portions of the composition had separated from the metallic plate, and that the casting was thereby utterly spoiled. Making the prepared plate something hotter than the hand could bear to handle, had a tendency to insure a good casting. As before observed, it was extremely difficult to make the composition adhere firmly to the whole surface of the metallic plate: if there was too little flour therein, it possessed little or no adhesiveness; and if too much flour, it would sometimes swell up or become spongy I found that very smooth plates of steel and of iron seemed best for the purpose, as in the course of two or three days after the composition had been spread over them, a slight degree of oxidization would take place, which had the effect of making the composition adhere more firmly to the iron and steel surfaces, than it would to the surface of any other of the metals. This suggests to me, that perhaps a finely-powdered ferruginous oxide mixed with the whiting and plaster of Paris, might have the effect of attaching the composition more firmly to the metallic surfaces on which the drawings and castings should be made.

I have here given a circumstantial account of my attempts at type-plate casting; and the practical illustration here detailed of the difficulties attendant on these experiments, will, I think, without any disparagement to Mr. Woone, if he be a young man, not only convince him that his discovery is no new affair to me, but also that I was well acquainted therewith long before he could have thought of it at all. I only wish that Mr. Woone may be more successful in type-plate casting than myself; and although I have just read the splendid account of Mr. Woone's very ingenious discovery in the *Weekly Dispatch* of last Sunday, my opinion, founded on personal experience therein, does not incline me to expect the very brilliant performances that some persons appear to anticipate; neither do I believe that it is likely to supersede the long-established mode of engraving portraits and other works of the fine arts on plates of steel and copper. I should conclude it may prove very useful in casting types for mathematical diagrams, such as are found in Euclid's Elements and in other geometrical works where the lines are neither required to be very close, nor yet very fine.

Invention of making Lead, Block Tin, and other Metal Pipes, without a Seam and without soldering.—At the opportunities offered by visits to goldsmiths' workshops before mentioned, I had often seen straight parallel slips of sheet silver, brass, &c., turned up until both the edges thereof met, then taken to the draw bench and drawn through the draw plate into tubes, which were often soldered in the seam or meeting of the two edges of the metal. And having seen square ingots of gold, silver, brass, and copper

cast, I reasoned within myself, and said, why not cast round ingots of these metals with a core or plug in the middle, which could be taken out when the casting was cold? Thus a great quantity of the hollow tube wire could soon be made that would not want soldering, and would do very well for the joints of tea and coffee pot covers, and of tobacco and snuff box lids. I also thought a great deal of making lead water-pipes by the same process. A few years after, a person, as I was told, about the neighbourhood of Norton Folgate or Shoreditch, took out a patent for the same invention; this I had much desired and intended to have done myself if I could have got the means of procuring the patent: indeed, if the cost of a patent had been no more in England than in America, where the expense is only 8*l.*, I should within these last thirty-two years have taken out patents for more than twenty useful inventions.

File cutting by Machinery.—About the year 1807, I invented several plans of machines for file cutting, the principal feature of which was a leading screw to each, to advance the cutter, and *vice versa*, of different degrees of fineness in the thread or worm thereof to regulate the distance between each cut, and thereby determine the fineness of the file. About a year ago, a person took out a patent for file-cutting engines, but I have never seen the machinery. I have still in my possession one of my plans, designed in 1807 or 1808, so that my invention was about thirty years prior to that of the patent just mentioned.*

Inventions and Improvements in Steam Navigation.—My attention was long ago turned to this department of the mechanical sciences; even in my early youth I thought of propelling vessels by steam; I turned my attention, previous to the year 1807, to the inventing of machinery for this purpose, without knowing at that time that any previous attempts had been made by any other person to effect the same object. My plan resembled that now generally in use, except that the axis

---

* Various patents have at different times been taken out for file-cutting machinery; among others we may mention the names of Nicholson, Cook, Shilton, Vickers, Stocker, and Ericsson. None of these inventions have, we believe, been found to answer, with the exception of Capt. Ericsson's, which is now in successful and extensive operation at one of the first houses in Sheffield.—Ed. M. M.

of the paddle wheels had two bevelled cog wheels upon it, fixed upon a collar or socket that would slide backwards and forwards when required, and was thereby brought to act upon either one or the other of two other bevelled cog-wheels upon the axis of the fly-wheel, by which arrangement the motion of the paddle-wheels could be instantly reversed. After three or four weeks, I may have more leisure and opportunity than at present, and will call on you, Mr. Editor, and show you a letter which I received in the year 1808 from the highest scientific authority in the kingdom,* being a reply to my proposal for navigating ships by steam; in which the very learned and illustrious personage told me that he could not hold out any hopes of the success of such a project, as various attempts had been made to accomplish the same purpose, but they had all failed; for, he said, it was not possible to make machinery strong enough to resist the rough waters of the ocean, &c. Thus we see titled persons, holding high offices, imbued with learned prejudices, are always ready to retard the march of useful improvements; it was thus in the year 1808, and is so still in 1838. Therefore, Mr. Editor, neither yourself nor your readers need be surprised when I state, that some of my inventions for steam navigation, designed by me these twenty years past, although superior to anything yet in use, as you may judge from the certificates I sent you on the 26th of last month†, still remain neglected for want of means, and may perhaps be forgotten, though my engines would not take up half the room, nor consume half the fuel, that the same power engines do, on board the very best steam-ships that have ever yet been constructed in this kingdom; and would, in such a ship as the *Great Western*, enable her to carry about 750 tons more, in freight and passengers, than on the present plan.

Loss of Power by the Cranks of Steam Engines.—I do not know of any publication having so great a number of very intelligent and talented correspondents as the *Mechanics' Magazine*; and though I have the greatest respect for their ge-

neral skill and intelligence, I must beg leave to remark that some of them do sometimes appear to write in great haste and upon the impulse of the moment, and thereby take either a partial or limited view of the subject under consideration. In reply to your correspondent "W. H. T." (in No 771) who very justly remarks upon the long circuit that the crank pin makes compared with the length of the stroke of the piston; I hope he will not feel offended when I assure him that I am as perfectly acquainted with that circumstance as himself or any engineer in the British Empire; but I must remind him that the circumference of the circle, and the leverage of the crank under different positions during its revolution, are totally distinct and different matters in mechanical science, and must not be confounded or mistaken one for the other. I could hardly help smiling at the remark of W. H. T. when he says there is a want of greater nicety in calculating the length of the leverage or average of the sines. To this I beg leave to observe, that the numbers, or natural sines, which I have taken from Hutton's Tables, are so very correct, that they will give amount of leverage to the thousandth part of an inch, even if the crank were ten feet in length. Were I disposed so to do, I could easily demonstrate that, considering its extreme simplicity, the crank is the most efficient mechanical contrivance extant; and I could further prove, that the amount of its performance would be on a par with various other contrivances; yet this is no argument that it might not be dispensed with, and something better substituted for it. That which my essays have endeavoured to prove, is, that its power is not equable, and that, in consequence thereof, the amount of that power is not near so great as it has generally been thought to be.

Reply to Objections on Davenport's Engine.—In No 772 of your Magazine, a gentleman of Manchester, who signs himself F., states what he considers very great objections against the powers and velocity that I have assigned to Davenport's Engine in No. 763 of your publication; this gentleman particularly objects to the great velocity of the wheel and he thinks it cannot exceed ten feet per second. He says that no increase of power can arise from increasing the diameter of the wheel,

---

'and that its power will depend entirely on the size of the magnets." The last thirteen words only, quoted from this gentleman are a perfect truism; but take the bearing and import of the whole quotation together, as above given, it is one mass of error. This correspondent has taken a very hasty, partial, and narrow view of the subject, and has totally overlooked some important considerations which should not be lost sight of: viz. that I had founded my calculations on the proportions and powers of Mr. Davenport's working model engine, as given by Mr. Davenport himself or his friends, and contained in No. 786 of the *Mechanics' Magazine*; secondly, that the velocity was not stated by me at all as the result of any calculations of mine, but is taken as a matter of fact from the statements of Mr. Davenport, who positively asserts that the wheel revolves one thousand times per minute. If a wrong statement has been made, I ought not to be blamed for that. But let your correspondent F. recollect, that if the statement be true, that the wheel turns round 1000 times per minute, although only six inches diameter, its velocity will by calculation be found to be 18,849 inches, or 1570,⅘ feet per minute, which is twenty-six feet six inches per second, nearly three times the velocity which F. says it is possible for the wheel to attain. Why F should limit the velocity to 10 feet per second, he has not made satisfactorily appear to me; for as far as I have observed, it appears to me, that the effects of magnetism and electricity travel with the velocity of lightning.

Thirdly, if your correspondent had closely examined my calculations and the dimensions I had given, No. 763 of your Magazine, he would have seen that there was such an increase in the galvanic batteries as was proportionate to the size of each wheel, and sufficient to act efficiently on magnets of a magnitude capable of acting with all the power required upon the wheel, however large the wheel might be; I can assure Mr. F., that if the wheel was increased to certain dimensions, that all the other parts of the engine were by my calculations allowed to be increased in the same ratio.

Fourthly, if F. had carefully examined these calculations, he would soon have discovered that I had allowed more than ten times the battery power that Mr. Davenport asserts would be sufficient to impel a great ship across the ocean; for Mr. Davenport is reported to have stated that a battery as big as a moderate sized barrel, consisting of a few thin sheets of zinc and copper, would be sufficient to drive a large ship over the seas. I smiled when I read this assertion, for really I did not believe it; such powers appeared to me as surpassing magic itself, and this was the cause of my making the aforesaid calculations, and soon convinced me that Mr. Davenport himself had not made any calculations at all on the subject, but had been influenced by hope and guided by conjecture, in his asserting that a battery the bulk of a moderate sized barrel, and a few sheets of zinc and copper, would be sufficient to propel a ship. I found by mathematical calculation that this was totally impossible, and that by comparing the dimensions of the batteries of his working model engine, with one the size of a barrel, that the increase of power to do this, would be far beyond any increase of power to be obtained either by the squares or cubes of the given dimensions; and therefore it would be quite irrational to expect any such great power from so small a battery. In fact, I found by my calculations, that it would require about 6500 superficial square feet of sheet zinc and copper to perform this. I have not my calculations by me just now, but I believe, from recollection, that this is very nearly correct.

Once for all, let me most respectfully assure your very numerous readers, that if the performances and dimensions of Mr. Davenport's working model-engine have been truly reported by him and his friends, then they may rest well assured that my calculations will give the sizes and capabilities of the engines which I have described in the former numbers of your Magazine; but also let them remember, that those persons who draw their judgments from supposition or conjecture, will always be found to differ widely from the conclusions founded on mathematical calculations. In conclusion, I will here remark, that if I do not shortly hear of some more satisfactory details and more minute descriptions of Mr. Davenport's engine, I shall begin to suspect that there has been very gross exaggeration and much misrepresentation from our Transatlantic friends concerning the powers and performances of this invention.

I remain, Mr. Editor,
    Yours most respectfully,
        THOMAS OXLEY.

Teacher of Mathematics, &c.
Elizabeth Place, Westminster Road.
30th May, 1838.

TOUCHING VARIOUS MODERN IMPROVEMENTS AND DISCOVERIES.

Sir,—Far be it from me to say to the stream or tide of improvement, "hitherto and no farther;" but on the legitimate grounds of discovery itself, there may be a right and a wrong application, and this is all I bring to the "rack" or the "question." To illustrate my position. I think *asphaltum* a very notable article of combustion, and, as *fuel*, a very *useful* one; but to *pave* our streets withal, here, indeed, is madness "without method." What could save our towns and cities from total destruction by fire, in such a case as this? Our streets would become lava torrents of liquid fire, as difficult to extinguish as the "Greek fire" in the olden time. Nay, the meteor in the thunder storm might kindle it, and the fate of the "Cities of the Plain" be ours, though the judgment in their case was specific and penal. Harper and Joyce's "wonder" is a parallel example; but the expence they have recklessly incurred is sufficient punishment, if none in the mean time have indeed fallen victims to their ignorance of the principles of chemistry. A few experiments satisfied me of the dangers of their pretension; and I will confess, that though a firm and unflinching advocate of the superior salubrity of open fire-places, I must say, that I think Dr. Arnott's invention one of the best I have ever seen. Dr. Arnott is an elegant writer, and a clever and judicious man.

Though you may, Sir, pronounce my *mellange "de omnibus rebus et quibusdam aliis,"* I pray you to allow me a paragraph for Perkins's pipes.

These "heaters," as they have been called, I never could attempt to approach except when they ceased to be so, and the fire beneath had been long withdrawn. The very idea of "red-hot water" terrified me and inflamed my

fancy; we cannot account for these idiosyncrasies, but so it was. "The proof," &c.—it is a homely adage, you can finish the sentence, and know the commentary.

Well then, permit me to ask, is there any one that has ever used these Perkins's *tubes*, *pipes*, or *heaters*, but would be most heartily glad to get rid of them? I fear, as far as my knowledge extends, I must answer by a decided *negative*. In the Manchester Botanic Garden, they burst, set the place on fire, and destroyed property to the amount of more than 300*l.* You therefore see, Sir, that my opinion, recorded in your former pages, was a valid conclusion, formed on a solid basis.

I am, respectfully, Sir,
    Your obedient servant,
        J. MURRAY.

London, June 11, 1838.

INDIAN STEAM NAVIGATION.

Sir,—I am sorry that Mr. Bayley (page 150,) should have found matter of offence in the few remarks I hazarded on his letter relating to Indian steam navigation, especially as his thanks rather than his resentment, might have been expected for calling his attention to the article on Messrs. Seaward's scheme in vol. xxi, so unaccountably overlooked by him, notwithstanding his qualification as a "constant reader" of the *Mechanics' Magazine*. Far from wishing to insinuate that there was any thing in Mr. B.'s "conduct" not "consistent with propriety," my sole intention was to impugn his "opinions" as to British supineness in the matter of steam navigation in the East, and to point out a few of the many facts militating against his sweeping condemnation of his countrymen's inactivity.

That these facts were quite conclusive, is evident from every paragraph in Mr. B's. last letter, which, indeed, would seem to have been written only to amplify and confirm them. How stands the case, according to Mr. Bayley's own showing? Simply thus. The Dutch, the active Dutch, *are building* some steam-vessels in the East; the English, the backward English, have only five steamers already on the spot, and three more building at home "expressly for the service." This, surely, is enough to quiet any immediate apprehensions for the security of our pre-eminence in that quarter,—but Mr. B. might have added, had he referred, as requested, to the recent pages of the *Mechanics' Magazine* (page 16,) that the English East India Company are building an experimental steamer at Bombay, which, if expectation should be answered, will soon be followed by others, and that the Indian and Arabian ports have been often visited by other steamers than those belonging to the Company. It could hardly fail to excite surprise to find a gentleman so conversant with such matters as Mr. Bayley, expressing a fear of the Dutch getting the start of us,—by means of their steamers in embryo—twelve years after the British "Enterprise" had borne witness to the existence of its namesake by making its appearance in the Indian Ocean,—long after the power of steam had become familar in every port of the British dominions, and also long after even the Burmese had been astonished at the giant strength of the monster, guided by British skill, in the very heart of their empire.

It is not easy to divine what is Mr. Bayley's meaning, when he accuses me of "overlooking the fact, that steam-navigation in India was common long ago." My former letter was written principally to call attention to that fact, of which I was well aware, before reading the instances brought forward by Mr. B.; which are certainly quite enough to convince any reader, of not more than common obstinacy, as to the real state of the case.

Mr. Bayley recommends the people of India and New South Wales to be on the alert to promote. the extension of steam navigation. His advice, good in itself, is probably quite supererogatory; the British residents in India have been long since fully awakened to the importance of the subject, and are already engaged in active measures for its accomplishment. As to the good folks of New Holland, they, according to a witness examined before the late parliamentary committee " out-Herod Herod" in their enthusiasm. According to this witness (Captain Barber), the Australians were, some time back, fully prepared to undertake their portion of the plan, and had, several months ago, several steamers actually built and ready for the voyage. It may, however, be as well to add, that

the Captain's enthusiasm seems occasionally to have run away with him, so that it is to be feared he saw those steamers "only in his mind's eye." There is, nevertheless, no reason to doubt that the Australians will show themselves quite as active as the Dutch, ere long, in navigating " the Indian Archipelago" by steam.

With regard to the speed of our home steamers, it is unnecessary for me to say much in reply to Mr. Bayley, as the excellent letter of " Piston," on the same subject, happens to appear in the same number. By referring to that, Mr. B. will perceive, that so far from "thirteen miles per hour" being the utmost limit of steam speed, our Thames vessels have actually reached, *"under the most favourable circumstances"* the astonishing rate of twenty miles an hour?

Mr. Bayley must not be offended if I remark, that his concession to the opinion that ten miles an hour might be regularly kept up on a steam voyage round the Cape, has been extremely sudden. On May 19th he holds it to be impracticable, on the ground that the best steamers in the home seas have not been able to effect it; on June 9th he has " little doubt" but that, if vessels " of a much larger class than the *Atalanta* and *Berenice*" were employed, the sticklers for the practicability of the ten-miles-an-hour, would be " found to be correct"! Query, how much larger are they to be than the *Great Western*?

I have now, with regret, to complain of a piece of disingenuousness on the part of Mr. Bayley, who represents that I " disapprove of the patent condensers of Mr. Hall, and would fain have it be supposed that they were the cause of the difference in speed between the *Sirius*, and the *Great Western*." My former letter passes no opinion, either way, on the merits of Mr. Hall's invention, nor does it lay the inferior speed of the *Sirius* at his door, although the ill-timed advertisements of that gentleman might have justified me in doing so, if no allowances were to be made for the rashness of an inventor, in the full confidence of success. Mr. Hall himself drew attention to the voyage of the two vessels, as a test of the utility of his condensers; and would probably have claimed all the merit, had the race been in favor of the smaller vessel. His condensers have of course suffered in public estimation by the result, for which he has only himself to thank; but no impartial observer would condemn such an invention *in toto*, on the strength of the result of two voyages only, under circumstances of great disparity in other respects. At any rate I did not, and it is therefore hardly fair for Mr. Bayley to represent that I did.

In conclusion, allow me, Sir, to disclaim the slightest idea of imputing to Mr. Bayley a " wish to discourage the praiseworthy efforts to increase the velocity of steam-vessels," or any other maritime improvement. Mr. B's numerous communications to the *Mechanics' Magazine* bear such ample evidence to the direct contrary, as to render such a notion untenable for a moment.

And, I remain, Sir, &c.,

         H.

London, 13th June, 1838.

ASPHALTE CEMENTS.

Sir,—Some of the Asphalte Companies make their material with pitch and lime, in a somewhat similar manner to that adopted by Lord Stanhope in his composition for roofing, &c., and which was used some years ago in the roofing of Buckingham Palace, the Pavilion at Brighton, and many other places. I have in the course of my practice, as a builder, used these pitch and lime compositions frequently; and having formerly tried many experiments to improve them, I at last adopted the method of using hot lime with the pitch, which I found to answer much better than when I put the lime in cold; the lime and pitch being both hot, the combination becomes much more perfect. As I have used this method with success, it may be worth a trial by some of the asphalte companies, if they have not already adopted the method.

AN OLD BUILDER.

BLOWING UP SUNKEN VESSELS.

Sir,—Allow me to suggest an alteration of the method lately adopted in blowing up the wreck of the *William*. In any future operations of this kind, would it not be better and more effective in entirely separating the wreck, to open the main hatchways, and place the cylinder in the body of the vessel? The cargo, whatever it may happen to be, seldom reaches up to the deck, and if it

did, a sufficient quantity of it could easily be displaced with the diving bell to admit the cylinder.

I am, Sir, yours respectfully,

         I. S.

Grafton-street, Soho, June 7, 1838.

LOSS OF POWER BY CRANK OF STEAM-ENGINES—DAVENPORT'S ELECTRO-MAGNETIC ENGINE.

Sir,—I have to request the favour of your inserting the following reply to the strictures of Mr. Oxley, on my remarks in No. 764 of your useful Magazine.

With reference to the " strictly mathematical demonstration" of the loss of power by employment of the crank, we will make use of the diagram in No. 770, and will take, in the first place, six natural sines, instead of ten, assumed by Mr. O., and by proceeding in the same manner, to take an average, we shall obtain 6094 as the leverage, instead of 6215.

Again, by taking 16 sines, as above, the result will be 6275, instead of 6215, effective leverage ; and proceeding thus, *ad infinitum*, it will be seen that the average of sines will constantly vary in its approximation to the truth, giving a greater amount of leverage than that estimated by Mr. Oxley, with a loss proportionably less.

But, since the variation of the angle contained by the crank and connecting rod, viz. from 0° to 180°, exerts, according to Mr. Oxley, a considerable influence on his results, will he favour us by computing, *de novo*, the *actual* power lost by the crank, taking this oblique action into account, and likewise the variation in the *force* exerted by the connecting rod ?—" for if we sum up the forces acting in the circle, we find them exactly equal to the mechanical power in the *straight line*, the additional friction excepted," which " never amounts to a twentieth part of the power of an engine:" hence, " there is no reason to hope for an equal degree, either of economy or simplicity, by using the *rotary action of steam* according to Fredgold.

Indeed, Mr. Oxley has conducted his argument, as if no other objectionable consideration existed in the steam-engine but that of the crank. What, may I ask, will be the remnant of the power of the machine, when all other deductions are made?

Again, with reference to the diagram, it is stated that, "when the crank is in the position CR or CP, or when the piston is at the *half-stroke*, the crank acts with the *greatest force* it receives from the piston ; and from *these two points* the power of the crank continually decreases, until it arrives at A and B, where its power is nothing."

Now, as the available force must be in the direction of a tangent, it remains for Mr. Oxley to explain, how the connecting-rod D R exerts "its greatest force" on the crank C R. And since the connecting rod at the *half-stroke* should be equal to the distance C D, the triangle DCR would be isosceles, and not right-angled, as will appear from the subjoined

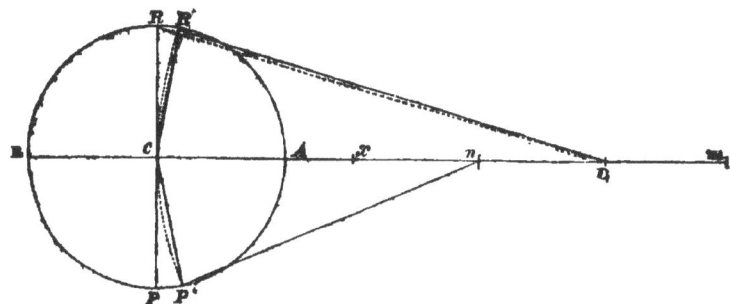

sketch, where *m s* represent the extremes of stroke, and D the piston at the half-stroke ; while C R' and D R' represent the crank and connecting-rod respectively, and not C R, D R.

Moreover, by taking *x* D as extremes, and *s* for the half-stroke of piston, a still greater variation will be apparent : the angles included by the cranks C P', C R', and the line C D, differing according to the length of their connecting rods.

After *repeating* that the "greatest force" is exerted at the *half-stroke* in C R, Mr. Oxley dares the "admirers of crank movements" to assert, that the piston would produce as great an effect as if its force had been applied at right angles to the crank. Where, pray, is the direction of the force, when the connecting-rod is a tangent to the circle described by the crank.

Now to the horse-power data. It is assumed that a horse-power will be equivalent to 200 lbs. to 230 lbs. raised 6 feet high per second ; then 200 × 6 × 60 = 72000 lbs. one foot high per minute ; but when qualified for convenience of the revised calculations, we must take 120 × 6 × 60 = 43200 lbs. one foot high per minute ; while, according to Watt, a horse-power is equal to 33000 lbs. one foot high in the same time, and this is the work of one and a half ordinary horses (Farey), compared with the lowest assumption of 200 lbs., while the highest

gives 82800 lbs., and 49680 lbs. one foot high per minute respectively.

Again, in referring to the "computed nominal," and the "real and effective," power of steam-engines, Mr. Oxley has taken the *Great Western*, rated at 450 horse-power ; and, by applying his standard of deduction, has reduced the power exerted on the paddles, to 270 horses. Query,—did the proprietors bargain for this ? I believe that they, in common with other purchasers of steam machinery, would expect that the *bonâ fide* amount of effective power stipulated for, should be furnished after all deductions were made. Indeed, the power, as exhibited by an indicator, which will answer to Mr. Oxley's "computed nominal," must have been very great in engines of such magnitude, even when the usual deductions were made, which, it is well known, are much too high,—7 1/4 lbs. per square inch being that which is usually allowed as effective pressure, on the piston of a low-pressure engine, while Mr. Farey estimates the effect in the best modern engines, as 12 1/2 lbs. per square inch, when all requisite deductions are made ; and hence, the surplus power is a bonus to the purchaser ; the *actual* power exerted being greater than the *nominal* horse-power, in proportion as the actual force exerted by the piston, is greater than the assumed standard of 7 1/4 lbs. per square inch.

Without adverting to the *suppositious* engines raising 15,000 lbs., and 69,444 lbs. 6 feet high per second, respectively, and liable to the concussions which it is stated that "Nauticus" has *unwittingly* admitted, at such speed, it will be seen, according to Farey, that "the crank, by the variable motion that it gives to the piston, prepares it for the changing direction of its motion. So that it *does not* come *suddenly* to rest, nor is the piston required to start suddenly into motion, in the opposite direction; but the change is effected imperceptibly."

We will now proceed to consider the electro-magnetic engines, against which there are "no such objections."

"Some persons" would say, that the power will increase as the squares of the diameters: that is, the *same* force being employed, and the diameter (or leverage) increased 30 times, the circle of 15 feet will be described in the same time as that of 0.5 foot; thus gaining both *time and power*. Suppose, for example, that such be the case: then the six-inch wheel of Davenport is stated to revolve 600 to 1000 times per minute;—say 600 per minute = 10 per second: the circumference of the wheel of 15 feet, at this velocity, would describe the space of 47.124 × 10 = 471.24 feet per second; while "a velocity of 33 feet per second at the rim, is about the *extreme* limit for a fly, even where the ring is of malleable iron," according to Tredgold. And, as the magnetic wheel, to operate on machinery, must be considered as such, what will become of the 25 feet wheel, which is not limited to a velocity of 2200 feet per minute, or 1000 revolutions even, according to Mr. Oxley?

Again, by the increase of size and *weight* of the wheel, with its essential coils of wire, &c., the cube of the effect of the model engine is assumed as a result; without considering the resistance of the air (which increases as the square of the velocity), and the friction due to the pivots.

Now, with reference to the action of electro-magnetic engines, it is observed by Mr. Watkins *(Phil. Mag. Feb.* 1838), who, it appears, has had much *practical* acquaintance with the subject, that "we certainly have mechanical arrangements which enable us to alter, many hundred times in a minute, the direction of the inducing electric current about the soft iron: but the *polarity* of the soft iron cannot be changed so rapidly, if Herschel and Babbage's law be just; for they say, *time is an essential element of induction*; and it is by the induction of the electricity in the wire coils embracing the soft iron, that the magnetism in the soft iron is induced, and thereby an attractive force gained." He observes, moreover, "that as it is necessary, for the constant employment of the magnetic attractive force in its *full effects*, that the polarity of each of the opposing poles of the fixed magnets should be in opposite states to the advancing poles of the mobile magnets, it is clear, that if the *time* has not transpired necessary for the transient magnet to acquire its full and proper polarity, there will not be the whole effective magnetic attractive force gained."

The space being limited through which the attractive force operates to a working amount, and the *distance* and *velocity* of the extremes of the radii increasing as their lengths, it would appear that Mr. Oxley has assumed a very questionable expression for the intermitting force of his proposed machines, more particularly when it is stated by Mr. Watkins, in continuation, that "the diminution of velocity is immediately perceptible when a very small portion of weight is added to a shaft which revolves rapidly without it;" and that "it is truly surprising how limited is the ratio of improvement in the power of a machine, by enlarging its magnets."

The foregoing considerations, it will be seen, would considerably qualify the estimated power alluded to, which Mr. Oxley may probably be sensible of, on review of the same in Nos. 763 and 770.

Now, with due deference to Mr. Oxley's experience, after several years of scientific application, I must submit, that comparisons with engines whose probable existence is disavowed, cannot be calculated to convey correct information; and, moreover, after an amusing appeal to public candour and judgment, the national insinuation conveyed in the allusion to the Chevalier de Pambour, does not much savour of "liberality,"—with the negative of which, my remarks, which were certainly not intended as "ill-natured," were characterized.

I am, Sir, your most obedient servant,

NAUTICUS.

Woolwich, May 25, 1838.

PREPARED FUEL—IMPROVED COFFEE-POT.

Sir,—As it would seem Messrs. Harper and Joyce mean to keep the secret of the precise method of preparing this fuel as long as they have the power, I will, with your permission, lay before your readers some experiments made to produce a fuel having some of the properties that Joyce's was said to have, and the reasons which led me to look for such a fuel.

Between five and six years ago, I constructed a coffee-pot, combining the properties of the common boiler and the percolator. Externally, the form was that of a common boiler, having the interior divided into an upper and lower compartment by the diaphram as shown by the dotted lines at *a a* in the annexed figure. The only communication between these compartments is by a tube *d* passing through the division *a a*, where it is soldered, and reaches to within a

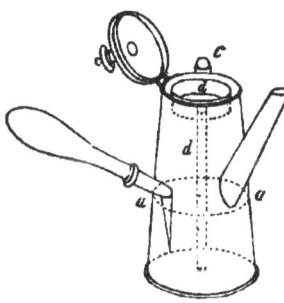

quarter of an inch of the lower bottom. To the upper end of this tube *b*, a box is soldered, open at the top, which serves as a funnel, in which to pour water to fill the lower compartment, and likewise to contain the coffee-powder, the powder being previously put into a similar box, having the bottom pierced with fine holes, and a moveable cover pierced in a similar manner, pressed lightly over the coffee, to keep it in a bed of uniform thickness. This box is to be turned upside down, and fixed in the box *b*. When the boiler is placed on the fire, and the water boils, the steam having no exit but through a tube having a valve at *c*, equal to a column of water 4 inches higher than the boiler, the steam acts upon the surface of the water and forces it up the tube *d* through the coffee in the box *b*, extracting its soluble parts; the

extract falling over into the upper half of the boiler, beautifully clear and nearly boiling hot.

After this pot had been in use for some time, I lent it to a friend in Lichfield-street, Birmingham, to assist him in constructing one of Britannia metal, to be used on a table, making use of spirits of wine as the generator of heat. After constructing one, and having used it in his own family for some time, he found that the expence of the spirits would be a great drawback on the sale of such pots; and I accordingly turned my mind to the production of a fuel that would generate heat at a small cost, and free from deleterious gases. I first tried oils, but could not entirely get quit of the smell during their combustion. I next tried a mixture of fresh burnt lime, nitre and charcoal, made into a cake and well dried; but when burned, carbonic acid gas was given off freely. I next tried different mixtures of charcoal, lime, common salt, nitre and litharge, but the heat generated in a small pot without a chimney, was not sufficient to decompose the salt, so that no soda was set free to take up the carbonic acid from the combustion of charcoal. I then rendered some soda caustic by lime, filtered, and evaporated till much concentrated, into which some red-hot charcoal was plunged,—the charcoal being well dried and lighted, was put into a flower-pot admitting air at the bottom to keep up combustion—the gases passing off were collected by a common bellows, placing the valve over the mouth of the pot, and moving up the handle, the nozle having a thin piece of leather tied, so as to form a valve. On blowing the gases through lime-water, the carbonate of lime precipitated was at first in very small portions; but after combustion had gone on for some time, carbonate of lime was precipitated in abundance. This, no doubt, arose from too small a quantity of soda being combined; but if the whole of the carbonic acid could be got rid of, there still remains the nitrogen. For the purpose of boiling a coffee-pot, this would be of little consequence; but the nitrogen passing off from a stove sixteen or eighteen hours continually, would dilute the air in the apartment so much, as to render it very unfit for healthy inspiration. When I had experimented thus far, I left Birmingham, and have not again resumed my researches; but I have no doubt, but that a fuel may be made to burn without giving off carbonic acid gas, by using a very porous charcoal combined with a sufficiency of caustic soda having a proper proportion of nitrate of potass to assist the combustion by supplying its oxygen, and thereby reducing the quantity of air that would be otherwise necessary, so that less nitrogen would be given off. If it is a fact, as reported of Joyce's stove, that no noxious gases are given off and that very little residuum is left, the basis of the fuel must be hydrogen, which, combining with the oxygen of the air, forms water, leaving the nitrogen to mix with the air in the room.

J. × J.

Clevedon, May 4, 1838.

RAILWAYS IN FRANCE.

A report was lately made to the Chamber of Deputies, by its distinguished scientific member, M. Arago, on the part of the commission appointed to examine the ministerial project for a system of railways throughout France. The document, although chiefly of local interest, possesses also, in some of its features, considerable attraction for the English reader; while, in the would-be gaiety of its tone, and the absolute *flimsiness* of some of its remarks, it presents a glaring contrast to our House of Commons' Reports on the like grave subjects,—more, perhaps, in the former than the latter.

The report pronounces most decidedly against the ministerial plan, according to which the principal lines were to be executed under the direction of the government at the national expense, and the branches only left to be undertaken by private capital. The commission hold that the whole may safely be left, under certain suggested conditions, to the enterprise of private companies; and that the reasons against the interference of the government in the matter, are so numerous and so cogent, as to leave not the slightest doubt which way the question ought to be decided. As the chamber has adopted this view, it may be considered as settled, that the plan of the Ministers is rejected. That plan comprised the construction of the following grand national lines :—

1. To the frontier of Belgium.
2. Havre.
3. Nantes.
4. The Spanish frontier, by Bayonne.
5. Toulouse, through the centre of France.
6. Marseilles, by Lyons.
7. Strasburg, by Nancy.
8. From Marseilles to Bourdeaux, by Toulouse.
9. Marseilles to Basle, by Besançon.

Besides branches to Dunkirk, Calais, Boulogne, Amiens, Metz, Tarbes, and Perpignan; without reckoning which, the system would extend to a distance of eleven hundred leagues, or upwards of three thousand miles. The ministers did not propose to commence the whole at once, but had selected 375 leagues—the lines from Paris to the Belgian frontier, and to Bourdeaux, and from Marseilles to Avignon, as proper to be begun upon immediately. The report, of course, is against the *government's* commencing either of these lines, or any other, now or at any time; and, in stating the reasons for this, the Commissioners, or M. Arago, in their names, enter at some length into both the theory and the history of railways. In the course of doing this, M. Arago shows that he is by no means an enthusiastic admirer of the railway system; in fact, he dwells so much on its defects, and adopts altogether so depreciatory a tone, as to appear almost in the light of an advocate against it; until, at last, he reluctantly, as it should seem, allows that its advantages in point of quickness are so great, that France ought not to be without them! There is one point, on which he dwells at much greater length than would be thought necessary in almost any other than his own glory-loving country,—the military facilities which railways may be expected to afford. From the space and labour devoted to this part of the report, it is evident that this is considered one of the most important points for consideration, and that military affairs still take the precedence of mercantile in France, even when a question which *we* should consider so exclusively connected with commerce as that of railways, is under discussion! M. Arago takes considerable pains to demonstrate, that the railway system will not realise a hundredth part of the advantages, in military operations, which many of his sanguine countrymen have anticipated from it, without due reflection on its peculiarities,—and has thereby deprived it of its strongest hold on the *affections* of the French public.

Another of the considerations advanced by M. Arago, sounds strangely enough in English ears. The promoters of railways in France urge, as a strong recommendation, that it will greatly increase the transit of foreign merchandise through the kingdom. M. Arago admits this, but endeavours to show, that the saving effected will be all on the side of the foreign merchant, who, by the shorter time required for the passage through France, will be spared the necessity of disbursing two-thirds of the sum now required for incidental expenses, of which the French innkeeper, and so forth, will be *minus ;* while, as the goods will be conveyed quite *through* the country, no advantage of any kind will be reaped by France from the increased celerity of their transmission. This may be all very well, but why not carry out the principle, and insist on a return to the packhorse system, or any other which would cause greater delay, and of course greater benefit to the innkeepers,—so far, at least, as all foreign goods are concerned? M. Arago's argument is, nevertheless, not without its weight; and shows, at least, that he has considered the subject with great minuteness.

The ministers, in bringing forward their plan, by way of depreciating the idea of leaving companies to form the great lines, triumphantly enquired,—" Where are we to look for extensive works, completed satisfactorily by private associations ?" M. Arago answers by referring them across the channel. "The objection," says he, " would have great force, if it would apply to countries where the spirit of association has long existed, and met with strenuous support. But, forsooth, France alone is held up to view ! By that means, the necessity is avoided of enumerating the overwhelming list of roads, railways, bridges, canals, ports, wharfs, docks, and industrial establishments of every kind, which, in a neighbouring country, demonstrate at every step that association is the most powerful resource of which modern nations can make use, to increase their welfare, their riches, and political importance !" The hit here given, it must be allowed, is a "palpable" one; and M.

Arago follows it up by enquiring, in his turn, whether France, on examination, might not be found to exhibit traces, in its public works, of the powerlessness of even the mighty hand of government itself ?—a question easy enough to answer, when the state of the principal roads is a daily subject of lamentation in the Chamber.

Another of M. Arago's points is the difficulty of distinguishing between the principal and secondary lines in many instances. The ministers, as one grand reason for government interference, advance the position that, if the principal lines were left open to companies, they might charge so excessively, as to prevent an influx of travellers, and, regardless of the loss to the nation, so that their own interests were served, drive them, where practicable, to other countries, in preference to France. M. Arago shows, that it would be highly probable, that the *branch* of the Belgian railway to Boulogne would, on account of its convenience to the English, enjoy a larger traffic than the main line; and that, consequently, a private company would there have greater influence over the national welfare than the government itself, after all its trouble to secure it ! The importance of the railway traffic with this country, seems, indeed, to have been strangely overlooked in France; for we question whether the line best suited for transit from London to Paris, would not turn out the best frequented, and by far the best paying, line in the whole country : and yet it is looked on, by the government at least, as only of secondary importance.

NOTES AND NOTICES.

Needle-making Machinery.—Messrs. Cocker and Son, of Sheffield, have obtained a patent for, and commenced working, a machine for making needles, which draws out the wire, straightens it, cuts it into the exact length, points it, grooves it, drills and counter-sinks the eye, files off the rough edges, and finally drops the needle into the box, at the rate of 40 needles in one minute. The proprietors expect that 50 machines may be attended by five persons, and that these will produce *one million two hundred thousand per day.* The employment of grinding needles has hitherto been very injurious; but by this machine, the operation is performed in such a manner as not to injure the health of the most delicate person. Patents for the invention, which will work a revolution in the trade, have been taken out in the principal kingdoms of Europe.

Jonathan's Description of a Steam Boat.—It's got a saw-mill on one side, and a grist-mill on the t'other, and a blacksmith's shop in the middle; and down cellar there's a tarnation great pot, boiling all the time.—*American Paper.*

Prospect of a change in the Patent Law.—Mr. Hall begged to give notice that he should on Wednesday next ask the right honourable gentleman the President of the Board of Trade whether it was his intention to introduce any bill for the improvement of the law relating to patent inventions; and in the event of the answer of the right honourable gentleman being in the affirmative, he should ask him what day it was probable he would introduce the measure.—Mr. C. P. Thomson would state now, as he had always done, that he did propose to bring in a bill to amend the Letters Patent Act of last session, but he must say that it was quite out of his power to state when the measure would be discussed. —Mr. Hall begged to give notice that unless the bill was brought in during the present week, he should proceed in a course which suggested itself to him.—*Parliamentary Report, Tuesday, June* 12.

Steam on Canals.—A trial was lately made before the Navigation Committee of the City of London, of Captain Ericsson's ingenious invention for propelling vessels by means of machinery fixed at the stern, by Messrs. Robins and Co., the Canal Carriers of London-wall, the owners of the patent. The experiment was attended with the most complete success. The boat, which was a common fly-boat, such as is ordinarily used on canals, left the wharf of Messrs. Robins and Co., Paddington, shortly before nine o'clock, and having arrived at Bull's bridge, upon the Grand Junction Canal, at an average speed of five miles an hour, proceeded to the Thames, along the Brentford Cut, and having taken on board at Kew-bridge the Chairman and other members of the Navigation Committee and the Water-bailiff, continued her progress to Queenhithe, a distance of fifteen miles, which she accomplished with ease in one hour and forty minutes.

Animal Magnetism Outdone.—It is said that Mr. Perkins has invented a compound which he calls the "concentrated essence of the sublimated spirit of steam." A person has only to put a vial of it into his pocket, and it will carry him along at the rate of fifty miles an hour; or by merely swallowing three drops when you go to bed at night, in the morning you will wake up in any part of the world you choose.—*U.S. Paper.*

Railways in France.—The French Railway Commission continues sitting daily, and gravely *considering* the multiplicity of plans propounded to it on all hands by projectors, capitalists, and the authorities of towns situated near the great proposed lines. This is almost all that is doing, however, in the matter; of consideration there is enough and to spare, but very little is effected in the way of actual execution. It is expected, that a fillip will be given to the Dieppe Railway, by a proposition which, it is said, has been laid before the authorities by the British consul, on the part of the Brighton Railway Company, who consider the extension of their line on the French side of so much importance to their interests, that they have offered to subscribe for shares to the value of twelve millions of francs (fifty thousand pounds) on condition of its being immediately commenced. The affairs of the first railway opened in France,—that from Lyons to St. Etienne,—are not in the most flourishing condition, the shareholders realizing only two per cent. on their capital; but the highly-popular one from Paris to St. Germain is in a different condition, the shares being now at a premium of just 100 per cent.

Architects in want of a House.—The Royal Institute of British Architects applied to Government, without success, in 1835, to be placed on a footing with the Royal and Antiquarian Societies, and the Royal Academy, by the grant of a suite of apartments at the public expense. The application was unsuccessful; this, however, did not prevent a second application to the same effect on another opportunity occurring by the opening of the National Gallery, which set free Somerset House for disposal; but the "Royal Institute" met with another refusal! Why do they not "shame the rogues," and show the resources of their profession at the same time, by *building* a magnificent house of their own. Are they afraid their own estimates might happen to be exceeded?

British Museum.—The number of visitors to the great National Museum, during the Whitsun holidays, has been much less than at the same period last year. On Whit-Monday, 1837, the establishment was visited by no less than thirty thousand persons, by far the largest number ever known, the preceding Easter-Monday having fallen short of it by no less than six thousand. Last Whit-Monday the amount was only twelve thousand, showing a decrease of sixteen thousand from the corresponding period of last year.

Nothing New under the Sun.—There is in the British Museum an old French pamphlet, a dissertation on Asphaltum, published at Paris in 1621—two hundred and seventeen years ago. Its author, a certain Monsieur d'Eyrinys, states that he had discovered the existence of this substance in large quantities in the vicinity of Neufchatel, and he proposes to make use of it in a variety of ways—principally in the construction of air-proof granaries, and in protecting, by means of arches, the water-courses in the city of Paris from the intrusion of dirt and filth, which at that time found their way in to such an extent as to render the water unfit for the use of the inhabitants. He expatiates also on the excellence of this material for forming level and durable terraces—apparently with an idea of increasing by that means the convenience and agreeability of the palaces of the great, the notion of forming such terraces as public footpaths in the streets being one not likely to cross the brain of a Parisian of that generation. All these plans are brought forward and advocated with a vigour that would do honour to the projector of a modern asphalt company, and the pamphlet concludes with a list of the different places in Paris where the new article was for sale. M. d'Eyrinys states, that previously to his discovering it at Neufchatel, asphaltum was only known to exist in the Dead Sea, which covers the ancient cities of the vale of Siddim, and hence, had only been made use of by the inhabitants of Syria, who availed themselves of it for various purposes. We wonder, by-the-bye, no " Dead Sea Asphalt Company" has yet made its appearance in the market. It is a fact that, we are afraid, rather tells against the new material, that its merits should have been brought forward in so able a manner more than two centuries ago, and yet that it should never have come into general use.

Pinner's (not Grant's) Improved Lithographic Press.—We have received a letter from Mr. Pinner, lithographic press-maker, of Crown street, Finsbury, (which we must apologise for having overlooked) in which he states that "the press designated Grant's improved lithographic press described in No. 743 of the *Mechanics' Magazine*, consists of improvements made wholly by himself"—that the first he made was purchased by Messrs. Standidge and Lemon, of Cornhill, and that Mr. Grant, is their foreman. Mr. Baker the correspondent, who furnished us with the description, confirms Mr. Pinner's statement.

☞ *British and Foreign Patents taken out with economy and despatch; Specifications, Disclaimers, and Amendments, prepared or revised; Caveats entered; and generally every Branch of Patent Business promptly transacted. A complete list of Patents from the earliest period* (15 *Car. II.* 1675,) *to the present time may be examined. Fee* 2s. 6d.; *Clients, gratis.*

LONDON: Printed and Published for the Proprietor, by W. A. Robertson, at the Mechanics' Magazine Office, No. 6, Peterborough-court, between 135 and 136, Fleet-street.—Sold by A. & W. Galignani, Rue Vivienne, Paris.

Mechanics' Magazine,

MUSEUM, REGISTER, JOURNAL, AND GAZETTE.

No. 776.]   SATURDAY, JUNE 23, 1838.   [Price 6*d*.

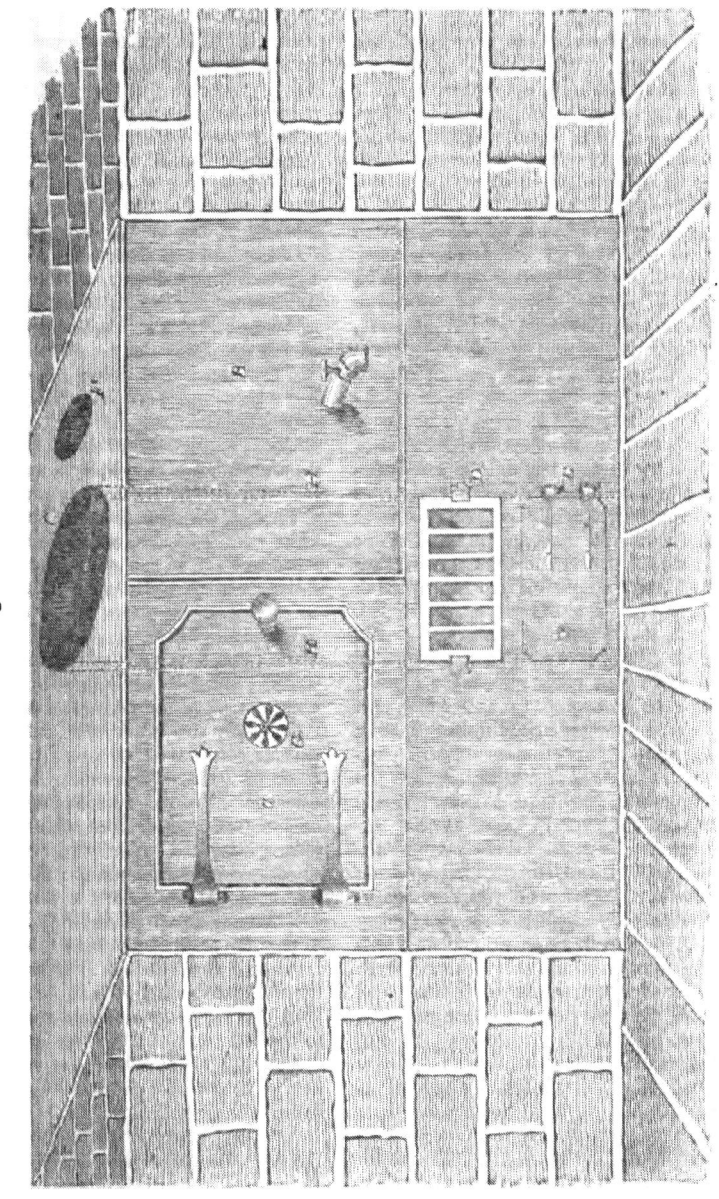

IMPROVED DOMESTIC COOKING STOVE.

Fig. 1.

IMPROVED DOMESTIC COOKING STOVE.

Sir,—Some years since, when making a short tour through part of France and Belgium, my attention was directed to the stoves used for cooking in those countries, and it appeared to me that a modification of the plans adopted there could be introduced, with great advantage, in this country. I was deterred from recommending any plan to public notice, by the impression that popular prejudice was too strong in favor of the present modes of producing heat, to permit of any change. The recent improvements of Dr. Arnott in the construction of stoves, and the new and curious stove of Harper and Joyce, have excited a degree of curiosity and attention, which may be followed by important results, and may lead to considerable changes in a very important branch of domestic economy. The present period appears, therefore, a favorable moment for directing attention to the present modes of applying heat in the process of cooking, with a prospect of success.

It is a well-known fact, that from two-thirds to three-fourths of the fuel consumed in heating apartments is wasted without producing any benefit, and with the serious evil of loading the atmosphere of London and every large town with a heavy smoky air, which is detrimental to the health and comfort of the inhabitants. The process of cooking is also conducted with an equal waste of heat and fuel, and yet is capable of being effected on principles equally economical. A great part of the consumption of coal takes place in cooking, and if every family were to calculate the expense of fuel consumed, in the kitchen alone, they would find it to form a very serious item in their annual expenditure.

To remedy these defects in the common mode of cooking, I send you the plan of a stove which is capable of effecting every object required in cooking, except roasting by an open fire. It will keep a large quantity of water constantly boiling, boil a number of separate vessels, steam, bake, fry, and broil, all at the same expense of fuel, and with great cleanliness and accuracy. The great objection to the use of this stove consists in its not roasting by an open fire; but a proper attention to the process of baking would render meat cooked by this process, equal to meat roasted in the usual way. The difference of flavor, between baked and roasted meat, appears to depend principally on two causes; one is, that baked meat is hardly ever basted, and it would be found that if this was neglected in roasting, that the flavor of meat would be more injured than even by baking. The other cause is the want of due ventilation of the oven, to carry off the vapours formed. This defect may be remedied in this oven, as the powerful heat produced will admit of an occasional admission of pure air.

Where it may not be desired to dispense with the ordinary open range, especially in large families, the present stove could also be adopted with great advantage, for all the other processes of cooking, as well as heating the kitchen, thus rendering the use of the open range necessary only when actually roasting, and which, in most families, will not exceed a few hours in a week.

I am aware that several kinds of cooking apparatus have been introduced to public notice; none of them have been generally adopted, partly in consequence of the prejudice in favor of an open fire, but more particularly on account of their great cost. This stove may be constructed at such a moderate expense as to place it within the reach of every family, it consisting of little more than an oven, boiler, and fire-place, as in a common kitchen range.

The simplicity of construction in this stove, renders it not liable to be put out of order, and its certainty of action is sufficiently proved, by the general adoption of this mode of applying heat for cooking on the Continent. As before observed, this is a modification of the continental stove, from which it differs principally in a boiler being constructed on one side, and in placing the fire vessel more in the centre, it being, in the continental stove, placed half in front, by which much of the heat is lost for cooking, and the kitchen is kept too hot. From the annexed plan it will be seen, that this stove consists of an oval vessel, which contains the fuel, an oven, and a boiler. The fire-vessel for a three-feet stove should be of cast iron, of good thickness, and eleven inches in the long diameter and nine inches in the short diameter. The oven should be twenty-two inches wide, and the boiler fourteen inches; each to be cast to fit accurately the

Fig. 2.

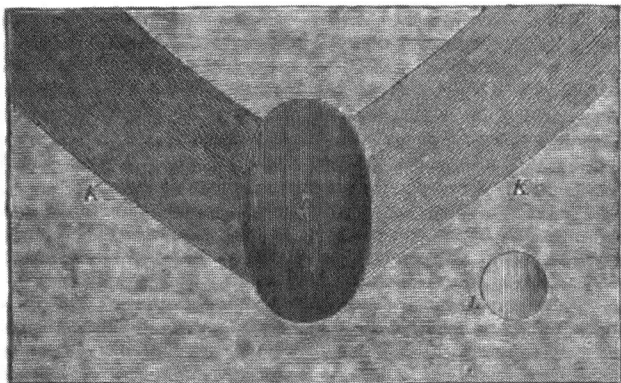

sides of the fire-vessel, which is placed equally between them. The construction of the oven would be improved by

Fig. 3.

being lined with wrought iron, as in the best ovens. On the upper surface of both oven and boiler is placed a flue, each diverging towards the back, and each being one, or one inch and a half deep, and twelve inches wide; these form a hot plate of sufficient extent to boil several vessels (the whole forming a level surface); the fire-vessel and boiler are to be fitted each with an iron lid. Underneath the oven and boiler is the regulator, for the supply of air, which consists of two plates, one brass, the other iron, both having bars and openings, each an inch wide; the brass plate moving one inch over the iron plate opens or shuts the regulator at pleasure. Underneath the regulator is a small door leading to the ash pit; in the cheaper construction of stoves the regulator may be dispensed with, the same effect being produced by the use of the damper of each flue. The construction of the flues in brick work, with dampers, requires to be the same as in the common kitchen range.

J. R.

Description.

Fig. 1.—*a* oven; B boiler; C fire-vessel; D regulator; E ash-door; F opening to boiler; G regulator to oven; H dotted lines shewing the place of fire-vessel.

Fig. 2.—I top of fire-vessel; K K position of flues : L opening to boiler.

Fig. 3.—The fire-vessel; *n* flues; *o* grate.

COLES'S FRICTION-WHEEL CARRIAGES.—THEIR UTILITY QUESTIONED.

Sir,—The "knowing ones" of the scientific world have been so completely "taken in" upon several recent occasions, that *a tyro* may be pardoned for examining more critically than usual, the pretensions of each new plan that is brought forward, in this wonder-working age. I have read with some attention, the notice of Mr. Coles's recently patented railway carriages, inserted at page 136 of your 773rd number, as also his own pescription, in a recent number of the *Civil Engineer and Architect's Journal*, and I must confess, Mr. Coles's claims

N 2

appear to me, to be of a very startling description. Although *theory* would seem to justify the assumption of credit for a certain amount of advantage in the application of (*anti*)-friction wheels to the purposes of transport, yet even this quantity, large as it is, falls far short of Mr. Coles's claim; whereas, in *practice*, I very much doubt if Mr. Coles's gain would not turn out to be a loss.

In the first place, the large (anti)-friction wheels being placed perpendicularly over the axle, are not in the true line of the force to be neutralized, which arising from two forces (gravity and traction) acting at right angles to each other, is a diagonal between the two. A good deal of friction will therefore arise, from the rubbing of the axle against one side of the moveable nut or collar, varying with the weight of the load and the velocity of transit. In the second place, I have heard it stated by skilful mechanicians, that anti-friction wheels always wear into facets, forming the rim of the wheels into polygonal figures, and so far as my own experience goes, with a large driving-wheel (made in a superior manner by Clements), this fact is fully confirmed. When this effect takes place, I fancy the *friction-wheels* might be advantageously dispensed with.

In Mr. Coles's communication before alluded to, he says "the two-wheeled carriages appear to me to possess a decided advantage over those with four. My friction-wheel carriages, whether two-wheeled or four-wheeled, are evidently adapted for use with any kind of power, whether steam, horse, or hand. To test the value of my invention I have constructed various models, to which I have given motion by means of two clock-springs acting upon the ground axle of the first carriage. With this apparatus I have made many experiments, and obtained highly satisfactory results; so that I do not hesitate to assert *my belief* that the above carriages will carry any weight, *with less than half the power* usually employed, or that they will travel *twice as fast* as carriages of the ordinary construction, *if the same amount of power* be exerted."!

I am sure your readers will agree with me in designating this a startling proposition, and I am at a loss to conceive how Mr. Coles could have been so egregiously deceived as to put forth such a statement. To reduce the power *one-half*,

or to just double the velocity at once, is "no joke,"—mighty magic this, truly. Suppose we take a railway-carriage with its load at six tons, will Mr. Coles continue to assert that the friction on one pair of axles carrying three tons each (even mounted after Mr. Coles's plan) is less than while running on two pair of axles bearing one and a half ton each?

The course adopted by Mr. Coles for "testing the value of his invention" is of a most fallacious character, and although models worked by springs *may* give "highly satisfactory results," a practical application of the principle on a proper scale, would, I calculate, rather go to justify the title Mr. Coles has given to his invention, and prove them to be in reality, "friction-wheel carriages"

I shall be most happy to learn that I have under-rated the value of Mr. Coles's invention, and that his plan has been tried and found practically useful; but there is so little ground for hope, and so many reasons for fearing the reverse, that I think the caution likely to arise from these remarks cannot be considered either impertinent or ill-timed.

I am, Sir, &c.

WM. BADDELEY.

London, June 16, 1838.

CAOUTCHOUC SPRINGS.

Sir,—The description by Mr. Baddeley in your 772nd number, of a buffer for fire-engine levers, has reminded me of an application of caoutchouc which occurred to me some time ago, and which I do not remember to have seen mentioned anywhere: I mean to the formation of very powerful springs, by preventing its *lateral* expansion. To illustrate my meaning I will suppose a cylindrical hole bored in a block of metal, 2 inches diameter and 12 inches deep; into this let a cylinder of caoutchouc, 4 inches long, be accurately fitted, above which let a solid plunger be placed, also turned to fit the hole exactly; the plunger being kept always in contact with the caoutchouc, by a collar at the top of the hole.

It seems to me that the result of this arrangement would be a very effective spring; which theory I must leave to others to experiment upon, if they should think it worth the trouble.

I remain, Sir, your obedient servant,

J. R.

London, 28th May, 1838.

SUGGESTION OF A NEW CARRIAGE FOR HEAVY LOADS.

Sir,—I send you herewith the suggestion of a plan for a new carriage for the removal of heavy goods, which seems to me to possess some advantages. May I request some of your scientific readers to give me an opinion thereon. I enclose you the opinion of one scientific gentleman of Salisbury, which is not very favorable to the scheme.

Your very obedient servant,

MECHANICUS.

In all carriages or vehicles that carry weight, there are three frictions, namely, first the friction on the axle, caused by the weight it bears; secondly the friction on the axle, caused by the resistance in the draught; and thirdly the friction caused by the wheels on the ground: but the principal friction is in the first,—that caused by the weight on the axle.

Now, if all weights were made to roll, instead of being carried, the first friction would be entirely done away with, as the weight then would come immediately on the ground, requiring no axles for the support of this weight; the only frictions then remaining are those caused by the draught and rolling on the ground. This principle may be carried into effect by a vessel much the same as a common cask, drawn in the manner of a common garden-roller, the cask having two broad and deep hoops driven on, which would bear on the ground, and prevent the cask itself touching. This cask could be made of any size that would be considered advisable; of course, this mode of conveyance is only applicable to carrying heavy weights that would not be injured by rolling, such as thrashed corn, earth, stone, &c. With respect to the loading, unloading, &c., and also any other minutiæ that may arise, it is not necessary to explain. The great question to decide is, whether the principle here put forward is correct or not, which is this: that it is easier to draw a weight that rolls, than the same weight in a carriage. If this principle is correct, all the minor details can be shown to have greater facilities than are now in any kind of vehicle; and it must not be considered that there is any difficulty in carrying this into operation.

Opinion upon the above Plan.

One of the great advantages of the wheel and axle is, that the friction is confined, as it were, to a point, which point is completely under control, so as to be overcome by acting upon it with the force of a considerable lever, which increases as the diameter of the wheel increases. Iron or steel axles, working in iron boxes, and well greased, occasion but little friction, and the pressure at the axle does not appear to amount to *more* than $\frac{1}{4}$th, or to *less* than $\frac{1}{6}$th of the load. If we take it at $\frac{1}{6}$th, and suppose, in a large two-wheeled cart, that the diameter of the wheel is to that of the axle as 20 : 1, then the whole resistance due to friction at the axle is equal to $\frac{1}{6}$ of $\frac{1}{20} = \frac{1}{120}$. So that in the latter case, to move one ton would not require a force of traction greater than $2240 \div 120 = 18\frac{8}{12}$ lbs. In this case we have considered the friction at the axle only.

This mode of viewing the nature and extent of the friction at the axle, is important to the present question, because, if that friction is small, it necessarily diminishes the advantages which could possibly be derived from the employment of the proposed cask, even supposing the principle assumed concerning the latter to be correct.

A large number of experiments upon friction generally have been made at various times; but the results of different experimentalists are so contradictory, and so little has yet been done in deducing fixed laws respecting friction, that a feeling prevails among mechanical philosophers, to ground *special* deductions on experiments only, and not at all on theory, until *general* deductions can be relied on. It would, therefore, be premature to pronounce as to the effect of a certain combination of circumstances, until they have been submitted to actual experiment, or until the laws which regulate friction are more perfectly known. I cannot, however, see sufficient reason for believing, that a saving of tractive power would result from the employment of the hollow cask. If the diameter of the bands or hoops were the same as that of the wheels of a cart, the pressure on the ground by the periphery of each wheel, and the nature of the friction against it (omitting the weight of the carriage and cask), are the same in both; and as the moving power is, in both

M 3

cases, applied to the axis of the equal circles, there seems no reason why one should preponderate over the other.

Two men can roll a hogshead of sugar along the pavement of a street, and this may be considered as a case in point; but a little reflection will show that it is not applicable, since the pavement acts as a tangent to the curve formed by the cask; whereas the proposed barrel will, in fact, be a cart moving on two wheels: and since the men who roll the sugar obtain a powerful leverage by applying their force at the circumference instead of at the axis.

Should the proposed principle be granted—of the truth of which I have strong doubts—it appears to me to be utterly unattainable in practice, at least to any useful extent.

The proposed plan is, however, ingenious; but I am cautious not to give a decided opinion until certain obvious experiments have been made.

C. T., Salisbury.

12th April, 1838.

KYAN'S ANTI-DRY-ROT PROCESS.

Sir,—It does not appear that Mr· Kyan's dry-rot scheme promises to be a winning game for the speculators on his "patent," judging, at least, by the *price of shares* in the market, that have at no time risen above par. So that, the public seem to consider the adventure very much in the same light that I do. In the use of the chloride and sulphate of copper, there is no risk whatever, and the one is just as efficient as the other, not to take into the estimate the difference of expense.

It was certainly a farce for Dr. Birkbeck to volunteer an attack on my chemical knowledge, on the basis of a gratuitous assumption, taking for granted the very principle that remained to be proved,—namely, that the *albumen* of the sap was "at fault" in the case. But, though a question " *ad hoc sub judice;*" be it so, *causa argumenti*; animal albumen is coagulated, &c. by the chloride and other salts of copper, as well as by the chloride of mercury; and with Lord Bacon I would therefore only say, "*experimentum fiat.*" On the other hand, by what means, in his vaunted superior chemical skill, does Dr. Birkbeck find albumen in sail-cloth and cordage?

" I believe" that in many cases to which Kyan's scheme (abandoned by DAVY for the very reason I now contend for) has been applied, it amounts to MADNESS,—a " creed" that will not speedily be shaken by *facts*. Besides, I defy any one, on the same principles of definite proportions, to adjust the metre of quantity in the chloride of mercury to the assumed measure of albumen; an excess there may or must be. Is, therefore, an *excess* of perchloride of mercury dangerous or not by contact? Is it, or is it not, volatile in tropical climes, and decomposable by alkalis and alkaline earths, iron, and its carburet, &c? The chloride being decomposable, it is sufficiently proved that at *common* temperatures, mercury produces salivation; how much more, therefore, must it be enhanced in tropical climes, and when the chloride is subjected to the agency of a highly electric condition of the atmosphere? I have, in this communication, nothing but the weal of the community in view.

Believe me to be, Sir, &c.
J. MURRAY.

London, 11th June, 1838.

CONSUMPTION OF FUEL IN THE "SIRIUS" AND "GREAT WESTERN."

In the various accounts which have been published of the successful voyage to and from America, by the *Sirius* and *Great Western* steam-vessels, it is stated, that the consumption of fuel was only about a ton per hour, which cannot be true, provided their engines were working up to the power of more than four hundred-horse, which they are announced to be. It is an easy thing to work such engines with that coal, or less; for there are times, when a steam-vessel is going with a favorable wind, where the ship will drive the engine without burning much coal. It is also asserted that the vessel went against the wind most of the voyage, making 7½ knots: had that been the case, they would have required a third more time to make the voyage between London and New York. The truth is, that about a ton of coals per hour is commonly consumed by a 200-horse power engine, if the labour of 200 horses be performed; and in propelling, by having the area and velocity of the paddles in proportion to that of the piston, which in many vessels lately built is no the case. Had they no other fuel on board but coal? A little resin, &c. will save a deal of coal. It is rather singular that the *Sirius* (whose engines are of the same kind as those of the *Great Western*,) acknowledges to burn about a ton of coals per hour, besides quantities of resin, &c. at different times, although their engines are only about three hundred horse power. You see they are all fond of saving coals, (which no doubt is true,) but they must use some other kind of fuel to do so. The voyage to America, which has now become possible, will soon be rendered, no doubt, more profitable to the proprietors, by the improvements which are constantly making in steam-engines. Amongst others of much importance, I have heard mentioned Mr. Dickson's, whereby a second use of the caloric and steam are stated to be obtained, and that whatever may be the consumption of coal or other fuel, by the best engines now in use, a reduction of 25 per cent. will be effected under his system.

Yours respectfully,
P.

London, 28th May, 1838,

FIRE-PROOF CEILINGS.

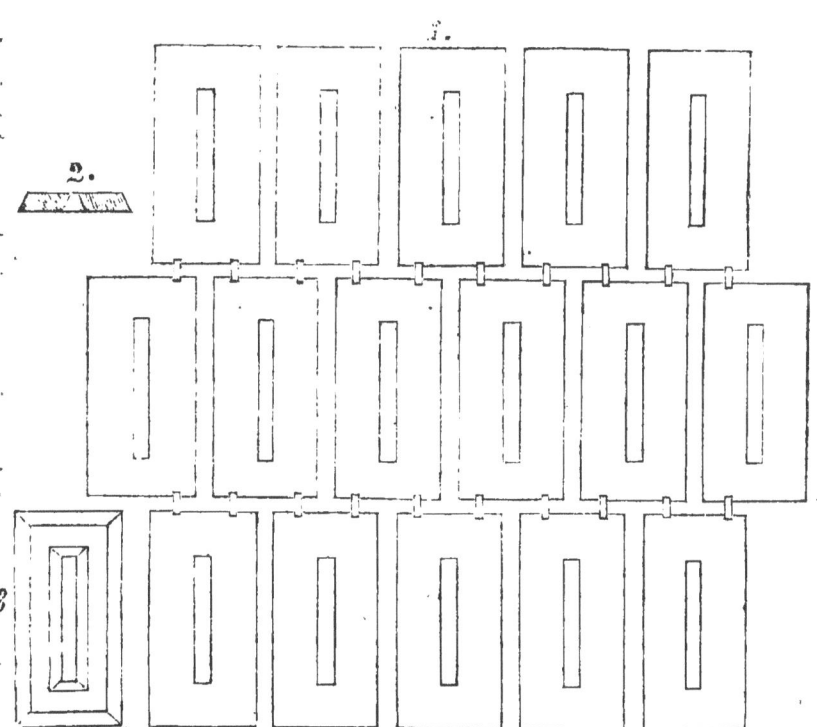

Sir,—Much discussion has taken place in your pages, respecting the manner of rendering fire-proof the ceilings of rooms; but as all the different methods proposed appear to me to be open to objections that would be fatal to their adoption, I beg to forward a plan of my own, which, I think, is calculated to answer the end in view, and be at the same time practicable.

I shall observe, that the method proposed of using sheet iron, either nailed to the naked timbers or on plastering, would present such an unsightly appearance as would prevent its being adopted in any but the most common apartments; in fact, it would be impracticable in ceilings required to be ornamented. Iron hooping used in place of laths would be preferable to the sheet iron; but it is to be feared that the hooping would bend with the excessive heat, and thereby throw off the plastering, and leave the timber exposed.

I propose the use of tiles manufactured for the purpose, about sixteen inches long and eight wide, with an opening through the centre half an inch wide and ten long—the tiles to be nailed to the joists with T nails, leaving a space half an inch wide all round between each tile; the upper surface to be made smaller than the under, with the edges of the opening in the centre, and the outside edges to be levelled off, so as to afford a complete dove-tail or key to the plaster. The tiles are to be laid in such a manner, that the openings in the centre of one row may be in a line with the outer edges of the tiles in the next course, or, as it is technically called, "breaking the joint." These tiles may then be plastered in the usual way, with two or more coats of plaster, and would, I think, afford a very good fire-proof ceiling.

I would also recommend, that for the future, instead of using lath and plaster partitions between rooms, four-inch brick walls should be substituted; as it is quite absurd to make fire-proof ceilings, and leave other parts vulnerable. For still greater security, it would be desirable to use cement skirtings instead of wood, to be put up before the floor boards are laid, so that the cement may extend below the surface. The idea of using cement floors laid on boards is not to be entertained, since, besides the great additional weight, it would, I think, be very soon smashed into pieces by the furniture, and the shrinking of the boards. The accompanying drawing of these tiles, and of the method of placing them, will make the thing the more easy to be understood.

I am, Sir, your obedient servant,
WALTER CADE.
32, Little Russell-street, Bloomsbury.

WHITELAW'S AND BADDELEY'S PLANS FOR FEEDING STEAM-BOILERS.

Sir,—The apparatus for feeding high-pressure and steam-boat boilers which is in most general use, consists of a single-acting pump wrought off the large steam-engine, a stop-cock, and a loaded valve; and my feeding apparatus, when it is wrought by means of the large en-gine, and has this very same number and construction of parts, will answer as well in every respect as this form of the old feeding apparatus; only in my plan, two slide-valves are used in place of the stop-cock which forms a part of the other apparatus. In my apparatus I prefer using *two* slide-valves, as marked *l l*, in the cut given in No. 769, although *one* valve will answer the purpose, especially if it is made to slide sideways, and not up and down. If my apparatus had no more parts than now mentioned, it would, like the other apparatus noticed above, require the constant attention of the engine-keeper to adjust (not to work) the slide-valves, in order to regulate the quantity of water admitted into the boiler; but if an eccentric to work the slide-valve (or valves) is, in my plan, added to the parts already mentioned, then the attention of the engine-keeper will not be wanted. As an eccentric appears to me to be a very simple part of any apparatus in which it is needed, your correspondent, Mr. W. Baddeley, will oblige me much, if he explains to me the meaning of the word "complexity," used in his notice of my feeding apparatus which appeared in No. 774 of your Magazine.

Does Mr. William Baddeley know any thing of a Mr. Whitelaw, who sent a drawing and description of two forms of a feeding apparatus, dated May 5, 1830, to the Society of Arts, and who got a reward from this society for his plan; one form of which is given in the volume of their Transactions published in 1833? Both of Mr. W.'s forms act on the same principle, and the one which was not published by the Society of Arts, but which is yet to be seen in their museum, is exactly the same in principle, and its form is the same, as the plan which Mr. B. calls his; only Mr. B. has put two slide-valves into his sketch, and Mr. W., in his drawing, has two hinged valves. Mr. W. has made a slight mistake in his drawing, and I believe that Mr. B. knows so little about the matter, that he will not be able, within three weeks from the date of this letter, to point it out to me. I would ask Mr. B. another question or two similar to this last, respecting some other of his *discoveries*, if I thought that the good resulting from my doing so would counterbalance the evil occasioned by filling up the pages of your useful Magazine with a subject very unimportant.

Mr. B. seems to think that *simplicity* is every thing in a machine; but it will not do for him to entertain, any longer, notions which might lead him to believe, that the old and *simple* form of the single-acting condensing steam-engine, without an air-pump and condenser, and having a boy to work its valves, is a preferable machine to the double-acting condensing engine in its most improved form.

I am, Sir, your's very respectfully,
JAMES WHITELAW.

London, June 19, 1838.

THE ENGINES OF THE "GORGON" STEAM FRIGATE.

On Monday last the engines of the new steam frigate *Gorgon* were put in action for the first time in the City Canal, adjacent to the factory of Messrs. Seaward and Co., at Limehouse. They were kept at work nearly the whole day, and were visited by numerous parties connected with steam navigation, and science generally. The engines are of 320-horse power,—that is, two engines, each of 160-horse power;—they were made by Messrs. John Seaward and Co. and are upon a very novel construction, being remarkable for their compactness, strength, and lightness; they have none of the usual cast-iron framing, sway-beams, side-rods, or cross heads; but the line of shafts being placed directly over the centre line of the cylinders, the rod of the piston is connected directly to the crank, by means of a connecting-rod of moderate length, without the intervention of any other part or piece of machinery. The piston-rod is preserved in its vertical position by a strong parallel motion, of peculiar construction,—which serves, at the same time, to work the air-pump, as also the feed and bilge pumps. In consequence of dispensing with the parts above-mentioned, there is a saving in weight of upwards of sixty tons. The sway-beams, and cross-heads, for engines of this power in themselves would have weighed about forty-five tons, which, vibrating from between 15 to 20 times per minute, is the principal cause of the tremulous motion given to steam-vessels. Although firmly fixed by her moorings, which gives a greater strain to the working than if the vessel were free and in motion in the water, the

vibration of the *Gorgon's* engines was barely perceptible.

The main carriages, which carry the line of shafts, are supported by eight bright wrought-iron columns, of seven inches in diameter, which rest immediately upon the tops of the cylinders, so that the whole strain and force of the engines are confined entirely between the cylinders and the main carriages; and no strain or force of the machinery is thrown upon any part of the vessel. Each engine is supported upon a very strong foundation plate, which, with the condenser and lower part of the hot-well, is cast all in one piece, and weighs about 10 tons. The space occupied by these engines is remarkably small, being little more than half what is required for engines of the same power made upon the ordinary plan with sway beams. The *Gorgon*, in fact was built for 220-horse engines, and Messrs. Seaward's engines are, as before-mentioned, of 320-horse power, with plenty of room to spare.

There are four copper boilers for supplying steam to the engines, which are quite detached from each other, and can be used separately, or in conjunction, as may be required. This is an important convenience, as it admits of repairs being made to one or two boilers while the others are in use. The boilers stand in pairs, side by side and back to back; so that two of the boilers stand with their fronts towards the engines and the bow of the ship, and the other two with their fronts towards the stern of the vessel. There are 12 fire-places, and two stoke-holes, one in front of the boilers and one abaft. The two stoke-holes communicate by passages going all round, and over the boilers, by means of which a free circulation of air is kept up throughout the engine-room. Any person may walk along these passages and touch the boilers, when in full work, without the least inconvenience.

On each side of the engines and boilers are ranged the coal-boxes, which reach on each side of the vessel from the after bulk-head to the fore bulk-head. The boxes average about eight feet wide on each side, and afford ample stowage for 400 tons of coals, being adequate to sixteen days' consumption of the engines; so that the engines and boilers stand between two solid beds of coals eight feet thick. No shot could pass through such

M 5

a thickness of coal, and do any material injury to the machinery. Moreover, the more vulnerable parts of the engines, as well as the boilers, are below the water line, and quite out of the reach of shot.

The diameter of cylinder is 64 inches; length of stroke 5½ feet; diameter of paddle-wheel 27 feet; length of engine-room from the fore bulk-head to the after bulk-head 62 feet.

We hope shortly to be enabled to give our readers engravings and a further description of these engines, as, should their action be found to equal the expectations formed by a witness of their present working, it will be a most important step towards the perfection of the marine engine.

The *Gorgon*, for which these engines were built, is the largest and most powerful steam vessel belonging to the British service, her tonnage, according to the old mode of computation, being 1150 tons. The length on deck, 183 feet; breadth between the paddle-wheels, 37 feet 6 inches; full breadth of deck, 45 feet. She was built in the dock-yard, at Pembroke, from the designs of Sir William Symonds, the Surveyor General of the Navy; and for her excellent properties as a steam-vessel of war, for her strength, symmetry, and durability, is unrivalled by any vessel in the British, or any other navy. She combines also, in a most eminent degree, the necessary qualities of a sailing vessel with those of a steam ship. The whole of the timbers, the planking, the beams, and the deck, are formed of East India teak;— the sleepers for the engines, and the main-beams, are of very hard durable African oak; the whole secured in the most complete manner, by a profusion of copper bolts and stout iron knees and riders. The partitions and doors of the cabins are composed of South American cedar, in general appearance equal to Spanish mahogany, taken from the hull of the *Gibraltar*, a Spanish man-of-war of 80 guns.

The *Gorgon* will be fitted with sixteen 32-pounders (long guns), of which, twelve will be on the gun-deck, and four on the upper-deck. She will also be provided with two of those newly-invented tremendous engines of war the 10-inch guns, intended to propel hollow shot of 96 lbs. weight. One of these guns will be placed forward, and the other aft, on the upper deck, on sliding swivel beds, which will range entirely round the horizon; the bulwarks all round are so constructed, that they can be thrown down in a moment to admit the guns being pointed in any direction. The gun-deck of the vessel is fitted up in the commodious manner for the accommodation of the officers and crew, amounting altogether, with the engineers, in war time, to 190 men. The orlop-deck, fore and aft, is appropriated entirely for the reception of troops with their stores and baggage; and the ample hold will receive abundance of water, provisions and stores, for a long voyage.

MODE OF GENERATING THE INTERIOR EPICYCLOID.

Sir,—In the November Number of your very useful work, you inserted an original paper of mine on the construction of the exterior epicycloid, together with a general theorem for determining the length of the entire (or of any part of the) curve. Herewith I beg to hand a few remarks on the interior epicycloid, the originality of which will, I trust, entitle them to a situation in your valuable columns. They are submitted, with much deference, to the consideration of the practical machinist.

The interior epicycloid may be determined by the same general principles, and method of construction, as the exterior curve—the several chords of the generant being always assignable from the number of teeth in the semi-generant. The epicycloidal line may be drawn by intersection, as the examples herewith indicate, and is generated by the motion of a point in the periphery of the rolling circle or wheel moving on the interior of the base circle, which is stationary—the axis of each circle being always in a right line with each other. Consequently, the length of the several chords constantly indicate the position of the tracing point; and this suggested the accompanying method of construction. This curve is somewhat singular in its modifications; in some cases the line is concave to the base, in others convex, and in one particular case it is a straight line. Attention to these circumstances must be of the utmost importance where precision is an object.

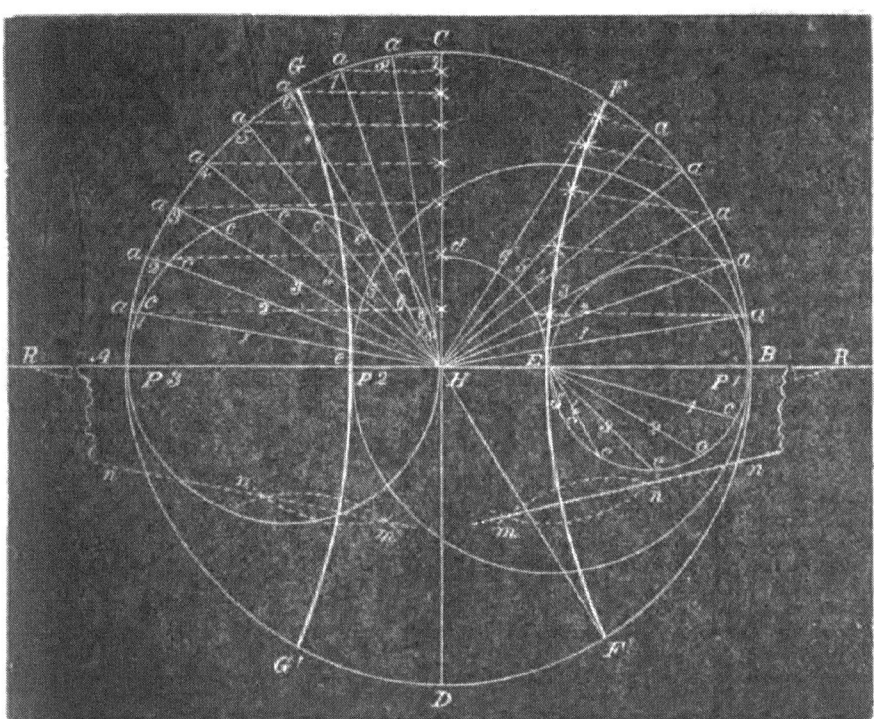

Let ABCD represent the interior of the base circle, and P1, P2, P3, the generant circles, which are to the base AB in the ratio of three to one, two to one, and three to two successively. AB is the diameter, AH radius; FF′ the interior epicycloid generated by P1 concave to the base BF; GG′ is the curve generated by P2 convex to the base BFG; CH = radius of the base is the line generated by P3 moving on the interior of the curve AGC.

For the curve described by P1 set off 6 divisions equal to the semi-circumference of the generant on the base from B to F; draw the chords c 1, c 2, c 3, c 4, and c5, and with these distances in the compasses, beginning with c 5, mark the intersections for the line EF, by placing the point first at E, then at the foot of a1, a2, a3, &c., on the curve Ed; and with the same distances on the curve BF, set off the faintlines from a1, a 2, a3, &c., which will exhibit the intersections for the epicycloid.

For the generant P3 set off 9 divisions on the base curve from A to c, equal the semi-circumference on the generant,

which mark a 1, a 2, a 3, a 4, &c.; then draw the chords c1, c2, c3, &c., and with the distances of the chords taken successively mark the intersections on the radius, placing one point of the compass at the centre H. Then, as the generant rolls on the point H, and against the base curve AGC, the points c 1, c 2, c 3, &c., will come in contact with a1, a2, a3, &c., on the base; and the training point H will mark the intersections on the line HC, as it moves from H to C. The faint lines from a1, a2, &c., are severally equal to the chords of the generant, demonstrating the epicycloid to be in this instance a straight line equal to the radius.

The principle of generating the epicycloidal lines by a succession of chords, dividing the circumference of the rolling wheel into teeth, suggests an easy method of general application for producing the line by the determination of the radius of curvature. As in the case of P2; the base circle being shewn, draw the generant; set off the length of the semi-generant on the base (by small chords for exactness) from B to G; then, w[i] any convenient distance from the points G and e, describe the intersections m n, and draw the line m n n until it touch the diameter of the base produced, and the locus of that point is the centre, from which draw GG', the epicycloid generated by the motion of P2. This method will apply to P1, or any other case of determinate ratio between the generant and the base.

From the principles of construction herewith adopted, we conclude, that in all cases, when the generating circles are to each other in a ratio greater than two to one, the interior epicycloid will be concave to the base circle on which it rolls; and when the ratio is less than two to one, it will be convex to the base. But when the proportion is that of 2 : 1 (exactly, in that case only) the epicycloid is a straight line, equal radius of base.

H. S. RAYNER.

OBSERVATIONS ON THE BURSTING OF THE STEAM-BOILERS ON BOARD THE "VICTORIA."

Sir,—The captain says, "that 6lb. per inch was all the pressure they worked at; and yet they found great difficulty in procuring steam." He also says, "that the other boiler was red hot, and without water!" Here is a frightful state to be in. If it was found the pumps did not supply sufficient water to work at 6lb. per inch, why not lower the pressure and decrease the intensity of the fire, so as to work at 4lb. per inch?

The engineer ought to have known, that in proportion as the density or expansibility of steam is increased, so is the quantity of water taken up by the caloric it contains. For instance, steam at atmospheric pressure is as 1711 to 1 of water, but as 1.17 atmospheres, its force is increased to 2.44lb. per square inch, and contains 8 grains per cubic foot of steam, more water than before, and so on in proportion.

Now, suppose the pumps were set (on starting from Hull) to supply water to the boilers under the pressure of 4lb. per inch, is it not egregious folly to expect them to deliver water sufficient to work at 6lb. to the inch, unless the length of the stroke is increased so as to deliver a proportionate quantity of water? For, as I have before stated, and it ought to be universally known, that the higher the pressure the greater the quantity of water and latent caloric is absorbed or taken up by the steam; consequently it is of the first importance to be very careful in regard to the pumps being of a fit and proper size, and kept in the best possible order for supplying water according to the intensity or expansibility of the steam, or the evaporation required. It would, perhaps, be easy to show, that the pumps at starting did supply sufficient water; but by increasing the evaporation without altering the stroke of the pumps, the water kept decreasing in the boiler continually during the twenty-four hours voyage from Hull, until it evaporated nearly to zero; when, of course, as the intensity of the fire was not diminished, but, perhaps, increased, the flues would become red hot, and then the water from the pumps would in such case naturally flash into steam; and the safety valves of all boilers being much too small to discharge so large a volume of steam formed instantaneously, an explosion must of course take place. The stronger the boiler under such negligent circumstances, the more disastrous will be the effect, as was the case of the Union at Hull not long since, and which, I was satisfied at the time, bursted from want of water, and neither from bad iron nor defective workmanship.

If the public would attach less weight to the opinions of those learned M.D.'s, D.D.'s, L.L.D.'s, and other paper and pasteboard artists and evidence-mongers, who are so fond of calling themselves engineers, and put a little more trust in practical manufacturing engineers and boiler-makers, it would be a public benefit; for one practical fact is worth a hundred theoretical opinions, filled and interlarded with ifs, and buts, and suppositions.

No doubt a host of the above theorists will be ready to come forward with their opinions on the present occasion, and will be thrust forward by their various partizans and admirers accordingly, to the exclusion of those practical men whose opinions ought to have greater weight than is attached to them in general.

Now, it would be very easy to find a remedy for such unfortunate occurrences as those of the *Victoria* and others, and that is by attaching a glass guage to every boiler, such as are affixed to the patent boilers of Upton, Nicholls & Co., of Battersea.

If this instrument had been attached to the boilers of the *Victoria*, any one on board might have seen the water and steam in the boilers by a glance, the water and steam being always visible; for if the water was a hair's breadth higher or lower than the proper level assigned, it would be visible, not by any index or other uncertain guage, but the water itself is seen in its boiling state, and the steam inside the boiler also.

Any person desirous of directing their sight to this safe, neat, and most important little instrument, could, on perceiving the water decreasing below its assigned level in the boiler, say instantly, " Stop the engine, open the safety valves, and lower the fires; the water guages show the pumps are deranged," &c.

At the same place may be seen one of the safest boilers, and the quickest in getting up *steam*, that has yet been invented; and which is by far the best for a ship, inasmuch as it is smaller and lighter, and, by not carrying the water in one boiler, but in several compartments, safe beyond all comparison.

This boiler would do well at sea, if external condensation was adopted; and it could be very easily repaired if required, even at sea. As to its saving properties, a ten-horse power one has been known to produce steam of 45lb. to the inch in fifteen minutes, and the boiler is proved to bear a pressure of 1000ths to the square inch.

A rupture in such a boiler could not be attended with any bad consequences. If any rent was to take place, as those of the *Victoria*, and the *Union* at Hull, it would only put out the fire. Nor is it possible for it to explode altogether, and disperse the water instantaneously, as is the case with *all those boilers which carry their water in bulk.*

Now, so long as the owners of steamers continue to follow the plan of rejecting the best boilers and engines for the sake of getting the lowest priced ones, and which are the least to be depended on, the public must expect to have their lives put in jeopardy.

Even the simple water guage abovementioned would have prevented all those disastrous effects that have happened both in England and America. In fact, Mr. Editor, no boiler, whether for sea or land service, ought to be suffered by the owners to work without it, let the boiler be whatever shape or make it will.

Now, as all common boilers are liable to similar accidents, I would strongly urge the necessity of fitting them up with large and very capacious safety valves, capable of allowing the escape of much greater volumes of steam than is at present the case. Besides which precaution, a metallic alloy, fusible at any number of assigned degrees of heat, might and ought to be used on board of every steamer. This being appended to the lever of a very capacious valve, would, by allowing the steam to escape, prevent the bursting of every kind of boiler. This was mentioned to me by Mr. Upton as the plan to be adopted by them for all sea-going boilers.

I am, Mr. Editor,
Your obedient servant,
SCRUTATOR.

MILLS'S MERCURIAL PUMP.

Sir,—Some time since I constructed a mercurial pump, on what I conceive to be a new plan. I presented a working model to Mr. Grier, lecturer of Natural Philosophy in the Baronial Hall, who exhibited it to his class, and the action was so satisfactory to the lecturer and his audience, that I have been solicited to transmit you an account of the pump, which I hope you will not consider unworthy of notice in your excellent periodical.

The pump is of the suction kind, A A is a pipe not more than 30 feet in length, open at both ends, the undermost of which is inserted in the well to be drained. At B there is a clack valve opening upwards, immediately above which a branch pipe C leads off, and opens into an air vessel D, of the ordinary construction. The top of the pipe C is furnished with a valve E, opening upwards into the air vessel, and the ejection pipe is terminated at the required height F. Immediately above the branch pipe C, the main pipe A A is begirt with a cylinder G G of iron or glass. The cylinder is of greater diameter than the pipe, but screwed to it at the bottom, H H, so as to be perfectly air-tight. The cylinder rises to the same height as the pipe A A, and the space between them is nearly filled with mercury. A cylinder open at the bottom, and of a diameter intermediate between the cylinder G G, and the pipe A A, is immersed in

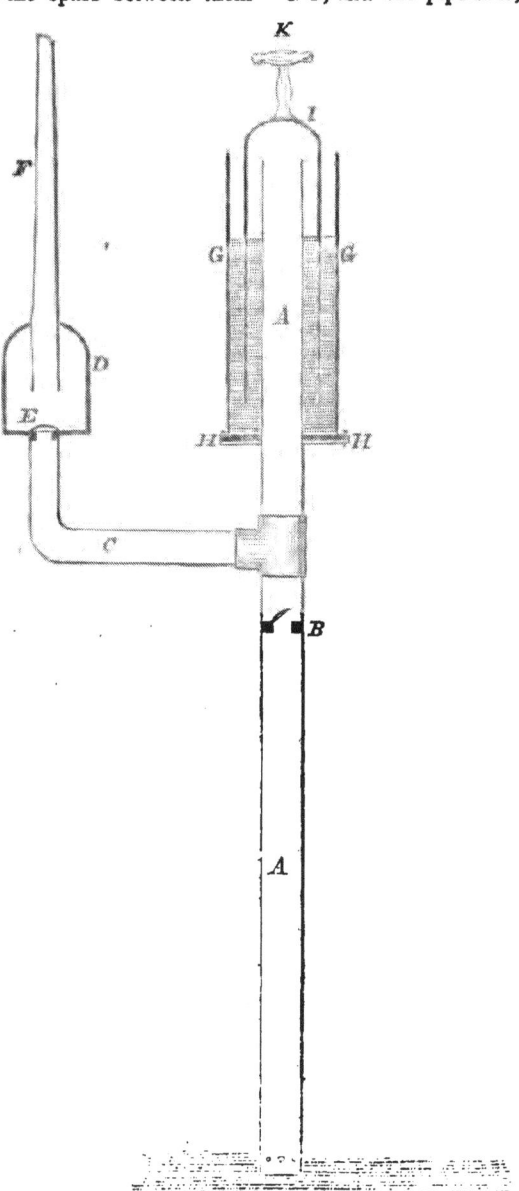

the mercury over the pipe, after the manner of a gas holder receiver, but so as to be capable of an easy motion upwards and downwards. The top of this cylinder is furnished with a handle K. In consequence of the mercury in the cylinder G G, and of the valves B and E, no external air can enter the main pipe

A A, which enters the well; but the cylinder I being lifted by the handle K, yet not so far as to come out of the mercury, the air within the pipe A A will be rarefied, and the pressure of the atmosphere will force the water from the well up the pipe A A, so as to pass the valve B, which opens for its passage. When the cylinder I is brought down, the valve B shuts, the air is compressed, and the water having no other way of escape, passes through the tube C, through the valve E, and into the air vessel D, thence up the pipe and becomes discharged at the orifice F.

The advantage of this pump is, that little friction is encountered, and for every inch of stroke of the handle K, the water will be raised one foot high.

JAMES MILLS.

Glasgow, 13, Clyde Terrace,
March 30, 1838.

AMERICAN STEAM-BOAT RACES.

* * That these steam-boat *accidents* mainly arise from a headlong impetuosity, and childish rivalry, seems clear enough. The *Ben Thersod* caught fire in *running a race*. The American public ought to put down this practice: on the contrary, it is sanctioned, and stimulated by paragraphs like this:— "There was a beautiful trial of speed last night between the steam-boat *Swallow* and *Rochester*, which are undoubtedly the two fastest boats in the world. They came out of their berths in New York together, *and for twenty miles ran neck and neck, neither gaining or losing a foot.*" This voyage, which is about 150 miles, appears to have been made in *between eight and nine hours!* We have, in another paper, a description, by a passenger on board the *Franklin*, from Louisville up the Ohio to Cincinnati, of *a race carried on the whole of that distance*, which is also about 150 miles, by this boat with a rival one, named the *Phillips*. In this case, there was a wager of 100 dollars between the captains that the *Franklin* would beat by an hour. The other boat had a half-hour's start. At fifty miles she was nearly "over-hauled;" at thirty more she was passed (having slight stoppages to make with the mails), but by only five or six lengths. The passengers of the leading boat, some sixty, including ladies, now entered into the sport, which they had hardly understood before:—"The contagion spread —'Go, ahead, captain—keep her in the wake—huzza for the *Phillips!*' was in every mouth. Nothing could exceed the spirit of the firemen and deck hands. The hatches were thrown open, pine knots covered the

deck, and two or three axes kept going in splitting and breaking them; the deck passengers were huddled into the bow, to give the boat more dip; the chain waggons were hauled from the tops of the chimneys, while dense clouds of black smoke filled the atmosphere over us. It was plain that no less excitement prevailed on board the *Franklin*. Thus far she had been queen of the waters." And so they keep on for the next twelve or fifteen miles. "In passing Warsaw, the two boats were 'neck and neck,' and we were saluted with loud and continued cheers. No response was sent back from either boat—not a sound was heard save the sonorous breathings of the scape-pipes, and the whirl of the water-wheels."—After this, "the boats, which till now had been abreast, and from ten to fifty feet apart, struck each other with a slight concussion. The ladies, of whom there were twelve or fifteen on board the *Phillips*, became alarmed, and besought their husbands to interfere. While this consternation prevailed in the ladies' cabin and state rooms, a different scene was witnessed without: the two boats seemed to be lashed together, the officers of each shaking hands across the railings, and the firemen and crew looking defiance. The river in front of the boats, from the light of the furnaces, seemed a sheet of fire, while the sky continued overclouded with the dense volumes of smoke which poured forth from the chimneys. In passing Petersburgh, the boats again struck with a more violent concussion than before; the alarm of the ladies increased,"—and so on. Now, what an atrocious game is this to be played with human life! That the passengers encouraged it, only aggravates the case; and so do the cheers from the shore. We fear that the Americans are too careless of life. Their driving habits of business, and the adventurous frontier character of a part of their population, may account for it. The great number of their steam-boats has familiarized them with scenes such as we have here described. Think of more than forty boats on Lake Erie alone—of nearly 400 on the Mississippi—for it must be allowed, as we said of the burning of buildings, that the Americans are as enterprising in one way, as destructive in another. But none of these circumstances can excuse the practices referred to, though they go some way to account for them. On the contrary, the great number of the steam-boats, and the usual comparative lightness of their construction, is the strongest argument for a more careful management on board, and for the interference of the public and the government.—*Athenæum*.

M 3

ON THE FALLACIES OF THE ROTATORY STEAM-ENGINE. BY JOHN SCOTT RUSSELL, ESQ., M.A., F.R.S., ED., LECTURER ON NATURAL PHILOSOPHY.

[Abridged from the Second Part of the Transactions of the Society of Arts for Scotland.]

It has been represented to me by the secretary, that the objects of this society will be materially promoted by any disquisition in which the fallacious views that are sometimes entertained upon important mechanical subjects shall be clearly analysed, and the errors pointed out into which the authors of supposed improvements have been drawn, either by reasoning accurately on false grounds, or making erroneous deductions from established principles. I feel it, therefore, to be my duty to make such contributions to the efforts of this most valuable association, as my humble abilities enable me to produce: and I have selected for this purpose the rota'ory steam-engine, as a subject upon which erroneous views are widely prevalent, upon which much ingenuity and mechanical skill is every day expended, and which belongs to the same category of fallacies to which the quadrature of the circle and the perpetual motion have long been assigned.

To any one who compares the state of the mechanical arts in Great Britain at this instant, with their condition at the commencement of the century, the progress of these arts will undoubtedly appear more rapid in their approach to perfection, and more extensive in their range of application, than during any former period in the history of civilization; but if he will direct his attention more closely to these wonderful effects, and, looking below the surface of events, will examine into their causes; if he will consider how large and wealthy a portion of our population have directed their whole talents and energies solely to the purpose of attaining perfection in these arts, he will be disposed to question whether the results have been at all proportioned to the means, and whether, by such mighty interests judiciously directed, more would not have been judiciously achieved, had these resources been devoted exclusively to legitimate problems of real improvement, instead of being expended on the *ignes fatui* of mere visionary speculations; and had the talents which have been permitted to daviate from their proper channel been devoted to such ends only as should permanently benefit society, and form decided steps in the advancement of civilization, or valuable additions to the truths of science.

To direct the enterprise and resources of one part of this empire into the legitimate avenues of valuable improvement, and to afford the means of distinction and encouragement to the mechanical talent of Scotland, is the object of this society: and when I reflect how many men there are, even within the limited sphere of my acquaintance, whose inventive genius is of the highest order, and whose labours are yet abortive, I cannot but feel convinced that there must be either a misapplication of talent to objects which others with better opportunities, and possessed of peculiar advantages, have better accomplished, or a misdirection to subjects containing in their own nature something either impracticable or impossible. Were it possible on the other hand, for such men to unite their exertions for promoting the real advantage of society, and were every individual, by a proper division of mental labour, to direct his mind to the object most congenial to it, I cannot imagine but that, with such means, so directed, changes and improvements in the state of the arts would be produced in this country much more rapid and astonishing than all that we have already witnessed.

I am led to make these general remarks by their applicability to a series of inventions which have successively appeared under the generic appellation of *rotatory steam-engines.* Their principle has assumed various forms and modifications, and has seduced, and still continues to seduce, many a bright genius from the straight path of useful industry and accurate invention. I have the pleasure of personal acquaintance with several men of eminent talent, who have sacrificed the energies of great minds to this ruinous fallacy. With one or two, my arguments have been successful in dissuading them from a pursuit sure to end in disappointment, but there still remain others of them, and many beyond the sphere of my knowledge, of whose talents and exertions the world is still deprived by the *fallacies of the rotatory steam-engine.*

It is the object of this paper to show that the whole principles of the rotatory engine, as an improvement upon the common reciprocating engine, whether condensing or non-condensing, is radically false, and mechanically fallacious: that it is false in its mathematical principles, fallacious as a mechanical structure, and can never be attended with any mercantile advantage in its application; and thus to dissuade men of mechanical talent from devoting themselves to so unworthy an object.

Before requesting acquiescence to be given to me on any opinion so decided as this, I ought to premise, for the purpose of obtaining the confidence of practical men, that, although the views which I am about to develope were first suggested to me in the course of an investigation where I found it necessary to bring the battery of the higher analysis to bear upon this subject, and employ the powers of the calculus to raze the foundations of prevalent error in the steam-engine; yet, as such men are apt to use the word "practical experience," as antithetical to scientific skill, I ought to mention that, during the last ten years, I have been continually engaged in the practical solution of the most difficult problems of the steam-engine,—that I myself invented, and had constructed for me, several rotatory engines, which were sufficiently successful to convince me that *the principle*, and not the mere *application* I had made of the rotatory principle, was radically wrong. I have also had the opportunity of examining and working the most successful engines of this kind ever produced, and therefore conclude that, had theory never led me to any such result *a priori*, I must have been convinced that practical experience was opposed to the rotatory construction of the steam-engine. In what follows I shall endeavour to adduce my arguments in a form as little technical as is consistent with precision.

1. It is first of all my wish to show that the subject of the rotatory steam-engine is *not so new and untried* an invention as some who attempt the problem for the first time may be led to imagine;—for this purpose I adduce the names of more than ninety inventors, most of them patentees.

2. By an arrangement of these inventions, I have endeavoured to show that *five different classes comprehend them all*, and that the others are mere repetitions of the same principle, and attended with the same failure; so that an inventor may know whether his invention contains an entirely new principle, and if it do not, that it has already been tried and failed.

3. By showing, in one view, the names of inventors of unsuccessful rotatory engines, I endeavour to convince the inventor that the five classes already invented have *not failed from want of genius, skill, or practical experience*, in those who have made the trial, for the list contains the names of eminent practical men.

4. I endeavour to show that the *ordinary crank engine does not possess the defects attributed to it*, and which it is the sole object of the rotatory engine to remedy,—that the use of the crank causes no loss of power.

5. In a practical point of view the *rotatory engine is every way inferior* to the reciprocating engine;—in simplicity, and cheapness, and ease of construction,—in durability and economy in use,—in uniformity of action and equable motion.

6. The rotatory engine is *peculiarly inapplicable to the great purposes* of terrestrial locomotion and steam navigation—objects to which it has been considered peculiarly suitable.

7. That the *present steam-engine is practically perfect* as a working machine, being within ten per cent. of mathematical perfection.

8. That the *crank* of the common steam-engine possesses certain *remarkable properties* of adaptation to the nature of matter, of motion, of steam, and the human mind; from which its supremacy as an elementary machine is derived,—properties which cannot possibly belong to any species of rotatory engine.

The common or reciprocating steam-engine is distinguished from the rotatory steam-engine by the nature of certain parts of its mechanism, which convey the motion of the steam to the machinery which is to be moved. There are a cylinder, a piston-rod, and a crank-axle. Now, the root of the whole of the fallacies of the rotatory engine will be found in certain radical misconceptions of the nature of the crank, as the simple elementary instrument by which the revolving motion of the axis, or great wheel of the steam-engine, is immediately produced. Nothing can be simpler than the crank. We wish to turn an axle round; we bend a part of the end of it at right angles to itself; we take hold of this end, and by this means turn round the axle. The bent part is the crank, and may be seen every day in winding up a clock, or in turning any wheel on its axle, by holding a spoke; likewise in the handle of a coffee-mill, at the top of a draw-well, or in the handle of any winch or crane for raising weights. Now, in the same manner as the hand of the operator takes hold of the handle, and, by drawing it towards him or pushing it from him, makes the axle or wheel turn round,— so does a rod from the piston of a steam-engine take hold of the end of a crank, and alternately draw and push it round in its circle of revolution. The crank is indeed so simple that it can scarcely be called an addition to the axle of which it forms a part; it is merely a bend or *crook* in it, which the word *crank* originally implies, and has been used to move the pistons of the cylinders of common pumps, since the days of Aleotti, in precisely the same way as it now moves in the steam-engine. Now, it is owing to a radical misconception of the nature of this elementary machine, that hosts of schemes have arisen for the production of circular motion, without the intervention of the crank, either by giving to the steam itself an immediate circular action, or by the substitution of some other less elementary mechanism, between the reciprocating piston and the revolving axis, as the means of producing its rotation. In the rotatory engine, on the other hand, the cylinder, piston, rod, and cranked axle are superseded, in the most common form, by a cylinder, valves, s'op, and axis. In the same way as a mill-wheel is compelled to move in a circle, either by the direct action of water or wind upon it, so is the drum or wheel, with valves, fans, or other projections on its circumference, urged round by the force of the s'eam, and, enclosed in an outer cylinder or cse, gives revolution to an axis to which it is atached. This direct rotating action of the steam will, it is imagined, give out its effect more powerfully, uniformly, and economically, than the common mode of repiprocating action, when converted by the crank into revolution.

Rotatory engines may be arranged according to the mode of action into four classes.

Class I.—Rotatory engines of simple emission.

Class II.—Rotatory engines of medial effect.

Class III.—Rotatory engines of hydrostatical reaction.

Class IV.—Rotatory engines of the revolving piston. As closely connected with the rotatory engines in the fallacy which has given rise to both of them, we may add a series of inventions forming,

Class. V.—Revolving mechanism substituted for the crank.

Class I.—The rotatory engine of simple emission forms the earliest, as well as the most rude and elementary method of giving motion to mechanism, by the escape of vapour or steam. It is described by Hero of Alexandria, in his *Pneumatika*, upwards of 120 years before Christ, and depends, for its effect, upon the same principle which gives to a rocket its career, and makes a fire-wheel revolve in giving off its beautiful lights. In these, as in all instances where fire, or steam, or any fluid or gas is genera'ed in a chamber from which it is permitted to issue with violence, it will, in its exit, drive the vessel from which it issues away from it in the opposite direction, and is, in fact, merely an application of the principle of recoil,—where the gas, generated by the explosion of the powder, urges the ball outwards in one directiou, and forces the breech of the gun backwards in

the opposite one. The same recoil is felt in all cases of simple emission of a fluid from a reservoir; and if it be so arranged that water, steam, air, or the gaseous productions of gunpowder, shall rush out of a chamber through the arms of a revolving wheel, the openings of escape being properly directed, the recoil will urge round the wheel, and we shall have a revolving engine of simple emission. By availing himself of this principle, the mechanist of Alexandria produced an efficient engine, merely by heating a vessel containing water and air, and allowing the vapour to rush from the two opposite orifices at the end of two arms proceeding from a sphere which the emission was employed to move.

Instead of using the principle of recoil, the force of steam issuing with violence as we see it from the mouth of a kettle or boiler, may be directed upon the vanes of a wheel, so as to blow them round; and thus we have a second variety in the manner of converting the simple issue of steam into a moving power. This second species of the rotatory steam-engine of simple emission was invented by Branca, in 1629.

Since that time the engines of this class have been frequently re-invented and slightly modified.

Inventors of Rotatory Steam-Engines of the First Class.

1. Hero of Alexandria	B.C.	130
2. Branca	A.D.	1629
3. Kircher	—	1643
4. Daslesme	—	1699
5. Kempel	—	1785
6. James Sadler	—	1791
7. Richard Trevithic	—	1813
8. Alexander Craig	—	1834

The theory of machines of simple emission has been frequently and fully investigated, and the result is, that there is no possibility of obtaining, by simple emission, more than one-half of the whole power of the steam, so as to make it available to useful mechanical effect. The other half is wasted in giving off its impulsion to the air, or is expended in a current equally unavailing.

Practical experience corroborates the predictions of theory. Smeaton and Pelletan made the machines of simple issue the subject of careful experiment, and found that 3 parts out of 11, 8 parts out of 27, and 2 parts out of 5, are the highest measures of practical effect that it has been found practicable to attain, and by no possible improvement can more than one-half of the whole power be turned to a useful effect.

Class II.—Rotatory engines of medial effect are those which do not immediately give revolution to an axis by the action of steam upon the wheel, but have a *medium of communication* between the power and the effect, which medium is the direct agent in circular motion. This class of engines will be well understood by taking as its type any simple steam machine, such as Savary's and Newcomen's, used for raising water, which water by falling on the floats of a common mill-wheel will then give rotatory motion to it. The engine of Savary raises water by pressing directly on its surface, and it is only necessary to allow this water to fall on a wheel, when it will be made to revolve and form an engine of the 2nd class.

A variety of this class has been invented of which the fire-wheel of Amontons is a type. The stream pushes water through certain channels that form the arms of the wheel, from a set of chambers on one side of the wheel, to a corresponding set of chambers on the opposite; and thus the side filled with water preponderates over the other, and the wheel revolves. The water being constantly driven off by the steam from a given side of the wheel to that opposite, uniform revolution is the result of the weight of the water. In this state, although steam is the agent, water is the medium of communicating the rotatory motion.

Solids have also been made the medium of effecting rotation in this manner; weights of solid matter, in the form of pistons, have been transferred by the force of steam to a considerable distance from the centre on one side of a wheel, and drawn nearer to it on the other side, so as, by bringing about a continual preponderance on one side, to effect revolution. Watt and Witty have designed rotative mechanism of this nature.

Inventors of Rotatory Steam-Engines of the Second Class.

1. Guillaume Amontons ...... A.D. 1699
2. Leopold of Plainitz .... — 1723
3. Champion of Bristol ...... — 1752
4. James Watt .... — 1769
5. Davidson & Hawkesley.... — 1793
6. Richard Witty .... — 1816
7. Sir W. Congreve .... — 1818
8. John Moore .... — 1820
9. Sir W. Congreve .... — 1821
10. Thomas Masterman ...... — 1822

In this class of engines the loss of effect is manifest, for it is necessary that the steam, in order to produce circular motion, shall give out its force in setting the medium in motion, and, in overcoming the very great resistance of the liquid in all the pipes, passages, and valves, through which it is transmitted to alternate sides of the wheel in every revolution; the whole of this force is subtracted from useful effect, and becomes power lost.

In those which move weights from and towards the circumference, there are mere groups of reciprocating pistons without cranks, and share the evils to be explained in Class V.; in fact, in the engines of Watt and Witty of this class, we have *a series* of reciprocating engines ranged round a wheel to do the work of one.

In the case of the fluid medium, we have not only a loss of all the power expended in moving the medium itself, but also the additional loss of effect encountered in all modes hitherto adopted for applying a fluid to the rotation of a wheel, a loss, in the best examples ever presented, amounting of itself to more than one-sixth part of the power.

Class III.—The engine of hydrostatical reaction is more effective than either of the former classes. As invented by Watt in 1769, it consisted of steam-vessels in the form of hollow rings, or circular channels, with proper inlets and outlets for the steam, mounted on horizontal axles, like the wheels and buckets of a water-mill, and wholly immersed in some fluid. This wheel was made of iron, six feet in diameter, and the reaction of mercury was employed to give revolution to it; the engine moved, but was found to be inefficient, and abandoned, although it had been tried in very favorable circumstances.

The principle of action is this : steam is admitted into a circular channel or chamber on the circumference of a wheel; this chamber is partially filled with some liquid, the pressure of the steam is expended in pushing the mercury in one direction, and the end of the chamber in the opposite way, so that while the liquid is thus forced out of the chamber, the chamber is by an equal force pushed away from the liquid; the wheel is thus turned round.

It is apparent that a part of the force is employed in propelling the wheel, and the remainder is expended in overcoming the resistance of the liquid of reaction, and expelling it from the chambers, which remainder is a large portion of the power withdrawn from useful effect.

Inventors of Rotatory Steam-Engines of the Third Class.

James Watt .... A.D. 1782
Bryan Donkin .... — 1803

Class IV.—Rotatory engines, having a revolving piston, are constructed on a much better principle, and hold out much fairer prospects of a successful competition with those having the ordinary reciprocating piston, than any of the species of the three first classes that have been already considered. In these classes the steam is not confined in rigid vessels, but its action is applied to producing currents in fluids, and force is expended in medial effects which are useless, and therefore waste power. This is not the case with the steam-engine of the revolving piston. The steam is confined in a close and rigid chamber, and acts only on a solid inflexible surface, and makes its escape by confined passages, so that its full effect may be obtained in useful work. Abstractedly considered, it is an engine capable of giving out the full power of the steam, and therefore may fairly be imagined to come into competition with the ordinary reciprocating crank engine. The objections to it are entirely of a practical nature, and regard the engine not in its abstract mathematical form, but as a machine made of destructible matter, of matter imperfectly elastic, of surfaces opposing resistance to motion, of matter obeying the known laws of motion and rest. These objections are not the less valid that they are of a sensible and tangible, rather than a speculative description. But as a natural consequence of the more plausible deceptions held out by this species than by any of the three preceding ones, it has followed, that the fallacies of this class have been more widely seductive than any of the others. The Patent-office presents us with the names of more than forty victims, including some of the highest fame.

Inventors of Rotatory Steam-Engines of the Fourth Class.

1. James Watt .... A.D. 1782
2. James Cooke .... — 1787
3. Bramah & Dickinson .... — 1790
4. Edmund Cartwright...... — 1797
5. Jonathan Hornblower .... — 1805
6. William Murdoch........ — 1805
7. Jonathan Hornblower .... — 1805
8. John Trotter............ — 1805
9. Andrew Flint .... — 1805
10. William Lester........ — 1806
11. Richard Wilcox........ — 1806
12. Thomas Read .... — 1808
13. Edward Jane .... — 1808
14. Samuel Clegg .... — 1809
15. William Chapman....... — 1810
16. John Trotter.......... — 1811
17. William Onions .... — 1811
18. Richard Trevithic...... — 1813
19. Joseph Turner......... — 1816
20. John Mallam .... — 1818
21. Joshua Routledge...... — 1818
22. William Carter........ — 1818
23. John Rider .... — 1820
24. Robert Delap .... — 1821
25. Bambridge & Thayer .... — 1821
26. William Foreman....... — 1824
27. Lord Cochrane .... — 1825

28. L. M. Wright .... — 1826
29. F. Halliday .... — 1825
30. Joseph Eve .... — 1825
31. John Costigin .... — 1826
32. Marquis de Combis ..... — 1826
33. Elijah Galloway .... — 1826
34. Paul Steenstrup .... — 1827
35. John Evans .... — 1828
36. John Strut .... — 1830
37. E. & J. Dakeigne....... — 1830
38. William Morgan .... — 1831
39. Samuel Hobday .... — 1831
40. John Ericson .... — 1832
41. Robert Stein.......... — 1833
42. Elijah Galloway .... — 1834
43. Edward Appleby .... — 1835
44. John F. Kingston....... — 1835
45. John Yule............ — 1836
46. John White .... — 1836

The fallacy of this class of engines we shall expose in conjunction with the next class, as the same misconceptions lie to a considerable extent at the root of both.

Class V.—Revolving mechanism substituted for the crank of the common steam-engine, for the purpose of obtaining from the reciprocating piston a rotatory effect otherwise than by the crank, and in a better manner than by the crank, forms a class of inventions involving fallacies similar to those in which the revolving piston has originated. These two may therefore be considered together.

Inventors of Rotatory Mechanism as a substitute for the Crank.

1. Jonathan Hulls........ A.D. 1737
2. Keane Fitzgerald ...... — 1757
3. Gautier of Nancy....... — 1757
4. John Stewart.......... — 1769
5. Dugald Clarke .... — 1769
6. Matthew Washborough ... — 1779
7. James Watt .... — 1781
8. Thomas Burgess........ — 1789
9. Matthew Murray .... — 1779
10. William Lander....... — 1799
11. Phineas Crowther...... — 1800
12. George Medhurst....... — 1801
13. Edmund Cartwright..... — 1801
14. Matthew Murray .... — 1802
15. Richard Witty .... — 1811
16. J. Dawes .... — 1816
17. Tobias Mitchell....... — 1810
18. Henry Penneck........ — 1827
19. William Aldersey...... — 1821
20. Robert Barlow .... — 1827
21. Thomas Peck .... — 1827
22. Samuel Clegg .... — 1828
23. William Lucy .... — 1836
24. Charles Schafhautl ..... — 1836

Although the name of Watt has been included in this list of inventors of substitutes for the crank, it should be observed, that he was only driven to the invention of such a substitute by the circumstance of a patent having been previously obtained for the crank in its simple form, and that he abandoned this beautiful, but more complex, mechanism on the instant that the elementary crank was released from fetters of monopoly.

In exposing the nature of the fallacies of the two last classes of inventions, we shall avail ourselves of the accounts of their misconceptions on the subject of the common reciprocating crank-engine, which formed the ground of the preference given by the inventors of these improvements to their own mechanism, as these conceptions have been given by the inventors themselves, and those who have adopted their view of the subject. Fortunately for us, they have been particularly full in explaining their views.

Thomas Masterman, patentee, of a rotatory engine, says, "that the steam-engine on the reciprocating principle *absorbs about half the power of the steam.*"

William Aldersey, in his patent substitute for the crank, observes that—

"The object of this invention is to equalize the motion, and principally to save the *force which is unnecessarily thrown away* in steam-engines, and all other machines in which a reciprocating or backward and forward motion is converted into a circular one; and the simple manner in which it is here effected, will, it is presumed, be found a great desideratum by all who have occasion to use such machines, since a saving of power is a pecuniary saving of coals, which in the constant use of a machine is of much more importance than its first cost. That this saving is really effected in the present machine, will be sufficiently evident to those who possess mechanical knowledge; and for the conviction of those who do not, I have subjoined the diagram by which the action of the ordinary crank may be demonstrated. If the crank rod be so placed as to act either from above or below, it will have no power at all (figs. 1 and 3) to turn the crank round, while it is, in either of the two situations where the crank and rod are in one line, as at A and B, but it will have the greatest possible power upon it at those instants when it is at two other intermediate points (M and

Fig. 1.

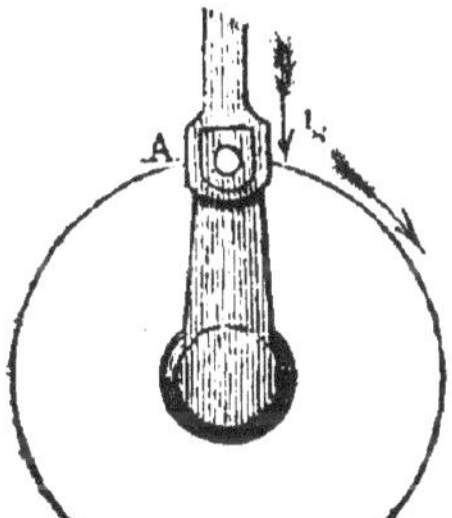

Fig. 2.

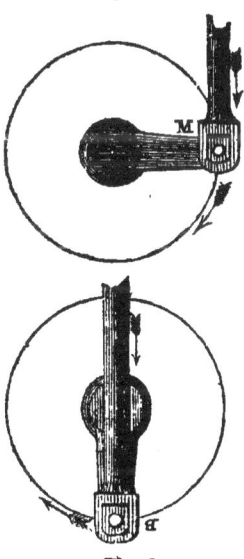

Fig. 4.

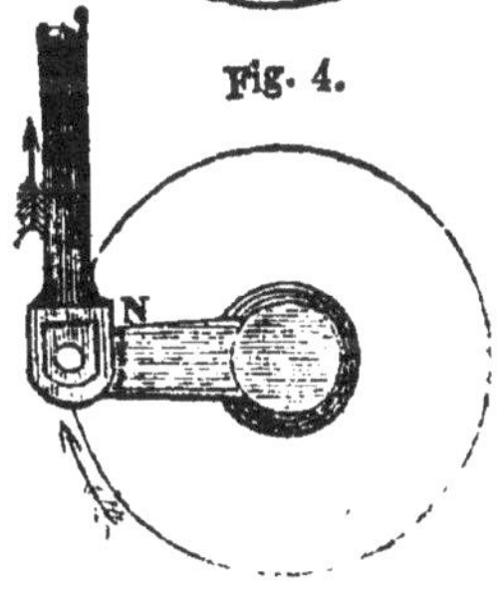

Fig. 3.

N, figs. 2 and 4), the consequence of which is, that while the power forces the crank to revolve, it increases in the first quarter revolution from zero to a maximum, and diminishes in the second quarter from the maximum to zero, and so on for each half revolution. The loss of power attendant on the use of the crank, is found in figures to be nearly one-third of the whole,"

Mr. Aldersey expresses clearly the senti-

ments of a host of inventors, all of them pursuing the main object of doing away the imaginary loss of power occasioned by the crank. I am sorry to add, that some eminent standard writers on the steam-engine have advanced the same doctrines.

I shall now, then, proceed to show, that the pressure produced by the crank is not a loss of dynamical force; that, where the apparent loss is greatest, there is no loss at all ; and that, at every point, the effect produced is directly proportioned to the quantity of steam producing it.

Let it be recollected, that at the two extremes of the lines of the centres, the greatest *apparent* loss of force takes place.

But it is not seen that at this instant there is in reality no loss at all, because there is no expansion of steam, no consumption of the elements ? The supply has been closed, the communication with the boiler is cut off, the steam has done its work, and only waits to be dismissed from the chamber, which it leaves on the instant that the eductive valve is thrown open for egress, and access is given to to the fresh supply which is forcing its way inwards to the other side of the piston.

The entering steam finds the piston almost in contact with that end of the cylinder at which it enters. It insinuates itself into the vacant disk, and powerfully expanding, swells out its thickness, propelling the disk of the piston towards the other end of the cylinder. At first its progress is but slow ; it gradually accelerates till the piston reaches the middle of the cylinder, when it moves with the full velocity of the crank in the centre. But, as the motion of the piston must altogether cease on arriving at the end of the cylinder, it is prepared for this event in a manner most exquisitely beautiful ; for, the moment of reaching the point which is half way from the end of its course, the piston begins to be retarded, the steam expands more and more slowly, the final stoppage is gradually prepared for, and at last the rectilineal motion, having dwindled to nothing by insensible shades, altogether ceases ; the steam has expanded by a continually dimin-

ishing movement, and now ceases to produce any effect, and is released from its confinement. Such is the history of the elemental power in its transit through the cylinder,—first communicating motion to the piston by gradually increasing increments, and then bringing it to rest by decrements of motion in the reverse order.

Let us now trace, with equal minuteness, the simultaneous phenomena of the joint which, by its connection with the piston, is carried round in the circumference of a circle, while] its mover progresses in its reciprocal strokes in the cylinder.

To trace the simultaneous positions of the point describing the circle of the crank, and the point describing the straight line in the cylinder, it is necessary that we have recourse to a simple diagram. You are requested to conceive a circle with its centre and radius placed at a given distance from the end of the cylinder, so that a piston moving in the given straight line of its piston-rod, at a given distance from it, is so connected with it that the motion of the one produces the motion of the other.

Let figs. 5 and 6 represent a cylinder, and the circles 1, 5, 10, 15, and 20, the path of the crank, the numerals on the cylinder and on the circles representing corresponding places of the crank and the piston at given instants of time. In fig. 5 the motion of the crank is supposed uniform, and the circle divided into equal parts, while in fig. 6 the axis of the cylinder is supposed to be divided into equal parts to represent a hypothetical case of uniform reciprocating motion in the piston ; so that the piston, when elevated and depressed by the steam,

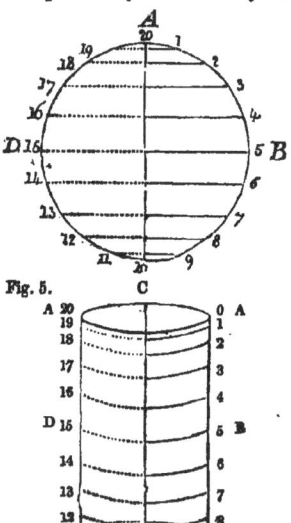

Fig. 5.

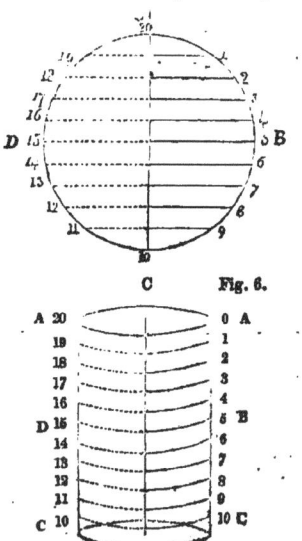

Fig. 6.

draws the crank down with it from A to B and C, and raises it up with it from C to D and A. Let the orbit of the crank be divided into twenty equal parts, the first ten numerals being placed on the descending side, and the other ten on the ascending side of the circle. Let the length of the stroke of the piston, which is equal to the diameter of the circle, be divided into ten parts, shewing the place of the piston at every instant of its stroke, contemporaneous with the points of the crank in its orbit; the first ten numerals corresponding both to the circle and the cylinder with corresponding points of reciprocation and of revolution.

Now, at each of these points, let us examine into the relation which exists between the pressure of the steam on the piston, and the quantity of the effect produced in revolving the crank, and that part of the pressure of the steam which produces no motion, and which is therefore erroneously said to be lost. The pressure of the steam acting obliquely on the crank produces two effects—pressure towards the centre through the crank, and motion in the direction of the circle tangentically. See figs. 7 and 8, in which the arrows placed as tangents represent effective rotating force, the vertical lines the power of the steam, and the lines directed to the centre the apparent loss. Let the whole pressure of the steam be taken at 100 lbs., then, by ascertaining the proportion which the lines a, b, and c, in the direction of those parts bear to each other, it will be seen that, at the first division, the force

Fig. 7.

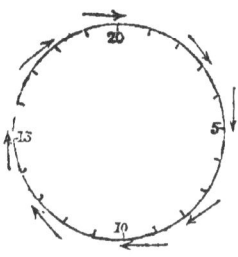

Fig. 8.

in the direction of the circle is only 31 per cent. of the force on the piston; at the second division it will be found to amount to (51.78) 59 per cent.; at the third to (80.90) 81 per cent.; at the fourth to (95.11) 95 per cent.; and at the fifth division, having completed one quarter of a revolution, the pressure is for an instant equal to 100 per cent., or the whole power on the piston; but the action has now become a maximum. In its next point a diminution of circular force takes place: at the sixth division the force has diminished by 5 per cent.; at the seventh 19 per cent. are lost (apparently); at the eighth 41 per cent.; at the ninth 69 per cent. are lost; and at the tenth the piston has reached the end of its stroke, and the whole pressure applied to the crank, in this position, would produce no effect at all on the circular orbit, or the apparent loss would be 100 per cent. Equal diminutions take place through the remaining semicircle during the returning stroke of the ascending piston.

The following table of the part of the power directly available to the production of circular motion at ten points in the semicircle, may therefore be found.

Points in the Fig.	Are moved over by Crank.	Force in the direction of revolution.	Relative velocity of Crank to Piston.
0 and 20	0°	0.00	Infinite.
1 .. 19	18	30.90	3.236
2 .. 18	36	58.78	1.701
3 .. 17	54	80.90	1.236
4 .. 16	72	95.11	1.051
5 .. 15	90	100.00	1.000
6 .. 14	108	95.11	1.051
7 .. 13	126	80.90	1.236
8 .. 12	144	58.78	1.701
9 .. 11	162	30.90	3.231
10 .. 10	180	Mean 63.138	Infinite.

Such is the reasoning by which, with apparent correct steps, many have been led to the conclusion, that in the crank the mean effect is less (by more than one-third) than the pressure exerted in the cylinder by means of the piston.

I have gone into analysis of this false reasoning the more fully, as it puts more perfectly before the mind of the reader the circumstances in which the error of the conclusion lurks in concealment. I shall proceed immediately to lay open the source of error, and the means of arriving at the truth.

Let it then be recollected, that, in all

calculations of power, we must attend to *space passed over*, as well as to the force exerted in that space. And that a force of *two* pounds moving a weight of two pounds through *three* feet a second, is equal in effect to a force of *three* pounds moving a weight of three pounds through a space of only *two* feet a second; or that, in calculating the quantity of effective power, a greater velocity is equivalent to a greater force. Thus much being premised of the principle of virtual velocities, as applied to uniform motions, if we find that, in the case of the crank, the force acting on the piston produces an effect through the crank, in which, although the force may be less, it is exerted through a space equivalently greater than that through which the piston is moved, then we have a right to infer that there is no loss of ratio of its effect on the crank; so that, at the instant when the power, but that what is lost in force is gained in velocity. Now, this is precisely the case.

While the piston moves through the length of the cylinder, which is equal to the diameter of the crank circle, it moves the crank through the circumference of a semicircle; now, the length of the diameter is to the length of the semicircumference as follows: Diam. :—semicirc. : : 2 : 3.14159, being a little more than the ratio of 63 : 100.

If, then, we find that the mean force exerted through the crank is not less than in this proportion, we shall be able to shew that the loss is imaginary. Now, the mean force on the crank obtained from the third column of the preceding table, is also 63 to 100; that is to say, *the force in the piston is greater than the mean force in the crank, in precisely the same ratio in which its velocity is less than it*.

There is another view of the matter to which I would direct particular attention. It is said that, at the top and bottom of the stroke, the position of the crank is so unfavorable to the production of circular motion, that no force of steam, however great, would produce any good effect towards causing revolution. This leads me to trace the progress of the steam itself in the cylinder, in connection with the motion of the piston and of the crank.

The steam, when the piston is at the top of the cylinder, has not yet been admitted to press upon the piston, and, therefore, none of its force can at this moment be lost. On the instant of leaving this point, the steam enters, and at the end of the first 18°, presses round the crank with a force of only 12.80 per cent.; but let it be observed, that the steam only carries the piston through a space of about one-eighth part of that through which the crank revolves,—so that, in pro-

ducing this effect, the motion of the piston is just so much slower than the motion of the crank, as the power on the crank is less than that on the piston; so that here again we have a dynamical equivalent of a greater force and a slower motion to a higher velocity with a less force.

As the piston descends and the pressure increases, it will be observed that the velocity of the piston increases exactly in the pressure on the crank and piston is equal, their velocities are also equal, and during the subsequent decrease of pressure on the crank, the velocity of the piston diminishes in the same ratio. The motion of the piston is not therefore an uniform but a variable motion, its velocity varying according to the pressure on the crank; and the two dynamical effects are not only equal in ultimatum, but they are equal at every instant of time; and if, on the other hand, the motion of the piston had been uniform, the motion of the crank must have been a variable quantity, as it is represented in fig. 6, a case which does not occur, and would be unsuitable at once to the nature and laws of matter, and to the practical application of mechanical power.

It appears, therefore,—1. That the mean pressure on the crank during the whole revolution, is less than the pressure on the piston, just in the proportion in which the space moved over by the latter is less than the space described by the former, so that the total of all the power in the one is equal to the total of all the effects in the other; —2. That the steam is not at all expended at the neutral points, and that its expenditure is at every point exactly proportioned to the power it gives out in useful effect;—3. That the velocity of the motion of the piston is in the ratio of the force acting at each instant on the crank.

These conclusions, here derived from obvious and elementary views of the relations of position and velocity, are originally deduced from the same data, by the more rigid method of the calculus. In the numerical exemplification I have endeavoured to give here of that more correct process, I have been compelled to select only a few points in the circuit, and the result is only approximately correct; but as the same might obviously be done at any point, the result is equally satisfactory.

The study of the higher analysis cannot be too strongly recommended to those who wish to avoid errors in invention.

In the reciprocating piston, therefore, acting through the crank, the whole power is found by multiplying the stroke and backstroke, or twice the stroke of the piston, by the pressure upon it, and this is equivalent to the whole effect produced in the entire revolution of the crank; the pressure of the steam, and the space it moves through, are therefore the measure of the power.

In the revolving piston, the effect of the steam must be precisely the same, if the revolving piston be of the same size, and moves through the same space as the reciprocating piston; and if the revolving piston have a pressure on it equal to the mean pressure on the crank, and move through a circle equal to the circle of the crank, the effect will be the same in both cases.

Since there is no loss incurred by propagating the action of the steam on a reciprocating piston through the crank of a revolving axle, and since it is not in the power of machinery of any kind to augment the quantity of power given out by any mover, but merely to arrange, dispose, and modify that power to suit any given purpose, it follows that the rotatory piston can have no purpose to accomplish, unless it excel the reciprocating one in simplicity and economy of construction, diminished bulk, durability, and economy in operation, facility of repair when deranged, diminished friction, or a peculiarity of adaptation to some individual purpose, such as steam navigation or inland transport.

I. As regards simplicity of parts, the engine with the rotatory piston cannot excel the simplest forms of the reciprocating engine; take, for example, that form which merely consists of a cylinder, piston, and crank axle; where the cylinder, mounted on an axle, oscillates with the revolutions of the crank, which is immediately attached to the end of the piston-rod, and which requires no moving valves of any kind, the steam being admitted and emitted through ports in the axle of the cylinder, which open and shut by the motion of the cylinder itself. Neither as regards facility and economy of construction does it possess superiority; for it will be readily granted to me, that whether the piston and channel in which it moves be rectangular or circular, they are more difficult of construction than a straight, round cylinder and piston, which, being derived from the straight line and circle, are the simplest of forms, while an annular chamber, if the piston be rotatory, is a surface of double curvature, of difficult construction and imperfect completion; if square, the construction of a rectangular piston is a still more troublesome attempt, the increased surface being increased expense and labour.

II. In point of bulk, the common reciprocating piston has a decided advantage; the annular cylinder of the revolving piston must be (to give equal power) about two-thirds of the area, and about three times the length of the reciprocating cylinder, being a bulk of cylinder nearly double. But even this is an estimate too favourable to the piston of rotation; the diameter of the axle requires to be very considerable; there are various reasons for this,—one is, that it is frequently a steam-passage; another is, that it is much larger than is required for the mere purpose of communicating the force, because any force of steam applied near the centre is of little value in producing an effect, from the smallness of the circle which that part of the piston describes; and for this reason also, that the portion of piston exposed to leakage and wear is in proportion to the effect gained; the piston is therefore removed to a considerable distance from the centre, to answer the purpose likewise of rendering the revolution of the parts more nearly equal. These points will, however, have our attention at another time; it is sufficient for our present purpose, that these circumstances render it imperative to increase the bulk of the engine.

III. In point of durability and economy in its use, the most conclusive arguments lie against the rotatory engine. I have seen many of them perfectly constructed, working beautifully, but they went very soon out of order. They invariably work best when new. This may appear to some to arise only from the defects incidental to particular modes of construction. I admit that many have had peculiar elements in their construction not indispensable to the principle. But, on the other hand, I shall now go on to show, that, independent of the idiosyncracy of peculiar engines, the necessary mode of action involves elements of self-destruction very rapid in their operation, by means of which every rotatory piston must soon wear itself out of condition.

It is a received principle in constructing machines, that, in a good engine, the parts should wear equally, and that even the very working of their parts should make them fit each other better. This is truly the case with the piston and cylinder, and other appendages of the reciprocating steam-engine. So true, that old engines of Messrs. Watt and Bolton—some of their earliest—are still working better than they ever did, or than some more recently made. To this the reciprocating engine necessarily presents a contrast: and it will not be difficult to show that its parts *must* wear unequally, so as to become unfit for use, and be rendered by each day's work less fit for the duty of the succeeding one.

To show the cause of this :—Suppose two perfectly flat plates of metal, perfectly round, to be laid one upon the other, so as exactly to coincide at every point. Let the undermost rest upon a table, and let the uppermost be so made as to turn round on an axis while in contact with the other, and let a rapid motion be communicated to the uppermost,—let me ask what will be the result of the attrition of the one of these upon the other? Will they wear equally, so as to remain in a state of mutual adaptation, or will they not? Experience furnishes an answer which exactly quadrates with reasonable expectation;—they will *not* wear equally,—they will *not* retain their forms. Let it be considered that the outer edge performs a larger circuit than any part nearer the centre; that, therefore, as all the parts revolve in the same time, those nearer the circumference move with a greater velocity than these towards the centre; that the attrition is most rapid at the circumference, and uniformly diminishes towards the centre of the plates; then it inevitably follows that *the plates must become conical*, with a continual tendency to become more so. This is a most incontestible truth. It is one which has caused the failure of many beautiful inventions; it is the reason why conical bearings have been universally abandoned for cylindrical ones; and it is the cause that has rendered a most beautiful class of inventions totally useless to the improvement of the reciprocating engine. I allude to the flat *revolving valves* introduced by Oliver Evans, and afterwards brought into this country, but now universally abandoned, in spite of simplicity, efficiency, and economy, on account of this very attrition from a centre, which we consider to be ruinous to every steam-engine on a revolving principle.

The application of the result of this illustrative experiment to the subject in question, is abundantly obvious, the circumstance of rotation from a centre, with pressure on bearing surfaces of which the parts are at unequal distances from the centre, implies the excessive attrition of the circumferential surfaces above those which are near the centre, and which move with less velocity. Hence the circumferential surfaces wear more rapidly, and are unfit for use long before the central parts have suffered any sensible effect. Where extensive metallic surfaces are in contact, their repair is a matter of much expense and delay.

To diminish this cause, or to delay its effect, the revolving piston is removed far from the centre of action. By this means, however, the bulk of the machine, and its friction, are very much increased, and the evil only partially remedied. It is obvious, however, that in this way, by increasing the radius, the engine is brought more nearly to the principle of the straight cylinder; so that perfection would just be attained if the circular cylinder were made straight, or, in

other words, if the rotatory engine were converted into an ordinary reciprocating engine.

When a piston reciprocates in a straight cylinder, all its points, and those of the cylinder, move equally, being in lines parallel to the axis; and to prevent accumulation of eccentricity, the piston may have its position on the circumference altered by part of a turn.

The essential nature of *rotatory attrition* is therefore fatal to the success of the revolving principle,—a cause of expensive repairs, and speedy destruction.

IV. There are other defects to which this species of engine is peculiarly liable;—to vacuities and losses at the valves and passages —to irregular action, and collisions and shocks from the action of the parts upon one another; but these will be the subject of consideration as they occur in individual machines.

V. Unless, therefore, we shall find that there is some peculiar applicability in this form of engine above the common one, to certain important purposes, such as steam navigation and inland transport, we must abandon the hope of deriving practical advantage from the engine of rotation.

Now, it has been proposed for steam navigation, but to this is peculiarly inapplicable. In a steam-vessel, it is useful to have the axis of rotation as *high* and the weight of the engine as *low* as possible. Now, if the engine be placed on this axis, as it would be in the case of the rotatory engine, one of two evils would follow; the axis would either require to be much lowered, or the weight of the engine would be so high as to make the vessel the very reverse of steady. By such a disposition of its parts it must necessarily be rendered crank, and have its power greatly diminished. In the present engine, the weight is immediately above the floor of the vessel, and the axis in contact with the deck.

Applied directly to the axis of a steam-carriage or locomotive engine, there are insuperable objections to the rotatory engine. As there would be no spring between it and the wheels, every jolt would derange the machinery. The weight of the engine, rigidly connected to the axle, would reciprocate the evil, and knock the wheels to pieces. These evils are prevented in the reciprocating engine, by the detachment of the engine from the axle, and the propagation of power through rods, wheels, or chains, to the propelling wheel or axis. It is indeed a radical defect in some of the existing forms of the locomotive engine, that the detachment is less perfect than might be desired. This very adjustment, so impracticable with the rotatory engine, was, even with the superior facilities presented by the form of reciprocating locomotion, one of the greatest impediments to the success of elemental locomotion.

VI. In addition to the above-mentioned advantages possessed by the reciprocating engine above the rotatory one, it presents facilities (altogether wanting to the latter) for working directly the subordinate appendages of the steam-engine, such as cold water pump, its own feeding pump, &c. If the engine be a condenser, the simplicity of the reciprocating mechanism of the air-pump puts the rotatory engine altogether *hors de combat.*

VII. All these considerations, of the most important practical bearing, demonstrate clearly to us, that if there be no very considerable loss of power in the reciprocating engine, we have little inducement to make the substitute of the rotatory chamber and revolving piston for the cylinder and reciprocating piston.

It appears, on the contrary, both from theory and the practical working of the steam-engine of ordinary construction, that, with a very small allowance for friction, the piston gives out through the crank, in actual work done, all the power of all the steam applied to it in the cylinder. Mechanism can do more.* And since neither simplicity of action, compactness of form, condensation of bulk, nor economy, either in first cost or operation, give it a superiority to the common engine, but that, on the other hand, from the very nature of its movement, it possesses the elements of rapid detrition and unequal deterioration, and is, by the necessary arrangement of its parts, rendered peculiarly inapplicable to such important objects as the purposes of steam navigation and land transport, I do not see what motive can possibly remain for devoting a single thought to its further improvement, or the alteration of its form, when its very principle holds out

no higher premium than that, if brought to its utmost perfection, it might possibly approach in durability and efficiency the ordinary reciprocating engine, but in no point of view could ever excel it. To expend more time and mind on such a subject, is therefore merely sowing the wind to reap the whirlwind.

VIII. The force of the exposure I have now been induced to make of the fallacious nature of those attractions by which the rotatory motion has drawn aside ingenious mechanists from the direct path of legitimate invention into the fruitless pursuit after ingenious trifles, will have considerable weight added to it, if we turn our attention to the *peculiarities of the crank* as one of the elementary machines for the conversion of reciprocating into rotatory action.

The crank, as the means of converting the reciprocation of the piston of a steam-engine into a continuous rotatory action, possesses singular and beautiful properties, which distinguish it from every other means of producing that conversion, and which appear to be so perfectly adapted to the nature of steam and the constitution of solid matter, that we are indebted to it materially, although indirectly, for the very great advantages we derive from the modern steam-engine as a source of mechanical power. Ingenuity has been taxed to the utmost to find substitutes for it, which should remedy the (imaginary) defects of the crank, but the mighty element has disdained them all, pounded them to powder, and thrown them from her. Like unskilful keepers, they have attempted to control a power by means which have only encountered the force they were designed to direct; and, after many vain efforts, it is found that the crank is the magic rod under which alone the mighty force of the element becomes peaceful and docile. Wheels, sectors, and racks, in various combinations, have been made to assume the functions of the crank, but they have uniformly been declared incapable. Once or twice it has happened that a substitute was obtained, but it was soon found that these (the sun and planet motion, for example) were only cranks in disguise; and the useless mask was speedily dispensed with when the cause of its assumption had ceased to exist. It was an invidious patent alone that induced the immortal Watt to give the name of sun and planet to two wheels, placed one at the base and another at the apex of the crank. The disguise disappeared as the patent expired, and the simple unencumbered crank resumed its well-merited station.

The peculiarities of the crank which give it its unapproachable perfection as an elementary machine, I shall now go on to describe.

* We have before us the printed reports of last year, in which the duty done by the crank engines of Charlestown and Wheal Kitty, constructed by Mr. Sims, is given. We have also before us the indications of pressure in the cylinder, as obtained by a very accurate indicator applied in the course of last summer by Mr. Smith, of Manchester, who visited the mines for that purpose, and has been kind enough to favor us with a copy of his observations. We have thus the means of comparing the power actually exerted on the piston with the work done, and find the result of the comparison to be, that *the work done is within ten per cent. of being perfectly equal to the power employed.* Here, then, we arrive at this conclusion, that the utmost conceivable reach of improvement in the rotatory engine, if it attained even to perfection, would not save more than a few per cent. That the crank engine, therefore, as at present used, is as near the perfection of mechanism as any thing we can hope to obtain, is, we think, satisfactorily established.

1st, I would observe, that in the reciprocating piston in a steam-engine the following things occur :—The piston is to be put in motion in one direction, then stopped ; then put in motion in the opposite direction, stopped again ; motion in the original direction begun and once more made to cease. At the commencement of the motion downward, a valve is to be opened for the entrance of the steam above the piston, which valve must be closed at the end of the stroke, and at the same instant in which one steam-valve closes, an opposite one must be opened to admit steam below the piston ; at the same instant, also, a valve of eduction for the first portion of the steam must be opened, and a second valve of emission on the opposite side of the piston closed. At one and the same instant, therefore, the motion of the piston has to be stopped in one direction and commenced in the opposite direction, one steam communication closed, a second opened, a third of eduction cut off, and a fourth renewed, and all this (for the perfection of the engine) must be done with the most absolute precision.

But these processes, which produce the change of state from rest to motion, and from motion to rest, require time. Matter acquires momentum which must be gradually removed, otherwise that matter is subjected to concussion, as if by the stroke of a hammer, and either suffers or produces injury. And, on the other hand, when in motion, matter requires a force to stop it equal to the force that gives it that motion. These effects, therefore, cannot be instantaneous ;[*] and it is necessary that while the motion which the steam gives off be uniform and continuous, the parts of the engine itself shall be allowed time to be brought to a state of rest, without shock, concussion, or jolt, and as gradually and gently be again urged to their greatest velocity in the opposite direction. *All these with exquisite adjustment the crank effects* ; it stops the piston as gently and softly as if it placed beneath it a cushion of eider down, and afterwards as gradually begins and accelerates its motion to its highest velocity in the opposite direction. The valves, too, are opened with the same perfect adjustment, being performed with that gradual motion which proportions the largeness of the aperture to the supply of fluid required to be transmitted. An adjustment so complete could only take place by such a relation as subsists between the crank and piston, the one describing uniformly the circumfer-

ence of a circle, while the other moves by simultaneous gradations of alternately increasing and diminishing extent. But this is not all that distinguishes the crank.

2d, It is one of the highest recommendations of a piece of mechanism, that any very slight error in its construction shall not very materially prevent its usefulness, nor any slight derangement of its adjustment be attended with immediate destruction, but that on the other hand, the *efficiency of the mechanism shall be consistent with such degrees of correctness as ordinary workmen can accomplish, and with such care as ordinary attendants can be trusted to bestow* ; also, that the progress of disrepair shall be so gradual as to give timely warning of the necessary readjustment. Just such a piece of mechanism *is* the crank. It is at the top and bottom of the stroke, or in the line of the centres, as it is technically called, that the opening and shutting of the valves should take place ; and it is just at this point that pressure on the piston can produce any effect on the crank ; but suppose the valves not to open with obsolute precision, suppose them to open and shut too soon or too late, then will the error at that part of the circuit be of comparatively small importance, because, *just then*, the motion of the piston is so slight, that, through an arc of twenty degrees, it does not describe one hundredth part of a stroke, and the effect of any error in that space will not effect the crank by more than one hundredth part of its amount ; any *error of adjustment is therefore diminished in effect to one hundredth part* of what would be produced, were the motion of the piston to be uniform in portions corresponding to the arc of description, as would be the case in any other species of rotatory conversion.

3d, In like manner, errors arising out of construction, management, or wear, are diminished one hundred-fold by transmission through the crank. It has been to me matter of frequent astonishment, that although I have seen at the mouths of coal-pits, small mines, and quarries, mere remnants of engines, frail rusty old fragments of iron and wood, working so loose as scarcely to remain upright upon their basements, they were still working within 30 per cent of their full power.

4th, To all these circumstances, I may add, that the constitution of the crank is one reason why an engine may be constructed of enormous weight, and of the most unwieldy dimensions, without being thereby much injured in its working ; because the crank acquires so slow a motion at the commencement and termination of the stroke, that it equally slowly communicates motion to all parts of the machine, and in a like

* " On sait que pression ne peut pas produire tout-à-coup une vitesse finie."—Lagrange, Mech. Analyt., p. ii. sec. x.

manner receives from them the impetus which they give out in the act of being again slowly brought to rest towards the end of the stroke. The impetus, therefore, given to the reciprocating parts of the machine is *lent* not *lost*.

We have thus endeavoured to expose the nature of the fallacy under which they labour, who imagine that the present steam-engine, as derived from Watt, is a machine which "destroys" or "absorbs" a larger portion of the power it is designed to transmit, and who looked to the rotatory engines as a means of increasing the amount of the power given out in useful effect. That the rotatory engines, which appear day after day, are not new, we show from the fact, that the five great classes which comprehend them all have been invented and re-invented by upwards of ninety individuals. That their inventions have been unsuccessful, is manifest from the non-existance of their machines in the daily use of ordinary manufactures. That the failures of these contrivances did not arise from defects accidental to the peculiar arrangements and contrivances of the engines, is rendered probable by the great variety of forms in which they have been re-invented, tried, and abandoned. That they have not failed from deficiencies in the workmanship and practical details, is rendered still more probable by the circums'ance of finding among the names of inventors, those of the most eminent practical engineers We have next shown that in theory, the crank of the steam-engine in common use, cannot as has been supposed, be attended with a loss of power, as such loss would oppose the established doctrines of virtual velocities ; it is shown also from very simple and elementary considerations, that what appears to be lost in force, is resumed in velocity—that, in proportion as the mean force on the piston is greater than the mean force on the crank, in that proportion is the space described by the latter greater than the space described by the former. That the dynamical effect produced in a given time is exactly in the proportion of the steam expended in that given time ; and thus have we arrived at the conclusion, that the common reciprocating crank steam-engine has not the faults attributed to it in theory, and which the rotatory engines have been designed to remedy. We have next taken the practical view of the subject—in simplicity of parts the rotatory piston has no advantage over the reciprocating piston ; in difficulty of construction the rotatory piston far exceeds the reciprocating engine —it is more expensive at the outset—it has more friction—it is more bulky, and less compact—it is inferior in precision and uniformity to the crank engine—and there

is a radical fault inherent in the very nature of rotatory mechanism, from which it follows that the rotatory engine can never be rendered either an economical or a durable machine. We have further shown that, even if rotatory engine could be made economical and durable, its very nature renders it unsuited to the great purpose of steam navigation and inland locomotion,—objects to which it has been considered peculiarly applicable. We deemed it an appropriate and instructive conclusion to our inquiry, to examine into the action of the crank, for the purpose of discovering what those remarkable qualities are which have given to the crank of the common steam-engine, its unrivalled superiority as an element for the production of circular motion, and a degree of perfection unattainable by any other mechanism. We heve seen that well-constructed crank steam-engines are daily performing duty, which is within ten per cent. of the therotical maximum of possible effect— of obsolute perfection— that this practical perfection arises from the simplicity of the crank, from its wonderful adaption to the nature and laws of matter and of circular motion in connection with rectilineal motion— from its reduction of errors either in construction, adjustment, or management, so as to work well without the obsolute necessity of greater intelligence, expertness, and precision, than belongs to ordinary workmen; and from the compensating nature of the arrangements of its structure, by which it is accommodated, in a remarkable degree, to the necessary imperfections of all human mechanism.

It is my earnest desire, that this exposure may have the effect of inducing some of my ingenious countrymen to direct their exertions for the advancement of the arts and industry of Scotland, to other and more promising subjects of invention. A wide field is open to their exertions in the useful *applications* of the mechanical powers of the common steam-engine to the wants ef growing civilization, and to the improvement of the condition of the human race. Let them direct their exertions to these objects, with the industry and unity of purpose which they have already displayed in the pursuit of the facinating fallacy of a rotatory steam-engine, and they will one day be reckoned in the glorious list of those who have been the benefactors of their kind, and the ornaments of Scotland.

RECENT AMERICAN PATENTS.

(Selected from the *Franklin Journal* for March.

MANUFACTURING SADDLE-TREES, *William Kelley, Pennsylvania.*—" My improved mode of manufacturing saddle-trees consists in the substitution of raw-hide for the wood, usually employed for that purpose; to effect which, I proceed in the following manner: After the hair has been removed from the hide, in the usual way, and the hide is properly broken, I draw, or strain it, whilst wet, either over a wooden saddle-tree, or over a mould properly shaped and prepared for that purpose, where it is to remain until it is perfectly dry and hard. Having in this way brought two or more such pieces of hide into the proper form, I unite them together at their edges, by means of rivets, or otherwise; preferring, however, the employment of rivets to any other mode. The pieces of hide are, of course, cut to the proper size and shape for the intended purpose. I sometimes form the tree, or foundation of the saddle, of a single piece of raw-hide, in which case I turn the edges of the hide over, all round the outer and inner edges of the tree, and rivet through the double thickness. To this foundation, or tree, the irons usually employed may be fastened, as to trees of wood. Strips of spring steel, also, may be rivetted on, whenever it may be deemed requisite, so as to increase the stability and elasticity of the whole: I usually affix such a spring all round the under side. After my tree, thus made, has received its proper form, and is ready for covering, I give to it a thick coating of any good water-proof varnish, such as shellac, copal, or gum-elastic. In finishing the saddle, any of the known modes of procedure may be adopted, according to the fancy or judgment of the workman."

RAIL-ROAD CARS, *Anthony Planton, Philadelphia.*—This contrivance exhibits a railroad car upon castors. The running wheels are to be grooved to embrace both sides of the rail, and these wheels are embraced between, and have their gudgeons in two cheeks of metal, which unite at top, forming part of a vertical swivel upon which the wheel, with its embracing cheeks, may revolve horizontally. The claim is, to "the substitution for the axle now in use, of four upright pivot standards, as above described, which contain the wheels, and possess the power of rotation; also their mode of construction and their application to any form of car or locomotive that may be used on railroads."

There is no probability that a car upon this plan will ever be essayed, and should it be, we are convinced that its career would end there. The idea that such a wheel would readily adapt itself to curvatures, is manifestly fallacious. It is to swivel round by the action of the two flanches of the wheel upon the rail, and that under the weight of the car and its burthen.

STOVE FOR HEATING IRONS FOR HATTERS, TAILORS, &c., *Bartholomew W. Taber,*

Falmouth, Massachusetts.—This stove is intended to be used with anthracite as fuel, but other kinds may be burnt in it. The most convenient form is rectangular, the plates being, in general, of cast iron, and put together in the usual manner; The fuel is contained in a grate with front and bottom bars, such as are commonly employed in open fire places, and frequently in close stoves, there being a door in front by which the grate may be enclosed, and another above it for replenishing the fire. The receptacles for the irons to be heated are at each side of the fire, and consist of small compartments, like ovens, which are closed by doors that slide up and down; each of these compartments must be sufficiently long and deep to contain the goose, or pressing iron, which is to be laid upon its side within it, the handle standing out, so that when a door or shutter which closes the compartment is slid down, the handle of the iron is without, exposed to the air, there being two notches in the lower edges of each of these sliding shutters, to allow it to close over the two ends of the handle.

The distinguishing feature of this stove, as applied to the heating of irons is, that the irons are exposed to the direct action of the fire, there being bars at each end of the grate, which bars constitute the division between the fire and the compartments, so that the faces of the contained irons are exposed to it, as they would be if exposed against the front bars of an open grate, whilst, at the same time, they are confined within a small oven, or enclosed compartment, in which they will be rapidly heated.

PROTECTING TIMBER FROM DESTRUCTION BY WORMS AND DRY ROT, *August Gotthilff, New York.*—The patentee states, that he saturates the timber with either of the following articles, either alone or combined with common salt; or uses two or more of them so mixed, or combined, as may be preferred; that is to say, take common vegetable tar, pitch, the tar-like residuum from the manufacture of illuminating gas, in gas works where animal or vegetable oil, resin, a mixture of oil and resin, or any vegetable oleaginous or resinous substance is employed for the production of the gas, and melt or combine them together in such proportions as may appear best, adding, in most cases, to these resinous materials, and more especially when the timber to be saturated is of a very porous kind, from one-eighth to one-fourth part of their weight of common salt.

As these materials are to enter, and fill the pores of the wood, by the aid of heat, it may be necessary, sometimes, to dilute them, and this is done by means of spirits of turpentine, or of an analogous solvent distilled from any of the above enumerated materials; this, however, will rarely be necessary. To effect perfect saturation, the timber and the resinous materials are placed together, in suitable metallic troughs, or tanks, the quantity of the resinous matter being sufficient to cover the timber; the whole is then submitted so a temperature of from three to four hundred degrees of Fahr. scale, for a term which may vary from one to twelve, or more, hours, dependant upon the size and nature of the timber; after which the redundant heated fluid is to be drawn off, when it will be found that the timber will be saturated throughout. The well known processes of exhaustion and pressure may be applied to promote the saturation, but it is not believed that this will ever be required.

He claims the application of the tar, pitch, and other analogous materials, obtained from vegetable substances, by the agency of heat, to the various kinds of timber, in the manner described, so as completely to saturate the same; using these various materials, in some cases, in combination with common salt; the saturating of timber with the vegetable products within mentioned, by submersing the timber therein, in a heated state, without, as well as with, the addition of common salt.

MACHINE FOR BREAKING AND DRESSING FLAX AND HEMP: *Harvey Lull, New York.*—Upon a main shaft, the gudgeons of which are sustained in any suitable frame, I fix (says the patentee) two circular heads, which for an ordinary sized machine for hemp may be three feet in diameter, and three feet six inches apart. Between these heads there are to be fluted breaking rollers, which have their bearings near the peripheries of these heads, or in circular plates. These rollers may be of cast iron, or of wood covered with metal; they extend from one circular head to the other, and may be ten inches in diameter. They are fluted from end to end by deep angular flutes, each of which may constitute two sides of an equilateral triangle, and of these there are upon each roller usually ten in number. Two or more such rollers are placed at equal distance apart, with their teeth projecting beyond the edges of the plates in which their gudgeons revolve. Knives for dressing the hemp, or flax, extend across from head to head, there being one in advance of each roller, nearly in contact with it, and having its blade in the direction of the peripheries of the circular heads, and on a level with them, whilst they are strengthened by a strip on their backs at the under sides of them.

The breaking is to be effected by means of metallic plates, or slats, with the aid of the above-named fluted rollers, within the flutes of which they are to be received, their conjoint action effecting the object. These slats may be of the same length with the rollers, four or five inches wide, and one-fourth of an inch thick; and they are to be so fixed that they may be made to pass to a greater or a less depth within the roller flutes, as the breaking proceeds; the rollers also must be made to revolve on their own axes, and both of these objects I effect in the following manner.

I prepare two flat circular plates, or hoops, usually of cast iron, which are to be of such size, and so attached to the frame of the machine, as that they shall surround the fluted rollers, near each of their ends. One of these hoops is round on its inner edge, and the opening therein of such diameter as just to allow the fluted rollers to revolve, and to be carried round by the main shaft within, without touching it; this plate or ring, is about three inches wide. The opposite plate differs from this first in being furnished with teeth on its inner edge, which mash into the flutes, or teeth, of the fluted rollers, which play with freedom in them. The effect of this arrangement is, that when the main shaft, carrying the cylinder of fluted rollers and knives, is made to revolve, the individual rollers will likewise revolve on their own axes.

The slats which are to pass between the teeth of the fluted rollers are received between the two last described hollow circular plates, extending from one of them to the other, and sliding in and out, in notches or groves prepared for that purpose, their planes pointing towards the centre of the main shaft and standing in the middle of each of the teeth, by which the rollers are turned. The number of these slats may vary, but eight will usually answer the intended purpose; they occupy the upper portion of the machine, commencing about twenty degrees from its top on the feeding side, and extending about one-fourth of the way round.

I have said that these slats are made to slide in and out, as may be required, and this sliding I effect by making a projecting tongue on each end of them, which tongues are received into grooves upon moveble curved plates adapted to the inner sides of the hoops, or rings, by which the slats are sustained; the grooves, above named, form inclined planes, so placed that when the curved plates are made to slide back or forth within the circle, the slats are simultaneously forced in or out: they are made to slide by means of a cranked lever attached to their ends, and which crosses the machine. Instead of tongues, there may be notches on each end of the slats, having inclined tongues, or fillets fitted into them; and the sliding of the slats also may be effected in other ways.

When this machine is used, the main shaft is to be made to revolve by any competent power; the tow or flax is to be held in the hand, or in a gripe made for the purpose, and fed in upon the revolving rollers, by which it will be carried under the slats, which by means of the cranked lever, are forced down as the breaking proceeds, whilst it is at the same time dressed by the knives, which separate the shivers from it, and clean it in a very perfect manner. When one end of the handful has been thus dressed and cleaned it is withdrawn, and the other end is fed in and cleaned in a similar manner. For flax the machine should be of smaller size than that designated; but considerable latitude may be allowed in this particular.

NOTES AND NOTICES.

Smoky Chimneys,—It has often occurred to us that one very common cause of smoky chimneys, where no apparent cause can be discovered, arises from the practice of using boys to sweep them, and thus the sin against humanity is partly punished by a large amount of continuous annoyance. For a flue to draw well, it is essential that there should be only two openings into it—one at the bottom and the other at the top. Now, chimney flues are divided from one another by single courses of bricks in width, or half bricks, as it is technically termed. Those flues are built with lime mortar, which is an absurdity in the outset, as the heat of the fire restores the mortar to the state of quick lime, which falls out in powder, and leaves gaping chinks for misdraught between the bricks, destroying the continuity of the flue. To provide in some measure against this evil, the practice is to coat the inside of the flue with a composition of lime mortar with cow-dung, called "pargetting." This is, in fact, a luting to make the flue air-tight. The climbing boys, by frequent ascents, break the luting away, and the chimney, opening into chinks, produces an imperfect draught. This is an evil for which there is no remedy, except rebuilding the chimney. Were it the practice to use iron tubes built into the thickness of the walls, or better still—as more economical of heat—to introduce hollow iron columns upon the face of the wall, covering them in the apartments with perforated screen partitions, the great source of evil would cease, and the still greater evil—the crime—the degradation of humanity—would cease also.—*London and West. Review.*

Quick Adventures of a Bale of Cotton—A bale of cotton was shipped on board the *Great Western*, at New York, on the 6th ult.; arrived in King Road on the 22nd; was sent to the new cotton factory at Bristol on the 23rd; and on the 24th, part of it manufactured into yarn, was exhibited, at a public meeting of the inhabitants, as a specimen of the first cotton ever manufactured in that city.

Dr. Lardner and Animal Magnetism.—Dr. Lardner has recently taken occasion to announce his conversion to a full faith in the wonders of animal magnetism, on which he is delivering lectures at various scientific institutions, besides giving it the support of his *powerful* pen. He scruples not to avow his belief that persons in the "sixth stage" of magnetism are gifted with the faculty of foretelling coming events. What a pity, then, the Doctor himself was not magnetised to this degree before he undertook to prophecy the fate of the Atlantic steamers! Another faculty with which the magnetised are gifted, is that of reading with the eyes shut; but it has not yet been stated whether they are able to read an article which ought to have appeared, but *did not,* in a scientific magazine. If this might be hoped for, it would be worth while to submit to be "treated" by the Doctor, taking care to have the last number of the *Monthly Chronicle* to practise upon. The reading of the missing article on "Ocean Steamers," would no doubt afford plenty of amusement,—especially to the magnetiser!

The Prepared Fuel again.—The inventors of the celebrated "Jerusalem Coffee-House stove" have a new project on the anvil, for applying their prepared fuel to the generation of steam, and other similar purposes, by way, it may be supposed, of counterbalancing its utter failure for domestic uses. Query,—if the death of any party had taken place in consequence of full reliance on the assurances in the prospectus of the "new stove," as to the innocuous nature of the prepared fuel, would not the patentees have been indictable for manslaughter, at the least?

Channel Steaming.—Boulogne has now decidedly taken its place as the chief port of transit between England and France, having for some time far surpassed Calais in the number of passengers landing and embarking. She will not lose ground during the present season—a splendid new steamer, the *City of Boulogne,* having been built expressly for the station between that port and our own metropolis, while another has been started to run daily from Rye, in addition to the old-established packets from Dover.

Retirement of Dr. O. Gregory.—We understand that Dr. Olinthus Gregory, who has for the long period of thirty-five years presided over the Royal Military Academy, Woolwich, with so much credit to himself and advantage to the public service, and whose numerous scientific works have contributed so much to the promotion of practical science, has been permitted to retire from the Professorship of Mathematics at Woolwich. He is succeeded in the professorship by Mr. S. H. Christie, Secretary to the Royal Society, who took a high degree at Cambridge many years ago, and who has been connected with the Royal Military Academy, we believe, about 32 years. He is succeeded as first Mathematical Master, by Mr. Peter Barlow, whose name is well known to our readers. Mr. Barlow, who was Second Master, is succeeded by Mr. Thomas S. Davies. The remaining Mathematical Masters are, Mr. James Christie and Mr. W. Rutherford, late of Berwick-upon-Tweed. An additional Mathematical Master, it is expected, will be immediately appointed. We hope he will be one whose talents and acquirements will, with those of the other gentlemen named above, keep up the distinguished reputation of this institution, now, in many respects, more important than ever, and especially from the circumstance that the military engineers trained at Woolwich, have of late been much employed in dock-yards, and other of our public works.

Complete Sets of the Mechanics' Magazine may now be had, twenty-seven volumes, half-cloth, price £11. 7s.

☞ *British and Foreign Patents taken out with economy and despatch; Specifications, Disclaimers, and Amendments, prepared or revised; Caveats entered; and generally every Branch of Patent Business promptly transacted. A complete list of Patents from the earliest period (15 Car. II. 1675,) to the present time may be examined. Fee 2s. 6d.; Clients, gratis.*

LONDON: Printed and Published for the Proprietor, by W. A. Robertson, at the Mechanics' Magazine Office, No. 6, Peterborough-court, between 185 and 186, Fleet-street.—Sold by A. & W. Galignani, Rue Vivienne, Paris.

𝔐𝔢𝔠𝔥𝔞𝔫𝔦𝔠𝔰' 𝔐𝔞𝔤𝔞𝔷𝔦𝔫𝔢,

MUSEUM, REGISTER, JOURNAL, AND GAZETTE.

No. 777.]   SATURDAY, JUNE 30, 1838.   [Price 3*d.*

WILCOX'S REVOLVING SLIDE-REST.

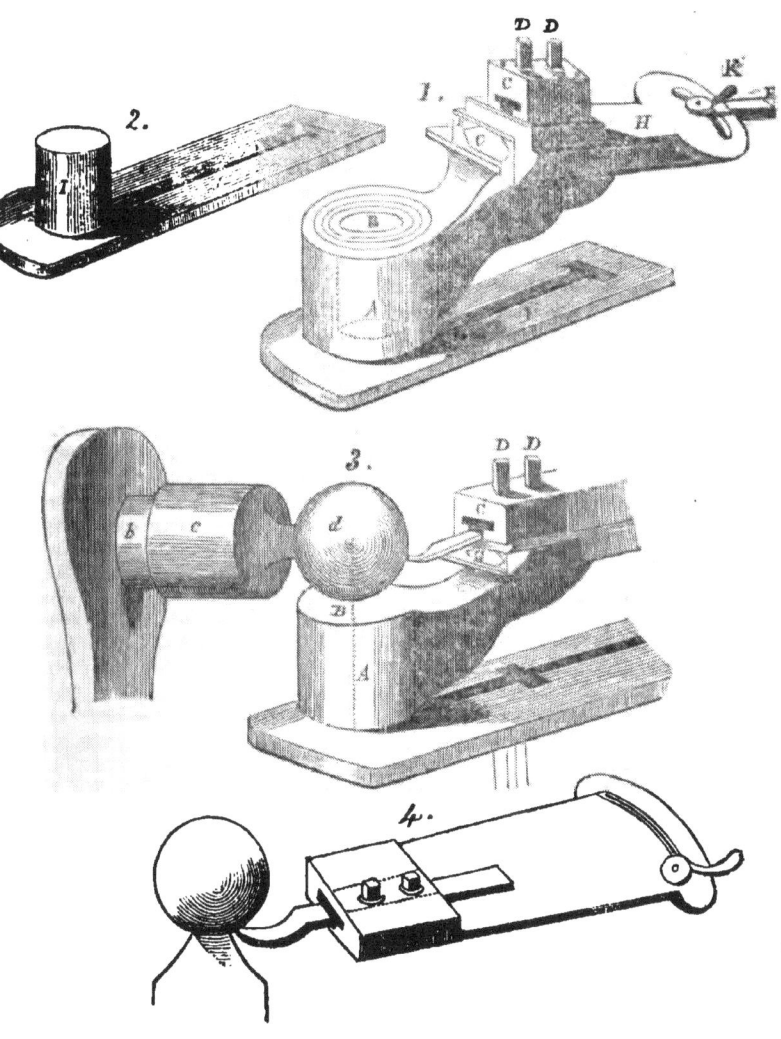

WILCOX'S REVOLVING SLIDE-REST.

Sir,—The accompanying drawing of a revolving slide-rest may probably be useful to some of your readers, as a ready means of accomplishing ball-turning. I have no idea of the principle of the tool revolving by means of a centre under the ball, being new, but with the addition of a slide-rest I do not believe it has ever before been used. I find it in practice a very efficient tool, by which a perfect ball can be turned in a few minutes.

A A (figs. 1 & 3) is made of beech wood, bored out, as shown by the dotted lines in A, to fit very true on to I fig. 2 (which is in fact, the lower part of my slide-rest); it has a plate of brass screwed on to it; E E two side plates, with grooves in them, to receive the slide G. On to G is screwed a plate H, with a quadrant at one end turning upon the screw as a pivot; carrying immediately over the pivot a box to hold the tool in the mortice C, where it is held firm by the screws D D; the screw F advancing or retiring the slide G, as may be required, and the thumb nut K fixing the quadrant at any inclination. The peculiar value of this quadrant may be seen at fig 4, where we will suppose the ball finished, and requiring cutting off,—in the position shown. The quadrant being turned back, allows the tool to be advanced in the mortice so far, that when it comes round, it separates the ball perfectly true to the rest of the work.

Fig 3 shows the revolving slide-rest in application; b is the mandril; c the wood fixed on to it; d the ball being turned. In fixing the rest under the ball (which for convenience should previously be rough turned,) it is requisite that the centre it revolves on at B should be perfectly true under the ball;—this may be proved by turning the rest round upon the upright I, and observing that the point of the tool is equidistant to the three sides. If then, it be firmly screwed down on the bed of the lathe, it is clear when motion is given to the lathe and the point advanced, that by being moved round by the hand, it cannot do otherwise than cut a perfect circle. The shape of the tool is sufficiently shown in fig. 4.

With the help of this apparatus, and a crooked tool, I have succeeded in turning four hollow balls, one within the other, after the manner of the Chinese balls. I wish to carry the operation to a greater extent, but this is all at present I am able to succeed in. Some of your readers may be acquainted with a more perfect way of doing it, and I should feel myself greatly obliged by any information they would have the kindness to give through the medium of your valuable Magazine.

I am, &c.,

JAMES WILCOX.

WOONE'S NEW MODE OF ENGRAVING.

Sir,—Mr. Oxley, who undertakes in your last number to prove that "Mr. Woone's substitute for wood-engraving" is not new, refers to the process as if it were one with which the readers of the Mechanics' Magazine were perfectly familiar: yet, I do not recollect meeting with any account of "Mr. Woone's" invention in your pages.* Mr. Oxley's allusions to it are, therefore, somewhat obscure; but if, as appears probable, the process is analogous to that of stereotyping, it is assuredly no novelty, as will be found by reference to the Mechanics' Magazine, for February 4th, 1832, where there is a description of a mode of "engraving in stereotype," in some detail, with an anticipation of its beating the old system of wood-engraving out of the field. From its never having been heard of since, we may take it for granted that it did not answer the expectations of the inventor. Whether Mr. Woone's is more likely to succeed, it is of course impossible to predict, from the very slender data afforded by your correspondent.

I am, Sir, your constant reader,

OBSERVATOR.

20th June, 1838.

DAVENPORT'S ELECTRO-MAGNETIC ENGINE.

Sir,—I am truly sorry that Mr. Oxley does not understand the principles which I laid down in No. 772, relating to the power of the electro-magnetic engine. As this is perhaps owing to a want of perspicuity in that communication, you will much oblige me by inserting the following additional observations.

The position which I maintain is this: that it requires a certain quantity of time

---

* We shall give the substance of the specific tion of Mr. Woone's patent in our next number.

to put iron into a state of magnetic polarity. On this part of my subject I find I am in some measure anticipated by your correspondent "Nauticus," in No. 775. This is a well-known fact in electro-magnetic science, and it is impossible for Mr. Oxley to maintain the contrary without overturning a principle established by experiment.

I therefore still assert that the power of the electro-magnetic engine is in the ratio of the weight of the iron employed; provided, firstly, that the galvanic battery be increased with the size of the engine in some ratio which remains to be determined by experiment; and secondly, that the poles of the magnets be at equal distances from each other, whether the wheel is great or small; for if the poles are disposed at considerable distances from each other on the wheel, they will be almost inactive during a great part of each revolution, in consequence of the attraction of magnets being in the inverse ratio of the squares of the distances. Now, in Davenport's engines, this last condition is not observed: it will be seen on inspecting the figure in No. 758, that the distances between the poles M N O P, will vary in the same proportion as the diameter of the wheel; and in an engine with a wheel 15 feet in diameter, these four poles would be only useless lumber to the engine during the $\frac{99}{100}$ part of a revolution.

I shall be very glad if a velocity at the rim of the wheel of 26$\frac{1}{2}$ feet per second has been attained; it is my opinion, however, that 10 feet per second is the utmost hitherto reached, *with the weight attached :* Mr. Oxley will perceive from the former part of this letter, why the velocity is thus limited.

Mr. Oxley need not wait for further news from our transatlantic friends on the subject of this invention, for I believe that the experiments of Mr. Callan, in Ireland, and of Jacobi and others on the continent, are in a state of forwardness; and those who wish to read a general history of the engine will be supplied with it in the July number of *Sturgeon's Annals of Electricity.*

I am, Sir, yours respectfully,

F.

Manchester, June 20, 1838.

COMMON ROAD STEAM CARRIAGES—MR. HANCOCK'S PERFORMANCES.

Sir,—In your valuable miscellany No. 775, you state that Mr. Walter Hancock, when detailing his travelling on the Paddington road in 1835, in your Number 685, mentioned that he was then preparing calculations to prove that even that traffic, unfavourable as the attendant circumstances were, *was carried on at a profit :* and you state that since that time he has assured you, that taking *interest of capital, wear* and *tear,* expenses of *fuel, stations, steersmen, engineers* and *every thing else,* into consideration, *it was carried on at a profit.* Now, my dear Sir, it was a very cheering announcement to all the advocates and friends of steam locomotion on common roads, to hear this promise given in 1835; but I am sorry to say, that Mr. Hancock having failed in realising the hopes he then held out, did such injury to the cause of steam locomotion on common roads, as has considerably more than counterbalanced all the good he had done before. It was a general remark to us his advocates, "Oh! There is Mr. Hancock, your main support, when he had closed his traffic on the Paddington road for the season, published an account of miles he had travelled, and the money he had received, and promised an account of expenses and receipts, which would show to the public that, unfavourable as the circumstances were, yet that he had worked at a profit; and as he has not produced this statement, so publicly promised, the conclusion must be he had worked at a loss ; for most assuredly if he could have truly shown that he only realised one or two per cent. to begin with, he would then, and now, find plenty of supporters, for *not one of them have yet shown a profit.*" Now Mr. Editor, as the time is opportune, and as I believe it impossible that Mr. Hancock could not, after all his experience and improved boiler, and other improvements, have realized at least one or two per cent., I would request you, if you had any interest with him, to urge him to put forth the promised statement. I am sure that if he can truly show even only one per cent. profit, he will quickly find plenty of supporters ; *notwithstanding the Steam Waggon Company, who I am pretty confident (from the sight of their boiler) will* not much impede his progress. *Public opinion,* and every thing now, is in Mr.

Hancock's favour; there is plenty of capital ready, let him only show *one per cent. clear profit* in his last traffic, and an ample fortune will quickly be at his disposal, and he will confer a real pleasure on all advocates for the introduction of steam on common roads, and particularly on one who has suffered no small annoyance in advocating his cause, and who hopes quickly to be enabled again to do so successfully. With thanks to yourself Mr. Editor, for your advocacy of all that tends to the welfare of the community,

I remain, your most obedient servant,

AN ADVOCATE OF
STEAM LOCOMOTION.

Holborn, June 18th, 1838.

ON IRON BEST SUITED FOR RAILWAYS —BEING THE SUBSTANCE OF A PAPER BY MR. MUSHET, READ BEFORE THE MECHANICAL SECTION OF THE BRITISH ASSOCIATION AT LIVERPOOL, 1837.*

The following conclusions at which I have arrived on the important subject of the nature and habitudes of malleable iron, particularly that adapted to railway purposes, are the result of many experiments, and of forty years unremitted application to iron making.

1st. I consider that a crystalline arrangement of the fracture of bar iron is incompatible with great strength and fibre, and that it is essential to railway iron that it should be hard and fibrous.

2nd. The more frequently iron is heated or melted in the course of its progress towards its completion as bar iron, the greater is its tendency to crystallize and become brittle when cold. This is in some measure prevented by repeated rollings; but fibre acquired in this way, is to a certain extent artificial, for where native fibre is absent, heating and cooling will restore the crystalline arrangement and weaken the tenacity of the iron when cold.

3rd. Excessive decarbonization, commonly called refining, which tends to deprive the iron of its last portion of carbon, produces a quality of malleable iron, soft, and easily abraded by rubbing or friction, and therefore, in point of durability, not well calculated for rail iron.

4th. Conversely, iron manufactured so as to retain the last, and consequently, the most intimately united portions of carbon, or to have this substance communicated to it in minute portions in working, is upon two accounts better calculated for rail-making (provided the fibre is not injured) because it will wear less by rubbing, and be subject to less waste from oxydation.

5th. Bar or malleable iron has a tendency to crystallize in the cooling, in proportion to the size of the manufactured mass, a circumstance deserving the greatest consideration on the part of the engineer, in determining the form or shape of his rails.

6th. Continued vibration, such as is produced by the motion of an engine or waggon travelling on a railway, causes iron to crystallize, and to a certain degree become brittle. Hence the importance of making rails from iron full of fibre, so as to postpone the time of crystallization, to as remote a period as possible.

7th. Unless impaired or destroyed, by the repeated heatings and fusions to which iron is subjected in the progress of its manufacture, the quantity and strength of fibre developed, will mainly depend upon the proportion of carbonaceous matter, originally contained in the pig-iron from which it is manufactured.

8th. It is essential in rail-making, to have a quality of iron, which, without dropping or opening at the rolls, will stand a degree of heat capable of compactly and adhesively welding the piles together, so as to prevent exfoliation or separation of the parts when subjected to rail-road traffic.

Considering the foregoing conclusions to be well founded, it has often been to me a matter of surprise, that the two most important qualities of iron for rails, namely, fibre and hardness, have seldom or never formed a condition in any railway contracts for rails. Certain manipulations or stages of operations, which

---

* In the report of the proceedings of the British Association at Liverpool (see page 43 of our present vol.), Mr. Mushet's paper upon railway iron was dismissed with a brief notice. Mr. M. has since forwarded us the manuscript of his memoir, requesting its publication; and as it is upon a subject so important and interesting to the public at the present time, we most readily comply with his request.—ED. M. M.

may be necessary in making iron for smiths, or indeed for general purposes, are usually stipulated for without its being taken into the account, that the properties required in railway iron may be quite the reverse. The consequence of this oversight, has been to withdraw the attention of the manufacturer from these important desiderata, and induce him to follow the letter of the engineer's specification as to process, leaving the properties of fibre and hardness to the chapter of accidents.

The present process of bar iron making, is in some measure incompatible with the production of the abovementioned requisites for railway iron, and this may serve to account for the difficulty of obtaining fibrous masses, such as rails of 60 to 75 lbs. per yard, as well as for the want of hardness in the body of the rail itself. The whole process is one of severe decarbonization. The pig iron for the refinery is in most situations chosen with as small a portion of carbon as will enable it to melt. In this furnace in order to separate, about 4 per cent. of carbon marganese, silica, &c., from 12 to 15 per cent. of the whole quantity of iron is lost, by being converted into a slag or scoria of a most deleterious quality. After the pig iron has by melting passed under the blast, and penetrated the body of cinder, it is then literally set on fire by the action of the blast pipes on its surface, and the decarbonization is carried on, not by fermentation as in puddling, but by a true combustion of a part of the iron, and by a change of surface produced by an alteration in the specific gravity of the particles of the iron. Should the quantity of refinement have been limited, the new arrangement resulting from the fusion of the iron, in so high a temperature, will be found unfavourable to fibre in the ultimate result. So, that to produce any certainty in this respect, it becomes necessary to prolong the refinement until a new and steelly arrangement takes place, and this arrangement is indicated by the extreme levity of the iron in running from the furnace, intense combustion, greater waste, and a porous or honey-combe fracture of the metal when cold.

This com-mixture of crude iron and steel, is again melted by flame in the puddling furnace, where it undergoes, by the addition of cinder, a process of fermentation, which carries off the last portion of carbonaceous matter, and leaves the iron comparatively soft when cold.

The reverse of this takes place in the manufacture of charcoal iron. In this operation the pig iron, during the single process which converts it into malleable iron, is always in contact with fuel. This prevents that total decarbonization which takes place with puddled iron that has passed through the refinery. Hence the superior hardness and tendency towards steel in Sweedish and Russian iron.

To the subject of fibre my attention has for some years been directed. At various times I have made numerous experiments, and it has been gratifying to find, that the same means employed to obtain fibre, to a certainty produced a superior degree of hardness and durability, and altogether avoided the process and waste of the refinery. In the method I have adopted (and for which I have lately taken out a patent) the charge of pig iron is at once introduced into the puddling furnace, where it is subjected to an imperfect though uniform fusion, the temperature being no more than is barely necessary to melt it. In this state a portion of finely ground rich iron ore, as a subsitute for cinder, is from time to time thrown upon the iron and worked into it by the puddler. In a short time considerable fermentation takes place, and gas is evolved. In twelve or fifteen minutes pig iron of the most crude and fusible description, is converted into malleable iron, which appears in a flakey and divided state. The heat being increased, the iron coalesces and is formed by the puddler into what are called balls of puddled iron. These are, in the usual way, taken to the hammer or rolls, and elongated into bars called No. 1, or puddled bars. These again are cut into certain lengths, piled upon each other and re-heated, and for the purpose of railway iron rolled into broad bars or slabs, known by the name of No. 2 iron. These in their turn, are either piled alone a second time, or mixed with narrower iron, re-heated and rolled into rails in that state, which is called No. 3 or best iron.

The quantity of iron ore required to decarbonate the pig iron, depends upon the fusibility of the latter, and varies from one-tenth to one-twentieth the weight of pig iron; and the fusibility principally depends on the quantity of carbonaceous matter contained in the iron, which is as various as the numerous shades between white iron and dark grey foundry iron.

By following this process a considerable saving of pig iron is effected, at a very trifling increase of expense for ore and additional labour beyond the expense of the usual mode of working. This is one great advantage of the process, but the most important consists in being able at all times to develop, in the first stage of the manufacture, a certain quantity of strong fibre, which is increased during the ulterior operations, and conjoined with great hardness.

Iron ore when used in the puddling furnace, whether with pig iron or with refined metal, decarbonates the iron by means of oxygen which it presents to the carbon united with the iron; and at the same time it calls into existence an unusual display of fibre. This remark applies as well to refined metal as to pig iron, and no degree of fusibility on the part of the pig iron retards the full and beneficial effect of the iron ore, provided it be applied in proper quantity.

I consider pig iron, and not refined metal, as the true source of strength, hardness, and fibre in bar iron, particularly when cold, and as these qualities can at all times be obtained by a judicious selection of pig iron, and the use of iron ore, we may consider ourselves in possession of a method by which these three great requisites to the production of railway iron are secured. I have only further to remark, that it is probable the piling and rolling in the first instance may be done away with in the making of railway iron, by hammering the puddled balls into large and solid blooms, to be afterwards rolled into rails. By following this line of operation the great evil of lamination, as it is called, or a separation of the piles hitherto so injurious to durability, would be got rid of.

PORTER'S PROGRESS OF THE NATION.

When the first volume of Mr. Porter's work appeared, somewhat more than a twelvemonth ago, we ventured a few strictures on the general characteristics of the undertaking. Those strictures

are still perfectly applicable, as the second volume,* in the mode of handling its subjects, varies in no essential respect from the first, though the subjects are of course of a different nature, the former being devoted to "Population and Production," while the present refers to "Interchange," including conveyance by sea and land, and all the ramifications of trade and commerce,—and the less congenial heads "Revenue and Expenditure." As before, Mr. Porter has recourse for nearly all his materials to those inexhaustible storehouses of statistical lore, the parliamentary reports; and, also as before, he may be complained of for the wholesale manner in which he has converted them to his own purposes, and the too little pains he has taken to discriminate between the good and the bad, —the well and the ill-founded, which, in statistical reports, are often separated by, as "thin partitions as do the bounds divide" between wit and madness in the moral world. With all its faults, however, the work is a valuable one, if not for any higher excellencies, for bringing a multitude of previously-scattered facts within a convenient space for reference and examination.

The first chapter is on "Internal Communication" generally; and here, almost at the very outset, we meet with a brilliant specimen of statistical exaggeration. It is introduced when the roads of France are under discussion, in comparison with those of England, and seems to be intended as a preparative for certain amazing details which follow, as to the loss of iron from horse-shoes on the French roads, which are even more incredible, if that may be. The reader may well be tempted to exclaim, "Who'd have thought it!" on meeting with such *nice* calculations as the following:

"In the first report of Messrs. Villiers and Bowring on the commercial relations between France and Great Britain, the following curious calculation is given, in order to show how severe a loss is entailed by the high price of iron upon one class of persons

---

* The Progress of the Nation, in its various Social and Economical relations, from the beginning of the nineteenth century to the present time. By G. R. Porter Esq. F. R. S.—Sections 3 and 4, Interchange; and Revenue and Expenditure. London. 1838. C. Knight and Co: small 8vo. pp. 379.

in France, the cultivators of the soil. ' The lands cultivated in France are supposed to amount to 22,818,000 hectares, equal to 57,045,000 acres English, and it is calculated that a team of oxen would cultivate 15 hectares : hence the quantity of ploughs employed in France is estimated at about 1,500,000. M. de la Rochefoucault represents the annual use and waste of iron at 40 kilogrammes per team, but it has been more frequently estimated at 50 kilogrammes, making for the whole consumption 75,000,000 kilogrammes of iron, which, at 90 francs per 100 kilogrammes, consumes 67,500,000 francs, equal to 2,700,000l. sterling. Now, though this estimate is too high for an average calculation, it is undeniable that the iron could be imported from foreign countries at half the price, and the loss to agriculture alone must be taken at above one million sterling per annum!' "—p. 3.

All this is circumstantial enough, at any rate—for a "rough calculation," in which a few odd thousands may be thrown out of the reckoning, if convenient, without endangering its general correctness. But would it not have been as well to have been a little more particular in laying down the authorities for the main fact—that on which all the rest depend—the astonishing waste of iron in French farming? One authority, whose name is given, it will be seen, guesses forty kilogrammes per team; but this does not answer the purpose; anonymous estimates, therefore, are adduced to raise the amount (high enough already) to fifty,—and this alone, in so extensive a calculation, makes a difference of something more than *five hundred thousand pounds* in the gross total! Yet, of such stuff is the matter of our statistical works too often made,—and, whether the estimate had been ten kilogrammes or a hundred, the calculation would have been relied upon—(and copied)—as quite authentic. Dr. Bowring is a practised hand in the line, and always sufficiently sweeping in his assertions, notwithstanding he has ever and anon met with some awkward contradictions in the course of events. We remember his sending forth a well-paid-for and bulky report on the French system of keeping the National Accounts, in which he strongly insisted on the absolute impossibility of official depredation, owing to the ingenious checks imposed by the methods pursued, and the

general clearness and publicity of the whole affair. No sooner, however, had this report been issued, than the news arrived that one of the cashiers had absconded, after having pursued a system of peculation *undetected* for several years, taking with him a quantity of public money, the amount of which was unknown, in consequence of the impossibility of unravelling the very "clear" accounts of his department. This singular occurrence Dr. Bowring has evidently consigned to a mental oblivion, and, in spite of it, he still flourishes as the most imperative and infallible of government commissioners.

A little further on, we find a still richer bit from the reports, referring to the roads of Ireland, and, we must take it for granted, the production of a native writer, though Mr. Porter, who quotes it very seriously without any comment on its peculiarities, is not, we believe, a gem of the Emerald Isle. It is, perhaps, necessary to assure our readers that we quote *verbatim* :

" The fertile plains of Limerick, Cork, and Kerry, are separated from each other by a desolated country, hitherto nearly an impassable barrier. This large district comprehends upwards of 900 square miles ; in many places it is very populous. As might be expected, under such circumstances, the people are turbulent, and their houses being inaccessible for want of roads, it is not surprising, that during the disturbances of 1821 and 1822 this district was the asylum for whiteboys, smugglers, and robbers, and that stolen cattle were drawn into it, as to a safe and impenetrable retreat. Notwithstanding its present desolate state, this country contains within itself the seeds of future improvement and industry."—p. 11.

This fairly beats Dr. Bowring! He never ventured to tell us of a " deserted country" which in many places is " very populous," nor did he speculate on what " might be expected" under *such* (very extraordinary) circumstances; though, even if he had, he would probably not have anticipated the knowing procedure of the rapparees, in taking advantage of the places being *inaccessible* to drive their cattle into it, at the same time securing a snug retreat for themselves in the houses of the *inhabitants* of the *desolate* waste! Of a verity, it takes many strange themes to make up a "report" of the orthodox dimensions ; but we do not see why Mr. Porter should be driven to such matter to fill his more slender and select miscellany. He should have made a more unsparing use of the crucible, and rejected without remorse all such self-evident trash as that we have quoted.

After chapters severally on "Turnpike Roads" and on "Canals," the information contained in which is less novel than important, we arrive at the most interesting in the volume;—those on "Steam Navigation" and on "Railways." The succeeding ones in the division "Interchange" are devoted to details connected with shipping and commerce generally; and as to the remaining division "Revenue and Expenditure," *that* deals too much with the awful theme of "Taxes" to be at all pleasant to any but a thorough-bred political economist. We shall therefore restrict the remainder of our notice to the two chapters in question.

· The following summary view of the present state of water conveyance by steam is at once neat and comprehensive.

"The facility in moving from place to place, joined to the great economy both of time and of money that have accompanied the adoption of this mode of propelling vessels, have excited the locomotive propensities of the English people in a most remarkable degree. The countless thousands who now annually pass in steam packets up and down the river Thames, seem almost wholly to have been led to travel by this cheap and commodious means that have been thus presented to them, since the amount of journeying by land is by no means lessened. The number of passengers conveyed between London and Gravesend by steam packets in 1835 was ascertained by the collection of · the pier dues at the latter town to have been 670,452, not one in a hundred of whom would have been induced to make use of the Dundee boats just described. It was stated in evidence before a committee of the House of Commons in 1826, that at least 1,057,000 passengers, including those to and from Gravesend, pass Blackwall in steam vessels every year. In confirmation of the fact, that the establishment of additional facility in travelling is embraced by persons who would not otherwise be induced to quit their homes, we may refer to the continually increasing number of licenses for stage-coaches issued every year from the stamp-office, and to the great and constantly-increasing number of omnibusses which are continually traversing the great thoroughfares of London, without displacing the hackney-carriages

which were previously in use. The number of passengers conveyed by the Hull and Selby steam-packets in the twelve months which preceded the opening of the Leeds and Selby Railway was 23,882, whereas, in the twelve months that followed that event, the number conveyed was 62,105.

"The published lists of steam-vessels belonging to different ports in the United Kingdom show the extent to which this new mode of voyaging is adopted by the public. Scarcely any two ports of conveyance can be pointed out between which steam communication is not maintained as well for the conveyance of passengers as for the transmission of goods. Besides this, the communication is regularly maintained with all the principal neighbouring ports on the continent of Europe. From London vessels proceed to the French coast almost every day; to Holland three times a week; to Belgium as frequently; to Hamburg twice a week, and to Lisbon and Cadiz every week. From the coast of Kent, Sussex, and Hampshire daily departures takes place for France. From Hull three vessels depart every week for Hamburgh, and one is dispatched to Rotterdam; the greater part of the important traffic which formerly was carried on in sailing vessels between those ports is now conveyed through the more quick and certain agency of steam."—p. 48.

There is indeed no part of the world in which steam navigation has been so assiduously cultivated as in our own country. Even the United States, with its thousands of miles of "seaboard," and its endless length of navigable rivers, cannot stand the comparison for a moment; while all other nations are a century behind the Yankees. The English steamers, indeed, far exceed in number those belonging to the rest of the world put together, brother Jonathan included, who contributes a hundred and fifty-seven out of three hundred and sixty-six, composing the entire list of foreign steamers. The English list alone exhibits a total of just *six-hundred* vessels, exclusive of the steamers,—now a very numerous class—in the employ of government—thus exhibiting a majority of two hundred and thirty-four in favour of England over all the rest of the world!

The table exhibiting these results, which is compiled from information furnished by the British Consuls at the various ports, contains many other particulars of interest. As might be expected, France is the most active of the continental nations in steam navigation,—her number of vessels amounting to not less than seventy; the three next highest, Holland, Sweden, and Russia, are neck-and-neck in the race, a fact highly creditable to Sweden, where steam must have been enthusiastically welcomed to have produced such a result. While commercial Holland owns but twenty-eight steam-vessels, and powerful and extensive Russia only twenty-six, it could hardly have been anticipated that Sweden, without either of these qualifications in any thing like the same degree, should number twenty-seven. Yet, such is the fact; a fact highly honorable to the activity and energy of the Swedes of the present day. It appears in even stronger relief, when contrasted with the backwardness of some other countries of as high, or higher pretensions—Spain and Portugal, with their four steamers each, Prussia with its three, or Belgium—industrious, manufacturing Belgium—with its solitary *one!* Even Turkey, it appears, has two (are these the Egyptian steamers? they do not appear elsewhere in the list); and Barbary no less than eight, a number which appears incredible, until it is explained that they all belong to Algiers, and might, therefore, be more properly given to France. In the new world, brother Jonathan reigns paramount; since, notwithstanding the adaptation of South America for this species of transit, the incessant and ridiculous revolutions among the numberless "independent states" into which the country has been split, have cast such a damp upon improvement, that the whole of that immense continent,—we might add, also, the states of Spanish origin in the northern one—can only boast of three steam-vessels, the whole of which belong to Brazil. Steam *must* work its way in that quarter ere long, however, and a few years will probably witness a peaceful "revolution" produced there by its agency, more important, and beyond all challenge more gratifying, than the miserable squabbles which have so long disgraced and degraded it.

The English are probably destined to have the chief hand in working this change, as they have had hitherto in introducing steam to the old world. It is not in England alone that the works of the English engineer in marine machinery are to be seen, though that he must have

been tolerably active at home, is evident from the plain fact of the increase in our number of steamers from two in 1814, with the burthen of 456 tons, to six hundred in 1836, carrying *sixty-eight thousand tons!* His handy-work has also appeared in every part of the globe where steam has penetrated; as witness again the consular returns:—

"Among the particulars which the Consuls were required to give relative to this subject, was the place where the engines were manufactured. The returns made from Russia do not comply with this part of the order, which has been otherwise pretty well attended to. In the United States of America, the machinery, as might be expected, is almost wholly the production of native engineers; only six out of 157 steam-vessels belonging to the States being furnished with English engines. If we exclude from the account these vessels, and also, for the reason just given, the 26 Russian vessels,—although there is reason to believe that the greater part, if not the whole, of the machinery of the latter is of English construction—there will remain on the list 183 vessels, of which 97, or more than one-half, are indebted for their machinery to English engineers."—p. 61.

So much for the powers of steam directed by British ingenuity on water; turn we now to similar triumphs on dry land. Mr. Porter's chapter on "Railways" commences with a condensed view of the rise and progress of the system. This we extract, though perhaps some objections might be raised on account of its sins of omission, rather than of commission. It must be taken for no more than what it professes to be—a very rapid sketch of a very extensive subject. If our author could have spared more room, he would doubtless have entered at greater length into the *history* of the invention; as it is, he dismisses it in a few lines:—

"It has been said that railways were first brought to use in this country at the beginning of the seventeenth century, when they were employed in some of the Newcastle collieries. The railways then constructed were very different from the scientifically-constructed works to which we are now accustomed to apply that name, and it was long before any progress was made towards their improvement. They were first constructed altogether of timber, and it was not until 1767 that the first experiment was made, and that upon a very small scale, to determine the advantage of substituting iron for the less durable material. Nor does it appear that this experiment was successful, or followed by any practical result; for in a volume published by Mr. Carr, in 1797, he sets up his claim to be considered the inventor of cast-iron railways. The railways which were constructed up to the beginning of the present century, were all private undertakings, and each was confined to the use of the establishment—generally a colliery—in which it occurred. The public railways of England are strictly creations of the present century. It was in 1801 that the first Act of Parliament for the construction of a work of this kind, obtained the sanction of the legislature. The number passed since that time has been—

1801 .. 1	1816 .. 1	1829 .. 9
1802 .. 2	1817 .. 1	1830 .. 8
1803 .. 1	1818 .. 1	1831 .. 9
1804 .. 1	1819 .. 1	1832 .. 8
1808 .. 1	1821 .. 1	1833 ..11
1809 .. 2	1823 .. 1	1834 ..14
1810 .. 1	1824 .. 2	1835 ..18
1811 .. 3	1825 .. 5	1836 ..35
1812 .. 2	1826 .. 6	1837 ..14
1814 .. 1	1827 .. 6	
1815 .. 1	1828 ..11	

making in all 178 Acts.—p. 62.

No great invention has perhaps been so much indebted for its progress towards perfection, to unforeseen circumstances, as the railway. It may be said to have forced its own importance and utility on the attention of mankind by its own unassisted efforts. It does not seem, now that we are accustomed to be wheeled along by a steam-engine at the rate of forty miles an hour, that the Liverpool and Manchester line—the parent of a numerous and flourishing progeny—could ever have been looked upon as a medium for the mere transmission of cotton-bags and coal-sacks, and that, too, at the pace of a fly-waggon, and (can this be possible?) by the help of horse-flesh! Yet these things were even so. Fortunately, whatever were the ideas of the projectors, the work was undertaken; and, once undertaken, each successive improvement *evolved itself* (with *a little* assistance, of course), until the whole system had attained to its present perfect condition,—perfect, that is, until the next improvement points itself out to public attention. Among other matters, the railway was obliged in person to convince its originators, that they knew absolutely nothing of its destined uses.

"It is a singular fact, that of all the railways hitherto constructed and contemplated up to the opening of the Liverpool and Manchester line, not one was undertaken with a view to the conveyance of passengers. In the prospectus published by the projectors of that work, it was indeed held out as probable that half the number of persons then travelling by coaches between the two towns might avail themselves of the railway in consideration of the lower rate for which they would be conveyed, and the Directors expected to realise an income of 20,000l. per annum from this source; but the chief inducement held out to subscribers was the conveyance of raw cotton, manufactured goods, coals, and cattle. The great success attending this splendid work being in a principal degree attributable to the passengers conveyed by it, the chief inducement thenceforward to embark in similar undertakings has been the number of passengers, and not the amount of goods to be conveyed. Hitherto it has been found, in nearly every case where a railroad adapted for carrying passengers has been brought into operation, that the amount of travelling between the two places has been quadrupled. In the case of the Liverpool and Manchester railway, the income derived from this source has enabled the company to meet a large amount of extraordinary expenses, and to divide regularly 10 per cent. annually upon the capital, although the outlay in the construction of the work has been more than double the sum contemplated in the original estimates."—p. 65.

What a pity that a railway cannot make its own estimates, as well as lecture (practically) on its own advantages! With this extract we take our leave of Mr. Porter's present volume, though we shall probably again pay our respects to him when the third appears, which, according to present appearances, will complete his task.

———

ANALYSIS OF MILK—SUPPLY OF PURE MILK.

Sir,—As you have so recently had a paper on the milking of cows (vide No. 765, page 6), perhaps a few remarks on the article milk itself, will not prove inopportune. They are extracted from a valuable essay, by M. Barreul, lately published in Paris.

"By the extension of the use of coffee (*caffè au lait*), the quantity of milk now consumed in Paris, is at least double that which was used eighteen or twenty years ago. But the number of milch cows in the vicinity of the city, has not increased in any thing like the same proportion. Much of the milk sold by certain milk-men at the corners of the streets, has none of the properties common with milk, except the whiteness.

"The quantity of the milk which proceeds from the same cow, is very different at different times; and that of different cows varies also in quality.

"Some of the more wealthy inhabitants who obtain their milk directly from the dairies, at a good price, have it pure;—but the mass of milk sold in Paris is always more or less altered.

"The most common adulteration is that of water. But as this can be detected by the taste and colour, brown sugar is added to restore the sweetness, and wheat or some other kind of flour, the whiteness and consistency.

"Hence the *areometre* which merely determines the specific gravity of the fluid, is of no use in detecting these impurities; and besides, milk which is rich in butyraceous matters is much lighter than that which is less rich in butter, but more rich in caseous ingredients.

"To prevent the flour which is used in thickening the skimmed and watered milk from settling to the bottom, it is previously mixed with water and boiled, which renders it when cold, soluble in the milk.

"Thus flour is easily detected by the *tincture of iodine*, which gives it a wine or violet colour.

"More especially, if this floured milk be heated with a little sulphuric acid, and the coagulum separated by a filter, the serum acquires a fine blue colour by the tincture of iodine.

"Thus detected, the milk sellers sought for some substance which would not produce the blue colour with iodine, in which they doubtless obtained the aid of some chemists. They resorted to an emulsion of sweet almonds, with which, for the cost of about one franc, they can give a milk white to thirty pints of water, and communicate no unpleasant taste.

"Some of these pretended milk dealers, less scrupulous, employ hemp-seed in lieu of almonds, because of its greater cheapness. They thus dilute the milk of cows to almost any extent they please, without altering its colour or opacity, and correct its taste by a little coarse sugar.

"This factitious milk may be detected, however, by the oily nature of its curd. When the latter is pressed between the fingers, or on paper, the oil exudes from it, which is not the case with the curd of pure milk.

"That portion or part of milk which is least influenced by variations of food, &c. in the cow, is the caseous portion or curd.

"Four specimens of milk were obtained by the author from dairies on different sides of Paris, and one other was taken from a cow and brought immediately to him. Three hundred grammes of each of these were warmed and treated with equal quantities of vinegar. The curd of each being drained, and equally pressed between folds of soft paper furnished, namely, those from the dairies, each twenty-nine grammes of cheese, and that from the cow, thirty grammes.

"A second experiment gave within a small fraction the same result.

"Taking the quantity of this caseous matter as a type of the purity of milk, other equal portions of milk were mixed, each with an equal weight of water, and treated in the same manner, when it was found that the quantity of cheese was exactly one-half.

"In a third experiment, the milk was diluted with twice its weight of water, and the cheese was precisely one-third.

"The last experiment was repeated, with the addition of sugar to the milk and water; when the cheese was extracted, the whey cautiously evaporated to the consistency of extract, treated with boiling alcohol, filtered and evaporated, the sugar which had been added was recovered.

"To distinguish the milk which is adulterated with emulsion of almonds or of hemp-seed, one hundred and fifty grammes of pure milk were united with one hundred and fifty grammes of emulsion of sweet almonds, and the curd was separated by vinegar with the aid of heat. Being well pressed, it weighed sixteen grammes five-tenths. Then another mixture was made, in the proportion of one hundred grains of milk to two hundred of emulsion, and this furnished ten grammes and eighteen decigrammes of curd, which it will be observed is proportionate to the prior quantity.

"Besides, the curd or caseous of pure milk can be easily distinguished from that with the emulsion, by its consistency, and by the grease which the latter yields when exposed for some time to white paper.

"To prevent the milk from turning sour and curdling, as it is so apt to do in the heat of summer, the milkmen add a small quantity of *sub-carbonate of potash or soda*, which saturating the acetic acid as it forms, prevents the coagulation or separation of curd; and some of them practise this with so much success, as to gain the reputation of selling milk that *never turns*. Often when coagulation has taken place, they restore the fluidity by a greater or less addition of one or the other of the fixed alkalies. The acetate which is thus formed has no injurious effects—and besides, milk contains naturally a small quantity of acetate of potash, but not an atom of free or carbonated alkali.

"It is proposed, from the result of these investigations, that the authorities should ordain, *first*, that no milk should be sold *except in sealed measures*; and, *second*, that in each quarter of the city, one or two pharmaceutists should be charged with the duty of examining, from time to time, the quality of the milk offered for sale, and that penalties should be enacted for every fraudulent alteration of *quantity or quality*."

I cannot quite agree with the first of M. Barreul's propositions mentioned in the last paragraph. How such an article as *milk*, for which there is so extensive and constant a demand, is to be sold in "*sealed measures*," is to me a puzzle.

The second is a little more reasonable, and I have no doubt, if brought into operation, would be the means of insuring to the city of Paris a supply of much purer milk than it appears to be favored with at present.

A similar regulation would certainly prove very beneficial if introduced into England, and enforced in the city of London, as well as in large towns, such as Manchester, Liverpool, Sheffield, &c.

I am, Sir, yours very respectfully,

JOHN FORDRED.

Brighton, May 18, 1838.

LONDON AND BIRMINGHAM RAILWAY, AND THE PYRAMID OF EGYPT.

[From Lecount & Roscoe's History of the Railway.]

The London and Birmingham Railway is unquestionably the greatest public work ever executed either in ancient or modern times. If we estimate its importance by the labour alone which has been expended on it, perhaps the great Chinese wall might compete with it, but when we consider the immense outlay of capital which it has required,— the great and varied talents which have been in a constant state of requisition during the whole of its progress,—together with the unprecedented engineering difficulties, which we are happy to say are now overcome, the gigantic work of the Chinese, sinks totally into the shade. It may be amusing to some readers, who are unacquainted with the magnitude of such an undertaking as the London and Birmingham railway, if we give one or two illustrations of the above assertions. The great pyramid of Egypt, that stupendous monument which seems likely to exist to the end of all time, will afford a comparison. After making the necessary allowances for the foundations, galleries, &c., and reducing the whole to one uniform denomination, it will be found that the labour expended on the great pyramid was equivalent to lifting fifteen thousand seven hundred and thirty-three million cubic feet of stone, one foot high. This labour was performed, according to Diodorous Siculus, by three hundred thousand, and by Herodotus, by one hundred-thousand men; and it required for its execution twenty-years. If we reduce in the same manner the labour expended in constructing the London and Birmingham railway to one common denomination, the result is twenty-five thousand million cubic feet of material, (reduced to the same weight as that used in constructing the pyramid) lifted one foot high, or nine thousand two hundred and sixty seven million cubic feet more than was lifted one foot high in the construction of the pyramid; yet, this immense undertaking has been performed by about twenty-thousand men, in less than five years. From the above calculation has been omitted, all the tunnelling, culverts, drains, ballasting, and fencing, and all the heavy work at the various stations, and also the labour expended on engines, carriages, waggons, &c.; these are set off against the labour of drawing the materials of the pyramid from the quarries to the spot where they were to be used—much larger allowance than is necessary.

As another means of comparison, let us take the cost of the railway and turn it into pence; and, allowing each penny to be one inch and thirty-four-hundredths wide, it will be found that these-pence laid together so that they all touch, would more than form a continuous band round the earth at the equator.

As a third mode of viewing the magnitude of this work, let us take the circumference of the earth in round numbers, at one hundred and thirty million feet. Then, as there are about four hundred million cubic feet of earth to be moved in the railway, we see that this quantity of material alone, without looking to anything else, would, if spread in a band one foot high and one foot broad, more than three times encompass the earth at the equator. It will be evident, that such a work as this could only have been undertaken in a country abounding with capital, and possessing engineering talent of the highest order. The steps by which the science of railways has arrived at its present position were slow, yet progressive. Railways of wood and stone were in use, as well as the flat iron or tramrail, in the middle of the seventeenth century, particularly among the collieries of the north, and were gradually improved from time to time; they still, however, retained a character totally distinct from those structures which will soon form the means of transport through all the principal districts of the kingdom.

RECENT AMERICAN PATENT.

(From the *Franklin Journal* for March.)

DIVESTING CAOUTCHOUC, OR INDIA RUBBER, OF ITS ADHESIVE PROPERTIES, AND ALSO OF BLEACHING THE SAME, AND THEREBY ADAPTING IT TO VARIOUS USEFUL PURPOSES, *Charles Goodyear, New York.*— The specification states, that this patent is for a process of divesting Caoutchouc, Gum Elastic, or India Rubber, of its adhesive properties ; not at the surface merely, but for some distance below it ; and, under certain circumstances, throughout its whole thickness ; which process is applicable to that material either in its natural state, or after it had been dissolved in any of the known solvents thereof, and made into sheets, or employed as a covering to cloth, or other substances.

I employ (says the patentee) the various acid solutions of the metals, either saturated or partially saturated, and with such metallic solution I wash over the surface of the caoutchouc, of which I mean to destroy the adhesive property ; or instead of washing the surface of the caoutchouc, I dip it, or the article coated with it, into such a solution. If the article is cloth, coated on one side only with the solution, it is necessary, in general, to protect the uncoated side from the action of the acid solution, more especially when the more corrosive acids are used ; the cloth may, in this case, be united together at the edges, and at the ends, so as to form a sort of bag, capable of being dipped into the metallic solution without its interior being brought into contact therewith.

The metallic solutions are not, by any means, equally effective in destroying the adhesiveness of the caoutchouc ; the stronger acids being in all cases preferred, as being perfect in their action ; nor is it indifferent what kind of metal is employed. The strong nitric acid, undiluted, is that which I in general prefer ; and among the metals I prefer either copper or bismuth, forming a nitrate of copper, or a nitrate of bismuth, as the full effect is produced by these solutions in from one to five minutes. After the action is thought to be complete, the article acted upon is to be washed with water, so as to remove the whole of the acid solution, and it will be found, that not only the surface of the caoutchouc will resemble that of a soft cloth, but that this surface may be worn off to a considerable depth, and the new surface not manifest the slightest tendency to adhesiveness ; it is indeed so far altered in its properties as to resist, to a considerable extent, the action of those menstrua by which it is ordinarily dissolved ; it may, for example, be washed in spirits of turpentine, or in

the oil of sassafras, without being rendered stickey ; and it will equally resist the action of solar or of artificial heat, under all ordinary temperatures.

I have thus fully described what I believe to be the best modes of carrying my discovery into effect, by the use of metallic solutions, and have said that they are not equally efficacious ; some of them, I am well convinced, would not answer the purpose at all, as the acetate of lead, for example ; and probably all the solutions of metals in the vegetable acids ; and there are some which will produce the effect in a less perfect manner than the nitrates which I have named, or which will require a much longer time for their complete action ; but these are differences which it is not necessary, or possible, to particularize ; neither is it essential to a full knowledge of the means which I have adopted to produce the intended effect. I have also spoken of dipping the article to be acted upon into a metallic solution, or of washing its surface therewith, but other modes may be devised of producing the same effect by means substantially the same. I have sometimes covered the surface of the caoutchouc with the metallic powder known by the name of bronze, and have afterwards washed it over with nitric acid, which has produced the same effect as the washing it with, or dipping it in, the metallic solution, such a solution being in this case immediately produced by the action of the acid upon the metal.

It is a common practice to add some of the absorbent earths, or some pigment, to the dissolved caoutchouc, and when this is done the metallic solution may be readily made to operate to a greater or less extent throughout the whole mass of a sheet of considerable thickness.

Instead of the process above described, or preparatory to it, I combine the caoutchouc with quick lime, as I have found this earth preferable to either of the others in fitting the sheet caoutchouc to be acted upon throughout its whole thickness by the metallic solution ; but besides this, the lime has the property of bleaching the caoutchouc, and of giving to it a surface and texture adapting it to the receiving impressions from copper plates, or by other modes of printing, rendering it, either alone, or when used as a coating for cloth, applicable to the purpose of printing charts, or other devices. The caoutchouc, so prepared with lime, will, however, be rendered adhesive by the action of heat, or of solvents, unless the metallic solutions be applied to it ; in which case much of the whiteness communicated to it by the bleaching property of the lime, will disappear. I, however, view my discovery of the action of lime, in the way in which I have applied it, as of great importance, and therefore proceed to point out the manipulation which I have found necessary to its successful use.

I slake a portion of the finest quick lime, and then mix and agitate it with so much water, as that it shall not be thicker than milk, when on allowing it to stand at rest, all the coarser particles contained in it will rapidly subside; the upper portion, containing the finer particles, is then to be poured off, and the fine lime allowed to subside, the water left on the surface of this being then poured off, it is obtained in a state fit for incorporation with the caoutchouc when in that form of thick paste into which it is brought by the manufacturer preparatory to its being rolled into sheets.

LIST OF ENGLISH PATENTS GRANTED BETWEEN THE 25th OF MAY AND THE 25th OF JUNE, 1838.

Thomas Ridgway Bridson, of Great Bolton, Lancaster, bleacher, and William Latham, of Little Bolton, machine-maker, for improvements in machinery or apparatus for stretching, drying, and finishing woven fabrics. May 26; six months to specify.

Stephen Geary, of Hamilton-place, New-road, Middlesex, architect, for improvements in the preparation of fuel. May 28th; six months.

Thomas Ridgway Bridson, of Great Bolton, Lancaster, bleacher, for certain improvements in the construction and arrangement of machinery or apparatus for stretching, mangling, drying, and finishing woven goods or fabrics, and part or parts of which improvements are applicable to other useful purposes. May 29th; six months.

Miles Berry, of 66 Chancery Lane, for certain improvements in the means of economizing heat and fuel in furnaces or closed fire-places, being a communication from a foreigner residing abroad. May 31st; six months.

Joshua Wordsworth of Leeds, machine-maker, for certain improvements in machinery for heckling and dressing flax, hemp, and other fibrous materials, May 31st; six months.

Peter Walker, of Liverpool, brewer, for an improved apparatus to be used in cleansing beer, or other fermented liquors. May 31st; six months.

Luke Hebert, of Camden town, C. E., for a new and improved method or methods of uniting or soldering metallic substances. May 31st; six months.

George Nussey, of Leeds, dyer, for a new vegetable preparation, applicable to dyeing blues and other colours. May 31st; six months.

William Rattray, of Aberdeen, North Britain, manufacturing chemist, for certain improvements in the manufacture of the preparations called gelatine, size and glue. May 31st; six months.

Edouard François Joseph Duclos, late of Samson, Belgium, but now of Church, Lancaster, gent., for improvements in the manufacture of zinc, copper, tin, and antimony. May 31; six months.

William Needham, of Manchester, gent., for an improved machine called the silkworm, for the purpose of spinning, twisting, and doubling silk. May 31; six months.

Nicholas Raper, of Greek-street, Soho, Middlesex, gent., for improvements in rendering fabrics and leather water-proof. May 31; six months.

Thomas Walker, of Birmingham, clock-maker, for improvements in steam-engines. May 31; six months.

James Hardy, of Wednesbury, Stafford, iron master, for certain improvements in rolling, making or manufacturing shafts, rails, fire-irons and various other heavy articles of metal and machinery, or apparatus used in the same. June 2; six months.

Joseph Green, of Ranelegh-grove, Chelsea, Middlesex, gent., for an improvement on ovens. June 2; months.

Francis Sleddon, of Preston, Lancaster, machine maker, for certain improvements in the machinery or apparatus for spinning and doubling cotton, silk, flax, wool, and other fibrous substances. June 2; six months.

David Cheetham, junior, of Hollins Mill, Staley Bridge, Chester, cotton spinner, for certain improvements in the machinery applicable to the preparation of cotton, and other fibrous substances for the purpose of spinning. June 5; six months.

Thomas Beck, of Little Stonham, Suffolk, gent., for new or improved apparatus or mechanism, for obtaining power and motion, to be used as a mechanical agent generally, which he intends to denominate Rotæ Vivæ. June 5; six months.

Samuel Parlour, of Croydon, Surrey, gent., for improvements in paddle-wheels, and in communicating rotary motion from steam or other power where change of speed and power are required. June 5; six months.

Thomas Hammond Fiske, of Portsmouth, Hampshire, watch and clock maker, for improvements in apparatus for measuring and indicating the depth of water in a ship's hold. June 5; six months.

Charles Knight, of Ludgate-street, in the city of London, bookseller and publisher, for improvements in the process, and in the apparatus used in the production of coloured impressions on paper, vellum, parchment, and paste-board, by surface printing. June 7; six months.

Samuel Clegg, of Sidmouth-street, Gray's Inn Road, Middlesex, engineer, for improvements in gas meters. June 7; six months.

John Coope Hadden, of Duke-street, Westminster, gent., and John Johnston of Cursitor-street, Chancery-lane, London, brass founder, for certain improvements in warming, in lighting, and in ventilating. June 7; six months.

Herman Kessels, Major in the Belgian Artillery, now residing in St. Mary Axe, London, for certain new and improved means or apparatus for the saving of lives and property from fire, which he denominates "the Salvator." June 7; six months.

Robert Thomas, of No. 36, St. James's-street, Westminster, boot maker, for certain improvements in apparatus to be attached to carriages for the purpose of preventing horses from starting, and for stopping or restraining them when running away or descending hills. June 7; six months.

Edward John Massey, of Liverpool, Lancaster, watch-maker, for certain improvements in chronometers and other timekeepers. June 9; six months.

Archibald Richardson, of Hackney, Middlesex, distiller and wine-merchant, for a new and improved mode of producing a pure spirit from malt and all kinds of grain, and from vegetable substances of every description containing saccharine matter. June 12; six months.

James Reed, of Bishops Stortford, Hartford, stone-mason, for improvements in joining slate, stone, and marble, for cisterns and other purposes. June 12; six months.

Benjamin Ledger Shaw, of Henley, near Huddersfield, York, clothier, for improvements in preparing wool for, and in the manufacture and finishing of woollen cloths, part of which improvements are applicable to the weaving and stretching of other fabrics. June 12; six months.

Samuel Parker, of Argyll-place, Middlesex, lamp-maker, for improvements in lamps and apparatus connected therewith. June 12; six months.

Richard March Hoe, late of New York, but now residing at No. 66, Chancery-lane, Middlesex, C. E., for certain improvements in machinery or apparatus for grinding and polishing metal surfaces. June 12; six months.

Richard March Hoe, late of New York, but now residing at No. 66, Chancery-lane, C. E., for certain improvements in machinery or tools, and apparatus for chipping, levelling, smoothing, and polishing the surface of stone, slate or other materials. June 12; six months.

Henry Robert Abraham, of Keppel-street, Bloomsbury, Middlesex, civil engineer and architect, for new or improved apparatus for regulating the supply of water or other liquids, and the quantity delivered into reservoirs. June 14; six months.

Joseph Winter, of Fountain Court, Cheapside, London, glover, for improvements in painting, printing, and otherwise ornamenting the surfaces of leather, silk, cotton, or linen, which improvements are particularly applicable to the manufacture of gloves, stockings, and such like articles. June 14; six months.

Joseph Bolton Doe, of Hope-street, Whitechapel, Middlesex, iron-founder, for certain improvements in apparatus used in the manufacture of soap. June 14; six months.

Charles Davis, of Wednesbury, Stafford, engineer, for certain improvements in engines or machines to be used for obtaining mechanical power, also for raising or impelling fluids. June 14; six months.

Joseph Bennett, of Deptford, Kent, engineer, for improvements in steam-engines. June 14; six months.

George Price, of Cornhill, London, Esq., for improvements in clarifying water and other liquids, being a communication from a foreigner residing abroad. June 14; six months.

Richard Goodridge, of No. 7, Bell's Buildings, Salisbury-square, London, purser, R.N., for a new or improved apparatus for lifting or raising fluids on water or on land, and for marine propelling purposes, without steam. June 14; six months.

John White, of the New Road, Mary-le-bone, Middlesex, architect, for certain improvements in the construction of railroads, bridges, and viaducts. June 18; six months.

William Gossage, of Stoke Prior, Worcester, manufacturing chemist, for certain improvements in manufacturing iron. June 18; six months.

William Garnett, of Haslington, Lancaster, dyer, for certain improvements in machinery for spinning and doubling wool, flax, cotton, silk, and other fibrous materials; being a communication from a foreigner residing abroad. June 19; six months.

William Edward Newton, of Chancery-lane, Middlesex, mechanical draftsman, for improvements in diving apparatus; being a communication from a foreigner residing abroad. June 19; six months.

John William Fraser, of Arundel-street, Strand, Middlesex, for improvements in raising or floating sunken and stranded vessels and other bodies. June 22; six months.

Eliezer Chater Wilson, of Skinner-street, Snowhill, London, printer, for improvements in evaporation; being a communication from a foreigner abroad. June 22; six months.

Thomas Joyce, of Camberwell New Road, Surrey, gardener, for certain improvements in the mode of erecting heating and ventilating buildings. June 22; six months.

Peter Fairbairn, of Leeds, machine maker, for certain improvements in looms for weaving ribbons, tapes, and other fabrics; being a communication from a foreigner residing abroad. June 22; six months.

Peter Fairbairn, of Leeds, machine maker, for certain improvements in the machinery or apparatus for roveing, spinning, doubling, and twisting cotton, flax, wool, silk, or other fibrous substances. June 22; six months.

Robert Sandiford, of Tottington, Lower End, Lancaster, block printer, for certain improvements in the art of block printing, and in certain arrangements connected therewith. June 22; six months.

John Nathaniel Larkin, of Wellington-street, Pentonville, Middlesex, gent., for improvements in machinery for cutting corks and bungs. June 25; six months.

George Holworthy Palmer, of New-cross, Deptford, civil engineer, for certain improvements in steam generators and engines applicable to locomotive and stationary uses, and in the carriages to be used therewith and otherwise. June 25; six months.

Thomas Dowling, of Chapel-place, Oxford-street, Middlesex, gent., for improvements in preparing metals for the prevention of oxidation. June 26; six months.

LIST OF SCOTCH PATENTS GRANTED BETWEEN THE 22nd MAY AND THE 22nd JUNE, 1838.

William Neale Clay, of West Bromwich, Stafford, manufacturing chemist, for improvements in the manufacture of iron. May 28; four months to specify.

Charles Hullmandel, of Great Marlborough-street, Middlesex, lithographic printer, for a new mode of preparing certain surfaces, for being corroded with acids, in order to produce patterns and designs for the purpose of certain kinds of printing and transparencies. May 28.

Jeremiah Grime, of Bury, Lancaster, engraver, for certain improvements in manufacturing wheels which are applicable to locomotive engines, tenders, and carriages; and to running wheels for other useful purposes, and also in the apparatus for constructing the same. May 28.

John Upton, of Battersea, Surrey, engineer, for an invention of an improved method or methods of generating steam power, and applying the same to ploughing, harrowing, and other agricultural purposes, which method or methods is or are also applicable to other purposes to which the power of steam is or may be applied. May 23.

James Hill, of Haley Bridge, Chester, cottonspinner, for a certain apparatus applicable to machinery used in the preparation of cotton and other fibrous materials, for the purpose of spinning. May 29.

Edmund Shaw, of Fenchurch-street, London, stationer, a communication by a certain foreigner residing abroad, for improvements in the manufacture of paper and paper boards. May 29.

Alexandre Happey, of Basing-lane, London, gent., a communication by a certain foreigner residing abroad, for a new and improved method of extracting tar and bitumen from all matters which contain these substances, or either of them. May 29.

William Ketland Izos, of Cambridge, for improvements applicable to steam-engines. May 29.

John Wilson the younger, of Hurlet, Renfrew, North Britain, coal-master, for an improved process of manufacturing Prussian blue, prussiate of potash, and prussiate of soda, and other substances into which prussine or cyanogen enters as a constituent. June 1.

Thomas Hancock, of Goswell Mews, waterproof cloth manufacturer, for improvements in the method of manufacturing or preparing caoutchouc, either alone or in combination with other substances. June 5.

Francis Sleddon, of Preston, Lancaster, machine-maker, for certain improvements in machinery or apparatus for spinning and doubling cotton, silk, flax, wool, and other fibrous substances. June 5.

Robert Thomas, of 86, St. James's-street, Westminster, boot-maker, for certain improvements in apparatus to be attached to carriages for the purpose of preventing horses from starting, and for stopping or restraining them when running away or descending hills. June 5.

Charles Button, of Holborn Bars, chemist, and Harris Grey Dyar, of Mortimer-street, Cavendish-square, Middlesex, gent., for improvements in the manufacture of white lead. June 7.

John Potter, of Ancoats, Manchester, spinner, for an improvement or improvements in the process of preparing certain descriptions of warps for the loom. June 7.

William Neale Clay, of West Bromwich, Stafford, manufacturing chemist, and Joseph Denham Smith, of St. Thomas's Hospital, in the borough of Southwark, student in chemistry, for certain improvements in the manufacture of glass. June 7.

Samuel Clegg, of Sidmouth-street, Gray's-inn, Middlesex, engineer, for an invention of improvements in gas meters. June 7.

John Melville, of Upper Harley-street, Middlesex, Esq., for improvements in the generation of steam, and in propelling vessels by steam or other power. June 11.

Miles Berry, of Chancery-lane, Middlesex, in consequence of a communication from a foreigner residing abroad, for certain improvements in the means of economising heat and fuel in furnaces or closed fire-places. June 15.

David Cheetham, jun., of Hollinsmill, Staley Bridge, Chester, cotton-spinner, for certain improvements in the machinery applicable to the preparation of cotton and other fibrous substances for the purposes of spinning. June 15.

Edmund Butler Rowley, of Chorlton-upon-Medlock, Lancaster, surgeon, for certain improvements applicable to locomotive engines, tenders, and carriages to be used upon railways, and which improvements are also applicable to other useful purposes. June 19.

William Sanford Hall, of Strathearn Cottage, Chelsea, Middlesex, Lieutenant Royal Army, for improvements in paddle-wheels. June 21.

Joseph Rock Cooper, of Birmingham, gun-maker, for improvements in fire-arms. June 21.

John William Fraser, of Arundel-street, Strand, Middlesex, for improvements in diving or descending and working in water, and for raising or floating sunken or stranded vessels and other bodies. June 21.

LIST OF IRISH PATENTS GRANTED IN MAY, 1838.

Eugene Richard Ladisas De Breza, of Paris, now of St. Martin's-street, London, for a chemical combination or compound for rendering cloth, wood, paper and other substances indestructible by fire, and also for preserving them from the ravages of insects.

William Newton, of Chancery Lane, London, for certain improvements in preparing on textile plants, either indigenous or exotic, to be used in the place of hay, or hemps.

William Herapath and James Fitchew Cox, both of Bristol, for certain improvements in the process of tanning.

NOTES AND NOTICES.

An Apology for Gin.—It has been remarked, in extenuation of the usual wholesale condemnation of "Gin Palaces," that at any rate they have contributed to the spread, as well as improvement of the arts. Gin-shops assuredly contribute more to the architectural splendour of the streets of London, especially in neighbourhoods where a display of taste of that kind is most rare, than shops of any other description. Decorative painting has of late years received its most effective encouragement from the same source, and so also have gas-fitting, letter writing and cutting, and many other of the artistico-mechanical trades; while wood-carving, which had become nearly obsolete, has experienced a considerable revival from the *spirited* demand for the decoration of bars and counters. To sum up all, science itself is indebted for the discovery of the magnetic pole, and the extension of our knowledge of the arctic regions, to the munificent aid afforded to Captain Ross by the greatest gin-distiller of the day, Sir Felix Booth. Who shall venture to say, after all this, that the effects of gin-drinking are uniformly and essentially pernicious?

The Asphalte Mania.—Thirty-two French patents have been granted for different descriptions of bitumen and asphaltum since January.—*Paris paper.*—As many have been applied for in England, but being opposed were refused—the *pseudo* patentees' inventions being all so much alike.

Patents.—The past month has been a busy one in the patent world. The number granted for England and Scotland is unprecedented,—being, for England 52 and for Scotland 23, and this notwithstanding the enormous cost of obtaining the fourteen years' monopoly. Taking the lowest average, including the specification, not less than £150 is expended in obtaining each patent.

Hancock's Steam Cab.—On Friday last (22nd inst) in the afternoon, Hyde-park presented a more than usually gay appearance, in consequence of a crowd of fashionables being assembled to witness the trial of a newly-constructed steam-cab. Among the many splendid equipages, were observed those of the Dowager Countess of Sutherland, the Marquis of Salisbury, the Marquis of Northampton, the Earl of Winchelsea, the Earl of Warwick, Lord Howick, Lord Holland, and many other distinguished personages. About 3 o'clock the object of attraction moved forward at a slow pace from the old foot-guard barracks, Knightsbridge, and threaded its way through the various vehicles into the park, passing through the centre gate of the triumphal arch, and making, in the open space opposite the statue, several turns within its own length. The vehicle was then propelled, with apparent ease, for three or four hours, round the park, and, from the slight noise it made, the horses passing did not appear to be frightened. The average speed of the cab was about twelve miles an hour. The vehicle was guided by Mr. Hancock the inventor.

A New Light.—Among the new discoveries in science there is one at Paris which is said to be likely to do considerable injury to the existing gas companies. It is a lamp which generates its own gas, of a very superior quality to that supplied by coals, and which, being obtained at a moderate expence and without a complicated apparatus, can be had by all persons who can afford the cost of an ordinary lamp. It is applicable also to public lighting. The mixture employed is spirits of wine and turpentine, both of which are cheap in France. The light is beautiful, and there is no danger of explosion.

Railway Map of England.—On the first of August will be published the Title, Index, and Contents to vol. 28 of the *Mechanics' Magazine*, and as a frontispiece to the volume a large map of the Railways in England and Wales, price 6d. The map alone on fine paper, price 6d. Also the volume complete, in half-cloth, price 8s. 6d.

Complete Sets of the Mechanics' Magazine may now be had, twenty-seven volumes, half-cloth, price £11. 7s.

☞ *British and Foreign Patents taken out with economy and despatch; Specifications, Disclaimers, and Amendments, prepared or revised; Caveats entered; and generally every Branch of Patent Business promptly transacted. A complete list of Patents from the earliest period (15 Car. II. 1675,) to the present time may be examined. Fee 2s. 6d.; Clients, gratis.*

LONDON: Printed and Published for the Proprietor, by W. A. Robertson, at the Mechanics' Magazine Office, No. 6, Peterborough-court, between 135 and 136, Fleet-street.—Sold by A. & W. Galignani, Rue Vivienne, Paris.

Mechanics' Magazine,

MUSEUM, REGISTER, JOURNAL, AND GAZETTE.

No. 778.]   SATURDAY, JULY 7, 1838.   [Price 3*d.*

SLACK'S METHOD OF BUILDING AN OBELISK WITHOUT SCAFFOLDING.

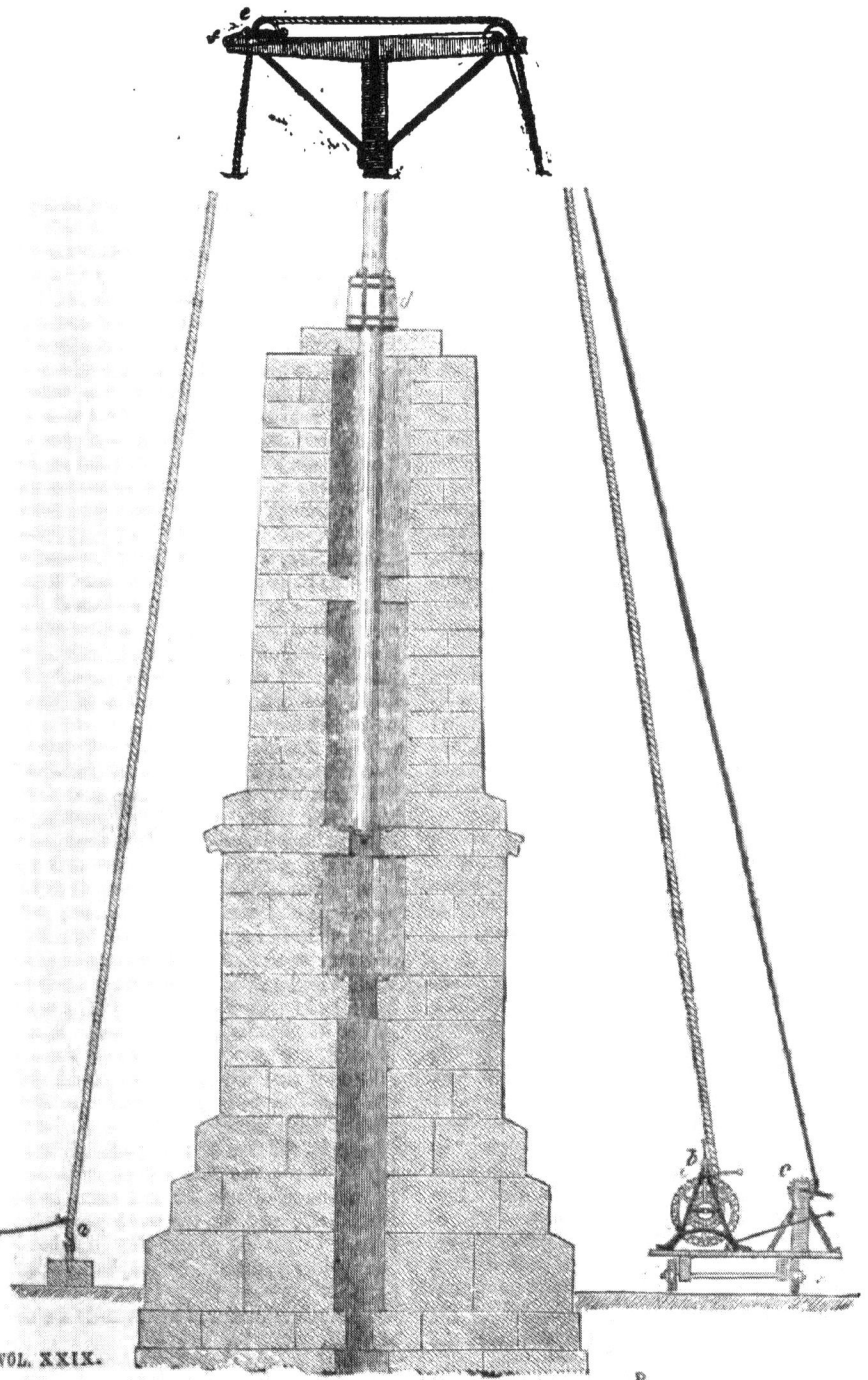

VOL. XXIX.

SLACK'S METHOD OF BUILDING AN OBELISK WITHOUT SCAFFOLDING.

[From the Transactions of the Society of Arts, Vol. LI. Part II.]

The gold Isis Medal was voted by the Society of Arts to Mr. Slacks of Langholm, mason, for his invention of a method of building as obelisk without the use of scaffolding.

This apparatus was used, for the first time, in erecting an obelisk of handsome white sand-stone, 100 feet high, not including its foundation, on the summit of Whitaw, a mountain overlooking the town of Langholm, in the district of Eskdale, Dumfriesshire, which was built by subscription, in honour of the late Major-General Sir John Malcolm, G.C.B., K.L.S., &c. &c., a native of that district.

Colonel C. W. Pasley, Director of the Royal Engineer Establishment, at Chatam, was appointed by the committee of management to employ an architect, or other competent person, to prepare a design and working drawings for the obelisk, which was done, at his request, by Mr. Robert Howe, clerk of works and professor of practical architecture at the said establishment; and having decided, pursuant to the advice of Mr. Burn, an eminent architect of Edinburgh, that the obelisk should be built hollow, with thorough bond-courses at intervals, the drawings and a specification were put into the hands of some respectable masons of Langholm, who offered to execute the work by contract, at an expense not exceeding the funds at the disposal of the committee of management, provided that they could obtain permission to cut holes of ten inches in diameter in the centre of each of the thorough bond-courses; as they stated, that by means of these holes they would be enabled to raise their materials in a new mode, which would be a great deal cheaper, and not less efficient, than the usual system of scaffolding. To this trifling deviation from the original plan, which would not injure the stability of the work, Colonel Pasley and the committee immediately assented; and, in consequence, the simple and ingenious machinery, which forms the subject of this paper, was brought into use.

General Description of the Machinery. (Fig. 1, front page.) — A pole with a cross-beam at top, in the form of the capital letter **T**, erected in the centre of the masonry whilst in progress, answered the purpose of a crane for lifting the stones and other materials, which were hooked on to the fall of a rope, at *a*, fig. 1, which passed over the top of the beam, and from thence was let down to a crab *b*, on the other side of the obelisk, capable of raising five tons with ease. This crab, and a small windlass *c*, were placed on a carriage, having four iron wheels, with axles converging towards the centre of a circular railway surrounding the base of the obelisk, upon which this carriage moved.

Pole.—The pole was 40 feet long, and ten inches in diameter, and was kept upright in the centre of the obelisk, by means of the holes in the three thorough bond-courses, as shewn in fig. 1; the two lowest of which served as stays, whilst the uppermost supported its whole weight, bearing a collar of hard wood *d*, which embraced the pole, and was so firmly bolted to it, that it formed an integral part of it. Between the collar and the thorough bond-course immediately below it, seventeen balls, each $3\frac{1}{2}$ inches in diameter, were introduced, to enable the pole to turn round with ease in all directions; and the under surface of the collar, as well as the upper surface of the thorough bond-course, were each prepared with a circular groove, to suit the form and guide the motion of these balls.

First Position of the Pole.—A hole, 2 feet square, was left in the foundation, at the bottom of which a large stone had been previously placed, supporting a block of hard wood, with a small hole cut in the centre of it for afterwards receiving the gudgeon at the bottom of the pole, which was lowered down and stepped in the aforesaid block by means of a pair of shears, after the masonry had been raised a little higher than the surface of the ground, the foundation being rather more than 10 feet deep. In this portion, the pole turned upon its own gudgeon, as a pivot, when required, until the masonry was raised to the level proper for placing the thorough bond-course in the die of the pedestal, upon which course the pole was made to rest, by means of the collar and balls before described; and, as the work proceeded, it rested upon every new thorough bond-course in regular succession, being raised for this purpose, from time to time, in the manner that will afterwards be described.

Cross-Beam.—The cross-beam was about 12 feet long, and 12 inches square in the centre, where it was mortised down upon the head of the pole, and from thence tapered upwards on both sides. It was further strengthened and connected with the pole by two strong iron braces, one from each end of it, and by an iron strap passing over the top and down both sides of the pole; this strap, as well as the braces, being secured by transverse screw-bolts driven through the pole (fig. 1). The arm of this beam nearest to the crab was solid; but, on the other side, at the distance of 18 inches from the centre, a vertical groove was cut through the wood to within 2½ inches of the end, which was strengthened by an iron hoop and screw bolt. Over this groove a sort of railway was formed, by two iron rods placed on different sides of it, upon which a small cast-iron carriage *e*, 20 inches in length, travelled, by means of wheels 4 inches in diameter. The stones were hooked on to the fall of the lifting rope of this sort of crane by means of lewises. This rope, which, at its other end, communicated with the crab, passed over two iron wheels at contrary ends of the cross-beam, each 10 inches in diameter, one hung near the solid end of it, in a mortise cut for the purpose, the other in the centre of the small iron carriage, the movements of which it participated, in order that the stones or other materials raised by the rope might be brought further from or nearer to the centre of the masonry, as required. This matter was regulated as follows :—

Two small ropes made fast to the outer ends of the carriage, passed round two small cast-iron pulleys *f*, fixed outside of the adjacent end of the beam, and from thence passed over two similar pulleys, fixed outside of the other end of the beam (fig. 1.); and, at some distance lower, these two ropes were united into one, and led down to the small windlass *c*, placed on the same carriage with the crab. On winding up this rope round the barrel of the windlass as far as it will go, the carriage is made to travel out upon its little railway to the extreme end of the beam; and if the rope be now made fast, the carriage is prevented from moving. Consequently, when a stone is raised by the crab, under these circumstances, it is kept out to the greatest possible distance from the centre of the masonry; but if the windlass rope be slacked, the weight of the stone, in being raised by the crab, forces the carriage to move towards the middle of the beam, and, consequently, the stone is itself brought nearer to the centre of the masonry.

The workmen were also raised and lowered by the crab, after putting one foot into a loop at the end of the rope. Whilst being lowered, a man always stood at the break of the crab, who allowed them to descend rapidly, but without acceleration.

Mode of raising the Pole to a higher level.—This was always done after the masonry had been carried up by the above apparatus about 10 feet higher than the thorough bond-course on which the collar rested for the time being, that is, as soon as a new thorough bond-course was ready to be placed. Two half trestles were then set up on different sides of the pole, upon the last finished course of masonry, having a semicircular hole in the top of each; after which they were connected, by four strong iron screw bolts, into one complete trestle, with its cap embracing the pole. Two planks were then placed transversely in the same alinement, but on contrary sides of the pole, each having its upper end resting on the cap of the trestle near the pole, and its lower end projecting over the sides of the masonry; and, to prevent them from separating, these planks were chained together at the head. Near to each end of these planks was hung a cast-iron pulley, about 4 inches in diameter, so that two of these pulleys were near the pole on contrary sides of it, whilst the two others projected a little way beyond the outside of the masonry.

The rope used for raising the pole and beam was passed through a hole in the former, a little above the collar, and the middle of it being brought to this point, the ends of the rope were led up along the two opposite sides of the pole, and passed over the pulleys in the planks; from whence they were led down respectively to the crab on one side, and to a windlass on the other side, of the base of the obelisk. The winches of both, being carefully and regularly worked at the same time, raised the pole the whole height necessary, by means of the upper pair of pulleys in those two planks, whilst the lower ones prevented the rope from rubbing against the masonry. The balls were then extracted from below, which was accomplished with ease by means of a spring forceps, made of hoop iron, and having a handle 9 feet long. The new thorough bond-stones, which had previously been laid towards the outside of the obelisk, were then moved inwards by crow bars, until they met; after which they we cramped together, and the balls placed as before in the circular groove prepared for them,

and then the pole was lowered a little, till the collar rested on the balls, which, being done, the trestle was taken to pieces and removed, and the whole thorough bond-course completed, and the work proceeded as before. The whole time consumed by raising the pole and beam to a higher level, in the manner that has been described, did not exceed two hours.

Hanging Scaffold for finishing the top of the Obelisk, figs. 2 and 3.—When the work had attained the height of 95 feet, and the first sloping course of stones

Fig. 2

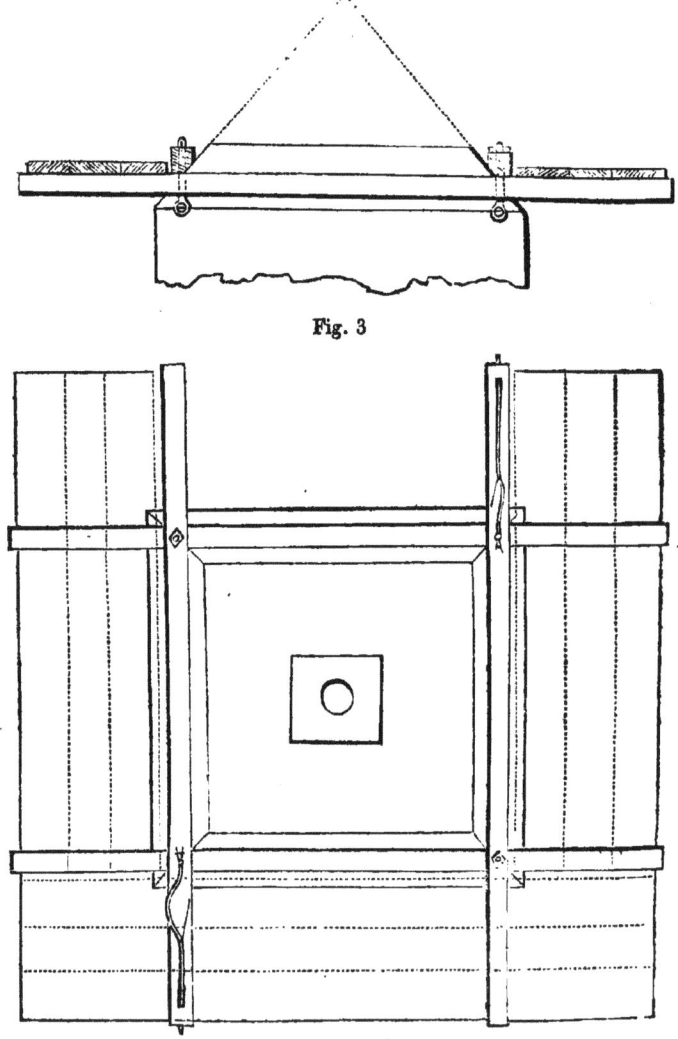

Fig. 3

forming the base of the pyramidal apex of the obelisk had been placed, a light hanging scaffold was formed, consisting of four strong wooden bearers, each 12½ feet long, fitted to the slopes of the said course, and bolted together at four points, so as to form a square frame, having its ends projecting about 3 feet each way beyond the outside of the masonry. Planks were bolted down upon these projecting ends on three sides of the frame, but the fourth had a pulley attached to it for a rope and bucket, by which the workmen were to be drawn up and let down. This scaffold was held down and kept in its proper position by a pair of guy-ropes made fast below, on contrary sides of the obelisk, each branching out into two parts at top, like the capital letter Y, in order to act upon all the angles of the frame.

Mode of removing the Pole and Cross-beam.—As soon as the hanging scaffold was completed, all the materials necessary for finishing the remainder of the work were got up and piled upon it, after which, the upper part of the pole, having the cross-beam attached to it, was sawed off, and lowered down to the ground below, whilst the lower part of the pole was left standing, and is now buried within the masonry.

Mode of removing the Hanging Scaffold.—The four bearers composing the frame of this scaffold were fixed together by four bolts, as before stated, each of which was fitted as an eye-bolt for receiving a rope at its lower end. Two of these bolts, at opposite angles, were screw-bolts, but the two others, at the alternate angles of the frame, were slip-bolts with their upper ends keyed, and the head of each of these keys was provided with a ring for receiving a rope, and at their other ends, they themselves were secured by a second pair of smaller keys, as shown in fig. 4.

After the masonry was finished, the planks of the scaffold were disengaged and lowered down, and at the same time ropes were made fast to the eyes of the four bolts, and to the rings of the two principal keys, the former being led straight down to the base of the obelisk, but the latter being first passed in a horizontal direction over pulleys at the ends of two of the bearers. The ropes from the bolts were passed through snatch-blocks, near the base of the obe-

Fig. 4.

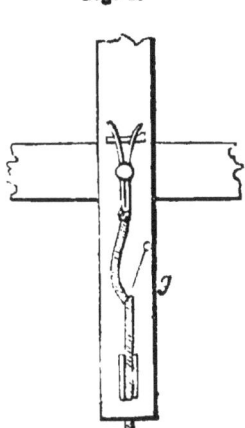

lisk, and from thence led out to such a distance that they might be acted upon by a windlass, without danger to the men. These preparations being taken, one active mason, who remained the last, disengaged the second pair of small keys from the first, and then descended by the bucket; after which the two principal keys were drawn out by means of the ropes fixed to their rings, as before described. The slip-bolts were then pulled out, by acting in like manner on the ropes attached to them.* This being done, the four bearers ceased to form a connected frame, being separated into two parts, each part consisting of two pieces of wood, held together at right angles to each other, in the form of an irregular cross, by their respective screw-bolts. The ropes attached to these bolts were then acted upon, and the parts of the scaffold pulled down, which descended along two opposite angles without injuring the masonry; for the projecting cornice, which was the most exposed part of it, had previously been covered with sods, and further protected by eight long poles, leaning against the sides of the shaft above it.

---

* Two small lines, one of which is shown at *g*, in fig. 4, were used, in a very ingenious manner, to relieve these keys from the weight of their own ropes, which, if not thus counteracted, might have drawn them before the proper time, with great danger to the mason who remained last on the scaffold. As soon as this man had descended, these small lines, which had just sufficient strength to prevent an accident of this kind, were broken by a strong pull of the windlass, acting upon the key-ropes, by which the keys themselves were at the same time extracted.

Mr. Thomas Slacks, the inventor of the above ingenious arrangements, is an operative mason, who was previously employed as foreman of masons under the able engineer of the Carlisle and Newcastle railway, in constructing a remarkably fine skew-bridge over the small river Gelt, in Cumberland, in which the machine called a Hercules was used. Mr. Slacks states, that he took the idea of his own machinery solely from the Hercules, which he modified by changing a straight into a radiating movement. It will be seen, however, that the principle adopted by him is much more similar to that of the balance-crane used by Mr. Stevenson more than twenty years ago, in the erection of his justly celebrated work, The Bell Rock Light-house, Hence, in recommending Mr. Slacks to the favourable notice of the Society of Arts, the writer of this article has no wish to claim for him the merit of priority of invention, so far as regards the principle of his machinery. But it is hoped that the following observations will show, that Mr. Slacks' arrangements involve a considerable practical improvement upon the balance-crane. That very ingenious machine was constructed entirely of iron, of the very best workmanship, and the whole of the wheels, pinions, &c. acting upon it, formed an integral part of the crane itself, which was erected first upon the solid part of the masonry, and afterwards in each of the successive chambers of the light-house, previously to their being covered in. This machine could not have been used in the Malcolm Obelisk at all, because the hollow spaces allowed in the centre of that work were much too small to admit it; besides which, the expense of such a machine would have far exceeded the funds at the disposal of the managing committee. In fact, it is much too costly ever to be used at all, except in very important and arduous works, where nothing simpler will answer equally well, and where expense is a secondary object. Mr. Slacks' crane, on the contrary, was of the cheapest and simplest possible form, consisting chiefly of a larch-tree, cut in the neighbouring woods, and a short piece of square timber, besides some other very simple wood-work, iron-work, and ropes. In respect to his machinery, it consists of a crab and small windlass, such as every

builder must necessarily be provided with, and which, by not forming an integral part of his crane, but being entirely separated from it, saves superfluous expense ; and, so far as regarded the peculiar nature of the Malcolm Obelisk, this arrangement also was much more convenient, since, by being worked from below, the machinery, as well as the men employed at it, were entirely out of the way of the masons whilst in the act of building. Moreover, by placing his crab below, Mr. Slacks gets rid of the necessity of using a suspended and movable weight as a counterpoise to the materials raised, which is so very essential a part of the balance-crane, that it has derived its name from it. In short, instead of that very ingenious but expensive machine, which certainly was much better adapted for the work of the Bell Rock Light-house than any other that could have been used, but which is only capable of being made by first-rate iron-founders and mechanists, Mr. Slacks has contrived an apparatus no less efficient for the purpose he had in view, but infinitely cheaper, and so much simpler, that the same might be fitted up by common country carpenters and blacksmiths in any part of the United Kingdom, or of the British colonies. In respect to his arrangements for finishing the work by the hanging scaffold fixed upon the first course of the pyramidal apex of the obelisk, which scaffold was taken to pieces from below after all the workmen had descended, this part of his plan is still more ingenious, if possible, than the former, and appears to be perfectly original.

By the process that has been described, this obelisk was executed, without the smallest accident, in rather less than twelve months, in a manner highly creditable to the contractors, and satisfactory to the committee by whom they were employed.

———

KNIGHT'S ILLUMINATED ENGRAVING.

Mr. Charles Knight, the indefatigable publisher to the Society for the Diffusion of Useful Knowledge, has just taken out a patent for a new invention in engraving, which, if but a small part of his glowing anticipations in regard to it should ever be fulfilled, will create quite a revolution in the world of art. Certain it is, that the invention could not be in better hands, so far as the bringing it fairly before the public is concerned; Mr. Knight is not the man to sleep on his post, and, should the new process of "illuminated engraving" fail at last, it will assuredly be for no want of effort to give the world an opportunity of judging of its capabilities. Two or three series of coloured engravings, portraits and historical pieces, are already announced, as well as two series of maps, a species of illustration for which the new process is said to be peculiarly fitted. As the specification is not yet enrolled, it is not known in what way Mr. K. proposes to effect his object, but that it must be rapidly and easily attained is evident from the low prices at which these commencing series are to be published,—two or three large coloured maps, for instance, at ninepence, or of the largest size for a shilling. It is conjectured that the whole of the colours are printed at once, probably from a block consisting of as many separate pieces as there may be colours required, the invention consisting in the method of unlocking those with facility to perform the inking, and locking them again to take the impression; this has, we believe, often been attempted, but never hitherto with success. Illuminated printing of engravings is of course already well-known, as witness the splendid specimens produced of late years by Mr. George Baxter, the eminent wood-engraver, especially in his beautiful "Pictorial Annual." Mr. Knight cannot be expected to compete with such finished productions as these, the only objection to which consisted in the expensiveness of the method by which they were produced. Economy is to be the grand feature of the new plan, but it will hardly succeed unless due attention be paid at the same time to excellence in an artistical point of view.

CAOUTCHOUC SPRINGS.

Sir,—I beg to inform J. R., whose suggestion for the employment of caoutchouc in the construction of "powerful springs" appeared in your last Number, (page 80,) that the peculiar properties of this curious substance render it wholly unfit for the purpose recommended. It is perfectly true, that by confining a solid cylinder of this material in a suitable cavity, and using a very accurately fitted piston or plunger, "lateral expansion" might be prevented; there are other difficulties, however, not so easily got over, among others, to wit, the decomposition by heat, of the caoutchouc, which would be the certain consequence of powerful concussion. This is a very inconvenient effect, and I fancy it would be no easy task to find a practical method of preventing its occurrence.

It appears to me that nearly all the purposes to which the caoutchouc-rod spring would be applicable, are already fully met by the employment of spiral and other metallic springs, some very ingenious applications of which have recently been made in the buffers of railway-engines and carriages, and for some other purposes. For my own part, I cannot perceive what important advantages the application of caoutchouc in this form holds out, to compensate for the numerous inconveniences that would inevitably attend its employment. Under no circumstances would the result of this arrangement be "a very effective spring," as J. R. would find should he take the trouble to experiment thereon.

I am, Sir, yours respectfully,
WM. BADDELEY.
June 26, 1838.

MILLS'S MERCURIAL PUMP—A FALLACY.

Sir,—I think it right to offer a few remarks on "Mills's Mercurial Pump," which you have "not considered unworthy of a notice in your excellent periodical;" vide No. 776, p. 189.

I know nothing of Mr. Grier, (lecturer on natural philosophy in the Baronial Hall,) to whom the working model of Mr. Mills's pump was presented; but I cannot compliment him on his discrimination, that he did not at once detect and point out to Mr. Mills, the thorough fallacy of his contrivance. On the contrary, we are told, "its action was so satisfactory to the lecturer and his class," that a publication of the invention was solicited.

In Mr. Mills's description, his pump is said to be "of the *suction kind*," but in the engraved illustration which accompanies it, is represented to be a *lifting force-pump.* Mr. Mills is somewhat explicit in giving a limit for the length of the feed-pipe, viz., 30 feet; but he gives no idea of the length required for the play of the mercury in the cylinder, a circumstance that would interfere most prodigiously with the efficiency of the pump, if the feed-pipe approached any way near the assigned limit.

The close-topped intermediate moving cylinder, is directed to be so placed as to be capable of easy motion upwards and downwards, but without hinting at the manner in which this is to be effected, or by what means the parallelism is to be preserved, so as to secure the promised advantage of "*little friction.*"

If we suppose a pump constructed upon this principle, in the very best manner possible, with a clear perpendicular lift of 26 feet, the working cylinder would require to be nearly three feet high; for on raising it, the mercury would fall on the outside and rise within, in proportion to the extent of vacuum induced. Again, on depressing the handle, the mercury would, in the first instance, return to a state of equilibrium, and then, if the pressure of a column of water, air-vessel, &c., has to be encountered, the mercury would fall in the inner, and rise in the outer cylinder, until the height of the column was equal to the opposing pressure. It is this play or oscillation of the mercury that I have before alluded to, and which would, in practice, render almost nugatory more of the motive force, than the friction of any ordinary well-made pump.

The second advantage claimed by Mr. Mills for his mercurial pump, is, " that for every inch stroke of the handle, the water will be raised one foot high!" Now, this effect depends entirely upon the relative sizes of the respective parts of the apparatus, without any reference to the fact of the pressure of one inch of mercury being about equal to one foot of water, a fact illustrative of the inconveniency to which I have adverted.

There are other objections to this form of pump to which I need not now advert, but only observe in conclusion, that this is by no means a solitary instance, even in recent times, of clever men being imposed upon by the fallacious character of *models.*

I remain, Sir, yours respectfully,
WILLIAM BADDELEY.
London, June 28, 1838.

FIRE-PROOF HOUSES. — DE WITTE'S FIRE-PREVENTIVE COMPOSITION.

Sir,—From the extreme interest I have ever taken in the best methods of preventing the occurrence of calamitous fires, and for arresting their progress—with the share I have had in the discussion of these topics in your pages—you may very well suppose I have not been inattentive to the recent proceedings of Mr. G. J. De Witte, with his Patent Fire-preventive Composition. In a prospectus issued a short time since for the formation of a "Fire-preventive Company," the patentee very justly observes, that "the prevention of so dreadful a calamity as fire will always be considered of the first importance to society, and the discovery of a composition which effectually renders timber and other materials indestructible by that element, will form a new era in the building of houses, shipping, and every erection in which wood is employed." He then goes on to state, that "the experiments which have been already submitted to the public, have convinced the scientific world of the extensive utility of this invention, and of the impossibility of burning timber when covered with this preparation. By a cheap and easy process, walls, ceilings, partitions, staircases, &c., can be covered with this fire-proof material. It is alike applicable to houses under repair as well as when building,—a slight coating being sufficient to secure the wood-work from burning."

Having been informed that the patentees were preparing a house in Dorset-street, Clapham-road, for an experimental illustration of the perfect efficacy of their plan, I took an opportunity of inspecting their progress. The house, which was a small one, in connection with another adjoining, had been built in the usual way, with the intention of being fitted up in the ordinary style; it had a very liberal allowance of timber in its construction, but was a mere shell when taken up by Mr. De Witte and his colleagues, who proceeded to protect the boards and other timbers, the floors, ceilings, stairs, and wood-work generally, with their patent fire-proof composition, without in any way disturbing the original foundation or superstructure.

Their composition in appearance very closely resembles grey or slate-colored mortar; it is exceedingly pleasant *to* work, dries extremely hard, is free from expansion or contraction under all variations of temperature, and preserves its cohesive properties to the last. When dry it is susceptible of as fine a polish as marble, and forms a better ground for the reception of paint than any other substance I am acquainted with; it can be stuccoed with ornamental devices in the usual manner, in accordance with the taste of the architect or builder.

The preventive process having been completed, Wednesday, the 6th of June, was appointed for the experiment, which was to put to a conclusive test the efficacy of the preparation. A great crowd collected near the spot, which was favourable for the accommodation of a large assemblage, on account of the open space afforded by the fields in the vicinity. An inclosure was made behind the premises for those persons who had been invited by the Directors. The company assembled, consisted of men of science, practical builders, several directors of insurance companies, and persons of importance and property, all of whom appeared to take a deep interest in the result of the experiment.

The upper floor was covered with shavings in great abundance, to which a number of deal planks were subsequently added. The first floor front room was fitted up as a chamber, with bed and furniture, chairs, tables, &c., as nearly as possible in the usual style of furniture, although, perhaps, less valuable, certainly not less combustible; on the contrary, this floor was likewise embedded with, at least, eighteen inches deep of dry shavings, with a plentiful supply of planks, &c. In consequence of the suggestion of some of the visitors, (who, on going over the premises had objected to the composition being exposed on the surface of the floor as offensive to the eye,) the floor, which had been prepared with the non-conducting composition, was covered over with a veneering of thin deal, which caused the flooring to present the usual appearance. Soon after two o'clock the scientific incendiary perpetrated an act which would have brought certain destruction upon any ordinary building; the shavings, wood, &c., on the upper floor were first fired, and burned with great rapidity, but laying low upon the floor, the appearances to those persons on the outside of the build-

ing was not such as to prove altogether satisfactory. On igniting the combustible, in the first floor furnished room, however, a different effect was produced; the shavings, as a matter of course, were soon in a blaze, the bed and other furniture rapidly took the infection, and the windows being without sashes, a strong wind blew through the house, which caused the flames to rage with a degree of fury one might, have supposed to be altogether beyond the ordinary means of relief. The immense volume of fire that poured from the window, produced a semblance of what might, in common parlance, be designated "a dreadful fire." At this moment the interest of the spectators was raised to the highest pitch: the furniture, &c., was entirely consumed, but the flames did not communicate to the adjoining apartment upon the same floor, nor to those above or below it. Fully proving what it was the object of these experiments to establish, viz., that fire can be confined to the apartment in which it originates by means of this composition, which effectually prevents contagion.

The only sign of injury to any portion of the building was exhibited by a lintel over one of the windows, the wood-work of which being charred by the intense heat directed upon it, a small quantity of gas escaped through a minute fissure in the composition and burned for a few seconds only. The other apartments of the house were then subjected, in succession, to tests equally severe, by heaping shavings on the floor, which were fired, and more fuel added, until each of them might have been compared to the atmosphere of so many ovens; the result, in every case, proving equally successful.

Some iron hooping had been introduced into the ceiling of the first floor room, the expansion of which, by the excessive heat it was subjected to, caused the displacement of a considerable portion of the plastering; but the composition remained entire, and duly performed its office as was proved by several parcels of gunpowder which had been deposited between the ceiling and the floor above remaining untouched. This effect of iron hooping, is exactly that which has been anticipated by Mr. Cade, in his letter at page 184 of your last No., and, I think, Mr. C. will be disposed to give the preference to the patent composition, as being, in all respects, much superior to *tiles* for giving the protection required.

After the combustible matters had fairly exhausted themselves, several gentlemen minutely examined the premises, and reported that they found the fabric perfectly sound. Indeed, every person who witnessed the experiment, must have been satisfied of the great value and importance of this discovery; of its efficacy there is no doubt, and the additional expense of the composition will not, it is said, exceed 20*l.* in a ten-roomed house, so that the public have the opportunity whenever they choose, to put an end to those disastrous conflagrations which every now and then spread dismay and ruin among the inhabitants of populous towns and cities.

Several of the fire-brigade were in attendance in Dorset-street, to watch the progress of the experiment; among them was a fireman of thirty-five years standing, who came primed with natural prejudice, having witnessed several unsuccessful attempts of a similar class, and even he pronounced the " arrangements to be very good; the best he had ever seen." Mr. Sylvester, who accompanied Dr. Farraday, acknowledged, that " he had come to see the experiment, prejudiced against it, but the result had changed his mind, and he was satisfied that the inventors had satisfactorily established their principle." Mr. Shepperd, Architect, (Royal Exchange,) expressed himself in similar terms.

I may, hereafter, resume this subject, but for the present,

I remain, Sir, yours respectfully,
WILLIAM BADDELEY.

London, June 21, 1838.

———

ON THE TANNING PROPERTIES OF ELM BARK.

Sir,—No tree grows in more profusion in this country than the elm; it forms a feature of embellishment to every diversified aspect of rural domain; it is one of the most hardy of the vegetable tribes, and grows to a size of great beauty and luxuriance, and, although not a favourite tree of the poets, it is frequently seen towering above their much-vaunted and venerated "monarch," the oak, which

in many soils bears but a stinted and mediocre appearance. However, the purport of this paper is to inquire of any of your correspondents, (who may have turned their attention to the subject,) what degree of utility and importance the elm tree may be said to possess as regards the tanning properties of its bark. The late Sir Humphrey Davy has given us a comparative analysis of its astringent properties, as compared with the staple commodity of oak bark; but Sir H. D. was a philosophical experimentalist, and tanners (many of whom I have conversed with upon the subject) seem to be wholly unaware of elm bark possessing any serviceable qualities *as a basis* for their business. Oak bark has become a plentiful article since the opening of the continental trade to us, say, from 1814 to the present time, but prior to that period, having no other than our home growth to supply the tanner's wants, it had not only reached a most exorbitant price, but had become so exceedingly scarce, (especially in some parts of the north of England and Scotland,) that many tanners were seriously impeded in their business, owing to an inadequate and precarious supply. When I visited Morpeth, in Northumberland, in 1813, Messrs. Benjamin Woodman and Robert Hall, tanners of that place, informed me that their supply of bark was so inadequate to their wants, that they could not work more than three-fourths of their yards in consequence. When I travelled in the foreign hide and skin line in 1811, 1812, and 1813, (a time when English oak bark was exceeding scarce and dear, I think 38*l.* the load,) I made inquiries of several tanners, as to whether they had ever made any experiments, successful or otherwise, elucidatory of any tanning development evinced by the elm bark, and their uniform reply (with one exception) was, *that they knew nothing at all about it, and had never tried it.* Now, the person I gained some information from, was the late Mr. Cousins, tanner, of Five Head, near Curry Rivell, in Somersetshire. He informed me he was then trying elm bark, upon a small scale, upon some dressing hides, but that he found it did not answer; for although, he said, he was satisfied it possessed sufficient astringency and power to penetrate into the animal pores, and to transform the substance into leather, still, he said, he perceived so many discolourations and stains arising on the surface of these hides during the process of manufacture, that he expected when he had brought them into a state of thorough tannage, to be a considerable loser by his experiment. I forgot, at the moment, to point out to Mr. C. what I am well satisfied was the sole cause of the discolouration and stains he complained of. They must have been owing entirely to his having used the said elm bark in its rough or unprepared state, (i. e. without its first being made clean by shaving; and sure enough, if it had been the finest Sussex oak bark that was ever put into a tan-pit, and so used, the article it assimilated with would have been sure to be proportionally deteriorated. When we consider how many years, centuries, that most useful tanning stimulant, larch bark, remained unknown, and was brought to light by a mere rustic depradator,* in the county of Durham, it is extremely probable that many other vegetable acids may, ere long, be discovered, suitable to act as an efficient substitute, or, at least, as a valuable assistant to oak bark, as a tanning stimulant; for although the banners of peace are at the present moment pleasingly flaunting between us and the continental nations, the time may come when war will again supersede our friendly intercourse and barterings. Independent of this, we know it to be one of the wisest principles of national economy, never to purchase an article at a foreign market, when we can procure it upon cheaper terms, and better in quality at home.†

I remain, Sir,
Your most obedient servant,
ENORT SMITH.
Marlborough Terrace, Albany Road.

* This is a literal fact, although a person in highly superior circumstances got the credit of it.
† It is an incontrovertible fact, that our English oak bark is of a much superior quality to that imported from Holland and other parts of the continent. The tanning business, although "as old as Joppa," still appears to be in its infancy, for if we may believe the statement of Messrs. Herapath & Cox, heavy butt hides, such as used to require six to eight months to perfect, through the kindly assimilation of the animal and vegetable juices, will now be ready for the shoemaker's lapstone in three weeks! Surely some more expeditious mode of wearing out shoes ought to be discovered, to keep pace with this *leathern* wonder of modern times.

GREAT WESTERN RAILWAY.

Sir,—From the various reports and opinions that are in circulation on the above undertaking, it is perfectly clear to me that the subject is not generally understood by the public, and that very erroneous conclusions have been drawn from unwarrantable data, probably arising from the absence of correct information. Your valuable journal being a source of substantial facts, the following remarks may probably not be uninteresting at the present moment.

A writer in the *Railway Times* says, that this railway and carriages, being nearly double the width of ordinary lines, the expenditure in the formation must be twice as great. It is evident this writer either does not understand the subject, or if he does, that he wishes to continue a system of misrepresentation, and which a very few words will be sufficient to prove. The distance of the rail being 7 feet instead of 4 feet 8 inches, the extra width of the two lines will also be 4 feet 8 inches; and as I presume that the middle and side ground will be about the same as on other roads, the above extra width will be the total extra expense in the earth work. To show by figures what this would amount to, I will instance a piece of cutting for an ordinary railway in ground requiring the slopes to be what is called "two to one," (that is, that every foot in depth requires 2 feet for its horizontal base,) the depth of cutting being 20 feet and the width of road 30 feet. The width of this cut at the top would be 110 feet, and the sectional area 155 yards. The cost of a mile of such cutting, at 1s. per cube yard, would be 13,640l. Now, let the width of this road be increased to 34 feet 8 inches, the sectional area will be 166 yards, and the cost of a mile 14,608l., making a difference of 968l., which is, certainly, far from being double. This remark on comparative expense applies to excavations, embankments, and tunnels.

With regard to the extra width of the rails which is said to be such a disadvantage in working, it is easy to show that the reverse is the case. In the first place, as the centre of gravity need not be higher in these than in other carriages, it is almost, if not altogether impossible, that such carriages can be overturned by any thing being inadvertently left or maliciously placed on the rails.

The width of the carriages on the respective roads being governed by the width of base, it is evident that the capacity of the carriages will be in the proportion of two to three, or that two of the Great Western carriages will carry as many persons or as much goods as three of the ordinary width, the lengths being equal; therefore, the number of axles and pairs of wheels, and consequently the friction in running, will be reduced in the same proportion. Another advantageous result is, that the wide trains (to carry the same quantity) being so much shorter than the narrow ones, the abrasion or rubbing of the flanches against the rails on the curves of the road, will reduce the resistance arising from that cause.

It has been remarked to me, that such a width of rails and carriages is a disadvantage on the curved parts of the road, causing friction, by the wheels sliding on the rails; but as the curves have a radius of not less than two miles, such an objection, though correct in theory, is too insignificant to be entertained; and I will venture to assert, that the trifling and unavoidable inequality at the junction of the rails, assisted by the elasticity of the sleepers, will always relieve any tendency of "gathering" that may take place in the position of the axles; and the only retardation of velocity produced by curves, will be caused by the rubbing of the flanches as described above. The imaginary centre of the curves being distant 1500 times the width of the rails, it is obvious that the obliquity of the axles, *if set for curves*, would be $\frac{1}{14}$ of an inch from parallelism, a nicety not in practice to be expected.

There being a greater load to be supported, and a greater length of axle between the wheels, it is important to consider how these conditions are provided for. First, the strength of revolving shafts being as the cubes of their diameters, while the friction of the bearings is only as the weight or circumference of the bearing, it is clear, without detailing the calculation, that to increase the strength of bearing from 2 to 3 will require but a very trifling addition in the diameter, and, consequently, the increase of circumference or rubbing surface will also be of almost insignificant amount. In the next place, to compensate for the increased length of axle to prevent de-

flection, without at the same time increasing the quantity or weight of materials, the plain parts of the axles between the wheels, are *hollow cylinders*, by which means great strength and stiffness is obtained with the least possible quantity of iron, being an application of that beautiful principle of nature developed in the formation of pillar bones, grasses, reeds, &c.

I need not prolong this article by entering very minutely into the locomotive department of this work, but at the same time I cannot omit to acknowledge the proof of judicious design in using larger engine wheels than ordinary, not for the purpose of travelling at a greater speed, for, I think, that people ought to be satisfied with a velocity and impetus of a great load at 30 miles an hour, but because it is very desirable that the velocity of the piston and alternations of the engines should be reduced as much as possible to obtain the maximum effect of the steam by its flowing less rapidly through the passages, besides lessening the wear and tear of the various parts subjected to the reciprocating action.

With your permission I will advert to some other parts of the subject in the course of a few days.

I am, Sir, your obedient servant,
J. R., ENGINEER.

Old Kent Road.

WOONE'S PATENT METHOD OF ENGRAVING.

We last week promised that we should publish the substance of Mr. Woone's specification for this object, which we now do. The resemblance between this patent method, and that referred to by our correspondent "Observator," is very striking indeed; and we cannot see in what the processes so far differ, as to render Mr. Woone's patent a good one. We shall, however, be happy if we are mistaken, and that Mr. Woone's shall turn out to be not only a good patent, but a good invention. As Mr. Oxley experienced, so we have heard that Mr. Woone's main difficulty has occurred in the *casting*, and we know not whether he has overcome that difficulty. We have been shown some extremely beautiful impressions of plates made in the patent method in the style of wood engraving; but the main point is not beauty of execution, but speed and economy in the operation, and we were not supplied with information upon these particulars.

Mr. Woone, in his specification states, that his invention consists in improvements in forming moulds or matrices, from which casts are to be taken in metal or other substances, capable of receiving a sharp impression, having on their surface the relief of the pattern, engraving, writing, or design, intended to be printed. He obtains his moulds by the following methods, according to the nature of the pattern, engraving, or design desired to be obtained in relief. For the finer patterns used in calico, or other printing, or paper-staining, or for engravings, such as are usually cut on box-wood, and printed at a type-press, he takes white lead and plaster of Paris, in different proportions, about two parts of white lead, and one of plaster of Paris, mixed with water, to the consistence of cream; he then pours this mixture, or composition, on a well polished, and perfectly even plate, or block of metal, or other hard substance of the required size, varying the depth of the composition to the height of the required relief. For work to be printed at the type press in the manner of wood engravings, the thickness of the layer, or composition need not exceed the twenty-fourth part of an inch; but for coarser patterns or designs, as for calico-printing, the thickness of the composition must be increased to about the eighth part of an inch. The plate, or block, covered with the above composition, must be left to dry gradually, or baked until it is entirely dry; or in order to give this coating a more even and perfect surface, and obtain with greater exactness the required thickness or height, the composition or coating on the plate or block is laid on thicker than is intended to be worked upon. After the coating has been well dried, the surface is scraped or smoothed down to the required thickness with a piece of metal, having a perfectly true and even edge. On this composition or coating, the design or pattern is traced in the usual manner now employed by engravers or artists. The artist then proceeds to engrave, etch, scratch, or draw, with a steel point, or other suitable instrument or machine, all the lines or parts of the design, through the composition or coating, down to the metal

or substance on which the composition or coating is laid.

For forming moulds or matrices, preferable for the coarser patterns or colouring blocks used in calico or other printing, a piece of metal, wood, pasteboard, stone, or composition of plaster of Paris, of the height of the intended relief, is glued or otherwise fixed on a block of wood, metal, or other suitable material; the outline or pattern is then cut, engraved, or etched, with acid, in the usual manner employed by engravers. When the outline only has been done, it is necessary that those parts that are within the outline of the pattern or design should be taken out or removed, in order to form a perfect mould or matrice of the pattern or design to be obtained in relief. If acid is used for obtaining this mould in metal, stone, &c., the plate of metal or stone, &c. may be fixed on a block of wood, pasteboard, or any other substance that is not liable to be corroded by the acid used for biting in the mould of the design or pattern.

It is necessary, in order to procure a perfectly clear impression from the casts to be obtained from these moulds, that some parts should be lowered or depressed, in order that those parts may not receive the printing-ink or colour when applied to the relief, and so produce a blurred or imperfect impression on the paper, calico, or other substance to be printed on. In order to effect this, a cast is either taken from the mould immediately after it is finished by the methods before described, and the cast finished ready for receiving the ink, colour, &c., by the usual methods employed by wood engravers, of cutting, engraving, scooping or lowering those parts of the cast, which, in consequence of the distance between parts of the design, &c. require to be deeper than the rest. Or the following method may be adopted: after the whole of the design, engraving, or pattern has been engraved, cut, or etched through the composition, there is laid on those parts of the mould required to be heightened (for the purpose of obtaining a corresponding depression on the cast or impression to be taken from it,) with any convenient or suitable instrument, modeller's clay, or other fine earth or composition to the height required, taking care not to injure or interfere with the design or pattern which has been drawn, cut, or executed on the mould or composition. Or, the heightening matter may be laid on in the following manner: mix chalk, white lead, or any similar substance with water, as thick as can be conveniently laid on with a brush, and apply this composition or mixture to those parts of the mould which require to be raised. When this last-mentioned mixture is to be applied to the layer or composition of white lead and plaster of Paris, the mould or design drawn on the plate and layer of composition, must be first carefully and slightly oiled. In order to prepare the moulds for the operation of casting, they must always be perfectly dried, which may be effected either by allowing them to dry gradually or baking them. These moulds may be cast, stamped, or moulded in metal, *papier-maché*, or other substances now in use, for obtaining casts of fine work for ornamental or other purposes, capable of being cast, stamped, or moulded, and receiving a sharp and clear impression from the mould, and at the same time sufficiently hard for the purposes of printing.

THE "GORGON" STEAM FRIGATE.

On Monday, July 2nd, the steam frigate *Gorgon* made an experimental cruise down the river to Gravesend, and back, with Lord Minto and other Lords of the Admiralty, and a number of naval and scientific gentlemen on board.

The vessel proceeded down the river in gallant style, and notwithstanding her immense bulk and her draught of water, 13 feet forwards, and 14 feet 6 inches abaft, she speedily attained a velocity through the water of 11¼ miles per hour, the engines making 19½ strokes per minute; and yet with this great speed there was not the least sensible vibration on board; a tumbler of water placed on the taffrail, as well as one on the paddle beam, right over the engines, remained undisturbed; it was remarked by all on board, that the motion of this vessel was exactly that of a sailing ship, no sensation of the immense power that was propelling her forward being perceptible, except the great velocity with which she glided through the water.

The total freedom from vibration or concussion in this ship, may be attributed to two important causes; first, to the judicious and excellent plan adopted by the surveyor of the navy in the construction, by which this vessel may be said to be from stem to stern like one solid piece of timber, so admirably is she fastened and secured; and, secondly, to the important improvement adopted in the engines, whereby a mass of moving material of 45 tons weight is dispensed with, and the energy of the piston is at once carried to the paddle-shafts, and the whole force of action and reaction confined within the base of the cylinder upon which the engine stands.

The *Gorgon* proceeded at once to the Mile Ground, as it is termed, in Long Reach, when after four trials, two with the tide and two against it, the average was found to be as above stated, eleven and a quarter miles per hour, through still water. Their lordships then proceeded to Gravesend, where they had ample opportunity of witnessing the ease with which this splendid ship was worked; her steerage was perfect, one man at the wheel being found sufficient for all ordinary purposes. She was turned round repeatedly in the river in about four times her own length, occupying in the evolution from two and a quarter to two and a half minutes; on her voyage down she easily passed all competitors except the Gravesend clippers, and on her return from Long Reach she overtook the *Albion* river steamer, and in a run of one hour and a quarter, passed her and gained two miles upon her between Gravesend and Woolwich, where she finally arrived at five o'clock.

The consumption of fuel, ascertained by weighing, was one ton of Welsh coals per hour, equal to 7 lbs. per horse per hour at full speed,—of course, when under canvass, or when going slow with head winds, the consumption will be considerably less. The coal boxes holding 400 tons of coals in the engine-room, will be sufficient for seventeen days' consumption at full speed; 10 days more coal may be occasionally stowed in the fore and after hold, making in the whole, fuel for twenty-seven days; this at an average speed of nine miles will carry her a distance of 5,800 miles by steam alone.

Now, as this steam frigate will carry beside the crew, 1,000 troops with stores and provisions for two months, it is evident that we might at pleasure transport a regiment to Odessa, Constantinople, or any of the ports in the Mediterranean, or to St. Petersburgh, or any of the northern cities, or to the West Indies and principal American ports, at once, without waiting for wind or stopping for fuel, and there is no doubt, but that with ships like these, with true British tars on board, England's superiority on the waters will be long maintained.

RECENT AMERICAN PATENT.
(From the *Franklin Journal* for March).

BOILERS FOR GENERATING STEAM: *James J. Rush, Machinist, Philadelphia.*— The general principle upon which I construct my boilers, (says the patentee,) is that of combining together two, three, or more sections of cylinders, in lieu of two or more perfect cylinders, placed side by side ; such sections of cylinders having tubes within them, constructed and operating in the manner of those ordinarily used in locomotive steam engines. The accompanying sketch is a cross section of two such cylindrical sections united together, by rivets or bolts, *a, a,* and to the diaphragm, or plate, *b, b,* extending the whole length of her boilers. The cylindrical parts of such a boiler may be three feet six inches in diameter, and their conjugate diameters six feet, more or less. Such boilers do not differ in the general mode of arranging the tubes for the passage of heat, from those in general use. I intend in general, to surmount these boilers by steam chambers. Three or more sectional cylindrical boilers may be connected together in the same way, with the former. The combining together of boilers consisting of sections of cylinders as herein described, constitutes my first improvement.

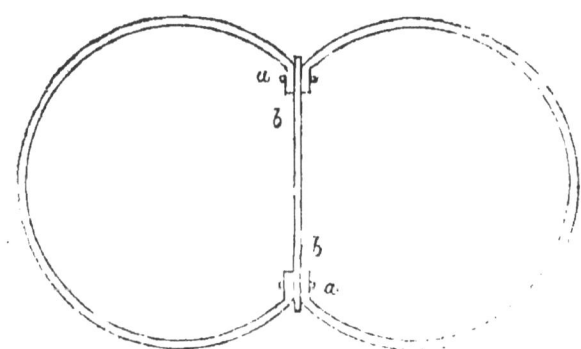

My second improvement consists in the using of sheets of wove wire, or wire gauze of a fine texture, similar to that employed in bolting machines, to prevent the rising of the water into the steam chamber, and the consequent throwing of a quantity thereof into the cylinder, intermingled with the steam. For this purpose I stretch sheets of wire gauze upon suitable frames, which frames are allowed to float upon the surface of the water in the boilers ; or I stretch such sheets of wire gauze across the tubes which connect the boiler with the steam chambers, or I place them in any other manner which convenience or the particular construction of the boiler may suggest, so that the sheet, or sheets, may be interposed between the water in the boiler, and the steam chamber or reservoir ; where it will have the effect of breaking the rising bubbles, and of separating the water and steam from each other.

I am aware that wisps or tangles of wire have been placed in steam pipes, with a view to the obtaining of the end proposed by me, but my plan of interposing a sheet of wire gauze, just above the surface of the water, which I have found to answer the intended purpose in the most perfect manner, is, as I believe, essentially new.

NOTES AND NOTICES.

The New Copyright Bill.—We are by no means sorry at having to announce that Mr. Serjeant Talford has thought proper to *withdraw* his Copyright Bill "for the present Session," notwithstanding its triumphant progress to Committee. It is understood that the learned Serjeant's reason for this proceeding was, that the Government would have exerted its influence against the Bill, if it had been proceeded in,—moved, perhaps, by certain of the great publishing houses, who had commenced a vigorous opposition, at the eleventh hour, to those parts of the measure which they were apprehensive would interfere with their "vested interest" in copyrights already purchased. It still seems to be held that the public is a party having no concern in the matter, as Mr. Serjeant Talfourd, when withdrawing the Bill, spoke in the most confident terms of his hopes of ultimate success, not on the ground of its public utility, but because—"alterations had been introduced which were likely to remove the objections of the publishers to its provisions." It is devoutly to be wished that, the learned Serjeant will take a more enlarged view of the subject previous to his next attempt at legislation.

A British Architect.—The present Rajah of Tanjore, who is remarkable for the zeal with which he promotes the study of the English language and literature throughout his dominions, has just proved himself an active corresponding member of the Institute of British Architects by transmitting, in return for the Transactions of the Institute, a number of highly-finished drawings of the most celebrated buildings in his territory, especially the ancient temple of Avidiar Coil. The letter enclosing these drawings, in the handwriting of "Seevajee Rajah" himself, does honour to his highness's reputation as an English scholar.

Novel Pleasure Excursion.—The navigation of the Atlantic by steam bids fair, in a short time, to cause the trip to America to be looked upon as a mere trifle. We are told that the people of New York, on the arrival of the *Sirius* and *Great Western*, began to talk forthwith of the pleasure and propriety of taking an excursion to England, by way of seeing something of the old country," and enjoying a short holiday. Not to be behind hand, a Liverpool company which has just started, and has chartered a Dublin steamer, the "Royal William" for the voyage, advertises that she will not start on her return for ten days after her arrival at New York, in order to afford her passengers an opportunity of viewing "the beautiful scenery of the Hudson, and the stupendous Falls of Niagara," previous to their return! This is "going a-head" rather too fast; even in these march-of-intellect times we should think there were but few folks wise enough to take a voyage of at least a month (there and back) for the sake of ten days' pleasuring,—to say nothing of the expense. It will be well if these steam-speculators do not progress too rapidly in other particulars. It is to be feared that in the eagerness to rush into the market, steamers of a class ill-fitted to breast the Atlantic will be employed in the service, and that accidents may perhaps occur, from this cause alone, calculated to cast a damp on ocean steaming which it may require many successful voyages of better adapted vessels to remove.

Progress of Journalism.—The empire of Persia is no longer destitute of a newspaper, an official Gazette having made its appearance in the capital, Sehrauu, regularly since the commencement of the present year. It is printed from stone, the Persian metropolis not yet boasting of a letter-press printer, and, by way of decoration, each number is surmounted by an imposing representation of the arms of the empire.

Common Road Steamers.—Sir,—In your last number (777), a correspondent who signs himself "An Advocate of Steam Locomption," expresses much interest in that department of science. If he will apply to Mr. Alexander Gordon, civil engineer, No. 22, Fludyer-street, he may see something in the locomotive boiler way, that will please him. Further, I can give him such information on the subject as will settle his ideas on the subject. I fully agree with him, that Sir James Anderson's plagiarism on Mr. Hancock's boiler will still further bring common road steam travelling into contempt. I am, &c.
July 2, 1838.   F. MACERONI.

Locomotive Villages.—The Messrs. Lyons, coach-makers of this city, are building a small moveable village for the Utica and Syracuse railroad. This company have now on their road two steam-engines, which drive the piles upon which the road is built, and saw them off at the proper level, the rails are then laid and the road completed as they go along. The "village," consisting of a number of neat-looking cottages, is to be placed on the road in the rear of the pile drivers, for dwelling houses for the mechanics and labourers on the road. Improvements will never stop; and we shall yet see the time when one may take a tea kettle in his hand, put a few chips in his pocket, get astride a broom-stick and go where he pleases. *Utica Democrat.*

Railway Speed Extraordinary.—It is stated that an engine on the Great Western Railway, sent to the assistance of another engine performed twelve miles in the most incredible time of five minutes, being at the rate of 144 miles per hour.—*Salisbury Herald.*

Railway Casualties. — For 471 detentions on the Grand Junction Railway, the following causes are assigned:—Broken axles of engines, tenders, and waggons... 19
Failures of pumps, eccentrics, connecting-rods, cotters, &c.. 34
Bad coke and fires burnt out, &c.......... 42
Heavy trains............................... 59
High winds................................ 25
Obstructions from cattle waggons, and breaks down... 13
Detentions from goods and second-class trains, &c. on Liverpool and Manchester Railway.... 107
Engines more or less out of order, the number not being sufficient..................... 63
Rails slippery............................. 26
Detentions in watering.................... 22
Horses kicking out the sides of horse-boxes 4
Waiting for London Mails at Birmingham (time deducted)............................. 7
Engines and waggons getting off the road at points.. 6
Waiting for Manchester train at Warrington. 39
                                           ———
Commons' Paper, No. 257.   471

Field Piece Wanted.—A correspondent requests us to "invite offers to construct a field piece of wrought-iron, either iron wire rolled round a cylinder and hammered solid, or a solid bar of iron to be bored out. It must be about three and a half feet long, nine and seven inches in diameter at the ends, and weigh (when bored out) about 4 cwt."—Address to P. A., H. A. care of our publisher.

Railway Map of England.—On the first of August will be published the Title, Index, and Contents to vol. 28 of the *Mechanics' Magazine*, and as a front-ispiece to the volume a large map of the Railways in England and Wales, price 6d. The map alone on fine paper, price 6d. Also the volume complete, in half-cloth, price 8s. 6d.

☞ *British and Foreign Patents taken out with economy and despatch; Specifications, Disclaimers, and Amendments, prepared or revised; Caveats entered; and generally every Branch of Patent Business promptly transacted. A complete list of Patents from the earliest period (1b Car. II. 167b,) to the present time may be examined. Fee 2s. 6d.; Clients, gratis.*

LONDON: Printed and Published for the Proprietor, by W. A. Robertson, at the Mechanics' Magazine Office, No. 6, Peterborough-court, between 135 and 136, Fleet-street.—Sold by A. & W. Galignani, Rue Vivienne, Paris.

Mechanics' Magazine,

MUSEUM, REGISTER, JOURNAL, AND GAZETTE.

No. 779.]   SATURDAY, JULY 14, 1838.   [Price 3*d*.

LOSH'S PATENT RAILWAY CARRIAGE-WHEELS.

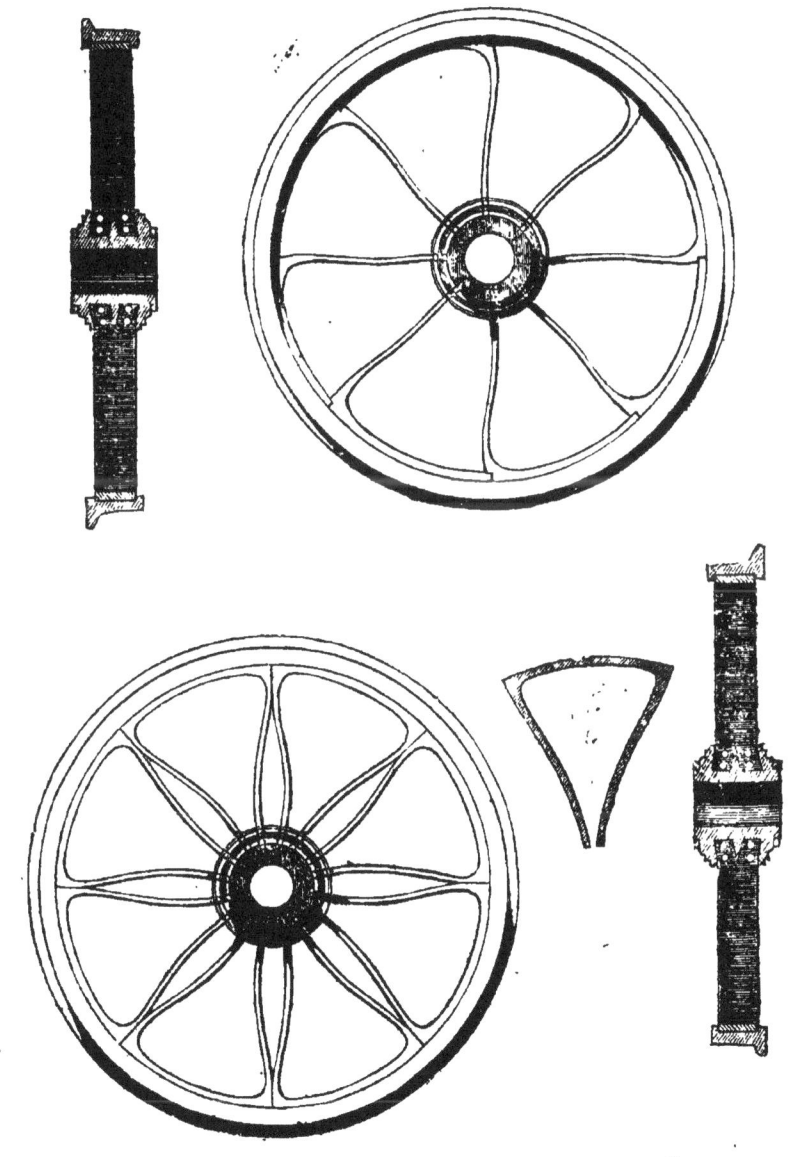

PATENT RAILWAY CARRIAGE-WHEELS
—LOSH'S, HAGUE'S AND PATON'S.

In August, 1830, Mr. William Losh obtained a patent for " certain improvements in the construction of wheels for carriages to be used on railways ;" and the improved wheel formed according to this patent has come very extensively into use. Mr. Hague, the engineer, of Wellclose-square, having lately been making wheels for railway carriages upon a plan which Mr. Losh considered to be the same as that which he had patented, Mr. Losh applied to the Court of Chancery for an injunction to restrain Mr. Hague from making the wheels in question, and the case was argued in the Vice Chancellor's Court on the 9th of last August, an injunction granted, and the question of the validity of Losh's patent referred to a jury in a court of law. This reference was tried in the Court of Exchequer on the 4th inst., when a verdict was returned in favour of Mr. Hague, and against Mr. Losh's patent right. The arguments used, both in the Courts of Chancery and Exchequer against Losh's patent were ; 1st, that a patent had been obtained as long ago as September 1808, by a Thomas Paton, of Christ Church, Surrey, for iron wheels in which the same mode of construction was used as that patented by Losh ;' 2nd, that Mr. Losh himself, in conjunction with Mr. Stephenson, had previously taken out a patent for an invention similar to the one in question. It was also argued, on behalf of Hague, that the wheels which he made were not the same as Losh's patent; and that Losh's wheels would not answer if made according to his specification, he having materially departed from it in the wheels which he now constructed. We shall lay before our readers the substance of Losh's and Paton's specifications, and a description of Hague's wheel, alleged to be an infringement of Losh's patent.

Mr. Losh states in his specification that the object to be attained by his improvements is, to render wheels more durable and less liable to be damaged or broken by the violence of the shocks to which they are liable, than the wheels hitherto in use upon railroads, and more particularly when propelled with rapid motion. The spokes, the rims or felloes, and the tires of his wheels are to be made wholly of malleable-iron,

and to be joined one to another, and to a cast-iron central nave, in the manner afterwards described, whereby all the parts are so firmly fixed and united one to another, that they will all act simultaneously to support or sustain the cast-iron nave in the centre of the wheel, and to preserve the true form of the wheel in every respect.

Fig. 1 (opposite page), is a side elevation, and fig. 2 a section of a wheel. A is a central nave of cast-iron. a, b, c, are the spokes made from bars of flat iron. In the formation of such a wheel, the bars for the several spokes are wrought with elbow bends, p, q, t, near the middles of their lengths, the prolongations beyond those elbow-bends being curved, as represented at p, r, in the engraving; so that when the proper number of such spokes are put together, their curved prolongations beyond the elbow bends will form a complete circle, and their *straight* parts within these elbow-bends, will form the radii of that circle. To unite all these spokes together to form a wheel, the proper number are laid round in a suitable mould, prepared for the purpose of casting the central nave, in the manner usually practised by ironfounders. The central ends of the spokes which project into the cavity of the mould for the nave—being heated before laying them in the mould, according to the usual practice of iron-founders when they intend to run cast-iron around wrought-iron ;—the cast-iron for forming the nave, A, is run around the inner or central ends of all the spokes; these ends had been previously indented or cut dove-tailed, so that they cannot draw out of the cast-iron which is run around them ; or a hole may be pierced through these ends about which the cast-iron is to be run.   For security against splitting the cast-iron nave, circular hoops, v v, of malleable iron, may be put on around both the projecting ends of the cast-iron nave A, these hoops being applied hot, so as to shrink on the cast-iron and bind it very firmly. The outer ends or curved prolongations of the spokes beyond the elbow-bends (which prolongations fit together, as shown in the engraving, to form a circular rim) overlap each other sufficiently to enable them to be united one to another: for instance, the extreme end r, of the curved prolongation of the

Mr. Losh's Wheels.

Fig. 1.   Fig. 3.   Fig. 4.

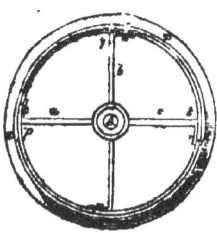 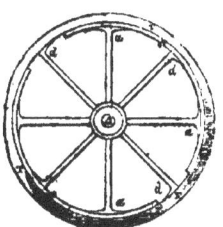 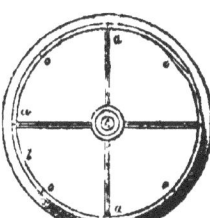

Fig. 5.   Fig. 2.

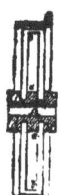 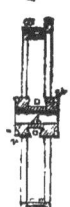

Mr Paton's Wheels.

Fig. 6.   Fig. 7.

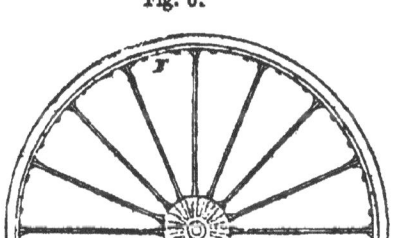 

Mr. Hague's Wheels.

Fig. 8.

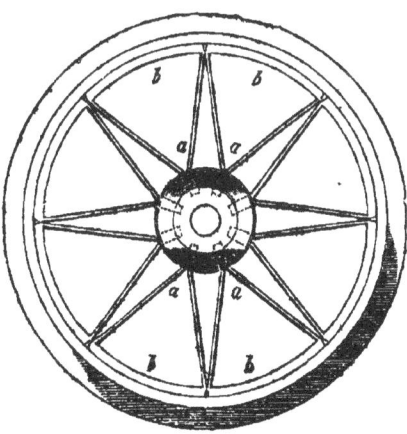

Fig. 9.

spoke a, is accurately fitted into and upon the recess, at q, which is formed like a double-crank bend in the elbow-bend of the spoke b, and the extreme end, s, of the curved prolongation of the spoke b, is in like manner received into a similar recess, t, at the elbow-bend of the spoke c, and so of all the others. The extreme end of each prolongation, when it thus overlaps and rests upon the elbow-bend of the next spoke, must form a good joint in the recess, which is secured by welding, or a strong rivet or rivets put through the recessed or double-cranked part of the elbow-bend. The curved prolongation of the spokes when thus rivetted together at their several joinings, form a firm circular rim p, r, q, s, t, to the wheel around which the wrought-iron tire T, that runs upon the rails of the railway is fixed, by the same means as is usually taken for applying the hoop-tire on wheels of carriages, viz.; the said tire is a circular hoop formed of a wrought-iron bar, rolled into the proper shape for travelling upon the rails. A proper length of such a bar is curved into a circle, and the ends welded together, and the hoop being applied whilst hot around the circular rim (made by the curved prolongations of the spokes), the shrinking or contraction of the hoop in cooling, firmly embraces the said circular rim and forms a strong and secure wheel. The hoop of tire may be fastened on the rim formed by the prolongations of the spoke, by conical pins put through the tire and the said rim, in a direction pointing towards the centre of the wheel; the pins being fitted into corresponding holes bored through the tire, with their longest ends on the outside thereof, that the pins may hold the tire tight without any projecting heads on the outside The small ends of the pins which project through the inner rim, may be rivetted or have nuts screwed on them; or, in order to make the tire hold very securely on the outside of the rim formed by the prolongations of the spokes without any pins.

The iron bar for the tire may be rolled with a head projecting about $\frac{1}{16}$th of an inch from each edge of the bar on that side which is to form the interior of the hoop for the tire; the breadth or space left vacant between those heads being sufficient to receive the edge of the rim formed by the prolongations of the spokes. The expansion of the hoop of tire when heated, will allow it to be applied around the said rim, but when it contracts thereon by cooling, the projecting beads will overlap each edge of the rim, and effectually prevent the tire coming off therefrom. Or otherwise for the same object, the bars of which the spokes are formed may be rolled rather concave on one side, like a shallow gutter or trough, the other side being either convex or flat; and when those bars are wrought into spokes with elbow-bends, as before described, their concave sides should be outwards on the circumference of the circle that is to be formed by the prolongations of the spokes beyond those elbow-bends; and in that case the bar of which the tire is formed should be rolled with a corresponding convexity on that side which is to form the inside of the hoop, which hoop being made of a proper size, and then heated in order to expand it, and get it on around the rim formed by the prolongations of the spokes. The convex inside of that hoop, when it contracts by cooling, will fill the concave on the circumference of the prolongations, and effectually prevent the tire coming off therefrom.

Instead of making each of the spokes and its prolongation out of the same piece of iron-bar, the spoke may be made of a piece of one bar, rolled to any pattern of transverse section judged most suitable for the spokes of the wheel, and the prolongation made from another bar, rolled to any different pattern of transverse section, judged most suitable for the circular rim that is to be formed by the said prolongations. The said two pieces of different bars being firmly welded together at the elbow-bend, so as to be as strong as if both spokes and prolongation were made by bending one piece of iron-bar. This mode of making the elbow-bend will facilitate the formation of the recess or double-cranked bend, into which the extreme end of the next prolongation is to lodge.

Fig. 3, represents a side elevation of a segment of another wheel. The ends of the spokes are put into a mould and hammered into the form or forms shown at a, a, a, a; or they may be spread out into any other form that will be found most convenient for welding them to the rim. A circular rim *s, s,* of wrought iron is then made of the proper diameter to receive the tire, and the spokes are welded to it. To make this rim perfectly circular, and of a proper diameter to fit accurately to the inside of the hoop of tire T, which is intended to surround it, the said rim may be fitted upon a mandril or circular mould which has openings or slits in its circumference, at proper distances to receive the arms; the rim is then put upon the mandril by the common expedient of expanding the rim by heat, dropping it on the mandril, and whilst the rim is contracting again in cooling, it is retained at the required diameter by the resistance of the mandril; this mandril may be made in two halves, or in three or more parts so kept apart as to form a true circle of the proper size, by the interposition of suitable wedges, or by screws, which, being withdrawn or unscrewed, the parts will collapse, and facilitate the taking off of the wheel from the mandril when cold.

Spokes may be welded to a bar of wrought-iron at proper distances apart, and at right angles to that bar, and then turning the bar into a circular form, by hammering it into a circular mould, (which should be the segment of a circle of the diameter of the inside of the tire); when the rim is thus formed into a circular shape, and the ends of the bar forming the rim are brought together, they should be welded. To make this rim, to which the arms have been previously welded, of the exact diameter required for the rim, it should be fitted upon a circular mandril prepared with openings or slits to receive the arms, in the manner before described. Or otherwise the said rim, to which the arms are previously welded and its ends welded together, may be heated red and hammered down into a true circular mould, which is made bell-mouthed to facilitate the entrance of the rim into it. The spokes may be immediately welded to the rim or hoop of tire, as shown at *a, a,* without the intervention of an interior rim.

Fig. 4 represents another wheel, in which each spoke is formed of two bars of iron laid together at one end, as at *a a a,* to form one bar; and the prolongations of each of the single bars of the spokes beyond the elbow bends, *b b b,* of each of the bars, being blended in op-

posite directions, as shown in the engraving, they form a curved prolongation of the compound spoke on each side of it; those prolongations of the different spokes meet each other, as at *o o o,* in the middle of the spaces between the spokes, and where those ends overlap, they may be rivetted together to form a circular rim, around which the tire is applied; or the overlap at the ends of the spokes where they meet may be welded together as at *c;* a mode of junction which will add much to the support of the tire. The bar of which each spoke is formed may be blended with two elbow bends, the middle part between those two elbow-bends forming a portion of the circular rim, and the two ends of the bar being straight thus ▽, so that each bar forms a sector of a circle; and a proper number of such sectors being put together with the straight parts in contact, will form a wheel, whereof each spoke is composed of two bars; the circular rim of the wheel so composed must be surrounded by a circular hoop of tire. The spokes in figs. 3 and 4 must be attached to the nave, in the same manner as before described in figs. 1 and 2.

Fig. 5 represents a section of another form of wheel, the spokes of which are made by bending a bar of iron into the shape shown at *a a, b b.* The end *b b,* forming a double elbow-bend, is placed in the transverse direction of the bar of iron, constituting an inner rim, such as hereinbefore described, and is joined to such rim by rivets, or by welding. The ends *a a* are to be fixed in the nave by running cast-metal around them, in the manner described in fig. 1. Upon the spokes and rim thus combined, the tire is put, in the manner directed in the description of figs. 3 and 4.

Mr. Losh claimed,—First, the improvement described and represented in figs. 1 and 2, "of making the wheels of carriages to be used on railways, with wrought-iron spokes, having elbow-bends and curved prolongations from such spokes, which prolongations join one to another, in the manner hereinbefore described, so as to form a circular rim of wrought-iron to support and give strength to the hoop of wrought-iron tire which is applied and fixed around that circular rim."

Secondly, the making the circular hoop of iron-tire out of bar-iron, rolled with projecting beads at the edges, or with a convexity, the rim of the wheel having a corresponding concavity on that side which is to form the inside of the hoop of tire, in order that the hoop of iron may, after it has been put on in a heated and expanded state, be retained securely from coming off, either by the overlapping of the projecting beads of the tire over the edges of the rim of the wheel, or by the interlocking of the convexity and concavity of the tire and rim of the wheel.

Thirdly, the improvement described and represented in fig. 3, of making wheels with wrought-iron spokes, moulded at their outer ends into the form shown in the engraving, fig. 5, as at *a a a a*, or having elbow-bends at the outer ends to form feet, as at *d d d*, which ends of the spokes are joined by welding, or by conical bolts or rivets without heads, at the outside, either to a complete ring of wrought-iron, around which a hoop of wrought-iron tire is to be applied and fixed, or else to a hoop of wrought-iron tire, made of sufficient strength to retain its circular curvature without any such inner ring.

Fourthly, the improvement described and represented in fig. 4, of forming each spoke of two bars of iron laid together at one end, as far as the elbow-bends, and the parts beyond those elbow bends being bent in opposite directions to form curved prolongations of each of the compound spokes on each side thereof; and which prolongations when united together form a circular rim, upon which the tire is laid.

Mr. Losh, finding that his plan of fastening on the tire of his wheel by shrinkage of a convex over a concave surface, claimed secondly in his specification, was not new, disclaimed that part of his patent in 1836, so that that point was not argued before the court.

Mr. Paton's patent for improvements in the construction of wheels, was granted September 24th, 1808. *Railway* carriages were not contemplated in this patent, and Mr. Losh's is particularly confined to railway carriages; nevertheless, the resemblance between the modes of construction described is very striking.

Mr. Paton states in his specification, —First, that instead of making wheels of wood, as has been generally done heretofore, he makes the stocks or naves

of wrought-iron, lined with steel in the inside, or of bell-metal, hard brass, gunmetal, or of cast-iron, with or without steel bushes inside, or even of cast-steel.

Second, in the wrought-iron stock or nave, in place of wood spokes, as in wheels in general, he inserts spokes made *of wrought-iron, or any other metal not liable to break with a sudden jerk,* by wedging, screwing, keying, or by turning the end of the spoke to fit the hole in the nave exactly, and drilling holes through both nave and spoke to receive a transverse pin to prevent their coming out.

Third, in the least iron bell-metal, gun-metal or least steel naves, he fixes the spokes in the same way, but he has also another method, which is by laying the spokes in the mould and running the metal round them; which is much sooner done.

Fourth, in the least iron naves he fixes the steel bushes by wedging, or by putting them in the mould and running the metal round them; the same may be done with the bell-metal, &c.

Fifth. He makes the felloes, or the external circle that the tire fixes on, of iron or other metal, and makes them and the spokes of one solid piece; or fixes the felloes to the spokes with rivets, screws, and nuts, or any other way, as convenient; and when the wheel is wider than common, he puts two or even three rows of spokes in the nave to receive them, or makes them in one piece with the spoke, with brackets on each side projecting from the side of the spoke to the edge of the felloe.

Fig. 6 represents a wheel for a gig, chaise, &c. showing the method for connecting the spokes to the nave of the wheel, when the metal is to be run round them; the cavities *a,* in fig. 7, are to fix the spokes more securely to the nave; the joint of the felloe at F shews the dowell.

Fig 7 is a view of the spoke and felloe by itself, which may be of one solid piece or fixed to the felloe with rivets, screws, and nuts, or any other most convenient way. The tire or exterior ring to be fixed to the felloe with rivets or screws and nuts, &c.

There is a contrivance described in this patent to keep oil in the bushes; but, as it does not bear upon the question in dispute, we have omitted to describe it.

The wheels which Mr. Hague constructed, and which were assumed by Mr. Losh to be an infringement of his patent were made in the following manner:—Bars of wrought-iron were bent and formed into the shape shown by fig. 9, and the ends welded together at the points *a*. A series of such bent bars of wrought-iron were made into wheels thus: a number of the bent bars fig. 9, and the parts *a*, combined together by means of a cast iron nave, as shown at fig. 8, and the parts *b b*, produced a ring or felloe for the wheel, on to which a wrought-iron flanched hoop or tire was shrunk, by first heating, in order to expand it, and render it capable of being placed on the outer periphery of the parts *b*, of the bent bars of wrought-iron, fig. 9, and when on and shrunk by cooling, such flanched tire or hoop tightly embraced the wheel, *a b*.

The engravings on our front page show the last improvements of Mr. Losh on his wheels. The bending of the spokes for the purpose of giving more elasticity to the wheels was the variation from the specification brought forward by Mr. Hague's counsel.

DR. LARDNER AND ATLANTIC STEAM-NAVIGATION.

Dr. Lardner's long-announced article on "Ocean Steamers" has at length seen the light in the pages of the *Monthly Chronicle* for July. It is needless, perhaps, to observe, that the article is evidently an entirely new one. What may have been the contents of that which was withdrawn, at the very moment of publication, from the preceding number, must of course be matter of conjecture; but it is at least plain enough that it would not have been occupied, as this is, with the details of the voyage of the *Great Western*, whose arrival just in the nick of time, deprived the world of the proofs it probably contained that she never could arrive at all! Be this as it may, the article as it stands is of a sufficiently remarkable character.

It is now Dr. Lardner's cue to persuade the world that he was never adverse to the scheme of the steam-navigation of the Atlantic! In pursuit of this object he displays a very considerable degree of ingenuity as well as the most enviable hardihood. Thus, after commencing with a flaming panegyric on steam, from a book of his own, and following it up by some reflections on the same subject in a most grandiloquent strain, he comes to close quarters in a style which at once shows how "cunning of fence" he has become. "The general expression of astonishment and mutual congratulation," quoth he, "which has followed the recent accomplishment of the voyages of the steam-ships, the *Great Western* and the *Sirius*, though natural and excusable on the part of the public generally, would, if shared by men of practical science, betray a culpable breach of allegiance to the sovereignty of steam, and an unpardonable ignorance of the actual state of that power." Could it be believed that the writer of this sentence was himself one of the (so-styled) "men of practical science" by whom this "unpardonable ignorance" had been shown? That he was the only one of the genus who had made himself conspicuous by denouncing the idea of steaming across the Atlantic as impracticable?—or that he had actually taken great pains to demonstrate the absolute *impossibility* of the voyages whose accomplishment created a "natural and excusable feeling of astonishment on the part of the public generally?" Yet are these things so. Dr. Lardner has done all this, and the self-same Dr. Lardner is the avowed author of this very article! *O tempora! O mores!*

The Doctor, indeed, dexterously interpolates a note, comprising an extract from the *Times'* report of his speech at Bristol in 1836, by way of proof positive that he never expressed an opinion adverse to the plan, but on the contrary always thought it practicable; and it may be allowed that the extracts, *as they stand,* may be made to bear that interpretation. But the Doctor does not give the whole of that report. He leaves out the middle portion, as being matter of no consequence,—merely "some calculations of the performances of Admiralty steamers, from which the speaker is represented as recommending the coast of Ireland as a point of final departure." We have had the curiosity, as well as Dr. Lardner, to refer back to this report, "published at the time," and we find that these omitted calculations are of rather more consequence than the Doctor now affects to think them. *In that re-*

port Dr. Lardner is represented as producing these calculations in support of his assertion that the steam-navigation of the Atlantic at one trip is impracticable!

Dr. Lardner, be it remembered, brings forward this report in a tone of great candour, to rebut the assertion that he had ever pronounced "a steam voyage from England to New York a physical impossibility." He alludes to it with the air of injured innocence in the moment of its vindication. Yet what are the facts?—*he* merely quotes a few general remarks from the beginning of the report, and a few words from the conclusion, unintelligible without the context, and studiously leaves out the main body, which, as it happens, contains the most full and satisfactory evidence that the charge against him is perfectly true and well-founded! In *that* part of the report we find it stated that the Doctor laid down the position, that the extreme distance to which a steam-vessel could be propelled, without halting for fuel, was 2080 miles, and that, consequently, a voyage like that from Bristol to New York, of 3,500 miles (sic) was flatly impossible! We find him, after adducing this fact, and others of the same calibre, calmly and complacently observing that it would be a "waste of time" to discuss further the practicability of the plan, and that it became reduced to "a mere geographical question" as to where the steamers should halt for coals! We find him approving or rejecting various proposed routes because the distance to be run was, as the case might be, within or without the "steam-limit" which he held to have been established by his calculations! We find him, moreover, taking great credit to himself for the accuracy of these calculations, stoutly maintaining that the performances of the government steamers, on which they were founded, could not be exceeded, and finally, by way of covering the promoters of Atlantic steam-navigation with inextinguishable ridicule, and displaying the absurdity of their ideas in the most glaring light, demonstrating, perfectly to his own satisfaction, that the coals and machinery of a vessel of 1600 tons, intended to run the whole distance, would weigh 1748 tons, and that consequently it would be impossible for such a vessel to cross the Atlantic, even could she *go alone*, to say nothing of crew, passengers, or cargo!!!

What, after all this, are we to think of the Doctor's dictum, that the "natural and excusable" astonishment of the public at the voyage of the *Great Western*, would, "if shared by men of practical science, betray an *unpardonable ignorance?*" Shall he be allowed to pass sentence on himself, and for the future be styled, by his own consent, the Doctor "unpardonably ignorant?"—And then again, what are we to think of the moral attributes of the man who could have the hardihood to refer to this very report of the *Times*, in proof of the groundlessness of a charge which it fully substantiates, and the perverse ingenuity to suppress the only passages which bear directly on the question, and which turn the scales on that question so decidedly against him?—Is not this, also, and in a higher degree than his self-proclaimed "ignorance"—UNPARDONABLE?

The whole of the article in the *Monthly Chronicle* is distinguished for its evasive and equivocating tone. How could it be otherwise, considering that its author still endeavours, in spite of fate, to retain a rag or two of that reputation for "practical science" which the voyage of the *Great Western* has reduced to tatters? The situation of that individual must, indeed, be pitiable, despite all the resources of broad assertion and suppressed quotation, whose every prediction has been so thoroughly falsified by the result. Let us only imagine the situation of a man who has laid it down that the voyage to America will require 2¼ tons of coal per horse power, when a vessel arrives which has performed it with the expenditure of *one ton:*—who has been ready to stake his all that the speed of 7.8 miles per hour cannot be exceeded, when that vessel traverses the ocean at the rate of 8.2 miles per hour, in spite of adverse circumstances which might have been expected to retard her course 25 per cent.:—who has affirmed that the quantity of coals taken out would be only sufficient for half the voyage, when the whole voyage is performed, and a couple of hundred tons are left unconsumed.—All these circumstances must necessarily be not a little annoying, and must be expected to generate an ardent wish that the prophecies, *founded on the most authentic practical data*, of the last two years, could be recalled: they can hardly justify, nevertheless, a garbling of the truth, or a misrepresentation of actual fact.

The whole course of Dr. Lardner's proceedings in this affair is pregnant with instruction. The overweening confidence of his assumptions, previous to their being brought to the test of experiment, is amusingly contrasted with his attempts to escape from the disgrace of having ever uttered them, when that test has proved their hollowness. His theory professes to be founded on the most thoroughly practical data; yet every one of his inferences from these data, (which, at the Liverpool Meeting of the British Association, he would hardly permit to be questioned) has proved to be wrong,—egregiously, totally wrong,—wrong to such an extent as to make their propounder a mark for ridicule, and even to cast discredit for a time on all conclusions professing to be deduced from "practical grounds." Yet, in spite of all this, the Doctor, for the present at least, shows a bold front; and, *perhaps*, in spite of all this, will, for some time longer, continue to be consulted as an oracle of mechanical science by Parliamentary Committees, and other grave deliberative bodies. Nay, more, he will possibly still continue to superintend the scientific portion of the *Monthly Chronicle*, and, (as in the last number,) while he, in one page, reluctantly allows that it may be possible to steam across the Atlantic, he will avow his firm belief in all the wonders of animal magnetism, from reading with the eyes shut to the gift of prophecy, by the mere agency of "twiddling the thumbs." Truly, "practical science"— and theoretical too,—may well be proud of such a votary!

We believe Dr. Lardner stood pretty nearly alone in his opposition to the grand scheme which has now been consummated. He, indeed, with matchless effrontery, says, in the article in question, that "of its practicability no doubt, so far as we have heard or read, has ever been expressed by any one who has taken a part in the discussion of the question," and this passage occurs on the very leaf preceding that on which the mangled quotation from the *Times* is given,—a quotation which could not have been so mangled without the writer's becoming acquainted with the de-

cisive portions so carefully suppressed. But the idea of Dr. Lardner's being unaware of the existence of "doubts" on the matter! Did he never hear of such doubts being contained in a certain Treatise on the Steam Engine, of which Dr. Lardner was the author? Or in a critique in the *Edinburgh Review*, also by a Dr. Lardner? Or in a pamphlet—pamphlet on Steam Communication with India, from the pen of a Dr. Lardner? Or in divers lectures at scientific institutions, delivered by a Dr. Lardner? Or in a pseudo-scientific periodical called *The Railway Magazine*, again by a Dr. Lardner? Or, finally, at both the Bristol *and* Liverpool meetings of the British Association, a Dr. Lardner being the speaker?—Certain it is, that "doubts" in abundance have been thrown upon the scheme in all these ways, and through all these media, and all, strange to say, have been traceable to no other than— Dr. Lardner!

LOCOMOTIVES FOR COMMON ROADS.

Sir,—By a paragraph which has been going the round of the papers, and was copied into your 769th Number, we learn that Mr. Hancock, the most enterprising and the most persevering of common-road locomotionists, has been trying his hand at steam-carriages of a smaller class than heretofore. In lieu of a steam-omnibus, he now astonishes the city with the speed and tractability of his steam-gig. Although we have proof, by his progresses, that the steam is "up"—I know there are some persons who consider this motion of Mr. Hancock's as retrograde, and speak disparagingly of steam-carriages as "looking down." Permit me to express my firm belief in the good sense and propriety of Mr. Hancock's proceeding. All common-road locomotives, *on a large scale*, have hitherto failed; witness the results—or non-results if you please—of Dr. Church's protracted labours at Birmingham, on a scale that might well be termed magnificent; observe the termination of the short but splendid career of the ingenious Heatons, his townsmen; who accomplished more in the character of their performances, with their first steam-carriage of small power, than any of their competitors—and yet, in attempting to carry out the very same principles upon an extended scale, they completely failed. In spite of all the ingenuity of man, the *weight* of the locomotive increases in a much quicker ratio than the *power;* and the evils consequent upon this increase of weight, are of such a magnitude, as greatly to diminish—nay, wholly to extinguish—all reasonable prospect of success.

Mr. Hancock may very judiciously disclaim all connection with the "Steam Carriage and Waggon Company;" for in reasoning upon the experience of the past, it would appear that vehicles of a smaller class are most likely to succeed, and I am quite of opinion, that locomotives of moderate power, will be in general use, and travelling at satisfactory speed on common roads, long before steam-waggons shall have proceeded beyond *experiments.*

I remain, Sir; yours respectfully,
WM. BADDELEY.

London, July 5, 1838.

MR. HANCOCK'S STEAM-CARRIAGE EXPERIENCE.

Sir,—In the letter to which your correspondent, "An Advocate of Steam-locomotion," refers, I stated that "I have now in preparation calculations founded upon actual practice, which, when published, will prove that steam-locomotion on common roads is not unworthy of the attention of the capitalist;" and I now beg to inform him that those calculations are in the press, and will shortly be published.

I am, Sir, your obedient servant,
WALTER HANCOCK.

Stratford, July 7, 1838.

SIR JAMES ANDERSON'S STEAM-CARRIAGE COMPANY.

Sir,—Your observations on my steam-carriage and boiler have just been placed before me. Without in the slightest degree detracting from the many and great merits of the gentlemen named by you, who have given so much time and talent to the subject of locomotion upon common roads, I claim for myself *merely whatever merit the public may find me entitled to when I have placed my carriage before them.* You accord to others much and deserved credit for their efforts, —pray do not detract from *mine,* on mere supposition. We all know that some of the most valuable improvements have been made by the most unpretending persons.

I have spent nearly *two apprenticeships* to this undertaking, and have, unaided by any company, expended above 30,000*l.* on my experiments. These have never been brought before the public, or its aid sought; for I did not consider my carriage, until the present time, equal to the difficulties to be overcome. And I now give the measure into the hands of a company, *because it is of paramount importance to the country that locomotion on common roads should be introduced as widely and expeditiously as possible,* which cannot be done individually: otherwise, my partner and myself would have worked it for our own benefit.

I have sought no money from the public to enable me to try my experiments, nor ask any benefit for which I do not give a *"quid pro quo."* I produce and prove my steam-drags before I am paid for them, and I keep them in repair: consequently, neither the public nor the company run any risk.

There is room enough, sir, in England for us all. If the public find my steam-drag answer, it will but prepare the way for those of greater talent to introduce theirs. Capital can never be wanted for what is really good; and the public are now awaking *to the necessity* for locomotion on common roads.

Is it not a little singular that you attack myself and the company, and still state that *"you will not give an opinion pro or con. on my invention?"* It is wise, however, and I am glad, for the sake of the leading mechanical journal of England, you have so determined.

I shall not trespass on public expectation much longer; the first steam-drag built for the company is now nearly complete. It will speak for itself.

I am, Sir, your obedient servant,
JAMES C. ANDERSON.

Buttevant Castle, July 3, 1838.

HONORARY FIRE-BRIGADE AT CHELTENHAM——EXTENSIVE FIRE AT BOLTON, &c.

Sir,—I mentioned, a short time since, the circumstance of an honorary fire-brigade having been established at Southampton: I have now the pleasure to announce the formation of a similar corps at Cheltenham. The Southampton brigade have only one engine, but the Cheltenham company will be more extensive; the three town-engines have been put into a state of thorough repair by Mr. Merryweather, who is now building for them a new and powerful engine on the patent principle, which will combine all the latest improvements, with every necessary accompaniment. This corps is already provided with a set of Mr. Merryweather's portable fire-escape ladders, and they promise to be shortly in a highly efficient state. In addition to the protection afforded by this association, the Phœnix Fire-office have a large engine stationed in Cheltenham, in charge of an experienced fireman; so that this town may be considered very adequately protected against the spread of calamitous fires.

In the absence of a properly organized and efficient fire-police, these voluntary associations are likely to be productive of incalculable good; and the successful results of their well-directed energies will, I doubt not, form a pleasing contrast to the sickening details continually afforded by the provincial press, of places where these matters are entirely disregarded, and where fires are left to glut their ruthless fury upon unprotected premises of the largest dimensions, frequently stored with the most valuable contents. No longer ago than last week, a striking exemplification of this incredible recklessness was presented at Bolton, in Lancashire, by the destruction of a considerable portion of the splendid spinning-mills of Messrs. Ormrod and Hardcastle, the damage of which is estimated at upwards of fifty thousand pounds. In the published particulars of this fire, it is stated that "the destruction of this fine property is highly disgraceful to the authorities of the town, as well as to the fire-offices, in a place where such immense mill-property is at stake, covering many millions in value. It is scarcely credible, but such is nevertheless the fact, that out of three engines belonging to the town, not one was in a condition to work, nor seemingly a single soul who understood how to work them!"

That a similar apathy prevails in many places to a lamentable degree, is a fact notorious to all, and I see no better remedy for this cruel neglect of the "proper authorities," than the immediate formation of honorary fire-associations, after the transatlantic fashion, throughout the kingdom. This course pursued with spirit, in connexion with a judicious and extensive application of the best known *preventives*, would, although not wholly prevent the recurrence of accident, yet so effectually limit the extent of danger, as to give a security against the loss of life and property by fire, to a degree scarcely anticipated by the most sanguine.

Although the places and persons obnoxious to the charge herein brought forward are exceedingly numerous, there are yet many honorable exceptions, as shown by the large number of fire-engines continually building by the London makers. It was remarked at the Bolton fire, that the most efficient services were rendered by the "stranger engines," and it will very often be found, that the fire-engines belonging to private individuals are kept in better working order, are sooner brought out, and more skilfully directed, than those of towns not having a regular fire-establishment. I am, therefore, glad to observe an increase in the number and power of the engines kept by the proprietors of extensive manufactories in various parts of the kingdom. I may here mention, that Mr. Merryweather has just finished a very excellent carriage-engine for Messrs. Clarke, Murze and Co.'s "Great Western Cotton Mills," at Bristol, and he has already sent two engines to another manufactory in the same city.

Other establishments, both public and private, have lately renewed or increased their fire-extinguishing machinery, and it is to be hoped this important subject will receive from all, the share of thoughtfulness and attention it so imperatively demands.

I remain, Sir, yours respectfully,
WM. BADDELEY.

London, July 4, 1838.

THE THAMES TUNNEL WORKS—MR. WALKER'S REPORT.

[From the *Times* of July 7th.]

We publish to-day, certainly beyond all comparison, the most singular report of an engineer that was ever before made public in this age for schemers and engineers. It is the report of Mr. James Walker, dated December, 1837, on the works and prospects of the celebrated Thames Tunnel Company. The view which this report presents to the public of the work in question is, we have no hesitation in saying, prodigious in absurdity. Would we could add, that the work itself was not also equally prodigious, or, rather, prodigal, in its drafts upon the public purse, and, in fact, in every species of dupery and imposition. Mr. Walker, it will be seen, in his abstract of his own report, gives as a head that Parliament should agree to Mr. Brunel's proposal to proceed with the works on the Middlesex side, if it be the resolution to complete the works "*without present inquiry as to the cost.*" We could hardly believe our eyes when we read these last words. Was ever such a thing heard of as continuing works "without any previous inquiry as to what they might cost?" Of what faith, or what religion, we should beg leave to ask, is Mr. Walker? Did he ever read his Bible? "Which of you, intending to build a tower, sitteth not down first and *counteth the cost*, whether he hath sufficient to finish it? Lest, haply, after he hath laid the foundation, and is not able to finish it, all that behold him begin to mock him, saying, this man began to build, and was not able to finish."—Luke xiv. 28, 29. Well, then, we ask, if, according to Mr. Walker's proposition, the works may, perhaps, ultimately be finished (if Government will continue them without making any present inquiry as to the cost), in what way are they to be continued? First of all, notwithstanding daily accidents are happening on the river from the superabundance of traffic and the rapidity of steam-boats, these are all to be compressed into the narrow space which is already tunnelled under by the present progress of the undertaking. And for what purpose is the passage thus to be compressed? Why, in order that a new bed of clay may be formed for the rest of the river, in the place of its present bed of silt; and this new bed, whereon Father Thames is to rest one part of his body, is to be completed, before the wondrous machine called Mr. Brunel's shield, be advanced one inch farther. Here, we think, we may repose ourselves, and the public may repose with us; for that such a clay-bed will ever be made, or ever can be made, notwithstanding Mr. James Walker's admirable scheme of "two rows of close whole timber piles, one row on each side of the Tunnel," is as impossible as that two rows of trees should be planted and form an avenue from this sublunary globe to the satellites which attend it by night. Mr. James Walker and Mr. Brunel, in the contemplation of such a scheme, may well say, that it should be attempted "*without making cost an element in the question.*" Will nothing put an end to this absurd and even murderous project? We say *murderous*; for, in addition to the four irruptions which have been made into the Tunnel, some with loss of life, Mr. Brunel also mentions "the impregnation of the water with sulphurated hydrogen, *which has proved very injurious to the health of the workmen.*"

Of the causes assigned by Mr. Brunel which had retarded the progress of the Tunnel in May, 1837, one was, the excessive rains of the preceding autumn; which he says, "liquified the ground between the ceiling of the shield and the river." How the rain got in there we cannot tell; or how the ground lying between the bottom of the river and the top of the shield could possibly be more "liquified" than it was from its natural position, we defy philosophy and all the dabblers in hydrostatics and hydraulics to discover.

RETURN TO AN ORDER OF THE HON. THE HOUSE OF COMMONS, DATED JUNE 27, 1838, FOR COPY OF MR. WALKER'S REPORT TO THE TREASURY ON THE WORKS AT THE THAMES TUNNEL.

I duly received a letter from Mr. Baring, under date 7th of October, 1837, informing me "that the Lords Commissioners of her Majesty's Treasury had under their consideration a report from the clerk of the Thames Tunnel Company of the 13th September, with an account of the breaking in of the river of the 23d of August, 1837, and various papers relating thereto, which, with the former report from the same party, and special reports from Mr. Brunel of the works proposed to be carried on at the Tunnel, were referred to me for my consideration and report, previous to their Lordships giving any direction on the application for consent to the several propositions made by the engineer and directors of the Company for continuing and facilitating the progress of the works."

I gave the subjects my immediate attention, and was preparing a report thereon, when on the 2nd of November another (the fourth) irruption of the Thames took place, and on the 6th, when I visited the works of the Tunnel, Mr. Brunel, the engineer, and Mr. Charlier, the secretary, requested a postponement of my report for a short time, until they should complete an expected arrangement with the navigation committee of the river Thames, from which they expected increased facility and security. This request I communicated to Mr. Baring by letter on the 9th of November.

I have since seen Mr. Spearman's letter of the 2nd of December, transmitting to me, by command of the Lords of the Treasury, a copy of a letter from the secretary to the Thames Tunnel Company, dated 15th November, together with a report of Mr. Brunel on the present state of the Tunnel, and the best mode of proceeding, and also a plan of the works, with a request that I would communicate to their Lordships my opinion upon the several points referred to in the papers, previous to their determining on the proposals and recommendations of the company.

Since receiving the above instructions, Mr. Spearman has stated to me the desire to be, that every point, *particularly as respects cost or estimate, which I consider of importance in the general question of the Tunnel, should be included in my report, so as to bring the whole fairly under the consideration of their Lordships.*

That Mr. Brunel's different reports, in which the same recommendations are repeated, may be brought to their Lordships' recollection, I shall give a short abstract of the main points in the order of date.

In his report of May 2, 1837, Mr. Brunel ascribes the difficulties which had retarded the progress of the Tunnel for the last five months to the excessive rains of the preceding autumn *liquifying the ground between the ceiling of the shield and the river, and causing it to run into the works;* he states that this has been augmented by his being deprived of the pumping-well and drain from Wapping, which is stated to have been originally intended, and to have been considered the most efficient means of drainage, particularly as the dip of the strata is to that side, and that before any satisfactory progress can be calculated on the proposed pumping-well, with a drain or drift-way, should be made, but that a preferable plan would be to sink the 50 feet shaft for the foot passengers' descent, which would, he considers, be a better means of drainage, and would give employment to the workmen when not in the shield. The fact of the pumping at the entrance of the London Docks having dried the wells in that neighbourhood, is adduced as a proof that a pumping-engine on the Middlesex side would diminish the land-springs in the Tunnel.

Mr. Brunel estimates the expense of the shaft, including the steam-engine, pumps, &c., at 6,844l., and the pumping-well alone at 2,990l., independent of the drift-way or drain, which he calculates at 4,310l., making together 7,000l., which sum he presumes would be saved by forming the shaft rather than the well at the present time, exclusive of keeping the workmen and establishment employed, and thereby reducing the amount which is now charged to the tunnel account. *He also mentions the impregnation of the water with sulphurated hydrogen, which has proved very injurious to the health of the workmen,* as another reason for making the drift-way, as it would be the most effectual means of drawing it off. The report states, that "the fact of 16 feet of the Tunnel having been completed under the described difficulties, is a proof that it can be accomplished, though, owing to the disadvantages, at an enormous price, and that it never could be intended in the conditions of the Treasury that he should be deprived of the means of completing the work at the estimated cost."

Mr. Brunel's report, dated 9th of August, 1837, recapitulates the substance of his previous report, and adduces the successful result of pumping-engines and drift-ways erected for the purpose of taking off the land-springs that impeded the formation of the Kilsby tunnel, in the line of the Birmingham railway, as a proof of the good effect that would be felt in the works of the Thames Tunnel, by a pumping-engine on the Middlesex side. He states also, as an argument for the works he proposed in his former report, the importance of giving the disturbed and artificial ground time to consolidate, and now proposes, on the completion of the Middlesex shaft, to commence the tunnel on that side also, with a view to greater expedition and economy, and to keep the full complement of men more regularly employed by having the two ends to work at. This, it is stated, would reduce the cost of conveying the men, materials, and excavation to the shaft on the Surrey side. In this report Mr. Brunel further states, that so soon as the plan he has proposed is in satisfactory operation, the formation of the carriage-roads might be commenced simultaneously with the tunnel, and that by the various means he now proposes, a saving might be effected in the time of four and a half years, which in my report of April, 1837, I considered requisite for the completion of the tunnel and approaches, and that consequently there would be an earlier receipt of toll, and a saving of current expenses and machinery to the amount of 15,000l., by the works being completed one year and a quarter within the time I had calculated. Various accounts and calculations in proof of his several positions are appended to this report of Mr. Brunel, and an estimate that to carry on the works as he recommends, the sum of 94,000*l.* will be required during one year from August, 1837.

The Lords Commissioners of her Majesty's Treasury having refused their assent to the tunnel being begun on the Middlesex side, Mr. Brunel in his report, dated the 7th of September, 1837, repeats the other recommendations of his former reports.

The last report of Mr. Brunel that is referred to me is dated the 15th of November, 1837, *the fourth irruption of the Thames* having taken place on the 2nd of that month. In this report he considers the third irruption (that of the 23rd of August) as not having been unfavorable in one point of view, as it would enable substantial ground to be substituted for the loose silt that had been worked into the tunnel by the irruption, in proof of which he states that the work done before the third irruption cost 900*l.* per lineal foot, while what was done between the third and fourth irruptions cost only 630*l.* The former recommendations and arguments are repeated, and in addition it is now stated that the fourth, or last irruption, was caused in a great degree by the part of the tunnel then in progress being under the portion of the river chiefly used for navigation, and that the depth being small, the artificial bed of the river, or roof of the tunnel was liable to be disturbed by passing vessels. *This Mr. Brunel now proposes to remedy by deepening a part of the river where the tunnel is formed, moving some of the ships in the tiers near the tunnel from the northern to the southern side of the river, according to a plan which accompanies his report, throwing the space which is required to be kept clear for the navigation, from the north side towards the middle of the river over where the tunnel is formed, so as to leave the space which is in advance of the works free for tunnelling operations, and then substituting a thicker roof of clay and gravel raised above the present level, to which, from the navigation not being then over that part, there would not be the same objection as at present.* This thicker roof Mr. Brunel proposes to make 100 feet in length, or in advance of the shield, and 100 feet on each side of it. He calculates on a great saving in the end from this artificial covering, which he estimates at 1,800*l.*, and ascribes much of the late trouble and expense to the passing ships, *and the want of a sufficient thickness in his roof,* which the navigation prevented his having.

The reports are drawn up in great detail, and the above abstract is to be considered not as a substitute for them, but only as bringing the leading points to recollection in one view, without the repetitions which the reports themselves, being of different dates, naturally contain.

It is now my duty to state my opinion, which is, to recommend Mr. Brunel's proposals to be adopted, as the most economical and creditable way of executing the works, if it be the determination that the Thames Tunnel (a work which for many years has attracted much of the public attention in this, and *still more in other countries,* and upon which upwards of 80,000*l.* of public money has been advanced) shall be completed, *without making cost an element in the question.* I would then even advise more effectual works in front of the shield than Mr. Brunel's description and estimate of 1,800*l.* contemplates; for if the work is to be considered a national or Government work, a repetition of the danger, the late irruptions, and the enormous expense of the work, would be discreditable, and as it may be, it ought to be prevented. In addition to Mr. Brunel's proposals, I would recommend, after the removal of the clay that has lately been thrown in, and a portion of the silt, that two rows of close whole timber piles should be driven between where the ground begins to rise and the present shield, one row on each side of the line of the tunnel, with space between sufficient for the shield to travel, and to as great a depth as they can conveniently be driven, the heads being level with low water. These, with a return of shorter piles at the end, would form a dam against the silt. The piles being driven, I would continue the dredging of the silt in the space enclosed by the piles, and then fill up with clay, gravel, &c., as at present, to a sufficient height, and afterwards give the mass time for consolidation before attempting to advance the shield, which in my report to the commissioners for the loan of Exchequer-bills, I stated to be an essential element for success in the undertaking. In the progress he has made through very bad strata, Mr. Brunel has fully tried and proved the great power of his excellent shield; *but the strata, rendered worse by the irruptions and the causes assigned by Mr. Brunel, are now too bad for even the shield to overcome.* By the substitution of good artificial soil to work through, and keeping the silt or sand back by the piles, there would be much less difficulty or danger; and with proper precautions, my decided opinion is, that the tunnel may be completed notwithstanding the late irruptions, and with comparatively little difficulty or risk.

Here the question naturally presents itself, at what cost? and to answer it with the probability of accuracy is still very difficult.

The amount of the company's capital expended previous to any advance of public money was 180,000*l.* On the 27th of February, 1837, when (64,600*l.*) received from the Commissioners for the Loan of Exchequer-bills had been expended, I estimated the addition then required to complete it, at 310,600

| | 64,600 |

Making, exclusive of the company's capital......... £374,000

Between the 27th of February and the 2nd of November, 19,300*l.* have been expended, making 83,900*l.* of public money expended to the 2nd of November, but the quantity of work done with the above 19,300*l.* is only 19 feet six inches, making (inclusive of 1,400*l.* for pumping, excavating, and claying, after the third irruption), *nearly* 1000*l. per foot, which very much exceeds all previous estimates,* and proves what I stated in evidence before the Select Committee of the House of Commons, that no prudent man would commit himself to the accuracy of an estimate of this work, while it shows also the impolicy of attempting to drive on the shield through the present bad soil without a sufficient covering and time for consolidation.

In the present situation, I consider that the sum of 150,000*l.* should be taken as the estimate for completing the tunnelling; and that the shafts and other works remaining to be done, together with the purchases, should not be estimated under 200,000*l.*, making, with the 84,000*l.* of public money already expended, and the company's capital previously expended, a total of 614,000*l.* for the estimate of the work, or *upwards of triple the original estimate,* and this *is allowing but a moderate sum for contingencies,* WHICH HAVE HERETOFORE BEEN VERY HEAVY.

I have estimated the great descents at double Mr. Brunel's estimate, and yet I have, from the nature of the work, as much doubt as to the sufficiency of that sum as of any other item in my estimate.

If, however, in place of determining to complete the tunnel *without reference to cost,* which the foregoing observations suppose, the Lords of the Treasury resolve, as heretofore, to confine their operations to the advance of the tunnel, so as to remove any doubt of its getting through, before they sanction a further heavy outlay, then, although I agree with Mr. Brunel that the pumping-well or the shaft with the drift-way or drain would lessen the springs, I do not by any means think them so essential to the progress of the work as to agree in recommending their being proceeded in at present. Up to the time of the second irruption, in January, 1828, the works were under the uncontrolled management of the directors and engineers, and during that period nothing had been done on the Middlesex side with a view of draining the water from the tunnelling, although it had been advanced to the middle of the river, only 155 feet having been done since; but in the report of 1831 the drift-way or adit is proposed and estimated, with the pumping-well, at 6,000*l.* Mr. Brunel informs me that the drainage in the tunnel is now very small, and the short time in which the water, after irruptions, has been taken out, proves that the present pumping-engine is fully equal to the work.

More rain by two inches fell during the last six months of 1836 than of 1835[*], an increase, but not such as to cause a very important difference in the workings, which I ascribe almost entirely to the ground towards the Middlesex side being of a looser and more sandy and silty nature than towards the south side; this, it has always been said by the Trinity officers and others acquainted with that part of the river, would be found to be the case; so that, although the spring-water has been an evil and an hindrance, the Thames water has been another and probably a greater, and is the present enemy, which makes the cases of the London Dock or the Kilsby Tunnel parallel to a certain extent only. It is not in preventing the communication with the spring, but with the river water, that the artificial roof of clay, &c., has been useful.

I agree that the air for respiration would be improved by the drift-way, and probably the present air-pump, which is worked by the steam-engine, rendered unnecessary; but this pump, ingenious as all Mr. Brunel's applications are, appears to completely answer the purpose, and would probably be found quite as effectual in abstracting the sulphurated hydrogen as a drift-way at the bottom would be.

I cannot agree as to the saving of expense by the shorter distance to the Middlesex shaft; the difference of distance in the present situation of the shield would be only 70 yards, and as an excellent railway is laid, and machinery attached for working it by the steam-engine, I am sure that the conveyance of the excavated soil along the bottom of the tunnel to the low ground on the Surrey side must be at least as cheap as to the Middlesex side, where the ground is chiefly covered with buildings, and does

---

[*] The quantity of rain that fell in the last six months of 1835 (as kept at the Royal Society's Rooms) was 10¼ inches, and in the corresponding period of 1836 it was 12¼ inches. In the same period of 1834, a very dry year, it was only six inches.

not require to be raised, and that, as a passage to and from their work, the workmen would generally prefer the spacious lighted tunnel to a drift-way until the difference of distance is much greater than at present.

That the well or shaft on the Middlesex side would give employment to the miners and other workmen when they cannot be employed in the shield, and thus lessen the amount now charged to the tunnel, I entirely agree; but my opinion at the same time is that they may be fully employed in securing the ground in advance of the shield, according to Mr. Brunel's plan, or with the additional piling, such as I have suggested. It appears to me that sinking the shaft, driving a drift-way, making a new shield, and proceeding from the Middlesex side, would amount to a committal to go through with the undertaking, and ought not to be begun until that, as a previous question, has been determined.

In stating this, I am in some measure influenced by the opinion *that Mr. Brunel's estimate for the works on the Middlesex side is too low.* He estimates the pumping-well and drift-way at 7,000*l.*, and the shaft-engine and pumps at 6,844*l.*, and gives a decided preference to the shaft. Now, the shaft on the Surrey side is stated in the account to have cost 20,000*l.*, and evidently the drift-way, 4,310*l.*, should have been added to the shaft as to the well plan. The Middlesex shaft may, and probably will, be less expensive than the Surrey one was; I think it unsafe to trust calculation against experience, so far as to take one-third of the actual of the Surrey as the estimate for the Middlesex shaft.

Of the propriety and importance of changing the channel for the passage of vessels, from the part of the river in front of the shield which has yet to be tunnelled through, over to the part which is tunnelled, and forming a body of compact gravel and clay in front of the shield, in the way Mr. Brunel proposes, to a greater thickness than is now compatible with navigation, there can be no question; and I am glad to learn, by a letter received from Mr. Charlier, that the Navigation Committee have agreed to the proposal, and as Mr. Brunel considers that this will remove much of the cause of the late irruption, by enabling him to have a better covering of clay, and preventing vessels grounding upon the artificial bed, and estimates the necessary work at only 1,800*l.*,

I have no hesitation in recommending to the Lords of the Treasury to sanction it, even with the addition I have proposed, should Mr. Brunel be disposed to adopt it. I think the expense of the piling and clay may be taken at about 10,000*l.*, and I feel assured that, if the completing of the tunnelling be the object, this outlay will be more effectual, and much less in amount, than proceeding with the works on the Middlesex side; from the length of the river proposed to be covered with clay, if done according to Mr. Brunel's plan, being three times greater than with piling suggested by me, I think the difference of expense of the two plans would be small.

Having now given my opinion on the various points that have been referred to me, I would beg to add, that as the Thames Tunnel is Mr. Brunel's work *as respects design and responsibility*, any measure that may be proposed for executing the work should, in my judgment, have his approval. If that approval is refused, unless the Lords of the Treasury will consent to works which exceed the amount they have yet thought proper to agree to, almost any course would be better than letting the complaint be repeated, "that the engineer has been deprived of the proper means of completing the work at the estimated cost."

JAMES WALKER.

December, 1837.

LIST OF IRISH PATENTS GRANTED IN JUNE, 1838.

John Melville, of Upper Harley-street, for improvements in the generation of steam, and propelling vessels by steam or other power.

Alexandre Happey, of Basing-lane, London, for a new composition applicable to paving roads, streets, terraces, and other places, which improvements are applicable to the different purposes of building, and also in the apparatus for making the said composition.

Ambrose Ador, of Leicester-square, for improvements in lamps or apparatus in producing or affording light.

Pierre Armand Lecompte de Fontainemoreau, for improved methods of preventing the oxidation of metals.

Ambrose Ador, of Leicester-square, for improvements in producing or obtaining motive power.

Railway Map of England.—On the first of August will be published the Title, Index, and Contents to vol. 28 of the *Mechanics' Magazine,* and as a frontispiece to the volume a large map of the Railways in England and Wales, price 6*d.* The map alone on fine paper, price 6*d.* Also the volume complete, in half-cloth, price 8*s.* 6*d.*

☞ *British and Foreign Patents taken out with economy and despatch; Specifications, Disclaimers, and Amendments, prepared or revised; Caveats entered; and generally every Branch of Patent Business promptly transacted. A complete list of Patents from the earliest period* (15 *Car. II*: 1675,) *to the present time may be examined. Fee* 2*s.* 6*d.*; *Clients, gratis.*

LONDON: Printed and Published for the Proprietor, by W. A. Robertson, at the Mechanics' Magazine Office, No. 6, Peterborough-court, between 135 and 136, Fleet-street.—Sold by A. & W. Galignan Rue Vivienne, Paris.

Mechanics' Magazine,

MUSEUM, REGISTER, JOURNAL, AND GAZETTE.

No. 780.] SATURDAY, JULY 21, 1838. [Price 3*d*.

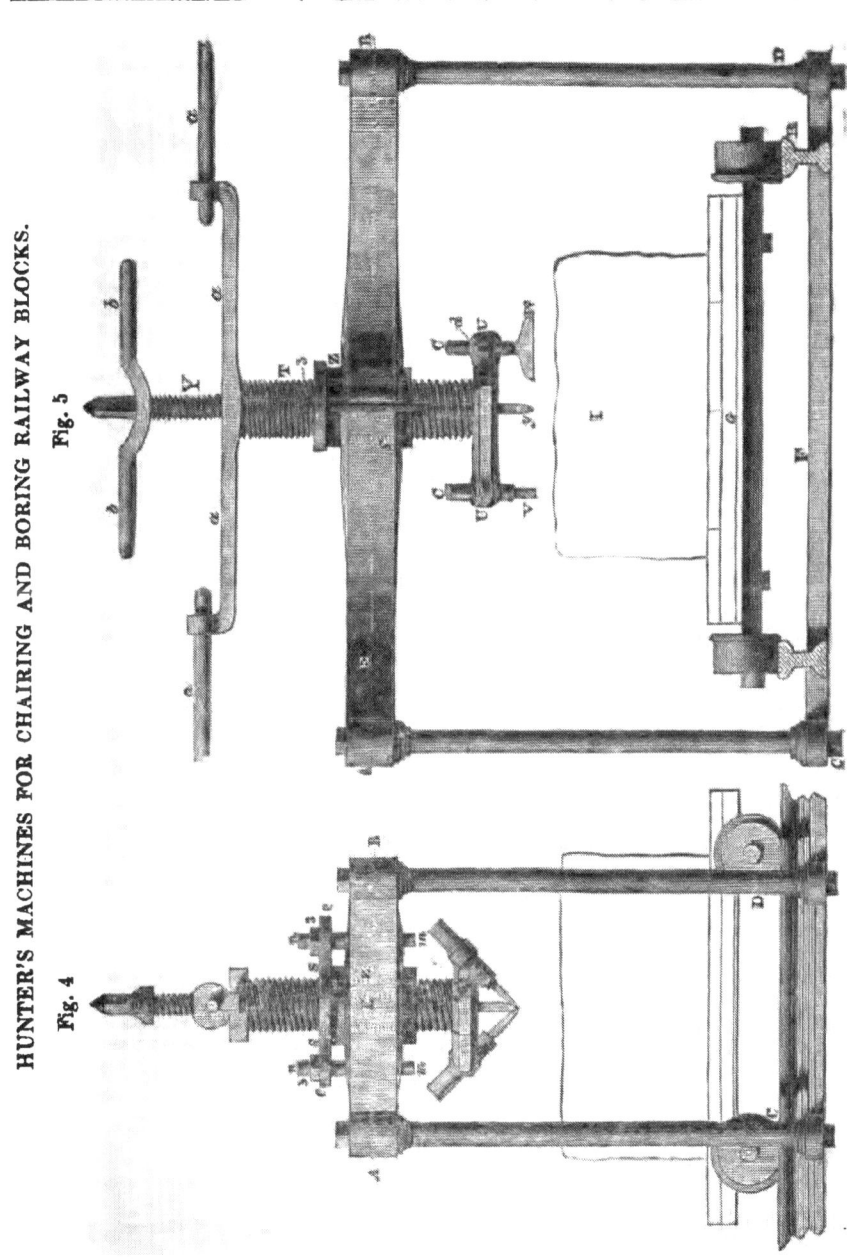

HUNTER'S MACHINES FOR CHAIRING AND BORING RAILWAY BLOCKS.

Fig. 5

Fig. 4

HUNTER'S MACHINE FOR CHAIRING AND BORING RAILWAY BLOCKS.

Mr. Hunter, of Leysmill, Arbroath, whose ingenious stone-planing machine was described in our Magazine for Oct., 1836, (No. 636,) and which has since that time continued to work with complete success, has lately invented and patented a machine for cutting out in stone railway blocks, the beds for the reception of the chairs, and for boring holes to receive the wooden pins into which the spikes are driven, by which the chairs are fastened to the blocks.

We shall proceed to describe the machines, and afterwards make a brief mention of the success which has attended their operation. Now that it appears to be a question amongst railway engineers, whether stone blocks or wooden sleepers are most worthy of adoption, whatever may tend towards the economical formation of either the one or the other, must be of interest to all connected with this novel and important branch of inland transit. Taking this view of the matter we shall be explicit in our description, and careful as to the authenticity of the statements of working which we publish. The principle of action of the cutting tool, in Mr. Hunter's boring and chairing machines, is precisely similar to that of his planing machine, and its application in the present instance is most ingenious. Fig. 1, is a front elevation of the boring machine; fig. 2 an end elevation; and fig. 3 a ground plan and top section through the line A B of figures 1 and 2. S S S S is the framework of the machine, consisting of four iron uprights and connecting pieces. The top-piece E, composed of two somewhat flexible plates of iron, by having semicircular bends at o o, clasps the boring tools K^1 K^2, and holds them firmly at the height at which they are placed, by the screws N^1, N^2, N^3. M^1 M^2, fig. 1, are augers of a spiral form, which instead of having centre-bits like the common auger, terminate in two broad-faced points, turning in opposite directions. L^1 L^2 are male screws, into sockets in the lower ends of which the heads of the augers M^1 M^2 are inserted and secured. K^1 K^2 are female screws or sheaths, into and through which the male screws L^1 L^2 work. The winch or cross-tree R, being placed upon the head of either of the

screws L^1 or L^2, on being turned, works the auger. G is a railway truck or carriage, for conveying the stone block which is to be perforated, under the boring tools; and H H the rails on which the truck runs. The sheaths K^1 and K^2 are fastened in the head-piece E, at a height corresponding to the depth of holes required to be bored in the block, by the screws N^1 N^2 N^3.

On examining this arrangement it will be seen, that on the tool being turned, the points of the auger must scoop out or chip off at each revolution a portion of stone, as great, at least, as the distance the screw has descended. Thus, there is no scraping action, (in all hitherto invented stone-cutting machinery found so destructive to the tool,) but, as in the stone planing machine, pieces or chips of stone are removed by the great and steady power applied to the tools. Were the thread of the screw which regulates the descent of the tool very fine, or were the augers merely kept pressed against the stone by a weight or spring, (as has been hitherto tried,) the tool would merely grind away the stone, and at the same time its own edge; but by Mr. Hunter's arrangement the stone must either yield to the descent of the auger, the rate of which is to an extent incompatible with a grinding action, or the tool must break. The chips ascend through the spiral channel of the auger, and are thrown off at top.

The chairing machine is somewhat similar, in general construction, to the boring machine. Figs. 4 and 5, (see our front page,) are front and end elevations. Fig. 6 a ground plan and top section through the line A B of figures 4 and 5. S S S S the framework. The top cross-piece E, is of the form shown in the top section, fig. 6. Z is a sheath, plain on the outside, but tapped through the centre with a female screw, inserted in the top E, and with broad shouldered pieces S S, having orifices e e, so that when the long tails m, of the pins z z are passed through these orifices, the said long ends pressing against the sides of the cross-head F, fix the sheath Z in its position, and prevent its turning. T^1 is a male screw, which works in the female screw of the sheath Z, and has a cross-piece fixed to its lower extremity, the two arms of which carry the tools or chisels U W and U V. Y is another male screw which

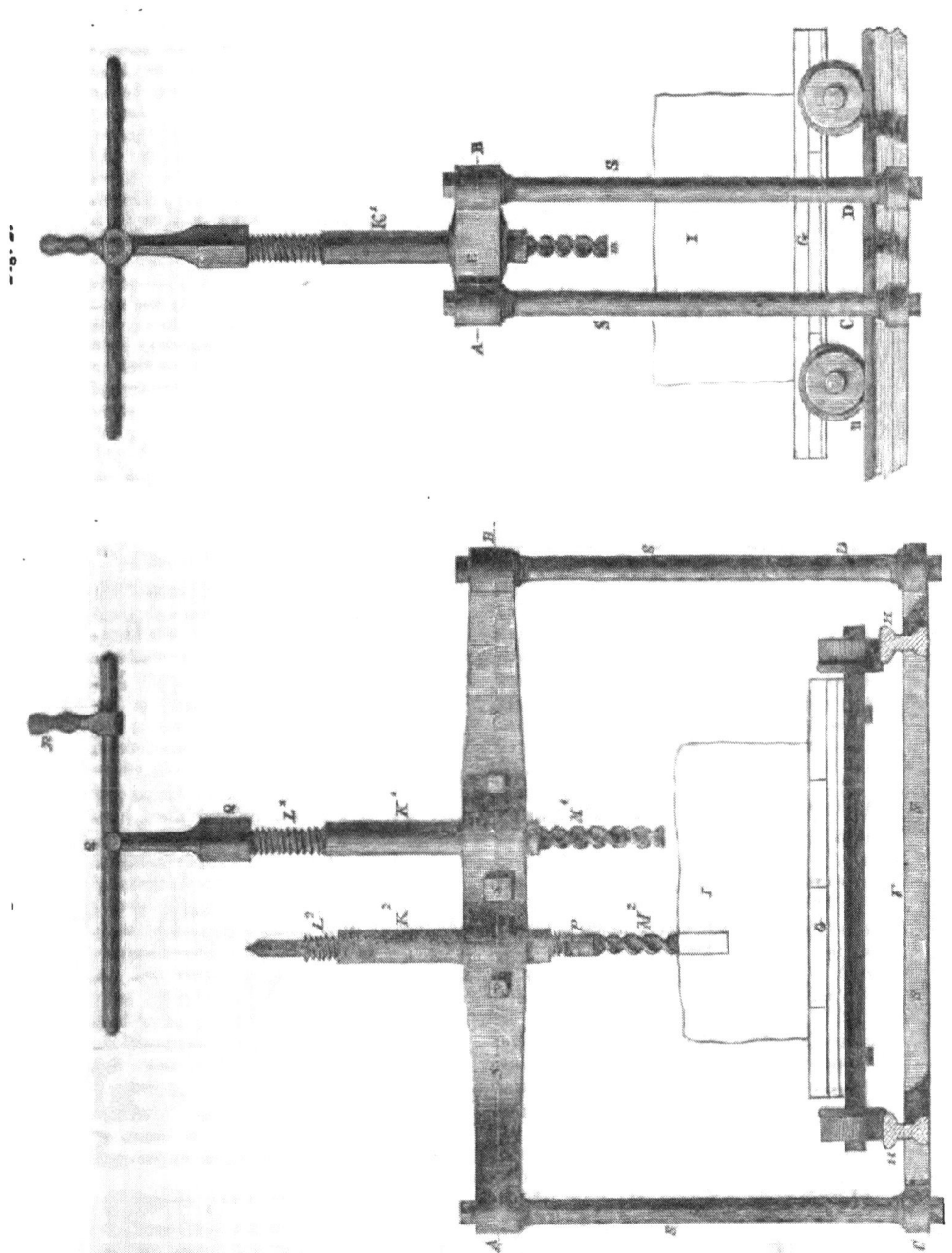

works through a female-threaded cavity in the centre of the screw TT.

The mode of operation is as follows : the block being brought on the truck and railway under the chairing tools, the centre-bit Y, armed with the tool *y*, is screwed down by means of the arms *b*, to the full depth of the chair-seat, and which will give sufficient strain or pressure, to hold the block firmly in its place during the operation of excavating the seat for the chair. The male screw T is then set in motion by the arms *a a*, the centre tool Y remaining stationary while the tools or chisels U W and U V traverse round it. When the chisels are considered to have penetrated deep enough into the stone, the pins *z z*, by which the sheath Z is prevented from turning in the cross-head E, are taken out and reversed in the orifices *e e*—that is, the short tails or ends, *n n*, are inserted in the ears *e e*, leaving the long ends *m m* sticking up ; so that the arms *a a* will, on being turned, press against them, and carry round the sheath Z, and with it all the tools, but without, at the same time, descending, there being no screw on the outside of the sheath. One or two turns thus will grind a smooth face to the bottom of the chair-seat. When the chisels require sharpening, they can be removed from their sockets by loosening the screws *d d*. Separate and enlarged representations of the tools are given at figs. 7, 8, and 9.

The operations of the chairing and boring machines are carried on conjointly thus :—A railway runs under a set of machines, consisting of two for boring and one for chairing, and the rails are fixed correctly at right angles with the machines. As soon as a block is bored upon its truck, the tools are removed, and the truck with the block upon it drawn by the workmen under the chairing machine, where the chair bed is formed, and the block is completed. By these means the holes are to a certainty obtained at right angles to, and the bottom of the chair-bed parellel with, the base of the block.

With regard to the successful operation of the machine, we have been favored with various documents, from which we have selected the following certificate from Mr. Grainger, the engineer of the Dundee and Arbroath, and Arbroath and Forfar railways :—

"Edinburgh, 9th July, 1838.

"The machine invented by Mr. James Hunter, of Leysmill Quarry, in the county of Forfar, for boring, as well as that invented by him for chairing, railway blocks, have been in use upon the Arbroath and Forfar Railway for upwards of ten months, during which time more than thirty thousand blocks have been bored and chaired by them. At present four machines are constantly in use in boring, and two in chairing the blocks. By these machines the work is done in a much more perfect manner, and at much less expense, than by hand labour. They have also been employed to a considerable extent upon the Dundee and Arbroath Railway. The blocks which have been bored and chaired by these machines consist of hard sandstone. The holes have been sunk to the depth of six inches ; the diameter thereof 1¼ inches; the bed upon which the chair is to rest is 9 inches diameter, and in point of smoothness is equal to polished work, and is made perfectly parallel to the sole of the block. Five workmen, employed about ten hours a day, finish with ease from 450 to 500 blocks per week.

(Signed)   "THOMAS GRAINGER."

The above certificate, proceeding from the high authority it does, appears very satisfactory as to the utility of Mr. Hunter's invention. From other documents before us, it would appear that Mr. Grainger speaks under the mark as regards the quantity of work done ; the contractors on the railways mentioned are, we are informed, often in the practice of finishing one hundred blocks per day. The cost of a set of machines, consisting of two boring and one chairing, is not more than sixty or seventy guineas.

On the Arbroath and Forfar Railway the wooden pins for plugging the blocks are turned in a lathe, and pierced with a hole, less, of course, than the thickness of the iron spike to be driven in. A much firmer hold is thus obtained with less force of driving, and the great loss by splitting of blocks altogether avoided.

We need hardly observe, that the chairing machine may be easily adapted to cut holes or tubes of any diameter and depth in stone quarries, by steam or any other power, with great speed and economy.

We are informed that Mr. Hunter has completed a great improvement upon his planing machine, adapting it to dress the hardest Yorkshire flag with very great economy. This improved machine will shortly be at work in Yorkshire, and we hope to be soon enabled to give our readers a description and statement of its performances.

Fig. 3.

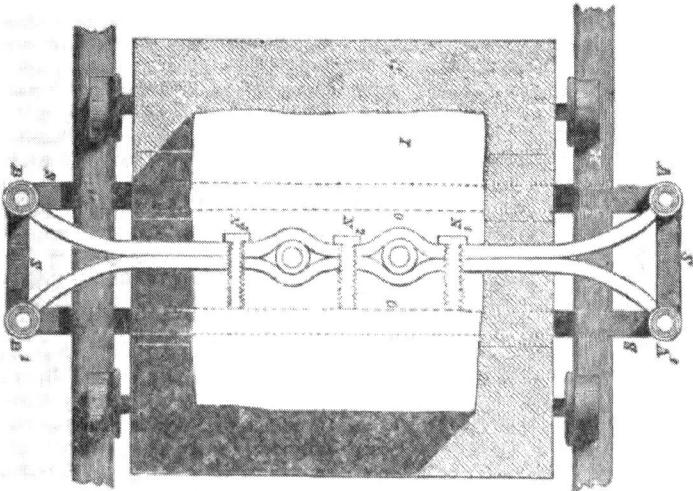

Fig. 6.

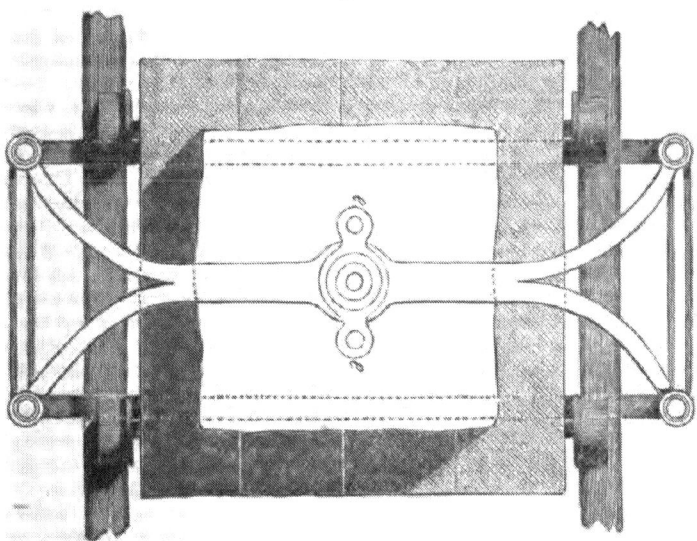

Fig. 7.

Fig. 8.      Fig. 9.

STEAM NAVIGATION TO INDIA.

Sir,—Your correspondent "H," seems inclined to pick a quarrel with me for venturing to differ in opinion from him, and recording my dissent to his views in your valuable miscellany. His last letter produces no change in my opinions, nor does it explain away any one of the facts to which reference was made in my former letters.

I am still decidedly of opinion, that the supineness of our East India Government is affording the Dutch and other nations an opportunity of acquiring a superiority over us, by means of an extensive line of steam navigation in the Indian Archipelago, and that the "*steam flotilla*" in the service of the company, if not altogether contemptible, is yet quite inadequate to the wants of that part of the British Empire. Hitherto the earnest remonstrances of the mercantile residents, and the strenuous exertions of the East India Steam Committee in England, have failed to produce their proper effect. Individual enterprize has been paralized by an influence which may not be described, and the general good sacrificed to a narrow and mistaken policy.

I am not aware that in any part of my correspondence upon the subject of East India steam navigation, that any statement has appeared to countenance "H.'s" misrepresentations of my sentiments, relative to the exertions now making by the Dutch, to establish steam navigation in India for commercial purposes,—nor the flourish about the English being "about to reinforce the steam flotilla which they have *long ago* (*sic orig.*) introduced in the East Indies from home, by a number of steamers built and equipped in the country itself." Will "H." condescend to inform your readers of the names of those steamers "*long ago*" introduced into the East Indies from this country? The *Enterprize* was sent out from this country about twelve years since. What others are there sent out from this country "*long ago?*" The *Atalanta, Berenice,* and *Semiramis,* were sent out last year. The *Hugh Lindsay* was built in India. If the "steam flotilla" goes on increasing at this rate of five in twelve years, it will be many before it is equal to the increasing wants of India; and will afford, in reality, an opportunity to our Dutch neighbours to

monopolize the steam navigation of the Indian Archipelago.

But "H." charges me with veering round as to the speed of steam-vessels. If he had read my remarks with ordinary attention, such a charge would not have been made by him. In page 98 my statement was, that I had "not at present met with any steam-vessel (meaning, of course, sea-going steam-vessels, of which I was then speaking,) in the course of my somewhat extensive observation, that had been able to maintain such an average speed (10 miles) for several consecutive days." * * * * "Some few boats will maintain 10 miles an hour for 30 or 40, or even 80 hours." Now I still maintain this to be the fact. The *Berenice* is said to have attained the speed of 14 miles per hour when tried in Scotland, but what was her *actual* performance when on her passage to India? not ten miles an hour, nor any thing like it. If "H." will refer to the logs of the two vessels as given in the *Nautical Magazine,* he will find that he is mistaken as to the speed of sea-going steamers, even of the first class; and it must be obvious that he has misrepresented my meaning.

Whilst I am writing this, I have been informed that the *Great Western* arrived at Bristol on the 7th, having left New York on the 25th ult. This, indeed, would show a speed of rather more than 10 miles an hour; but it is to be remembered that this speed is acquired by a vessel of a very much larger class than any of those formerly afloat, and is in perfect consistency with my remarks in former letters,—that with larger ships a greater velocity would be attained.

The Dutch are doing what the East India Government have been openly or covertly opposing—endeavouring to introduce steam navigation for commercial purposes into the East Indies.

The reference to the experimental steamer *to be built at Bombay,* confirms my previous remarks. "Strong representations have been sent home of the necessity for immediately placing a greatly increased number of steamers on this service, and the greatest anxiety is evinced for the accomplishment of the object. The company have at length given orders that the experiment should be tried of building a steam-ship at Bombay." Now mark, Mr, Editor, it is not said that she is building, but that "*the company have at length* given orders" that she should be built at Bombay. Are these reluctant orders gone out? Are they couched in such terms that the executive government will understand that they are to be complied with? Or are they like some other orders of the honourable court only meant to be disregarded? In 1834 a Committee of the House of Commons passed some strong resolutions on the subject, and recommended that a steam communication should be attempted. Private individuals attempted to establish one, but were prevented carrying their intentions into effect, by the same power that determined Indian idolatry should be supported at the expense of government, notwithstanding their orders to the contrary.

"H." speaks of "Indian and Arabian ports," having "been often visited by other steamers than those belonging to the company;" will he be kind enough to enumerate them, with the date of their visit?

The reference of "H." to my letter, page 150, is so obviously incorrect, that it exposes him to the suspicion of disingenuousness; for had he read the paragraph with ordinary attention, he must have perceived that the pronoun "he" was an error of the press, and should have been "we," as is clearly seen by the concluding part of the sentence, which is "and that *we* (myself and others) should have been impressed with the belief that steam navigation was still in its infancy in that part of the British Empire, &c." Against whom does the charge of disingenuousness lie? Your impartial readers will acquit *me* of it.

The sneer about my advice being "good in itself" comes with an ill grace from "H.," as in my first communication I had referred to the fact, that the British residents in India were long since awakened to the importance of the object which they had been prevented from attaining, although actively seconded by Captain Grindlay and a committee in England. And here, Sir, I trust you will pardon my expressing the sense which I entertain of the valuable services which Captain Grindlay has rendered to the cause of East Indian steam navigation. He has ventured to advocate it, when in high quarters it was deemed an Utopian

scheme, and its advocates but little removed from insanity. Messrs. Seaward, in 1824, struck out a plan and demonstrated its practicability, but they m with but little attention—they were too much in advance of the age: and Dr. Lardner then appeared in the field as the presiding genius of steam navigation, Messrs. Seaward would have been crushed beneath the unmerciful load of wet blankets which he would have applied to cure them of their insanity.

The excellent letter of "Piston" confirms my statements relative to the speed of some of the river boats, but does not apply to sea-going vessels. "Piston" states, that some steamers, which he names, did reach the speed of $13\frac{1}{4}$, $13\frac{1}{2}$, and $13\frac{1}{2}$ miles per hour, when tried under favourable circumstances (without passengers, or more than a moderate supply of coals on board, mind); from this "H." ventures to assert, that they have reached the astonishing speed of 20 miles per hour.

Whatever "H." may think of my concession, as he terms it, that an average of 10 miles an hour might be maintained during a steam voyage round the Cape, I confess there does not appear any inconsistency; for on reference to my letter, page 98, it will be seen that I was then speaking of existing steam vessels, and remarked that improvements were still required. My opinion expressed, June 9th, is quite consistent with this, as "H." must know, if at all conversant with nautical affairs; for in two vessels of the same form and proportions, the larger is always found to be the faster of the two.

If "H." will refer to his own letter, page 122, he will see the propriety of sparing any further regret about my disingenuousness. He there uses such a form of expression that would even now impress me with the belief that he did intend to convey his disapprobation of Mr. Hall's Patent Condensers; however, as he denies any intention of doing so, I must believe him, though he now admits that "the ill-timed advertisements of that gentleman (Mr. Hall) might have justified" him "in doing so, if no allowances were to be made for the rashness of an inventor in the full confidence of success."

It appears from a recent parliamentary return, that there are about 600 steam-vessels belonging to the British empire, exclusive of government vessels. Of these 600, there are only 39 in all the colonies and possessions, which contain an aggregate population six or seven times larger than the mother country. Is the monstrous flotilla of five steam vessels in the East Indies at all commensurate with the wants of the population, or proportioned to the importance of that part of our dominions?

Since my first letter referring to the want of steamers in the East Indies, and the tardy stinted compliance with the reasonable claims of the British residents there, upon the merchant-princes in Leadenhall-street, I am informed, that two other steam-vessels have been contracted for, to be built in England, which will probably arrive out at the end of 1839, or during the early part of 1840, and add to our numerous and efficient steam flotilla already existing in the East Indies.

As an illustration of the greater velocity acquired by large vessels over smaller ones of the same form and proportions, I will just mention, that by advice from the *British Queen* off Falmouth, she was going through the water at the rate of eight knots, with a light breeze. This circumstance justifies the general expectation that she will prove a very fast vessel when steaming, if her machinery be properly adapted for her, and is equal to its reputed power.

Apologizing for having trespassed so much with a subject which cannot but interest your readers, I take leave of the controversy, and subscribe myself,

Your obedient servant,

GEORGE BAYLEY.

July 10, 1838.

STEAM-BOILER EXPLOSIONS--THEORY AND PRACTICE.

Sir,—Your correspondent "Scrutator" has assigned a probable, and certainly most efficient, cause for the bursting of the *Victoria's* boiler, or more properly the collapse of the internal flue,—the manner in which similar boilers, containing high steam, nine times out of ten, explode.

The steam-room in cylindrical boilers with a large flue is, proportionally to the water space, much less than in rectangular boilers,—a defect which must be met, either by an increased steam-chest or pipe, or by keeping the steam higher in the boiler, and throttling it down into the cylinder. My object, however, is to point out, that the connection of scientific and practical knowledge is alone of value.

The practical man will blunder on till he is right at last, if he has common sense and sufficient funds. Theorists are equally subject to blunders, to the great delight of the practicists—parties, by the bye, who are often alone in possession of correct data, and who, by experience derived from observation, are enabled to guess at, rather than to exhibit reasoning for probable results, under different conditions—theorists, in fact, without a language to express their ideas. This, and the limits of power and correction, under different conditions, so as to lead to the highest possible results by the shortest path, are the legitimate objects of theory. Another class are sometimes called theorists in contempt,—persons not more remarkable for their reckless assertions without proof, than the absence of both practical and scientific knowledge. "Scrutator" very properly objects to "if's" and "but's,"—conditions, in fact, not clearly expressed—loopholes for erroneous opinions,—and gives an example of their misuse in his own letter :—" *This boiler would do well at sea, if external condensation was adopted.*" What has the boiler to do with the means employed by the engineer to produce an assigned vacuum, as long as that assigned vacuum is produced?* The boiler has only to perform its allotted task. If the meaning is that a better condensation is afforded, as its advocates assert, by external condensation—for instance, to the extent of one inch of mercury,—then it amounts to an admission of inferiority, to be estimated on the principles of heat required to evaporate water at about 16 and 16½ lbs. pressure respectively, into steam, as used in the cylinder.

Theoretical, like practical, opinions are sometimes at variance, and in such cases one at least of the theoretical opinions will be oftener traced to false, or

---

* We are surprised that our correspondent, who appears to understand his subject upon other points, should put such a question. The advantage of external condensation alluded to by "Scrutator" had no reference to the production of a vacuum, but to the condensing of the steam and the returning it in the form of pure water to the boiler, whereby tubes or small chambers may be used without their being liable to be choked up by the incrustations of saline or other deposits incident to the use of sea water. —ED. M. M.

the omission of important, data, than to incorrect reasoning.

Success and failure were both theoretically predicted of the direct unknown voyage of the *Great Western* to New York, from arguments founded on known voyages performed ; the failing theory has attracted most attention, like a bad hole in blasting rocks—much noise and no work. The successful theory is remarkably well expressed in a report to the committee at Bristol, dated January 1st, 1836, and signed Christopher Claxton, managing director, which silently effected its purpose. The pleasure I felt on reading this report, as given in the *Nautical Magazine* in January, 1837, was only equalled by a comparison of the estimated, with the actual results, of the first voyage.

Previous to the opening of the Manchester and Liverpool railway, theory arguing from known performances, foretold that a speed greater than ten or twelve miles per hour would be impracticable, and quite forgot a possible condition—increased evaporation in the same space, without any great increase of boiler-weight. The method of forming numerous flues of small tubes—the reverse of the common steam-coach boiler—seems to have been suggested by the treasurer —evidently a theorist respecting heat— to the engineer, whose adoption of the plan is as creditable as the suggestion, and who fairly earned the competition and renown.

Theory, at least, did good service here, but sooner or later it would have been effected by some person, who might have had pretensions to have been dignified with the more coveted title of being a practical man.

If any difficulty was ever found to occur in not getting the lower tube to draw as much air as the upper, theory would suggest that a proportionate contraction of the upper flues at either end would effect this object. Practice might find out some objection relative to a soot deposit. I have alluded to this merely to show the connection between theory and practice without any knowledge whether it has ever been done, or required to have been done.

The theory of fusible plugs, to melt at assigned temperatures, is very pretty, and was introduced with Trevethick's high-pressure boilers, and is still often used in the mining modification of these boilers. Recent experiments have shown that on continued heat they melt at lower temperatures ; but for this allowance can be made. It was lately mentioned to me that these plugs have been abandoned in steamers, where they will not do, especially in the weather flues, which are apt to get hot when the vessel heels. This is a specimen of a practical argument from a defect, not of the plug, but of the boiler : they must meet the real objections how they can—fixing difficulties, and liability of failure on a lee shore.

For smooth water craft, partitions in a single boiler, with a separate feed-pipe to each division, will obviate the first objection ; but the large boiler top is exceedingly objectionable to passengers, as on explosion the whole flies off together. It is their interest to have separate boilers—then the flues become the weakest parts, and the enginemen must keep a bright look-out for themselves, as the only persons likely to suffer on an explosion. Partitions are not sufficient in sea-going vessels to prevent, under some circumstances, the effect of the constant flush of the water to leeward. Three or four separate boilers alone will enable the weather-boiler to be forced, and the sea one eased, by which means a great increase of stability is afforded—a point of as much importance in crank steamers as trimming to windward in crank pleasure-boats.

Theory, judging from the disposition to obtain power in a small space, and the eventual tendency of expansion, at present only used with low steam, may safely predict the rapid approach of a most dangerous era in steam navigation, —the transition period from low to higher steam. Competition will induce the attempt, and (whether successful or not) considerable danger will exist, until the safety conditions are fully ascertained. As for the United States, they seem simply distinguished, in the inland waters especially, by an engineering recklessness, in utter defiance of theory and practice.

Legal enactments are likely to prove futile. Two points alone perhaps would prove efficient,—increase of knowledge among the enginemen, which time only can effect, and a deodand on the vessel for each death of 100*l.*, to be doubled on neglect being proved, so as to render an explosion an expensive operation for the owners.

I remain, Sir, yours respectfully,

N. S.

BADDELEY'S AND WHITELAW'S PLAN FOR FEEDING STEAM-BOILERS.

Sir,—I am sorry that I should so grievously have roused the ire of Mr. James Whitelaw, by the opinion I entertain of his plan for feeding steam-boilers, promulgated in your 769th Number. As I am by no means singular in my opinion, it is just possible that I may be right, and Mr. Whitelaw wrong. I would refer to "Nauticus's" letter at page 107, as the best answer that could be given to Mr. Whitelaw's epistle.

Mr. Whitelaw asks if I "know any thing of *a* Mr. Whitelaw who sent a drawing and description of two forms of a feeding apparatus to the Society of Arts, and who got a reward for *his plan;* one form of which is given in the volume of their Transactions published in 1833 ?"

In reply, I know nothing of this gentleman, but I have just procured a copy of the Society's Transactions for that period, from which I have extracted, verbatim, all the information relative to Mr. George Whitelaw's plan, which, in fairness to both the Messrs. Whitelaw, and in justice to myself, I send for insertion in your Magazine with this letter. With the form not published in the Society's Transactions, I am wholly unacquainted; but as Mr. James Whitelaw says it is exactly the same in principle and plan as the one I call mine, I take it for granted that it is so, with the difference mentioned by Mr. W.; but I presume the Society considered the plan they have published in their Transactions *the best of the two.* I candidly admit the identity of principle in Mr. G. Whitelaw's apparatus, with that which appeared as mine in your 572nd Number, and only beg to add, that at the very time Mr. Whitelaw was addressing his communication to the Society of Arts, I was exhibiting a working drawing of my plan at Birmingham and elsewhere, with a view to its being taken up and patented. Not succeeding in this object, I subsequently published a description of my plan in your 21st volume. So that, while I admit *perfect originality* both in plan and principle to Mr. Whitelaw, I likewise claim the same for myself. I cannot help adverting to the statement in Mr. Whitelaw's communication that water was supplied to steam-boilers through the agency of the engine-man alone !" whereas, a force-pump wrought by the engine—and, therefore, self-acting, so far as the engine-man was concerned—had been employed a long time previous.

By comparing the arrangement given in No. 572, with that now extracted from the Society's Transactions, I think it will generally be conceded that the action of *one* slide-valve (for the *second* can be very advantageously dispensed with) is preferable to the revolving of a hollow stop-cock; especially if made large enough to hold twice the quantity of water required by the boiler during one revolution of the stopper. Although, as the stopper is made to revolve by connexion with the engine, by means of wheel-work, it seems strange that this *size* should be insisted upon as necessary.

The subject at present at issue, "the supply of water to steam-boilers" is most important; one, at this time, invested with solemn interest, and deserving the best attention of all, both as a matter of economy, and also as a preventive against those melancholy accidents, of late so lamentably frequent.

Any discussion, therefore, which brings into juxta-position the various plans proposed from time to time for attaining this object, cannot fail to prove useful. Whether the propounders are actuated by selfish and interested, or disinterested and benevolent motives, will signify but little: facts, those "stubborn things," will speak for themselves, and by gathering a little from one and a little from another, practical men will soon obtain the means of effecting the object sought, with certainty, economy, and safety.

I remain, Sir, yours respectfully,
WILLIAM BADDELEY.

London, July 5, 1838.

"*Method of Feeding a High-Pressure Boiler.*

"Glasgow, May 5, 1833.

"Sir,—I take the liberty of forwarding to you, that you may lay before the Society for the Encouragement of Arts, &c., the drawings of a new method for regulating the supply of water in steam-boat and high-pressure engine boilers. At present this is done through the agency of the engine-man alone, which is not only troublesome, but unsafe, as, from neglect or carelessness on his part, too much or too little water might be admitted into the boiler, so as in one case to be hurtful to the working of the engine, or in the other to endanger the bursting of the boiler. . The self-acting apparatus, of which drawings are herewith sent, and a description given below, would obviate the trouble and insecurity attending the present method; and I shall be happy if it be found worthy the attention and remuneration of the Society.

I am, Sir, &c.

(signed)   GEORGE WHITELAW.

A. Aikin, Esq., Sec., &c.

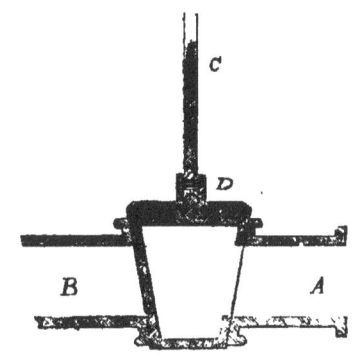

" The plan consists merely of a common stop-cock, with the key or stopper made hollow, and open only on one side. Let the branch A be the one leading to the hot-well of the engine, and the branch B the one going to the boiler. The stopper can only communicate with one of these branches at a time. The rod C is for conveying a rotatory motion to the stopper from the engine. This may be easily done by means of wheel-work. The spiral spring D is for keeping the stopper in its place.*

" *To explain its Action* —Let the stopper be in the position shown in the diagram, that is, having its opening opposite the branch leading to the hot-well. In this case, the water from the hot-well would fill the hollow part of the stopper, and as the stopper would be revolving, the communication with the hot-well would come to be shut off, and the opening of the stopper to be opposite the branch B going to the boiler. This would allow the water in the stopper to pass into the boiler, till the water in the stopper came to a level with that in the boiler.

" The stopper again turning to the opposite side would receive another charge, and again deliver the proper quantity into the boiler. In constructing this feed-regulator

(as it may be named), the hollow part of the stopper would be required to contain full twice the quantity of water which the boiler would require during one revolution of the stopper. The pipe that leads to the hot-well should be made pretty wide, and the hot-well must be high enough, so that the water may run into the stopper of its own accord. The pipe for conducting the water from the hot-well must on no account have any bends in it turning downwards, as they would prevent the uncondensed steam, or air, that is displaced from the stopper, from escaping."—*Transactions of the Society of Arts, &c.*, vol. 49, 1833.

ON REVOLVING SLIDE-RESTS.

Sir,—Mr. James Wilcox, whose revolving slide-rest forms the frontispiece to your 777th Number, will perhaps pardon me, when I state that his contrivance (evidently the production of an amateur) embodies nothing that is new, and little that is really useful. There is a want of firmness and stability, both in the plan and in the materials employed by Mr. Wilcox, that would render his apparatus wholly unfit for either large spheres, or hard materials; inasmuch as the smallest vibration would cause a serious deviation from truth. I strongly suspect the existence of several very beautiful tools of this description, but if so, the owners keep them so profoundly secret, as to render the fact very difficult of being ascertained with any degree of certainty.

Having lately invented a new manufacture, in which it became absolutely necessary to have the power of turning, both *internally* and *externally*, spheres of metal, of considerable size, with perfect accuracy, I have designed and executed a revolving slide-rest which performs this office with great facility. My rest combines all the powers of Mr. Wilcox's, with more besides, in a very convenient manner; it accomplishes what is required with astonishing precision, and will turn *balls* of any material from an eighth of an inch to four or more inches in diameter.

As the manufacture to which I have alluded is not yet made public, I cannot, without injury to the parties who are engaged in it, enter into a more minute explanation at present, but I hope shortly to be able to send you further parti-

---

* How it fulfils this office is not very evident.— W. B.

culars. In the mean time, if Mr. Wilcox will send to your office for a letter directed to him there, he will have the opportunity afforded him of obtaining more of the information he solicits than I can conveniently communicate " through the medium of your valuable Magazine.'

I remain, Sir, yours respectfully,
WM. BADDELEY.

London, July 10, 1838.

THE BOOMARANG.

Sir,—In a former Number of your Magazine I gave an account of the boomarang, a missile used by the natives of New Holland, in the hope that some scientific gentleman would be induced to examine the causes of its very singular gyrations when thrown into the air; but although I have read several explanations of the supposed causes, none of them appear conclusive. In my opinion, the best form to give the missile in order to cause it to return, is half, or something more than half a circle, it is difficult to find a piece of timber sufficiently strong to prevent breaking when cut into this form; the best part of a tree is the fork; that, for instance, of an old apple tree, the grain then runs somewhat circular. I have thrown two or three boomarangs at a time; they were made perfectly flat on each side in order to lie the better in my hand, when all have returned after going forward about fifty yards, giving me sufficient time to select and shoot at two of them with a double-barrel gun. This kind of practice would soon make a man a good flying shot; I have tried various kinds of ballistas or cross-bows for projecting the boomarang, and with satisfactory results. Stiffness is essential in the missile, whatever substance it may be made of.
JOHN NORTON.

July 14, 1838.

BARREL CARRIAGES.

Sir,—If my humble approbation to the ingenious suggestion of "Mechanicus" is of any importance, I freely give it. There would doubtlessly be a saving of friction, and also of weight. The machine would, in fact, be a carriage consisting of one broad and hollow wheel, and this would be the whole.

All that friction which in ordinary carriages arises from the weight pressing upon the axle, would be saved. I do not consider the friction of the axle to be much impediment to the motion of carriages, but still it is something which is better to be got rid of if possible. The chief impediments to the motion are the obstacles, asperities, and softness of the ground; the truth of which appears from the comparative small force which is required to move carriages on wheels which step over obstacles (these having been a long time before the public under the appellation of Icapus).* But with respect to the barrel carriages, they would require always to be quite full or quite empty, and loaded with matter of the same specific gravity, otherwise much friction, irregularity, and loss of force would be propagated within, by the material which would tumble about.

With respect to the ideas of " C. T. Salisbury," I am sorry to differ from him. According to my view the weight on the axle is not only one-eighth of the load, as he conceives, but is the load itself; yet the friction is diminished according to the ratio its circumference bears to that of the wheel, *not on the principle of a lever*, but merely because there is less motion and rubbing. The rolling friction must, however, be added to the amount, and this is not so trifling as is generally believed; in proof of which, if a brass wheel of a quarter of an inch in diameter be fitted up with an iron axle of an eighth of an inch in diameter, and an attempt be made to roll the wheel over a smooth piece of box-wood (pressing on the axle), the wheel will not turn, but will slide along; consequently, in this case, the rolling friction is more than half as much as that which the ground would cause if there were no wheels, and rather more than that of the axle itself,—because the wheel chooses to slide on the ground instead of undergoing the sliding of the axle, added to the rolling of the periphery. It has, indeed, been an error too general to consider the rolling friction nothing. Another popular error, though perhaps foreign to the subject, is the idea that carriage

* See Repository of Arts, March 1815, and June 1821; also Dr. Jamison's Dictionary of Mechanical Science; also the 3rd number of " The Animals' Friend," by Cotes, 139 Cheapside, for the best improvements.

wheels act as levers in surmounting obstacles: wheels do nothing more than reduce the friction; but with regard to overcoming obstacles, nothing whatever is gained by employing them, and, excepting the friction, a carriage would surmount every obstacle quite as well if the wheels were chained fast as if they were allowed to revolve. This may appear strange, but it is the fact, and will appear when borne in mind that the body of a carriage, or the centre of a wheel, always describes a circle, *in space*, when the wheel rises over the obstacle, whether the wheel turns round or not, and this is the same circle in both cases —namely, the same size as that of the wheel, but with this difference, that when the wheel revolves over a prominent point, the centre describes the circle about that point by means of the radius; and when the wheel is fixed, it describes it by means of its periphery being drawn over the prominence, and the larger the wheels the more gradually are the obstacles overcome; sledges overcome them still better, and if it were not for friction would be greatly superior to wheels.

LOCOMOTIST.

June 28, 1838.

ROYAL CORNWALL POLYTECHNIC SOCIETY—FIFTH REPORT.

The Report for the year 1837 of this Society evidences that it is still in a prosperous condition. The principal objects of attention are, of course, of local interest,—and this is as it should be: were such institutions general throughout the country, the more entirely confined to the scientific wants and capabilities of the particular district their reports were, the more likely would they be to contain correct and authentic information. The steam-engine, however, is now confined to no district or country; and all that relates to it is interesting, as well to the philanthropist as to the man of science. Cornwall has ever been prominent, from necessity, in its eagerness to adopt improvement, and thus it has become itself prolific in inventors and improvers of this great instrument of civilization.

The name of Sims has, no doubt, often been observed by our readers, as the engineer to the mines whose duty stands amongst the highest in the tables we have from time to time published. This gentleman is thus mentioned in the Society's Report, in connection with an important improvement in the expansive working of steam.

"Mr. Sims, (the engineer to whom this county is indebted for the enormous increase (from 25 to 58 millions) of duty, performed by the single stamping engine acting directly on a crank,) exhibited at the meeting of the society, the drawings of an engine, in which the steam is allowed to expand partly in a small cylinder, in the down stroke, and afterwards in the up stroke in a larger cylinder, placed with a view to apply the expansive action of steam through the greater proportion of the revolution of the crank. The organized system of competition on known conditions, afforded by the monthly report, will become the best practical test of its merits; and the society would feel gratified by the success of an engine, the drawings of which were, by the liberality of the engineer, first made public at their annual meeting."

We hope to be enabled to lay before our readers a description of Mr. Sims' engine when its performances have been tested. From the invention of an engineer of so much experience, there can be but little doubt of most satisfactory results.

We had looked with considerable interest for the result of the competition for the prize offered by H. H. Price, Esq., for "the best method of applying to steam navigation the Cornish method of working steam expansively"—and are sorry that none of the plans sent in were found "fully to comply with the conditions required." Were none of the competing plans even worth publication? We observe that an ingenious correspondent of ours, and a practical engineer, (Mr. James Whitelaw of Glasgow) received a bronze medal on account of the beauty of his drawings. Judging from Mr. Whitelaw's contributions to our pages, we should have thought that there was more than mere pictorial beauty in his plans; and that the pages of the report which are filled up with subscribers names in large and leaded type, would have been better occupied with the designs of this gentleman and others, which, although not in the opinion of the judges deserving of the prizes offered, yet might be considered worthy of publication, as giving hints to be improved upon. Mr. Price's offered premium, we are sorry to observe, has been withdrawn.

Looking at the reports of the judges upon the plans sent in to compete for the various prizes offered, we think that they are too particular in their requirements. Out of six prizes, only one is adjudged as having been deserved by a candidate. The judges cannot expect an inventor will, for the sake of a premium of at most ten guineas, give up an invention which might make his fortune. In the case we have mentioned above, that of Mr. Price's premium, an arrangement that would have " fully complied with the conditions required"—that is worked marine steam-engines expansively in the best method,—would be a fortune to any man; and we cannot wonder at the plans sent in being found somewhat deficient, where the requirements are so large. The withholding the premiums held out as an inducement to exertion, must tend to discourage and weaken the endeavours of men of moderate inventive capacity— whilst a liberal judgment upon, perhaps, even questionable merits, would induce others to come forward and compete, whose designs might perhaps be found " fully to comply with the conditions required."

In referring to the endeavours now making to effect the removal of the tax upon tin, the committee make an interesting comparison between the scientific characters of the Elizabethan and the present age—making an extract from Davies Gilbert's History of Cornwall, lately reviewed in our pages.

" 'The incidental allusion to former impositions, naturally invites an estimate of the social and intellectual condition of the county, at distant periods of our history. Confining the comparison, then, to those pursuits which challenge the principal attention and countenance of your society, it may be questioned, whether any part of the United Kingdom has made a more signal and conspicuous advance than the county of Cornwall. We have high contemporary authority for all matters of local interest and information, in the most complete antiquarian history of the Elizabethan age, of which any district in England can boast. It will readily be inferred, that allusion is here made to Carew's Survey of Cornwall; a work which has, of late years, attained a celebrity in some degree commensurate with its merits, from the edition put forth by the first patron of your society. In that valuable and amusing provincial history, the worthies of Cornwall are of course enu-

merated; who are classified as divines, civilians, common lawyers, physicians, statesmen, and warriors. The last place is assigned to those who had attained eminence in mechanical science. A single name is all that is inserted in this part of the catalogue; and it must be confessed that the varied accomplishments of this worthy, savour so strongly of the marvellous, as almost to transfer him out of the region of fact into that of the fabulous. ' For mechanical sciences,' says the author of the Survey, 'the old Veale of Bodmin might justly expostulate with my silence, if I should not spare him a room in this Survey, while he so well deserves it. This man hath been so beholden to Mercury's predominant strength in his nativity, that without a teacher he is become very skilful in well-nigh all manner of handicrafts; a carpenter, a joiner, a mill-wright, a freemason, a clock-maker, a carver, metal-founder, architect, *et quid non?* yea, a surgeon, physician, alchymist, &c.; so as that which Georgias of Leontium vaunted of the liberal sciences, he may profess of the mechanical; viz.: to be ignorant in none.' It may be suspected that this Roger Bacon of the 16th century, was beholden to the influences of Mercury in his nativity, in one other particular at least, which has not found a place in the above enumeration. Admitting, however, that this testimony is of any worth, what shall we think of the state of science in the county, when all that can be told of it is comprised in a notice, so meagre, suspicious, and unsatisfactory?

" In harmony with this statement, are the graphic accounts furnished from the same source, of the manner of working the mines, and the primitive methods resorted to, in order to overcome the obstacles which presented themselves. When we learn that the last resource against 'a hard country, was burning faggots and furze to break the rocks ;' that among the most approved machines for conveying away the water, were wheels driven by a stream, and interchangeably filling and emptying two buckets; (what a contrast, by the way, to the present unrivalled efficiency of our Cornish steam-engines !) that from their inexpertness in the use of the needle, and their ignorance how to drain their ground, the miners were compelled to carry their adits open to a considerable depth—' a practice costly in charge and long in effecting;' our surprise will not be that so little was done, but that so much was accomplished, notwithstanding the rudimental state of mechanical and philosophical expedients in facilitating their labour. It was not indeed till long after the period now referred to, that working with the dial under ground was generally understood and adopted; whilst even within the memory of man, as was stated by an eminent member of your society at the last exhibition, whatever skill might have been attained in working with the dial, Cornwall did not furnish an artist capable of producing the instrument, which was not to be purchased in the whole county. The accuracy, beauty, and elegance, conspicuous in many of these instruments, made by Cornish artists and displayed in the Polytechnic Hall, clearly show that such a reproach no longer attaches to us; nay, more, instead of being dependent on other parts of the kingdom for philosophical and mechanical instruments, we are enabled to supply the most delicate and elaborate that can be required, even for the highest branches of scientific research and experiment."

We have marked for extract an interesting paper by Mr. Enys, on "Duty and Horse-power"—and various other articles which shall appear in our pages in due season. We take leave of the Report, wishing well to the Society, and trusting that our observations will be taken in good part, as we are assured, that if they are acted upon they will tend to the prosperity and increased usefulness of the Association.

ON A LARGE AND VERY SENSIBLE THERMOSCOPE GALVANOMETER. BY JOHN LOCKE, M.D., PROFESSOR OF CHEMISTRY IN THE MEDICAL COLLEGE OF OHIO.

[From the *London and Edinburgh Phil. Mag.*]

The chief novelty of the instrument which I am about to describe, consists in its proportions and the resultant effects. The object which I proposed in its invention, was to construct a thermoscope so large that its indications might be conspicuously seen, on the lecture table, by a numerous assembly, and at the same time so delicate as to show extremely small changes of temperature. How far I have succeeded, will, in some measure, appear by a very popular, though not the most interesting experiment which may be performed with it. By means of the warmth of the finger applied to a single pair of bismuth and copper disks, there is transmitted a sufficient quantity of electricity to keep an eleven-inch needle, weighing an ounce and a half, in a continued revolution, the connexions and reversals being properly made at every half turn.

The greater part of this effect is due to the *massiveness* of the coil, which is made of a copper fillet about fifty feet long, one-fourth of an inch wide, and one-eighth of an inch thick, weighing between four and five pounds.

This coil is not made in a pile at the diameter of the circle in which the needle is to revolve, but is spread out, the several turns lying side by side, and covering almost the whole of that circle above and below. The best idea may be formed of the coil by the manner in which it is actually modelled by the workman. It is wound closely and in parallel turns on a circular piece of board eleven and a half inches in diameter, and half an inch in thickness, covering the whole of it except two small opposite segments, of about 90 degrees each. The board being extracted, leaves a cavity of its own shape to be occupied by the needle.

The copper fillet is not covered by silk, or otherwise coated for insulation, but the several turns of it are separated at their ends, by veneers of wood, just so far as to prevent contact throughout. In the spreading out and compression of the coil it is similar to Melloni's elegant apparatus, though in my isolated situation in the interior of America, I was not acquainted with the structure adopted in his prior invention. In the *massiveness* of the coil, my instrument is, perhaps, peculiar, and by this means it affords a free passage to currents of the most feeble intensity, enabling them to deflect a very heavy needle. The coil is supported on a wooden ring furnished with brass feet and levelling screws, and surrounded by a brass hoop with a flat glass top or cover, in the centre of which is inserted a brass tube for the suspension of the needle by a cocoon filament. The needle is the double astatic one of Nobili, each part being about eleven inches long, one-fourth wide, and one-fortieth in thickness. The lower part plays within the coil, and the upper one above it, and the thin white dial placed upon it, thus performing the office of a conspicuous index underneath the glass.

I have not yet made any very extensive experiments with this instrument, being only just prepared to do so. It is very sensible to a *single* pair of thermo-electric metals, to the action of which it seems peculiarly adapted; but the efficiency of such metals is increased by a repetition of the pairs, as in the thermo-pile of M. Melloni, especially if they be massive in proportion to the coil itself. With a battery of five pairs of bismuth and antimony, the needle was sensibly moved by the radiation from a person at the distance of twelve feet, without a reflector, the air being at the temperature of $72°$.

In a recent interview with M. Melloni, to whose politeness I am much indebted, he expressed his opinion that with a thermopile, massive in proportion to the coil, my galvanometer might be made to exhibit his thermo-experiments advantageously to a large class. Some idea may be formed of its fitness for this purpose from the result of a single trial on transmission. The heat from a small lamp with a reflector, at the distance of five feet, passed through a plate of alum, and falling on a battery or pile of five pairs of bismuth and antimory, deflected the needle only a fraction of one degree, but on substituting a similar plate of common salt, the same heat produced, by impulse, an immediate deflection of 33 degrees.

Although the instrument is finely adapted by its size for the purpose for which it was intended, class illustration, yet, from the weight of the needle, and the difficulty of bringing it to rest after it once acquires motion, it is not so suitable for experiments of research as the Mellonian galvanometer. When a massive thermo-pile, such as has lately been made by Watkins and Hill, of Charing-cross, is connected with the coil and excited by a heat of about 200°, the needle being withdrawn a distinct report is obtained on interrupting the circuit ; in producing this effect it is less efficient however than the ribbon coil of Professor Henry. The tube for suspension, placed over the centre of the instrument, is so constructed, as to admit of bing turned round by means of an index, which extends from it horizontally over the glass cover, and thus any degree of torsion may be given to the suspending filament or wire. A wire of any desired thickness may be easily substituted for the cocoon filament, when the instrument becomes adapted to measuring the deflecting forces of the galvanic battery. By using a thick wire it was ascertained that the calorimetor of Professor Hare, having forty plates, each 18 inches square, acted on the needle with a force equal to 92 grains, applied at the distance of six inches from the centre. In attempting to force the needle by torsion into a line parallel to the coil, where the deflecting current acts with the greatest strength, I accidentally carried it too far and reversed its *position*, when instantly it became reversed in *polarity*, that which had been the north pole becoming the south. This showed how unfit is the magnetic needle to measure such a quantity of electricity as was then flowing through the massive conductor. The instrument is well adapted to show to a class the experiments upon radiant heat with Pictet's conjugate reflectors, in which the differential, or air, thermometer

affords, to spectators at a distance, but an unsatisfactory indication. For this purpose, the electrical element necessary is merely a disk of bismuth as large as a shilling, soldered to a corresponding one of copper, blackened, and erected in the focus of the reflector, while conductors pass from each disk to the poles of the galvanometer. With this arrangement the heat of a non-luminous ball at the distance of 12 feet will impel the needle nearly 180°, and, if the connexions and reversals are properly made, will keep it in a continued revolution.

I have thus given you a brief sketch of an instrument which seems to supply a desideratum on the lecture-table, when the common thermometer is too small to afford to a class that direct and full satisfaction which, in a subject so important as that of heat, is very desirable to every professor. I have not, so far, attempted to use it extensively as an instrument of research, yet it shows evidently the importance of massiveness in conductors for feeble currents, such as those produced by thermo-combinations ; nor am I certain that I have arrived at a maximum in this particular, for so far as I have proceeded in using thicker conductors for the coil, the deflecting effects have been increased.

I am, &c.
JOHN LOCKE.

London, August 30, 1837.

NOTES AND NOTICES.

Iron Welding.—A practice has for some time prevailed at Keswick, of welding iron and steel with a mineral which is said to be very abundant in that neighbourhood, and is found to answer the purpose much better than sand or borax, inasmuch as it affords a decidedly better protection to the fusing metals. It is used in the same common or simple way as sand, requiring no further care or management. Two, three, or more pieces of cast steel may be welded together, and drawn out, hardened, and broken across the junctures, which cannot be observed; or iron or cast steel can be welded together in the same way, as perfectly, and with as much ease as the mildest steel or iron.—*Carlisle Patriot.*

Premium for Bottle-washing Measuring Machine. —Two or three of the designs offered seem of such equal merit, that it has been thought proper to make an actual trial of them, before deciding which is the best. We hope in a week or two to be able to announce the award of the premium.

Railway Map of England.—On the first of August will be published the Title, Index, and Contents to vol. 28 of the *Mechanics' Magazine*, and as a frontispiece to the volume a large map of the Railways in England and Wales, price 6d. The map alone on fine paper, price 6d. Also the volume complete, in half-cloth, price 8s. 6d.

☞ *British and Foreign Patents taken out with economy and despatch; Specifications, Disclaimers, and Amendments, prepared or revised; Caveats entered; and generally every Branch of Patent Business promptly transacted. A complete list of Patents from the earliest period (15 Car. II. 1675,) to the present time may be examined. Fee 2s. 6d. ; Clients, gratis.*

LONDON: Printed and Published for the Proprietor, by W. A. Robertson, at the Mechanics' Magazine Office, No. 6, Peterborough-court, between 135 and 136, Fleet-street.—Sold by A. & W. Galignani, Rue Vivienne, Paris.

𝔐𝔢𝔠𝔥𝔞𝔫𝔦𝔠𝔰' 𝔐𝔞𝔤𝔞𝔷𝔦𝔫𝔢,

MUSEUM, REGISTER, JOURNAL, AND GAZETTE.

No. 781.]   SATURDAY, JULY 28, 1838.   [Price 3*d*.

GARBUTT'S NEW MODE OF MOUNTING TELESCOPES.

Fig. 2.

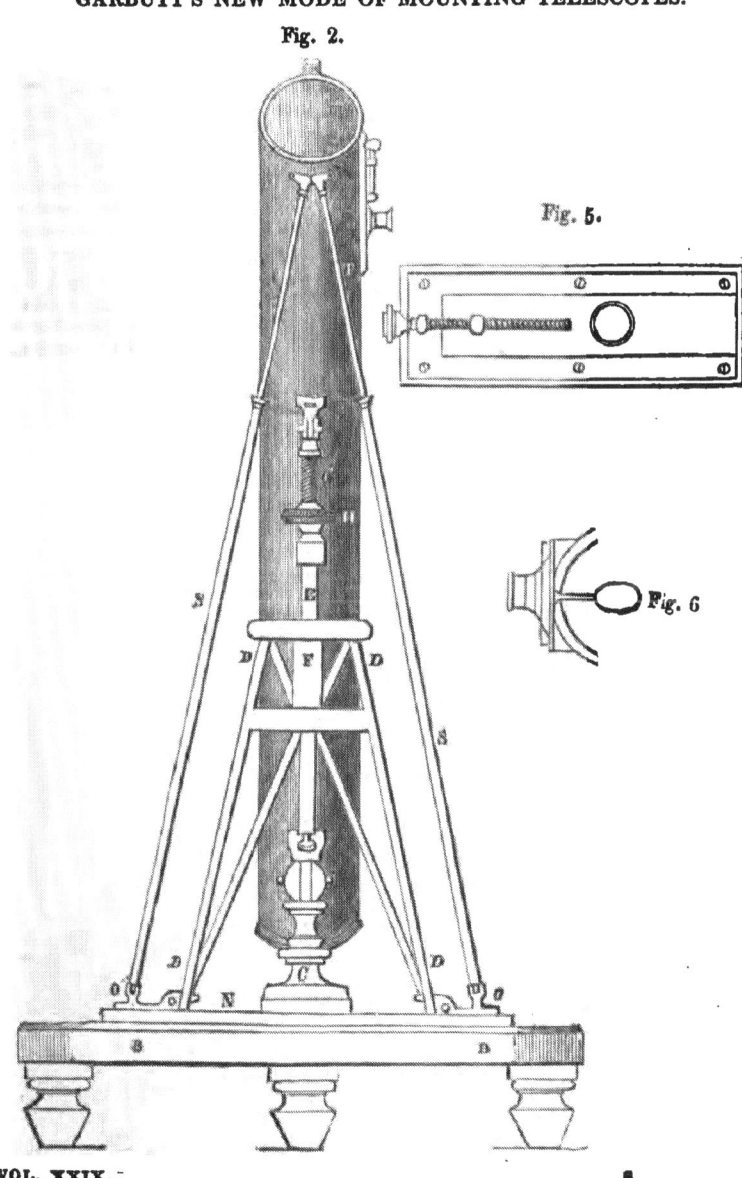

Fig. 5.

Fig. 6

GARBUTT'S NEW MODE OF MOUNTING TELESCOPES.

Sir,—I beg leave to hand you a drawing and description of a Newtonian telescope which I have now finished, mounted on a new principle, and if thought worthy of a place in your Magazine is at your service for that purpose.

I am, Sir,
Yours very respectfully,
C. GARBUTT.

21, Bridge-street, Gateshead,
July 4, 1838.

A A, figs. 1 and 2, is the tube, 6 feet 3 inches long; 5 inches diameter inside, made of half-inch deal, and veneered with mahogany : hooped at the ends with brass, and provided with a proper cell for the large speculum at the lower end, marked X.

B B, figs. 1, 2, 3, 4, represent views of the stand or base of the instrument; framed of mahogany and supported upon three turned feet.

C, the pedestal, turned of mahogany 8 inches high, with a rule joint and a brass bracket, screwed fast to the underside of the tube, by two mill-headed screws, the nuts of which are on the inside of the tube. The lower end or base of the pedestal is fixed to a radius arm marked N, which rests upon a washer on the stand ; and terminates with a conical spindle, 1¼ inches diameter, and accurately fills the hole in stand M, fig. 4, and secured by a cap and pin on the underside.

D D, fig. 1 and 2, the stage or principal support of the telescope, framed and braced as represented in fig. 2; it is 2 feet high, and rests upon the radius arm N, where it moves upon two pivots O O, to allow for the vibration in elevating or lowering the tube. The top end of this stage is fitted up with a box and sliding piece E, 18 inches long, 1¼ inch square, and made hollow to receive the iron screw marked G, through a brass milled screwed nut and socket H, fixed to the

Fig. 1.

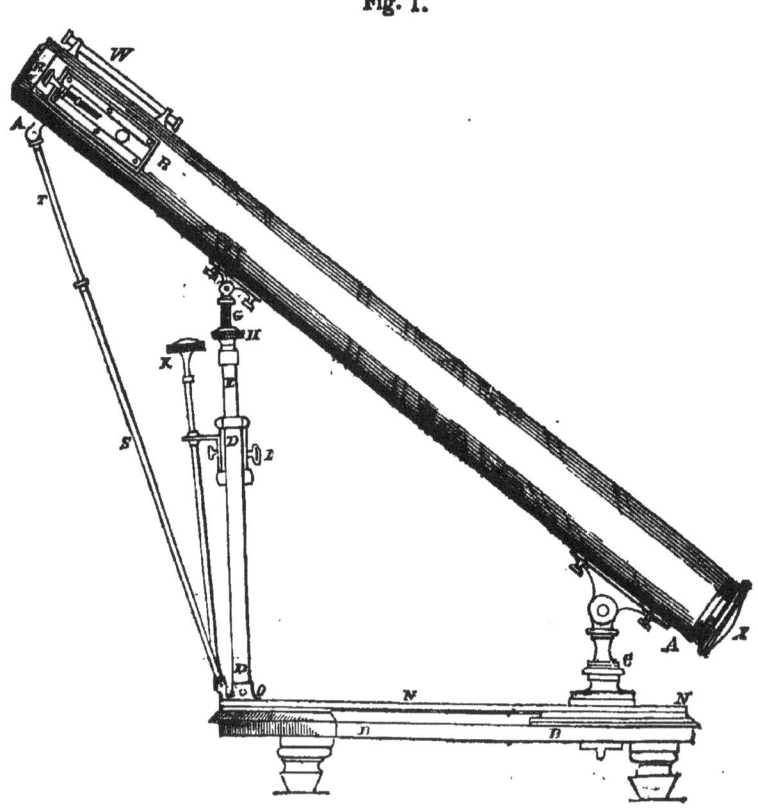

slide represented in fig. 1 and 2; this sliding piece is to extend the elevation of the tube, by drawing it through the box, and is secured by a thumb-screw marked I. The iron screw G, with rule joint and bracket fixed to the underside of the tube, passes through the brass nut H into the hollow of the sliding piece, and by turning this nut, the tube can be raised or lowered with precision and correctness, affording a complete adjustment in its vertical motion for variation of altitude.

F, is the box at top of the stage where

Fig. 3.

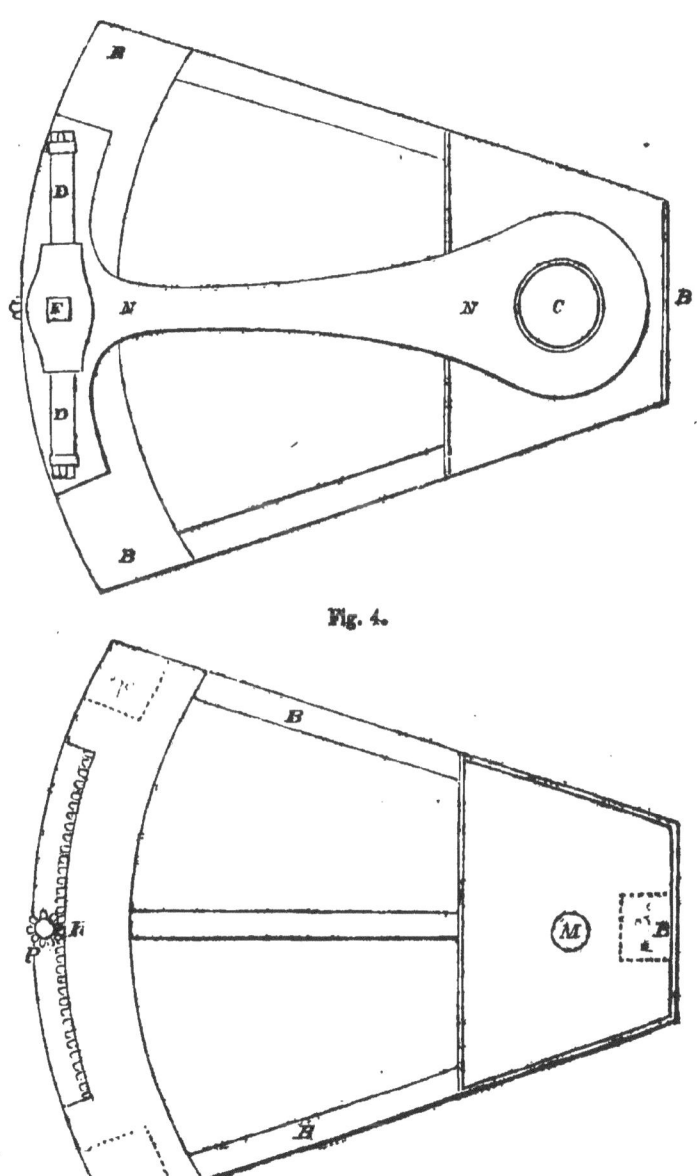

Fig. 4.

the slide passes through with a thumb screw I, to fasten the sliding piece, as is more fully shown in fig. 2, where the braces cross or meet each other.

K, fig. 1, represents a brass rod with large milled head, suspended to the front of stage by a bracket and socket, and terminating with an universal joint; to which is attached a pinion-wheel fixed to the underside of the radius arm, in such a manner as to act upon the teeth of a sector firmly screwed to the front of the stand, and shown by L P fig. 4. By turning this rod the pinion acts upon the sector, and carries the instrument with a steady horizontal motion.

S T, two sliding brass rods to steady the tube, and free it from vibration; they are in two lengths, one sliding within the other, and are attached to the high end of the tube, with a double joint, and to the cross part of the radius arm near the feet of the stage also, by joints as more fully shown in Fig. 2, S S.

R, a brass plate, and dove-tailed slide with eye-glasses, and arm carrying the small speculum as shown on a large scale at fig. 5 and 6. The slide is moved by the screw with milled head, to adjust to the focus of the eye-glasses.

W, a small telescope finder fixed to the tube, and adjusted parallel to its axis, to enable the observer to find his object in the field of view of the large telescope, with greater readiness.

From the preceding description it will be observed that this instrument has two vertical motions; viz., that of the slide piece E, used where extensive changes of altitude require a speedy elevation, (which can be held in any position by the thumb-screw I); also that of the screw G for the finer adjustment. A horizontal motion is obtained by turning the brass rod K. In using this instrument it is necessary to place the tube, pointing as near as possible to the object, then by using any or all of the above-described motions; bring the object into the centre of the cross wire contained in the finder or small telescope; and as its axes are adjusted parallel with the large tube, the object is in the field of view there also; and from the complete steady command over the instrument can be easily retained in that situation.

———

EXPLOSION OF THE "VICTORIA" BOILERS—EXAMINATION OF THE PRINCIPLE OF THEIR CONSTRUCTION.

Sir,—I have thought much of the *Victoria* flues; and it appears to me so extremely probable, that such flues as they are described to be, will collapse sooner or later, even if a full and sufficient quantity of water is kept in the boilers, that I have determined on publishing my opinion, and the reasoning by which I have arrived at that conclusion.

If we were to put an elastic fluid into a flexible cylindrical vessel of equal strength and thickness all over; and then by extraneous force alter the form of the vessel; the pressure of the fluid would tend to restore it to its original shape.

If we subjected such a cylinder to the pressure of an elastic fluid on the outside, it would bear any force *less* than one sufficient to crush the material of which it was composed. But that is only on the supposition that the form is perfect, and the strength and texture exactly alike in every part. For if its form were altered, although in ever so trifling a degree, by any extraneous force, the pressure of the elastic fluid would flatten it, or crumple it up, or tear it, according to the direction of the extraneous force, and the nature of the material of which the cylinder was made. And the same effects would follow from some parts being weaker than other parts, although no extraneous force were used to change its form.

These are properties which belong to the figure, may be demonstrated, and I suppose will not be disputed. The following observations apply to circular flues having the pressure outside.

I shall state three propositions, the truth of which I think cannot be doubted by those acquainted with the subject.

1st. The flue is not, and cannot be made, of exactly equal strength in all its parts.

2nd. Its form is not that of a perfect cylinder, but a rough approximation to it; it is full of dents and irregularities.

3rd. Any given flue may be placed in such circumstances of heat, and pressure, as will render it flexible.

Now we know that circular flues are made, and are placed in such circum-

EXPLOSION OF THE "VICTORIA" BOILERS.

stances, that although they are not inflexible, strictly speaking, their original form never suffers any permanent alteration. Hence it appears, that *the degree of stability of any given circular flue, depends upon the degree of heat and pressure to which it is subjected ; upon the extent of the deviation of its figure from that of a perfect cylinder ; and upon the difference in the strength of the different parts.*

But there is yet another cause of weakness and of change of form—the unequal heating of the flue. The flame and hot vapour will always act more directly, and with more effect upon some parts of the flue, than upon other parts ; unless the flue is very small.

Now let us imagine a flue to be of such strength and form, and in such circumstances, that when it is at the temperature T, and the pressure of the steam = P, it suffers a very small permanent *change* of form; and that the temperature and pressure at which it is commonly worked, are very nearly = T and P; and consider the consequences that are likely to ensue.

By the fortunate combination of a variety of different circumstances, such as the water used leaving little or no deposit—the flue never getting hotter in some parts than usual from shortness of water, alteration of furnace, or any other cause—the steam never getting to so high a pressure as that we have taken as the limit of the flue's strength, &c., such a flue might last a considerable time ; in fact, until it got sufficiently weakened by fair wear and tear, to allow of ordinary circumstances changing its form, when it would collapse, and probably cause loss of life. This seems to have been the case with the flue of the boiler on board the *James Gallocher.* See the *Times* of June 30.

A flue of this kind may be placed in such circumstances, that when the steam and temperature get unusually high, or as high as the safety-valve will permit, it suffers a minute permanent change of form. Under these circumstances it will inevitably collapse sooner or later, according to the extent to which its form is altered at each time it is unusually heated, and the frequency of that occurrence, *let it be surrounded with as much water as it may :* and I have not the least doubt, that both the *Victoria*

flues have collapsed from this cause alone. I state this opinion with all due deference to that of Mr. Seaward ; but that gentleman says he could not satisfy himself that the flue had been red hot ; and that, although it opened at the bottom, the mischief might have begun at the top. Now it appears to me, that if the top of the flue had been softened by heat, so as to cause the immediate failure of the flue, that it would have been forced *inwards,* and the flue would have failed in that part ; or if not, that it would have exhibited a very sharp bend *outwards,* and thus have proved its having been overheated in that particular part. All the other circumstances which would occur in the case supposed by Mr. S., seem to me very accurately described.

I will not occupy more of your valuable space in considering what would happen to these flues under the various circumstances in which they might be placed. But I must observe, that if we wanted to know what such flues would bear, the only way we could ascertain it would be by actual experiment. Such experiments have, unfortunately, been tried on a large scale. We know that each of these flues that has failed has exhibited certain peculiarities in the circumstances of its failure ; and our theory has pointed out the particular circumstances that would lead to such peculiarities as have been exhibited in each of the failures we have spoken of, and would do so by them all. Have we not therefore a right to conclude, that the circumstances we have supposed, and those which actually occurred, are precisely alike ?

I must observe, that it is totally impossible to ascertain the strength of these flues by calculation, and any pretence to do so would be absurd, or something worse; because, to make such a calculation, we must have the exact form, strength, and temperature of every part of the flue when *at its highest temperature.* And that the flue which would be safe with one furnace, might very likely fail, in a short time, with a different one ; although the weight on the safety-valve remained the same.

But is proposed to *prove* the remaining boilers of the *Victoria* and thereby establish their character for safety. How would they prove them ? Doubtless, by the same means they have proved the whole four—HYDRAULIC PRESSURE.

Now really, if ignorance were not the best excuse for this proposal, and therefore, that it might seem uncharitable to believe the parties knew better, it would be out of my power to suppose they did *not*. According to their own account of the matter, the water in two of these boilers has been allowed to get too low, although they were under the care of most experienced engineers, who well knew the consequences of such inattention,—and the last of whom could not have forgotten the dreadful punishment the first victims suffered for their alleged neglect. It is therefore sufficiently established, that these boilers, from some cause or other, are liable to this accident; and one would think the advocates of these boilers *must* know, that after the flue has once been overheated from this accident, and its figure altered by this or any other cause, that its strength is lessened; and that under such circumstances it is monstrous, to talk of the hydraulic pressure it *has* sustained, being any assurance of its present safety.

I have written thus much, because I hear other boilers are making on the same plan, and I feel very desirous of warning all concerned of their danger. But I trust no more lives will be sacrificed to an obstinate perseverance in the use of these most incongruous boilers; which will most certainly be the case if their use is persisted in.

Yours, &c.

C. G. JARVIS, Engineer, &c.

July 14, 1838.

P.S.—Fourteen people have been killed by the collapsing of these flues; and yet, a certain person has deemed it wise to declare, they are "the very best boilers that can be made;" and that "the Company are more than ever convinced of their safety," notwithstanding the fact of every engineer, except the unfortunate person who designed them, condemning them as highly dangerous?

It certainly behoves all persons who have any regard for their lives, to be very cautious how they entrust themselves to the care of the servants of a "Company" of persons whose judgments are so singularly and so conspicuously perverted.—July 19.

Your intelligent correspondent "N. S." page 265, says, "the enginemen must keep a bright look out for themselves," &c.

I am decidedly of opinion that all possible attention could not have prevented the collapse of the *Victoria* flues.

High steam, is as safe as low steam, when those who construct and manage the apparatus for its application, know all they *ought* to know, before they meddle with it. But if any company should choose to employ any one who is not fit for the task, the credit of that company must suffer, and the safety of the public will be endangered.

C. G. J.

MR. WALTER HANCOCK'S, AND SIR JAMES ANDERSON'S PATENT BOILERS.

Sir,—To the *Mechanics' Magazine*, more than to any other journal, is the cause of steam-locomotion on common roads indebted, not only for its liberal advocacy, but its impartial insertion of the performances, plans, and pretensions of all those who have, in the course of their career, made out any tolerable title for such a distinction, admitting at the same time, through the medium of its columns, "a clear stage and fair play" for such as may have misrepresentations to complain of, or explanatory communications to offer; thus affording to the scientific competitors of the present day an arena more facile and available than has fallen to the lot of their predecessors in any age or country.

Such, Mr. Editor, having been your course hitherto, I trust you will not deny me an opportunity of answering a letter which I have received from one of your readers (besides various verbal interrogations) respecting a boiler, described in your 775th Number, purporting to be the patent of Sir James Anderson, and to form the principal feature in a steam-carriage for common roads, building or built by him for a public company. I have examined the wood-cut and description referred to, and find that the boiler is composed of flat chambers, for which invention I obtained a patent in the year 1827; and, as I have never granted a license to any person whatever to use my said invention for steam-carriages, no person can have a legal right to adopt it.

I should not have taken any notice of this circumstance if I had not been called upon to do so; because, until a boiler composed of flat chambers is publicly used, there is no legal invasion of my right; and it is by no means the first time that I have been placed in precisely the same situation in regard to these flat chambers; but, as the parties alluded to employed my invention only in experimental, and, ultimately, *abortive attempts*, I had no occasion to interfere;—and with regard to these experiments of Sir James Anderson with my flat chambers, I fully expect they will have the same result. I tried the flat chambers, placed so as to form one continuous flue, in a carriage eight or ten years ago, and therefore know well the merits of such a mode of arranging them. If Sir James Anderson had had one-twentieth part of the practice with flat chambers that I have, he would not have ventured any public announcement, *even of experiments with them, thus arranged*, until he had tried how his carriage would perform over a good run of new-laid gravel or a rugged steep. I quite agree that "there is room enough, Sir, in England for us all;" but let every one in so noble a race bring *for himself* the resources of his *own talent only*, and make it a point *scrupulously and honourably to stand clear of the discoveries and combinations wrought out by his competitors;* and if these discoveries and these combinations have resulted from years of labour and expense, let that circumstance *render them so much the more sacred* in the estimation of a keen but generous rivalry, whether they belong to a Gurney, a Maceroni, a Sir James Anderson, or

Your obedient servant,

W. HANCOCK.

MR. HANCOCK'S STEAM-GIG.

Sir,—Being in the park last Tuesday afternoon, I had, for the first time, the gratification of seeing Mr. Hancock's steam-gig, and of noticing its perfect operation and evolutions, during the whole time it was there. This brought to mind an inquiry I wish to make:—is the theory laid down by Mr. Baddeley in your last Number correct—that "the *weight* of the locomotive increases in a much quicker ratio than the *power*"?

I must confess my disbelief of this; surely an engine and boiler of 80-horse power does not weigh so much as two separate engines and boilers of 40-horse power each. I have always understood, that the little dependance to be placed on the results of small working models, arose from the very reverse of his position.

Residing in the district, I have frequently rode on Mr. Hancock's carriages, on the Paddington Road, and I most cordially wish him a due reward for his ingenuity, and years of perseverance, which perhaps he may now stand some chance of, as, I understand, the gig was worked in the park by the express desire of some of the distinguished foreigners now in London. Prince Puttbuss, the Prussian Ambassador, the Prince of Hanover, the Hanoverian Ambassador, and several ladies, rode upon it at different times; it was also minutely inspected by Prince George of Cambridge, Duke de Nemours, Marquis Milleflores, Prince Pattrass, and many other foreign nobles, whose names I did not hear, and who all expressed their admiration of this neat and effective little piece of powerful mechanism.

Most heartily do I hope that, now Mr. Hancock has brought his carriages to a state of perfection fit for public use, he will not be surrounded by a host of pirates, as is too frequently the case; but of this I have my fears, from perusing your pages of the 16th ultimo, in which a description of Sir James Anderson's boiler, composed of "broad flat water-chambers," is given.

This boiler differs from Mr. Hancock's only in two points—the steam-chest, or separator, and the direction given to the heat, both of which are so disadvantageous, that Mr. Hancock, or any other practical man of talent, would not adopt either of them; and this anticipation or fore-knowledge of failure, I suppose, accounts for Mr. Hancock's supineness in not noticing the invasion of his invention.

I am, Sir, your very obedient servant,

AN AMATEUR MECHANIC.

Islington, July 19, 1838.

UNEXAMPLED PLAGIARISM—MR. BADDELEY'S FLOATING FIRE-ENGINE.

"*Reddite cuique suum.*"

Sir,—I know not if you are acquainted with the existence of a cotemporary publication called the *Penny Mechanic*—whence babes in science endeavour to draw a *weakly* stock of knowledge. Sympathy would suffice to prevent my being too hard upon the " Tyros," who occasionally try the strength of their pinions in this atmosphere, and their puerile attempts would have passed unnoticed and uncommented upon by me, had not one audacious stripling endeavoured to fire off a great gun, to astonish his compeers by the magnitude of his calibre. This daring performance has been achieved by pilfering a " ready made article" from one of your back numbers of four years standing.

In No. 588 of the *Mechanics' Magazine*, published November 15, 1834, there appeared two engravings and a description of an " improved floating fire-engine," which I had designed some time previously. The last number of the *Penny Mechanic* contains a copy of these two engravings on the frontispiece, with my article appended, almost verbatim from your pages. All the circumstances which I enumerated—all the alterations I proposed—and all the improvements I suggested—have been re-stated, re-proposed, and re-suggested by a Mr. J. E. Goddard !

The deviations from my words are few and unimportant: there is one paragraph, however, which this wholesale plagiarist has not had the effontery to transcribe. It is that which sets forth the fact of my being employed by Mr. Buston to examine and improve the floating fire-engine of the London Assurance Corporation, of which he was foreman. I suppose Mr. J. E. Goddard thought that to repeat *this* statement as his own, would at once stamp him " the lying'st knave in Christendom," though for my own part, I can see but little difference in criminality between this and what he has really done. In reiterating my words Mr. Goddard subsequently says, " the floating engine I allude to, &c," forgetting that *he had omitted the allusion* referred to ! His reference to " the late tremendous conflagration at the House of Lords," looks particularly silly at this distance of time; especially after the building of a powerful floating fire-engine by the London fire-establishment, together with the occurrence of several serious water-side fires, at which it has been eminently useful.

In consequence of some errors in the punctuation, that which was originally sense, is converted into nonsense, and taken as a whole, this is one of the most disgusting and disgraceful acts of plagiarism I ever met with.

Although for the present superseded, my plan assumes considerable importance, inasmuch as I have been informed, that in some respects the new floating engine has disappointed the expectations of its designers, and that in the event of another being built, several of the improvements I have suggested would be adopted.

I remain, Sir, yours respectfully,
WM. BADDELEY.

London, July 17, 1838.

———

HONORARY FIRE-BRIGADES IN SWITZERLAND.

Mr. Baddeley, whose numerous contributions to your valuable Magazine are distinguished for their usefulness, and their constant tendency to promote the public interest, as well as for a propriety of language, is very likely to be correct in his expectations, when he asserts, in mentioning the formation of an honorary fire-brigade at Cheltenham, that " these voluntary associations are likely to be productive of incalculable good." These associations, which have been known on the continent for some time, are certainly worthy of every encouragement which public confidence can bestow on them. Some details respecting their organization in Switzerland, which have come to my knowledge during a residence in that country, may perhaps not be deemed unworthy of notice at the present moment.

Honorary fire-brigades are already organized in Switzerland, not only in small towns and cities, but even to a great extent in villages. The most reputable citizens vie with each other in eagerness and zeal to become members of so useful associations, which, however, consist of a fixed number of men. In some places the members are divided, some devoting themselves exclusively to the management of the fire-engine, while others are charged with the not less important task of taking immediate possession of the house on fire, in order to carry off, and convey to places of safety, the furniture and other moveable property which it may contain. Large and very convenient bags, with which they are often provided, enable them to save also most of the minor articles, which would probably otherwise become a prey to the flames. None but members of the brigade are allowed to enter the house; by this wise regulation, men of a bad character are entirely prevented from exercising their disgraceful industry on such occasions, while the order and method with which the praiseworthy exertions of the fire-brigade are conducted, are certainly productive of the greatest benefit to the poor sufferers. It is but justice to state, that on all occasions these exertions meet with due encouragement from every one capable of appreciating the self-devotion and generous feelings of the spirited citizens forming the honorary fire-associations.

Before I conclude, I beg to be allowed to make one more reflection. It sometimes happens in this country, that fire-engines cannot be put in action immediately on their arrival, because no water can be procured, the man who has charge of the key of the water-plugs not being on the spot. Now, in Switzerland, two or three keys are distributed to an equal number of persons living near the house where the fire-engines are kept; so that, in want of one key, there may always be procured another in any case of emergency. It is evident that the application of this principle to the water-plugs of the metropolis would be as beneficial as easy. It would, indeed, be quite needless for me to dwell on the advantages which would undoubtedly accrue from such a practice being adopted. I shall, therefore, only add, that

I have the honour to be, Sir,

Yours respectfully,

P. OBER.

Twickenham, July 20, 1838.

SINGULAR FACT IN FALLING BODIES.

Sir,—I have observed that a piece of stiff writing-paper, three inches long by an inch wide, held up as high as a man can reach, and extended between the fore finger and thumb of each hand, and then let loose in a room, when the doors and windows are shut, will always revolve on its long axis. This fact I mention in the hope that, in this age of mental exercise,

and easy communication of thought, the knowledge of it may lead to some useful practical result in science.

Your obedient servant,

JOHN NORTON.

London, July 21, 1838.

SEEKING THE SUN'S PARALLAX FROM THE TRANSIT OF VENUS.

Sir,—The following is to show the fallacy of seeking the sun's parallax from the transit of Venus.

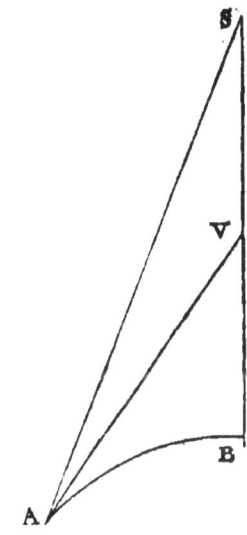

In all such observations, the annual motions must be allowed for, and so reduced as if there were no such motions. Let this be done, and let A B be an arc of the Earth; V, Venus; and S, any point in the sun with which V is in conjunction, as seen from B; but from the observer at A, the point S appears in the direction A S, and Venus in the direction A V, where V will fall on a different part of the sun. Here angle A V B is the parallax of Venus, and angle A S B that of the sun. Now angle S A V is the only observed angle, and its position is unknown; whence A S was treated as if parallel to B S, making the alternate angle A V B = angle S A V, and whence the sun's distance as if infinite; but since the sun has a parallax, A S and B S must meet at S, and form a triangle A S V, whose outward angle, A V B, is greater than either of the inward angles, S A V or S, ∴ the angle S is equal to the angle A V B, less by angle S A V, which gives the difference of the parallaxes, and not the parallax of either the sun or Venus. Thus treating A S as parallel to B S, the angle A V B measures too little; and hence A V or B V are too much for venus's distance; which, compared with the known ratio of the distances of the primary planets from the sun, make their distances and magnitudes too great: but if S was a fixed star, then A S would be parallel to B S, and angle S A V, and angle A V B would be equal, and would be the correct parallax of Venus. The ancients found the earth's distance from the sun to be 81 millions of miles, and this I find correct; and am, Sir, your humble servant,

WILLIAM SHIRES,
Teacher of Mathematics.

May, 1838.

———

MILLS'S MERCURIAL PUMP NOT NEW, AND USELESS.

Sir,—Perhaps it would be too much to expect that every projector who may send his little nursling to encounter the rough ordeal of your Magazine, should previously be conversant with the history of the branch of science to which it may belong; nay, even the most absurd pretension to originality may be treated with indulgence, provided it be put forward with a due degree of modesty and diffidence; but the case is otherwise when we are told that a learned lecturer on natural philosophy, who ought, ex officio, to be deeply read in his vocation, has adopted the invention as a class-subject, and edifies his pupils by a model of the discovery!

It is almost needless to say, that this observation bears reference to Mr. Mills's account of his mercurial pump, contained in your 776th Number, page 190. Had Mr. Mills read an article on pumps in the Encyclopædia Britannica, (which book I particularize because there is scarcely any person to whom it is not accessible), he would have soon found that he has not a single particle of claim on the pump he has so charitably adopted as his own;—that it was invented and abandoned for its many defects upwards of a century ago;—and that the only difference between the pump there described and that invented by Mr. Mills is, that the arrangement of the parts is slightly different,—the moving part in Mr. Mills's being an empty, unweighted, unsteady vessel; while in the original invention (by Mr. Haskins) the vessel containing the mercury, rendered steady by its great weight, is the moving part; —the latter arrangement being so greatly superior, and so much more elaborately contrived, that it is an almost unavoidable inference that the plan used by Mr. Mills was first tried, and the other afterwards adopted as an improvement upon it. But, as if to deprive Mr. Mills of the loop-hole of escape which even this slight difference of arrangement might afford him, the description of Haskins's pump concludes with the following remark:— "It is on precisely the same principle as the cylinder bellows described under the article Pneumatics;" and the cylinder bellows, so referred to, is the exact counterpart of Mr. Mills's pump, the arrangement being there not so objectionable.

But the concluding remark in Mr. Mills's communication is of such transcendent genius, that it throws the rest far into the shade: he says, that one advantage possessed by his (?) pump is, that "*for every inch of stroke of the handle K, the water will be raised one foot high!*" This piece of unmitigated absurdity proves, as clearly as the noon-day, that Mr. Mills *has seen* the description of Mr. Haskins's pump, and has copied it as his own invention, without understanding its principles: in the said description it is stated, that for every inch difference of height between the inner and outer columns of mercury, there must exist a difference of a foot in the columns of water, the former being twelve times heavier than the latter. Now, does not the sentence from Mr. Mills's letter, quoted above, furnish internal evidence that this part of the description of Haskins's pump must have been travestied in Mr. M.'s brain, without his having understood its meaning? else, why should he adopt one foot and one inch—13½, and not 12, being *now* the acknowledged specific gravity of mercury?

In fine, although Mr. Mills's model may form a very pretty squirting-toy for Mr. Grier's lecture-table, it is equally valueless, whether as an original invention or as a practical machine.

NAUTILUS.

———

Sir—From the non-appearance of my letter of the 3rd inst., respecting Mr. Mills's pump, I conclude that you considered it anticipated by Mr. Baddeley's communication on the same subject in No. 778, page 231. I freely acknowledge that Mr. B. was fully entitled to the preference, as well from priority in the date of his letter, as from his known experience in the world of hydraulics. I took, however, quite different ground from him; he confining himself to objecting to the practical efficiency of the pump, while I directed my remarks to its total want of originality; in fact, all the objections adduced of Mr. Baddeley may be found in any of the many treatises wherein the pump of Haskins is described.

There is, however, one most extraordinary blunder, into which Mr. Baddeley has fallen, and which I sincerely regret, as it may afford a peg to Mr. Mills or his friends whereon to hang an apparently successful answer to his letter. It is that part wherein Mr. Baddeley says that Mr. Mills's pump is of the *lifting*, and not of the *suction* kind, as stated in Mr. Mills's description.

Now, that the contrary is the case, is an axiom so palpable to any one who has glanced at the rudiments of hydraulics, that to attempt to prove it by any serious argument is almost puerile; but, when such an authority as Mr. Baddeley is supposed to be, writes it, not as a random assertion, but as a grave accusation of want of correctness in description, a few words in proof of his egregious mistake may be excused.

A lifting pump, then, is that wherein the piston acts entirely *beneath* the surface of the water to be raised; for, if the piston act in the least *above* such surface, the pump partakes of the suction kind. Ordinary pumps, with a valve in the piston, are of this mixed nature, —the water beneath the piston being sucked, or supported by atmospheric pressure, while that above the piston is lifted.

Now, it is evident, that in the mercurial pump, described at page 190, the piston being 30 feet above the surface, it is, in its up-stroke, altogether of the *suction* kind, and, in its down-stroke, of the *force* kind: the term *lifting force-pump*, which Mr. Baddeley has conferred on it, is, therefore, glaringly wrong; while the

original description of Mr. Mills is, in this instance, correct: and I can only repeat my regret, that this opportunity of triumph should be given to the latter, in a subject wherein he certainly did not deserve such a chance.

I remain, &c.,
NAUTILUS.

July 17, 1838.

STEAMING ON CANALS—ERICSSON'S PROPELLERS.

We copy from the *Manchester Guardian* the following account of a very successful experiment made on the Duke of Bridgewater's canal with Mr. Ericsson's propellers, described in our 751st Number. The account is defective and erroneous in many particulars, and in none more so than in the ascription of all "the merit" of the affair to Messrs. Robins and Co. (the well-known carriers), and the apparently studious omission of the name of the ingenious and indefatigable inventor, Captain Ericsson. We have subjoined, therefore, some notes which may help to set the matter in its true bearings before the public.

As our American neighbours would say, we are "going a-head" in the use of steam as a locomotive power. But a few weeks ago we noticed the starting of a small steam boat to ply on the Irwell, with passengers, between this town and Warrington; and we have now to announce the application of steam to carriers' canal boats for the transit of goods between this town and London. In canal navigation in this country, a long period of time has elapsed since any alteration or improvement of any great importance has been made. The boats are of the same construction, and so inartificial is the mode of working them, that the only means in practice, at the present day, for propelling them through the immense tunnels, of which one is nearly a mile in length and another three quarters of a mile, is for the boatmen to lie on their backs on the tarpaulin which covers the goods with which the boats are deeply laden, and, by pushing their feet against the roof of the tunnel, work the boats onwards at a tediously slow rate, with great labour and fatigue, amidst the smoke from the boats' chimneys or funnels, which, to any one unused to its effects in a long tunnel, would seem wholly unendurable. This is what the boatmen term "*legging* through;" and in this way every boat-load of goods is worked onwards through the tunnels on every great water-line of internal navigation in the country. The first application of steam on canals has been made, not on a new form or construction of boat, nor even on an iron boat of similar form, but on one of the long narrow canal boats, with sharp stem and stern, which had for some time before been plying on the canals in the usual way. The experiment which has been tried, at little cost, and which, at best, is an imperfect one, has, however, been eminently successful; and there appears very little doubt that its results will be a revolution as complete in canal navigation as the introduction of marine steamers has worked in our coasting packets. *The merit of making this experiment* belongs to Messrs. Robins, Mills, and Co., carriers, of London, and of Castle Field Wharf, in this town. Into one of their canal boats, near the stern, *they* introduced a small high-pressure marine steam-engine, of *only four* horses' power, to which a boiler *that had been used for one of the locomotive engines on the Liverpool and Manchester Railway* was adapted (1.) As the narrowness of canal tunnels and the injury likely to result to the banks from the use of side paddles must always have thrown a difficulty in the way of applying steam power, in the ordinary mode, to canal navigation, it became necessary to substitute some paddle which should not be in the way, while it should not be liable to the objection of injuring the banks. This difficulty has been surmounted, as it seems to us, very satisfactorily and completely, by an ingenious application of the principle of the *old fish-tail paddles* (2.) These paddles are placed at the extreme stern of the boat, and this terminating in a sharp point, it was *necessary to lengthen the boat*, and make a square box to contain the paddles (3.) They consist of two small wheels, placed *side by side*, not working parallel to

the boat, but transversely, and revolving contrary ways (4.) The paddle-boards or plates of iron, of which there are six on each wheel, have an inclination of about 45°. When in action, therefore, it will be seen that, as one wheel of paddles *strikes the water on the starboard side* of the stern, the other *strikes it on the larboard*, thus producing an action on the water resembling that which sailors call " *the double scull*," and which is the best effort of art that we have seen in imitation of the mechanical action of the tail of a fish when swimming (5.) The *defects* of the present experimental engine, &c. seem to be rather in its *adaptation and arrangement* than in itself. In the first place, we should think a *more powerful engine necessary* to the fair development of the power of steam in this species of navigation, considering the great length of the boat and the bulk and weight of its cargo, which is probably eleven or 12 tons (6.) Then we have no doubt, that *that* form of boat which has hitherto sufficed for the slow dragging of horses and a towing line, is not precisely the shape and build, nor, perhaps, is timber the best material for canal steam navigation. Again, it appears to us that the engine was rather *too far from the paddles to exercise its full available motive power* (7.) But these and several other points, into which we have not time to enter, will, doubtless, receive a *full and sagacious* consideration from *scientific and practical* men when once their attention is directed to the subject (8.) That the time for this, we think, bearing in mind the power and force of competition in every branch of trade and mode of communication, cannot be far distant. But to return to the *Novelty*, which is the new name the

---

(1) The boiler is *not* one that has been used for locomotive engines—it is one invented by Captain Ericsson, and of quite a peculiar construction. It is besides only 5 feet 10 inches long, while locomotive boilers are never less than 12 feet. The cylinder is 12 inches in diameter, with a 10-inch stroke, making about 70 strokes per minute; the steam always kept at 30 lbs. per square inch. The scientific reader will allow that such power is *good measure* for "*four horses*."

(2) The propeller is by no means on the principle of the "old fish-tail paddles." See description in *Mechanics' Magazine*, No. 751. The *Guardian's* process of reasoning seems to be this; the tail of a fish is (commonly) behind the rest of its body, Captain Ericsson's propeller is placed behind; *ergo* Captain Ericsson's propeller and a fish's tail are very much alike. By the same sort of logic it might with great ease be shown to be very like the famous pigtail at Charing Cross.

(3) The boat has *not been lengthened*. A square

piece of wood has been attached to the stern part, but which does not project more than 10 inches further aft than the point of the stern of the ordinary fly-boats.

(4) The paddles are not placed " side by side." See above Number of *Mechanics' Magazine*.

(5) The paddles do not " *strike the water*;" the propulsion being perfectly uniform, a gradual sliding of the water takes place from the stern.

(6) The *engine* is by no means a defective one, nor has it been found *not* powerful enough; on the contrary, its power is full 20 per cent. *too great* for the paddles, which ought, in point of fact, to have been much larger.

(7) The power of the engine is communicated to the paddles by means of a straight shaft of about 12 feet in length. Does the *Guardian* suppose that if this was reduced to 6 feet the power of the engine would be increased?

(8) The inventor, Captain Ericsson, being neither scientific nor practical!—and all "the merit" in the case consisting in the introduction by Robins and Co. of the "old fish-tail paddles!" if our cotemporary will but condescend to advise with some of the many "sagacious, scientific, and practical men" to be found in his own neighbourhood, he will be surprised to find how little he really knows about the whole matter.

boat received when from a [tow] *liner* she became a steamer, the first voyage she made very recently from London to this place with very considerable success. Like her great prototypes, the Great Western and the Sirius, a log was kept of her rate of steaming during this her first outward voyage; but we have not been able to obtain a sight of this log, and can, therefore, only very generally notice her performance, which, we understand, was at the rate of nearly eight miles per hour. She left Paddington on Thursday week, at noon, with about eleven tons of goods, but was detained for several days on the Grand Junction canal, waiting her turn to proceed: notwithstanding this delay, she reached here about half-past three o'clock on Wednesday afternoon last, without having sustained the least injury, except that, having been lengthened, she was a little too long conveniently to pass some of the locks; and the result was, that her paddle-boards were a little bent and put out of order. They were speedily put to rights; and, on Monday last the proprietors, with a party of friends, proceeded with the boat on an excursion down the canal, we believe as far as Runcorn, when her speed was tried, with the favourable results already noticed. On Monday evening she took on board a cargo of bale or pack goods for London, and, we believe, started on her homeward voyage the same night. We understand that when going at the rate of eight miles an hour she does not occasion the least swell. It is anticipated that she will be able to deliver goods in London in three days from her departure from this place. On one occasion shortly before her first canal voyage, the *Novelty* towed the city barge, on board of which were a hundred and fifty gentlemen, up the Thames as far as Teddington Lock, at the rate of about eight miles an hour; and her performance then gave the highest satisfaction to all who witnessed it.

Since penning the preceding notes, we have seen a subsequent notice in the *Guardian*, which we also insert, in which we are glad to observe tardy justice is done to Captain Ericsson, and the character of the improvement is a little more correctly appreciated. It is not a little amusing, however, to note the pertinacity with which our contemporary sticks to his fish-tail resemblance, while in the same breath he does his best to show that there is no resemblance at all.

(Second notice in the Manchester Guardian.)

In an article under this head in the *Guardian* of Saturday last, we noticed the first down voyage to this town from London, through the canals, of a steam-boat named the Novelty.

We have already stated that the Novelty is the hull of an old canal boat. Her form, to those unacquainted with the build of these boats, will be better understood when we state that her length is about 74 feet, with a seven feet six inch beam; she is heavily constructed, and when loaded draws about two feet water. We noticed that her engine was high pressure, and of four-horse power, supplied with steam from a small locomotive boiler. The boat is fitted with a species of paddles, already described, but perhaps better known as "Ericsson's" propellers, in substitution of the side paddles of the old steamers, which are constructed so as to propel without raising a surge injurious to canal banks, and so as to pass through the narrow locks with ease and safety — objects hitherto unattained, and deemed impracticable. The main peculiarity of this invention is the construction of the paddle, so as to secure an action resembling that of a fish's tail, or of a perpetual sculling through the water. The difference between the operation of these propellers and that of the fish or double scull is, that instead of the force being alternate from side to side, the propellers' strokes upon the water are simultaneous. As these propellers work with the greatest effect when submerged, no waste of power is incurred, and no shaking motion communicated to the boat. When in motion, with her propellers submerged, there is little to distinguish the Novelty from other canal boats, the old wooden funnel being retained; there being little smoke, as coke is the fuel consumed: the engine and boiler being out of sight, and the only variation in her form being the elongation and widening of the stern, about 14 inches, with the addition of a slight stage for the helmsman.

We noticed the fact of an experimental trip having been made by this boat on Monday week upon the Duke of Bridgewater's canal. The party on board consisted of some of the principal canal proprietors and water carriers in this town and neighbourhood, and their friends. The Novelty started from the Manchester end of the canal about six minutes before one o'clock; passed the Worsley branch at twenty minutes past one o'clock, and reached the wharf at Altrincham at half-past two o'clock, having performed the eight miles in one hour and 36 minutes. The speed of the boat, and the fact of no towing horses being visible, caused no small astonishment to various rustics on the canal banks; and some of the more cunning of these people, hearing the panting of the engine, and seeing the bubbling of the water in her wake, at length decided that there was "summat aloive in her tail." At twenty minutes before five o'clock the boat started on her return from Altrincham bridge, and on her way came up with the Wellington fly-boat, which, having just been freshly horsed, kept a-head for about two miles, but was then obliged to yield with a bad grace, the horses being half killed under the unwonted exertion. The Novelty passed "his grace" in fine style, and arrived at Messrs. Robins, Mills, and Co.'s wharf at ten minutes after six o'clock.

Owing to the construction and form of the boat, the propellers being only partially immersed, to the engine being out of repair, and to the utter disregard of her "trim" during the experiment, it was observed that the propellers had not a fair chance; nor could the boat attain that higher rate of speed which her due emergence from the water must have produced. During the trial trip no injurious ripple was produced by the propellers; but where the water was shallow a ripple, caused by the displacement of water by the boat, followed midway, and considerably impeded her progress. With deeper water her speed accelerated, and on the Thames she is said to have attained a rate varying from eight to nine, and even up to and exceeding ten miles per hour.

We understand that the American government, ever on the alert, has availed itself of this invention. An iron steamboat, built by Mr. John Laird, of North Birkenhead (under the inspection of Mr. F. B. Ogden, the United States consul at Liverpool), and fitted with these propellers, was launched on the 7th instant. She is at present waiting for her boilers, and it is expected will be tried on the Mersey in the course of next week. She is intended to be worked as a steam tug to tow ships upon the Delaware and Raritan Canal (New Jersey), which is forty-four miles in length.

LIST OF ENGLISH PATENTS GRANTED BETWEEN THE 26th OF JUNE, AND THE 26th OF JULY, 1838.

Nathan Defries, of Paddington-street, engineer, for improvements in gas meters. June 27; six months to specify.

John Ferry, of Leicester, Woolcomber, for certain improvements in combs for combing wool. June 27; six months.

Charles Green, of Birmingham, gold plater, for improvements in the manufacture of brass and copper tubing. June 27; six months.

Daniel Beckham, of No. 22, Sussex-place, Old-Kent-road, Surrey, stereotype founder, for an improved mode of obtaining castings in gold, silver, and others. June 27; six months.

James Robinson, of Huddersfield, merchant, for an improved method of producing, by dying, various figures or objects of various colours in woollen, worsted, cotton, silk, and other cloths. June 27; six months.

Edward White Benson, of Birmingham, chemist, for certain improvements in the manufacture of carbonate of lead. June 27; six months.

Richard Bednall, of Cotton Hall, Stafford, gent., for a certain improvement in the manufacture of carpets, and other similar woven fabrics, which improvement is effected by the introduction of a certain article of commerce not hitherto so employed or used in such manufactures. June 27; six months.

George Round, of Birmingham, lock filer; and Samuel Whitford, of the same place, die sinker, for a new and improved method of manufacturing certain of the parts of gun and pistol locks. June 30; six months.

Henry Grey Dyar, of Cavendish-square, gent., and John Hemming, of Edward-street, Cavendish-square, gent., Middlesex, for improvements in the manufacture of carbonate of soda. June 30; six months.

Augustus William Johnson, of Upper Stamford-street, Lambeth, for certain improvements for preventing the incrustation of steam boilers or generators, or evaporating vessels. June 30; six months.

Matthew Uzielli, of Fenchurch-street, London, merchant, for improvements in locks or fastenings, being a communication from a foreigner residing abroad. June 30; six months.

William Dobbs, of the Penn-road, Wolverhampton, brass founder, for certain improvements in the construction of racks and pulleys for window blinds and other useful purposes. June 30; six months.

George Carter, of Lombard-street, London, gent., for improvements in saw mills. July 2; six months.

Joseph Needham Taylor, of Red Lion-square, Bloomsbury, captain R.N., for a certain method, or certain methods of abating or lessening the mischiefs arising from the shock or force of the waves of the ocean, lakes, or rivers, and of reducing them to the comparatively harmless state known by the term "broken water," and thereby preventing the injury done to, and increasing the durability of break-waters, mole heads, piers, fortifications, lights, houses, docks, wharfs, landing-places, embankments, bridges, or ponton bridges; and also of adding to the security and defence of harbours, roadsteads, anchorages, and other places exposed to the violent action of the waves. July 2; six months.

Edward Davy, of Fleet-street, London, chemist, for improvements in apparatus for making telegraphic communications or signals, by means of electric currents, parts of such apparatus being applicable to obtaining, regulating, or measuring electric currents for other purposes. July 2; six months.

Frederick Joseph Burnett, of St. Mary-at-Hill, London, ship insurance agent, and Hippolyte Francois, Marquis de Bouffet Montauban, colonel of cavalry, now residing in Sloane-street, Chelsea, Middlesex, for certain improvements in the manufacture of soap. July 4; six months.

Henry Elkington, of Northfield, Worcester, gent., for certain improvements in engines to be worked by steam, air, or other fluids. July 6; six months.

Cornelian Alfred Jaquin, of Huggin-lane, Wood-street, London, for improvements in the manufacture of buttons. July 7; six months.

William Knight, of Chichester, ironmonger, for improvements in machinery for raising and forcing water and other fluids. July 7; six months.

George Salter, of West Bromwich, manufacturer, for improvements in apparatus for weighing. July 9; six months.

Claude Schroth, of Leicester-square, gent., for an improved method or methods of making or manufacturing the tools or apparatus employed in the process of pressing, or embossing the surface of leather or other substances; being a communication from a foreigner residing abroad. July 9; six months.

William Palmer, of Sutton-street, Clerkenwell, manufacturer, for improvements in lamps. July 10; six months.

William Barnet, of Brighton, ironfounder, for certain improvements in the manufacture of iron.—July 10; six months.

John Thomas Betts, of Smithfield-bars, rectifier, for improvements in process of preparing spirituous liquors in the making of brandy. July 10; six months.

Louis Cyprien Callet, late of New York, but now residing in Manchester, for certain improvements in machinery, or apparatus for producing motive power applicable to propelling boats and other vessels, carriages, machines, and other useful purposes, being a communication from a foreigner residing abroad. July 11; six months.

Henry Van Wart, of Birmingham, merchant, and Samuel Aspinwall Goddard, of the same place, merchant, for certain improvements in machinery, or apparatus applicable to locomotion on rail roads, and to steam navigation, parts of which improvements are also applicable to land or stationary engines. July 11; six months.

[John Bethell, of Mecklenburgh-square, gent., for improvements in rendering wood, cork, leather, woven and felted fabrics, ropes and cordage, stone and plasters, or compositions, either more durable, less pervious to water, or less inflammable, as may be required for various useful purposes. July 11; six months.

Job Cutler, of Lady Poole-lane, Sparkbrook, Birmingham, and Thomas Gregory Hancock, mechanist, of Prince's-street, Birmingham, for an improved method of condensing the steam in steam-engines, and supplying their boilers with water thereby formed. July 12; six months.

Joseph Bennett, of Turnley, near Glossop, Derby, cotton-spinner, for certain improvements in machinery for carding wool, cotton, flax, and other fibrous substances, which are, or may be carded, part of which improvements are also applicable to machinery for drawing, doubling, and roving, and spinning such fibrous substances as are, or may be subjected to those operations. July 12; six months.

James Milne, of Edinburgh, gas meter manufacturer, for improvements in apparatus employed in transmitting gas for the purpose of light and heat. July 13; six months.

Alexander Cochrane, of Arundel-street, Strand, Middlesex, gentleman, for improvements in umbrellas and parasols. July 13; six months.

Thomas Robert Sewell, of Carrington, Nottingham, lace manufacturer, for improvements in manufacturing white lead. July 14; six months.

Richard March Hoe, late of New York, but now of 66, Chancery-lane, civil engineer, for a new or improved instrument or apparatus for ascertaining or determining the latitude and longitude of any place, or the situation of ships or other vessels at sea, and the dip and variation of the magnetic needle, which new or improved instrument he intends to denominate "Sherwood's Magnetic Geometer," being a communication from a foreigner residing abroad. July 18; six months.

Henry Ross, of Leicester, worsted manufacturer, for improvements in machinery for combing and drawing wool and certain descriptions of hair. July 18; six months.

Henry Bridge Cowell, of Lower-street, Islington, ironmonger, for an improved apparatus answering the purpose of a press, for retaining and keeping leaves or pieces of paper, or of cloth or of other thin substances folded or unfolded in a flattened condition, under gentle pressure. July 18; six months.

John Robertson, of Great Charlotte-street, Buckingham-gate, for improvements of architecture in its forms and combinations, and also in the superficial figures which may be employed; also for an improvement or improvements in the surfaces of buildings. July 18; six months.

Richard Treffry, of Manchester, chemist, for certain improvements in the method of preserving certain animal and vegetable substances from decay, and also in the apparatus for and mode of impregnating substances to be preserved. July 28; six months.

George Richards Elkington, and Oglethorpe Wakelin Barratt, of Birmingham, manufacturers, for improvements in coating and colouring certain metals. July 24; six months.

Joseph Price, of Gateshead, Durham, flint glass manufacturer, for certain improvements in constructing and adapting boilers for marine, stationary, and locomotive engines, and in adapting and applying boilers to steam-vessels. July 26; six months.

Charles Wye Williams, of Liverpool, gentleman, for certain improvements in the means of preparing the vegetable material of peat, moss, or bog, so as to render it applicable to several useful purposes, and particularly for fuel. July 26; six months.

John Gray, of Liverpool, engineer, for certain improvements in steam-engines and apparatus connected therewith, which improvements are particularly applicable to marine engines for propelling boats or vessels, and part or parts of which improvements are also applicable to locomotive or stationary steam-engines and other purposes. July 26; six months.

William Madeley, of Manchester, machinist, for certain additions to, and improvements in, machinery used for spinning and forming into cops upon spindles, cotton, and other fibrous materials of the like nature. July 26; six months.

Sir William Burnett, knight, of Somerset House, for improvements in preserving wood and other vegetable matters from decay. July 26; six months.

Alexander Croll, of Greenwich, manufacturing chemist, for improvements in the manufacture of gas for the purpose of affording light. July 26; six months.

Frederic Edouard Fraissinet, of Covent Garden-square, Westminster, for certain improvements in the machinery for propelling vessels by steam, by which their speed will be much accelerated with a diminished power and with a diminished action in the water, being a communication from a foreigner residing abroad. July 26; six months.

LIST OF SCOTCH PATENTS GRANTED BETWEEN THE 22nd OF JUNE, AND THE 22nd OF JULY, 1838.

Joshua Taylor Beale, of No. 11, Church Lane, Whitechapel, Middlesex, engineer, for certain improvements in, and additions to his former invention known by the title of "A Lamp applicable to the burning of substances not hitherto usually burned in such vessels or apparatus." Sealed the 26th of June, 1838; four months to specify.

Edward Cobbold, of Long Melford, Suffolk, clerk, master of arts, for certain improvements in the manufacture of gas for affording light and heat, and in the application of certain products thereof to useful purposes. June 27.

Stephen Geary, of Hamilton-place, New-road, Middlesex, architect, for improvements in the preparation of fuel. June 27.

William Gossage, of Stoke Prior, Worcester, manufacturing chemist, for certain improvements in manufacturing sulphuric acid. June 29.

Francis Thorp, of Knaresborough, York, flax spinner, for certain improvements in machinery or apparatus for heckling, preparing, or dressing hemp, flax, and other such like fibrous materials. June 29.

Peter Fairbairn, of Leeds, York, machine-maker, for certain improvements in the machinery or apparatus for roving, spinning, doubling, and twisting cotton, flax, wool, silk, or other fibrous substances. July 6.

Henry Davies, of Stoke Prior, Worcester, engineer, for certain improved apparatus, or machinery for obtaining mechanical power, also for raising or impelling fluids, and for ascertaining the measure of fluids. July 11.

Edward Davy, of Fordton, near Crediton, Devon, merchant, for certain improvements in saddles and harness. July 11.

Frederick Joseph Burnett, of St. Mary-at-Hill, London, ship insurance agent, and Hippolyte Francois Marquis de Bouffet Montauban, colonel of cavalry, now residing in Sloane-street, Chelsea, Middlesex, in consequence of a communication from a foreigner residing abroad, for certain improvements in the manufacture of soap. July 11.

William Rattray, of Aberdeen, in North Britain, manufacturing chemist, for certain improvements in the manufacture of the preparations called gelatine size and glue. July 12.

Henry Count de Crony, of Picardy, France, now residing at No. 14, Cambridge-street, Edgware Road, Middlesex, for a new and improved method of filtration, communicated partly by a foreigner, and partly invented by himself. July 13.

Francis Pope, of Wolverhampton, Stafford, fancy iron worker, for certain improvements for making or manufacturing pins, bolts, nails and rivets, applicable to various useful purposes. July 13.

Bennet Woodcroft, of Mumps, Oldham, Lancaster, gent., for improvements in the construction of looms for weaving various sorts of cloths, which looms may be set in motion by any adequate power. July 19.

Charles Bourjot, of Coleman-street, London, merchant, in consequence of a communication made to him by a certain foreigner residing abroad, for improvements in the manufacture of iron. July 19.

Jean Leandre Clement, of Rochfort, France, but now of Jaunay's Hotel, Leicester-square, Middlesex, gent., for improvements in apparatus for ascertaining and indicating the rate of vessels passing through the water. July 19.

Thomas Nicholas Raper, of Greek-street, Soho, Middlesex, gent., for improvements in rendering fabrics and leather waterproof. July 19.

Luke Hebert, of High-street, Camden Town, Middlesex, in consequence of a communication from a foreigner residing abroad, for a new and improved method or methods of uniting or soldering metallic substances. July 19.

NOTES AND NOTICES.

Cheap Education for the Poor.—The friends to the rising generation of the working classes at Liverpool will be glad to learn that it has been determined to open a preparatory school in connexion with that already existing at the Mechanics' Institution. When the moderate charge for instruction is considered—only *six guineas* per annum, with a few extras—there cannot be a doubt that the labouring men of the "northern hive" will hasten to avail themselves of the advantages so completely within their reach, especially when it is remembered that the education so begun may be completed at the easy rate of *ten guineas* per annum.

Steam Navigation to Russia.—The St. George Steam-Packet Company advertise that their vessel, the *Sirius*, now absent on the voyage to New York, will, immediately on its return, proceed direct to Saint Petersburgh. This is, it is believed, the first instance of a direct steam voyage the whole way through, between the capitals of England and Russia, the usual route having been from London to Hamburgh per steamer, thence on land across Holstein (36 miles) to Lubeck or Travemendes, and thence by steamer again to Saint Petersburgh. The new route will be " the furthest way round," but will possess all the advantages attendant on single trips. The *Sirius* will stand a better chance of success in consequence of the comparative absence of competition caused by the recent destruction by fire of the Russian steam-vessel " Nikolay; I." which traded regularly between Luebeck and the city of the Czar,

Preventing Incrustations in Steam Boilers.—The following method employed by Captain Kennedy, commanding Her Britannic Majesty's steamer Spitfire, to prevent the incrustations or deposits of saline matter on the inside of the boilers of steam-engines, has been communicated by him in a letter to M. Gautier, of the French consulate at Malta. Captain Kennedy recommends, after having well cleaned the boilers and tubes, to coat those parts of their interior surface most exposed to the action of the fire with a mixture composed in the proportion of 18 pounds of melted suet and 3 pounds of powdered black lead. He states that the advantages of this application have been so fully tested by experience, that the Lords of the Admiralty have resolved that all the Government steamers shall for the future be provided with a sufficient quantity of the above-mentioned ingredients.—*French Paper.*

Railways.—As an evidence of the great increase of travelling attributable to the formation of railways, at present the number of passengers through Selby, on a moderate calculation, amount to 600 daily, whilst the number at a corresponding period of the year, previous to the Leeds and Selby Railway, did not exceed 50. The regularity of the departure and arrival of the trains, together with the facilities afforded for passengers' luggage, &c., are deservedly raising the management of the undertaking in public esteem, and we are happy to understand the business of the line is considerably and steadily on the increase.—*Leeds Intelligencer.*

Enterprise.—Mr. Mackintosh, the contractor for the line of the Midland Counties' Railway between this town and Rugby, and who is now supposed to be worth a million of money, was some years ago a gauger, or sub-contractor, in Scotland.—*Leicester Herald.*

Railway Map of England.—On the first of August will be published the Title, Index, and Contents to vol. 28 of the *Mechanics' Magazine*, and as a frontispiece to the volume a large map of the Railways in England and Wales, price 6d. The map alone on fine paper, price 6d. Also the volume complete, in half-cloth, price 8s. 6d.

☞ *British and Foreign Patents taken out with economy and despatch; Specifications, Disclaimers, and Amendments, prepared or revised; Caveats entered; and generally every Branch of Patent Business promptly transacted. A complete list of Patents from the earliest period (15 Car. II. 1675,) to the present time may be examined. Fee 2s. 6d.; Clients, gratis.*

LONDON: Printed and Published for the Proprietor, by W. A. Robertson, at the Mechanics' Magazine Office, No. 6, Peterborough-court, between 135 and 136, Fleet-street.—Sold by A. & W. Galignani, Rue Vivienne, Paris.

Mechanics' Magazine,

MUSEUM, REGISTER, JOURNAL, AND GAZETTE.

No. 782.]   SATURDÀY, AUGUST 4, 1838.   [Price 3*d*.

PEACOCK'S METALLIC PISTON.

Fig. 1.

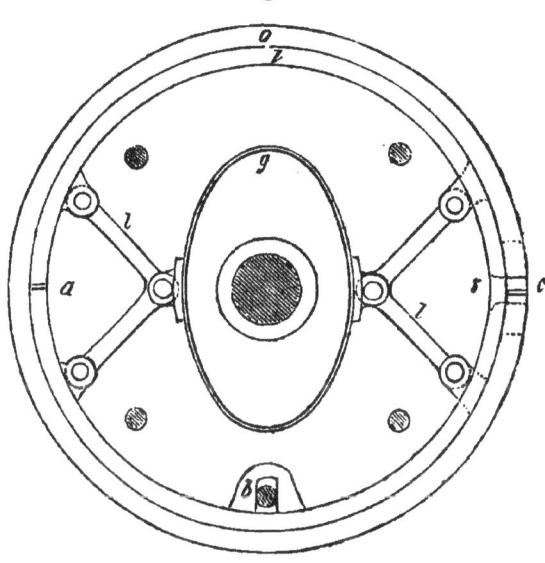

Fig. 2.

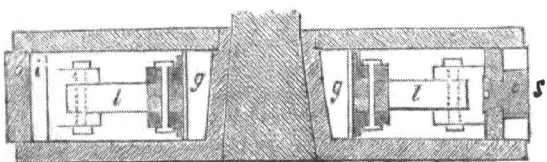

Fig. 3.

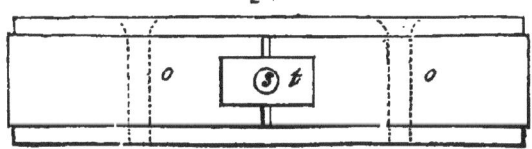

PEACOCK'S METALLIC PISTON.

Sir,—I have lately made a full-sized drawing of a metallic piston invented by a working engineer, Mr. Alexander Peacock; by his permission I have reduced it to the size of your page, and beg to hand it to you with the accompanying description, with a view of giving the public the benefit of his invention, through the medium of your extensively circulated Magazine.

The merit of this piston consists in the simplicity of its construction, having but one spring, which from its form and position cannot fail of acting.

He considers it peculiarly adapted for engines subjected to uneven work, and particularly for horizontal cylinders, and therefore very applicable to locomotives. Fig. 1 is a plan with the top lid or cover off. Fig. 2 a central section, and Fig. 3 an edge view; the same letters apply to the same parts in all the figures. o, the outer ring, is cut at c, and the tongue t is held in its place by the screw s, from the inner ring i; this inner ring is cut at a, on the opposite side. g is the elliptical, and only spring, put loose between the lower and upper covers; ll are two pairs of levers extending from the sides of the spring to the rings, one pair pressing immediately upon the outer, and the other upon the inner ring; these levers are connected at either end by a plain rule joint.

It will be readily seen that as the outer ring wears, the spring proportionally opens or extends, and pressing on the radial levers, and these against the ring, keeps it up to its work.

As it is material that a piston, particurlarly for a horizontal cylinder, should be always replaced in the same relative position to the cylinder, provision is made to ensure this by the screw b working in a slot cast upon the inner ring.

There is no necessity for occupying your columns by describing the other well-known parts of a piston, Several to whom I have shown it, agree in declaring this to be a good practical invention.

I remain, Sir,

Your very obedient servant,

WM. VERE.

Ratcliffe, July, 1838

THE USEFUL ARTS IN CHINA.

The literary labours of Protestant Missionaries have added but little to our knowledge of the countries in which they have been stationed, or the manners of their inhabitants. Many of them, indeed, seem to have held it a point of conscience to deprive their journals—such, at least, has been the case with those which have seen the light—as much as possible of all interesting information on mere mundane affairs; so that we have been presented with accounts of a residence in Siberia, or a tour in India, which, for aught of "special matter' contained in them, might as well have been written within the purlieus of Camden Town or Chelsea. There are symptoms abroad, however, of a change in this particular, and our stock of geographical knowledge has been not a little increased during the last few years, by the publications of English and American Missionaries. Another work of this better kind has just been added to the list,* and not at all too soon, if our modern missionaries may be expected to contribute to our acquaintance with China and the Chinese in anything like an equal ratio with their Catholic predecessors, to whom the "barbarian" world is indebted for all the most valuable information it possesses with regard to the Celestial Empire.

The greater portion of Mr. Medhurst's volume is occupied with the details of his proceedings in his mission, and especially of the celebrated voyage to the north of China, in the course of which Mr. M. persisted in repeatedly landing, in defiance of the constituted authorities, and distributing to the astonished natives a plentiful assortment of religious tracts, in their own language. What good purpose was likely to be served by this irregular proceeding does not very plainly appear; certain it is, that, as might be expected, it effectually roused the attention of the Chinese government; and, it is equally certain, that not a single step towards a freer intercourse has ever been gained by any of the numerous attempts

* China, its State and Prospects, with special reference to the Spread of the Gospel; containing Allusions to the Antiquity, Extent, Population, Civilization, Situation, and Religion of the Chinese. By W. H. Medhurst, of the London Missionary Society. Illustrated with Engravings on Wood by George Baxter. London, 1838. Snow. 8vo., pp. 596.

which have been made from time to time to carry matters with a high hand, and, in a manner, coerce the Chinese into liberality. On the occasion in question, the government was evidently taken by surprise, as it well might be,—but we question whether, now that its vigilance has been roused, a similar voyage, with similar proceedings on landing, would be at all practicable. Wonderful progress has often been made, for a short time, in forcing an intercourse in opposition to the Chinese authorities,—but it has uniformly happened that, in the end, those authorities have carried every contested point, and placed the assailing party in its former, if not even in a retrograde position. There is little reason to doubt that such would also be the result of any attempt to renew the strange transactions commemorated in Mr. Medhurst's work. The experiment will, most probably, be soon tried, and then *nous verrons!*

The narrative portion is preceded by several chapters devoted to the other subjects mentioned in the title-page, and among the rest, when " civilization" comes to be considered, to the state of the arts and manufactures—the truest touchstone of a nation's real position in the social scale. The whole of this part of the volume abounds in interest, and a few pages, extracted at random, would be almost certain to give a favourable opinion of our author's labours. Although, we are afraid, no inventions of equal importance to those of printing and gunpowder remain in the exclusive possession of the Chinese, some advantages might, nevertheless, accrue to the useful arts from a closer investigation than has ever hitherto been made into the processes which resemble in the main those of our western world, but which, from their having been necessarily perfected without any acquaintance with our corresponding methods, may very possibly present points of difference well worthy of notice and imitation, and at the same time not likely to be hit upon amongst those who have long looked on their own way as *the* way, and have, perhaps, from inveterate habit, never dreamt of the possibility of the existence of any other. In this manner the study of the long-established industrial processes of the Chinese may be turned to account; but there can be no question that, if a "re-

ciprocity system" were established to-morrow, the Chinese would have a thousand times more to borrow of the *outer barbarians* than the outer barbarians of the Chinese. The steam-engine alone would be a contribution from this side of the world which our tea-growing friends would find it rather difficult to balance, to say nothing of its endless applications to purposes of utility,—the printing-machine, for instance. This brings us to an interesting point. Notwithstanding all he has to say in its favour, the Chinese process of printing, as described by Mr. Medhurst, presents a striking contrast to the speedier operations with which the use of moveable types, combined with the indefatigable labours of the steam-press, have made us familiar. We quote Mr. Medhurst's description, as well for this reason, as from its being a fair specimen of his style of handling the subject.

" The mode of printing adopted by the Chinese is of the simplest character. Without expensive machinery, or a complicated process, they manage to throw off clear impressions of their books, in an expeditious manner. Stereotype, or block printing, seems to have taken the precedence of moveable types in all countries, and in China they have scarcely yet got beyond the original method.

* * * * *

" The use of wooden blocks has not been without its advantages; among which we may enumerate speed and cheapness. The first part of the process is, to get the page written out in the square or printed form of the character. This having been examined and corrected, is transferred to the wood in the following manner:—The block, after having been smoothly planed, is spread over with a glutinous paste; when the paper is applied and frequently rubbed, till it becomes dry. The paper is then removed, (as much of it as can be got away,) and the writing is found adhering to the board, in an inverted form. The whole is now covered with oil, to make the letters appear more vivid and striking, and the engraver proceeds to his business. The first operation is, to cut straight down by the sides of the letters, from top to bottom, removing the vacant spaces between the lines, with the exception of the stops. The workman then engraves all the lines which run horizontally; then, the oblique; and, afterwards, the perpendicular ones, throughout the whole page which saves the trouble of turning the block round for every letter. Having cut round the letters, he proceeds to the central parts; and, after a while, the page is completed. A workman generally gets through one hundred characters a day, for which he will get sixpence. A page generally contains five hundred characters. When the engraver has completed his work, it is passed into the hands of the printer, who places it in the middle of a table; on one side is a pot of liquid ink, with a brush; and on the o'her a pile of paper: while, in front, there is a piece of wood, bound round with the fibrous parts of a species of palm, which is to serve for a rubber. The workman then inks his block with the brush: and taking a sheet of dry paper, with his left hand, he places it neatly on the block; and seizing the rubber with his right hand, he passes it once or twice quickly over the back of the paper, when the impression is produced, the printed sheet hastily removed, and the workman proceeds with the next impression, till the whole number is worked off; and thus, without screw, lever, wheel, or wedge, a Chinese printer will manage to throw off 3000 impression in a day. After the copies are struck off, the next business is to fold the pages exactly in the middle; to collate, adjust, stitch, cut, and sew them; for all of which work, including the printing, the labourer does not receive more than ninepence a thousand. The whole apparatus of a printer, in that country, consists of his graves, blocks, and brushes; these he may shoulder and travel with, from place to place, purchasing paper and lamp-black as he needs them; and, borrowing a table anywhere, he may throw off his editions by the hundred or the score, as he is able to dispose of them. Their paper is thin, but cheap; ten sheets of demy size, costing only one half-penny. This, connected with the low price of labour, enables the Chinese to furnish books to each other for next to nothing. The works of Confucius, with the commentary of Choo-foo-tsze, comprising six volumes, and amounting to four hundred leaves, octavo, can be purchased for nine-pence; and the historical novel of the *three kingdoms*, amounting to 1500 leaves, in twenty volumes, can be had for half-a-crown. Of course, all these prices are what the natives charge to each other; for all which Europeans must expect to pay double.

"Thus books are multiplied, at a cheap rate, to an almost indefinite extent; and every peasant and pedlar has the common depositories of knowledge within his reach. It would not be hazarding too much to say, that in China there are more books, and more people to read them, than in any other country of the world."—p. 103.

Many of the praises here bestowed by Mr. Medhurst on the Chinese practice, must be taken with a very considerable allowance. We cannot very well see why the attribute of "speed" as well as "cheapness" is to be ascribed to it. From his statement it would appear that a workman is occupied five days in producing a block for a single page of a common size. What sort of "speed" is this, compared to that attained by the use of single types? And by what miracle would the Chinese, with their "speedy" method, manage to get out such a sheet as the double *Times*, in the course of a few hours? The thing is clearly impossible; and Mr. Medhurst would therefore have done better to adduce rapidity as one recommendation of a process, which in its very nature must be slow. The "cheapness" is also rather problematical. True, the expense of engraving a page does not strike the English reader as any way alarming; but engravers are not to be had everywhere for sixpence a day. The process is only comparatively, not positively cheap,—cheap not from its inherent simplicity, but merely on account of the cheapness of labour in China, from the overstocked state of the labour-market. Did the Chinese language admit of the introduction of moveable types, (which a former Emperor once attempted,) and were the Chinese acquainted with the art of typefounding, our system would be far cheaper than their own, it being recollected that where wood-engravers are to be had for sixpence a day, type-founders must be procurable at a proportionate sum. To make the matter clear, let us only imagine the reverse to take place,—the introduction of the Chinese method into England. Supposing our artist to be as expert as his Eastern prototype, and to be satisfied with six shillings a day, (no very extravagant wages, it will be owned,) here are at once thirty shillings for the labour alone of "setting up" a single page—and that, too, a page only of the extent of one of our *columns*, reckoning every "character" to represent a word. This, indeed, is allowing nothing for the casting of the types, but this may be set against the value of the Chinaman's block, which, it should be borne in mind, will serve for only one page, while the more expensive type may be distributed and set up again *ad in-finitum.*

The mode of obtaining the impression is a different matter altogether; in this case something is likely to be gained from an observation of the Chinese fashion. Our ideas are so bound up with "the press," that it appears to us an essential of "the glorious art;" and we are so often in the habit of toasting "the Liberty of the Press," that is seems almost sacrilegious to compass and imagine the printing of a book without its aid. Yet the Chinese have printed for ages without having heard of "the Press" at all! The great simplicity of their process is a most striking feature, while even the limited experience which has been had of it in England, (where a similar method is adopted for taking engravers' proofs, &c.,) is sufficient to demonstrate that it is compatible with the highest degree of typographical excellence. Would it not be worth the while of some of our ingenious mechanics to turn their thoughts in this direction? Ingenuity has been lavishly bestowed on the improvement of the printing press, until the maximum of power in that engine may be presumed to be attained. Why not try invention on another tack, and apply English skill in machinery to the perfecting of a mode of printing on the Chinese plan, where the impression is obtained by gentle friction, instead of a tremendous direct impression? Could this be achieved, it would probably be one of its not least important results, that type might be made of a much less valuable material than at present, and by a much less expensive and elaborate method. At any rate the attempt is worth making,—though it would probably be necessary to commence by introducing a much softer texture of paper than that now used, and, perhaps, to print, like the Chinese, on one side only.

Mr. Medhurst is again, towards the conclusion of our extract, rather too solicitous to exalt the cheapness of Chinese literature. The number of volumes to be had for a few pence may seem rather startling, but then he should have stated, that volumes of Chinese books are by no means of such substantial dimensions as our own. For instance, the six volumes of Confucius, it appears, contained altogether only four hundred leaves, (that is, four hundred *pages*, being printed on one side only,) containing only about half as much as a common English volume of the octavo size. Nine-pence certainly seems low enough for this quantity of matter, but then this sum of nine-pence in China, be it remembered, forms the whole earnings of an artist for a day and a half; so that, all things considered, it is evident that our own standard works are sold at a much lower rate than this much-vaunted and inconceivably cheap edition of the great Chinese classic. If books, therefore, are sold in China for "next to nothing," what are we to think of the price of such commodities at home? It would be as well for Mr. Medhurst to avoid such mystification for the future.

The present work, in all its mechanical details, is well got up. It is illustrated by several well-executed wood-cuts; the frontispiece especially, which represents the author seated opposite to a learned young Chinese, (who accompanied Mr. M. to England, and addressed a number of public meetings in his own language,) is remarkable both for the interest of the subject, and the excellent style in which it has been engraved and printed in colours by Mr. Baxter's patent process.

INDIAN STEAM NAVIGATION—REPLY TO MR. BAYLEY.

Sir,—Mr. Bayley (page 262) seems so obstinately bent on taking the alarm at the *intended* progress of the Dutch in Indian steam navigation, that it would be useless to waste any more discussion on that subject, especially as Mr. B. is probably the only "constant reader" of the *Mechanics' Magazine* who remains in the same state of needless excitement, after the perusal of the facts admitted by that gentleman himself in his former letter. There are one or two things, however, in his last, which call imperiously for observation.

For one thing, Mr. Bayley intimates that no such vessel as a private steamer has been heard of in India. To convince him of the fact, nevertheless, recourse need only be had to the pages of a work of which he calls himself a "constant reader," although, if he be so, he is certainly a most forgetful one. I have before taken the liberty to refer him to the 21st vol. of the *Mechanics' Magazine* for an article on that very plan of the Messrs. Seaward, as to which he had avowed his entire ignorance. I now beg him to turn to page 272 of the same volume, where he will find a notice of an intended voyage of the steamer *Forbes*, from Kedgeree to Suez (an Indian and an Arabian port) so "long ago" as the year 1834. Nor was she then by any means a novelty, on the contrary, she had been a familiar visiter for years before at many of our Indian ports, besides her native one of Calcutta; and, as she was built expressly for her owners, Messrs. Mackintosh and Co., and employed on their account, I suppose she may be taken as an example of a steamer "not belonging to the Company." Is this instance satisfactory; if not, what will be?

Mr. Bayley would do well to study the work above referred to a little more closely than he has been accustomed to. This will save him many a blunder, and his readers many a smile at his expense. It would have prevented him, for in-instance, from talking so learnedly of the attempt to render steam navigation available in "the Tigris," a river as yet never disturbed by the revolution of a paddle-wheel. The "Euphrates Expedition," has, indeed, often been noticed in the *Mechanics' Magazine*, but the discovery that much valuable time and talent had been wasted in the endeavour to steam along the *Tigris* was reserved for Mr. Bayley,—and much honour may it do to his name!

. Mr. B. is very wroth with the East India Company for standing in the way of the steam communication project, as recommended by the Committee of 1824, in opposition, as he appears to think, to "the Government." Here, again, I need only refer him to the *Mechanics' Magazine*, at page 183 of the last volume of which, he will find a statement, abridged from that made before the Parliamentary Committee of 1837, by the President of the Board of Controul, from which it is evident, that the delay in carrying that recommendation into effect was caused by "the Government" in opposition to the East India Company. Mr. Bayley will then perceive that his high-sounding tirade has been completely thrown

away, and only served to make him ridiculous in the eyes of those "constant readers" who have a rather better memory than himself. That he is a "constant reader," there is, of course, no doubt :—he says so; and therefore "I must believe him,"—but most certainly, his memory must be very treacherous!

There is yet another point, on which a re-perusal of your "valuable journal" might be useful. Mr. B. alludes to a late Parliamentary return as showing the great want of steam navigation in our colonies. But why stop there? Why not tell us the number of steamers possessed by Holland—that country of which we are to hold ourselves in fear? This is done in the Magazine, No. 277, page 217, where it appears the Dutch actually own *twenty-eight* steam vessels, while the supine English, as Mr. Bayley horrifies us by telling, have only *six hundred* at home, and no more than *thirty-nine* in the colonies! Is it not high time to better ourselves, if we would hinder the Dutch from "monopolizing" steam altogether? Recollect, we have only eleven more vessels of the kind in our colonies, than they have in their colonies and at home into the bargain! Will Mr. Bayley be kind enough to inform us *how many* of these are already employed in navigating the Indian Archipelago?

Mr. Bayley has displayed such amazing ignorance on every part of the subject, that it may be possible that he thinks the five vessels whose names he gives compose the whole of our East Indian steam flotilla. This, however, is as egregious a blunder as any of the rest, since the arrival out of Col. Chesney's expedition, the *Euphrates* may of course be added to the number, and a gentleman of Mr. Bayley's pretensions ought also to have known that four large iron steamers were "sent out from this country" so "long ago" as the year 1834, for the navigation of the Ganges, adding not a little to the strength of our aforesaid "steam-flotilla." The *Hoogly* and the *Burrampooter*, he will find upon inquiry, were members of the "steam flotilla" at a still earlier date. Thus, then, we have at least twelve vessels instead of five, besides five more (accord to Mr. Bayley's own account) in preparation; and all these to balance "*some*" steamers which the Dutch "*are build-*

ing in the Indian Archipelago! Is this a state of things to raise alarm, or to justify it when created? I may as well spare the endeavour to beat Mr. Bayley from his position, when he has the courage to maintain it in the face of such facts as these.

I come now to the alleged "error of the press" in Mr. Bayley's former letter; and here I must object to his proposed correction, for two good reasons. The first is, that the substitution of "we" for "he" in the sentence referred to, would make bad English of the whole passage: this is not much, to be sure, but the second objection is fatal. If the new reading be admitted, Mr. Bayley must be taken to have alluded to *himself* as a person having "access to the sources of early and accurate information upon maritime subjects." Now, how was any one to suspect that this description could possibly be intended to apply to the perpetrator of all the blunders I have just exposed? The poor compositor at any rate is not to blame for restoring something like grammar and common sense to a paragraph, which, according to its author, was originally destitute of either.

I need not take up your space in exposing once again Mr. B.'s sudden conversion to Messrs. Seaward's ten-miles-an-hour theory. The facts are before your readers, all of whom, probably, are not blessed with such a singular mnemonic conformation as Mr. Bayley. I will only observe, that he has "veered round" on more points than one: for instance, he grounded his opinion originally on the performances of our home steamers, while now he refers exclusively to the performances of the *Atalanta* and *Berenice* on their voyage to India, and states that he founded his calculations on the data they afforded. Was this from shortness of memory again?

Once more, and I have done. In this case I only think it necessary to contrast a representation in Mr. Bayley's last communication with a verbatim extract from the letter of "Piston's" to which the passage refers. Let them appear opposite to each other, and Mr. B.'s unhappy failing will show itself in so strong a light as not to need a word of comment.

Mr. Bayley, page 263.	'Piston' (not 'H') p. 149.
"'Piston' states, that some steamers, which he names, did reach the speed of 13¼, 13½, and 13¼ miles per hour, when tried under favourable circumstances (*without passengers*, or more than a moderate supply of coals on board, mind); *from this* H. ventures to assert, that they have reached the astonishing speed of twenty miles an hour."	"On three different occasions last season, the *Ruby* made the passage from London to Gravesend *with passengers*, including stoppages, in one hour and thirty-five minutes, which, allowing five minutes for stoppages and interruptions, would make the time of running 1½ hours; the distance is computed to be thirty miles, here then, Mr. Editor, is *twenty miles per hour!*"

So much for "misrepresentation," and "disingenuousness," leaving the readers of the *Mechanics' Magazine* to decide *with whom* these charges ought to rest.

Yours most respectfully, H.

July 25, 1888.

CHAPLIN'S NON-ELASTIC LEATHER BANDS.

Sir,—It may, perhaps, be interesting to some of your readers to be informed, that a method has at length been discovered of manufacturing leather, for machine straps or bands, which is nearly or quite free from any tendency to stretch. This is accomplished by the new method of tanning, which lately attracted some notice in your pages, and of which I am the inventor. The hide, in its elastic state, before it is tanned, is made into a bag, by sewing the edges together, and then filled with tanning liquor, the pressure of which forces it through the pores, so that it comes out on the other side, leaving the tannin which it contained in combination with the hide—the result sought by the tanner. In this way the hide is, of course, completely opened and extended, and kept so during the whole process; so that, when the leather is afterwards subjected to strain or pressure, very little further extension can be obtained.

The singular difficulty experienced in various applications of this very peculiar kind of leather, where the workman is accustomed to take advantage of the elasticity of ordinary materials, has suggested its application to the purposes of machinery; and the experiments which have yet been made, fully justify the expectation I was induced to entertain—that leather so prepared would be, to a very considerable extent, free from the common and very inconvenient objection. Whether this may be confirmed, or the contrary, by more varied and extensive trials, I cannot of course say; but if any of your readers should think it worth their while to put it to a practical test, I shall be happy to supply, at a price not exceeding the cost of ordinary leather, either hides ready dressed for the purpose, or straps made ready for use, of any required dimensions. Yours, &c.

FRED. CHAPLIN.

Bishops Stortford, July 23, 1838.

METHOD OF CUTTING OFF THE HEAD OF AN IMAGE WITHOUT REMOVING IT.—BY THE LATE MR. W. ETTRICK.

Sir,—As the image exhibited at the Adelaide Rooms in the Lowther Arcade, London, whose head is apparently severed from the body by a knife, and after such operation cannot be removed, must have been seen by wondering thousands, it may not be amiss to show how the thing may be accomplished—though I do not

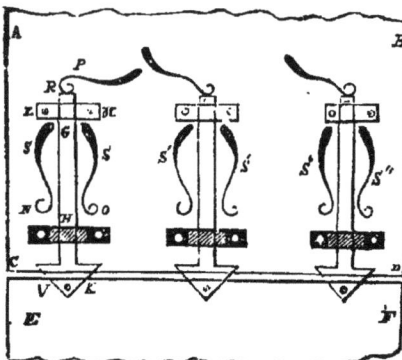

pretend to say that the method, here given, is the one there used; but if not, I make no doubt it would answer equally well. It may be thought by some, that the publication of such trivial things, occupy the pages of a valuable Magazine uselessly; but I must beg to dissent from

such an opinion, as it shows a neat method of locking and unlocking pieces of machinery.

Description.—A, B, C, D, part of the head, or rather, upper part of the neck,—and E, F, part of the body, or rather, lower part of the neck, there being a small distance between the two parts to allow of the passage of the blade of the knife: G, H, K, a slide, or solid piece of iron, one-eighth of an inch thick, made to slide in pieces of iron L, M, N, O. The sliding piece G, H, K, has no side-motion in L, M, only vertical; but in N, O, it has, both; the side-motion being from one dark part or side to the other, these acting the part of banking-pins. The slide is forced down by a spring, P, but it is stopped by a pin, o, near R. The slide has a spring at each side S, N, S, O, which *just touch it* when in the middle between the banking pins N, O, but apply no force till the slide is forced to one side, so as to touch, or nearly touch, the banking pins. There is a *flat* pin in G, H, K, at o near K, which is for the purpose of laying hold of a similar pin in the neck, or lower piece, E, F. The pin in G, H, K, has hold of the pin in E, F, when the slide is in the centre between the banking-pins; but when forced a-side so as to touch either of the banking-pins, it is let loose, and then has a free motion upwards. If we take a thin knife, and introduce it at C, E, it will strike against the inclined plane V, and force the slide G, H, K, against the banking-pin o, when, not being allowed to go further to the right, the inclined plane V will cause the slide to rise upwards, and allow the knife to pass under the point of K, so as to go on to the next slide. The knife must clear one slide before it takes another, consequently, two have always hold of their pins.

W. ETTRICK.

High Barns, Sunderland, Dec. 16, 1837.

ENGRAVING BY MACHINERY.

Mr. Bate's medal-engraving machinery has not been allowed to be idle, although we are not daily greeted with puffing paragraphs and flaming advertisements, as was the case in respect to the publications of his foreign rivals. In the able hands of Mr. Freebairn justice will be done to British fine art, and mechanical genius. The invention has lately been applied, with success, to engraving in re-lief, and the medallion head of the Queen in that beautiful specimen of typography the *Golden Sun*, was executed by Mr. Freebairn with Mr. Bate's apparatus. That the relief must be good is evidenced by the immense number which has been issued of that publication.

In steel engraving, by the machine, two beautiful works have lately been pub-lished, one the bas-relief design from a salver, by the celebrated Jean Gougou, and the other a head of the Duke of Wellington. Gougou's salver, of which the engraving is a fac-simile, is nineteen inches in diameter, and one of the most elaborate and beautiful specimens of the art of metal-chasing, executed at a period when that art was practised to a far greater extent than in the present day, and by none more successfully than Jean Gougou. The design is divided into se-veral compartments, containing groups of figures, emblematical of the four quarters of the globe, their principal conquerors, and the four seasons; the intermediate spaces being filled up with exquisitely-finished ornaments of the style which prevailed in the 16th century, the era in which Jean Gougou flourished. Mr. Freebairn's engraving is the most clear, distinct, and brilliant representation of this rare work imaginable; the effect of the relief is beautifully deceptive, and is heightened by the metallic colour of the ink in which the engraving is printed; the most minute details are given with perfect accuracy, and the drawing, both of the figures and ornaments, is pre-served with a fidelity that reflects the highest credit on the skill of the artist, and the accurate working of the machine.

MR. NUTTALL'S MODE OF ENGRAVING IN RELIEF.

Sir,—In your Number for the 7th of July, you have inserted an abstract of Mr. Woone's patent for what he calls a new method of engraving. Now it hap-pens, that the very same system was practised by myself upwards of five years ago; but I found the plan did not an-swer for the purposes of shading, or de-signing minute objects; nor do I believe that it can ever be made to answer, not only on account of the difficulty of drawing fine lines and shades on the composition Mr. Woone recommends, but also the utter impossibility of producing perfect

casts on metallic substances, as any caster of stereotype plates will inform him; for the moment his composition, mould is subjected to the heat of the furnace, it will crack, and fly from the body to which it was attached, whether wood, stone, or iron. Attempts at the above, however, eventually led to ano-ther mode of engraving, by which I have been enabled to produce fac-similes of shaded designs, maps, plans, &c.; some of which have appeared in the *Gentle-man's Diary, Gentleman's Magazine, Ar-cheologia*, and other works, with which I happened to be editorially or typogra-phically connected.

At this time, I only want the co-operation of a skilful and confidential artist, not being one myself, to bring the invention into full operation. As to a patent, I am convinced, it would be no protection; and therefore, secrecy alone likely-to secure any future advantage.

The inclosed are two roughly printed specimens.

Yours, &c.

P. NUTTALL.

1, Gough-square, July 16, 1838.

[The specimens sent us by Mr. Nut-tall, consist of a view of an ancient gate-way, and a head of Virgil, under which is printed the following note, "This HEAD of VIRGIL, as being the first rude specimen of a new chemico-mechanical art, invented by the editor of these Bucolics, and executed without the agency of wood, stone, or metal of any kind, is given as a curious graphic novelty. Thus, from a simple drawing myriads of copies may be produced with almost the same ease and certainty as common letter-press printing." The specimens prove that Mr. N.'s plan is one capable of being carried to great beauty of execu-tion, in experienced hands; the relief appears from the indentation upon the paper impressed, to be considerable—and the lines are fine, and clear. As we mentioned of Mr. Woone's plan, however, the object to be obtained is not beauty, but rapidity of execution.—ED. M. M.]

ON THE CLASSIFICATION OF PUMPS.— MR. BADDELEY'S REPLY TO "NAU-TILUS."

Sir,—I am much obliged to "Nau-tilus" for pointing out an error into which I had fallen, while endeavouring to set Mr. Mills right with reference to his mercurial pump. (vide page 281.) As "Nautilus" very justly observes, in your last Number, I certainly did make a "most extraordinary blunder," in calling that machine a *lifting* force-pump; it is in reality a *force-pump*.

By common consent it has become the practice to divide pumps generally into three classes, viz., the common suction-pump, the force-pump, and the lifting force-pump. The first class are distinguished by a valved piston working in an open-topped cylinder; the second class have a solid piston; while the third description have a valved piston working in a close-topped cylinder, the piston rod moving through a stuffing box, and thereby converting the machine into a forcing-pump to any extent in the lift.

Most of the pumps in common use are readily assigned to one or other of these classes; but, among the philosophical toys of the lecture-table nondescripts are of frequent occurrence. It should be borne in mind, that by far the greater number of pumps depend for their first action upon *suction* (I am quite content to use this expressive and well-understood term in the absence of a better), and it is only after the barrel has been filled by suction that the peculiar office commences which fixes the character of the pump, and assigns it to one of the three classes enumerated above. The term "common suction pump," is exclusively applied to the simplest form of pump, having one valve in the piston and another at the bottom of the working barrel, and only capable of raising water to the top of its own barrel.

Although I have sadly blundered, I think "Nautilus" will see that, after all, my mistake will not afford a peg for Mr. Mills to hang a rejoinder upon—especially after the dressing he has received at the hands of our lynx-eyed friend.

I remain, Sir, yours respectfully,
WM. BADDELEY.

London, July 31, 1838.

OBSERVATIONS ON DUTY AND HORSE POWER.—BY J. S. ENYS. ESQ.

(From the Cornwall Polytechnic Society's Report.)

The origin of the term *duty* in Cornwall, and *horse power* in the rest of the kingdom, may be readily traced to the different circumstances under which Watt's low pressure engine was introduced, and the different nature of his agreement with the miner, and manufacturer. The former was in possession of a powerful but expensive machine, by whose means a new era of mining had been commenced, and the reduction of the coal expenditure was his object; while the latter was in want of means of entering into competition with water power, and of rendering the coal itself, and the fertile districts in which it is often found, available for manufacturing purposes.

In several of the deepest Cornish mines of that period, the exertions of the adventurers were paralysed, since the water charge approximated to, or even exceeded the returns of ore, while favorable mining symptoms urged on an extended trial. The characteristic caution of miners in the introduction of new machinery on property, whose value was not above two or three years' purchase, is apparent, in the agreement that Watt should receive one-third of the savings accruing in the performance of an equal amount of work by his engine in comparison with Newcomen's. The range of load of the latter engine, is nearly as great as in Watt's low pressure engine; and in both the number of strokes per minute are regulated by the same means, and it remained in nearly general use in coal mines until after the expiration of Watt's patent, and even then the most essential parts of the patent—the air pump, and condensing pipe for the injection water—were often added to old engines of Newcomen's construction.

The atmospheric engine thus improved, would not be much inferior to Watt's engines, when worked at full pressure, in the performance of mining duty, if equally well constructed. The determination of Messrs. Boulton and Watts, to force their steam pressure engine into use, instead of consenting to receive a share of the savings of coal, on a similar agreement for the application of the air pumps and condensing pipes to the old atmospheric engines, caused a large outlay of capital in Cornwall, from the necessity of taking these engines, at first, at prices far above their value, and of erecting the patent engine at a moderate charge, with a view to repayment, by the annual payments of the coal savings; with the exception, that these savings might be redeemed at ten years' purchase, Watt steadily adhered to the terms originally proposed, which proved exceedingly favorable to the patentees, inasmuch as the duty due to improvements in the pitwork and boilers, which were equally applicable to Newcomen's engines, more than counterbalanced the disadvantage in many shafts, which was unavoidably caused by their increase of depth, arising from the lessened coal expenditure, the patentees are supposed to have received nearly £189,000.

continue of the profit of erecting engines during the latter years of their patent.

In 1781, three years after these arrangements, Hornblower, a descendant of one of the engineers brought into Cornwall by Newcomen, took out a patent for the double cylinder engine, to work steam expansively; and in the ensuing year, Boulton and Watt's second patent appeared for a similar application of steam in a single cylinder, together with six patent contrivances for equalising its effect. This patent included the double acting engine, a contrivance which by lightening the fly-wheel, and from its compactness and double power in the same space, facilitated the introduction of the steam engine for manufacturing purposes. It also seemed a favorite with its inventor for mines, though now totally abandoned, as it either requires a balance, or a double column of pumps in the shaft, and hence increased friction, with a double chance of stoppages from accidents. By means of double action, however, a considerably greater power was obtained by a double acting 63-inch cylinder, than had been before afforded by a 72-inch atmospheric engine, which was necessarily single acting. Probably Messrs. Boulton and Watt had not tools capable of boring cylinders larger than 63-inches in diameter, with sufficient accuracy—at least, they never ventured to erect any of a larger size; and even then, only single acting—though after 1800 double acting 63's were used.

Expansion in the last fourth part of the stroke, and even to a greater extent with a light load, was soon used by Watt in pumping engines, often as much to guard against too great an acceleration of the piston towards the end of the stroke—from the reduced resistances of the pitwork, as soon as its inertia, and that of the water in the bucket pumps of that period, had been overcome by the constant steam pressure—as for economy of fuel.

The requisite conditions for the coincidence of the practical and theoretical advantage of the expansive action of steam, were not ascertained until a more recent period, when high steam was used expansively, to produce a mean pressure equivalent to, and often exceeding, that of steam of 2½ lbs. above atmospheric strength, used at full pressure. After a sharp contest of about fifteen years, during which Watt's counter was again used to decide on the relative performances, by registering the number of strokes made per bushel of coal, between Woolf, in a double cylinder engine, and the other mining engineers, in Watt's engine, assisted by Trevithick's cylindrical boilers, —all using high steam expansively—a preference has been given to the single cylinder

engines, which are now alone used in Cornwall for pumping. Woolf himself was often obliged by the managers of mines, to erect single engines; and the engine bearing his name at Consols, took a leading place in the performance of a duty above 60 millions, but was soon excelled by Wilson's engine at Wheal Towan.

During a period of 70 years, the method of estimating the work performed by the load in the shaft, and by the space through which it is lifted by the steam produced during the average time of the consumption of each bushel of coal, has been in constant use,—the result is an expression in lbs. lifted one foot high, which was termed by Watt, the duty of the engine.

The recent act of parliament for the substitution of the imperial bushel (94 lbs.) instead of the Winchester of 90 lbs, both weighed damp from open yards, has caused a change that should not be neglected—and Watt's duty of 27 millions in the Cornish mines, must be increased to about 30 millions.

The manufacturer is unable by equivalent methods to ascertain the work performed in lbs. one foot high, and moreover his object was a moving power within certain limits of expense, which would afford him a choice of situation free from winter floods—or deficient power in summer, and capable of unlimited extension.

The obvious basis for the supply of such power, was that which could be exerted by a horse, and this had been estimated from actual work in pumping water,—exclusive of friction, &c., &c., by Smeaton, at 22,000 lbs. one foot high,—and by other persons at a higher rate,—but whether exclusive or inclusive of machinery or pitwork resistances, (a point too much neglected in technical terms at least,) is not quite clear.

To prevent disputes on this point, Watt seems to have added one half to Smeaton's estimate of horse power, and fixed the surplus steam pressure,—which should be considered equal to a horse power, after engine resistances were deducted, at 33,000 lbs. one foot high, which is equal to a steady draught of 150 lbs. like a weight over a pulley, for 8 hours, at 2¼ miles per hour.*

The power of a horse is always partly expended in overcoming the resistances of the machinery necessary for its conversion into the pressure and velocity required, and even in the simplest case, the weight of the waggon employed in the conveyance of goods.

---

* The nomical HP. of engines has been sometimes × by 3 for the relays of Horses requisite for constant work during 24 hours—and again by 1½ to allow for the inferiority of Cornish horses, by this process, mining engines of 200 HP. have been called 900 HP.

The essential distinction of duty is, that it is founded on the load either actual, or calculated exclusive of such resistances.

When these are included, the power to produce motion being always one of them, to reduce it to a simple statical question, the term *effect* would prevent confusion, and it would be equal to the H.P., as measured by the surplus or effective steam pressure, after the engine resistances are deducted, by the space of action of the piston per minute.

In mining engines, the duty has always been calculated from the weight of a column of water, equal in diameter to the working part of the pumps, without any allowances for short strokes and other causes, and the practice seems occasionally to have been adopted, of considering the resistances of the pitwork balanced by the deficiency of the actual, in comparison with the calculated delivery of water,—in which case, by substituting the space passed over per minute, instead of the space per bushel of coal—the effect = the H.P. of the engine will be obtained in lbs. one foot high from the calculated load for duty. Suppose for example, that Davey's engine, an 80-inch cylinder, Consols, makes 400 strokes, and consumes 4 bushels of coal per hour, a close approximation to the facts— the space of motion in the shaft is 58¼ feet per minute,—and 875 feet per bushel of coal—the pump stroke being 8¼ feet.

Load in the shaft in lbs.   Feet.   Effect H.P.
    Hence 85530 ×   58¼ = 4,87925 = 148
                           875 = 74.827750 Duty,
or 2.54lbs. of coal per H.P. per hour.

In consequence of greater attention to the full length of the strokes, and the improved state of the pitwork, the deficiency of water delivery is less than at any former period,— the friction has been greatly decreased, where main and pump rods are of equal lengths,—but the depth of many shafts have been nearly trebled, since Watt's engines were first erected. Possibly the following estimate of the effect, H.P., in deep shafts, will be a fairer approximation than the first method. Davey's engine works in a shaft 290 fathoms deep from the surface, in which about 300 tons are put into motion at each stroke, though all, except the load, is balanced—

Calculated load 85·530lbs.
¼Deficiency.. 10·691 from various causes.

Actual load ... 74·839
¼Resistances.. 18·709

Effect Load .. 93·548 + 58¼ft. = 171 Effect
                                              H.P.
2·08lbs. of coal per H.P. per hour.

It is obvious that the denomination of the units of which duty is composed, may be changed at pleasure, and that either of them may be made the varying quantity : thus a duty of 70·000·000, the average of the 12 or 13 best engines reported, may be expressed, as a bushel of coal (94lbs.) lifting its neighbour 146 miles high—and the largest known moveable unit,—an 120 gun ship, fully equipped, if left by the tide, would be lifted off the beach, 7 feet high, by a bushel of coal.

In the railroad form, which is strictly a duty, though the term does not seem to be yet applied, it becomes, on the supposition that 1 ton is equal to 8lbs. over a pulley—1 ton, 1 mile per ·057lbs. of coal—in such estimates the weight of the locomotive engine should be taken as part of the neat load, and under such circumstances, if the duty was 1 ton, 1 mile, per 1lb. of coal, it would be expressed in the Cornish method by 3·969·560lbs. one foot high, or just four millions duty.

As the importance of the economy of fuel became felt in manufactories, the comparative estimate of the quantity expended, was commenced in the form of lbs. of coal per H.P., per hour ; a method well known, from its general application to steam boats—but neither this, or any expression derived from this source, such as the number of miles 1 ton of coal will impel 1-horse power—ought to be termed a duty ; at least, if an usage of more than 60 years can give any claim to the use of the technical word, with a defined meaning.

The load for duty would be the draught in lbs. due to the area of the midship section, with the given stern and bow angles.

The load for effect, would be the pressure due to the area and number of the paddles × by the difference of the squares of the velocities of the wheel and vessel + the friction of the levers and the shaft—the difficulty of ascertaining these points, which would be very great in smooth water, and which would be much enhanced in rough weather, has probably led to the adoption of the nominal H.P., as an unit in the comparative estimate of the fuel expended—the H.P. exerted would afford a better test—since the former is obtained from an estimated surplus steam pressure on the piston, notoriously less than that which is exerted in modern engines × by the space of action of the piston, which is taken at from 200 to 220 feet per minute.

In fine weather, these engines are generally worked from the above cause, at one fourth more than their nominal horse power, and this difference is greater whenever a a load exceeding 2¼lbs. per square inch, is placed on the safety valve.

In rough weather, however, from the reduction in the number of strokes, the actual H.P. exerted is less than the nominal.

Public attention seems fully directed to the reduction of the coal expenditure, which is of the utmost importance to steam boats, whose power of making distant voyages increases inversely as their coal consumption is lessened, either by improvements in the forms of the vessels,—lessened engine's resistances,—improved boilers or paddle-wheels,—or from obtaining a greater power from a given quantity of steam.

This latter cause, expansion, will probably be first found advantageous in steam tugs, where steam of 10 or 12lbs. above atmospheric strength, might be used at full pressure, for large ships, which might be reduced by expansion as required, for smaller vessels, or even as at present, throttled before expansion with a light load: the power of such engines is easily adapted to the work to be performed, and if well managed, the coal used would be proportional to the work performed; but like the large Cornish engines, which use steam of 20 or 30lbs. above atmospheric strength, from 3 to 6 times expansively in the cylinder, the usual methods of estimating the nominal horse power from the load on the safety valve, are inapplicable. The load, on the safety valve, particulary in Cornish engines, where no escape of steam is allowed, is sometimes from 10 to 12lbs. above the steam pressure requisite to work the engine.

MARSHAL SOULT'S VISIT TO THE BIRMINGHAM WORKSHOPS.

At the late visit of Marshal Soult to Birmingham, he was escorted by some of the first manufacturers of the town, over its workshops. The Marshal observed, that his friends in the iron and coal districts were so kind and pressing for him to remain there longer, and he was so struck with the wonders produced by their industry and ability, that had he staid a week, there would have been at the end of it still much to be seen and admired. "You are an extraordinary people," observed the Duke, "your ingenuity and activity know no bounds." The Marshal declined all refreshment, and expressed his anxiety to visit at once those extraordinary magazines of invention, the Birmingham workshops. Three carriages were in readiness, into which the Marshal and his suit were conducted, and, attended by the High and Low Bailiffs, F. Lloyd, Esq., and G. R. Collis, Esq., (the French Vice-Consul,) set off in the first place to the manufactory of the last-named gentleman, in Church-street. Here, it it well known, are struck some of the most beautiful specimens of English medals, and every species of bronzes, vases, plate, and lamps, are manufactured. With the "Warwick Vase," and its splendid proportions, the party were much pleased, and expressed their admiration very warmly. In the Marshal's presence, and in less than two minutes was struck, by Mr. Collis, a large three-inch coronation medal, bearing an excellent likeness of her Majesty, and Mr. Collis presented his distinguished visiter with a similar one in silver. After spending nearly an hour amidst the various branches of this manufactory, the whole of which drew from the Marshal expressions of surprise and pleasure, the party were taken to the extensive gun-barrel manufactory of the Messrs. Sergeants,—and here his Excellency made numerous inquiries, as to the kind of metal used in the manufacture—the time of completing a barrel—the cost of it—the charge to the government—the charge to the merchant and the exporter—the locks—whether percussion was thought of as likely to answer, &c. &c., to all which queries the Messrs. Sergeants gave him the fullest answers: and he appeared to listen to his interpreter (Mr. Manby) with greater interest on this branch of trade than any other he visited during the day. Most of the gentlemen composing the Marshal's suite being military men, and not unacquainted (at least the elder ones) with the efficiency of English muskets, availed themselves of the opportunity of learning all they could about their manufacture. With the sword-grinding, also carried on extensively at this manufactory, they appeared likewise highly interested. The party were next taken to the establishment of Messrs. Jennens and Bettridge, the celebrated *papier maché* manufacturers, where they staid some time, and were much gratified while intently surveying the workmen as they fabricated the beautiful tea trays, screens, work-tables, boxes, and other highly-finished ornaments of japanned ware. From hence they drove to the Britannia nail works, belonging to T. M. Jones, Esq., and the transition from the delicate and ornamental, to the powerful, ponderous, and useful, appeared to gratify them very much. The machinery, worked by steam, which keeps employed some hundred hands, making above a thousand nails a-minute, of all sizes, from the small boot-tack to the ten-penny nail, (five inches in length,) was, as might be expected, the amazement of the foreigners; and the din of so many machines working at one time, rendering any conversation entirely inaudible, made the Marshal remark, that " he could almost fancy himself amidst the roar of British cannon, instead of those mighty emblems of England's power in peace." From hence they were escorted to the button manufactory of Messrs. Turner and Sons, and saw another source of Birmingham's wealth. His Excellency having expressed a strong desire to see the manufacture of button shanks by machinery, again visited Mr. Collis's establishment, where he had an opportunity of witnessing this ingenious process. Previous to his departure he wrote a few lines in French in the visiter's book, expressive of his admiration of all he had seen, and the courtesy and attention he had experienced from the proprietor. Thence to the Town Hall, which building the Marshal declared he had seldom, if ever, seen surpassed for classic beauty of design. Mr. Hollins performed some pieces on the magnificent organ, for the purpose of affording his Excellency an opportunity of witnessing its powers, and all the company expressed themselves greatly delighted—*Midland Counties' Herald.*

TRIAL OF ANTHRACITE COAL IN LOCOMOTIVE ENGINES.

We understand, that, on Friday last, a trial was made, on the Liverpool and Manchester railway, of the applicability of anthracite coal, as a fuel for locomotive engines, under the superintendance of Mr. Woods, the talented engineer of that line, and with the approbation of the Board of Directors. Mr. E. O. Manby, an engineer connected with the South Wales anthracite district, who has devoted his attention most successfully to the introduction of this fuel, was present, and assisted in the trial.

The engine employed was the "Vulcan", one of the smaller engines, used for conveying goods. The general result of the trial was highly satisfactory. In the first instance, the engine ran out without a load about six miles, and the coal was found to do very good duty, without any difficulty being experienced either with the tubes or in getting up the fires. It was noticed, that the fuel burnt nearly without dust from the chimney, and entirely without smoke. The engine brought back a load of coal waggons from the Huyton colliery, and acquired a speed, thus loaded, of twenty-one miles an hour, which is about the duty of the "Vulcan," with an equal load on coke.

Another trial was made in the evening, with the same engine, for the whole distance to Manchester, taking five loaded waggons. The journey was performed in one hour and

twenty-nine minutes. The consumption of anthracite was only five and a half cwt., although a large portion was wasted, from the fire bars being too wide apart for the economical use of this fuel. The engine would have used upwards of seven and a half cwt. of coke for the same journey, with the same load.

We regard the success of this trial as likely to prove, in its result, a most important public benefit. The price of coke, as the demand for it for use in locomotive engines, on railways, has extended, has increased, in some places, almost fifty per cent.; and in districts which produce no coal, this enhanced cost of coke will be seriously prejudicial to the success of railway undertakings. If anthracite can be generally applied in locomotive engines, we are given to understand that a saving of thirty to forty per cent., in cost and quantity, will be effected. We have no doubt that the Directors of our leading railways will instruct their engineers to follow up these experiments, and introduce such modifications into the form and working of the fire-boxes as the use of a new fuel may naturally be supposed to require.

The application of anthracite to marine engines is the next object most deserving the attention of practical men. The journalists of the United States appear to claim for their country almost the exclusive production of this invaluable fuel, which is destined to play so great a part in the iron manufacture, in railway locomotion, and in steam navigation; but the western part of the South Wales coal field, with reference to which Liverpool is, geographically, so favourably situated, contains stores of anthracite of much superior quality to those specimens from America which we have seen, and can produce it at a much smaller cost.—*Liverpool Albion.*

IMPROVEMENT IN CARPETS.

The public in Edinburgh is occasionally gratified with exhibitions of the carpets of Messrs. Whytock and Company, executed upon a peculiar principle, the subject of a patent, and which we shall try to give our country readers some idea of. Externally, these carpets resemble the richest velvet, the upper surface having a thick nap, like plush, but not so deep in the pile as the usual Turkey carpets and hearth-rugs. The pile of the Turkey carpet, as is well known, is produced by a laborious process of building in bits or tufts of coloured wool, fixing the tufts with a cross thread and lay, as in weaving, and then shaving the tufts to a smooth surface. In another fabric the usual process consists in weaving the carpet with threads of different colours, throwing up certain coloured threads to form the patterns, and keeping down those coloured threads in parts where they do not require to be shown. For example, in order to throw up a small pink rose-bud, within the compass of a yard in length, threads of a pink colour must go along the warp of the whole web, and be kept out of sight every where but at one spot in each yard. It is clear that the one process is extremely tedious, and consequently expensive, and that by the other a great loss of materials is incurred, which also has the effect of increasing the price of the article. The plan followed by the copartnery above mentioned obviates both disadvantages. We are not at liberty to describe their process minutely; but we may state that, by a mechanical arrangement of the most ingenious nature, the threads of the warp are separately dyed beforehand in such a way as ultimately, when woven, to produce the desired appearances. Each thread is tinctured in a particular manner along its whole length of several hundred yards, a little bit green, a little bit yellow, another little bit red, and so on, so as to perform its part in the general effect—each thread, of course, different from another. An unskilled visiter, taking up one of those threads, and being told that each bit of colour had its share in the designed composition of perhaps a series of flowers, or even of some more formal pattern, would be lost in wonder to think of the ingenuity which could plan and provide for such a result. And yet, when the threads are arranged and put into the loom, every little bit of colour is found to take its own proper place, and fulfil its end in the general design. The pile is produced by a knife which runs across the web, and cuts open the raised loops; and thus the carpet is completed without a single inch of thread being any where lost. The figures shine out in harmoniously blended tints with unparalleled brilliancy, and the appearance is that of the richest painting on velvet. As works of art, or rather, we should say, the fine arts—for they are as much so as the famed Gobelins of Paris—these productions of the loom afford a striking testimony of the improvement which has of late years taken place in Scottish manufactures of the more tasteful kind.—*Edinburgh Journal.*

RECENT AMERICAN PATENTS.
(From the *Franklin Journal* for May.)

WEATHER STRIPS TO THE BOTTOMS OF DOORS: *Isaac D. Brower, New York.*—The weather strip used is a strip of metal, let into a groove along the lower edge of the door, and closing, when down, against a re-

bate along the sill. The strip is attached in the middle, to a sliding-bolt enclosed within the framing of the door, and it is raised by the action of the knob which moves the spring-bolt of the lock, by attachments contained within the frame-work. The closing of the strip is effected by a sliding rod, which projects out from the hinged edge of the door, the pressure of which, against the rebate in the door-frame, insures the descent of the bolt and the strip to which it is attached.

The arrangement is made with much ingenuity, and we perceive but one difficulty in the way of its action; we feel assured that the appendages to the sliding-bolt of the lock, by which the strip is to be raised, will cause the handle to turn with some difficulty. We apprehend, also, that the application will be two costly for general adoption.

LOCOMOTIVE POWER MACHINE, FOR REMOVING HOUSES, &c.: *Stephen Compton, New York.*—This machine consists of a combination of wheels and pinions, upon suitable shafts, operating upon a windlass; from this windlass a rope, or chain, is to be extended to a house, stump, or other body to be removed. The machine is mounted upon wheels, and is so constructed that " the end of the frame towards the resisting body, may be brought into contact with the ground, this end being armed with iron, and so formed that it will enter, and form a bearing against the earth, with a power of resistance proportioned to that applied. The claim is to " the mounting of such a machine upon a carriage, constructed in the way described, so that it may readily be removed from place to place, and that it shall anchor itself, or take firm hold in the ground, by the action of the power applied, substantially in the manner shown."

REMOVING WOOL AND HAIR FROM SKINS: *Benjamin F. Emery, Bath.*—This improvement is effected by the application of steam of the proper temperature to the hides and skins, instead of water, acids, or other materials.

For the purpose of softening dried sheep-skins, for pulling the wool and tanning the skins, a room should be provided large enough to contain, suspended, as hereafter described, as many skins as it may be required to operate upon at one time, and made as nearly air-tight as it can be without much expense, say by tight boarding and shingling; with several small windows, or openings, with shutters, to admit or exclude the air, as occasion may require. I employ racks, consisting of rails, or strips of boards, or planks placed about three feet apart, and having tenter-hooks inserted about four or five inches from each other, precisely as the are now commonly used for drying sheep skins after they are tanned. As many of these may be put up in the steam room as will consist with the objects of not having the skins touch each other, and of permitting passages through them, to hang up, and take down the skins. The steam may be generated in any kind of boiler, and conveyed by pipes from the boiler into the steam room; it is most advantageously discharged only a few inches from the floor, in the centre of the room. For a room about 12 by 15 feet square, and 9 feet high, a common potash boiler, having the steam secured, and forced into the room by a tin or copper pipe, of about two inches diameter would be sufficient, although an iron boiler resembling those used for steam-engines is more convenient. Two windows of about two feet square, placed opposite each other, would well answer for such a room : with the temperature of blood heat, the skins in such a room would be sufficiently steamed in about three hours, unless they were much harder than usual. It is easy to ascertain, however, by going into the room, when the wool is loose, and the skins are sufficiently pliable, taking care to lose no more steam, by keeping the door open, than is necessary. The process may be somewhat expedited by raising the temperature a little higher, although I should not advise raising it above 150 degrees of Fahr. for fear of injuring the skins. The softening will be expedited by wetting the skins or hides, before hanging them up.

Hides of neat cattle, and other large animals, may be softened for tanning in the same way; the rails and tenter-hooks being larger and further apart, in proportion to the size of the skins, or hides. The time required for softening, will also be longer in proportion to the thickness and hardness of the skins, or hides. In all cases, the skins and hides should be affixed to the tenter-hooks by the shanks, so as to keep them moderately stretched.

Slaughtered hogs, instead of being scalded in the usual way, for the purpose of scraping off the bristles, may, also, be more conveniently scalded by steam, in a similar way, where the business of dressing them is carried on to a large extent. The hogs may be hung up by the gambrils, only far enough apart to permit the butcher, or dresser, to work between them. Hot steam should then be rapidly thrown into the scalding room; until it rises to the temperature of about 175 or 180 degrees, and if very rapidly done, to the boiling point, (although this is rather dangerous,) when the room should be immediately ventilated sufficiently to admit of the operation of dressing. In order to keep the labourers employed, there may be two steam rooms, so that they may operate in one room while the preparation of the hogs, and the scalding, is going on in the other.

NOTES AND NOTICES.

Joyce's Apparatus for Heating by Steam.—A mode of heating a small greenhouse by steam from a portable apparatus placed within the house, has lately been invented by Mr. Joyce. The apparatus is a copper cylinder, with the fire placed in the centre, the fuel being supplied from the top, and the ashes coming out below, through the grating which admits air to the fire. The fuel is charcoal, and the little smoke which it produces is delivered into the same tube which conveys away the steam. At the further extremity of the steam-pipe the fumes of the charcoal are allowed to escape outside the house, through a tube; which, for ordinary apparatus, need not exceed an inch in diameter. As the steam-pipe is placed so as to return all the condensed water to the boiler, the loss of heat by this mode is extremely small, but it will not answer well for any other fuel except charcoal, which is expensive.—*Loudon's Suburban Gardner.*

Plagiarism.—Sir,—I deem it right to state, that in the *Penny Mechanic* of last Saturday, upon the remonstrance of a correspondent, (Mr. Richard Darling) the Editor, "begs to assure him we were entirely ignorant at the time, that *J. E. Goddard* had *pirated* the article of the Floating Fire-engine, which was originally written by Mr. Baddeley for the *Mechanics' Magazine* [vide page 279 of your last volume] ; to the proprietor of which publication, and also to Mr. Baddeley, we beg to offer an apology." In addition to which, an article on " Literary Poaching" appears in the number, conveying the severest possible censure upon the party who had been guilty of this barefaced piece of imposition. I remain, &c.
August 1, 1838.   WM. BADDELEY.

Hollow Shot.—A correspondent, " Mariner," inquires whether " the hollow shot, proposed for service in the *Gorgon* steam frigate, are to be filled with water, plugged and safety plugged, as proposed some years ago by Sir Robert Seppings, to the Admiralty, or whether they are to be only metallic shells, to save powder and recoil in close action." We have made inquiry, and are informed that the hollow shot in question have nothing inclosed in them—the object being to make the largest hole with the lightest weight of metal.

Erratum.—In the article on "Russian Exchange in London," vol. xxvii, p. 61, for "consequently by a pound sterling," read, "consequently an hundred pounds sterling."

The twenty-eighth volume of the *Mechanics' Magazine* is now published, price, in half-cloth, 8s. 6d., with a Railway Map of England and Wales. The Railway Map may be had separately, price 6d., and on fine paper, coloured, price 1s.

☞ *British and Foreign Patents taken out with economy and despatch; Specifications, Disclaimers, and Amendments, prepared or revised; Caveats entered; and generally every Branch of Patent Business promptly transacted. A complete list of Patents from the earliest period (15 Car. II. 1675,) to the present time may be examined. Fee 2s. 6d.; Clients, gratis.*

LONDON: Printed and Published for the Proprietor, by W. A. Robertson, at the Mechanics' Magazine Office, No. 6, Peterborough-court, between 135 and 136, Fleet-street.—Sold by A. & W. Galignani, Rue Vivienne, Paris.

Mechanics' Magazine,

MUSEUM, REGISTER, JOURNAL, AND GAZETTE.

No. 783.]   SATURDAY, AUGUST 11, 1838.   [Price 3*d*.

WHITELAW'S IMPROVED EXPANSION GEAR AND SLIDE-VALVES.

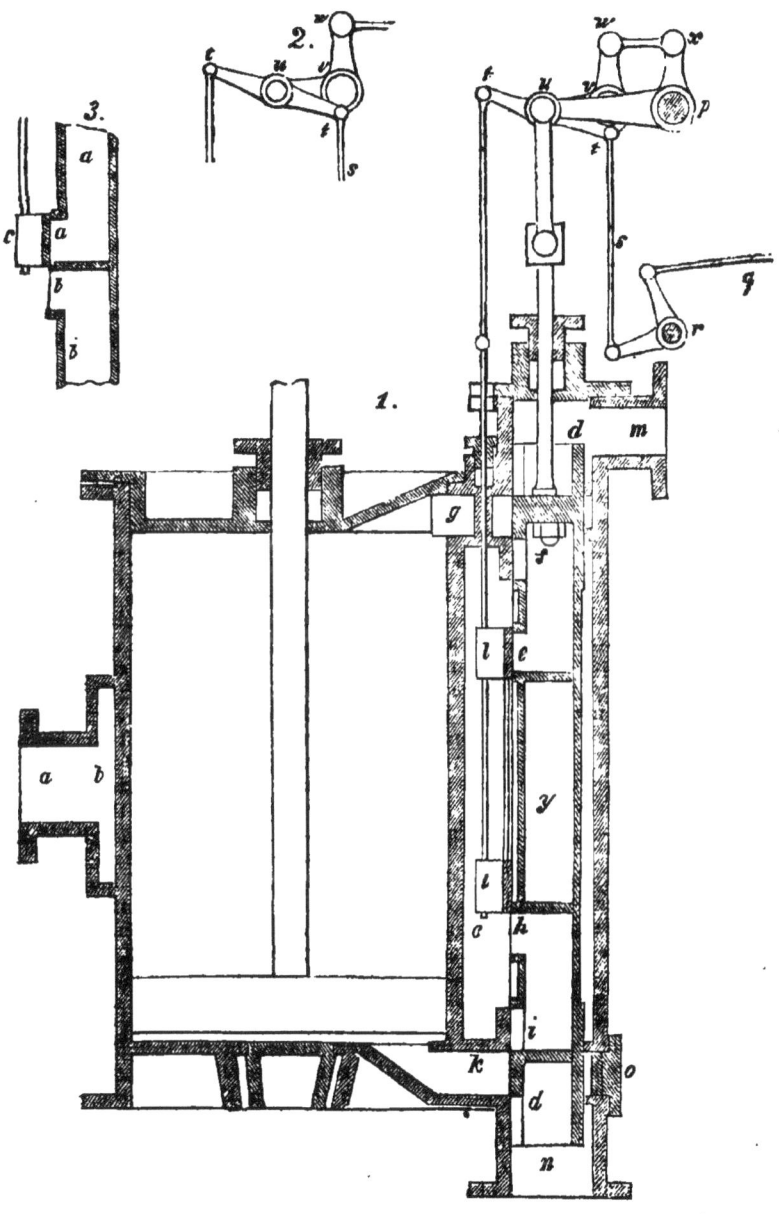

MR. WHITELAW'S IMPROVED EXPANSION GEAR AND SLIDE-VALVES.

Sir,—I send you herewith an account of my plan of expansion gear, for insertion in the *Mechanics' Magazine*, for which I received from the "Royal Cornwall Polytechnic Society for the *encouragement* of the sciences, arts, and industry," their first bronze medal, in order that your readers may know to what extent this society *encourages* improvement. I sent the medal back to the *Royal Cornwall Polytechnic Society*: as my plan of a governor for regulating the time of cutting off the steam, is alone, in my opinion worth twenty times its value, I could not think of keeping such a trifle.

It is a pity that Mr. W. Baddeley, in his letter dated 5th July, 1838, was not able to answer my last letter fairly, but was obliged to prop up his notions respecting my feeding apparatus, by what were once the opinions of "Nauticus;" as the latter gentleman, at the time he entertained the same notions on the subject as Mr. Baddeley now does, believed also that the old feeding apparatus, in ordinary use, to be perfect; and of course, a person entertaining such ideas must laugh at every attempt at improvement,—even the feeding apparatus of Mr. B. must, then, have appeared worthless in the eyes of "Nauticus." I have something more substantial than the opinion of others in favour of my plan, as Mr. B. will perceive, when I let him know that I was asked by a gentleman in London, about a month ago, to get a feeding apparatus on my plan made for him: and from letters which are at present in my possession, I have every reason to believe, that there are two sets of this apparatus now making in one of the most extensive steam-engine factories in the kingdom.

Description of Improved Expansion Gear and Slide-Valves.—Figure 1 shows one form of my plan of expansion gear: in this fig. the steam pipe is shown at *a*, and the steam passes through a hollow belt *b*, cast round the cylinder into the chest *c*. *d d* is the slide valve which is of the D shape, so that outside the valve has the appearance of a pipe having a flat side with four ports in it, and a part of it taken away at each end. *e f* shows the passage through the valve by which the steam gets into the port *g* at the top of the cylinder, and *h i* is another passage through the valve, by which the

steam gets into the bottom port *k* of the cylinder. The cut off valves *l l*, are both fixed upon one rod. When the steam is cut off on the top side of the piston, the top valve marked *l*, then covers the uppermost of the two middle ports on the flat side of the valve *d d*; and when the steam is cut off on the bottom side of the piston, then the bottom valve marked *l* is upon the undermost of the two middle ports on the flat side of the valve. The eduction-pipe for the top end of the cylinder is seen at *m*, and *n* is the bottom eduction-pipe. The top end of the valve *d d* is packed by lifting off the top of the valve chest, and its bottom end is packed by taking away the cover *o*. The top port *g* into the cylinder has a part cast inside of it for the rod of the cut off valves to pass through; but this part being small it will not contract the port, as it (the port) may be made a little wider opposite the part. The slide valve *d d* is wrought by means of an eccentric, and *p* is the rocking shaft: the cut-off valves are wrought by means of a wiper fixed upon the crank shaft, which communicates motion to the rod *q*. *r* is a small rocking shaft with two levers on it, the same as shown in the fig.; and the rod *s* communicates the motions of this shaft to the lever *t t*, which works upon a centre at *u*. If there were no more levers, &c. to work the cut off valves than now described, then, on account of the slide valve *d d* being always in motion, and the cut off valve making only one move in a half revolution of the crank shaft, the motions of the valve *d d* would shift the cut off valves from their proper positions on its face: but as the centre *u*, of the lever *t t*, works upon a stud fixed into the bell crank lever *u v w*, the centre *v*, being placed at a horizontal distance from the rocking shaft *p*, equal to the distance of the centre of the rod of the valve *d d*, from the centre of the rod for working the cut off valves; and the part *v w* of the bell crank lever *u v w* is connected to the lever *p x*, fixed upon the rocking shaft, by means of the link *w x*; and as *v w* is of the same length as *p x*, the end of the lever *t t*, to which the cut off valve rod is attached, will move through the same space as the slide valve, its other end being kept from rising or falling by the rod *s*. For these reasons the cut off valves can never shift from their positions on the slide valve *d d*, into which they are put by the wiper upon the crank shaft which works them.

Fig. 2 shows the bell crank lever *u v w*, and the parts in connection with it.

By lengthening the steam passages *e f* and *h i*, so that there will be only one division betwixt these passages, and no space as shown at *y* left, you will get one cut off valve to answer instead of two, if every thing else remains as in the fig.; only by doing so you will have a considerable waste of steam, although there will be nothing like so much waste in this as in the plans in most general use for cutting off the steam. Fig. 3 is the middle part of a slide valve similar to *d d*, in fig. 1, and shows this plan. In fig. 3, *a a* is the passage through the valve into the top port of this cylinder, and *b b* is the passage leading to its bottom port; *c* is the cut off valve.

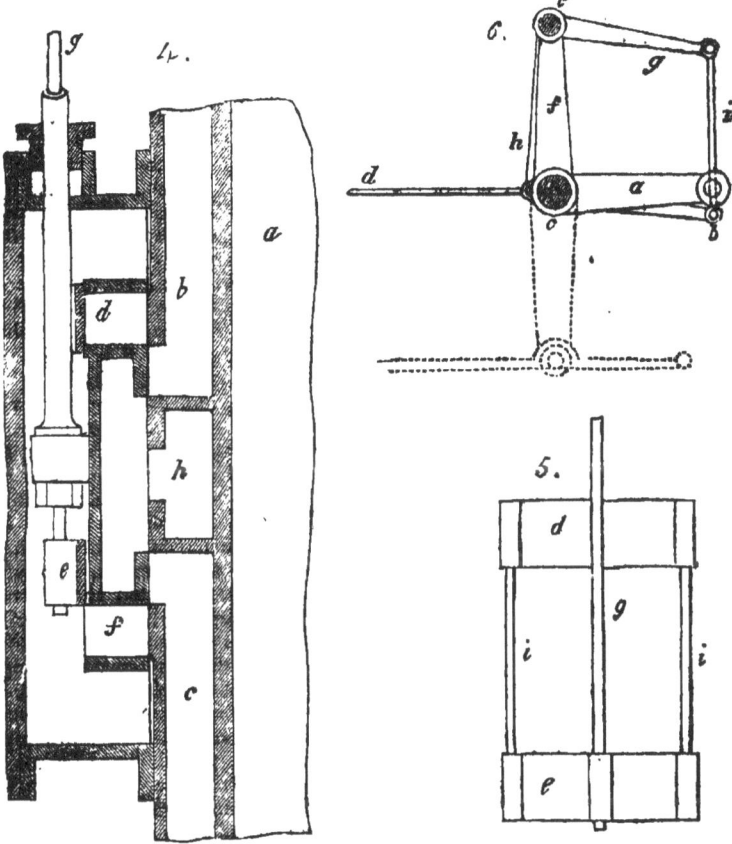

Fig. 4 shows how my plan of expansion gear can be applied to the short slide valve; in this fig. *a a* shows part of the cylinder; *b* is the steam port leading to the top end of the cylinder, and *c* is the port leading to its bottom end; *d* is the cut off valve which opens and shuts the passage through the slide valve which leads to the port *b*, in connection with the top end of the cylinder; and the cut off valve *e* opens and shuts the passage *f*, leading through the slide valve into the bottom port *c* of the cylinder. The rod *g*, which works the cut off valves, passes through the rod of the slide valve. *h* is the eduction port. Fig. 5 is a front view of the cut off valves; the rods *i i*, shown in this fig. form the connection of the one valve with the other. Fig. 6 shows an arrangement of shafts, rods, and levers for working the valves: in this fig. *a* is the lever, which works the slide valve, and the lever *b* communicates motion to the cut off valves; *c* is the rocking shaft, and the lever *b* is fitted so as to work loose on it. The lever shown by dotted lines is the one into which the rod from the eccentric for working the slide valve gears; *d* is the rod which receives its motions from the wiper for working the cut off valves, which is fixed upon the crank shaft of the engine; *e* is a rocking shaft, the journals of which work into two levers fixed upon the rocking shaft *c* : one of these levers being placed exactly behind the other ; *f* shows them both; *g* is a lever fixed upon the rocking shaft; *e* and *h* is another lever fixed upon the same shaft. The levers *g* and *h* communicate the motions of the rod *d* to the lever *b*, by means of the rod *i*. A similar arrangement of rods, &c., as now described, may be used for working the cut off valves when they are placed in figure 1.

Fig. 7 shows another form of my plan of expansion gear. In this fig. it will be seen, that the cut-off valves work upon the back of the face-part of the large slide-valve of the engine : *a* is a small rocking-shaft, supported upon brackets which may be fixed at a convenient distance, above or below the rocking-shaft *b*, which works the large slide-valve. The rocking-shaft *b* is cranked, in order to let the end *c*, of the lever *d c*, be so near to the centre of motion of the shaft *b*, as that the motions which this shaft gives to the large slide-valve, will not shift the cut-off valves from any position on the large slide-valve into which they may be put, by means of the wiper on the crank-shaft. The centre of the lever *d c* works upon a pin, which pin is fixed into the levers in connection with the links which work the large slide-valve. *e* is part of the rod which communicates the motions of the wiper, fixed upon the crank-shaft, to the rods, &c., shown in the fig., which carry its motions to the cut-off valves : *f* is the eccentric rod.

Fig. 8 shows the crank-shaft, and the wiper upon it which works the cut-off valves. The large valve, shown in fig. 7, is a modification of the D leech-valve. The pipe *h* which forms the connection with the top and bottom ends of the valve is stationary, and the valve slides past it. The eduction pipe *h* rests, and is prevented from rising by means of narrow flanches cast near its bottom end, which are guided by means of similar flanches cast inside of the bottom part of the nozles. As the working part of this slide-valve is very light, it may be made entirely of brass, and cast in one piece. Behind the rod which connects the top and bottom cut-off valves a light rib is shown : one of these on each side connects the top and bottom parts of the valve.

In a factory engine, the part of the stroke at which the steam is cut off must be regulated by the governor. Fig. 9 shows a plan of a governor, which shifts the wiper for working the cut-off valves, so as to cut off the steam later, whenever the engine goes too slow ; and if the engine happens to work above its proper speed, it puts the wiper into a position to give the piston the full pressure of the steam during a shorter portion of its stroke ; and, in this way, the governor keeps the engine going at nearly the same speed, whether it is doing much or little work. The wiper *a* gives motion to the cut-off valves by means of a similar arrangement of rods, levers, &c., as shown in fig. 1, 6, or 7; and it is of the same form as the wiper shown in fig. 8. *b* is a spur-weeel, and *d* is a pinion which gears into it. The part *e* of the governor is connected to the pinion *d* in such a manner that, if the part *e* rises or falls, it will carry the pinion *d* along with it; but the connection of these parts does not hinder the pinion from revolving on the governor shaft or rod. The wheel and pinion are calculated so as to cause the shaft *c*, upon which the wiper *a* is fixed, to make the same number of revolutions as the crank-shaft of the engine. The pinion *d* is bored out and fitted to the governor-rod, so that it can revolve and work up and down on it; and the feather, which forms the connection betwixt the rod and the pinion, runs in a spiral direction, as shown in the cut, and not, as in ordinary cases, straight up and down. By this arrangement, if the pinion *d* is raised or lowered, by means of the governor, the screwed feather will carry it round upon the rod, and shift the position of the wiper, so as to cut off the steam sooner or later, according as the balls are up or down—if the screwed feather winds in the proper direction. If the teeth of the spur-wheels *b* and *d* wind in a spiral direction on the surface of their rims, as in White's wheels, the pinion *d*, as it rises or falls along-side of the wheel *b*, will cause the

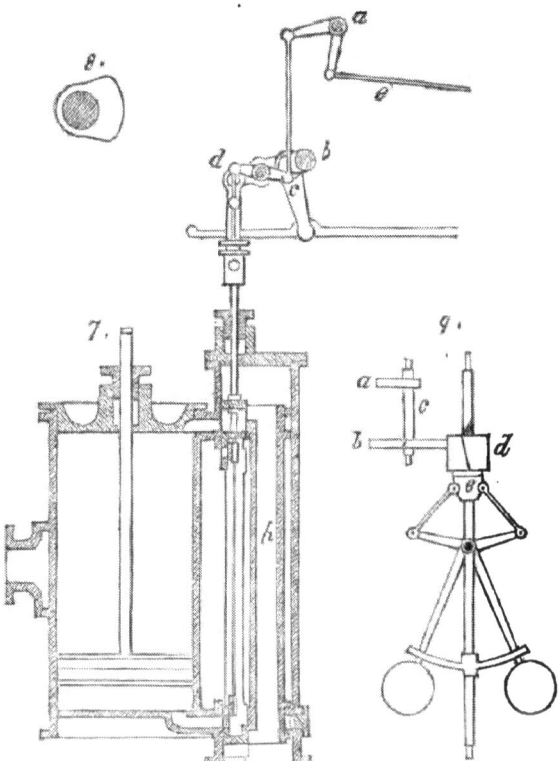

wiper and its shaft to revolve still further than with the screwed feather simply—if the teeth of the wheel and pinion have the directions as per the angled lines drawn upon them. It will be evident that, if the governor was driven at the same speed as the crank-shaft, then the shaft c, as well as the wheel b and the pinion d, are not needed; as, in this case, the wiper a would act as before stated, if it was fitted upon the governor rod at the same place, and in the same manner, as the pinion d is fitted.

This last paragraph is taken mostly from the *Popular Encyclopædia,* for which work I made a drawing and description of one form of my plan of expansion gear, as also a drawing and account of my governor.

I am, Sir, yours respectfully,

JAMES WHITELAW.

London, 27th July, 1838.

DIRECTIONS FOR MAKING AND MANAGING THE BEST MARINE STEAM BOILERS.

Sir,—I beg to submit to your readers, directions for making, managing, &c. the best of all possible boilers for steam-engines in general, and marine engines in particular.

1. Let your chief care be to make the boilers very complicated, and of such form and strength that the most trifling accident shall eventually cause them to explode.

2. Connect them all to one steam-pipe; and take care that the openings into it are so formed that it is almost impossible for the steam to pass through; and then, to make the steam obedient to your will, put in immense fires, and thereby gene-

rate steam very fast, and, by that means, *oblige* it to pass through the aforesaid awkward openings, somehow or other.

3. Be sure to form the flue so that a great part of the heat is appropriated to scorching the hull of the vessel, instead of to boiling the water; it *may*, perhaps, set the vessel on fire, which will cause an amusing excitement among the passengers, and relieve the dull monotony of the voyage.

4. Do not by any means neglect to place the chimney in such a situation as will give the engine-men a lively idea of the heat of the abode of a certain old gentleman, whose name is commonly abreviated to the first syllable.

Having made all these admirable arrangements, you may expect an explosion every hour. After it has occurred,

5. Employ some clever engineer to examine the boilers; and make a great parade of your own anxiety for a full and fair inquiry; if the engineer says the boilers are every thing they ought to be, all well; if he does not say so, bring forward as many persons as you can, who may safely swear they do *not* know *why* the boilers are not every thing they ought to be, and that, *therefore*, they consider they are;—declare you *know* they are—and mystify the jury until they return a verdict which amounts to saying they have tried to understand the matter, and have failed in the attempt.

You may, however, think it prudent to make a few alterations, which you can easily do by sticking a few steam chests on the tops of the boilers, which will enable you to assure the people that, although they were perfectly safe *before*, they are a vast deal safer *now*; and that you are decidedly certain no accident can possibly happen. You may say all this with a safe conscience, because you will take care to be profoundly ignorant of every thing which would render your opinion worth one straw.

But you will prudently provide for contingencies : that is, as you will not know whether the boilers are any safer or not, you will prepare yourself, as well as may be, to encounter another explosion; for which purpose the following hints may be useful :—

Impress upon the mind of some one on board that, as soon after the explosion as possible, he is to go and look at the feed-cocks, and call some one else to look too; if they can see that all the cocks are shut, and the boilers red-hot all over, it will be glorious; if not, the more red they can see the better.

Be prepared to state, that the men who have been killed, were very carefully chosen—that they were the most sober, experienced, and efficient engineers that could possibly be selected—that they were never guilty of inattention until they were employed on board your vessel; but that, when that was the case, they formed a perverse determination to do what they had manifestly no motive for doing, and which they must have *known* would end in their own destruction. You can intimate a suspicion, that they had agreed among themselves to commit suicide; or that they were quarrelling, and that some of them exploded the boiler for the purpose of giving the others a more effective "blowing up"; or any thing else that may occur to you, and which you think may do your cause some service, however monstrously inconsistent it may happen to be; for you must not think of sticking at trifles.

Possibly, about this time, the coroner will be kind enough to tell the jury, that he thinks *they know as much of the matter as they ever will know*, and the jury *may* think so too, and return much such a verdict as the first jury did—in which case you can try again, and kill a few more.

But if the case happens to be before a jury who are most inconveniently determined to arrive at the *truth*,—declare most emphatically, *that* is your only object; if you can make them believe this, you will have the better chance of leading them wrong. To assist you in doing so, bring forward some one who will declare, that the strength of a steam-boiler is "merely a matter of fancy." And do not by any means neglect to try *figures*; tell the jury " there is a matter of figures to go into," and do your best to bother them that way. For, if any one should be unkind enough to declare in print, that " any pretence to calculate the strength of your boilers would be absurd, *or something worse*," and give good reasons why,—you have nothing to do but to say no more about the " figures," and you are but where you were before you made the attempt.

If an eminent engineer should be called upon to give an opinion of your boilers, and should disapprove of them, write him a blustering letter, in the hope that his answer may lessen the effect of his opinion on the minds of the jury. (N.B. This last direction is to be used with *extreme caution;* because his answer *may be* any thing but such as you wish, and he may *insist on its being read to the jury.*)

If another eminent engineer gives a clear and decided opinion against your boilers, listen to him with all the patience you can; you will naturally feel very glad when he has said his say, and will not be so foolish as to ask him any questions—you will have had quite enough of him without that.

Throughout the whole business, you will take every opportunity of declaring that your boilers are *the very best boilers in the world*; and that *the more boilers that burst, and the more people they kill, the more you and the company they belong to will feel convinced of their safety.* This will make a forcible impression on the jury in favour of your good sense and discretion.

But there is yet a *last* resource when all other hopes fail. If you can only bring forward some one who may be supposed to know something about the matter, but who, from illness, or being nearly scalded to death, or any other trifling cause, has been unable to appear before the jury until the last stage of the proceedings, you need not despair. You may sooth yourself with the hope, that what *he* will say, may obliterate from the memories of the jury and the public, the unanimous opinion of all the engineers in the world,—much less in such a paltry place as London.

But, if the jury persist in refusing to be persuaded to think as you wish,— why, you will, of course, conclude, they are the most obstinate set of men that could be collected together; and you have nothing left for it, but to yield to your fate with the best grace you may.

I am, Sir,

With due commiseration,

Your obedient servant,

S. Y., an Engineer.

2nd August.

LONDON MECHANICS' INSTITUTION— CLASSIFICATION OF THE MEMBERS.

Sir,—Widely differing opinions, havbeen very frequently circulated as to the description of persons constituting the members of the London Mechanics' Institution, I beg to hand for insertion in your Magazine the following classified list, recently made out by a sub-committee specially appointed to conduct this investigation.

A similar analysis has been made upon previous occasions by individual members of the institution, but the present is the first *official* document of the kind that has been prepared. The constitution of some provincial Mechanics' Institutions having appeared in your previous volume, I trust that of the parent establishment will be received with some degree of interest.

Had the particular occupation of the members been more carefully inquired into, from the commencement of the institution, I am confident that the accompanying table would have shown more favourably for the *mechanics;* but I apprehend, as it now stands, it will bear examination, and is such as can hardly fail to prove satisfactory to all the advocates of general education. The high integrity of the members forming this sub-committee is a sufficient guarantee for the accuracy of their report, which is also to a certain extent corroborated by the results of previous investigations.

The report says, "Your sub-committee have been at much pains, to render their report as accurate as possible; in order to effect this, they have gone over the whole list of members three times, and the result of their investigation will be found in the following report:"—

"Some little difficulty has been experienced in classifying the trades, but where several members were found belonging to different branches of one trade, they have all been included in that trade. Thus, for instance, all the various branches of watch-making, have been included under that head; and the same course has been adopted with other businesses.

"In consequence of such a classification as the present not having been probably expected, all the members, on entering, have not been particularly required to describe their trade or profession. Hence it happens, that a considerable number have given no description at all; and amongst the number included under this head, must also be reckoned many students,—young persons who are at present engaged in no occupation."

The number of members at the present time is one thousand one hundred and forty-four, and they will be found to belong to the different trades in the proportions detailed in the following summary :—

Trade	No.	Trade	No.	Trade	No.	Trade	No.
Artists	15	Chemists and Druggists	6	Merchants	3	Silversmiths	20
Agents, auctioneers	3	Drapers	7	Masons	10	Stationers	13
Architects, surveyors	13	Die-sinker	1	Music masters	3	Smiths	7
Attorneys	2	Dentists	2	Musical instrument makers	2	School-masters and teachers	4
Accoutant	1	Dyer	1	Mangle-maker	1	Shoemakers	15
Artificial flower maker	1	Engravers	28	Medical students	3	Shopmen	3
Book-binders	14	Engineers	12	Muslin manufacturer	1	Surgeons and apothecaries	2
Braziers	2	Enameller	1	Millwright	1	Salesmen	1
Bakers	6	Engine-turner	1	Mercer	1	Scale-maker	1
Butchers	6	Fishmonger	1	Messenger	1	Strop-maker	1
Bricklayers, builders	11	Furriers	4	Mineralogist	1	Surgical instrument makers	2
Brewer	1	Fire-screen maker	1	Mechanic	1	Steel-pen maker	1
Bacon-drier	1	File-maker	1	Mariner	1	Tailors	23
Booksellers	4	Floor-cloth maker	1	Naval Officer	1	Toy-maker	1
Brass-founders	6	French polishers	2	News agents	2	Type-founder	1
Brush-makers	3	Grocers	6	Opticians	6	Tin-plate workers	6
Brass-workers	2	Gold-beaters	3	Oilman	1	Turners	2
British plate-maker	1	Glass-cutters	5	Optical turner	1	Truss-maker	1
Broker, furniture	1	Gunsmiths	2	Perfumers	3	Tallow-chandler	1
Compositors	20	Gentlemen	3	Pewterers	3	Watch-makers and clock-makers	27
Carpenters	45	Hatters	7	Printers	57	Warehousemen	8
Cabinet-makers, upholsterers	18	Hotpresser	1	Painters	14	Wire-weaver	1
Coppersmith	1	Ironmongers	8	Plumbers	9	Wheelwrights	5
Carter	1	Ivory-workers	2	Piano-forte makers	7	Whitesmith	1
Coach-builders	13	Iron-founders	2	Philosophical instrument-makers	14	Members with no description	187
Carvers and gilders	11	Iron-plate worker	1	Publican	1	Students and apprentices not entered in the Alphabetical Book, from which the list has been made	102
Coopers	6	Jewellers	25	Pawnbroker	1		
Coffee-house keeper	1	Japanners	2	Pastry-cooks and confectioners	4		
Curriers	3	Looking glass-maker	2	Paper-hangers	2		
Coal-merchant	1	Lamp-makers	2	Pencil-makers	2		
Cutlers	3	Lightermen	4	Plate-glass maker	1		
Chasers	8	Leather-gilder	1	Quill cutter	1		
Corn-merchant	1	Law-stationers	10	Rule-makers	2		
Colour-makers	2	Lapidarys	2	Ribbin-dressers and dealers	2		
Cheesemonger	1	Locksmith	1			Total	1144
Carpet-planer	1	Letter-founder	1				
Clerks	124	Labourer	1				
		Lithographers	5				

Whatever may be the deficiencies of this document, its preparation evidences a disposition to free and fair inquiry, which must eventually lead to a very accurate and highly useful epitome, of the class of individuals who are wise enough to avail themselves of the immense advantages afforded by institutions of this description.

I remain, Sir, yours respectfully,

WM. BADDELEY.

London, July 30, 1838.

FLAT CHAMBER BOILERS—SIR JAMES ANDERSONS' AND MR. HANCOCK'S.

Sir,—Mr. Hancock states (page 278), that he has examined the wood-cut and description referred to, in No. 775 of your Magazine, of a patent boiler, and finds that the boiler (Sir James Anderson's) is composed of *flat chambers*, for which he obtained a patent in the year 1827; and he adds, that as he "has never granted a license to any person to use his said invention for steam-carriages, no person can have a legal right to adopt it." Now, Mr. Editor, this sounds very well; but I will, with your leave, endeavour to show, first, that Mr. Hancock has no patent which gives him a legal right to attempt to restrain any person from adopting *flat chambers* for *boilers*; secondly, that he has no legal patented right to prevent any person adopting or arranging such flat or any other sort of chambers, in a vertical position, side by side, with spaces between for the caloric and smoke to pass through; and, thirdly, that he has no legal patented right to prevent any person strengthening such chambers in any way he may please, whether by having bolts or rivets through each particular chamber, or by having link-bolts externally round one or more chambers.

In 1824, a Mr. Smith, of London, patented a boiler, for evaporating fluids, composed of two narrow flat chambers, he having previously obtained a patent for a single flat chamber, each composed of thin metal, which were strengthened by having a number of bolts and nuts through the said narrow flat chambers, such bolts being placed about nine inches apart, over its whole surface* (I believe nine inches is mentioned in Mr. Hancock's specification). Again, in 1825, a Mr. J. C. C. Baddaly† obtained a patent for a boiler for evaporating fluids, which boiler was to be composed of several flat narrow chambers, placed vertically side by side, with spaces or flues between them for the caloric and smoke to pass through, with fire and furnace underneath the chambers.

Mr. Hancock, therefore, whose patent is said to have been obtained in 1827, being two or three years later than the above, cannot legally claim either flat chambers, or the mode of arranging them side by side, with flues or spaces between them, or the mode of strengthening them by bolts, or the fire or furnace underneath,—all these principles being combined and claimed in the above two patents.

I am, Sir,

Your obedient servant,

A SHAREHOLDER IN THE STEAM-

CARRIAGE COMPANY.

July 31, 1838.

---

* Smith's (Furnival and Smith's) flat boiler we are acquainted with; it is totally different from Mr. Hancock's. Smith divided his boiler into two flat horizontal chambers, both of which contained water, but the fire was only in contact with the lower chamber, the steam in the upper being generated by the heat of that in the lower. As the partition dividing the boiler into two chambers was of thin metal, cross-ties of iron were used to strengthen it, as well as the top and bottom of the boiler, somewhat in the manner patented by Mr. Russel, and described in our 22nd volume, p. 386.—ED. M. M.

† Will our Correspondent give us a more particular reference to this alleged existing patent of Mr. Baddaly's? We have examined the register of patents kept in our Patent Agency Office, (for the accuracy of which we think we can vouch,) and can find no such patent as "A Shareholder" mentions. Fearing the existence of a flaw in our list, we likewise caused search to be made at the Inrolment, Petty Bag, and Rolls Chapel offices, in which all specifications are enrolled, but no invention by any one of the name of Baddaly, or of any name at all similar to it, had been specified. We hope that this is an error on the part of our correspondent, and not a wilful attempt at deception, as we were at first inclined to think.—Ed. M. M.

REPORT AS TO THE SAFETY AND EFFICIENCY OF JOYCE'S PATENT HEATING APPARATUS: BY J. T. COOPER, ESQ., &c. AND WILLIAM THOMAS BRANDE, ESQ. F. R. S. PROFESSOR OF CHEMISTRY IN THE ROYAL INSTITUTION.

In compliance with your letter addressed to me on the 10th of March last, I have undertaken an investigation of Joyce's Heating Apparatus, in relation to its heating powers, the quantity of fuel consumed in a given time to produce in an appropriate room a certain increase of heat, also the amount of contamination the air of the room sustains in a certain time, as likewise the deterioration of the air by the combustion of oil, tallow, spermaceti, stearine, and gas, with the view of estimating the comparative injurious effects of Joyce's stoves, and of other methods, by which heat as well as light are produced; and also of the amount of contamination the air undergoes, in places where a number of individuals are congregated, and in which no injurious effects are found to occur.

In the outset I may state, that the room in which the experiments have been conducted, is nearly 14 feet long, 13 feet wide, and 12 feet high, and, consequently, contains about 2000 cubic feet. It has a chimney, and a peculiarly accurately fitted and well constructed register stove, which, when shut, effectually closes its lower aperture. Whenever a particular trial was to be made, bags of sand were placed on the junctions of the window sashes, and also at the bottom of the doors, and every precaution taken to make it as air tight as could be.

I find that one of Joyce's stoves, the internal cylinder of which is six inches in diameter and fifteen inches high, with an inverted cone, having twelve holes, each a quarter of an inch in diameter, burns three ounces of the prepared fuel per hour, when the regulating apertures at the top are quite open; in one instance, with a particular kind of fuel (such as is not commonly sold) it burnt three ounces and 4-10ths.; but taking the average of a great number of trials carried on for days, its rate of burning is a fraction less than three ounces per hour; but in all cases the combustion proceeds without producing any of the unpleasant odour that occurs when charcoal of the ordinary kind is burnt in a similar manner.

In one instance, the stove was kindled, and at eleven o'clock in the evening was placed in the above-named room, the temperature of which was 62 degrees Fahr.; the room was then closed, and not entered till ten o'clock the following morning; I then remained in the room about an hour, the doors and windows being kept closed, and found that exactly thirty-six ounces avoirdupoise of the fuel had been consumed; and on testing the air taken from the upper, lower, and middle parts of the room, the greatest quantity of carbonic acid contained was three quarters per cent. The temperature had increased to 72¼ degrees Fahr.

In another experiment, the stove was allowed to burn fifteen hours in the closed apartment, and at the end of that time, it had consumed forty-four ounces and a half of fuel; and the air of the room on being tested for carbonic acid, as before, was found to contain less than one per cent, and the temperature had increased 13 degrees.

These experiments have been made repeatedly, and always with the same results, excepting some slight differences in the increase of heat.

It can be demonstrated as follows, that each ounce of pure charcoal, when burnt, will produce a little less than two cubic feet of carbonic acid: for, one hundred cubical inches of carbonic acid is estimated to weigh 47 grains, and every 22 grains of carbonic acid is known to contain 6 grains of carbon; then as 22 is to 6, so is 47 to 12·82, which is the weight of the carbon contained in 100 cubical inches of carbonic acid; then if 100 cubical inches of carbonic acid contain 12·82 of carbon, 1728 cubical inches, or one cubic foot, will contain 221·53 grains of carbon; again, if 221·53 grains of carbon be contained in one cubic foot of carbonic acid, one ounce avoirdupoise or 437·5 grains will be contained in 1·97 cubic feet, which is so nearly two cubic feet, that, for my present purpose, it may be said that one ounce of pure charcoal will produce two cubic feet of carbonic acid.

If no change in the air of the apartment had occurred in the two cases before related, there should have been present in the first instance 72, and in the latter 89 cubic feet of carbonic acid, which would have made the per centage 8·6, and 4·45; whereas, in both cases, it was less than one per cent, thereby showing, that whatever care may be bestowed to render a room air tight, that it is not possible to accomplish it so completely as to prevent the escape of the warm air, through minute pores and crevices from the upper parts of the room, and the entrance of the cooler air at the bottom, for in no other way am I able to account for the difference observed in the quantity of carbonic acid produced, and that detected in the air of the room.

An imperial pint of good sperm oil will burn, in a well trimmed Argand's lamp of the ordinary size, about twelve hours; but I find by my analysis, that a pint of such oil contains 6333 grains of carbon, or nearly 14·5 ounces avoirdupoise, making the quantity of carbon consumed in one hour, a trifle more than 1·2 ounce; which, as I have shown above, is equivalent to the production of 2·4 cubic feet of carbonic acid. It will follow from this, that two such table lamps burning together will produce nearly as much carbonic acid in the same time, as one of Joyce's stoves, such as I have used in my experiments, and which I have before stated to be adapted for warming an apartment, containing about 2000 cubic feet of air.

A moulded tallow candle (long four) burns, on the average of some hours, 12½ grains of tallow per hour; but in 122 grains of tallow there are about 95 grains of carbon, consequently, about fourteen such candles burning together, would produce as much carbonic acid in the same time as the Joyce's stove to which I have before alluded.

A spermaceti candle of the same size, will burn in one hour 129 grains of spermaceti; but in 129 grains of spermaceti there are about 100 grains of carbon, consequently, about thirteen such candles burning together will produce in the same time as much carbonic acid as the Joyce's stove.

A stearine candle of the same size will burn in an hour 156 grains of that substance; but in 156 grains of stearine, there are about 121 grains of carbon, consequently, eleven of such candles burning together will produce as much carbonic acid in the same time, as the Joyce's stove.

Another stearine candle from a different maker with a larger wick, but of the same weight, (long four) will burn 175 grains in an hour; but in 175 grains of stearine there are about 136 grains of carbon, consequently, between nine and ten of such candles burning together, will produce as much carbonic acid in the same time, as the Joyce's stove.

Coal gas of average quality, I have found to produce by burning, 0·6 of its bulk of carbonic acid; an ordinary coal gas burner on the Argand's principle, having fifteen holes, will consume 5 cubic feet of gas per hour; six tenths of five are three, therefore, three cubic feet of carbonic acid would result from one such light, consequently, two such gas lights burning together, will produce exactly the same quantity of carbonic acid as the Joyce's stove.

But, independently of the formation of carbonic acid, all the common combustibles last named, contain such excess of hydrogen as tends to the further deterioration of the air, by the abstraction of an additional portion of its oxygen, so as to leave an excess of residuary nitrogen, which, of itself, is nearly as deleterious as carbonic acid; the air, therefore, which issues from the glasses of Argand, oil, or glas lamps, or from the flames of candles, will, if received into a proper vessel, by which the entire products of combustion may be collected, prove equally, if not more, deleterious to animal life, than that which results from the combustion of an equivalent quantity of charcoal.

With a view to determine the amount of deterioration the air underwent in crowded assemblies, I obtained some air from a chapel in my neighbourhood, towards the close of the evening service, and, on examination in the ordinary way, it was found to contain a little more than one and a half per cent. of carbonic acid. In another instance, I collected some air from the gallery of a crowded theatre, at eleven o'clock in the evening, about four hours after the commencement of the performances, and this I have found to contain about three per cent. of carbonic acid.

The advantage which I conceive Joyce's stove to possess over the ordinary methods of burning charcoal for warming apartments, is the perfect control over the rate of combustion of the fuel; for while, in a common chafing dish or brasier, almost an unlimited quantity of charcoal may be consumed in a comparatively short space of time, and liberate very suddenly a large volume of carbonic acid, which might be prejudicial to health, if not absolutely dangerous; in these stoves, by their peculiar construction, and arrangement of proper-sized apertures, the fuel can be consumed only at a certain given rate; and, if they be properly adjusted to the size of the apartment they are intended to heat, my experience leads me to believe, that no injurious consequences can arise from their employment.

JOHN T. COOPER.

82, Blackfriars Road, London,
June 14th, 1838.

Having been present at the experiments made at Mr. Cooper's house, with a view of determining the degree of deterioration which the air suffers by the employment of Joyce's stoves in close rooms, and having examined, in conjunction with him, the composition of the atmosphere under such circumstances, I can certify, that after burning for twelve hours, in a close room of the dimensions above stated, that less than one per cent. of carbonic acid was, in all cases, found in the air of the room; that such proportion of carbonic acid cannot be considered as deleterious, or in the least degree dangerous, in reference to respiration; that it falls short of the relative quantity of carbonic acid found in crowded and illuminated rooms, or in buildings in which many persons are congregated, such as churches, theatres, and assembly rooms, in which ventilation is generally imperfect, and in which, as far as my experience goes, the relative proportion of carbonic acid always considerably exceeds

one per cent. I am, therefore, of opinion, that the said stoves, which are so constructed as to consume only a limited quantity of pure charcoal in a given time, may be employed with perfect security, for all the purposes for which they have been proposed, and I consider the grounds of this opinion sufficiently detailed by the experiments above given.

WILLIAM T. BRANDE.

London, June 14, 1838.
To Mr. William Harper.

Note on Mr. Cooper's Letter to Mr. Harper, respecting Joyce's Stove.

(From Sturgeon's Annals of Electricity.)

Having made a very careful perusal of Mr. Cooper's letter to Mr. Harper, on "Joyce's Stove," we are prepared to furnish our readers with some additional information respecting the use of that apparatus. We shall premise by observing, that the first impression which the reading of Mr. Cooper's letter left on our mind was this: that, sanctioned as it is by Professor Brande, it is much better calculated to be serviceable to the venders of Joyce's stoves than to the purchasers of them; for it is sufficiently obvious, even at first sight, to a scientific man, that Mr. Cooper's experiments are not only deficient in point of number, but appear to us, whether selected or not, to be eminently calculated to convey to the unwary, an exceedingly partial view of the real value of the apparatus.

It might seem necessary to inquire, why Mr. Cooper's experiments were made in a natural atmosphere which required no artificial heat to make it agreeable? Are the purchasers of these celebrated stoves to understand that they are to be used only at those times when the natural temperature of the room is 62° Fahr.? Is this the information they receive at the sale rooms? If, on the contrary, Joyce's stove be intended to be more generally useful, and to compete with other modes of warming apartments, we readily perceive that Mr. Cooper's experiments would have afforded a much more perfect view of the *real* value of the stove: and, consequently, would have been of far more importance to the public, had they been made at those *natural temperatures* of the atmosphere in which artificial heat is generally wanted.

If proper experiments had been made during the severe weather of last winter, and that no other artificial source of heat than that produced by the combustion of three ounces of charcoal per hour had been in the room, Mr. Cooper knows very well, that the results would have been very different to those stated in his letter.

It is here we find that the investigation is imperfect, or partial; and that there is a blank at the very point from which the only really important information is to be derived. But as it is our intention to dispose of that which *has been* done, before we offer any remarks on that which *ought to be* done : we will now endeavour to apply the data which Mr. Cooper's *summer* experiments have afforded, to the solution of some of those problems which a winter's atmosphere and Joyce's stove might probably produce.

If the charcoal burned at an equable rate from "eleven o'clock in the evening" till "ten o'clock the following morning," the temperature of the air of the room would be at a maximum at the latter period. Hence, from this fact, combined with other data furnished by Mr. Cooper's letter, we are led to understand, that, in order to elevate the temperature of 2,000 cubic feet of air from 62° to 72·5°; or through a scale of about 10°, requires 33 "ounces of the *prepared* fuel," and eleven hours of time. And, according to the other experiment, an increase of 13° of temperature would require "forty-four ounces and a-half of fuel," and "fifteen hours in a closed apartment." With many persons *time* is as valuable as *fuel;* and the economizing the former of far more importance than that of the latter.

Let us now assume, for the convenience of illustration, that the conducting faculty of air, and other bodies in the apartment, for heat, is a *constant quantity* at all temperatures. Then, according to Mr. Cooper's experiments, we are led to understand, that, in order to elevate the temperature of 2,000 feet of air, in a close room, from 32° to 72·5°, would require *four* of Joyce's stoves, 132 ounces of fuel, and eleven hours of time; and at some periods of the severe frost of last winter, no less than *six* such stoves, 198 ounces of fuel, and eleven hours of time, would have been necessary to raise the temperature to 72·5° Fahr.: or, it would have required *five* stoves, 165 ounces of fuel, and eleven hours of time, to have heated the air of Mr. Cooper's room to the temperature at which he found it previously to the introduction of the *experimental stove.*[*]

Respecting the formation of carbonic acid, the per centage would be proportional to the quantity of the charcoal consumed in the standard period of eleven hours; so that by adhering to Mr. Cooper's data it appears, that by raising the temperature to 72·5° from the freezing point, the air of the room will contain about four per cent. of carbonic acid: and during cold weather, such as we experienced last winter, the air of the experimental room heated to 72·5° Fahr. by the *new mode*, would be charged with carbonic acid to no less than one-seventeenth of the whole mass.

It will have been observed that, in the above calculations, one per cent. of carbonic acid has been taken for every 33 ounces of fuel consumed, which is something more than that which Mr. Cooper's experiments will allow. According to one experiment, the carbonic acid would be 4·5 per cent., and according to the other, a little more than 4 per cent., for the combustion of 198 ounces of fuel.

The comparisons which Mr. Cooper has made respecting the carbonic acid formed by the combustion of oil, tallow, spermaceti, stearine, and gas, necessarily stand on the same footing as those already noticed, for if one stove give as much carbonic acid as two table lamps, for an elevation of 10° of temperature, then for an elevation of 40°, or from the freezing point to 72°, the stove or stoves would produce as much carbonic acid as eight such lamps; and during such weather as we have experienced in the present year, the "new mode" of heating would produce as much carbonic acid as twelve such lamps. The candles and gas would, of course, follow the same ratio.

The influence which the names of Messrs. Cooper and Brande may have on the public mind on this important topic, calls forth the judgment of every uncompromising scientific man: and humanity demands that a full and faithful investigation of the extent to which the use of Joyce's stove may, probably, deteriorate the air of rooms, be immediately laid before the public in the most efficient manner, to guard the ignorant from imposition, or the timid from fear.

We entertain no doubt whatever of the accuracy of Mr. Cooper's experiments, as far as they have extended; but they fall sadly short of that degree of importance which would have been attached to them had they been carried on at the temperatures of our usual winter seasons, or under circumstances in which the article in question is most likely to be in use. The few calculations we have made are the mere obvious inferences derivable from the scanty data which have been placed before us; not venturing even a single conjecture relatively to the *probable* consequences which might result from any variation of the experiments. But, we should hold ourselves highly culpable of a serious neglect of duty, as Editor of a scientific journal, were we not to warn our readers of the imperfect views which Mr. Cooper's partial investigation of a topic

[*] The number of stoves here mentioned is merely for convenience of calculation; Mr. Cooper's experiments affording no other means.

of such vital public importance is calculated to produce ; and we earnestly solicit the attention of Mr. Harper to these candid remarks ; and suggest to him the absolute necessity of a complete experimental investigation of the matter, and that it be proceeded with as early as the temperature of the atmosphere will admit.

An investigation such as we should recommend would require at least two rooms, of different sizes. The smaller one not be less than that in which Mr. Cooper made his experiments, and the other much larger.

The experiments should be made at intervals of 10° of temperature, from 50° downwards to the freezing point at least ; and as much lower as our winter seasons would allow. The standard elevated temperature to be 60°.

The rooms ought to be no further closed that what is usual whilst warmed by ordinary fires, or stoves in common use.

Thermometers ought to be suspended in various parts of the room, and at different altitudes. The experimenter ought to remain in the room for several hours at a time, at intervals, during the whole period the stove is kept in play. The thermometric observations, and test experiments for carbonic acid, ought to be made as frequently as convenient : and the latter on air taken from various altitudes in the room; and the character of the air at each individual altitude should be distinctly stated.

There might be one stove or more in each room, as found necessary ; and the total consumption of fuel in each stove ought to be strictly noted.

BELL'S IMPROVEMENTS IN HEATING AND EVAPORATING FLUIDS.

[The following extract from an article in the *Scotsman* supplies the information requested by Mr. Gyfford in No. 752, page 232.]

With the view of putting the principle of his invention to the test, Mr. Bell made numerous experiments on a small scale, in which it was invariably found that there was an increase of evaporation when the hot air was used. In experiments afterwards conducted by Dr. Fyfe, at the request of the patentee, on a larger scale, and with an apparatus of a totally different construction— viz. a small waggon boiler, with flues through the centre—similar results were obtained. Many long trials were more lately conducted under the superintendance of the same chemist, at the manufactory of Mr. Morton, engineer, Leith Walk, who also superintended, on an eight horse engine boiler, with

a flue through the centre, and surrounded also by flues. The ordinary average performance of this boiler, without the use of hot air, was 6.22 pound of water steamed off, to each pound of Newcastle coal. These, therefore, may be considered as trials applicable in practice, and in them the results were equally satisfactory. Of course, these results varied according to circumstances. In the most unfavourable, there was, when the hot air was propelled through the boiler, a saving of fuel to the extent of 17 per cent.; but the general result amounted to from 20 to 30 per cent. Taking the average of all the experiments, the saving was 23 per cent. In the apparatus last used, by which the above results were obtained, there is an iron box, situated immediately behind the fire, connected in front with a circular blower, by which air is propelled into the box, and from which it is conveyed by tubes through the boiler, where it gives off its heat to the water. By this means the air has been heated to 600 and upwards, in which state it enters the water, and, traversing it, comes off at 212 or thereabouts, having communicated the heat, necessary for raising it from 212 to 600 or 700, to the water, and by which the evaporation was increased.

It must, however, be evident that, by the transmission of air in this way, part of the heat must be lost; because it is given off from the boiler at the temperature of the boiling water. With the view of saving this, the patentee has adopted means by which the hot air, after having done its duty in the boiler, may be returned under the ash pit, so as to serve for combustion ; thus, along with his own method, also applying a well-known principle, of aiding combustion by a hot-blast, and by which. it is well known, there is a manifest advantage. When the hot air was thus returned into the ash-pit, it was found that the saving of fuel was greater than has been already stated ; on an average, it amounted to upwards of 33 per cent.

In trials which have been made, also under the superintendance of Dr. Fyfe and Mr. Morton, by passing the hot air in tubes through water, but without mixing with it, and under which there was no fire, it was found that the water was made to boil, and was kept boiling. On one occasion, the steam from a low-pressure engine boiler, passed in pipes through a large trough with water, did not act so powerfully as 100 feet of air, at about 600 degrees of heat, propelled through the fluid per minute. Now, from this boiler there must have passed about 250 feet of steam in the same time.

We are aware that objections may be, and indeed have been, urged against this plan. It is supposed that the box in which the air

is heated, will soon be destroyed, by the great heat to which it is exposed; but that is not the case. It seems to be protected from injury by the constant currents of cold air introduced into it; the box employed in the trials at Mr. Morton's, though it has been long in use, is not in the least injured. Another objection brought against the plan is, the power required for propelling the hot air through the system of tubes, and by which it is of course supposed that a part, or even the whole of the saving effected, must be consumed, and consequently that there can ultimately be no saving. But this objection, though plausible, does not hold true. Those who have advanced it seem to have had in their minds, at the time, the propulsion of the hot blast in furnaces for smelting iron; but the cases are very different from each other. In the latter, the air has to pass through a mass of semi-fused materials in the furnace, and consequently requires a considerable power to do it; but in the latter, the air has merely to travel through tubes, in which it meets little or no resistance, so that the power required is trifling. But even this is not necessary; for, in those cases where the hot air is to be returned into the ash-pit for combustion, the ash-pit is closely shut, and it has been proved that the draft up the chimney is all that is required to maintain a constant and adequate current of air through the heating box; so that, by this mode of using it, no additional power whatever is required.

It may also perhaps be urged, that, as the air has to pass over hot iron, its oxygen may be abstracted, and that thus its utility for the purposes of combustion may be expended or destroyed. In all the trials, however, that have been made, it was found that this was not the case. The air has been analyzed by Dr. Fyfe, and never found to have lost more than three or four per cent. of its oxygen, while in other trials, there was little or no change in its composition.

GREAT SEAL OF ENGLAND.

Our attention has been frequently called by patentees to the disgracefully imperfect and mutilated impressions of the great seal of England, attached to the grants of Royal Letters Patent. From the nature of the composition on which these impressions of the great seal are taken, before it reaches the hands of the patentee, nearly the whole of the figures or design becomes obliterated, leaving the patentee nothing but a tin box full of some material which appears like a mixture of yellow soap and rosin.

Several attempts have been made by us

to correct this matter; and the propriety of using a better quality of wax, has been frequently urged and several times discussed between us and the "officials," on which occasions the beautiful wax used in Edinburgh, in taking the impression of the seal of Scotland, have been compared, and, as we understand, submitted to his Lordship, the Chancellor. Hopes were consequently entertained that the Scotch wax would be adopted in England; but in this we have been disappointed.

It is but justice to Mr. Ruscoe, the clerk of the great seal, under whose direction her Majesty's Royal letters patent are now prepared, to say, that as far as his exertions are concerned, those documents are now executed in a style of elegance and taste, which reflect great credit upon his exertions; and appear suited to the important nature of the grants; and, if accompanied with good impressions of the great seal, would carry that character of "*official importance*," which they ought to possess. But at present we have a deed highly embellished, and beautifully written on vellum, with an unsightly lump of wax, bearing no intelligible device, nor any perceptible meaning. We trust his lordship, the Chancellor, will take this into his immediate consideration.

The new great seal of England of our amiable young Queen is now in use, and we have within these few days received several letters patent, with the impressions appended thereto; but however beautiful the seal may be, either in design or execution, no one can judge of its merits, for the "*was*" is really worse than ever, and looks more like bird-lime and rosin; it is sticky to the touch, and so soft, that it could not retain the impression for one hour. The seals invariably stick to the tin boxes in which they are enclosed, and cannot be removed, so that the patentees must content themselves with viewing only the outer tin case, or, at most, one side of the wax; with an obliterated impression; for if the seal was to be removed from the box, it would be broken in pieces, or present a blank face, the counterpart impression of the surface of the tin.

For the information of our readers, we subjoin a short description of the seal, which has been executed by Mr. Benjamin Wyon, chief engraver of her Majesty's Mint and Seals, in his usual style of excellence.

Her Majesty's new great seal is a most beautiful specimen of art, and reflects the highest credit on the talent, skill, and professional taste of the artist:—Obverse: An equestrian figure of her Majesty, attended by a page. The Queen is supposed to be riding in state; over a riding habit she is attired in a large robe, or cloak, and the collar of the order of the Garter; in her right hand she carries a sceptre, and on her head is placed a royal tiara or diadem. The attendant page, with his hat in his hand, looks up to the Queen, whilst gently restraining the impatient courser, which is richly decorated with plumes and trappings. The inscription, "Victoria, Dei Gratia Britanniarum Regina, Fidei Defensor," is engraved in Gothic letters, and the spaces between the words are filled with heraldic roses.—Reverse : The Queen, royally robed and crowned, holding in her right hand the sceptre, and in her left the orb, is seated upon the throne, beneath a rich Gothic canopy ; on either side is a figure of Justice and Religion ; and in the exergue are the royal arms and crown ; the whole encircled by a wreath or border of oak and roses.—*London Journ.*

RECENT AMERICAN PATENTS.
(From the *Franklin Journal* for May.)

SMELTING IRON ORE, BY A COMPOSITION OF ANTHRACITE AND CLAY AS A FUEL : *Joseph Lyon, Pennsylvania.*—This improvement consists in the employment of a mixture, or composition, of anthracite and clay, as a fuel, which is to be called "clay-coals," of which the following is an exact description:

Anthracite is reduced to a coarse powder, or screened, mixed, or mingled, either by hand or machinery, with such portions of clay and water as may be requisite to bring the mass, or aggregate, to a consistence that may be readily made into balls, or be taken up by hand, or machinery, in portions of any shape, or size ; when these "clay-coals" are dried, they can be used as fuel in the manner that coke or charcoal is commonly used in the reduction of iron ores. Portions of the limestone, or other fluxes, may be mingled in the composition of the mixture, and also some of the finer portions of the ore, when either, or both of these additions, may be considered useful.

PREPARING OLEAGINOUS SEEDS FOR PRESSING : *James Crisswell, Pennsylvania.*—This invention consists in conveying steam by means of a tube into a chest, flat on the top, with rim round it ; within which rim the seed is placed in such a manner as to expose it to the heat from the steam within the chest; the chest may be of any given size, dimensions, or construction, to suit the convenience of the manufacturer.—The patentee claims, as new, the application of flax-seed, or other oleaginous seeds, preparatory to the expressing the oil therefrom, by means of any apparatus so constructed as to expose the seed to the heating influence of the steam.

MANUFACTURING WHITE LEAD, AND OTHER SALTS OF LEAD: *Homer Holland, Massachusetts.*—The invention consists, 1st. In an improvement in the method of applying the conjoint action of friction, air, and water, to metallic lead, by placing fragments of this metal in revolving lead cylinders, or chambers, so as to produce a fine powder or pulpy suboxide of lead, for making or producing the commercial salts, nitrate, and acetate of lead.

2nd. In combining carbonic acid, from the atmosphere, directly with this suboxide, as it is formed in the cylinder by the addition of carbonate of soda, or other alkaline carbonate, so as to produce, or make, the carbonate of lead, or the pigment known as white lead. To effect the oxidation of the lead, I put coarse shot, or other fragments of unalloyed lead, into a leaden cylinder, or chamber, about four feet in length, and three in diameter, made to revolve, horizontally, upon an axis of flanches. The leaden cylinder, or chamber, is enclosed in a strong and tight wooden case ; air is admitted by perforations of the cylinder, at the ends, near the axis ; soft water is put in the chamber, sufficient to cover the charge of shot or fragments. The cylinder is made to revolve eighteen or twenty times in a minute, by the application of any force, and the electro-chemical action of the friction, air and water, produces a fine, pulpy suboxide of lead which is strained out by removing a bung from the side of the cylinder, and placing therein a hollow tube, leading to a sieve, or strainer, resting in a canal, or trough, which conducts to a reservoir.

This pulpy suboxide sufficiently freed from water, is readily combined with acetic acid, this giving "sugar of lead," and, with nitric acid, producing nitrate of lead. To make carbonate of lead, the process is identical with the above-described for the suboxide, with the addition of about six or eight ounces of the carbonate of soda to each gallon of water used in the cylinder. The cylinder is revolved several hours in producing the suboxide for the salts of lead, and from twelve to sixteen previous to straining out the carbonate, or white lead, which is conducted, as above described, to a vessel armed with an agitator and washed by decantation with pure water, once or twice, to free it from alkali, when it is to be dried by any convenient means, becoming the pure carbonate, "or cream," white lead of commerce. In this process, for white lead, the use of vinegar and of acetic, or acetous acid in any shape is avoided, and the health of manufacturers is preserved from the fumes of the volatile peracetate of lead so deadly in the ordinary process. The foregoing process the patentee prefers : but the revolving chambers may be cylindrical, square, or polygonal of any size and length. The lead lining of a wooden cylinder may be of sheet lead, or cast in cylinders to fit the wooden case, or carcass, and the cylinders are to be renewed from time to time, as they frit away. The number of cylinders, their weight, and the charge, will depend on the force employed, and the extent of the manufacture. Each cylinder (principally the lead chambers) may weigh six hundred pounds. The charge added, from one hundred to one hundred and fifty pounds of fragments, and the necessary water and carbonate of soda. The lead fragments may be shreds of sheet lead, shot, or fragments produced by pouring melted lead through a colander into water. Antimony and other alloys of metals are often mingled with lead in the shot of commerce, and unfit them for this process. The alkali preferred is soda, as this has the strongest affinity, or attraction, for oxygen and carbonic acid, and is less liable to form an hydrate. The pulpy suboxide may also be conveniently carbonated in the vessel employed for decantation, as it it armed with agitators, by passing into the pulpy suboxide, as it is withdrawn from the cylinders, carbonic acid produced by the combustion of charcoal, from fermentation, or from the decomposition of carbonate of lime, or chalk, by sulphuric, or hydrochloric acid. The decanting vessel, again, may be used conveniently in removing a disagreeable yellowness from pure carbonated lead by minutely mingling a trifle of indigo, or blue smalts, with the carbonate of lead.

NOTES AND NOTICES.

Honours to Men of Science.—Sir John Herschel is, we believe, the first Englishman who has ever received a baronetcy purely on account of his scientific acquirements. His father was only a Hanoverian knight, which was also the honour enjoyed by himself previous to the late coronation. Sir Edward Lytton Bulwer is only the second *literary* baronet, having been preceded by Sir Walter Scott. No great inventor has ever received a similar honour; Sir Richard Arkwright was indeed knighted, but that was not on account of his mechanical merits, but in the usual routine, as the bearer of an address of congratulation on His Majesty's escape from the knife of Peg Nicholson, or some equally important occasion.

A Cheap Voyage.—Such is the competition at present among the steamers between England and France, that passengers are actually taken from Boulogne to London for *one shilling*, or sometimes, it is said, for even less!

Enormous Plate of Iron.—We were lately shown in Messrs. Fawcett, Preston, and Co.'s yard, two plates of iron, which are said to be the *largest ever made*. They measure 10 feet 7 inches long, 5 feet 1 inch wide, and 7-16ths of an inch thick, and weigh between 7 and 8 cwt. They are intended for the bottom plates of two steam generators on Mr. Howard's plan, and were made by the Colebrookdale Iron Company, Shropshire; who, we were informed, are the only company in Britain (we may say in the world, that can make plates of this size, or even approaching to it.—*Liverpool Standard*

Woolf's Engine Re-invented.—Mr. James Duncan, watch-maker at Glenluce, has lately constructed a small steam-engine on the high pressure principle, the novelty of which consists in the steam acting twice in the cylinder before it escapes into the atmosphere, by which there is a saving of half the fuel, and half the water, which a common engine of the same power would require.—*Ayr Observer*

British Association.—The arrangements for the meeting of the British Association in August are going on rapidly under the direction of the local committee, who have entered into contracts for preparing the various places to be occupied on the occasion. In fitting up the riding school, where the dinner ordinaries are to be held, considerable progress has been made; as also at the Assembly Rooms, where a spacious apartment is about being built, to connect the great room with the racketcourt behind, so as to furnish ample accommodation for a promenade and refreshments for 3000 persons. The Green Market will also be fitted up with great splendour as a promenade. Amongst the distinguished men of science expected are Sir John Herschel and M. Arago, who, with many others, will be accommodated in private houses.—*Newcastle Journal.*

Wheatstone's Electrical Telegraph.—On the bank by the side of the Great Western Railway the directors are now laying down iron tubes containing wires, for communicating with the various stations by means of Wheatstone's electrical telegraph. The advantages, if it succeed, will be immense; the expense we have heard is about 100*l.* per mile.

New Cordage.—The brothers Landauer, of Stuttgard, have obtained a patent for a new species of cordage; the threads of which are not twisted one over the other, but united in a parallel direction. A cord, 1¾ inch in circumference, sustained a weight of 1300lb. without breaking; and when at last an additional weight caused it to break, the fracture resembled a cut with scissors, which proves that each thread was of equal strength. A cord of 504 threads, $3\frac{2}{16}$ inches in circumference, 111 feet long, woven in this manner, only weighed 19lbs; whilst an ordinary cord of the same circumference and length, and as many threads, weighed 51½lbs.

The twenty-eighth volume of the *Mechanics' Magazine* is now published, price, in half-cloth, 8s. 6d., with a *Railway Map* of England and Wales. The *Railway Map* may be had separately, price 6d.; and on fine paper, coloured, price 1s.

☞ *British and Foreign Patents taken out with economy and despatch; Specifications, Disclaimers, and Amendments, prepared or revised; Caveats entered; and generally every Branch of Patent Business promptly transacted. A complete list of Patents from the earliest period (15 Car. II. 1675,) to the present time may be examined. Fee 2s. 6d.; Clients, gratis.*

LONDON: Printed and Published for the Proprietor, by W. A. Robertson, at the Mechanics' Magazine Office, No. 6, Peterborough-court, between 135 and 136, Fleet-street.—Sold by A. & W. Galignani, Rue Vivienne, Paris.

𝔐𝔢𝔠𝔥𝔞𝔫𝔦𝔠𝔰' 𝔐𝔞𝔤𝔞𝔷𝔦𝔫𝔢,

MUSEUM, REGISTER, JOURNAL, AND GAZETTE.

No. 784.] SATURDAY, AUGUST 18, 1838. [Price 3d.

ROWLEY'S PATENT ROTARY ENGINE.

Fig. 1. Fig. 2.

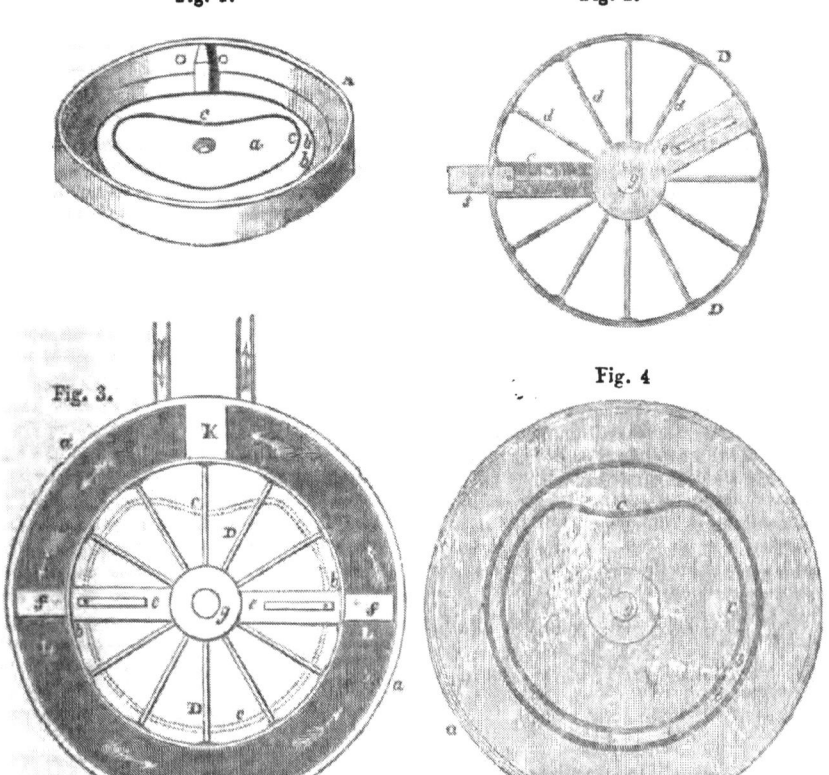

Fig. 5.

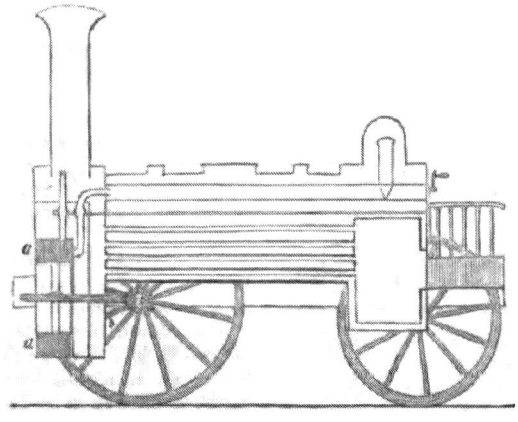

ROWLEY'S PATENT ROTARY ENGINE.

Sir,—I herewith send you a copy of the specification and plans of the *last*, and as it appears in my humble opinion, about the *best* patent ever taken out for a rotary steam-engine, the production of Edmund Butler Rowley, Esq., Surgeon R. N., of Manchester. Although it comes upon the heels of your extracts from Mr. Russell's voluminous and powerful article condemnatory of this application of steam power, I think it will stand well in the estimation of most practical men, and may not perhaps escape a compliment from Mr. Russell,(should it meet his eye) embracing, as it does completely, the most favourable principle that he professes under any circumstances to tolerate, as compared with the reciprocating engine.

I also send you an account of Mr. Rowley's patent buffing apparatus for insertion.* He is likewise the inventor of the pneumatic telegraph, favourably noticed some months ago in your Journal, but, being as diffident as he is ingenious, he takes little pains himself, to give his several inventions even common publicity. An engine of 6-horse power will soon be constructed according to his plan, to test the merits of his patent, and he will in the mean time be happy to show the model to any gentleman favouring him with a call, as well as glad to obtain, through the medium of your pages, the opinion of any of your scientific contributors, of its general merits.

I am, Sir,

Your obliged, and obedient servant,

RICHARD EVANS.

7 Portland-street, Manchester,
    July 9th, 1838.

Description of Mr. Rowley's Rotary Engine, abridged from his specification.—Figs. 1, 2, 3 and 4, are representations of the various parts composing Mr. Rowley's rotary engine, which should be mounted in frame-work, for stationary purposes; it is shown as applied to a locomotive engine at fig. 5.

The engine is composed of a cylinder A, whose top and bottom or side-plates *a a* are precisely similar in every respect, and which are bolted to the said cylinder by means of the flanches with which they are provided; in the interior of each of these plates, or cylinder sides, there are

* It shall be published in a subsequent number. ED. M. M.

two grooves or races, formed as at *b b* and *c c*, the outer groove *b* being perfectly circular and concentric, whilst the inner groove *c* is partly circular and partly eccentric, as represented. There is a circular apparatus D D, formed with a rim and spokes or arms, similar to a wheel (or the same may be formed of one solid piece,) having two or more steam-tight chambers *e e*, formed in it, for the purpose of lodging the pistons *ff*, and allowing them to slide in or out. The whole of the apparatus is keyed firmly upon the central shaft *g*, which shaft revolves in proper bearings, and passes through and extends beyond the side plates *a a*; the outer rim D D D, of this revolving wheel fits exactly into the circular grooves or races *b b*, and forms the inner side or wall of the steam-chamber L L, whilst the guide-pins of the pistons *i i* (which guide-pins may be furnished with rollers) travel in the eccentric grooves or races *c c*. Thus it will be seen, that as the expansive force of the steam introduced through the inlet pipe *j* exerts itself against the pistons, it will drive round the wheel D D, and as the guide-pins of the pistons travel in the eccentric grooves *c c*, the pistons will be alternately drawn in towards the centre of the wheel, to enable them to pass the abutment K, after which they are gradually forced into the steam-chamber, and so again allow the steam to act against them; the steam, after exerting its force upon the pistons, escapes by the exit pipe *k*.

In order to assist the parallel motion of the pistons, the guide-pins *i i* run in parallel grooves, or mortises *m m*, in the pistons chambers; each piston is also furnished with a guide-rod *h*, which works in an opening in the central shaft *g*.

It will be readily seen by reference to fig. 5, that if this revolving wheel or engine be applied to a locomotive carriage, as at *a a*, the central shaft *g* will drive the wheels of the said carriage, by means of the bevelled gearing *b b*, and if applied to stationary purposes as at figs. 1, 2, 3 and 4, the main driving-wheel must be keyed upon the central shaft *g*, and revolve with it.

The sides of the pistons and the abutment are to be furnished with suitable metallic packing.

The reason for having two or more pistons is very obvious, for if the wheel had been furnished but with one, it might so happen as to be arrested when opposite the abutment, in which case, the steam would enter and escape without producing any effect upon the piston; but as it is here proposed to construct the apparatus with two or more pistons, and as it is impossible for more than one of them to be retracted at the same moment, the steam must act against some one of them, and thus produce a continuous rotatory motion.

Fig. 6.

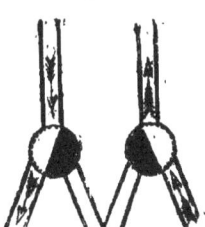

Fig. 6 represents an induction and eduction-pipes, constructed with two branches, one of each proceeding from and leading to both sides of the abutment. At the division of the pipes there is a stop-cock, or tap, which is so constructed as to allow the steam to enter and escape through one of the branches of the induction and eduction-pipes only. It is intended that both pipes shall be worked by one rod, and which, when turned to the right, allows the steam to enter on the right side of the abutment, and escape on the left; when turned to the left it allows the steam to enter on the left side of the abutment and escape on the right; and thus the steam-wheel is caused to revolve to the right or left at pleasure; so that, when applied to locomotive purposes, the engine may be driven either backwards or forwards, as may be required.

Mr. Rowley states, that his improvement in the rotary engine consists in inclosing a wheel, having two or more pistons encased in it, in a cylindrical steam-tight vessel; and which pistons work in a circular path-chamber or steam-chamber—and which steam-chamber has a division or partition in it, constituting an abutment for the steam; and to enable the pistons to pass this abutment they are gradually drawn in, or retracted within the wheel, and often passing the said, they are as gradually pushed forward into the steam-chamber; and this

gradual retraction from, and protrusion into the steam-chamber is self-acting; and is effected by causing the two guide-pins with which each piston is furnished to travel in the two excentric grooves, or races, contained in the interior of the said cylindrical vessel—also the admission and escape of the steam from either side of the abutment, and which can be regulated at pleasure.

THE THAMES TUNNEL WORKS.

Sir,—The report of Mr. Walker on the Thames Tunnel (No. 779, p. 252,) may well be styled an " extraordinary" document. It is extraordinary in all its features, but the measures it recommends to be taken for the completion of the work are most extraordinary. It now appears that it is impossible to carry the tunnel through with the means at present employed;—that Mr. Brunel's shield, of which all the world has heard so much, has met with more than its master in the oozy bed of the river;—that a most egregious blunder has been committed from the first, in endeavouring to tunnel under the Thames at so short a distance from its bottom,—and that, if the undertaking is ever to be completed, it must be not as a tunnel under the Thames, but as a tunnel through a mass of clay thrown for the purpose, where the Thames ought to be! Truly, these matters alone are sufficient to make the report " extraordinary" enough, without the addition of the many others which Mr. Walker adds, with a prodigal hand, in every sentence of his singular production.

Mr. W. was desired, in the letter from the Treasury, to attend particularly to the question of cost, but the chief gist of his report seems to be to recommend the completion of the work, as he phrases it, " without reference to cost," that is, without at all considering what it may come to. He observes, indeed, that " no prudent man would commit himself to the accuracy of an estimate of this work," yet, strangely enough, he almost immediately proceeds to calculate that the total expense (supposing those measures to be adopted whose cost *cannot be calculated*) will be 614,000*l.* or triple the original estimate. It is pretty certain, we may take it for granted, that the tunnel could not be completed *under* this estimate; and yet we are told, in the last paragraph of the report, that "almost any course would be better than letting the complaint be repeated," (it has been once made,) " that the engineer has been deprived of the proper means of completing the work at the estimated cost." The meaning of this complaint of Mr. Brunel's it is impossible to fathom. From the passage above quoted it would appear, that the " original estimate" was about 200,000*l.* Mr. Walker tells us that " the amount of the Company's capital expended" amounted to 180,000*l.* previous to any application to Government, and that " 83,900*l.* of public money" have been " expended up to the 2nd of November." From this it follows that the engineer has already expended upwards of 60,000*l. over and above his* original estimate for the whole of the works, although he has not yet completed one half of his task, and has brought the tunnel to such a pass that it cannot possibly be finished without impeding the navigation of the river to a most serious degree, and at an expense, at the very least, of 350,000*l.* more!! What on earth, such being the position of affairs, can be the meaning of this complaint of Mr. Brunel's, backed as it is by Mr. Walker? It passes the philosophy of common folks to find it out. One would think it far more natural for the Government to complain of the engineer, than the engineer of the Government.

Another of Mr. Brunel's proposals is a little more modest than this grand one, that the public purse should be handed over to him without controul. This is, that he should be allowed to commence his great bore again on the Middlesex side of the river: in plain English, having got over all the plain sailing on the Surrey shore, and finding himself in a dilemma from which his wonder-working shield will not extricate him, he proposes to get rid of his present miseries by leaving the middle of the river, where all the difficulty lies, and very comfortably commencing *de novo* on the other side, where all would be plain-sailing again, for some months to come at any rate. But where would be the utility of all this? In due time the inevitable middle of the stream would be again approached, and precisely the same difficulty would occur,—the projecting en-

gineer coming precisely to the same conclusions that *the navigation prevented his having sufficient thickness in his roof,* a conclusion, pretty well founded, probably, but one which he would have done well to have come to *before,* rather than after, it was quite evident to the world at large; and which might have been arrived at even previous to the commencement of the works, seeing that the Thames was just as deep then as now, and was even in those times a navigable river. The only difference, were the new plan acceded to, would be that we should then have two holes to look at, instead of one as at present, and a still deeper hole in the public purse, affording a stronger argument than ever of the *necessity* of completing the work " without reference to the cost," if we would not become the laughing-stock of Europe for twice beginning that which we knew not how to finish. The lords of the Treasury are surely provided with a sufficient answer to Mr. Brunel. The point is now arrived at when the practicability of the plan is to be put to the test: let the tunnel be conducted past the middle of the river before the funds for its completion are applied for. As to commencing again on the opposite shore, that is not required, as the part already finished demonstrates quite satisfactorily that a tunnel under the *side* of the Thames is quite practicable, and the proposed excavation from the Wapping shore could prove no more.—*Let Mr. Brunel get past the middle, and then* ——.

But, if the tunnel is to be proceeded with, why not take the work out of the hands of Mr. Brunel? It is hard to say for what reason he should be continued as its engineer, dissatisfied as he seems to be with the backwardness of the Government in matters pecuniary. It will be said that Mr. B. is entitled to the preference, as the projector of the undertaking. This, however, is a small merit. It would be easy enough to propose a suspension-bridge from Dover to Calais, but rather difficult to execute it, notwithstanding Smeaton pronounced it possible, *if no regard were had to the cost.* Besides, the idea of tunnelling under the Thames is every thing but a novelty, so that Mr. B. can bring forward no very valid claim on that score. His principal other claim rests on his being the inventor of " the shield," of which so much has been said, and which was to have rendered the performance of the work perfectly easy. But the shield, we have Mr. Walker's authority for saying, is not able to overcome the difficulties that now present themselves. Is Mr. B., therefore, to be continued in his office, because he is the inventor of a machine whose inefficiency is proved just at the pinch?—Again, it will be laid down as unfair that the work should be completed by another hand, after Mr. Brunel had overcome all its difficulties. The publicity of this objection, however, is evident from every line of Mr. Walker's report. So far from getting over the difficulties, Mr. Brunel has only brought the work to the most difficult part—and there left it—at least unless it be determined to proceed regardless of expense. Mr. B.'s own admission, that he finds his roof *too thin*, is itself a strong condemnation of his capabilities as an engineer, backed as it is by his monstrous proposition to fill up the Thames with an artificial bed purposely for the tunnel to be worked in! It hardly requires a first-rate engineer so to miscalculate, as to render the prosecution of his proposed work, in its proposed form, absolutely impossible; and assuredly first-rate abilities are not required to work a tunnel through a bed made for the especial purpose. In no point of view does it appear necessary that Mr. Brunel's services should be retained, expensive as they have already been to the Company and the country. It is needless to remark, that Mr. B.'s estimates for the future are just as likely to be realized as those for the past have been. It even seems rather too gross an experiment on public credulity to estimate that the Middlesex shaft to be made, would only cost one-third of the sum which that on the Surrey side has actually been found to come to, and Mr. Walker only acts prudently in taking the expense of "the great descents" at double Mr. Brunel's estimate. To talk of estimating the cost at all, where the tunnel is concerned, is indeed altogether ridiculous—but more than ever to talk of it in Mr. Brunel's style. He estimates the cost of his artificial roof, for instance, at 1,800*l.*, a sum, the total inadequacy of which must be evident at a glance. The reference, however, to the Kilsby Tunnel, was probably meant to

put the reader on his guard,—the actual expense in that instance being only just *six times* the original estimate!

If the Thames Tunnel is to be completed at all, the Government had better grapple with the work at once, and begin by taking it into their own hands: it has surely been quite long enough in those of its present directors, of whose doings the public only hear through the almost periodical accounts of fresh irruptions in the newspapers. It may indeed well admit of question whether it be worth while to finish it at all. It serves very well for one of the "lions of London" as it is, and it would probably be no more when quite completed—its utility as a medium of communication between the opposite shores of the river being very problematical, when the necessity of going down the "great descent" on one side, and up the equally "great ascent" on the other, is taken into consideration. It would, perhaps, be best for all parties, (John Bull among the number) to let matters remain as they are: the work might continue to exercise its principal functions of "attracting much of the public attention in this, and still more in other countries;" Mr. Brunel might repose in the enjoyment of his fame as the inventor of the highly-effective shield, and as the engineer who *would have* finished the tunnel at the original estimate, if he could have got the money from a niggardly Government; and, better than all, John Bull would keep his cash where he best likes to keep it,—in his own pockets, instead of seeing it literally *sunk* in the bottom of the Thames.

And, I am, Sir,
Your most obedient servant,
AQUARIUS.

London, August 8, 1838.

CYLINDRICAL STEAM BOILERS.

Sir,—I freely acknowledge my blunder (see No. 780, p. 264); it never occurred to me that a recommendation of a boiler should be dependent on distilled or non-deposit water: especially as tubular or chambered boilers often claim an entire exemption from the injurious effects of either deposit or over-heated flues, in consequence of the supposed rapid water circulation.

The rapidity of getting up steam is generally due either to fire intensity or reduced water space; the first is not favourable to economy in its generation for use—and the latter is apt to allow less time, on a deficient water supply previous to the destruction of part of the boiler, which seems dangerous in proportion to the size of the tubes.

I have observed Mr. Jarvis's opinion respecting large circular fire flues, and should feel obliged to him to state whether he extends its operation to the old railway (see Wood) and to the Cornish mining boiler; the former I believe is still used in some coal railways; and 500 or 600 of the latter are in constant work, their respective conditions are nearly as follow:—

	Length feet.	Flue diameter ft.	Length flue feet.	Steam above Atmosphere.	Steam in Atmosphere.	Temp.	
Victoria........	38	8	9	10	1½	275	Salt water.
Old Railway....	9	2½	3	50	4½	340	} Fresh water.
Cornish Mining..	35	3½	5	35	3½	290	

The last are likely to afford good data for the investigation of this subject; the facts attendant on their explosion, are generally an assertion of the engineman of a sufficient water supply. Yet, they almost without an exception take place either soon after the engine has been started, on being idle for some hours, or as soon as additional feed water has been given.

They are often not fatal, as the engineer and boy, the only attendants on the largest engines, sit in the engine-house for the greater portion of their time,—since the consumption of four or five bushels of coals per hour in three or four boilers requires to great time for attendance.

A record of the ascertained facts (in the *Mechanics' Magazine*) respecting the the *Victoria's* explosion, as a reference for the future, would aid practical science, especially if accompanied with a section of the boiler.

I am, Sir, yours respectfully,

N. S.

MR. WALTER HANCOCK'S AND SIR JAMES ANDERSON'S PATENT BOILERS.

Sir,—The misrepresentations contained in the letters signed "W. Hancock," and "An Amateur Mechanic," in your 781st Number, at pages 278 and 279, have just come under my observation; and, conceiving that they are calculated to injure an absent individual, who is, probably, unaware of their existence, and therefore unable to counteract their evil tendency, I feel it to be incumbent upon me, as the London agent of that individual, as well as from a regard to truth and " fair play," to address you on the subject,— and I do so in perfect confidence, that the compliments so universally bestowed on you, for impartiality, are not without foundation.

About twelve months since I received a letter from Sir James Anderson, instructing me to obtain for him Letters Patent, for " Certain Improvements in Locomotive Engines," and not until three days before the English specification became due had I the slightest intimation, or knowledge, of the peculiar nature of those improvements. At this latter period Sir James Anderson came to London, and, having explained to me the exact construction of his apparatus, he desired me, (with that generous confidence with which he has always favoured me,) to prepare the specification according to my own judgment; and, in making out the claims, he enjoined me to use the pruning-knife as freely as I might think expedient—entirely disregarding any feelings of vexation that he might experience from the loss of contrivances which had cost him great labour and anxiety—if there were, in my opinion, any reasons for supposing that he had been anticipated therein by others.— These, Sir, were Sir James's instructions to me: if, therefore, there are any pretensions made to " the discoveries and combinations wrought out by others," as stated by Mr. Hancock, *I* am to blame, and not Sir James Anderson.

In a consultation with Sir James, I mentioned those boilers which occurred to me which had, in one feature or other, the nearest relationship to his. As respects that particular feature upon which Mr. Hancock exercises his eloquence—

the *flat chambers*—I mentioned, among several others, Furnival and Smith's patent in 1823, Dr. Alban's in 1825, James's in 1832, Hebert's 1833, not excepting Mr. Hancock's in 1827. All these were discussed without any true resemblance being found; and, as respects Mr. Hancock's, that was soon dismissed—from the notion, *then* entertained, that it was the kind of boiler which he *used*, and not that which he *abandoned, as useless*. By the one "used" I mean, of course, that which Mr. Hancock described himself as using in your 534th Number, pages 67 and 69; and that boiler, I am sure, every *mechanic* will acknowledge to be the very antipodes of Sir James Anderson's in its entire construction, arrangement, and action. Sir James's water-chambers *are flat*, like Salisbury Plains,—Mr. Hancock's (in proportion) more mountainous than the Alps; Sir James's are *independent* of each other,—Mr. Hancock's *dependent*; Sir James's are individually so *strong* that they are proof against the highest pressure of steam that it is possible to generate in them,—Mr. Hancock's individually so *weak* as to be useless, unless combined together for mutual support, and even then are very unsafe, as experience, indeed, has most lamentably proved—while Sir James's, were they to burst, could, obviously, do no harm whatever. I could pursue the comparison to a dozen other material points, and show much greater differences; but, as those already instanced show the impossibility of identity, either in construction or arrangement, I shall for the present quit this part of the subject.

I have now to entreat the attention of the reader to a few remarks on the subject of the patent taken out in the year 1827, which gave to Mr. Hancock the exclusive right, according to his assertion, of using *flat chambers* for the generation of steam. The specification of the patent referred to is enrolled in the Petty-bag Office, Chancery-lane,—I have just been there to read it, and found, that the real claim therein made was *not* to every kind of flat chambers, but to the particular construction of those described. Could Mr. Hancock be ignorant of this fact? Did he make the unqualified assertion to impose upon your readers—that he was the first person to use flat chambers of any kind? Has

Mr. Hancock calmly reflected upon all the consequences of making such unfounded statements in the widely-circulated pages of the *Mechanics' Magazine*, for the obvious purpose of injuring an honourable competitor? Is not this conduct exactly in keeping with placarding his steam "gig" with the words "*No connection with the Steam Carriage and Waggon Company?*" thus servilely copying the miserable expedient of the lowest tradesman, "no connection with the next shop," in order to throw odium upon his respectable neighbour. Does this practice of Mr. Hancock's accord with his preaching, when he deprecates in moving terms, applied to another, the very conduct he is pursuing himself? "Let every one, (says he,) in so noble a race, bring for himself the resources of his own talent only, and make it a point scrupulously and honourably to stand clear of the discoveries and combinations wrought out by his competitors," &c.; and, in the same breath, Mr. Hancock accuses others of pirating from him the very thing which he virtually acknowledges, in his specification, never belonged to him! It is evident, that Mr. Hancock knew of prior patents to his own, wherein flat chambers were used, without even being claimed as new at the time, (which they were not, as I saw them in use eighteen years ago,) and therefore prudently kept the broad claim out of his specification—wherein unfounded pretensions would be fatal.

Mr. Hancock likewise endeavours to depreciate the labours of Sir James Anderson, by pretending that the Baronet had not had a twentieth part of his experience. On this point I think it fair to observe, that the experience of these gentlemen commenced within a year of each other, and that the boast, on the part of Mr. Hancock, is rather ill-timed when he makes allusion to his patent of 1827—the contrivances in which are of such a character, as to render the new construction almost impracticable, and, when made, incompetent to remain steam-tight for an hour, in actual practice.

In stating these and other facts, in defence of an absent person, it is far from my wish to detract from the real merits of Mr. Hancock, who, apart from these untoward proceedings, to which he has been instigated, I regard as a man of genuine talent and respectability.

It has been a rule with me never to answer an anonymous letter, but the classic pen of the *reverend* gentleman who signs himself " An Amateur Mechanic," is as well known to me as if he had appeared in his proper person. He states, that Sir James Anderson's boiler " differs from Mr. Hancock's only in two points—the steam chest or separator, and the direction given to the heat." Well, though that is obviously incorrect, it is quite enough; for I am quite ready to leave the question to the readers of the *Mechanics' Magazine*, whether the situation of the steam-chest, and the manner of producing the steam, are *trifling* matters or not, in the construction of steam generators?

I am, Mr. Editor,

    Yours respectfully,

        L. HEBERT.

Camden Town, 11th August, 1838.

MR. HANCOCK'S AND SIR JAMES ANDERSON'S FLAT-CHAMBERED BOILER.

Sir,—I am exceedingly sorry to see the mistake which has been made in *copying the name* of the patentee mentioned in my letter of the 31st of July—which should have been *J. C. C. Raddatz*, who, in his patent method of generating steam, uses flat chambers placed vertically, side by side, over the fire-place, with spaces between each chamber, as described in my letter to you—in which letter, I do assure you, I had no wish to do any more than to show, that Mr. Hancock had no exclusive legal right to flat-chamber boilers, nor to the mode of strengthening or arranging them. I only cited Mr. Smith's patent to show, that flat chambers, strengthened by bolts, had been used and patented before the date of Mr. Hancock's patent—Mr. Smith's previous patent being for one chamber so strengthened; and I cited Mr. Raddatz's patent to show, that he not only used flat chambers for his steam-boiler, but had arranged them side by side vertically, with spaces between, and fire-place underneath—which said arrangements Mr. Hancock claims in his patent two years afterwards. Besides, Mr. Hancock not having used his patent for eleven years it would be invalidated on account of *non-utility, and non-fulfil-*

ment of the stipulations,* even though its principles had not been previously patented or used by others. Nor can his subsequent patent give him any such privileges, it being specified, I believe, as improvements on his former patent, which is *nil*. This latter important fact, and part of my letter to you has been omitted I trust in mistake; but, after such an open uncalled-for attack on Sir James Anderson's claims to his patent boiler, I trust you will omit nothing that may be necessary for his complete justification.

I am, Sir,

    Your obedient servant,

    A SHAREHOLDER IN THE STEAM CARRIAGE COMPANY.

CHINESE BOOK-MAKING.

Sir,—The reviewer of Mr. Medhurst's recent work on China, in your 762nd Number, has fallen into a slight error, while contrasting the relative cheapness of Chinese and European literature.

The works of Confucius are said to contain altogether only four hundred leaves, " *that is*," says the reviewer "*four hundred pages*, being printed on one side only."

The fact is there are eight hundred pages, for Chinese books, like most others, contain two pages per leaf,

*Our correspondent is in error in stating that a patent becomes forfeited by not being put in operation. There is no "stipulation" to work the invention in a patent-grant; and, in fact, it is not an unfrequent circumstance for a manufacturer to patent an invention which might interfere with an established business, for the sole purpose of preventing its being worked, and to keep it out of the market. In all foreign countries there is a proviso in the grant, that the invention is to become public property if not put into operation within a certain time, usually two years, but not so in Great Britain. The remark, however, is not at all applicable in the present instance. Has " A Shareholder" been asleep these twelve years past? or did his steam-carriage experience commence with taking shares in the Steam Carriage and Waggon Company? Mr. Hancock has been constantly, from a considerable time previous to the date of his patent to the present day, (as appears from a "Narrative" of his steam carriage labours we have just received) using, both experimentally and practically, privately and publicly, his flat-chambered boiler, modified in various ways, but always preserving its principal distinctive features. The question of the sufficiency of Mr. Hancock's, or any specification, is one which could not be discussed in our pages, except at a great sacrifice of space, which the mechanical character of the age will enable us to occupy to better purpose. The remarks in this note apply equally to some parts of Mr. Hebert's letter.—Ed. M. M.

although only printed on one side. This curious people use a thin smooth paper, which being printed on one side, is doubled together to form a leaf, the fold forming the fore-edge of the book, which is knocked up very true, and after being stitched through, is *cut at the back*. In the extract from Mr. Medhurst's work, given at page 292, it is stated that " after the copies are struck off, the next business is to fold the pages exactly in the middle; to collate, adjust, stitch, cut and sew them." I have seen a considerable number of Chinese books at different times, but never met with one yet that did not contain two pages per leaf by means of the doubled form; some thin paper writing books are put up with doubled leaves in the same manner, but when a thick paper is employed they are made up singly like our own.

The extreme care which the Chinese book-binder bestows in adjusting his folded leaves, gives an evenness to the fore-edge, fully equal to that which we obtain by means of the cutting-plough, but in respect of his sewing, Mr. Chinaman might take a lesson from the " barbarian eye" with great advantage.

I remain, Sir,
Yours respectfully,
WM. BADDELEY.
London, August 13, 1838.

STEAM COMMUNICATION WITH INDIA.

Now that the homeward passage from India by the Red Sea has become so popular, it has been judged necessary to make better arrangements than have hitherto existed for crossing the Isthmus of Suez. When the improvements are fully carried into effect, it is expected that the whole journey will be accomplished in twenty-four hours, and the requisite steps have been taken for establishing a regular house of entertainment half-way across the desert, where the travellers are to stop and dine like stage-coach passengers in England, the principal of a respectable hotel at Cairo—an Englishman—having entered into a contract for that purpose. The last passage out was effected in only forty-three days, but there is unfortunately too much probability of the regularity of the steam communication being interrupted, in consequence of the impending rupture

with Persia, to which country the *Semiramis* steamer, which was to have composed part of the line. has been ordered, with a fleet of sailing vessels. This, however, would have interfered much more seriously with the *Euphrates* line, if that had been adopted.

SPEED ON RAILWAYS.
[From the *Monthly Chronicle*.]

Among the many benefits which the human race has derived from the combination of the discoveries of science and the resources of art, the facility and rapidity of intercommunication between distant centres of population and industry by the application of steam power on railways, stands out in prominent relief.

This great advance in the art of transport over land was sudden and unforseen,—unlike other improvements, which proceed gradually to perfection through a series of partial failures. A speed was attained in the earliest trials which produced unqualified astonishment in all who witnessed it, not excepting the engineers themselves. How much these first results transcended previous expectations, and how small a part of them can be fairly ascribed to contrivance or design, may be judged by comparing them with the reports and estimates previously furnished to the railway company by engineers most experienced in this application of the steam engine.

Mr. J. Walker, the present president of the Institution of Civil Engineers, and Mr. J. U. Rastrick, one of the soundest men of practical science in the profession, made a report before the opening of the Liverpool and Manchester Railway, in which they estimated the speed of locomotive engines at ten miles an hour, and the loads they would carry at twenty tons gross. Mr. R. Stephenson, engineer of the Birmingham Railway, and Mr. J. Locke, engineer of the Grand Junction Railway, also furnished a report, in which they assigned twelve miles an hour as the speed, and thirty tons gross as the load, of a locomotive engine. In the first performances a speed of more than thirty miles an hour was obtained, and not long afterwards we witnessed a single engine drag the enormous load of two hundred and forty tons gross, at a speed of sixteen miles an hour on some parts of the line, and at an average rate of twelve miles an hour from terminus to terminus.

These early performances have hitherto not been much exceeded, when load and speed are considered; but cases have occured with engines travelling either unloaded or drawing a less than usual weight, in which much greater speed has been attained. We have ourselves witnessed a velocity of above forty miles an hour with a considerable load, and nearly sixty miles an hour with an unloaded engine.

For various reasons, however, the full power of speed of the locomotive engine has not yet been developed. It is evident that on short lines of railway, especially when it is necessary to stop at various intermediate stations, very considerable average speed cannot be obtained. On approaching each station the action of the impelling power must be suspended, and the train of carriages allowed to come to rest by a gradually declining motion. The sudden stopping of the rapid progressive motion of a heavy mass would be attended with the destruction of the carriages and machinery; and even the common brakes provided to bring the train to rest should be sparingly used, as they are always attended with more or less injury. It must also be considered, that any delay at a station produces a greater diminution of the average rate of motion when great speed is attained than with a slower rate of travelling. If in a trip of thirty miles a speed of thirty miles an hour be the rate when actually in motion, and the stoppages at the stations, and delay in coming to rest and getting up the speed, amount to fifteen minutes, the *average* speed will be reduced to twenty-four miles an hour; the loss of speed being six miles an hour, or one fifth of the regular rate. If in the same trip a speed of ten miles an hour be the rate when in motion, and the same delay of fifteen minutes be produced at the stations, the average speed will be reduced to about nine miles and a quarter an hour; the loss of speed being only three quarters of a mile per hour, or about one thirteenth of the actual speed when in motion.

To develop, therefore, to their full extent, the actual powers of speed of railways worked by steam engines, we must wait for the completion of some of the great lines of communication now in progress of construction between the metropolis and the more distant points of commercial intercourse, and for the complete organisation of the traffic and intercourse upon them. When that is accomplished arrangements will doubtless be made for despatch trains, which will communicate between the termini of the longest lines, without any intermediate stoppage. The only indispensable cause of stoppage, at present, is to take in water and fuel. Now the consumption of both of these is in the direct proportion of the amount of the load carried. If we can now transport a gross load of fifty tons thirty miles without a

relay of water and fuel, we could transport twenty-five tons twice that distance, or sixty miles, without any relay. But, independently of this, nothing can be more easy than to provide, if desirable, tenders sufficiently capacious to carry the quantity of water and fuel which would be required for the transport of a light despatch train from terminus to terminus of any line of railway now projected.

Seeing the vast amount of national capital which has been, and is about to be, absorbed by these enterprises, and the large portion of all classes of persons in this country whose well-being will be directly and indirectly affected by them, we feel assured that we shall not be regarded as performing an unacceptable duty in attempting to unfold, in familiar language, the means whereby those great improvements are likely to be effected, and to investigate the probable extent to which they may be carried.

The impelling power of the steam is applied, in the first instance, to drive a piston backwards and forwards in a cylinder, which rests in an horizontal position on the axle of one pair of the wheels which support the engine. The rod of this piston is attached by a joint to a bar which lays hold of an arm, called a *crank*, placed on the axle of another pair of the engine-wheels, called the driving or impelling wheels. As the piston is driven through the cylinder in each direction, this arm is made to revolve by the bar which the piston rod moves. Now, the arm being fixed on the axle of the driving wheels so as, in fact, to be part of that axle, when it is made to revolve the axle must revolve with it. If the wheels were placed on this axle, like the wheels of common road carriages, the effect of this operation would be merely to cause the axle to revolve within the naves or boxes of the wheels, and the engine with its load would stand still. But, on the contrary, the wheels of the engine are firmly keyed upon the axle so as to form one solid piece with it. The axle, therefore, cannot revolve without compelling the wheels to revolve with it.

Now, if one pair of the wheels which support the engine be in this manner compelled to turn round, either of two things will happen: the engine will advance along the road, the tires of the wheels *rolling* on the surface; or the engine will stand still, the tires of the wheels *rubbing* on the surface of the road. So long, however, as the resistance which holds the engine back is less in amount than the resistance which the pressure of the tire on the road produces to the rubbing motion, so long will the engine advance and the wheels roll. It is found, in practice, that, on a level railway, a load amounting to more than twenty times the amount of the pres-

ears on the wheels will be insufficient to stop the progressive motion of the engine, when the axle of the wheels is made to revolve by the steam power.

Each motion of the piston, backwards and forwards in the cylinder, causes one revolution of the arm driven by the piston rod, and, therefore, one revolution of the driving wheels of the engine. This produces a progressive motion of the train through a distance equal to the circumference of the driving wheels. In accomplishing this, the cylinder must then be twice filled with steam by the boiler, and, therefore, to propel the train through a distance equal to the driving wheels consumes a measure of steam equal to twice the capacity of the cylinder.

But in the successive attitudes into which the revolving arm is thrown, the power of the piston-rod upon it is subject to great variation. When the elbow forms a right angle the power acts with its full effect; and according as the angle of the elbow becomes more extended and obtuse on the one hand, or more contracted and acute on the other, the effect of the power is diminished, and this diminution is continued until in one extreme position the arm is stretched directly against the end of the piston-rod, and in the other it is doubled down upon it. In both of these extreme positions the piston loses all power over the revolving arm, and therefore, for the moment, its influence in impelling the engine and train is suspended. This happens twice in every revolution of the arm.

Under such circumstances it is evident that the train would be impelled with an unequal motion, being urged by starts. Besides this, if, by chance, the train should come to rest when the arm is in one of those attitudes in which the piston has no power over it, no motion could be produced by the engine, and to put it in motion it would be necessary to push the train by some external force until the revolving arm should alter its position.

To avoid this inconvenience a second cylinder and piston are provided to drive a second arm, placed on the same axle as the first, but fixed upon it so as to be always in a position at right angles to the first. Thus, when the first is horizontal, the second is vertical, and *vice versa*. By this arrangement an impelling power is obtained which is very nearly uniform in its action. By the relative position of the two arms it will be seen that, at the moment when one is in the attitude in which the piston loses all power over it, the other is in the plenitude of its energy; and according as the efficiency of the latter is diminished, that of the former is increased. By this means the sum of the

effects of the two pistons on their respective arms is very nearly of an invariable amount. Nor is any power lost by this expedient, since the combined effect of the two pistons will be equal to that of a single piston of twice the magnitude of either, and which in each stroke would consume twice the quantity of steam. The measure of steam, therefore, necessary to draw the train through a distance equal to the circumference of the driving wheels will be four times the capacity of either cylinder.

When these preliminary principles are understood, the circumstances which determine the speed of the progressive motion will be easily comprehended. In the engines which have been generally used for several years on the Liverpool and Manchester Railway, the impelling wheels have been five feet in diameter. The circumference is then 15·7 feet. Each stroke of the piston then impels the train over 15·7 feet, and ten strokes carry it the distance of 157 feet. The number of strokes necessary to carry the train a mile will therefore be 336. It is a matter, then, of easy calculation to show, that if the piston make 168 strokes per minute, the train will move at the rate of 2640 feet per minute, which is equal to thirty miles an hour.

Assuming for the present that steam can be produced by the boiler with sufficient rapidity to supply the cylinders, let us inquire what are the circumstances which place practical limits on the further increase of speed. The very rapid reciprocating motion of the pistons, and of every part of the working gear and machinery connected with them, is attended with much concussion and vibration, and is certainly one of the most formidable sources of wear and tear, and therefore of expense, in the locomotive engine. While the mechanical connection at present used between the pistons and the driving wheels is retained, it is evident that there is only one method of obtaining increased speed without increasing the rapidity of this vibration of the pistons; and that method is by increasing the diameter of the impelling wheels. If, instead of being five feet in diameter, the impelling wheels had diameters of ten feet, each revolution would carry the train through twice the distance; so that with the same number of strokes per minute of the piston, the actual speed of the motion would be doubled. Either of two advantages would thus be placed at the option of the engineer: increased velocity without increased vibration, or the same velocity with greatly diminished vibration.

Why then, it may be asked, has not this very obvious expedient been long since resorted to? To answer this, we must bring

one or two other points under the reader's
attention.

On a railway the engine and carriages are
confined to the rails by ledges, called *flanges*,
raised from the inside edges of the tires of
the wheels. These flanges, when the tires
rest upon the rail, descend on the inside below the level of the rail; so that if from any
cause the wheel acquired a tendency to roll
off the rail *outwards*, the flange would immediately press against the inside of the rail,
and prevent the escape of the wheel. The
same expedient being provided on the wheels
at both sides, the engine and carriages are
strictly confined to move upon the rails in
the same manner as a thing would be compelled to move in a groove.

For the same reason that a large wheel
passes with greater facility than a smaller
one over any obstacle which comes before it,
large wheels on railway carriages and engines
would be less effectually protected by their
flanges from escaping from the rails. The
rail may be regarded as an obstacle over
which the flange must roll before the engine
or carriages can run off the road. Now, in
proportion as we enlarge the wheels, it is
clear that we facilitate the passage of the
flanges over the rails, and therefore impair
their protective power.

The most fruitful source of railway accidents, and these accidents of a very dangerous kind, being the liability of running off
the rails, the Directors of the Liverpool and
Manchester Railway were excusably cautious
in allowing any change in their arrangements
which appeared to increase this danger, and
for this reason they have pertinaciously adhered to the five feet wheels. In one instance, we believe, wheels five feet six inches
in diameter were placed on an engine, and it
happened unfortunately to run off the road,
the accident being attended with loss of life.
Although it did not appear that this misfortune was owing to the enlargement of the
wheels, still it served to strengthen the determination of the board of directors to adhere to the lesser dimension.

An improvement, however, has been more
recently introduced in the construction of
locomotive engines, which has in a great degree, if not altogether, removed this ground
of objection to augmenting the magnitude of
the driving wheels. The engines formerly
were supported on four wheels. The *flanges*
of each pair were therefore indispensable to
keep the engines on the rails; and it is necessary to observe, that from the operation
of the pistons on the axle of the driving
wheels, these have a greater tendency to run
over the rails, than the other wheels of the
engine or of any of the carriages. The engine builders have now very generally placed

these machines on three pairs of wheels, two
pairs of which are usually of small diameter,
the pair of driving wheels being larger. The
axle of the driving wheels is generally in the
centre. Now it will be evident, on the
slightest consideration, that with such an
arrangement the engine will be kept upon
the rails by the flanges of the first and last
pairs of wheels; and that those of the middle
pair need never come into action, unless indeed the rails be so curved as to produce a
deflection inwards between the first and last
wheel; a circumstance which very rarely
happens on a railway, and when it does, it
were better that the middle wheel had no
flange.

It is evident, therefore, that in the ordinary operation of the engines thus constructed, the flanges of the driving wheels
are unnecessary, and can be only useful in
the possible case of the fracture of either of
the other wheels or axles, or in the event
of their having a tendency to run over the
rail.

The engine being thus kept upon the
rails independently of the driving wheels,
the objection to their enlargement is removed.*

Nevertheless, such has been the con-
servative spirit of directors and engineers,
that notwithstanding the obvious advantage
derivable from driving wheels of an increased size, the six-wheeled engines recently placed on most of the lines have still
the five feet driving wheels. In one or two
instances they have ventured an increase of
six inches. On the Great Western Railway only has the principle of large driving
wheels been carried out to its full extent.
The engines constructed for that line are
impelled by wheels varying from seven to
ten feet in diameter.

It must not, however, be inferred that,
with the enlarged wheels, the same load
can be drawn with the same force of steam;
and as this is not a very uncommon mistake, it may be worth while here to explain
the point. By increasing the diameter of
the driving wheel, we increase the lever
against which the power has to act in drawing the load. The lever *upon* which the
power acts is the arm or crank placed on
the driving axle; the lever *against* which
it acts is the lowest spoke of the driving
wheel. Now the most elementary percep-
tions in mechanics will enable any one to
see that if we increase the length of the

---

* Another advantage of three pair of wheels is,
that, in the event of one axle breaking, the engine, connected as it is with the tender, will be
supported by the other two. The driving axle is
very liable to fracture, being weakened by the
cranks.

latter lever, the power and the crank remaining the same, *we must diminish the load in the same proportion.* With the same force on the piston, and the same length of crank, therefore, a ten feet driving wheel will draw only half the gross load which would be drawn by a five feet wheel.

But it will perhaps be asked, how the mere difference of magnitude of the wheels can change the actual effect produced by a given amount of the moving power? The answer is obvious: no such change of effect is produced. The actual quantity of steam necessary to transport a given load over a given distance is the same, whether we use a five feet wheel or a ten feet wheel. If a ten feet wheel be used, the load being the same, the resistance to the force on the piston is doubled, for the reason already explained. Therefore the moving force which has to overcome that resistance must be doubled; that is, the force of the steam on the piston must be doubled. Now this may be done either by doubling the superficial magnitude of the piston, or by doubling the pressure of the steam per square inch upon it. In either case the quantity of steam consumed in each stroke of the piston will be doubled. In the one case it will be twice the measure of steam of the same density; in the other case, it will be the same measure of steam of double the density.* Each revolution of the ten feet wheels will, therefore, cost as much steam as two revolutions of the five feet wheels. But since the circumference of the former is double the circumference of the latter, the load is drawn by one revolution of the former the same distance as by two revolutions of the latter. Therefore the transport of a given load a given distance requires the same power of steam, whatever be the diameter of the wheels. If then, in fine, it be asked what is the advantage gained by increasing the wheels, we answer, in a word, that it enables us to carry light loads at very much increased speed without increasing the rapidity of vibration of the working parts of the engine.

The practical experience which we possess already of the working of ordinary locomotive engines has demonstrated that an engine with five feet wheels in good working order will draw six first class carriages, each accommodating twenty passengers, on a tolerably level line of railway, at the average rate of thirty miles an hour, supposing no stoppage at stations from terminus to terminus.

The carriages will weigh about three tons each when unloaded. One hundred and twenty passengers will weigh about eight tons; and if we allow for mails, parcels, and other objects of transport six tons, we shall have a gross load of thirty-two tons. The engine, with its tender, water, and fuel, may be taken at eighteen tons, which gives a total weight transported of fifty tons.

All other things remaining the same, let us now suppose the five feet wheels replaced by ten feet wheels, and for the six carriages a single one substituted, which, with its load, shall weigh seven tons. The total weight transported will then be reduced to twenty-five tons; the same power will move it at double the speed, or sixty miles an hour, except so far as the increased resistance of the air may absorb the moving power. The extent of this effect has not yet been satisfactorily ascertained by experiment, but we have no doubt that some persons who have devoted attention to this inquiry have greatly overrated it, while, on the other hand, it has been as erroneously disregarded by others.

It is the opinion of some engineers of considerable practical knowledge, that greater durability of the working parts, and increased speed, would be better and more effectually obtain d by totally changing the nature of the mechanical connection by which the force of the piston is conveyed to the driving wheels. They contend that the cranks by which the continuity of the working axle is broken in two places is a monstrosity in engineering, and a complete violation of every principle of sound mechanical science; that the working axle on which the chief part of the weight of the engine *must* be thrown, in order to give the driving wheels sufficient adhesion, is thereby rendered the weakest part of the machine; and that this glaring error is most clumsily and unmechanically compensated by throwing into that axle an enormous weight of metal; that even this is a very imperfect remedy for the evil, as is proved by the frequent fracture of the cranked axles coming from workshops of the highest character;* but above all, that the rapid vibration of the piston, slides, and other working parts, which, even with the largest practicable driving wheels, is necessary when high velocities are attained,

* These remarks of the writer in the *Monthly Chronicle* are strikingly borne out by recent facts.—At the late general meeting of the Grand Junction Railway Company, (see report in *Railway Times,* Aug. 4.,) it was stated, that "all the axle of their engines were too weak, whether cranks or otherwise, and had *all in consequence broke.*"

is utterly destructive of the machinery, an incalculable source of expense, and exposes the public to constant danger by liability to fracture and other accidental derangement. To the increase of the magnitude of the driving wheels there is also an obvious and narrow limit. Their unwieldy dimensions and enormous weight would soon be productive of evils which would much more than counterbalance any benefit which could be derived from them, either by increased speed or diminished vibration. It is still doubtful how far the ten feet wheels intended to be tried on the Great Western Railway will be attended with success; and though we have not ourselves great misgivings on the subject, a large majority of the engineering profession is decidedly opposed to them.

It is contended that the motion of the piston should be considerably slower than in the present engines. A slow motion would not only remove the present formidable evils arising from the reciprocating motion of the working parts, but it would also render the power in other respects more effective. Mr. Watt and other eminent practical men held, that a steam-engine works with best effect when the speed of the piston does not exceed two hundred and forty feet per minute. Now a five feet wheel driven by an engine having an eighteen inch stroke would require the piston to be moved at the rate of above five hundred feet per minute, to give a progressive motion of thirty miles an hour, being more than double the most effective speed.

Those evils above mentioned which arise from the working axle being weakened by the cranks, have been already attempted to be removed by placing the cylinders outside the wheels of the engines, and connecting the piston rod with a pin attached to one of the spokes of the wheel. This expedient, however, has totally failed; and as the practice has, we believe, been on all hands given up, it is not worth while here to occupy our limited space with a statement of the reasons of its failure. Meanwhile it will be observed, that it in no degree abated the main cause of mischief—the rapid vibration of the piston.

One of the methods by which it has been proposed to render a moderate velocity of the pistons compatible with the extreme speed of progressive motion, which, having once been enjoyed by the public, has become an indispensable necessity in railway transit, is to convey the power of the piston to the working wheels by tooth and pinion gear. If the practicability of applying this species of mechanism, under the peculiar circumstances of the case of a lo-

comotive engine, be once admitted, we can hardly discover any practical limit to the speed of transit which may be obtained on railways. Even now, with all the difficulties and defects of the present mechanism, we think that for a light load—say a single carriage carrying the mails with their guards or couriers—sixty miles an hour may be demonstrated to be practicable, and even an hundred miles an hour is not altogether beyond the sphere of possibility. But once admit the practicability of applying toothed gear, and it will be difficult indeed to say where may be the limit of mechanical possibility, whatever may be said of the limit which prudence may prescribe:

In the application of this method, it is proposed to place on the working axle a toothed pinion or small wheel, which shall be keyed on so that it cannot revolve without causing the axle to revolve with it. The teeth of this pinion shall be engaged in those of a larger wheel by which it shall be driven; and which, being on a second axle, shall itself be driven by the pistons of the engine. This second axle, not having any other weight to support than its own weight and that of the larger wheel just mentioned, may without objection or difficulty be constructed with two cranks or arms, to be driven by the pistons of the two cylinders as formerly explained.

Now let us suppose the pinion fixed upon the axle of the working wheels to be eighteen inches diameter, and the larger toothed wheel by which it is driven to be four feet six inches in diameter; one revolution of the latter will produce three revolutions of the former, and, therefore, three revolutions of the driving wheels. But the large-toothed wheel being impelled by cranks on its axle, one revolution of it will be produced by one stroke of the pistons; therefore one stroke of the pistons will produce three revolutions of the driving wheels, and will therefore cause a progressive motion equal to that which would be produced by engines of the present construction having wheels three times greater in diameter.

With six feet working wheels a speed of thirty-six miles an hour would, under these circumstances, be produced, if the piston vibrated at the rate of fifty-six strokes per minute, whereas in the present engines the same speed requires one hundred and sixty-eight strokes per minute. All injurious vibration proceeding from the machinery would, in fact, be removed.

The same motion of the piston which, in the present engines, with six feet wheels, produces a speed of thirty-six miles an hour, would with the mechanism above described, other things being the same, produce a speak of one hundred and eight miles an hour!

Such a mechanical arrangement is so obvious, and founded upon mechanical principles and expedients so well understood, that it cannot be supposed to have escaped the attention of engineers; but its practical application has been attended with difficulties so formidable, that hitherto it has been unattempted. These difficulties arise chiefly from the necessity of placing the cylinders and other machinery on springs, while the axle of the working wheels, to which the machinery has to impart motion, must act upon the road, and be acted upon by it without the intervention of the springs. Thus the machinery partakes of one set of motions and disturbances, the working axle moved by the machinery of another. As the locomotive engine is constructed at present, the inconveniences arising from this are avoided, since there are no tooth and pinion gear; the unequal motion of the working wheels is shared by cranks, piston rods, and pistons; but there it ends, the elasticity of the steam intercepting its effects.

A contrivance, however, has recently been patented by Mr. T. E. Harrison, engineer of the Stanhope and Tyne Railway, for a method of applying tooth and pinion gear to locomotive engines. Mr. Harrison connects the large-toothed wheel and the axle by which it is turned with the axle of the working wheels by means of iron straps, by which both axles are firmly held together, and compelled to partake of a common vertical motion; all jolts, therefore, received by the action of the driving wheels are equally imparted to the cranked axle above them, the effect of which is, that the teeth of the large wheel are always equally engaged in those of the pinion; meanwhile the general framing supporting the cylinders and other parts of the machinery is placed, as usual, on springs, chairs being being provided to confine laterally both working axles.

The height occupied by such machinery renders it impracticable, as in other locomotive engines, to place the boiler above it on the same carriage. The boiler, therefore, with its furnace and appendages, is placed on an independent carriage behind the machinery. The pipes which supply steam to the cylinders, and reconduct the waste steam to the chimney, are supplied with peculiar joints, which admit of as much longitudinal and lateral play as the relative motions of the carriages bearing the machinery and boiler require. One of these joints is, in fact, the common telescope joint; and the other the ball and socket; the former permits the two carriages to approach to and recede from each other; and the other to vibrate from side to side in contrary directions, within limits which, though small, are sufficient for the circumstances under which such carriages are placed when connected together and confined between the rails.

The removal of the boiler to an independent carriage seriously diminishes the weight which rests upon the working wheels, and in applying the machine, to draw a heavy train, the adhesion would be insufficient to give progressive motion. To obviate this, the wheels of the carriage bearing the machinery are *coupled*, that is, they are united by a bar attached to corresponding pins placed upon their spokes, so that one pair of wheels cannot revolve without at the same time compelling the other pair to revolve. In this way the adhesion of both pairs of wheels is brought into action, and the weight of the machinery is or may be made sufficiently great to render this adhesion proportionate to the load.

The extreme caution observed by railway engineers and directors in the management of these undertakings has hitherto imposed a check, amounting almost to a dead lock, on the progress of mechanical invention in this department. We are not prepared to say that such caution may not have been defensible; but whether defensible or not, it has undoubtedly retarded the progress of improvement. A conspicuous exception to it, however, is presented in the management of the Great Western Railway, which has gone so far in the other extreme as to retain, in the circumstances of the structure of the road, scarcely a feature in common with other lines of railway throughout the country, and which has ventured most startling departures from established usage in the machinery to be worked upon it. As, however, we shall notice this enterprise more at large in a future number, we shall now merely observe, that among the many other novelties intended to be tried upon it is an engine, constructed on the above principles, by Messrs. Hawthorn, of Newcastle-upon-Tyne. However such experiments may affect those who first institute them, they cannot fail to accelerate the progress of practical science and to advance the interests of the public.

NOTES AND NOTICES.

Davenport's Electro-Magnetic Railway Locomotive.—Mr. Davenport has at length gratified the curiosity of the English sceptics to a certain extent, by sending over a model of a locomotive engine, which is now exhibiting at the Adelaide Gallery, in the Lowther Arcade, worked on the same principle as his larger stationary engines. This carriage runs on a circular railway, and draws after it two other carriages, which move, by the aid of two small galvanic batteries, at the rate of about three miles an hour. The weight thus propelled is nearly 80 lb., and the carriage containing the apparatus is about one foot square. The manner in which the electro-magnets are arranged, is kept a secret for the present; but the principle on which the application of the power depends is well known, and the chief superiority in Mr. Davenport's invention, consists in his having, by some peculiar contrivance, brought into exercise a greater amount of power within a given space and weight, than has been hitherto accomplished. Though we do not anticipate that Mr. Davenport's invention, as exhibited in the working model, would be found applicable on a large scale with any practical advantage; yet what he has accomplished is sufficient to show that important results may be expected from future improvements in the application of the same principle. We are informed by an American gentleman who has recently arrived in England, that he witnessed a two-horse power electro-magnetic engine, of Mr. Davenport's construction, employed in printing a newspaper in New York, and that it performed the work most satisfactorily. Whether or not, however, this was done at a cheaper rate than the same power might be obtained from steam, we are not able to ascertain.—*Morning Herald.*

Midland Counties' Railway.—The neighbourhood of Spondon, near Derby, has presented a busy scene for the last week. A diversion of the canal had to be made by the Railway Company, which could not be effected without stopping the navigation, for which there was a penalty of 2l. per hour. The contractor, Mr. Mackenzie, taking advantage of a stoppage of the canal, mustered his forces from the other parts of the contract, and has succeeded in executing the diversion while the repairs of the canal were going on, to the astonishment of the natives. Between 200 and 300 men were employed in a very small space, and when all busily at work, presented a very animated spectacle. To induce the men to persevere and work an extra number of hours, Mr. Mackenzie supplied them with a substantial dinner of beef and ale, in addition to their wages, which was served and eaten on the works.—*Railway Times.*

Menai Bridge.—We have been assured of the truth of the following singular anecdote of Telford, the great architect of the bridge, whose monument, it has been well said, "hangs over the Menai Straits." A small cottage had been fitted up for his (Telford's) use, and on the day on which the hopes and expectations of his life were to be realised or blighted, when the first chain was to be fixed, connecting the two shores together—when thousands had assembled to witness the scene, and as the time approached, were watching in breathless silence, Telford, unable to bear it any longer, and utterly incapable, from agitation, to give any orders, retired to the little cottage, and there, with the blinds down awaited the result. At the appointed hour, slowly, but securely, the immense chain rose from the raft, and the bolt was fixed. A loud and long-continued huzza from the multitude told the event to the happy Telford; and, when the narrator of this incident entered the cottage, Telford was on his knees, returning thanks to God for the fulfilment, thus far, of the grand scheme of his life.—*Birmingham Paper.*

Artesian Well.—The bore which has been going on for so long a period near Paris, has now reached the depth of 410 metres, (or about 1345 feet,) and the funds being exhausted, M. Elie de Beaumont has been requested to examine the matters lately brought up by the augur, and to say whether they afford any indication by which the thickness of the bed to be pierced, before arriving at the sand, may be gathered. M. de B. has accordingly given his opinion, that the bore has reached the lower beds of the chalk formation, and that the maris and gault which still intervene between the bore and stratum where the water will be found, will probably be less than 100 metres thick, (328 feet.) If M. de Beaumont's anticipation should prove correct, the well should have a depth of 1600 feet, at which depth, according to recent calculations, the water should have a temperature sufficiently high to furnish Paris with an abundant supply of hot water for baths, and for many other purposes.

Effects of Prussic Acid Counteracted.—A numerous body of gentlemen of this town, consisting of members of the medical and legal professions, were last week invited to attend a series of experiments of a physiological and chemical nature, illustrative of the important subject of forensic medicine, by John Robinson, M.D., which afforded much instruction and the greatest satisfaction to the audience. The most important feature of these demonstrations, was the Doctor's method of resuscitation from the effects of hydrocyanic acid, of which we will give a brief outline. Two strong rabbits being selected for experiment, four drops of powerful hydrocyanic acid were applied to the tongue of each—the effects were instantly apparent—the animals were for some minutes motionless, and apparently dead, when Dr. Robinson administered his restorative, cold water poured from an eminence over the occiput and spine, (the temperature of the water being previously lowered by nitrate of potass and common salt.) The effect was magical; for by this resuscitative process it was remarked that each animal in turn skipped about the floor as if in the enjoyment of good health and spirits. We need scarcely remark, that such facts as we now record, cannot be too prominently placed before the public.—*Sunderland Paper.*

The Victoria Boiler Explosion.—The lengthened inquest into the cause of this melancholy event has at length been brought to a close, the jury having returned the following verdict,—" They consider that the death of Andrew Brown was accidentally occasioned by the explosion of the boiler on board the Victoria steam-vessel, on the 14th of June last. The jury consider that the construction of the boilers was unsafe, the water spaces too small, and the plates too thin. The jury further consider, that the engineers having no immediate controul over the safety-valve in the engine-room is highly reprehensible, and the *jury levy a deodand of 1,500l. upon the boiler and steam-engine of the Victoria.*" We shall next week publish a double number with the whole of the evidence taken before the coroner, and engravings of the boilers.

The twenty-eighth volume of the *Mechanics' Magazine* is now published, price, in half-cloth, 8s. 6d., with a *Railway Map* of England and Wales. The *Railway Map* may be had separately, price 6d.; and on fine paper, coloured, price 1s.

☞ *British and Foreign Patents taken out with economy and despatch; Specifications, Disclaimers, and Amendments, prepared or revised; Caveats entered; and generally every Branch of Patent Business promptly transacted. A complete list of Patents from the earliest period (15 Car. II. 1675,) to the present time may be examined. Fee 2s. 6d.; Clients, gratis.*

LONDON: Printed and Published for the Proprietor, by W. A. Robertson, at the Mechanics' Magazine Office, No. 6, Peterborough-court, between 135 and 136, Fleet-street.—Sold by A. & W. Galignani, Rue Vivienne, Paris.

Mechanics' Magazine,

MUSEUM, REGISTER, JOURNAL, AND GAZETTE.

No. 785.]   SATURDAY, AUGUST 25, 1838.   [Price 6d.

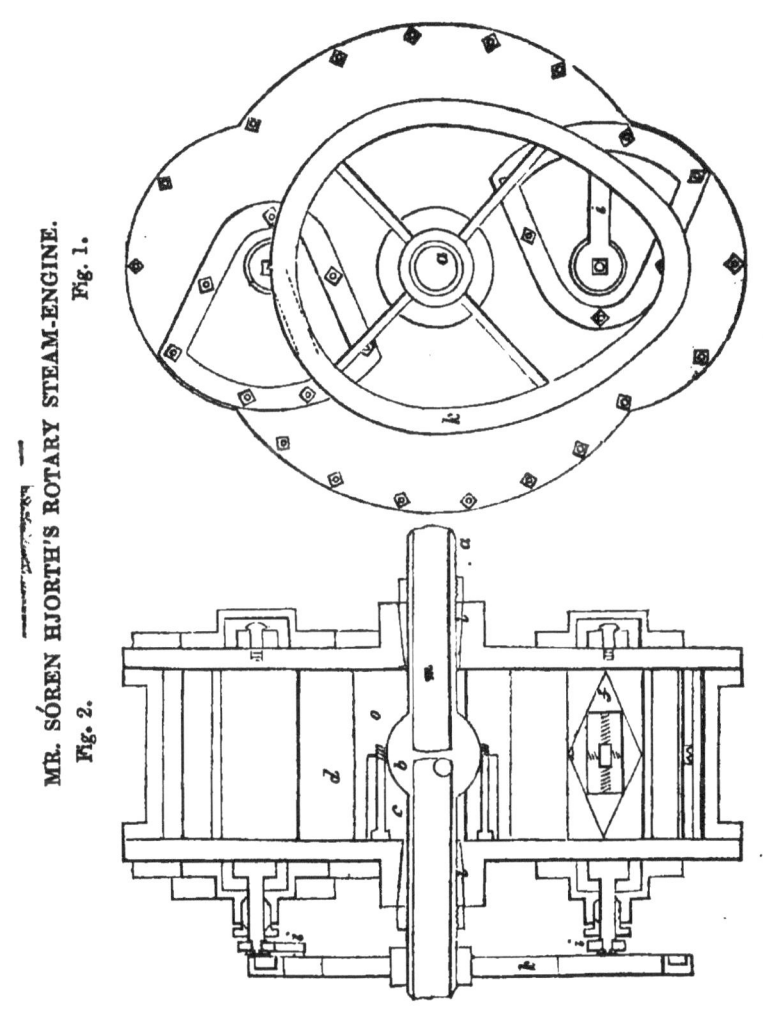

MR. SÓREN HJORTH'S ROTARY STEAM-ENGINE.

Fig. 1.

Fig. 2.

MR. SÓREN HJORTH'S ROTARY STEAM-ENGINE.

Few objects have engaged the attention of machinicians more than the endeavour to obtain a direct rotary motion from the power of steam; and, as the pages of the *Mechanics' Magazine* from time to time witness, the greatest ingenuity of mechanical arrangement has been evinced in these numerous, and, as yet, unsuccessful attempts.

The inventor of the rotary engine now to be described is Mr. Sóren Hjorth, of Elsinore.

Fig. 3.

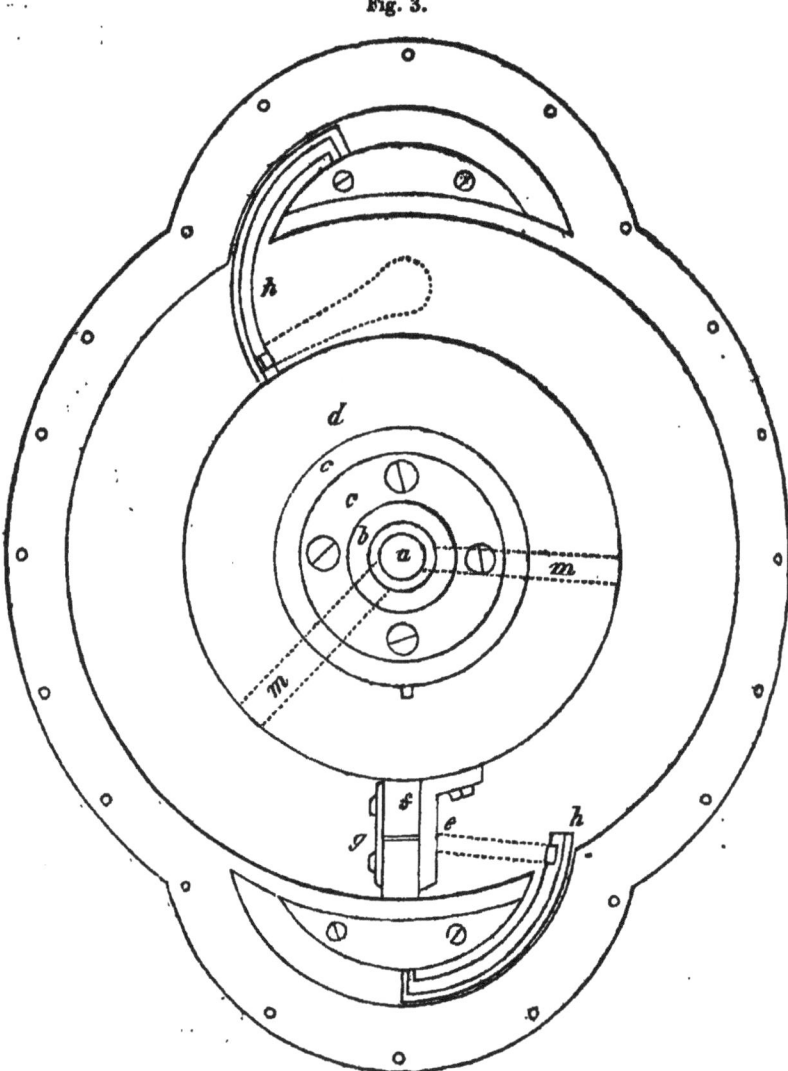

Figs. 1 and 2 (see front page) are a side view and section of the engine; fig. 3 is an enlarged side view, with the outer parts removed, to show the interior apparatus; fig. 4 a separate view of the piston, showing the mode of packing, or keeping all its edges against the sides of the steam-chamber. Similar letters refer to similar parts in all the figures.

a is the axle or shaft of the engine. *b*,

a ball which is fixed thereon, in order to allow the piston and the other moveable parts to move independent of the axle, if not perfectly rectangular to the side abutments. *c, c,* two rings, which are connected by screws, and form upon the ball a cylindrical foundation to *d,* two ring-formed wedges, which, by a spring, or by a little wedge between, are pressed towards one another by degrees as they wear away. The one of these wedges and the rings *c,* are, in driving the working axle, combined therewith by nuts. They are separately and more clearly represented in figs. 5 and 6. *e,* an angular piece, or elbow, which is fixed to the wedges *d,* which are attached to *c. f,* the piston; constructed as represented in fig. 4. *g,* a plate, which covers the piston. *h, h,* two slides, constructed, as re-

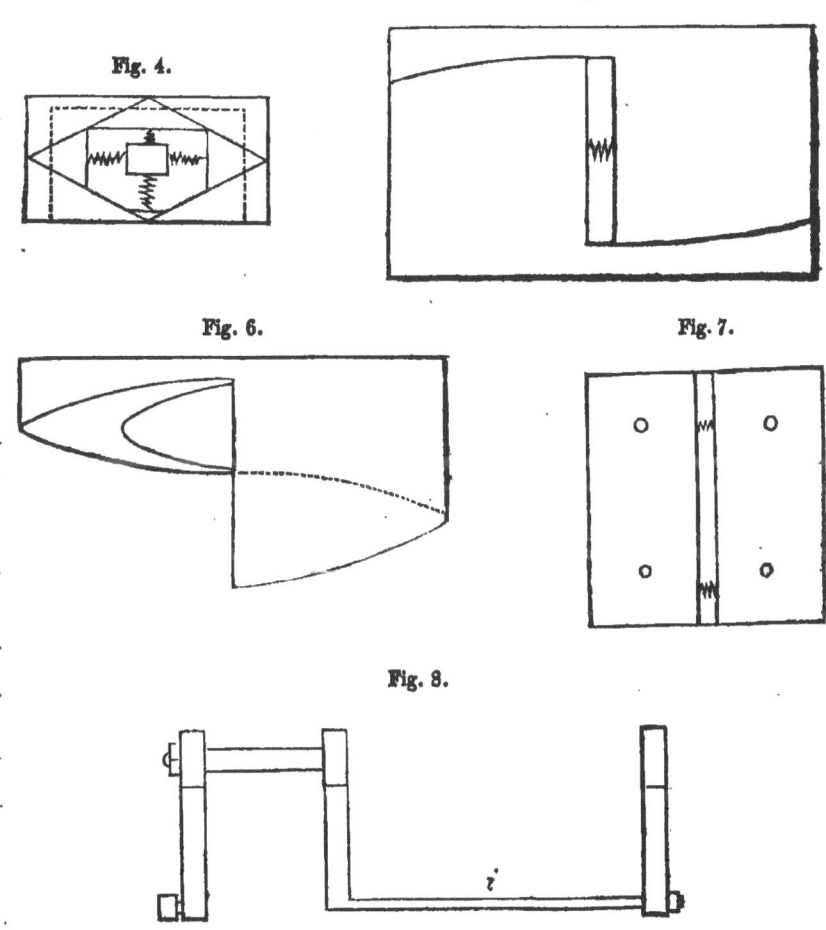

Fig. 5.

Fig. 4.

Fig. 6.

Fig. 7.

Fig. 8.

presented in fig. 7, of three pieces, of which two are pressed by a spring towards the side abutments by degrees, as they wear away. *i,* three combined cranks, which move and support the slides; shown separately at fig. 8. *k,* an eccentric guide to move the cranks. *l, l,* two steel rings, which are made conical in order to form a steam-tight stuffing-box; they are, of course, moved with the axle. *m,* the passage for the steam, which also can pass through the side abutments, *n.* It will easily be understood by the drawing that the centre can constantly be kept filled with oil, which, together with the therein accumulated steam, will counteract the steam which might escape between the round wedges and the side abutments. The sides and the piston are made of steel, but the tightening wedges of soft cast-iron. The inventor claims as new all the moveable parts in the engine, and especially the method by which the tightening parts extend themselves by degrees as they wear away, and move independent of the position of the axle, in case of not being perfectly rectangular to the side abutments.

VICTORIA BOILER EXPLOSION.—THE CORONER'S INQUEST.

SIR,—So the jury have made "something of it" at last, I see, and although they "can never ruin steam-boat travelling," their verdict will go far towards preventing further loss of life by the use of such *infernal machines* as have been employed on board the *Victoria* in place of steam-boilers.

I should like to know how it happened that, at the beginning of the inquiry, the coroner had no power to call for the opinions of such persons as could assist the jury in coming to a correct opinion—that is, according to *his own declaration* as reported in the papers —and that afterwards, when it was found the jury were *determined* to have such opinions, the coroner discovered he could call before him such persons as Mr. Seaward, Mr. Field, &c. Did not the coroner at first know the extent of his own authority, and the duties of his office? or did he afterwards stretch his authority? or is there an error in the reports?

Yours, &c. &c.

S. Y., an Engineer.

London, August 20, 1838.

VICTORIA EXPLOSION INQUEST.

This protracted investigation having been at length brought to a close, we, at the request of numerous correspondents, now publish a complete account of the proceedings—more particularly as regards the evidence upon the construction and management of the boilers and engine. We have abstained from publishing any parts of the proceedings hitherto, as the newspapers of the day gave them sufficient publicity,—but as the melancholy event will be a black letter day in the history of steam navigation, we judged that by bringing all the evidence together we should enable our readers the better to form a correct opinion upon the subject, as well as furnishing a record for after reference. The conversations, discussions, and wranglings between the coroner, jury, counsel, and witnesses, we have altogether omitted; the repetitions of various witnesses as to the circumstances of the collision and explosion; and also the oft-repeated descriptions of the boilers, which are rendered unnecessary by the evidence being prefaced by engravings and descriptions from the drawings of Mr. Ewart, the engineer appointed by government to examine them, and for which we are partially indebted to our cotemporary, the *Civil Engineer and Architects' Journal.*

We take the opportunity of referring to the following letters from correspondents which have appeared in our pages upon the subject of this explosion; viz., by Scrutator, p. 188, No. 776; by "N. S.," p. 264, No. 780; by Mr. C. G. Jarvis, engineer, p. 276, No. 781; by "S. Y., an engineer," p. 309, No. 783; by "N. S.," p. 325, No. 784—and by "S. Y.," in our present Number.

Description of the Engravings of the Victoria Boilers. — Fig. 1.—Longitudinal section of the wing boiler, exhibiting the ruptures.

Fig. 2.—Plan, showing the exterior of two adjoining boilers; the interior of the third, the upper half being removed; the fire flue of the fourth (the collapsed one), the upper half of the other case being removed.

Fig. 3.—Elevation; the left hand boiler is shown with the fire doors removed; the second, with them in their places; the third, at a section behind them, exhibiting the bridge of the furnace; the fourth with the bridge and bars removed.

Fig 4.—Cross section of collapsed boiler at *b a*.

Fig. 5.—Cross section of collapsed boiler at *d c.*

Fig. 6.—Cross section of collapsed boiler at *f e*.

Fig. 7.—Cross section of collapsed boiler at *h g*.

Fig. 8.—Cross section of the *Victoria* boiler.

Fig. 9.—Cross section of Cornish boiler.

A.—Principal flue, or fire tube. B—Water tube. C—Pipes of ditto to top of M. D—Brick bridges of the furnaces. E—Water spaces round the fire tube. F—Steam and water chambers. G—Steam connecting-pipes. H—Cross connecting-pipes. K—Water connecting-pipes; connecting each boiler with the adjoining one. L—Feed-pipes. M—Feed-cocks. N—Outer flues of bricks. O—Opening from fire tube to flues N. P—Boiler seat of brick-work. R—Furnace bars. S.—Funnel. T.—Man holes to water tubes. W.—Water line. *x*—Steam pipes. *r*—Ruptures; *rp*, Principal rupture ; *s*, Detached piece.

The boilers are 38 feet long, and 6 feet 5 inches in diameter.

Fig. 1

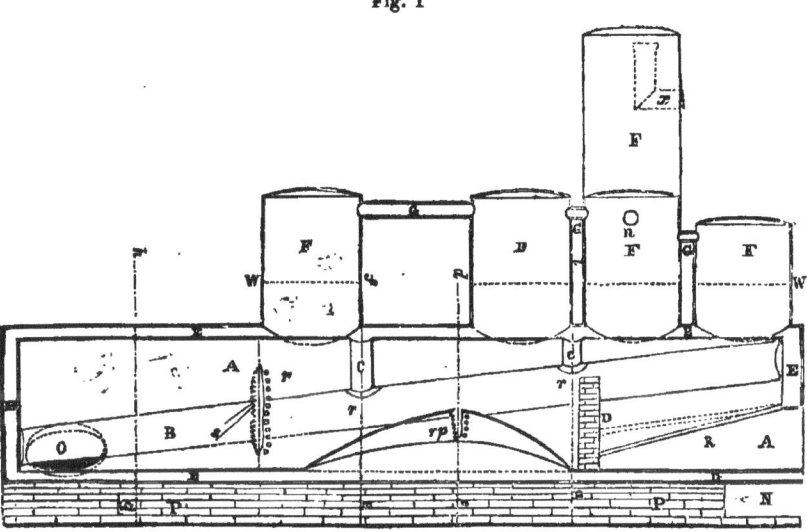

Fig. 2.

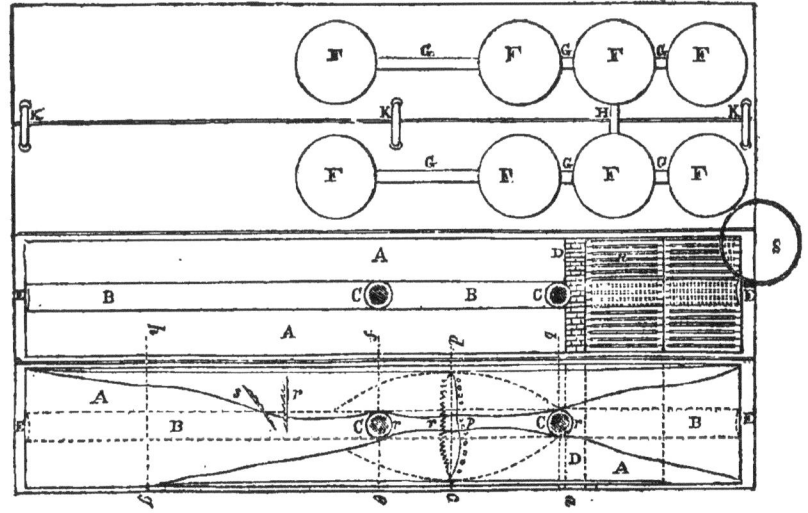

Fig. 3.

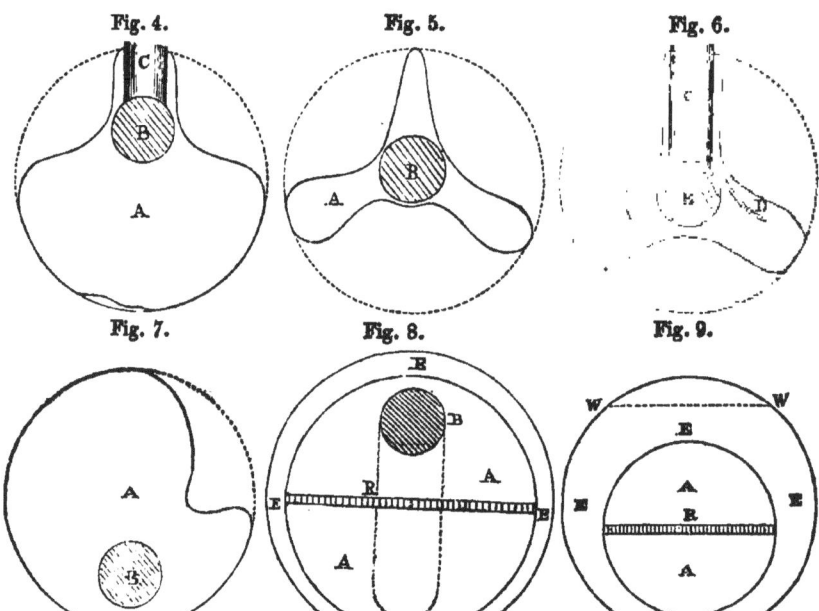

Fig. 4.   Fig. 5.   Fig. 6.

Fig. 7.   Fig. 8.   Fig. 9.

The Inquest.

On Saturday the 16th of June, the inquest commenced. After the jury had viewed the bodies of the sufferers, the coroner addressed them at great length. Without at all referring the jury to any facts connected with the very awful calamity into the circumstances of which they were met to inquire, he thought it his duty to call their attention to the law as connected with such cases, especially as they might affect any person or persons engaged in the construction of the boilers and machinery, and in managing the vessel in which the deceased met their deaths. There was one important fact which the jury would not overlook, that a similar accident had occurred to this vessel in March last, when five persons lost their lives in a like way. These facts would no doubt come out in evidence. Now, it was clear that any man employed in any enterprise of any description, was bound to bring into it his best physical and mental powers, both in the preparation and execution of the undertaking, and if accident then occurred he might be held excusable, but not otherwise. When a person was engaged in a dangerous business, but took such precautions as to make the occurrence of accident improbable, he would be excused; but want of caution and unskilfulness would be taken as homicide, and the jury would be careful particularly to consider the construction as well as the management of the engines and boilers of the steam-ship, and to ascertain if there was any defect in their construction, and if any want of necessary caution and attention was apparent. As a guide he would refer them to the case of "the King against Carr," reported in Carrington and Paine, 163 which was analogous. An iron-founder was employed to cast some pieces of cannon for a pleasure boat; one of the pieces burst, and was sent back. It was, however, repaired and returned to the sailing vessel, when it again burst and killed a man. This was held to be manslaughter against the founder of the cannon. There was another circumstance connected with this case to which the attention of the jury should be directed. The steam-packet in which the accident occurred, and another belonging to a rival company, left Hull about the same time, and they arrived in the river both nearly at the same moment. Now, when they knew well the very serious results that had occurred from what was termed steam-boat racing, it would be their imperative duty to ascertain if any such act had taken place between the two vessels, and whether there had been an unnecessary increase of the fires in order to propel the boat forward in the race, and whether danger had incurred thereby. The jury would also consider if the engines were fit to be worked, and whether they were kept in that condition. The jury, he was sure, would not take up any preconceived notions, but would attend solely to the evidence. The state of the law as respected steam-boats was just the same as that respecting a vehicle on land, and if accident occurred from want of care or from furious proceeding, it little mattered whether the force was a horse or steam. The latter, however, was the most dangerous, as it was the most powerful, and therefore required attention in the management. The jury would, however, remember, that those engaged in increasing the speed of a steam vessel were themselves in the greatest danger, and if any accident occurred, they would be the first sufferers. This would no doubt go far to prevent the jury returning a verdict of

manslaughter against the surviving engineers[*] who had been so frightfully burnt and scalded by the explosion. But there was another and most convenient mode of inflicting punishment, namely, by deodand. If this should be the conclusion of the jury, they would take care not to make it exorbitant, as it was controllable by the Court of Queen's Bench. The operation of this mode of punishment might be to induce more care in future. In conclusion, the jury would consider that the trade of the port of London required expedition, and this might be an excuse for increasing the speed of such vessels in general. The jury would see the vessel and the boiler, and would have the evidence of scientific men upon their nature and safety.

Mr. W. J. Hall, the company's agent, and Mr. Clarkson, attended on behalf of the Hull Steam Packet Company, to whom the vessel belonged.

Thomas Smith was the first witness called. He deposed that he was a coal trimmer and fireman on board the *Victoria*, which left Hull about half-past 4 o'clock on Wednesday afternoon, the 13th June, and arrived in the port of London about half-past 3, off Shadwell. We met with no accident until we arrived here. We started before the *Wilberforce*, and she came up with us in the Yarmouth-roads. She was then about two miles or a mile and a half astern of us. She was never any nearer than that. The speed of the *Victoria* was about the same as it had been on former occasions. If any thing her speed was less. During the last trip the engines did not work well, and we could not get sufficient steam. That difficulty lasted during the whole voyage. There is no way of overcoming that difficulty but by increasing the fires, and that was what we did. The principal engineer gave the directions for that to be done. As the steamer came up the river she got foul of a collier brig. I was on the engine floor when the collision happened, and remained to stop the engines, after which I went on deck to see what was the matter. The engines were stopped in consequence of the collision. The *Victoria* was brought up immediately afterwards. The explosion took place about three minutes after the collision, and the *Victoria* cast anchor immediately afterwards. The engines were stopped in the ordinary way, and promptly. I observed nothing wrong at that time. I cannot tell what caused the explosion. There was not much noise when it occurred. There was a sudden hissing noise like the turning of a tap, and the whole of the en-

---

* Not one, alas, survived.

gine-room was immediately filled with steam and scalding water, causing the instantaneous death of M'Donald, Young, Brown, and M'Kinley. The body of M'Donald, was blown into the stoke-hole; the others were on the engine-room floor. They appeared as if they had been roasted alive. All the steam and water escaped out of the boiler.

Mr. Clarkson then read the statement of Mr. W. C. Ellis, a passenger, as follows :—

"The *Victoria* left Hull on Wednesday, the 13th instant, at half-past five o'clock, and proceeded into the Thames without any accident having occurred until she arrived near to the Shadwell entrance of the London Docks, having just rounded a point in the river. It appeared evident that she could not escape coming in contact with the outside of a tier of colliers. The order from the paddle-box was immediately given to stop the engine, which was promptly done. The pilot called out instantly to a man who was in a boat at the head of the collier to get out of the way. At that moment the bowsprit of the collier came in contact with the starboard paddle-box of the *Victoria*, which was stove in with a tremendous crash. All was now a scene of confusion. I was standing at the head of the steamer, and saw the collision take place. I crossed to the other side of the steamer, and looking upwards the masts of the brig appeared to be tottering and ready to fall across the bows of the steamer, and, apprehending such to be the case, and not knowing what injury the brig had sustained, retreated towards the after part of the vessel, and when abreast of the engine-room, a dense volume of smoke proceeded forth, and in an instant I was enveloped in darkness. I then groped my way towards the stern, expecting every moment to be blown up, and upon looking back saw an immense body of steam bursting forth. After a few minutes had elapsed, and seeing so much steam escaping, I considered the boiler had burst, and consequently no danger could be now apprehended from an explosion. I pushed my way through the steam to the fore part of the vessel to ascertain the danger of our situation, and just at that moment one of the engine men was brought up a most awful spectacle. A second one was then laid upon the deck, and, after uttering two or three dreadful groans, expired. A third and then a fourth was brought up and laid upon the deck. At that time the captain was calling upon persons to come down to the engine-room to assist in bringing up the remainder of the sufferers. I had heard it mentioned by the engineers that they were unable to get up the full power of the steam during the whole day in consequence of an alteration in the furnaces, which had prevented the fires from burning. The captain appeared to be a very careful man, and frequently went below and examined the engines. An opposition steam-packet was close astern of the *Victoria*, but no disposition was evinced by the captain to endanger the lives of the passengers by causing additional pressure of steam in order to enable him to keep the lead; on the contrary, it was asserted that it was a matter of small importance if the *Wilberforce* did get up before the *Victoria*."

Mr. Ellis said the *Victoria* was 10 miles a-head of the other off the coast of Suffolk. No steam was blown off after the collision before the explosion took place. The brig run foul of, was the outer one of the tiers.

After some conversation it was agreed to adjourn until Tuesday afternoon, the 26th July, and the coroner and jury immediately proceeded to Blackwall in three boats provided by Mr. Hall, for the purpose of examining the boilers.

The coroner and jury, on arriving at Blackwall, where the *Victoria* was moored alongside the Bashemore hulk, were received by the agent of the company, who immediately conducted them to the engine-room, where they had great difficulty in finding their way to the stoke-holes. These places are the most confined of the sort that any of the jury had ever witnessed, and they expressed their astonishment at the men being able to work in them. The attention of the jury was directed to the feed-pipes which supply the engines with water. From the state of the bends it would appear that the supply was nearly or quite cut off, and this was also assigned as the probable cause of the accident. The taps which indicate the quantity of water in the boiler were then examined, and found to be in perfect order. Captain Bell explained to the jury the nature and use of the engine. Before they left Hull on the last occasion, two of the furnaces were provided with new gratings of a different construction to those generally used, and the consequence was that the fires could not be kept up, nor sufficient steam procured. Captain Bell's opinion was, that the men, having been disappointed in their expectation in getting up the usual supply of steam, had determined to effect it somehow, and had cut off the supply of water to the boilers, and had thus caused instant destruction. The coroner said that that was highly probable from the state of the supply pipes, but he could not but observe that several other parts of the boilers had been bent and torn in such a way as to appear very dangerous.

Captain Bell in reply to this said, "Oh, the others were going, and there is no doubt they were red-hot when the other burst."

The jury then withdrew, and were shown into the cabin, and

Mr. Hall said he should be happy to afford them every information in his power, and if they could discover there was any defect in the boilers, the Company would be very grateful for their knowledge. He had fitted up the vessel in a way that he thought not one thing was wanting to make her the most complete and commodious steam vessel on the waters, and if he had to remodel another he should take the *Victoria* as a pattern. He much deplored the melancholy accident which had occurred in the vessel, but it was his decided opinion that the supply of water must have been cut off by the men, and hence had occurred the explosion. If the men had properly discharged their duty no accident of the kind could possibly have taken place.

The coroner said, that what had particularly struck the jury from their view was the confined and inconvenient place for the men to attend the fires and the engines. There was no possibility of an escape from them if an accident occurred.

Mr. Hall said more room could not be spared, as they wanted space for the passengers' luggage, &c.

Mr. Jackson, a juror, said more attention ought to be paid to the comfort and convenience of the men engaged in such laborious duties.

The coroner asked Mr. Hall if he was, after this second accident, still in favour of cylindrical boilers?

Mr. Hall, in reply, said—Yes, I am more than ever convinced of their safety; it is not a new principle.

On the morning of the 26th of June the jury again met at Mr. Hammett's, the Watermen's Arms, Lower Shadwell, pursuant to adjournment. The following are the names of all the deceased persons, four of whom were killed in the engine-room when the boiler exploded; another died on the same night in the Dreadnought hospital-ship, and the others since that time, after enduring very great pain from severe scalds and burns:—Jacob Evans, chief engineer; William Colville, second engineer; Andrew Brown, James Young, William M'Kinlay, John M'Donald, George Clay, otherwise Hutchcroft, Jacob Asher, and James Wilcox Derrington, *alias* Burgess.

Mr. L. Jacobs, solicitor to the Hull Steam Packet Company, attended for that body. Mr. D. Napier, engineer, of Blackwall, and from whose designs the boilers and engines were made, was present during the investigation.

After the examination of a witness as to the state of one of the sufferers, and some desultory conversation, Mr. Napier was called upon to give evidence; but after he had been sworn, his examination was not proceeded with, as the boilers of the *Victoria* had been constructed according to his plans.

Charles Bell, of Hull, was then sworn. He deposed as follows:—I am Captain of the *Victoria*, and have been so ever since she was launched, on the 19th of June last. She was built at Hull. The engines were partly made at Glasgow and partly at Hull. The boilers were made at Hull by Messrs. Brownlow and Pearson, who are themselves engineers and boiler-makers. The tonnage of the *Victoria* is about 400 tons. The engines are two in number, and making 280 horse power. The engines are low pressure

condensing ones. There are two safety-valves several feet above the deck. The people in the engine-room have no controul over them, except by coming upon deck. When it was necessary to ease the valves to let steam off on too great a pressure arising, it was necessary for the engineers to send a man up on deck to do it. It might take about a minute to do it. In cases of sudden emergency or stoppage it might be necessary to do it. There are no means in the engine-room for the engineers to raise the valves without going upon deck. If the steam gets higher than required, it lifts the valve itself without the assistance of any one. We have always worked at a pressure of 10½lb. to the square inch; when the pressure is above that, the safety-valve rises, and the steam goes off. The safety-valves were behind the chimney, and no one had any right to interfere with them. They were so placed that any one could be seen touching them or placing an additional weight upon them, and a person was always on the bridge day and night, and he never left while the vessel was under way. I was on the paddle-box when the *Victoria* struck the brig lying at anchor off Cuckold's Point on the north side of the river. I gave orders to stop the engines when that occurred; that was always done by an intermediate man or boy placed over the engine-room, who reported the orders given by the captain or pilot to the engineer. The paddle-box struck was opposite to to me. As soon as the engine stopped, I am quite sure the safety-valve acted; I saw the steam passing off. It was the first time I had seen it since I left Hull, and took particular notice of it, not having been able to get up enough steam before. The collision caused the bowsprit of the brig to be broken short off, but did not stop the *Victoria*. It was the paddle-box which caught the brig, and when I found her clear, I gave the order to go ahead, and the engine was put in motion. After about three revolutions the accident happened by the explosion. She was worked by a lever at the time. There was an order given to reverse the wheels, but it could not be done owing to the way on the ship. The collision was quite unavoidable. We must have either gone over a loaded barge going up or touched the brig; of the two evils we chose the least. I cannot say whether the collision had any effect upon the engines. It was a sliding blow, and the shock was not great. The tide was going up; we were going at the rate of ten miles an hour in Limehouse-reach, below the Pool. There is no restriction there as to speed to my knowledge. We had no greater speed than that, and sometimes less. Our greatest speed is 13 or 13½ knots an hour. The wheels would then make about 17 revolutions per minute. There was a want of steam all the way from Hull. I attribute it to some new grating bars placed at the bottom of the furnaces. All the old ones, except two, were removed. The bars "drooped" at the after end lower than the mouth of the furnace in the original construction, and consequently gave more draught. The new gratings were made to droop less—not quite horizontal, but so as to greatly destroy the draught. I could not judge of the difference in the draught by the indicators. It is only a matter of opinion. My opinion is founded on the fact of our having got a better supply of steam before the alteration was made at Hull in consequence of the bars getting reduced by heat. No other alterations were made at that time. The difference in speed was not less than three or four knots an hour, or 10 miles in three hours. A similar accident happened before. The boiler on the starboard side collapsed and burst on the last occasion (Thursday, the 14th June); it was broken. The top and bottom of the boiler were broken from one end to the other at the top, but not quite so at the bottom. The consequence of this was, the water washed out of the boilers on to the fires, causing the doors to fly open and discharging the steam, fire, and boiling water on the men who were in the engine-room. The hot water ran into the bottom of the ship, but the coals and ashes lay all round the engine-room. The engine-room is the usual size of engine-rooms.

Coroner.—Now, Captain Bell, what was the cause of this melancholy accident?

Captain Bell, after considering awhile, said he might not be right, but he thought it was from want of water in the boilers. When he went down into the engine-room, a few minutes after the accident, he found the boilers red-hot; those on the starboard side were the worst.

The Coroner.—What was the cause of water not being in the pipes—feed pipes?

Witness.—I can't tell

Coroner.—What state did you find them in?

Witness.—I found all the feed-pipes shut. The concussion would not have caused that. I was the first person who went down below after the explosion, and I saw that the starboard boiler was ruptured, and I examined the others, which were red-hot. The feed-cock of the boiler which was ruptured was closed entirely, and the water cut off. The feed-cocks are to regulate the quantity of water into the boilers.

The water had been supplied by the working of the engine which propelled the vessel. There was also a small 4-horse engine erected on purpose to pump water into the boilers when the large engines were not in use, but on this occasion the small engine was not used or required.

The Coroner.—Is such an auxiliary engine used in other steam-vessels?

Captain Bell.—I believe not. I know of no other that is so provided.

The Coroner.—Is it the principle of these engines that renders such a provision necessary, or is it undoubtedly a provision of safety?

Captain Bell.—I am not in a condition to say?

The Coroner.—How were the other feed-pipes?

Witness.—They were all turned off. There were other means of filling the boilers by hand pumps.

A Juror wished to know what time elapsed between the collision with the brig and the explosion?

Captain Bell.—About five minutes.

The Coroner.—When you went down into the engine-room, were any of the deceased persons in a state to act?

Witness.—No, certainly not.

The Coroner.—Then you feel certain that the turning off of the feed-cocks had taken place before the rupture of the boilers?

Witness.—I do; but I cannot say when it was done; but I observed an increased speed off Greenwich. The *Wilberforce* was a little astern at that time. There was such an increase that the *Victoria* shot off in in instant. The effect of turning off the feed-cocks would be to increase the steam, and of course increase the speed. Did not know if that was a usual mode of getting an increase of speed. Did not understand sufficiently to say what course might be taken by engineers, but orders were often given to diminish or increase the speed, and they had means of doing it. We never exceeded the pressure of ten pounds and a-half on the square inch; if that pressure was exceeded, the safety-valve would come into action and carry off the steam. He believed the safety-valve was in good order.

Mr. Hall said, that the man who was now the only survivor had made a statement which was highly important, as he understood, relative to the valves, and he thought it was his duty to inform the jury.

Mr. Jackson said, if the magistrates had pleased, the jury might have had the benefit of the dying statements of the first and second engineers.

Captain Bell said the survivor's name was John Cordinow, and he then lay dangerously ill at Deptford-green. That man was third engineer,[*] and had charge of the third boiler; he had made a statement to him.

The Coroner.—And that statement we cannot hear. The man may yet recover and give evidence.

A man named Brown, who was in the engine-room a few minutes before the accident, was a fireman, and his brother, who was killed, had just relieved him in his duty, was next examined. There was a difficulty in getting up the steam all the way. And there was quarrel among the stokers who worked the hardest. This was in Sea Reach. The vessel went down to Hull in 20 hours and a half, and was 23 hours and a half coming up.

By Mr. Jackson.—There was no harm in turning off the feed-cocks when the boilers were well supplied with water, and he had observed them partially turned off during the first part of the voyage. The same boiler which burst on the former occasion is now used in the Victoria, but is not the one that burst on the last occasion.

The Coroner.—Was there any injury done to the other boilers on the last explosion?

Witness.—No, Sir, but Captain Bell can speak better to that.

Captain Bell said, no injury was done except to the boiler that burst on that occasion, but upon this another of the boilers has been injured, and is collapsed, but not broken. Fairburn and Murray, of Millwall, did the repairs to the boilers after the first accident. There was a certain pressure allowed on safety valves beyond which they never worked. Did not know what was high pressure engines, but the engines of the Victoria were of the common condensing kind. It would take two or more men to stop the engines. The engines were stopped before the Victoria struck the brig, or more injury would have been done.

The Coroner.—How did you know whether there was any water in the boilers?

Witness.—By trying the gauge cocks. There was no water from any of them. Could not say how much water was between the gauges, but the sides and tops of the boilers were red-hot. There was no tell-tale or bell to indicate when the boilers were short of water. The former accident was attributed to the same cause as the present. No person employed in the engine-room then was employed on the last occasion, and five of them

lost their lives by that occurrence. The chief and second engineers were employed in the Victoria about six weeks, the interval between the first and second accidents having been engaged in repairs.

Thomas Brown, brother of Andrew Brown who was killed by the fatal explosion, was then sworn, and he deposed that he was a fireman on board the Victoria, and only joined the day before the accident. He attended to the starboard wing boiler, the one which had burst, and he saw nothing to indicate any danger of explosion. They had, however, great difficulty in getting up steam during the whole voyage. We endeavoured to burn the fires, then to get more draft; but this did not succeed. We then burnt them heavier, but they did not burn well. We then kept the fires up so that the furnaces were nearly full. I went down below at Woolwich, and was not aware of any increase in the speed between that and Cuckold's Point, Rotherhithe, and heard no expression used indicating a wish to beat the Wilberforce, and did not observe any alterations made in the feed-pipes. Came upon deck about three minutes before the accident took place, and his brother Andrew Brown, one of the deceased, took his place. He went with Captain Bell into the engine-room after the explosion, and saw the wing boiler on the starboard side red-hot. Captain Bell said, look at the feed-cocks, and he saw that the water was turned off. He did not observe that the other boilers were red-hot, and the fire was drawn out and extinguished by the hose-pipe. Was quite sure that Captain Bell did not touch the feed-cocks. He asked me to look at them, and I told him they were shut, and he asked me to bear witness to it. There was fire in the furnace after the explosion. He went down to the engine-room as soon as possible after the explosion. He first saw five men come up and shortly after he went down. They waited till the steam had cleared away, but could not tell how long that was. No one but the engineers interfered with the feed-pipes. When I left the stoke-hole there was no particular smell, nor did I think there was any indication of danger when I left it to go upon deck. Was sure the boiler which burst was red-hot after the explosion had taken place.

Mr. Young said he could hardly understand how that could be after the steam and water had passed through the furnace.

The Coroner.—The witness may have been mistaken by the red appearance so common on iron after it has been heated.

The witness said he was not mistaken, the boilers were red-hot.

---

[*] For the evidence of this witness, who, it appears, was not an engineer, but a fireman, and who survived, see post, p. 366.

Andrew Murray, an engineer, residing in Park-street, Greenwich, was called by Mr. Jacobs on the part of the Hull Steam-packet Company. He stated that he was a partner in the firm of Messrs. Fairburn and Company, engineers of Mill-wall, and had been practically engaged in making boilers for the last seven years, and had repaired the boilers of the *Victoria* after the fatal accident in March last. The whole internal case of the boiler was renewed. The accident occurred from the same cause as the last—a want of water in the boilers; this was at least his opinion. The injuries were similar, the flues being in both instances in a state of collapse. The fact simply was, that in both cases the scantiness of water in the boilers had allowed the plates of which they were composed to get red-hot, and this rendered them susceptible of pressure from the steam and water.

The plates of the boilers are a quarter of an inch thick, and as far as strength goes, he thought that thick enough. There was a space of 2 inches and a half in the narrowest part for the water, and that was sufficient. It is necessary to keep a certain height of water in the boiler, and the neglect of this witness believed had caused the accident. He knew of nothing of any complexity in the machinery; it was simple, such as every engineer ought to understand. The *Victoria* boilers had no connecting-bolt, as some other boilers had, with their safety valves in the engine, but such machinery was upon deck. He believed that there was nothing faulty in the engines or boilers before the accident took place.

A model of the boilers and flues, representing a section of the two centre boilers, with the steam-chests above, neatly made in tin, was here presented to the view of the jury, and its construction was explained to the jury by Mr. Murray. Witness would have no objection to have worked those engines at a pressure of 25 lbs. on the square inch. He had tested plates of a quarter of an inch thick to ten pounds, but not higher. Cylindrical boilers were unquestionably the strongest, and the boilers of the *Victoria* were made of the best iron; at least some of the plates were stamped with the Lowmore mark.

Captain Bell was recalled to prove that the boilers of the *Victoria* were tested up to 30 lbs. on the square inch, but he could not tell of what description of iron they were made.

It being now ten o'clock the the jury adjourned.

At eleven o'clock the jury reassembled.

James Craig, an engineer, was then examined.—Was well acquainted with the *Victoria* boilers. He believed they would bear the strictest scrutiny both as to manufacture and construction, and there was nothing deficient or weak in their arrangements, which, in his opinion were perfect. He gave this opinion from an experience of seventeen years engaged in working marine boilers. He had worked similarly constructed boilers, of a cylindrical shape, but more awkwardly situated as regards water space. In the present instance of the *Victoria's* boilers, the water space is two inches at the smallest space and three inches in the largest. In similarly constructed boilers in the *Chieftain*, which trades to London, Cadiz, and Gibraltar, there was not so much water space as in the *Victoria*. There was no danger from a lurching of the vessel driving the water out of those spaces. The *Chieftain* was on fire once, but the witness did not know the cause. Had made a voyage on board the *Victoria* previous to the last as chief engineer. Had no hesitation in saying that the boilers and machinery were then most complete, and that if they were in a similar state, he should have no objection to sail in the *Victoria* again in the same capacity. The engines were as much under controul as any in the river. Considered the accident to have happened from the flues being overheated from want of water. It would entirely depend on the quantity of water in the boilers and the heat of the furnaces as to the time it would take to overheat the flues. It was considered as a *desideratum* that as the engines and boilers were of a peculiar construction he (witness) should go one voyage, having being used to similar boilers, and on his report the proprietors were perfectly satisfied. He thought the boilers as safe as any in existence; there was no more difficulty or danger in working them than in working any others in existence. I know the *James Gallacher*, and have heard of an accident which happened to her. Knew that an accident happened to the *James Ewing*, but her boilers were not similar to those of the *Victoria*. Knew the *Fingal* of Belfast. The boilers of the *Fingal* were designed by Mr. Napier. Did not know what two men had been killed in that vessel, but knew an accident had taken place. Would rather not answer the question about the *James Ewing*. Did not know the *Union* or the *Corsair*, but knew the *Earl Grey*. There was an explosion and loss of life in that vessel. They were Mr. Napier's boilers and engines. The *Earl Grey* had not got cylindrical boilers, but common ones, and they were now working and giving satisfaction. Accidents on board steam vessels were of daily occurrence. No steamer ever made 20 voyages without accidents, some more, some less. The safety-valves of the *Victoria* are quite safe; one is quite enough for all the boilers. Was now in the service of the Peninsular Steam-packet Company, and similar accidents occurred on their vessels. Not a day elapsed but accidents of fire and instances of boilers bursting were recurring.

The jury generally remarked that should such an opinion become public there would be little travelling by steam.

Mr. Hall.—You can never ruin steam-boat travelling.

Thomas Wickstede was next called, and stated that he was an engineer, fitting up boilers similar to those on board *Victoria* at the works of the East London Water Company, and he had seen similar boilers at work in Cornwall tested up to 50 lbs. on the square inch. He believed cylindrical boilers to be more safe than those of any other construction, and that if proper care was taken with them no accident could occur. He thought 2 inches and a half water space sufficient, but the moment that an engineer found no water from the lowest gauge-cock he ought to put his fires out. Cold water then admitted might cause instant explosion. The pressure on such boilers in Cornwall was from 40lbs. to 50lbs. on the square inch. Was a member of the Institution of Civil Engineers, and had recently been awarded the Telford medal for his report on Cornish engines and boilers. Was also chairman of the committee of mechanics of the Society of Arts, in the Adelphi. The boilers of the *Victoria* were as easily to be managed as any others; they might be left with perfect safety for an hour and a half, and he was sure the feed-pipes must have been neglected above that time before the accident took place.

Mr. Hall said that he owed a duty to the public and to science to defend this case. However they might regret the great loss of life that had taken place, it was his duty to see that a great principle was not prejudiced, and as he could prove that the boilers of the *Victoria* were of a superior description, that the principle upon which they were made was not new but had existed in Cornwall for half a century, and that no blame was to be attached to their design or execution, he naturally felt anxious that the general interests of steam navigation should not suffer by an accident the result of neglect and carelessness.

It being now nearly one o'clock, the jury rose and the inquest was adjourned to the following Tuesday, the 2nd of July.

On that day the inquest was resumed.

Richard West, a pilot, was examined. His evidence principally related to the circumstances of the collision with the brig. He stated, he went on board the *Victoria* at Gravesend. The steam was then very slack, which he could tell by its not blowing off through the steam pipe. The boiler burst about two or three minutes after striking the brig: was sure that was about the time. I heard a hissing noise and a report, but not a very loud one. After this there was a list, but could not tell what it was occasioned it. It might have arisen from the passengers on board going on one side.

Mr. Young, juror and engineer, said the question respecting the lurching of the vessel was highly important, as they had only circumstantial evidence as to there being a want of water in the boilers, which was stated to be the cause of the accident. The explosion of one boiler would of course cause a listing of the vessel.

Mr. John Penn, jun., was then sworn, and he deposed that he resided at Greenwich, and was a steam-engine maker and engineer. He had been in the business all his life, and was now thirty-four years of age. He was a practical man, and had always been engaged in the business. His father was engaged before him. He examined the boilers of the *Victoria* after the former accident, which happenened in March last, and killed five men. The cause of the accident on the former occasion was the collapse of the tube or inner circle of the boiler rupturing it, and causing the steam to escape.

The Coroner.—What is our opinion of the construction and efficiency of the boilers in the *Victoria*?

Witness.—I think they were bad; not safe ones. I consider the water spaces too small. They were then about 2¼ inches between the fire flue and the outside of the boilers. I think that the large fires of the *Victoria* would drive the water from such narrow interstices. I speak of the fires from the size of the furnaces. My opinion is, that the fire would drive the water into the receivers above, so as probably to mislead the men who are watching the feed. My opinion is, that if the water was driven up in the way I have described, the plates would get red hot in two minutes. The consequence of this would be, that the tube would expand endways or lengthways, and it would then be so disfigured that the pressure of the steam would put it out of form altogether, and it would become so weak that a very slight pressure would cause an explosion, the plates of the tube being so very thin—¼ of an inch in thickness. I speak from long and practical experience. I have made experiments with water in small spaces, and have seen it driven upwards by the fire. He had seen a tube filled with water, heated intensely at one end, by which the water was driven upwards, and finally out of it. In his opinion this happened from want of circulation, the water not being circulated freely from want of water over the heated surface.

The Foreman.—It is very important to know if, when a feed-pipe is at the bottom, and kept incessantly flowing with water, such an accident could occur.

Mr. Penn—I think it could; besides which they usually turn off the feed-pipes for a quarter of an hour. It is usual to keep 18 inches of water over the crown of the boilers.

The Coroner.—What is the principle of the boilers?

Mr. Penn.—The broad principle of the boilers is, that they are too confined, their spaces too narrow, and consequently the feed can't be depended upon. If 12 inches water space was at the sides, this would not have happened. He thought it was necessary to have at least 12 inches water in the sides of the boilers of the *Victoria*. In common boilers the lowest water space was 3½ inches, and the highest 6 inches; 4 inches was enough as established by ordinary practice.

The Coroner.—You foretold that a similar accident to the first would occur again, if the same boilers were used?

Mr. Penn—I did so. I said openly, and to Mr. Carter, the coroner for Kent, that another accident would take place if the same boilers were again used.

By Mr. Young.—If the water had receded from the crown of the tubes they would bend; it often happened with square boilers, but rarely did any harm, for it was the nature of square boilers, on such occasions, to collapse into a stronger shape, and of round boilers into a weaker shape. Never knew the tube of an ordinary boiler burst at the bottom, but had accounted for this occurring in the *Victoria's* boilers from the narrowness of the water spaces. In his opinion the boilers could not be fed with certainty, and the men might be deceived.

By the Coroner.—The usual pressure was 4lb. on the square inch in the boilers used on the river. Ordinary boilers were about 30 feet in length by 24 feet in breadth. The boilers of the *Victoria* were 39 feet long. Boilers of the form of the *Victoria's* boilers, of ½ inch thick, would bear a pressure of 10lb. on the inch much better than a square boiler of the same thickness, until they became red hot, when they would be displaced. He thought her boilers ought to have been

¼ an inch thick. Her boilers were not thick enough. Ordinary boilers were made strong enough in metal to resist the pressure of steam when they were red hot. The *Victoria* worked at a pressure above 5lb., and her boilers were not more than ¼ of an inch in thickness. Ordinary boilers were 3-8ths of an inch in thickness, and worked under 5lb. If the feed-cocks of the *Victoria* had been shut off the water would not be supplied, and the tubes would become red hot, when they might burst. The men might have been deceived in this case by the violent ebuilition of the water, and it was in consequence not safe to work boilers of that description. The deception he had alluded to might have caused the accident to take place.

Mr. Lovell.—There are three gauge cocks; would they not indicate the want of water correctly?

Mr. Penn.—The lower gauge might give water, and yet this accident occur, under the circumstances I have mentioned.

The model of the engine was here produced, and Mr. Penn explained his opinions respecting it. The water space was much less than he had been accustomed to; the connecting tubes were too small, and the boilers too long.

Mr. Hall.—If it can be proved that a vessel is now working, and has been working for two years, with similar boilers, with only 1¼ inch water space, what will you say for your theory?

Mr. Penn.—Why, I should say that there must be some material difference in the construction of the boilers, and that they work at a much lower pressure than those of the *Victoria*.

Mr. Hall said, that the evidence of Craig, the engineer, who made one voyage in the *Victoria*, had established the fact of such a vessel being worked.

The Coroner then read the whole of Craig's evidence, which was to that effect, with respect to the Cornish boilers, mentioned in this evidence, and upon which much reliance had been placed.

Mr. Penn said, that the tubes of the Cornish boilers were certainly very small, but that the cases were very large. He added, that he had made boilers of the cylindrical form, but the water spaces in such were always 18 inches.

Mr. Hall.—Do you consider your boilers perfect?

Mr. Penn.—Oh no; I do not consider I have arrived at perfection.

The Coroner.—Oh no; steam science is only in its infancy.

Mr. Penn then went on to say, that he thought such boilers as those in the *Victoria* very dangerous, from the incrustation which always took place, not only in salt water, but in fresh.

The Foreman.—From the view of the models, do you at all alter the opinions you previously expressed?

Witness.—Certainly not, they are confirmed.

By Mr. Jacobs.—He had never been applied to to repair the boilers on the occasion of the first accident, except that Mr. Napier had spoken to him upon the subject; he had, however, expressed an opinion in public, and to the coroner of Kent, that, if applied to, he would not repair the boilers for 10,000l.

By the Coroner.—A lurch of the vessel would never cause an explosion of the boilers.

By the Foreman.—It is not usual for a communication to exist in the engine-room with the safety-valve, but some engines are so provided.

By Mr. Jacobs.—He had manufactured six or eight boilers for sea-going vessels, besides numerous river ones. Thought fires 3 feet across would not be so strong as fires 6 feet wide against the sides, but this would depend on the structure of the boilers. If the water was forced up, it would go into the steam-boxes, and, though still partly in the boiler, it would leave the narrow spaces and the bottom of the boiler.

Mr. John Dickens, practical engineer, examined.—Had seen the boilers of the *Victoria* a week ago. The fracture in the tubes was caused by a want of water in the boilers, and had there been plenty of water the plates could never have become heated. The water receded from the crown of the flue, and, of course, the plates then became red hot and weakened, and when it lost its shape it went directly. The witness saw the fracture plainly, and he was convinced that it was from want of water in the boiler, and not a blowing off of water in the narrow interstices, which he thought were large enough. He considers the feed-pipes amply sufficient for the purpose of supplying the boilers with water.

The Foreman.—Would you use stronger materials in the construction of vessels?

Witness.—It's all fancy.

The Coroner.—Oh no; it's a matter of strength, witness.

Witness.—Oh! I might make them thicker.

The Coroner—But is it not necessary, Sir?

Witness.—I generally make boilers ⅜ths of an inch thick; the boilers of the *Victoria* are rather thinner.

On Mr. Hall asking the consent of the coroner to remove the vessel, the foreman said, before the vessel was removed that the coroner would write to the Home Secretary to appoint practical engineers to examine and report on the boilers and machinery.

The Coroner said, that as that was the wish of the jury he would certainly do so. It was highly desirable, after two accidents had happened with the same boilers, each attended with great loss of human life, that there should be a clear and scientific report from engineers appointed by the Government, unconnected with the Company.

The Jury said nothing else would satisfy them and the public.

Mr. John Seaward, engineer, of the firm of Seaward and Co., Canal Iron-works, Limehouse, said he was a practical man, and 50 years of age. He had been in the trade 25 years, and in business on his own account for 13 years, and the firm to which he belonged had supplied a great number of engine boilers and machinery to river and sea-going vessels. For 18 years he had been particularly engaged in boiler-making. He had seen the engines and boilers of the *Victoria* on the previous night, and on that morning, and had examined the boilers carefully; his foreman and a workman accompanied him, and they went into the boilers and water chambers. I think the water spaces between the casing a great deal too small for a boiler of that construction; I should certainly put 8 inches. There is a very large fire-place, and the water space is not in proportion to it. I never made a boiler exactly like it. I think there would be great danger of the water being driven out of the spaces by the large body of fire, and the plates would then get heated, and become distorted. I think by the rapid transmission of heat from so large a body of fire the water would be in a state of violent ebullition, much more so than if the water spaces were twice or thrice the size. The consequence of that violent ebullition would be, the water would rise up and swell in the boiler, and render it a matter of uncertainty as to getting up the feed regularly, and the engineer would be deceived as to the quantity of water he might have in the boiler. I will state a case. It is possible that a boiler may not generate steam fast enough to supply the engine while it is in full work; in a case of that kind it is possible for the pressure inside the boiler to be so reduced as to be below the pressure of the atmosphere. During that time the ebullition would be very great, and the less the pressure in the boiler the greater would be the ebullition. If at that moment the engines were to be suddenly stopped, as in the case

352 VICTORIA EXPLOSION INQUEST.

of the present accident, the pressure on the inside of the boiler would be increased in a very few minutes by 8lb. or 10lb. That would cause the water to fall in a boiler of that kind 12 or 15 inches, and then the upper part of the flue would be left without water. I state that as one reason why the boiler might become red hot at the top without any neglect on the part of the engineers or firemen. I think the water spaces are not large enough for a boiler of that capacity having such large fires. That is my opinion, from the best consideration I can give to the subject. My attention was afterwards directed to the plates of which the boiler was constructed. They are not sufficiently thick. If I had to construct a boiler of that kind I should not employ plates less than 5-16ths. I think they ought to be ⅜ths of an inch thick. The quality of the iron is good, but with the best plates they are not thick enough. Examined the safety valves; they are 9¼ inches at the bottom of the conical seating; the superficial area, 96 inches and 6-10ths. The whole weight on the valve was 1,033lbs., which gives 13½lb. on the square inch, within a fraction. I should observe that there is a counter-balance weight and lever attached to the valve, the net weight of which is 50½lb. If this weight had been extended to the end of the lever, it would have relieved the valve 2lb. on the square inch, and would have left the load on the safety valve 11½lb. Never saw a valve so adjusted before, and cannot account for its being so. One weight was confined in a box—the others were exposed, and could be meddled with by any one. I think an engineer ought to have a control over the safety valve in the engine-room, by pulling a handle. It was desirable in cases of emergency. Did not like the way in which the safety valve was fitted up in the Victoria. Examined the boiler that was ruptured, and from what I have seen, and from what my men described, I have made a rough sketch.

Mr. Seaward here produced a really well-executed drawing, and described to the jury the fissures made in the boilers, which were portrayed on it. The accident, he said, arose, in the first place, from the pressure of steam on the inside of the boiler being much greater than the plates were able to support; the boilers might have become red hot, but he could not satisfy himself as to that. It did seem to him extraordinary that the boilers should have burst at the bottom, as it was not likely the lower parts could get red hot; but the mischief might have begun at the top and altered the shape of the flue.1

The Coroner.—Well, what is your general opinion as to the cause of the accident?

Mr. Seaward.—The plates not being sufficiently strong in the first instance to resist the pressure of steam, I think the primary cause; the small water spaces might have aided. I think the engineer might have been misled by the steam being drawn off until it became weaker than the atmospheric pressure, and the ebullition being suddenly suspended by the sudden increase of pressure in the boiler. The boilers are high pressure. Any engine working at 10lb. and upwards, I think decidedly high pressure. In a popular sense high pressure is considered more than 10lb. to the inch. I have seen Cornish boilers, but nothing like these. The feed-cocks might have been turned off by the engineers, supposing the boilers to be full. I think the stoke-hole contracted; there ought to have been more space. The larger the fire-place the greater would be the heat evolved. He made the engines for the Water Witch and Vivid steam-ships. He understood that they ran between Hull and London, and belonged to an opposition company.

John Dawley, foreman to Messrs. Seaward, of the Canal Ironworks, Poplar, stated that he had been for 26 years engaged in boiler-making. He examined the engines of the Victoria, in company with Mr. Seaward, and described the nature of the injuries similar to that deposed by other witnesses. The rupture of the boiler, he said, had been caused by external pressure; the mischief had been caused by there being a greater pressure than the plates were able to bear, they not being thick enough to bear a pressure of 10lb. on the square inch. There was a way of testing plates by a force pump and cold water, and from such a mode of testing he thought the plates were not of sufficient thickness. The heating of the plates excessively would render them less liable to bear a pressure by one-third; but he was not of opinion that the plates had ever been red hot, or more heated than was usual for the generation of steam. He attributed the whole accident to the inefficiency of the plates in point of strength. He would have used plates of 3-8ths of an inch in thickness, to bear a pressure of 10lb. on the square inch, the boilers being 6 feet, or nearly so, in diameter. He thought that would be the proper thickness for the plates. He thought the water spaces not wide enough; he never made them less than 4 inches, and seldom less than 5 inches, in width. One evil of their being so narrow was, that they might corrode at sea with salt; they might fill up with salt. He could not speak as to the effect the fires might have on the narrow interstices in forcing the water out. The iron was good in those boilers; and the workmanship, also, so far as that went. He had never seen quarter plates in a cylindrical boiler tested, but he had seen plates of 3-8ths of an inch tested up to 75lb. to work safe with a pressure of 20lb. He never used quarter plates in the construction of a boiler, but if plates were tested up to 40lb. on the square inch, he would work them safely with a pressure of 14lb.

Mr. Hall said, every facility should be afforded for the examination of the engines and boilers, and the vessel should lie at Blackwall a few days longer.

The inquest was then adjourned to Wednesday, the 18th July.

On Wednesday, July 18th, the jury again met, when the coroner read the correspondence which had passed between him and the Home Secretary. The following is an extract from the Coroner's letter:—

"At the instance of the jurymen assembled to inquire into the cause of the deaths of the nine unfortunate persons who have lost their lives by the accident which happened on board of the Victoria steam-boat in the river Thames on Thursday, the 14th of June last, I am under the necessity of addressing your Lordship with a view of obtaining from Her Majesty's Government the assistance and evidence of some experienced person, competent, from his thorough knowledge of the manufacture and use of steam-engines and boilers, to guide them in their decision in a case involving great nicety and discrimination, and in which material difference of opinion has arisen in the evidence of the engineers and others who have been called before them.

"The jury as well as myself are aware of the reluctance on the part of Her Majesty's Government in interfering in a judicial inquiry of this nature, but they trust that in a case of such importance as the present, and adverting to the very recent accident of a similar kind on board the same vessel, whereby five other lives have fallen a sacrifice, and knowing, as your Lordship does, that there is no fund at the disposal of the coroner for the payment of scientific men (who must first examine the engines and boilers, and then lose a further portion of their valuable time in attending to give evidence), your Lordship will feel a disposition to relax the ordinary rule on this occasion, seeing how important it is that the very best evidence should be laid before them in a matter so essentially involving the lives and safety of her Majesty's subjects.

To his communication the coroner received the following answer from the Under Secretary of State:—

"Whitehall, July 6.

"Sir,—I am directed by Lord John Russell to acknowledge the receipt of your letter of the 3rd instant, and its enclosure relative to the accident which occurred on board the Victoria steam-boat, in the river Thames, on the 14th of June, and I am to inform you that Lord John Russell has considered your statement, and is disposed to concur in the opinion expressed by you and the jury, that the evidence of some scientific person or persons of experience may be useful, and his Lordship will make a further communication to you on the subject when he has ascertained in what manner this object may be attained.

"I am, Sir, your obedient servant,
"S. M. PHILLIPPS.
"To William Baker Esq.,

In a subsequent communication, the coroner was informed that Mr. Peter Ewart of Woolwich Dock Yard, chief government engineer, had been appointed to examine the boilers, make the necessary inquiries, and attend at the inquest to give his report.

The Coroner then read over the suggestions he had framed for the guidance of the gentleman who examined the engines and boilers.

Mr. Hall said that two perfect boilers now existed on board the Victoria, and the jury might test them, for they (the Company) were more than ever convinced of the goodness of the principle upon which they were constructed, and they would be glad to submit them to the test.

The coroner and jury objected to Mr. Hall saying anything more, as it was irregular and not evidence.

Mr. Peter Ewart deposed, that he was chief engineer and inspector of the machinery to the Admiralty. He had been so about three years, but had been intimately acquainted with the business generally for 48 years, and took the general management of the mail packets. In pursuance of the instructions he had received from the Home Office, he had made four separate examinations of the boilers. At the first visit to the vessel, he went into the stoke-hole, where he received every attention from Captain Bell, who explained everything to him. I found the boilers of the Victoria so constructed that the pressure might be varied from 3lb. on the square inch to 13½lb. The maximum of low pressure was 5lb., and commonly only 3lb. The boilers in the Queen's service are square, not circular. The pressure on the square inch, with the boilers used in the Queen's service, never exceeded 5lb.; the average was about 4lb., but the orders were never to exceed 5lb. With the same strength of metal the circular boilers are stronger than the square ones if the circular are not too large.

The Coroner—Do you consider the high pressure as safe as the low pressure?

Witness—It is too general a question.

The Coroner and jury then asked the witness several questions, but he said he could not answer such general questions.

The Foreman said, the jury had not sufficient experience in steam-engineering to ask proper questions. It would be better if the gentleman would give his evidence by way of report.

Mr. Ewart said, he would endeavour to answer the coroner's questions as to the relative safety of high and low pressure engines. There was a greater number of more serious accidents with high pressure engines than with low pressure. The high pressure engines had been used in Cornwall for many years, and latterly with very little accident. He produced a plan. According to the construction of boilers now adopted very few accidents had occurred. The boilers of the *Victoria* [see Engravings p p. 341, 342], were nearly of an oval shape, about 6 feet 5 inches in diameter, with 2½ inch spaces between the sides. It was more at other places. There was 9 feet of water pressing on the bottom of the boilers; making by its weight a total pressure of 17lb. on the bottom of the boilers. The weight of water made an additional pressure on that part of 3½lb. The water spaces of the Cornish boilers round the flues were much larger, being at least 6 inches. The external cylinder of the boilers was about 6 feet, and the internal 3 feet 9 inches, leaving a water space of 6 inches at the bottom, and instead of being filled with water, a space was left in the upper part of the boilers occupied by steam. The plates were generally half an inch in thickness, and the safety-valves were generally loaded 45lb. on the square inch. Those constitute the chief difference between the Cornish boilers and those of the *Victoria:* I attribute the superior safety of the Cornish boilers to the difference in their construction altogether. I wish to observe that almost all the towing vessels on the river Thames have high pressure boilers made very much upon the Cornish principles, and very few accidents have occurred to them of late years ; further, he considered the water spaces of the *Victoria's* boilers much too small, and their plates of insufficient thickness. He found them from a quarter of an inch to 3-8ths in thickness only. He produced a section of the boiler that burst. In the longitudinal section [see fig. 1, p. 341], the lower part of the fire tube had been originally straight, but was now bent upwards two feet, and torn asunder. The thickness of the plates at this part was little more than a quarter of an inch, but about five feet further forward; and where the iron had yielded very little to the pressure, the iron was about one-fourth thicker than where the fracture was. He ascertained it by boring a hole, and the iron at that part must have been subject to nearly the same pressure as the part which burst. That was one reason he thought it too thin. He endeavoured to discover the cause of want of steam during the last voyage, and he found that considerable alterations had been made in the two midship fire-places, which prevented the fires burning, from want of draught. The water spaces of the boilers were too small for any

fire, but the fire-places of the *Victoria* were very large. The one under the boiler which burst unusually so; it is capable of being urged to a very high degree of heat. The boiler adjoining having the same relative position to the one that burst, is a little out of shape, but had escaped in consequence of that furnace not being capable of being so much urged as the other. In consequence of the deficiency of steam, the furnaces in the wing boilers were required to be urged to a much greater degree than before the change was made, and he had been led to conclude that the furnace of the boiler which had burst, had been urged in a much higher degree than any other. The four transverse sections in the plan before him [see figs. 4 to 7, p. 342], showed the progress of collapse: the first showed the fire-door; the next, a little behind the bridge, showing the upper part of the fire-tube, greatly collapsed. The next was taken where the principal rupture was, and the tube collapsed in an extraordinary degree. The next was taken further on than the principal fracture, where there was a fracture, but not to the extent of the principal one. Three other sections of the flue showed smaller collapses, and that of the further end [fig. 8], showed the flue in its original state. As a matter of opinion, he should say that these collapses would not have taken place in the manner or degree they had, if they had been made upon the Cornish plan [fig. 9]. I do not think a lurch of the vessel would blow the water out of these narrow interstices, but that the excessive heat acting upon such narrow spaces might have caused the steam to blow the water out of some part of the water spaces, and have let the iron get red-hot.

The Coroner—Would the water be forced up so as to deceive the engineer ?

Mr. Ewart—No, but an ebullition would take place, which, from its violence, might certainly deceive them as to the feed-cocks and gauges.

Coroner—What is the cause of the collapse you have spoken of ?

Mr. Ewart—The external pressure of the steam and water is greater than the plates could bear when over-heated, which it is always subject to.

Coroner—Was any gas produced ?

Mr. Ewart—No, not in this case, neither was there a vacuum formed.

The Foreman—In her Majesty's vessels is it usual to have machinery in the engine-room by which the engineer might have control over the safety-valve ?

Mr. Ewart—Yes, Sir ; it is very wrong to send a vessel to sea without one.

The Foreman said, he had been induced to ask this question from observing that the engineer of the *Victoria* had no control over the safety-valve in the engine-room, and was in a situation in which he could not relieve himself, whatever occurred, or how great the danger might be.

Mr. Ewart—The safety-valves of the *Victoria* are placed in a highly improper manner. They are placed at a great distance from the engine-stage, and exposed on the top of the cook-house, so as to be accessible to every one, and liable to be tampered with, which, with lever weights, would be both easy and dangerous. In all the government steam-boats, and those which I have had any direction of elsewhere, the weight on the safety-valve was so placed that it could not be increased without taking part of the boiler apparatus away, which must occupy much time. I examined the glass gauges and gauge-cocks, which were of the usual construction, as were the feed-cocks also. The steam-cock was placed in a very inconvenient situation, being at a great distance from the proper place of the engineer. The situation of the feed-pipes was very convenient, but I cannot determine whether the iron was heated to a red heat or not. The discharge-pipes were placed in a very excellent manner, and this was an important point.

The Coroner—I have to ask you a very important question. Do you think all you have described might not have occurred by the turning off of the feed-cocks?

Mr. Ewart—I will try to answer it. The turning off the feed-cocks occasionally, and for a short time, does not endanger the boilers, and upon calculation it would take three hours to dry the boilers so as to expose the parts fractured to intense heat. The reason why I think the lower collapse must have taken place in the bottom of the flue as early as in any part of the boiler, was because it is the largest collapse, and because there is a second and a third collapse, about six feet further aft; and it appears to me that those two fractures must have taken place at the same moment, for this reason—if one had broken first, it would have relieved the other.

In answer to a question by the Foreman, Mr. Ewart said they tried iron plates for boilers by submitting them to a red heat, when, if they were unsound, they would blister. Some iron was very faulty. When iron becomes heated, it is softened and weaker. It would take three hours to evaporate the water in the boiler; but I do not say that really took place. I can never believe that ten men could be so blind as to leave the cock shut half-an-hour, much less

three hours. The engines required that number of men to stop her.

By the Foreman—The accommodation for the stokers is very confined indeed. There are none like it in her Majesty's service. What adds to the evil, the chimney passes through the stoke-hole, and there are no cases round the chimney, to prevent the radiation of heat, which must make the place very uncomfortable.

By the Coroner.—Could not say what the thickness of the plates ought to be for high-pressure engines; but the Americans had long persevered in their use, although an immense number of the most awful accidents had occurred: but of late, from the advertisements in their newspapers, I have seen that low-pressure engines were becoming favourite and popular. The fact was, the American people had, at length, become alarmed. Did not think it necessary to prove low-pressure engines. Had plates tested up to a high degree so injured by it, that they were spoiled. That injury could not be apparent.

Mr. Jacobs—Could not those boilers be so strengthened as to bear a pressure of 20lbs. or more?

Mr. Ewart—It is extremely painful for me to speak upon the subject, but I must say I would not do any such thing, I would use no such pressure.

By the Foreman—There would be a smell of burning when the water was low.

By Mr. Hall—If a vessel has been working two years with only an inch and a half water spaces, what should you be inclined to say respecting the danger of narrow water spaces.

Mr. Ewart would say nothing unless he had examined the boilers. He, however, thought if they were such, they must differ much in their construction to those of the *Victoria*. Had not examined the boilers that are now entire, and therefore cannot tell the thickness of their plates. Would examine them if ordered, but he should be sorry if any such duty should be imposed on the Coroner and jury.

Captain Bell was recalled, and asked if he heard the stokers urging each other to keep up the fires? He said he did, and that they quarrelled so much that he was obliged to check them, telling them that he did not allow such rows on board.

The ship's register, as entered at the Custom-house, was here produced. It stated the *Victoria* to be of 538 16-34 tons burden. William Bachelor Brownlow, of Hull, and numerous other persons in Yorkshire, Lincolnshire, and London, were stated to be owners.

Mr. Ewart then said, that as the Coroner

wished to be informed on the subject of prevention, there was an easy way of discovery whether there is sufficient water in the boiler, by means of a pipe, which dips to a certain depth in the strand-chest in the water.

Mr. Hall objected, that this had nothing to do with the question before the jury.

The Coroner—I know it has not, but you do not wish to profit by anything. The coroner and jury did, and so did the public.

Mr. Ewart said, he was instructed by her Majesty's Government to report any plan for the safety of the public which he might be able to suggest. He then produced a plan, by which it clearly appeared that if there was either a scarcity of water in the boilers, or too great a pressure of steam in the boilers, or that the safety valve was impeded in action, it would immediately call the attention of the engineer, in the first case, by a peculiar noise, and, in the last, by showing steam from a small tube. Four of the Admiralty vessels were fitted up with these tubes, and they had orders to supply them generally.

At the conclusion of Mr. Ewart's evidence, which lasted from 11 until 3 o'clock, he was complimented on the very great pains he had taken in the examination of the boilers, and his general solicitude to inform the jury.

The jury then retired for an hour and a-half, to get their dinners. On their return, Professor Fairy was called upon.

John Farey, of No. 67, Guildford-street, Russell-square, stated that he was an engineer. He had been engaged in that department of science which relates to machinery and steam-engines. He had seen and examined the two larboard boilers of the Victoria. He then described the collapsed state of the flue—the fractures, one at the bottom of the flue, 6 feet long, and another at the side, 4 feet long, and these two fissures had allowed the water to be ejected with considerable violence; there was a small crack in the conducting pipe, near to its connection with the upper part of the boiler, and a small crack near to the fireplace. The water and steam issued with great violence; that was apparent, as was shown by the brick-work being washed away. In the principal fissure above 40 rivets had been forced away. The thickness of the metal in the lower edge is only ¼ of an inch on an average, but the untorn edge is thicker by the 32d of an inch. About 9 square inches were torn away. From what he had heard of the water spaces, he should say that they were too small. In steam coaches the necessity of lightness has led to the making of small water spaces, and it has

been invariably followed by the boiling out of the water whenever the fire was disproportionate, when the iron always becomes red hot. I think that this has placed a limit to steam-coach travelling. The excessive bubbling which takes place on those occasions prevents the water being pressed upon the metal, and the consequence of this is, that steam is generated and mixes with the water. It should be observed, that these difficulties arise oftener with high-pressure steam than in low pressure, from the diminished bulk of the steam; and, consequently, high-pressure boilers do not require so wide water spaces as low pressure to be equally secure. When he spoke of the water spaces of the Victoria being too small, it was in reference to the condition under which they worked the boilers. The fires were unusually large, and the return flues being at the bottom of the boilers, all the steam generated at the bottom of the boiler had to pass up through the narrow spaces, and, consequently, the spaces must have been filled with water and steam mixed.

The Foreman—If the supply of water had been cut off for more than the proper time, what part of the fire-tube would first become red hot?

Mr. Farey—The deficiency of water so occasioned must have been progressive; and as less and less water remained above the internal flues, it would become a mixture of more steam and less water, allowing all the upper part of the boiler to get hot, the heat being greatest at that point where the greatest proportion of steam was mixed with water, which in these boilers would not be in the highest part, because that would be kept wet by the steam and water rising on both sides.

The Coroner—You attribute the evil to the narrowness of the interstices?

Mr. Farey—That is one reason. Another is the thinness of the plates; and another the extent of the fires. I never saw any fires so large; the general size is 2 feet 6 inches by 9 feet. Those of the Victoria are 6 feet wide and 9 feet long; besides which the boilers of such vessels are ¼ an inch thick in metal. The pressure, also, was great on the Victoria's boilers, being 10lbs. on the square inch, while the usual class of steamers have a pressure generally of not more than 4lb., and this is the regulation in government vessels, and amongst low-pressure engines generally. While there was nothing to prevent it, competition would force the conductors of steam-boats to use high pressure, and to increase it, and consequently the greater risk would be run. There were difficulties in the way of legislating on the subject, which had been several times before the House of Commons, from the fact of there being no standard of perfection, and from a laudable fear to prevent improvements. He believed this would have been the case if any legislation had taken place on the subject 20 years ago. In France regulations had been made, but they only respected the testing of the boilers, and the consequence was that fewer accidents had happened since.

Mr. Hall—The last witness said testing was injurious.

The Coroner—Mr. Ewart said he would only use those which were strong enough without testing.

Mr. Hall—What is your definition of a high-pressure engine?

Mr. Farey—High-pressure engines were invented by Trevethick, who gave the name to them, and they are used for locomotive engines. Since that Wolfe had applied the high-pressure principles to condensing engines, and they were now universally used in Cornwall. A high-pressure engine of Trevethick's blows the steam off into the air at every stroke of the piston. Low-pressure engines, worked on the high-pressure principle, had lately been called high-pressure, and this has led to some confusion. No one will undertake to fix the point at which high-pressure begins in such engines, but the extremes could not be mistaken. The low-pressure engines of 4lb. on the square inch are undoubtedly the best; they are better adapted to the vessel, and this is borne out by the government packets.

Mr. Hall—Should you call 5lb. a low pressure?

Mr. Farey—Yes, certainly.

Mr. Hall—What would you call the same engine if she was worked at 10lb.?

Mr. Farey—A low-pressure engine overworked.

Mr. Hall—What would you say if it was worked at 15lb. or 20lb.?

Mr. Farey—Still more overworked; and then an apparatus for the expansion of the steam in the cylinder must be provided.

Mr. Farey further gave a most minute description of the boiler that burst on board the *Victoria*; but as it entirely coincided with that before given by Mr. Ewart, it is unnecessary to insert it.

In answer to a question from Mr. Hall, Mr. Fairey said, that high-pressure engines, as applied by Wolfe, were very popular in France, and that the boilers of this sort were superior to the high-pressure boilers of England.

On the whole, he considered that the accident arose from a concurrence of unfavourable circumstances in the construction of the boilers, as they required very urgent fires to enable the engines to do their work; the water spaces were too narrow compared with the width of the gratings; the metal of the internal tube was too small, compared with its diameter; the load on the safety-valves greater than such a tube was qualified to work under; and a deficiency in the extent of the heads of water over the boilers, which ought to be continuous throughout.

A discussion here took place as to the propriety of adjourning, but it was at length determined to hear the evidence of

Mr. David Napier, from whose designs the boilers on board the *Victoria* were made. That gentleman being sworn, deposed as follows:—I reside at Blackwall, and am an engineer, and have been all my life engaged in that business. I am 47 years of age. I was brought up under my father, who was an engineer, and practised at Glasgow, where I had extensive works. I have ceased to follow the business for three years, owing to bad health. I have fitted a great number of boats with engines and machinery. I made the boiler for the *Comet*, the first steamer that was employed for practical purposes in Europe. I do not now recollect whether it was from my design or not. I was the sole owner of the *Rob Roy*, the first steamer that navigated the open seas.

Mr. Jacobs said he would put in a report of the committee of the House of Commons, in which was the evidence of Mr. Napier, relating to the employment of the *Rob Roy* between Greenock and Glasgow, the first time that a steamer was usefully applied in the open sea.

Mr. Jacobs—You made the engines for the *Talbot* and *Ivanhoe*?

Mr. Napier—I did. They were the first steamers that ran between Dublin and Holyhead. I constructed the engines for the *Belfast*, *Eclipse*, *Superb*, and *Majestic*. They were the first vessels of a powerful description that completely succeeded on the Liverpool and Greenock passage. They were employed by the government to carry the mails. About two years ago the engines of the greater part of the sea-going vessels out of the port of London, were made by me. Among these were the *Belfast*, *Mountaineer* and *United Kingdom*. Several belonged to the General Steam Navigation Company. Had made boilers of the width of those in the *Victoria* in the water spaces. The *Loch Lomond* upon this principle, had been plying for three years, and I never heard of the least inconvenience from the width of her water spaces, and not sixpence has been incurred in repairing them. They are precisely the same as those in the *Victoria*.

When I went to Glasgow a month ago, I found other engineers copying them, so satisfied were they of their efficiency. Two of the *Victoria's* boilers are now as perfect as they were when originally made. I made them all from one plan. I am a judge of the power of the engines from their practical use. When the *Victoria* came up, she was working at much less power than when she went down. Horse-power was an indefinite term, and depended on the pressure of steam.

. The jury said that they were receiving a new light; steam-vessels were generally set down as so many horse-power. When a vessel was advertised of 300 or 400 horse-power, could Mr. Napier say what was meant?

Mr. Napier—I really cannot. The engines of the *Victoria* might be worked up to 400 horse-power.

In answer to a question by the Coroner, Mr. Napier said he considered the blowing out of the water from the interstices all nonsense.

Some angry observations were here indulged in between the jurors and the steam-packet people, which was at length terminated by the coroner and foreman begging that the proceedings might be conducted with temper.

Mr. Napier then stated that he had made the engines of the *Chieftain* for the Mediterranean, with boilers of the same construction, but with only one inch and a-half water space. The boilers were a little less, and nearly five feet in the tube. The fire-places were five feet wide, and of the same description as the *Victoria*. The cylinders of the *Chieftain* were 48 inches, those of the *Victoria* 64 inches, and the plates of the boilers were a quarter of an inch thick.

· By a Juror—Did not know that the *Chieftain* had been on fire, or that she was now laid up.

· By Mr. Jacobs—No engineer who did his duty could be deceived by the boiling of the water. An engineer who did his duty would always keep the water at the same level, and so regulate the feed-cocks to effect that object.

By the Coroner—Did not know by whose orders the gratings were altered. He saw the *Victoria* coming up the river on the day the accident occurred, about five miles below Woolwich; the *Wilberforce* was astern of her, and witness was surprised to see them so close together. Considered the *Victoria* could beat the *Wilberforce*. At Blackwall the *Victoria* again began to go much slower; the *Wilberforce* was then gaining upon her. I watched them, and just above Greenwich the *Victoria* increased

her speed. I did not see her stop at all. When she passed the City Canal, I still had my eye on her, and she was then going much faster, and I saw steam blowing off, and I concluded that the engineers had been pinching the feed-pipes, and getting up more steam, in order to get to London first, when they saw the *Wilberforce* was gaining on her. I believe she would have gone to London safe, but for the collision with the brig. The engines were stopped, and the steam suffered to accumulate, which caused the explosion. The engineers were, in my opinion, neglectful of their business. They ought to have eased the safety-valve.

The Foreman—That is the reason why the engineer should have control of the safety-valve in the engine-room.

Mr. Napier—The boilers were overheated, and then a slight pressure of steam would injure them. The engineer ought to have removed the extra weight on the lever at Blackwall, going and coming, and the accident could not have occurred. It was excessively stupid his having it on; the difficulty in backing astern was accounted for by that. Recommended plates a quarter of an inch in thickness, and that they should be tested to three times the pressure intended to be used, and if they exhibited any signs of weakness, to use increased strength. Had made a boiler for the *Postboy* steamer, which had worked six years without accident, and the water spaces were only one inch and a half. The *Postboy* was in general use, and was of 24-horse power.

Mr. Napier then referred to his evidence respecting steam-coaches, and said that he had made one, and that the cause of their failure was not the blowing of the water out of the tubes, but the great weight of the carriage on a common road. He had wasted 1000*l*. in experiments with steam-coaches. With respect to the blowing out of the water from the narrow spaces of the *Victoria*, he was ready to give 10,000*l*. to the poor of the parish of Shadwell if any one could prove it could happen. If the plates had been double the thickness, and they had been allowed to get red hot, the same results would have followed. The plan recommended by Mr. Ewart for discovering deficiency of water in the boiler was used by him 20 years ago, and not found to answer in many vessels. The Cornwall land-boilers could not be used at sea. The safety-valves of the *Victoria* were, in his opinion, properly placed; they could not be better. The *Earl Grey* engines and boilers were made by me. She exploded in the Clyde, and lives were lost. Her boilers were square ones, and I recommended the owners of the *Victoria* to have four circular boilers, for I do not consider the square ones so safe. There was an explosion on board the *James Ewing*. The engines and boilers of that vessel were made by me, and a loss of life ensued. The boilers of the *James Ewing* were not constructed the same as the *Victoria*.

After a long discussion among the jurors, several of them declaring they had already heard enough, while a few said that in order to satisfy all parties, every person who offered himself should be heard.

Mr. Hall said he should go on calling engineers from all parts of England to prove the safe principle of the boilers, and when the jury said they were satisfied of that, he would leave off. He wished to convince the jury the boilers were the best that could be constructed.

Mr. Ralph, a juror—After two accidents have happened, and 14 men have been killed by them! you may convince us if you can, Sir, but you won't frighten us.

Mr. Hall—Oh! no; you are the wrong person to be frightened.

The inquest was then postponed till the afternoon of Tuesday, the 31st of July.

On Tuesday July 31st the inquest was resumed.

Mr. George Harman Barth, operative chemist, and lecturer on that science, deposed as follows :—I am a lecturer upon chemistry, but have for a considerable period paid very particular attention to the subject of steam-boiler explosions. I have passed the greater part of the last two years in the manufacturing counties, principally Staffordshire, Lancashire, and the West Riding of Yorkshire. I have had opportunities of examining boilers which have exploded, and ascertaining minutely all the circumstances attending boiler explosions in very many instances. I have likewise made all possible experiments which I could suggest in order to acquire a knowledge of the subject, and am of opinion that in most cases the explosions are not to be attributed to the pressure or expansive force of steam, but to the decomposition of the steam. I will explain this. It is well known that if the steam is shut off from the cylinder or generated too rapidly, more rapidly than it can escape, and the safety valves ceased to be safety valves from over weighting or from any other cause, the consequent accumulation of pressure will rupture the boiler; in this case the boiler will of course give way at the weakest place; and the steam will escape at the fissure or rupture made. I think this bursting could not possibly be attended with a collapse of any part of the boiler. By collapse as here applied I understand the squeezing the plates of some part towards each other from the exterior towards the interior of the boiler, which squeezing would not be produced by the steam pressure, as that presses from the interior towards the exterior. A boiler may be destroyed by collapse from external pressure. If the water and steam in a boiler are at a low temperature, and consequently at a low pressure, the furnaces being slack, and a quantity of cold water be suddenly injected, a partial vacuum will or may be produced, and the boiler be ruptured by collapse. I have known one instance of this happening; or it may be possible that a boiler will collapse from the cause assigned by Mr. Seaward in his evidence before this jury. I have never known a case, but I think it possible. I do not attribute the Victoria explosion to either of those causes, but I think it was owing to a decomposition of the steam, and consequent generation of gas or gases in the boiler. I examined the boiler which was ruptured, but as it presented the same appearance to me as to the many scientific gentlemen whose reports are now in evidence, unless wished, I will not trespass on your time by recapitulating the minutiæ. From the appearance of the largest fissure, I should suppose it produced by expansion or force acting from the interior to the exterior (not considering the fire-hole as the interior, but the exterior of the boiler); while the other fissures might be, and the collapse and distortion possibly were, produced by a vacuum being formed, and subjecting the plates to exterior pressure. When examining the boiler, I concluded, from the particular appearance of the plates, that they had been red hot; but wishing to have further satisfaction on this point than the appearance of the metal merely, I procured a heavy hammer and sheet of paper, and succeeded in detaching a small quantity of scales from the interior of the boiler. I took these scales home, and on subjecting them to the usual analysis, they proved what I suspected them—oxide of iron. Blacksmith's scales are oxide of iron. This satisfied me that the boiler had been red hot, either at the time of explosion or at some previous time; and, as an explosion would, I think, have taken place whenever the boiler was red hot, I conclude that it was red hot at the time of the explosion now in question. The iron having been red hot is a convincing proof of gas having been formed, as it is physically impossible that red hot iron and steam or water could be in contact without such being the case. I will endeavour to explain this. Water is a compound of two simple bodies or elementary principles—hydrogen and oxygen. Water may be decomposed by various processes, some of which will not only decompose but also recompose it—that is, turn it into two gasses or separate them from each other, and also make the gasses combine again and produce their weight of water. Red hot iron is one of those agents. When steam is in contact with red hot iron it parts with its oxygen to the iron, and hydrogen gas is set at liberty. The oxygen forms a crust upon and with the iron or scale, and will impair the strength of the plate, in the ratio of the thickness of the crust. Were iron, red hot, to be a long time acted upon by steam, it would be all oxide or crust, and very little stronger than a bread-crust of similar thickness. Oxide of iron is a compound of iron and oxygen gas, the oxygen losing its gaseous form. Oxide of iron cannot be reduced or deprived of its oxygen by that alone, but it may be reduced by heating it in contact with bodies having stronger affinity for it : charcoal is one ; hydrogen gas another. If we pass a small current of steam through a red hot iron tube, oxide of iron will be formed in the tube, and hydrogen gas escape at the other end. If we collect this gas and return it through the tube, it will take the oxygen from the iron, and water will be formed by the chemical union of the gases. If we reduce or deoxidize oxide of iron at the temperature of a low or dull red heat by the action of hydrogen gas, the combination of the gases will be effected slowly. If we increase the temperature, it will take place more rapidly. If the oxide of iron be intensely heated, at or above what is termed a bright red heat, the reduction of the iron oxide will take place very rapidly—almost instantly. If a sufficiently large quantity of hydrogen gas be present, a great degree of heat will be produced by the combination of the hydrogen gas and oxygen of the oxide of iron, with a sudden increase of volume, followed instantly by a decrease of volume, which decrease of volume would produce a vacuum. There are two ways or causes by which the boiler might be destroyed in this instance of the *Victoria*, gas being the immediate agent ; and as it is impossible, I conceive, for us to ascertain the degree of temperature to which the metal of the boiler was heated, so will it be impossible for me to say which of the two it is to be attributed to, particularly as the appearance in each instance would be nearly similar. Supposing that the iron was only heated to a dull redness, the steam in contact would be decomposed, and the iron oxidized ; the strength of the iron would be impaired by its temperature or heat, and further impaired by the oxidation ; the heat at the same time would greatly expand the hydrogen gas, which pressing on the weakened metal might rupture it. The hydrogen gas mixed with or followed by the steam in the boiler would

then rush through the fracture into the fire-hole, mix with the current or draught of atmospheric air there, combine with its oxygen, and explode violently. The explosion taking place in a confined place at the fire-hole, would not only drive out the cinders and ashes, but distort the iron of the boiler in contact, and thus occasion the collapsed appearance. If at the moment of explosion the iron had attained a bright red heat, we know it must previously have been at a low red heat, and decomposition of steam had taken place. I think part of the hydrogen gas generated would remain in the waterways, and when the previously oxidized metal received the higher temperature, would take away and combine with its oxygen so rapidly as to produce an expansion with immense force, instantly succeeded by a condensation, and that thus a vacuum must be produced. Should I be considered correct in my description that the boiler was heated to redness at the time of the explosion, then must it follow that one of those two causes produced the explosion. This is not merely an opinion, but based on facts depending on unvarying physical laws : establish the first position, and one or other of the effects described must necessarily be consequent. I will now advert to the cause of the iron being red hot. and am aware that I differ widely in opinion from several scientific gentlemen who have favoured the jury with their valuable assistance. I conceive they may have made their deductions from erroneous data—that in forming conclusions and forming experiments they have omitted taking into consideration every possible influencing circumstance. I do not believe that the waterways of the ruptured *Victoria* boiler could have been made red hot if there had been a supply of water above them as high as the bottom of the glass gauges. The action of heat will drive water rapidly out of narrow chambers ; but if the water is above them, and a communication exists, the heat will not prevent the return of the water ; and though it will be quickly ejected again, it will still carry with it enough caloric to prevent the iron attaining a red-heat, or even getting hotter than the boiling water. I will adduce an experiment which I consider proves this. The water in a tube with a perpendicular column is not ejected in a continuous stream, but by jets. I am, from these experiments &c., of opinion, that the heating of the iron was owing to a deficiency of the proper supply of water. Shutting the feed-cocks would, of course, occasion it, and I do not think an accurate calculation can be made of the time they must have been shut to allow the water to evaporate, as I consider there is not sufficient data. The quantity of water which the boiler contained may be estimated certainly, but it is necessary also to know exactly how much heat was applied—the heating power of the furnace ; this, I think, not very easily determined. 1st. The time necessary to vaporize a given quantity of water depends not only on the heat applied, but on the pressure on its surface. 2d. If an experiment had been made previously of the length of time necessary to get the boiler dry with the furnace urged to the utmost, we could form some opinion. A comparison with other boilers holding a similar quantity could not be depended on, unless the boilers were exactly similar in construction, and the same kind of coal used, &c. It may be worthy of inquiry to ascertain if the feed might have been suppressed from any accidental circumstance without closing the feed-cocks. The witness explained to the jury at great length his reasons for coming to the above conclusions, and referred to various authorities in support of his assertions. I do not say, but I think, that common prudence would dictate a thicker description of plates where there is a greater action of fire on them. A thick plate would not be so soon weakened by fire, or so much acted upon, as a thin one by oxidation. I understand very little of the practical part of steam engineering. I should not like to give an opinion as to the water spaces of the boilers, or the thickness of the plates. I think there would be an almost imperceptible difference in the heating of a plate a quarter of an inch thick and half an inch thick. They would be almost heated at the same moment. If they were an inch thick they would still burst.

I do not consider it possible to make iron red hot, with a proper supply of water, at an ordinary temperature, without a pressure of 1,000lb. on the square inch. The colour of the oxide of iron I collected from the boiler is black. It was not laminated. It had no appearance of lamination—not scale upon scale, only a rough scale. A copper boiler would not have burst under the circumstances I have stated of decomposition of steam. I do not consider iron boilers absolutely safe ; they are only relatively safe. The Legislature should not permit the use of any but copper boilers. If a boiler was tested at 40lb., I should think it strong enough to bear a pressure of 10lb. on the inch when at work.

The Coroner, after some preliminary conversation, then read the following correspondence between Mr. Hall and Messrs. Seaward ; and the jury expressed an anxious hope that it would obtain publicity, as the opinions of so respectable and eminent an engineer as Mr. Seaward were entitled to every consideration :—

"Canal Ironworks, Limehouse, July 5.

"Sir,—I deem it right to acquaint you, that I have received a letter from Mr. W. J. Hall, of Custom-house-quay, one of the proprietors of the *Victoria* steam-ship, requesting me to offer explanations on certain parts of the evidence given by me at the inquest on Tuesday last. Having complied with Mr. Hall's request, I think it due to you and to the jury to send you the enclosed copies of the correspondence, which I will thank you to communicate to the jury at your next meeting.

"I remain, Sir, your most obedient servant,
"To W. Baker, Esq."   "JOHN SEAWARD."

"Custom-house Quay, July 4.

"Sir,—Being one of the proprietors of the *Victoria*, I am very desirous of getting at the truth, for the information of the public, whether or not there is anything wrong in the construction of her boilers. As you have examined them and stated at the inquest yesterday that the water spaces being only three inches, you considered them too small ; that for a boiler of their construction, with one large undivided furnace, you would have considered eight inches necessary. When I sold the *Chieftain* to the Commercial Company, they applied to you to examine the machinery and boilers of that vessel, which you did very minutely, causing the man-hole doors to be taken off to discover if any faults existed, though she had previously made several long voyages. after this examination you gave in a written report that was anything but favourable; nevertheless, the narrowness of the water spaces was not one of the faults pointed out, although the *Chieftain's* boilers are of the same construction as the *Victoria's*, with one large undivided furnace, and the water spaces only 1½ inch, being exactly one-half of those of the *Victoria*. Will you therefore be so good as to explain that circumstance ? There is another part of your evidence on which I should like some explanation. You stated that the water spaces in the boilers which you made were from 5 to 6 inches. Your foreman boiler-maker, who was examined immediately after you, stated that the water spaces in the boilers he makes are generally 4 inches ; that slight variation is of no consequence, as you both agreed that there was a furnace on each side of that 4-inch water-space. Is it not a fact that in the *Victoria's* boilers, although the water spaces are only 3 inches, as stated by you, there are always two of these water spaces betwixt two furnaces, and consequently there are 6 inches of water between the fires, instead of 4, as in the boilers you make ? As the proprietors are desirous of making up their minds what course to pursue in the necessary repairs and alterations in the *Victoria*, and there being only one other engineer, Mr. Penn, who gave similar evidence to yourself, and who stated, that, although he had been all his life in business here, he could not direct our attention to any seagoing vessel furnished with machinery by him nearer than Austria, will you be so good as to point out some of those done by you of five or six years' standing, that we may inquire as to their performance ? Those plying out of the port of London would be most convenient for us to examine. There is another point I should like you to explain. When asked by the coroner what thickness you would have made such boilers as the *Victoria's*, had you made them, your answer was, not less than 5-16ths, probably ⅜ths of an inch. I believe it is an undisputed fact, that the boilers of the *Victoria* are full ¼th of an inch. Will you let me know what the difference is between full ¼th and 5-16ths, and how much more a boiler would bear of 5-16ths than one made of full ¼th inch plates.*   "Yours respectfully,
"Mr. J. Seaward.   "W. J. HALL.

---

* We have been favoured by Mr. Seaward with a copy of a letter addressed by him to Mr. W. J. Hall, on the the 20th instant, in answer to this question, containing "a plain practical rule for determining the relative strength of tubes," as also some observations respecting the idea descanted on

"P. S.—It is perhaps correct that I should state, that I am aware the *Chieftain's* boilers are at present out of repair in the same way as those of the *Flood* and *Water Witch's* were the very first year they ran. I do not individually point out those vessels, but it must be admitted that the boilers of most steamers, when they are between two and three years old, as the *Chieftain's* are, require more or less repairs."

"Canal Iron-works, Limehouse, July 5, 1838.

"Sir,—I acknowledge the receipt of your letter of yesterday, in which you request me to explain certain parts of the evidence given by me at the inquest held last Tuesday, on the unfortunate sufferers on board the *Victoria*. Now, although I believe that your request is unusual, I am, nevertheless, quite willing to comply therewith, provided the explanation I give you be also communicated to the coroner and jury, with this understanding I shall proceed to answer the questions contained in your letter. In the first place I beg to say, that I never was on board the *Chieftain* in my life, and I know nothing of the construction of her boiler; my brother, Mr. Samuel Seaward, was on board that vessel, and I have no doubt will be able to justify the report which he gave after making an examination of the machinery. I stated at the inquest that in boilers made at this place intended for sea-going vessels, it was usual to make the water spaces about 5 or 6 inches; you can convince yourself of the correctness of this statement, by inspecting the boilers of the *Gorgon*, the last steam-vessel fitted out at this place; or, if you prefer to pay a visit to this establishment, you may inspect three sets of boilers now in progress of making for sea-going vessels. The furnaces of our boilers seldom exceed 32 inches in width; for this a water space on each side of 5 inches, or even 4 inches, may be quite sufficient; but for a furnace nearly 6 feet wide, like those in the *Victoria*, I consider an 8-inch water space on each side indispensable. I did not state to the coroner that I would have made such boilers as the *Victoria's* 5-16ths, probably 3-8ths, of an inch. No inducement on earth would tempt me to make boilers at all upon such principles. What I stated was, that the plates ought to have been 5-16ths of an inch, or 3-8ths of an inch; but I ought also to have stated that even if the *Victoria's* boilers had been made of plates 3-8ths of an inch thick, with water spaces 8 inches all round, still I should have considered such boilers dangerous, working under a pressure of 13½lbs. to the square inch. I regret having omitted to state thus much at the inquest, as I fear, from the nature of your remarks, that my answer to the coroner on this part of the inquiry has led to some misapprehension, and I am therefore thankful to have this opportunity of supplying the omission. With respect to the actual boilers of the *Victoria*, as they are now made, it is my clear and decided opinion, that working with steam of even the low pressure of 4lb. upon the square inch, they never would have been safe, useful boilers. You state that the proprietors are desirous of making up their minds what course to pursue in the necessary repairs and alterations in the *Victoria*, &c. If this remark is addressed to me with the view of obtaining my opinion on the proper course which the proprietors should pursue, I cannot for a moment hesitate recommending to them the total abandonment of the present ill-fated boilers, and also the faulty principle on which they are constructed. I cannot for a moment conceive that it is contemplated to continue their use in the vessel. If any man, with a full knowledge of what has occurred on board the *Victoria*, should again employ those boilers, or others

similarly constructed, to work a pressure of 12lb. or 13lb. per square inch, I should pronounce his case to be that of decided insanity. ('Hear, hear,' from the jury.)

"I remain, Sir, your most obedient servant,
"JOHN SEAWARD.

"W. J. Hall, Esq.
"P.S. I must decline your invitation to point out boilers made at this place of five or six years' standing, for the purpose of affording you an opportunity of inquiring into their performance. I cannot understand what connection that can have with the present inquiry."

Mr. Napier said, the water spaces in the boilers of the *Victoria* were large enough; and he begged leave to add to his former evidence, that the *Victoria* had made seven voyages without anything happening.

William Harker, of Hull, foreman fitter to the owners of the *Victoria* and the Hull Steam Packet Company, deposed, that in September, 1837, he tested the boilers which exploded on the first occasion in March last. He made the test with an hydraulic pump to the extent of 41½lb. on the square inch. It stood that force very well, and did not strain either in the plates or the rivets. He did not think the boiler the worse for that test. The first test was a public one in the presence of the owners, and he afterwards tested it again privately, as high as 50lbs. It did not display any symptom of weakness. In consequence of the boiler having stood the test so well three others in the *Victoria* were made upon the same principle and the same description of metal. The boilers would have borne a greater pressure, in his opinion. The plates were from the Lowmore iron-works in Yorkshire. It was crown iron of the best quality. If he saw the plates draw or the rivets spring, he should think it gave way, but it did not do either. The plates were also tested. Has no means of ascertaining the dimensions of the boiler before and after testing. A few plates only were tested; they were taken indiscriminately from the mass, but all were used up.

Andrew Massey, foreman to Messrs. Fairburn and Co., engineers, of Mill-wall, said he superintended the repairs after the first accident, and put in a new flue. In order to repair the flue it was found necessary to enlarge the circle, which consequently diminished the size of the fire under it. We began with 3 inches, and gradually increased to 5 inches. We put in iron about 5-16ths of an inch think, of the Colnbrook Dale iron-works, the best we had. After the last accident I examined the boiler which we repaired after the first accident, and I found it had given way in a part I least expected. It had partially collapsed nearly at the top of the boiler. Where it has given way it is 9 inches, the largest part of the water spaces. It is alongside the one which last burst, and it is connected with

by Mr. Barth, (p. 359,) that steam-boiler accidents are attributable to the explosion of gases. We much regret that their length, and the late date at which we received them prevent their publication in our present number. Coming from so experienced and talented a practical engineer as Mr. Seaward, the opinions expressed therein are most important to the engineering world at the present juncture—ED. M.M

the other. If ruptured the water would come out of it to the next, and the consequence would be it would very soon become red hot, and that would cause it to collapse. I do not know from my own knowledge where the connection is. I found the boiler we repaired in the narrowest spaces, standing as firmly as ever where I had left it after the repair. The heat is the greatest at the sides, where it has not given way; and where it has given way the water spaces are free and uninterrupted. I always thought the first accident arose from the deficiency in the supply of water, and I think the second arose from the same cause. There are two boilers still entire which have more narrow water spaces, while the fire places are larger. They are as entire as when first put in. I have been a boiler-maker 20 years. I never put larger water spaces than 3 inches; we make square boilers generally for marine purposes; I have worked them from 5lb. to 7lb. on the square inch, with plates from ¼ to 5-16ths of an inch thick. The greatest pressure I ever saw on the square boilers was 7lb. on the square inch when at work. I never tested any of the square boilers I have mentioned. Last week we tried a spherical boiler with plates barely a ¼ of an inch thick. We tested it with an hydraulic pump, and were compelled by the owners to try it up to 50, with great satisfaction, and we afterwards put on 30 more, and it stood the test well. I do not think boilers are weakened by a test of this description. The witness considered that plates a ¼ of an inch thick were sufficient for the cylindrical boilers of the *Victoria*. Knew that contrary opinions had been given.

Mr. George Blaxland, of Swan-street, Southwark, superintending engineer of the packets of the Commercial Company, was next called to speak to the state of the boilers of the *Chieftain*, which it had been asserted by witnesses called by Mr. Hall, had water spaces similar to those in the *Victoria*. On the last occasion, however, it was asserted that the *Chieftain* had caught fire. Mr. Blaxland said, he had been an engineer 20 years. He had not seen the water spaces of the *Victoria* or her boilers. The lower part of the water spaces of the *Chieftain* was about two inches. The boilers of that vessel were about two or three years of age, and at that age all boilers are in want of repairs, some more and some less. He never found any deficiency in the water spaces. The iron is about a quarter of an inch thick. He could not tell the dimensions of the boilers. She once took fire. It originated in the bottom of the boilers; from the flues. The paving-bricks got red hot. He would not speak positively. It

was not uncommon for them to get hot. The witness's examination was continued at great length. He thought that circular boilers like those of the *Victoria*, were better able to resist the pressure than square ones, whether large or small. The *Chieftain's* boilers are circular, and are worked up to about 7lb. on the square inch. He did not think it at all advisable to work them above that. If they were new, he should not think proper to do so. It is intended to remove the boilers of the *Chieftain*, for two reasons. The first is, they are getting thin; and the next is, the bricks of the flues having become red hot, we don't consider them safe. The age may be another. We prefer water ways between the timbers of the vessel and the fires, rather than the boilers of the present construction. There were narrow water spaces in the *City of Glasgow*, three inch water spaces, and the most intense fires were used. They were of Collier's construction. The water was not displaced, but the iron was destroyed in about two voyages. I think there is more danger of water chambers worked vertically than horizontally. It is merely a matter of opinion. There was about 18 inches breadth of water the whole length of the boilers in the *City of Glasgow* steamer. His opinion was that the water could not be blown out of the narrow interstices or water spaces of the *Victoria*.

William Collick, of Ann's-place, Hackney, said he was an engineer, and had been trying experiments at the desire of Mr. Hall, to ascertain if water could be blown out of a narrow space by the application of great heat. The witness then produced a crooked gas-pipe, about three feet long, and a straight one 10 feet long, with the aperture at one end closed. He said the short pipe was filled with water with a head of nine gallons of water upon it. The pipe was put into a smith's furnace and the bellows blown for three hours, so that the heat was of the most intense description. The water did go out, but always returned again immediately, and the pipe could not be made red hot. It was greater than a continuous heat in a boiler furnace. No heat could be greater than that to which this pipe was exposed. The witness said he tried another experiment after that with the long pipe in a circular fire. The pipe was passed through the centre of the fire, composed of coals and coke. The water was blown out and returned directly. We had nine gallons of water upon it. It bubbled up a few inches high. It is only a common gas pipe, and we could not make a better fire. The pipe was an inch and a half bore, and is the eighth of an inch thick.

Mr. Barth, on being appealed to, said the tube was too long for a fair experiment. The same difficulty existed as regarded the smaller pipe, but not to so great a degree, and the experiment with that was fair.

Mr. Collick continued:—The water in the top of the tube was boiling, and the steam was allowed to evaporate. Incrustations would form on steam-boilers, and he was of opinion that 2½-inch water spaces were sufficient.

Mr. Joshua Field, of the firm of Maudslay and Field, engineers, and steam-engine makers, of Lambeth, was then sworn, and gave the following evidence:—I have been on board that vessel to make the examination necessary to enable me to form a judgment on the matter. On going into the boilers, and passing through the flues, I found that the fire-tube of the starboard outside boiler had collapsed to a very great extent, and had become fractured, so as to let the water escape, thus producing the loss of life which is the subject of the present inquiry. The immediate cause of the accident appears to me to have been that the strength of the fire-tube, from its large diameter and insufficient thickness, was incapable of bearing the pressure of steam and water to which it was exposed. I have examined the safety-valves, and find that with all the weights on they were loaded to 13lb. on the square inch, to which must be added the statical pressure of the water on the boilers, which is equal to about 3lb. more, acting on the lower part of the tube, about 15lb. on the middle, and about 14lb. on the top; thus taking the mean pressure of 15lb. on the square inch, the fire-tube, which is 6 feet in diameter, and very little more than a quarter of an inch thick, had to sustain a pressure of 2,160 lbs. on every square foot of surface, and every ring or hoop of it a foot wide, had to sustain seventeen tons, and on the entire length it had to bear 629 tons; such a pressure could only be sustained so long as the tube retained a perfectly cylindrical figure, and whilst the pressure and strength remained uniform throughout the circle. The pressure, as we have seen above, was not equal by fully two pounds on the square inch; so soon, therefore, as the tube departs from the true cylindrical figure, the key of the arch is disturbed, and an immediate collapse takes place. This, I think, is of itself sufficient to account for such a collapse having happened, which may also have been aided by other causes. I could not obtain any certain evidence as to the state of the water in the boilers at the time of the accident, but from an examination of the plates at the fractured part, I should not judge that they had been red hot, and it is clear that the lowest part, in which the greatest rupture has taken place, could not become red hot until the boiler was entirely empty, and had this been the case the upper part must have been red hot a long time, and would show evidence of that having been the case. The surfaces in the steam chambers, which stand on the boilers, from which the steam disengages itself from the water, are divided into 20 compartments; the total area of them is small compared with the size of the boilers and the quantity of steam rising in them: the ebullition is thereby increased, and this must render the water-line undefined, and make it difficult to keep the feed regular and uniform as in ordinary boilers, where the steam rises from the entire surface. The water spaces, especially at the sides of the fires, are the most contracted I have ever seen, being only 2½ inches, whilst the fire-places are the largest, being 6 feet wide by 8 feet 6 inches long. This renders the circulation of the water through those spaces confused and imperfect. The fire, after passing through the large fire tube above alluded to, is caused to descend through an oblique opening into the space between it and the neighbouring boiler, and passes back the whole length of the boiler, between the bottom of the boiler and the bottom of the ship, into the chimney situated at the front and between the two centre fire doors. This return flue is formed of plate iron, paved with brick, which arrangement I cannot help pointing out as very dangerous and quite unusual, being very likely to set fire to the vessel. The coals are not stowed in iron cases over the boilers, and detached from them, but lay immediately on the boilers. Consequently, for several hundred square feet they are within five or six inches of the most intense part of the flames; insulated, it is true, by the water in a high state of ebullition, when all is going right, but should the water, from any cause, become low, these coals would inevitably take fire.

On August the 14th the inquiry was continued, and the following letter read from Mr. Fairey:—

"67, Guildford-street, Russell-square, July 30.

"Sir,—In the newspaper report of the proceedings of the last meeting on the *Victoria* steam-ship, it was stated that Mr. Hall contended for the safety of the principle of the boilers, and that they are the best that can be constructed. If it is to be inferred therefrom that the use of the same boilers is to be resumed, the investigation now pending becomes more important than ever; and as further loss of life may incur from working the boilers again, I think it right to call your attention to the circumstance, respecting which no question was put to Mr. Ewart or to me, and therefore nothing was said—it is the danger of setting fire to the vessel by the flues under the boilers. You are probably aware that the universal practice of the best engineers is to include the whole of the furnaces with their flues, and also the lower part of the chimney as high as the deck, and above it within the interior of the boilers, in order that every part to which fire or flame, or sparks can have access, may be surrounded on all sides with water or steam. In the *Victoria* the returning flues under the lower part of the boilers, together with the lower part of the chimney, are not surrounded, and circumstanced as they are with very strong fires, having powerful draughts from them through those returning flues, I consider them to be very dangerous, from the liability of setting fire to the vessel. If the boilers are to be used again, that part of their construction requires full investigation. I have seen one similar instance, and that was destroyed by taking fire fortunately before she got out of the river. It should be kept in mind that the *Victoria* cannot be impelled at the speed she has been with her present boilers and engines, unless by excessive hard firing, and also in overworking in pressure of steam, whereby the risks incurred by the serious faults in her construction and proportions are aggravated beyond any example known to me; and when other instances of similar construction are cited (as the *Chieftain* has been), the circumstances should be inquired into; for, if the boilers and engines are competent to perform the work they are required to do without immoderate firing or overworking in pressure, there will not be a parity by which safety in the *Victoria* (from bursting) can be inferred from what has happened in other cases.

"There are many conditions which the best engineers invariably prescribe to themselves in constructing marine engines for the sake of safety and durability, but which conditions render engines expensive to make, and some are unfavourable to the attainment of the utmost possible speed. For instance, the boilers are made large, containing abundance of water, whereof a considerable portion under the boilers is of very little avail in producing steam, but by surrounding fire it protects the vessel from being burnt. The fireplaces are as small as they can be, and the metal is thick, and the safety valves are lightly loaded, to avoid subjecting that strength to any considerable pressure. The engines are proportionate, and executed with care; they make use of all the steam supplied to them, and waste none by leakage or misapplication, as they will perform their task without much pressure of steam. The best kind of valves are used without regard to cost, the best materials also, and ample strength is given to all parts. Such boilers and engines are necessarily heavy, take up much space, are expensive to build, but are safe and durable, and economical in fuel, which renders them safe in the end.

"By judicious observance of such conditions steam navigation has been carried on during several years with success and safety. The majority of all the vessels now in use in England, have been fitted with engines by the following engineers—viz., in London, Messrs. Maudslay, Field, and Co., Lambeth; Messrs. Barnes and Miller, Limehouse, who have separated, and are both carrying on business; Messrs. Seaward, of Limehouse; and Rennie, of Greenwich. In the country, Messrs. Bolton and Watt, of Soho, and Messrs. Fawcett, of Liverpool; the Buttery Company in Derbyshire, and the Horsely Company in Staffordshire. From an intimate knowledge of the engines made by the above engineers, and which are all really on the low pressure system, not overworked, I can undertake to say that accidents of any kind are extremely rare, and the bursting of boilers is quite unknown amongst them. I am not aware of any loss of life occasioned by marine engines made by the above engineers, and believe that a strict inquiry would prove that there has been none.

"Nevertheless, frequent accidents of a fatal kind have happened amongst engines made by a class of men, engineers who have evinced a want of knowledge of safe proportions, or a disregard of them, order to make cheap engines, which would perform the work of more expensive engines, by taking every advantage to gain the utmost speed at all hazards of blowing up, taking fire, breaking and becoming disabled, running foul of other vessels, or getting on shore: for instance, smaller boilers with but little water in them, and without any water under the flues, and made of thinner materials, may be rendered lighter and cheaper than the boilers used in the best vessels. But by giving them larger fire-places and flues, and urging the fires therein to the utmost, the requisite quantity of steam may be produced, and by loading the safety-valve that steam may be kept strong enough to enable very inferior engines to be overworked so as to do as much as more perfect and costly engines do with moderate pressure, but the latter do it with safety, while the others have been strained to the utmost, and are liable to accidents of all kinds.

"JOHN FAIREY.

"To Mr. W. Baker, Coroner."

Mr. Andrew Murray, an engineer, who was examined on a former occasion, then gave the following additional evidence :— There is in every boiler a greater pressure on the bottom than on the top; and therefore, had a circular flue of equal thickness, like the *Victoria's*, given way from a deficiency of strength in the plates, it would have done so at the bottom; but the moment a rupture did take place, the whole boiler would be relieved from any pressure, and the top, where there was the least pressure, would remain uninjured. This not being the case in the present instance, as the top of the flue was collapsed, and the strength of the cylindrical form lost, the bottom was forced upwards, and the rent took place there from the plates not being so able to bear a change of form as the plates of the top, which were rendered more ductile from being overheated from a want of water above them. In corroboration of the above, the flue of the boiler immediately adjoining the one that is ruptured is partially collapsed about 1 foot below the level of a pipe that connects the water spaces of the two boilers, and immediately over the fire, where the water is quite unconfined. This flue is composed of plates generally one-fourth thicker than the others, and it is at least 4 inches less in diameter in most parts; the water spaces are consequently thus much greater, and the furnaces thus much less, than in the two boilers which are still entire and in their original shape as first made. This circumstance of itself alone proves indisputably, that the tops of the flues of the two injured boilers must have been destitute of water at the time of the accident.

Mr. Robert Morton, engineer, of High-street, Wapping, was next examined, and after stating that he had been for the last 12 years engaged in the business of a boiler-maker, said, that he had, by the desire of the coroner and jury, examined the boilers of the *Victoria*. He found the boiler on the starboard side injured in the manner spoken of by the other witnesses—that was, ruptured and collapsed. The cause of the explosion was, in his opinion, a want of water in the boilers, which had been allowed to get red hot. The excessive heat weakened the iron, and caused the boiler to get out of shape, which would render it more easy of collapse. If water had been over the flues, the flue could not have become red hot. He thought the water spaces of 2½ inches were sufficient, and that their narrowness would not cause the water to be forced up from the bottom of the boiler, so as to allow the plates to become heated. As a practical man he should say, that the water spaces were large enough to allow the water to circulate, whether in a state of ebullition or otherwise. The engine sometimes draws the water out of the boilers by what is termed priming; that occurs when the water being near to the steam raises up the steam and passes into the cylinder, and passes through the valve into the condenser, and thence to the waste cistern from which the boilers are fed. Sometimes injury arises from its not passing freely through the valves. I do not know if this engine has valves to accommodate that. The safety-valve was, in his opinion, large enough for the size of the boiler, and it was regulated to a pressure of 12lb. on the square inch. There was nothing he could see to impede the operation of the safety-valve. It was certainly in an exposed situation, but then no one could meddle with it without being seen. There was no controlling power over the safety-valve in the engine-room; some vessels were so provided, but he did not think it material. In case of a stoppage the engineer might make use of such a provision to prevent danger, but the safety-valve ought to act of itself. He would not have made the plates of the *Victoria* so thin as they were for engines of so great a power; they were from ¼th to 5-16ths of an inch in thickness. The iron had the name of Bowling on it, and appeared very fair iron. He knew of nothing wrong in the construction of the boilers or engines. If the plates were double the size, they would not resist the power of steam when red hot; they would resist more, but not sufficient to prevent injury. He did not think that any danger would arise from the combustion of gases. He considered the boilers safe boilers if they were not allowed to get red hot; and he did not think them more likely to be overheated than other boilers.

John Cordinow, the only survivor of the firemen and engineers of the *Victoria* in the late accident, was here led into the room, and though still very weak from the effects of the dreadful injuries he had received, appeared in a very improving state. Having been sworn, he said he had been third engineer of the *Victoria* for about three months, and was in the engine-room at the time of the accident, on the 14th of June last. He had been employed on shore for some time before that as a smith in the engine line. I think it was wrong for the pilot to give three orders, "Ease her," "Stop her," and "Back her," in one moment. He felt the stroke of the collision with the brig. The engine did not back, and I know of no other reason than that the vessel had too much way on her. Did not see anything during the voyage which would tend to produce accident; the conduct of the men was the same throughout. There was a great difficulty in getting up steam, from want of draught in the two fire-places where the bars were altered. The men were obliged to work harder to keep the fires up. Every attempt was made to make the fires work well. To get the steam the fires must be urged, but this was done uniformly throughout the voyage. No part of the machinery was put in motion to get up the steam. I knew nothing of the *Wilberforce* being close astern, and did not hear any communication made to the engineer of that kind. If any such communication had been I must have known it. I was in the engine-room from Gravesend till the accident took place, and the work was conducted in the same way as it had been during the other part of the voyage; no greater efforts were made in the river than elsewhere. The number of strokes made by the engine was from 14 to 16 or 17 per minute. She sometimes made 18½ or 19 strokes in a minute, but never in the river. Captain Bell was pretty often in the engine-room, but not more than usual. I never saw the boilers red hot. When an order was given to stop the engine, the furnace doors were always opened, and the feed-cocks were turned off, to prevent the steam forcing the hot water of the boilers into the feed-pipes. I never knew of the feed-cocks being shut off, except when there was too much water in the boilers, and they were occasionally shut and opened, as necessity required. The feed-cocks were not shut before the collision took place. I shut the feed-cocks off myself at that time, and am quite sure they were not turned off before. Neither I nor the other engineers had been pinching the boilers; we had been regulating them. The water was always in a state of ebullition. I was at the larboard lever when the accident took place. The water was always bubbling. I was never certain how much water there was in the boilers. The water might have been below the gauge-cocks. The solid body of water being nearly as low as the lowest gauge-cock, would bubble up to the highest gauge-cock, and we could not tell where the water was. When the accident occurred the water was between the lower and the second gauge-cock. He could tell that by opening the cocks. They could never depend on the gauge-glasses, and the floats never acted. The river water fermented more than the sea water. He thought the water spaces were too narrow, the fire causing a greater ebullition. He considered the true water level which ought to be kept up in the boilers to be about 8 inches above the feed-cocks or the surface of the flue. That would be plenty of water, in his opinion.

A reference was here made to the plans left by Mr. Ewart, the government engineer, for the guidance of the jury, but they were found to be incomplete, inasmuch as the place of the gauge-cocks of the boilers had not been distinctly pointed out; it was generally understood, however, that the witness meant that the water was between the lowest and second gauge-cocks.

To a general question by the jury, the witness said he was quite sure there was plenty of water in the boilers when the accident happened. The water was between the lowest and second gauge-cock, and that was sufficient. If too much water came from it I should say the boiler was too full. The water-line, in my opinion, is below that level.

The witness here became so much exhausted that it was found necessary to adjourn to allow him time for refreshment and rest.

On the jury reassembling,

Mr. Hall asked the witness if he worked the boilers of the *Victoria* with water above the second gauge-cock.

The Witness.—Yes, I have with the fermented water. I never knew any real or solid body of water at all in the boilers, it always appeared in a state of ferment. I was always in bodily fear, but I thought there was no danger when there was plenty of water in the boilers. The other engineers had the same feeling. We were always examining them, every three minutes at most, and have known the water to lower from the top gauge to the second in less than five minutes. I have not measured what quantity of water the boilers could contain. I shut the feed-cocks off myself directly after the collision with the brig. The witness here pointed out the way in which the feed-cocks were situated, and the way in which they would be when turned off. He further said the chief engineer could not read the words "shut" and "open," but knew when the feed-cocks were open or shut by practice. He was in the habit, with the other engineers, of regulating the feed, and as the mid-

ship boilers would be supplied in their working by the wing boilers, the feed was generally turned nearly off in the midship boilers whilst they were kept fully open in the wing boilers. This was the case with them when the collision took place, and he turned the feeds off. This was not a regular mode of working boilers, but these boilers required great attention, and required to be worked in this way. Furnace plates of other boilers were generally half an inch in thickness. Witness never saw any so thin as the *Victoria's*, which are about a quarter of an inch thick.

The coroner was about to arrange the voluminous evidence, previous to summing up, when Mr. Hall requested that James Craig, an engineer, who had the charge of the vessel on one voyage, and who was examined in the early part of the investigation, should be recalled.

Craig was accordingly sworn; and in answer to questions by Mr. L. Jacobs, he said that he knew the witness Cordinow. He was chief stoker on board the *Victoria*. He was not an engineer. He instructed this man to keep the boilers perfectly fed, and not only him, but every other man in the engine-room. A person of the name of Tempest, a neighbour of Cordinow's, was also on board, and was also instructed, and they all expressed their satisfaction at the working of the boilers, but said they were not up to the mode of feeding till he pointed it out. He showed them exactly how to fix the lever. He always kept the water in the second cock, and steam in the top cock. To make her quite safe, he should always keep the water between the second and third cocks. The supply pipes were sufficiently simple to regulate the feed without opening the furnace doors or any other help. The stoke-hole was large enough. He considered the chief engineer a very competent man, but he had not so good an opinion of Colvill, the second engineer. He had been chief engineer of 37 different steam-boats. He never found any difficulty in managing any engines. The engines of the *Victoria* were as easily worked as any others.

The coroner said he had no doubt that they might supply the water very well, but the question was whether the engines worked well afterwards. He asked if the fire drove the water out of the narrow interstices?

Craig—As engineers we have been always taught that the steam will find its way through the water, which will find its level.

At 8 o'clock the coroner proceeded to read over the whole of the evidence taken in this case, which occupied upwards of three hours.

The jury retired at 12 o'clock to consider

of their verdict, and at half-past one they were prepared to deliver it.

Mr. P. Mellish, the foreman, rose and said, that he was never placed in a more difficult situation than he was that night. He had to contend with difficulties he never had to contend with before. He had now to declare the opinions of the jury. He believed he spoke their feelings when he said that they never saw a steamer fitted up with greater splendour and taste than the *Victoria*, or with greater attention to the convenience of the passengers. He must, however, say, and he was delivering the unanimous opinion of the jury, that they never saw a vessel in the river fitted up with so little regard to the comfort of the engineers and stokers who worked the engines, and the place where they were employed; in fact, it was a perfect pandemonium, at least such was his opinion. He never saw a place which realized his ideas of pandemonium so much before.

The Jury—It is our opinion generally it is not a fit place for the engineers and stokers.

The Foreman continued—I will now deliver the verdict of the jury.—"They consider that the death of Andrew Brown [and the other sufferers] was accidentally occasioned by the explosion of the boiler on board the *Victoria* steam-vessel, on the 14th of June last. The jury consider that the construction of the boilers was unsafe, the water spaces too small, and the plates too thin. The jury further consider, that the engineers having no immediate control over the safety-valve in the engine-room is highly reprehensible, and the *jury levy a deodand of* 1,500*l. upon the boiler and steam-engine of the Victoria.*"

NOTES AND NOTICES.

Magnetic Fluid.—During the late storm at Rochdale, a cotton-mill was struck by the lightening, and the bell which hung above the roof was destroyed. It was afterwards found that all the tools of a watchmaker residing in the neighbourhood, had become in a greater or less degree magnetic, and were wholly useless; they all attracted iron filings readily, and the hammer was polarized, the needle being neutral. —*Athenæum.*

London and Birmingham Railway.—On Monday last, a large party of the directors and Proprietors breakfasted at the Birmingham station, and at half-past six they left, with one of Mr. Bury's engines, to make the first excursion along the entire line to London, where they arrived at the Euston station at one o'clock, without any kind of accident or circumstance to interfere with the pleasure of the journey. The time occupied in travelling was exactly five hours, the other hour and a half being devoted to the examination of the stupendous and interesting works on the new part of the line, much of which is yet incomplete. The distance to Coventry (18½ miles,) was performed in 36 minutes; from Coventry to Rugby (11 miles,) in 22 minutes; from Rugby to Denbigh Hall (35 miles) in 2 hours and 10 minutes; and from Denbigh Hall to London (48 miles) in 1 hour and 54 minutes—in all 5 hours and 2 minutes. The Kilsby Tunnel has been constructed in defiance of immense of physical difficulties, and is a work which has excited the greatest interest and admiration. Arriving at the central shaft which has a diameter of 60 ft. they were saluted with hearty cheers from a number of workmen who had stationed themselves at its summit far above the subterranean travellers who responded to the welcome. The rocky excavations at Blisworth, extending through a very considerable extent of country, astonished the visitors, perhaps, as much as any other part of the line, and must be seen to enable any person to form an adequate idea of its character. The Wolverton viaduct excited great admiration, and many of the proprietors walked down the embankment to enjoy a view of the beautiful structure, from the meadows below. At the great Wolverton station, or central depot for the engines, the workshops, and arrangements were inspected, and refreshments were liberally provided. The remainder of the journey, although entitled to notice, presented fewer features of novelty. The jaunt gave much satisfaction.—*Midland Counties Herald.*

Steam-Boats beaten in Speed.—Mr. Jobard, of Brussels (says the *Nouvelliste*), has discovered a method, according to which it is asserted that the Straits of Calais may be crossed in eleven minutes, by means of a pyrotechnical composition, of which the chlorate of potash is the basis, but in a less proportion than in Congreve rockets. The whole apparatus consists in a boat, with the floating properties of the life-boat, long and narrow, crossed at its greatest diameter by one or more iron tubes charged with the pyrotechnical composition. By applying fire to these tubes, the openings to which should pass beyond the stern of the boat, the reaction is stated to be such that the boat will glide over the water with a swiftness never attained on any railway. The construction being upon the principle of the life-boat, the person embarking in it will run no other risk than that of getting a few momentary duckings, but will always rise again to the surface. The building of the boat will not cost more than about 1000 francs, and each voyage will require 100 francs' worth of gunpowder.

Flat-chambered Boilers.—We have received a letter from Mr. Hancock in reply to Mr. Hebert and A Shareholder; as we have not been able to publish it this week, it is but fair to state that he very clearly refutes Mr. Hebert's objections to the merits and originality of his invention of flat-chambered boilers, and shews that Raddatz's patent, referred to by A Shareholder is quite different from his.

The twenty-eighth volume of the *Mechanics* *Magazine* is now published, price, in half-cloth, 8s. 6d., with a *Railway Map* of England and Wales. The *Railway Map* may be had separately, price 6d.; and on fine paper, coloured, price 1s.

LONDON: Printed and Published for the Proprietor, by W. A. Robertson, at the Mechanics' Magazine Office, No. 6, Peterborough-court, between 135 and 136, Fleet-street.—Sold by A. & W. Galignani, Rue Vivienne, Paris.

𝔐𝔢𝔠𝔥𝔞𝔫𝔦𝔠𝔰' 𝔐𝔞𝔤𝔞𝔷𝔦𝔫𝔢,

MUSEUM, REGISTER, JOURNAL, AND GAZETTE.

No. 786.]   FRIDAY, AUGUST 31, 1838.   [Price 3*d.*

IMPROVED METHOD OF MINE VENTILATION.

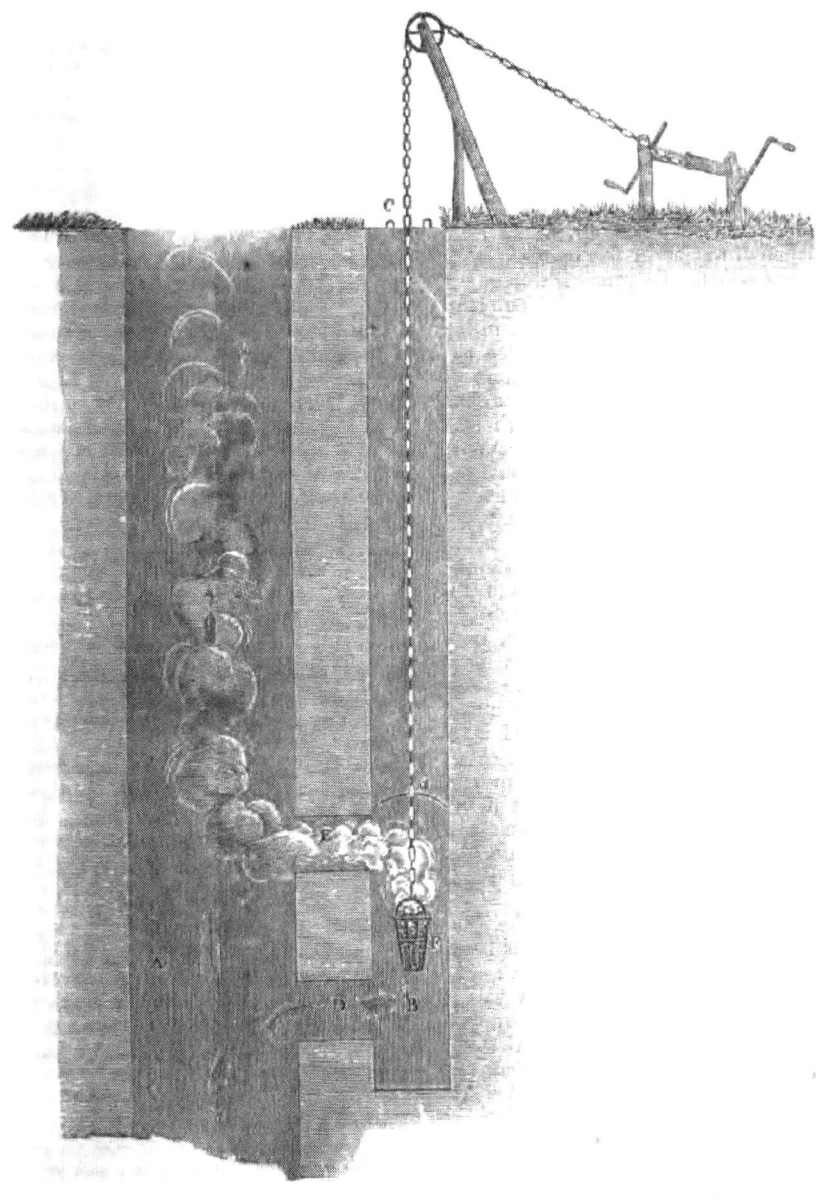

IMPROVED METHOD OF MINE VENTILATION.

SIR,—As you have always shown an anxious desire to promote the safety of the working miner, by disseminating, through the medium of your useful periodical, any information bearing on that object, I am induced to trouble you with the particulars of a plan for assisting ventilation, which I have introduced successfully at a colliery under my management in Derbyshire, and which has been tried at two neighbouring collieries with equal effect. It is, perhaps, necessary I should first state, that the principle of ventilation is simply that of a pneumatic balance, where one scale is made to preponderate, either by receiving an increased supply of air, or by a reduction of weight in the opposite scale by rarefaction. To promote this object of rarefaction in the north, powerful furnaces are placed at the bottom of the upcast shaft, the heat from which expands, and lightens the long column of air above, and thus promotes a constant circulation. This method, though efficacious, is open to several objections, amongst which are the danger and expense of feeding the fire, and the necessity of confining the upcast shaft entirely to the purposes of ventilation, as suffocation must inevitably ensue should any one attempt to descend through the smoke and vitiated air voided therefrom. The plan I have adopted, though, perhaps, not so powerful as that used in the north, is certainly much more simple and less expensive; and the result of three years' experience has proved it to be quite sufficient in all ordinary cases for the removal of those pests to the miner, carbonic acid gas, and the more dangerous hydrogen, both of which it has had to contend with in formidable quantities. My plan (see sketch) is as follows:—

At a distance of 4 feet from the side of the upcast shaft A, (which is here used for drawing coals,) I sink a small shaft B, 4 feet diameter, and 14 yards deep, the top of which is closely covered with a pair of folding iron doors C. At 2 feet from the bottom of this shaft an opening D is made into the upcast shaft 2 feet 6 inches high, and 2 feet 6 inches wide, the sides of which are secured with brick walls, and the top supported with broken cast rails. At 2 yards from the top of this hole another opening E of the same dimensions communicates with the main shaft, and is secured in a similar manner. A fire-lamp, F, 2 feet 6 inches high, and 18 inches wide is then filled with fire and lowered into the small pit to the space between the holes D and E; the doors are now closed, when the heat and smoke, with a portion of rarefied air, rushes through the top hole E, and mixing with the air in the upcast shaft, so lightens it as to produce a very strong and continuous current through the mine to the surface. A few weeks ago I effected a considerable improvement by suspending to the chain in the small shaft, at a little distance above the uppermost hole E, an iron cover G, which nearly fills the shaft, and thus preventing the escape of any portion of the heated air or smoke through the folding doors above, renders the whole available for the purpose of rarefying the air in the upcast shaft A. In practice I find the depth I have chosen for the small shaft B (14 yards), to be the most convenient, as one man can with ease wind up the fire and repair it, and there is no inconvenience to the workmen in descending for this distance through the smoke.

I am, Sir,
    Your very humble servant,
        THE BLACK DIAMOND.
Kilburne, near Derby, July 27, 1838.

ON THE COMPARATIVE STRENGTH OF CYLINDRICAL TUBES EMPLOYED IN HIGH-PRESSURE BOILERS; WITH A PLAIN PRACTICAL RULE FOR DETERMINING THE RELATIVE STRENGTH OF SUCH TUBES,—BEING IN REPLY TO A QUESTION OF MR. J. HALL IN HIS LETTER TO MR. J. SEAWARD OF THE 4TH JULY, 1838. (See p. 361.)

To W. J Hall, Esq.

(Copy)   Canal Ironworks, Limehouse,
                              August 23rd, 1838.

SIR,—In your letter to me of the 4th July last there was one question which I did not answer, viz., that respecting the difference of strength of plates employed in the construction of tubes; the reason of my not then replying to that question was, that it would have led into too much detail to be conveniently introduced in the then pending inquiry; the subject, however, being important, I now send you what I hope will be a satisfactory reply to your question. I also send you a few observations respecting the idea that steam boiler accidents are attributable to the explosion of gases. I propose to publish these documents, to which I presume you can now have no objection.

I am, Sir,

Yours most obediently,

(Signed)　　JOHN SEAWARD.

———

The strength of a cylindrical tube to resist an external pressure exerted on its outward surface, is a very different thing from the strength of the same tube to resist an internal pressure.

In the latter case, that is, when the force is exerted on the inside of the tube, and tending to burst or rend it asunder, the relative strength or power of resistance of the tube is very easily estimated, it is well known to be, under like circumstances, in the simple ratio of the thickness of the metal of which the tube is formed, and inversely as the diameter of the tube.

But in the other case, when the pressure is external, the strength of the tube to resist such pressure will depend upon very different principles :—it is generally supposed that the strength of a cylindrical tube under such circumstances must be immeasurably great ; and there is no doubt that such is really the fact, provided the pressure is uniform all round the tube, and that the true cylindrical figure is strictly preserved ; because in such case the tube is like a well-formed arch ; it cannot be destroyed except by the absolute crushing of the particles of metal one into the other, which is altogether improbable.　But if the true cylindrical or circular figure is not preserved, and indeed if the deviation from the true figure of greatest resistance is ever so trifling, the principle of the arch is gone at once, it is then like an arch without abutments ; and the tube under such circumstances, instead of being able to resist almost infinite pressure, will in fact be unable to resist a comparatively moderate pressure.

Now, practically speaking, it is almost impossible to form a tube that shall* be strictly cylindrical, or of any other figure of greatest resistance ; the very weight of the material is sufficient of itself to destroy the true figure; the circumstance of the tubes of steam boilers being formed of metal plates with lap joints rivetted together precludes the possibility of obtaining the true figure ; moreover, in the case of horizontal tubes, as they are employed in steam boilers, the pressure is not uniform; for while the pressure on the upper part of a tube six feet diameter may be only $13\frac{1}{2}$ lbs. upon the square inch, the pressure on the lower part of the tube will be nearly $16\frac{1}{2}$ lbs. to the square inch, because the weight of a column of water six feet high has to be added to the pressure on the lower part of the tube; therefore the cylindrical or circular form is not in that case the true figure of greatest resistance ; and it is not very likely that in the ordinary way of business, of boiler making, much care or correctness can or will be bestowed to the calculating, or afterwards in the making of the tube, agreeable to the true figure of greatest resistance.

Moreover, if all the above difficulties be overcome, and the tube is formed according to the true figure of greatest resistance, there is little chance that it will long remain so, in the practical working of a boiler; the unequal contraction and expansion of the plates by being partially overheated and then suddenly cooled, accidents of constant occurrence, will cause the plates to be drawn and buckled, and thereby soon destroy the true figure. And it should be borne in mind that however trifling the alteration of form may be at first, yet the moment a slight alteration has taken place, the destructive change then goes on in an accelerated ratio. And here a very important distinction should be observed, which is, that when the force is exerted within a tube tending to burst it outwards, the force exerted will not induce any change of form such as to render the tube weaker ; because if the tube was originally made tolerably near to the true figure of resistance, any change of figure which afterwards takes place, must be such as

* As a strong corroboration of this fact it may be stated that about fifteen years back some interesting experiments were made to ascertain the relative force which copper tubes were able to support internally and externally : the tubes were beautifully made, and as perfectly cylindrical as hands could form them, but it was found in every case that a much less force was sufficient to crush or collapse the tube than what was required to burst it asunder.

will render it in fact stronger—that is supposing the metal plates to have some degree of elasticity—it will cause the tube to assume the figure of greatest resistance. But it is not the same with a tube that supports an external pressure, because in this case, any change of figure must demonstrably produce a greater departure from the figure of greatest resistance, and thereby render the tube weaker and weaker; and this is a very important reason why a tube that has been proved to a pressure of 30 or 40 lbs to the square inch, may afterwards fail under a pressure of less than half that amount.

For the above reasons it is therefore clear, that a practical estimate of either the absolute or relative strength of tubes, supporting an external pressure, cannot be based upon the idea of these tubes being correctly formed agreeably to the figure of greatest resistance; the safe mode is to estimate the strength of the tubes by the capacity of the metal plates (of which the tubes are formed) to resist a transverse strain, in the same manner as we should estimate the strength of a flat plate, a bar, or a beam, the strength of which is known to be in the ratio of the square of the thickness or depth, in the direction of the strain.

Under this view of the matter, therefore, it would be correct to consider, that the strength of tubes under an external pressure would vary as the *square* of the thickness of the metal, but it is also clear that the strength will also vary *inversely* as the *square* of the diameter of the tube; because an increase of diameter not only increases the leverage, but also the absolute quantity of force in a like ratio.

But it would not be right to suppose that the absolute strength of curved plates in a tube is no greater than that of perfectly flat plates; this is not the case: there can be no question that the curved form enables the plates to sustain a much greater force than flat plates are able to support; and it is clear that the nearer the curvature of the plates approximates to the figure of greatest resistance, the greater force will they be able to bear; for although, as is stated above, the slightest deviation from the figure of greatest resistance destroys the principle of the arch, and thereby reduces the comparative strength of such tubes from almost infinity to a strength of very moderate limits, nevertheless curved plates will support a greater or less strain the nearer or the more remotely they approach to the true figure of greatest resistance.

It is therefore evident, that besides the capacity of resisting a transverse strain, there is also another element of strength in tubes subject to external pressure; that is, the strength derived from the curvature of the plates; but, as this latter strength depends entirely upon the greater or less approximation of the curvature to the figure of greatest resistance, and as the degree of approximation will vary in every individual case, and will also be liable to rapid alteration in the same tube, it is clear that no general rule can be given for determining the strength thereby gained. And, indeed, this is not requisite in the present instance, because it is not intended to offer a rule for estimating the positive strength of tubes, but simply the relative strength of different tubes; which, as above stated, is, in like circumstances, as the square of the thickness of metal, and inversely as the square of the diameter of the tube. The positive or absolute strength of such a tube can only be known by actual proof, but this once known the strength of other tubes may be estimated by the foregoing rule:—thus, if a tube 3 feet diameter and made of $\frac{1}{2}$ inch plate is capable of sustaining a given external pressure, what will be the relative strength of a tube 6 feet diameter made of $\frac{1}{4}$ inch plate? Answer—the former is 16 times stronger than the latter.

But, in the case of the force acting inside the tube with a tendency to burst or rend it asunder, the strength of the tube will be as the thickness of the metal directly and inversely as the diameter; therefore if a tube is 3 feet diameter and made of $\frac{1}{2}$ inch plate, it will be 4 times as strong as a tube 6 feet diameter made of $\frac{1}{4}$ inch plate.

The foregoing is a safe, easy, practical rule, and if employed by boiler makers in the planning of high-pressure boilers, I believe it will be the means of preventing many serious errors and fatal accidents.

JOHN SEAWARD.

Limehouse, August 29, 1838.

ON THE CAUSE OF STEAM BOILER EXPLOSIONS.

Sir,—An opinion has lately prevailed with many persons, that the frequent explosions of high-pressure steam boilers may be attributed to the igniting of explosive gases generated within the boilers themselves. The subject is highly important, and has engaged my attention for some time past; and the result of my observations and reflections is, that the above opinion is not based upon any satisfactory or valid foundation. I therefore offer a few remarks, in the hope of engaging more competent persons than myself, to investigate this interesting subject.

That under certain circumstances hydrogen gas may be formed inside a boiler in consequence of the overheated iron plates decomposing the water of the steam by abstracting and uniting with its oxygen, is a fact generally admitted; but the circumstances under which this process may go on, I conceive must be exceedingly rare, and the effect of very trifling amount. If it were possible for the gas to be formed in any considerable quantity, the circumstance must be immediately known by the very perceptible effect it would have upon the working of the engines, but which effect I have never been able to discover myself, nor have I ever heard of any well-authenticated account of such fact having been noticed by others: although I, as well as others, have had the opportunity of noticing many boilers in which a portion of the interior flue or fire-place plates, have become red hot.

It is quite certain, that even if a considerable quantity of the gas were formed, it must be carried off with the steam so rapidly, either through the cylinders or through the waste steam-pipe, that no great accumulation could ever remain in the boiler; in high-pressure boilers which alone are exposed to the accidents of explosion, the steam space is so limited that the whole quantity of steam contained in the boiler is carried off, and again renewed, at least every eight seconds, or about seven or eight times per minute; and as the gas is carried off with the steam, it is clear that the former must be generated at a most abundant rate, or otherwise the quantity at any one time in the boiler, must be very small indeed.

But admitting the fact, that hydrogen gas may be present inside a boiler, how are we to account for the presence of oxygen gas also, which is so essential to form the explosive mixture? It is true, some persons suppose that the latter is supplied from outside the boiler, from the atmospheric air; but this is an idea wholly untenable: others suppose that the oxygen is also formed inside the boiler by the de-oxidizing of a part of the metal plates that had been previously oxidized; but this idea is as difficult to conceive as the former; for either the two operations of oxidizing and de-oxidizing must be going on conjointly, or the one must cease before the other commences; if the latter, then it is certain that the whole of the hydrogen gas will have escaped from the boiler before the oxygen begins to be formed; and if we suppose the other mode, then we must admit that two opposite antagonist operations are promoted at the same time, under the same circumstances, and by the same means; a fact somewhat marvellous, though perhaps quite within the range of chemical affinities.

But, granting that the two gases may both be produced simultaneously in the boiler in sufficient quantity and proportion to form the explosive mixture, what will then take place? Why, the gas will be so saturated or diluted by the steam or vapour of the water, that it is difficult to conceive any other than that the compound will be inexplosive and wholly innoxious.

The above are some of the difficulties which militate against the opinion that steam boiler accidents are occasioned by an explosion of gases, difficulties that cannot readily be explained away; there is, however, one fact of so strong and irrefragable a character, that in my opinion it most conclusively decides the fate of this ingenious hypothesis; and clearly proves that steam boiler accidents cannot be attributed to an explosion of gases. The fact alluded to is this, that an explosion or a collapsing, in the numerous class of low-pressure boilers are things never heard of, while they are but too numerous among the class of high-pressure boilers; although it is most certain that the former boilers are quite as likely to form the gases as the latter; the plates of the fire-places and flues of the former boilers are probably quite as much exposed to the mischance of becoming red hot, and from the great capacity of these boilers are likely to hold the gases in greater abundance; but notwithstanding, in low-pressure boilers no explosions do take place,—no fatal accidents,—no loss of life.

JOHN SEAWARD.

Limehouse, August 20, 1838.

CHAPMAN'S STEAM-ENGINE IMPROVE-MENTS.

Sir,—Any plan for economising the fuel of steam-engines must be considered as of the utmost importance at the present day; more especially if the proposed plan be accompanied with the beneficial result of at the same time increasing the duty, or power of the engine to which it is applied. Take in particular the case of marine engines—it is not merely the saving of expense in the outlay for fuel that we are to take into account, but the saving of burthen and stowage room in the ship. The less fuel a ship of a given power requires, the longer voyage it will be able to undertake, or in a short trip more room will be left for passengers and goods.

To accomplish which, both a saving of fuel and gain of power, there are two very important things which must in the out-set be attended to; that is :—1st. To generate the greatest possible quantity of steam from a given quantity of fuel, with sufficient dispatch. 2nd. To apply the steam when generated, so as to effect the greatest possible duty, or quantity of work.

To effect the first requisite is the chief property of a good boiler, but there are two or three other things which are necessary in addition; that is—the boiler should be more than sufficiently strong to resist any strain that it is ever likely to be subjected to; it should be easy of access so as to be kept clean; it should also be made of a form to ensure its durability for the greatest length of time. But in order that it may generate the greatest quantity of steam with sufficient dispatch, with any given quantity of fuel, it should present the greatest quantity of water surface, to the greatest possible quantity of surface exposed to the flame and other heated gases.

A boiler, having, I believe, the above requisites has lately been patented by Mr. G. Chapman of Whitby, along with some other important improvements in the steam-engine (to which I shall afterwards advert). To give an adequate idea of the nature of the invention, I think I cannot do better than quote the patentee's own words, in an abridged form, as contained in his specification:

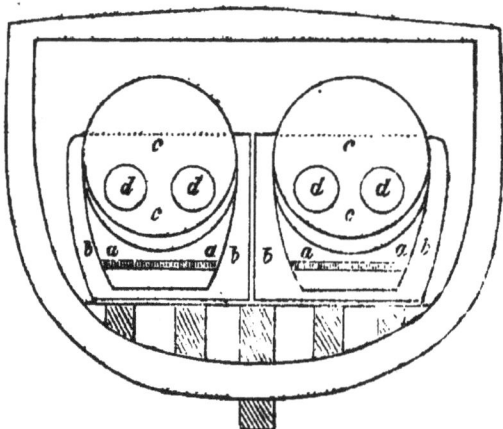

"With respect to my improved boiler or steam generator, I declare, that whereas it has hitherto been the practice (more especially in marine boilers) to enclose the furnace and boiler in one chamber, or case, which is subject to the same pressure of steam in every part, instead of this I make the furnace and boiler two separate and distinct vessels, which have no communication with each other, internally, except by means of a pump or pumps, or other equivalent apparatus, to extract the water from the furnace part below (where it has been partially heated) and force it into the boiler part above, to be more highly heated, to generate steam of sufficient elasticity to effect the purpose required. The figure annexed is a cross section of a steam ship, provided with furnaces and boilers on this improved plan, A A are the furnaces, B B outer casings to the furnaces, which are kept filled with water at a heat a little below the boiling point ; as these casings are not required to sustain any great pressure they may be made of a shape, externally, best suited to the place where they may have to be fixed, or to the fancy of the engineer. C O the boilers, or steam generators ; which I make of a cylindric, or other shape, (but I prefer the cylindric as being the strongest) and place them directly over the furnace ; D D return flues within the boilers. but which may be dispensed with if required, the furnace casings may be supplied with water by a pump or pumps, or other means, from any source convenient, or from the hot well of the engine, which being at a higher level the water will descend by its own gravity into the furnace casings, and after the water in the furnace casings has been heated to near the boiling point it is forced into the boilers C C by a pump or pumps. or other equivalent means, to be converted into steam ; the casings may be furnished with one or more outlets at the top, which outlets may either be covered with a light valve, or left open. The furnaces may be lined either all, or in part, with fire bricks. fire clay, or any fire resisting material but in many cases it will be found sufficient to line those parts only which are more directly exposed to the action of the fire."

So far I have given an abridgment of the specification, leaving out many of the technical expressions, &c , which the nature of such legal documents require ; but to explain the whole of the advantages, it requires something to be said in addition.

First. By making the furnace and boiler separate, the shapes best adapted to the duty and strain each has to undergo, as well as a shape best adapted to receive the greatest effect of the fire, can be adopted. For instance : the boilers in steam ships have generally an external form, which has large flat surfaces, which surfaces have to sustain the full pressure of the steam within them, however ill adapted that form may be to withstand it (else why so many lamentable disasters

as are almost daily taking place ?): Instead of this, the furnace part of Mr. Chapman's boiler, which is necessarily the weakest from its form, has only the weight of the water that is in it, and the weight of the boiler and water above it, to support, without at all being subject to any internal strain from the steam, however strong it may be in the boiler at the time. The boiler too, where the steam is generated, is in the best practical form possible to sustain the strain to which it is of necessity exposed, as well as of the best form, in conjunction with the furnaces, for exposing the greatest quantity of water surface, to t e greatest quantity of fire or heating surface (in this particular the patentee challenges all other forms of boiler which may in practice be applied) ; and further the most intense heat is applied to that part of the boiler (should the supply pumps cease to act) which would for the greatest length of time not injure the boiler; for as long as there is any water in the boiler it will occupy that part of it which is immediately over the fire on the grate. The common marine boilers are very faulty in this respect, as well as in others ; the fire being placed in a number of small square or other shaped boxes, side by side in the inside of the boilers, (which from their confined situation are miserably deficient in water and fire surface) with from six to twelve inches (more or less, according to the size of the boilers) of water above them, should the pump cease to give a sufficient supply, in a very little time the top of the fire boxes are boiled dry, the consequence is, the intense heat underneath soon burns the iron through, and the steam rushes out, however weak it may be at the time; and it is well known that the scalding power of the weakest steam is as great, or greater, than steam of a higher elasticity, and its effects equally as fatal.

The actual strain which the common square boiler is able to sustain in comparison with the cylindrical boiler, is totally out of the question. By a calculation which I have made of the pressure, a cylindrical boiler made of iron of a medium quality, six feet diameter, plate ¼ inch thick (the length immaterial) would be able to sustain, just at the bursting point, 583 pounds pressure on every square inch of its surface, if it could be made without seam; but as that is not the case, the plates have to be lapped over each other, and revits put through them both; we may allow, therefore, half the above strength, which leaves 291½ lbs resisting strength to the square inch. It is quite ridiculous to think of such a boiler exploding by fair means; if ever such a thing should occur it will be for want of water, and the fire will burn the iron through with the same facility, whether there be two pounds per inch pressure on the inside, or two hundred. To calculate the strain that a boiler of a square form would sustain, is impossible, without having the boiler in question to look at, as there is generally a number of cross bars in the inside; that go from side to side, to prevent the sides from bulging out with the pressure; with the exception of these stays the comparison of strength between a cylindrical vessel and a square one, turns on this—that the strain to break the iron in the cylinder is in a direction to pull it asunder in its length, and the strain in a square vessel is in a direction to bend or break it across; so it must be evident to any person who pays the least attention to the matter, that a great deal depends upon how the above stays are fixed, whether well or ill; it likewise requires a great attention, if they are well fixed at first, to keep them so, which is no very easy matter, by reason of the very great and unequal strain they have to undergo, which causes their fastenings at the ends to give way. I have seen a square boiler made with stays as above, and every time the boiler was opened, and that was very frequently, the stays were all adrift, either by breaking, or pulling their fastenings away, or some other cause; at length the boiler, by bulging out by the steam, and collapsing when cold, broke asunder at one time, at an angle to the length of three feet, and by the time that the boilers had been in use for twenty months (undergoing very frequent and expensive repairs in that time) they had to be replaced by entirely new ones, whereas if they had been good cylindric boilers, they ought, and would, have been in use three times as long at least, without any material repairs.

Secondly, to apply the steam when generated, so as to effect the greatest possible duty, or quantity of work, There is only two methods, in which steam can be applied, (properly speaking, whether it be what is called high, or low steam) that is,

letting it flow into the cylinder during the whole length of the stroke of the piston, through the steam admission, or throttle valve, which is opened to a width to admit the steam into the cylinder, at a proper elasticity to perform the duty required, which is the common method; or by opening the steam valve to the full width at the moment that the crank passes the dead points, and allowing it to remain open for a greater or less portion of the stroke of the piston, as the duty the engine may have to do, or the elasticity of the steam in the boiler may require; after which the further supply of steam from the boiler to the cylinder is shut off, allowing the steam that has already entered the cylinder, to expand, to effect the remaining part of the stroke. The latter method is allowed by engineers and others, in general, to be by far the most economical and beneficial; Mr. Watt, at an early period of his improvements, applied it with advantage in his single-stroke pumping engines; the principal reason that it has not been more generally made use of hitherto, has been the want of a simple and effective method of giving the proper supply. Watt's method as applied to his single-stroke pumping engines, is quite inadequate to a double-stroke rotatory engine. But this want for the future need not apply, as the principle may be acted on to the full extent by adopting Mr. Chapman's second improvement in steam-engines, that is, his newly invented expansion gear, which is both scientific and ingenious, simple and efficient, and is under most perfect command by the governor of the engine, where a governor is used, or may be clamped by the engineer in a moment, where there is no governor. It will always open the steam valve at the proper time, and likewise shut the steam from the cylinder at any fractional part of the length of the stroke, so as to keep the engine at any desired rate of motion, let the duty the engine may have to do, or the elasticity of the steam in the boiler, be what it may. The apparatus is applicable to any kind of steam engine, old or new, land or marine, fixed or locomotive.

Such an apparatus has been long wanted, and I have no doubt but it will become in great demand, as I am informed that the patentee intends to offer it to the public on the most liberal terms.

In support of my assertion of the advantages to be derived from working an engine expansively, it may not be amiss to quote some authorities in favour of it, that can be referred to, and whose evidence cannot be disputed.

The writer of the article "Steam Engine," in the 19th volume of the fourth edition of the *Encyclopædia Britanica*, page 671, after giving an algebraic solution in proof of his assertion in favour of working by expansion, says:—"Here Mr. Watt observed a remarkable result; the steam expended in this case would have been four times greater than when it was stopped at one fourth, and yet the accumulated pressure is not twice as great, being nearly five-thirds. One-fourth of the steam performs nearly three-fifths of the work, and an equal quantity performs more than twice as much work when thus admitted during one-fourth of the motion." Then he says further "let the steam be stopped at one-half of the stroke, its performance will be multiplied by one and seven-tenths; if stopped at one-third, its performance will be multiplied by two and one-tenth; if at one-fourth, by two and four-tenths; at one-fifth, by two and six-tenths; at one-sixth, two and eight-tenths; and one-seventh, three times as much work, &c.; in comparison to the steam employed, as it would do if the steam flowed into the cylinder during the whole stroke." Mr. Luke Herbert in his *Engineers' and Mechanics' Encyclopædia*, article "Expansion," after alluding to some other things relating to the expansion of the gases, says; "this property of elastic fluids has been turned to great advantage in steam-engines, by admitting steam of high-pressure into the cylinder during a portion of the stroke, and shutting off the communication with the boiler, the expansion of the steam in the cylinder, carries the piston with a constant decreasing force through the remaining portion of the stroke, by which mode of working, the whole effect produced during the expansion of the steam, is clear gain; for example, if the steam be stopped at one-fourth of the stroke, the gain would be 150 per cent of the steam employed." If further proof be required, I would refer your readers to the most astonishing duty performed by the Cornish mining engines, as is published in their reports, and other works, all which is effected by expansion.

Mr. Chapman's apparatus consists of a wheel fixed on the principal, or any other axle or shaft of the engine, having a rotatory motion, the circumference of which wheel is a spiral, or curve, generated by the ever-varying motion of the piston in the cylinder, in combination with the angle that the connecting rod forms in its different positions during the revolutions of the crank pin, which spiral acts on a lever which has an advancing and receding motion, effected by the governor, so as to be either a greater or less portion of the stroke in contact with each other, which at every stroke opens the valve at the proper moment, and retains it open for any length of the stroke which the duty of the engine requires, and then closes it suddenly, allowing the steam already entered to effect the remaining part of the stroke.

C. W. J.

SPEED ON RAILWAYS. — HEATON'S TOOTH AND PINION GEARING, &c. &c. &c.

Sir,—I have read with considerable attention the article copied into your last Number (784), from the *Monthly Chronicle*, headed "Speed on Railways." This article is in the writer's best style, and he is evidently not so much "at sea," as when dealing with "ocean steamers."

I apprehend there are few persons who have had an opportunity of observing the working of railway-locomotives, who will not readily coincide with Dr. Lardner's opinion, that the velocity of the *pistons* is much too great; a slower motion would not only obviate many serious evils attending the rapid reciprocating motion of the apparatus, but it would materially reduce the vibration experienced by passengers in the trains—to many persons a source of great annoyance. Whatever reduction may be effected in the relative speed of parts of the machinery, however, it is quite certain that the velocity of transit must at least be sustained. So far as the size of the driving-wheels affects this problem, I incline to the opinion of those engineers who would limit the size of these wheels to six, or at the utmost, to seven feet diameter. To ten feet wheels I am decidedly opposed; and I fancy those persons who advocate the employment of wheels of such insecure and unwieldy dimensions, will find their advantages altogether fallacious when tried by the unerring test of *practice*.

"One of the methods," says Dr. Lardner, "by which it has been proposed to render a moderate velocity of the pistons compatible with the extreme speed of progressive motion, which, having once been enjoyed by the public, has become an indispensable necessity in railway transit, is to convey the power of the piston to the working wheels *by tooth and pinion gear*. If the practicability of applying this species of mechanism, under the peculiar circumstances of the case of a locomotive engine, be once admitted, we can hardly discover any practical limit to the speed of transit which may be obtained on railways."

"Such a mechanical arrangement," continues this writer, "is so obvious, and founded upon mechanical principles and expedients so well understood, that it cannot be supposed to have escaped the attention of engineers; but its practical application has been attended with difficulties so formidable, that hitherto it has been unattempted." From this statement it would seem that Dr. Lardner is unacquainted with the mode of gearing invented and patented by Messrs. Heatons, of Birmingham, and employed by them in their justly celebrated common-road locomotive, whose unparalleled performances have been recorded in your pages.

The statement that "such a mechanical arrangement had not hitherto been attempted," is only true as confined to railroads; on common roads the Messrs. Heatons have not only *attempted*, but actually accomplished all that is mentioned as desirable in the foregoing quotation. By their system of gearing, the action of the springs in no way interfered with the free and efficient transfer of power from the pistons to the driving wheels: while wheels and pinions of several different sizes being employed, the power of traction, or the rapidity of transport, was capable of increase or diminution, as circumstances required. It was by means of this "mechanical arrangement" that Messrs. Heatons were enabled to skim the level roads in the vicinity of Birmingham, and to ascend the steepest hills of Warwickshire. It follows as a matter of course, that if

such an arrangement of mechanism proved thoroughly efficient, while subjected to the violent concussions of roughly-paved turnpike roads, there can be no chance of its failing under the more favourable circumstances of a railroad.

Dr. Lardner says, "but once admit the practicability of applying *toothed gear*, and it will be difficult indeed to say where may be the limit of mechanical *possibility*, whatever may be the limit which prudence may prescribe." The foregoing will, I presume, do something more than *admit the practicability* —it establishes the fact of its successful application under circumstances extremely unfavourable: and I venture to predict, that when this mode of gearing is introduced into our railroad locomotives, the common results, both as to weight drawn and speed attained, will greatly surpass our present average performances.

Dr. Lardner touches very tenderly upon the "extreme caution observed by railway engineers and directors;" he admits, however, that the result of this has been to impose "a check amounting almost to a dead lock, on the progress of mechanical invention in this department." Whatever difficulty Dr. Lardner may feel in giving his opinion as to whether this "caution" be defensible or not, I know there are plenty of competent persons who do not hesitate to pronounce it *indefensible*.

It happens, most unfortunately for all parties, that although this "extreme caution" has in most cases been exercised by railway engineers towards the plans and improvements of others, they appear to have applied but little of this caution in working out their own plans and experiments. Nay, so strikingly apparent is their want of caution in this respect, as to lead to the acquirement by certain railway companies, of a considerable stock of very dearly bought experience.

On railways generally, the door has been most pertinaciously closed against almost every individual who felt desirous of ascertaining, or of demonstrating, the extent of practical utility pertaining to sundry inventions or improvements. Had more liberality prevailed in this respect, I have no doubt that many important questions, at present in abeyance—such as the safest and most ad-

nomical form of boiler, the best construction and most eligible size for wheels, &c. &c. &c.—would by this time have obtained something like a satisfactory answer.

Had the ocean been no freer than railways, how many important facts would to this day have been undiscovered, how much theory would have remained unsifted. "The sea, the open sea," however, has offered an unrestricted field for the exercise of inventive genius, and the importance of the numberless experiments that have from time to time been made, with boilers of all shapes and sizes, with paddles and propellers of almost every possible variety, with every description of engine, both high and low pressure, &c. &c., the importance of these experiments, I say, may be best estimated, by referring to the present triumphant state of steam navigation.

No person, I am sure, would be found to advocate the admission of inventors to run as much on railroads, sans control, but the "extreme caution," or as less scrupulous persons term it, "the one-sided caution," is calculated to cramp the genius of skilful men, and to continue to the railway companies their present almost ruinous expenses for locomotive power.

Waiting the forthcoming explanation of the doings of the "Great Western" in "the other extreme,"

I remain, Sir,
Yours respectfully,
W. BADDELEY.

London, August 16, 1838.

FIRE ASSOCIATIONS.—THEIR DUTIES POINTED OUT.

SIR,—Permit me to thank your correspondent, Mr. P. Ober, for the flattering mention he has been pleased to make of my name at page 280, and to assure him that "the public interest" is the only object I have in view in my multifarious contributions to your pages.

I am extremely glad to find the general opinion is favourable to the advantages of Honorary Fire-brigades. I am well aware of the celebrated fire-associations of the continental towns: they have existed for many years, and it is to them we are indebted for several of the most valuable improvements which constitute the efficiency of our present fire-engines.

There is, however, one serious and too often fatal error in the working of some of these associations, which is partly illustrated by Mr. Ober, in his letter; speaking of the fire-brigades already organised in Switzerland, Mr. Ober says,—" In some places the members are divided, some devoting themselves exclusively to the management of the fire-engine, while others are charged with the not less important task of taking immediate possession of the house on fire, in order to carry off, and convey to places of safety, the furniture and other moveable property which it may contain. Large and very convenient bags, with which they are often provided, enable them to save also most of the minor articles, which would probably otherwise become a prey to the flames." It was a common practice, and still is in some places, a prominent object with fire-volunteers, to rescue as much property as possible from the burning building; and not only so, but even in London, up to a comparatively recent period, some of the Insurance companies maintained a corps of fire-porters, whose sole duty was to rescue goods, &c. from burning buildings. At numberless fires in our own metropolis, in many provincial towns, in America, and on the continent, the consequences of this mode of proceeding have proved most disastrous; many thousand pounds worth of property have been consumed, that would most assuredly have been preserved, had all the assistance present been concentrated upon extinguishing the flames. In Manchester, London, Edinburgh, or indeed wherever a skilful fire-police is formed, the attention is now exclusively directed to the suppression of the fire, and all the energies of the men being directed to this one point, their efforts are, nine times out of ten, crowned with extraordinary success. Where the reverse of this obtains, great efforts are often made, much property is got out of the endangered premises, and placed in fancied security a short distance off; meantime the unopposed flames are gaining such a tremendous ascendancy as to defy all subsequent efforts to arrest their course.

The remedy being too late, is applied in vain, and the triumphant element involves in ruin all the adjacent premises, with the property originally rescued. The New York fire was a melancholy instance of this kind. Mr. Braidwood in his excellent work on fires and fire-engines, very justly remarks, that "persons may often be seen toiling like galley-slaves at operations which a moment's reflection would show were utterly useless. I have seen tables, chairs, and every article of furniture that would pass through a window, three or four stories high, dashed into the street, even when the fire had hardly touched the element," and it is no uncommon sight to see glass, china, &c. precipitated from windows in like manner.

It very commonly happens that much greater risk is encountered in attempting to save goods than would be experienced in successfully combating the flames. An awful loss of life took place at Southampton, through the misdirected zeal of the volunteers who undauntedly endeavoured to bring out a stock of the most combustible description, while the most unwarrantable delay was permitted in getting the fire-engines to bear upon the flames.

The removal of property in case of fire is generally of little moment, for the manner of rescue is so hurried as to damage what is preserved so seriously as frequently to render it valueless.

I should be sorry to be supposed by these remarks to forbid entirely the preservation of any kind of property; on the contrary I know there is often time afforded, and assistance at hand for saving books, papers, and property of an invaluable description, which should not be thrown away. What I wish to insist upon in all cases is, that every *trained corps of firemen*, whether paid or honorary, should direct all their powers to the extinction of the flames; and upon no account to waste their time and labour in removing such unimportant articles as chance may place in their way.

This course is dictated by sound sense, and past experience fully proves its correctness.

I remain, Sir,

Yours respectfully,

Wm. BADDELEY.

London, August 17, 1838.

ENCKE'S COMET.

Extract from the ephemeris of Enck's comet, published by the Editor of the *Nautical Almanac*, whereby its apparent path may be traced.

Perihelion, 1838, Dec. 18th, at 23^h 6^m Greenwich time. Perigee, Nov. 7th, at noon, when its distance will be rather more than a fifth of the sun's. From Sept. 27th to Nov. 10th, the comet will be constantly above the horizon.

At midnight.		R.A.		Decl.
Aug. 20	..	2.^{h} 20.3^m	..	25.°51' N.
28	..	2 25.7	..	27 44
Sept. 5	..	2 30.0	..	29 51
13	..	2 32.6	..	32 20
21	..	2 32.7	..	35 20
25	..	2 31.5	..	37 5
29	..	2 28.9	..	39 6
Oct. 3	..	2 24.7	..	41 24
7	..	2 18.2	..	44 5
11	..	2 8.1	..	47 15
15	..	1 52.5	..	50 59
19	..	1 27.5	..	55 24
23	..	0 45.0	..	60 19
27	..	23 29.3	..	64 47
31	..	21 29.1	..	65 43
Nov. 4	..	19 27.4	..	59 29
6	..	18 42.9	..	53 59
8	..	18 9.2	..	47 39
10	..	17 43.6	..	41 2
12	..	17 23.8	..	34 30
14	..	17 8.2	..	28 21
16	..	16 55.5	..	22 43
18	..	16 45.1	..	17 37
20	..	16 36.2	..	13 3
22	..	16 28.7	..	8 59
24	..	16 22.2	..	5 20
26	..	16 16.5	..	2 3 N.
28	..	16 11.7	..	0 55 S.
30	..	16 7.6	..	3 37

J. W. W., 1838, 8, 18.

FLAT-CHAMBERED BOILERS.—MR. W. HANCOCK IN REPLY TO MR. HEBERT.

In your 784th Number I find a letter from Mr. L. Hebert, in which he advocates' the cause of Sir James Anderson, with that becoming zeal, which, considering the relative positions of the parties, appears to be perfectly requisite and commendable; nor does he forget to exercise the tact so common to advocates, of occupying a large space with matters of no importance to the question, and which, although easily answered, are not of sufficient weight to be worth troubling your readers about.

Nor can we blame him either (as far as regards his character of advocate,) for very speedily and completely changing his opinion, or rather *expressing* a contrary opinion to one already published. My boiler is precisely the same now as it was in 1837, when Mr. Hebert published his *Encyclopædia*, and I beg to refer those who have read his depreciation of the merits of my invention in comparison with Sir James's, in your Magazine, to what he says upon the subject under the article "Railways." His opinion then, was that of an impartial historian, having no interest on any part. Of course his change of mind is upon due consideration, and for good and sufficient reasons.

The patents alluded to by Mr. Hebert and "A Shareholder" of a date anterior to mine, do not bear any similarity whatever to my invention. Furnival and Smith's has been already disposed of by the note which you, Mr. Editor, were kind enough to append to the "Shareholder's" letter; but that there should be no doubt upon the subject, and that your readers may judge for themselves, I beg to refer them to the description of this plan in Mr. Hebert's work before mentioned, under the article "Boilers;" where will also be found Raddatz's, or Dr. Alban's, (which are one and the same, Dr. Alban being the inventor, a foreigner residing abroad, who communicated the invention for the purpose of the patent, to Mr. Raddatz in England). Your readers will hardly perhaps, believe, that this prior patent brought forward so confidently by your two correspondents as completely destroying my right, consists of a row of tubes closed at the bottom, and with a small hole at top, through which water is injected, which row of tubes is immersed in a flat vessel of fluid metal kept in a state of fusion by a fire underneath! It is mentioned that a series of these melted-metal pots containing tubes may be placed side by side—hence they cry, "behold Hancock's boiler!" Mr. Raddatz states his invention to be, and claims "the mode of generating steam by injecting water into vessels that are heated by immersion in fused or fluid metal."

The principal or only point on which Mr. Hebert seems to rely has reference to the import of the word "*flat*," adducing Salisbury Plain as an example. I would just ask him whether, if that celebrated spot should become half covered with mole-hills it would cease to be Salisbury *Plain?* When geographers describe the surface of a country as *flat*, do we consider there are no embankments, undulations, and rising grounds included? Does not Mr. Hebert very well know, that at Birmingham, the term "hollow" ware is commonly used to distinguish it from that which is flat, and in the Potteries, on the contrary, the term *flat* ware is used to distinguish plates and dishes from bowls and cups, although the said plates have rising edges, and the dishes cavities and depressions. Has Mr. Hebert never heard of a *flat* roof, or a *flat* casting; albeit the roof may have a dozen soldered ridges, or the casting any number of projecting facings or depressed fittings; possibly he never has had the misfortune to fall "flat on his face," and may never have been laid "*flat* on his back," but he must have heard of the "*flat*ness of pussey's face" and that some things are as "*flat* as a flounder," and that there are great varities of *flat* fish. Now only think, Mr. Editor, what a torture it would be in any of these last-mentioned cases, if by the word flat, we meant that the face, or the back, or puss, or the flounder and his brethren, were all to be reduced exactly to a plane mathematically true, or even to an approximation thereto!

If a steam chamber, three or four feet square, and only two inches thick, is not to be called a *flat* chamber, what other denomination could be given to such a vessel, although its sides may have any conceiveable or possible degree of unevenness?

There is a circumstance alluded to by Mr. Hebert, and in that kind of *inuendo* style which gives one a lamentable opinion of the good feeling of the writer, and were I to pass it over with the contempt which perhaps it deserves, it might lead to erroneous conclusions by those unacquainted with the facts. He states that my chambers "are unsafe, *as experience has lamentably proved.*" He doubtless alludes to the only serious accident that ever occurred throughout the whole of my steam-carriage experience, extending over a period of 14 years of constant activity. In Decem-

ber 1832, an engineer in my employment of the name of Outridge, *fastened
down* the safety-valve of a boiler *with
copper* wire—one of the chambers as a
necessary consequence rent, and Outridge was thrown down and died in about
an hour afterwards—from *fright* it is supposed, as there was neither wound, bruise,
nor scratch upon his person, and as he was
or in ill health at the time. Some imagined
he was choked by the rushing of the
steam into his lungs; but this was denied by the surgeon on the inquest. I
beg to refer your readers for a full account of the matter to your Magazine,
vol. 18, p. 204, or more particularly in
my " Narrative" * lately published. So
much for this most unfair misrepresentation of Mr. Hebert's, which I consider
the less honourable because couched in
terms correct in the main, but utterly
false in the impression intended to be
conveyed to the reader. I had rested
content had he mentioned the circumstances of the case.

With regard to the claim of invention
actually made by me in the specification
of my patent, Mr. Hebert charges me
with an attempt to " impose upon your
readers." The accusation recoils upon himself : the words of my claim are, the constructing narrow flat vessels in the form
and manner hereinbefore described; and
which are adapted to be placed vertically,
or edge-ways upwards, over the fire, for
producing steam for steam-engines. And
also in arranging and combining a series of such vessels together, with narrow vertical spaces between them for
the fire, so as to form one boiler, with
communications through their junctions
for the passage of water and steam from
one vessel to another."

Even had I not used the latter gene-
ralizing words, the law would assume
them, and protect me from all infringements by such a mere colourable modification of my plan, as Sir James Anderson's, I again assert, is.

I must make one more remark, which
will, I imagine, surprise your readers :
in my specification, the drawings of the
chambers happen to have the *favorite*

and *identical flatness, and rivets through
strengthening bars from side to side, as
specified and claimed by Sir James Anderson!*

In conclusion, Sir, I am perfectly satisfied with the result of this controversy.
If Sir James Anderson, his agent, his
company, directors, secretary and shareholders, can find, (and no doubt after
a diligent search,) no better grounds
upon which to invalidate my patent than
they have adduced, I consider that it
rests upon firmer grounds than before it
was attacked; and I thank them for
putting the matter to the proof. I shall
not again trouble you, Sir, unless some
other anterior patent be discovered, or
truth implicitly demands it. Those concerned, however, may rest assured, that
though thus silent, I shall not stand
tamely by, and see my right invaded. I
have fairly obtained a legal monopoly of
my invention of flat-chambered boilers,
and I shall assert that right, either at
law, or in equity, whenever I discover
that it is intrenched upon.

I am, Sir, your obedient servant,
WALTER HANCOCK.

Stratford, August 23, 1838.

———

LIST OF ENGLISH PATENTS GRANTED BE-
TWEEN THE 26th OF JULY AND THE
29th OF AUGUST, 1838.

Wilton Wood, of Liverpool, for an improved method of making bands and tackling to be used in
drawing, turning, or carrying machinery. July 26 ;
six months to specify.

George Holworthy Palmer, of New Cross, Surrey,
civil engineer, and George Bertie Paterson, of Hox-
ton, engineer, for certain improvements in the
mode of preparing, constructing, and adapting
certain parts of gas meters. July 28 ; six months.

Andrew Paul, of Doughty-street, Saint Pancras,
surgeon, A. B. and M. B., for an improved hydraulic pump, douche or jet obean, applicable to all the
purposes of lavement in medical operations. July
30 ; six months.

Robert Hendley, of Belgrave-street, St. Pancras,
doctor of medicine, for a metallic concrete capable
of being, by means of fire, cast into a variety of
forms, and applied to a variety of purposes for
which iron, lead, zinc, copper, and other substances have been heretofore used. July 30 ; six
months.

Samuel Hall, of Basford, civil engineer, for improvements in steam-engines, heating or evaporating fluids or gases, and generating steam or vapour.
July 30 ; six months.

Joseph Rayner and Joseph Whitehead Rayner,
of Birmingham, civil engineers, and Henry Samuel
Rayner, of Ripley, civil engineer, for improvements
of machinery for roving, spinning, and twisting cotton, flax, silk, wool, and other fibrous materials.
July 31 ; six months.

Edward Heard, of Bateman's-buildings, Soho-
square, manufacturing chemist, for certain improvements in oxydizing lead, and converting the

———

* Narrative of twelve years experiments (1824 to
18 6), demonstrative of the practicability an d
vantage of employing steam carriages on common
roads, &c., pp. 104. London: Weale, High Holborn, and Mann, Cornhill.

same into pigments, or white and red lead, and manufacturing part of the products arising from these processes into soda. August 1; six months.

George Marques of Tweeddale, for an improved method of making tiles for draining soils, house tiles, flat roofing tiles, and bricks; to extend to the colonies only. August 1; six months.

Edwin Whele, of Walsall, Stafford, tallow chandler, for an improvement or improvements in the manufacture of candles. August 1; six months.

John Dennett, of New Village, in the Isle of Wight, engineer, for improvements in war rockets, and in the methods and apparatus for applying the powers of rockets for the purpose of obtaining communication with vessels which are stranded or in other situations of danger; also an improved instrument and method for accurately pointing mortars for throwing shells, which may likewise be used for firing shot from mortars for the purpose of obtaining communication with ships. August 2; six months.

Samuel Sanderson Hall, of the Circus, Minories, for improvements in preserving certain vegetable substances from decay; being a communication from a foreigner residing abroad. August 3; six months.

Thomas Lund, of Cornhill, in the City of London, cutler, for improvements in extracting corks from wine and other bottles, with steadiness, facility, and safety. August 3; six months.

Charles Bourjot, of Coleman-street, City, merchant, for improvements in the manufacture of iron. August 3; six months.

Robert William Sievier, of Henrietta-street, Cavendish-square, gent., for certain improvements in looms for weaving, and in the mode or method of producing figured goods or fabrics. August 6; six months.

Pierre Armand Lecomte de Fontainemoreau, of Charles-street, City-road, for certain improvements in wool combing, being a communication from a foreigner residing abroad. August 6; six months.

Richard Rodda, of Saint Austle, Cornwall, assay master, for certain improvements in furnaces, fire-places, and stoves, for the consumption of smoke and the saving of fuel, and in the mode of applying them to the generation of steam, the smelting of metals, and other works. August 7; six months.

Eugene de Beuret, of Moorgate-street, City, for certain improvements in the construction of rail-roads and tram-roads to facilitate the ascent and descent of hills and inclined plains, being a communication from a foreigner residing abroad. August 10; two months.

Matthew Heath, of Furnival's Inn, London, gentleman, for improvements in preparing tobacco, and in making snuff; being a communication from a foreigner residing abroad. August 10; six months.

Thomas Corbett, of Plymouth, for certain improvements in heating hot-houses and other buildings. August 10; six months.

David Cheetham, jun., of Staley Bridge, Chester, spinner, for certain improvements in the means of consuming smoke, and thereby economising fuel and heat in steam-engine or other furnaces or fire-places. August 14; six months.

Charles Wye Williams, of Liverpool, gent., for certain improvements in the process or the mode of purifying or preparing turpentine, rosin, pitch, tar, and other bituminous matters, whereby he increases their power of giving out light and heat either when distilled or burnt as fuel. August 14; six months.

William Henry Porter, of Russia-row, Cheapside, warehouseman, for improvements in anchors. August 15; six months.

Ramsay Richard Reinagle, of George-street, London University, Royal Academican, and the Chevalier George Robert D'Harcourt, of King William-street, City, civil engineer, for certain improvements in the means of propelling canal boats, steamers, and other vessels. August 15; six months.

George Robert D'Harcourt, of King William-street, City, civil engineer, for improvements in the manufacture of paper; being a communication from a foreigner residing abroad. August 15; six months.

Charles Fox, of Gloucester place, Camden-town, engineer, for an improved arrangement of rails for the purpose of causing a railroad engine, carriage, or train to pass from one line of rails to another. August 15; two months.

Matthew Warton Johnson, of Buckingham-place, Middlesex, sculptor and stone-mason, for improvements in the construction of coffins. August 15; six months.

William Wainwright Potts, of Burslem, Stafford, china and earthenware manufacturer, for certain improvements in machines, applicable to the printing or producing patterns in one or more colours, or metallic preparations to be transferred to earthenware, porcelain, china, glass, metal, wood, cloth, paper, papier machie, bone, slate, marble, and other suitable substances. August 21; six months.

Samuel Stocker, of Bristol, machinist, for improvements in chimneys for dwelling houses, and in apparatus for scraping, sweeping, or cleaning chimneys, and in the manufacture of such apparatus, and of the materials of which such chimneys are formed. August 21; six months.

Richard Bradley, William Barrows, and Joseph Hall, of Bloomfield iron works, Stafford, iron masters and co-partners for an improved method or means of making iron. August 21; six months.

Nicholas Troughton, of Broad-street, City, gent., for improvements in the process of obtaining copper from copper ores. August 21; six months.

Jean Leandre Clement, of Rochfort, in the kingdom of France, but now of Jauney's Hotel, Leicester-square, gent., for improvements for ascertaining, and indicating the rate of vessels passing through the water. August 21; six months.

Pierre Armand Lecomte de Fontainemoreau, of Charles-street City-road, gent., for certain new and improved metallic allays, to be used in various cases as substitutes for zinc, cast-iron, copper, and other metals. August 23; six months.

George Dickinson, of Wood-street, Cheapside, paper manufacturer, for an improvement or improvements upon steam engines. August 23; six months.

Arthur Dunn, of Stamford-hill, gent., for certain improvements in the manufacture of soap. August 24; six months.

John Coope Haddan, of Basing-place, Waterloo-road, gent., for certain improvements in the construction of carriages to be used on railways, and in the method of forming the same into trains. August 25; six months.

Lawrence Heyworth, of Yewtree, near Liverpool, Lancaster, merchant, for a new method of applying steam power directly to the periphery of the movement-wheel, for the purposes of locomotion, both on land and water, and for propelling machinery. August 30; two months.

Miles Berry, of Chancery lane, for certain improvements in looms for producing metallic tissues, and also improvements in such tissues, applicable to the making of buttons, epaulets, tassels, and other purposes, for which gold and silver lace or braiding is commonly employed, and to the making of imitation of jewellery and other fancy articles; being a communication from a foreigner residing abroad. August 30; six months.

William Doller, of Liverpool, lecturer on education, for a certain durable surface or tablet for the purposes of receiving writings, drawings, or impressions of engravings or other devices, capable of being printed, which surface may be applied for roads or pavements, and part of which invention may also be used as the means of strengthening or beautifying glass. August 30; six months.

Joseph Davies, of Nelson-square, gentleman, for a composition for protecting wood from flame. August 30; four months.

John Grafton, of Cambridge, C. E., for certain improvements in the construction of retorts and other machinery for making gas from coal and other substances. August 30; six months.

Henry Knill of Eldon-place, Bermondsey, for improvements in cleansing the bottoms of docks, rivers, and other waters. August 30, six months.

John Earle Huxley, of Great Marlborough-street, John Earle Huxley, Jun., of the same place, and John Oliver, of Dean-street, Soho, stove-makers, for improvements in certain descriptions of stoves. August 31; six months.

Joseph Curtis, of Stamford-street, Blackfriars-road, C. E., for certain improved machinery and apparatus for facilitating travelling and transport on railways, parts of which are also applicable to other purposes. August 31; six months.

LIST OF SCOTCH PATENTS GRANTED BETWEEN THE 22nd OF JULY, AND THE 22nd OF AUGUST, 1838.

Joseph Bennett of Turnlee, near Glossop, Derby, cotton spinner, for certain improvements in machinery for carding wool, cotton, flax, or other fibrous substances, which are, or may be carded, part of which improvements are also applicable to machinery for drawing, doubling, roving, and spinning such fibrous substances as are, or may be subjected to their operations. Sealed 26th of July, 1838; four months to specify.

Richard March Hoe, late of New York, but now residing at Chancery-lane, Middlesex, civil engineer, in consequence of a communication made to him from Dr. H. H. Sherwood, of New York, aforesaid, for a new or improved instrument, or apparatus for ascertaining, or determining the latitude and longitude of any place, or the situation of ships or other vessels at sea, and the dip and variation of the magnetic needle, which new or improved instrument he intends to denominate, "Sherwood's Magnetic Geometer." July 26.

Richard March Hoe, late of New York, but now residing at Chancery-lane, Middlesex, civil engineer, for certain improvements in machinery, and apparatus for grinding and polishing metal surfaces. July 28.

William Barnett, of Brighton, Sussex, iron founder, for certain improvements in the production of motive power, and in the manufacture of iron. July 31.

Richard Badnall, of Cotton Hall, Stafford, gent., for a certain improvement in the manufacture of carpets, and other similar wooven fabrics, which improvement is effected by the introduction of a certain article of commerce not hitherto so employed or used in such manufactures. July 31.

Richard Treffry, of Manchester, Lancaster, chemist, for certain improvements in the method for preserving certain animal and vegetable substances from decay, and also in the apparatus for, and mode of impregnating substances to be preserved. Aug. 6.

Robert Sandiford, of Tottington, Lower end, Lancaster, block printer, for certain improvements in the arts of block printing, and in certain arrangements connected therewith. August 7.

John Thomas Betts, of Smithfield Bars, in the city of London, rectifier, in consequence of a communication from a person residing abroad, for improvements in the process of preparing spirituous liquors in the making of brandy. August 9.

Henry Bessemer, of City-terrace, City-road, Middlesex, engineer, for certain improvements in machinery, or apparatus for casting printing types, spaces and quadrats, and the means of breaking off and counting the same. August 9.

Peter Fairbairn, of Leeds, York, machine maker, in consequence of a communication from a foreigner residing abroad, for certain improvements in looms for weaving ribbons, tapes, and other fabrics. Augst 10.

Sir James Caleb Anderson, of Buttevant Castle, Cork, baronet, for certain improvements in locomotive engines, which are partly applicable to other purposes. August 18.

David Cheetham, junior, of Staley Bridge, Chester, spinner, for certain improvements in the means of consuming smoke, and thereby economising fuel and heat in steam-engines, or other furnaces or fire places. August 22.

James Robinson, of Huddersfield, York, merchant, for an improved method of producing by dyeing various figures or objects of various colours in woollen, worsted, cotton, silk, and other cloths. August 22.

IRISH PATENTS GRANTED IN JULY, 1838.

Joshua John Lloyd Margary, of Wellington-road, Middlesex, for a new mode of preserving animal and vegetable substances from decay.

William Holme Heginbotham, of Stockport, Chester, gent., for certain improvements in the construction of gas retorts.

NOTES AND NOTICES.

American Rotary Steam-Engine.—On the farm of Whittingham Mains, East Lothian, possessed by Mr. Hepburne, we witnessed on the 13th inst. an engine of six-horse power, made by Ruthven of Edinburgh, propelling a thrashing-machine in a manner which left no doubt of the power and ultimate success of the application of steam on this principle. Thus the American rotary steam-engine, after being so severely ridiculed, has been first adopted on this side of the Atlantic by a farmer, without aid or encouragement from his landlord, in separating grain from straw, and we have no doubt of its history amongst us arising from so unpretending an origin, long conveying a lesson of humility to the engineers and men of science in Britain. —*Correspondent of the Edinburgh Chronicle.*

Platina Wires.—A musical composer, named Fischer, has proposed the substitution of platina wires for those of steel or brass. It is (he says,) more elastic and ductile, and the sounds produced by this metal are sweeter; air and damp do not act upon it, and as it combines with iron, cords might be made of a composition of the two, which would present the advantages of each.—*Athenæum.*

It has been calculated that if the toll on Waterloo-bridge were raised in proportion to "the original cost of the construction, and the maintenance thereof," (the words of Sir James Graham's motion on railways), the charge for each foot-passenger would be one shilling, and for each carriage, with two horses, six shillings.

The twenty-eighth volume of the *Mechanics, Magazine* is now published, price, in half-cloth, 8s. 6d., with a *Railway Map* of England and Wales. The *Railway Map* may be had separately, price 6d.; and on fine paper, coloured, price 1s.

☞ *British and Foreign Patents taken out with economy and despatch; Specifications, Disclaimers, and Amendments, prepared or revised: Caveats entered; and generally every Branch of Patent Business promptly transacted. A complete list of Patents from the earliest period (15 Car. II. 1675,) to the present time may be examined. Fee 2s. 6d.; Clients, gratis.*

LONDON: Printed and Published for the Proprietor, by W. A. Robertson, at the Mechanics' Magazine Office, No. 6, Peterborough-court, between 135 and 136, Fleet-street.—Sold by A. & W. Galignani, Rue Vivienne, Paris.

Mechanics' Magazine,

MUSEUM, REGISTER, JOURNAL, AND GAZETTE.

No. 787.]   SATURDAY, SEPTEMBER 8, 1838.   [Price 6*d*.

HANCOCK'S STEAM-PHÆTON.

Fig. 1

Fig. 2.

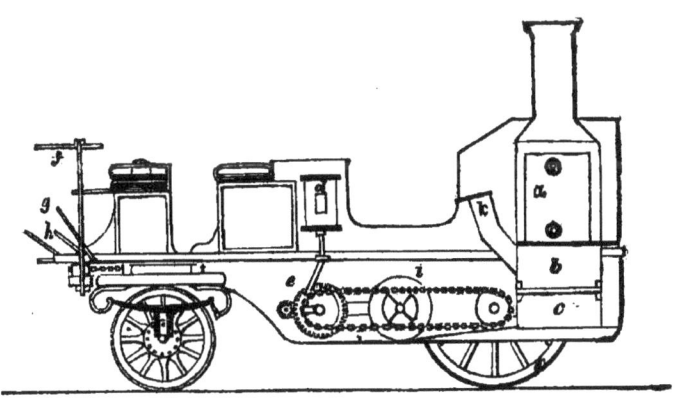

MR. WALTER HANCOCK'S NARRATIVE OF HIS EXPERIMENTS ON COMMON ROAD STEAM-CARRIAGES.

Few instances have occurred in which the public expectation has been kept so continually on tip-toe, and been so repeatedly disappointed, as in the endeavours of various inventors to perfect the common-road steam-carriage. Some nine or ten years ago, the newspapers of the day teemed with paragraphs upon the subject, in various shapes and guises, and amongst others it was stated that wagers to the amount of many thousands of pounds were depending—that there would be no other kind of vehicle in use on the western road within a twelvemonth! The experiments then made were, indeed, extremely promising in appearance, and seem alike to have deceived the sharpness of the knowing-ones of the sporting world, and the wisdom of a committee of legislators. But, with slight exceptions, if exceptions they can be called, the projectors have never gone beyond experiment, and, as far as can be judged from appearance, the carriages first brought on the road performed as well as those which succeeded them. The natural inquiry hence arises, what are the hidden causes which have prevented the application of these favourable experiments to actual public operation? How is it that steam-carriage inventors have, during the last fourteen years, one after another appeared upon the stage, each played his short part, received the plaudits or hisses of the spectators, and retired behind the scenes, either to be visible no more, or perhaps to return after an interval, and amuse the public with another ride across the stage, before his final exit? And, with one exception, this is the epitome of the history of all the steam-carriage projectors. For an answer to the above queries, we beg to refer our readers to the evidence given before the Parliamentary committee on Mr. Gurney's claims to a national reward for his exertions to introduce steam-carriages on common roads,*—as far as re-

gards that gentleman, and for further information, with regard to the inventor forming the exception we have just made, and who was first upon the stage, and still continues to play his part, we turn to the volume now under review.†

We believe it will be most satisfactory to our readers, and to Mr. Hancock, to allow him to speak for himself. We shall, therefore, extract largely from his Narrative, which, we hope, will give no offence, presuming his object in writing to be publicity, rather than profit.

It may be necessary to premise, that although the title-page bears the date of 1838, the body of the work is stated at the end to have been printed two years ago, and the introduction is dated from Stratford, October, 1836. The reason of this delay in its publication does not appear; and, it is certain, that had it been brought forward at the time it was written, it would have been more serviceable to the author than it can now be. The work was written at the time when Mr. Gurney applied to Parliament for compensation for his losses of other people's money, as the inventor of common-road locomotion; and it is to this Mr. Hancock refers, in the following extract from his introduction:—

"The author believes he should offend alike against truth and genuine modesty, were he to yield to any of the steam-carriage inventors who have appeared in his day, in a single particular of desert; he began earlier (with one abortive exception) and has persevered longer and more unceasingly than any of them; he was the first to run a steam carriage for hire on a common road, and is still the only person who has ventured in a steam vehicle to traverse the most crowded streets of the metropolis at the busiest periods of the day; he has built a greater number of steam carriages (if not better) than any one else, and has been thus enabled to try a greater variety of forms of construction, out of which to choose the best; and all that he has done, has been with his own means chiefly, while his rivals—the more prominent of them at least—have been largely assisted by others. He has never, however, been an obtrusive suitor for the favour of the public—neither pestered it with boastful pamphlets, nor with wild exaggerations; he has been all along more anxious that his works should speak for him, than he for them. His steam carriages running on the public roads, have been his best witnesses. He has been occasionally obliged to address the public journals, for the purpose of cor-

* See Mechanics' Magazine, vol. 22, pp. 308, 323.
† "Narrative of Twelve Years' Experiments—1824–36,—demonstrative of the Practicability and advantage of employing Steam-carriages on Common Roads; with Engravings and Descriptions of the different Steam-carriages constructed by the Author, his Patent Boiler, Wedge-wheels, and other Inventions. By Walter Hancock, Engineer. Weale, Holborn, and Mann, Cornhill." 8vo. pp. 104.

resting erroneous statements that had gone abroad respecting particular performances of his carriages; but beyond that he has hitherto troubled the press but little.

"Nor perhaps should he have been now inclined to depart from the quiet, yet earnest, course he has hitherto pursued, were it not that he sees himself in some danger of being thrust aside in public regard, through the extraordinary efforts made by others to arrogate to themselves all the praise, where they have at best had but a share of the merit.

"That neither the public may be the dupes, nor he the victim of false pretensions, he has at length resolved on publishing a complete and faithful narrative of his steam carriage experiments from their commencement, twelve years ago, to the present period, (1836) along with engravings and descriptions of all the carriages he has built, and of the particular mechanical improvements which have from time to time been embodied therein, and have led to that perfect success, which his performances have so often and so publicly attested."—Page 4—6.

We shall now proceed to the *Narrative.* The Messrs. Hancock might, with very good reason, be called the India rubber fraternity. Mr. Thomas Hancock, it is well known, obtained a patent simultaneously with Mr. Macintosh, the eminent manufacturing chemist of Glasgow, for India rubber waterproof cloth, and with whom he afterwards entered into partnership, and has since obtained numerous patents for improvements in the manufacture and application of that useful substance. Mr. William Hancock has a patent for India rubber book-binding (the *Narrative*, by the way, is bound in this manner). Mr. Charles Hancock, the well-known animal painter, has patented modes of engraving and printing with India rubber; and it now appears that Mr. Walter Hancock's first ideas of a common-road steam-carriage were founded on an *Indian rubber steam-engine.*

"The attention of the author of this Narrative was first turned to the subject of steam locomotion on common roads, by the circumstance of his having invented, in 1824, a steam engine of a very novel description, which seemed to him peculiarly well adapted to the purpose. Metallic substances enter but in a very limited degree into the construction of this engine, and in the prime movers are almost entirely dispensed with; instead of iron or copper, an article is used which is not only much lighter, but free from all liability to fracture; and hence both a great reduction of weight and great capability of resisting tear and wear, two of the most important desiderata in a steam carriage intended for common roads."

This steam-engine consisted of two flexible globular steam-receivers, composed of layers of canvass, firmly united together with coatings of dissolved caoutchouc, or India rubber, and capable of sustaining a pressure of upwards of 60 lbs. on the square inch. By the alternate expansion and contraction of these India rubber globes, by the admission and exit of the steam to them, a reciprocating motion was obtained, which was converted into a rotary by a crank, in the usual manner.

"Anterior to the invention of this simple application of steam as a motive power, the writer had casually met with a print of a steam carriage, built by Messrs. Bramah for a Mr. Griffiths; and it now occurred to him that his new engine was well adapted to sustain the concussions to which such a machine must necessarily be exposed. A model of a steam carriage on this plan he accordingly constructed which so far bore out his previous conception, as to determine him to commence the building of one on a larger scale. But after many trials and experiments, he found that the requisite degree of power for locomotive purposes could not be attained by means of his new engine.

"When once the mind, however, has been much exercised towards a certain point, it is no easy matter to apply it in a different direction; at least, it proved so in this case. Although his experiments demonstrated the inefficiency of his new engine as a locomotive agent, they left on his mind a strong conviction, that the application of steam power to the propulsion of carriages on common roads was decidedly a practical object. The great and essential desideratum seemed to him to be—a boiler that while it should generate steam rapidly, and produce a sufficient and continuous supply, should occupy but little space, be of small weight (comparatively speaking), harmless if it should burst, simple in its construction, and inexpensive in its manufacture; to construct such a boiler became now, therefore, his chief study."—p. 9—10.

After designing, experimenting with, and patenting, various tubular boilers, which are described in the *Narrative*, Mr. Hancock gave up the idea of constructing one on that principle; and he proceeds—

BB 2

"The unsatisfactory result of every attempt to produce a safe and efficient boiler, on the tubular principle, led the writer to consider of some arrangement by which the water, exposed to the action of the fire, might be less divided, and yet extended over a large surface; and the plan now occurred to him, which he has since successfully followed in the several steam carriages he has built, and applicable also to a variety of other purposes. For this invention, which he has denominated the chamber boiler, he obtained a patent in 1827."—p. 12.

The originality of this chamber-boiler, and the extent of Mr. Hancock's claim of monopoly,—whether it extends to all kinds of flat chambers in which fire, or rather hot air, and flame, and water, are in alternate layers, or whether it is confined to the particular method of construction specified by Mr. Hancock, has been lately the subject of discussion in our Magazine. We incline to the former opinion. If Mr. Hancock can show himself to be the original inventor and patentee of flat-chambered boilers, notwithstanding he has only described one method of making them in his specification, which is as *per example*, the law as at present interpreted will protect him from all mere colourable modifications, even although they may be improvements; and the patentee of such modifications or improvements can only work them under license from Mr. Hancock, until the term of his patent has expired.

It has been frequently observed that the discovery of mechanical arrangements and forms is often the result of accident, observed and applied by an inventive mind. We have here an additional instance to the many already on record.

"About four or five years ago, the writer tried various forms of projection in the sides of the chambers; some of them were channelled or corrugated the whole length, so as to form straight flues, and others were of irregular forms, to cause the heated air in its ascent to impinge on their lower surfaces, with a variety of other similar contrivances; but after giving the best consideration to all the forms, he was upon the whole induced to adhere to the hemispherical embossing, conceiving that form to possess the greatest advantages, although he is still of opinion, that the use of *vertical bars* to prevent the distension of the chambers, and to form the flues, will have advantages in some cases, and may hereafter be recurred to.

"The hemispherical projections on the sides of the chambers the writer has occasionally employed almost from the first; but the corrugated form was suggested to him accidentally, in a boiler composed of plain-sided chambers, with *vertical bars* between, which (through inattention to the due supply of water), being allowed to get almost red hot, instead of maintaining the shape shown in the horizontal section of two chambers at fig 1, the metal became so yielding by the heat, that the internal pressure

Fig. 1.

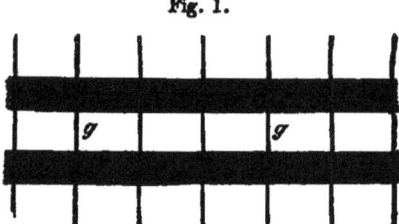

caused them to assume the form shown at fig. 2: by simply taking out the bars, and

Fig. 2.

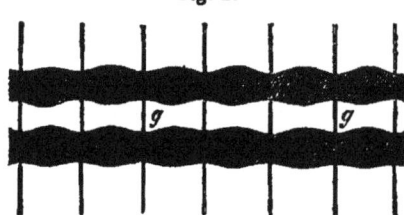

bringing the protruded parts in contact, the open spaces would, of course, allow a sufficient passage for the fire upwards, without the divisional bars or gratings *g g*: such is the arrangement of two chambers shown at fig. 3."—p. 13—14.

Fig. 3.

Upon the merits of his boiler as applied to various purposes as a prime mover, Mr. Hancock says:—

"The perfect safety of this boiler arises from the ample subdivision of its parts and power, and the weakness of the chambers, as compared with the bolts and braces by which the whole series is combined: the utmost that can happen is the rupture of one chamber, and this with a force equal to only one-fifteenth or one-twentieth of the whole ; and this rupture would release all : an explosion of the whole is impossible, because the bolts and braces by which all the chambers are held together, are of such size and strength, as to be capable of resisting a pressure twenty times greater than the chambers are calculated to sustain.

" In tubular boilers there is a confinement or throttling in the tubes, so that the steam is not freely disengaged, but goes off in gusts or starts, agitating or displacing the water, part of which it carries off with it ; but in the chambers of this boiler, steam is formed and separated in a more uniform manner, the whole surface of heated water giving out its volume of steam freely, whilst the body of water is in a state of comparative quiescence.

" Mr. John Farey, in his evidence before the Select Committee of the House of Commons on steam carriages, at page 42, says— ' Mr. Hancock has taken the middle course in subdividing the water in his boiler, having all that can be required for safety ; and the weight, I believe, on the whole to be less than that of any other boiler, which will produce the same power of steam : for owing to the freedom with which the steam can get away in bubbles from the water, without carrying the water with it, the surface of the heated metal is never left without water. Hence a greater effect of boiling is attained from a given surface of metal and body of contained water, and that with a much greater durability of the metal plates, than I think will ever be obtained with small tubes.'

" The writer believes this boiler to be superior to any that has yet been produced, whether for steam carriages on common roads, or for railways or steam-boats, and in many cases for stationary engines. They are lighter, take up less room, economise fuel, and are at once powerful and safe. They are also less expensive of renewal and repair. For places difficult of access they are particularly suited, as they may be taken in parts, so as to be carried by men or mules over mountains or in mining operations, and put together with facility by persons possessing little skill, as is the case also with repairs ; the substitution of a new chamber for a defective one is neither difficult nor tedious.

These facilities apply equally to sea-going vessels ; a spare boiler or spare chambers may be stowed in a small compass, and the means always at hand of putting in a new boiler, or replacing a chamber in the midst of the ocean at any time with comparative ease."—p. 15—17.

To proceed with the steam carriage experiments—Mr. H. thus continues :—

"Being satisfied that in this boiler he had at length attained the prime requisites of a boiler for locomotive purposes, namely, great steam producing power within a small compass, and entire safety from explosion ; the attention of the writer was next directed to a better construction and arrangement of the propelling machinery. Laying aside his propelling flexible engines, which he had despaired of rendering available, he determined to make those of the ordinary construction, subservient to his purpose."—p. 17.

His first steam carriage was one with three wheels, the power being applied by a pair of vibrating or trunnion engines to the fore wheel only, the bite of which upon the road was found sufficient to propel the carriage. Mr. H. performed journeys comprising many hundred miles with this vehicle.

" In the course of these early experimental trips, the writer experienced the usual fate of all who run counter to long standing usages and prejudices ; namely, to be ridiculed by the many, encouraged by but a very few, and fiercely opposed by all whose personal interests were threatened with injury by his proceedings. The popular mind had not yet become sufficiently familiarised to the notion of dispensing with horses in common road travelling. The newspapers had made mention about this time of some *private* trials made by Mr. Goldsworthy Gurney, in a steam drag of his construction ; but hitherto no *public* exhibition of anything of the sort. All had heard something of a scheme for riding by steam, but most persons with much the same degree of incredulity that we now listen to tales of journeying in the air. The writer was the first, or with the first, to offer, to all who chose to come and see, ocular demonstration of the practicability of the thing—to exhibit in the face of day, and on the public highways, a carriage propelled by steam. But though this was evidence not to be gainsayed, it was not a little mortifying to see how the force of it was evaded. Some would admit frankly that the carriage worked well ; but expressed as frankly their decided conviction, that it would never answer for a continuance. Others would depreciate its performances, exaggerate its defects, and exult, as it were, in every instance of accidental stoppage. If requiring temporary accommodation, through the failure of some part of the machinery,—a circumstance naturally enough of frequent occurrence in this early period of his locomotive career, he usually experienced the reverse of kind or considerat · treatment. Exorbitant charges were made for the most trifling services, and important facilities withheld, which it would have cost nothing to afford. If, again, he happened to be temporarily detained on the road from want of water, or from any other cause, he was assailed with hootings, yellings, hissings, and sometimes even with the grossest abuse. It is true, this latter description of treatment proceeded chiefly from the rabble; but he regrets being obliged to add, not exclusively so. Great obstruction was also continually experienced on those occasions from waggons, carts, coaches, vans, trucks, horsemen, and pedestrians, pressing so close on the carriage, as sometimes to preclude the possibility of moving. Altogether the writer's situation was in general anything but agreeable; often most irksome and irritating, sometimes very hazardous.

"No ways disheartened by any of these untoward circumstances, the writer persevered in his experiments; and as the novelty of such exhibitions wore off, so also did the excitement and the opposition which they at first produced Clearer-sighted views and kindlier feelings began gradually to prevail; more serious convictions of the practicability and advantages of substituting inanimate for animate power in common road travelling; and greater readiness to promote, by word and deed, the success of the project" p. 18—20.

We shall not further follow Mr. Hancock through his various experiments and statements of the workings of his carriages. They have been from time to time recorded in our pages, cotemporaneously with their occurrence. Encountering difficulties the most severe, and obstacles the most trying, he has continued his operations to the present day from his own resources. If any one deserves reward or compensation from the nation it is Mr. Hancock; but we have no doubt that he would prefer that his exertions should be acknowledged rather by a company of capitalists making a fair experimental working of his carriages, and remunerating him according to their success, than any government grant to enable him to live at ease. He wants the means of activity, not of retirement. We subjoin a list of the carriages constructed by Mr Hancock.

"Steam-carriages built in the order of their construction, and the number of persons they were respectively calculated to accommodate, exclusive of the steersman, engineer, and fireman:—

Experimental carriage	4 outside
Infant .. (trunnion engines).......	10 outside
Ditto (enlarged with fixed engines)	14 outside
Era .... (Greenwich)	16 inside, 2 out
Enterprise	14 inside
Autopsy.........................	9 inside, 5 out
Erin	8 inside, 6 out
German Drag.....................	6 outside, exclusive of those accommodated in the separate carriages behind
Automaton	22 inside.

We cannot help thinking that a very fair opportunity for a few capitalists of putting the practicability of steam- locomotives on common roads to the test here exists. It certainly would not cost a great sum to put these carriages already made into complete repair, and to place them on some moderately level road, between London and some town about twenty or thirty miles distant, where there is good passenger traffic. Let them run constantly at particular intervals each day for a certain time, say three or six months. A correct account kept of the receipts and expenses of this traffic would certainly set the matter at rest. We hardly think that less would satisfy the public. The difficulty which Mr. Hancock has now to overcome is greater than those he encountered seven or eight years ago. He has now to overcome the *indifference* of the public. The subject has been so long on the tapis, that a steam carriage on the streets is looked at as a passing show, and then dismissed from the observer's mind. The eagerness which follows a first experiment has passed off, and as those who were zealous in the onset have not succeeded, it is considered as a settled thing that the project never can succeed.

The following estimate appears in Mr. Hancock's work:—

"The estimate of expenses and wear and tear has been calculated from the actual working of the writer's steam-carriages during their running for hire on common roads, but principally from the "Automaton," this carriage being the only one he has hitherto built of sufficient magnitude to cope with the ordinary contingencies always to be found on a long line of road. To this estimate the writer has added another, showing the outlay necessary for an establishment on a large scale, and the probable pecuniary results.

ONE DAY'S WORK, OR ONE HUNDRED MILES.

EXPENDITURE.	£	s.	d.	REVENUE.	£	s.	d.
Coals, 1s. per mile	5	0	0	Fifty passengers, 1½d. per mile each	31	5	0
Repairs, and wear and tear	4	0	0	One ton of goods, 1d. per cwt. per mile	9	6	8
Oil, hemp, &c.	0	10	0				
Two engineers, two steersmen, two stokers, one guard	2	0	0		40	11	8
Rent of stations and offices, wages of attendants, &c.	3	0	0	Deduct 20 per cent. for light loads	8	2	4
Tolls	1	10	0				
Fund for renewal of carriages, 2l. each	4	0	0		£32	9	4
Contingencies	2	0	0				
	22	0	0				
Daily profit	10	9	4				
	£32	9	4				

ONE DAY'S WORK, OR ONE THOUSAND MILES.

	£	s.	d.		£	s.	d.
Say 20 steam-carriages, £1,500	120,000	0	0	313 working days, at £10 9s. 4d. per 100 miles, is for 1000 miles	32,760	0	0
— 50 common carriages, £120 each	6,000	0	0				
— Stations, &c.	14,000	0	0				
	£140,000	0	0				

Profit on Capital, nearly 25 per cent.

To the list of carriages before given, we have to add another constructed subsequent to the printing of Mr. Hancock's book, namely, his steam gig, or phaeton, which has been running most successfully about the neighbourhood of the metropolis for the last six months. On our front page, fig. 1 is an elevation, and fig. 2 a longitudinal section, showing the arrangement of the machinery. *a* is the boiler; *b* the furnace; *c* the ash-pit; *d* one of the cylinders; *e* the chain gearing to communicate the motion from the drum on the crank axle to the drum on the driving wheel axle; *f* the steering apparatus; *g* a lever to turn on, shut off, and regulate the supply of steam; *h* a lever acted on by the foot of the steersman to bring into operation the retarding apparatus; *i* the place for the engineer; *k* funnel to feed the furnace; *l* the blowing fan; the water tanks are under the two seats.

ON THE EXPANSIVE USE OF STEAM IN MARINE ENGINES.

Sir,—At the present day, when the economy of fuel in steam navigation is regarded as a matter of such transcendent importance, it appears surprising that so little attention should be paid to the practicability of rendering the expansive force of steam available in marine engines, which, if effected to any considerable extent, would contribute more than any thing else to reduce the present consumption of fuel.

Whatever may be the case in a *practical* point of view, *theoretically* speaking it is certain that steam is capable of exerting, *by expansion,* an amount of force *vastly greater* than can possibly be obtained from its usual mode of operation; and in marine engines, in which, of all others, economy of fuel is of the greatest importance, this expansive force is in general wholly neglected. Here then is scope for the most extensive improvement, greater than can possibly be expected from any other source, and the utmost exertions ought therefore to be used, to effect the removal of whatever practical difficulties may oppose its attainment in this quarter.

No doubt there is an insuperable difficulty in the way of employing the expansive force of *low pressure* steam to any considerable extent, its elasticity being so quickly reduced to an equilibrium with the friction of the engine, beyond which it can have no available power; but we have only to increase the density of the steam to render its expansive force available to a greater extent; and the more we increase its density the greater will be the available force afforded by its expansion. And it is to be observed, that besides the greater value of the *expansive* force of high pressure steam, its *generative* force, as it is usually called in contradistinction to its *expansive* force, is also capable of greater efficiency than that of low pressure steam; firstly, because owing to its higher temperature its volume is not diminished to the same extent that its pressure is increased; and secondly; because the friction attending its operation not being increased in the same ratio as the pressure, the available force, or excess of the pressure above the friction, is relatively greater than that of low pressure steam. High pressure steam, then, is in every respect capable of greater efficiency, and if we find that a given weight of high pressure steam can be propagated with the same expenditure of fuel as an equal weight of low pressure steam, we may look for the most beneficial results from its employment, expansively, in steam navigation, as well as in all cases where economy of fuel is of vital importance.

But here I shall be met with an exclamation against the *danger* of employing high pressure steam. Now my opinion is, that little or no increase of danger would ensue from its adoption, because there is no reason whatever why a high pressure boiler, if made proportionably stronger, should be more *liable* to burst than a low pressure boiler; and as to the *effects* of an explosion, if from the greater efficiency of the steam, and the consequent reduction in the quantity required, we should be enabled, as I believe we should, to reduce the size of the boiler in nearly the same proportion that we increased the pressure of the steam, the consequences of an explosion would probably not be more dreadful than at present.

It is to be recollected also, that the mere reduction in the size of the boiler would itself tend to increase its strength, or more correctly speaking, to diminish the aggregate pressure it would have to sustain, and would also lessen the risk of the occurrence of defective parts in its material and construction, and so contribute to increase its safety. And here I may observe that the reduction in the size of the boiler would be more than proportionate to the reduction in the consumption of steam, because that part of the boiler which is occupied by the steam, and which is usually about one-third of the whole, would be reduced in *a double ratio*,—first in proportion to the smaller quantity of steam it would have to contain; and secondly, in proportion to the greater density of

that steam. Nor would this further reduction in the size of the steam chamber in respect of the greater density of the steam, have any tendency to render the *priming* of the engine, as it is technically called, greater than at present, because the violence of the ebullition in the boiler would also be diminished in exactly the same degree that the density of the steam evolved from the water was increased. If, however, after all, boilers of the common construction could not be relied upon for steam of excessive pressure, tubular boilers might be substituted, the bursting of which can never occasion very serious mischief. Tubular boilers no doubt have their disadvantages, but would those disadvantages outweigh the enormous benefit to be derived from high pressure steam?

With respect to the relative consumption of fuel in the propagation of high pressure steam, it is now perfectly well ascertained that the quantity of heat required to produce a given quantity, or weight of steam, or in other words, to evaporate a given quantity of water, is always the same, whatever the density of the steam may be, for where the sensible heat is *greater*, the latent heat is *less* in the same degree, and *vice versa*. Unless, therefore, there be some increased practical difficulty in the way of communicating the heat to the water, it is clear that the efficacy of the fuel would not be impaired by increasing the pressure in the boiler, and that whatever saving might be effected in the consumption of the steam by increasing its pressure, would be attended with a commensurate saving of fuel. Whether or not any greater difficulty would be experienced in communicating the heat to the water would be best proved by experiment, but I shall here briefly state my reasons for believing that such increased difficulty would not occur, or at least not in any material degree.

The rapidity with which the heat of an engine furnace is communicated to the boiler, depends upon the disparity between the heat of the furnace and the temperature of that part of the boiler which is in contact with the fire, so that the heat of the fire being the same, the hotter the boiler, the less, in something like the same ratio, will be the quantity of heat communicated to it.

Now the quantity of heat communicated to the boiler is, of course, a measure of that which is transmitted to the water, so that we have only to inquire what effect the increase of pressure would have on the temperature of the boiler, to determine the difference in the quantity of heat which would be transmitted to the water. In the first place, then, the mere increase in the temperature of the water consequent on the greater pressure under which the steam might be generated would not add sufficiently to the heat of the boiler to produce any sensible approximation to that of the fire, so as materially to impair the efficacy of the fuel.

The only question then is, whether the part of the boiler in contact with the fire would be more liable than at present to acquire a temperature greatly exceeding that of the water within? Now, so far from this being the result of increasing the pressure, I conceive the very reverse would be the case, because since the steam produced in the boiler would be of greater density, and consequently of smaller volume, its formation at the inner surface of the metal through which the heat was transmitted to the water would displace the water to a *less extent*, and so render the contact of the water with the metal more perfect than it can be in a low pressure boiler. If it were necessary to increase the thickness of the boiler in order to give it the requisite degree of strength, that circumstance, no doubt, would have a tendency to cause the part of the boiler which was exposed to the fire to become unduly heated; but a boiler may be made of any degree of strength, without at all adding to its thickness, merely by multiplying the number of internal stays from side to side.

With regard to the greater loss of heat by the radiation of a high pressure boiler, that is a matter of very small importance, for by surrounding the boiler with a case of non-conducting material, the radiation may be reduced to a very trifling amount.

On the whole then, I can see no substantial objection to the introduction of high pressure steam, so far as its propogation is concerned; and now let us turn to the practicability of employing it *expansively*.

As far as I can see, the only appearance of difficulty which presents itself in this quarter, is to obtain an equable result from the varying force of the expanding steam. In pumping engines, as in those of the Cornish mines, where the expansive principle is adopted with such great advantage, this varying force is exactly what is wanted; but where a continuous uniform effect is to be produced, some means must be had recourse to for amalgamating the greater with the weaker force of the steam. A heavy fly-wheel is the usual expedient for attaining this object in expansive engines, and where the steam is not cut off at a very small portion of the stroke, it answers the purpose sufficiently well. But in steam vessels this method would be extremely inconvenient. In reality, however, marine engines as now usually constructed, do already possess the means of greatly equalizing the varying force of the steam when used expansively. For, where two cylinders are employed, as is almost universally the case in such engines, each receiving its steam at half the stroke of the other, the difference between the greatest and least *mean* pressure on the two pistons taken together, no matter at what part of the stroke the steam may be cut off, would only be one-half as great as the difference would be per square inch, if only one cylinder were employed. And if the steam were cut off at a very small portion of the stroke as at one-fourth or one-fifth, its power would be still further equalized by the operation of the cranks, which is the very reverse of their effect where the pressure of the steam is uniform.

The force thus obtained from two cylinders worked expansively would probably, with the assistance of the impetus of the paddle-wheels, be sufficiently uniform even to allow of the steam being cut off at so small a portion of the stroke as one-fourth or one-fifth; but if it should not be so, the addition of a third cylinder, adapted to act in proper rotation would, I think, produce the desired effect beyond a doubt.

If other practical objections do really exist, either to the propogation of high pressure steam, or to its employment expansively, I can only repeat, that the advantages to be derived from their removal are so enormous, that if they be not palpably insuperable, the most strenuous exertions ought to be used to subdue them. For my own part I am persuaded that if the value of the principle were appreciated as fully as it deserves, all practical difficulties, if such there be, would speedily be surmounted, and that steam would be used of a pressure which is now unheard of, and would be employed expansively to an extent which, under present circumstances, would appear perfectly unattainable.

It was with great pleasure that I heard Mr. Russell, at the recent meeting of the British Association, in his admirable address on the improvement of steam navigation, express opinions in favour of the same principle which I have recommended ; viz. the substitution of high pressure steam and its employment expansively.

W. G. A.

Newcastle-on-Tyne, 1st Sept. 1838.

PRICE'S ADJUSTING ROUND-SOLE PLANE.

Sir,—I am a carpenter and pattern-maker at the iron-works which are conducted at this place, and in the course of my business have practically found the great inconvenience and expense attending the plan at present in use of planing concave surfaces of different curves. You are no doubt aware, that for any change in the radius of the curve, it is necessary, with the circular planes or round-soles at present used, to cut away a certain portion of the plane in order to adapt it to the new curve required, and consequently by successive alterations the plane is destroyed. This evil I have remedied in my own case, and feeling the advantages which I have derived from my invention, I take the opportunity afforded me by your widely-circulated Magazine to draw the attention of my brother workmen to it. My plane (which may be called the adjusting plane) is fitted with a loose plate of elastic steel, the two ends of which are made to approach or recede from the convex surface of the wood by means of screws passing through holes near them. It will be at once seen that by merely turning the screws the curve of the plate may be varied from any convexity which may be given to the wood in the first instance, to the straight line which the plate would assume if left to its own elastic power. The part through which the groove for the iron passes,

is strengthened by an additional piece of steel, about a quarter of an inch thick, brazed across the inner side; which piece serves also to fix the plate in its due position, being let into the wood. The counter-sunk heads of the adjusting screws work also in small blocks similarly brazed and let in.

This description will, I trust, enable my fellow-workmen who have occasion to use circular planes or round-soles, to avail themselves of an improvement from which I have myself found great advantage. Should you agree with me in this, you will, perhaps, permit the insertion of this letter in your valuable Magazine.

I am, Sir,
Your obedient servant,
REES PRICE.

Varttg, near Pontypool, South Wales,
August, 1838.

EXPERIMENTS AND OBSERVATIONS ON THE COLOURS OF THIN PLATES.
BY CHARLES TOMLINSON, ESQ.

Sir,—The various modes of obtaining the rings of Newton and the colours of thin plates generally are well known : 1st, by the thin film which the soap bubble affords ; 2nd, by the thin film of air obtained by superposing two lenses ; 3rd, by laminated substances generally, such as talc, mother-of-pearl, selenite, &c. ; 4th, the ingenious method of Nobili by means of galvanic agency, as developed by him in his system of metallochromy ; and 5th, by films of oil upon the surface of water. These and other modes are so well known, that any new modes of multiplying them can only be regarded as new variations of old facts, and therefore not sufficiently important to present for publication.

My object in this paper is, to offer to the notice of scientific men some new facts connected with the colours of thin plates.

If a single drop of olive, rape, or castor oil, or of copaivi, Peru, or Canada balsam, be placed upon the surface of clean and perfectly still water, contained in a clean glass goblet, and placed in such a situation as to receive the light of day, a film will be formed upon the surface of the water, the thickness of which varies from about 0.36 to 57.75 millionths of an inch, and in some cases where white light only is reflected by the film, the thickness thereof is greater. Some of the oils and balsams require to be heated before they are dropped upon the water, because, at the temperature of the air, their viscidity is too great to allow of a diffusion over the surface of the water.

From the above oils and balsams I will select two, viz. oil or spirit of turpentine, and balsam of Peru.

A small portion of spirit of turpentine being taken up on a glass rod, a single drop is allowed to fall upon the surface of the water—this drop immediately expands into a circular form, the diameter of which is about 1½ inches—it reflects white light, but no colour whatever for a considerable time, until, by evaporation, the film becomes sufficiently thin. If, however, as soon as the drop of turpentine has fallen upon the water and expanded into a film, we hold over the film, at the distance of about one-sixth of an inch, a glass rod, or the finger well moistened with sulphuric ether, a splendid display of Newton's rings is instantly obtained, which continue until the ether has evaporated. The centre of the orders of rings is immediately below the end of the rod or finger; but their form is subject to variation according as the article dipped in ether varies.

The rings generally close up and disappear as soon as the influence of the ether is removed from the film; but as soon as the ether is removed, the rings lose their perfect form as circles or ellipses, become broken up, and a variety of colours is seen, which depend upon varying thicknesses of the film.

If, now, we dip a clean glass rod into nitric acid, and hold the wetted end over the film, the latter begins to contract in dimensions until a certain thickness is attained at which all colour disappears; and a film of the size of a crown piece is soon reduced to one the size of a sixpence. On again applying ether the film expands rapidly, and the rings are developed as before.

These results are also obtained when the film is formed from animal and vegetable oils and balsams. Liquor ammoniæ, pyroligneous ether, alcohol and naptha, have, the first by its gas, and the rest by their respective vapours, a similar effect upon the films as vapour of ether.

When a drop of balsam of Peru is allowed to fall upon the surface of water we instantly get a magnificent display of coloured rings: on applying vapour of ether, ammonia, &c. to any part of the film, its thickness is instantly reduced, so that the colour belonging to one order of Newton's rings is instantly exchanged for the colour of one of the series above it.

A magnet seems also to have an action upon the film, the north pole tending to repel it, and the south pole to attract it. But the magnetic, as also the galvanic and electrical results, which I have as yet obtained, are not sufficiently satisfactory for me to speak decidedly in this communication.

I have carefully abstained from all theory in this article: the above is a short extract from a large variety of results which I have obtained in an endeavour to substantiate a principle of chemical repulsion in contradistinction to chemical attraction. I wish to give immediate publicity to the above facts, and if you will oblige me by inserting them in your next number, I will send you another article on the same subject in a few days.

Salisbury, August 23, 1838.

ARTIFICIAL FUELS.—WELCH COALS.—MECHANICAL FLYING.

Sir,—You will have, doubtless, perceived by the newspapers that the authorities at Woolwich, have, like many others, taken a leaf out of your book, without any acknowledgement. In No. 170, Nov. 25, 1826, twelve years ago, may be seen a letter of mine in which I recommended the use of fat, oil, or coal-tar, combined with coal or cinders, (for a wick, as it were) for the use of sea-going steamers. I further suggest, that melted fat, oil, or coal-tar, might be injected into the incandescent coal or coke, through "little beaks in the sides of the furnace, and performed by the engine itself, under the complete control of the engineer." I add, that oil, either animal or vegetable, and wood, are often to be procured where no coal is to be had; and that a wood fire, with the regulated projection of oil upon it, would produce a clear flame and great heat. Coal-tar burns at a far lower temperature than oil or fat, and produces vast quantities of smoke and soot.

Some time in 1833, I think it was, another correspondent of yours, described his process for making an artificial fuel or coal, by working up coal-tar, dry clay in powder, and saw-dust, which were formed into brick-like shapes, just as the Woolwich gentlemen have now *invented*, for the *third* time, at least.

I take this opportunity of submitting to the consideration of those concerned in sea-going steamers, that from experiments I have made, I am decidedly of opinion that the real Welch stone-coal will be found to double the work of any other coal or coke; and consequently, that one ton of the former will propel a ship as far as two of the latter. With some furnaces, it may require a first charge of Staffordshire, or other quick-burning coal, to ignite it, but once well lit, its durability is quite surprising, and without any smoke whatever.

Should any one of your monied readers be desirous of immortal fame, he will patronise my invention of flying in the air by purely mechanical means, and so confer on mankind dominion over the air, as they already have over the sea, which will effect a greater change in our physical and moral condition than has any other invention of the last 3000 years. Ye closet doctors, remember the scoffers at gas—steam-printing—and the report of the seven British Admirals, who in 1805, solemnly declared steam navigation on the ocean to be *"impossible"!* Remember also our own illustrious Dr. Lardner, who pledged all his practical science against the possibility of steaming across the Atlantic, just at the moment that the feat was being achieved! Alas! the scorn with which the Doctors and the vulgar herd, both rich and poor, assailed poor Windsor and his "smoke lights!" Poor creatures—to apply the word "impossible" to the merely *varied application* of a simple mechanical action!

I have the honour to be, &c.,
F. MACERONI.

3 St. James's Square, August 22, 1838

ROCKETS AS APPLIED TO LOCOMOTION.—BADDELEY'S NAVIGABLE BALLOON, &c.

Sir,—A notice in your 785th Number, page 368, informs us that a M. Jobard, of Brussels, has proposed to apply the force arising from the burning of a pyro-technical composition, to the propulsion of certain vessels through the water, with great speed.

It must be quite evident to a majority of your readers, that in proposing to cross from Dover to Calais in eleven minutes! M. Jobard is propounding what is utterly impossible. It would take him nearly that time if blown from a mortar; but as to attaining anything like the velocity stated, while moving through so dense a fluid as water, it is quite absurd.

The immense resistance offered to bodies moving with high velocity through water is tolerably well known; but a body of *suitable form*, urged by such a force at a more moderate rate, might traverse the air at will. I have no hesitation in here stating, that one of three plans (the other two being mechanical) by which I proposed to give the necessary impetus to my "navigable balloon," was to employ the reacting force given out by the combustion of a suitable rocket.

The power thus generated is exceedingly great, while the material is comparatively light; and the rocket long since suggested itself to me as being by far the most eligible source of power that could possibly be applied to the purposes of aërial navigation.

A form of balloon susceptible of being thus impelled—and as a necessary consequence, of being guided—through the air, has been designed by

Yours respectfully,
WM. BADDELEY.

London, August 27, 1838.

FLOATING BREAKWATER.

Sir,—The Lotus forms a natural breakwater on a small scale, intended, perhaps, as a shelter for the spawn and young of fish, and the nestling and rearing of equatic birds. I have often thought that a hint might be taken from nature in this point, to form floating breakwaters, in situations where the formation of harbours would be impracticable, or attended with such expense as to preclude the possibility of undertaking their formation.

JOHN NORTON.

23, Upper Berkeley-street, West.

REMARKABLE MATHEMATICAL PROPERTIES OF A CERTAIN PARALLELOGRAM, WITH A SUGGESTED APPLICATION TO PURPOSES OF GENERAL UTILITY.

Sir,—At one of the meetings of the Royal Society of Edinburgh, in February last, an interesting paper was read by John Scott Russell, M.A., F.R.S.E., containing a notice of the remarkable mathematical properties of a certain parallelogram. The parallelogram which formed the subject of this communication was the rectangle whose sides are to each other in the ratio of the diagonal of a square to its side,—a figure well known to architects, sculptors, and painters, from its beauty, and frequently adopted in the practical arts.

The author showed, that if the given rectangle bisected by a line parallel to its shortest side, each segment will be a figure similar in all respects to the original rectangle; and if either of these halves be itself bisected in the same manner, their halves will be rectangles similar to the original rectangle; and so on *ad infinitum*. The sides of the primary figure and its halves are continual proportionals, represented by the series—

$$b, \frac{1}{\sqrt{2}}b, \frac{1}{\sqrt{2^2}}b, \frac{1}{\sqrt{2^3}}b, \frac{1}{\sqrt{2^4}}b, \ldots\ldots \frac{1}{\sqrt{2^n+1}}. b.$$

The author endeavours to trace an analogy between the properties of this parallelogram and the logarithmic spiral.

A class of figures may be obtained by trisection and by division into four, five, or any number of figures, all of them similar to the primary figure, and capable of division *ad infinitum* in the same manner.*

The following elegant and useful application of the foregoing facts, has been suggested by Sir John Robison, the talented secretary of the Royal Society of Edinburgh, and I think the advantages of the plan proposed, must be evident to all. Many of your readers will be aware, that it has been contemplated to sell stamped envelopes or franks, for the conveyance of letters at a reduced charge. In a letter recently addressed to the Lord Advocate for Scotland, Sir John Robison observes:—

" If the proposed change in the mode of charging the postage of letters should take place, the forms and sizes which may be adopted for the stamped covers will be a matter of some importance, as considerable inconvenience would arise from an injudicious form being selected, or from too great a variety of them being made requisite.

The endless variety both of *proportion* and of *dimensions* which the makers now give to the writing papers, renders it difficult to determine on a size of envelope which should suit all cases; but if the largest ordinary page of quarto post, be taken as a ground (say 10 by 8 in.) then it may be seen that letters written on such paper, and notes written on the octavo and sexto-decimo forms derived from it, may all be conveniently fitted by two sizes of envelopes. *e. g.* an envelope 5¼ by 4¼ will contain the quarto page folded twice transversely, across the middle; or octavo pages doubled in the same manner; and a smaller one, (4¼ by 2¾ will contain octavo notes twice doubled) as above; or sexto-decimo notes one doubled. A full sheet of folio post, if thin, and neatly folded three times instead of twice, may also be contained in the larger sized cover.

"A great advantage may, however be gained, by making a small change in the proportions generally given by manufacturers to their papers. The present average proportion of the sides of an expanded folio sheet of writing paper is in the ratio of 20 to 16. If this were to be slightly modified, and if the longer side was to bear to the shorter one *the proportion of the diagonal to the side of a square*, this convenient consequence would ensue, that, however often such a parallelogram should be doubled by folding across its middle, its subsidiary divisions would always have the same proportions, and be symmetrical; and two sizes of envelopes of symmetrical proportions would serve to contain all sizes of letters."

The differences between the present and the altered forms are as follows:—

	Folio page.	Quarto page.	Octavo page.	16mo p.
Present form ..	16 by 10 ..	10 by 8 ..	8 by 5 ..	5 by 4.
Proposed do. ..	14¼ × 10 ..	10 × 7¹⁄₁₁ ..	7¹⁄₁₁ × 5 ..	5 × 3³⁄₁₁.

---

* From proceedings of the Royal Society of Edinburgh.

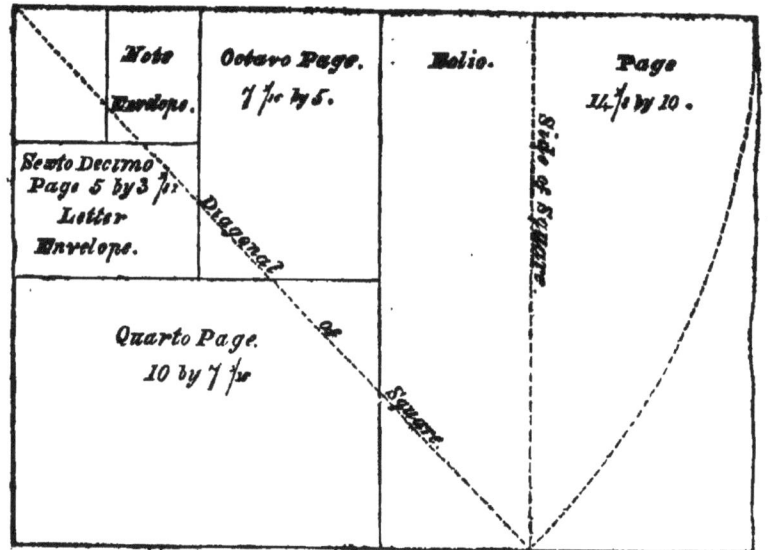

The accompanying diagram represents the proposed sheet of writing paper with its subdivisions marked off, at the same time showing the construction of the parallelogram by which the form is produced. Independently of the advantages that would attend this slight change in the proportions generally given to writing papers, the form is very agreeable to the eye, and it is to be hoped the suggested improvement will forthwith be reduced to practice.

I remain, Sir,
Yours respectfully,
WM. BADDELEY.

London, August 22, 1838.

NEW AMERICAN ACT FOR THE REGULATION OF STEAM VESSELS.

The numerous accidents and the immense loss of life in the United States from the bursting of the boilers of steam vessels, have produced in the last Session of Congress some attempt at a legislative remedy. As all hints of the kind must be valuable, when we ourselves are considering a proper remedy for the same evil, we subjoin the enactment on the subject which was passed by the American Congress on the 7th July last :—

CIRCULAR.

Custom-house, Collectors's-office, New York, Aug. 3, 1838.

The undersigned has received from the Treasury Department of the United States as a certified copy of a law approved the 7th day of July last, entitled " An act to provide for the better security of the lives of passengers on board of vessels propelled in whole or in part by steam," (a copy of which is annexed,) with instructions to take immediate and suitable measures within the limits of this district, to make the owners and masters of vessels propelled as above stated, acquainted with the nature of the provisions of said law, and of the absolute necessity of their being complied with on or before the first day of October next, and also of the settled determination of the department rigidly to adhere to all of these provisions so far as depends upon the power conferred by law upon the officers of the Government. In furtherance of the desire of the head of the Treasury Department to carry out the will of the legislature as expressed in said law, the undersigned hereby gives notice of its provisions, and of the instructions he has received in relation thereto, the execution of which, so far as devolves upon him, will be promptly enforced.

J. HOYT, Collector.

An act to provide for the better Security of the lives of Passengers on board of Vessels propelled in whole or in part by Steam.

Be it enacted by the Senate and House of Representatives of the United States of America in Congress assembled, That it shall be the duty, of all owners of steam-boats or vessels propelled in whole or in part by steam, on or before the first day of October 1838, to make a new enrolment of the same under the existing laws of the United States, and to take out from the collector or surveyor of the port, as the case may be, where such vessel is enrolled, a new license, under such conditions as are now imposed by law, and as shall be imposed by this act.

Sec. 2. And be it further enacted, that it shall not be lawful for the owner, master, or captain of any steam-boat or vessel propelled in whole or in part by steam, to transport any goods, wares and merchandise, or passengers, in or upon the bays, lakes, rivers or other navigable waters of the United States, from and after the 1st day of October, 1838, without having first obtained, from the proper officer, a license under the existing laws, and without having complied with the conditions imposed by this act; and for each and every violation of this section, the owner or owners of said vessel shall forfeit and pay to the United States the sum of 500 dollars, one half for the use of the informer; and for which sum or sums the steam-boat or vessel so engaged shall be liable, and may be seized and proceeded against summarily, by way of libel, in any district court of the United States having jurisdiction of the offence.

Sec. 3. And be it further enacted, that it shall be the duty of the district judge of the United States within whose district any ports of entry or delivery may be, on the navigable waters, bays, lakes, and rivers of the United States, upon the application of the master or owner of any steam-boat or vessel propelled in whole or in part by steam, to appoint, from time to time, one or more persons skilled and competent to make inspections of such boats and vessels, and of the boilers and machinery employed in the same, who shall not be interested in the manufacture of steam-engines, steam-boat boilers, or other machinery belonging to steam-vessels, whose duty it shall be to make such inspection when called upon for that purpose, and to give to the owner or master of such boat or vessel duplicate certificates of such inspection; such persons before entering upon the duties enjoined by this act, shall make and subscribe an oath of affirmation before said district judge, or other officer duly authorized to administer oaths, well, faithfully, and impartially to execute and perform the services herein required of them.

Sec. 4. And be it further enacted, that the person or persons who shall be called upon to inspect the hull of any steam-boat or vessel, under the provisions of this act, shall, after a thorough examination of the same,

give to the owner or master, as the case may be, a certificate, in which shall be stated the age of the said boat or vessel, when and where originally built, and the length of time she has been running; and he or they shall also state whether, in his or their opinion, the said boat or vessel is sound, and in all respects seaworthy, and fit to be used for the transportation of freight or passengers; for which service so performed upon each and every boat or vessel, the inspectors shall each be paid and allowed by said master or owner applying for such inspection, the sum of five dollars.

Sec. 5. And be it further enacted, that the person or persons who shall be called upon to inspect the boilers and machinery of any steam-boat or vessel, under the provisions of this act, shall, after a thorough examination of the same, make a certificate, in which he or they shall state his or their opinion whether said boilers are sound and fit for use, together with the age of the boilers; and duplicates thereof shall be delivered to the owner or master of such vessel, one of which it shall be the duty of the said master and owner to deliver to the collector or surveyor of the port whenever he shall apply for a license, or for a renewal of a license; the other he shall cause to be posted up, and kept in some conspicuous part of the said boat, for the information of the public; and for each and every inspection so made, each of the said inspectors shall be paid by the said master or owner applying, the sum of five dollars.

Sec. 6. And be it further enacted, that it shall be the duty of the owners and masters of steam-boats to cause the inspection provided under the 4th section of this act to be made at least once in every 12 months; and the examination required by the 5th section at least once in every six months; and deliver to the collector or surveyor of the port where his boat or vessel has been enrolled or licensed, the certificate of such inspection; and, on a failure thereof, he or they shall forfeit the license granted to such boat or vessel, and be subject to the same penalty as though he had run said boat or vessel without having obtained such license, to be recovered in like manner. And it shall be the duty of the owners and masters of the steam-boats licensed in pursuance of the provisions of this act to employ on board of their respective boats a competent number of experienced and skilful engineers, and in case of neglect to do so, the said owners and masters shall be held responsible for all damages to the property, or any passenger on board of any boat occasioned by an explosion of the boiler, or any derangement of the engine or machinery of any boat.

Sec. 7. And be it further enacted, that whenever the master of any boat or vessel or the person or persons charged with navigating said boat or vessel, which is propelled in whole or in part by steam, shall stop the motion or headway of said boat or vessel, or when the said boat or vessel shall be stopped for the purpose of discharging or taking in cargo, fuel, or passengers, he or they shall open the safety-valve, so as to keep the steam down in said boiler as near as practicable to what it is when the said boat or vessel is under headway, under the penalty of 200 dollars for each and every offence.

Sec. 8. And be it further enacted, that it shall be the duty of the owner and master of every steam vessel engaged in the transportation of freight or passengers at sea, or on the lakes of Champlain, Ontario, Erie, Huron, Superior, and Michigan, the tonnage of which vessel shall not exceed 200 tons, to provide and to carry with the said boat or vessel, upon each and every voyage, two long-boats or yawls, each of which shall be competent to carry at least 20 persons ; and where the tonnage of said vessel shall exceed 200 tons, it shall be the duty of the owner and master to provide and carry as aforesaid not less than three long-boats or yawls of the same or larger dimensions: and for every failure in these particulars the said master and owner shall forfeit and pay 300 dollars.

Sec. 9. And be it further enacted, that it shall be the duty of the master and owner of every steam vessel employed on either of the lakes mentioned in the last section, or on the sea, to provide, as a part of the necessary furniture, a suction hose, and fire engine and hose suitable to be worked on said boat in case of fire, and carry the same upon each and every voyage in good order ; and that iron rods or chains shall be employed and used in the navigation of all steam boats, instead of wheel or tiller ropes ; and for a failure to do which, they, and each of them, shall forfeit and pay the sum of 300 dollars.

Sec. 10. And be it further enacted, that it shall be the duty of the master and owner of every steam boat, running between sunset and sunrise, to carry _____ _____ _____ one or more signal lights, that may be seen by other boats navigating the same waters, under the penalty of 200 dollars.

Sec. 11. And be it further enacted, that the penalties imposed by this act may be sued for and recovered in the name of the United States, in the district or circuit court of such district or circuit where the offence shall have been committed, or forfeiture incurred, or in which the owner or master of said vessel may reside, one-half to the use of the informer, and the other to the use of the United States ; or the said penalty may be prosecuted for by indictment in either of the said courts.

Sec. 12. And be it further enacted, that every captain, engineer, pilot, or other person, employed on board of any steam-boat, or vessel, propelled in whole or in part by steam, by whose misconduct, negligence, or inattention to his or their respective duties, the life or lives of any person or persons on board said vessel may be destroyed, shall be deemed guilty of manslaughter, and, upon conviction thereof before any circuit court in the United States, shall be sentenced to confinement at hard labour for a period not more than ten years.

Sec. 13. And be it further enacted, that in all suits and actions against proprietors of steam-boats for injuries arising to persons or property from the bursting of the boiler of any steam-boat, or the collapse of a flue, or other injurious escapes of steam, the fact of such bursting, collapse, or injurious escape of steam, shall be taken as full *prima facie* evidence, sufficient to charge the defendant, or those in his employment, with negligence, until he shall show that no negligence has been committed by him or those in his employ.

Approved July 7, 1838.

A true copy compared with the Roll in this office.

A. VAIL, Chief Clerk.

Department of State, July 9, 1838.

MR. J. J. O. TAYLOR'S APPARATUS FOR PROPELLING STEAM-SHIPS.

Some very interesting models of vessels, propelled by an apparatus which is *meant* to supersede the use of paddle-wheels, and the inconvenient and unsightly appearance of paddle-boxes in steam-ships, have just been exhibited by the inventor, Mr. J. Jephson O. Taylor, at No. 51, Gracechurch-street, at which place the models are now open to the inspection of captains in the navy, engineers, and all persons connected with the shipping interest, or generally concerned in the improvement of science. The new apparatus, when adapted to actual steam-ships, is to be worked by the power of steam, in the same manner as the paddle-wheels attached to such vessels are now worked; in other words, steam is to be the power employed, but its operations are to be directed to different machinery. The difference is this :—The power of the steam-engine will be brought to bear upon a horizontal iron shaft, which will pass from the engine or closely in position with it, beneath the deck of the main cabin, through the stern-post of the vessel ; at the extremity beyond the stern-post two blades, in shape like the blade of an oar, will be fixed, not perpendicularly, but at an angle of

22 degrees to the perpendicular stern-post, and beyond these blades, which occupy but little space, will be affixed a false stern-post, secured to the real stern-post at top and bottom by transverse timbers and iron knees, &c., for the sake of strength, and to prevent accident in case of grounding. The rudder will of course be attached to the false stern-post. The space between the real stern-post and the false one will be very trifling; in the models it is not sufficient to destroy the symmetry of the vessel, though sufficiently large for the purposes required. The iron shaft being put in motion by the power of the steam-engine, revolves with great rapidity, and at each stroke drives the blades through the water. The vessel is thus propelled forward in precisely the same manner as a wherry is seen to be frequently propelled in the river by a man at the stern using one oar or scull to force it forward. The experiments are made on the models in a large tin trough of water, of about 30 feet long. The power used in them is that of the common clock spring wound up, steam being of course out of the question in models of a foot or two feet long. An experiment was first tried on a model with paddle-wheels to prove her speed; by using the same power, she moved from one end of the trough to the other in 115 seconds. An experiment was then tried on her, using the same power applied to the new apparatus of stern blades, and she performed the distance in 18 seconds. The patentee of this invention insists that the following advantages belong to it, and if in a large vessel it should prove as satisfactory on trial as it as on the experiments with the models, what he contends for must be admitted. He says there will be a great saving, not only of expense, but in the construction of the machinery, the waste of coals, and the employment of engineers, because an engine of 60 horse-power will be able to do as much under the new system as one of 80 under the old. There will be a great deal of room saved by removing the paddles and paddle boxes, and a straight uninterrupted gangway for guns in vessels of war. There will be no swell by the use of the blades, so that accidents to boats or small craft in rivers will be avoided, and the banks of canals uninjured in canal navigation by steamers. There will be space for masts and rigging to carry any quantity of canvass, and as the blades at the stern are beneath the surface of the water, there will be less chance, or rather no danger at all, of their being shot away in action, or in an attack by hostile vessels or batteries.

In the same room a naval officer has a model of a brig of war, to which he has attached blades on each quarter; they are

made to lie flat to the quarter when not required, and can be carried out in a few minutes by means of a very simple but efficacious apparatus, when required; they are to be worked by means of manual labour at a windlass. Nothing can be more "snug," to use a nautical term, than the whole apparatus; it is cheap in construction, simple in operation, and takes up scarcely any room whatever. Nevertheless, in keeping a vessel from drifting under a battery, or on a rocky shore, getting her head round, and enabling her to manoeuvre in a small space, it is of important use.—*Times.*

SAFE-PLUG FOR STEAM-BOILERS.

The Society of Arts lately voted a silver medal to Mr. Isaac Dodds, of Masborough, near Rotheram, for his safe-plug for steam-boilers; the following description of which we quote from the last part of their *Transactions.*

In some steam-boilers a hole is made at the bottom, and is afterwards filled up with a plug of lead or fusible metal, in order to serve the purpose of a safe-valve; for, by duly proportioning the ingredients of which the plug is composed, its melting point may be lowered from that of 612° Fah., the temperature at which pure lead becomes fluid, to 212° Fah., the ordinary boiling point of water, which is more than sufficient to melt common fusible metal, composed of eight parts bismuth, five lead, and three tin. Mr. Dodds objects to the usual position of such safe-plug, because, being inserted in the lowest part of the boiler, it will remain covered with water, even when so little is left in the boiler as to allow part of the bottom and sides to be uncovered, and therefore liable to become red hot. Now, since the plug in this position cannot acquire a higher temperature than that of the water by which it is covered, it may continue unmelted while the steam and other gaseous contents of the boiler are accumulating, till an explosion takes place. This hazard, in the opinion of Mr. Dodds, will be prevented by placing over the hole in the bottom of the boiler a cap of iron, of such height that its top shall be left uncovered, while the whole bottom of the boiler, and those other parts that are exposed to the direct action of the fire, shall still be under water. The top of the cap is to be perforated by a hole, which is to be filled up by a plug of fusible metal. When, therefore, from defect in the feeding apparatus, or from neglect on the part of the engine-man to work the supply-pump, the water in the boiler is so far evaporated as to be a little below the top of the cap, the heat, not being conveyed off by the water, will melt the plug, and the steam will be discharged through the hole into the fire.

The intention of the Society to reward Mr. Dodds for the above proposal having been made public, was the occasion of a letter from Mr. J. B. Humphreys, of Southampton, civil engineer, from which it appears that a plan, not differing in any essential particular from Mr. Dodds's, was put in practice by Mr. Humphreys in the boiler of a small steam-packet at Southampton, in the year 1828, and also more recently, in February 1835, in a boiler made by Mr. Hague, under the especial direction of Mr. Humphreys, as engineer to the Rio Doce Company.

In Mr. Humphreys' original arrangement there was no cap; but a boss, about five inches in diameter, was formed in one of the boiler-plates, projecting inwards about three inches, and in the top of this the plug of lead was inserted. Mr. Humphreys finds that when salt water is used the plug wastes by galvanic action, and cannot be depended on for more than fourteen days. When the weeping or oozing of water between the plug and side of the hole which it occupies has begun it continually increases, and thus gives notice to the stoker, and this will go on for some hours before the plug blows out. It is, therefore, necessary, from time to time, to renew the plug; for this purpose a hole, about an inch and a half in diameter, is made in the roof of the boiler, directly over the plug, is tapped with a fine thread, and is habitually closed with a square-headed screw and tapping. Through this hole the new plug is introduced, being first slightly set on the end of a ramrod to facilitate its insertion into the hole occupied by the former plug. When in its place, a light blow with an iron rod makes it tight, and the whole operation is done in less than five minutes. The only preparation required is to let down the steam to atmospheric pressure, and to lower the water in the boiler that it may not wash the plug seat. The fire may, in the meanwhile, be backed up, and in twenty minutes after the insertion of the new plug, the engine will be again in action.

Mr. Humphreys further states, that having been at first annoyed by the plug blowing out on unseasonable occasions he put a fine on every such occurrence, and the annoyance ceased ever after.

CHATTERING OF MILL-STONES.

Sometimes, after every possible care has been taken to suspend the upper stone so that its grinding surface shall in every part be equidistant from the surface of the lower one, the stones will *chatter;* that is, the upper one will lose its perfect parallelism with the lower one, and will become oblique; so that on one side the stones will knock against each other, and on the opposite side will be too far apart to make good meal. This is a very serious defect, as it is scarcely possible to remedy it. When at rest, the two stones are correctly parallel, and it is only when in motion that the grinding surface of the runner becomes oblique. To Mr. Donkin I am indebted for a very probable explanation of the phenomenon. From the very irregular size and form of the pieces of Buhr, and from their being cemented together by plaster—a substance that differs much in specific gravity from the Buhr itself—it is evident that the weight must be very unequally distributed through the mass: the consequence of this will be, that the plane of rotation will never strictly coincide with the horizontal plane, to which, alone, can the grinding surfaces be adjusted; and when these planes differ by a certain angular amount, the runner will come in contact with the bed-stone, in one part of its rotation, and produce chattering. The only very obvious remedy for this evil is, great attention to sorting the pieces of Buhr, and to arranging them within the frame of the stone, that the cement required shall be distributed as evenly as possible.—*Mr. Aikin's Lecture on Corn Mills, Trans. Soc. Arts.*

DOMESTIC FLOUR MILLS.

The popular charges against millers and bakers of adulterating flour, whether false or true, become, from time to time, epidemically prevalent; and then all the world runs wild for hand or family mills, as they are called. It is worth while, therefore, to consider what may fairly be expected of such mills. The main object proposed by the use of domestic mills, namely, an unadulterated material for bread, is unquestionably obtained. If the grinding is performed between stones, the meal, although coarse, harsh to the feel, and ill-ground in many respects, from want of the necessary knowledge and attention, which can only be expected of those who are millers by trade, will be sufficiently performed to allow of most of the bran being separated by the sieve, leaving a flour from which perfectly wholesome, though coarse brown bread may be made. The bran, with a considerable quantity of flour still adherent to it for want of being properly ground, remains; and in private families, resident in town there exists no use to which it can be applied. When, therefore, the loss in the article of bran and of flour not separable from the bran, is added to the current cost of labour for grinding and the prime cost of the mill itself, it will soon appear at what a price a family so supplied eat their bread : for the labour of the mill is such as not to admit of its being imposed as an extra on the ordinary duties of modern domestic servants. The noise, too, of the grinding, is a nuisance that deserves to be taken into account, unless it can be performed in an out-house, where the labourer employed, being out of inspection, has it in his power to adulterate your wheat with inferior grain, in the same degree as is charged upon the miller.

All the objections that I have just enumerated, apply to the use of steel mills ; with this in addition, that, as the action of metal plates is to cut rather than to rub down or grind the grain, a much larger proportion of flour will be left adherent to the bran. and a much larger proportion of this latter will be cut so fine as to pass through the sieve with the flour ; the only way, therefore, at all consistent with economy, of employing the meal produced by a steel mill is to use it entire, without any attempt at separating even the bran. I have had bread made of such meal, and. though dark in colour, and coarse to the look, it rose, with the usual quantity of yeast, quite as well as home-made bread of finer quality, and was not deficient either in palatableness or in wholesomeness.

As far as I can judge, by experiments made in my own family, and from those that have come to my knowledge made by others, it will take about two hours' continued hard labour for one man, to grind a bushel of wheat ; and if to this be added the time and labour of sifting and dressing the meal by hand, I believe that an average day's work will rarely exceed two bushels.—*Mr. Aikin on Corn Mills, Trans. Soc. Arts.*

IVESON'S PATENT PLAN FOR THE PREVENTION OF SMOKE AND SAVING OF FUEL.

Mr. Iveson's process consists merely in propelling steam into the furnace, immediately over the fire, and down upon the flame, by which the whole of the combustible materials, he states, are completely consumed, and there is not the slightest appearance of smoke at the top of the chimney. The actual result of the practical working with Mr. Iveson's furnace, for several months past, as proved by Dr. Fyfe, operating in conjunction with him, has shown that the saving of fuel is very great. We may state, and we do it by the authority of the above-mentioned gentlemen, that they have been enabled to save at least one-half of the quantity of coal ; in

other words they have, by the process followed, been enabled to make one part of coal do the work of two, when the object in view was the raising of steam, so that an engine consuming 10 tons of coal a-day, may do its duty with only 5 tons in the same time. Apart, however, from the saving of fuel, which is undoubtedly of the utmost importance, we consider in many respects the prevention of smoke as perhaps greater. We are aware that many processes have been recommended for effecting this, and though some have done it to a considerable extent, yet none have gained the object in view,—but the process now alluded to does it with the utmost degree of certainty. We were present, a few days ago, and witnessed the results with the apparatus at work. The fire being charged in the usual way, volumes of black smoke instantly issued from the chimney top ; but no sooner was the steam-pipe opened, and the steam allowed to flow upon the fire and flame, than the smoke ceased, and the chimney top was as free from it as if the fire had been completely extinguished,—and again on cutting off the steam, the smoke appeared as before. This was observed time after time, leaving not the slightest doubt with regard to the triumphant success of this simple process.

It is extremely important to observe that now, when steam navigation and railway travelling are becoming daily more and more extensive. every thing that can diminish the consumption of fuel must certainly deeply interest us, and to this town, in which it has of late been proposed to raise manufactories, surely it must be gratifying to know, that, place them where we may. we are not to be annoyed by the volumes of smoke which now issue from them ; indeed, so far from objecting to manufactories, we should rejoice to see them established, as the lofty chimneys may be so raised, as to add greatly to the appearance of the town. An act, we believe, was some time ago passed, to compel manufacturers to consume their smoke ; we trust that this act, if still in existence, will be put in force. In many places we know that police bills have clauses to this effect, and it is to be hoped, that if the act alluded to has become obsolete, clauses compelling the consumption of smoke will be introduced; and yet why should we wish for anything of the kind ? independent of the prevention of smoke, the saving of fuel is so great, that every one consuming coal to any extent must feel it to be his interest to adopt Mr. Iveson's process. While alluding to the prevention of smoke, we may state it as a remarkable circumstance, that the first to raise a factory in this town, and against which strong objections have been advanced, have been the first to disclose to the public a means of entirely consuming the fuel, and removing one of the strongest objections to them.

In most of the proceedings referred to, high pressure steam was used, the engine generally working under a pressure of 35lbs.; but in some, low pressure steam was employed with equal advantages,—indeed there is every reason for believing that it will be greater.

Fortunately the process is of easy application. All that is required, in those cases where a boiler is in use, is merely to carry a small tube from any part of it, and which is made to terminate in the furnace, by a sort of fan, perforated with a number of small holes, so as to throw the steam in all directions down upon the flame; this can be done for a trifling expense, compared with the immense benefit derived. Should there not be a boiler attached to the furnace, a small one can be raised at little expense. Of course, in stating the great saving effected, it must be kept in mind that part of the steam is consumed in accomplishing this, but it is small in comparison to the whole amount, not exceeding one-twelfth of the total quantity of steam raised from the boiler, and which must of course be deducted from the saving stated; but it is not always necessary to take the steam from the boiler. When high pressure engines are used, a pipe may be made to convey part of the waste steam into the furnace; and there are also many ways of generating steam, without any additional expenditure of fuel, which must occur to every engineer.—*Edinburgh Observer.*

SELECTIONS FROM THE PROCEEDINGS OF THE NEWCASTLE MEETING (BEING THE EIGHTH) OF THE BRITISH ASSOCIATION FOR THE ADVANCEMENT OF SCIENCE.

Upon the occasions of the previous meetings of the British Association we have given the proceedings of *all* the sections at considerable length; and many of our readers and correspondents have complained of our so doing—and perhaps justly—as filling up too great a proportion of our publication with matter not at all of a mechanical description. We shall avoid this fault in the present instance, and only give the proceedings of the Mechanical Section, and selections from that of the others bearing upon mechanics or manufactures. Altogether the meeting of the Association just past has been one of the most uninteresting —and in a mechanical point of view, the most meagre of the eight periodical assemblages that have taken place. The Reports that have been published are also very unsatisfactory and too general. We shall be most happy to receive any of the papers read at the Mechanical Section, of which mere mention is made, or only a scantling given in the Reports, for publication in our Journal.

"A Statistical View of the Recent Progress, and Present Amount of Mining Industry in France," by Mr. G. R. Porter.

Mr. Porter began by a general reference to the importance of the subject, and observed, that it is surprising that, among a people so proverbially practical as we are, such researches should be so little the subjects of inquiry as they hitherto have been: even the amount of one of the most important of our mineral products is so much left to conjecture, that the produce of our coal-mines at the present day is variously estimated by men conversant with the subject, at from 15,000,000 to 30,000,000 of tons per annum. In France, however, a law was passed, in April 1833, which gave authority to collect statistical details of the mining industry of France, and intrusted the execution of the duties subjoined to a public department, known as the 'Direction Générale des Ponts et Chaussées et des Mines,' and placed under the ultimate controul of the Minister of Commerce and Public Works. Attached to this department is a staff of well-instructed, able engineers, who make a personal inspection of every establishment connected with mining operations; and a report is carefully drawn up from materials supplied by these officers, and presented every year to the Minister of Public Works. These reports present a most elaborate view of every branch of mineral industry in each department of the kingdom; and from tables, the result of which will be given hereafter, it will be seen at what a rapid rate of increase the mineral resources of France have of late years been developed—a rate which Mr. Porter thought might reasonably suggest the probability of its being in some part owing to the public attention having been drawn to the subject, and still more to suggestions offered to the proprietors of works by accomplished engineers at times when the works have been inspected. The increase in the value of coal, iron, lead, antimony, copper, manganese, alum, and sulphate of iron, since the system of inspection was begun, has been from 105,750,995 francs, (4,230,039*l.*), in 1832, to 154,228,455 fr. (6,169,138*l.*), in 1836, or 45 per cent., as under:—

	1832.	1836.
	Francs.	Francs.
Coal, Lignite, and Anthracite .... }	16,079,670	26,607,071
Iron and Steel	87,312,994	124,384,616
Silver and Lead	856,673	821,534
Antimony.............	71,233	305,032
Copper	247,680	196,924
Manganese............	105,150	152,671
Alum & Sulphate of Iron	1,077,595	1,760,607
Total.........	105,750,995	154,228,455

The increase experienced in the same branches during the four years that preceded these inspections, viz. from 1828 to 1832, amounted to no more than 304,392 fr., or 12,175*l.*, while the increased experienced during an equal period under the system of inspection, viz. from 1832 to 1836, has been, as above stated, 48,477,460 fr., or 1,939,098*l.*

Coal.—There are 46 coal-fields *(Bassins houillers)* from which that mineral is obtained in France. These coal-fields are situated in the following departments, 30 in number, which are here arranged in the order of their productiveness, as shown by the quantity procured in 1835, and stated in English tons:—

	Tons.		Tons.
Loire	812,914	Rhône	7,463
Nord	531,605	Mayenne	6,206
Saône et Loire..	142,149	Ardéche	5,229
Aveyron	119,152	Pas-de-Calais	3,786
Gard..........	45,569	Moselle	3,015
Calvados	41,511	Corréze..........	1,763
Nièvre.........	30,162	Creuse	1,576
Haute Loire	21,863	Vosges	1,356
Loire Inférieure	21,742	Dordogne	1,000
Tarn..........	13,420	Haut Rhin	537
Hérault.......	16,201	Vendée.........	504
Haute Saône....	16,128	Bas Rhin........	177
Allier..........	13,826	Cantal	177
Maine et Loire ..	11,556	Lot.............	60
Puy-de-Dôme ..	11,387	Aude...........	22

There are forty-five separate mining establishments, which extend over an area of 42,038 English acres. A table is subjoined, in which are stated the quanity and value, in English measure and money, of the coal, lignite, and anthracite respectively, raised in all the departments of France in each year, from 1814 to 1826. It will be seen from this table that the produce has been increased from 675,747 tons, in 1814, to 2,583,587 tons in 1835, or 282 per cent. If this interval of time is divided into three nearly equal periods, the average annual produce in each period has been as follows :

7 years---1814 to 1820... 792,496 tons.
8 "   1821 " 1828...1,197,491 "   Increase, 51 per cent.
8 "   1829 " 1836...1,536,531 "   53 "
                                        from 2nd period.

The increase, comparing the 1st and 3rd periods, is 131 per cent.

The whole number of mines in operations in 1836 was,—

Coal.......... 189—employing 19,813 workmen.
Lignite 44   "   1,181   "
Anthracite 25   "   919   "

Total..... 258   "   21,913   "

Great as the increase has been of late years in the produce of French coal-mines, the inspectors predict that this branch of the national industry will shortly exhibit a more rapid progress than any hitherto seen. Large establishments are in the course of formation in the great field of the Loire, as well as in other localities ; and it is expected that the opening of cheaper means of communication will give an impulse to coal-mining in quarters where it has hitherto been scarcely attempted.

STATEMENT of the QUANTITY and VALUE of COAL, LIGNITE, and ANTHRACITE, raised in FRANCE, in each year, from 1814 to 1836.

Years.	COAL.		LIGNITE.		ANTHRACITE.		TOTAL.	
	Tons.	Value.	Tons.	Value.	Tons.	Value.	Tons.	Value.
		£.		£.		£.		£.
1814	636,835	261,112	23,086	9,161	5,689	1,824	665,610	272,097
1815	715,276	324,823	23,300	11,608	5,735	1,985	744,311	338,416
1816	764,785	322,648	25,504	11,239	4,723	1,646	795,812	335,533
1817	815,229	342,976	27,349	16,060	4,579	1,579	847,141	360,615
1818	723,471	313,704	29,600	14,562	5,018	2,120	758,089	330,396
1819	761,809	333,518	44,113	11,846	8,037	4,374	813,950	349,738
1820	871,980	376,114	43,977	21,464	7,405	3,827	923,362	395,405
1821	913,213	395,771	39,122	19,344	5,676	2,490	958,011	417,605
1822	950,899	400,842	48,603	21,316	8,220	3,773	1,007,722	425,931
1823	950,642	404,846	49,194	22,399	9,313	4,507	1,009,149	431,752
1824	1,065,016	435,695	41,032	19,897	13,222	6,481	1,119,270	462,073
1825	1,176,538	482,698	59,242	25,008	23,374	9,915	1,259,154	517,621
1826	1,217,963	520,812	68,116	29,201	14,966	5,992	1,301,045	556,005
1827	1,344,432	557,130	57,838	35,214	25,483	12,185	1,427,753	604,529
1828	1,403,239	565,733	64,939	26,764	29,647	14,969	1,497,825	607,466
1829	1,378,136	539,347	59,719	22,747	32,512	16,884	1,470,367	579,478
1830	1,477,313	582,118	64,348	24,600	30,761	16,221	1,572,622	622,939
1831	1,403,124	549,452	52,513	19,723	30,631	16,726	1,486,268	585,901
1832	1,540,636	600,389	69,177	22,314	39,898	20,483	1,657,211	643,186
1833	1,633,776	672,393	58,274	26,160	45,180	25,288	1,737,230	724,341
1834	1,962,085	748,946	86,064	31,166	53,987	30,715	2,102,136	810,827
1835	1,957,022	793,291	101,508	39,433	57,603	35,532	2,116,133	865,246
1836	2,394,299	1,000,018	96,340	36,514	54,296	27,750	2,544,835	1,064,282

In this Table metrical quintals are converted into English tons at the rate of 10,1455 metrical quintals to a ton, and francs are reduced to sterling money at the exchange of 25 fr. per pound sterling: fractions are discarded.

During the years embraced in the foregoing table the use of coal in France has increased in a greater degree than the productiveness of the mines, as will be seen from the following statement of the quantity imported for consumption (*commerce spécial*), in each year from 1815 to 1836 :—

	Tons.		Tons.
1815	245,658	1826	495,325
1816	315,815	1827	531,800
1817	235,269	1828	570,010
1818	277,624	1829	539,247
1819	284,102	1830	621,459
1820	276,795	1831	532,259
1821	315,785	1832	547,251
1822	392,192	1833	686,116
1823	321,497	1834	730,281
1824	456,644	1835	755,865
1825	499,325	1836	949,573

The greater importations of the last three years have been encouraged by a partial diminution in the rate of duty on consumption—a measure rendered necessary by the rapid extension of steam navigation.

Iron.—At the present time France occupies the second rank among nations as regards the production of iron, England being still immeasurably in advance of France, in which country the extension of this branch of industry is far less than has been effected of late years with us. There are at this time in France twelve distinct localities or districts, in which the making of iron is prosecuted, which are thus distinguished in the official reports :—1. Group of the North-east ; 2. of the North-west ; 3. of the Vosges ; 4. of the Jura: 5. of Champagne and Burgundy ; 6. of the Centre ; 7. of the Indre and La Vendée ; 8. of the coal-fields of the South ; 9. of Perigord ; 10. of the Alps ; 11. of the Landes ; 12. of the Pyrenees.

The actual and relative importance of these groups may be seen from the following particulars, given in the Report presented in the present year, and having reference to the working of 1836.

Group.	Number of Iron Works	Number of Workmen.	Quantity of Fuel in Tons and Steres.				Quantity of Products.			Value of Products in English Money.
			Wood. Charcoal.	Coke.	Coal.	Wood.	Cast Iron.	Bar Iron	Steel.	
			Tons.	Tons.	Tons.	Steres.	Tons.	Tons.	Tons.	£.
1	94	2,288	90,844	3,530	8,280	38,583	46,233	30,450	162	530,599
2	59	1,771	54,051	..	2,964	..	23,755	11,182	..	219,238
3	7	388	..	7,315	24,830	..	2,226	9,189	..	147,560
4	148	2,090	126,754	..	910	..	54,737	28,900	581	652,030
5	152	2,807	189,602	..	49,947	..	81,490	42,309	..	691,528
6	124	2,133	71,098	14,094	35,798	..	36,993	27,029	766	501,862
7	21	499	17,564	..	..	..	5,824	2,870	..	61,865
8	15	1,243	..	87,444	115,038	..	28,440	27,276	..	877,158
9	115	1,175	89,120	..	8,399	..	14,893	9,064	96	173,644
10	39	174	6,614	..	251	..	2,021	282	1,120	5,916
11	21	410	17,466	..	32	478	7,118	3,674	..	62,585
12	99	815	30,742	..	..	..	..	9,466	..	171,140
	894	15,738	593,855	112,386	232,399	34,061	303,739	201,691	2,725	3,585,737

The figures given in the foregoing table do not present in all their importance the extent of this branch of industry in France. The number of workmen employed for the production of pig-iron (*fonte*), malleable iron (*gros fer*), and steel, which alone are there included, does not much exceed one-third of the number engaged in all the various processes of the iron manufacture ; and the total value of the material produced, instead of being, as in the above statement, 3,585,739*l.*, amounted in 1836, according to the returns of the inspectors, to 4,975,424*l.* The following abstract contains all that it appears desirable to offer on this occasion, and presents under five principal divisions the total number of workmen engaged in the manufacture, with the value created by them in each of those divisions :—

	Number of workmen.	Value created.
		£.
1. Extraction and Preparation of the Ore	17,557	500,632
2. Production of Pig-Iron (*fonte*)	6,776	1,969,182
3. Production of Malleable Iron (*gros fer*)	8,678	1,506,247
4. Founding, Drawing, Rolling, &c.	8,615	812,466
5. Converting, Moulding, Casting, &c. Steel	2,149	186,927
Total	43,775	4,975,424

Rather more than 40 per cent. of the value here stated is made up of the cost of the fuel used in the various processes, viz.—

	£.
Wood Charcoal	£1,643,826
Wood	15,046
Coke	96,972
Coal	295,235
Peat	694
	£2,089,767

This sum is divided among the different processes in the following proportions:—

	£.	Decim. Propn.
1. Roasting the Ore	1,782	0.087
2. Smelting	1,152,039	55.508
3. Refining, Puddling Furnaces, &c. &c.	787,888	36.175
4. Casting, Drawing, Rolling, &c.	121,556	5.959
5. Moulding, Casting, &c. Steel	46.502	2.279
Total	2,089,767	100.000

It will be seen that four-fifths in value of the fuel is composed of wood. Coke was not used in the iron-works of France until 1821, and at the present time is employed almost exclusively for processes subsequent to smelting the ore. The proportionate value of different kinds of fuel consumed in the various processes in each year, from 1833 to 1836, has been :—

	1833	1834	1835	1836
Wood Charcoal	0.838	0.818	0.864	0.806
Coal	0.098	0.129	0.098	0.140
Coke	0.062	0.050	0.037	0.048
Wood	0.002	0.003	0.001	0.006
	1.000	1.000	1.000	1.000

The average prices of the different kinds of fuel in 1836, as stated in the Report, were—

Wood Charcoal	54s.	10d. per ton.
Coal	18	5
Coke	20	3
Wood	2	10 per stere.

The increased proportion of wood, observable in the working of 1836, is caused by the substitution in part, in some works, of wood dried by heat or partially carbonized. By the introduction of a proportion of dry wood in place of charcoal, a diminution in the cost of fuel has been attained, but against this advantage must be placed the smaller produce obtained from the furnace in a given time, as well as a diminution of metal from a given quantity of ore.— Where wood charcoal alone is used for smelting, it requires eighteen metrical quintals for the production of thirteen metrical quintals of iron. Where coke and coal are used in the proportion of ten of the former to nine of the latter, it requires about three quintals of fuel to produce one quintal of iron. In some cases, coke is used with charcoal in the proportion of one quintal of coke to two quintals of charcoal, and the produce has been eight quintals of iron for ten quintals of fuel. In the first case (where wood charcoal is used), the cost of the fuel has been 9.92 fr. per metrical quintal of iron, or 4l. 0s. 6d. per English ton. The cost when coke and coal are used, is stated to be 4.45 fr. per quintal, or 36s. 1½d. per ton; and in the third case, where coke and charcoal are mixed, the cost is said to be 7.60 fr. per quintal, or 3l. 1s. 8d. per ton. The value assigned to the produce is,—

	Per ton.
In the first case, 20.99fr. per quint., equal to	£8 10. 4
In the 2nd case, 11.13fr. " "	4 10 4
In the 3rd case, 20.32fr. " "	8 4 11

The mixture of coke and charcoal would, upon the whole, appear to be the most profitable in its result. Deducting from the value of the metal the sum expended for fuel, there would remain, when charcoal alone is used, 4l. 9s. 10d. per ton; when coal and coke are used, 2l. 14s. 2½d. per ton; and when coke and charcoal are used, 5l. 3s. 3d. per ton. These calculations are of course wholly inapplicable to the circumstances in which the manufacture is placed in this country, from the actual and relative cheapness of our mineral fuel. The use of the hot blast has been adopted in several of the furnaces in France. At first it was found that the iron thus obtained was not so well adapted for making bar iron as that for the smelting of which cold air had been used; but some modifications, which are not particularized in the Reports, have been introduced into the process, and this advantage has been remedied. No account is given of the quantity of iron made in France earlier than 1824; but from that year the account is regularly stated in the Reports from which the following abstract has been computed :—

	Pig-Iron.	Malleable Iron.
	English Tons.	English Tons.
1824	194,636	139,564
1825	196,588	141,896
1826	202,756	145,098
1827	213,175	146,671
1828	217,604	149,117
1829	213,868	151,319
1830	222,965	146,242
1831	221,423	139,942
1832	221,660	141,835
1833	232,559	149,967
1834	266,028	174,507
1835	290,378	205,396
1836	306,789	201,891

As in the case of coals, the importations of foreign iron into France have kept pace with the increase in the native production. The Custom House accounts of that country are detailed with great minuteness; but it is not necessary here to particularize the quantities of each description of foreign iron used in France. The value so consumed in each year since 1815, and the amount of duty collected on the same, were as follows:—

Years.	Value of Foreign Iron imported for use.	Amount of duty collected	Years.	Value of Foreign Iron imported for use.	Amount of duty collected.
	£.	£.		£.	£.
1815	87,556	29,848	1826	218,212	130,326
1816	98,963	45,690	1827	186,846	98,960
1817	202,305	122,024	1828	179,635	95,073
1818	163,173	89,491	1829	150,625	84,396
1819	164,238	94,180	1830	187,117	100,476
1820	162,107	81,517	1831	121,185	63,644
1821	226,571	126,945	1832	155,222	82,193
1822	144,193	74,540	1833	174,601	91,569
1823	141,501	86,258	1834	200,573	104,598
1824	164,812	94,167	1835	231,208	121,346
1825	150,690	86,904	1836	252,702	122,843

The production in France of metals, other than iron, is of little or no commercial importance at the present time. The whole value created in the articles of lead and silver, antimony, copper, and manganese, amounted in 1836 to less than 60,000l., and gave employment to only 1760 workmen. In noticing this fact, the inspectors encourage the hope that some considerable addition may shortly be made to the produce of mining industry applied to the articles just enumerated; they do not, however, explain the grounds upon which this hope should be entertained, further than by noticing the existence in the country of several promising fields for that industry hitherto allowed to remain unproductive, and by stating that they are occupied in collecting information which may serve to facilitate the future attempts of persons desirous of embarking their energies and their capital in this direction.

Lead and Silver.—There are eleven lead mines in operation in France, situated as under:—

		Tons.		£.
Hautes Alpes	2, produced in 1836,	46,	valued at	1,175
Finistere ...	1	504	"	11,692
Gard	1	4	"	80
Isere	1	54	"	848
Loire	1	22	"	260
Lozere	1	47	"	1,816
Puy-de-Dome	1	30	"	740
Rhone	3	6	"	98
	11	713		£16,209

The silver obtained from the soil of France is separated from the produce of some of the lead mines above mentioned: the quantity and value thus yielded in 1836 were—

Hautes Alpes	203 lb.	valued at	£660
Finistere	3,517	"	11,542
Lozere	1,028	"	3,388
Puy-de-Dome	324	"	1,060
	5,072		£16,650

The value put upon this produce in the Report is thus 5s. 6d. per oz.

The quantity of lead of native production supplies but a small part of the wants of the country. The importations into France from foreign countries, principally Spain, for consumption during the five years from 1832 to 1836, have averaged 14,800 tons per annum.

Antimony.—This mineral is produced in France from eleven mines, viz.

		Tons.		£.
Allier	1, prod. in 1836,	138,	valued at	3,864
Ardache	1	63	"	1,944
Gard........	1	23	"	628
Haute-Loire..	2	22	"	652
Lozere	4	35	"	960
Puy-de-Dame	2	130	"	4,073
	11	411		£12,121

Copper.—The produce of copper mines in France, five in number, is inconsiderable: three of these mines are in the department of Hautes Alpes, and two are in the department of the Rhone. The quantity of metallic copper which they yielded in 1836 was only 102 tons, and its value 7,877l. The yearly consumption of foreign copper, principally the produce of Russia and of England, during the five years from 1832 to 1836, has averaged 6,235 tons.

Manganese.—The manganese mines are situated as follows:—

		Tons.		£.
Allier	1, prod. in 1836,	365,	valued at	1,628
Aude........	1	148	"	570
Dordogne ...	3	215	"	951
Haute-Saone	1	39	"	31
Saone-et-Loire	1	900	"	2,926
	7 Mines.	1,667 Tons.		£6,106

The engineers to whom the task of inspecting the mining establishments of France is intrusted, have not confined their inquiries to the objects which have been noticed in this paper: they have included in their Annual Reports the statistics of various branches of industry in which mineral substances are produced or employed ; such as bituminous minerals—alum—sulphate of iron—and salt ; the produce of quarries—of glass-houses—of porcelain and pottery manufactories—of copper and zinc works—and of chemical processes. By this means, it is shown that the number of workmen who, in 1836, depended for subsistence upon mining operations and their consequences, amounted to 273,364 ; while the total value created by their joint labour amounted to 377,684,791 fr., or 15,107,392l. viz :—

	Esta-blish-ments	Work-men.	Value created.
			Francs.
Coal, Lignite, Anthra-cite, and Peat	2,219	55,735	30,533,922
Iron and Steel	—	43,775	124,385,616
Lead, Silver, Copper, Antimony, Manga-nese..............	—	1,770	1,476,161
Bitumens	6	245	192,128
Alum and Sulphate of Iron..............	19	1,141	1,760,667
Salt.................	—	16,615	10,397,164
Quarries.............	—	70,396	40,350,419
Glass Manufactures....	—	10,497	47,274,301
Porcelain, Pottery, and Earthenware........	—	20,485	27,418,122
Bricks and Tiles, and Lime	—	44,604	51,939,239
Plaster	—	4,298	14,713,796
Chemical Products....	—	2,216	22,043,732
Copper, Zinc, & Lead Works............	—	1,597	4,999,524
		273,874	377,684,791

Dr. Bowring observed, that this Report, like every report communicated by government agents, gave far too favourable a view of the mineral prosperity of France. Two of the institutions to which reference had been made—the mining establishments of Bassin du Creussot, and the iron-works of Decazeville—were not merely losing, but ruinous concerns; and the latter had been forced to import pig-iron from England. The injurious effects of the perversion of French industry to branches of production, for which the country possessed no natural advantages, was evidenced by comparing the number of ploughs in an agricultural district of France, with a district of the same extent in England, and the result would show that our country had the advantage, in the proportion of five to one. The cottagers in France, as most travellers have observed, were generally destitute of carpenters' tools, nails, and other little implements necessary to economy and comfort. Though the French engineers talked of the increased productiveness of their mines, they did not add, that iron in France was from 5l. to 7l. per ton dearer than in England; and as 300,000 tons of iron are annually consumed in that country, it followed that the French were taxed to the amount of more than a million and a half annually, to afford speculators in mines an opportunity of ruining themselves. — Mr. Felkin considered it of vital importance to have a correct statistical account of our mineral and manufacturing resources published to the world. Though the speculations to which Dr. Bowring had referred, had proved ruinous to the projectors, yet they were not abandoned; and it would be idle to deny, in reference to the competitive

situation of England and France, that machinery and fixed capital, accumulated on a spot, must be worked, even at a loss; and he believed that the Manchester manufacturers had already felt such establishments to be a thorn in their side. The workmen of France were a patient, industrious, and temperate race. The state of the Savings' Banks in that country reflected great credit on the character of the operatives, and was calculated to gratify every person who, laying aside the prejudices and jealousies of country, was gratified by the progressive improvement of our race, no matter in what locality, as a triumph of philanthropy.

" On a new Day and Night Telegraph," by Joseph Garnett.

The paper on this subject was accompanied by a model, to exhibit the construction and method of working the telegraph, which it is proposed should consist of two ladders, about forty-one feet long, framed together at about twenty-four inches asunder at the bottom, and twenty at the top, so as to constitute the frame for the machinery. There are two arms, one at the top, the other about midway up the frame-work, counterpoised by weights, and worked by machinery, consisting of eight bevel mitre wheels. At the bottom of the frame-work, is a dial plate, with a pointer, and the workman, in setting the pointer, brings the arm of the telegraph into the required corresponding position. The paper proceeded to describe the mechanical adjustments, and was accompanied by tables of the day and night signals, each of which contains fifty-six variations of the arms. The night signals are made by covering the lamps in a particular order. For instance, two vertical lamps covered designate twenty—two horizontal ones covered thirty—and so on.

" Description of an improved method of constructing large Secretaires and Writing Tables," by Thomas Sopwith.

The great loss of time to persons engaged in extensive official business, in consequence of the difficulty of arranging numerous sets of papers, and of obtaining access to them when so arranged, induced the author to take this opportunity of describing a table invented by himself, and which had been extremely serviceable to him. The principle is, that by opening a single lock, the whole of the drawers, closets, and partitions are opened. These are so disposed, also, as to admit of every thing being reached without the person stirring from his seat. They are all entirely closed again by a single spring lock. It would be impossible to convey a proper idea of this ingenious invention without sectional plans and elevations: but the President, and many present, expressed their admiration of the arrangements, and of the convenience which such a table must be to every person engaged in an extensive correspondence, or having many sets of papers on various subjects. One contrivance is peculiarly worth mentioning. Within this case Mr. Sopwith hangs up his various keys. On any key being removed, a small counter-balance weight, or bolt, drops down, and remains down until the key is replaced. This bolt effectually prevents the closing of the case. If, then, the person should forget to replace the key which has been removed, he is immediately reminded of it, by being unable to close the case. The principle and contrivances are applicable to many various arrangements of drawers and partitions.

"On the Power of Econ mising and Regulating Heat, for Domestic Purposes," by George Webb Hall.

The author insisted on the necessity of having the backs of the fire-places vertical, and the apertures of the chimneys as contracted as possible; and he described the results of his experiments. One principle to be universally attended to in close fire-places is, that the burning fuel be surrounded by a substance retentive of heat, and capable of radiating it back upon the fire itself. This is attained by covering the fire itself with a species of fire-brick, and only allowing a very small aperture for the escape of the heat thus forced off at the highest degree attainable, then to be economised by close confinement and regulation. The economy of heat when attained, consists in conducting the hot air through long and horizontal flues, so as to counteract as much as possible its tendency to ascend, which tendency is exactly proportional to the temperature. The author illustrated the preceding paper by details of the arrangements which he had adopted and alluded especially to the researches of Rumford on this subject.

Sir John Robison remarked, that he had paid considerable attention to this subject, and to its practical applications; but he had done nothing more than endeavour to follow out the principles which were laid down by Mr. Sylvester, in his account of Mr. Strutt's method of warming the Derby Infirmary. He would also call attention to the accounts in *Loudon's Cottage Economy*, and to two papers in the *Architectural Magazine*, (see *Mechanics' Magazine*, vol. 27, p. 12, 21, 47) the one by Dr. Ure, the other by Mr. Ritchie, on the subject of warming and ventilating. —The President remarked, that great care was requisite in all experiments on the above subjects, especially with reference to the heat of smoke in the flues. He had once observed the smoke, at two feet from the exit, to be 196° Fahrenheit, the water in the hot water apparatus being 260° Fahrenheit; the

slightest change in one damper caused the temperature of the smoke in the flue to fall almost immediately to 160° Fahrenheit, and that of the water to rise to 290° Fahrenheit. Thus, by a slight alteration in the damper, about 60° Fahrenheit was saved.

Sir John Robison, at a subsequent meeting, stated that he had omitted to mention a circumstance, which he considered of peculiar importance to the lower orders. Mr. Strutt, of Derby, to whom the country owed so much, had some years ago expressed to him an opinion, that coal-gas would be found, by the lower orders, the cheapest fuel for cooking. This he had applied; and the whole apparatus, which might be considered as the converse of the Davy safety lamp, consisted in fixing a piece of wire-gauze at the extremity of a gas-pipe of about six inches diameter. He referred to the account in Loudon's *Encyclopædia of Cottage Architecture*, for some valuable remarks and directions on this subject. The wire-gauze was liable to be destroyed under a long-continued intense heat: this, however, was obviated by sprinkling a small quantity of sand upon it. Bulk for bulk, gas was more expensive than coal, but the former was more economical and convenient for occasional use, and the smaller operations in cooking.

"Notices on the Resistance of Water," by John Scott Russell.

Mr. Russell stated, that the observations he had to offer might be considered as a sequel to what had been given at the preceding meetings of the Association (see *Mechanics' Magazine*, vol. 27, p. 448). He and Sir John Robison had been constituted a committee to prosecute the investigation of the motion of waves, and other problems in hydrodynamics, the results of which would be given in the Physical section. But, as they went on, they had met with some results of great value to the practical man; of these he now proposed to give a brief acount. The general problem was, the resistance of a fluid to a floating solid. Now, this is a department of science of which we are avowedly ignorant; so much so, that some of our best vessels are acknowledged to be constructed by the rule of thumb, as it is termed—that is, by knowledge gained from a repeated series of trials and errors, and not on any fixed scientific principles. It had been ascertained in previous investigations, that the action of a solid on the water is very different from the action of fluid when impinging on a solid. These actions had formerly been considered the same. The solid causes an elevation; the elevation puts the water in motion. Thus, the question of resistance resolves itself into that of the motion of waves. Waves are of various kinds. The laws of the great primary wave had been laid down in previous communications. Its velocity depends simply on the depth of the fluid. The old law of resistance, as the source of the velocity, is too small so long as the velocity of the solid is less than that of the wave, but too great so soon as the velocity of the solid becomes greater than that of the wave. Mr. Russell then detailed some experiments which had led to the above law, and from which it appeared, that the form of the vessel of least resistance depends as well on the velocity with which it is to move, as on the velocity of the wave; also, that the form which is best for moving with a velocity less than the velocity of the wave, may be worst for moving with a velocity greater than that of the wave. The consideration of the laws of this wave reconcile many of the discrepancies in experiments on this subject. Mr. Russell then proceeded to describe some remarkable facts, which they had observed on the motion of the particles constituting this wave; the particles had a vertical and a horizontal motion, and the extent of the motion depended on the force of the wave. Another remarkable result is, that the ordinates of the vessel should correspond with the ordinates of the wave; a form so constructed would separate the water without any apparent elevation or white ripple, which was common to all other forms. The form is that which belongs to the wave, which is to move with the particular velocity of the vessel.

The accompanying diagrams will serve to convey a more distinct idea of the nature of the motion of the particles of the water.

Fig. 1.

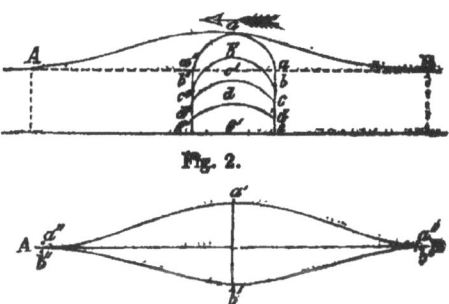

Fig. 2.

Fig 1 shows the form of the wave, and the lines of translation of the particles during the transit; A d′ B the line of the wave; a d′ d″, b b′ b″ c d′ c″, &c. lines of translation of the particles during the transit.

Fig. 2 shows how the lines of a vessel are to be formed so as to produce a displacement analogous to the displacement of the wave, and so move through the fluid with the least resistance.

"On the Principles of Oblique Bridges," by P. Nicholson.

The oblique arch, an invention of comparatively recent date, has been rendered necessary by the general adoption of railways, and by the necessity which exists for their being carried forward in lines as direct as possible. The theory of this arch is attended with some difficulty, and the author lays down in this paper the principles by which the engineer should be guided. Five of the faces of each stone are to be prepared in such a manner that four of them recede from the fifth, and when the stones are arranged in courses, the surfaces of the fifth faces form one continued cylindric surface, which is the intrados, and the other four faces form the beds and ends of the stones in which they join each other. In every course two of the opposite courses of the first stone, two of the opposite surfaces of the second stone, and so on, form two continued surfaces throughout the whole length of each course, and the edge of each of these continued surfaces in the intrados will be a spiral line. If a straight line be drawn through any point in one of the spiral lines perpendicular to the axis of the cylinder, the straight line will coincide with that continued surface which is a bed of that course, and the straight line thus drawn will be a tangent to the curved surface of the cylinder at that point in the spiral line; the straight line then drawn will be perpendicular to another straight line, which is a tangent to the spiral line at that point. The intrados being developed, the spiral lines which form the edges of the courses will be parallel, and their distances equal, and the spiral lines which are the edges of the ends of the stones will be developed in straight lines perpendicular to those lines which are the developements of the spirals of the edges of the courses. From these principles a simple geometrical construction may be deduced, such as the workman can readily use. To construct an arch on the above principle, it is only necessary to know the angle of obliquity of the acute-angled pier, the width of the arch within its abutments, the height of the intrados above the level of the springing, the perpendicular distance between the planes and the two faces, and the number of arch stones in each elevation. The author then detailed some examples illustrative of this method.

' Remarks on the Material and Mechanical construction of Steam Boilers," by W. Greener.

Mr. Greener is of opinion, that the accidents which happen to steam-boilers are principally due to defect in the material of which they are constructed; and he details several experiments made on slips of iron cut from plates of different quality. He found that slips cut latitudinally from a plate, bore less by 30 per cent. than slips of the same dimensions cut longitudinally; in some cases the difference was much greater. He also had immersed plates in a mixture of sulphuric acid and water, and found that the injury done in twenty-four hours varied from $6\frac{1}{4}$ to 15 per cent. of the original strength. Many boilers will stand so long as the form remains perfect; but should any part, as the crown of the arch in cylindrical boilers, collapse, an accident is inevitable.

A communication was read from Mr. Maule, "On a Substitute for the Forcing Pump in supplying Steam-Boilers, &c." It was the well-known contrivance of a hollow cock, having an orifice, which, being uppermost, the plug became filled with the liquid, and then, being turned half round by the motion of the piston, the liquid could run into the vessel below.

Sir John Robison explained a model of the bucket of a pump in use in Sweden, the peculiar feature of which was, that the pressure of the sides of the bucket outwards against the pipe is exactly proportional to the load to be raised. This bucket is peculiarly applicable for raising foul water.

"A New Rotatory Steam-Engine," by S. Rowley. (See *Mech. Mag.* No. 784.)

The inventor being absent, Mr. Evans undertook to bring this before the section; and having pointed out the construction, stated, that the only novelty in this consisted in the eccentric being on the inside. Many present condemned the rotatory engine as mechanically impracticable. Many of the most talented mechanics in this country had given up the attempt after repeated trials. It was argued, that no theoretical advantage can be gained by it; and that though there might be some circumstances under which economy of space and first cost were of such import-

ance that the most expensive wear and tear can be borne, yet no prudent man would purchase an engine which might ruin him in the repairs. It is not sufficient to have a good theory; the powers of mechanical construction must be considered. Many inventions which, thirty years ago, might have been lost, because they were antecedent to the march of the mechanical art, would now, in the wonderfully advanced state of this art, be generally introduced.

"Report on Railway Constants," by Dr. Lardner.

Dr. Lardner stated, that at the last meeting of the Association a sum of money had been voted for the purpose of ascertaining certain railway constants,—that is, the force of traction on a level plane; the resistance due to friction, to curves, to the atmosphere; how the force of the wheels and the carriages influenced the motion. He then explained the causes which had prevented the experiments being made, and that, consequently, he had nothing to report as experimentally determined on the above subject; but that he had that instant received a set of experiments on the above subjects, made, at his request, by Mr. Woods, the resident engineer of the Liverpool and Manchester Railway, a young man whose excessive modesty alone prevented his occupying the position which his talents could claim. Some of these results, especially those relating to the effect of the resistance of the atmosphere, he then alluded to. He then described the various methods which had been proposed for the determination of the constants in question. These differed in no respect from the statements which were made last year at Liverpool, and which were then fully reported in our pages. (See Vol. 28, page 76.) He also described a dynamometer, by which the traction might be measured with considerable accuracy; and concluded by adverting to the great experiment which was now trying on the Great Western Railway, with respect to the gauge of seven feet instead of four feet eight inches.

———

Tuesday evening was devoted to the description and explanation of some of the most remarkable mechanical models, exhibited during this meeting at the rooms of the Central Exchange; but it was not known until a late hour.

Professor Babbage, said, that when at Berlin, ten years ago, he was present at one of the German Associations, in which the sciences and arts were equally represented; and so delighted was he, that he laboured to impart a share of his pleasure to his friends, and from the letters he then wrote, the first impulse was taken, which led to the

models collected in the exhibition room were interesting, not merely to the mechanist, but to the higher classes, for it must be a great source of pleasure to know how the various articles of luxury and ornament were produced. The subjects which he had undertaken to illustrate, were the arts of engraving on copper and wood, and of taking impressions from hollow and raised plates or blocks. He then showed my models and diagrams, that the great difficulty in wood engraving or the raised die, was to obtain black lines crossing each other, and in copper-plate to obtain white lines crossing each other. Having noticed various mechanical contrivances for overcoming these difficulties, he described the art of printing in colours from wood blocks, and directed the attention of the members to specimens sent to the model room by Mr. Knight, declaring that the exertions of that publisher were likely to bring all the processes of wood engraving to a degree of perfection without parallel and beyond expectation. He then mentioned Mr. Woone's process, by which, in the raised die, black lines crossing each other had been obtained; a polished brass plate was thinly covered with plaster, and on this surface the process of sunk engravings could of course be easily performed, and then by taking a cast, the raised engraving might be obtained. He directed attention to the advantages resulting from the multiplication of engravings by the stereotype process, and particularly mentioned its application to the representation of the parts of machinery in detail. The Professor concluded by directing attention to a detector lock, which had been placed in the model room, but stated that its merits could only be understood by inspection.

The Rev. Dr. Robinson, of Armagh, then addressed the meeting. He felt great difficulty, he said, in following a person of such eminence as the President of the Mechanical Section; but when he looked at the model which he had undertaken to illustrate, that of the wooden viaduct over the Ouseburn, he felt that its architect was fairly entitled to the reward offered by the tyrant of old for the invention of a new pleasure. The stupendous edifices of Egypt, the splendid architecture of Greece, when compared with a bridge, were but specimens of magnificent barbarity. Although the art of constructing bridges had been long known, yet recent events had given it new developements; the destructive agents, fire and water, had been pressed into our service, and compelled to minister to our wants: like the evil spirits in the Arab tales, they had been forced to become slaves of the

lamp and the ring, and to obey the behests of the magician. Dr. Robinson then entered into a minute history of the various contrivances employed for bridges, which he illustrated by models, from the simple plank and rope, to the bridge of Schaffhausen, and the structure over the Ouseburn. In the latter, he said, a new element had to be provided for; the architect had not only to provide for the transit of weight, but for that of bodies coming with the velocity of the lightning, and the resistless force of the thunderbolt; stone could not be used in its construction, for the extensive mines in the vicinity might render the foundation insecure: iron was so elastic that it might suddenly break from the intensity and rapidity of the shock given by the locomotive engines. He then pointed out all the contrivances in the structure for the distribution of stress, assigning the use of almost every beam. He said that many might be inclined to lament that such an edifice had been built with perishable materials, but by a recent discovery—which, perhaps, more than any other, illustrated the connexion between the sciences—wood had been rendered durable. He then minutely described the Kyanizing process, with which, of course, our readers are familiar.

Professor Willis then exhibited a model of a new locomotive engine, and explained all its parts. The merit of the new engine consists in its having a contrivance for changing the direction of the valve without an excentric motion on the shaft.

Mr. Dent read a paper "On the Construction of a portable Mercurial Pendulum, accompanied by Experiments."

The mercurial pendulum having a glass cistern containing the mercury, is not well calculated for sending abroad. The use of glass is suspended, in the present case, by substituting a cistern made entirely of cast-iron, which not only possesses portability, but other advantages; for in this cistern the mercury can be boiled to expel the bubbles of air. Before adopting iron for the cistern, it was obviously necessary to ascertain, by repeated experiments, the effect of that metal on the enclosed mercury, as regarded variations in temperature, when compared with glass. In prosecuting these experiments, a remarkable effect of radient heat was observed on these materials, worthy of being brought before the Association, as well as the description of the new mercurial pendulum, to the construction of which these experiments were subservient. The cistern is made entirely of cast-iron: the adoption of this metal admitted of the cistern being turned perfectly cylindrical within and without, and of thus simplifying the elements of calculation for the height of a perfect cylinder of mercury requisite for compensating the effects of variable temperature on the rod, an advantage which the use of glass did not allow. The homogeneity of the material also facilitates the reductions for temperature, by equilizing this throughout, and also admits of the bearings being diminished in number, and simplified in construction, when compared with the usual mercurial pendulum having glass cisterns. The suspending rod passes through a hollow screw, and is secured by a pin going through both. The hollow screw passes through the axis of the cistern, and the cistern is constructed to move round this screw, which admits of shortening or lengthening the pendulum for alteration in time. The edge of the cap belonging to the cistern is graduated, which subdivides the threads of the screw on the cistern being turned round for alteration in time. There is an aperture on the top of the jar, which allows of mercury being added or removed without unscrewing the cap of the cistern. This aperture is closed by a screw, which, as well as that on the cap, has a leathern collar to render the joints perfectly air-tight. Before any experiment on variable temperatures could be proceeded with, it was necessary that an oven (or hot chamber) should be constructed. A wooden case was made, having the door glazed with double glass panes, to admit of reading off the arc of vibration, also the thermometers. This wooden case was lined with a tin casing, which admitted of a current of hot water or air to circulate : the latter, after some experiments, was adopted. Great difficulty was presented by the thermometers at the top and lower part of the case not being of equal temperature—an inequality which would be fatal to the experiments. The obstacle was eventually overcome by introducing into the middle of the cross space below a hemisphere of tin, into the lining of the tin casing, just above the flame of the lamp, the heated air, passed from this reservoir up the two vertical spaces, which were filled with tin cuttings. The quantity and distribution of these cuttings were arranged, by trial, till a thermometer indicated the same temperature at top and bottom of the enclosed space. The top of the vertical sides of the tin casing were closed by that kind of ventilator, technically called a " hit or miss," by which a nice adjustment for the equality of temperature could be obtained. The object, in the first instance was to determine, by experiment, the quantity of mercury to be put into the cistern, adapted to produce the necessary compensation for variation in the length of the rod. This quantity being found, by repeated experiments, to be greater than that which would have been given by calculation, the height being 7.9 inches, it became necessary to determine, by new experiments, what was the effect of the varying elasticity in the spring, by which the pendulum was suspended, produced by changes of temperature, and to separate this quantity from the effects of a variation in length, between the points of suspension and oscillation. To accomplish this, it was necessary that the pendulum should be preserved at a constant and low temperature, while the spring was exposed to a much higher one. For this purpose the pendulum was made to oscillate in a room in which the thermometer was at 52° Fah. ; while a current of heated air was conveyed to the spring from a lamp placed at the other end of a tube. The spring had a circular perforation made in it opposite the end of the tube ; and the bulb of a thermometer being placed opposite the aperture, the temperature of the spring was maintained at 95° for several hours. From this arrangement it was obvious, that if the pendulum was kept at the unvarying temperature of 52°, any change in its rate must be due to an alteration in the elasticity of the spring, and a small quantity due to its elongation, arising from the high temperature to which it was exposed ; and the result of the experiment, as shown by a table, was a loss of 1.9 sec. in twenty-four hours. To render the inquiry complete, it was essential that the error arising from a change in temperature, in the *pendulum rod*, should be determined. A pendulum rod of steel was suspended, 0.293 in. in diameter ; length, 3 ft. 7.1 in., from the spring to the point of attachment of the ball, which was suspended from the *end* of the rod : diameter of ball, 6.5 in., weight, 12.7 lb. The results shown by the table were, that the error due to the elongation of the rod alone, for 47° of Fah., is 12.0 secs. in twenty-four hours ; while that of the varying elasticity and elongation is 1.9 sec. for 48° of Fah. in twenty-four hours. The author believes he was the first who separated the effects on the rates of chronometers arising from the elongation of the balance-spring, from those produced by variations in its elasticity ; and in the present instance has completed the subject, by deducing the corresponding effects in the case of a pendulum In order to try the comparative effects of changes of temperature on mercurial pendulums, with iron instead of glass cisterns, two thermometers were selected, whose scales throughout their range were consistent with each other ; the glass and iron cistern were filled with mercury ; the thermometers immersed up to + 12° Fah., care being taken that the bulbs were in the axis of the cisterns. They were then placed on a table, at two yards from the fire, and the author's attention was first attracted to an inequality in the temperature of the mercury contained in the two cisterns indicated by the thermometers in them. The thermometers were changed, but still the same inequality appeared; that in the glass cistern always indicating a higher temperature by 5° than that in the iron one. To vary the experiment, a book was placed between the fire and each of the cisterns, when the inequality between the indications of the thermometers was reduced to 2°. The Argand lamp, used to observe with, was then removed, under an idea that this discrepancy would be still further reduced,—the room being left without other source of light or heat than the fire, after the lapse of three hours, the two thermometers indicated the same temperature nearly. On again exposing the two cisterns to the effect of direct radiant heat, the increased difference of temperature again appeared as before, between the glass and iron cisterns. These experiments are recorded in a tabulated form, as also is an experiment under similar conditions, with only this difference—that the *surfaces* of both cisterns were *blackened* by a mixture of lamp-black and spirits of wine. Under this arrangement, although exposed to direct radiant heat, no discrepancy appeared between the thermometers placed in the glass or iron cisterns. These experiments, it should be borne in mind. were not undertaken with any view to the effect of radiant heat, *but to determine the relative time of acquiring a certain increment and decrement of heat in the mercury contained in the cisterns* employed in the compensation pendulum, and the same as regards the *rod* of the pendulum. From the tables, which are very elaborate, the following results are deduced:—Mercury acquires increment of heat from 26° to 75° Fah. in 2h. 15m., and the pendulum rod from 30° to 82° in 0h. 34m. Therefore the mercury contained in the cisterns takes upwards of *four times* the interval to arrive at the same temperature as the rod, under similar circumstances. The rod experiment was conducted by taking three small thermometers, and placing them on the rod, one in the centre, and the others at each end, making the contact by an amalgam. A table showing the effect of a strong and weak *suspension spring* was exhibited, giving the time for every decrease of 15m. of arc; from which experiment it was proved, that the length of time a free pendulum continues in vibration, is in the inverse ratio to the strength of the suspension spring of

the pendulum; and that a pendulum suspended by too strong a spring will decrease in its arc to a greater extent than one supported by a weak spring, provided that any diminution of the maintaining force takes place.

Dr. Robinson was glad to see the iron cistern, for it rendered possible the boiling of the mercury in it, which he considered essential. However carefully the vessel was filled, there always remained minute air bubbles between its sides and the mercury, which were liable to changes of place, and could only be removed by this process. This was still more important when (as ought in all cases to be done) a correction depending on the state of the barometer was applied. Dr. R. had deduced this correction for his own clock, by the method of minimum squares. from actual observation; but it was far more easily done by swinging the pendulum in a vacuum apparatus. For the success of this, however, the total absence of air bubbles was requisite; and it had been found by a distinguished astronomer (whose researches, though not yet published, he took the liberty of quoting), that if this precaution were neglected. the same pendulum gave for a change of one inch in the barometer, a variation of rate from 0 to 1.5 seconds per day, the true value being 0.35. He would also profit by the opportunity, to suggest two other matters. The effect of high temperature on the pendulum consisted of two parts—one its own expansion, the other that of the air in which it vibrated. The first only was corrected by the usual compensation; but the other, varying according to a different law, required a separate compensation on a different principle, as the error resulting from its neglect was within the reach of observation. Another point was, the neglect of the old knife-edge suspension; which he considered, in many respects, superior to the spring suspension, as, indeed, was clearly shown by Berthoud, and which he anxiously wished to see on trial among us.—Mr. Dent considered the formation of a knife-edge difficult, and apprehended it would soon be blunted. —Dr. Robinson conceived that it would wear into a small cylinder, which would act as a roller, and still retain its good qualities.

(*To be continued.*)

NOTES AND NOTICES.

Mr. Seaward's Rule for Calculating Strength of Steam-Boiler Tubes.—Sir,—I do not see that Mr. Seaward has told us more about circular flues than we had previously been told by Mr. Jarvis in your 781st number, except that Mr. Seaward has given a rule which appears to me to be erroneous, as it attributes the greatest strength to the weakest form, which may be thus proved:—Suppose we have a flue whose thickness is one unit, and we find it will bear a pressure on the square inch of one unit on the outside, and of two units on the inside, with safety. According to Mr. Seaward's rule, if I understand it rightly, another flue, the same in all its dimensions, except that it is *three* times the thickness of the first, should bear *three* times the pressure inside, and *nine times* the pressure outside; or a pressure of *six* units on the square inch on the inside, and of *nine* units on the square inch on the outside, which is contrary to both reason and experience.—Yours &c.   S. Y., An Engineer.

Railway Signal.—We have recently had an opportunity of inspecting a railway signal erected at the Grand Junction station, Birmingham, which, from its great simplicity, and the unerring certainty with which it conveys the requisite information, as to the state of the points, to the drivers of locomotive engines, both by night and day, appears to be an invention highly important, not only to the proprietors of railroads but to the public generally, as it will greatly tend to prevent those accidents which have occasionally occurred in consequence of the points (or shunts as they are called) being left in a wrong position. The invention consists of two discs, about two feet in diameter, placed at right angles, surmounted by a lantern showing four lights, but of three distinct colours, viz., two red, one blue and one white; the discs, are painted to correspond. This apparatus is firmly attached to the top of the eccentric shaft employed in moving the points, and consequently turns with it with unerring certainty, and can be seen at a great distance, affording the enginemen or drivers ample time to govern the trains according to circumstances. The signal is the invention of Dr. Church, of Birmingham, and has been patented; and there is no doubt it will soon be adopted by the railway companies generally. —*Midland Counties Herald.*

Opening of the London and Birmingham Railway.—We are glad to learn, that, in consequence of the unexpectedly rapid progress recently made with the works of the London and Birmingham Railway, as announced by the engineer to the directors on Thursday, the opening of the line will in all probability take place a week earlier than had been previously arranged. *The 17th of September,* instead of the 24th, is the day now fixed upon; and, from what we have heard on the subject, we have no doubt the line will, on that day, be opened for passengers from end to end. We understand that the following are likely to be the times of departure from London, and of arrival in Birmingham, Manchester, and Liverpool:—*Eight in the morning:*— First-class train; to arrive at Birmingham at two; start from Birmingham at half-past two, and arrive in Liverpool and Manchester at seven.—*Nine in the morning:*—Second-class train; to arrive at Birmingham at four; to start from Birmingham at half-past four, and arrive in Manchester and Liverpool at ten.—*Eleven in the morning:*—Day mail train; to arrive at Birmingham at five; at Manchester and Liverpool about a quarter-past ten.—*Half-past Eight in the evening:*—Principal mail train: to arrive at Manchester and Liverpool at seven in the morning. In addition to the above trains, which will bring passengers for Manchester and Liverpool, there will probably be two trains from London to Birmingham, which will not meet any corresponding trains in the latter town, namely, a second-class train at two, and a first-class train at four in the afternoon.—*Manchester Guardian.*

Improved Coach Lamps.—Messrs. Kay and John-

ston, lamp-manufacturers, Edinburgh, have succeeded in producing a splendid article of the kind, for the use of her Majesty's mails. The form is circular, with a rather small reflector behind; a funnel and air-holes are attached for draught, which force and carry off smoke so rapidly, that dimming or dirtying the glass and plates within—the great defect of the old lamps—are very little, if at all, known. The front of the lamp is grooved, and the adjoining metallic plates so shaped, that they become in common with the reflector behind, foci of the purest lambent light. One of these lamps we saw on Saturday night, in the King's Arms inn yard, and were enabled to read a letter distinctly. In travelling from Edinburgh the road is illuminated from side to side, 100 yards in front, and of the Edinburgh mail thus furnished, it may be said, without a figure of speech, that she carries two harvest moons along with her.—*Dumfries Courier.*

Dangers of Steep Hills.—When expeditions travelling is the object, the rate of inclination that never should be exceeded in passing over hills, if it be practicable to avoid so doing, is that which will afford every advantage in descending hills, as well as in ascending them. For, as carriages are necessarily retarded in ascending hills, however moderate their inclinations may be, if horses cannot be driven at a fast pace in going down them, a great loss of time is the result. This circumstance is particularly deserving of attention, because the present average fast rate of coach driving over any length of road can be accomplished in no other way than by going very fast down the hills. But when the hills are very steep, and the coachman cannot keep his time except by driving very fast down them, he exposes the lives of his passengers to the greatest danger. Few travellers by stage coaches are aware of the risk they run of losing their lives in descending hills. A coachman must be thoroughly well skilled in his business, naturally cautious, and at all times sober. The wheel horses must be not only well trained to holding back, but very strong. If a pole breaks, or a pole-piece, or a hame, hame strap, or drag chain, when a heavily-laden coach is descending a steep hill, at a rate exceeding six miles an hour, an overturn is almost inevitable, by reason of the coach overpowering the horses. Hence it is that ninety-nine out of every hundred coach accidents which happen, are on hills. Nothing is more important for all turnpike trustees to pay immediate attention to, as the reducing of all hills to inclinations of at most 1 in 24.—*Sir H. Parnell's Treatise on Roads.*

The Compass in Iron Vessels.—The hitherto insurmountable obstacle to the employment of iron vessels in other than river navigation, has been the usefulness of the compass, in consequence of the attraction of the metal of which the vessel is constructed. Mr. Samuel Porter, in a letter to the Directors of the General Steam Navigation Company, proposes a plan by which the difficulty may be overcome. He says, "Having made upwards of 3000 of my magnetic sun-dials, and adapted them for all parts of the globe, my attention has been directed for 16 years to the variation of the needle. I think—I almost dare say, I know—if a compass were suspended by means of brass, a few feet above deck, like those in cabin ceilings, with the face downwards, even a deck as well as sides of iron would not divert the needle from that course which the Almighty has most wonderfully assigned to it there, is a point where local attraction ceases."

☞ *British and Foreign Patents taken out with economy and despatch; Specifications, Disclaimers, and Amendments, prepared or revised; Caveats entered; and generally every Branch of Patent Business promptly transacted. A complete list of Patents from the earliest period (15 Car. II. 1675,) to the present time may be examined. Fee 2s. 6d.; Clients, gratis.*

LONDON: Printed and Published for the Proprietor, by W. A. Robertson, at the Mechanics' Magazine Office, No. 6, Peterborough-court, between 135 and 136, Fleet-street.—Sold by A. & W. Galignani, Rue Vivienne, Paris.

𝔐𝔢𝔠𝔥𝔞𝔫𝔦𝔠𝔰' 𝔐𝔞𝔤𝔞𝔷𝔦𝔫𝔢,

MUSEUM, REGISTER, JOURNAL, AND GAZETTE.

No. 788.] SATURDAY, SEPTEMBER 15, 1838. [Price 3*d.*

COOPER'S PATENT RAILWAY.

Fig. 1

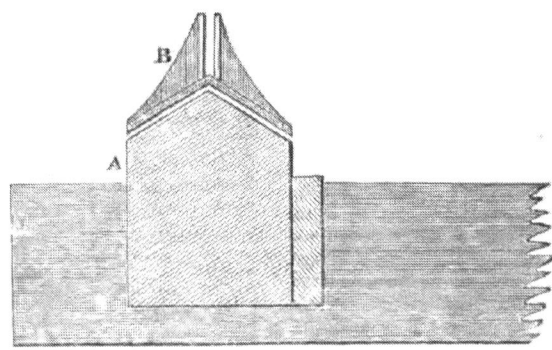

Fig. 2.

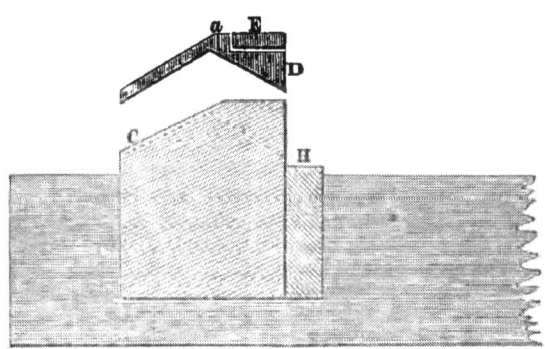

Fig. 3.

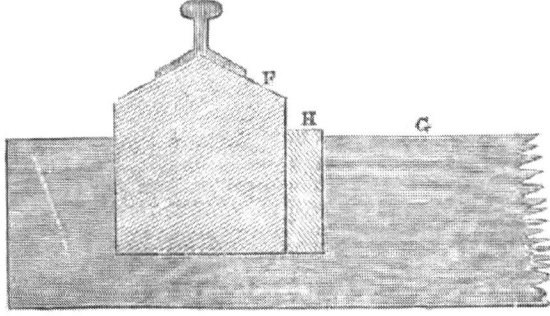

COOPER'S (AMERICAN) PATENT RAILWAY.

(From the *Franklin Journal*.)

Mr. Cooper's improvement consists, in part, in the form given to the upper sides of the string pieces upon which the rails, chairs. or plates are to be sustained, or to the upper sides of the block of wood, or of stone, used for the same purpose; in the form and construction of the chairs adapted thereto, and in the manner of combining and connecting the respective parts together, so as to form a more stable foundation and superstructure than have hitherto been obtained at the same cost.

The patentee sometimes makes his rails by taking string pieces of a peculiar form on their upper sides, and upon these putting edge rails, by means of chairs adapted to the form of such string pieces. Fig. 1, in the drawing (see front page), shows a cross section A, of one of the string pieces of timber, and a side view, B, of a chair adapted thereto. These string pieces may be of any convenient length and size, but it will be found best to make them larger than those ordinarily used. Twelve inches in height, and two in thickness, are the dimensions preferred. It will be seen by the section that the string piece is made ridge-shaped on the top; the angle formed by the sloping sides may vary considerably, but a descent of two inches and a half on each side will answer all the purposes intended. Instead of descending from the ridge, or middle part, in a straight line, it may do so in one which is somewhat concave, or convex; the chair, in this case, being adapted thereto. The same remark will apply to the blocks of wood, or stone, hereafter to be described. The chair B, is so formed on its under side as to adapt it to the ridge-formed string piece across which it is made to straddle. Such chair, so formed, and firmly attached to string pieces, will afford greater stability, being less liable to displacement, and resisting the lateral thrust more effectually than any mode of forming and fixing such articles, now in use.

When it is desired to use a plate rail, the top of the string piece must be adapted thereto. In fig. 2, is shown a section of such a rail and plate, together with the kind of chair Mr. C. has invented, and adapted to be used with rails of that description. The upper sides of the string pieces are, in this kind of rail, sloped towards the outer edge only, commencing from a point immediately under the outer edge of the iron rail plate; C, in this fig. is the section of the string piece; D, the chair, and E, the rail plate. The chair is made in the form shown in the drawing. The chair is to be let into the string piece, so that its top shall be flush with the top thereof. There is a

shoulder offset, or jog, at *a*, to steady the rail plate; this shoulder may be extended up within an eight of an inch of the surface of the plate. These chairs are made of cast-iron of such strength as is necessary to sustain the load; they, however, will be found but little liable to fracture when properly imbedded in the rail. The distance of these chairs from each other may vary from 18 inches to 3 feet.

The dotted line shows the depth to which the chair may be let in to the string piece.

Fig. 3 represents a cross section of a railroad, and exhibits an improved mode of construction, in which the rail, or the chair which supports it, is placed upon blocks of wood, or of stone, having the upper surfaces of such blocks ridge-formed, in the same way with the string pieces first described. F, are blocks of stone, or of wood, the upper sides of which are ridge-shaped, and their lower let into the cross tie-piece G, and secured there by means of wedges H. The tie-pieces may vary in size, but abundant strength is a point of much importance: The patentee recommends having them, usually, about 8 feet long, 14 inches broad, and 8 inches thick, and then making the notches to receive the blocks 4 inches deep. The rail may be made so as to be used without chairs, in which case its form will be somewhat like that of the T rail, the lower side, however, being rolled in such a shape as to adapt it to the ridge of the block, upon which shape its stability will greatly depend. Edge rails of any of the ordinary forms may be used by employing chairs adapted to them, and to the ridge-formed block. In a road so constructed a stone block foundation will possess the requisite elasticity, from its resting upon the wooden tie piece. If preferred, a similar advantage may be obtained by imbedding the stone blocks on a rubble foundation in the usual way, leaving their upper surface flat, and securing the tie pieces above instead of below them. The ends of the tie pieces are, in this case, to be notched, or cut, into such a form as to adapt them to the kind of chair, or rail, above described, that is to say, they must, when these are seated upon them, be ridge-formed.

ON THE CAUSES OF EXPLOSION OF STEAM BOILERS—GENERATION OF GASES IN BOILERS—BY G. H. BARTH, ESQ.

Sir,—I have before me in the last Number of your Magazine, a letter from Mr. Seaward, on gas explosions as connected with the bursting of steam boilers, and request permission to offer a few observations on the subject; not in a spirit of controversy, but cordially concurring with Mr. S., in the hope that it may lead to a full and adequate investigation of the gas theory. Should any of your readers suppose it a matter of trifling importance, I / beg to remind them—that if the gas theorists are not entirely in error, it is quite apparent that the means now in use to prevent boilers bursting from steam pressure, are no more efficient as a safeguard against a gas explosion than they would be against a gun-powder one.

May I ask why the idea of gas explosion has been at all entertained, or how it originated?—has it not being owing to boiler explosions having taken place, attended by circumstances which it was difficult to suppose were produced by the sudden liberation of pent-up steam, though under very high pressure. Allow me to advert, as a case, to the boiler explosion near Wigan, Lancashire, in the December of 1836, when a high-pressure engine at a coal-pit came to a dead stand; the engine-man not being able to perceive any cause, the boiler soon afterwards burst at the bottom, was torn from its fixings, and carried, or rather projected, over two chimneys, to a measured distance of 150 yards. I have conversed with persons who were present at the time, and will vouch for the truth of this statement. I cannot speak as to the exact weight of the boiler—but heard it calculated at from five to six tons. Again, see the boiler explosion at Stockport, last spring, by which nine persons were killed; in this case a heavy iron pipe was thrown completely over a five story mill, and a paving stone, or slab, 2 feet 8 inches diameter, (placed near to the boiler) through the second story window. Also a case in Derbyshire, last winter, where the top of the boiler and a mass of brickwork, weighing together more than ten tons, was projected over two streets, falling on and demolishing a frame-shop beyond. Many similar instances might be adduced—these may suffice. I conceive it difficult to show, in such cases, that the steam, when liberated, has sufficient projectile force to produce these tremendous effects; if this is allowed, the inquiry consequent is—what force then was in operation? and what the nature and capability of such force?

The answer would lead to the gas hypothesis. Before entering upon the details of such subject, perhaps, Sir, some gentleman amongst your many scientific correspondents may oblige the gas theorists by demonstrating that the presumed difficulty exists only in the imaginations of those who entertain it.

In the second paragraph of the letter in question, Mr. Seaward admits that hydrogen gas may be formed in a boiler from decomposition of steam, but objects, "that the circumstances under which this process may go on must be exceedingly rare, and the effect of very trifling amount." With all deference I suggest, that production of hydrogen gas must always go on with iron sufficiently heated and steam in contact. In proof of this we have the evidence of every chemist who has written on the subject since water was discovered to be a compound of hydrogen and oxygen. The temperature necessary to effect decomposition of steam is generally stated at about red-heat; I am led to suppose from experiments—that it commences, though the process goes on slowly, when the iron is heated to about 700°, or even less, and increases with increase of temperature. The effects I think would depend on the structure of the boiler and fire-places, or flues in some measure, as on other circumstances also; I cannot concede they would be trifling. If Mr. Seaward will not allow the possibility of oxygen being communicated to the hydrogen —I presume that gentleman will grant, if a boiler be red-hot, and burst at, or over the fire-place, the hydrogen gas must escape, mix with the air in the flue or fire-place, and explode; would its effect then be very trifling? I do not perceive, if Mr. Seaward intended from the concluding observation of this paragraph with respect to having seen boilers partly red-hot, that they were performing their usual amount of duty at the time; if such inference was intended, and the engines condensed their steam, I will allow it to be an extraordinary circumstance, and strong objection to the gas theory, unless we could also show that sometimes red-hot iron does not decompose steam *(a poser for the chemist)*—or what is more likely, that iron may be sometimes protected from oxidation by an encrustation of some substance or substances held by the water in solution.

c c 2

Mr. 'S. also objects, that if it were possible for the gas to be formed in any considerable quantity, it must be manifest, by the effect it would have upon the working of the engines; a very important objection, and one in which I perfectly concur; being of opinion from the circumstances connected with explosions which I have collected, that such effect has actually taken place in some instances of boilers bursting attributable to gas explosion. As one case amongst many, I refer to the boiler explosion at Manchester, on the 5th of November, 1836, fully detailed in the Manchester journals of that period, attended with loss of life. It appeared in evidence at the coroner's inquest, that the safety-valve was not over weighted, and that for a considerable time previous to the explosion the engineer had not been able to make the engine do its usual work—it had almost stopped. Seven experienced engineers, who were deputed to examine into the case and report thereon to the jury, were of opinion, *that something had got into the steam-pipe and thus stopped its passage to the cylinder, (though they could find no vestige of this supposed something,) and that the consequent accumulation of pressure burst the boiler, where they thought it required another stay.* It also appears, that in the majority of cases which have occurred, both in America and this country, the boilers have exploded either prior to the starting, or after the stopping of the engine, which would then not be effected by the presence of hydrogen gas in the boiler.

With respect to the difficulties pointed out in paragraphs four and five of Mr. Seaward's letter, I regret, that an attempted explanation, would necessarily, from its length, occupy more space in your valuable columns than I can venture to expect—at least in one number. That red-hot iron decomposes steam, and hydrogen gas oxide of iron, is known to most persons conversant with chemistry, who may not be equally well aware that oxygen will support the combustion of hydrogen gas, not only in an atmosphere of steam, but actually under water. Is it absolutely proved that a low-pressure boiler has never yet exploded? Granting this to be so, does it leave the gas theorist no new ground of inquiry as to the cause and circumstances why

such should be the case? An opinion is very generally entertained amongst engineers, that boilers often burst by being overheated from want of water—is this opinion fallacious? or is it not rather the result of observation? If it is admitted that boilers may become red-hot, and steam be in contact with their iron, the admission leaves a foundation for the gas hypothesis,—those gentlemen who dispute it, should show that gas cannot, under these circumstances, be generated; and when this is conclusively done, I will most cheerfully acknowledge the error, which, as one gas theorist, I have entertained. In conclusion, I will advert to two extraordinary cases of boiler explosion, one at Manchester, the other in Lincolnshire, each occasioning loss of life. In each case the *boilers had been a long time cold*, and *the fires extinguished.* The man-lid was taken off, and a man entered the boiler to examine the inside. On introducing a light an explosion took place, the man being killed; this could not be owing to steam-pressure—was it gas? if not, what was it that exploded?

I am, Sir,

Your most obedient servant,

GEO. H. BARTH.

University-street, Sept. 5, 1838.

***

FLAT-CHAMBERED BOILERS. — MR. HEBERT IN REPLY TO MR. HANCOCK.

Sir,—It was my anxious desire to avoid trespassing again upon your valuable space, on the above-mentioned subject; but the unfounded charges, suppressed facts, and general mystification which distinguish Mr. Hancock's letter contained in your last Number (786), seem to render some notice of them indispensable.

It is proverbially true, that when a disputant has the worst of an argument, he is apt to endeavour to prejudice his opponent by personal reflections which have nothing to do with the question at issue. Thus Mr. Hancock endeavours to make your readers suppose that I am a hired advocate, in order that my statements may receive no credit with your readers. All that I will or need say, in answer to the insinuation, is, that it is without the slightest foundation. There is, however, no need for any personal remarks whatever. If Mr. Hancock is as sincere as I am for the truth, the whole truth, and nothing but the truth, he will prove his sincerity by inserting (with your acquiescence) *a verbatim copy* of his specification, and drawings attached thereto. Then would the readers of the *Mechanics' Magazine* be able to estimate the value of Mr. Hancock's pretensions; then would they see that all his *patent claims in boilers* consist in the inventions of preceding machinists. (I would not hence infer that Mr. Hancock has effected nothing; on the contrary, I believe that some of his contrivances in locomotion are original and good.) If Mr. Hancock shall refuse to subject his pretensions to this fair ordeal, I may admire his prudence, but I shall sincerely regret that he should have so far committed himself, as to make charges that he has no means of substantiating, and to fulminate threats which he would not to execute.

It is a most singular feature in Mr. Hancock's letter, that he expresses his indignation at being charged with an attempt to impose upon your readers, and in the very next sentence proves, that such charge was well founded! In his first letter, it will be remembered that he stated himself to have invented, and that he possessed a legal monopoly in, *flat-chambered boilers*, without any limitation as to the *kind;* thus suppressing that portion of the truth, which was essential to forming a correct judgment of the real fact. *Now,* to avoid the claims of previous inventors, which would demolish his broad claim, he is obliged to qualify it down, first, to " constructing narrow flat vessels, *in the form and manner hereinbefore described.*" The *form,* be it observed, means flat and square (which was adopted by Smith, Dr. Alban, and many others); the *manner* means, chiefly, the tyeing of the thin flat surfaces together by stay bolts (which was the especial object of Captain Smith's patent, and which I saw, both in the process of manufacture, and in use; and it was, most likely, the interference of Captain Smith's patent that hindered Mr. Hancock from making boilers according to his specification.) Mr. Hancock goes on to say, that these narrow flat vessels are " adapted to be placed vertically, or edgeways upwards

over the fire, for producing steam for steam engines." Now, is there a reader of the *Mechanics' Magazine,* who will deny that Dr. Alban's square flat plates, of the same proportions too, were not previously *placed vertically,* or *edgeways upwards over the fire for producing steam for steam engines?* The third claim put forth is equally Dr. Alban's; but I will not exercise the patience of your readers by the needless repetition of the parallel.*

Although there is much more that might fairly be commented upon, I will here conclude my brief epistle, by observing, with respect to Mr. Hancock's allusion to my description of his boiler in the *Engineers' Encyclopædia,* that that description was chiefly supplied by himself, and that it had no reference to his *patented* boiler of 1827, which is an essentially different apparatus.

I remain, Sir, your obedient servant,
           L. HEBERT.

Camden Town, 5th Sept. 1838.

COLLIERY COMMUNICATION.

Sir,—Eight or nine months ago, having some spare tubing, and being rather inconvenienced by the distance which my workshop is from the front one, I thought of applying tubes to convey the voice from one place to the other, that so I might save unnecessary waste of time and labour. I therefore proposed my plan to some friends, and it met with decided opposition, " it had no chance to answer." However, I resolved to try it,—and my labours were completely successful. (*Note,* when I had my tubes put up I was not aware that the same plan had been in use many years before: —indeed I have since seen advertisements, offering to make "speaking tubes" at so much per foot.)

My present object is to suggest, through the medium of your useful pages, that such tubes would be very suitable for colliery purposes, obviating the necessity of either signals, or that unearthly yell which is ever and anon pouring

---

* As Mr. Hancock has declared his intention of not proceeding further in this controversy, it is perhaps necessary that we should append a few words to Mr. Hebert's letter. In our last we stated our opinion that if Mr. Hancock can prove himself to be the first inventor and patentee of flat-chamber boilers, his monopoly extends to all mere modifications thereof. As far as evidence has yet been adduced, and in particular, as regards the patents of Smith and Alban, we think decidedly that Mr. Hancock's patent would be legally upheld.—ED. M. M.

up the shaft, placing a small funnel to terminate each end—one near the head of the "brakesman," and the other below, near the "hanger-on;" by this method every order or message might be conveyed correctly.

My workmen are at the third story of the house, and when both parties are near the tubes, and attending, a whisper can be heard at the extreme end more distinctly than where it is spoken:—indeed, the sound is so much reverberated, that I think information might be conveyed by this means from *one stage* to another, if the terminations were in quiet, close rooms?

I remain, Sir, respectfully yours,

WM. PEARSON.

Bishop Auckland, Aug. 16, 1838.

THE SWISS PORTABLE FIRE-ENGINE.

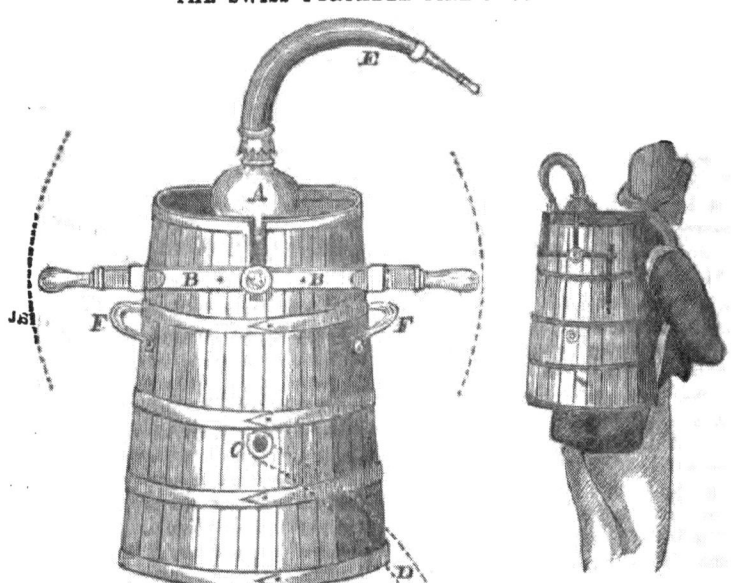

Fig. 1.   Fig. 2.

Sir,—The above sketches represent a Swiss portable fire-engine, manufactured by Messrs. Bramah and Robinson, Pimlico, for the use of private and public buildings, ships, gardens, &c. The working part consists of a horizontal brass cylinder, having a flanch at each end, to which two end-caps or covers are screwed. These caps have stuffing-boxes in their centres for supporting, in an air-tight manner, the working axis of the engine. Within the cylinder is placed a strong metal partition or radius, the lower edge being joined to the cylinder, and the uppermost edge, which is grooved, made so as exactly to fit the circle of the latter. The axis is armed with two wings or fans, on each of which is placed a valve opening upwards, to allow the water to pass through them.

These fans are made to move water-tight against the sides and ends of the cylinder, by means of leather on their edges. When the axis carrying the fans is fixed in its place, the groove in the metal partition, described above, is filled with hemp, or some other soft material, so as to press on the under surface of the axis, and cause it to move in a water-tight manner. The fans being a diameter of the cylinder, divide it into two parts, the lower of which is again divided by the radius partition into two compartments; in each of these an aperture is cut through the cylinder opening into the suction-passages; these apertures, like those in the fan, are closed by valves opening upwards. A vibratory motion being given to the fans by means of the lever on their axis, the capacity of the two lower compartments of the cylinder become alternately enlarged and diminished; the consequence of this is, that water becomes drawn up into the cylinder, gets above the fans on either side, and is then forced out through the exit-pipe, the stream being equalized by means of a spherical air-vessel placed above the working cylinder.

This engine is mounted in a wooden tub, as shown by fig. 1. The working cylinder is concealed by the side of the tub, but the air-vessel A is seen. BB are the lever handles by which the engine is worked; for the convenience of carrying about, they fold up, as shown at fig. 2.

If made so as to work by suction from a pond, reservoir, cistern, &c., as well as from its own tub, the suction-pipe is attached to a screwed orifice C, its course being denoted by the two dotted lines D. A short metal branch-pipe is affixed to the ascending tube of the air-vessel by means of a flexible leather hose E. FF are two handles by which the engine is lifted. As the weight of this apparatus is under 100lbs., it can be readily carried by a man; for this purpose two shoulder straps are permanently attached to the engine. The mode of carrying is shown by fig. 2. This is a very compact engine, of considerable power; it may be worked by one man, but when two are employed, about twenty imperial gallons of water are discharged per minute to a distance of nearly 70 feet horizontal, or 50 feet high.

To be really useful as a *fire-engine*, however, it is absolutely necessary that the machine should be furnished with a good length of leather hose, for it is next to impossible for any person to stand within an apartment where a fire is raging, and work the engine to any good effect; the labour and excitement, (leaving *fear* out of the question) would cause an increased respiration, which the heated and contaminated atmosphere of the apartment would very ill supply. One of the best authorities on this subject, Mr. Braidwood, in his treatise on fires and fire-engines, remarks:—"Much has been said about the convenience of conveying small engines up stairs, and into places where the fire is raging; but I fear that those who have so strongly recommended them have never made the experiment. I have generally found that all the fresh air to be had in a burning apartment is required, to enable a man to lie on the floor, and direct the water from the hose, while the engine is being worked by those on the outside."

Portable engines have advantages enough to recommend their general adoption, without attributing to them powers which they can never possess; they are calculated to be eminently serviceable at the infancy of a fire, but it is not by placing them in an unpleasant and even dangerous situation, that their advantages can ever be fully realised. It is a misunderstanding of this kind that has operated to limit the adoption and practical application of many ingenious machines that have from time to time been constructed for the speedy extinction of fires; I trust, however, that the time has now arrived, when a more general diffusion of the proper mode of proceeding in case of fire will tend to nip these accidents in the bud, and render available the several mechanical aids which have been designed for this important purpose.

I remain, Sir, yours respectfully
WM. BADDELEY.

London, August 30, 1838.

TRANSPOSING PIANO-FORTE.

Sir,—I have had an idea of extending the range of amateurs' singing, by means of a transposing piano-forte, for many years. Various have been the attempts at simplifying transposition: an instrument was once attempted to be introduced, in which all the keys were alike with respect to fingering, but were placed black and white alternately. This, however, presented so many difficulties to those who had acquired a knowledge of the usual mode of fingering, that it did not succeed.

My plan is as follows:—Let the instrument be strung with five additional wires above and also below the compass of the keys; let the key-board move on rollers, by means of an adjusting screw, and an indicator made to show whether the key-board is screwed 1, 2, 3, 4, or 5 semitones above or below the pitch (suppose concert pitch) of the instrument.

I need not point out to an instrument-maker the alterations in bridges, hammers, &c. contingent on this plan.

I am, Sir, yours,
AN OLD CORRESPONDENT.

Hitc in Herts

PRACTICAL SQUARING OF THE CIRCLE.

Sir,—Understanding that contributions connected with mechanics are acceptable for the columns of your Magazine, I send you the accompanying demonstration of the square of the circle, as applicable to the measurement of trees and other cylindrical bodies.

The mathematician will not object to a subject of scientific study since the days of Euclid and Archimedes, as it affords, *I believe*, the readiest and nearest *practical data*, as a relative proportion between the square and circle, ever yet offered to the public in integers, and the young arithmetician, or humble artisian, will be able by it to make his calculations free of decimals and fractional parts.

To the private gentleman wishing to ascertain the dimensions of the beam that he can get from a tree; to the merchant in purchasing timber; to the builder, the mechanic, and in short, for numerous purposes, it may be found useful in simplifying and shortening calculations.

The author, Captain Cortlandt Taylor, of the Madras artillery, when on a mission in 1837, from the Madras government to the Malabar coast, to procure teak timber for the government gun-carriage manufactory, forwarded it with some calculations in the reduction of logs, to the military board of that presidency.

.I am, Sir, your obedient servant,

EXODUS.

London, July 23, 1838.

The square of the circle, and its adaptation to measuring of timber and other cylindrical bodies.

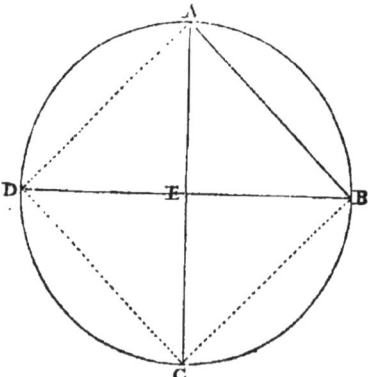

Let A B C D be a circle, and the dia-

meters |A C, and B D perpendicular to each other; then are the triangles A E B, B E C, C E D, and D E A (formed by the radii of the circle and the points A, B, C, and D being joined), right angle triangles and similar; having the common centre E a right angle in each; the legs A E, B E, C E, and D E (or circles radii,) equal; and the lines or hypothenuses A B, B C, C D, and A D, also equal, and together forming an inscribed square to the circle A B C D.

Then, as the circumferences of all circles are to their diameters, as 3.1416 is to unit. So 3.1416 is to 1, as the circumference of any given circle A B C D, is to its diameter, D B: but D B the diameter is the double of E B,—the radius; and E B is one leg or side of the right angle triangle A E B, of which A E is the other leg, and A B, is the third side, or hypothenuse.

Then, as in right angle triangles, the square of the hypothenuse is equal to the sum of the squares of the other two sides, in the right angle triangle A E B, $B E^2 + A E^2 = A B^2$: but as B E, and A E are equal, their squares are equal also, therefore $2 E B^2 = A B^2$, or $\sqrt{2} E B^2 = A B$, the *one-fourth* of the perimeter of the required square.

Thus, knowing the circumference of any circle, the perimeter, or measurement of the inscribed square can be easily ascertained; and *vice versa*, knowing the square the circle can be obtained, and the difference, (or loss on the latter being squared,) is known.

Practical Illustration.—To illustrate this demonstration by numbers: In the above figure, assume the measurement of the *inscribed square** A B C D at 100, (one hundred, say inches,) of which the side A B is one-fourth or (twenty-five,) 25. Then in the right angle triangle A B E, (as before). the square of the hypothenuse (or side A B), or 25^2, is equal to $A E^2 + E B^2$, that is $625 = A E^2 + E B^2$; but as A E and E B are radii of of the same circle and equal, their squares are equal also, and $625 = 2 E B^2$, or $\frac{625}{2} = A E^2$, or $\sqrt{\frac{625}{2}} = E B$, or again $\sqrt{312.5} = E B$. (Extract root of 312.5—)

312,5)17,6776 the root.

```
         |1
         |————
    27|  212
         189
    ————————
   346|.2350
         2076
    ————————
  3527|.27400
         24689
    ————————
 35347|.271100
         247429
    ————————
353546|.2367100
         2121276
```

That is, 17.6776 is equal to E B; but E B, or radius of the circle, being half the diameter D B, then the diameter D B is equal to 35.355 (inches).

Again, (as before,) unit is to 3.1416 as diameter D B or 35.355, is to the circumference of the circle A B C D; or thus, 1 : 3.1416 :: 35.355, (by common rule of three), to 111.072 (inches) Q E D.

So, as an average for any general purposes of the department to which I belong, or for any merchant or artisan in his vocation, 11 *per cent.* may be used as the difference between any cylinder and its square; or by the common rule of three, as 111 is to 100, so is the measurement of any circle to the square of that circle.*

Cochin, July 1837.

PERKINS'S HEATING APPARATUS.

Sir,—In your Magazine, No. 775, p. 168, I notice a letter from a Mr. "J. Murray," in which he deprecates the use of "Perkins's pipes." I have seen the heating apparatus by those pipes successfully used for many years, without having produced any of the evils he ascribes to them, evidently because his "knowledge" does not "extend" to their efficient practical application.

The term *red-hot*, as applied to iron, conveys an idea of *ignition*, but I have yet to learn that this term applied to water, excites any such association or its consequent alarm. *Red-hot water* could not have set the building at the Manchester Botanic Garden on fire—of this his knowledge of its elements should have prevented him giving credence or publicity to any such an allegation.

I am desirous he should have the practical benefit of the maxim "*audi alterum partem.*" That his mind may be disabused of the mere abstract impression of this subject which it has received, and if he will call upon me, I shall be able to show how an heating apparatus formed exclusively of these pipes, which have for years been used with uninterrupted safety, and that the owner does not wish "to get rid of them," but deems them a valuable improvement. Any defective pipe is always discovered on being *first* properly tested by the workmen that construct the apparatus, by noticing any fissure therein, or emission of steam, so that no danger need afterwards be apprehended if superintended with common care.

Yours most respectfully,
JOHN DORNING.
Wavertree, near Liverpool, Sept. 8. 1838.

P S.—Will thank you to inform me if the writer of the letter alluded to be Mr. J. Murray, the chemist and lecturer, of Hull, or some other gentleman of the same name, as probably I shall write to him on this subject.—J. D.†

---

* The decimal .072, or $\frac{72}{1000}$ *per cent.* may, for any practical purposes be omitted as insignificant, but should a greater degree of accuracy be required, it may be obtained, I may say to *fractional nicety*, by the addition of unit to the *sum of percentage* of every 1400,—which would so be $14 \times 11 = 154 + 1 = 155$; or as 1400 is to 1555. The *proof* of the correctness of this demonstration is, that decimal .7071 is the side of an inscribed square, the diameter of the circle of which is unit:—Then, as 1555 is to 1400, so is 3.1416 to its inscribed square = 2.8884, the side or one-fourth of which, is .7071.—Q E D.

† Mr. Murray, of Hull, we believe.—ED. M. M.

SELECTIONS FROM THE PROCEEDINGS OF THE NEWCASTLE MEETING (BEING THE EIGHTH) OF THE BRITISH ASSOCIATION FOR THE ADVANCEMENT OF SCIENCE.
[Continued from page 415.]

Mr. Russell, of Edinburgh, brought up the "Report of the Committee (consisting of Sir John Robison and himself) on Waves."

This report was a continuation of that of last year, published in the volume of the Transactions just issued. The following were the duties of the Committee :—1. To examine the phenomena of a certain kind of wave generated in a fluid, with the view of enabling us to understand the mechanism of its propagation, and so advance this department of hydrodynamical science. 2. To examine the nature of the connexion which exists between the generation of these waves in a fluid, and the resistance of the fluid to the motion of a floating body moved through it, as in the instance of a ship. And, 3. To investigate the nature of the connexion which exists between this wave, which Mr. Russell has called the "Great Wave of Translation," and the tidal wave, remarkable analogies having been already ascertained to exist between them ; and to determine the effect of the wind on the propagation of the tide wave. In regard to the first department, the phenomena of the great wave of translation, the report of the preceeding year contained a great portion of what had been done this year ; but the observations were such that they would probably not be completed in several years. What they had done this year, had been to complete, as far as they possibly could, the second of these departments of investigation—that which related to the physical investigation of waves ; and he was happy to think that all that could be done had, he believed, been done, towards an understanding of the mechanism of the wave. He should, first of all, show what had been done in regard to the physical mechanism. They had previously determined the *formal* law of the wave ; that was to say, they had determined that the velocity of the wave was totally independent of the manner in which it was generated, and depended only upon one circumstance—namely, the depth of the wave. But this was a merely formal result, and his present object was to investigate the physical constitution of the wave. In the formal investigation, they experienced considerable difficulty in ascertaining its form. The nature of a wave was such, that it was exceedingly difficult to detect its form, because it required an instantaneous observation, made with great precision, by a number of observers, in a small space, and with a minuteness which exceeded any means of

ordinary observation. The method proposed by Prof. Stevelly had been satisfactorily applied, to determine the length of the wave, which they found little more than six times the depth of the fluid. But they also found that this did not hold in all cases ; for when the wave was very high, the quantity was much greater ; but when it was low, it was exactly the same. So that just when the wave was about to disappear, it was found that its length was six times the depth of the fluid. Now they could not define a form, unless by fitting it into some form already known ; and from all that he could learn, the only class of curve to which there was any liklihood of fitting this wave, were the trochoidal curves, of which the cycloid was the limit. Now the form, as observed by him (Mr. Russell,) was almost precisely cycloidal ; but of double the length which the circumstance of its being the cycloid would have given, because it was manifest that taking the limits, and supposing the wave to be a cycloidal wave, it would only be the circumference of a circle, of which its height was the diameter, or little more than three times the depth of the fluid. But the true length was six times that quantity. Thus another set of curves became necessary. They found that the curve which the wave would fit was not a cycloid, but an analogous curve, which he (Mr. Russell) should be disposed to call the *semi-circular cycloid*. He should now state the results which they had come to. For the purpose of ascertaining the physical constitution of the wave, and how it was propagated, the reservoir which they had previously constructed was formed in a certain part of plate glass, the object being to float particles in water, and to observe the phenomena which took place among these particles while the wave was passing over them. He had previously examined many observations which had been made in Germany and elsewhere. Weber had described the oscillating wave and the ocean wave in all their phenomena ; but neither the Webers nor any other investigator appeared to have recognized the existence of this great solitary wave of translation ; they seemed to have limited their observations to the oscillatory and gregarious waves. He (Mr. Russell) called his the primary wave, or great wave of translation of the fluid. The glass side of the vessel was carefully divided, so as to enable the eye to determine the results ;

and the following phenomena took place among the particles so invariably, that on the slightest observation he could calculate the results. Suppose that the particles were in a particular plane, at right angles to the direction of the motion of the wave, when first the wave came to that place, the particles would begin to move in the direction of that motion. They would move with accelerating velocity; they were at their maximum when the top of the wave was immediately over them; and from that moment the particles began to move forward with retarded velocity, and, at the instant when the wave left the place, they were at rest in precisely the same position to one another as they occupied previously to the translation. They were put forward without the slightest displacement. The next question was the path of translation, which was a curious and yet simple matter. While these particles were in their progress forward, they were also raised. They were transferred forward horizontally to a distance equal to twice the height of the wave; and the curves, which the uppermost particles described, were as exactly as possible semi-circles, described on a radius equal to the height of the wave; and of the other particles, at greater depths, each of them described a semi-ellipse, whose major axis was equal to the diameter of the semi-circle, and whose minor axis was to the radius of the semi-circle in the same ratio as the height of the particle above the bottom to the whole depth of the fluid; the path of the lowest being a straight line. Considering, next, the vertical motion of the particles, it appeared that during the transit of the great wave, each particle was lifted upwards from a state of rest with an accelerated motion, left at its highest point for an instant at rest, from which it descended with a motion first of all accelerated, and then retarded, so as to be left perfectly at rest at its original height at the instant when the wave had passed away. Supposing, then, an elevation of fluid of this kind to have been once generated, the manner in which it propagated the wave might be adequately conceived to take place thus: any given series of particles, in the same vertical plane, would be more pressed forwards than a similar series behind them, under the anterior part of the elevation, and the difference of pressures would be the differential of the vertical ordinates in those planes; and this excess of pressure necessarily produced two effects, it forced the particles in one plane nearer to those in the other, and thus caused progression or horizontal translation of the particles; then the same excess of pressure diminishing the distance

between the particles, elevated the intervening column of fluid to a height inversely proportional to the distance of these planes from each other. The planes situated in the latter part of the elevation of fluid, were in a situation the reverse of this, and the difference of pressure permitted the particles to descend, and diminished the velocity of translation; and the sum of these increments and decrements being equal and in opposite directions, the particles were successively accelerated and elevated, retarded and depressed, by the same law. The curve which the wave described, was a very remarkable one. It was very nearly related to the cycloid, yet differed essentially from it. It was also related to the curve of sines. The ordinates of the cycloid consisted of the ordinates of a curve of sines, added to those of a circle. The ordinates of this wave-curve consisted of the ordinates of the curve of sines, added to those of a semi-circle, whose diameter was double that of the circle. He, therefore, should designate this curve as the semi-circular cycloid. It was the only one which appeared to represent the observed phenomena. The next part of the subject to which he directed attention, was the relation which the translation wave bore to the phenomena of resistance of fluids. He had previously ascertained that the displacement of a fluid by a vessel took place, not in the body of the current, but solely by the generation of waves. Now, the manner in which they were generated, appeared to throw light upon the subject of the resistance of fluids; because they wished to have exactly the same transference for particles of matter which was required for transference of waves. They wished to remove the particles of fluid from a state of rest, and admit the vessel to pass through, and then allow them to return to their former places, just as in the wave the particles were first elevated above the surface, and then permitted to subside. Now they found that whenever the displacement took place, as in the wave, they had the phenomena of least resistance. So that, in forming a floating vessel with this wave-line disposed on alternate sides of the keel, so as to give such motion to the particles as to displace nothing more than was necessary, nor for a greater distance than was necessary to allow the vessel to pass, they obtained the solid of least resistance. Since that time, a variety of experiments on large vessels had been performed; steam vessels were now constructing on this form; and it was a remarkable fact, that the fastest vessel on the Thames was one to which this form had been given. Several other vessels had since been built on a large scale on this construction, and he was happy to find that a great number of ship-builders had adopted and were building vessels with great success on this line. It was scarcely credible, that a vessel should move at the rate of fifteen miles an hour, and not raise a spray—not raise anything like that high mass of water which was always found at the bows of vessels going at speed, but enter the water perfectly smooth, and leave it smooth, and as much at rest in the direction of the displacement as it was before the floating solid passed. This phenomenon had invariably accompanied all the vessels formed on this line. Now this appeared to him (Mr. Russell) to show the correctness of a remark made by D'Alembert, who, in his *Opuscules*, had given a demonstration, from the mathematical theory of fluids, that the resistance to a solid body, if properly formed, was nothing. He challenged the mathematicians of the day to disprove his assertion, which was never done; though what the proper form necessary for this purpose was, had not been assigned. Now he (Mr. Russell) thought he had quite manifested the possibility of a vessel moving through the water with little or no resistance. On making allowance for adhesion to the sides of the vessel, (which they knew might be done correctly, from experiments made by others,) they found that the resistance of the vessel was not one-twentieth part of the mere adhesion of the water to the sides of the vessel; so that the resistance from displacement of transference was nearly nothing. A large vessel having been made in this form, the following experiment was performed. Two oranges were placed in the direction in which the vessel moved; the person steering, after many attempts, at last succeeded in insinuating the prow of the vessel between the oranges; they rolled along the side of the vessel, remained in contact therewith, and returned at the wake, and when the vessel passed they remained at rest; they had been transferred horizontally, in the manner of a wave, and remained at rest in precisely the same position as they were when the transference commenced. This appeared to him to be the strongest test; and if this vessel was not a solid of least resistance, it was closely allied to it. [The Chairman: I should say it was a vessel of no resistance.] There was another thing which he might mention—namely, that as steam vessels built on this line did not produce the waves which were at present so injurious to the banks of rivers, &c. perhaps its introduction would be attended with great advantages in this respect. He felt certain, indeed, that this was a form to

which ship-builders must ere long be driven. It was the theoretical form of least resistance, which he (Mr. Russell) gave at Dublin three years ago; but it was not until he discovered the law of transference of the wave, that he found he had hit upon the very form of displacement of the wave. Ship-builders had been in the habit of saying,—Whatever you do, let us have no hollow lines. The maxim now would be, at least of those ship-builders who had carefully examined the subject,—Let us have the hollow lines where we want them, and then we shall have plenty of scope for making fuller lines where they will not injure the progress of the vessel. He (Mr. Russell) should now have entered upon the connexion of the subject with the theory of tides, because he thought he had identified the theory of this wave with that of the tidal wave; and whatever influence the celestial mechanism might have upon the tides, they must yet depend upon terrestrial mechanism for bringing it to their doors: he thought they could get a great deal more knowledge about the theory of waves by tidal observations, because there they had a large, long, slow wave, which could be examined with great minuteness. Time, however, would not then permit him to enter upon the subject.

Sir W. R. Hamilton congratulated the section on the increasing interest excited by these valuable researches of Mr. Russell on waves. It was now evident that they had a most important and direct relation to the doctrine of the tides; and he had no doubt, from the many imperfect glimpses which he was enabled to catch of their relation to the undulatory propagation of light, that they were in progress towards elucidating some of the mysteries of that mysterious physical process.—Mr. Whewell felt peculiar interest in that part of Mr. Russell's communication in which he described the internal motion of the molecules of the fluid during the progress of the wave, and traced each from its first disturbance of position to its return to rest after the passage of the wave; and he felt confident this was only the first step towards the solution of a most important problem in general hydrodynamics, by which we should at length be led to know the manner in which motions were propagated through fluids as perfectly as we at present know how forces communicate motions to cohering masses of matter. In describing the form of the curve of the wave Mr. Russell had proposed to call it the semi-circular cycloid. He would be inclined to suggest the propriety of the term hemi-cycloid, in which both parts of the term are borrowed from the Greek, and the term semi-cycloid had already another acceptation.—The Rev. Prof. Chevallier asked, whether it was not necessary to vary the dimensions of the several curves of a vessel built on his principles to suit the velocity with which she was intended to move.—Mr. Russell answered that it was necessary.—Sir John Herschel was anxious that Mr. Russell should describe minutely to the section the manner in which his experimental waves were generated; before, however, he gave Mr. Russell the opportunity of doing so, by resuming his chair, he would state the reason why he was anxious on this point. Prof. Weber, as Mr. Russell had informed the section, had some time since traced with much accuracy the motions of the several particles of the fluid mass during the transit of a wave; and had assigned the circular motion of each near the top, and the elliptic motions varying as you approached the bottom; but from his researches it would appear that each particle during the transit of a wave described the full circuit of its own curve, so as to return, as soon as the transit of the wave was completed, to the spot from which it had started when its equilibrium was first disturbed on the approach of the wave; whereas, if he understood Mr. Russell rightly, he had described cases in which the particles only described semi-curves, beginning with the semi-circle at the surface of the fluid; and did not describe the under-half of their curves, so as to return to the places from which they had started at the commencement of their motions. If he had apprehended this rightly, it furnished a case in the propagation of undulations in water very analogous in its physical circumstances to the loss of a half-wave of light at the change from refraction to reflexion, and might perhaps lead to some conception of the origin of the distinction between positive and negative polarization in the luminous waves.—Mr. Russell said that he would describe the manner in which he generated the waves in his experimental canal, by which it would appear that he could at pleasure produce either a positive wave, or that which consisted of an elevated ridge only passing along the surface of the canal, or a negative wave consisting of a depression alone, similarly progressing, or a wave compounded of a positive and a negative wave, or one in which there was a ridge accompanied by a depression to constitute the wave. By penning up an elevated column of water at one end of his experimental canal, which was separated from the rest of the fluid by a sluice or diaphragm placed across it, when he suddenly opened this sluice the positive wave was generated; by depressing cautiously into the end of the canal a mass of foreign matter, as, for instance, a block of wood, a positive wave was also generated; by slowly and cautiously

drawing out the same block the negative wave was generated; and by letting fall a considerable body of water from some height above the surface at one end of the canal, a compound wave was generated. During the transit of a positive wave each molecule of the fluid only passed through the upper half of its semi-curve, and thus only passed forward by the length of its longer axis without returning to its place; during the transit of a negative wave each molecule described only the lower portion of its curve, and thus went backward by the length of its axis, without returning again to the place from which it had been disturbed, while, during the transit of a compound wave, each molecule of the fluid described both the upper and under portion of its own curve, and thus returned at the conclusion of its transit to the place from which it had begun its motion when first disturbed.

———

Mr. Robert Mallet read his report of the experiments, instituted at the command and with the funds of the Association, " On the Action of Sea and River Water, whether clear or foul, and at various temperatures, upon Iron, both cast and wrought," by himself and Prof. E. Davy, of Dublin.

This subject is one of great interest to the engineer, as well as the chemist, as the former has no knowledge of the rate of action, relative or absolute, of water on iron under various conditions; and the chemist does not know precisely the changes which ensue during this action. The report is comprised under four principal sections, viz. :—First, a brief "*précis*" of the actual state of our chemical knowledge of the subject, *i. e.* of the reactions of air and water on iron. This embraces the following subdivisions of the subject: A. of the action of pure water free from air on iron, at various temperatures, and the nature of the compounds formed, which are at low temperatures, $(Fe_2O_3) +$

HO according to Berzelius, or $FeO + Fe_2O_3$

according to Gay-Lussac. The latter is the oxide formed at a red heat according to Robiquet. B. Perfectly dry air has no action, or none below a red heat; the oxide then formed is $4FeO + Fe_2O_3$; or, according to

Mosander, $6FeO + Fe_2O_3$. C. Air and

water together,—viz. air combined with water, or moist air, act most rapidly on Iron, producing when the vessel is shallow, Fe^2O_3

$+ HO_2$, but if deep, Fe_2O_3 mixed with a large

quantity of magnetic oxide. The second section of the report is devoted to a statement of the nature and extent of the experiments, which have been made on the great scale for the use of the engineer, as well as chemist, on the action of water on iron; for this purpose, boxes containing regularly formed specimens of nearly all the makes of iron in Britain,—have been sunk,—1. in the clear water of Kingstown Harbour; 2. in the foul water of the same; 3. in foul river Liffey water; 4. in clear water of the same; and 5. in sea water maintained constantly at a temperature of 125° Fah.   These will be examined twice a year for four years, and will give the relative and absolute rates of corrosion of the included specimens, which are contained in boxes so contrived as to allow free access of air and water to them. The third section contains a refutation of the method proposed by Mr. John B. Hartley, at Liverpool, for preserving iron by brass, which is shown by numerous and careful experiments, chiefly by Prof. Davy, and by appeal to the results of actual use, as well as the results of Schœnbein and other continental philosophers, to be wholly erroneous, and contrary to all theory, and to be productive of a most rapidly increased corrosive action of water upon iron when present.   Fourthly, a new method, founded on electro-chemical agencies, is proposed for the protection of wrought and cast iron, now in progress of experiment; and, lastly, the report concludes with the statement of various desiderata upon this subject.   All the details of the subject, such as the action of sea water in converting iron into a plumbaginous material, and the nature and properties, &c. of this subject, are necessarily omitted in a mere abstract.

"On the Construction of Apparatus for solidifying Carbonic Acid, and on the elastic force of Carbonic Acid Gas in contact with the liquid form of the Acid, at different Temperatures," by Mr. Robert Addams.

Mr. Addams prefaced the communication by adverting to the original production of liquid carbonic acid by Dr. Faraday, in 1823, and also to the solidification of the acid by M. Thilorier, and then exhibited three kinds of instruments which he (Mr. Addams) had employed for the reduction of the gas into the liquid and solid forms.   The first mode was mechanical, in which powerful hydraulic pumps were used to force gas from one vessel into a second, by filling the first with water, saline solutions, oil, or mercury; and in this apparatus a "*gauge of observation*" was attached, in order to see when the vessel was filled.   The second kind of apparatus is a modification of that invented and used by Thilorier.   The third includes the mechanical and the chemical methods, and by which, as stated, a saving of a large

quantity of acid formed in the generator is effected; whereas by the arrangement of Thilorier's plan, two parts in three are suffered to rush into the atmosphere, and are lost.   With this set of instruments are used two gauges of observation—one to show when the generator is filled with water by the pumps, and consequently all the free carbonic acid forced into the receiver; and the other to determine the quantity of liquid acid in the receiver.   He likewise exhibited other instruments for drawing off and distilling liquid carbonic acid from one vessel into another, and mentioned some experiments which were in progress, and especially the action of potassium in liquid carbonic acid, —an action which indicated no decomposition of the real acid, but such as implied the presence of water or a hydrous acid.   A table of the elastic force or tension of the gas over the liquid carbonic acid, was shown, for each ten degrees of the thermometer, beginning at zero, and terminating with 150 degrees.   The following are some of the results:—

Degrees.	℔ per sq. inch.	Atmospheres of 15℔ each.
0	279.9	18.06
10	300.	20.
30	398.1	26.54
32	413.4	27.56
50	520,05	34.67
100	934.8	62.32
150	1495.65	99.71

Mr. Addams announced his intention of examining the pressure, at higher temperatures, up to that of boiling water, and above; and asserted his belief that it may be profitably employed as an agent of motion—a substitute for steam—not directly, as had been already tried by Mr. Brunel, but indirectly, and as a means to circulate or reciprocate other fluids.   The solidification of the acid was shown, and the freezing of pounds of mercury in a few minutes, by the cooling influence which the solid acid exercises in passing again to the gaseous state.

"An Improved method of Constructing Railways," by J. Price.

This method consists in fixing rails on a continuous stone base, a groove having been made in the stone to receive a flange or projection of the lower side of the rail.   The stones and rails are to break joint with each other, and the chair by which the rails are to be secured is to be made fast to the rail by a bolt, not rivetted, but slipped in.   The chair is to be sunk until the top is level with the top of the stone, and fastened to it by two small wooden pins.   Any sinking of the road is to be obviated by driving wedges of wood underneath the stone until it is raised to the required height. The chairs are to be fixed at about 4 feet apart, and to weigh, if of malleable iron, 14 lbs., but if of cast iron 20 lbs. : the rail to weigh 50 lbs. per yard.

"On the Construction of a Railway with Cast-iron Sleepers, as a substitute for Stone Blocks, and with continuous Timber Bearing," by T. Motley.

The cast-iron sleepers, which are wedge-shaped, and hollow, having all their sides inclined inwards towards the under side, are to be laid transversely, and the timber is to pass longitudinally through the centre, and to be secured by wedges of iron and wood. The sleepers are to be six inches apart, and the timber of such a thickness as to prevent any perceptible deflexion betwixt the rails. The road is to be ballasted up to the top of the sleeper, and the timber to stand out sufficiently, and to have any approved rail laid upon it.

Mr. Stephenson considered the plan too expensive.—Mr. Donkin observed, that a certain portion of elasticity was beneficial.

"Machine for raising Water by an Hydraulic Belt," by Mr. Hall.

In this machine an endless double woollen band, passing over a roller at the surface of the earth, or at the level to which the water is to be raised, and under a roller at the lower level, or in the water, is driven with a velocity of not less than 1000 feet per minute. The water contained betwixt the two surfaces of the band is carried up on one side and discharged at the top roller by the pressure of the band on the roller, and by centrifugal force. This method has been in practice for some time in raising water from a well 140 feet deep in Portman Market, and produces an effect equal to 75 per cent. of the power expended, which is 15 per cent. above that of ordinary pumps. This method would be exceedingly convenient in deep shafts, as the only limit is the length of the band, and many different lifts may be provided.

Mr. Hawkins had seen a machine very similar, fifty years ago.—Mr. Donkin, without entering on the question of originality, stated that he had seen a machine of this description working with a beneficial effect of 75 per cent., the beneficial effect of ordinary pumps being about 60 per cent.

"On Clegg's Dry Gas-Meter," by Mr. Samuda.

This instrument consists of a pulse glass, that is, two thin glass globes united by a tube. These globes are partially filled with alcohol, and hermetically sealed when all the air is expelled from their interior. In this state, the application of a very slight degree of heat to one of the globes will cause the alcohol to rise into the other. The pulse glass is fixed on an axis, having a balance weight projected from it, and the axis works in bearings on the sides of a chamber through which the gas to be measured is made to pass in two currents, one of which is heated and the other cold. The hot gas is made to enter opposite to, and to blow upon the lower globe of the pulse glass, while the cold gas blows upon the other. The difference of temperature thus established between the globes causes the alcohol to rise into the upper one, and the glass turns over on its axis, thus varying its position, and bringing the full globe opposite to the hot stream of gas. This stream, with the assistance of the cold gas, which condenses the vapour in the top globe, repeats the operation, and the speed at which the globes oscillate will be precisely in proportion to the quantity of gas which has been blown upon them, provided a uniform difference of temperature is always maintained between the two streams of gas. The difference of temperature is established and rendered uniform by a small flame of gas, which heats a chamber through which the lower current of gas has to pass, and the arrangements for securing an equality in the difference of temperature are very ingenious. The instrument is first tested by making a given quantity of gas pass through it, and observing the number of oscillations of the pulse glass. This once established, the instrument registers the quantity passed with inconceivable accuracy.

Considerable discussion ensued, during which many objections were raised, to which Mr. Samuda replied.—Mr. Liddell observed, during the progress of the discussion, that a flame consuming one-fifth of a cubic foot of gas per hour would burn in a chamber, and not be liable to be extinguished by the opening and shutting of doors; and that if due precaution were used, a flame might be preserved with a consumption only of one-eighth or one-tenth of a foot per hour.

"On the construction of Geological Models," by Thomas Sopwith.

Mr. Sopwith lays down a method by which the commonest workman can make geological models, showing not only the position and thickness of the strata in a vertical section, but the actual surfaces and imbedding of the strata lying in different planes; so that one tray of the model being taken from above the other, we may consider that we have the stratum in miniature, with every undulation and indentation upon it. There was exhibited a model of the Forest of Dean, constructed in the following manner: The plan of the district was divided by lines crossing each other at right angles, and at the distance of a mile from each other. A vertical section was then prepared corresponding with each of these lines. These sections were drawn upon thin pieces of wood in the ordinary manner of a vertical geological section, and the several pieces of wood were then united by being half-lapped together, forming a skeleton model of vertical sections. After being thus united, the several sections were taken separately, and cut into as many portions as were required to illustrate the successive layers of strata ; the intersection of each of these portions having been first marked by a number at the several corners. After each section has been divided into its several parts, these respective portions are again united, and formed the exterior boundary of a square mile of rocks. The interior of this is filled with wood, and carved so as to coincide with the sections. Any intermediate portion can be fitted in with great exactness, first by a thin or skeleton section, and afterwards by wood, which any workman can carve with the most exact accuracy as quickly and as surely as any ordinary mechanical operation ; and thus at once a connexion between the most complicated section and the art of a common workman is accomplished. The outline of the surface, and the general contour of the country, is obtained, partly by means of the skeleton sections, and partly by the use of a gauge, or graduated pencil, sliding in a frame, in the same manner as practised by sculptors in transferring the dimensions of a cast to a block of marble.

(*To be continued.*)

NOTES AND NOTICES.

Davies's Fire-proof Composition.—Sir,—Among the list of patents given in your 786th Number (p. 383), there is a notice of one granted to " Joseph Davies, of Nelson-square, Blackfriars-road, Gentleman," *for a composition for protecting wood from flame.*" I feel myself called upon to state, that it was this composition which formed the subject of the highly interesting experiment in Dorset-street, Claphamroad, detailed at page 233 of your 778th Number, in which I erroneously described it as *De Witte's* fire-preventive composition. Mr. De Witte being associated with Mr. Davies, and having taken an active part in the several public and private trials that have been made with this patent composition, some other writers besides myself have been led into a slight mistake, which I take this opportunity of correcting. In an affair so truly humane, and of

such national importance, it is necessary that the public generally, and the scientific world in particular, should be rightly informed, both as to the invention and its inventor ; the former has been repeatedly demonstrated to be worthy of universal adoption—the latter is, consequently, deserving of public gratitude. I remain, &c.

London, Sept. 7, 1838.   WM. BADDELEY.

Belgian Railroads.—In the course of last month the number of passengers on the Belgian railroads was 269,086 ; the receipts amounted to 409,679 francs 80 cent. There is no other instance of such a result. It is, therefore, very unjustly that the establishment of iron railroads has lately been looked on in a more unfavourable light, on account of some accidents, which are of very trifling importance relatively to the number of persons who have travelled by these roads. We have received the following letter on the subject from Aix-la-Chapelle :—" The accidents which have lately taken place on the Belgian railroads, and which, as usual, have been amplified in proportion to the distance that the news has travelled, since the two persons killed have been multiplied to 200 by the time the news reached Prussia, do great injury to the shares in the iron railroads from Cologne to Elberfield. The public fearing the prejudices that may ensue, the shares have fallen to 92. The directors wishing to obtain all possible information on so important a subject, and to profit by any useful advice proceeding from other persons, have caused letter-boxes to be put up in the principal towns, through which any person may communicate his ideas anonymously."

The Great Western.—The success which has attended the steam navigation to America, and the preference given to it, exceed all expectation. It appears that before the arrival of the *Great Western* from New York, all her berths amounting to 130, were engaged for the return voyage fixed for the 8th instant. So numerous were the applications, and of course the number disappointed, that premiums of 20 guineas have been offered, and would be given, for berths on the first refusal of vacancies from parties who by any accident might be prevented from going. In an instance a party having engaged a double berth, was written to in Devonshire to request accommodation for a passenger, if the whole were not absolutely wanted. The directors have fitted up every yard of disposable space on deck, as well as below, in order to make room for the number stated. Upon the 87 passengers home, and the 130 out, at 40 guineas passage money per head in saloon, and 35 guineas cabin, each way, the directors of the *Great Western* will have received, therefore, upwards of 8,000*l.* exclusive of the benefit derived from the conveyance of goods, of which the *Great Western* brought from New York to the extent of about 200 tons measurement.

Taylor's patent Propeller.—We have received a letter from Mr. Lowe, of King-street, Old Kentroad, (for which we have not room this week) claiming the invention of the propeller described in our last Number, p. 400, as his, and stating that it was surreptitiously obtained from him by Mr. Taylor. Mr. Lowe states, however, that his patent was sealed in March last, two months prior to Mr. Taylor's : his right is therefore secure as against all subsequent patentees.

The *Railway Map* of England and Wales continues on sale, in a neat wrapper, price 6d. ; and on fine paper, coloured, price 1s.

☞ *British and Foreign Patents taken out with economy and despatch; Specifications, Disclaimers, and Amendments, prepared or revised; Caveats entered; and generally every Branch of Patent Business promptly transacted. A complete list of Patents from the earliest period (15 Car. II. 1675,) to the present time may be examined. Fee 2s. 6d.; Clients, gratis.*

LONDON: Printed and Published for the Proprietor, by W. A. Robertson, at the Mechanics' Magazine Office, No. 6, Peterborough-court, between 135 and 136, Fleet-street.—Sold by A. & W. Galignani, Rue Vivienne, Paris.

Mechanics' Magazine,

MUSEUM, REGISTER, JOURNAL, AND GAZETTE.

| No. 789.] | SATURDAY, SEPTEMBER 22, 1838. | [Price 3*d*. |

JONES'S MINERS ASCENDING AND DESCENDING MACHINE.

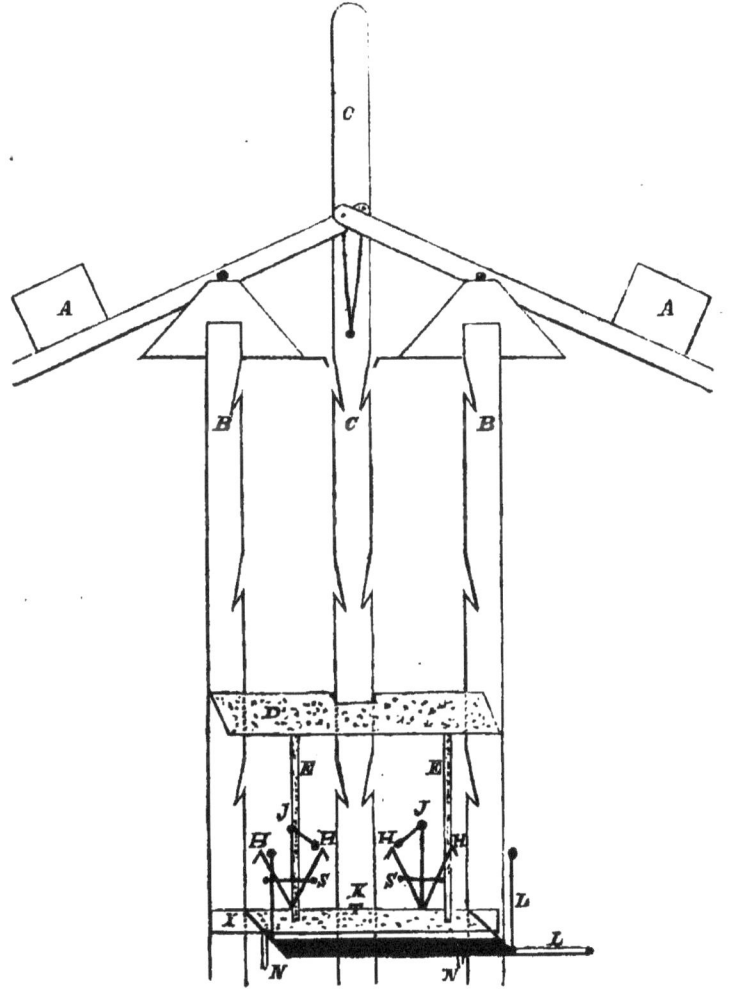

JONES'S MINERS ASCENDING AND
DESCENDING MACHINE.

Sir,—Much of the time and attention
of the good people of Cornwall, and elsewhere, has been directed toward the
construction of a machine for abridging
the arduous toil of the miner in going
to and from his work; and which, owing
to the great depth of many of the mines,
can only be worked at great expense to
the adventurers, and serious injury to
the health of the miners.

A large working model, of which the
annexed is a rough drawing, was exhibited at the last meeting of the Royal
Cornwall Polytechnic Society, and was
said by the judges, in letter which I received from them, to overcome four difficulties not met by any previous plans,
and for which they awarded their first
bronze medal.

B B C, are three stout rods of timber,
with notches or gaps at every twelve
feet; X is a strong piece of timber, in
which the four iron catches H H H H
work, and to which the car is attached.

J J, are two upright pieces of wood,
which, with the two handles J H, and
cross pieces S S, which are for working
the catches and governing the machine.
AA, two balance bobs.

N N, are two strong pieces of timber
tapering to one side, and shod with iron,
and which can be thrown out in an instant
by placing the foot upon the treadle K,
which, by encountering the side catches
must infallibly check any sudden descent; K depresses a strong elliptic spring.

To produce the motion, the middle
rod C is made to alternate, up and down,
by the mine engine, in strokes of 13 feet,
that is, 6 inches each side of the points of
suspension, insuring in the ascent a firmer
hold, and in the descent, easing the
catches required to be withdrawn. L L,
serves as a door when folded up, or for
a foot-path for getting in and out at the
different levels.

In making the ascent, the engine does
all the work, nothing more being necessary, on the part of the persons in
the car, than to put forth the middle
catches when the order to start is given.

The descent is effected in the following
manner: in every stroke of the rod,
whether up or down, two sets of niches
pass the middle catches, observing in
the descent you drop the middle catches
into the last niches upon the up-stroke,

and immediately withdraw the side catches,
when the car will be suspended from the
middle rod, and follow it in its descent.
Any negligence upon the part of the
guide, will be productive of no harm,
but will take the car a stroke higher, and
give him the trouble of doing his work
over again.

It is calculated that it might be worked
in its ascent, as the engine does all the
work with great ease at six strokes per
minute, and at 12 feet per stroke, or
216 fathoms in 18 minutes.

Yours most respectfully,
WM. JONES.

ON THE DANGERS OF FIRE FROM LO-
COMOTIVE AND MARINE FURNACE
FLUES.

Sir,—Considerable discussion has at
different times taken place, as to the probable extent of danger, in the shape of accidental conflagrations likely to arise from
the sparks of railway locomotives. Experience has shown that the actual amount
of danger has, in general, been greatly
overrated, although accidents of this kind
have been rather numerous, and in some
cases sufficiently costly, (the late case of
the Manchester mail-bag for instance) to
render every expedient desirable by which
the liability of accidents may be decreased.
A good deal of care has been bestowed
upon this subject, and your 26th volume
contains a report of the Lords' Committee, on the danger by fire likely to
arise from locomotive engines passing
through narrow streets, with extracts
from the evidence; but with respect
to steam-boats, which would seem to
be in many respects more dangerous,
very little caution seems to obtain. I
have several times witnessed, what I am
given to understand is a frequent occurrence, the soot in the funnel in a
state of intense combustion, pouring
forth showers of sparks on the deck,
and all around. Returning over London bridge, one night in particular, I
saw a large steam-boat (from Gravesend
I believe) lying at Nicholson's Wharf,
the chimney of which was belching forth
fire, both "fast and furious." Large
flakes of ignited soot were falling thickly
on the deck and rigging of this and some
adjacent vessels, and part were carried
on to the wharf; the settlement of these
particles on dry combustible matter would
seem likely enough to occasion a tre-

mendous conflagration—such as usually occurs in places of this character, when once fired.

By advices recently received from New York, we learn there has been a most destructive fire in the city of Hudson, sixty houses are reported to have been consumed, and the property destroyed is valued at upwards of two hundred thousand pounds. This catastrophe is said to have been originated by *a spark from the steam-boat "Congress,"* which was at the time lying in the dock.

The practice of burning out the flues, though a common, is decidedly a bad one; some other method of cleansing should be employed, and in the event of the soot taking fire, instantaneous methods of extinction should be resorted to. The introduction of a small jet of water, or a cartridge, within the funnel, would soon remove all chance of mischief.

The small number of cases in which any serious consequences arise from the foregoing causes may induce a sort of apathy in those who are frequent observers, that may in some cases lead to serious loss. The foregoing narrative shows what has happened, and may happen again, and should be a sufficient warning to persons in charge of steam-boats lying in tiers of shipping, in docks, or at wharfs, to be careful of flying *sparks*.

I remain, Sir, yours respectfully,
WM. BADDELEY.

London, Sept. 8, 1838.

"EXCELLENT FIRE-ESCAPE."

"Patriæ sis idoneus."

Sir,—In that highly respectable paper the *Sunday Times* of August 26th, is a paragraph under the above title, abridged from a letter by myself. I should be very glad, on public grounds, to give it additional extension. The subject may interest every one of us at some period or other, and has, like the "steam explosions," derived a more painful and pressing interest, from frequent recent accidents; to an instance of which, involving four deaths in the street where this is dated, in November, 1835, is owing the existence of the numerous fire-escapes now kept in different parts of London.

The fire-escape which I first saw and tried in the year 1818,—the only one of the kind I ever saw, and the owner could

not tell the name of the inventor, and whether it had been ever patented,—was in the form of a pipe or. trough, with sticks on the upper surface like a ladder, or like the heavy *wooden* trough moveable on wheels, lately invented,[*] and probably pirated, from it; differing, however, essentially in being constructed of canvass, and of course both flexible and portable; rolling up, to the best of my recollection, in a circle of 2½ or 3 feet diameter, about the circumference of a fore coach-wheel. I believe it fastened at the top by grappling-hooks, but it has since been suggested to me that a transverse bar of iron wire, having a purchase against the inner side of the window, would be more sure. Of course this escape is let down from a window, &c., and the party to be rescued gets in at the top and slides down. Down indeed he *must* go when he has entered, no misgiving, or drawing-back, can prevent his being saved; but if the rapid transit has a breathless and unpleasant effect, he can moderate and regulate it, by laying hold of the successive sticks above him.

I have heard it remarked by an eminent mathematician, and popular London clergyman, that "all fire-escapes which presuppose much dexterity and *presence of mind* in the parties who are to be rescued, have a strong chance of failure." This I believe; but the security of this is so self-evident, and may be so carefully and leisurely considered before-hand, that there is as little scope for *nervousness* as in anything of the kind hitherto broached.

The weight, I should imagine, for a length of 60 feet would not at the utmost exceed 30 lbs., and the cost might be between 3 and £4. In almost every respect, therefore, I think it preferable to the *wooden trough.* It is impossible for the latter to be used "within" a house, or to be used without much communication and probable delay from external power; and when the canvass one is adapted for being raised from without (of which I am going to speak) it will have about the same advantage in portability and celerity that a "watering-pot" would have over a "butt."

This "Escape," which I saw at Woburn, in Bedfordshire, where it be-

[*] If our correspondent refers to Wivell's fire escape, he is mistaken; the trough is of canvass. See *Mech. Mag.* No. 723.—ED. M. M.

longed to a celebrated poet, a native of that place, and librarian to the Duke of Bedford, Mr. Wiffen, may have been formerly better known, and may be now known to many, but I am convinced it is not generally so; whilst, therefore, it may be laudable to extend its notice, it would be culpable not to do so.

After anxious consideration and some experience, I have proposed the following three improvements.—1st. That it should be periodically washed with a solution of potass and other ingredients (which some of your readers can specify) to enable it to withstand the flames. 2nd. That in case persons should not be at hand to receive and firm it below, a *weight* (attached to the lower end by a short cord) should be thrown out with it to steady it, at a sufficient distance from the wall; probably from ¼ cwt. upwards, would be sufficient for this purpose. 3rd. That as he would be no friend to his species who should recommend the neglect of external means, this escape might be raised from without, by means of a *rod* in pieces, jointed after the manner of a fishing-rod, the lower pieces of course longer than the upper ones, and of a length corresponding to the escape—from 50 to 70 feet, many houses requiring such a height to their summits. Whether, if there was awkwardness in fixing it at the top, this rod would bear the weight of a person descending without bending or snapping, I doubt, though I think it possible; however, a pole might be often at hand to be substituted. Of course any one might *ascend* by this escape when fixed, with as much ease as by a ladder. The weight of the rod I have estimated at 18 lbs.; and I suppose there may be woods even better than larch for the purpose.

Commending this necessarily long statement to kind and judicious public consideration,

I am, Sir, yours respectfully,
J. D. PARRY.

Tottenham Court Road, September 4, 1838.

P.S. Would it be possible to construct a *portable staircase* with wire railings and a "landing" of 2 feet square, not exceeding 3 or 4 cwt., and nearly as easy of transfer, on wheels, as the wooden trough, being, of course, much lighter than an engine?—If so, there might be cases of infirmity, &c., where it would be invaluable.

LOCOMOTION BY ROCKETS—COUP DE DE GRACE ROCKET.

Sir,—General Andreosi, who has written the best works extant on practical artillery, &c. did many years ago suggest the use of large rockets for propelling a boat loaded with shells, gunpowder, &c., along the water, against the sides of an enemy's ship. In 1825, Colonel Paixhaus rementions the subject, and in 1824, Colonel Ravichio, in the French service (engineers), promulgated the same idea. In 1824 I constructed a kind of little boat, which inclosed a large shell rocket (32 lbs.) which floats on the water, and being fired by a particular contrivance of my own, the boat-like envelope is blown to pieces, and the rocket skims along, or close to the surface of the water, good fifteen hundred yards, so as to enter the enemy's ship between wind and water. My method of giving them the proper direction is simple, easy, and exact, and may be effected from an open boat. I could construct rockets of one hundred to five hundred pounds weight each, which, containing from thirty to two hundred pounds of powder in their cast-iron conical heads, for explosion in a ship's sides, may merit the name of *coup de grace* rockets. They may be allowed to remain on the water, washed over by the waves, for hours, or days, without injury, or any chance of missing fire. One of my shot-proof steam ships provided with a few such rockets, armed with a twelve-inch bomb-cannon for horizontal projection, and a frame for throwing fifty of my *prehensile* incendiary rockets into the sails and rigging of a ship, such as I proposed to the Lord High Admiral of England in 1828, will constitute a formidable antagonist to any ship of war, if manœvered in the proper way, at a proper distance.

I am, &c.,
F. MACERONI.

WOODEN PAVING—HINTS ON ROAD MAKING.

Sir,—You see, how the paving people are going on with their layers of loose gravel,—then loose broken granite—then new large stones,—then ramming with their absurd hand rammer,—then liquid mortar,—then a corfortable cover of sand and rubbish. And then—after a few weeks—holes and bumps as bad as ever—and then anon—the whole *job* to do over again! Glory be to the paving boards, and to the vestry boards that can invent so much capital work for paving-men, and granite-mongers—and for the wielders of the "Lady Griffins" who grunt in vain to give the stones and the subjacent mass compression enough to stand the shock of even a Tilbury's wheel! Pray, Mr. Editor, do remind the people who have to pay for such vagaries, that from the pages of your valuable periodical for 1825,—they will learn how to form a carriage pavement that shall be as level as a billiard table, and remain so under any pressure from carriages, as long as the stones shall last, becoming better and better, the longer it is used—and any part of it being taking up for pipe laying, immediately restored to uniformity of hardness with the rest. Moreover, that all these advantages may be secured—with the old small stones, and without any application of the gravel, broken granite, and mortar, so expensively and absurdly applied by the present paviours. I would again befriend the public, by calling their attention to your observations on my *Hints to Paviors* (2nd edition, 1833), a copy of which I sent to the members of the Oxford-street Committee. By the bye the *Monthly Repository* for February or January 1834, ridicules my suggestion of paving certain streets, and the vicinity of churches, with blocks of wood; and portrays the citizens of St. Giles's holding out their dusky hands before a good Christmas fire, furnished from the carriage way; he puts into their mouths a song of praise to me, of which the following is a fragment:—

"London streets are paved with wood,
　Long live Maceroni;
For we'll blow out with summut good,
　Saved out on our coal money."

I trust that the *Repository* will indite a new song to his old tune, in honour of the wooden paviours who are now about to gladden the hearts and warm the bodies of the St. Giles's songsters. Seriously speaking, Sir, it is infamous that the public should be duped and robbed for so many years, by the jobbers in a most expensive, silly, inefficient mode of paving this great metropolis, when the only method which can suit all the con-

tingences and features of the case, is offered them at less than half of the expense. It may be as well for me, with your permission, just to state the main principle of my paving plan:—First, the earth is levelled and then hardened by a machine consisting of a frame on wheels, supporting a block that weighs 3 or 500 pounds, worked like a minor pile-driving monkey; the stones are then laid, and beaten down by the broad flat head of the stone driver. After a short time, if any inequalities of surface appear, the *protuberances* are beaten down,—and these can be distinguished with great accuracy by pouring water over the surface. Thus, the pavement *must* become better and better, and if any part is taken up, that part can be immediately reduced to any degree of solidity by the machine. The stones that were used some years ago were much smaller than the new ones lately introduced to complete the paving *job*, and the smaller the stones, the better the pavement. Amongst other advantages, they do not become round-headed. The stones should be square-ended of equal sizes. Mortar is ridiculous, unless it be used as at Rome and Naples, especially at the former place, where the pavement is a thick horizontal wall, the small deep parallopepoidal stones being built in, and supported by, above a foot thick of the best puzzolana mortar. But, as I have shown in my *Hints to Paviors*, such a pavement will not do for London, where it has to be frequently disturbed, for sewers, pipes, &c. Of course the substratum would be improved by an admixture of brick and mortar rubbish, with a little chalk—but the earth and gravel already under it, is much disposed to harden by the formation of carburet of iron, and with my due mechanical compression, will produce a far better, and quite durable level, which all the fuss and expense of the new-fangled jobbers will not secure for a week. Without the application of my means the wooden pavement will speedily become as uneven as the stone.

Inviting those whom it may concern to wipe the dust off the copies of *Hints to Paviors* that I have sent them,

I remain, Sir,
　　　Your obedient servant,
　　　　　　F. MAOBRONI.

Sept. 11, 1838.

EARTHENWARE WASH-HAND STANDS.

Sir,—We have all seen, and many have purchased, the wash-hand stands fitted with marble slabs, the clean and comfortable appearance of which must strike everybody, as also must their manifest superiority over the ordinary stands with wooden tops and sides, which soon loose their paint, disclosing the naked deal underneath; and if mahogany the surface rapidly becomes stained and spotted. Now it seems to me that it is very possible to secure all the neatness, cleanliness, and comfortable appearance of the marble, without going to the expense of £4. 4s., and upwards.

I propose lining the top and sides with earthenware, which can be accomplished with ease, combining a neat appearance with a low price. If the slab in which the circle for the basin is made (and which I shall call the slab to distinguish it from the back and sides) be considered too large to be made conveniently in one piece, it can be made in two pieces, thus :—

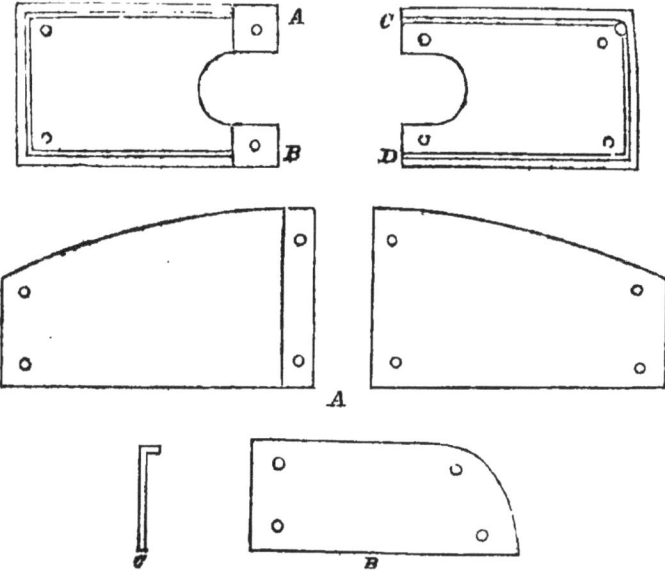

The ends A B being made with a shoulder, the ends C D made to correspond, will wrap over, and if bedded in plaster of Paris, the joint will be made impervious to water.

These slabs should be screwed on to the deal top with neat brass-headed screws, the holes in the slabs being, of course, countersunk to receive them. The back can, in like manner, be made in two pieces, as A; the sides B can be easily made in one piece; the crevices between the back, sides, and slabs should be pointed with plaster of Paris, or any other cement, as it is important that no wet should find its way between the earthenware and wood, as in that case the wood would rapidly decay. The back and sides should be made with a turn-over edge, as may be seen at C, which is a perpendicular section of B. The shoulders of the slabs and backs, which wrap over, should not be glazed, in order that the cement may take a firm hold.

The stands, if fitted with earthenware in this manner, may be made of fir, and neatly painted in the usual manner, there is no fear that the stand will grow shabby, as the paint will in no part be subject to any rough wear and tear. If a little channel be made to run round the edge of the slab, communicating with a hole in the corner E, and from which an earthenware tube one inch long be continued downwards, all the slop will run off into a mug placed under it upon a little shelf.

I am, Sir, your humble servant,

                      E. R.

Mile End.

FLAT-CHAMBERED BOILERS.—ON THE
EXTENT OF MR. HANCOCK'S CLAIMS.

Sir,—We feel much interest in this
neighbourhood in the discussion on
Hancock's and Anderson's steam boilers.
If Mr. H. can claim Sir J. A.'s boiler,
it appears to me that he may claim also,
almost every existing boiler of a subsequent date to his patent; for there are
few that do not possess some feature of
similarity; but it does not follow that
they are infringements, nevertheless, even
if such features were suggested by the
labours of another, as it would be too
much to assume that what one man has
effected, however intricate and profound,
could not be equally accomplished by
another.

Mr. Hebert asserts that he found the
"real claim of Mr. Hancock was not for
every kind of flat chamber;" and, a little further on, that "Mr. Hancock prudently kept the broad claim out of his
specification." Mr. Hancock in reply,
after much unnecessary play on the term
flat, has given his claims as follows:—
"Mr. Hebert charges me with an attempt to impose upon your readers: the
accusation recoils on himself. The
words of my claim are, the constructing
narrow flat vessels in the *form* and *manner* hereinbefore described, and which
are adapted to be placed vertically edge-
wise upwards over the fire for producing
steam for steam-engines; and also in
arranging and *combining* a series of *such
vessels* together with narrow vertical
spaces between them for the fire, so as
to form a boiler with communications
through their junctions for the passage
of water and steam from one vessel to
another."

Nothing, certainly, can be more clearly
and concisely defined than are these
claims, and they corroborate most completely Mr. Hebert's assertion, that Mr.
Hancock is limited to the particular
construction of the vessels "therein described;" and also to the one particular
mode of *combining a series of such vessels.* They demonstrate most decidedly
that Mr. Hancock did not, on the occasion, contemplate the possibility of any
variation or modification of form, or
mode of connection, otherwise such contingency would have been provided for.
The law of patent right does not
grant a monopoly of a principle, and in
the case of steam boilers, it can only

give protection to the patentee of a particular conformation, mode of construction, or combination; and to these means,
which are specified and described by him
to be essential or conducive to the exercise
of his invention, is the patentee rigidly
confined: to quote from an author, "He
must not be allowed to bring within the
meshes of his monopoly contrivances
which he has not made, and which are
already perhaps, or may chance, in ordinary course, to come from other sources
to common property."

Mr. Hancock's invention consists of
flat chambers, each of which is complete
in itself; and is not his boiler formed by
combining a series of such chambers
together through the medium of two
bolts, round which, by means of collars,
or some such arrangement, a water and
steam communication is formed throughout the series?

Now, how does Sir J. A.'s invention
accord with this? His boiler is composed of a bottom and top chamber,
connected together by partitions of alternating water and flue spaces; these
spaces are not chambers, properly speaking, they only form a part of a whole,
solidly riveted together. None of these
spaces before riveting are complete in
themselves, like Mr. Hancock's chambers, they having one side wholly open,
and the other partially; therefore, until
they are riveted to the body, they cannot, like Mr. Hancock's chambers, be
used individually for the purpose of
generating steam. Further, if Sir J.
A.'s boiler were laid on its side, an
horizontal section of the spaces would
present a fac-simile of the flue and water
spaces of a marine boiler; that the flue of
such boiler is much wider in proportion
than the water spaces, is most true, but
we cannot patent the width of a flue,
nor that of a water space.

He must be a bold man, and no mechanic, who will say that the conformation of these inventions are the same, or
that they bear a greater similitude to
each other than boilers generally do, or
indeed than is justifiable. So much,
then, for the "appropriation of the labour of others."

I had written thus far, when I received the last number of the Magazine,
wherein you review Mr. Hancock's
Narrative, and in the course of your
editorial remarks you observe, (page

388), "That the originality of this chamber boiler, and the extent of Mr. H.'s claim of monopoly, whether it extends to all kinds of flat chambers in which fire, or rather hot air and flame, and water, are in alternate layers; or whether it is confined to the particular method of construction specified by Mr. H., has been lately the subject of discussion in our Magazine. We incline to the former opinion. If Mr. H. can show himself to be the original inventor and patentee of flat chamber boilers, notwithstanding he has only described ONE *method of making them* in his specification, (which is as *per example*) the law as at present interpreted, will protect him from all mere colourable modifications, even although they may be improvements, and the patentee of such improvements or modifications can only work them under license from Mr. Hancock, until the term of his patent is expired." If this new reading of the patent laws be correct; if Mr. Hancock's right extends to all flat chambers, whatever may be the form of construction, in which fire, or rather hot air and flame, and water, are in alternate layers, to which "your opinion inclines," notwithstanding it is not so specified, patentees must use their most strenuous exertions to oppose an extension of the term of an expiring patent; and which extension cannot evidently be granted, without manifest injustice to those whose patents this new interpretation thus makes dependent. But what if the public should object to Mr. Hancock's claim, and reply in something like these terms—" We, the public, have for a long period previous to the existence of your patent, Mr. Hancock, been in the habit of using boilers in which water and heated air are ranged in alternate layers, as shown in marine boilers above noticed. But you seek by this new doctrine to deprive us of that which has already become public property, for it must extend to all."

Would not Mr. H. naturally reply, " I do not claim the monopoly of generating steam by hot air and water in alternate layers, I claim only the *particular mode of construction* set forth in my specification, thus disposing at once of his high pretensions, and allowing poor Sir J. Anderson to continue the even tenor of his way.

The recent amendment of the patent laws has removed several of the unjust restrictions to which patentees were subject; but I do conceive that, if the opinion you have expressed were law, patentees would labour under difficulties a thousand times greater than before, and which would sap patent property to its very foundation. As if a patentee is to travel beyond the record—if he is to be allowed to bring within the meshes of his monopoly contrivances which he never made or contemplated, and provided not for in his specification, and a simple description of the invention, as *per example*, is to suffice, it is tantamount to obtaining the monopoly of a first principle; hence we should have, as has been well observed, but one patent spinning machine, one patent loom, one patent steam-engine, and so on—thus the patent would be granted for the end, not for the means, and which would be destructive to ninety nine patents out of a hundred in existence, and therefore the question as to limit is one of the gravest import to patentees ever mooted.

I am, Sir,
Your obedient servant,
JOHN SIMMONS.
Birmingham, Sept. 13th, 1838.

———

MR. HANCOCK'S AND SIR JAMES ANDERSON'S PATENT BOILERS.

Sir,—I quite agree with your remarks in No. 784 of your Magazine, that it is not the proper place to discuss the legal rights of patentees. It would have been much better if Mr. Hancock had refrained from making any attack on Sir James Anderson's patent right until he brought it before a court of law; but as you did (I have no doubt from the best and most liberal motives) insert the attack, which from the immense circulation of your Magazine had such a powerful tendency to prejudice the interest of Sir James; and as you have allowed Mr. Hancock in his last letter to reiterate the statement, I hope you will also allow me a short reply. In No. 783 of your Magazine, I stated, that Mr. Hancock had no legal right to restrain any person from adopting flat chambers for boilers, nor for the modes of strengthening or arranging them in any way they thought proper; and I stated my reasons for such opinion in No. 783, and 784, and as I had legal statements on the subject I still retain the same opinion, notwithstanding your kind remarks on behalf of Mr. Hancock. I omitted, however, to state, that although acts of commission or omission existed which would invalidate his patent, yet it required a wr.t of *scire facias* to issue actually to annul them; which course could be adopted by any parties who might be interfered with. Thus far in explanation I conceive requisite by your notes appended to my two letters. Mr. Hancock now having published his claim in No. 786, and having thus made known to the world, that his patent (if good and valid) is only for constructing narrow flat vessels in the *form* and *manner described* in his specification, and that he also claims for his mode of arranging and combining a series of *such* vessels together, with narrow vertical spaces between them for the fire, so as to form one boiler, with communication *through their junctions* for the passage of water from one vessel to another; having done this, it is clear from his own statement, that his claim is only for a boiler whose chambers or vessels are of the form and manner described in his specification, and for the method of combining and arranging *such* chambers; so that, according to his own showing, *any* person may make a different form of chambers, and may combine and arrange such different form in any way they please, without in the least entrenching on his claim. I trust, Mr. Editor, you will now allow me to show that Sir James Anderson's boiler is so essentially different in all its parts and arrangements from such described patent, that no similarity can be found to exist. In the first place, Sir James's chambers are flat parallel chambers;—Mr. Hancock's are near double the size at each end that they are in the middle. Mr. Hancock strengthens his chambers by a series of bolts passed through them at various places, the plates being bulged inwards to admit of the heads of such bolts being brought below the surface;—Sir James strengthens his by peculiarly constructed frames inside, to which the perfectly flat plates are rivetted. Mr. Hancock has a number of *vertical* flues (by his arrangement of his chambers) for the fire and smoke

to pass through;—Sir James's chambers are arranged to form only one continuous flue. Mr. Hancock's arrangement only admits of the water occupying a portion of his chambers,—Sir James's chambers must be at all times full of water. The upper part of Mr. Hancock's chambers are his reservoirs for steam;—Sir James's has a separate chamber for that purpose at the top of his boiler. Mr. Hancock has a clear and nearly direct passage to the atmosphere for his fire and smoke; while Sir James's has a flat *water* chamber over the whole of his and connected with them. Mr. Hancock's fire-place is *underneath* his chambers;—Sir James's is at *one end*. Sir James relies for keeping all his joints steam-tight by having all iron or copper joints;—Mr. Hancock invariably in his specification says, he uses and recommends lead tin foil and *soft solder* for all his joints. Mr. Hancock connects the water and steam in each of his chambers with the others by means of two or more hollow bolts, which pass through the whole of the chambers;—Sir James has no such bolts, nor any connection through his chambers. Having now shown that Sir James Anderson's boiler is in no respect constructed or arranged so as to incroach on Mr. Hancock's claims as shown by himself, I remain, Mr. Editor, with many thanks for your impartial conduct.

Your obedient servant,
A SHAREHOLDER IN THE STEAM CARRIAGE AND WAGGON COMPANY.

OBSERVATIONS ON THE LAW OF PATENTS, AS REGARDS THE EXTENT OF AN INVENTOR'S CLAIMS OF MONOPOLY—MR. HANCOCK'S AND SIR JAMES ANDERSON'S PATENT BOILERS.

In inserting the two preceeding letters we have swerved from our intention not to admit of a discussion of the legal rights of patentees in our pages; but the temporary interest excited as regards the parties whose patents are in question, and the importance of the general point at issue, must be our excuse. We hope, however, that our correspondents will not strain the character of impartiality which they are pleased to give us, by entering further into the discussion. The opinions after expressed are the result of considerable experience in patent matters, and mature consideration of the existing law upon the subject.

In supporting the validity of Mr. Hancock's patent we rest upon the hypothesis that he is the original inventor and patentee of flat-chambered boilers, as we shall hereafter more particularly define, leaving out of sight the common marine boilers, referred to by Mr. Simmons, and Smith's patents, referred to by Mr. Hebert, the bringing forward of which is a mere begging of the question.

Our observations upon the question of law as to the extent of Mr. Hancock's monoply (see page 388) are in consonance with the opinions of all writers on the law of patents for inventions. It is not a new, but a very old reading, and one held to be correct and just by the first legal authorities, even under the old administration of the patent law, when every point was construed in the strictest sense, as against a patentee, and every objection to a patent considered to be good until its force was explained away by indubitable evidence.

In the most generally received work, of authority on the law of patents, it is laid down that,—

"A person may take for the foundation on which he intends to erect the superstructure of his improvements, either a thing that has been long known, or one that has lately been made public; either the subject of an expired patent, or that of one which is void. But if the improvement cannot be used without the subject of an existing grant, he must wait until it is expired. He may, however, at once take out a patent for the improvement by itself, and sell it. In all these cases he must claim nothing more than the mere addition."—*Godson on the Law of Patents.*—p. 74.

Now, Mr. Hancock's invention was simply, (and if it had been properly specified would have been so described) the construction of a steam boiler, in which there should be alternate vertical thin laminations of water, and heated air or flame from a furnace. This, it appears to us, was the invention for which Mr. H. obtained a patent,—and referring to his *Narrative* this view of the case is borne out. He commences his experiments with tubular boilers, but finds the division of the water too minute for practical purposes, he is consequently led to "consider of some arrangement by which

the water exposed to the action of the fire should be less divided, and yet extend over a large surface." He accordingly invented the "flat-chambered" boiler, and for this he obtains a patent. The mode of joining together the plates and chambers of his boiler were mere subordinate points as regarded him, but might certainly be the subject of subordinate patents under his license, during the term of his patent right, or by himself or others, after its expiration. According to the requirements of the proviso in the patent, he is bound to declare in his specification "the nature of his invention and the manner in which it is to be performed." What we consider to be the nature of Mr. Hancock's invention we have just stated,—and that is what he claims; "the manner in which it is to be performed," is necessary to be described according to the best of the inventor's knowledge and experience—but he is not to be bound by, and confined to, the precise method of putting the parts together, which he details. He must specify the most efficient means for carrying his invention into effect, as far as he has the power, either as resulting from experiment, or from mental consideration and design;—and this best means, in the inventor's opinion, is, as we have stated, only as *per example.* The process of manufacturing an article may legally and justly be the subject of a patent, where the article or thing to be manufactured is already public property; or, where patented, under license from the patentee;—but, it would strike at the root of a majority of the patents granted—of that class which are most worthy of protection, if any one, by merely contriving a different way of making an article, or a mere alteration or modification of that described by the first patentee in his specification, could make the patented article, and perhaps put the real inventor out of the market. Great and important inventions very frequently issue from persons unacquainted with the minor details of the branch of manufacture in relation to which the invention is made. The artisan is confined to some particular routine of operation, and is prejudiced in favour of it, or it never enters into his mind to strike out of the beaten track. A novice, perhaps for a single time, sees the operations of the factory; the relations and connections of the various manipulations and proceedings one with another are made clear to him; and in the process of ratiocination, a more simple and direct means of obtaining the object suddenly occurs to him. He patents his invention, but being unacquainted with the minutiæ of the proceedings of the manufacture, he cannot himself describe every rivet, bolt, screw, nail, shaft, lever, wheel, pinion or pulley, that is necessary to be used to carry out his invention; in this he must either trust to hired workmen, his patent agent, or make the best he can of it himself. He satisfies the law if he describes one way, the best to his knowledge, in which his invention can be carried into effect; and hard upon him would it be indeed, and most unjust, if one well skilled and experienced in the manufacture in question could turn upon him, and say that as he can perform the operation in a better or in a different manner from the patentee, he will deprive him of the fruits of his genius.

These latter remarks may not be exactly applicable to the case of Sir James and Mr. Hancock in the particular, but in the main they are. We are not in possession of the specifications of either of these gentlemen: our observations are founded on the same information which our readers possess—the various particulars which have been published in our pages.

The distinction between the principle, which is not patentable, and the application of the principle which is, in Mr. Hancock's case is clear: the principle would be the division of the water to be evaporated into small portions, the better to expose it to the influence of the heat; Mr. Hancock's application of the principle is the so doing by flat thin chambers. The first inventor of division by *tubes*, could have sustained a patent for all ways of placing the tubes together. We question whether the principle of construction above-mentioned, viz. division of the water into a number of small portions might not have been the subject of a valid patent in the early history of the steam-engine, as distinguished from the large dome boiler containing one mass of water over the furnace; this would class Mr. Hancock's invention as the third step from the unpatentable principle.

It has been repeatedly brought forward by Mr. Hancock's various anta-gonists as a fatal ground of objection to his patent that the boiler which he now uses is an improvement upon that described by him in his specification. Upon this point we will again turn to the same authority as we have before quoted:—

" If it appear that a better mode of using the manufacture be a subsequent discovery; that the patentee has since the date of the grant found out this new means of carrying on his own invention to a better effect, then the grant will continue valid."—*Godson on Law of Patents*, p. 124.

That the boiler which Mr. Hancock now uses is better than that which he originally patented is unquestionable, as it is also in our opinion that he has retained and adhered to the main and distinguishing features of his patent. It would be absurd to suppose that during fourteen years' experience " no new means of carrying on his invention with better effect" should occur, and it would be unjust to say he shall not use it.

Whether Sir James Anderson's patented boiler be an improvement upon Mr. Hancock's we have not yet heard of any experiments from which to judge: so great have been the expectations raised by his friends, perhaps injudiciously, that we have hesitated to give an opinion based upon theory alone, and have anxiously waited the starting of his embryo carriage. It was promised to be on the road before the coronation, but three additional months have elapsed without any sign of life. Only let Sir James perform a tithe of what has been done by Mr. Hancock, and he shall have our cordial support. Sir James, say his friends, has failed in twenty-nine carriages to succeed in the thirtieth—but we fear that twenty-nine stumbles are poor evidence of the thirtieth step being a sure one. Mr. Hancock has built ten vehicles, and every one has, in a measure, succeeded. Steam travelling on common roads we have always considered as a doubtful mercantile speculation, but we would very willingly have our doubts removed. Mr. Hancock we have praised and supported as persevering to effect his aim against no ordinary difficulties; and should Sir James, who boasts of having started about the same time, outstrip him in the race, we shall not be backward in awarding him the palm of victory, and his due meed of praise.

SYMINGTON'S PLAN FOR THE PREVEN-
TION OF EXPLOSION OF STEAM-BOAT
BOILERS.

The alarming extent to which this awful
calamity has of late arrived, particularly in
America, is certainly horrifying in the extreme to the reader. In fact, we can scarcely
take a newspaper into our hands, but an account of one or more of those fearful accidents, attended with extensive loss of human life, meets our eye. It is, therefore,
to be feared, that if government do not interfere, and endeavour to put a stop to such
accidents, by passing a law to compel steam-
boat proprietors to use the most efficient
safety apparatus on board these boats, it
cannot fail to act very prejudicially against
this cheap, speedy, and indispensable mode
of communication. An inspector could be
appointed at all the principal sea-ports, at
no great expense, with full power to examine the machinery, and see that the law
was strictly attended to. This would do
much for humanity, and give great satisfaction to the public.

We have lately seen a paper, written by
Mr. Andrew Symington, son of the origi-
nator of steam navigation, " On the cause
and Prevention of Steam-Boat Boilers' Explosion," which he intends to lay before the
Society of Arts. As it contains some ingenious and original suggestions on the subject, we consider a few extracts from it to
be well worth our attention. Mr. S. is
of opinion that the causes of explosion are
by no means numerous nor intricate, and
quite within the power of man to prevent.
The first and greatest cause which he notices
is the want of a regular supply of water to
the boiler, in consequence of which it falls
below the level of the flues ; of course, the
top of them gets red-hot, and the boiler
being in this state, if any agitation of the
vessel should cause the water contained in
the spaces between the flues to be thrown
over the extensive surface of hot iron, the
generation of steam at the instant is so
rapid, that the safety-valve is not capable
of allowing it to escape, although it be in
good working order, and of course, the boiler
must explode. This, in all likelihood, was
the cause of the late catastrophe on board
the *Victoria* steamer in the River Thames,
the evidence of Captain Bell, the master of
that vessel, being to this effect :—That he
experienced a difficulty in getting steam all
day, and had never been able to work the
engines more than six pounds on the inch ;
and also from the circumstances of his finding the boiler that was not burst to be red-
hot immediately after the explosion, which
took place only a few seconds after the collision with the collier brig. Such evidence

as this certainly warrants the conclusion,
that the accident originated from the above
mentioned cause.

The remedy for this evil is a newly-invented float of Mr. Symington's, by the
use of which the boiler is self-supplied with
water, in a similar manner to that applied
to land-engine boilers. The great difficulty
which has been overcome by this invention,
was the impossibility of using the common
float in a steam-boat boiler, owing to the
agitation of the water therein, caused by
the motion of the vessel. Mr. Symington's
float is enclosed within a cylindrical case,
and suspended from the roof of the boiler ;
this case is entirely close, with the exception of a small hole in the top and bottom
of it, to allow the ingress and egress of the
water. The case preserves the float from
being agitated by the water,—a rod is attached to it that communicates with a cock
in the supply pipe, and by this contrivance
the boiler is supplied independent of the
engineer.

The second risk of accident is by the
safety-valve getting corroded and cemented
to its seat. To prevent this, Mr. S. proposes to connect the valve in a simple way
to any moving part of the engine, so as to
give to it a slow revolving motion. This
valve should be locked up in a case and
loaded with a weight not to exceed the working pressure of the steam for the engine.—
Scotch Paper.

OPENING OF THE LONDON AND BIRMING-
HAM RAILWAY.

Monday, the 17th instant, was the first
day that the complete line of rail-road from
the London to the Birmingham terminus
was opened. The portion of the road which
was traversed for the first time on this occasion was that which extends between the
old station at Denbigh-hall and the station
at Rugby. The station at the former place
now no longer exists; but there are on this
extent of 35 miles stations at Wolverton,
Roade, Blisworth, Weedon, and Crick. The
first train started from the Euston-square
station at seven o'clock, having in the carriages the proprietors of the undertaking
and their friends. The next train which was
open to the public, left Euston-square station at ten minutes after eight o'clock, but
did not get fairly under weigh with the steam-
engine until twenty-five minutes past eight.
This train reached Birmingham, by the Birmingham clocks at the terminus, at ten minutes to two, but by the watches of those
who went by it, at two minutes before two.
Watford was reached in 38 minutes from
the Euston station. The train halted there

three minutes. Tring was reached in 73 minutes, and the train halted four minutes and a half. Wolverton, the first new station, was reached by 28 minutes past 10, then the train halted 25 minutes. At this place a great crowd of persons were assembled, and preparations were made for a rural feast and celebration of the opening the line. Roade was reached at 17 minutes past 11, the train stopped 10 minutes at this station, which is 60 miles from London. Weedon, which is nine miles further, was reached at seven minutes to 12 o'clock, and Rugby, which is 83 miles from London, at half-past twelve. The train stopped here eight minutes. Coventry was reached at six minutes past one o'clock, and here the train remained for 15 minutes. The next place was Birmingham. The portion of the line just opened, from Denbigh-hall to Rugby, appears to be equally good with any other part of the road. It is in this division of the road, shortly before entering Rugby station, that the trains pass through Kilsby tunnel. It is one of the most extraordinary pieces of road in the whole line. The length of this tunnel is 2,400 yards in length, and does great credit to the skill of Mr. Foster, the engineer by whom it has been completed. The train which left Birmingham for London at half-past twelve was delayed, by some means or other, on the road for nearly two hours, in consequence of which, the train next in succession, which left Birmingham at half-past two, was delayed nearly two hours when almost close to Euston station; this last train arrived in London about 20 minutes to 10, instead of a quarter-past eight, the hour stated for the arriving in the public announcements. It does not appear that any accident whatever occurred on the road; indeed so excellent were the arrangements, that the possibility of accident was provided for in every way that could be imagined. The road, as most persons know, passes through six of the most beautiful counties of England—Middlesex, Hertfordshire, Buckinghamshire, Bedfordshire, Northamptonshire, and Warwickshire, and through a line of country abounding with fine prospects, historical recollections, and antiquities. One drawback to travelling by the railroad however, is, that for many miles it is so buried between lofty embankments, that nothing can be seen but the sides of the trench, and this is more particularly the case where a prospect of the seats and parks of the nobility and gentry would be most desirable. Another disagreeable is the passing through the tunnels, of which in the whole line there are seven. The road is crossed by numerous bridges, all of excellent workmanship, and some of considerable elegance. That part of the road which has been open some time has been repeatedly described, but that portion which was opened yesterday for the first time is of course less known. One of the principal places through which it passes is Weedon. This place is 67 miles from London. The Roman Watling-street comes close to it, the rail-road of 2,000 years ago. From the rail-road the traveller looks down upon the barracks of the town, which are very spacious, containing an hospital, parade, &c. This extensive depot is, as a military establishment, not surpassed by any in the kingdom: it is capable of receiving 200,000 stand of arms. A great quantity of warlike stores and artillery are generally deposited here. The Grand Junction Canal communicates with the storehouses, and close to them the rail-road passes. The Grand Junction Canal is carried across the valley by means of a very noble embankment on the left. At Dodford, which is a little beyond Weedon, the labourers held a *fête* in honour of the day. There were nearly 800 persons assembled, enjoying themselves in various ways; their festivity and good humour greatly enlivened the scene. The most beautiful town, or rather city, on the whole line is, however, Coventry. The spires of St. Michael's Church, 300 feet high, of the Holy Trinity, and of the Grey Friars, are the great ornament of the neighbourhood, and are seen to great advantage from the road. There is a splendid station here, with staircases of stone, and every accommodation for the landing and departure of travellers. Taking this line of road as a whole, it is one of the most stupendous undertakings of modern times, and will ultimately lead to results of which it is difficult to foretell the extent. Human labour and human ingenuity appear to have outstripped even the operations of nature. When the celebrated Duke of Bridgewater was intersecting the country with canals, Brindley, the engineer, was asked in his examination before the House of Commons what he supposed Providence to have made so many rivers for? He replied, to supply the canals with water. In the same spirit it may be replied to those who ask for what were all the roads now in existence made, they were made to bring passengers to the stations of the rail-roads, and supply customers for seats in the interminable trains by which they are traversed.

Birmingham, Monday Evening, Sept. 17.

The first train (being of the second class), that from Wolverton, arrived at the Birmingham station-house at a quarter to 10 o'clock, having performed the distance (59 miles and three-quarters) in two hours and three-quarters, half an hour under the time allowed by the Company's regulations. This was the first train for the conveyance of passengers that ever passed through the celebrated Kilsby tunnel, (one mile and a half in length,) and the passengers describe it, from its shafts, as much more pleasant in the transit than those of a shorter length. As this train came only from Wolverton, it was much lighter than those which subsequently arrived from London. The stations from which the Wolverton trains take up passengers are, Roade, Blisworth, Weedon, Crick, Rugby, Brandon, Coventry, Hampton, all of them places, with the exception of Coventry, of very small population, and from which, except supplied by tributary coaches from the surrounding country, few passengers could be expected.

Soon after 12 o'clock, an emission of smoke announced the approach of a special train, conveying a number of the directors and officers of the company, amongst whom were—Mr. R. C. Glynn, chairman; Mr. Calvert; Mr. Stephenson, the engineer; Mr. Berry, contractor for locomotive; Mr. Creed, secretary; Mr. Baxter, &c. His Royal Highness the Duke of Sussex, suite, and two carriages, were conveyed by this train from Euston-square to Rugby, and appeared throughout the whole of the journey to be highly delighted with railway travelling. The following is an account of the time occupied in the journey, furnished by Rootes, No. 123, the guard who accompanied the directors :—

The train left Euston-square at 15 minutes past 7, but did not take on locomotive until 20 minutes past. It arrived at Tring station at 25 minutes past 8, where there was five minutes delay. Arrived at Wolverton 16 minutes past 9, where the directors alighted and changed engines. The train arrived at Rugby at 11 o'clock, where the Duke of Sussex and his suite alighted, and proceeded by carriage to the place of his destination. The directors remained at Rugby 10 minutes, and arrived at Birmingham three minutes past 12, having performed the whole journey, including stoppages, in four hours and 48 minutes, and, exclusive of stoppages, in four hours and 14 minutes. This is unquestionably the shortest time in which the journey between London and Birmingham has ever been performed, being upwards of two hours less than the time occupied by Marshal Soult and attendants a few weeks ago.

The speed at which the directors' special train proceeded being considered no test of the rate at which a numerous train of heavy carriages would be able to travel the same journey, considerable anxiety was manifested by the directors and company in attendance, as to the time the first class train, which left London at 8 in the morning. The directors brought word that in all probability it would be a heavy train, and such it proved to be. The table of hours of arrival and departure stated that it would arrive in Birmingham at 37 minutes past one ; and precisely at a quarter to two, eight minutes after it became due, it arrived at the station. The train consisted of 16 first-class carriages and mails, and 4 gentlemen's carriages, and must in the aggregate have conveyed at least 200 passengers. The success of this, the first journey, throughout the entire line, gave unequivocal delight to all persons who witnessed the arrival of the train, and the bustle of so large a number of passengers alighting from the carriages and mixing with friends and spectators added greatly to the interest and excitement of the scene. The passengers generally spoke in the highest terms of the comfort and speed with which they had performed the journey ; the only delay being on the new and unsettled part of the road between Rugby and Denbigh-hall. As soon as time had been allowed for the transfer of the passengers from the carriages of the London and Birmingham to those of the Grand Junction, those whose destination was Manchester or Liverpool proceeded forward, and would, in the ordinary course of travelling on the latter line, after leaving London at 8 in the morning, arrive at Liverpool or Manchester at half-past 6 o'clock the same evening.— *Abridged from the Times.*

LONDON ELECTRICAL SOCIETY — MR. CLARKE'S EXPERIMENTS.

(Communicated by the Assistant Secretary.)

On Tuesday, the 4th September, at the ordinary meeting, very numerously attended, a paper was read by Mr. Clarke, " On Experiments in Magnetic Electricity."

The experiments, so perseveringly conducted, and on a more extensive scale than hitherto, may, by increasing and extending the boundaries of our experimental observations, be of great utility. To theorise, it is true, is to cause people to think, but to register experiments is to cause others to sift and test, and thereby establish data for fixed laws. Upon experiment must chiefly depend the reduction of the wonderful phenomena of electricity to laws. The importance of this desideratum requires no advocacy. For many years the attention of electricians has been directed to this point, and the discovery of the identity of electricity and magnetism has considerably augmented the chances of its attainment; yet, they are far from success, and probably because, from want of experiments on a large scale, certain phenomena constantly observed, and invariably occurring within the limits of past investigations, so miscroscopic in comparison with the wonders of the mighty agent under examination, have been considered sufficiently established to form a sure foundation for the superstructure.

The experiments were performed with a machine greatly exceeding in dimensions any other that has yet been constructed. The magnetic battery being separated into two parts, connected together by the inductors rotating at their sides—the quantity arrangement being at one side, and the intensity on the other. The results, with the machine in this form, were so opposite to what has been anticipated, that the arrangement was supposed to be defective. As usual, the quantity-inductor was furnished with a short coil of thick insulated copper wire, and the intensity-inductor with 15,375 yards of fine copper wire. On trying the voltameter with the intensity arrangements, no decomposition took place, although the shock obtained by it was most excruciating, nay, even dangerous. The decomposing power of the quantity-inductor was next tried, and one cubic inch of gas obtained in four minutes. This, being a novel fact, was supposed to be caused by a compound action, produced by the rotation of the inductors. Mr. Clarke, therefore, determined to arrange the magnets similarly to those of the machines he had been in the habit of constructing. The only difference consisting in the size of the instrument, and the means of communication to the inductors, namely—by a crank and treadles similar to the lathe. The battery consists of ten bent steel bars, each four feet long, the whole weighing 156lbs. Ivory was made use of to retain the wires on the inductors, in lieu of brass plates, which gave uncertain results, owing to their conducting power. The novel results of the experiments were, first—the great amount of gas obtained by the quantity-inductor, in one instance, one cubic inch in one minute and a·half, which result confirmed the correctness of the original arrangement. The second was—the trifling decomposition obtained from the intensity-inductor. The voltameter employed in the experiments was furnished with two slips of platina, one inch in length, and three-eighths of an inch in breadth. The decomposing power was, however, increased at least fifteen times, by the substitution of fine-pointed wire of platina. The next experiments briefly alluded to, referred to the different appearance of the spark with various modifications of the in-

ductors; with the intensity-inductor a long straggling noiseless spark is obtained, having much resemblance to the spark which passes from the prime conductor of an electric machine, to a body placed in what is called the striking distance. The quantity-inductor gives a spark which not only has the usual stellar form, but is accompanied with a loud snapping, resembling the discharge of a leyden jar. Although these distinctions exist between the sparks, they appear equally luminous. The experiments were most brilliant.

NOTES AND NOTICES.

Captain Norton's Percussion Lead, for exploding charges of Powder at the bottom of Harbours and Rivers.—A sea lead is charged at its heavy end with a small iron tube, having a percussion cap at each end, filled with gunpowder; the lead has two eyes or rings on its side, in a straight line, through which a cord is run, one end being attached to the box of powder, at the bottom of the water; the lead is allowed to slide along the cord, and on striking the box, explodes it; a thin piece of sheet lead or copper being fixed to the box, when the percussion primer strikes. Captain Norton successfully tried his percussion lead at the Polytechnic Institution, Regent-street, on the 19th instant; he proposes this means as a substitute for the fuzes at present in use, being more simple, less costly, and easy of application.

Prevention of Smoke from Steam-ships.—Mr. Iveson's apparatus is now being applied to the furnaces of the *Royal Adelaide* steam-ship, preparatory to her sailing to-day for London. The enterprising proprietors of this vessel, the London, Leith, Edinburgh, and Glasgow Shipping Co., deserve great credit for having been the first to introduce this improvement to steam-ships, and the result of its application on this voyage will be looked forward to with considerable interest, not only as to its effects in entirely consuming the smoke, but in the more important one to the proprietors—the economising of fuel. During the last ten days, great numbers of engineers, manufacturers, and men of science, from different parts of the country, have visited the Silk Mills to witness the apparatus in full operation, and one and all of them have expressed themselves highly pleased with its efficiency.—*Edinburgh Evening Post.*

Blowing up of the brig " William."—It appears that this operation, described in our No. 773, has proved a failure. " The brig *William* is still at the bottom of the Thames. It is true there was a pop, and a splash, and a bushel or two of coals thrown into the air, but as to the brig herself she remained fast where she was, or, if moved at all, it was only a little further down the river. After a little time some over-curious impertinent persons began to express a doubt whether the thing had really been accomplished; inquiry and investigation followed, and, although a tree nail or two might have been loosened, and a plank or two detached, the vessel was found to be still snugly reposing in the mud. The Colonel's astonishment may be easily conceived. There was nothing, however, to be done, but to set to work again at the business; and, the Colonel and his sappers have been mightily busy for the last two or three weeks in their endeavours to complete the job. Last week there were three puffs and three failures."—*Correspondent of the Morning Herald.*

Glass Cloth.—A new and curious fabric has been manufactured by Mr. Richard Baker, of Ossett, near Dewesbury; it is a web of glass cloth, which has a very splendid appearance. The ingenious manufacturer has so far succeeded in annealing this very brittle substance as to admit of its being wove like cloth. It is deposited for inspection in the North of England Society of Arts, together with a slipper made of the same material.—*Liverpool Standard.*

Dr. Davidge, of Saratoga, has invented a steamboat for canal navigation, in which flexible floats or paddles, operating beneath the water, are substituted for wheels.

Messrs. Dean, iron-founders, of Bolton, are manufacturing an iron gate, twenty-seven feet high, for the grand seraglio of the Pacha of Egypt.

Iron Steamers for the Nile.—The iron steamers destined to ply on the river Nile are at present building at Greenock. The models are of the most approved description, and when ready for plying will draw from 22 to 24 inches of water. A neat handsome steamer, named the *Hope,* built and fitted out at Greenock, is to sail some of these days from Greenock for the Cape, where she is to run as a constant trader and packet. Almost every quarter of the globe have Clyde-built steamers plying on their rivers.—*Glasgow Chronicle.*

Night Travelling on Railroads.—A writer in the *National Intelligencer* states, that Mr. Herron, a distinguished civil engineer on the Gasten and Raleigh Railroad, proposes to illuminate railroads during night travel, by a light shed in front of the locomotive so strong and brilliant as to illuminate objects to a considerable distance ahead.

Another Enormous Steam-ship.—Messrs. Curling and Young, of Limehouse, the builders of the *British Queen,* have begun a steam-ship of 2000 tons; being 400 tons more than the *British Queen*; she is not to be so long as that vessel, but much wider.—*Mining Journal.*

Bitumen Pavements.—Robinson's bitumen pavement is about to be employed at Brighton. At Herne Bay a handsome promenade has been made of it, formed of blocks cemented together; and it is also to be used at Canterbury. The company are also engaged laying down a large floor or area, from three to four hundred feet, in Bunhill-row. The Commissioners for paving Kensington have given permission, and selected a spot, for a foot pavement to be composed of it; a good pavement is much required there.—The Rotunda of the Bank of England is being paved by the Bastenne Company, as also a portion of the Strand, in front of Northumberland House. The piece of pavement in front of Whitehall, laid down by Claridge's company, continues in good order.

Tubular Flue Boiler Explosion.—Another boiler explosion, fatal to seven persons, has taken place at Newton-in-the-Willows, at the viaduct foundry of Messrs. Jones and Co. The rupture was in the flue, and the attendant circumstances appear to have been of a similar nature to that of the *Victoria* explosion. The boiler was a new one, just started, and cylindrical, with a tube flue; the size of the water spaces is not mentioned. Mr. Jones stated, "that he had endeavoured to ascertain the cause of the accident, and he was of opinion that there was not sufficient

water in the boiler, which caused the flue to get red hot; and when the engine pumped in the cold water, the boiler (flue) collapsed. In his opinion hydrogen gas was formed in the boiler, the moment the water was let in." The circumstance of this, as well as the *Victoria* boiler, being new, seems to favour the gas theory. The iron plates were clean, and free from the oxide or incrustation which exists on an old boiler, and which might tend to prevent the sudden generation of hydrogen, on the flues becoming red hot, by its interposition between the iron and the water; on a stream of water coming in contact with this clear red hot iron, hydrogen certainly would be generated.

American Inventions.—Mr. Thos. Blanchard.—The *New York Advertiser,* of August 24, has the following communication from a correspondent:—Thomas Blanchard, well known in the history of inventions in this country, has produced a model to prevent steam-boat explosions. It is so contrived that when the water is reduced below a given quantity, the door through which fuel is supplied closes, and cannot be opened until the compliment of water is made up. There is, therefore, no possibility of an explosion arising from a deficiency of water, even if the engineer is ever so much disposed for it. It is in this particular a complete guard against carelessness, intoxication, and that fool-hardiness which scatters destruction. Mr. Blanchard is a member of the American Institute, and has promised to make a full exhibition of his contrivance, and have it tested at the eleventh annual fair [which commences on the 15th of October next. It is an exhibition of machinery, models, manufactures, &c. in New York, resembling the "Adelaide Gallery" in London]; and he will offer a premium to any one who will cause this boiler to explode. There are few men living whose inventive powers will compare with Thomas Blanchard's. His education is limited, but the faculty of discovering unexpected means to accomplish desired ends strikingly characterises his mind. It was he who invented the wonderful machine for turning irregular forms, which, ever since he brought it forth, has been used in the armory of the United States, for manufacturing gun stocks. Hat blocks, lasts, &c. are turned with this machine. The history of this invention is somewhat curious. Mr. Blanchard had made some improvement in constructing the metallic part of fire arms, which dispensed with a portion of the labour before required, whereby several workmen were thrown out of employ. The gun-stock manufacturers observed, "Thank fortune none of your inventions can deprive us of our employment." "You are not so certain of that," said Mr. B., and in a few weeks he produced his famous lathe, which readily gave an exact *fac simile* of any pattern. The boats successfully used in ascending flats, particularly on the Connecticut river, which before were deemed insurmountable, are from the same inventive source. We have written this to call public attention to a most important object, and to induce a thorough investigation of this invention, which, if successful, will save thousands of lives, and will rank Mr. B. among the list of benefactors.

The *Railway Map* of England and Wales continues on sale, in a neat wrapper, price 6d.; and on fine paper, coloured, price 1s.

☞ *British and Foreign Patents taken out with economy and despatch; Specifications, Disclaimers, and Amendments, prepared or revised; Caveats entered; and generally every Branch of Patent Business promptly transacted. A complete list of Patents from the earliest period (15 Car. II. 1675,) to the present time may be examined. Fee 2s. 6d.; Clients, gratis.*

LONDON: Printed and Published for the Proprietor, by W. A. Robertson, at the Mechanics' Magazine Office, No. 6, Peterborough-court, between 135 and 136, Fleet-street.—Sold by A. & W. Galignani, Rue Vivienne, Paris.

Mechanics' Magazine,

MUSEUM, REGISTER, JOURNAL, AND GAZETTE.

No. 790.]　　　SATURDAY, SEPTEMBER 29, 1838.　　　[Price 6*d*.

DR. ROGER'S IMPROVED MODE OF ARRANGING A SAND BATH.

Fig. 3.

Fig. 2.　　　　　　　　　　Fig. 1.

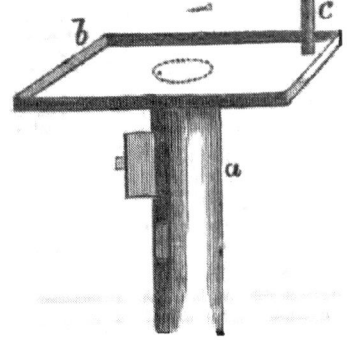

ROGERS'S DESCRIPTION OF A CONVE-
NIENT MODE OF ARRANGING A SAND
BATH.

(*From the Franklin Journal.*)

The practical chemist is always more
or less incommoded by the corrosion of
the balances and other delicate pieces of
apparatus in his laboratory, by the gases
and vapours evolved during the processes upon his sand bath. He is moreover subject to uncomfortable heat in
the apartment from the necessity of
keeping his bath at an elevated temperature. To obviate these inconveniences,
I have devised an arrangement, the description of which may be useful to
those pursuing the subject. The accompanying figures represent the construction of one which I have now in use.

a, figs. 1, 2, represents a nine inch
sheet-iron stove, without its ordinary
top, while *b* shows a rectangular sheet-
iron bath, two feet long by 18 inches
wide, made to fit as a top upon the
stove; the heated air from the stove is
then made to circulate under the sand
bath, before it can pass out through
the pipe. *c*, fig. 3, represents the stove
and sand bath, in place, surrounded by
brick-work. *d* is a chamber in which
the stove is placed, and corresponding
in size to that of the sand bath. The
fuel is introduced into the stove through
the hole *e*, and the ashes removed
through *f*. The chamber is made to
communicate with the external atmosphere, by holes in the outer wall,
against which the arrangement is built.
The effect of the body of air circulating around the stove is to prevent
entirely the wall of the chamber from
becoming heated. *g* represents a window in the wall of the building occupied by wire gauze, through which the
vapours pass out, while their escape
into the apartment is prevented by the
moveable sash, seen in front. Thus at
the same time that the operator has
completely under his eye and control all
his process, he is entirely exempt from
the inconveniences of the common forms
of sand baths.

R. E. ROGERS, M.D.

MINING EXPERIMENTS NEAR HAY,
BRECON.

During a visit which I paid to the
little romantic town of Hay, in Brecon-
shire, South Wales, in November 1831,
I was informed that several explorations
had been made in that great range of
mountain land denominated "the Cusup
Hills," and that the explorers had succeeded in extracting both coal and iron.
I understood a bar of metal had been
made of extremely good quality; but of
the quality and quantity of coal extracted from the same depot I cannot
speak. Hope was flattering the minds
of the inhabitants, that the little, neglected, and obscure town of Hay would
speedily become a mart of the first-rate
traffic and wealth; but seven years have
since rolled on without producing, as
far as I know, any verification of the
expectation. I have just perused the
last part of the *Penny Cyclopædia*, (although a work of by no means safe
authority to quote) which says, speaking
of Hereford, that "no coal or productive
ore has been discovered here," so that
in the absence of better sources of information, I am constrained to suppose
that the above-mentioned enterprise has
turned out an unlucky and abortive undertaking.

Perseverance and capital are necessary features in all mining transactions,
although chance will sometimes put her
hand upon a prize, which the most untiring industry will fail to possess itself
of. This was the case in that remarkable development of natural wealth,
which was exhibited in the copper works
at the Parys mountains in Anglesea,
North Wales, and which was brought to
light by one of the merest accidents
which could possibly occur. A countryman (so says village tradition), travelling across a piece of ground which
he had traversed hundreds of times before, by chance struck his foot against
something which he felt to be a hard
substance, which caused him "to measure his length upon the ground;" upon
recovering his equilibrium, and looking
for the cause of his fall, he perceived
upon the surface of what appeared to
him to be a large rough stone, some
peculiar shining marks or scorings, which
were caused by its having come into
contact with the iron nails of his shoes.
Curiosity prompted him to examine
this specimen more minutely: and on
stooping down with the intention of
lifting it from the ground, he found he
could hardly move it; but with considerable exertion he got it upon his

shoulder. As the village curate's house was only a few roods off, he determined to take it to that gentleman for his inspection. This was no other than the late Rev. Mr. Hughes, father to the present Lord Dinorbin, who was then living in extreme poverty upon a paltry stipend of thirty pounds a year. This worthy person's optics being better adapted for metallic discoveries than those of the simple countryman, soon discovered it to be a lump of the purest copper ore. If he was pleased in the first instance at such an unexpected discovery, how much were those pleasurable sensations increased, when he learned from his untutored companion that the spot upon which he had found this treasure formed a portion of his own paternal estate! The immense subterraneous wealth now soon brought to light, has been the source of all the subsequent riches of the Hughes family, and the house of Dinorbin now flourishes among the loftiest peers of the highest house of Parliament.

I remain, Sir,
Your obedient servant,
ENORT SMITH.

Marlborough-terrace,
Albany-road.

REPORT ON LONDON FIRES, &c.

Sir,—At the recent meeting of the British Association, at Newcastle, Mr. Rawson read a report before the statistical section, "On the fires of London," comprising a detailed account of the character, causes, &c., of 3,359 fires which have occurred in and about the metropolis during the five years that the London Fire-engine Establishment has been in operation; viz.: from 1833 to 1837, both inclusive. This report, which is founded upon my annual papers on this subject in your pages, has since appeared in No. 5 of the *Journal of the Statistical Society of London.*

At the conclusion of Mr. Rawson's reading — "Reference was made to the great excess of fires in the southern counties of England over the midland counties. This was attributed, by Sir Charles Lemon and Mr. Felkin, to the use of thatched roofs. It was also stated, that Newcastle, notwithstanding the vast consumption of coal in that town, is remarkably free from fires of dangerous magnitude: and it was suggested

whether, as the greater number of fires occurred in London about eleven o'clock at night, the practice of raking out the fire at bed time, which is not done at Newcastle where coals are cheap, might not have some connexion with these conflagrations."[*]

Had Mr. Rawson studied the "analysis given of the presumed causes" of fire, I should think he would have had little difficulty in refuting this hypothesis. From the list of causes given in my annual reports, it will be seen, that a very large portion of each year's fires originate from carelessness in the use of candles; the bringing of which too near to bed, and window curtains, &c., cause numberless accidents about bed time.

I know that many well-informed persons hold an opinion, that raking out a fire is a dangerous and absurd practice, yet the number of conflagrations that can be traced to this cause is infinitely small. The accidents from unextinguished coal fires, although comparatively few, are much more numerous than the preceding.

Mr. Rawson "observed, that the number of fatal fires had *greatly increased*," which is not the fact; there is an *apparent increase,* which I have explained, by stating, that in consequence of the prompt application now usually made for the firemen's assistance in every case of fire, they are frequently called out to accidents arising from the ignition of wearing apparel on the person, which terminate fatally,—these cases, being reported, swell the number of fatal fires, although they do not in reality constitute what is generally understood by this expression. Had all the accidents of this kind last year, been attended by the firemen and reported, they would, being upwards of *one hundred* in number, have given the appearance of a frightful increase in *fatal fires.*

I remain, Sir,
Yours respectfully,
WM. BADDELEY.

London, Sept. 11, 1838.

ROWLEY'S PATENT BUFFING APPARATUS FOR RAILWAY CARRIAGES.

In our 783rd Number we described the rotary steam-engine patented by Mr. Rowley, of Manchester, and we now,

* Vide *Athenæum,* No. 566, page 637.

E E 2

according to promise, publish an account of his buffing apparatus, contained in the same patent. Mr. Rowley states in his specification that his buffing apparatus consists of pneumatic or vacuum springs, either alone or in connection with steel springs of an elliptical or other form; together with a novel plan for connecting the buffing apparatuses of the carriages by means of a bolt in the centre of the apparatus; and the being enabled to raise this bolt by a pulley or lever, and so detach a carriage or carriages from the train when the same is *en route*, and thus avoiding the necessity of stopping at any station.

Fig. 1 is a plan, or horizontal view of the improved buffing apparatus as attached to the frame-work of a locomotive engine, tender, or passenger car-

Fig. 1

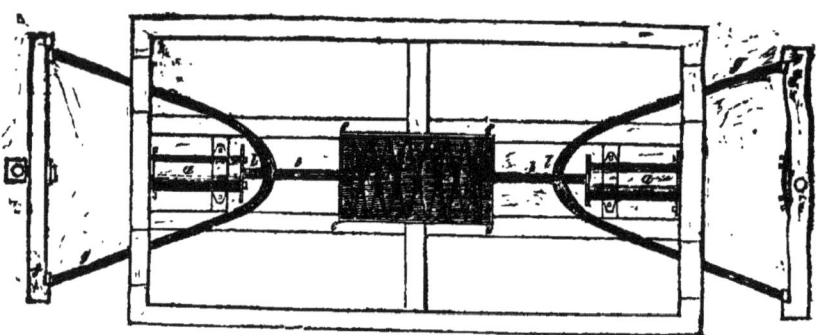

riage. *a a* are two cylinders fitted with pistons and rods *b b*, and made perfectly air-tight to constitute pneumatic springs, and fixed at each end of the frame-work of the carriage; *c c* are the heads of the piston rods, connected with the first of the elliptical springs *d d*, which is the traction spring, and which is contained in the box *e*; *f f* are bars of timber constituting the buffers, and connected to the above system of springs by the rods *g g*: these rods pass through oblong square holes formed in the end of the carriage frame, and are connected to the piston-rods by compass joints at *h h*, in order to allow of lateral motion. Thus it will be seen, that when any concussion takes place the piston is driven by the shock towards the centre of the carriage, thus forming a vacuum in the opposite end of the cylinder, offering a powerful resistance, and constituting a vacuum spring. After the receipt of the shock the piston is forced back to its former place by atmospheric pressure, aided by the metallic springs.

Figs. 2 and 3 exhibit the contrivance for connecting and disconnecting two carriages; fig. 2 being a front view of the buffer bar *f*, and fig. 3 a section taken through, when connected; *a* is a strong piece of iron inserted in the cen-

Fig. 2.

Fig. 3.

tre of the buffing bar *f*, and having an eye formed in it to receive the connecting bolt *b*, which also passes through the other buffing bar *c*, and forms a swivel joint working in the metal bush *d*. It will be seen that there is a space or opening left in the buffing bar *f*, to allow of the vertical action of the connecting link *a.* The connecting bolt *b* has a passage or groove formed upon its head, to allow a small spring to act upon it with just sufficient pressure to keep it in its place. Now, in order to disconnect any one carriage from the train while the whole is in motion, the connecting bolt may be lifted or raised by pulling the cord *e,* which may be either attached to a pulley or lever, and thus any number of carriages may be disconnected without stopping the whole.

RUSSIAN WEIGHTS AND MEASURES.

Sir,—As you have been pleased to insert in your vol. 27, the article I sent you from hence concerning Russian weights, as calculated with such great accuracy by my late father, I now send you a summary statement of various measures, and something more concerning weights. I am aware that the subjects are not such as to interest the generality of the readers of your valuable and scientific publication, and that they may *partly* be found in other works, but most certainly not in your pages.

Your readiness in inserting what I sent you, shows your wish to impart every species of knowledge to every class of your readers, the *very many*, in consequence of the instructive contents and reasonable purchase of the *Mechanics' Magazine*, are most certainly under very great obligation to its enlightened conductors, though I am sorry at times to read so much petulancy (to use the softest word) inserted in your pages by gentlemen of science and education; certainly no man can be censured for expressing his sentiments, but it is the manner the opinion is expressed which is objectionable. Excuse this digression.

I am, Sir, your obedient servant,
BENJAMIN HYNAM.

St. Petersburg, July 12, 1838. O. S.

Russian Lineal Measure.

The verst.... contains 500 sagenes .. 7 feet English = 1 sagene.
The sagene .. do. 3 archenes.
The archene .. do. 16 verschokes .... = 28 English inches.
The verschoke is .... = 1¾ ditto.

To reduce the Russian archene into English inches, multiply by 7 and divide by 9.

Example.

9 : 7 : : 36 inches, an English yard.
7
———
9)252(28 inches, a Russian archene
18
———
. 72
72

Liquid Measure.

The vedro, which was definitely determined at 750 cubical English inches for its contents, is the standard liquid measure, it contains about 30 Russian pounds of river water; 13 English wine gallons contains about 4 vedros; 152 beer gallons contains 57 vedros.

Dry Measure.

1 bag of rye flour, weighs 9 pounds, or 360 Russian pouds.

1 bag of wheat flour weighs 5 pounds, or 200 Russian pouds.

60 Russian tschverics contain about 14 English Winchester bushels.

Superficial Measure.

The desateen, is in length 80 sagenes, and in breadth 30 sagenes, making 2,400 square sagenes, or 117,000 square feet.

Weights.

For weighing precious stones, gold or silver, the troy weight is used.

The heavy goods, such as iron, hemp, tallow, &c. they weigh by the bercowitz, a nominal weight containing 10 one poud weights.

	berc.	poud.	funt.	zot.
1 ton (20 cwt.) makes Russian weight	6 ..	2 ..	8 ..	85⅓
1 cwt. (112 lb.) ditto	0 ..	3 ..	4 ..	42⅓
1 stone (14 lb.) ditto	0 ..	0 ..	15 ..	53⅓
1 pound (16 oz.) ditto	0 ..	0 ..	1 ..	10⅔
1 ounce (16 dr.) ditto	0 ..	0 ..	0 ..	6⅔
1 am ditto	0 ..	0 ..	0 ..	0₁₇⁵

At the same rate	cwt.	lb.	oz.	dr.
1 bercowitz makes English (avoirs.)	3	25	11	14⅝
1 poud ditto	0	36	1	13¼*
1 funt ditto	0	0	14	7½
1 zototnic ditto	0	0	0	2½

IMPROVED CARPENTER'S BENCH.

Sir,—The benches which joiners and carpenters use in this neighbourhood, and probably elsewhere, are of so defective a description, that they afford, indeed, a matter of surprise in a country so highly eminent for its improvements in every branch of mechanics. The accompanying sketch will, perhaps, give you an idea of a carpenter's bench, such as I have had occasion to see in general use in several foreign countries. I do not pretend to say that it is the best that could be contrived, but I take it to be an evident improvement. Should you, therefore, consider it susceptible of being of service to any of your numerous mechanical correspondents, I should feel much obliged to you for making them acquainted with it, through the medium of your valuable Magazine.

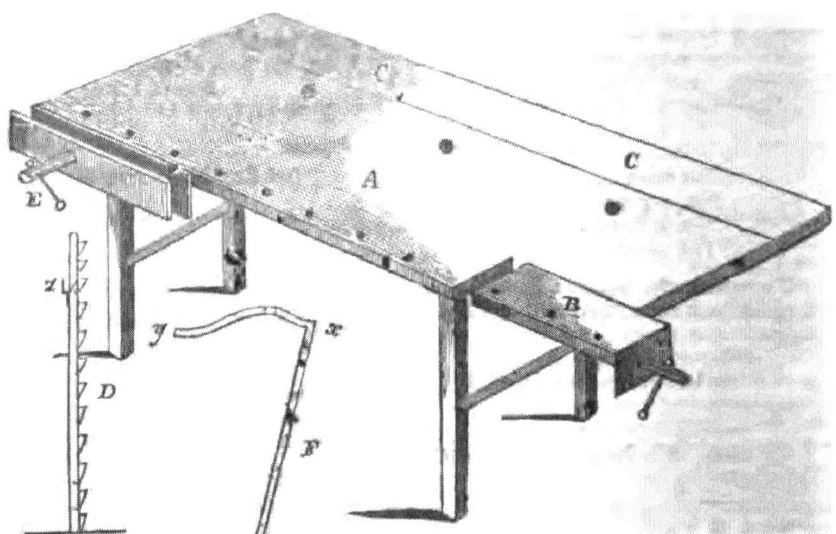

☞A is a stout bench, constructed on the usual principles, except that B is a moveable apparatus, by means of which boards may be fixed on the bench, for planing, &c.; it is also found very convenient for many other purposes. C C is a kind of hollow or trough, which takes up nearly the whole length of the bench; nails, chisels, and other small tools may be placed in it, in order to avoid unnecessary encumbrance on the bench. D is a ratchet stave to support, at any given height, the hook z, on which boards to be planed edgeways are allowed to rest, whilst one end is engaged in the screw E. F is a stout cramp-iron, which, being put in one of the holes in the middle of the bench, will, by means of two or three blows with the mallet on the projecting part x, acquire a firm hold of every object placed under its extremity y.

I remain, Sir, yours respectfully,
P. O.

Twickenham, Sept. 5, 1838.

---

* Though in all mercantile concerns they calculate that 36lbs. avoirdupois makes one poud.

REPORT OF THE COMMITTEE OF THE FRANKLIN INSTITUTE ON THE EXPLOSION OF STEAM BOILERS.

(From the *Franklin Journal*.)

[Continued from vol. xxvi., page 375.]

[We now resume our publication of the American experiments upon steam boiler explosions. The subject has, by recent events, assumed a character of melancholy and paramount importance ; we hope, therefore, that our readers will not think that so large a portion of our pages as it will be necessary to devote to them, is done so needlessly. The late act of the American Congress was founded upon these reports, and as it is in contemplation to enact some measure of a similar nature in Great Britain, the experiments detailed will be examined by all interested in steam machinery, with interest. As we have so recently published the Act of Congress itself, we shall only now insert those parts of the proposed bill which were not adopted by the American Legislature, and which referred to proposed arrangements of machinery.]

49. *Second.—The undue heating of parts of a boiler may be produced by deposits.—* No cause of undue heating is better made out than this one, and the remedy is of the most simple kind.

The water of all rivers contains, in suspension, in greater or less quantities, the muddy particles detached from their banks or beds, and may contain in solution, salts derived from the same sources, or from the springs which supply the stream. The water of springs generally contains so large an impregnation of saline matter, as to decompose soap. The rivers of our Atlantic States, where perfectly fresh, contain few dissolved impurities, while many of those of the Western States are highly charged with calcareous matter. When waters holding substances in suspension, or solution, are evaporated, a sediment is deposited, varying in nature with the water employed. As the quantity of solid matter contained in the water varies, so the time required for such a deposit to take place, from the feeding water of a steam boiler, must be very variable. If a deposit is allowed to remain in a boiler it gradually increases in thickness and in density ; the heat which before passed rapidly from the metal to the water, is now impeded by a mass of viscid or of solid matter, which is a bad circulator or conductor of heat, and the temperature of the metal rises. The sediment thus heated increases in denseness, and may even form a hard crust upon the bottom of the boiler. A complete non-conducting coat is thus formed, which, is from its nature liable to crack or fissure, may allow water to have access to the heated metal below, and produce an explosion. This supposition is, however, as will be seen, by no means necessary to such a result. The most usual action of the sediment would seem to be as follows : When it has accumulated in thickness, sufficiently to produce a temperature in the metal, at which its strength is inadequate to bear the pressure without extending, it yields, and becoming more and more attenuated, finally bursts. It seems that the first yielding may bring water in contact with the metal so as to cool it, when the steam produced is not sufficient materially to increase the pressure within the boiler. Thus the attenuation may increase for a considerable time and gradually, and at last the bursting not produce any more injurious effect than to stop the working of the engine.

Accidental circumstances of figure, heat, &c., seem frequently to determine the places of deposit of these masses of sediment, but it is principally observed at the fire-end of the boiler, where its presence is most dangerous.

50. The committee have derived much information of a practical kind on this subject, and coming as it does from entirely different quarters of the country, where the water depositing the sediment was of different qualities, the details agree very remarkably.

Col. S. H. Long* describes a deposit found in one of the boilers of the *Western Engineer*, a boat used in the exploring expedition of 1818. The sediment had collected in less than two days so as to be two inches thick, and was found in parts of the boiler, where, from its construction, the heat was greatest. A difficulty in making steam enough for the supply of the engine, was observed, and induced an examination of the boilers, in one of which, the metal at a particular spot was found to have been made to project an inch and a half. In this case timely precaution prevented further evil consequences.

51. The plan of "blowing off" the lower parts of the fluid in a boiler, which is very generally used in turbid streams to the West, is, no doubt, of considerable service while the boat is running, but should never be used as a substitute for cleaning the boilers, when opportunity is afforded for this complete operation. Indeed it must be carefully executed, since, if the flues are bared by it,

---

* Replies to Circular of Com. on Expl. No. II.

any deposit upon them may become hardened before the boiler is replenished with water.

52. A practical engineer of New Albany, Indiana, Mr. Benton,* states that he has found deposits in boilers, used on our western waters, "almost as hard as the iron itself." These consist of a mixture of calcareous matter with the ordinary mud of the rivers.

The very consistent and satisfactory accounts given of the explosion of a boiler of the steam-boat *Caledonia*, on the Mississippi, show that the disaster had its origin, at least in part, in the deposit within the boiler. The boat had eight connected cylinder boilers of wrought iron, for high steam, 30 inches in diameter and 20 feet long, with interior flues. The engine had been in operation for seven consecutive days prior to the accident, and had, just before its occurrence, been stopped for about eight hours, to repair the machinery. During the time of stopping, the boilers were not blown out, and two hours after resuming the working of the engine the explosion occurred. On subsequent examination, it was found to have occurred in a patch, which had been put on the year before with *copper* rivets; the sediment on the bottom of the boiler was found to have been heated, so as to render it very hard. The rent began at about one-third of the diameter of the boiler from the bottom, that is, at, or near, the fire line, and passed upwards. The sediment had caused the heating of the copper rivets, and, it is probable, that the working pressure of the steam accomplished the rest.

53. The effect of a deposit of a different kind, in a boiler, near Richmond, Virginia, is well described by Mr. Burr.† The boiler was of wrought-iron, five-sixteenths of an inch thick; the water used for its supply was a chalybeate, but not so strong as to prevent its common use, as a beverage, by the workmen. A few weeks after the engine had been put in operation, a crack was observed in the boiler, just over the fire, and on examination, a deposit of oxide of iron found in this place. The fire-end is stated to have been lowest in the setting of the boiler. A plate of wrought iron was substituted for that which had cracked. In four or five weeks a swelling began to form upon this plate, which continued to increase until it attained a considerable size, and in ten days from the first on which the protuberance had been observed, the boiler

burst. No great damage was done. The iron was found to have been diminished in thickness, at the spot where the rent occurred, to one-eighth of an inch.

54. The deposits in boilers using salt water are no less dangerous. Mr. Lester* gives an account of the case of the boilers in the steam-boat *Eagle* of Boston, which leaked after being in use two or three weeks, and on examination were found to contain a deposit of from two to three inches thick, and which, in some parts, was so hard as to require the use of a hammer and chisel to remove it.†

55. Various other cases are on record of the effects of deposits in boilers, but the characteristic ones which have been selected convey all the information necessary. They show that no rule as to the time of cleansing a boiler can be general, and fully enforce the necessity for care upon this point. Farinaceous substances introduced into a boiler may tend to render frequent cleansing less necessary in cases of sedimentary matter, but cannot dispense with it.‡ Sound economy, as well as safety, require frequent cleansing of a boiler using hard or muddy water. The least that can happen, after the accumulation of sediment, is the injury of the boiler, perhaps its bursting, and a true explosion may result. Two violent explosions, at Bowen's mill,‖ and at McMickle's mill in Pittsburgh, are fairly attributable to the effect of sediment; and there does not appear, in either case, to have been a deficiency of water at the time of the explosion.

---

* Reply to Circular of Com. on Expl., by Erasmus W. Benton, No. VIII.

† Jour. Frank. Inst., vol. vi., p. 334.

---

* Letter to Sec. Treas. U. S. Replies to Com. on Expl., No. XVII.. See also Jour. Frank. Inst., vol. vii. p. 289, &c.

† In a letter to the Editor of the Jour. Frank. Inst., a gentleman of Boston states, that in a boiler using salt water, a deposit of more than two inches in thickness occurred in less than twenty days. Mr. West states that deposits, chiefly of sulphate of lime, occur in from one to six weeks of use, in the boilers at Manchester. See Jour. Royal Institution, vol. i. p. 42. See also F. Naested's Letter to Sec. Treas. U. S., Doc. H. Rep. U. S.. 1832-3, No. 478, p. 52.

‡ It was stated on the authority of Sig. Ferrari, that coarse charcoal prevents or removes deposits in boilers.—Jour. Frank. Inst. vol. ix. p. 420. The Society of Arts of London awarded, in 1833, a premium to Mr. James Bedford for rendering deposits readily removeable by introducing sperm oil into the boiler. We are not aware to what extent this device has been tried.—Trans. Soc. Arts. vol. xlix. part.II. p. 88. The use of grease for the same purpose is recommended in the London Mechs'. Mag. vol. vi. p. 308; and in the same journal, Vol. ii. p. 206, it is stated that the radicles of barley produced in the process of malting prevent deposits. These act on the same principle as the fecula of potatoes. They merely retard the formation of a deposit, and by rendering the fluid viscid, no doubt ultimately affect the generation of steam.

‖ Replies to Circular, &c. No. XII. Letter of Thos. W. Bakewell, Esq., to Sec. Treas. U. S.

56. The accidental introduction of materials which are bad conductors of heat within a boiler, may produce the same effect as the deposits just described. Mr. Benton* suggests that loose packing from the steam cylinder is sometimes passed through the force-pump, and collecting under the flues, causes them to be highly heated. M. Arago mentions an instance of a rent made in a boiler, at Paris,† by the accidental resting of a rag on the bottom of the boiler.

57. Frequent cleansing of the boiler, or blowing out the lowest portions by small quantities at a time, are the true preventives to accidents from deposits. Besides them, however, the use of chemical reagents has been proposed for limestone water, and filtering in the case of muddy water. The former of these would prove but a partial remedy, and in unskilful hands would be dangerous; and the latter would probably be objected to on the score of its considerable expense. When the escape steam is allowed to run to waste this would be especially the case.

58. It has been also proposed to use boxes for collecting the sediment, but from them the committee would not anticipate any very good result, though they might, in part, facilitate the cleansing of a boiler.

59. *Third.—The careening of a steam-boat may expose parts of the boiler to heat without their being covered by water, and a subsequent return to its level will bring water in contact with the heated metal.*

There is no evidence known to the committee that the careening of a boat has ever produced accident in any other than the small connected cylinder boilers, so extensively used in the boats navigating the western waters. In these, the danger has been forcibly pointed out by several correspondents,‡ and means of remedying it suggested.§ These boilers communicate by pipes below the ordinary water level, and are supplied by the same forcing-pump. The fire is most generally applied to the exterior of the boilers, and they have besides interior flues. Being placed side by side, the length of the boiler being parallel to the keel of the boat, they occupy according to their size and number a more or less considerable portion of

its breadth. The six contiguous boilers of the steam-boat *Helen McGregor*, and the eight of the *Caledonia*, occupied certainly not less than 22 feet in breadth of the boat. Calculating upon the dimensions of the boilers in the first-named boat, and taking into view the circumstances under which the water has access to the heated metal, we find that a depression of 9 inches, at the extreme boiler, taking place about the axis of the set of boilers, would expose a surface of boiler and flue together competent to supply, when the water returned upon them, one-third more steam then the ordinary working of the boiler could furnish: this supply being kept up, at an average, during the cooling of the elevated boilers, to their ordinary working temperature. This danger might easily be met by an increased area of safety-valve, if indeed those commonly used would be insufficient, for the escape of the extra steam.* But the danger from even the working pressure acting upon the metal, of which the tenacity has been much decreased, is the real source of danger, and is not thus to be parried. There are but about 440° of Farenheit's scale between the working pressure of eleven atmospheres and a red heat visible in the dark.

This careening of the boat is liable to occur at every landing place, and to last for a considerable time. Whenever a passing boat, an engaging view, or accident, shall call the passengers to one side of the boat it will be thrown out of trim.

60. In the small boats on our Atlantic rivers there are heavy carriages used to keep the deck level; these are also used in the English steam-packets which carry sails, but the committee are not aware that they are employed in the boats of our western waters.

61. *Different modes of remedying the evil under discussion, and to be applied to the boilers themselves have been suggested.*

The first of these which came before the committee, and which we believe has been applied in practice, was by Mr. James J. Rush. Doors are placed in the flues, at a point furthest from the fire-end, which, when opened, check the draught through the furnace and flues, and consequently prevent their becoming unduly heated. These are to be thrown open at each landing place. They do not, however, meet the case of accidental careening of the boat, unless made self-acting by expanding rods, as was proposed by Mr. Rush. They expose

* Replies, &c. No. VIII.
† Used in producing steam to heat the exchange.
‡ The first communication made to the committee on this subject was by James J. Rush, Esq., of the firm of Rush and Muhlenberg; by some accident the drawings presented by him were not deposited among the papers of the committee, and a similar diagram to that of Mr. Rush being afterwards presented by Mr. C. Evans, was published among the Replies to the Circular of the Com., No. XXII.
§ Replies to Circular, &c. No. XXII. Earle on Explosions, Jour. Frank. Inst. vol. vii. p. 154.

* We are not able to make the calculation corresponding to this remark, not having the dimensions of the safety-valve or valves, of the boilers of any one of the western boats.

the flues to the action of air containing its full supply of oxygen, and must tend therefore to oxidize them more rapidly than in the ordinary wear of the engine.

62. The other devices before the committee are those of Mr. C. Evans,[*] and of Mr. J. S. Williams.[†] The first places the mouth of the feeding-pipe just below the proper level of the water in the boiler, so that it shall be laid bare by a change of level, and the water be prevented from escaping from the higher boilers. This would remedy the evil, except in cases where the careening was sufficiently long continued to exhaust the upper boilers of water by the ordinary working of the engine; those boilers of which the supply pipes are bare not being likely to receive any supply from the pump. Mr. Williams places the supply pipes below the boilers and feeds through valves opening upwards, which of course prevent any return of water. The valves in this machine, and also those proposed by Mr. Evans, to prevent any escape of water from the higher boilers, would be objectionable. The method of cleansing the pipes proposed by Mr. Evans is very ingenious.

63. After a careful examination of these devices, the committee are of opinion that they present but partial remedies for the evils which they are intended to meet, and they consider that nothing less than detaching these boilers from each other, and feeding them singly, or at most in pairs, will prove effectual. They would therefore, respectfully, but earnestly, urge this upon constructors and owners.

64. *Fourth. Are there cases in which the metal of a boiler may become unduly heated when in contact with water?*

After much reflection and examination the committee are of opinion that such cases *may* occur. They believe that such have occurred, though not frequently, and that with the common thicknesses of iron and copper boilers, and modes of arranging the furnaces, there is very little liability of their occurrence. Still it is well to recognise that such may be the case, as it may prevent accident by watchfulness in the use of a new construction of boiler, or application of the fire.

65. Mr. F. Graff [‡] mentions specially an instance "in which the heads of the bolts burning off over the fire-place, and the joints parting," "the boiling water passed into the ash pit." From his known carefulness, there is no reason to suspect that there was sediment in this boiler, which was one of the low pressure boilers used at the Philadelphia water-works.

66. Mr. Hebert [*] gives two cases; in the first, three different rents of an iron boiler occurred at the same spot, at different times. Previous to the first "disruption, there was observed a bulging, or swelling out, of the metal, which gradually increased until it became nearly of a hemispherical figure, when it burst open and let the water out of the boiler into the fire. The boiler was repaired by putting a thick patch of malleable plate iron over the hole, when, after about six weeks wear and exposure to the fire, this metal bulged out again, and burst asunder; a third patch was substituted, and in about a similar period of time was destroyed in like manner." "The cause of these ruptures appeared upon investigation to be owing to a partial and very intense heat impinging against that particular spot where they took place." If to this detail had been added proofs that the first rupture was not caused by sediment, nor by a defect in the metal, the evidence would have been complete. It is not, however, probable, that either of these causes were actually operative, since the second and third plates are stated to have bulged out, in the manner of the first, and if sediment had collected at this spot, it could not thrice have escaped notice. The defect in malleable iron, to which the committee alluded above, is the want of connection in parts of a plate, resulting from imperfect welding before rolling, and which sometimes separates the plates into distinct layers, for a considerable extent.

In the communication just referred to, Mr. Hebert further states, that the disruption of a boiler, occurring twice in the same place, was traced by Mr. John Martineau, a respectable engineer of London, to the impinging of a current of air upon this spot.

67. A case apparently of the kind now under discussion, but which was found subsequently, to be due to the imperfect union of the parts of a sheet of metal of the boiler is as follows: Part of a boiler belonging to Messrs. Merrick and Agnew, of this city, was observed to be protruded, in a similar way to that described by Mr. Hebert. Suspecting the presence of sediment, the boiler was examined and found to be clean. It

---

* Replies to Circular, &c. No. XXII.
† Jour. Frank. Inst. vol. viii. p. 289. The method adopted by Mr. W. C. Redfield, places the means of feeding separately, or in the connected way, within the control of the engineer. This was not presented to the committee, but may be found alluded to in the Documents of the House of Representatives of the United States, 1832-3, No. 478, p. 17.
‡ Letter to Councils. Replies to Circular, &c., 4th of No. I.

* Replies, &c. No. XL.

was a cylindrical boiler of wrought iron, the fire applied on the exterior and at one end, and without interior flues. The fuel was anthracite coal. The effect was next attributed to the intense local heat produced by this fuel, and the grate bars being lowered the swelling made no further progress. It has been since ascertained that there was a separation into laminæ of the iron, at this place, requiring the removal of part of the sheet.

68. While, then, the evidence in the cases preceding the last is certainly incomplete, the committee conceive that they are leaning towards the side of safety by admitting the possibility of the occurrence of danger, to the engineer and fireman at least, from peculiarities in the arrangement of a boiler, or of the fire which heats it.

69. In these remarks it has been supposed that there is a considerable column of water over the metal; if that should not be the case it may well happen that the steam-bubbles will form so numerously on, or near, the iron as to allow it, while they rest there, to become heated above what it would be, if the water were in absolute contact with the metal.* This will especially occur with a viscid fluid, such as salt water, or water with much sediment suspended.

70. The views suggested by the several sections of the preceding head are the following :—

1. The feeding of a steam-boat boiler should not be done at intervals, but go on throughout the working of the engine.

When the engine is stopped, as at a landing, or to take up passengers, &c., the water should still be supplied by the engine itself, or by a subsidiary one, or by hand. In this case the free safety valve should be raised. The practice of wasting water by opening a valve, when the forcing-pump is not in action, is considered dangerous.

2. If the water should by any accident get down so as to expose a flue or flues, the fire should be in part extinguished, to cool the boiler before adding water. If the engine is at rest, in such a case, it should not be put in motion. If it is in motion it should be slackened, or stopped, the furnace doors opened, and the heat got down. Then water may be thrown in. The opening of a safety-valve should in such a case be avoided. The engineer should remember that his life is at stake, he cannot be too prudent.

Such a condition of things, however, ought never to be allowed to occur, and the responsibility for the danger which results

must rest upon the master, the engineer, and his assistants.

3. If a self-regulating apparatus for the supply of water is used it should be closely watched, and on no account be implicitly trusted to. It may be a convenience, but can, in no case, be a substitute for human care.

4. For ascertaining the level of the water within a boiler, the committee recommend the glass tube water-gauge, a form of which is shown in the foregoing pages (vol. xxv, pp. 83, 87, 97.)

5. The committee recommend for every boiler a fusible metal apparatus, the metal of which shall be inclosed in a tube, so as not to expose it to pressure.

In boilers without flues it should be attached at the water-line; in those with flues, at the highest part of the flues; or if level, at the part likely to be most rapidly heated, as at the juncture of several flues into one, a sudden change of direction, or the place of most active combustion of the fire.

The form described in the report (vol. xxv, page 118), is convenient, and the lever should act upon a bell, and upon a small cock. The apparatus should be inclosed, the master of the steam-boat having the key of the inclosure, which should further be so arranged as to protect the apparatus from the weather.

The quantity of metal should be no greater than is required to keep the rod in its place. The metal should be regulated so as to melt at a temperature of fifteen degrees * above that corresponding to the working pressure. Tables for this purpose will be found annexed.†

---

* This difference of pressure corresponds at a pressure of two atmospheres, to half an atmosphere or one-half the bursting pressure, and at eleven atmospheres to rather more than two atmospheres, or one-fifth of the bursting pressure. The difference is not, however, too great at low pressures, because an excess of strength may rather be expected in the low pressure boilers as now made, and the alloys, containing bismuth, pass through the different states from solidity to liquidity, by slow degrees.

† While correcting the proof sheets of this No. of the Journal, we notice in the *London Magazine of Popular Science*, for last month, (September, 1836,) a paltry criticism of this proposition of the committee—" to enclose the fusible metal in a case in which it shall not be exposed to the pressure of the steam, but only to its heating effect."—After quoting the sentence, the Magazine critic, triumphing in the fancied discovery of a good American bull, exclaims—"but *cui bono?*—for what purpose?—the metal is in a case! not exposed to the pressure of the steam! How then is it to act efficaciously as a means of relief to a boiler dangerously increasing in temperature? *How is it to act at all*, though fluid as in a crucible?" The conclusion he then arrives at is,—" There must be a district in Pennsylvania where the Shamrock is worn!" And he further thinks, that our sage com-

---

* Replies, &c., No. II. Communication of "an Engineer." Philos. Mag. vol. i. p. 405.

If the metal is melted, the injection of water, or the opening of the furnace doors, will reduce the temperature of the heated parts ; or lower the pressure of the steam if that should have been too high, and the safety valves be out of order.

By sounding with the rod, it will be ascertained when the metal is about to recongeal, as it becomes a soft solid into which the rod may be forced. If, accidentally, the metal congeals without taking in the rod, the end of the latter being heated, will melt the fusible alloy.

If the safety-valves do their duty, this metal will never be melted by increase of temperature, caused by an increase in the elastic force of the steam.

6. The true remedy for undue heating of boilers by deposits is frequently cleansing them. When this is impracticable, blowing out should be cautiously resorted to, so as not to lay the flues bare of water. The danger from these deposits is especially great in salt water, and muddy water mixed with calcareous matters. It should be

guarded against by ascertaining the time required for the water used, to make a sensible deposit. No general rule in regard to this can be given, since boilers in different places and even those fed by springs at short distances apart, are liable to deposits in different times.

Negligence on this point will always produce the rapid destruction of a boiler, and may cause it to burst, or even to explode.

No substitute for the care just recommended, has yet been found.

7. The following table of fusible alloys applicable to boilers working at pressures from one to thirteen atmospheres, is deduced from the experiments of the committee.* The alloys are those determined approximately, which at temperatures severally 15° Fah. above the working temperatures will allow a metallic stem to be drawn out from the mass. The principles which guided the committee in their experiments may be seen by referring to Part I. of their Report (vol. xxv, p. 103, &c.) The proportions are given in parts by weight.

Table of alloys for use in closed tubes, and with a metallic stem.

Working pressure in atmospheres.	Tin.	Lead.	Bismuth.	Working pressure in atmospheres.	Tin.	Lead.	Bismuth.	Working pressure in atmospheres.	Tin.	Lead.	Working pressure in atmospheres.	Tin.	Lead.
1¼	8	8	7.5	4	8	8	3.4	8	8	8	12	8	12.3
2	8	8	6.2	5	8	8	2.2	9	8	9.8	13	8	13.2
2½	8	8	5.3	6	8	8	1.2	10	8	10.6			
3	8	8	4.6	7	8	8	0.5	11	8	11.4			

71.—III. *Explosions may arise from defects in the construction of a boiler, or its appendages.*

This comprehensive division includes the discussion of the form, material, and mode of manufacture of the boiler and of its appendages. The committee have, however, no desire to interfere with the present or future state of the engine in these respects,

further than as their duty requires them to give candidly to the public, their opinion of facts which are on record.

72. 1st.—*Form.* The influence of the form of a boiler in producing danger is of course very great ; but to consider the numerous varieties of form would be impossible, even if their minute differences were known to the committee. Every boiler should be required to stand frequent proofs, as a test of its sufficient strength, but the working properties of each, with originally adequate strength, may be very different.

73. It may, in general, be remarked, that the old waggon-boiler of Watt, should be only used when very low steam is employed. The varieties of the cylinder boiler, with or without interior flues, are in most common use

mittee would be likely to propose, as the best means of preventing the loss of a key which would alone open a box, to *shut it up in the box!* We recommend to this ingenious critic to read this part of the report of the committee carefully over again, and try whether he can discover no good reason suggested for enclosing the fusible alloy in a tube,— and no substantial answer to his *cui bono?*—If his own vision should fail him, perhaps he will do us the favour to borrow that of some *intelligent* friend. We are not aware that the "Shamrock" is at all indigenous to this country, though we have thistles and thorns a plenty.   G.

* Report of Com. on Expl. Part I. p. 36. Jour. Frank. Inst. vol. xvii. p. 36. *Mech. Mag.*, vol. xxv, p. 104.

in the steam-boat engines of this country. Of these experience, both abroad and at home, has shown those without flues to be the more safe, and those with them the more economical. The heads of these boilers are, in this country, plane surfaces; in England, frequently, hemispherical, and in France, are required by law, to be of the latter named figure. There is no reason, however, to doubt the sufficiency of strength of the thick plane wrought-iron heads. Of the flues used, those in the smaller cylinders, which pass directly through both heads of the boiler are the more safe;* the flues passing through the convex surface, called L flues, and those which in the larger boilers return without passing through both heads, add nothing to the strength of the cylinders. Observation has shown that boilers with interior furnaces, or flues, commonly give way by the yielding of the flues, or by blowing off the heads. The tubular boilers of Woolf, have, but in one case, as far as the knowledge of the committee extends,† been used in this country. Other forms of tubular boilers, in which very small tubes contain the water to be vaporized, have, in no case, to their knowledge, on full trial been found successful. The case is very different when, as in the locomotive boilers, the tubes are used as flues: and for obvious reasons. Such boilers have, however, only lately been applied to steam-boats.

There does not seem to the committee, evidence to show that any of these forms are essentially dangerous, though, as before remarked, there are grades among them as to impunity from careless management. From this remark, however, in some degree, should be excepted the L flue-boiler, which is incident always to a source of danger, hereafter to be pointed out. The remarks apply to single, or detached boilers.

74. Connected boilers, on board of steam-boats, are incident to a source of danger which has already been pointed out, (art. 59, &c.) and after examining the remedies which have been proposed to meet these circumstances, the committee are of opinion that they are of so varied a kind that the use of these boilers cannot be continued without certain danger, and therefore ought to be laid aside. Those at present in use could easily be detached, so as to connect only two boilers at most, and have a separate supply-pump for each pair.

* Experience seems to warrant this conclusion, and it does not appear probable that the difference of temperature between the flue and outer shell, even in boilers with interior furnaces, can be sufficient to injure a wrought-iron head, by the excess of the expansion of the flue. The case is different when cast-iron is used for a boiler-head.

† At Richmond, Virginia. See Burr on Explosions. Journ. Frank. Inst. vol. vi. p. 384.

75. In a former division of the subject, (II.) the committee showed the great danger which is produced in a boiler by highly heated metal; any boiler, therefore, which has parts exposed to heat, without being in contact with water, is essentially defective. The L flue-boiler is of this kind, though as it is only used in small cylinders, the exposure is not considerable.* The boiler with a steam-chimney presents an extension of this exposure, the boiler being continued up vertically at one end, so as to inclose the flue.† The idea is to economise the heat found in this flue, by heating the steam which is around it, and thus producing a small surcharge of heat which prevents condensation in the steam-pipe and cylinder. But the flues which the chimneys inclose, are thus exposed to become unduly heated. Two explosions which have occurred in boilers with steam-chimneys‡ have torn the

* A curious case of the overheating of a flue by the accumulation, and subsequent taking fire, of soot, is described by Mr. Hebert in No. XI. of the Replies to the Circular of Committee on Explosions.

† It should be recorded to the credit of the liberal minded patentee of this boiler, that he has afforded every opportunity to investigate its defects, and appears no sooner to have been convinced of the danger to particular parts of it, than he has applied his skill to produce a remedy.

‡ In justice to the force of this conclusion, the committee feel it necessary to give extracts from the excellent accounts of the explosions on board of the *Ohio* and of the *William Gibbons* steam-boats, by Thos. Ewbank, Esq., of New York. The first of these explosions occurred on the Hudson, in 1832, and the second in New York harbour in 1846. The

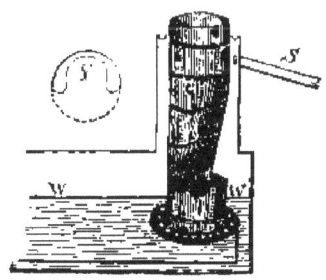

annexed figures represent in plan and section the ruptured flue of the *Ohio*. W W, in the elevation, is the water line, C, the flue, around which the steam chimney is placed, and S, the steam-pipe leading from the steam-chimney. The rent took place from 15 to 20 inches above the water line. This part of the flue is always exposed to the heated air from the horizontal flues which unite in the flue E, and is never covered by water. The line of fracture does not deviate more than six inches from a horizontal line. It is partly along a line of rivets, but chiefly through the centre of the sheets. In portions of one sheet, the metal is reduced from its original thickness of one-quarter of an inch, to one-eighth, and even to one-sixteenth of an inch. Jour. Frank.

same portion of the flue, and were so similar, as to show that they are to be attributed to an inherent defect in this construction. Indeed the presence of metal through which a highly heated draught is passing, while it is in contact only with steam, which cannot carry off the heat rapidly, is sufficient to warrant a decision against such a form of boiler, even if facts had not spoken so loudly in regard to it.

76. The committee feel constrained to recommend to constructors to discontinue the making of connected boilers, of those with L flues, and with the extension constituting a steam chimney.

77. It would be improper to leave this part of our subject, without calling attention to another point in the construction of boilers, which is to be avoided. It is the formation of small spaces intended to contain water and surrounded by fire.* All expe-

Inst.; vol. x. p. 226, No. XXIX. Replies to Circular, &c. The *William Gibbons* has one boiler of wrought iron, and similar in construction to those of the *Ohio*

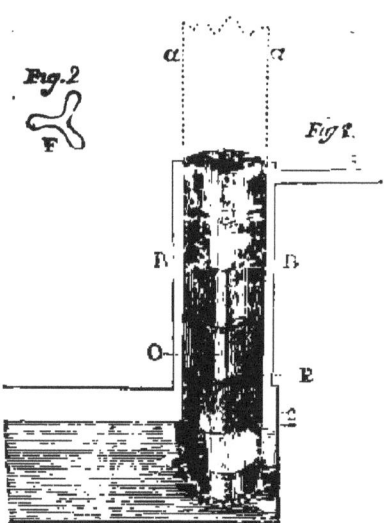

Fig. 2

Fig. 1.

and *New England*, but having a greater number of horizontal flues. The flue BB, within the steam-chimney, was collapsed so as to form a three cusped figure, as shown in fig. 2. The rent R, thus produced, was four inches above the roof of the boiler. It was in one of the horizontal seams, and confined almost wholly to it, extending nearly three feet, or about one-third of the circumference of the flue. The flue was iron, one-fourth of an inch in thickness, and its thickness was not sensibly diminished previous to rupture. Jour. Frank. Inst., vol. xvii. p. 298. The fuel used ordinarily, was a mixture of anthracite coal and wood, but, on this occasion, it appears that the fire had been urged with quantities of wood.

* Ewbank on the explosion of the boilers of the steam-boat *New England*. Jour. Frank. Inst., vol. xiii. pp. 292, 293.

rience has shown that steam cannot be generated in small tubes without driving out the water, and these arrangements are equivalent to tubes ; and besides being liable to the accumulation of deposits, they are exposed to have the water carried from them unless when under considerable pressure. The weakness of boilers of these irregular forms should never be lost sight of.

78. 2nd.—*Material and manufacture*. As early as 1818 a committee of the British House of Commons, on the authority of practical and scientific men whom they examined, recommended the disuse of cast-iron as a material for steam-boilers. This material has now so generally been abandoned, for this purpose, that remarks upon its defects are not necessary. Even the cast-iron heads for boilers which were used a few years since on the Mississippi, are, the committee believe, now giving place to wrought-iron ones. The materials in common use for steam-boilers, are wrought-iron and copper.

79. The committee have made, by the arrangement stated in the preface to the first part of their report, an extensive series of experiments on the strength of the different varieties of wrought-iron and copper, manufactured for steam boilers in the United States. These experiments they hoped to have presented before making this report, but circumstances not now necessary to be made public, have prevented them from doing so, and they deem it inexpedient longer to delay on this account. They must refer, therefore, to a report, specially upon this subject, for a complete development of their views, as well as for information in regard to the proper thicknesses for steam boilers, working under different pressures. They ought, however, to remark here, that the views usually entertained of the importance of working iron, have been entirely confirmed by them. The ultimate strength of a bar, or sheet of iron, coinciding more nearly with the strength which the whole bar exerts to prevent a first fracture, or the bar or sheet being rendered more uniformly strong, and therefore better adapted for use in the construction of steam-boilers, the more it is worked. Iron which has been heated nearly to redness has its tenacity permanently injured, being affected, though in a less degree than copper, the weakness of which, in such a case, has long been well established.*

80. There can be no doubt that the strength of boilers may be diminished by

* On both these points, see also the remarks of Mr. Lester in Replies to Circular, &c., No. xvii. where the fact is stated both in regard to iron and copper, as resulting from his own experience.

constant, and often unequal pressure, by which the material is injured so far as to give way under a less strain, than that which it may; once have borne.* By ordinary wear, from oxidation, &c., their strength is necessarily much impaired.

81. When salt water or spring water highly charged with saline matter, is used to feed boilers, iron is very rapidly acted on, and extreme care should be used in frequently cleansing them.† Careful owners would resort to more frequent proof by the forcing pump than in other cases. This would serve to detect corrosion in particular spots, to which the material is so liable. Copper boilers not being similarly acted on, are more safe in such situations, but these seems no reason to suppose that iron may not be safely used, with due precaution.

82. Instances of dangerous defects in construction, or arising from use, in boilers are but too well attested. The awful explosion on board the steam-boat *Helen McGregor*,‡ by which more than thirty persons lost their lives, took effect by forcing off the cast-iron head of a wrought-iron boiler, throwing the boiler in the opposite direction: the head was known to be cracked before the explosion occurred. It is not clearly made out whether this result was produced by a gradual increase of pressure,§ or by the return to its level of the boat, which had been eased by stopping at a landing place. The steam was not let into the cylinder to propel the engine, when the explosion happened. The boiler was one of six connected boilers of 3 feet diameter. A cast-iron head should never be united to a wrought-iron boiler with flues,‖ since, independently of the defects to which the metal is liable, the inequality of expansion is very likely to crack it.‡

83. A defect in a wrought-iron boiler head was detected by one of our correspondents, which we are surprised that any boiler maker should have allowed to pass. In turning the flanches by which the head is riveted to the cylinder, the iron was turned so sharply as to crack it more than half-way

through. This was one of four boiler heads belonging to the same set, found by Mr. H. W. Benton to be unsound. They could not have stood proving.*

There can be no doubt but that the repairs to the boiler of the *Caledonia* were improperly made,† an iron plate having been fastened upon the boiler with copper rivets: this seems, at least in part, to have been the cause of the accident which subsequently occurred.

84. The idea seems formerly‡ to have been entertained that dangerous explosions could not occur in wrought-iron boilers, which were merely rent without doing injury. It is almost needless to remark that the whole tenor of the evidence before the committee contradicts the idea. Wrought iron may even be separated into fragments, but the great source of danger is in the escape of the hot water, which, with the steam generated by it, produces death in one of its most painful forms.

85. Steam-boilers should not only be proved when originally made, but from time to time, to guard against their gradual wear or accidental injury; and especially after every important repair made to them. In the intervals care must be secured by other means. These proofs have been recommended by most of our valued correspondents.

86. In the attachment of sheets of metal to each other to form boilers, and in the fixing of heads to boilers, constructors appear to have lost sight of the fact that the metal which is taken out for the rivet holes weakens the sheet, and that materially. In examining cases of explosion from direct pressure, and where no undue heating or special weakness has led to the result, the lines of rivets appear to determine the direction of the first fracture.§ A very neat example of this was given in the bursting of an iron cylinder in the experiments of the committee.‖ The head of the cylinder was forced off, carrying with it the metal which projected beyond the line of rivets. The rivet-holes had cut out rather more than half of the circumference of the metal forming the convex surface, along the circle passing through the centres of the rivet-holes, and thus had made the strength of the convex surface to resist rupture in a direction per-

* See Replies to Circular, &c., Nos. ii. and xii. Col. S. H. Long and T. Bakewell, Esq.; also evidence of Mr. Bramah before Com. of House of Commons, 1817, Dodd's Collections.

† An instructive description of the action of salt water on iron will be found in the evidence of Professor Faraday before the Com. H. Commons of Eng. on steam navigation, 1822.

‡ Nos. III. IV. and XXI. of Replies, &c.

§ Replies to Circular, No. IV.

‖ See also explosion of *Atlas*, Replies, &c. No. VIII. and No. XXI., Car of Commerce, No. XXI.

‡ Evidence of John Taylor, Esq., before Com. of House of Commons, A cast-iron boiler head, affixed in his shops to a wrought-iron boiler, and originally proved with a pressure of 100lbs., cracked by heat when only exposed to a pressure of steam of 20lbs.

* No. VIII. Replies, &c. Boilers of *Tally-ho* Steam-boat.

† Replies, &c., Nos. V., VI., VII., VIII., XXI.

‡ Evidence before Com. of House of Commons, Dodd's Collection.

§ Ewbank on the Explosion of the Boilers of the *New England* Steam-boat. Jour. Frank. Inst., vol. xiii. p. 293.

‖ Report of Committee on Explosions. Part I. p. 67. Jour. Frank. Inst. vol. xvii. p. 224.

pendicular to the axis of the cylinder, less than its strength to resist a rupture in the direction of the axis.*

87. The exposure of joints, formed by the junction of boiler plates, to the fire, may be mentioned as liable to produce very rapid wear. The heat is not conducted off as rapidly as by the other parts of the boiler, and the lower sheet is exposed to rapid oxidation.

88. 3rd.—*Appendages to the boiler.* Of these the principal ones have already been made the subject of remark and recommendation by the committee. The forcing pump, as one of the most important, deserves further notice in this place. It is not the intention to recommend any particular form of this pump, especially as the committee believe that most commonly in use to be entirely adequate to all its objects. They may remark, however, that they consider several valves between the supply reservoir and the pump, and also between the pump and the boiler, as of the greatest importance. They would further recommend to be placed on eduction pipe a cock similar to that used in locomotive engines. A rod and handle connected with this should be placed in a convenient position, for the engine-man to ascertain, by turning the cock, if the pump is in action. Although this apparatus cannot dispense with due attention to the means of ascertaining the level of the water within a boiler, it may give notice of a defective supply, in time to apply a preventive, instead of a remedy.

89. The committee consider that their remarks already made in relation to the mode of applying heat to a boiler have been sufficient. They do not see that the use of a fusible metal or fluid bath can be applicable, in practice, to the heating of a steam boiler, or would, if applicable, realize the advantages which have been claimed for them. The recommendations embodied in the present division of the subject will be found carried out by the suggestion of appropriate enactments in the project of a law which is appended to this report.

90. IV. *Carelessness, or ignorance, of those intrusted with the management of the steam-engine.*

It might be supposed that the fact once known that the engineer or fireman who, from carelessness, or other cause, allows a boiler under his charge to explode, is in almost every case the first victim of the disaster, would produce care in those intrusted with the engine. But experience shows that this is not so; and the committee, in proposing remedies, do but the duty which has been confided to them, and proved indispensable by examples not to be mistaken or disregarded.

91. Familiarity with any sort of danger is so sure to produce callousness to it, and due caution is so apt to be considered as timidity, that a tendency to carelessness must be considered as the natural consequence of the situation of an engineer or fireman. The subject of the causes of explosions in steam-boilers has been so little investigated, that men well versed in general science might be excused for ignorance of it, and steam-engineers should not therefore be too harshly or hastily blamed for what is incident to the nature of the subject, rather than the fault of the profession. The fact of carelessness or ignorance has, however, been so much insisted upon by our correspondents* that it must be assumed, and endeavours made to apply a remedy.

92. In the present state of general education in our country, it would obviously be impracticable to insist that firemen, or even steam-engineers, should be versed in the scientific principles which regulate the use of steam. The public have, however, a right to expect from employers, that their agents, who are intrusted with human life, shiuld have a thorough practical acquaintance with the steam-engine, and to demand that those who have information of the sources of danger, should lay down plain rules for the guidance of those who have been referred to. As a guard against carelessness, the public have a further right to expect from the higher authorities, beginning with the chief engineers, and rising to the captains of steam-boats and masters of ships, that they should exert all the moral influence which vigilance can produce. And from the law, that it should constrain all these, by appropriate penalties, to the discharge of their responsible duties.

This view the committee have carried out in the project of a law which accompanies their report.

93. V. *Cases of collapse from a partial vacuum within a boiler, or its flues.*

These cases are so little applicable in the state of the steam-engine in this country, that the committee have postponed their discussion until the last.

It is certain that the boiler of a high pressure engine of proper strength for ordinary purposes, would also be able to sustain the

---

* With an equal thickness of metal the strength in the former case would have been double that in the latter.

* Replies to Circular, &c. Nos. III., VIII., IX., XVII., XIX., XX., XXI., XXIII., XXVIII. Also, Remarks by "An Engineer," Philos. Mag. vol. i. &c. &c.

action resulting from even the sudden formation of a vacuum within it. Low pressure boilers have been crushed by the pressure of the atmosphere when a vacuum has been formed within.* These accidents are effectually guarded against, as far as experience has shown, by a valve opening inwards, with which Watt's boilers were provided.

94. A case of explosion at the Mold Mines, in Flintshire, which has been circumstantially detailed by John Taylor, Esq.,† seems to prove that a rarefaction produced in the interior flues of a high pressure engine, may determine an explosion of the most violent description. The boiler which exploded, belonged to a set of three, feeding the same engine. The fuel used was bituminous coal. The furnace doors of all three of the boilers had been opened, and the dampers of two had been closed, when a gust of flame was seen to issue from the mouth of the furnace of these latter, and was immediately followed by an explosion. The interior flue of this boiler was flattened from the sides, the flue and shell of the boiler remaining in their places, and the safety valve upon the latter not being injured. Mr. Taylor states it as probable, that the steam pressure at the time of this accident did not exceed thirty pounds, and that the water was at its proper height. He assigns as the probable cause which determined the collapse of the flue, the ignition of a mixture of gas from the coal with atmospheric air, the contents of the furnace not being carried up the chimney on account of the closing of the damper, by which a partial vacuum was produced. If the strength of the flue was but little more than sufficient to resist a steam pressure of thirty pounds, it is plain that the cause assigned is adequate to have produced the effect. It must be admitted, however, that the testimony of the fireman who escaped injury by the explosion, and who would have been subjected to all the blame of the accident, if any attached, his comrades having been killed, is of that kind which induces a doubt whether the steam pressure and height of water, were exactly as stated.

The accident, however, suggests the precaution as necessary with coal, and with some kinds of wood, not to close a damper soon after fresh fuel has been added; if the furnace is within the boiler, the injurious

effects may be very serious, even more so than in the cases already referred to, where the furnace is not so placed.

95. That a vacuum can occur within a steam-boiler which is in action, as has been propounded within a few years' past, is a supposition too palpably contradicted by the facts of the case to require any examination here.

96. VI. Having closed the subject of the means of preventing explosions in steam boilers, the committee have yet to consider *whether it is possible to provide protection against their effects when they occur.*

The very respectable scientific and practical men who have at different times drawn the attention of the public to this matter, give undoubted authority to the suggestion. The means proposed are, by carrying the passengers in a separate boat from the engine, or by placing the boilers on the guards of the boat, and separating them from the parts occupied by the passengers, by a suitable bulwark.

97. In regard to the first of these plans, it has been attempted, and for want of sufficient patronage by the public, has been laid aside. Public opinion seems to set strongly towards precautions which shall render the engine safe, without crippling its power of giving speed.

98. The larger steam-boats on our Atlantic waters have generally the boilers upon the guards, * but without any obstruction between them and the inner parts of the boat. This affords but a partial security, diminishing probably the extent, but not preventing, the destruction of human life. That a bulwark of sufficient strength to protect against explosion, without adding too much to the weight of the boat, can be devised, the committee are not prepared to assert positively, though they believe that it could.

99. Their views incline entirely to the protection of the hands, as well as passengers by rendering the boiler safe, and they fully believe that this may be done without encumbering the boats now in use, or requiring, in a majority of cases, an entire change of structure in the engine.

They have, however, to meet opinions which they hold in so much respect, introduced a clause in the proposed bill, annexed to this report, by which a bounty is, in fact, offered upon a boat constructed with suitable bulwarks between the interior part and the boiler.

* Arago on Explosions. Annuaire du Bureau des Long. 1830, pp. 148, 169, and 170; also Journ. Frank. Inst. vol. v. pp. 404 and 412.
† On the accidents incident to steam boilers. Philos. Mag. vol. 1. See also remarks upon the same by "a practical engineer," and by W. J. Henwood, in the same volume.

* We are pleased to see that a boat in which the boilers are placed upon the guards has been put in operation upon the Mississippi. This, we trust, is only the first of many of this kind to be hereafter constructed.

166. The committee having now completed their examination of the causes of explosion, with their preventives, as far as they are informed upon the subject, and made all the recommendations, which this examination has suggested to them, refer to the accompanying project of a law for the regulations of the boilers and engines of steam-vessels, for the means of carrying the more important of these suggestions into effect.

The provisions of this law refer only to the means of preventing the explosions of boilers of steam-boats, or of affording protection against their effects. With the regulations in regard to the navigation or police of the boats, however important, this committee do not feel warranted in interfering. They believe that the experience necessary to frame such regulations will be found in the appropriate committees of Congress, upon whose attention they would respectfully urge the annexed provisions relating to the engine.

That such an enactment will contribute to the safety of the public, without interfering injuriously with those interested in the navigation by steam or in the manufacture of the steam-engine, is the deliberate opinion of this committee.

Respectfully submitted,
In behalf and by direction
of the Committee, by
ALEX. DALLAS BACHE,
Chairman of the Com. on
Explosions, &c.

Presented to the Board of Managers of the Franklin Institute of Pennsylvania, for the Promotion of the Mechanic Arts, and approved, September 21st, 1836.
M. W. BALDWIN,
Chairman of the Board of
Managers.

WILLIAM HAMILTON, Actuary.

Proposed Bill for the regulation of the Boilers and Engines of vessels propelled in the whole or in part by steam.

SECTIONS I* to 4.—[The same as the Act. See *Mech. Mag.*, No. 787.]*

SEC. 5.—That each and every boiler of a steam-boat, or vessel propelled in the whole or in part by steam, shall be constructed, and arranged, so as to comply with the following provisions:—

1. There shall be two safety-valves, each of which shall be competent to discharge the steam made in the ordinary working of the boiler.

2. The first of said valves shall be graduated by the maker of the engine, and

have stamped upon the lever, by which it is weighted, the pressure at which it will by calculation open, when the appropriate moveable weight is placed at the several marks. Said pressure to be the difference between the pressure of the steam within, and atmospheric pressure on said valve.

3. When the moveable weight exerts its greatest pressure, the total pressure upon said valve shall not exceed the pressure as certified according to the provision of the fourth section of this act.

4. The second of said valves, denominated the lock-up valve, shall be immoveably weighted, the total pressure upon it not to exceed said certified pressure.

5. Said lock-up valve, with its lever and other attachments, shall be inclosed in a grated box, or otherwise duly arranged as that it can be raised, but not pressed down, except as above provided, upon its seat.

6. Said inclosure, or arrangements, shall be secured with a lock, of which the captain or master of said boat shall alone have the key.

7. Said inclosure or, arrangements, shall admit a rise in the valve of at least one-fourth of the diameter of its seat.

8. The lever of said valve shall be so constructed as on the rising of the valve, to diminish the effect of the acting weight, by at least one-tenth of the ordinary pressure derived from said weight.

9. When two boilers, each of not more than forty inches diameter, are connected by a steam-pipe, each pair of said boilers may be furnished with safety-valves, as described in this section, for a single boiler.

10. When the certified pressure provided in section fourth, does not exceed two atmospheres, each and every boiler shall be furnished with a mercurial-gauge, indicating by a float or rod, upon a duly graduated and marked scale, the excess of pressure within the boiler over atmospheric pressure, in inches of mercury.

11. Said gauge and scale shall be so placed as to be readily examined by any and every passenger on board of said boat.

12. Each and every boiler shall be provided with a fusible metal apparatus of suitable form and dimensions, to be applied to the boiler itself, or to its flues, at the place which may be considered that of greatest heat, or most liable to exposure from a deficient supply of water.

13. Said fusible metal shall be contained in a tube to prevent its exposure to pressure, and shall on softening, communicate an alarm by some suitable device.

14. Said apparatus shall be duly secured from being rendered ineffective, in the manner of the lock-up safety-valve hereinbefore provided.

* Sect. 1 of the bill reported in Senate U. S.

15. The fusible metal hereinbefore referred to, shall be compounded by the inspector, who shall place it in the apparatus as aforesaid, and shall satisfy himself that the whole is duly arranged as heretofore prescribed.

16. The said alloys shall be compounded according to the certified pressure of steam within the boiler, by the following table of parts, by weight, of the ingredients.

Table of alloys for use in closed tubes, and with a metallic stem.

Certified pressure in atmospheres.	Tin.	Lead.	Bismuth.	Certified pressure in atmospheres.	Tin.	Lead.	Bismuth.	Certified pressure in atmospheres.	Tin.	Lead.	Certified pressure in atmospheres.	Tin.	Lead.
1½	8	8	7.5	4	8	8	3.4	8	8	9.0	12	8	12.5
2	8	8	6.2	5	8	8	2.2	9	8	9.8	13	8	13.2
2½	8	8	5.3	6	8	8	1.2	10	8	10.6			
3	8	8	4.6	7	8	6	0.5	11	8	11.4			

SEC. 7.—That any person or persons whatsoever who shall wilfully overload or otherwise render inoperative said safety-valve or valves, or render ineffective said mercurial-gauge or gauges, by plugging up or stopping off, or in any other manner preventing their action, or shall in any manner impair, or interfere with the usefulness of said fusible metal apparatus, shall for every offence be subject to the penalty of —— dollars, and to an imprisonment at the discretion of the court, not to exceed ——, and in case of accident to said steam-boiler, resulting from said offence, by which life is lost, shall be deemed to have been guilty of manslaughter, and punished according to law for said offence.

SEC. 8.—That not more than two boilers of a boat, or vessel, propelled in the whole or in part, by steam, and those immediately contiguous, shall have connected water pipes, nor shall the license heretofore provided for, be issued until the inspector has satisfied himself, and has certified, that the provision of this section is complied with.

SEC. 9.—That for each and every bursting of the boiler of a steam-boat or vessel propelled in the whole, or in part, by steam, which shall occur from a deposit of sedimentary matter within a boiler, the master of said vessel shall forfeit the sum of —— dollars, and that in case life shall be lost by the same, he shall be deemed to have been guilty of manslaughter, and shall be liable to prosecution accordingly.

SEC. 10.—That no boat or vessel propelled in the whole or in part by steam, shall be licensed until the inspector has certified on examination, that no part of the boiler of said boat is, ordinarily, directly exposed to flame, or to heated air from the draught, without the immediate contact of water.

SEC. 11.—That it shall be the duty of the person who shall be called upon to inspect the boilers and machinery of any steam-boat or vessel, in conformity to the provisions of this act, carefully, fully, and thoroughly, to inspect and examine the engine and machinery of said boat or vessel, and to state his opinion of their soundness: and he shall, moreover, provide himself with a suitable hydraulic pump, and, after examining into the state and condition of the boiler, or boilers, of said boat, or vessel, it shall be his duty to test the strength and soundness of said boiler, or boilers, by applying to the same a hydraulic pressure equal to three times the certified pressure which the boilers are to carry in steam.

SEC. 13.—That whenever the master of any boat, or vessel, or the person or persons, charged with the navigating said boat or vessel which is propelled in the whole or in part by steam, shall stop the motion, or headway of said boat, or vessel; or the said boat or vessel shall be stopped for the purpose of discharging, or taking in cargo, fuel, or passengers; he, or they, shall keep the engine of said boat, or vessel, in motion sufficient to work the pump, and give the necessary supply of water.

SEC. 14.—That no other than a practical mechanic who shall be of the age of twenty-one years, or upwards, shall have served two years in a steam-engine factory, or general machine making establishment, and who shall have a thorough knowledge of the working of an engine, and shall produce satisfactory testimonials of steady habits, shall be employed as an engineer on board of any boat or vessel propelled in whole or in part by steam.

SEC. 18.—That any boat or vessel propelled in the whole or in part by steam, which shall have its boilers upon the guards of the boat, and shall have between them and the interior of the boat, or vessel, a sufficient bulwark of timber, or other suitable material, so that passengers shall be protected effectually from injury in the event of explosion, shall be, on a certificate to the foregoing effect from the inspector heretofore provided, exempted from the payment of fees for the taking out of the license of navigation, and shall have remitted one-half of the fees for proving and for other purposes of precaution heretofore provided. The fees remitted in such case to be assumed and paid to the respective officers by the United States.

SELECTIONS FROM THE PROCEEDINGS OF THE NEWCASTLE MEETING (BEING THE EIGHTH) OF THE BRITISH ASSOCIATION FOR THE ADVANCEMENT OF SCIENCE.

[Continued from page 432.]

" Description of an improved Levelling Stave, for Subterraneous as well as Surface Levelling," by Thomas Sopwith.

The method of reading the figures of the stave itself, instead of the sliding vane, as adopted by most experienced engineers and surveyors, is used in Mr. Sopwith's improved staves. The figures are engraved on copper-plate, on an enlarged scale, so as to contract in drying to their proper length, which is fixed by a very accurate gauge. The arrangement of the scale is that of feet, divided into hundredth parts, alternately black and white; and in the form of the figures, clearness and distinct vision at a distance are chiefly aimed at. Mr. Sopwith's improvement consists in the mechanical arrangement of the slides, which are held in any fixed position by means of a catch or spring. The stave for mining purposes has also an entirely new arrangement. It has a glass shield or cover to protect the face of it from wet and dirt; and is hinged, so as to work in any seam of from three to five feet; but the principle may be adopted for any greater or less extent.

" On a Suspension Bridge over the Avon, Tiverton," by T. Motley.

The peculiar feature of this bridge, is, that each chain is attached to the roadway, and the suspending bars are carried up through each chain above it. The length of the bridge is 230 feet, the breadth 141, and the cost, including the towers and land abutments, under 2,400l. This bridge is superior to the common suspension bridge, in that it is more firm, and experiences much less friction, owing to the absence of vibration.

Models were exhibited and partially explained of a suspension bridge of wire, erected over the river Avon, near Bath, by Mr. Dredge. The bridge is upwards of 230 feet in length, the breadth of the roadway is fourteen feet, and the whole, including land abutments, &c., was completed for less than 2,400l.—A method of Pumping Water from Leaky Vessels at Sea, by Mr. Dalziell. The machine is worked with a piston, the motion of the vessel being given by the stream when the vessel is sailing, to paddle-wheels on the sides.—An instrument for Measuring Timber, by J. Smith.—A peculiar Combination for the Wheel Work of a Crane, by W. Horner.—A peculiar form of Steam-engine Boiler, in use at the Glass Works at Gateshead, by J. Price. The principal advantages of this boiler were said to be, the impossibility of collapsing, the rapidity with which it generates steam, and the small consumption of fuel.

Dr. Reid gave a brief notice of his researches " On the quantity of air required for respiration." He pointed out imperfections in previous experiments, particularly that consisting in the small number of individuals experimented on. A great difficulty existed in attempting accurate conclusions, from the diversity of constitutional temperaments, different states of humidity of the atmosphere, the state of insensible perspiration, and also from the admixture of small quantities of foreign gasss; in one instance the admixture of $\frac{1}{3000}$ part sulphureted hydrogen, was enough to " knock up" a whole room, producing very serious effects. The degree of light was also an important element; ten per cent. of carbonic acid produces much oppression in the dark; but, if strong light be admitted, it becomes tolerable. Dr. Reid stated, that at St. Petersburgh, he was informed by Sir I. Wily, that the cases of disease on the dark side of an extensive barrack, were in the proportion of three to one, to those on the side exposed to strong light, and this uniformly so for many years. Dr. Reid explained the mode he had adopted to ventilate the House of Commons, which he illustrated by diagrams, and demonstrated by the exhibition of a glazed model of the House. The current of fresh air could be introduced either from below or from above, diffused uniformly, and not by violent draughts, but as it were insensibly, and was under the most exact control as to quantity. The air, when used for the purposes of respiration and combustion, was conveyed away in an opposite direction to that in which it had been introduced. In answer to a question, Dr. Reid said, that he had taken no account of the products of the combustion by which the heat and light were produced, as these products should be omitted in all calculations on the subject. They, if possible, should be carried off so as not to interfere with the immediate supply to each individual. For the purpose of raising the temperature, hot water was used in iron tubes, not raised above 150°. Dr. Reid also stated, in answer to other questions, that he had not made any particular observation on the modifying influence of different articles of clothing, but he believed they did modify considerably the question, those being preferable that were of a very porous nature, allowing an *insensible* application of the atmosphere to the cutaneous surface.

" Substitute for the Mountain Barometer in Measuring Heights, " by Sir John Robison.

Mr Russell said, that all persons who had used the mountain barometer, when measuring heights, would admit that it was a very cumbersome instrument, put out of order by very slight accidents, and only to be used by persons well skilled in observing. Now, the principle of Sir John Robison's contrivance was simple, and such that the most ignorant person might be intrusted with the preparatory manipulation of it, and might be sent up mountains when the philosopher could not leave his study, and bring back the air to be experimented upon; and, since he could not go to the air with his barometer, to cause it to come to him. It consisted of a wooden box, containing simply a thermometer and a number of tubes, of a bore something wider than those of self-registering thermometers, open at one end, and blown into bulbs at the other, also a small vessel of quicksilver. All the person who went up the mountain had to do, was to note the thermometer, and immerse the open end of one of the tubes into the mercury at each station, and then bring down the whole. The examiner then places each bulbed tube, into the stem of which a considerable quantity of mercury will, of course, be found to have entered, under the receiver of an air pump, either along with a barometer or with a well-made gauge : and on pushing the exhaustion until the mercury stood within the bulbed tube as it did upon the mountain, making certain simple allowances for temperature, the height at which the barometer would have stood at the station on the hill can be deduced ; and thence, by the usual calculation, the height of the station. The stem is previously graduated by the maker, so that bare inspection shows the density of the air at the elevated station.

Prof. Chevallier said there was a very portable instrument, the Sympiesometer, the principle of which seemed to him to be the same as that contrived by Sir John Robison.—Sir J Herschel presumed Prof. Chevallier meant Adie's Sympiesometer ; if so, he would find, on consideration, that the principle of Mr. Adie's Sympiesometer was the compression of a confined portion of gas, and not at all the same as that of Sir John Robison.—Prof. Stevelly said, he was glad to find the air pump thus beginning to be made subservient to such inquiries ; he trusted its use would yet be extended to ascertaining, roughly at least, the heights of the clouds in different states of the weather, by a method which, if the time of the section were not so precious, he would have alluded to ; it was founded on a well-known fact, the appearance of cloud in the exhausted receiver of an air pump.

" On the Foreign Substances contained in Iron," by Thomas Thompson, M.D.

The best Dannemora iron, common Welsh iron, and Low Moor iron, were found to have the following specific gravities :—

Dannemora iron...... 7.9125, or 1000
Low Moor iron...... 7.3519 — 929
Welsh iron.......... 7.4359 — 939.7

Dannemora iron was composed of

Iron....................	99.56
Carbon	0.26
Manganese	0.05
Silicon..................	0.03
	99.90

Low Moor iron of

Iron....................	98.060
Manganese	1.868
Silicon..................	0.090
	100.018

Welsh Iron of

Iron, with a little Manganese	99.498
Phosphorus..............	0.417
Silicon..................	0.085
	100.

"Of Chemical Combinations, produced in virtue of the presence of Bodies which remain to continue the process," by Mr. Exley.

It has been observed, said Mr. Exley, that in many instances, powerful chemical affinities have been brought into activity by the presence of certain bodies which remain insulated. This Berzelius attributes to a peculiar force, which he calls catalytic force. Several reasons are adduced to show that this catalytic force is but one species of the general effects which occur usually in chemical actions, all of which are modifications of universal gravity arising from circumstances. The actions of this force were illustrated in four instances:—First, said Mr. Exley, a piece of spongy platina, about the size of a pea, is placed before a fine jet of hydrogen: this produces the combination of oxygen and hydrogen, raising the temperature till ignition occurs. To explain this by my general principles, it must be observed, that, as in all metals, so especially in platina, because of its great density and atomic weight, the sphere of repulsion is very small. Hence, the ethereal atmospheres of its atoms are very dense, on which account the atoms of other bodies are drawn very nearly into combination, and thus, by its influence, the atoms of oxygen and hydrogen are brought so near together as to effect their union; caloric is given out; this favours the like union of other atoms, till ignition is produced. The effect of a clear surface of platina in causing the combination of a due mixture of oxygen and hydrogen, depends on the same conditions. 2nd, Another example given, was the conversion of starch into sugar, by means of dilute sulphuric acid. 3rd, The conversion of sugar into alcohol. 4th, The conversion of the alcohol into ether, by means by sulphuric acid. . . . .

"On a new process for Tanning," by Mr. William Herapath.

The author assumed that the great cause of obstruction to rapid tanning, is, that the weakened ooze is retained by the capillary attraction of the fibres and blood vessels so long, that when it shall have passed out by exosmosis, it will have produced the same effect upon the soluble gelatin as is produced by maceration. Hydraulic pressure was too expensive to obviate this difficulty, and he accordingly thought of employing pressure by the roller. When 100 hides are to be tanned per week, it is necessary to have eight pits, over each of which should be affixed a pair of rollers, the upper ones to be loaded by weights fixed on two levers. For each pit, fifty hides or butts would be made into an endless band by ligatures of twine.

Upon introducing each band between a pair of rollers, each hide would be in succession pulled from the bottom of the pit, squeezed by the rollers, and then returned again into the pit for a fresh supply of tanning liquor. Each liquor becomes exhausted about two degrees of the barkrometer in twenty-four hours, when it is pumped to the next pit backwards of the series; and by the time it arrives at the last pit (eight days), it will have lost from sixteen to twenty degrees by the same instrument. The eight pairs of rollers require one horse-power to work them, and two boys, at 2s. 6d. a week each, to superintend them, when two bands, or 100 hides, will be taken off weekly. We believe a patent has been taken out for this process.

"On the application of Gas obtained from Water to the Manufacture of Iron," by Mr. J. S. Dawes.

The method of application is as follows:—Jets of steam are made to pass through red-hot cast-iron pipes filled with small coke or charcoal, (the riddlings from the coke-hearth answer every purpose, and are of little value); decomposition immediately takes place; the base of the carbon of the coke combines with the oxygen base of the steam, forming, in the first instance, carbonic acid, but, by passing this over a further portion of the red-hot carbon, it is converted into carbonic oxide, sensible heat at the same time becoming latent on combining with the hydrogen base, producing hydrogen gas, which, together with the oxide before mentioned, is applied to the furnace by means of a jet inserted within the blast-pipe tuyere, the pressure upon the gas, of course, being equal to that upon the blast. The pipes require to be replenished with the brays about every twelve hours, which is conveniently effected by means of a plug fitted to the top of each of them. At first, some difficulty arose from destruction of the pipes, but as the melting point of cast-iron is so much higher than the temperature required to decompose water, it was presumed that the cause of the mischief lay in the construction of the heating furnace; this has been remedied, and the apparatus seems now to be very durable. The present one, at Oldbury, has been in operation for several months, and the pipes are apparently little the worse for wear. The quantity of fuel required to keep them hot, is from 12 to 15 cwt. of small coal for 12 hours; and as the steam is obtained from the engine-boilers, and the fireman of the hot air apparatus has time enough to attend to it, the expense, with the exception of wear and tear, is comparatively trifling; and as this also, in every probability, will be very moderate, it may be concluded that the cost will not exceed 3 or 4 shillings per 1000 feet.

Dr. Buckland " On the application of Small Coal to Economical Purposes."

He referred to the well known enormous annual waste of coal at the mouths of the various pits near Newcastle; and that, in consequence of what has been said on the subject in his Bridgewater Treatise, the attention of a benevolent individual had been called strongly to the subject. That individual had succeeded in agglutinating the small particles of coal into a firm mass by a process at once simple and cheap; and he believed he had taken out a patent for the method. The individual was Mr. Oram. There would be even an economy in using this coal for many purposes, as it occupied one-third or one-fourth less space, when packed in boxes, than coal in its ordinary state. Specimens were exhibited, which had a firm compact appearance; and Dr. Buckland stated, that, by the directions of government, trials had been made under the inspection of competent persons, and that success had been complete, the combustion being, at least, as productive as that of coal in its common state.

Prof. Sedgwick read extracts from a statistical return by Mr. Wharton, which went to show that the waste at the pits' mouths, particularly at Hetton and other great collieries, was much less than is commonly imagined, and indeed insignificant. To which Mr. Buddle replied, by stating, that the great waste was underground. A vast quantity of coal was thrown aside as useless, and never saw the light.

" On the use of Wire Ropes in deep Mines," by Count Augustus Breunner.

There had been introduced into the silver mines of the Hartz Mountains, about seven years ago, ropes composed of twisted iron wire, as a substitute for the flat ropes previously in use. Since that time they have been adopted throughout the mines of Hungary and most of those in the Austrian dominions, to the almost total exclusion of flat and round ropes made of hemp. These iron ropes are of equal strength with a hempen rope of four times the weight. One has been in use upwards of two years without any perceptible wear, whereas a flat rope performing similar work would not have lasted much more than a single year. The diameter of the largest rope in ordinary use in the deepest mines of Austria is one inch and a half. This rope is composed of iron wires, each two lines in diameter; five of them are braided together into strands, and

three of those strands are twisted tightly into a rope. Great care is requisite in making the rope that the ends of the wires be set deep in the interior of the rope, and that no two ends meet near the same part. The strength of these ropes is little less than that of a solid iron bar of the same diameter. The usual weight lifted is 1000lb. The rope on leaving the shaft must be received on a cylinder of not less than eight feet diameter, and be kept well coated with tar. There is a saving of about one-third of the power in one case mentioned, for *four* horses with a wire rope are doing the same work as *six* horses with a flat rope. It was suggested by the distinguished foreigner, that the introduction of iron ropes for the flat ropes in our deep mines and coal-pits would be attended with the same, if not greater advantages than has attended their introduction into the mines of the Austrian dominions.

" On Steam Navigation and a self-recording Steam Journal," by Dr. Lardner.

Dr. Lardner said, no one could be more deeply impressed with the importance of the observations which had just fallen from the President than he was; and there was not any member of the Association more willing to admit the error into which he had fallen than he should be found to be. It was, however, a matter of no real importance how far any opinion which he might have formerly expressed on extended steam navigation was right or wrong, except so far as it had been made a personal question. The subject was first broached at the Bristol Meeting of the British Association, when a discussion arose upon it, and he then remarked, that it was a great experiment which had not yet been attended with any satisfactory result. Unquestionably, he did express a discouraging or unfavourable opinion as far as regarded the probability of ever maintaining an unbroken intercourse by means of steam navigation between Great Britain and New York. But he had been charged with declaring that the transit by steam navigation between Great Britain and New York was a physical impossibility. He never had given expression to such a statement, or to anything equivalent to it; and, as a proof, he read a passage from the article on Steam Navigation which appeared in the *Edinburgh Review* soon after the Bristol meeting, and which expressed the opinions he then held. He must, however, now acknowledge that the success of the *Great Western* steam ship had shaken the opinions he then entertained, and should the same success continue throughout the various seasons of the year, he would be the

472 SELECTIONS FROM THE PROCEEDINGS OF THE NEWCASTLE MEETING

first to come forward and acknowledge himself completely in error. Dr. Lardner then proceeded to the proper subject before the section, namely, the duty of marine engines, for ascertaining which a sum of money had been last year granted by the Association. He had been in communication with many steam navigation companies, and found that it would be a hopeless task to attempt to get the men on board the vessels to register with accuracy all the various facts required to be registered. He had consequently considered how this might be done by machinery, and the result was the construction of the instrument before them, and which he termed a steam journal. By this he proposed to register every five minutes the following varying phenomena, on which the efficiency and performance of steam-engines depend:—the pressure of the steam between the slides and the steam valve,—the pressure in the boiler,—the vacuum and the quantity of water in the boilers,—the saltness of the water in the boilers,—the velocity of the paddle-wheels,—the draft of the vessel,—the trim of the vessel,—the rate of the vessel,—the course of the vessel,—the apparent force of the wind,—the apparent direction of the wind. All these, excepting the course of the vessel, it is intended to register by self-acting mechanism. The methods by which this was proposed to be effected he then explained by reference to detailed drawings.

"On Steam Navigation," by Mr. J. S. Russell.

The object of this communication was to endeavour to point out the means which might be attempted, with the greatest probability of success, for improving steam navigation. It was of importance to consider whether they should look to some new, and as yet untried, method, or to improved combinations of the means already in common use. The latter was the better course; and these improvements might be in the vessel itself, in the machinery, or in the nature and application of the fuel. Mr. Russell then adverted to the fallacy of maintaining, as some persons did, that the form of the vessel was alone to be considered, while others held the directly contrary opinion, that an increase of power alone was to be considered. Mr. Russell, however, considered, that in the present state of steam navigation, the opinions of the former were most to be attended to. With reference to these questions, two great experiments had, he said, been made. Two fifty-horse power engines had been taken out of a vessel, and two sixty horse power engines put in their place. When the propelling power was two

fifties, the velocity of the vessel was ten miles and three quarters per hour. When it was two sixties, the velocity with which the vessel moved was ten miles and six-tenths per hour. Here then was an increase of power, a greater expenditure of fuel, and the increase of the velocity was only three-tenths of a mile. Another experiment was made on two vessels, one of 450 tons, and the other of 500 tons burthen. The larger vessel was propelled by two engines of 300-horse power, and the smaller one by two of 150-horse power. The larger vessel, with the double power, proceeded at the rate of nine miles and a half an hour, whilst the smaller one moved at the rate of nine miles and a quarter an hour. This instance he thought extremely satisfactory; the smaller vessel had the proper form that a vessel should have, and the larger one had not. He was, therefore, of opinion, that the form of the vessel was the direction in which we should look for improvement. Indeed, he thought it probable, that ere long we should have vessels of double the length, for a given breadth, that they at present generally are. The objection to an increased length, from the danger of what is called "breaking the back," might be in a great measure removed by a proper system of diagonal framing. Another important consideration is, that the linear dimensions of a vessel being doubled, the capacity is increased eight-fold, but the increase in the resistance need not be more than two-fold.

Mr. Whewell read a letter from the Astronomer Royal, G. B. Airy, Esq. "On the means adopted for correcting the local Magnetic Action of the Compass in Iron Steam Ships."

"Royal Observatory, Greenwich, Aug. 21, 1838.

"Dear Whewell,—Among the causes which have prevented me from attending the meeting of the British Association, the principal is, the trouble of carrying on a series of observations and experiments (at the request of the admiralty) for correcting the local magnetic action on the compass, in the iron steam ship the *Rainbow*. Perhaps by communicating the principal results to the proper section of the Association, you will more than compensate for my absence. The compass was placed in four different stations near the deck, and in four stations about 13 feet above the deck; and for each of these the ship was turned round, and the disturbance observed in many positions. The disturbances even at the upper stations were great, but at all the lower stations they were very great and at the station next the stern they were enormous. The whole amount there was 100° (from—50° to + 50°); and on one occasion, in turning the vessel about 24°, the needle moved 74° in the opposite direction. I should have perhaps found some difficulty in reducing these to laws if I had not made some observations of the horizontal intensity at the four lower stations, in different positions of the ship. From these I was able to infer the separate amounts of disturbance due to the permanent magnetism of the ship, and to the induced magnetism, and to construct correctors. These correctors I tried yesterday, completely at the sternmost station, and imperfectly at two others. The correction at the sternmost station was (speaking generally) complete; the extreme of deviation, which formerly exceeded 100°, did not, with the corrector, exceed 1°. At the other stations I had not leisure to adjust the apparatus: but I fully expect to-morrow to produce the same accordance at them. This result is, I should think, important in a practical sense. Some theorical results, which I did not anticipate, are also obtained. At the stern position, the disturbance is produced almost entirely by the permanent magnetism, the inductive magnetism producing only $\frac{1}{25}$ of the whole effect. Going towards the head, the effect of the permanent magnetism diminishes, and that of the inductive magnetism increases, till the latter produces about $\frac{1}{3}$ of the whole effect. The resolved part of the permanent magnetism transverse to the ship, varies little, increasing somewhat towards the head): the part longitudinal to the ship decreases rapidly from the stern to the head (where it is less than the transverse part). I must not omit to mention that Mr. Baily took one department of the observations for one day, and will therefore be able to give you a complete account of the method of conducting the compass observations. In this, however, there is nothing very important: the principal object being to contrive methods of observing, in a place where no distant object could be seen, and where there seemed to be, at first, great reason for suspecting considerable local attraction peculiar to the place, and independent of the ship.

"G. B. AIRY."

Mr. Baily described the method of observing the deviation of the needle, caused by the immense mass of iron in this vessel, the *Rainbow*, by theodolites fixed in proper positions on the shore; the deviation of the needle, as the ship's head was veered round, was ascertained, when the needle on board was placed in different parts of the vessel.—Sir John Herschel said, that Barlow's compensating plate having been found inapplicable to the correction of the effect of such large masses of iron, it became a problem of much interest to find out an adequate correction, when the following principle was suggested by the Astronomer Royal:—After the effect of the vessel upon the compass while on board had been determined, as described by Mr. Baily, the compass was removed to the shore, and placed in the neighbourhood of a large mass of iron, in such a way that the effect of this mass was the same as that of the vessel, a compensation for this was then applied to the compass; and, upon removing the entire apparatus on board, it is obvious the ship, which is an exact equivalent for the mass of iron (now left on shore) must be exactly compensated also. A ludicrous circumstance had occurred, proving the necessity of this compensation. When they were bringing the vessel round from Glasgow, where she had been built, they had hazy weather, and at the Land's End they were under the necessity of hailing a vessel to know where they were. The crew of the other vessel were in amazement to conceive why a ship of such magnitude had been intrusted to such a set of land-lubbers.—Capt. Johnson, R.N. said, that Barlow's compensating plate was fully adequate to the compensation of such a mass of iron as that in the *Rainbow*, as he had frequent opportunity of proving; in fact, the maximum deviation of the needle would not be more than 13° when the compass was suspended 18 feet (we believe) from the deck.—Sir John Herschel begged not to be misunderstood: he had no intention to undervalue or disparage the compensating plate of Barlow, which was unquestionably a most valuable discovery.

"On Riveting Boiler Plates by Machinery," by W. Fairbairne.

Mr. Fairbairne described the machinery which he had invented for making boilers. By this machine, two men and two boys can fix eight rivets three-quarter inch diameter per minute, or nearly 500 per hour, whereas, by the ordinary operation, with an additional man, not more than forty can be inserted; thus, the advantage is as about 120 to one, besides the saving of one man. By this machine an ordinary locomotive boiler, ten feet six inches by one foot diameter, can be riveted, and the plates fitted in *four* hours; whereas the time required, besides extra hands, without this machine, would be *twenty* hours. The work is also much superior. The rivets being hot, the holes are completely filled, and the rivet by its contraction draws the plates so closely together, that the joints are perfect. On testing a high-pressure boiler made by this machine, to 200lb. on the square inch, there was no leakage; but in a boiler made by hand, very many of the rivets would be found to leak.

"On the Construction of Timber Viaducts," by B. Green.

The timber viaducts constructed by Mr. Green on several lines of railway, consist of arches on stone piers. These arches consist of three ribs, and every rib is put together with three-inch deck deals, in length of from twenty to forty-five feet, and two of the deals in width. The first course is composed of two whole deals in width, and the next of one whole and two half deals, and so on alternately until the rib is formed. Each rib consists of sixteen deals in height or thickness, their ends making joints, so that no two of the horizontal or radiating joints shall come together. The three ribs are connected together by diagonal braces and iron bolts; the spandrils are strutted in a peculiar manner; the whole of the timber was subjected to Kyan's process, and between every deal is a layer of brown paper dipped in tar. The same principle of constructing arches of iron by laminated plates, has been adopted by Mr. Green. Wrought iron bars from one and a half to four inches square (according to the span of the arch), from fifteen to twenty-five feet long, grooved on the under, and tongued on the upper side, are laid one over the other and bent over a centre, until the rib is formed. The iron bars are bound together at intervals of from four to six feet apart, with iron straps and keys round the rib. The spandrils are fitted with iron struts. A considerable saving of expense and great lightness, as compared with stone or ordinary iron bridges, may thus be attained.

"On an Improved Method of Working the Valves of a Locomotive Engine."

Professor Willis described the method recently introduced by Mr. Hawthorn, for working the valves of a locomotive without the usual eccentrics. The motion is derived at once from the connecting rod, by means of a pin placed at the centre of the connecting rod, and giving to a frame a reciprocating motion in a vertical direction, at every revolution of the crank. To this frame are attached arms, by which motion is communicated to the slides. It is necessary that the slide should be open for the admission of the steam into the cylinder, a little *before* the piston has completed the stroke; this, which is technically termed the *lead* of the slide, must be provided for with great care, so as to correspond with the various speeds of the piston; this arrangement cannot be made where eccentrics are used without considerable difficulty, but

this is provided for in Mr. Hawthorn's method, by simply changing the angle at which the frame is set—an operation which can be performed by adjusting a screw.

"On Methods of Filtering Water," by J. T. Hawkins.

In this paper the author detailed the various essentials for a durable and simple filter for obtaining pure water. The charcoal must be perfectly well burnt, and kept from exposure to the atmosphere; a test of good charcoal is, that when pulverized, it sinks rapidly in water. The charcoal must be supported on an indestructible material, as a plate of burnt clay perforated with holes. The filter may consist of a common garden-pot, or similar vessel with holes at the bottom. The lower part may be filled with round pebbles, then some smaller pebbles, then some coarse sand, and finally a stratum of pounded charcoal, of about three or four inches in thickness. It is a great mistake to put any material, as sand, above the charcoal, with the view of arresting the grosser particles of impurity, as the sand will quickly stop up and be impervious to water. A filter thus prepared will render water perfectly clear and sweet for many years.

"On the Effect of Sea and River Water on Iron," by Mr. R. Mallet.

Mr. Mallet stated, that he and Professor E. Davy had, at the request of the Chemical Section, been associated in a series of experiments on the action of sea and river water on iron. They had come to results of great importance to the civil engineer, some of which he would mention. They found that pure oxygen and pure water are both neutral bodies in regard to iron, and only act on it together; that the larger the quantity of uncombined or suspended carbon in cast iron, the more is it acted on by these agents, so much so, that soft Scotch or Irish cast iron may be used to protect grey or chilled cast iron from all corrosion. With respect to the protection of iron by electrochemical agency, zinc will only protect iron for a time; the oxide of zinc becomes transferred to the surface of the iron, when all protection is at an end. Brass, as proposed by Mr. Hartley, will not protect iron, and he showed some specimens brought from the Liverpool Docks, in which the corrosion had clearly been promoted by the adoption of this method. Other very important results on this subject are detailed in the report to the Chemical Section. [See p. 429, No. 788.]

"On Steam Navigation," by Mr. J. S. Russell.

Mr. Russell resumed the above subject, the continuation and discussion of which had been adjourned from Thursday. He recalled attention to the following points—that, by doubling the three dimensions of the vessel, eight times the space, at an expense of only double the power, might be obtained—that the form of the vessel must be especially attended to—and that the objections on account of sharpness, which are applicable to sailing vessels, do not apply to steam vessels. He insisted on the propriety of making steamers sharp. Nautical men had great objections to extremely sharp vessels, and preferred full bows. He did not wish to do away with the fulness, but to leave the fulness in its proper part, and add a sharp prow to full bows. By this means, great advantages might be obtained in the proper stowage of the cargo, and proportioning of the load. Breadth and fulness in the centre are absolutely indispensable, and this can only be obtained by lengthening out the extremities. Mr. Russell next proceeded to the subject of power, especially with reference to that of the boilers, which depends on the surface. The points especially to be attended to are, extent of surface, thickness and quality of material, and modes of strengthening. Iron boilers, with copper tubes, possessed considerable advantages; the form of boilers is of little consequence, provided extent of surface be obtained.

Friday was the day fixed on for the Association attending the opening the Durham Junction Railway. The object of most interest was the " Victoria Bridge"—the entire length of which is 270 yards, and its width, within the parapet walls, 21 feet. There is a double line of railway over the bridge, with a flagged causeway for foot passengers. According to the *Newcastle Journal*, the arch over the river Wear is 160 feet span; from the foundation of the pier to the spring of this arch is 72 feet; from the spring to the crown of the arch the distance is also seventeen feet; and from the crown of the arch to the parapet wall, is 13 feet; making in all 157 feet. From this, to obtain the height for the ordinary water level, we must deduct the solid masonry buried beneath the weaves, which makes the observable walling 130 ft. This is considerably higher than the celebrated Sunderland Bridge, and (as Mr. Ingham, the chairman at the banquet observed), taken as regards *height* and *span*, is the largest arch in Europe. True it is that the arch of the bridge over the river Dee, near the city of Chester, is wider, and the Spanish bridge at Alcantara, near Lisbon, is more

lofty; but, taking into consideration the united difficulties of extent of span, and height from the water level, the " Victoria Bridge" must stand unrivalled.

The following grants for the advancement of science were agreed to :—

Section A.—Mathematics and Physics.

	£	s
For the reduction of meteorological observations	100	0
For the reduction of observations on the stars	200	0
For improving the nomenclature of the stars	50	0
For comparing the level of Bristol with that of the English Channel	150	0
For tide discussions at Bristol	100	0
For continuing reduction of stars for a new catalogue of stars, preparing under the direction of a Committee of the British Association	500	0
For similar reductions in the catalogue of Histoire Céleste	500	0
For the preparation of instruments for magnetical observation, to be claimed only on the refusal of her Majesty's government to undertake the expense	500	0
For continuing observations on waves	50	0
For the translation and speedy circulation of foreign scientific memoirs	100	0
For tabular meteorological observations	15	0
For repairing the anemometer at Plymouth	8	10
For meteorological observations at ditto	40	0
For hourly meteorological observations in various parts of Scotland, selected by Sir D. Brewster	100	0

Total amount of grants to Physical Sect. £2263 18

Section B.—Chemistry.

	£
For continuing Mr. West's experiments on the atmosphere	40
For observations on the effect of sea-water on cast and wrought iron	50
For the effects of hot water on organic bodies	10
For continuing the table of chemical constants	30
For conducting galvanic experiments near Newcastle	20

Total amount of grants to Chemical Section £150

A grant of 260*l.* to enable the Section to bring to this country Alexis St. Martin, the American, whose stomach is so peculiarly circumstanced as to afford opportunities for observations on organic chemistry and vital physiology (See *Athenæum*, No. 338.) was refused. The Committee of the Medical Section joined in the recommendation.

Section C.—Geology.

	£
For researches in fossil ichthyology	105
Ditto quantities of mud and silt in rivers	20
For a report on British fossil reptiles	200

Total amount to Geological Section.... £325

Section D.—Zoology and Botany.

	£
For experiments on the preservation of animal and vegetable life	8

Section E.—Anatomy and Medicine.

	£
For continued observations on the sounds of the heart	50
For similar observations on the lungs and bronchiæ	20
For construction of medical acoustic instruments	25

Amount of grants to Medical Section £100

Section F.—Statistics.

For continuing statistics of English schools	£150
Ditto .. .. of working population..	100
For statistics of collieries on the Tyne and Wear.......................................	50

Total amount of grant to Statistical Section £300

Section G.—Mechanical Science.

For ascertaining duty performed by Cornish engines	£50
Ditto .. speed of American steamers ..	50
Ditto .. duty of engines not in Cornwall	50
Ditto *the* best form of sailing vessels	200

(Mr. Webster moved, and Mr. Babbage seconded a resolution, that this vote should be increased to 300*l*., but the proposal was negatived.]

For experiments on the hot and cold blast on iron......................................	100
For ascertaining railway constants..........	20
For inquiries into marine steam engines....	17
For instruments to ascertain the duty of marine steam engines—to Dr. Lardner.......	50
Mr. Fairbairne....	28
Mr. Russell	33

Total amount to Section of Mechanical Science £598

Total amount of grants....... £3742 10

The principal recommendations not involving grants of money, were—

That Prof. Bache should be requested to report on the meteorology of the United States.—That Prof. Johnstone should report on the connexion of Geology and Chemistry.—That the Council should prepare a general report on the progress of Geology.—That J. E. Gray, Esq. should prepare a report on British molluscous animals and their shells.—— Selby, Esq. V.P., a similar report on British ornithology.—Dr. Forbes a report on the pulmoniferous mollusca of Great Britain.—And that Prof. Faraday, aided by a Committee, should report on the specific gravity of steam.

The recommendations involving applications to the government and other public bodies, were—

That the astronomical establishments at the Cape of Good Hope should be extended.—That an arc of the meridian should be measured in India, and the standard of English and Indian observations verified.—That observations should be made on the effect of refraction in the Himalaya mountains, and also in Bombay.—That magnetic observatories should be erected in India.—That, in continuation of the Ordnance survey, the mine and mineral wealth of each district should be in some way indicated on the map.—And that an office should be instituted for the preservation and collection of mining-records.

TABLE OF GRADIENTS.—BY C. BOURNS, A. INST. C. E.

(From the *Franklin Journal*.)

						per chain.
1 ft. per mile	=	1 in 5280	=	.15	of an inch
2	"	= "	2640	=	.30	"
3	"	= "	1760	=	.45	"
4	"	= "	1320	=	.60	"
5	"	= "	1056	=	.75	"
6	"	= "	880	=	.90	"
7	"	= "	754.2	=	1.05	"
8	"	= "	660.0	=	1.20	"
9	"	= "	586.6	=	1.35	"

					per chain.
10 ft. per mile	=	1 in	528.0	= 1.50	of an inch
11	"	= "	480.0	= 1.65	"
12	"	= "	440.0	= 1.80	"
13	"	= "	406.1	= 1.95	"
14	"	= "	377.1	= 2.10	"
15	"	= "	352.0	= 2.25	"
16	"	= "	330.0	= 2.40	"
17	"	= "	310.6	= 2.55	"
18	"	= "	293.3	= 2.70	"
19	"	= "	277.9	= 2·85	"
20	"	= "	264.0	= 3.00	"
21	"	= "	251.4	= 3.15	"
22	"	= "	240.0	= 3.30	"
23	"	= "	229.5	= 3.45	"
24	"	= "	220.0	= 3.60	"
25	"	= "	211.2	= 3.75	"
26	"	= "	203.1	= 3.90	"
27	"	= "	195.5	= 4.05	"
28	"	= "	188.6	= 4.20	"
29	"	= "	182.1	= 4.35	"
30	"	= "	176.0	= 4.50	"
31	"	= "	170.3	= 4.65	"
32	"	= "	165.0	= 4.80	"
33	"	= "	160.0	= 4.95	"
34	"	= "	155.3	= 5.10	"
35	"	= "	150.8	= 5.25	"
36	"	= "	146.6	= 5.40	"
37	"	= "	142.7	= 5.55	"
38	"	= "	138.9	= 5.70	"
39	"	= "	135.4	= 5.85	"
40	"	= "	132.0	= 6.00	"
41	"	= "	128.8	= 6.15	"
42	"	= "	125.7	= 6.30	"
43	"	= "	122.8	= 6.45	"
44	"	= "	120.0	= 6.60	"
45	"	= "	117.3	= 6.75	"
46	"	= "	114.8	= 6.90	"
47	"	= "	112.3	= 7.05	"
48	"	= "	110.0	= 7.20	"
49	"	= "	107.7	= 7.35	"
50	"	= "	105.6	= 7.50	"
51	"	= "	103.5	= 7.65	"
52	"	= "	101.5	= 7.80	"
53	"	= "	99.6	= 7.95	"
54	"	= "	97.8	= 8.10	"
55	"	= "	96.0	= 8.25	"
56	"	= "	94.3	= 8.40	"
57	"	= "	92.6	= 8.55	"
58	"	= "	91.0	= 8.70	"
59	"	= "	89.5	= 8.85	"
60	"	= "	88.0	= 9.00	"

SUBURBAN CEMETERIES.—HEALTH OF THE METROPOLIS.

(From the Trans. Inst., C. E.)

We have, for the first time, walked through the intended cemetery at Highgate, and a spot more healthful for the living we never beheld. But before this joint-stock speculation be consecrated, we humbly suggest to those placed in authority over us, and particularly to our diocesan, the propriety of pausing, re-considering, and coming to a different conclusion. Running the risk of being ranked among the benighted, besotted, or bigoted, we take leave to object to that species of cannibalism produced by the "march of intellect," and which drinks, instead of eating, the dead bodies of mankind. London may be truly said to be the vale of Highgate; and, although the inhabitants of Highgate pay so much a-piece for buckets of water, yet, however unscientific it might be, Highgate supplies gratuitously the city of London with that commodity. Yea, verily, even the inexhaustible pumps of Gray's-inn, and Whitecross-street prison, are alike supplied from the springs which gush from Highgate. Now, it seems to us that an admixture of decomposing animal matter with pure spring water, however scientific, is somewhat unwise. if not unpalatable. The question then is, would the intended cemetery at Highgate produce the results we speak of? Unhesitatingly we say, Yes. And as even infidels believe that facts are stubborn things, take some facts:—The city of New York is situated on a hill, forming part of Manhattan Island, about the size of our Isle of Wight, and the drainage from the city finds its level in the East river and the Hudson river, which surround Manhattan Island, just as the drainage of London, the vale of Highgate, finds its level in the Thames. Now, it so happens that New York was formerly visited periodically with contagious diseases, particularly with the yellow fever; and these awful visitations were considered the effect of the annually decaying vegetable matter of the natural forests about the city, and it was said that so soon as the country should be cleared and cultivated, there would be no more yellow fevers, &c. The yellow fever, &c., however, did continue even after the whole state of New York had become what it still is, one gorgeous modern garden of Eden. The sensible men of the city—none of your self-conceited scientific stock-jobbing modern humbugs, but really sensible men—set about investigating the subject, and they found that from the drainage from the churchyards were engendered myriads of animalculæ, and that where there was most drainage, there was most disease, and they boarded off what they called "infected districts," not so much on account of actual disease, as from ascertained practical knowledge that those districts were all liable to infection. What was the remedy? They made a cemetery some miles from the city, not on an inclined plane, as the intended one at Highgate is, but on a flat piece of ground, whose drainage is below the level of the rivers. What is the consequence? The city of New York is now probably the healthiest city in the universe,

and notwithstanding the intense heat there of the present summer no case of yellow fever has occurred, and even the quarantine laws in respect of ships from diseased parts of the Southern States have been relaxed. Had New York been excavated with sewers as London is, the drainage from the churchyards would, as it does in London, find its proper outlet, but as no such outlet was obtained, it found its way partly into their wells, and made the water unwholesome, and partly to the banks of the rivers, awaiting for the swelling of the tide, and such as was not carried off by the tide became a living pestilence. Apply all this to the intended cemetery at Highgate, and a child will understand that the decomposing matter of such as might be buried there must naturally, if not scientifically, find its way to, and become incorporated with, the springs under the surface, and also ooze out upon the surface, and poison the air of that valley in which Kentish-town and Holloway are situated, which air we once heard Abernethy say was worth a fee a sniff. —*John Bull.*

STEPHENSON'S THEATRICAL MACHINERY.

To whatever department of mechanical science we direct our attention, one uniform impression is conveyed—we become continually surprised by a mass of modern contrivances which, through the ingenuity and talent of our countrymen, (especially,) are in course of increasing improvement.

The subject recurs to us more forcibly from an opportunity we have lately had of examining a new and extensive series of designs for constructing, in our modern theatres, an entire system of machinery, by which the operations are rendered less complex, and the instantaneous effects produced are unlike anything which has heretofore appeared upon the stage of any theatre. There is, in this arrangement, one distinctive characteristic, which is rarely attendant upon an extended scheme of improvement —namely, it appears to have provided for every contingency, and to embrace every circumstance which can be anticipated as in any way controlled by, or affecting its action. In lieu of having the stage, as at present, inconveniently crowded with scene-shifters and others, to the manifest inconvenience of the performers, they are scarcely upon the stage beyond half an hour during the evening's performance. The machinery is constructing upon cast-iron columns, in preference to the usual practice of suspending every thing from the roof, and the entire construction being of metal, is beyond the reach of apprehension of accident by first. The operations are performed by toothed wheels, at the ends of vertical or horisontal iron bars put into motion by a windlass at the back of the stage, which can be worked by one man. The wheels when put in gear, or when the teeth are made to act one upon the other, will work with extraordinary precision and ease; the drop scenes are drawn up and let down from the top of the stage, and the side scenes are shifted without noise or confusion; the whole works quietly and evenly.

All machinery which, like the present, is intended to perform a diversity of duties of considerable extent, must be, to a certain degree complicated; it is, however, so greatly simplified, that its management only requires common care and attention on the parts of those who have charge of it.

The blunders to which the present methods of scene-shifting are constantly exposed have long called for revision; but the subject presented so many difficulties, so many conflicting interests, and so much to discourage any ordinary person, who might be qualified, from undertaking such a task, that we are not surprised it has so long remained unimproved. The task is one requiring much care, labour, and discrimination, to disentangle the collected heaps of useful from the superfluous materials; the result is, however, a saving of seventy per cent. in the expense of working the theatre.

Great credit is due to the contriver, Mr. Macdonald Stephenson, for his undertaking, and for the ability with which he has been enabled to overcome obstacles of no ordinary description, upon which, we believe, he has been upwards of two years engaged.

Mr. Stephenson, we understand, has received the encouragement he deserves from the authorities of Paris, where the circumstance of the machinery being fire-proof has been considered almost as important as the other advantages which attach to its application.—*Abridged from the Morning Herald and Times.*

LIST OF ENGLISH PATENTS GRANTED BETWEEN THE 31st OF AUGUST AND THE 27th OF SEPTEMBER, 1838.

John Keys, of Sutton, copper smelter, and William Thompson Clough, of Eccleston, Lancaster, for a method or process for the manufacture of sulphuric acid from copper ore, copper regulus, and sulphuret of sinc. August 31; six months to specify.

Morton Balmanno, of Queen-street, Cheapside, merchant, for a new and improved method of making and manufacturing paper, pasteboard, &c., and tissues. September 6; six months.

John Frederick Bourne, of Manchester, engineer, and John Barthey, jun., of the same place, engineer, for certain improvements in the construction of wheels to be used upon railways and other roads, and which improvements are also applicable to the construction of wheels in general. September 6; six months.

Miles Berry, of 66, Chancery-lane, mechanical draftsman, for certain improvements applicable to certain parts of the process generally used for the manufacturing and refining sugars; a communication from a foreigner. September 6; six months.

Timothy Burstall, of Leith, engineer, for certain improvements in the steam-engine, and in apparatus to be used therewith, or with any other construction of the steam-engine, or other motive power, for the more smooth and easy conveyance of goods and passengers on land and water, part of which will be applicable to water power. September 6; six months.

Henry Gibbs, of Birmingham, button manufacturer, for an improved perforated button. September 6; six months.

Joseph Brown, of the Minories, upholsterer, for improvements in beds, sofas, chairs, and other articles of furniture, to render them more suitable for travelling and other purposes. September 8; six months.

James Ulric Vaucher, of Geneva, in Switzerland, but now of Manchester, gent., for certain improvements in fire-engines, watering-engines, and other hydraulic machines and apparatus for raising or propelling water and other fluids; some of which improvements are also applicable to steam-engines. September 8; six months.

Henry Dunnington, of Nottingham, lace manufacturer, for improvements on machinery employed in making frame-work knitting or stocking fabrics. September 10; six months.

Alexander Southwood Stocker, and Clement Heasley, manufacturers, of Birmingham, for improvements in straps for wearing apparel. September 13; six months.

Ambrose Ador, of Leicester-square, for certain improvements on lamps or apparatus for producing or affording light. September 13; six months.

Joseph Hall, of Over, Chester, plumber, for improvements in the manufacture of salt. September 13; six months.

John Chanter, of Earl-street, Blackfriars, Esq., and John Grantham, of Liverpool, engineer, for improvements in furnaces for steam-boilers. September 13; six months.

Edwin Bottomley, of South Crossland, York, clothier, for a certain improvement or improvements applicable to power and hand looms. September 13; six months.

Edward Massey, of King-street, Clerkenwell, watchmaker, for improvements in watches and machines for keeping time. September 13; six months.

Thomas Swinburne, of South-square, Gray's-inn, Esq., for certain improvements in water closets and other conveniences of the kind. September 13; six months.

James Wapshare, of Bath, gent., for certain improvements in the application of heat for the purpose of drying wool, woollen yarns, woollen cloths, and other articles, and other improvements connected with the use of the press, in the process of dressing or finishing woollen cloths. September 13; six months.

Thomas Wilkinson, of the Quadrant, Regent-street, ironmonger and engineer, for certain improvements in the construction of tram or railways, and in the carriages to be used thereon. September 13; six months.

Archibald M'Lellan, of Glasgow, coach builder, for certain improvements upon the springs and braces of wheel carriages, and upon the mode of hanging such carriages. September 13; six months.

Frederick Le Mesurier, of New-street, Saint Peter's-Port, Guernsey, gent., for a certain improvement or certain improvements in the construction of pumps for raising water or other fluids. September 13; six months.

Sir Hugh Pigot, of Foley-place, knight, for a certain engine or engines useful as steam-engines, pumps, or propellers of vessels or machinery. September 13; six months.

William Day, of Gate-street, Lincoln's-Inn-Fields, lithographer, for an improved mode or method of applying and combining timber and other materials used in the construction of ships or vessels, masts, yards, beams, piers, bridges, and various other purposes. September 20; six months.

James Nasmyth, of Patricroft, near Manchester, engineer, for certain improvements in machinery, tools, or apparatus for cutting or planing metals and other substances, and in securing or fastening the keys or collars used in such machinery, and other machinery where keys or collars are commonly applied. September 20; six months.

Robert William Sievier, of Henrietta-street, Cavendish-square, gent., for certain improvements in rigger pulley bands for driving machinery, and ropes and lines for other purposes. September 20; six months.

John Thomas Betts, of Smithfield Bars, rectifier, for improvements in the manufacture of gin, which he intends to denominate Betts' patent gin, or Betts' patent stomachic gin. September 21; six months.

James Walton, of Sowerby-bridge, Halifax, cloth dresser and friser, for certain improvements in machinery for making wire cards for carding cotton, wool, silk, tow, and other fibrous substances of the like nature. September 21; six months.

Emile Alexis Fanquet Delarue, of Bacon's-hotel, St. Paul's Church-yard, calico printer, for certain improvements in providing and fixing red, and other colours in which red forms a constituent part, upon cotton, silk, woollen, and other fabrics. September 27; six months.

John Hughes Rees, of Penymaes, Carmarthen, Esq., for certain improvements in machinery applicable to raising water for propelling boats, carriages, and other machinery. September 27; six months.

John Joseph Charles Sheridan, of Ironmonger-lane, chemist, for an improvement in the manufacture of soap. September 27; six months.

Edmond Henze, of Fenton's Hotel, St. James's-street, merchant, for improvements in the manufacture of dextrine. September 27; six months.

John White, of Haddington, North Britain, ironmonger, for certain improvements in the construction of ovens and heated air-stoves. September 27; six months.

LIST OF SCOTCH PATENTS GRANTED BETWEEN THE 22nd OF AUGUST AND THE 22nd OF SEPTEMBER, 1838.

Charles Dod, of 21 Craven-street, Strand, Middlesex, gent., in consequence of a communication made to him by a foreigner residing abroad, for certain improvements in the construction of railway tram roads, and in the structure of the carriages to be used on the said railways or tram roads; and also of certain apparatus applicable to the cleaning and preserving of railways and tram roads. Sealed 28rd of August, 1838; four months to specify.

Arthur Dunn, of Stamford Hill, Middlesex, gent., for certain improvements in the manufacture of soap. August 24.

Ambroise Ador, late of Leicester-square, now of 29, Rue de Faubourg Montmartre, Paris, chemist, for certain improvements on lamps, or apparatus for producing or affording light. August 28.

Charles Phillips, of Chipping Norton, Oxon, surgeon, for improvements in apparatus or machinery for punching, bending, cutting and joining metal, and for holding or securing metal to be punched, bent, cut, or otherwise operated on, parts of which

machinery are adapted to perform some of those operations on other materials. August 30.

Job Cutler, of Lady Pool-lane, sparkbrook, gent., and Thomas Gregory Hancock, of Princes-street, Birmingham, mechanist, for an improved method of condensing the steam in steam-engines, and supplying their boilers with the water thereby formed. August 31.

Charles Fitton, woollen manufacturer, and George Collier, mechanic, both of Cumberworth Half, Wakefield, York, for improvements in power looms. September 6.

Charles Hancock, of Grosvenor Place, Hyde Park Corner, Middlesex, animal painter, for certain improved means of producing and applying figured surfaces, sunk and in relief, and of printing therefrom, and also of moulding, stamping, and embossing. September 13.

Samuel Hall, of Basford, Nottingham, civil engineer, for improvements in steam-engines, heating or evaporating fluids or gases, and generating steam or vapours. September 15.

William Joseph Curtis, of Stamford-street, Blackfriars Road, Surrey, C. E., for certain improved machinery and apparatus for facilitating travelling and transport on railways, parts of which are also applicable to other purposes. September 17.

Thomas Robinson Williams, of No. 61, Cheapside, C. E., for certain improvements in machinery for spinning, twisting, or curling, and weaving horse hair, and other hairs, as well as various fibrous substances. September 18.

Archibald McLellan, of Glasgow, coach builder, for certain improvements upon the springs and braces of wheel carriages, and upon the mode of hanging such carriages. September 21.

LIST OF IRISH PATENTS GRANTED IN AUGUST, 1838.

Bennett Woodcroft, of Mumps, Oldham, Lancaster, for improvements in the construction of looms for weaving various sorts of cloths, which looms may be set in motion by any adequate power.

Charles Pierre Davaux, of Fenchurch-street, London, for a new and improved apparatus for preventing the explosion of boilers and generators of steam.

Hippolyte Francois, Marquis de Bouffet Montauban, Sloane-street, Chelsea, for improvements in the means of producing gas for illuminations, and in apparatus connected with the consumption thereof.

Stephen Geary, of Hamilton-place, New Road, for improvements in the preparation of fuel.

Michael Wheelwright Iveson, silk spinner, of Edinburgh, for an improved method of consuming smoke in furnaces, and other places where fire is used, and for economising fuel; and also for supplying air, heated or cold, for blasting or smelting furnaces.

Michael Wheelwright Iveson, for an improved method of preparing and spinning silk waste, wool, flax, and other fibrous substances, and for discharging the gum from silk, raw and manufactured.

John Thomas Betts, of Smithfield Bars, London, rectifier for improvements in the process of preparing spirituous liquors in the making of Brandy.

Charles Button, of Holborn Bars, and Harrison Grey Dyer, Cavendish-square, for improvement in the manufacture of white lead.

NOTES AND NOTICES.

The *Highlandman's Almanack.*—Bend the first and third fingers of the left hand—and, commencing with March at the thumb, count on—the bent fingers will indicate the months which contain only 30 days.—*Scotsman.*

A Fact for Framework-knitters.—Under the heading of "Hosiery," the *Penny Cyclopædia* contains the following interesting observations, which are already, or will presently be, applicable to every branch of cotton manufacture:—"At this moment, (July, 1838,) stocking frames, with a rotatory action, in which 12 fashioned stockings are made at the same time, superintended by only one man and a boy, and worked by steam-power, have been successfully brought into operation at Nottingham, and bid fair to supersede the use of the reciprocating engine, in which but one stocking can be made at once by a single workman. The economy in the process of manufacture that will be thus effected is very great, and may be the means of securing to our manufacturers for some time longer the supply of foreign countries—a branch of trade which was fast leaving us. The principal seat of the cotton hosiery manufacture abroad is at Chemnitz, in Saxony, where, owing to the low rate of wages, as compared with the earnings of the weavers of Nottingham, goods are made with yarns imported from Lancashire, at prices which have excluded English goods from third markets, and have even brought them into consumption in this country after paying a duty of 20 per cent.!"

Railway Travelling in France.—We arrived at St. Germain-en-Laye at a quarter past seven o'clock; landed, walked to the railway station-house in eight or ten minutes, and obtained there tickets in return for cheques, which were put into our hands as we quitted the steamer. The charge for these tickets, which I believe is half a franc, was included in our fare; so, of course, we had nothing to pay. The station-house is a magnificent building, and the arrangements for the accommodation of passengers appeared to me in every respect unobjectionable. There were a great many applicants for places; but no rude contentions—no pushing about—no disorder of any kind. We entered the carriage indicated by our tickets, a roomy and well-constructed vehicle, without much show about it, and set off to the sound of a trumpet, slowly at first; the speed then was gradually increased until it attained a velocity, at no time, I think, exceeding 15 miles an hour. The trumpeter kept on sounding the whole way—a precaution that might be introduced into our railway arrangements with the most useful effect. The warning would be heard to a considerable distance; and, if it had been in use here these last two years, it would undoubtedly have prevented many accidents of a most disastrous nature. The vibration of the train of carriages was somewhat more than I had been accustomed to in England. We traversed the distance from the point of our departure to Paris in 27 minutes. At the terminus, omnibuses were in waiting for passengers to all parts of the capital.— *New Monthly Magazine.*

Congreve Rockets—War Machinery.—The very flight of the Congreve rocket is startling; it springs from the ground in a volume of flame, and then rushes along with a continued roar, with its large head blazing, and striking point-blank, and with a tremendous force, at the distance of a mile or more. In a siege it is already extremely formidable. It bursts through roofs; it fixes itself wherever it can bore its way; and it inflames everything that is combustible. Stone walls only can repel it, and that not always. This weapon may be regarded as almost exclusively English in its use, as well as its origin.

It will be like the English bow in the fifteenth century. In the next war what an extraordinary change will take place in all the established instruments of putting men out of the world! We shall be attacked at once from above, around, and below. We shall have the balloon showering fire upon us from miles above our heads; the steam-gun levelling us from walls and ramparts, before we can come within distance to dig a trench; the Congreves setting our tents, ammunition waggons, and ourselves, in a blaze in our first sleep; and the steam-boat running and doing mischief every where. But of all those mischief-makers I should give the palm to the rocket. No infantry on earth could stand for 5 minutes within 500 yards of a well-served rocket-battery. Half-a-dozen volleys of half-a-dozen of these fiery arrows would break the strongest battalions into fragments, lay one-half dead on the ground, and send the other blazing and torn over the field. The heaviest fire from guns is nothing to their effect. It wants the directness, the steadiness, the flame, and, resulting from all those, the terror. If the British troops shall ever come into the field without an overwhelming force of rocketeers, they will throw away the first chance of victory that ever was lost by national negligence. Nothing can be more obvious than that this tremendous weapon has not even yet arrived at its full capacity for war on a great scale.—*Blackwood's Magazine.*

French Steam Plough.—Among the new inventions in France, is one that is much talked of among speculators and manufacturers. It is a steam plough of very peculiar construction, with which it is said four miles of ground can be excavated with an engine of only eight horse power, to the depth of a foot, and the breadth of two feet, in a single hour. The projector of the canal from Orleans to Nantes, which under ordinary circumstances would require at least five years for its construction, pretends that in one year the whole would be completed by the use of this machine, and that the saving in mere interest of capital would amount to forty thousand pounds sterling. A friend of mine, who is one of the best engineers in Europe, tells me that he has seen the instrument, and that with some ameliorations he believes it would accomplish all that has been stated. The earth as it is turned up is thrown into a sort of sail, which throws it to a distance of sixty feet.—*French Paper.*

New American Printing Machine.—We copy the following from an American paper, *The Peoria Register and North Western Gazetteer.* Mr. Thomas French, of Ithaca, New York, is constructing his patent printing-press, at the Speedwell Works, near Middletown, which is to be attached to one of the paper-mills in that place. This press takes the paper immediately from the paper-machine, prints it on both sides, and passes it through drying cylinders, which press it smooth. Thus, in one operation, and within the space of 3 minutes, the pulp is taken from the mill, and a book of 356 pages is ready for the binder. The paper is printed in one continuous sheet, and a whole edition can readily be printed, rolled up, and sent to any distance. Mr. French has on his press *Cobb's Juvenile Reader*, of 216 pages, of which he presents us a sheet of about 70 feet long, neatly printed, and which can be examined at our office.

The *Railway Map* of England and Wales continues on sale, in a neat wrapper, price 6d.; and on fine paper, coloured, price 1s.

☞ *British and Foreign Patents taken out with economy and despatch; Specifications, Disclaimers, and Amendments, prepared or revised; Caveats entered; and generally every Branch of Patent Business promptly transacted. A complete list of Patents from the earliest period (15 Car. II. 1675,) to the present time may be examined. Fee 2s. 6d.; Clients, gratis.*

LONDON: Printed and Published for the Proprietor, by W. A. Robertson, at the Mechanics' Magazine Office, No. 6, Peterborough-court, between 135 and 136, Fleet-street.—Sold by A. & W. Galignani, Rue Vivienne, Paris.

END OF THE TWENTY-NINTH VOLUME.

INDEX

TO THE TWENTY-NINTH VOLUME.

PRINTED BY W. A. ROBERTSON, 6, PETERBOROUGH-COURT, FLEET STREET.

Lightning Source UK Ltd.
Milton Keynes UK
UKHW05f1812300918
329793UK00004B/32/P